MW00682514

The Penguin

AUSTRALIAN ENCYCLOPAEDIA

The Penguin
AUSTRALIAN ENCYCLOPAEDIA

General Editor: Sarah Dawson

VIKING

Viking
Penguin Books Australia Ltd
487 Maroondah Highway, PO Box 257
Ringwood, Victoria 3134, Australia
Penguin Books Ltd
Harmondsworth, Middlesex, England
Viking Penguin, A Division of Penguin Books USA Inc.
375 Hudson Street, New York, New York 10014, USA
Penguin Books Canada Limited
2801 John Street, Markham, Ontario, Canada L3R 1B4
Penguin Books (N.Z.) Ltd
182–190 Wairau Road, Auckland 10, New Zealand

First published by Penguin Books Australia Ltd 1990

10 9 8 7 6 5 4 3 2 1

Copyright © Penguin Books Australia Ltd, 1990

All rights reserved. Without limiting the rights under
copyright reserved above, no part of this publication may
be reproduced, stored in or introduced into a retrieval system,
or transmitted, in any form or by any means (electronic,
mechanical, photocopying, recording or otherwise) without
the prior written permission of both the copyright owner
and the above publisher of this book.

Produced by Viking O'Neil
56 Claremont Street, South Yarra, Victoria 3141, Australia
A division of Penguin Books Australia Ltd

Typeset in Malaysia by Typeset Gallery Sdn. Bhd.
Printed in Australia by Griffin Press

National Library of Australia
Cataloguing-in-Publication data

The Penguin Australian encyclopaedia.

   ISBN 0 670 83148 4.

   1. Australia – Dictionaries and encyclopaedias.
   2. Australia – Handbooks, manuals, etc.
   I. Dawson, Sarah. II. Title: Australian encyclopaedia.

994.003

PUBLISHER'S NOTE   In 1968 Andrew and Nancy Learmonth
produced an *Encyclopaedia of Australia* (Frederick Warne
& Co.; 2nd edn 1973). That book provided the starting
point for *The Penguin Australian Encyclopaedia*, and the
Publishers wish to acknowledge the Learmonths' founding
contribution to this publication.

FOREWORD

I grew up with encyclopaedias and as a child used them incessantly to make sense of newspapers and radio and to create my own window on the world. I have never lost the habit.

In an era of instant global communication, with computerised databases, I believe that the need for accessible 'hard copy' in book form, with an extended shelf life, is greater than ever. Books, especially encyclopaedias, are basic instruments for developing personal autonomy, giving each reader opportunities to pursue the multiplicity of connections between entries – to stop, note, review, compare and question. *The Penguin Australian Encyclopaedia* will fulfil an important national function, not least if it is used in schools and tertiary institutions to encourage students to become accustomed to checking detail and then pushing themselves on to enlarged understanding and new perspectives.

For decades, we complacently accepted the concept of Australia as 'the lucky country' where prosperity and production depended on chance factors alone, missing the irony in the title of Donald Horne's famous book. Reliance on raw materials will not carry Australia through to the 21st century: we must become a brain-based society, 'the intelligent society' (or 'the clever country' as Bob Hawke calls it). We have never been fanatical in our pursuit of knowledge – getting it right, making informed judgements and acting on them. Competitors in our region will eat us alive unless we make a national commitment to knowledge, both as understanding and as a precondition for action. Our future depends on it.

This one-volume reference is a guidebook for a journey of discovery about ourselves and our capacity to make our mark in the world. It stands alone, in range and depth.

Barry O. Jones
April 1990

CONTENTS

Foreword   *v*

Consultants and contributors   *viii*

Conventions and abbreviations   *x*

Editor's note   *xii*

A–Z   *1*

Appendix: government of Australia   *532*

Maps   *541*
    Australia and the Pacific rim
    Geological formation
    Geology of Australia
    Weather patterns in the major centres
    Australian soil types
    Natural vegetation
    Australia's unique wildlife
    Voyages of discovery
    The great inland explorers
    How the six States developed
    Population growth 1788–1986
    Population distribution
    Aboriginal population by State, 1986
    Agricultural land use
    Major mineral and energy resources
    National parks

Extended entries

Aboriginal art *22*
Aboriginal culture and society *2*
agriculture *7*
architecture *18*
Australian English *30*
aviation *34*
ballet and dance *39*
banks and banking *42*
broadcasting *69*
business *78*
climate *100*
colonial administration *106*
Constitution *110*
defence *135*
defence forces *137*
discovery voyages *142*
drugs and drug use *146*
economy *152*
education *156*
electrical energy *160*
environment and conservation *166*
ethnic groups *170*
eucalypts *173*
exploration by land *175*
fauna *181*
film industry *186*
flora *193*
foreign policy *201*
forests and forestry *202*
fossils *205*
geology and major landforms *217*
gold *222*
government *227*
grasses and grasslands *230*
health and health services *245*
housing *257*
immigration *263*
land rights *288*
law and legal system *292*

libraries *298*
literature and writing *302*
magazines and periodicals *316*
manufacturing industries *321*
medical research *327*
mining industry *331*
museums *346*
music and musical composition *347*
New South Wales *357*
newspapers *359*
Northern Territory *362*
oil and natural gas *368*
painting *375*
police *390*
population *392*
post and telecommunications *397*
publishing and bookselling *404*
Queensland *407*
racial conflict *410*
railways *412*
religion *416*
roads and road transport *421*
science and technology *432*
ships and shipping *442*
social services *449*
soils and soil conservation *450*
South Australia *452*
sport and recreation *455*
Tasmania *471*
taxation *472*
theatre *475*
trade *483*
urban planning *492*
Victoria *496*
water and water resources *504*
Western Australia *511*
women in Australian society *520*
women's movement *522*
World War 1 *525*
World War 2 *526*

CONSULTANTS AND CONTRIBUTORS

GENERAL EDITOR: SARAH DAWSON
DEPUTY EDITOR: MARGARET GEDDES   **SENIOR EDITOR:** BETTINA STEVENSON

DON AITKIN, MA, PhD, chairman of the Australian Research Council.

RICHARD APPLETON, editor and writer.

PETER H. BAILEY, OBE, MA, LLM, barrister and solicitor ACT; former deputy chairman of Human Rights Commission.

RONALD M. BANNERMAN, LLB, former chairman of Trade Practices Commission.

MARGARET BARCA, writer.

PETER J. BAYNE, LLB, JD, barrister and solicitor Vic. and PNG; reader, faculty of law, ANU.

DANIEL BICKEL, PhD, entomologist, Australian Museum, Sydney.

VERITY BURGMANN, BSc(Econ), PhD, senior lecturer in political science, University of Melbourne.

SHANE CAHILL, MA, DipEd, journalist.

MARGARET CARNEGIE, OAM, author.

KEITH CONNOLLY, film critic (*Herald*).

MARK CONSIDINE, PhD, lecturer in politics, University of Melbourne.

LAURIE COSGROVE, BA, MEnvS, DipEd, lecturer in school of environmental planning, University of Melbourne.

BRIAN COSTAR, BA, PhD, principal lecturer in political studies, Chisholm Institute of Technology.

ROBIN M. CREYKE, LLB, lecturer, faculty of law, ANU.

GEOFFREY D. DAWSON, BE, DipAppSc, FRAS; former director of quality assurance, Department of Air.

RHONDA DREDGE, BSc, journalist.

DAVID EVANS, MSc, DipAppSc, reader and director of environmental studies, University of Melbourne.

IAN FERGUSON, BScF, DF (Yale), professor of forest science and head of forestry section, University of Melbourne.

EVE MUNGWA D. FESL, AM, PhD, director of Koorie Research Centre, Monash University.

DON FOREMAN, MSc, PhD, botanist, Royal Botanic Gardens and National Herbarium, Melbourne.

ROBERT S. GEDDES, LLM, barrister and solicitor ACT; senior lecturer, faculty of law, ANU.

T. T. GIBSON, MA, BSc, PhD, senior lecturer, department of meteorology, University of Melbourne.

ISOBELLE GIDLEY, writer.

JIM GOODSPEED, BSc (Hons), research fellow, CSIRO Division of Water Resources.

BARRIE HUGHES, author.

BRIAN JOHNS, MA, emeritus professor; deputy chairman of Trade Practices Commission.

JAMES JUPP, BA, MSc (Econ), PhD; director of the Centre for Immigration and Multicultural Studies, ANU.

ROSS KING, MArch, DipTCP; senior lecturer and deputy head of school of environmental planning, University of Melbourne.

KAREN KISSANE, journalist.

ALAN KOHLER, journalist.

PATRICIA LAUGHLIN, dance critic and author.

J. BARRY LEAN, BSc, DUP, ASTC, FAusIMM, FAIE, MAIME.

FRANK LUCAS, BA, tutor in political studies, Chisholm Institute of Technology.

STUART MACINTYRE, MA, PhD, FASSA, reader in history, University of Melbourne.

NOEL McLACHLAN, MA, PhD; reader in history, University of Melbourne.

DUGALD McLELLAND, art consultant and writer.

JOHN D. McMILLAN, BA, LLB, barrister and solicitor ACT; senior lecturer, faculty of law, ANU.

KENNETH J. MADDOCK, MA, LLB, PhD, associate professor of anthropology, Macquarie University.

ANDREW MARKUS, BA, PhD; senior lecturer, department of history, Monash University.

JOHN MENADUE, AO, former ambassador, secretary of Department of Prime Minister and Cabinet, and chief executive of Qantas.

WENDY OAKES, BSc, medical journalist.

DESMOND O'CONNOR, BA, LLM, PhD, barrister NSW, and barrister and solicitor ACT; former reader, faculty of law, ANU.

TONY O'GRADY, MA, DipEd, principal lecturer in political studies, Chisholm Institute of Technology.

STEPHEN J. PARKER, LLB, PhD, solicitor England and Wales.

DENNIS C. PEARCE, LLM, PhD, barrister and solicitor SA and ACT; professor, faculty of law, ANU; Commonwealth Ombudsman.

RUDOLF PLEHWE, BA, LLB, PhD, senior lecturer in politics, La Trobe University.

LEONARD RADIC, MA, theatre critic (*Age*) and playwright.

THERESE RADIC, MMus, PhD, music historian, biographer and playwright.

IAN REINEKE, BA, PhD, director of centre for information technology research, University of Wollongong.

ANN RENNIE, BSc, DipEd, Equal Opportunity Officer, Chisholm Institute of Technology.

PAUL RODAN, MA, academic secretary, Chisholm Institute of Technology.

TONY RODD, BSc, botanical consultant, writer and photographer.

SHIRLEY SAMPSON, BA, BEd, PhD, senior lecturer in education, Monash University.

PHILIP SARGEANT, BArch, architect.

MARIAN SAWER, PhD, visiting fellow on secondment to the research school of social sciences, ANU.

STUART SAYERS, journalist and author, formerly literary editor of the *Age*.

VINCENT SERVENTY, AM, BSc, BEd, conservationist, naturalist and author.

CHRIS WALLACE-CRABBE, MA, former professor of Australian studies, Harvard University; poet and critic, director of the Australian Centre, University of Melbourne.

CHRIS L. WATSON, PhD, scientist, CSIRO Division of Soils.

PHILLIPA C. WEEKS, BA, LLM, barrister-at-law NSW, barrister and solicitor ACT; lecturer, faculty of law, ANU.

DOUGLAS J. WHALAN, LLM, PhD, barrister and solicitor NZ and ACT, FAIM; emeritus professor, faculty of law, ANU.

SALLY WHITE, BA (Hons), lecturer in journalism, Royal Melbourne Institute of Technology.

GREG WHITWELL, BEc, PhD; senior lecturer in economic history, University of Melbourne.

ROBYN WILLIAMS, science broadcaster.

ERIC WILLMOT, BSc, MEd, DLitt, LLD, MACE, secretary of ACT Department of Education.

MICHAEL ZIFCAK, MBE, executive chairman, Collins Booksellers.

CONVENTIONS AND ABBREVIATIONS

Cross-referencing has been planned to lead the reader to entries providing further relevant information. The symbols used are > within or instead of entries, meaning *see*; and >> at the end of entries, meaning *see also*. Common or familiar names, where existing, are used for botanical and zoological groupings, although the scientific nomenclature is also given. Population is given in brackets for each town; figures are based on the 1986 census, unless otherwise stated. Common abbreviations used in the text are as follows:

AAP – Australian Associated Press
ABC – Australian Broadcasting Corporation
ACT – Australian Capital Territory
ACTU – Australian Council of Trade Unions
AD – Dame of the Order of Australia; Australian Democrats
AIDS – acquired immune deficiency syndrome
AIF – Australian Imperial Force
AK – Knight of the Order of Australia
ALCOA – Aluminium Company of Australia
ALP – Australian Labor Party
AM – Member of the Order of Australia; amplitude modulation
AMA – Australian Medical Association
AMP – Australian Mutual Provident Society
ANA – Australian National Airways; Australian Natives' Association
ANU – Australian National University
ANZAAS – Australian and New Zealand Association for the Advancement of Science
Anzac – Australian and New Zealand Army Corps
ANZUS – Australia, New Zealand, United States treaty
AO – Officer of the Order of Australia
ASEAN – Association of Southeast Asian Nations
ASIO – Australian Security Intelligence Organization
AWA – Amalgamated Wireless (Australasia) Ltd
AWU – Australian Workers Union
BBC – British Broadcasting Corporation
BHP – Broken Hill Proprietary Limited

c. – circa
C – Celsius
CAE – college of advanced education
CBA – Commonwealth Bank of Australia
cm – centimetre(s)
CMF – Citizen Military Forces
CPI – Consumer Price Index
CRA – CRA Ltd (formerly Conzinc Riotinto Australia)
CSIR – Council for Scientific and Industrial Research (now CSIRO)
CSIRO – Commonwealth Scientific and Industrial Research Organisation
CSR – CSR Ltd (formerly Colonial Sugar Refining Company Limited)
CWA – Country Women's Association
cu.m – cubic metre(s)
DFC – Distinguished Flying Cross
DFM – Distinguished Flying Medal
DFSM – Defence Force Service Medal
DSM – Distinguished Service Medal
F – Fahrenheit
FAO – Food and Agriculture Organisation
FM – frequency modulation
g – gram(s)
GATT – General Agreement on Tariffs and Trade
GC – George Cross
GDP – gross domestic product
GMH – General Motors Holden's Ltd
GMT – Greenwich mean time
GNP – gross national product
Gt – gigatonne(s)
GW – gigawatt(s)

GWh – gigawatt hour
ha – hectare(s)
HMAS – Her (His) Majesty's Australian Ship
HMS – Her (His) Majesty's Ship
IAC – Industries Assistance Commission
IBM – International Business Machines
ICI – Imperial Chemical Industries
ILO – International Labour Organization
IMF – International Monetary Fund
INTELSAT – International Satellite
  Organisation
IVF – in vitro fertilisation
kg – kilogram(s)
kJ – kilojoule(s)
km – kilometre(s)
kmh – kilometres per hour
kW – kilowatt(s)
kWh – kilowatt hour
lat. – latitude
lbs – pounds
LCP – Liberal Country Party
long. – longitude
LTAA – Lawn Tennis Association of Australia
lt – lieutenant
m – metre(s)
MIM – Mount Isa Mines
ML – megalitre(s)
MLA – Member of the Legislative Assembly
MLC – Member of the Legislative Council
mm – millimetre(s)
MP – Member of Parliament
MW – megawatt(s)
n/a – not available
NATO – North Atlantic Treaty Organization
NCP – National Country Party
NDP – Nuclear Disarmament Party
NG – New Guinea
NIDA – National Institute of Dramatic Art
NSW – New South Wales
NT – Northern Territory
NZ – New Zealand
OAM – Medal of the Order of Australia
OECD – Organization for Economic
  Co-operation and Development
OM – Order of Merit
OPEC – Organization of Petroleum Exporting
  Countries
OTC – Overseas Telecommunications
  Commission (Australia)
PAL – phase alternation line
PNG – Papua New Guinea
POW – prisoner of war
Qld – Queensland
QANTAS – Queensland and Northern
  Territory Aerial Services

QC – Queen's Counsel
RAAF – Royal Australian Air Force
RAC – Royal Agricultural College; Royal
  Armoured Corps; Royal Automobile Club
RAF – Royal Air Force (UK)
RAN – Royal Australian Navy
RBA – Reserve Bank of Australia
RSL – Returned Services League of Australia
SA – South Australia
SEATO – Southeast Asia Treaty Organisation
SEC – State Electricity Commission
SPEC – South Pacific Bureau for Economic
  Co-operation
sq. km – square kilometre(s)
STD – Subscriber Trunk Dialling
t – tonne(s)
TAB – Totalizator Agency Board
TAFE – Technical and Further Education
Tas. – Tasmania
TEAS – Tertiary Education Allowance Scheme
Telecom – Australian Telecommunications
  Commission
TNT – Thomas Nationwide Transport Ltd
TWU – Transport Workers' Union
UAP – United Australia Party
UHF – ultra-high frequency
UK – United Kingdom
UN – United Nations
UNCTAD – United Nations Conference on
  Trade and Development
UNDP – United Nations Development
  Program
UNESCO – United Nations Educational,
  Scientific and Cultural Organisation
UNICEF – United Nations International
  Children's Emergency Fund
US – United States
USSR – Union of Soviet Socialist Republics
VFL – Victorian Football League
VLF – very low frequency
Vic. – Victoria
WA – Western Australia
WEL – Women's Electoral Lobby
WHO – World Health Organization
WRAAC – Women's Royal Australian Army
  Corps
WRAAF – Women's Royal Australian Air
  Force
WRANS – Women's Royal Australian Naval
  Service
YMCA – Young Men's Christian Association
YWCA – Young Women's Christian
  Association

EDITOR'S NOTE

The Penguin Australian Encyclopaedia is an encyclopaedia for the 1990s and beyond. It recognises that modern readers want quick access to essential information, guidance in complex areas, and forthright comment. In it we have attempted to meet all the requirements of a good encyclopaedia – breadth of content, scrupulous attention to fact and depth of historical detail – but we also offer informed opinions and cogent analyses that are intended to help readers grasp the fundamentals of a subject or theme under review.

The prime task of any encyclopaedist is selection – both of topics and of scope. Inevitably there is some subjectivity involved, but we have tried to ensure a proper coverage of the broadest possible spectrum of subjects: arts and sports; business and industry; flora and fauna; geography and history; law and politics; science and technology. In compiling the information we have drawn on advice and contributions from authorities in a wide variety of fields. In editing the material we have accepted that brevity and concision are the essence of encyclopaedia entries, but we have been expansive wherever we felt a deeper analysis or comment was necessary.

The Penguin Australian Encyclopaedia is concise, up to date, and easily accessible. We trust that it incorporates specialist and historical information that will be of enduring worth and provide stimulating discussion relevant to our future.

Sarah Dawson
General editor

A

abalone A large marine gastropod of the genus *Haliotis,* which lives pressed to rocks below the tidal zone, the abalone has a curved spiral shell with a row of holes through which water circulates. Three species are commonly found in the cold waters of southern Australia. The large muscular foot of the abalone is particularly prized in oriental cuisine, and Australian abalone fisheries are based on a large export market to Japan and other Asian countries; Tas. produces about half of the total catch and is the site of an experimental abalone hatchery. Abalone is harvested by divers operating from small boats; catches and size limits are regulated by a licensing system administered by the States.

ABC The Australian Broadcasting Corporation was established by federal parliament in 1932 as the Australian Broadcasting Commission, with control of twelve radio stations; it was reconstituted as a corporation in 1983. By 1989, with 400 television channels and 350 radio transmitters, the ABC was the world's largest English-speaking broadcaster; Radio Australia, catering for overseas listeners, has an audience exceeding 50 million people. The ABC manages the State symphony orchestras and sponsors concerts with Australian and international artists; it has also developed as a highly successful marketing entrepreneur, producing television and radio programs, books, records, music and catalogues. The ABC is a statutory corporation financed primarily through a direct grant from the federal government: it is independent as regards programming policy although the managing director (who, like the board, is appointed by the government) can strongly influence the balance, quality and direction of programs. Notable administrators have included > *Sir Charles Moses* 1935–65, who was largely responsible for the establishment of the orchestra network and for services such as independent news, in which he was supported by > *Sir Richard Boyer* (chairman 1945–61). The ABC charter requires it to provide innovative and comprehensive services that contribute to a sense of national identity, inform and entertain, and reflect the cultural diversity of the Australian community. Internal conflict, lack of funds, and at times an apparent lack of direction have periodically marred its progress, however, and an appropriate balance remains to be found between the demands for popular and quality material; it is noteworthy that only a handful of programs, notably 'The Science Show', combine both attributes and these are invariably produced on slender budgets. Recently, a range of organisational and programming improvements appears to have improved the quality of material and arrested audience decline. Funding continues to be a problem, although a major review of resources in the late 1980s may offer hope for the future. >> *broadcasting*

à'Beckett family, prominent in law and the arts. **Sir William** (1806–69), b. England, immigrated to NSW in 1837. Following service as resident judge of Port Phillip, he became first chief justice of the Vic. Supreme Court in 1852 but ill health forced his retirement in 1857. He was also a poet and literary journalist. His brother **Thomas Turner** (1808–92), b. England, trained as a lawyer and was a member of the Vic. parliament 1858–78. Sir William's eldest son, **William Arthur Callender** (1833–1901), b. England, was also a lawyer and member of the Vic. parliament. One of his daughters, **Emma Minnie** (1858–1936), b. England, was a talented artist; she married Arthur Merric Boyd and was thus matriarch of the talented > *Boyd family*. **Sir Thomas** (1836–1919), b. England, son of Thomas Turner, was a leading equity lawyer; he was appointed to the Vic. Supreme Court in 1886, retiring two years before his death.

Abeles, Sir (Emil Herbert) Peter

(1924–), business entrepreneur, b. Austria. One of Australia's most successful businessmen, Abeles in 1950 founded Alltrans, a small transport company which merged with the much larger Thomas Nationwide Transport Ltd (TNT) in 1967. In 1979 Abeles acquired aviation interests when, jointly with Rupert Murdoch, he acquired Ansett Transport Industries Ltd; today the TNT group is one of the world's largest integrated transport companies. A director of the Reserve Bank since 1984, Abeles is also chairman of the Australian Opera Foundation.

Aboriginal culture and society In 1988,

the bicentenary of European settlement of Australia, the nation's Aboriginal communities decided to dispense with the terms 'Aborigine' and 'Aborigines' and define themselves in names from their own languages. Those now in common usage are Koorie (meaning 'our people'), which is widely used in the eastern and southern States; Yolngu (in the NT); Anangu (in central Australia); Nyunga (in WA); and Nungga (SA). While this preference is acknowledged, the more conventional expressions Aborigine(s) (for the noun) and Aboriginal (for the adjective) are used throughout this encyclopaedia.

Origins Aborigines believe that the life of their people began in Australia. Certainly their oral history points to an antiquity stretching back beyond the Pleistocene period, which began about two million years ago. European scientists support a claim to antiquity by their own methods, which at this stage place Aboriginal occupancy of the continent at 30 000–40 000 years. The most ancient human skeletal relic is a female skull found at Lake Mungo in southwestern NSW, which was carbon-dated to that period.

Based on the available archaeological evidence, many theories have been presented concerning both Aboriginal immigration to the Australian continent from other parts of the world and the people's racial origins. It is generally held by European anthropologists that the Aborigines derive from Southeast Asia, with successive waves of migration from different parts of that region. There is, however, as yet no irrefutable evidence to substantiate these claims.

Culture and beliefs The religion of the Aboriginal people is integrally bound up with the land. The land is the 'mother' from whom all life springs and to whose source the spirit returns at physical death, for rebirth. Aborigines do not own the land, but rather the land owns them: their religous obligations entail custodianship, so that while utilising the land they must ensure that it is protected from over-exploitation.

In Aboriginal mythology, ancestral beings – religious deities and agents of the mother earth – moved across the land creating places, people, flora and fauna. Some of the places at which they halted are held sacred to either men or women, or to both; women have religious autonomy in Aboriginal society. The religious ceremonies and sacred places of both men and women relate to the paths of the ancestral beings and through them to the mother earth.

Kinship is a core element in Aboriginal society – it is the pivot around which the sacred and secular lives of clan members revolve. The place at which a person is born determines that person's position within a clan group. From this place, the person derives a secret name restricted to close family knowledge and use because of its association with the sacred.

Economy and lifestyles Before European settlement of Australia, Aboriginal communities utilised the land as hunter-gatherers. The Aboriginal calendar was seasonal and cyclical: food was harvested from nature as the seasons permitted; harvesting and fire-stick farming were controlled to promote growth and avoid the over-exploitation of food resources. Such harvesting required static settlement for short periods only: eel traps were set and stone houses built in the western parts of Vic., for example, but the dwellings were occupied only during the months in which the eels were allowed to be harvested. Most housing was built for more temporary occupancy – the dwellings were therefore able to be erected quickly from local resources such as bark and brush, and were not transported. As communities often moved in response to harvesting patterns, material possessions were few and those that were needed could be obtained from local materials – animal, vegetable and mineral – as required.

Despite the lack of fences and permanent housing, there were definite boundaries within which Aboriginal communities moved and lived. When moving into another's territory, permission to enter was obtained by such means as the sending of a message stick. Land boundaries were determined by the ancestral beings and, being sacred, the land within was of worth only to the prescribed group. It was therefore not necessary for Aboriginal peoples to develop warlike skills or equipment with which to take or defend land.

Aboriginal groups in different parts of the continent had diverse lifestyles, which evolved in adaptation to the needs of different regions – from the tropical north to the inland deserts or the snow-capped mountains of the south. Their cultures and languages reflect these differences. Little clothing was generally worn in hot areas, but thick possum-skin cloaks were worn in cold, wet climates. Hunting implements were designed also to meet environmental conditions. Implements fashioned for long flight, such as woomeras and boomerangs, were used on the plains and in the open; killer sticks and specialised spears were employed in densely foliaged parts of the terrain. Canoes made from the bark of trees were fashioned by those who lived near waterways; here also, nets and spears specially designed for catching fish were an essential part of a hunter's kit.

In areas of marginal rainfall, and during periods of drought when large game was scarce, the economy of a community was dependent almost entirely upon the women's digging stick, which was (and still is) used for obtaining the staple foods of the area such as yams and honey ants. Bags made from hair, and wooden dishes (coolamons), were also important women's utensils for carrying or crushing vegetable foods, fruits and seeds.

The trade routes which encircled Australia enabled skills and small items, as well as songs and history, to be passed to distant parts of the continent.

Education The education of Aboriginal children proceeded as they grew up and took part in the life of their community. Stages of knowledge were tested and attested to by specific ceremonies throughout the various stages of their lives. The ultimate acknowledgment of their graduation to adulthood and full knowledge was a very formal, and sometimes painful, initiation ceremony. During this ceremony initiates were taught about the sacred and secret matters which until then had been the province of initiated adults. Such knowledge and ceremonies were gender-specific.

History was passed on to all members of a community via song cycles, which incorporated new events as they occurred. Their content ranges from creation myths to relatively simple cautionary tales, or narratives which describe such events as the melting of the ice and the rising of the seas at the end of the last ice age. Inheritance of land, and the right to sing certain songs, paint particular paintings and dance specific dances are passed on to both male and female children within their respective clan groups. For some items inheritance is patrilineal, for others matrilineal.

Particularly where marriage is exogamous, clan members are at least bilingual, but most are multilingual. At the time of European settlement, it is estimated that there were 230 distinct Aboriginal languages with more than 500 dialects being spoken: today, half of them are extinct and many more are disappearing.

European contact Before European settlement, the Aboriginal population is estimated to have been at least 300 000; between 1788 and the 1930s it was reduced by more than two-thirds, to about 67 000. Despite their linguistic and cultural diversity and because of their attitude to land, Aborigines lived in comparative harmony for thousands of years. They were, therefore, both physically and psychologically unprepared for the advent of the British on their territories in 1788. Besides bringing with them hidden dangers such as venereal disease, influenza, smallpox and other European diseases against which the Aboriginal community had little immunity, the British carried with them attitudes, customs and beliefs which – along with their weapons – were instrumental in bringing about the physical and cultural extermination of many Aboriginal groups.

Forcible take-overs of land, and the rape of Aboriginal women and children, were major causes of early conflict. Having only hunting spears with which to defend themselves, Aborigines were far outmatched by the militarised and well-armed British; poisoned food left for Aboriginal families caused further deaths. Those who did survive had to battle against starvation as they were increasingly denied access to their hunting grounds; they were spiritually impoverished by being alienated from lands of sacred and ceremonial significance.

The Christian missionary activity which attended British expansion across the continent was largely unsuccessful by its own standards. In addition, in attempting to impose 'order' on a society which they did not understand the missions undermined the cultural and linguistic foundations of many Aboriginal groups. With the exception of a few humanitarian individuals and the early Lutherans, churches and the state generally co-operated to divide and segregate Aboriginal communities. Successive pieces of legislation, namely the Protection Acts which began to be introduced from the 1860s and were in force in all States by 1911, were ostensibly to provide physical protection and social justice for Aborigines. In practice they were largely restrictive and became a means of forcing Aborigines to provide free or cheap labour. Part-Aboriginal children were at particular risk and were commonly removed from their mothers to serve as domestic or apprenticed workers. The Assimilation Act of 1963 did little to change the order of things. A referendum in 1967 voted to recognise Aborigines as citizens, but their right to vote under the same conditions as other Australians was not enacted until 1984.

Postwar immigration schemes, which allowed many more people from non-English-speaking backgrounds to enter Australia, and the 1960s Black Power movement in the US were instrumental in providing Aborigines with the impetus to work towards cultural revival. Political activity in support of award wages and for Aboriginal rights over their traditional lands, which had commenced in the 1930s, grew in intensity during the 1960s and 1970s.

The 1980s and beyond Many Aborigines still live in third-world conditions that often resemble refugee camps, underlining their difficulty in entering white society. Because of the loss of access to their lands, fundamental to their material well-being, the life expectancy of Aborigines is the lowest in Australia (averaging 55 years by the 1980s, compared with 73 and 79 for white males and females respectively); infant mortality, unemployment and school attrition rates are, on the other hand, the highest in the country. Alcoholism in some areas is a further reflection of the continuing trauma of transition.

While some Aborigines still live in remote areas and a few are still able to practise earlier norms, the majority live in country towns or cities. Although their lifestyles vary according to the situation in which they find themselves, kinship – the central core of Aboriginal culture – still dominates; their relationship with the land is also still very strong, even among those who live in large cities.

Departments of Aboriginal affairs have been established in most States, but all are run by non-Aborigines. At the national level, moves to abolish the federal department in favour of a policy-making body elected by Aborigines met with strong opposition from administrative officials and the conservative Opposition parties in parliament in 1988.

The future of Aborigines in the 1990s and beyond will depend, as it has in the past, very much upon Aboriginal initiative and the support of a large number of non-Aborigines. The proposed establishment of an Aboriginal and Torres Strait Islander Commission, recently announced by the Hawke government, may be the first step towards the regaining of the self-determination which the Aboriginal community lost 200 years ago. >> *archaeology*; *art, Aboriginal*; *education*; *food plants, native*; *health and health services*; *land rights, Aboriginal*; *missions and reserves*; *racial conflict*

acacias > *wattle*

academies, national Australia has four national academies, which act as independent advisers to government and publish widely in their fields as well as organising conferences. All are based in Canberra and their members, known as Fellows, are recognised as having the highest distinction in scholarship. The Australian Academy of Science, established 1954, aims to promote science, maintain high standards of research and practice, and alert the community to scientific matters of public concern. The Australian Academy of the Humanities, established 1969, promotes and encourages scholarship in the humanities, with particular emphasis on the study of Australian culture and of languages in the Pacific region. The Academy of Social Sciences, founded 1971, promotes teaching and research in all branches of the social sciences in Australia; major topics of research have included women in Australia, and Aborigines in Australian society. The Academy of Technological Sciences (ATS), incorporated 1975, promotes the practical application of knowledge in such fields as physical and engineering sciences, and applied biological sciences.

ACTU Formed in 1927, the Australian Council of Trade Unions is the main organisational body of the trade-union movement in Australia; in 1987, more than 90% of all unions were affiliated with it. Over the years the ACTU has won acceptance as the representative of the Australian worker, and its original blue-collar image has been broadened to include white-collar and professional unions. Its most notable president was Albert Monk

(1900–75), who held the position 1949–69 and made the ACTU a body to be reckoned with by both government and employers; during his term of office the ACTU became the central body for the settling of industrial disputes. Another notable president was Bob Hawke, who streamlined the organisation, developed associated retailing and travel businesses, and strengthened links with overseas labour institutions such as the International Labour Organisation (ILO) and the International Confederation of Free Trade Unions. >> *trade unions*

Adaminaby NSW (pop. 283) A former gold-mining town in the Snowy Mountains, Adaminaby now serves a grazing and mixed-farming district and is a base for tourists, particularly cross-country skiers. It was important as a centre for workers on the Snowy Mountains hydro-electric scheme, which partially flooded the town in 1957. The original town is 9km away from the present one.

Adams, A.H. (Arthur Henry) (1872–1936), author and journalist, b. NZ. Adams arrived in Australia in 1898. Although his work is little read today, he criticised the current Australian scene with cultivated skill and acute observation. His political farce, *Mrs Pretty and the Premier*, was performed in London in 1916; his poems appeared in *Collected Verse* (1913) and of his wide range of fiction the novel *Galahad Jones* (1909) is among the best.

Adams, George (1839–1904), businessman, b. England. Adams arrived in Australia in 1855, and was a sheephand and a butcher before leasing O'Brien's (later Tattersall's) Hotel, Sydney, in 1878. He organised sweepstakes originally for hotel patrons and subsequently for the general public. Anti-gambling legislation forced him to move to Brisbane in 1893, and then to Hobart in 1895. After his death the business was carried on by his trustees, and now operates both in Hobart and in Melbourne. >> *gambling*

Adams, Phillip Andrew (1939–   ), columnist and film producer, b. Maryborough, Vic. Adams was a major force behind the revival of the Australian film industry in the 1970s, as both adviser to the government and producer of films such as *Don's Party* (1976) and *The Getting of Wisdom* (1977). He is also an irreverent social commentator through his regular columns

in the *Australian* and the *Bulletin*, and a co-founder of Monahan Dayman Adams, a major Australian advertising agency. He was appointed chairman of the Australian Film Commission in 1983.

Adelaide SA State capital of SA and Australia's fifth-largest city, Adelaide is regarded by many as the best planned capital in Australia and is characterised by spacious parks and gracious colonial architecture. Built on an alluvial plain, Adelaide lies between the Mt Lofty Ranges in the east and the sand-dunes of Cape St Vincent in the west, and is bisected by the Torrens River. The climate is temperate, with temperatures ranging from 7°C to 30°C; the rainfall is poor to moderate, varying from 450mm to 650mm annually and falling mainly between May and September. Because of low humidity and strong winds, Adelaide's outer suburbs are periodically at risk from bushfires.

Adelaide was named after Queen Adelaide, consort of King William IV of Great Britain. Little is known of the area's original Aboriginal population, as they were killed or driven away in the early years of British settlement. Based on the theories of E.G. Wakefield, the settlement had unpromising beginnings despite the planning abilities of its surveyor, Colonel > *William Light*. The discovery of copper, lead and silver in the 1840s boosted SA and thus Adelaide. After the Vic. gold rushes, both city and colony thrived for a time as the granary of Australia, but economic stagnation followed. At the close of World War 2, large-scale immigration led to further agricultural expansion and a growth in secondary industry – mainly the manufacture of motor vehicles and household durable goods in Adelaide and shipbuilding at Whyalla. This expansion boosted the city, but recession followed and by the 1980s Adelaide was again declining economically.

At the census of 1986 the Adelaide Statistical Division had a population of 977 721, which showed a growth rate of 4.92% over the five years between censuses, about 27% of residents being overseas-born. From the 1960s, new suburbs grew out to the northwest and southwest of Adelaide, but the city has generally preferred to concentrate on urban consolidation rather than to develop extensive dormitory suburbs with their attendant transport and service problems.

Steel-processing and oil-refining are the city's large-scale secondary industries, along with the smaller-scale production of consumer goods; the newer factories have been established in industrial estates away from the city centre. Tourism, boosted by the biennial Festival of Arts and the Australian International Grand Prix, together with wine-growing in the Barossa Valley, is also of economic importance. Despite its comparative lack of heavy industry, Adelaide operates under stringent environmental legislation aimed at preventing pollution; it is, however, largely dependent on the highly polluted Murray River for water, and this scarce resource seems likely to limit the future growth of the city, even if its economic problems are overcome.

Adelaide Festival of Arts > *festivals*

administrative law Administrative law defines the methods by which the decisions of government agencies may be contested. There are three principal avenues for such challenges: judicial review by the State Supreme Court, the Federal Court or the High Court; administrative review by a tribunal; or complaint to the > *ombudsman*. Another important right embodied in administrative law is that of access to government documents (> *freedom of information*).

Judicial review The right to judicial review of a government decision is enshrined in both federal legislation and common law. The Commonwealth Administrative Decisions (Judicial Review) Act 1977 defines the grounds upon which the Federal Court determines whether a government decision was lawfully made, and gives the affected person the right to be given reasons for the decision. This process has been used successfully in a number of appeals by immigrants against deportation orders. Complaints may also be made by means of judicial review under State and Territory common law; the main difference between the two forms of review is procedural, common-law processes being more technical.

Review by tribunal This form of review is increasingly common and there are now many administrative tribunals in Australia, covering such diverse fields as urban planning, the environment, discrimination, social security, and veterans affairs. The process is usually less formal than that of the courts, and the tribunal's powers are usually wider (including the authority to substitute their own decisions for those of the agency under challenge). Review before tribunals is also generally cheaper,

easier to pursue, and quicker than judicial review.

An Administrative Appeals Tribunal (AAT) exists in Vic. and under Commonwealth legislation. At the federal level the AAT has jurisdiction under nearly 300 Acts, ordinances and regulations; the Vic. body has jurisdiction over decisions made by administrators who have a duty to apply the rules of natural justice.

Admiral's Cup > *sailing and yachting*

advertising industry Advertising is the display-window of the free-enterprise system. In Australia, with its mainly advertising-based media and widespread commercialism, the industry is large and lively, with a total annual expenditure of over $5 billion.

Advertisements were carried in the earliest colonial newspapers and by the late 19th century were the business of agents who both sold advertising space and designed the notices. Radio and later television provided a great boost to the industry and commercially sponsored stations soon proliferated. Today there are more than 500 advertising agencies in Australia, all operating on a commission basis by extracting a percentage of their 'billings' (or turnover) from both clients and media. The largest agency is George Patterson, which in 1988 had billings of $540 million, or 10% of the Australian total. Like the rest of the large agencies in Australia, Patterson is foreign-owned. Other large agencies are Clemenger BBDO, Ogilvy and Mather, and Mojo-MDA; the last was once the largest Australian-owned agency and the first to become a public company, but was taken over by the US Chiat/Day group in 1989. Some smaller agencies which have made a name for themselves are the Campaign Palace (part-owned by George Patterson), Mattingly (once part of Mojo-MDA, but now controlled by a US/French/Japanese consortium), and John Singleton Advertising.

As all the large agencies are owned or controlled by overseas (mainly US) agencies, the advertisements seen by consumers – particularly on television – are of US extraction. Although the Australian Broadcasting Tribunal prohibits the use of television commercials not made in Australia or filmed by Australian crews, the prohibition is only cosmetic and an Australian Coca-Cola commercial, for example, is usually just a locally made copy of a US original. Mojo and John Singleton pioneered a blatantly nationalistic form of advertising in the 1970s which, while often jingoistic, was a relatively successful antidote to this practice.

Multinational companies such as Coca-Cola, Procter and Gamble, and Colgate-Palmolive are Australia's largest advertisers. The major Australian-owned advertiser is the retailer Coles-Myer, which spent an estimated $140 million on promotion in 1988; other large investors in advertising are retailers such as David Jones, the motor-vehicle industry, airlines, government agencies such as Telecom, and the federal and State governments. About half of all outlay on advertising is spent in the print media, a further one-third going to television and the remainder to radio and other outlets. A growing percentage of advertising expenditure is directed to direct ('junk') mail, which has been seen as particularly cost-effective in an era of falling newspaper circulation and rising television advertising costs.

As advertising is so omnipresent in our lives, it attracts a great deal of comment. Arguments in its favour claim that it creates demand for new products and as a result creates jobs and, provides information; its opponents claim that it is parasitic and wasteful, enticing consumers to switch products rather than creating demands for new ones, and helps large firms gain a monopoly hold on the market. Advertising is also seen as a powerful force in inhibiting its outlets, such as newspapers, which was clearly illustrated in the 1980s when the NSW Wran government withdrew all State government advertising from the Fairfax press after a series of critical articles. In addition, by constantly reaching for the largest market, advertising has had the effect of lowering general standards, particularly in television and radio.

Regulation of the industry There are few controls over the number and timing of advertisements played on the Australian airwaves. There are, however, some legislative restrictions on all forms of advertising to ensure that it is not false, misleading or unduly offensive; in addition, all governments have recently introduced restrictions on the advertising of tobacco and, to a lesser extent, alcohol. The advertising industry also has its own code of standards (established in 1967), which is overseen by the Advertising Standards Council.

aerial medical services Australia has one of the most comprehensive and best organised systems of aerial medical services in the world. The Royal Flying Doctor Service – founded by Presbyterian missionary > *John Flynn* in the 1920s – is a voluntary organisation financed by government grants, contributions and subscriptions; in 1987, the federal government contributed $6.5 million to its operational costs. Beginning operations in 1927, its first base was at Cloncurry in outback Qld, using a DH50 plane provided by Qld and NT Aerial Services. Today, it operates aerial ambulances and mobile clinics in all States except Vic., utilising an elaborate radio and landline network linking remote outposts with base hospitals and planes. This network also provides a general communication service and facilities for the School of the Air. Other services include the Aerial Medical Service operated by the NT and the Flying Surgeon Service operated by the Qld government. In addition, all States operate aerial paramedical services utilising planes and helicopters.

Afghans Some 2000 Muslim camel-drivers worked throughout inland Australia between 1860 and the 1920s. Although they were commonly called Afghans or Ghans, many also in fact came from the northwest of the Indian subcontinent (now Pakistan) and the Middle East. Their experience in desert terrain made them invaluable to transport in outback Qld, NSW, SA and WA; their pre-eminence engendered much rivalry from white bullock drivers, however, who tried to have them banned in Qld. The Afghans' desert skills were imparted to Australian troops from the end of the 19th century and were invaluable in the Middle East during World War 1.

agriculture Despite the problems of long-distance transport to unreliable markets, Australia is a major exporter of wool, wheat, meat, sugar, dairy products, barley, rice and cotton. Agriculture generates 35–40% of Australia's export earnings and is thus vital to the country's economy. Because much of the continent is not well suited to European styles of agriculture, however, just over half the area in agricultural or pastoral use requires treatment for land degradation if its productivity is to be maintained. This dilemma is central to the problems facing Australian agriculture today – and, in a sense, has been so since European settlement. Droughts and floods, which both reduce productivity and make soils vulnerable to erosion, are normal manifestations of Australia's climatic cycle: attempts to make the land amenable to European-style farming, while successful at first, have in the longer term resulted in erosion (caused by the clearing of trees and ground vegetation), dry-land salinity and, in irrigation areas, increasing wetlands salinity.

Historical development From the time of European settlement in 1788, it took more than a century for NSW to become self-supporting in basic foodstuffs. The early settlers had to contend with heavily wooded country, unsuitable crops, and very variable soil quality. Once the Blue Mountains were crossed and pastoralism established, wool became the main export and has remained so ever since except for the relatively brief primacy of gold 1850–70. NSW imported farm-grown foods from Tas. and later SA and Vic. until the end of the 19th century, although the advent of railways in the 1860s allowed increasing quantities of agricultural products to be transported from the inland to the coast.

Problems of transport and soil quality were less severe in Tas. and Vic. than in NSW, but the clearing of forests was necessary before grain crops and dairy products could be produced. Tas. rapidly became self-sufficient in foodstuffs, but exports were limited until the advent of refrigerated ships. Vic. was compelled to import wheat until the 1870s, although it rapidly became Australia's main wheat producer when railways reached its wheatlands in the 1880s. Also in the 1880s, dairy products began to be exported in refrigerated ships. In SA, crop farming grew rapidly – partly because the system of land settlement adopted there prevented the growth of a squattocracy – and it was Australia's leading wheat producer from the 1850s to the 1870s; barley and wine began to be produced there in the 1890s. Qld's production of grain crops was limited to its southern regions by climate: beef was exported from the 1860s, first in cans but then frozen from the 1890s; by 1900, sugar accounted for almost 25% of the area under crop. In WA, agriculture was limited by the size of the local market until the discovery of gold at Coolgardie in 1892 and the consequent construction of railways. In all six colonies, the major factors in agricultural growth were the availability of British markets and three major inventions: the > *stripper harvester* (1843), which enabled one person to harvest a grain crop; the > *stump-jump plough* (1876), which made possible the ploughing of partly cleared paddocks; and the use from the 1890s of superphosphate to improve soil quickly.

Since Federation in 1901, Australian agriculture has steadily improved in yield per hectare

but markets have fluctuated – farming was and still is a precarious way of earning a living. Research by universities (the first chair of agriculture was established at the University of Sydney in 1910), by the > *Waite Agricultural Research Institute* in SA (from 1925) and by the > *CSIRO* (from its establishment as the Council for Scientific and Industrial Research in 1926) led to selective breeding and produced crops and livestock more suited to Australian conditions. Irrigation increased from 1914, especially along the Murray River; and pasture improvement was much more widely used by graziers, reaching 28.6 million ha in the 1970s before declining again to 27.1 million in the 1980s. Pest control also was achieved to some extent.

Despite these advances the Australian yield per hectare for many crops is still only half of that in Europe. Government intervention, especially after Federation, after both world wars, in the 1970s and again in the 1980s has aimed to encourage closer settlement and also to rationalise the industry, but subsidies and debt-deferment schemes have almost always been necessary. Poor prices in the 1920s, during the depression of the 1930s and again in the late 1970s and 1980s have led many farmers to increasing debt, worsened by the need to acquire expensive agricultural machinery in order to compete at all in the world market. The place of agriculture in the Australian economy has in fact been declining since World War 2: by the 1980s it accounted for less than 5% of gross domestic product (compared with a figure of nearly 30% in 1950–1), and furnished little more than one-third of the nation's export income (a huge drop from its 92% contribution 30 years earlier). Since Britain's entry into the EEC, Europe's protectionist policies have made agricultural markets even more uncertain and more recently import restrictions have been applied by the US and Japan as well. Rural exports to Japan, the Middle East, the US, the USSR, China and Southeast Asia, however, have increased over the past two decades.

Since agriculture in Australia relies heavily on government support and government policies to survive, rural property owners have always been involved in politics. The Country Party (now the > *National Party*) was formed in 1920 to press for farmers' interests, but today is seen by many farmers as no longer adequate for that purpose. Other organisations, especially the National Farmers' Federation, now also

press for policies favourable to agriculturalists.
>> *soils and soil conservation*

AIDS An acronym for acquired immune deficiency syndrome, this is the popular name for a disease that is known as the human immunodeficiency virus (HIV). Although apparently originating in Africa and first identified in the US homosexual community, it has rapidly become the cause of worldwide concern as a major epidemic of the 20th century; it is transmitted by infected seminal secretions and by HIV-infected blood. In Australia the first death from AIDS occurred in 1983. By 1989, 1239 cases had been diagnosed, of which 591 had died: the majority of reported cases were among homosexual/bisexual men; others involved blood-transfusion recipients, heterosexuals, haemophiliacs and intravenous drug-users. The disease has a gestation period of many years; to date it is invariably fatal, and a vaccine is thought to be at least ten years away. Since 1984, the federal and State governments have spent about $50 million on the provision of preventive measures and research, and there are also a number of government-sponsored task forces and committees to advise on social and educational matters related to the disease. >> *medical research*

AIF > *defence*; *World War 1*; *World War 2*

aircraft production > *aviation*

airforce, Australian > *defence forces*

airlines > *aviation*

Albany WA (pop. 16316) The town of Albany is the port and regional centre for the State's southwest, handling the wool, cereal crops, beef, fruit and vegetables produced locally. Bulk grain has been the main export since the shipping of sheep and wool was centralised in Fremantle. The site of the earliest white settlement in the State, in 1826, Albany was originally named Frederickstown after the Duke of York and Albany, brother of King George IV.

albatrosses > *sea-birds*

Albury–Wodonga NSW/Vic. (pop. 37164) The twin cities of Albury (NSW) and Wodonga (Vic.) straddle the Murray River some 305km north of Melbourne. They were together designated a 'regional urban growth centre' in 1974, as part of a decentralisation program by the NSW and Vic. governments; their development, which has been rapid since that time, is co-ordinated by the Albury–Wodonga Development Corporation, established by the federal and two State governments. Albury–Wodonga lies near the place where Hume and Hovell crossed the Murray in 1824. Wodonga was once a Vic. customs post and Albury began as a small settlement around a police post at the river crossing. Progress was rapid after 1855, when the steamer *Albury* opened up the river traffic; rail links with Melbourne and Sydney were completed in 1883. Albury was proclaimed a city in 1946, and Wodonga in 1973. The cities are an important regional centre for a successful rural district based on dairying and pastoralism as well as a range of agricultural industries. Manufacturing and service industries have developed apace since the 1970s, and further urban expansion is planned to the southeast and northeast.

algae Simple plants which are comparable in structure to fungi but are able to photosynthesise, algae evolved in the sea and still account for the bulk of all plant life in the oceans; they are also well represented in freshwater and dryland habitats. The larger marine forms, generally brown or red, are the common seaweeds of coastal areas.

Brown algae, *Phaeophyta*, are diverse in form and include many seaweeds of Australia's shoreline. Familiar species include the aptly named Neptune's necklace, *Hormosira*, whose beads are in fact sacs bearing eggs or sperm. The giant kelp masses common to the intertidal regions of Australia's temperate shores also belong to the brown-algae group. Red algae, *Rhodophyta*, include many common seaweeds of the subtidal zone: Australia's southern coastline is home to more than half of the world's known species, many of which are endemic to the region. Other major algae groups include diatoms, *Bacillariophyta*, which are common in both marine and freshwater environments.

Algae, and seaweeds in particular, have a number of economic uses, from food to fertilisers. Red and brown seaweeds are important in several Asian cuisines and yield the gelling agents agar, alginates and carrageenin. In recent years attention has also been drawn to the potential use of algae in biotechnology, as they produce useful proteins, carbohydrates and lipids under large-scale artificial culture. Algae, on the other hand, can contaminate water and waterways: a growing problem in many parts of Australia is eutrophication, an excess of nutrients in the surrounding water – often due to run-off from settlements, agriculture and industry – which causes excessive growth of algae and results in choked waterways and the death of other aquatic life through oxygen depletion. Some blue-green algae are poisonous to stock and their presence in farm dams in many rural areas is a cause of serious concern. >> *seagrasses*

Alice Springs

Alice Springs NT (pop. 22 759) 'The Alice' is the chief town of central Australia and lies 1535km south of Darwin; in recent years – largely in response to greatly increased tourism – it has grown from a dusty outpost into a lively and relatively sophisticated centre. The town is traversed by the Todd River (dry except after floods), which was named by surveyor William Mills in 1871. The town itself was named Stuart until 1933, the name Alice Springs – honouring the wife of Sir Charles Todd, then SA postmaster-general – being reserved until that time for the nearby waterholes. The first settlement was established for a repeater station serving the Overland Telegraph line; a mission was founded in 1916, but the white population still numbered fewer than 50 until in 1929 the advent of a narrow-gauge railway from SA made the town a rail centre. The main local primary industry is beef production, although a limited expanse of irrigated land supports small-scale dairying and fruit-growing. Alice Springs was still a modest country town until the early 1970s, but since then has undergone dramatic development to cater for the area's flourishing tourist trade and now boasts hotels and motels, a casino and art galleries. It has retained nevertheless the long-standing tradition of an annual 'Henley-on-Todd' regatta, in which the boats are carried or wheeled on the dry river bed.

Alligator rivers NT In the northwest of the NT are the three rivers known as East, South and West Alligator – a misnomer, since the reptiles that infest their mangrove-swamp estuaries are crocodiles. All three run northwards to Van Diemen Gulf; the South and East rivers rise in the uplands of Arnhem Land and each flows for about 160km, but the West river is a shorter, coastal stream (80km). The courses of the South and West rivers run through Kakadu National Park and the region is outstanding for its Aboriginal rock art.

ALP The Australian Labor Party, Australia's oldest political party, emanated from the trade-union movement in the late 19th century, when strikes failed to secure better working conditions and political action was deemed necessary. Labour leagues were formed in NSW in 1891, pledged to electoral reforms, improved working conditions, government aid to education and agriculture, and a 'white Australia'. In that year more than 36 candidates were elected and labour held the balance of power in NSW, a situation repeated soon after in Vic., SA and Qld.

There were brief federal Labor governments in 1904 and 1908, but the party's first major period in power was 1910–13 under > *Andrew Fisher*. Growing more rigid and doctrinaire, this government was narrowly defeated in 1913 but resoundingly returned in 1914 owing in part to Fisher's immediate commitment to World War 1. The party became disillusioned by the progress of the war, however, and lost faith in Fisher's successor, > *W.M. Hughes*, over his stand on conscription. The resulting party split led to the virtual eclipse of the ALP as a parliamentary force for some years: between the world wars, Labor held office only once – in 1929–32 under > *James Scullin*, whose ineffective administration was defeated by a combination of economic depression, the resignation of Joe Lyons, and a split with the NSW ALP engineered by premier Jack Lang.

In October 1941, Labor won government of an Australia at war and the party's greatest period began. The strong wartime leadership of > *John Curtin* was followed in 1945 by that of > *Ben Chifley* who, in the immediate postwar years, launched far-reaching reforms in the fields of unemployment relief, immigration, medical benefits and education. Opinion began to turn against Chifley in 1948, however, following the government's attempt to nationalise civil aviation and banking, and with resentment growing at continued controls and high taxation. Labor was defeated in 1949 and did not hold federal office again until 1972. A major cause of this long period out of office was a disastrous split within the party in the 1950s (chiefly over communism) and the formation in 1961 of a breakaway right-wing party, the > *DLP*, which henceforth directed its preferences away from Labor. Although the

ALP under > *Arthur Calwell* came within one seat of winning the 1961 election, by 1969 – for the first time since 1910 – there was no Labor government in office anywhere in Australia.

A resurgence of the ALP began under the leadership of > *Gough Whitlam* from 1969 (in which year it won a respectable minority of 59 seats in the federal parliament). After electoral victories in SA in 1970 and WA in 1971, the ALP was returned to federal power in December 1972 with a majority of nine seats. The Whitlam government immediately completed the withdrawal of Australian troops from Vietnam, ended conscription and recognised communist China; it also undertook sweeping domestic reforms, many of which were much needed after the complacent final years of the Liberal administration. The Whitlam government was dismissed in controversial circumstances in November 1975 (> *constitutional crisis 1975*).

A more pragmatic Labor government under > *Bob Hawke* was elected in 1983. It has retained office since, owing principally to its adoption of the political middle ground and ineffective opposition from a disoriented Liberal Party lacking strong leadership. While this government's stringent economic policies and a resulting drop in living standards have created widespread disenchantment, in 1990 all States but NSW had Labor governments and the ALP won its fourth consecutive federal election. >> *political parties*; *trade unions*

aluminium Aluminium, often called the 'wonder metal' of the 20th century, was not producible in commercial quantities before the development of the Hall-Heroult electrolytic reduction process in 1896. To make aluminium, alumina (aluminium oxide) is first extracted from bauxite, after which it is sent to a smelter to be refined into aluminium. The process is a complex one, necessitating extremely high temperatures and large amounts of electrical power, some 16 000–17 000kWh being required to produce one tonne of aluminium. Australia is the world's largest producer of both bauxite and alumina and – owing mainly to its relatively cheap electrical power – is now also a major supplier of the finished product, aluminium.

In terms of the traditional mining industry, bauxite is a newcomer, the first commercial mine being brought into production by Alcoa in 1963 in the Darling Range near Perth, with alumina being refined at Kwinana; additional mines and refineries were later opened in the area, at Pinjarra and Wagerup. Australia's highest-grade bauxite is found in northern Australia, at Weipa in Qld (developed by Comalco Ltd) and Gove in the NT (developed by Nabalco Ltd). Bauxite from Weipa is transported to Gladstone, Qld, now one of the world's largest alumina-processing centres, which supplies Australian aluminium producers such as Alcan's Kurri Kurri smelter (NSW) and Comalco's Boyne Island smelter (Qld) as well as the export market. Bauxite from Gove is either exported directly or refined into alumina on site. Other Australian aluminium smelters are at Port Henry and Portland in Vic., Tomago in NSW and Bell Bay in Tas., which was opened in 1955 and was Australia's first.

The future for the industry seems assured given Australia's immense resources of bauxite and cheap power, but some concern has been expressed about the environmental impact of mining and smelting, the low prices charged to producers for electricity by State governments, and the close-knit structure of the few multinational companies that control the industry worldwide.

American bases > *US bases in Australia*

America's Cup > *sailing and yachting*

amphipods An order of shrimp-like crustaceans which have a distinct head, stalkless eyes, and a segmented body without a carapace, amphipods include both aquatic and terrestrial forms. The front legs are much shorter than those in the rear, and jumping is achieved by a sudden straightening of the curved body. A familiar group is the sandhoppers, common beach scavengers of the Australian genera *Orchestia* and *Talorchestia*. Marine species include *Caprella*, a predator of sea anemones, and the wood-boring *Chelura* which is a pest of wharf timbers. Australian freshwater genera include the *Neoniphargus*, some species of which (notably the well-shrimp) have adapted to living in underground water and are blind. The landhopper, *Talitrus*, is a terrestrial form, which lives among the leaf-litter of forests and is also common in damp gardens. > *Krill* are close relatives of amphipods.

ANARE > *Antarctic Territory*

Andamooka SA (pop. 402) A lonely opal-mining centre west of Lake Torrens, 610km northwest of Adelaide, Andamooka is noted particularly for the fact that many of its residents live in dugouts to protect themselves from the harsh desert heat.

Anderson, Jessica Margaret (1925–), novelist, b. Gayndah, Qld. Anderson was educated in Brisbane but has spent most of her adult life in Sydney. An ironist who aims for poetic brevity, she turned in the 1960s from short stories and radio drama to novels. Anderson won the Miles Franklin Award and the Australian Natives' Association Literature Award for *Tirra Lirra by the River* (1978). *The Impersonators* (1980) won the Miles Franklin Award and the 1981 NSW Premier's Award; set in Sydney of the 1970s, it is an ambitious study of an Australian family and the pursuit of money. *Stories from the Warm Zone* was named 1987 *Age* Book of the Year.

Anderson, Dame Judith (Frances Margaret) (1898–), actress, b. Adelaide. Anderson went to the US in 1918, where she pursued a successful stage career in classical theatre, her most famous roles being those of Lady Macbeth and Medea. Films include *Laura* (1944), *Cat on a Hot Tin Roof* (1958) and, most notably, *Rebecca* (1940), in which she played the demented housekeeper, Mrs Danvers – a role perfectly suited to her aquiline features and severe appearance. She was created a DBE in 1960.

Andrews, Gordon (1914–), designer, b. NSW. An exemplary talent and a pioneer of modern design in Australia, Andrews has worked in various fields (from packaging, furniture and cookware to exhibition display), but is best known as designer of Australia's decimal-currency notes, introduced in 1962. He bears the honorary title Designer of Industry, Royal Society of Arts, London.

Andrews, John Hamilton (1933–), architect, b. Sydney. Andrews has designed notable public and academic buildings in Canada, the US and Australia, including Miami seaport terminal (completed 1972), Harvard Graduate School of Design (1972), and Sydney's King George Tower (1977). He is also noted for his recent residential work in NSW, characterised by geometric formality and imaginative interpretation of traditional

homestead architecture using new technology; his iron-clad house at Eugowra (1981) is a prime example.

Angas family, prominent in the colonisation of SA. **George Fife** (1789–1879), b. England, was variously a coachmaker, shipping entrepreneur and banker who helped found the South Australian Co. He also lobbied the Colonial Office on behalf of SA, recruited Nonconformist ministers, and dispatched some 620 dissident Lutherans from Germany to be tenants on his Barossa Valley properties. In 1851 Angas himself settled in SA, becoming a leading political and philanthropic figure, though in his latter years strongly anti-Catholic. His elder son **George French** (1822–86), b. England, was an artist and naturalist who published *South Australia Illustrated* (1847) and *Views of the Gold Regions of Australia* (1851), as well as many other works on Australia and NZ. He was secretary of the Australian Museum, Sydney, 1853–60. George Fife's younger son, **John Howard** (1823–1904), b. England, was a pastoralist, politician and philanthropist who preceded his father to SA, managing the Angas properties there from 1843. He was a member of the SA parliament 1871–6 and 1887–94.

angler-fishes These fish, of which there are two main groups (ocean and inshore), all have a 'fishing rod' or lure in the form of an extended spine of the dorsal fin that is waved to attract smaller fish towards the large mouth. The numerous inshore species of the family Antennariidae include the rags-and-tatters fish, *Rhycherus,* named from the filaments and nodules all over its body and fins; and the smooth-skinned mouse-fish, *Pterophrynoides,* which is often found on floating seaweed. The hand-fish, *Brachionichthys hirsutus*, of south-eastern Australia and Tas. is often caught by trawlers and is well known for its habit of 'walking' on its pectoral and ventral fins. The various ocean species are usually dark in colour and with luminous lures. In some species, parasitic males – small, almost eyeless, and with vestigial 'fishing rods' – are attached to the females: their sole function is to produce milt when the female is ready to spawn.

Anglican Church The Anglican Church of Australia was originally called the Church of England but was renamed officially in August 1981, signalling Australian independence from the English church. It has always been the largest faith in Australia (23.9% of the Australian population in 1986), although the flood of non-English immigrants since World War 2 has lowered the proportion. The Anglican Church has never been the legally established church in Australia, although in the early years it had a monopoly in religion and education. The church is still actively involved in education at independent schools (especially at secondary level), as well as social welfare work.

On 3 February 1788, the second Sunday after the arrival of the First Fleet, the Rev. Richard Johnson held the first church service in the colony. He built the first church in 1793, and was joined in 1794 in NSW by the Rev. Samuel Marsden. In 1824 Sydney was created an archdeaconry under the Rev. T.H. Scott, within the see of Calcutta. In 1836 it became a diocese, with William Broughton as the first bishop, and bishops were appointed in Tas. in 1842 and in Melbourne and Adelaide in 1847. The 'bush parson' was often a lonely but important figure in remote communities; the Bush Brotherhood, established in 1897, is composed of separate groups of celibate clergy dedicated to working in sparsely populated areas; the Sisters of the Church is the best-known of the orders for women.

A new constitution for the administration of the Anglican Church was adopted in 1962. Although the national general synod (comprising clergy and lay people) has considerable power to make church laws, dioceses (under the jurisdiction of a bishop) retain substantial autonomy. The ordination of women – long a vexed and controversial question within the church – appears to be inevitable by the early 1990s. >> *religion*

Angophora A genus of trees in the myrtle family, *Angophora* is closely allied to eucalypts (indeed regarded by some botanists as one of the major eucalypt sub-groups). There are seven species, all of eastern Australia, ranging from far eastern Vic. through NSW into Qld as far north as the Atherton Tableland and inland to the Warrego River. Most attractive is the only species with deciduous bark, *A. costata*, known as smooth-barked apple. 'Apple' is applied to most species, possibly because of their spreading, crooked-limbed habit of growth.

Angry Penguins This modernist arts movement of the 1940s was founded at the Univer-

sity of Adelaide and published an eponymous journal 1940–6. Although principally literary, it attracted adherents from both art and music – notably painters such as Sidney Nolan, Albert Tucker and John Perceval. The magazine, edited by Max Harris and John Reed, published and promoted the avant garde but opposed the radical nationalism of the period. The focus of the > *Ern Malley hoax* in 1944, the magazine – and the movement – did not survive the ensuing controversy and conservative cultural backlash.

Angus, Samuel (1881–1943), theologian, b. Ireland. Angus was professor of theology at St Andrew's Presbyterian College, Sydney University, 1914–43. He made widely recognised contributions on the origins of Christianity in *Religions and Christianity* (1925) and other works. Angus's views on Christian orthodoxy were the subject of heated controversy among Presbyterians and he was charged with heresy in the early 1930s; although he was cleared by a church commission, the controversy and allegations persisted throughout the decade.

animal liberation This comparatively recent movement campaigns against the systematic exploitation of animals – particularly their use in experimentation (especially vivisection), blood sports, 'factory' farming, the fur trade, and maltreatment in zoos, circuses and homes. The founder of the movement in Australia was Peter Singer, who published *Animal Liberation* in 1975. As elsewhere in the world, the tactics of the group range from aggressive confrontations with farmers and hunters to lobbying for legislative change.

animals, introduced A number of animals introduced to Australia – some accidentally and some on purpose – have become established in the wild. Whether imported for human service, for sport, for nostalgic reasons, or as predators of existing pests, these creatures have in the main had a profound impact on the Australian environment: their unwanted effects include the destruction of native vegetation, the loss of native wildlife through direct predation or through competition for food and habitat, and incalculable economic losses as the result of the damage to farm lands and crops. Although quarantine laws now restrict the importation of live plants and animals, the effects of existing populations of feral animals are still felt in both urban and rural areas.

The earliest introduction was that of the semi-domesticated > *dingo*, which is thought to have been imported by Aborigines or Asian fishermen about 5000 years ago and subsequently became naturalised across the mainland. Animals which arrived in association with European settlement include livestock (pigs, goats, sheep, cows and buffaloes), domestic pets (most notably cats and dogs), > *rats and mice*, foxes, deer, poultry and perching birds, > *cane toads*, freshwater fish such as trout and carp, and numerous insect species. Numbers of all the mammals, with the notable exception of sheep, have since run wild in rugged and remote regions: > *rabbits* are probably the most renowned feral pest of rural Australia, but many other groups also spread rapidly after their introduction. Foxes, for example, which were introduced for hunting in Vic. in the 1840s, thereafter proliferated and dispersed; while they proved useful in the control of rabbits and hares, they remain a serious threat to many native mammals. Hoofed animals such as horses, cattle, goats and camels have caused sustained damage to native vegetation by both trampling and overgrazing; similarly, water buffaloes (and to a lesser extent pigs) have wreaked havoc in wetland areas by their trampling and wallowing habits. In urban areas throughout the continent, feral cats and dogs continue to prey on local wildlife. >> *birds, introduced*; *camels*; *deer*; *fishes, introduced*

Annear, Harold Desbrowe (1866–1933),

architect, b. Bendigo, Vic. Annear was the first Australian-born designer to reject imported historical styles, and arguably the most innovative local architect 1900–20. His functional domestic designs in that period were well ahead of their time in adopting features such as open planning, built-in cupboards, and modern gadgetry; Troon (1916) in Toorak, Vic., was hailed as Australia's first Modern house.

Ansett, Sir Reginald Myles (1909–81),

businessman, b. Inglewood, Vic. Ansett began a Hamilton–Melbourne air service in 1936 and formed Ansett Transport Industries (ATI), incorporating airline and coach operations, in 1946. In the 1950s he took over Australian National Airways, Butler Air Transport and other aviation companies, to make Ansett Airlines the largest private-enterprise airline in Australia. Later expansion included a television network, tourism and accommodation,

freight services and manufacturing. ATI was taken over in 1979 by TNT Ltd and News Ltd.

Antarctic Territory

Antarctic Territory Nearly twice the size of Australia, Antarctica is regarded as the world's last great wilderness continent. Australia holds the largest territorial claim of any country, thus playing an important and often difficult role in this unique theatre of international interests, which in recent years have focused on exploitation of the continent's vast marine and mineral potential.

Australia's associations with Antarctica go back to its own early history – to James Cook's great Southern Ocean voyage of 1772–5, the first to cross the Antarctic Circle. In 1933 Britain transferred to Australia claims based on 19th-century British exploration and Sir Douglas Mawson's expeditions 1911–14 and 1929–31. The Antarctic Territory administered by Australia covers 6 400 000sq.km (42% of the landmass). Part of the old Precambrian base of the east portion of the continent, it is covered with Palaeozoic sediments containing some coal. Although largely covered by ice, there are some ice-free areas of rocky islands and peninsulas on the coast.

Research establishments Since 1943, exploration and research have been undertaken by ANARE (Australian National Antarctic Research Expeditions). The first research stations were set up on Heard and Macquarie islands (1947–8), followed by Mawson in 1954 – the oldest continuously operated of all Antarctic continental stations. Australia currently has four permanent stations: Mawson, Davis, Casey and Macquarie Island. Summer bases have been set up at Cape Denison, Scullin Monolith, the Larsemann Hills, the Bunger Hills and Heard Island. About 120 Australians are based at the permanent stations, while up to 400 visit over the summer for short-term programs. Major areas of research include studies of the Southern Ocean ecosystem, focusing on the role of krill, seals and sea-birds; land and coastal marine ecology; cosmic ray physics, from an underground observatory at Mawson; upper atmosphere physics, including auroras and global pollution measurement; and the dynamics of the Antarctic ice sheet, to yield information on world climatic trends.

Administration In 1961 twelve nations – including seven which claimed territory – signed the Antarctic Treaty, which dedicated the region to peaceful and scientific research and placed it under international management. A number of protective conventions have been adopted since then, the most important being the Convention on the Conservation of Antarctic Marine Living Resources (CCAMLR) and the Agreed Measures for the Protection of Flora and Fauna. Against widespread protest, these have been ignored by some signatories: the French, for instance, built an airstrip at Dumont D'Urville, and CCAMLR has not been able to extract information on fishing catches from Japan and the Soviet Union, to confirm if overfishing is occurring.

The latest agreement, the Convention for the Regulation of Antarctic Mineral Resource Activity, was announced in Wellington in 1988. Substantial deposits of coal and iron ore and traces of gold, platinum, copper, cobalt, nickel and uranium have been found in the ice-free rocks since the days of the early explorers, and over the past fifteen years expeditions have surveyed geological formations under the shallow seas, which may bear oil. However, while some nations favour mining, conservationists argue that it could pollute oceans, kill wildlife and affect the weather. Nations had twelve months from November 1988 in which to determine whether to sign the agreement. Australia, as one of the seven claimant states, must be a signatory for the agreement to be ratified, which places the country in a quandary as to the best means of safeguarding the environment.

anteater, spiny > *monotremes*

antechinus > *marsupial mice*

Anthony, (John) Douglas (1929–), farmer and politician, b. Murwillumbah, NSW. Anthony succeeded his father, H.L. Anthony, as the Country Party member for Richmond, NSW, in the federal parliament in 1957; in the coalition government of 1949–72, he was minister for the interior 1964–7 and minister for primary industry 1967–71. He became deputy leader of the Country Party in 1966, and was deputy prime minister 1971–2 and 1975–83. He resigned as leader of the party (by then called the National Party) in 1984 and soon afterwards retired from politics.

Antipodean Group, a group of painters in Melbourne in the late 1950s who vigorously defended figurative art against abstractism. The founding members of this group, formed in 1959, were Arthur and David Boyd, John

Perceval, Clifton Pugh, John Brack, Robert Dickerson, Charles Blackman and Bernard Smith. They held a joint exhibition in August 1959, the catalogue for which incorporated their manifesto attacking the various prevailing forms of abstract painting and promoted in their place a return to figurative images. The manifesto dealt with a range of theoretical issues and has often been interpreted as a call for a national style of painting. The movement was short-lived, but achieved some notoriety in the UK and helped give Australian painting a stronger identity.

antlions > *lacewings and antlions*

ants Related to bees and wasps, ants belong to the family Formicidae of the order Hymenoptera. They usually live in colonies with a reproductive queen and large numbers of wingless, non-reproductive female workers and soldiers variously directed to tend the offspring, forage for food and protect the colony. Foraging workers collect a variety of nutriments, including animal prey, nectar, seeds, and plant exudates. Communication between individuals within a nest is facilitated by secreted scents, known as pheromones.

At certain times large numbers of winged males and virgin females emerge from a nest; mated females start new colonies, while the males disperse and die. In reproduction, queens are able to determine the sex and 'castes' of offspring by varying larval food composition and glandular secretions. Some species of ants tend and protect aphids and scale insects, feeding on the secreted honeydew. The Australian yellow honeypot ant, *Melophorus bagoti*, utilises the swollen abdomens of special workers as living storage vats for liquid nectar.

The ubiquity and abundance of ants makes them ecologically important in food chains, and even in soil aeration. Apart from causing casual annoyance, some ants are either pests of foodstuffs or seriously irritating; examples are sugar ants and meat ants, of the genera *Camponotus* and *Iridomyrmex*, and especially the introduced Argentine ant, *Iridomyrmex humilis*.

Australia has an estimated 4000 ant species. Notable among them are the stinging bulldog ants of the genus *Myrmecia*, the rare *Nothomyrmecia* – the world's most primitive ant – and the green tree ant, *Oecophylla*, which constructs elaborate nests of leaves bound together with larval silk.

ANZAAS The Australian and NZ Association for the Advancement of Science draws its membership from all scientific disciplines. Established in 1888, it was initially modelled on the British Association for the Advancement of Science to provide a platform for scientists to present their work for critical comment by colleagues. Since then, both science and ANZAAS have changed dramatically. Most scientific disciplines are now represented by specialised societies of experts. ANZAAS has moved in the opposite direction – to emphasise general issues affecting the scientific estate and to encourage interdisciplinary exchange. More recently, it has concerned itself with issues of national significance and of general interest to the community at large. Since the first meeting in Sydney (1888), congresses have been held regularly in the principal cities of Australia and NZ. The association awards two medals at each congress: the ANZAAS Medal for service in the advancement of science and the Mueller Memorial Medal for important contributions in anthropology, botany, geology and zoology. A bimonthly journal, *Search*, addresses current topics of scientific debate and recent advances.

Anzac This acronym for the Australian and New Zealand Army Corps, coined in 1915 when the troops were training in Egypt, was eventually applied to all Australian and NZ troops in World War 1, where its chief association was with the Gallipoli campaign and the tenacity and courage of the antipodean troops. Although the term was used to a lesser extent in World War 2, its identity with Australia (in particular) has persisted. It is enshrined in Australian and NZ culture in the annual holiday, Anzac Day on 25 April, which commemorates all those who have represented the nation in military conflicts. More recently it has acquired ironic significance in its application to the mythical qualities of the Australian male.

Anzac Day > *Anzac; holidays and national days*

ANZUS treaty This pact, signed in 1951 by Australia, NZ and the US, declared that the three countries would provide combined support in the event of an attack against any one of them. The treaty was initiated by Australia, which (like NZ) was concerned about the World War 2 Allies' 'soft' peace treaty with Japan, and was signed by the US as a concession to these fears. Despite numerous strains over the years and much local scepticism about actual US interpretation of the treaty, ANZUS remains the lynch-pin of Australia's defence policy; a by-product of the treaty has been the establishment of > *US bases in Australia*. Following the banning of US nuclear-powered or nuclear-armed warships from NZ ports by the Lange government in 1985, the US suspended its security commitment to NZ.

aphids > *bugs*

Apiaceae > *carrot family*

Apocynaceae This plant family consists mainly of tropical and subtropical trees, shrubs and climbers; their stems contain latex and are often poisonous, familiar examples being the oleander and frangipani. About 65 species (in fourteen genera) are native in Australia, of which 29 are climbers of the silkpod genus *Parsonsia*. The genus *Carissa* has four or so species of thorny, sprawling shrubs common in the northern inland. The genus *Alstonia* includes the milky pine, *Alstonia scholaris*, of Qld rainforests and the bitter-bark or quinine tree, *A. constricta*, of inland Qld and NSW.

apostle-bird > *mudlarks and allies*

aquatic plants and weeds Freshwater aquatic plants have three different growth forms – submerged, emergent and floating. The submerged forms are by necessity the most highly specialised, obtaining essential gases such as carbon dioxide and oxygen from the water and in the case of flowering plants requiring special mechanisms for cross-pollination and seed dispersal.

Some plant groups consist entirely of aquatic plants. In others, only a minority are aquatic, as is the case with some members of the > *sedge family* such as the floating clubrush, *Isolepis fluitans*, which forms masses of green threads at the water's surface; most other species of this genus are more conventional sedges found in damp ground. The river buttercup, *Ranunculus inundatus*, has fine-lobed leaves when growing submerged, unlike those of most land-dwelling buttercups; like many aquatics, it produces leaves of quite dissimilar shape in its terrestrial phase. Another group of aquatics with this characteristic is the water-milfoils of the family Haloragaceae, of which 36 species are native to Australia.

Some floating aquatics lack any connection with the bottom mud: one of the most remarkable examples is the duckweed family, Lemnaceae, consisting in Australia of three worldwide genera, *Lemna, Spirodela* and *Wolffia* which all occur as thin green films at the edge of still water. A floating liverwort, *Ricciocarpos natans*, sometimes occurs with duckweeds, as does the floating fern *Azolla* (although this often grows in reddish sheets) whose small flat plants consist of minute curled fronds. The other common floating fern, *Salvinia*, is an introduced plant that can form thick masses which clog waterways; in warmer climates it is thus regarded as almost as great a menace as the notorious water hyacinth, *Eichhornia crassipes*, another floating aquatic of South American origin. Many other aquatics, including some natives, are also regarded as weeds because they impede boating, clog pumps and other machinery, and greatly reduce the capacity of irrigation canals. Control measures are difficult, as it is often undesirable to introduce herbicides into the water.

Native genera consisting wholly or predominantly of aquatic plants include *Brasenia, Ceratophyllum, Alisma* and *Damasonium, Aponogeton, Ruppia* and *Najas*. The Podostemaceae is a remarkable family of moss-like flowering plants occurring on rocks in fast-flowing tropical streams. >> *algae*; *nardoo*; *seagrasses*; *waterlilies*

Arafura Sea This relatively shallow, tropical sea lies directly north of Australia. To the east of it is Torres Strait and to the west the Timor Sea; to the north is Irian Jaya and a string of Indonesian islands, and its southern shores are the coasts of NT and northern Qld, including the Gulf of Carpentaria. In past geological eras, the present sea floor formed a land bridge between Australia and the islands to her north; for the most part, the sea is less than 70m deep. This area was exposed during Pleistocene glacial periods, when sea-levels dropped as much as 120m.

Ararat Vic. (pop. 8015) Ararat is a commercial and service centre 203km west of Melbourne, and the base for tourists to the nearby Grampian Ranges. The area was first developed after a brief but intense gold rush in 1854–6. Today wool, wheat and wine are the main regional products, the last most notably from the Great Western vineyards; the steady industrial development is based on textile manufacture and timber-milling.

arbitration, industrial > *conciliation and arbitration*

archaeology Archaeology is a relatively recent discipline in Australia. The first major scientific excavation was made in SA in 1929; further work followed in NSW in the 1930s, but techniques and analytical methods were unsophisticated. Aboriginal prehistory was taught in universities from the 1950s, and historical archaeology from the 1960s. In the last 20 years the number of recorded archaeological sites – both historic and prehistoric – has multiplied a thousandfold.

Prehistoric archaeology Aboriginal prehistory is the principal object of archaeological study in Australia. Aided by radiocarbon dating and newer techniques such as thermoluminescence dating, prehistorians now consider that Aboriginal occupancy dates back 30 000–40 000 years.

Many white anthropologists believe that the Aborigines migrated from the Southeast Asian region; they are assumed to have entered Australia from the north and only gradually spread southwards. (Many Aborigines contest this view of their origins, holding that in fact they evolved in Australia: > *Aboriginal culture and society*.) Ancient sites of importance include those at Upper Swan in WA (38 000 years old), Koonalda Cave on the Nullarbor Plain (20 000 years) and Lake Mungo, NSW (30 000 years). These dates indicate that Aborigines were already in Australia when Homo sapiens was replacing the Neanderthals in Europe.

Archaeological methods have also been used in the study of prehistoric Aboriginal art. Estimating the age of ancient rock art has proved difficult because there are no appropriate techniques for dating the pigments, but recent analysis of the surface varnish of petroglyphs in the Olary district of SA verified their age as about 31 500 years. Other notable rock-art sites include Laura in Qld (13 000 years old), numerous locations in Arnhem Land, NT (7000–8000), and the Cleland Hills, NT (5000–7000).

Historical archaeology Historical archaeology – the archaeology of Australia since 1788 – provides objective evidence of the past and thus is often seen as a useful means of countering the alleged bias inherent in written records. Sites and relics of settlement, of maritime activities and of industry are the main focus of Australian historical archaeologists.

Archaeological remains include > *shipwrecks*, houses, factories, public buildings, gardens, and agricultural and mining landscapes, examination of which has added much to the store of knowledge about society and technology during the 200 years of white settlement. Achievements have been many and varied: information has been gathered on activities ranging from life in the first Government House in Sydney to work practices at the Irrawang Pottery, NSW, and the cement works at Fossil Beach, Vic., as well as changing architectural styles and methods. Maritime archaeologists have investigated many of the thousands of wreck sites around the Australian coast, which have provided details about technology and living conditions on ships from both the 17th and 18th centuries. Pioneering work was carried out in WA in the 1960s, where important sites include the Dutch vessels *Batavia, Vergulde Draeck, Zuytdorp* and *Zeewijk*; other excavated wrecks include the British naval vessels *Pandora*, off Qld, and *Sirius*, off Norfolk Island, and the trading vessel *William Salthouse*, off Vic. Like land-based historic and prehistoric sites of cultural or scientific significance, declared historic shipwrecks are protected by legislation.

Archer, John Lee (1791–1852), architect and civil engineer, b. Ireland. Archer arrived in Tas. in 1827. As government architect in Hobart 1827–38, he was responsible for many well-designed public buildings including churches and gaols, and was an early local exponent of Greek Revival. Among his most notable structures were the three-arched bridge at Ross (1836) and Parliament House, Hobart (1835–40), originally designed as a Custom House.

Archer, Robyn [Robyn Smith] (1948–), singer, b. Adelaide. A singer of jazz and folk music, Archer attracted particular attention in the early 1970s for her interpretation of the works of Bertold Brecht. She made her London debut in this capacity in 1977 and left Australia in 1980 to travel and work in the UK, US and Europe. She has written and performed numerous shows, including the resoundingly successful 'A Star is Torn' (1982), as well as making regular concert tours during the 1980s; her work is typically feminist and political. She

published a children's book, *Mrs Bottle Burps*, in 1983.

archer–fish These fish, of the genus *Toxotes*, are also known as rifle-fish and are found in tropical Australia and Southeast Asia. Deep-bodied yellow fish with brown side markings, they are named for their ability to 'shoot down' insects with a jet of water propelled accurately by means of a groove in the roof of the mouth. They are often found in billabongs of the monsoonal north.

Archibald, J.F. (John Feltham) (1856–1919), editor, b. Kildare, Vic. Archibald was baptised John Feltham but adopted the Christian names Jules François in the 1870s. As co-founder with John Haynes of the *Bulletin* in 1880, and its editor 1880–2 and 1886–1902, he had an important influence on Australian writing by his selection, editing and encouragement of promising authors, including Henry Lawson and Banjo Paterson. His love of France is seen in his assumed Christian names and also in the Archibald Memorial, a bronze fountain in Sydney's Hyde Park provided for by his estate to commemorate the Australian–French alliance in World War 1. He left the profits of one-tenth of his estate for the Australian art award, the > *Archibald Prize*.

Archibald Prize Australia's most controversial and prestigious art prize, the Archibald Prize has been awarded since 1921 through a bequest by *Bulletin* editor > *J.F. Archibald*. It is conducted annually at the Art Gallery of NSW and is awarded for a portrait of an Australian, preferably 'a man or woman distinguished in art, letters, science or politics'. William Dobell's winning portrait of Joshua Smith (1943), reviled by disgruntled losers as 'a caricature', resulted in a celebrated lawsuit. The Wynne and Sulman Prizes are held in association with the Archibald Prize. >> *art awards*

architecture The egalitarian ideals of Australian society are reflected, in its architecture, in the predominance of small-scale, private development. The absence of both powerful patrons and strongly implemented urban planning has meant that large civic and housing projects are the exception, and the works of individual architects often conflict with each other. In addition, Australia's architecture – and in many cases the architects themselves – derive from other countries and eclecticism has persisted over two centuries of rapid change in building technology and architectural theory. Often only the superficial aspects of an overseas architectural fashion have been copied; occasionally, however, a technical or stylistic influence from abroad has been taken up with passion and intelligence, adapted to local aspirations and conditions, and resulted in buildings which are significant for their time.

Early colonial buildings The First Fleet brought neither trained builders nor materials, and few tools: the earliest European buildings were crude palm-thatched huts, most commonly of wattle and daub. Bricks and mortar were soon produced, but – like stone and glass – were initially reserved for the houses of the wealthy and for public buildings. Inland, the squatters had to make do with earth-floored bark huts until prosperity and some security of tenure allowed the construction of more permanent homesteads.

The first buildings, being necessarily simple, benefited from the Georgian style then fashionable in England, which valued fine proportions above ostentation. This is illustrated by the simple symmetry of Elizabeth Farm in Parramatta, NSW (1793–4), one of the earliest homes constructed in the colony. The architecture of Lachlan Macquarie's governorship reflected both his breadth of vision and the talent and energy of the colony's principal architect, > *Francis Greenway*: notable extant examples include Hyde Park Barracks (1819) and St James church (1820–4). The addition of eaves and verandahs was a concession to local conditions.

Good design persisted into the Regency period, fine examples including Elizabeth Bay House (1832–7) and Camden Park House (1834), both designed by > *John Verge* and John Bibb. In Tas., the elegant legacy of architects such as > *John Lee Archer* and > *James Blackburn* testified not only to their design skills but also to that colony's abundant convict labour and fine building stone.

Victorian architecture From the mid-19th century, architecture responded to the affluence generated by gold. Allied with the intrinsic pomposity of the Victorian era – a celebration of Empire, material success, and morality – this resulted in a plethora of dignified but pretentious public buildings, of which the town halls of most capitals are prime examples. Banks, museums, grand hotels, churches,

theatres and private mansions also proliferated throughout the colonies, their characteristic ornateness made possible not only by the fruits of the industrial revolution – cast and galvanised iron, pressed tin, and sheet glass – but also by the abundance of cheap labour. Other useful technical developments included lifts (after 1880), which made it possible to construct buildings ten and twelve storeys high.

The neo-classical style was generally adopted for public buildings, and Gothic for churches. The Independent Church (1868) in Collins Street, Melbourne, demonstrated the eclecticism for which both its architect, > *Joseph Reed*, and the period, were noted. An Italianate style with asymmetrical massing was popular for mansions and terrace houses – the latter ranging in style and station from squalor to luxury. By the end of the century, ornamentation had become increasingly fanciful and often vulgar: high-Victorian fantasy architecture is typified by the Queen Victoria building (1893–8) in York Street, Sydney, designed by George McRae.

'Federation' style After the 1890s depression, a reaction to Victorian exuberance and historical styles was expressed in a new enthusiasm for the picturesque. Influenced by the English arts and crafts movement and Art Nouveau, it took the form of asymmetrical planning, much red brick, and elaborate terracotta roof shapes; this 'Federation' style affected the suburbs of Melbourne in particular. Other styles were also imported, often via the US: the Romanesque favoured by Boston's H.H. Richardson, for example, was introduced by > *John Horbury Hunt* when he arrived in Australia in the 1860s.

The free planning and irregular massing of the English and Californian styles made them adaptable to a site's levels and aspects, and were a continuing influence on residential design. The bungalow style for suburban dwellings was imported from California before World War 1; its low, spreading rural character demanded a 15–18m frontage, and in taking more land per block contributed to the sprawl of the suburbs as its popularity increased. Noted architects of the early 20th century included > *Harold Desbrowe Annear*, > *William Hardy Wilson* and Raymond Dods, although their influence was minimal at the time. The American influence became stronger, largely through the work of expatriate Americans such as > *Walter Burley Griffin* (who brought the architectural principles of Frank Lloyd Wright to Australia), and local architects who had worked in the US. In Sydney, > *Lesley Wilkinson* drew on Mediterranean traditions and introduced the 'Spanish mission' style for domestic architecture.

Early modernism > *Roy Grounds* worked on the US west coast during the 1920s: his work of the 1930s, in partnership with Geoffrey Mewton, was a precursor of postwar developments in Australian architecture – favouring function (rational planning, aspect, and outdoor living) over visual style. The influence of Dutch modernism can be seen in MacRobertson Girls High School, Melbourne (1934), by Seabrook and Fildes, and in the Mechanical Engineering building (1938) at Sydney University, designed by Harry Rembert. Some of the best buildings in the modern style before 1940 were hospitals, including the Royal Melbourne Hospital, Parkville (1939–43), by Stephenson and Turner; the work of Edward Billson was also notable, particularly the Sanitarium factory (1936) at Warburton, Vic. In general, however, the influence of the modern movement at this time was seen mainly in 'moderne' features such as rounded corners and horizontal windows.

Austerica A hiatus in home-building during the war created a housing shortage which was exacerbated by greatly increased postwar population. The period 1945–55 witnessed prolific construction, but material and labour shortages combined to produce smaller, increasingly similar and less interesting homes.

In 1960 the architect and critic Robin Boyd (> *Boyd family*) coined the term Austerica (= Australia, America, austerity, hysteria) to describe the Australian ethos in the postwar period. The architects who were able to intervene were influenced by 'Scandinavian Modern' and 'Festival of Britain'. Any style other than Georgian was eschewed, and Frederick Romberg's vigorous and thoroughly European Stanhil was designated 'Blot of the Month' by fellow-architect Neil Clerehan in 1952. Sydney Ancher was one of the few architects who made something out of the financial and artistic austerity of the time, his houses on Sydney's North Shore bearing witness to his earlier visit to Stuttgart; further north, John Dalton breathed life into the Qld vernacular. The prevailing notion of originality for its own sake was evidenced in triangular plans and elevations, by cable, bridge and concrete-shell structures, and by lots of bright paint.

Doctrinal Bauhaus arrived with Harry Seidler's house at Turramurra (1948–50). This became an era of rectangular buildings and glass walls, noted exponents including Bates, Smart and McCutcheon: Wilson Hall at Melbourne University (1956) typified the trend towards glass boxes, and their ICI and MLC buildings in Melbourne and Sydney (both 1957) heralded the rectangular city skyscrapers which symbolise the architecture of the 1960s. The curtain wall, another characteristic of the period, even appeared in domestic architecture in the form of Stegbar's 'window wall'. Rectangular elevations were applied to supermarkets and service stations; sometimes louvres, murals or a sculpture decorated the sober facades.

The Sydney school The reaction to glossy international functionalism first appeared in Sydney. Architect Ken Woolley adopted a rectangular treatment for the Fisher Library (1963–7) at Sydney University, but by contrast he designed a house in Mosman (1962) with several levels that followed the sloping site, and with details such as roof tiles, clinker brick and exposed timber beams; Mediterranean simplicity in the form of whitewashed walls and rough timber was employed by Bruce Rickard in Sydney. The idiom spread to other materials, such as off-form concrete, and to larger schemes such as the Newcastle University Union building (1965) by Ancher, Mortlock and Woolley. This concrete style derived from the later works of the noted Swiss-born architect Le Corbusier and its sculptural form expresses (or is excused by) the building's interior function and human traffic. It occasionally became monumental in scale, notably with the National Gallery in Canberra (1973–82). Generally, however, the style deteriorated into folksiness, and exposed brick and stained wood and glass became ubiquitous in the 1960s.

The 1970s and beyond The 1970s witnessed a new concern for more human architecture and for energy and heritage conservation, typified by the rise of resident-action groups and > *green bans*. Projects such as the redevelopment of Woolloomooloo, NSW, with renovated and infill housing, schools and pedestrian ways characterised this idealism. Recycling became a new architectural idiom, although the conflicting interests of conservation and development often resulted in unsuccessful compromises such as facadism, where only the shell of an old building was preserved. Civic schemes such as the Allendale Tower in Perth by Cameron, Chisholm and Nicol (1976) and Sydney Square by Ancher, Mortlock and Woolley (1977) were designed above all for pedestrians; similarly, the complicated low shape of an office complex (1980) in Belconnen, ACT, by > *John Andrews* was determined above all by the movement and comfort of its inmates. In housing there was increasing emphasis on low-rise and medium density, and a number of developers brought in architects to design individual 'project homes'. Parallel to the concern for sculptural expression of internal function was the influence of British 'hitech', epitomised by lightly clad steel structures. These were used by a number of architects, including Phillip Cox in the stadium at Bruce in the ACT (1977), and Glen Murcutt.

In the prosperous 1980s, architects seemed less concerned with social conscience or 'structural logic'; post-modernism allowed them to explore references to other buildings and periods, to be decorative and non-rational. This licence for invention resulted in some enjoyable buildings and parts of buildings, but the limited repertoire of square grids, fat columns and pastel colours too often degenerated into shallowness. By the end of the decade, a combination of factors including shrinking households and rising house prices began to encourage a new sobriety in architecture. There was increasing pressure for medium and high densities in housing, and for new and economic building techniques. >> *housing*; *urban planning*

archives The collection and storage of Australia's historical records was not carried out systematically until the 20th century. This work was at first largely the preserve of libraries, but today archives are held by the federal and State governments, and by many universities, local councils, churches, businesses and research organisations. This combination of private and official annals constitutes an invaluable history of Australia.

The *Historical Records of NSW* (published 1890s) and the *Historical Records of Australia* (1914–25) contain original records and dispatches documenting Australia's colonial history. The Australian Joint Copying Project, started in 1945 by the National Library and the Library of NSW, has recorded the most important historical documents on microfilm.

The Australian Archives, established by the federal government in 1961 and called the Commonwealth Archives Office until 1974, is the national authority responsible for the evaluation, preservation and provision of public access to official Commonwealth records. Based in Canberra, it has regional offices in all

capital cities and by June 1987 its holdings totalled more than 435 000 'shelf metres' of records. The Freedom of Information Act 1982 and the Archives Act 1983 provide for public access to Commonwealth records more than 30 years old, and information about government organisations is now held on computer. The > *Australian War Memorial* is a valuable repository of both private and public archival material relating to war and defence. These records are supplemented by the National Film and Sound Archives, established in 1984; by 1987 it included almost 500 000 record albums, 25 000 audio tapes, 50 000 film and TV productions, and 600 000 posters, photographs and advertising memorabilia. Some of the material is accessible to the public, and exhibitions and film screenings are held regularly.

Arecaceae > *palm family*

Argyle prospect > *gems and gemstones*

Armidale NSW (pop. 22 000) This city in the New England district of the northern tablelands lies about 562km northwest of Sydney. It is set in a rich agricultural area long famous for its wool and meat, and is also noted for the pleasing landscape surrounds which incorporate mountains and forests. Often described as the 'cathedral city', Armidale has two cathedrals; it is also an educational centre of long standing, with a university, tertiary colleges and four private schools. The area's first European settler was William Dumaresq, from the 1830s; the town was gazetted in 1849 and proclaimed a city in 1885.

Armstrong, Gillian (1950–), film director, b. Melbourne. After studying at the Australian Film and Television School, Armstrong made a number of documentaries including *A Busy Kind of Bloke* (1980) and *Not Just a Pretty Face* (1982). Her first feature film was *My Brilliant Career* (1978), one of the great successes of the revived Australian film industry and the winner of numerous awards. Subsequent feature films, *Starstruck* (1982) and the US-produced *Mrs Soffel* (1984), have not lived up to expectations.

army, Australian > *defence forces*

Arnhem Land NT Australia's largest Aboriginal reserve, covering about 97 000sq.km of the central peninsula of northern Australia,

Arnhem Land is a spectacularly scenic region of which a large part is set aside as > *Kakadu National Park*. Extending from Gove Peninsula in the northeast to Cobourg Peninsula in the northwest, it encompasses the western shore of the Gulf of Carpentaria and the offshore islands of > *Galiwinku* and Groote Eylandt.

Arnhem Land was named by Matthew Flinders in 1803, in honour of the Dutch ship *Arnhem* whose crew made the first recorded sighting of the northern coastline in the 1620s. The region contains the earliest archaeological evidence of Aboriginal occupation of northern Australia, which dates back at least 25 000 years, and innumerable 'cave galleries' of prehistoric rock art. The area was declared a reserve in 1931 and entry by non-Aborigines is by permission only. Except for mission stations, white settlement in the region was forbidden until the 1970s, since when mining has been allowed by the Aboriginal community in exchange for royalty payments. Mining is the area's major industry: bauxite is mined and processed at Nhulunby on the > *Gove Peninsula*; manganese ore is extracted on Groote Eylandt; and uranium is mined in the Alligator rivers area. Proposals to develop Arnhem Land's substantial mineral deposits – which were first detected in the 1950s – were the focus of early battles for Aboriginal land rights. Mining in the region remains a controversial issue, many Aboriginal landholders and some non-Aboriginal Australians being strongly opposed to further exploration and exploitation – particularly of uranium. In 1987 the NT government legislated to prevent Aboriginal communites from barring mining operations once they have agreed to exploration. Tourism is of major – and increasing – economic importance in Arnhem Land, particularly since the establishment of Kakadu.

Aroona Valley SA A starkly beautiful region north of Wilpena Pound in the Flinders Ranges, this valley is widely known through the paintings of Hans Heysen. The name comes from an Aboriginal word meaning 'flowing water'. In the 1850s it marked the most northerly pastoral settlement in the ranges, the permanent springs giving the title Garden of the North to the homestead. The Aroona dam and Mt Aroona lie 90km to the north.

art > *art, Aboriginal*; *art galleries*; *craft*; *painting, Australian*; *sculpture*

art, Aboriginal The art of Australian Aborigines is inextricably linked with their spiritual life and thus with the land; like dance and music, it has allowed a widely scattered population to communicate ideas and images across the continent since prehistoric times. The media of Aboriginal art are dictated by the geography of the continent: rock engravings, the most enduring form, are found in every State; the hard sand of the desert provides an alternative but ephemeral drawing-board in arid regions, as does the bark of trees in more fertile areas.

Aboriginal rock art is believed to be the oldest in the world; the most ancient petroglyphs known so far in Australia are in the Olary district of SA, recently verified as being 31 500 years old. The most outstanding sites are in the north of Australia – on Cape York Peninsula in Qld and in Arnhem Land, NT, where hundreds of caves and galleries contain a myriad of engravings and paintings under ledges and on the rock walls and roofs. The first recorded observations of rock art were made in 1803, by the artist William Westall who accompanied Matthew Flinders on his circumnavigation of the continent; the creation of rock art declined, however, as the nomadic life of the Aborigines changed after European settlement. Early records also demonstrate that the custom of drawing and painting on bark was originally widespread throughout the continent. The Aborigines of northeast Arnhem Land have traditionally used bark as the paper on which their petitions for land rights were presented.

Materials, methods and meanings The evidence of early descriptions and sketches indicates that the form and content of Aboriginal art have remained relatively constant throughout the ages. The artists use four principal colours – white, yellow and red (provided by the ochres of the desert), and black (from charcoal). White is associated with mourning and grief, black with revenge and death, yellow with anger and lust for combat, and red with joy and love.

The principal methods of rock painting are the stencil, where the palm of the hand is spread out and the colour squirted or blown over it; an impression, where the hand is dipped in colour mixed with liquid and then pressed on to the rock; and an independent outline. For bark paintings, the smooth inner layers of bark are first flattened and the pigments then applied with or without prior engraving. Artworks from ridged sculptures to colourful mosaics are also created on the desert sand; as with body painting, fingers, twigs and feathers are used to apply the pigments.

The content of Aboriginal art is essentially sacred and ceremonial, providing a continuous link between the ancestral past and the present. Many prehistoric petroglyphs comprise designs of arcs, dots, curves and U-shapes which appear to be abstract but have symbolic meaning often restricted to the initiated. Certain designs are specific to particular groups, whose art attests to their authority over ancestral lands. Aborigines must be initiated before being allowed to paint sacred symbols, which generally portray ancestral beings or some aspect of Aboriginal creation mythology, although styles and techniques vary widely. The huge painted Wandjina figures of the Kimberley region of WA, which bear large haloes but have no mouths, are unlike any other rock art in the world.

Portrayals of the myth of the Rainbow Serpent – the creation spirit deriving from the serpent-like form of the rainbow – occur throughout Australia. Naturalistic motifs are also widespread: notable sites include Mootwingee Cave in northwestern NSW, where engravings depict boomerangs, lizards, a 1.25m kangaroo, birds, and the arrow-like tracks of emus and bustards; they also portray human figures. Western Arnhem Land is particularly noted for its dancing Mimi figures, and polychrome 'x-ray' paintings of animals and fish in which the internal organs are depicted in decorative designs. In Arnhem Land, subjects such as Macassan praus, smokehouses, and Dutch clay pipes were incorporated with traditional motifs as foreign contact occurred.

Functional art is also ubiquitous, ranging from decorated containers and weapons to the small carved and painted wooden direction markers (called *toas*) at Lake Eyre in SA, which were first described in 1917. In most cases, however, objects are decorated for sacred or ceremonial purposes: tall, carved and painted *pukimani* burial poles occur on Bathurst and Melville islands; carved and painted mortuary figures, and hollow log coffins are found in parts of Arnhem Land.

Papunya – a bridge between past and present In recent years, Aboriginal artists from the Central and Western Deserts have begun to render traditional designs and images with modern materials, inspired by a young art teacher, (Robert) Geoffrey Bardon, who worked at Papunya from 1971. The acrylic works on boards and canvas now being produced have their origins in the traditional designs of sand and body painting: often described as 'dot paintings', the mosaic-like works are topographical maps with many layers of meaning. The precursor of this movement was > *Albert Namatjira*, who embraced the western watercolour tradition and whose work was later copied by several of the older men of Papunya, who recognised that painting offered them an opportunity to present their history and culture to a wider audience.

The critical and commercial success of Papunya painters such as Clifford Possum Tjapaltjarri and George Milpurrurru encouraged others to follow their example. A major showing of some 600 works by contemporary artists from central Australia was held at the Australian National Gallery in Canberra in 1989 and exhibitions have also been staged in Britain and the US. Representing social and political statements as well as works of art, the best of these paintings are helping to both restore Aboriginal self-esteem and increase the white community's understanding of their culture. >> *archaeology*

art awards Australia is well endowed with prizes and awards which provide critical and financial encouragement to artists. The > *Archibald Prize* for portraiture, probably the nation's best-known art award, is held simultaneously with the Wynne and Sulman Prizes. The Wynne, endowed by Richard Wynne (d. 1895), is for the best landscape painting of Australia scenery or the best figure sculpture. First awarded in 1897, to > *Walter Withers*, it is Australia's oldest extant prize. The Sulman, endowed by the estate of prominent Sydney architect Sir John Sulman and established in 1936, is for the best subject or genre painting, or design for an intended mural. The Blake Prize for religious painting, first awarded 1951, was instigated to bring about 'closer co-operation between the church and the artist in the modern world'. A more recent major prize – inaugurated in 1988 on a biennial basis – is the Doug Moran National Portrait Prize, established by a NSW businessman and philanthropist to encourage traditional portraiture. The Moët et Chandon Art Fellowship for painters under 36, first awarded 1987, is already acknowledged as providing exceptional encouragement, in 1989 entailing a cash prize of $50 000 plus a year's stay in France. In addition to individual and corporate awards, there are a number of regional and State prizes.

artesian water > *water and water resources*

art galleries Australia's first private gallery opened in Hobart in 1846 and the most of the major State galleries were established by the late 19th century. The greatest development of both commercial and public galleries has nevertheless occurred in the 20th century, in step with increasing art knowledge and curatorial professionalism. Growing interest in and patronage of art in the last two decades has stimulated further expansion of the major public galleries, the spread of regional galleries, and the proliferation of commercial galleries (the main exhibitors of contemporary art). Major international exhibitions such as 'The Entombed Warriors' and 'Modern Masters' have attracted corporate sponsorship and increased gallery attendances dramatically.

Like its museums, however, Australia's art galleries are today faced with a number of challenges. The purchase of major works, for example, is now increasingly difficult because of soaring prices on the world market, and there is also a recognised need for much higher standards of conservation, storage and display. In addition, there is growing pressure for gallery administrators to make art more accessible, through the provision of better interpretive services and initiatives such as travelling exhibitions.

The Australian National Gallery The most important new public gallery, the Australian National Gallery in Canberra houses the national collection – started in 1911 as a collection of portraits of prominent Australians – in a monumental building (completed 1982) overlooking Lake Burley Griffin. Ancient Egyptian, Black African, Pre-Columbian, central and southern American art, and international art movements and periods to the present day are all represented. Australian painters and sculptors figure prominently; craft, photography and film are also included. In 1989 the National Gallery staged a major exhibition of Aboriginal art, considered to be the first to convey the diversity of styles and concerns of contemporary Aboriginal artists.

NSW The Art Gallery of NSW, founded in 1875, still occupies a 'temporary' building erected in 1895, extended 1896–1909 and 1972. Its comprehensive Australian collection, notable for some fine colonial and > *Heidelberg School* paintings, includes many contemporary works. British art of the Victorian era and early 20th century dominates the European collection. Regional galleries dot the State; of special note are the Howard Hinton Collection in Armidale and the Power Gallery of Contemporary Art at Sydney University.

Vic. The National Gallery of Vic., Australia's first public art gallery, opened in the Melbourne Public Library in 1861. It was housed in its own building from 1875 until it moved to the Vic. Arts Centre in 1968. Assisted by the > *Felton Bequest*, the gallery has European masterpieces from the 17th, 18th and 19th centuries, and Greek vases and decorative arts; it is particularly noted for its pre-Raphaelite, glass and ceramic collections. Acquisition of works by Australian artists is given high priority. Notable regional galleries, some with significant collections, include Ballarat, Benalla and Geelong, the McLelland Galley in Langwarrin and the Latrobe Valley Arts Centre in Morwell.

Qld The Qld Art Gallery, opened in 1895, has been located in the Qld Cultural Centre since 1982. It houses many European works of note and a fine Australian collection.

SA The National Gallery of SA held its first exhibition in 1881. The present building, initially funded by a bequest from Sir Thomas Elder in 1900, was extended in 1936, 1962 and 1979. The gallery's strength is Australian and European paintings and Southeast Asian ceramics, but a large print collection and some notable sculptures are also held.

WA The WA Art Gallery in Perth, founded in 1895, now occupies a building opened in 1979. The emphasis of the collection is on Australian artists, although it features a substantial body of Aboriginal and Melanesian works.

Tas. The Tas. Museum and Art Gallery opened in the present building in Hobart in 1863 and was extended in 1889, 1901 and 1965. Many fine Australian colonial paintings form the core of the collection, which also has a fine range of works by Australian and European artists of the 20th century.

NT The NT Museum of Arts and Sciences opened in Darwin in 1981. Curatorial policy is to represent every major Australian artist since 1788, with particular emphasis on works relating to the NT and tropical Australia, and the Asia-Pacific region. The Araluen Arts Centre in Alice Springs is an important showcase for Aboriginal art.

Arthur, Sir George (1784–1854), colonial administrator, b. England. Arthur was lt-governor of Van Diemen's Land for twelve eventful and formative years (1824–36) covering separation from NSW (1825), removal of the penal settlement from Port Macquarie to Port Arthur (1832), establishment of the model prison for young convict boys at Point Puer nearby (1835), and creation of the Van Diemen's Land Co. (1825). Arthur was high-minded and efficient, but also autocratic and intolerant; these characteristics involved him in the long fight against Andrew Bent to curtail freedom of the press. Arthur planned the 1830 'Black Line' operation, which was intended to capture every Tas. Aborigine but in fact was a fiasco, capturing only two at a cost of £35 000. He also initiated the policy – ultimately fatal – of segregating Aborigines on Bass Strait islands. He was not above making considerable profit from land deals but was nevertheless a notable public servant of his day, serving also as governor in British Honduras (1814–22), Canada (1837–41) and Bombay (1842–6).

Arthur Range Tas. A rugged, glaciated chain of mountains running northwest–southeast for 32km in southern Tas., this range is part of the South West National Park. It extends from Mt Hayes (1118m) in the north to Federation Peak (1224m) in the south, and is the watershed between the Huon River basin and those of the Old and Crossing rivers, which drain into Port Davey.

Arthur River Tas. About 160km long, in the State's far northwest, the Arthur River rises in ranges near Waratah and flows north and then west to the sea. Its headwaters – in rough, glaciated rainforest – are noted for trout fishing; the upper and middle reaches lie in wilderness country and extensive State forest, while the coastal region is used for livestock grazing.

Arthurs Lake Tas. On the unglaciated east part of the Tas. central plateau, lying southeast of the Great Lake to which it has been connected by the construction of a dam, Arthurs Lake forms part of the Great Lakes hydro-electric power project. It is a popular summer fishing and tourist area, sometimes referred to (incorrectly) as Arthurs Lakes – there is but one body of water.

Arts Council of Australia This government-funded but independent arts organisation was established in 1946. Originally founded to arrange tours of the performing arts to rural areas, its scope has since widened to include the visual arts and education activities in both fields. There are now some 260 branches throughout Australia and local communities are increasingly encouraged (and funded) to initiate their own festivals, performances, exhibitions and workshops. >> *Australia Council*

asbestos Australia was formerly an important, though small, producer of asbestos, but all mining and use of the mineral has ceased in the wake of the link established between asbestos and the diseases 'asbestosis' (a form of pneumoconiosis) and mesothelioma (a deadly lung cancer caused by blue asbestos dust). In 1988, following a prolonged court battle, CSR Ltd agreed to pay $50 million in compensation to former workers (or to their surviving relatives) of its blue asbestos mine at > *Wittenoom* in WA, which closed in 1966. It is estimated that some 2000 workers and residents of Wittenoom have been or will be affected by mesothelioma, which can have a gestation period of 30–40 years and is invariably fatal.

ascidians > *sea-squirts*

ASEAN Initially comprising Indonesia, Malaysia, the Philippines, Singapore and Thailand (later joined by Brunei), the Association of Southeast Asian Nations was formed in 1967 with the stated aim of promoting economic growth, social progress and cultural development. Its main purpose is probably to achieve greater economic influence for its member nations by their acting in unison. In this it has not so far been notably successful – probably because the economies of its members are too similar and are thus in competition – and it has gained no new members from the region other than Brunei. ASEAN has, however, been involved in international discussions on the fate of Cambodia. It holds annual ministerial conferences, and has a permanent secretariat in Jakarta.

Ashburton River WA With headwaters in the Ophthalmia and Collier Ranges of the Pilbara region, in the wet season the Ashburton flows northwest for some 650km through gorges and then through wide floodplains to mudflats near Onslow. In a area of low rainface, its flow is intermittent, and it is navigable for only about 3km from its mouth.

Ashes, the > *cricket*

Ashmore and Cartier islands These four small, sandy coral islands, which lie some 800km west of Darwin, were transferred by the British government to Australian control in 1931; they were annexed to the NT in 1938. The three Ashmore Islands (known as Middle, East and West) abound in wildlife, notably birds, turtles and sea-cucumbers (or bêche-de-mer), and were declared a nature reserve in 1983. Although there is no permanent population, the Ashmore Islands are staffed during the March–November fishing season for the purpose of monitoring the activities of visiting Indonesian fishermen.

Ashton, Will (Sir John William) (1881–1963), painter, b. England. Ashton studied art in Adelaide and later in England and Europe. A prolific painter, he exhibited successfully in Europe and Australia. Although best recognised for his picturesque representation of European subject matter, he won the Wynne Prize for his paintings of the Australian landscape in 1906, 1930 and 1939. Ashton was director of the Art Gallery of NSW 1937–44.

Ashton family, associated with art in Australia since the 1880s. **Julian Rossi** (1851–1942), b. England, arrived in Australia in 1878. He worked as an artist with the *Illustrated Australian News* and other journals before founding the influential Sydney Art School in 1896 and becoming a distinguished teacher and tireless promoter of Australian art. His outstanding students included Sydney Long, Elioth Gruner and George Lambert; his espousal of *plein-air* painting was a prime influence on the young Melbourne painters who evolved the Heidelberg School. His brother, **George Rossi**, (1857–79), b. England, a competent draughtsman, lived in Australia 1879–93, working on the staff of the *Illustrated Australian News* and the *Bulletin*. Julian Rossi's son, **Julian Howard** (1877–1964), b. England, was a landscape painter and noted art critic. **Julian Richard** (1913–   ), b. Sydney, son of Julian Howard, is a painter of seascapes, a war artist and was principal of the Julian Ashton School (originally the Sydney Art School) 1963–77.

Ash Wednesday > *bushfires*

ASIO Australia's main counter-intelligence organisation, the Australian Security Intelligence Organization was established in 1949 by the Chifley government. It was only formalised by legislation in 1956, however, following the first of its major operations – handling the defection of the Soviet intelligence officer, Vladimir Petrov, in 1954. ASIO has been the subject of a number of controversies, and of two royal commissions (both chaired by Mr Justice Hope) whose subsequent reports (1977 and 1985), while critical of a number of aspects of ASIO's operations, upheld the necessity for the organisation, and redefined certain of its powers. >> *intelligence services*

ASIS > *intelligence services*

Askin, Sir Robert (Robin William) (1909–81), politician, b. Stuart Town, NSW. From a traditional Labor background, Askin entered the NSW parliament as a Liberal in 1950. Elected leader of the State party in 1959, he led the Liberals to power in 1965, ending 24 years of Labor government. He formed a coalition government in which he was both premier and treasurer until his retirement in 1975. Politically shrewd and noted for his conservative policies, he consistently opposed federal moves towards centralism and took a strong stand against public demonstrations. Askin's reputation has been tarnished by allegations that he permitted widespread corruption to flourish under his administration.

assignment system This system was first employed in 1789, when Governor Phillip allotted convicts to civil and military officers to grow food on their land and thus augment that produced on the government farms – on the argument that an individual employer would have a more material interest in the crops. Convict discipline was retained but the employer was responsible for the convicts' housing, clothing and food. Though the system was subject to abuse, particularly in relation to female convicts, it continued until transportation ceased. It eventually freed enough convicts to make some of the free settlers apprehensive that the social hierarchy was being undermined. The system played an important part in the adverse report by > *J.T. Bigge* in 1821 against Macquarie, who was trying to restrict assignment to the towns in favour of dispersing the convicts to farms.

Asteraceae > *daisy family*

Astley, Thea (Beatrice May) (1925–),
novelist, b. Brisbane. A teacher by training,
Astley is a three-times winner of the Miles
Franklin Award, for *The Well Dressed Explorer*
(1962), *The Slow Natives* (1965) and *The
Acolyte* (1972). She also won the Steele Rudd
Award for short stories, with *It's Raining in
Mango* (1988), and the Patrick White Award in
1989. Astley's Catholic upbringing in Qld has
provided a central theme in her novels, as has
small-town life, most notably in *A Descant for
Gossips* (1960) which was filmed as a mini-
series by the ABC in 1983. An indefatigable
lecturer on Australian writing, she was presented with the Gold Medal of the Australian
Literature Society in 1986.

Astley, William > *Warung, Price*

astronomy Australia's geographical position
in the southern hemisphere, together with its
advanced technology, political stability and dry
climate, has made it one of the world's major
astronomical centres.

The first observatory in Australia was a
private venture set up at Parramatta in 1821 by
Governor Brisbane, whose main work – with
two noted assistants, Carl Rümker and James
Dunlop – was to map the southern stars. With
official recognition of the need to provide
information such as accurate time for ships'
chronometers, star positions for geodetic surveys, and tidal, seismological and meteorological data, observatories were set up in
Melbourne (1853), Sydney (1856), Adelaide
(1874) and Perth (1896). One outstanding early
astronomer was the amateur, John Tebbutt,
working in his private observatory near Sydney.
He received worldwide recognition for his
observations of comets, particularly for his
discovery of the great comet in 1861.

The Great Melbourne Telescope, a 48-inch
reflector, was acquired in 1868 and for many
years remained the world's largest telescope,
but faulty design resulted in operational problems and it fell into disuse. Sold as scrap in
1945, it was modified, restored and put into
service again at Mt Stromlo Observatory
which, as the Commonwealth Solar Observatory, had been established in 1923; later a 74-
inch reflector was installed at Mt Stromlo.
After World War 2 the Australian National
University became the nation's centre for optical
astronomy and subsequently a major project
was developed – away from the lights of developing Canberra – at Siding Spring Mountain

in the Warrumbungles, northwest of Coonabarabran. This now includes the 3.8m Anglo-
Australian telescope, built jointly by Australia
and the UK. One of the first major achievements using this instrument was the discovery
of the optical counterpart of the Vela pulsar,
only the second optical pulsar to be found and
the faintest optical object to be measured.

Radio-astronomy has been particularly strong
in Australia. A CSIRO radiophysics laboratory
was opened in Sydney in 1939 to study and
develop radar, and progress was particularly
rapid after World War 2. The world's first
interferometer used for radio-astronomy was
set up at Dover Heights in 1946, soon followed
by the first Mills Cross radio-telescope. Other
important instruments include the 64m dish at
Parkes which identified the first known quasars
(1960) and a radio-heliograph, designed and
built in Australia, which produces radio pictures of the sun. The Australia Telescope, an
array of six mobile radio-telescope antennas at
Culgoora, NSW, with links to Parkes and
Siding Spring, was opened in 1988: one of the
world's largest facilities, it will be able to map
the universe in detail as well as link with overseas instruments. Computerised, X-ray and
satellite astronomy, and ultraviolet space tele-
scopy, are likely to be the basis of astronomic
observations and discoveries in the future.

Atherton Tableland Qld Part of the Great
Dividing Range, this tableland is a large
basaltic plateau in northeast Qld with an elevation of some 700m and an area of about 80 sq.
km. The chief townships are Mareeba and
Atherton. Much of the original rainforest was
cleared for dairying, and tobacco, peanut and
vegetable production. Timber-milling has
declined, and much of the remaining rainforest
is to be protected under World Heritage listing.
The tableland contains the headwaters of the
Barron River and (in the west) the catchment
area for Mitchell River headwater tributaries;
there are several national parks, notable points
of interest being the volcanic crater lakes,
Eacham and Barrine, and the Barron Falls.

athletics In the late 1980s there were more
than 17 000 registered athletes in Australia.
Since its establishment in 1980 the Australian
Institute of Sport has provided coaching, and
scientific and medical support, for budding
champion athletes.

Athletics in Australia was initially dominated by professionals. The first amateur club

was formed in Sydney in 1872 and other local and school clubs followed quickly; the first State association was formed in NSW in 1887. National championships were held in Melbourne in 1893 and the Amateur Athletic Union of Australasia was formed in 1897; the leading figures were administrators Richard Coombes and E. S. Marks, who oversaw Australia's entry into the modern Olympic Games. National championships were at first biennial but have been held annually since 1947. The first women's events were organised by Flora Drennan and Muriel Eacott in 1926 and the Australian Women's Amateur Athletic Union organised the inaugural national championships in 1932.

In international competition Australia has had most consistent success in men's middle-distance races and women's sprints, although there have been notable achievements in other track and field events. Edwin Flack (at the time resident in England) won the 800m and 1500m at the 1896 Olympics. After 1901, no gold medals were won by Australian men in track events until Herb Elliott's victory in the 1500m in 1960; the most recent Olympic win was Ralph Doubell in the 800m in 1968. Although they won no Olympic gold medals, other eminent male athletes have included runners John Treloar, Hector Hogan and > *John Landy* in the 1950s and > *Ron Clarke* in the 1960s. In field events, Nick (A.W.) Winter won the hop, step and jump at the 1924 Olympics and John Winter the high jump in 1948.

In 1952 the 'Lithgow flash', Marjorie Jackson, won the 100m and > *Shirley Strickland* the 80m hurdles. At the Melbourne Olympics in 1956, > *Betty Cuthbert* won both the 100m and 200m, Shirley Strickland won the 80m hurdles again, and the 4x100m relay team was also victorious. In 1964 Cuthbert won the 400m, and in the 1968 Mexico Games Maureen Caird won the 80m hurdles. Glynnis Nunn won the heptathalon in 1984, and in 1988 Debbie Flintoff-King won a narrow victory in the 400m hurdles. Leading sprinter Raelene Boyle won silver medals in the 200m in 1968 and in both the 100m and 200m in 1972. Robert de Castella won the world marathon title in 1983 and in 1988 became the first man to finish in the top ten at three successive Olympics. Lisa Martin won the marathon silver medal.

Atkins, Richard (1745–1820), colonial lawyer, b. England (as Richard Bowyer). Atkins arrived in Australia in 1791 and largely

through influence was appointed deputy judge-advocate (without legal training) 1796–8 and 1800–02; he was then judge-advocate 1802–09, with an interval when he was supplanted during the Rum Rebellion. Constantly assailed by alcoholism and insolvency, he nevertheless played a part in the anti-governor activities of John Macarthur. He supported Bligh and was arrested with him by the dissidents, but later agreed to support the 'rebel' George Johnston with evidence about Bligh's misconduct. He was a witness for Bligh in the London trial of Johnston, after which obscurity descended.

Atrichornis > *scrub-birds*

aurora australis Also known as the southern lights, the aurora is a spectacular display of shimmering light visible in the night sky, often in the polar regions and sometimes in southern Australia. It can appear as an arc, a wide, curtain-like band, a glow, or the 'corona' display in which rays radiate from a focal light high in the sky. Colour can vary from pale yellowish-white to deep red or green. It is believed to be caused by the influence of the earth's magnetic field on streams of electrified particles from the sun, and is usually most prominent in periods of sunspot activity.

Ausinet An Australian computer network which provides subscribers with text information from some 25 databases, Ausinet was established in 1976 by the National Library; it was taken over by ACI Computer Services in 1980. It contained Australia's first computerised newspaper index (1982), and has expanded to include full text of non-newswire stories in the *Australian Financial Review* and other business publications, as well as Australian directory and reference databases. The service operates through a normal telephone line and modem.

Aussat > *communications technology*; *post and telecommunications*

Austral, Florence [Florence Wilson] (1894–1968), opera singer, b. Melbourne. Making her debut at Covent Garden as Brunnhilde in *The Valkyrie* in 1922, Austral went on to become a renowned Wagnerian soprano, singing the complete *Ring* cycle in London and Berlin. A successful career in grand opera followed, both on stage and in concert performance. Returning to Australia after World War 2, she taught at the Newcastle Conservatorium in NSW 1952–9.

Australia The name Australia derives from *australis* (southern), which was used very early in reference to the supposed South Land, and in several linguistic forms after its discovery. The form 'Australia' came into wide use – especially in the colony itself – after the publication of Matthew Flinders's *Voyages* in 1814; Flinders had suggested its adoption after it had been finally proved that the western section, New Holland, and the eastern section, NSW, indeed formed one landmass. Lachlan Macquarie officially promoted the name in 1817, but acceptance in London was slow.

Australia Council The Australia Council was originally established (as the Australian Council for the Arts) in 1968 to advise the federal government on arts issues and policy. It has been restructured, and its responsibilities expanded, periodically since that time, becoming a statutory authority in 1975. Since 1987 it has comprised six boards, which dispense financial assistance in their particular fields: the Performing Arts Board, which covers dance, music, poetry and theatre; the Visual Arts/Craft Board; the Literary Arts Board; the Design Committee, which covers fields as diverse as architecture, engineering and fashion; the Aboriginal Arts Board, which supports the culture of both Aborigines and Torres Strait Islanders; and the Community Cultural Development Unit, which encourages community, multicultural and youth arts. The Australia Council is responsible for arts policy as well as funding, and is committed to stimulating and promoting all fields of Australian artistic endeavour. Certainly it has overseen a dramatic increase in government support for the arts since the 1970s and a new confidence on the part of Australia's creative artists.

Australia Day > *holidays and national days*

Australian Agricultural Co. Australia's oldest pastoral company was formed in London in 1824, prompted by the recommendation of J.T. Bigge that private settlers be encouraged to employ convict labour in return for land grants. The company began with a grant of 405 000ha in the Manning Valley and later took land on the Peel River under its subsidiary, the Peel River Co. The family of John Macarthur were leading promoters in the enter-

prise, which in 1831 also acquired coal-mining interests from the colonial government. In the intervening years the company has surmounted difficulties of labour, management and environment to play an important part in Australia's mining and pastoral industries.

Australian Alps This section of the Great Dividing Range was first seen and referred to as the 'Australian Alps' by Hamilton Hume and William Hovell, in 1824. A discontinuous group of mountains and high plateaus, it stretches roughly from the Brindabella Range in southeast NSW, south to Vic. and southeast across that State to Mt Baw Baw and Mt Donna Buang in the Vic. alps. Within it are Australia's highest mountains: Kosciusko (2228m), Townsend (2209m), Bogong (1986m), Feathertop (1923m) and Hotham (1862m), the last three located in Vic. Snow-covered in winter, the alps are the source of major rivers including the Murray, Murrumbidgee and Snowy, all of which are vital components of projects developed for irrigation, conservation and hydro-electric power. As a recreation area, the mountains hold the nation's major skiing resorts and are a popular summer attraction for climbers and bushwalkers. Much of the region – including lowland, mountain and alpine areas – is reserved: Kosciusko National Park (625 700ha) in NSW, Gudgenby Nature Reserve in ACT and Cobberas-Tingaringy, Wabonga Plateau and Mts Baw Baw, Bogong and Buffalo in Vic. The alps contain glacial lakes, glaciated rock pavements and moraines; much of the evidence of the ice age in Australia is found in the Kosciusko region. The mountains were explored in 1840 by Paul Strzelecki, who named Mt Kosciusko, and were settled by early pastoralists; summer grazing is now prohibited, because of its ecological drawbacks.

Australian Broadcasting Corporation > *ABC*

Australian Broadcasting Tribunal (ABT) Successor to the Australian Broadcasting Control Board (1949–76), the tribunal is an independent statutory authority responsible for regulating broadcasting in Australia. Its powers to grant, renew or revoke commercial and public broadcasting licences, formulate program and advertising standards, authorise changes to licence ownership or control, and hold inquiries into aspects of broadcasting have always made it controversial, if not as powerful as some people may wish. Because it has the unenviable task of overseeing the implementation of the federal government's changing media policies in times of technological change, its controversial image is likely to last through the 1990s.

Australian Capital Territory (ACT)

The federal territory of the ACT comprises an irregularly shaped wedge of land 2357sq.km in area, situated between Goulburn and Yass in NSW; it was transferred from NSW to the Commonwealth on 1 January 1911. Within it lies > *Canberra*, the seat of the federal government. The ACT also incorporates a separate area of 72.5sq.km at > *Jervis Bay* on the NSW south coast, which was ceded to the Commonwealth (for unrealised development as the federal port) in 1915. At the census of 1986 the population of the ACT was 249 407, of whom 248 441 lived in Canberra.

The residents of the ACT have consistently eschewed self-government, most recently at a referendum held in 1979, but in 1988 the federal government imposed independence upon them. Elections to a seventeen-member ACT legislative assembly were held in 1989: despite the fact that a simple majority was held by the forces opposing self-government, the ALP formed a government with the support of the Liberals, and Rosemary Follett was elected first chief minister. In December 1989, a no-confidence vote led to the defeat of this government and its replacement by an alliance of Residents Rally and Abolish Self-government representatives. The ACT also elects two representatives each to the Senate and House of Representatives.

Australian Children's Television Foundation > *broadcasting*

Australian Conservation Foundation
> *environment and conservation*

Australian Council of Churches This

association of Australian churches was constituted in 1946; its members include the Anglican, Uniting and Orthodox churches as well as the Salvation Army and various minority sects. It works to improve church understanding of issues in contemporary society and to strengthen Christianity in Australia and overseas. It is also actively involved in social and human-rights issues such as nuclear disarmament, racism, and Aboriginal and refugee

welfare. The organisation is funded by contribution and is affiliated with the World Council of Churches.

Australian Council of Trade Unions
> *ACTU*

Australian Defence Force Academy
> *defence forces*

Australian Democrats This political party

has held a balance of power in the Senate since 1980 and has representation in the upper houses of some States. Originally seen as a centrist party aiming to 'keep the bastards honest', it is now on many issues more radical than the ALP. The Democrats came into being in 1977 when Don Chipp – a minister in the Holt, Gorton and McMahon governments and a backbencher under Malcolm Fraser – resigned from the Liberal Party. Joined by most former members of the Australia Party and some former Liberal and Labor supporters, he formed the Australian Democrats; in the election of that year, he and Colin Mason were elected senators.

Unlike the major political parties, the Democrats elect their leader and decide their policies by a secret vote of all party members, although Chipp's election as leader in 1977 was a foregone conclusion and his dominance over the party through the 1980, 1983 and 1984 elections was unquestioned – hence his ability to force compromises in turn on the Fraser Liberal government and the Hawke Labor government. On his resignation in 1986 his place was taken by Senator Janine Haines, the first female leader of an Australian parliamentary political party. She led the Democrats in the federal elections of 1987 and 1990, the party each time winning an increased number of Senate seats. Despite an overall swing of more than 5% to the Democrats in the 1990 election, reflecting the community's jaundiced view of both major parties, Haines failed in her bid to win a place in the lower house and announced her resignation from the leadership forthwith. >> *political parties*

Australian English The bulk of Australian

vocabulary and usage is common to British and, to a lesser extent, American English, but there is also a distinctive Australian English. This language had evolved sufficiently by the end of the 19th century to lead to several published collections, including *Austral English*

(1898) by E.E. Morris and an *Australian Slang Dictionary* (1895) by Cornelius Crowe. Australian English, like the Australian accent, is remarkably homogeneous across the continent, although there are some regional variations: some would ask for a schooner, middy or pony of beer, others for a pot or pint; many shorten the 'a' in 'castle'.

Vocabulary Distinctively Australian words can be grouped: those borrowed from Aboriginal words most commonly refer to flora and fauna (boobialla, kangaroo, budgerigar); other words, while neologisms, were mostly made up from English words (outback, offsider, bottle-brush, saltbush); and a few were completely invented (jackeroo). Confusingly, many English names were given to species totally different from the European (ash, cedar, robin). The greatest number of peculiarly Australian words, however, derives from English words of two categories: slang, either that specific to the convict language as recorded by convict > *James Hardy Vaux* early in the 19th century (new chum, swag), or from regional dialects spoken by early convicts and settlers, some of which have died out in their place of origin (ringer, larrikin); and standard English words, which in Australia acquired extended, often completely new, meanings (paddock, run, creek, mob, station). Some English words, at first transplanted, were soon completely replaced (meadow, field, wood and stream). Words of American origin include a number associated with land survey (block, section, township) and many associated with the gold rushes (digger, prospect, cradle). Other Australian words resulting from the gold era include gutter, reef and fossick. Further words were coined or acquired during the two world wars, such as deener, dekko, buckshee and bint. European immigrants and their languages have had little direct linguistic impact, but many words were coined or adopted to describe them (balt, reffo, gyppo, wog). Other words, mostly derogatory, to describe nationalities or races included boong, chink, dago, pom, slope (US) and shine (1930s US for a negro, now defunct, popularised in a song sung by Louis Armstrong).

Usage and idiom The present trend is for increased American usage (scam, ballpark) and spelling, although there is no consistency of approach and much confusion. The Australian Government Publishing Service *Style Manual* (1987 reprint) recommends the US spelling 'program' but retains the English usages 'colour', 'favour', etc.; the 1988 edition recommends using the Macquarie Dictionary as a guide (the Macquarie uses 'program' but also 'programme music'). The ABC uses 'colour', the commercial television channels 'color'. The *Age* newspaper uses mainly American spelling but, inter alia, retains 'centre'. It is worth noting that the Australian Labor Party has used the US spelling since its name was adopted in 1908. In a world increasingly reliant on the computer, and where computer software is predominantly of US creation, it is probably futile to fight the increasing use of American spelling; even the London *Times* has accepted 'jail', 'gaol' being notorious for misprints.

Australia also has a colourful colloquial language – although now disappearing, smothered in part by the spread of American English. Surprisingly, in 20 years of decimal currency not a single familiar name has appeared for any denomination, whereas sterling currency had numerous nicknames including 'trey' (3d), zack (6d) and deener (1s). Australianisms such as 'dinkum', 'drongo', 'bonzer', 'bludge', 'dunny', 'galah', 'humdinger', 'no-hoper', 'troppo' and 'woop-woop' are still heard, as is 'chook' (an old British word, but unrecognised in Britain as referring to a domestic fowl). The comedian > *Barry Humphries* has through his characters – notably Barry McKenzie – virtually single-handedly preserved the rich lexicon of Australian colloquialisms: 'a four by two' (= Jew); 'to chunder', 'technicolour yawn' or 'to park a tiger' (= to vomit); 'to nudge the turps' or 'to get stuck into the La Pérouse' (= to booze). 'Stone the crows', and 'starve the lizards' are still used as exclamations, and 'bastard' can still be heard as an expression of great affection (although never when preceded by 'pommy'). In addition, Australia has a vast lexicon of scatological sexual slang, probably unique in the English-speaking world for its expressive power. The truncation of words is also common, with the ubiquitous addition of an 'o' or 'ie' (journo, muso, pollie, garbo, tinnie, barbie); more than 200 examples of such diminutives are listed in *The Dinkum Dictionary* (1988) by Lenie Johansen.

The Australian accent There is a distinctive Australian accent which varies little across the continent. In 1946, Professor A.G. Mitchell noted the common criticisms that the Australian accent was ugly, lazy, nasal, drawling, unclear, monotonous and flat; in fact, many of these characteristics are common to slovenly speech anywhere in the world. The Australian accent can be divided into three categories: broad, cultivated and general, the last being the accent of the bulk of the population. While there is considerable gradation from cultivated to broad speech, this is less marked than in the UK. The frequently alleged similarity to Cockney is only partial. Typically, the Australian voice is rather light, the intonation has little range, and delivery is slow and unemphasised. Vowels show the most characteristic features: mate (typically pronounced mite), home (howm), paint (pint); elision is also common. Amusing illustrations of the Australian accent can be found in *Strine* (1982) by 'Afferbeck Lauder' (= 'Alphabetical Order') [Alistair Morrison]. One unfortunate recent development in the Australian accent is the use of 'd' instead of the 't' in such words as 'quarter'.

Since the 1970s there has been a greater pride in the Australian accent, with advertising agencies exploiting its use as a selling point and with directives to ABC announcers to forsake Received Pronunciation (RP) – often defined as BBC English or Home Counties English. In the current climate of 'ockerism', Australians who speak well – that is, attempt an adapted RP by enunciating clearly and giving due weight to words – are often said to have 'a plum in the mouth' and are suspected of being 'pommy bastards'. On the other hand, many Australian expatriates (or, as Barry Humphries has defined them, traitors) and politicians find it expedient to cultivate broad Australian accents.

Australian Film Commission

This statutory authority was established by the federal government in 1975 to encourage Australian film production. In 1987, the commission spent more than $28 million in the development and production of films, and in its capacity as an advisory and marketing service to the industry. It also controls Film Australia, the film and video production arm of the Commonwealth, which makes about 80 documentaries each year on a range of social, educational and scientific subjects. >> *film industry.*

Australian Heritage Commission > *heritage conservation*

Australian Inland Mission

This mission was established in 1912 by the Presbyterian Church to provide spiritual, medical and social services to people in isolated areas of Australia. It resulted largely from a report by the Rev.

> *John Flynn* on the needs of outback settlers and Flynn was the mission's first superintendent 1912–51; the first outposts were Oodnadatta in SA, Pine Creek in the NT and Port Hedland in WA. In 1928, with the assistance of electrical engineer Alfred Traeger, Flynn established Australia's first aerial medical service, the original Flying Doctor Service, at Cloncurry in Qld. The mission's extensive network of facilities includes nursing homes, kindergartens, churches, and preventive-health courses. When the Uniting Church of Australia was formed in 1977, the mission came under the administration of the new church and was renamed the Uniting Church National Mission.

Australian Journalists' Association (AJA)

Formed in 1910 by Vic. political journalist B.S.B. Cook, the AJA is the federal union representing journalists and newspaper contributors such as artists and photographers. It is notable in Australian industrial history for its 1917 award, the first with provisions applying equally to male and female members, although many would argue that the union did not subsequently press the spirit of equality. Internationally, the AJA was a pioneer in applying self-regulatory ethical codes: under its 1944 Code of Ethics (revised 1983), members can be charged with unethical behaviour.

Australian Labor Party > *ALP*

Australian Medical Association (AMA)

A voluntary organisation of doctors and the profession's major lobby group, the AMA was formed in 1961 from the various Australian branches of the British Medical Association; its expressed function is to serve the interests and safeguard the freedom of the medical profession. A staunch defender of private medical practice, the AMA negotiates with governments and international bodies on matters such as medical fees, the remuneration of salaried doctors, and the structure and implementation of the national health system. In addition, it publishes the highly regarded *Medical Journal of Australia* (1914), promotes scientific and cultural aspects of medicine, holds national medical congresses, maintains medical libraries for members and generally encourages high ethical standards of professional practice. One of the most frequent criticisms of the AMA has been its conservatism and elitism, and factionalism has seen various other medical groups established in the last 20 years, notably the

General Practitioners' Society (1968) and the Doctors' Reform Society (1973).

Australian Natives' Association (ANA)

A patriotic association of native-born Australians, the ANA was founded as a friendly society in Vic. in 1871. For some time it exerted considerable political influence, actively concerned in the movement for Federation (many of its proposals were eventually embodied in the Constitution), women's suffrage, the one-man-one-vote principle, and later such vital national issues as defence, immigration, conservation, social welfare, and the eligibility of native-born citizens for high office. Since the 1950s, the ANA has been known mainly for its role in health insurance.

Australian Press Council This organisation was established by the newspaper industry in 1976 to uphold freedom of the press and to adjudicate public complaints about press performance. It was originally a tripartite organisation, comprising some publishers, the Australian Journalists' Association (AJA) and public representatives. The council has periodically been criticised for putting the interests of newspaper proprietors before those of the public and in 1987 the AJA withdrew its membership after the council failed to take a firm stand against News Ltd's take-over of the Herald & Weekly Times Group, which gave it a majority control over Australia's press media. >> *media ownership and control*

Australian Red Cross Society > *Red Cross Society*

Australian Rules football This innovation in the game of football was established in Melbourne in 1858 by T.W. Wills and H.C. Harrison. Wills, who had played football at Rugby School in England, sought to develop a code that would exclude some of the violent excesses of rugby and incorporate aspects of the football already evolving in Melbourne. The game developed quickly, and with the rules codified became the dominant form in Vic., Tas., SA, WA and the Riverina area of NSW. Crowds of 30 000 were common at the games by the 1890s, and support for Australian Rules developed in all sections of the community; by 1900 the distinctive features of marking and long-kicking had been established.

The Vic. Football Association (VFA) was formed in 1877, and regulatory bodies were established in other colonies. In 1897 a breakaway group set up the Vic. Football League (VFL), which became the strongest competition in Australia. The Australian Football Council was formed in 1906 as a co-ordinating body, but the game's real base lay in loyalty to local clubs. In the VFL Collingwood was the most significant club, winning successive premierships 1927–30. Vic. dominated interstate competition, and with its greater population and the wealth of its clubs was able to lure many players from other States. By the 1970s play had become faster, with greater emphasis on handball and running, and the drop kick had disappeared. In recent years a national competition has slowly evolved: the South Melbourne club transferred to Sydney in 1983, and clubs from Perth and Brisbane joined the competition in 1987. In tandem with these developments, by 1990 the VFL had changed its title to the Australian Football League (AFL).

There are 500 000 registered players, modified rules being used in junior and school games. Despite the absence of overseas competition, the game remains healthy and popular, the 1970 VFL Grand Final holding the record for sporting attendance with a crowd of 121 696.

Australian Security Intelligence Organization > *ASIO; intelligence services*

Australian War Memorial Situated in Canberra, the Australian War Memorial commemorates the 102 000 dead of all the wars and engagements in which Australia has fought, from the Sudan to Vietnam. Opened in 1941, it is built around a central courtyard and pool flanked by galleries containing the exhibits, with casualty lists placed along arched cloisters leading to the Hall of Memory. It also serves as an art gallery and museum, housing 12 000 paintings and sculptures, a collection of 50 000 war relics, more than 100 000 photographs, and thousands of books and official and personal documents. More than a million people visit the memorial each year.

Australian Women's Weekly Brainchild of English journalist George Warnecke and newspaper proprietor Frank Packer, the *Weekly* became the flagship and principal money-spinner of the expanding Australian Consolidated Press empire (> *Packer family*). First published in June 1933, the magazine was selling 450 000 copies by 1941. Its success in its first 40 years was due to clever use (from 1936) of colour photography of national and international news events, and the uncanny ability of successive editors – Warnecke (1933–8), Alice Jackson (1938–50) and Esme Fenston (1950–72) – to tap the mood of middle Australia. The social turbulence of the 1970s, and a change in editorial emphasis under Ita Buttrose (1975–80), caused a hiccup in growth. Increasing costs and stiffer competition prompted format changes: in December 1982, the *Weekly* became a monthly publication; a year later circulation topped one million and in the late 1980s the *Weekly* was still Australia's most widely read magazine.

Australia Party This party was formed in 1966 by dissatisfied Liberals and titled the Liberal Reform Group; its initial concerns included opposition to Australia's involvement in the Vietnam War and a desire for party members to contribute to policy. It was subsequently renamed the Australian Reform Movement (1967) and the Australia Party (1969). Its greatest electoral success was in NSW, where its founder Gordon Barton resided, but even there its highest vote was only 5.5% (1970), and with the advent of the Australian Democrats in 1977 most of its members joined that party.

Australind WA (pop. 2864) This resort 145km south of Perth has more recently developed as a commuter suburb of nearby Bunbury. It was named after an abortive land settlement scheme attempted in 1841 by the WA Land Co. to establish a trade link between Australia and India. Dairying and tourism are its main industries today.

australwinks > *gastropods*

aviation With its great internal distances and remoteness from major overseas centres, Australia is one of the most airminded countries in the world. It has an enviable reputation for both the quality and safety of its air services and there has not been a major disaster involving an Australian commercial plane since 1968. Within Australia, fatalities involving registered civil aircraft averaged 46 per annum in the late 1980s, an excellent record given that in 1987 there were more than 7000 aircraft – from airliners to gliders – registered in Australia.

Since 1952, Australian domestic aviation has operated under what is commonly called the 'two-airline policy', whereby two airlines (one government-owned) monopolised air services. The federal government announced the end of this arrangement in 1987, and from 1990 Australia will adopt an 'open skies' policy similar to that operating in the US. Some concern has been expressed about this development, particularly regarding safety and maintenance standards, and the ability of the present airports to handle the extra traffic that deregulation is expected to generate. Sydney's Kingsford Smith airport, Australia's premier air gateway, is already experiencing serious passenger and aircraft delays, but being virtually in the centre of the city has little room for expansion. On the other hand, genuine competition between airlines may result in better service, less duplication of timetables, and lower airfares.

Pioneer aviation Some early contributions to the development of flight were made in Australia, notably by Henry Sutton, > *Lawrence Hargrave*, and G.A. Taylor (who in 1909 made the first heavier-than-air flight in Australia in a motorless glider of his own design). World War 1 stimulated the development of aviation; in 1919, the > *Smith brothers* proved the practicality of intercontinental flight, flying from England to Australia in 28 days. Other pioneers were H.J.L. (Bert) Hinkler, Charles Ulm, > *Harry Hawker*, > *P.G. Taylor* and, most notably, > *Charles Kingsford Smith*. The attrition rate, however, was high; Ross Smith, Ulm, Hawker, Hinkler and Kingsford Smith all died in plane crashes.

As aviation progressed, it became clear that safety and quality controls were necessary and the 1920 Air Navigation Act instituted a civil aviation branch within the Department of Defence; this body was replaced by a separate Department of Civil Aviation in 1938. Since the 1970s, aviation has been under the control of the Department of Transport and Communications, which has wide powers to regulate the industry and does so with notable thoroughness.

Domestic airline services Intrastate services were begun in 1921 with a Geraldton–Derby route flown by WA Airways. This route was later expanded to Perth and Adelaide. In 1920, Qld and NT Aerial Services Ltd was formed by a group of Qld pastoralists in association with two World War I pilots, P.J. McGinness and W. Hudson Fysh. Known by the acronym

Qantas, it began a regular airmail service from Charleville to Cloncurry in 1922. In 1929, Kingsford Smith and Ulm started the first Australian National Airways (ANA), operating between capital cities, but the economic depression and the loss of an Avro X aircraft, the *Southern Cloud*, in the Snowy Mountains in 1931, bankrupted the company.

In 1936 a new ANA was formed, with the Tas. Holyman family and the Huddart Parker shipping line as major shareholders. It quickly became the main force in domestic aviation, taking over numerous smaller companies. ANA introduced the American DC2 and, later, the DC3 into local aviation, a break from the previous preponderance of British aircraft. After World War 2, the Chifley government unsuccessfully attempted to nationalise civil aviation; having failed to do so it established the Australian National Airlines Commission to operate a competing airline, Trans-Australia Airlines (TAA). For a time ANA and TAA divided the market equally, but a rapidly expanding general transport company, Ansett Transport Industries (ATI), started by > *Reginald Ansett*, was beginning to put pressure on this comfortable duopoly. By substantially cutting fares, Ansett Airways Pty Ltd (the aviation arm of ATI) began eroding ANA's market share.

In 1957, following the death of ANA's founder, Sir Ivan Holyman, the company was sold to ATI for £3.3 million, an extraordinary business coup; the resourceful Ansett – with assistance from the Menzies government, which was concerned about the success of TAA – then set about taking over most of Australia's private airlines. In 1979, ATI was purchased by a consortium of TNT Ltd and News Ltd. Today, Ansett Airlines and the government-owned Australian Airlines (TAA's new name from 1986) share the market between them, using fleets of American Boeing jets and European Airbuses. The only independent airline of any size remaining after Ansett's original take-over spree, the NSW-based East-West Airlines, was absorbed by TNT Ltd and News Ltd in 1987.

As well as Ansett Airways and Australian Airlines and their subsidiaries, there are 46 commuter airlines in Australia, which provide a valuable feeder service for small towns or remote destinations. These airlines carry more than a million passengers annually, flying mainly Piper, Beechcraft and Cessna aircraft.

The two-airline policy The two-airline policy was instituted by the Menzies government through the passage of legislation assuring TAA and ANA (later Ansett Airlines) of an equal share in airmail contracts and major trunk routes; any potential competition was effectively eliminated by the government's use of customs regulations to refuse licences for the import of necessary aircraft. By the late 1980s the proposed dismantling of the system was still a matter of public debate; given Australia's small population and the costs involved in establishing an airline, it is possible that the fruits of deregulation may not be as dramatic or as beneficial as anticipated.

International airline services In 1987, 30 overseas carriers serviced Australia, most under bilateral agreements which give Australia's international airline, Qantas, reciprocal landing rights. In 1986, 2.8 million passengers entered Australia, more than half of them carried by Qantas.

Qantas grew out of the Qld and NT Aerial Service founded in 1920. In partnership with Britain's Imperial Airways, it flew its first overseas service from Brisbane to Singapore in 1935 using a DH86; this was the first stage in a route to London, the rest of which was flown by Imperial Airways. In 1937, Qantas moved its headquarters from Brisbane to Sydney and began flying luxurious Empire Flying Boats on its Singapore route. During World War 2, most Qantas aircraft were commissioned for active service, although routes were kept open to Karachi and Colombo.

Postwar, Qantas and the British Overseas Airways Corporation (BOAC), the new name for Imperial Airways, resumed the service to the UK. In 1947, Qantas began an independent service to London operating Lockheed Constellation aircraft. In the same year, the Australian government nationalised Qantas, buying out the shareholdings of BOAC and the airline's founders. Qantas soon established routes to Hong Kong, Japan, South Africa and, following its take-over of the short-lived British Commonwealth Pacific Airlines, the US. Today, Qantas is a reliable operator with a modern all-Boeing fleet of 747 and 767 aircraft; it has the best safety record of all the world's major airlines, not having lost a plane since 1953. Qantas has made a profit in most years of its operation, an unusual situation in the airline business and helped by government policy which precludes charter airlines from intruding on its territory. Although it is the national flag-carrier, Qantas has for more than 30 years been in the unique and invidious position of not being permitted to carry domestic passengers in its own country, because of the two-airline policy.

Aircraft production Aircraft design, research and manufacture were carried out on a relatively modest scale until just before World War 2. During World War 1 the Central Flying School at Point Cook in Vic. constructed and repaired trainers, but an ambitious government proposal to construct 200 DH9A bombers was scrapped at the end of the war. In the early years of aviation, a number of small planes were built privately. Many small firms were established in the 1920s, providing aircraft for a market where demand was beginning to exceed supply. Planes were also being built under licence: Qantas constructed de Havilland aircraft at Longreach, Qld, and the Australian Aircraft and Engineering Co. assembled Avro planes at Mascot in Sydney. Also, an RAAF experimental station was established at Randwick, NSW, under Squadron Leader (later Sir) Lawrence Wackett; its production included Warblers and Widgeons. In 1927, the British de Havilland company established an Australian subsidiary at Mascot, assembling DH60 Moths. With another war just over the horizon, the government formed the Commonwealth Aircraft Corporation (CAC) in 1936. Based at Fisherman's Bend, Vic., it was placed under the command of Wackett. During World War 2 the CAC, de Havilland, and a third organisation, the Department of Aircraft Production, formed the nucleus of Australian aircraft production, providing planes for the RAAF when few were available from traditional overseas sources. The CAC produced Wirraways, Wackett trainers, Boomerang fighters and, later, US-designed Mustang fighters under licence; de Havilland produced mainly Tiger Moth trainers and more than 100 DH89 Mosquito bombers; the Department of Aircraft Production produced Beaufort bombers and Beaufighters. Overall, the industry supplied the RAAF with more than 3500 planes during and immediately after the war.

The industry was restructured postwar, with the Government Aircraft Factories (GAF) replacing the Department of Aircraft Production. Planes constructed or assembled by GAF and CAC included Lincoln and Canberra bombers and Sabre jets. In 1950 GAF produced Australia's first home-designed jet, the Pika, a prototype for the pilotless drone, the Jindivik.

Construction or assembly of overseas-designed military planes and helicopters today is the main function of AeroSpace Technologies of Australia (a proprietary limited company which replaced GAF in 1987), CAC and Hawker de Havilland: their products include the Mirage, F-111, F/A-18 Hornet, Pilatus PC9 trainer, and Sikorsky Seahawk and Black Hawk helicopters; components are also made for most major overseas aircraft companies, including British Aerospace, Boeing, Fokker and Airbus Industrie. Australia's most important locally designed non-military plane is the Nomad, a small general-purpose aircraft originally built by GAF, which has had substantial overseas sales. Aircraft manufacture is a relatively small but vitally important part of Australia's economic and defence structure, providing both an essential base for a specialised workforce and immense savings in foreign exchange through offset arrangements.

avocets > *waders*

Avon Valley WA An agricultural and pastoral region chiefly producing wheat and sheep, the Avon Valley is one of the earliest settled rural areas of the State. Through it runs the Avon River, which rises to the west of the Darling Range, traverses it through deep gorges, and east of the range is known as the Swan River.

Ayers Rock NT One of the world's great natural monoliths – an oval, dome-shaped mass some 9km in circumference rising 335m above a level plain – Ayers Rock is composed of vertically dipping strata of pinkish-red conglomerate. The fluted effect of the steep lower slopes is the result of the erosion of softer layers by seepage and sudden downpours. The region is arid, with extremes of temperature, and the low rainfall is irregular, but numerous holes and gullies on the rock summit retain storm water, overflowing to create 'White cataracts ... high-veiling the sun-baked walls'. The rock is of sacred significance to Aborigines (who call it Uluru), and Aboriginal paintings decorate its cave walls. Together with nearby Mt Olga (> *Olgas*), it is now part of Uluru National Park and is a major tourist attraction, probably one of the best known features of Australia. Freehold title to Ayers Rock and the national park was transferred to the Matitjula community in 1985, although the region has since been leased to and managed by the federal government. The rock was noted by Ernest Giles in 1872, but visited and named after the premier of SA, Sir Henry Ayers, by William Gosse in the following year.

Ayr Qld (pop. 8639) This town in the Burdekin shire, 1255km north of Brisbane, was founded in 1882 as the centre for the region's burgeoning sugar industry and has maintained that role to the present day. A bridge links it with the other delta centre of Home Hill, 11km to the south. The surrounding district is now the principal rice producer in Qld.

B

Babbage, Benjamin Herschel (1815–78), explorer and scientist, b. England. Babbage arrived in Australia in 1851. Employed by the SA government to survey for gold, he led two official explorations (1856 and 1858) which helped to prove that Lake Eyre and Lake Torrens were separate; alleged incompetence led to his being superseded. He was involved to a considerable degree in surveying the route of the Overland Telegraph Line.

babblers and allies The family Timaliidae comprises three groups of forest-dwelling birds – logrunners, babblers and whipbirds. Among the logrunners, *Orthonyx*, are two species found in Australian rainforests. They are solidly built birds; to feed they scratch the forest floor, and while doing this they support themselves with their tails, a habit that causes the tail feathers to wear away, leaving only the shaft and so bringing the birds their alternative name, spinetails.

The true babblers, *Pomatostomus*, comprise five Australian species of mainly inland forest birds, about the size of thrushes with large heads and tails and rather large, sharp, slightly down-curved beaks. They are generally brown with whitish underparts, though some have a conspicuous white eye-strip and tail-patch. They are highly social, usually seen busily turning over forest litter in search of grubs, and chattering loudly. The babbler's nest is a large, superficially untidy, dome-shaped structure with a side entrance, often in a high fork of a tree, and the bird lays three to six brownish eggs.

The whipbirds, *Psophodes,* represent two uniquely Australian species, generally dark-green and black birds with white-edged throats; the name derives from their remarkable call of soft whistles, an explosive, whip-like crack, and melodious cheeps.

Bacchus Marsh Vic. (pop. 7640) This shire and town grew at a coach crossing of the Werribee River, 49km from Melbourne, on the route to the central Vic. goldfields in the 1850s. The Border Inn, which opened in 1850, is thought to be Vic.'s first coaching stop. The town is now a dairying and orchard centre, and is a nascent commuter base for people working in Melbourne.

Badham, Charles (1813–84), classical scholar, b. England. An Anglican minister of somewhat unorthodox views, Badham arrived in Australia in 1867 to become professor of classics and logic at the University of Sydney, which position he held until 1884. A brilliant Greek scholar, he was noted for his eloquence and erudition. He maintained exacting educational standards and was the first to advocate access to the university through correspondence and evening classes.

Bailey family, botanists and horticulturalists. **John** (1800–64), b. England, arrived in Australia in 1839 and was briefly colonial botanist in SA before establishing a nursery. He was accompanied to Australia by his son **Frederick Manson** (1827–1915), who was appointed Qld colonial botanist in 1881. He published many articles, made botanical collections in north Qld and NG, and published his six-part *Queensland Flora* 1899–1902 (which was largely extracted from Bentham's *Flora Australiensis* of 1863–78). Frederick's son **John Frederick** (1866–?) was Qld government botanist 1915–17 but resigned to become director of the Adelaide Botanic Gardens. A grandson of F.M. Bailey, **Cyril Tenison White** (1890–1950), succeeded J.F. Bailey as government botanist in Qld and held the position until his death; he published much original work on the plants and vegetation of northern Australia, NG and the Pacific.

Baillieu family, prominent in Australian finance and industry. **James George** (1832–

97), b. Wales, arrived in Queenscliff, Vic. in 1853. In 1881, with his third son **George Francis**, he opened the Ozone Hotel; each later became mayor of the municipality. George's daughter, **(Margery) Merlyn** (1900–82), married Sidney Myer (> *Myer family*). The second son, **William Lawrence** (1859–1936), became a successful auctioneer before the 1890s depression; he then acquired banking interests, which allowed him to invest in lead and zinc mining at Broken Hill in NSW. He directed many Melbourne companies and encouraged the development of new technology – particularly the flotation process which revolutionised metallurgical development and revitalised Broken Hill. He later fostered Australian electrolytic zinc smelting and Tas. paper production. As a member of the Vic. parliament 1901–22, he supported free enterprise but was skilful in negotiating with industrial groups. His eldest son, **Clive Latham**, 1st Baron Baillieu (1889–1967), continued the family's support of industry and represented Australia on many international committees.

Bairnsdale Vic. (pop. 10 500) This industrial and tourist centre for east Gippsland is situated on the Mitchell River 280km east of Melbourne. The area was settled in 1844 by a squatter, Archibald Macleod, and later developed briefly as a port. Today the main industries are farming, fishing and sawmilling; tourism is also important, with the Gippsland Lakes 5km to the south and mountains to the north.

Baker, Richard Thomas (1855–1941), botanist, b. England. Baker joined the Sydney Technological Museum in 1888 and was both curator and economic botanist there until 1921. With H.G. Smith he founded a school of eucalypt taxonomy and investigated the economic aspects of Australian plants, most notably essential oils. Although their pioneering analyses in this field heavily influenced their approach to plant classification, in some instances leading to unjustified conclusions, a number of important eucalypt species were first distinguished by Baker.

Baker, Snowy (Reginald Leslie) (1884–1953), sportsman, b. Sydney. Baker was an all-round athlete: he is alleged to have played more than 20 sports throughout his career, with particular achievements in swimming, boxing, rugby and rowing. In 1902 he won the Australian middleweight and heavyweight boxing titles on the same night; he later became a successful boxing promoter through his company Stadiums Ltd, eventually retiring to the US.

baler shells > *gastropods*

Ballarat Vic. (pop. 65 000) This thriving rural city, about 113km west of Melbourne, was the hub of the Vic. gold rushes for 20 years from 1851, to which its fine Victorian architecture, parks and cultural life still bear witness. The gently rolling countryside was opened up by Thomas Learmonth for emergency grazing during the drought of 1837. By 1851, when gold was found, Ballarat held only a few scattered workers' huts – three years later it had a population of 27 000, which rose to more than 60 000 by 1870. Although gold-mining declined from that time, primary and secondary industries developed in its stead and persist today – most notably wool, cereals, fruit and vegetables, and a broad manufacturing base. Tourism contributes much to the local economy: about 450 000 people visit nearby Sovereign Hill (a reconstruction of a 19th-century gold-mining town) each year, and the city has a fine art gallery as well as a substantial architectural heritage. The original spelling of 'Ballaarat' is still used for official purposes.

ballet and dance For the first 150 years of European settlement, ballet in Australia was generally small-scale and performed on an amateur basis. While the influence of touring Russian companies occasioned increased interest and professionalism in ballet from the 1920s, the first major national company was not formed until the 1960s.

Classical ballet remains the most widely popular form of dance in Australia. There are more than 2500 ballet schools throughout the country and nine tertiary courses which include dance. Major senior courses are held at the Australian Ballet School (entrance by audition), the WA Academy of Performing Arts, and the Queensland Dance School of Excellence.

Historical development Australia's first dance academy opened in Sydney in 1833 and the first ballet was performed two years later. Romantic ballet was at its height in Europe in the mid-19th century and dancers from England and France introduced the colonies to masterworks such as *La Sylphide* (1845), and

Giselle and *La Fille Mal Gardée* (both 1855). The popularity of ballet waned during the latter part of the 19th century, however, and from the 1870s it was most commonly performed only as an adjunct to plays and operas. Interest in classical ballet revived in 1913 when the Danish dancer Adeline Genee toured with a company from the Imperial Russian Ballet. Tours by Anna Pavlova and her company in 1926 and 1929 were enormously popular and prompted many young Australians to study ballet. > *Robert Helpmann*, then aged 14, was accepted by Pavlova as a pupil and travelled with the company during its first Australian visit, before making his professional debut in Sydney in 1927.

The most formative decade for Australian ballet was undoubtedly the 1930s. In 1934 another great Russian dancer, Olga Spessivtzeva, toured with the Dandre-Levitoff company. It was the subsequent visits by the Ballets Russes companies of Colonel de Basil (in 1936, 1938 and 1940), however, which laid the foundations of professional ballet in Australia. The legacy of this company was a new and widespread public enthusiasm for ballet and the formation, in the early 1940s, of ballet academies and professional companies by the dancers Helen Kirsova and Edouard Borovansky, who remained in Australia; a third member of the Ballets Russes, Kira Bousloff, formed the WA Ballet in 1952. Modern dance was introduced by Gertrud Bodenwieser, a creative-expressive dancer and pedagogue from Vienna, who settled in Australia in 1938 and formed a ballet company and school. She died in 1959, but her work lives on at the Bodenwieser Dance Centre in Sydney.

Borovansky's company, touring under the auspices of the theatrical entrepreneur J.C. Williamson, enjoyed enormous popularity until the late 1950s. After his death in 1959, however, the company survived only for another two years. Despite the formation of a number of State and commercial companies from the 1940s onwards, there was still no truly national ballet company until, with government assistance, the Australian Ballet made its debut in November 1962. The company is now firmly established and has made many successful tours to the UK, Europe, the US and South America, the USSR, Asia and Southeast Asia. The company's founding artistic director was > *Peggy Van Praagh*, followed by Robert Helpmann, Anne Woolliams, > *Marilyn Jones* and Maina Gielgud. Its repertoire is eclectic,

representing most of the great choreographers – from the classics of Petipa and Ivanov to 20th-century works by Balanchine, Ashton and Bejart. Fine dancers of the Australian Ballet have included Marilyn Jones, > *Kathleen Gorham*, Marilyn Rowe, Lucette Aldous, Christine Walsh, Lisa Pavane, Fiona Tonkin, Garth Welch, > *Kelvin Coe*, John Meehan, Gary Norman, Jonathan Kelly, David Ashmole, Paul de Masson, Greg Horsman and Stephen Heathcote. Like the other large companies, the Australian Ballet now relies mainly on box-office receipts for its survival (some 70% of its income in 1989).

As well as the Australian Ballet, and the major State companies noted below, there are numerous small companies and groups throughout the country, the more notable including Tasdance in Tas.; the Meryl Tankard Company in Canberra; One Extra and Dance Exchange in Sydney; Dance North, Australian Youth Ballet, and Expressions in Qld; Dance Works in Melbourne; and 2 Dance Plus in WA. The Aboriginal/Islander Dance Theatre and School (formed in Sydney in 1975), combines the dance forms of these peoples with mainstream modern dance.

State companies The Sydney Dance Company has enjoyed great success both at home and abroad since 1976, when it acquired its present form, title, and artistic director > *Graeme Murphy*. Under Murphy the company has developed an idiosyncratic style which is neither classical nor conventionally modern, but strikingly theatrical. Janet Vernon, the company's principal dancer, is considered the supreme interpreter of Murphy's choreography. The Qld Ballet was founded in 1962 by Charles Lisner and in 1967 was the first regional company to receive State government subsidy. The company's aim, then as now, was to encourage Australian dancers, choreographers, musicians and designers, and although classically based it has a mixed repertoire of traditional and new works. The WA Ballet has had several noted artistic directors since its foundation by Bousloff in 1952, including Rex Reid and Garth Welch. Under its present director, Barry Moreland, a prolific choreographer, the company's repertoire is a mix of classical and contemporary dance. The Australian Dance Theatre of SA was founded in 1965 by Elizabeth Dalman as a modern dance company. It has largely remained so since, and under Jonathan Taylor (1976–86) made successful tours to the UK in 1980 and 1982.

Ballina NSW (pop. 12 500) A coastal resort and port at the mouth of the Richmond River, Ballina is situated 800km north of Sydney on the Pacific Highway. It is a busy tourist centre, with excellent beaches frequented by both fishermen and surfers; it has also become a popular retirement destination. The surrounding district supports mixed farming and Ballina is a regional business and commercial centre.

ballooning > *sky sports*

Balls Pyramid NSW A sheer pinnacle of Tertiary basalt, the 'pyramid' rises some 550m above the Tasman Sea, 19km southeast of Lord Howe Island. It was named for its discoverer, Henry Lidgbird Ball.

Balmain bug > *crayfishes and allies*

Balonne River Qld A seasonally flowing 280km continuation of the Condamine River in southeast Qld, the south-flowing Balonne forms anabranches (including the Culgoa) before crossing the NSW border to become part of the Darling River system. In 1972 the Beadmore dam was constructed at the confluence of the Balonne and Maranoa rivers; this regulates the river flow and provides water for irrigation. The valley's main pastoral pursuit is sheep grazing.

Balranald NSW (pop. 1398) A former ferry point on the Murrumbidgee River, near its junction with the Murray, Balranald is both a shire and a town and lies some 865km southwest of Sydney. It was developed originally as a potential centre for the river trade as well as surrounding pastoral properties, but the decline of steamboat traffic by 1900 ended the town's trade link. When the early summer floods spread over the surrounding hollows, the town is plagued by mosquitoes and graced by many beautiful waterfowl.

Bancks, James Charles > *cartoons*

Bancroft family, eminent in medical science. **Joseph** (1836–94), b. England, established a medical practice in Brisbane but was best known for his medical research. In 1877 he revealed the cause of the serious tropical disease elephantiasis; he also studied the transmission of insect-borne diseases and was the first to show the prevalence of leprosy in Australia. His son, **Thomas Lane** (1860–1933), b.

England, continued Joseph's work on disease transmission and in 1905 proved that dengue fever was carried by a mosquito. He was acclaimed for his studies of the Qld lungfish, and his large collection of natural-history specimens led to the recognition of many new species. He also made pharmacological studies of more than 1000 plants.

banded anteater > *numbat*

bandicoots These long-snouted marsupials form two families, the Peramelidae and the Thylacomyidae, and are found in a variety of habitats in Australia and the NG region. Coarse-haired and with a short tail, the bandicoot has snout, claws and teeth adapted to its feeding habits; much of its diet – in which insects, other arthropods and small mammals predominate – is obtained by digging, although some plant material is taken. The bandicoot is a solitary animal active only at night, spending daylight hours in nests hidden below bushes or grass tussocks; the nest is a shallow depression scraped out of the ground and lined with grass and leaf litter.

Genera within the family Peramelidae include *Perameles*, long-nosed bandicoots, of which one, the desert bandicoot, may now be extinct; *Isoodon*, short-nosed bandicoots, including species brown, golden and brindled; *Echymipera*, the spiny bandicoot, the sole species of this genus; and *Chaeropus*, the pig-footed bandicoot, considerably different in appearance from other family members, believed to be almost entirely vegetarian, and also now presumed to be extinct.

The family Thylacomyidae, the rabbit-eared bandicoots, contains one genus only – *Macrotis*, of which the two species are usually known as bilbies. They also differ from typical bandicoots; they have long, delicate ears, fur that is long and silky, and a long furry tail.

The name of these marsupials is a corruption of *Bandicota*, signifying a rodent genus of southern India, but the two animal groups are entirely unrelated.

Banfield, E.J. (Edmund James) (1852–1923), journalist and natural-history writer, b. England. Banfield lived for 25 years on Dunk Island off the north Qld coast. His fame rests on the personal but observant descriptions of his secluded tropical existence, notably in *The Confessions of a Beachcomber* (1908) and *My Tropic Isle* (1918).

Banks, Sir Joseph (1743–1820), botanist, b. England. Already a noted naturalist, Banks volunteered to join James Cook on his *Endeavour* voyage in 1768, at great personal expense. He initially described the Australian coast as barren and of little value, but after his return to England he changed his views sufficiently to recommend Botany Bay as a penal settlement. He subsequently retained his interest in both the politics and natural history of the colonies and was instrumental in obtaining a British ship for Matthew Flinders' 1798 expedition. His Australian correspondence and *Endeavour* journal are held in the Mitchell Library, Sydney; his journals, edited by J.C. Beaglehole, were published in facsimile in 1962; and engravings made by Sydney Parkinson on the *Endeavour* voyage were published as *Banks' Florilegium* in 1978.

banks and banking Despite its small population, Australia has long had one of the most stable and efficient banking systems in the world. In 1986 it comprised a central government bank (the Reserve Bank), 28 trading banks, 17 savings banks and three development banks, as well as numerous specialised non-bank institutions such as building societies and merchant banks. Six main groups dominated Australian banking for more than a century, until the financial system was deregulated in the 1980s: since that time, a number of new banks have been established and the distinction between bank and non-bank financial services has become increasingly blurred.

Historical development Australian banking began in 1817, with the establishment of the Bank of NSW in response to continuing finance and currency problems in the young colony. Banking practice followed the English system and the Bank of England performed central banking functions for the colonies throughout the 19th century. The number of banks increased dramatically during and after the 1850s gold rush, reaching a peak of 34 before the collapse which attended the economic depression of 1894. Twelve of the 21 surviving banks were forced to suspend payments, and although most were soon able to reopen their doors the losses to shareholders and depositors was estimated at £21 million.

In 1911 the federal government established its own bank – the Commonwealth Bank of Australia. Initially a trading and savings bank, it began to appropriate the central role of the Bank of England, to the general resentment of the longer-established private banks with which it still competed for deposits and loans. The Commonwealth Bank gradually relinquished its commercial functions as its role as a central bank increased, particularly during the 1930s depression and World War 2, and this position was formalised by legislation in 1945. An attempt by the Chifley government in 1947 to nationalise all the private banks was declared unconstitutional.

The next major reorganisation came in 1960 following the passage of the Reserve Bank Act and the Banking Act in 1959. The first established the Reserve Bank of Australia, which took over the central banking functions of the Commonwealth Bank and allocated tradings and savings bank functions to the new Commonwealth Banking Corporation. The second piece of legislation introduced tighter regulations on the private banks, which fostered tremendous growth among non-bank financial institutions such as finance companies, building societies, merchant banks and credit unions. While the banks retained some privileges, such as a monopoly over foreign exchange dealings, the other finance institutions had the advantage of being completely unregulated for nearly two decades. In 1974, however, the Financial Corporations Act empowered the Reserve Bank to examine and regulate their activities as well as those of the banks, not only to ensure that the Reserve Bank had complete control of monetary policy but also to protect depositors and promote competition.

The 1980s and beyond By the late 1970s it became apparent that strict regulation of the increasingly competitive financial system was causing market distortions and in some cases (as with limits on interest rates) discriminating against bank customers. The banks pressed for deregulation to allow them to compete more effectively, and their demands were supported by the 1980 interim report of the Campbell Committee, an inquiry into the financial system led by Sir Keith Campbell. The process of deregulation began in December 1980 with the removal of most controls on bank interest rates, which immediately allowed the banks to compete more effectively for funds. By mid-1984 all controls on banks had been removed, with the exception of the limit on interest rates for housing loans.

Controls over participation in the banking system were also lifted. A number of new trading and savings banks have since been established, often based on former building societies or created through mergers, as was the case with the Westpac Banking Corporation (an amalgamation of the Bank of NSW and the Commercial Bank of Australia) and the National Australia Bank (formerly the National Bank of Australia and the Commercial Banking Company). Sixteen foreign banks were also admitted, including a cross-section of the world's largest financial houses from the US, UK, Japan, Canada, Germany and Hong Kong. In the event Australian institutions have held their own against the overseas banks, owing in part to their greatly increased efficiency and competitiveness as the result of deregulation; several of Australia's leading banks have in fact embarked on an aggressive campaign of overseas expansion, especially in Europe and the US.

While the prospects (and profits) of Australian banking look secure, the long-term impact of deregulation remains to be seen. Factors such as the more cautious financial climate which characterised the late 1980s, and the continuing political debate over interest rates, will undoubtedly encourage further changes in the industry in the 1990s. >> *building societies*; *economy*

banksias Named after botanist Sir Joseph Banks, the *Banksia* genus of 73 tree and shrub species belongs to the > *protea family*. Only one species is found outside Australia (in NG) and all but fifteen are endemic to WA; most of the eastern species are found in temperate coastal regions. Banksias have distinctive cylindrical spikes of densely crowded narrow flowers, some of which give way to woody fruits; the leaves are mostly narrow, leathery and serrated. The nectar-rich flowers attract birds and even small marsupials.

Bannon, John Charles (1943–), politician, b. Bendigo, Vic. A State Labor MP since 1977 and SA premier since 1982, Bannon was formerly president of the Australian Union of Students (1968), industrial advocate for the SA branch of the AWU (1969) and special adviser to Clyde Cameron, federal minister for labour and immigration in the Whitlam government. As a member of parliament he rose rapidly from the back bench to cabinet, and with the defeat of Labor in 1979 he was selected by caucus to replace former party leader Des Corcoran. Reflecting a general trend in the ALP, his administration is

commonly considered both moderate and pragmatic, with emphasis on efficient management rather than reform.

baobab The baobab (or boab), *Adansonia gregorii*, a remarkable tree with a hugely swollen trunk, is endemic to the Kimberley region of WA and an adjacent small area of the NT north of the Victoria River. It belongs to the genus *Adansonia*, family Bombacaceae, of which seven other species occur in Madagascar and one in Africa. The baobab should not be confused with the Qld bottle tree, which belongs to the > *sterculia family*.

Barak, William (1823–1903), elder of the Yarra Yarra tribe in Vic. and early artist. Barak received some education 1837–9 and settled at Coranderrk Aboriginal station near Healesville in Vic. in 1863. Both a Christian and a progressive leader of the Coranderrk community, he became a noted spokesperson for Vic. Aborigines during the 1870s. He later outlined a plan (never implemented) for the establishment of autonomous Aboriginal communities.

Barcoo River Qld The Barcoo, part of an inland river network, flows for some 530km through the semi-arid grazing country of southwest Qld before joining the Thomson River to form Cooper Creek. This is a region of low and irregular rainfall, and variation from year to year can result in severe flooding of the plains in a wet year or reduction to a series of waterholes – or complete disappearance – in a period of drought. The upper course was discovered by Sir Thomas Mitchell in 1846, who wrongly thought it to be the 'great northern river' which his expedition was seeking.

Barkly Tableland NT/Qld A large grassy plateau reaching an average 300m elevation inland south of the Gulf of Carpentaria, this tableland covers some 130 600sq.km; it stretches about 500km west from Camooweal (Qld) to the central NT, east of the Stuart Highway, and has a monsoonal climate. William Landsborough discovered the region in 1851 and named it after Sir Henry Barkly, then governor of Vic. An early attempt to establish sheep in the area failed, and now it is devoted to cattle; among a number of cattle stations is Alexandria, the largest in Australia. Camooweal is the only settlement of note in the region.

bark paintings > *art, Aboriginal*

Barmah Forest Vic. A State forest bordering the Murray River, Barmah is composed principally of red gums but also contains a stand of yellow, grey and black box, and some grassland. Seasonal floods create swamplands that provide a rich wildlife habitat, especially for waterfowl. The area is controlled and supervised by the Vic. Forests Commission.

barnacles Australia has about 60 species of these highly modified crustaceans, which live attached to hard submerged surfaces such as rocks or ship hulls, or even large fish. As adults they have a hard shell-like body and long, jointed feathery gills used for feeding; the larvae are free-living. Australian barnacles belong to two major groups. The several genera of stalked or goose-necked barnacles, which look like small clams at the end of flexible stalks, are often found on pieces of driftwood. The sessile or acorn barnacles are among the most common creatures of the Australian seashore and also constitute the principal fouling organisms of ship hulls, considerably slowing their passage and increasing fuel consumption. Special anti-fouling paints developed in recent years release toxic chemicals to inhibit the growth of barnacles; their widespread use is now of concern, however, as it is thought to be a possible cause of the poisoning of major oyster beds along the eastern Australian coast.

Barnard, Marjorie Faith > *Eldershaw, M. Barnard*

Barnet, James Johnston (1827–1904), architect, b. Scotland. Barnet was NSW government architect 1862–90, during which time his office carried out more than 12 000 building projects. He had a powerful influence on 19th-century Australian architecture and pioneered the use of new construction methods and electricity in buildings. Large-scale assignments included the Renaissance-inspired Sydney GPO (1866–91), the outstanding Lands Department building (1876–91) and the handsome Goulburn courthouse (1887). He resigned in 1890 following public censure for alleged inefficiency.

Barossa Valley SA One of Australia's major wine-producing districts, situated about 60km northeast of Adelaide in a shallow north–south depression of the Mt Lofty Ranges, the valley was settled by German immigrants in the 1840s. It first supported wheat and sheep, until three major family vineyards were established 1847–51. The light soils, reliable winter rain and dry, sunny summers provide excellent conditions for wine-grape production; other agricultural pursuits include market gardening and poultry farming. The valley was named after Barossa in Spain by the State's first surveyor-general, William Light; its main townships are Nuriootpa, Tanunda and Angaston.

barracouta Like gemfish, the barracouta belongs to the snake-mackerel family, Gempylidae, of southern-hemisphere waters. Both are long-bodied, fast-swimming fish which prey on smaller fish such as sardines. The barracouta or snoek, *Leioneura atun*, is caught mainly with trolling lines; while it is an important commercial species, only a small proportion of the potential catch is harvested by this method and trawling is increasingly preferred. The gemfish or hake, *Rexea solandri*, is common in southern Australian and NZ waters and a popular food fish.

barracuda > *pikes*

barramundi Two unrelated tropical fishes are known by this name. The better known is *Lates calcarifer*, the silver barramundi or giant perch, much sought after as a table fish. It can weigh up to 50kg and measure 1.8m; a freshwater inhabitant, it travels to estuaries to breed – for this reason its future is of some concern, owing to the threat posed to rivers by widespread dam construction. In Qld a closed season from November to January has been introduced to protect nursery areas, and precautionary regulations imposed on fishing operations. The second barramundi, *Scleropages leichardti*, is also known as the Dawson River salmon.

Barrier Range NSW A low mountain system in the far west of the State, this range in some sections reaches a height of 430m. The range is notable for examples of Aboriginal rock engravings; the southern end encompasses the mining town of > *Broken Hill*, the site of rich silver, lead and zinc deposits.

Barrier Reef > *Great Barrier Reef*

Barrington, George (?1755–1804), sometime actor, b. Ireland. Barrington was educated for the Church, but became a notorious – though charming – thief and was transported in 1791. Emancipated, he became superintendent of convicts at Parramatta (1796–1800), but went insane. He has been falsely credited with several accounts of the colony and also with the *Barrington Prologue*, supposedly written for the opening of the first theatre in 1795.

Barrington Tops NSW A high basalt-capped plateau at the southern end of the Mt Royal Range, about 95km northwest of Newcastle, the Tops reach elevations of up to 1586m; they receive high rainfall, and form the headwaters of rivers in the Manning and Hunter drainages. The rugged plateau supports dense forests – which include snow gums and Antarctic beeches – and abundant wildlife, and is protected as part of the Barrington Tops National Park.

Barron River Qld The Barron River rises in the Atherton Tableland and flows north for about 110km, turning east to empty into Trinity Bay, north of Cairns. The upper river northeast of Atherton provides water for irrigation at the Tinaroo Falls dam, and hydro-electric power is generated at the Barron Falls, where the river plunges 250m to the coastal plain. A scenic railway follows the river and gorge as far as Kuranda.

Barrow Island WA Lying off the northwest coast, 96km north of Onslow, Barrow is the largest island in the Monte Bello group and the site of the first commercially producing oilfield in WA; production commenced in 1967 and in 1970 the oilfield yielded 26% of Australia's total crude-oil product. The island has an unusual mammal fauna, and is a wildlife refuge.

Barry, Sir Redmond (1813–80), lawyer and arts patron, b. Ireland. Barry settled in Melbourne in 1839 and was appointed judge of the Vic. Supreme Court in 1852, in which capacity he presided over the trial of bushranger Ned Kelly (whose hanging he survived by only twelve days). First chancellor of the University of Melbourne and instrumental in its development (1853–80), Barry also played a leading role in the founding of Melbourne's other major cultural institutions – the Public Library and the Art Gallery. His statue stands in Swanston Street, Melbourne, outside the State Library.

Barton, Sir Edmund (1849–1920), politician, b. Sydney. A classics scholar and successful barrister, Barton had a distinguished career in politics in NSW until 1898. An ardent supporter of Federation, he devoted himself tirelessly to the federal movement and led the delegation to London which secured approval for the founding Bill. Appointed first prime minister of Australia (and minister of external affairs) 1 January 1901, he resigned in 1903 for health reasons; he subsequently became a High Court judge (1903–20) in which role he was noted for his scrupulous impartiality and acuteness. A passionate patriot, Barton is alleged to have coined the term 'White Australia Policy'.

Barwick, Sir Garfield Edward John (1903–), lawyer and politician, b. Stanmore, NSW. A barrister from 1927, Barwick became a QC in 1941 and subsequently appeared in several famous constitutional cases. He entered federal parliament as a Liberal in 1958 and was attorney-general 1958–64, during which time he was responsible for various statutory reforms including the Matrimonial Causes Act and the Trade Practices Act; he was also minister for external affairs 1961–4. Barwick was chief justice of the High Court 1964–81, during which period the court handed down several decisions later regarded as unduly favouring tax avoiders. He was also an outspoken president of the Australian Conservation Foundation 1965–71.

Barwon River NSW Part of the Barwon–Darling system, this river is known as the Macintyre in its upper section and as the Darling downstream from its confluence with the Culgoa. It forms a section of the NSW–Qld border, and the name is derived from an Aboriginal word meaning 'great river'.

baseball After visits by US baseball teams in the 19th century, intercolonial matches were played in Australia but the game was not organised formally until 1900. Interest fluctuated, reviving with sporadic visits by US teams and naval squadrons; many cricketers adopted baseball as a winter sport. In 1933 the Australian Baseball Council (ABC) was formed and the Claxton Shield was donated by a SA patron, to be awarded annually to the champion State. In the 1950s the ABC affiliated with international bodies, and in Australia promoted baseball at the junior level and as a mass public entertainment. In the 1980s there were more than 100 000 registered players, and the proposed provision of training facilities and a 7000-seat stadium in Melbourne should ensure further development.

Basedow, Herbert (1881–1933), anthropologist and geologist, b. Adelaide. Basedow was a controversial champion of Aboriginal rights in the early 20th century. While leading mining and geographical expeditions to the Kimberleys, Petermann Ranges and Arnhem Land, he became greatly interested in the Aborigines and subsequently lived among them for some time, recording rare examples of their culture. His government-funded health study of central Australian Aborigines called for a reservation to protect tribes from extinction; his book, *Knights of the Boomerang*, published in 1935, castigated Australians for their 'racial homicide'.

basic wage > *wage determination*

basketball With more than 200 000 registered players in Australia, many of whom compete in more than one league, basketball is a major and rapidly growing sport. At the 1988 Olympic Games, of the 40 eligible nations, Australia was one of only five to have both men's and women's teams qualify for the medal rounds, in which each finished fourth.

The sport was introduced in the 1920s and the Amateur Basketball Union of Australia was established in 1939. A substantial boost in popularity came with the 1956 Melbourne Olympic Games, and a network of leagues and stadiums developed across the country. The formation of the National Basketball League (NBL) in 1979 moved the sport to a new level of public recognition; in 1988 the NBL had attendance of nearly a million, and a huge television audience. The rise of the brilliant Andrew Gaze through NBL, Olympic and US competitions has created even more interest in the game .

bass > *fishes, freshwater and marine*

Bass, George (1771–1803), surgeon and explorer, b. England. In addition to his achievements in exploration, Bass became a scientific observer of some merit. He arrived in NSW on the *Reliance* in 1795, on board befriending > *Matthew Flinders*. With remarkable courage and seamanship they explored the coasts south of Sydney in tiny boats, and confirmed the existence of coal on the Illawarra coast (1796). In 1798 they proved the existence of the strait

bearing his name, and sailed round Van Diemen's Land. Bass disappeared without trace on a trading voyage to South America in 1803.

Bass, Tom (Thomas Dwyer) (1916–   ), sculptor, b. Lithgow, NSW. Bass is known for his many civic commissions, whose stylised blending of cubism and realism received wide recognition in the 1950s and 1960s. The impressive sculpture *Ethos* (1959–61) for Canberra's civic square, the bronze relief *Trial of Socrates* (1954–6) for the facade of Wilson Hall (University of Melbourne) and the monumental 2.1m long bronze *Entrance Sculpture* (1966–8) for the Australian National Library in Canberra are especially notable. Bass started a sculpture school in Sydney in 1974.

Bass Strait Separating Tas. from the Australian mainland, the strait ranges from 130km to 210km in width. It is relatively shallow, averaging a depth of 60m; it once formed a land bridge when sea-levels were lowered during the ice ages. King Island and the Furneaux Group are the main islands – indicating the link between the highlands of Tas. and those of the eastern mainland. The strait is currently producing > *oil and natural gas* from platforms located off Gippsland. It is named in honour of George Bass who, with Matthew Flinders, sailed through the strait in 1798 to prove that Tas. (then called Van Diemen's Land) was an island.

Batemans Bay NSW (pop. 6492) This small resort town at the estuary of the Clyde River, 294km south of Sydney, also supports local industries including fishing, dairying, oyster farming, and timber-cutting. It was named by James Cook in 1770.

Bates, Daisy (1863–1951), legendary worker among the Aborigines, b. Ireland. Born Daisy May O'Dwyer, Bates arrived in Australia in 1884 and is believed in the same year to have married (albeit briefly) the bushman and balladist 'Breaker' Morant. She subsequently married cattleman John Bates, but returned to England in 1894 and worked as a journalist. In 1899 she returned to Australia to investigate reports of cruelty to Aborigines in WA. She lived among Aboriginal communities almost exclusively 1912–46, learning more than 100 dialects and becoming known as *Kabbarli* ('grandmother', 'friend'). She provided white

Australians with much information about Aboriginal customs and lore, publishing her experiences and accumulated knowledge in newspaper articles and in *The Passing of the Aborigines* (1938), which title reflected her belief that Aborigines were dying out and that neither proselytising nor white education was in their interest. Her attitudes and anthropological findings have since been questioned, both by the Aboriginal community and by scientists, and are alleged to have discouraged past governments from developing constructive welfare policies.

Bathurst NSW (pop. 22 237) The city of Bathurst is the industrial, educational and service centre for its surrounding wheat and sheep country; it lies 209km west of Sydney on the Macquarie River. It was named after Henry, Earl Bathurst, secretary of state for the colonies 1812–27, soon after the first crossing of the Blue Mountains in 1813. Like many other towns in the area, it was boosted by the gold rushes of the 1850s. The original site was changed in the 1830s and the town laid out along the present attractive lines of streets and gardens, with public buildings of great range and character, from the 19th-century post office to verandahed inns and shops. Motor races held at nearby Mt Panorama attract many visitors. Local industries include the processing of farm products (notably cereals, vegetables and fruit) and other small manufactures such light engineering and the production of cement pipes.

Bathurst Island NT A densely wooded island west of Melville Island, from which it is separated by the narrow Apsley Strait, Bathurst is a reserve for the Tiwi Aborigines; in 1978 the Crown ceded ownership of the island to the Tiwi Land Council of tribal representatives. Timber-getting and sawmilling have been established around the Catholic mission at the main settlement, Ngulu. The island was first sighted by Abel Tasman in 1644, but was named by Phillip Parker King in 1819 after Henry, Earl Bathurst, secretary of state for the colonies.

Batman, John (1801–39), co-founder of Melbourne, b. Parramatta, NSW. The son of a convict, Batman settled near Launceston, Tas. in 1821. In 1830 he was granted further land in recognition of his capture of the bushranger Brady, and of his conciliation attempts with Aborigines. He unsuccessfully applied to Governor Darling for a land grant at Westernport, then formed the Port Phillip Association. In June 1835 he made a 'treaty' with the Dutigalla tribe of Aborigines, acquiring some 243 000ha in return for articles such as blankets, knives, mirrors, scissors and flour; he alleged that the chiefs fully understood what they were doing. While he was back in Tas., John Pascoe Fawkner landed and settled on the spot Batman had selected, which became the nucleus of Melbourne.

Governor Bourke proclaimed Batman's purchase void, but settlement by squatters continued and had to be recognised, Batman retaining his land. He established himself as farmer and storekeeper, but by 1837 ill health limited him to storekeeping and investment.

bats Bats are one of two groups of placental mammals native to Australia; their power of flight enabled them to disperse readily from Asia to the Australian plate as it drifted northwards from the Antarctic supercontinent. Of the order Chiroptera, they are classed in two major suborders: Megachiroptera, fruit bats (or flying foxes) and blossom bats; and Microchiroptera, insectivorous bats.

The fruit bat or flying fox of the genus *Pteropus* has, as its name implies, a fox-like face, and in comparison with insectivorous bats it has relatively good eyesight. Fruit bats occur across northern Australia and down the eastern coast, especially in rainforest. They often form great roosting colonies or 'camps' in large, emergent trees, where they rest during the day; at dusk they fly often long distances in search of fruiting or flowering vegetation. Although sometimes causing serious damage to orchards, they usually feed on native rainforest species; previously they were regarded as pests, but now they are often protected, especially at their roosting sites. The blossom bats, *Syconycteris* and *Macroglossus*, feed exclusively on blossoms and nectar and as such are important pollinators of rainforest trees.

The insectivorous bats are generally small and are found in a variety of habitats across the continent; species roost variously in such places as caves, tree-holes and old buildings. They all navigate by means of a form of sonar known as echolocation, in which the position of objects is determined by emitting sounds and judging the echoes bounced back from them – in the case of the bat it is ultrasound, and the echoes are picked up by their large, sensitive ears.

Using echolocation they can avoid obstructions and locate flying insect prey in total darkness. The Microchiroptera include 50 species, the bulk of the Australian bat fauna. Representative groups are the sheath-tailed bats of the genus *Taphozous*; the ghost or false vampire bat, *Macroderma gigas*, the largest Australian specimen, which feeds on small mammals, frogs and other bats as well as insects; the horseshoe bats, of the genus *Rhinolophus*, which have a horseshoe-shaped nose designed to direct the outgoing echolocation calls; and the free-tailed bats of the family Molossidae.

As with other wildlife, many bat populations have declined through habitat destruction, and in particular some cave-dwelling species are threatened by limestone quarrying.

Baudin, Nicolas Thomas (?1754–1803), navigator and naturalist, b. France. Baudin was in charge of a French scientific voyage to complete the charting of Australia (1800). He commanded *Le Géographe*, on which two of his officers were François Peron and Louis de Freycinet, whose record of the expedition is the only one published. After some charting of the west coast of Australia and then of Tas. in April 1802, he met Flinders making eastwards on his historic circumnavigation. The French expedition was hampered by illness, Baudin himself dying on the way home.

Bauer, Ferdinand (1760–1826), botanical artist, b. Austria. Bauer was appointed by Sir Joseph Banks to accompany Matthew Flinders on his 1801 expedition to Australia. He amassed a large number of detailed drawings from this voyage, of which a small number were published as colour plates. Bauer subsequently helped botanist > *Robert Brown* collect plants around Sydney and in 1804 journeyed to Norfolk Island where he made the first significant collections of its flora. His name is commemorated in the Australian endemic plant genus *Bauera* and in the names of various plant species; his paintings of Australian flora were published in 1976.

Bauera This endemic Australian genus of attractive shrubs forms the family Baueraceae; all three species are confined to the east of the continent. The most widespread is the native dogrose or river rose, *B. rubioides*, a mainly pink-flowered shrub found in damp places along the coast and mountains from south-eastern Qld to eastern SA. *B. sessiflora*, which occurs only in the Grampian Ranges in Vic.,

bears long sprays of crimson flowers; *B. capitata* is limited to southern Qld and northern NSW.

Bauhinia > *legumes*

bauxite > *aluminium*

Baxter, Sir (John) Philip (1905–), chemical and nuclear engineer, b. Wales. A strong advocate of nuclear power, Baxter was chairman of the Australian Atomic Energy Commission 1956–72. He came to Australia in 1950 after leading a British team involved in the US Manhattan Project – the production of the Hiroshima nuclear bomb. Appointed professor of chemical engineering in the newly established New South Wales University of Technology, he became the university's first vice-chancellor in 1955. He was knighted in 1965.

Baynton, Barbara (1857–1929), author, b. Scone, NSW. Baynton took up writing after her second marriage, to Thomas Baynton in 1890. Of her two published works the best known is *Bush Studies* (1902), a collection of six grim stories of life in the Australian bush. After the failure of her third marriage (1921) to Lord Headley, she divided her time between England and Australia, becoming a notable Melbourne character.

Bean, C. E. W. (Charles Edwin Woodrow) (1879–1968), historian, b. Bathurst, NSW. Educated in England, Bean trained as a lawyer but practised only briefly before joining the *Sydney Morning Herald* as a journalist in 1908. At the outbreak of World War 1 he became official Australian war correspondent and served at Gallipoli and with the AIF. In 1919 he was appointed official war historian; he wrote six of the twelve volumes of the *Official History of Australia in the War 1914-18* and edited the others. The work is a distinguished record of Australia's endeavours and a fine military history. Bean was instrumental in establishing the Australian War Memorial in Canberra.

Beaurepaire, Sir Frank (Francis Joseph Edmund) (1891–1956), swimming champion and businessman, b. Melbourne. The first Australian swimmer to sustain international success over a period, Beaurepaire competed in the Olympic Games in 1908, 1920 and 1924. He used an individual stroke, transitional between the old trudgen and the new crawl, and in the course of his career he broke fourteen world records. Subsequently lord mayor of Melbourne, he was influential in bringing the 1956 Olympic Games to his city, but died just before they took place. A successful businessman, he founded the Beaurepaire Tyre Service in 1922, an enterprise which expanded under the trade name Olympic – the Olympic Tyre and Rubber Co. was established in 1933.

Beauty Point Tas. (pop. 1064) This small town, 48km northwest of Launceston, is a fishing and holiday centre. Its deepwater port was built to serve the Beaconsfield gold mines from the late 1860s.

bêche-de-mer > *sea-cucumbers*

Becke, Louis (George Lewis) (1855–1913), author, b. Port Macquarie, NSW. Becke travelled and traded in the Pacific region for 25 years before returning to Sydney and taking up writing in the 1890s. He was best known for his short stories about his experiences in the Pacific, such as *By Reef and Palm* (1894), but his 35 published books included historical and scientific works.

Bedford (George) Randolph (1868–1941), journalist and author, b. Sydney. A bohemian of large appetites and diverse talents, Bedford was also a politician, mining promoter and impassioned advocate of a white, socialist and republican Australia. He worshipped physical health and strength, and wrote with unexampled verve five novels, many short stories, poetry, travel and descriptive works and the play *White Australia: Or, the Empty North* (1909). Bedford's best book, published three years after his death, is the racy autobiography, *Naught to Thirty-Three* (1944).

beeches > *Nothofagus*

Beechworth Vic. (pop. 3252) This beautifully preserved former gold-mining town lies in the Ovens valley about 270km northeast of Melbourne. In the 1850s it had a population of 8000; it yielded some 85 000kg of gold in fourteen years. Today it is a tourist centre with more than 30 classified buildings, and serves as a base for visitors to the surrounding Vic. alps.

beef cattle > *cattle industry*

beer > *brewing industry*

bees and bee-keeping The bee is a hymenopterous insect of the superfamily Apoidea. All bees feed their young on pollen, in marked contrast to related wasp groups, whose offspring are fed with arthropod prey. Most bees are solitary; the female will construct and tend her own nest without help from other females. Social species have overlapping generations of related, non-reproductive female 'workers' that tend the nest of the reproductive 'queen', who is usually the mother of the workers. Some parasitic or 'cuckoo' bees lay their eggs in the nests of others; the larvae are fed by the host bee and they eventually destroy the host's offspring.

Aside from the naturalised honeybee, *Apis mellifera*, Australia has a very rich fauna of natives, estimated at some 3000 species. Short-tongued bees of the families Colletidae and Halictidae are mostly small and solitary, and nest in the ground or in plant stems; large, black carpenter bees, family Anthophoridae, excavate burrows in wood, and sweat bees of the family Apidae are dark-coloured and stingless, found mostly in tropical Australia where they form large colonies in hollow trees and produce a sweet honey favoured by Aborigines.

Honey production Honeybees were introduced to Australia in 1822, and successive stocks of Italian, Carniolan and Caucasian strains predominate in the apiculture industry. Honeybees have also become feral and 'naturalised' as part of the native fauna.

Because of its dry, sunny climate and nectar-rich flora Australia is a major honey producer, ranking fourth among honey-exporting nations. Annual production averages about 20 000t, mostly stemming from commercial apiculture. Production and inspection is regulated by the States, although the Australian Honey Board controls exports, sets prices and promotes the industry. Bee importation is subject to strict quarantine regulations to avoid accidental introduction of hive parasites. In Australia commercial apiculture is a migratory occupation – beekeepers often move their hives long distances to take advantage of the periodic blossoming of eucalypts; prime sites in State forests are usually leased. Although the ground crops clover and lucerne are important sources in some areas, most honey comes from eucalypt nectar; Tasmanian leatherwood, of the genus

Eucryphia, produces the most distinctively flavoured Australian honey, and the world's record honey production came from a flow of karri in WA.

The introduced weed Salvation Jane, *Echium plantagineum*, is favoured by apiculturists for its abundant nectar and pollen production. However, it is poisonous to stock and graziers regard it as a noxious weed, calling it Paterson's Curse; proposals to eradicate the plant through biological control have therefore placed these two rural industries in conflict.

beetles Of the order Coleoptera, beetles are found in a wide range of habitats. Adults are characterised by hard, modifed forewings, or *elytra*, which are folded over the body to form a covering for the membranous hindwings; the protective elytra have enabled beetles to exploit a variety of cryptic habitats while still maintaining their ability to fly. Both adult insects and larvae have chewing mouthparts, and the larvae, or 'grubs', usually have a sclerotised head capsule. Many beetles are serious pests of crops, stored products, wood, leather and natural fibres.

Not only is the Coleoptera the largest insect order, it is estimated to contain two-thirds of all described animal species. More than 20 000 Australian species in some 120 families are already described, and considerably more await description. The prominent representatives are mentioned here, with the family name and the number of Australian species recorded in each case.

Ground beetles of the family Carabidae – in which there are 1800 Australian species – are active predators; they include the swift tiger-beetles often found in sandy areas, and the bombardier beetle which emits a defensive cloud of hot, caustic vapour when disturbed. Whirligig beetles (family Gyrinidae, 28 species) are usually found swirling in groups on the surface of creeks, and rove beetles (Staphylinidae, 800 species) are distinguished by short elytra and are usually associated with dung and carrion; some of the smaller species occur in large numbers and secrete a blistering skin irritant when accidentally crushed. Male stag-beetles (Lucanidae, 75 species) often have grotesque, horn-like protuberances on their heads.

The dung beetles, scarabs, chafers and Christmas beetles (Scarabaeidae, 3000 species) are stout insects with a characteristic elbowed antenna and strong, digging legs. Dung beetles

and scarabs typically bury balls of dung, in which they lay their eggs: because native dung beetles were unable to utilise large, moist cattle droppings, South African species were introduced in an attempt to reduce breeding sites for bushflies. The chafers have C-shaped larvae, commonly known as 'white grubs', which feed on plant roots and can be serious pests of pastures, sugar cane, vegetable crops and eucalypts; the metallic-coloured Christmas beetles are often serious defoliators of eucalypts.

Jewel beetles (Buprestidae, 800 species) are beautifully coloured, boat-shaped insects whose larvae bore into wood. Fireflies (Lampyridae, 16 species) produce luminescent flashes from special abdominal organs as a means of attracting mates (and are not to be confused with glow-worms). Click beetles (Elateridae, 600 species), when upside down, are able to right themselves by flipping over with an audible 'click'; their larvae , known as wireworms, are root pests. Ladybirds (Coccinellidae, 260 species) include species that are active predators on aphids and scale insects; several Australian species have been introduced successfully for biological control of these pests in California and Hawaii. The long-horned beetles (Cerambycidae, 1200 species) have unusually long antennae and produce wood-boring larvae. Leaf-beetles (Chrysomelidae, 3000 species) are leaf-feeders, both as larvae and as adults; although many leaf-beetles are pests of crops, some have been introduced to Australia for biological control of weeds such as lantana.

The weevils, with more than 8000 species and belonging to the family Curculionidae, constitute the largest group of all and are characterised by a curved snout; they are plant-feeders, and include a number of introduced pest species. >> *bugs*

Bega NSW (pop. 4294) Situated on the far south coast of NSW, Bega is the regional centre for the valley's dairying industry. It is famous for its cheeses and is home to a large milk-processing factory that supplies fresh milk to Canberra. Other activities include timber and beef production, furniture-making, and brick and plaster manufacture.

Bell, George Henry Frederick (1878–1966), art teacher and painter, b. Melbourne. A leading figure in the first generation of Australian modernists, during the 1930s Bell wielded great influence in the Melbourne art world. He founded both the first art school to teach 'modern' principles (1932) and the Contemporary Art Society (1938), and was a key figure in the battles between modernism and the naturalistic and nationalistic traditions of the art establishment.

Bell, Graeme Emerson (1914–), jazz musician, b. Melbourne. Trained as a classical pianist, Bell worked as an insurance clerk before joining his brother's jazz band in 1935. Turning professional in 1943, Bell formed the Dixieland Band. In the late 1940s his Australian Jazz Band toured in Britain, Asia and Australia. Bell formed the All Stars in 1957, for many years Australia's most popular traditional jazz band. He has made numerous recordings, some on his own label, Swaggie.

Bell, John > *theatre*

Bellarine Peninsula Vic. Lying between Port Phillip Bay and Bass Strait, and extending eastward from Geelong, this peninsula is a popular beach and holiday resort. Point Lonsdale, in the southeast, is the promontory of the western head at the entrance of Port Phillip Bay. The 'wild white man', escaped convict William Buckley, lived in the region with Aborigines for 32 years until 1835.

bellbirds > *honeyeaters*

Bellenden Ker Range Qld This granite massif northwest of Innisfail extends for about 40km generally parallel to the coast, the precipitous south and east faces rising through dense rainforest. The range includes Qld's two highest peaks, Mt Bartle Frere (1611m) and Mt Bellenden Ker (1591m). On the eastern slopes, 31 000ha are reserved as Bellenden Ker National Park.

Bellinger River NSW This river drains the rainforest country of the New England and Dorrigo National Parks, and forms the Bellinger Valley before joining the Tasman Sea near Urunga. The town of Bellingen, in the valley, is the centre of a rich dairying and farming district.

Benalla Vic. (pop. 8490) A market and service centre 195km northeast of Melbourne, on the Broken River, Benalla is in the heart of country ranged by the notorious Kelly gang. It developed on an overland stock route after Thomas Mitchell's exploration of the region in 1836 and the surrounding region is flourishing

grazing and agricultural land. It is a base for visitors to the region's numerous natural attractions, including lakes and the Vic. snowfields, and has a fine art gallery housed in a striking modern building on the shores of the river.

Benaud, Richie (Richard) > *cricket*

Bendigo Vic. (pop. 53 944) A former goldmining 'boom town' 150km northwest of Melbourne and originally known as Sandhurst, Bendigo is now a major service centre for the Vic. central highlands. Like many other goldfields settlements, Bendigo was little more than a sleepy sheep run until transformed overnight following the discovery of gold in 1851; in the following few years, production reached £1 million a month. When the easily accessible alluvial goldfields were exhausted, company-based deep-lead mining continued until excessive costs forced its abandonment in 1954; in the 1980s, mining again became important to the city. Grazing and agriculture are important regional activities and Bendigo is the State's major egg-producer. Tourism has long been important and the city has more than 50 buildings classified by the National Trust; its Chinese heritage (dating from the gold rushes) is substantial and includes a well-preserved joss-house.

Ben Lomond Tas. A large flat-topped mountain, Ben Lomond more nearly resembles a plateau, of which the highest point is 1574m, at Legges Tor. In northeastern Tas., south of Launceston, it is included in a national park of the same name and is a major winter sports area. The mountain was named by William Paterson, who founded the first settlement in northern Tas. in 1804.

Bennelong (?1764–1813), an Aborigine captured and 'civilised' by Arthur Phillip in the first months of European settlement. Having taught Bennelong English and encouraged him to wear European dress, Phillip took him to England in 1792. There, and on his return to the colonies in 1795, Bennelong lived almost as an exhibit. He returned often to the bush, where he was rejected by his own people. His subsequent drunkenness and violent death made him the first of many tragic failures to reconcile Aboriginal and European culture. His name was given to Bennelong Point on the south side of Port Jackson, where he lived in

Phillip's time in a brick hut and which later became the site of the Sydney Opera House.

Bennett, (Henry) Gordon (1887–1962), soldier, b. Balwyn, Vic. Following distinguished service at Gallipoli and in France during World War 1, Bennett was given command of the 8th Division at the outbreak of World War 2. The division was captured at the fall of Singapore in February 1942, but Bennett made a daring escape, returning to Australia with much valuable information on Japanese tactics. Bennett's action in abandoning his troops was criticised, however, and he was never given another field command. A royal commission after the war censured Bennett in principle for escaping, but ruled that his motive for so doing had been patriotic.

Bent brothers, early colonial lawyers. **Ellis** (1783–1815), b. England, arrived in Australia in 1809 with Lachlan Macquarie, to serve as deputy judge-advocate. Although relations were initially cordial, disagreements developed due to the governor's predominance over the judiciary. Bent held commendable views on law reform and permitted emancipist lawyers to appear before his court (although his brother later encouraged him to recant from this view). His brother **Jeffrey** (1781–1852), also b. England, was in NSW 1814–17 as judge of the newly created Supreme Court. An arrogant man, he too quarrelled with Governor Macquarie, especially over the rights of emancipist lawyers to practise. Macquarie removed him from office in 1816 because of his refusal to open the Supreme Court without English solicitors; he was recalled to England in the following year.

Beresford, Bruce (1940–), film director, b. Sydney. An important figure in the revival of the Australian film industry, Beresford made short films while at Sydney University. Between 1966 and 1972 he was head of film production at the British Film Institute. His first feature film was *The Adventures of Barry McKenzie* (1972); others include *Don's Party* (1976) and *The Getting of Wisdom* (1977). Now based in the US, Beresford is perhaps best known for the successful *Breaker Morant* (1980) and the disastrous *King David* (1985).

Bergner, Josl (Vladimir Jossif) (1920–), painter, b. Austria. Born of Jewish parents, Bergner arrived in Australia in 1937, where he worked in factories before becoming a full-time painter. His social-realist works depicted his anguish at the plight of Europe's persecuted Jews, and he was one of the first to portray Australia's dispossessed Aborigines. He migrated to Israel in 1947, where he has established himself as a leading painter.

Berri SA (pop. 3502) This town and irrigation centre on the Murray River, 222km from Adelaide, is best known for its fruit products. It also has a substantial winery and distillery, and has recently developed rapidly as a regional service centre.

Bertrand, John > *sailing and yachting*

BHP Since the 1930s, Broken Hill Proprietary Ltd has virtually monopolised Australian steel production. The company is now also a major producer and exporter of iron ore and coal, and is involved in oil exploration and production, mineral extraction and processing, metal fabrication, engineering and transport. It has operations in 40 countries through its three main business arms: BHP Steel, BHP-Utah Minerals International and BHP Petroleum.

The company was incorporated in Vic. in 1885 to exploit a silver, lead and zinc deposit which had been discovered the year before by a boundary rider, Charles Rasp, at Broken Hill, NSW. Early this century, as the original silver deposits began to run out, the company diversified into steel-making, opening its first steelworks in 1915 at Newcastle, NSW, followed by further mills at Port Kembla, NSW, in 1935 and Whyalla, SA, in 1941. It is Australia's largest company, with a market capitalisation of over $10 billion in mid-1989, a figure twice the size of that of the next largest company, BTR Nylex. In 1988, BHP had net assets of $6.398 billion, employed 51 000 people and reported an operating profit of $985 million (slightly down on the figure for 1986, when it became the first Australian company to record a profit of over $1 billion).

In a joint venture with Esso, BHP has been the main developer of the Bass Strait oil and gas field since the 1960s and also has major interests in the newly developing Timor Sea oil field and in the North West Shelf natural-gas project. Overseas interests include oil and gas in the US, PNG and the North Sea, coal in the US, iron ore in Brazil and copper in Chile. A subsidiary company, BHP Gold Mines Ltd, was floated in 1987 to exploit BHP-Utah's Australian and overseas gold interests.

Within Australia, the health of BHP very much reflects the economic robustness of the country as a whole, partly because of the company's sheer size (it produces nearly 10% of Australia's total export receipts) but also because its range of mining and manufacturing businesses represents a cross-section of Australia's intrinsic wealth (excluding agriculture).

Bigge, J.T. (John Thomas) (1780–1843), judge, b. England. In 1819 Bigge was appointed commissioner to inquire into conditions in NSW and Van Diemen's Land. In addition, he was to provide an assessment of the effectiveness of transportation, the conduct of officials, judicial systems, religion, education, revenue and trade. Bigge spent seventeen months gathering evidence and travelling widely, then wrote three reports which he submitted to the British parliament (1822–3). He was soon at odds with Governor Macquarie, differing fundamentally, though honestly, with the latter's views on emancipists, the employment of convicts and industrial development. Bigge offered suggestions for governing NSW during the transition from prison to colony, and accepted John Macarthur's proposals for a large-scale pastoral economy using convict labour, while Macquarie envisaged more agricultural development. Bigge's reports had a profound influence on colonial policy in London.

bilbies > *bandicoots*

billiards and snooker The game of billiards was first played in Australia by the military as early as 1801, and by the 1820s was widely established; at this time – as indeed would occur later – it was often thought of as the pastime of idlers. In 1853 Henry Alcock began manufacturing tables locally and this, together with the arrival of overseas champions, gave the sport an enormous boost. In 1887 the game of snooker – which, played on a billiard table, had been invented by British officers in India – was introduced to Australia, again by Alcock but in conjunction with Frank Smith.

Two outstanding players were Horace Lindrum and Eddie Charlton. Lindrum showed apparently effortless skill in both billiards and snooker, winning national and world championships in a long career; in 1941 he scored the highest possible snooker break (147 points).

Snooker champion Eddie Charlton won the NSW and Australian titles respectively in 1964 and 1966, and has been the dominant figure in this sport ever since; he became World Open champion in 1968, and was the first Australian to play in the UK television series, 'Pot Black'.

Walter Lindrum, elder brother of Horace, dominated billiards as few others have done in any sport. He set 57 world records and created a world record break of 4137; as a result, international rules were changed to prevent the use of Lindrum's 'nursery cannon' cue, which had produced his enormous scores.

There are 44000 registered players in Australia, and many hundreds of thousands of others who play informally on smaller tables in private homes, hotels and clubs.

Billings, John and Evelyn, pioneers of the highly successful Billings method of natural contraception. **John** (1918–), neurologist, b. Melbourne, began research on the ovulation method of contraception – which relies on women detecting changes in their cervical mucus and avoiding intercourse when fertility is indicated – in the late 1950s. He was joined in this work by his wife **Evelyn Livingston** (1918–), paediatrician, b. Melbourne, in 1966. Her studies of breastfeeding mothers and women approaching menopause made a major contribution to development of the Billings method, which by the late 1980s was estimated to be used worldwide by more than 50 million couples.

biocides The use of biocides – any chemicals capable of killing living organisms – has long been widespread in Australian agriculture. While without herbicides and pesticides Australia's agricultural output could fall by as much as 40%, there is increasing concern about their effects on both the environment (particularly soils) and health. The heavy metal pesticides in common use 40 years ago were abandoned in favour of organochlorines such as dieldrin when it was found that they built up rather than broke down in the soil; now organochlorines are severely restricted and hundreds of farms have been quarantined because of stock contamination. These in turn are being partially replaced by organophospates, whose effect on the environment is not as long-lasting. A herbicide that in recent years has provoked much controversy is Agent Orange, which penetrates leaves and is absorbed into the plant system, but which is now known to be extremely dangerous to humans subject to high levels of exposure. >> *insect pests*; *pollution*; *weeds*

biotechnology As old as the art of bread-making, biotechnology involves the use in production of biological organisms and their components. In the 1980s the technology has taken on a new meaning, as advances in genetic manipulation offer immense potential in fields as diverse as medicine, agriculture, waste management, and food manufacturing. Australia is a small but potent force in biotechnology, with about 90 companies using the new techniques to develop or manufacture products. About half operate in the medical and veterinary health-care areas; many are already selling diagnostic test procedures, but most are fledgling companies with few marketed products. About $200 million is spent annually on research and development, more than half in the public sector. This is small expenditure by international standards, but Australian researchers nevertheless have some notable achievements solving the problems of pests, weeds, diseases of plants and animals, and agricultural production. In 1983 CSIRO scientists were the first in the world to isolate 'jumping genes', transposable elements that could be used to introduce new traits into maize and other crops. This team, led by Dr Jim Peacock, has also synthesised a gene that gives tobacco plants resistance to the virulent ringspot virus; work is now under way to build resistance genes for viral diseases in cereals. A University of Adelaide team received world acclaim in 1986 for developing a 'superpig' breed which contains additional copies of the porcine growth-hormone gene; the results have been dramatic, with major increases in feed efficiency, lean meat deposits and improved carcass quality. Australia's largest co-operative effort in the field of biotechnology has been to develop a vaccine for malaria. This is based on work at the Walter and Eliza Hall Institute of Medical Research in Melbourne – the first to produce protein antigens of the human malaria parasite. Other promising approaches already undergoing commercial development include the cloning by Melbourne's Florey Institute of the relaxin hormone which facilitates childbirth, and work by Biotechnology Australia, in Sydney, on a unisex contraceptive pill based on the hormone inhibin.

Rapid advances in the field have caused concern about the impact on the environment of genetically engineered organisms, should they be released. The formation of the federal Recombinant DNA Monitoring Committee in 1981 arose as a result of a voluntary moratorium by scientists themselves, who perceived potential hazards from the technology. The committee, renamed the Genetic Manipulation Advisory Committee in 1988, has permitted the release of three genetically altered organisms, including a live bacterium for the control of the disease crown gall on stone fruit and roses. >> *medical research*; *science and technology*

Birch, Arthur John (1915–   ), scientist, b. Sydney. While a postgraduate student at Oxford University, Birch – in collaboration with his tutor, Sir Robert Robinson – was instrumental in the development of the oral contraceptive pill. In 1948 he made the first synthetic male sex hormone, a development that led to the production of norethindrome, an analogue of progesterone. Birch has been professor of organic chemistry at the Universities of Sydney (1952–5) and Manchester (1955–67), and dean of the research school for chemistry at the Australian National University 1967–70 and 1973–6. In 1982 he was elected president of the Australian Academy of Science.

birds, introduced At least fifteen imported species of birds have become established in Australia, either through deliberate introduction on the part of acclimatisation societies wanting to establish European flora and fauna in this country, or through the imported birds escaping from cages or aviaries. The house-sparrow, *Passer domesticus*, is regarded as a pest by wheat farmers in WA; its cousin, *P. montanus*, the slightly smaller tree-sparrow, is less common and less obtrusive. The starling, *Sturnus vulgaris*, dark blue-black with some iridescence in the plumage, is almost universally considered to be a vermin-harbouring pest. Two introductions from India – the mynah, *Acridotheres tristis*, and the red-whiskered bulbul, *Pycnonotus iocosus*, are often abundant. The song-thrush, *Turdus philomelos*, and the slightly larger blackbird, *T. merula*, were introduced for their songs (as once were nightingales, but without success). The finches – of a different family from that of the indigenous weaver-finches – are on the whole successful introductions; they include the gold-finch, *Carduelis carduelis*, the greenfinch, *Chloris chloris*, and the southeast Asian spice finch, *Lonchura punctulata*. Two pigeons, the Senegal and Indian turtledoves, *Streptopelia* *senegalensis* and *S. chinensis*, are regarded as causing little harm except for local raiding of poultry-feed. Feral ostriches, which have been reported from SA, are possibly escapees from ostrich farms.

birds, native Out of the estimated 9000 species of birds in the world Australia has approximately 700, and of these 430 are endemic; families missing from Australia include woodpeckers, vultures and flamingoes. As with the rest of the continent's fauna, the indigenous birds of Australia have their origins in > *Gondwana* or Southeast Asia; several new species – such as fairy wrens (> *wrens*), the western rosella and the eastern spinebill – evolved during Australia's long isolation from other landmasses. While, for example, the > *emu*, > *lyrebirds*, > *scrub-birds* and many > *honeyeaters* and > *parrots* are endemic to Australia, each has affinities with other groups of Gondwanan origin: the emu is closely related to both the South African ostrich and the NZ kiwi; and lyrebirds, honeyeaters and fairy wrens are thought to derive from a single corvid (crow-like) group which derives from Gondwana. Many unusual species, such as magpies, birds of paradise, bower-birds and the spangled drongo, are found also in NG.

There is nevertheless a distinctively Australian bird population. Many groups have adapted to the Australian environment by, for example, nesting in termite mounds or holes in the ground to provide protection from weather extremes; a few species, including the lyrebird, breed in winter rather than spring or summer. Curiosities include the flightless emu and cassowary, three species of > *mound-building birds*, the black swan, and a number of birds noted for their singular calls – ranging from the raucous laugh of the kookaburra (> *kingfishers*) to the ringing tones of the bellbird and the brilliant mimicry of the lyrebird.

Many Australian birds are migratory, some land birds ranging long distances within the continent in search of food or water. More regular is the seasonal movement of > *seabirds* and > *waders*: from the northern hemisphere for the Australian summer, from Antarctica during winter; from NG and nearby islands to breed during spring; and occasionally between the Australian mainland and Tas. or NZ. A few species – such as the > *muttonbird* – migrate between the northern and southern hemispheres so as to summer in both regions.

Explorers and artists were important early observers and recorders of Australia's rich birdlife. *Birds of NSW* (1813) by artist-naturalist J.H. Lewin, was the first illustrated book printed in Australia. The first great scientific workers in the field were > *John Gould* and his assistant John Gilbert from 1838; much important classifying work was also done by zoologist Edward Ramsay at the Australian Museum in Sydney for two decades from the mid-1870s. The Royal Australasian Ornithologists' Union was founded in 1901 and the study of Australian birds became increasingly scientific and specialised. The results also began to reach a wider audience, the multi-volume works of Gould and later Gregory Mathews (published 1910–27) having paved the way for a plethora of popular illustrated bird books. Great strides were also made in the identification and recording of the Australian avifauna, through such projects as the *Atlas of Australian Birds* (1984), and the national photographic index of Australian wildlife (from 1969) which provided the basis for a series of books on different bird groups. A definitive three-volume catalogue of Australian birds is expected to be published by the Bureau of Flora and Fauna in the early 1990s. >> *birds, introduced*; *fauna*

birds of paradise > *riflebirds*

birds of prey > *eagles and hawks*

Birdsville Track This famous stock route, some 500km long, runs between Birdsville in southern Qld and the railhead town of Marree in SA, from where cattle are entrained to Adelaide. The track traverses Sturt's Stony Desert and the only water to be found is from artesian bores. In recent years the track has been improved and cattle are now transported by road train. Nevertheless, as an important part of Australian popular mythology, it has become synonymous with the courage and tenacity of outback pioneers, and attracts many tourists.

bitterns, egrets and herons These large wading birds are closely related. The sturdy bitterns hold their necks retracted except when they are alarmed, when they may stretch out neck and bill as camouflage to merge with the adjacent reeds of their swamp environment; some species have a booming call, often associated with lonely swamps. Herons are large, long-legged birds, with long bills and necks; they fly with their necks curved back in the shape of an 's'. The most common Australian species is the white-fronted heron, or blue crane, found in marshes and other freshwater habitats; others are the reef herons – two forms of a tropical species – and the nankeen night-heron, a striking, cinnamon-coloured bird bearing two long white plumes. Egrets are white herons, often with ornamental head plumes which in the past were much sought-after by the millinery trade. Australia has four species, the native plumed, white and little egrets, and the introduced cattle egret.

bivalves This is a class of molluscs – also known as pelecypods, meaning 'hatchet-footed' – in which the adults possess a shell in sections (valves), hinged at the 'beak', near which are interlocking teeth to keep the halves fitted together. The larval stage is shell-less and often shaped rather differently from the adult, sometimes living as a gill-parasite on fish; most species feed by filtering particles from water or mud. Bivalves include a number of well-known and commercially important species such as scallops, oysters and mussels.
Marine bivalves The well-known group of jingle shells includes the orange jingle, *Anomia descripta*, of southeastern Australia – translucent orange, golden or silvery, and irregularly shaped. One of the brittle but sharp-shelled razor shells is Menke's razor, *Pinna menkei*, often found anchored by thread-like processes and almost buried in mud or sand between tides or in shallow water in southeastern Australia. File shells are named for the fine-toothed, radial ridges they display; among them is Strange's file shell, *Stabilima strangei*, found in shallow water along much of the southern coast. The edible mussel, *Mytilus planulatus* is a familiar inhabitant the same coastal waters and is of increasing commercial importance. Giant clams, of the genus *Tridacna*, are found on coral reefs; the largest grow to a width of about 130cm, but despite popular belief there are no confirmed cases of giant clams trapping divers. The well-known pipi, *Plebidonax deltoides*, is one of the wedge-shells, a somewhat stout, surf-edge burrower, much 'fished' – by toe-wriggling – for bait and for food; the Chinaman's fingernail, *Solen correctus,* is a common representative of the finger oysters or fingernail shells. The boring bivalves, able to burrow in rock or wood with their shells, include the angel's wing, *Pholas*

australasiae, and the teredo, *Teredo austini*, which has two small, white burrowing shells at the front of a long, worm-like body which leaves behind it tunnels lined with a limy substance.
Freshwater bivalves These include the fresh-water mussels, such as the large *Alathyria jacksoni* of the Murray–Darling system and the small *Hydridella narracanensis*, which has an attractive mother-of-pearl interior, and the tiny pea-shells among which are various species of the genus *Sphaerium*, often found as early invaders of newly dug dams. >> *fishing industry*; *oysters and oyster culture*

Bjelke-Petersen, Sir Joh (Johannes) (1911–   ), politician, b. NZ. A peanut-farmer, Sir Joh entered the Qld parliament as a Country Party member in 1947 and was premier 1968–87; aided by a gerrymander, his National Party governed in its own right from 1983. Extremely conservative and consistently controversial, he strenuously opposed causes such as Aboriginal land rights and was as strongly pro-development as he was anti-union and anti-Labor. His political career ended in a forced resignation after an ill-judged campaign to enter federal parliament in 1986, which fuelled discord within the National Party.

Blackall Range Qld This is a small range of volcanic origin in the southeast of the State, which together with the Cooyar Range separates the drainage of the Brisbane River from those of the Mary and the Burnett. With rich volcanic soils the area is noted for citrus fruits, pineapples and bananas. The range was named in honour of a former governor of Qld.

blackberry > *weeds*

blackbirding This was the term colloquially applied to the system that brought South Sea islanders (Kanakas) to Australia c.1860–1900, chiefly to work on Qld cotton and sugar plantations. Legislation 1868–85 regulated conditions on the canefields but could not check abuses in recruiting, and 50 000 Kanakas had been imported by 1890. The abolition advocated by Samuel Griffith to be effective from 1890 reflected growing Labor concern over jobs as well as humanitarian motives, but was repealed in 1892 because of the prevailing depression; the northern planters threatened secession on the issue. By this time, smaller holdings were replacing plantations and mechanisation removed the need for so much labour. Abolition of the system followed Federation and recruitment ceased in 1904. Meanwhile, the employment of white labour was supported by a sugar subsidy. All Kanakas were repatriated by 1907.

blackbirds > *birds, introduced*

blackboy > *grass-trees*

Blackburn, James (1803–54), engineer and architect, b. England. Transported to Tas. in 1833 for forgery, Blackburn was pardoned in 1841. Although not formally trained he became a talented and original architect as well as a leading colonial engineer. The Holy Trinity Church in Hobart (1840–7) and the Lady Franklin Museum (1842–3) established him as a pre-eminent exponent of Greek Revival architecture. He was also responsible for extensive surveying, building, irrigation and engineering in Tas. (although many schemes were never implemented). As the city surveyor in Melbourne from 1849, he conceived and designed the ingenious water supply system for Melbourne from the Yan Yean Reservoir.

blackbutt > *eucalypts*

Blacket, Edmund Thomas (1817–83), architect, b. England. One of the leading 19th-century Australian architects, Blacket arrived in NSW in 1842 and was appointed government architect in 1849. A master of the Gothic Revival style, he designed some 58 churches including the attenuated St Mark's at Darling Point (c.1846). His design for Sydney University included the Great Hall (1854–60), arguably the finest Gothic Revival building in Australia. His commercial buildings were more conventionally classical and his domestic architecture frequently eclectic but unexceptional; Bishopscourt at Darling Point (c. 1855) is, however, notable.

Blackman, Charles Raymond (1928–), painter, b. Sydney. One of Australia's best known contemporary painters, Blackman worked as a newspaper artist before settling in Melbourne, where his 1953 one-man exhibition, 'The Schoolgirls', created considerable controversy, aligning him with 'modern art' and helping to establish his reputation. 'The Schoolgirls' represented a continuing theme in his work and led to the lyrical 'Alice in Wonderland' series. Blackman's work is charac-

terised by monumental, often silhouetted shapes, and bold colour.

Black War > *racial conflict*

blackwattle *Callicoma serratifolia* is a shrub or small tree with blackish bark and toothed leaves; it is native to coastal NSW and southern Qld, and is the sole species in a genus of the family > *Cunoniaceae*. Once common along creeks and in freshwater swamps around Sydney Harbour, its flexible canes were used as wattles by early settlers in the construction of wattle-and-daub huts, whence came its common name. The later application of the term 'wattle' to species of acacia probably resulted from the similar cream flower-heads of both groups.

blackwood > *wattle*

Blackwood River WA Rising east of Collie, the Blackwood River flows southwest through agricultural and pastoral land for 300km to Flinders Bay on the south coast, east of Cape Leeuwin. The town of Augusta stands at the estuary mouth.

bladderworts This is the common name of insectivorous plants of the family Lentibulariaceae, found in shallow water or boggy ground; small insects and other aquatic invertebrates are trapped in the delicate bladders of their highly modified leaves and digested as a supplementary source of nitrogen. The genus *Utricularia* is cosmopolitan in distribution, with about 55 species native to Australia: the most common is the purple bladderwort or fairy apron, *U. dichotoma*, with fine-stemmed showy mauve or purple flowers. The endemic genus *Polypompholyx* consists of three species, differing from *Utricularia* only in floral details.

Blainey, Geoffrey Norman (1930–), historian, b. Melbourne. Since 1984 Blainey has been a controversial figure because of his questioning – in newspapers and in his book *All for Australia* (1984) – Australia's continuing large intake of Asian immigrants. His standing as an Australian historian is indisputable, his major works including *The Rush That Never Ended* (1963), *The Tyranny of Distance* (1966) and *A Land Half Won* (1980).

Blair, Harold (1924–76) singer and teacher, b. Murgon, Qld. An Aborigine raised on a mission near Ipswich in Qld, Blair was a farm worker before being encouraged by noted Australian soprano Marjorie Lawrence, among others, to develop his excellent tenor voice. Having studied at the Melbourne Conservatorium he became the first Aborigine to succeed as a professional classical singer, touring the US and Europe as well as Australia 1949–62. By the late 1950s his professional appearances became less and less frequent; his diverse business and public activities included the inauguration of a scheme for bringing Aboriginal children from rural reserves to Melbourne for holidays.

Blake Prize > *art awards*

Blamey, Sir Thomas Albert (1884–1951), soldier, b. Lake Albert, NSW. After teaching, Blamey entered the army and trained in India 1911–13. During World War 1 he fought at Gallipoli and afterwards served as chief-of-staff to Sir John Monash (then lieutenant-general) in France. Blamey was Vic. police commissioner 1925–36, and following the outbreak of World War 2 was appointed general officer commanding the AIF in the Middle East. In 1942, he was commander-in-chief of all Australian military forces under US general Douglas MacArthur. He was a field marshal from 1950.

Blaxland brothers, explorers and pioneer farmers. **John** (1769–1845) and **Gregory** (1778–1853) immigrated to NSW in 1806–7. They were the first free settlers under Viscount Castlereagh's scheme to give land and convict labour to desirable men of status and capital. While both became involved in political affairs, opposing first William Bligh and then Lachlan Macquarie, their contributions were to farming and exploration. Gregory developed winemaking, John cattle-fattening. When insects, drought and land hunger made the discovery of fresh pastures essential after 1810, Gregory, with William Lawson and W.C. Wentworth, made the first Blue Mountains crossing in 1813 by following the ridges. His journal is an imaginative – if rather overstated – record.

Bligh, William (1754–1817), naval officer and colonial administrator, b. England. Bligh's governorship of NSW 1806–10 was a stormy interlude in a successful and colourful naval career. At 21 he commanded the *Resolution* on Cook's last voyage (1776); in 1789 he was in command of the *Bounty* when the crew mutinied, placing him with eighteen men in an open boat which he successfully navigated over 5800km to Timor in six weeks.

Recommended by Sir Joseph Banks as the governor to replace King, he found the colony in a state of chaos, debauchery and profiteering – especially by the officer elite of the NSW Corps, whom he soon antagonised by stopping payment in spirits for services and goods. Matters came to a head in the > *Rum Rebellion* of January 1808; Bligh was kept under arrest for almost a year, refusing to leave for England as a prisoner. Released in 1810 on condition that he return to England aboard HMS *Porpoise*, he was subsequently completely exonerated, and later promoted to rear admiral.

Bligh's courage, seamanship and administrative ability are beyond dispute; his temper and character are more open to controversy. He did much for NSW in both administration and agriculture, encouraging new methods, use of improved seeds, and even soil conservation.

bloodwood > *eucalypts*

blowflies These are large flies of the family Calliphoridae, metallic blue-green in colour, whose larvae develop on carrion, living hosts or excrement. Noteworthy among Australia's 200 species is the Australian sheep blowfly, *Lucilia cuprina*, a serious pest costing pastoralists millions of dollars annually in sheep deaths and spoilt fleeces. Sheep become predisposed to fly-strike when fleeces are soiled with urine or faeces, especially in wet weather; the flies then lay their eggs around the crotch – or elsewhere, on body wounds – and the hatching larvae emerge to feed on exudates from irritated skin, causing further irritation and possible secondary infection; further strike may prove fatal.

Preventive measures include mid-season 'crutching' – shearing around the breech and tail – and application of insecticidal sheep dips. There has been considerable research by the CSIRO on the control of blowflies by importing blowfly parasites, by genetic manipulation and by swamping wild populations with millions of sterile males irradiated with X-rays. However, none of these approaches has met with much success, and the problem remains.

bluebells Among Australian plants this common name is used chiefly for members of the genus *Wahlenbergia* (family Campanulaceae), of which Australia has 26 species. Most are delicate herbaceous plants with pale to dark-blue flowers; they occur in open country and in mountain woodlands and grasslands. A widespread and conspicuous species is the tufted bluebell, *W. communis*. The ACT's floral emblem is *W. gloriosa*.

bluebottle > *hydrozoa*

bluebush > *saltbush family*

Blue Lake SA The largest of the Mt Gambier crater lakes, Blue Lake is named for the brilliant colour of its waters at the height of summer. It is about 80m deep, covers 70ha and the sheer walls of the volcanic crater rise 80m above the water level. A popular tourist resort, it is also the source of Mt Gambier's domestic water supply.

Blue Mountains NSW These mountains in fact form a plateau of 600–1100m elevation, emerging abruptly from the plain 65km west of Sydney and thence rising gently further west; they are dramatically dissected by the Nepean and Cox rivers and their tributaries, the valleys of which are often steep-sided and crowned by precipices. The rocks are sedimentary, the uppermost a massive, resistant sandstone underlain by weaker shales and coal measures which, when eroded by river water, fall away to reveal sheer cliffs. The Blue Mountains were a barrier to expansion from Sydney until the crossing in 1813 by Gregory Blaxland, William Lawson and William Charles Wentworth. Their route, keeping to the ridges rather than to the impassable valleys, was followed by the road built by William Cox at the direction of Governor Macquarie and subsequently by modern rail and road routes. The string of towns which line this transport corridor have been combined administratively to form the City of Blue Mountains, covering the greater part of what is now a major tourist area. Most of the mountains are forested, and are reserved in the large national parks of Blue Mountains, Kanangra-Boyd, and Wollemi. Sydney derives much of its urban water supply from the mountain reservoir of Lake Burragorang, formed by the damming of the Warragamba River.

Boake, Barcroft (Henry Thomas) (1866–92), b. Sydney. Although well educated, Boake was drawn by the harsh romance of the outback and chose to work as a boundary rider and drover. He is mainly remembered for his ballad 'Where the Dead Men Lie' (1897), published in a volume of the same name: it conveys memorably the grim harshness of the outback and attacks the exploitation of bush people by absentee landlords. A pessimist by nature, and faced with financial problems, Boake committed suicide.

Bodalla NSW (pop. 291) A dairying town on the Tuross River, 335km south of Sydney, Bodalla (and its surrounding district) was noted particularly for cheese production until the town's factory closed in the late 1980s because of inadequate milk supplies. The town developed from a model farm established by T.S. Mort in the 1850s.

Boer War (October 1899–May 1902) When war broke out between Britain and the southern African Boer republics of the Transvaal and Orange Free State, the Australian colonies made individual offers of troops. After the formation of the Commonwealth in January 1901, these forces were consolidated as the Australian Commonwealth Horse. The bushcraft and horsemanship of the Australians assisted them in a war that proved to be one of movement and guerilla tactics. Of a total of 16 175 men sent, 518 died, more than half from disease. Six Victoria Crosses were awarded to Australians during the campaign, and the experience gained proved invaluable to the AIF during World War 1.

Bogan River NSW Rising on the western slopes of the Great Dividing Range, the Bogan is part of the Darling River system, flowing generally northwest for about 600km to join the Barwon River 40km upstream from Bourke. North of Nyngan, in an area of low and unreliable rainfall, many billabongs and anabranches develop, and flow is seasonal. The name Bogan is an Aboriginal word, meaning 'birthplace of a king (or headman)'.

Bogong High Plains Vic. An undulating plateau 1400–1800m above sea-level, the High Plains are part of the Vic. alps and include the State's highest peak, Mt Bogong (1987m). The plains were formerly used as summer grazing for beef cattle, but this is no longer permitted as it presents a threat to native flora and the danger of soil erosion. The plateau forms the headwater catchment for the Mitta Mitta and Kiewa rivers; waters of the latter contribute to the Kiewa hydro-electric scheme. The region supports three national parks – Mt Bogong, Mt Buffalo and Baw Baw – and is a popular recreation area, especially for skiing. The name Bogong is an Aboriginal word.

Bogong moth The dark-coloured adult of the cutworm, the Bogong moth, *Agrotis infusa*, breeds in vast numbers in the pastures and grasslands of western mountain slopes in Qld and NSW, emerging in early spring to migrate to the alpine areas of southeastern Australia. There they cluster in rock crevices and caves for the duration of the summer, returning to the interior to mate and lay their eggs. The Aborigines of southeastern regions used to make annual summer treks to the mountains to feast on the moths, considered to be a great delicacy. The Aboriginal name for them is reflected in one region of their summer sojourn: the Bogong High Plains.

Boldrewood, Rolf [Thomas Alexander Browne] (1826–1915), author. b. England. Boldrewood arrived in Australia with his family in 1836 and after his father's bankruptcy in the 1840s depression he worked variously as a farmer, goldfields commissioner and police magistrate. Taking his pen-name from Walter Scott's *Marmion*, he began contributing articles to literary magazines in the 1860s. He is best known, however, for his classic bushranging novel *Robbery under Arms* (1888), first serialised in the *Sydney Mail* 1882–3. Its huge popularity in Britain and the US as well as Australia encouraged publication of many more novels by Boldrewood, none of which has endured.

Bolte, Sir Henry Edward (1908–90) politician, b. Ballarat, Vic. Vic.'s longest-serving premier (1955–72), Bolte entered parliament in 1947. His Liberal government oversaw a great expansion in tertiary education (recognised with honorary degrees conferred on Bolte by Melbourne and Monash Universities). He supported the States' right to impose taxes, vigorously opposed the abolition of capital punishment, and his ministry of Aboriginal affairs was the first in Australia to grant specific rights to Aborigines. Throughout his record term of office he proved himself to be an astute tactician and a shrewd judge of public opinion.

Bond, Alan (1938–), business entrepreneur, b. England. One of Australia's most flamboyant businessmen, Bond started as a signwriter in Perth before going into real estate, which provided the foundation for the Bond Corporation. By the 1980s this was a worldwide conglomerate with interests in brewing, hotels, mining, property, television and communications. Bond became a national celebrity when his yacht *Australia II* won the America's Cup in 1983. By 1990, however, his brinkmanship and the level of debt carried by his diverse businesses were of growing concern in financial circles and major creditors launched debt-recovery actions against some of his companies.

Bonner, Neville Thomas (1922–), politician and Aboriginal advocate, b. Tweed Heads, NSW. The first Aborigine to enter federal parliament, Bonner was a Liberal senator for Qld 1971–83. He fought strongly against racial discrimination and was outspoken on Aboriginal issues such as land rights as well as environmental matters. Placed an unwinnable third on the Liberal Party's Qld Senate ticket in 1983, Bonner resigned from the party and stood unsuccessfully as an independent. He subsequently became a director of the ABC and has been an active public representative and adviser on Aboriginal affairs. He was made AC in 1984.

Bonwick, James (1817–1906), historian, b. England. Bonwick lived in Australia 1841–84 as teacher, digger, land agent and schools' inspector. He was a tireless – if untrained and not always reliable – researcher into historical records, and a compiler and profilic writer of school texts, encyclopaedia articles and booklets on the colony.

Bonynge, Richard Alan (1930–), musical conductor and director, b. Sydney. Initially trained as a pianist, Bonynge turned to the study of opera, particularly the lesser-known works of the 18th and 19th centuries. In 1954, he married opera singer Joan Sutherland. His conducting debut was in Rome in 1962, followed by Covent Garden in 1964. Since then he has conducted in most major opera houses of the world, usually appearing with his wife, for whom he has been both voice coach and arranger. He was musical director of the Australian Opera 1975–86.

Bonython family, notable in SA commerce and politics. **Sir John Langdon** (1848–1939), politician and philanthropist, b. England, was chairman of the Commonwealth Literary Fund 1908–29 and owner-editor of one of Australia's best known newspapers, the Adelaide *Advertiser*. His son, **Sir (John) Lavington** (1875–1960), b. Adelaide, was publisher and director of Advertiser Newspapers Ltd and an eminent figure in SA civic affairs and welfare organisations. **Kym (Hugh Reskymer)** (1920–), b. Adelaide, son of Sir Lavington, is a businessman and jazz promoter and a director of the Bonython Art Gallery, first in Adelaide and from 1972 in Sydney.

boobiallas This is the Aboriginal name for a number of small-flowered shrubs in the Pacific genus *Myoporum*, of which sixteen species are native to Australia. Some are found mainly in coastal regions, most notably the hardy southern shrub *M. insulare*, which bears small blue fruits. The corkwood, *M. acuminatum*, which reaches 8m in height, is common on the NSW coast and rainforest margins; its close relative the native myrtle, *M. montanum*, is a sparse shrub extending to drier inland regions. Predominantly inland species include the dogwood, *M. desertii*, which has sweet yellow fruits but foliage which is poisonous to livestock.

boobies > *sea-birds*

boobook > *owls*

bookselling > *publishing and bookselling*

Booth, Peter (1940–), artist, b. England. Booth is the leading exponent of neo-expressionism in Australia. His early textural paintings, almost completely black, gave way in the late 1970s to more figurative works showing terrified figures and fantastic monsters in post-Holocaust landscapes. He is a prolific draughtsman, his drawings combining prophecies of doom and bizarre fantasies. Booth exhibits regularly in Australia and has been represented in major group shows in Paris and New York.

Border, Allan (1955–), cricketer, b. Sydney. By the end of the 1989 cricket season, 'AB' had become the highest run-getter in Australian Test cricket history; in 102 Tests he had scored 7831 runs (including 23 centuries), had taken more Test catches than any other Australian, and had played in a world-record number of international one-day matches.

Border's record is the greater for having been achieved during a lean period in Australian cricket; he played his first Test in 1978, when the Australian team had been decimated by the introduction of World Series cricket. He played many fighting innings after assuming the captaincy in 1984, but victories were infrequent until in 1989 he led the Australian team to a record-breaking Ashes win.

Bordertown SA (pop. 2318) Situated in the Ninety Mile Desert, 19km west of the Vic. border, Bordertown originated in the 1850s as a gold-escort depot between Vic. and Adelaide. The town now depends on wool, wheat and dairy farming, and vegetable and wine-grape production.

boree > *wattle*

boronias This near-endemic group of Australian plants, which belongs to the > *citrus family*, is a major component in the diverse array of colourful shrubs abundant in sandy or rocky ground in the moist southeast and far southwest. There are almost 100 species in the genus *Boronia*, including the rare native rose, *B. serrulata*, of the Sydney sandstone and the brown boronia, *B. megastigma,* of WA, commonly cultivated for its rich fragrance. Outside Australia, this genus occurs only in New Caledonia. The related waxflower genus *Eriostemon* is endemic, its 30 species being divided between the southeast and southwest of the continent; all have profuse starry flowers, mostly white or pale pink. The genus *Correa* is also endemic; most of its eleven species have colourful tubular flowers and all are eastern except for the most widespread species, *C. reflexa* (commonly known as the native fuchsia), which extends to WA. This genus is remarkably concentrated in the far south of SA, especially on Kangaroo Island. The genus *Zieria*, of 26 species, is restricted to eastern Australia except for one New Caledonian species; it includes tall rank-smelling forest shrubs as well as some lower, heathy ones. Also predominantly eastern is *Phebalium*, with 45 species many of which have silver or brown leaves and twigs; the satinwood, *P. squameum*, is a tree of 12m or more in wet Vic. forests.

Borovansky, Edouard > *ballet and dance*

Bosisto, Joseph (1827–98), research chemist, b. England. Bosisto came to Australia in 1848.

He set up practice in Richmond, Vic. and established a laboratory in which he conducted experiments on native flora. He began distilling eucalyptus oil, and was among the first to take advantage of its pharmaceutical properties. This made Bosisto a household name and the parrot pictured on a yellow disc a famous trademark. Bosisto founded the Pharmaceutical Society in 1857; he was a member of the Vic. parliament 1874–89, where he was chiefly responsible for the 1876 Pharmacy Bill.

botanic gardens Many of Australia's major botanic gardens were well established by the late 19th century. While deriving from a long European tradition, modern botanic gardens reflect in particular the zeal for scientific collection and display which developed from the 17th century; in the 19th century, they were viewed chiefly as places for the introduction and acclimatisation of plants, particularly those of economic usefulness. Today, the emphasis has changed to a mix of public recreation and education, research and conservation. Since the 1970s, most States have established regional centres concentrating on local flora: these include annexes at Blackwood and Mt Lofty in SA, at Cranbourne in Vic., at Mt Tomah and Mt Annan in NSW.

The National Botanic Gardens in Canberra, which formed part of Walter Burley Griffin's design for the national capital in 1914, were not developed until the 1940s. Opened in 1970, they occupy more than 40ha and are devoted entirely to Australia's native flora; research activities also focus on indigenous plants, particularly the cultivation of endangered species. Similar research is undertaken by the State herbariums, most notably those of NSW and WA.

The major State gardens The botanic gardens of Sydney, Hobart, Melbourne, Adelaide and Perth are under the control of the respective State governments; those of Brisbane are the responsibility of the city council.

The botanic gardens in Sydney – which today cover about 30ha – were the earliest in the colonies and the third to be created in the southern hemisphere. Originating in a farm established on the shores of Sydney Cove in 1788, the gardens were established as a series of walks and shrubbery by 1816. They evolved gradually under a series of directors, the most notable of whom were > *Charles Moore* (1846–96) and > *Joseph Maiden* (1896–1924). The greatest scientific progress occurred under Maiden, who developed systematic garden plots, made great improvements to the site's drainage and landscaping, developed the herbarium and constructed the still-extant aviary. The herbarium was rehoused in 1981.

Also derived from a garden-farm, the Tas. botanic gardens were established within the Queen's Domain in Hobart in 1818 and remained the responsibility of the colony's Botanical and Horticultural Society until they were transferred to the Crown in the 1850s. Now covering 16ha, their greatest period of expansion was the late 19th century and they were substantially remodelled in the 1980s.

Melbourne's 35ha botanic gardens have their origins in a site of 2ha set aside in the 1840s. > *Ferdinand von Mueller*, director 1857–73, brought great botanical expertise to the gardens and established the herbarium; the park-like expanses and planting of the gardens today are owed to his successor > *William Guilfoyle* (1873–1909).

The Adelaide gardens were opened on a 16ha site beside the Torrens River in 1857. While they have been extended by only 2ha since that time, they were greatly developed in the late 19th century and again under the directorship of T. Lothian from 1948.

In Perth, a 2.5ha site near Government House was set aside for botanic gardens in 1829 but it remained little more than a park until the mid-20th century. New gardens extending over 17ha were opened in 1965, with particular emphasis on WA flora.

Brisbane's original botanic gardens also emanated from a government garden, which was established in 1828 and covered 9ha by 1836. The gardens were developed separately from the 1850s and were gradually extended into nearby Queen's Park and the Domain; separate gardens now also exist at nearby Mt Coot-tha.

Gardens were first created in Darwin in the 1870s. Ravaged by the 1974 cyclone, they have since been reconstructed and extended and are noted for their tropical plantings.

botany and botanists The earliest known botanical collections in Australia are those of William Dampier in 1699, who described and illustrated several Australian plants in the published account of his voyage; accompanying James Cook, Joseph Banks and Daniel Solander collected numerous specimens but failed to publish their results. In the period 1788–1810, many plants of the Sydney district were sent back to eager growers in England

and quite a number were illustrated and named. A major landmark was the publication in 1810 of Robert Brown's *Prodromus Florae Novae Hollandiae et Insulae Van Diemen*. In 1844 a work of equivalent size, *Plantae Preissianae*, was published in Germany describing the plants collected in WA by Ludwig Preiss.

The next landmark was the appointment in 1853 of German immigrant > *Ferdinand von Mueller* as government botanist in Vic. This marked the beginning of a 43-year career of remarkable industry in the description and cataloguing of the Australian flora. His published output was formidable, although much of it betrays a certain eccentricity, confusion in detail, and excessive formalism. Mueller's industriousness was perhaps exceeded by that of George Bentham, who never set foot in Australia but who between 1863 and 1878 published his comprehensive *Flora Australiensis* in seven volumes. Mueller, while aggrieved at not being chosen for this task, co-operated generously with Bentham by sending his specimens and manuscript descriptions; this was acknowledged by Bentham on the title page, although he stressed that the taxonomic arrangement of the flora was entirely his own.

Mueller excepted, few resident Australian botanists achieved distinction in the 19th or early 20th centuries . Charles Moore in Sydney and Richard Schomburgk in Adelaide were able botanic-garden directors with a sound grasp of the native flora, but neither published much. > *Joseph Maiden*, who succeeded Moore as director of Sydney's Botanic Gardens in 1896, contributed greatly to the understanding of eucalypt taxonomy and was a foremost populariser of botany. In Qld F.M. Bailey, government botanist 1881–1915, named many new plants especially from the tropical north (> *Bailey family*). In SA the talented amateur botanist J.M. Black singlehandedly wrote and illustrated the *Flora of South Australia*, published in four parts 1922–9 (since revised twice). In Vic., Professor Alfred Ewart published a bulky but inaccurate *Flora of Victoria* in 1931; fortunately this was superseded by the work of Jim (H.J.) Willis, whose two volumes of *A Handbook to Plants in Victoria* were published in 1962 and 1973.

The second half of the 20th century has seen a great upsurge in floristic work (involving many highly trained systematic botanists) as well as the maturing of plant ecology as a related discipline. The pace and coverage of botanical collecting has increased hugely, mainly due to the activities of the State and Commonwealth herbariums and other government agencies such as soil and wildlife conservation bodies. A government-sponsored program, the Australian Biological Resources Study, was initiated in 1973. This is now part of the federal Bureau of Flora and Fauna, which provides grants for systematic research, publishes indexes and other compilations, and since 1981 has been engaged in the publication of a new *Flora of Australia* in 50-odd projected volumes (of which nine had been published by 1988). A recent volume devoted to the lily and allied families indicates that 110 out of the 404 described species have been recognised and named only since 1960 – a reflection of the great growth in knowledge of Australia's flora.

Botany Bay NSW An inlet on the east coast, 8km south of Sydney, this was the site of James Cook's first landing in Australia. The entrance to the bay is flanked by La Pérouse and Kurnell peninsulas, now reserved as historic sites; the remaining shores are occupied by industrial and residential (Sydney suburban) areas, and in the northwest by Kingsford Smith international airport of which the longest runway, built on reclaimed land, projects into the bay. Although Cook first used the name Stingray Bay, he later altered it in recognition of the plant collections made there by Joseph Banks. Botany Bay was the planned destination of the First Fleet under Arthur Phillip who, however, found it to be a shallow harbour too exposed to easterly winds and lacking adequate fresh water. Supplanted thus by Sydney Harbour, only in 1955 did Botany Bay undergo significant development with the construction of an oil refinery at Kurnell. In 1961 the decision was made to develop Port Botany as a supplement to Sydney, and major enlargement of port facilities has included construction of a 2km breakwater projecting from the north shore. As a result of this development, pollution of the bay has become a continuing problem, and marine life has been seriously affected.

botflies Belonging to the families Gasterophilidae and Oestridae, botflies are parasitic within the bodies of mammals; some species were introduced to Australia in association with their hosts. All feeding takes place in the larval stage, the adults having only vestigial mouthparts. The eggs of the horse botfly are laid in the animal's hair and when licked are carried to its stomach where they hatch, feeding on secretions; they are then passed through the digestive tract. The sheep botfly deposits tiny larvae in nasal passages and the larvae eat their way through the nasal sinuses, often being sneezed out before pupating. There are also native botflies associated with kangaroos and wallabies.

bottlebrush > *myrtle family*

bottle tree > *sterculia family*

Boulder WA > *Kalgoorlie*

Bourke NSW (pop. 3018) This outback town on the Darling River in far west NSW was formerly a river port and is now an important wool railhead and agricultural and pastoral centre. It was named after Fort Bourke, a stockade built by Thomas Mitchell in the 1830s as protection against possible attack by Aborigines. Cotton, fruit and vegetable crops are irrigated by water from the Darling River.

Bowen Qld (pop. 7705) The port and town of Bowen lies on Port Denison, a fine natural harbour some 1149km north of Brisbane. The hinterland is a major producer of export beef and the town has a State coking plant (which services the Mt Isa and Townsville metal works) using Collinsville coal and solar-salt evaporation. Tomatoes, bananas and mangoes are exported and tourism is becoming more important to the town, which is near the Whitsunday islands and is home to the North Qld Cruising Yacht Club. A 331-berth marina was under construction in the late 1980s. Named after Sir George Ferguson Bowen, then governor of Qld, the town was first settled in 1861.

Bowen Basin > *coal; oil and natural gas*

bower-birds The family Ptilonorhynchidae is unique to Australia and NG and contains sixteen species in seven genera. Most species present remarkable mating displays by males, perhaps combined with some pleasure in ornamentation; this takes the form of building – and sometimes painting – a bower separate from the nest, although not all species have been seen to carry out this ritual. All bower-birds hop rather than walk and tend to mimic other birds in addition to their own variable calls and alarm cries. The best known species is the blue-black satin bower-bird of eastern Australian rainforests; the cock makes an almost tunnel-shaped grass bower, often lined with vertically placed sticks and decorated with any available blue or pale-yellow objects. The bower is sometimes painted with charcoal or perhaps dark fruits mixed with saliva. Females and immature males are greenish.

Other species include the regent bower-bird, also of eastern Australian rainforests, the cock being a spectacular gold-and-black; the beautiful golden bower-bird of northeastern Qld; and the brown- and buff-striped tooth-billed bower-bird of eastern Qld, which lays a carpet instead of creating a bower. The green catbird, a relative in which bower-building has never been observed, is so named because of its extraordinary, miaowing call.

bowls With more than 284 000 players in 2240 registered clubs, lawn bowls is a popular sport for all ages throughout Australia, and in recent years it has become popular television viewing. The first official match was played in 1845 in Hobart, where the first club was formed the following year. Intercolonial matches were instituted in NSW in 1880 by John Young, 'the father of bowls', and the Australian Bowling Council was formed in 1900, followed in 1907 by the Victorian Ladies' Bowling Association. International competition commenced in1900 with a tour of Britain by an Australian team, and the first British team to visit Australia came in 1925. The inaugural world championships took place in Sydney in 1966, and bowls has been a regular feature of first Empire and then Commonwealth Games. The most celebrated player Australia has produced is Glyn Bosisto, who was national champion 1949–53.

Bowral NSW (pop. 7390) A commercial and tourist centre 125km southwest of Sydney, Bowral is noted for its fine gardens and attractive surrounding farmlands. Already the retail and commercial centre for the southern highlands, Bowral is much sought after by retirees, hobby farmers and even commuters, particularly since the opening in 1980 of a freeway from Sydney. Nearby Moss Vale (pop. 5016) and Mittagong (pop. 4237) are centres for dairying, market gardening, wool and fat-lamb production.

box > *eucalypts*

boxing Bare-knuckle fights were conducted in Australia during the first years following white settlement; earliest extant accounts are of a 56-round bout at Sydney in 1814. Boxing according to Marquess of Queensberry rules was introduced in 1884, and in this period Larry Foley, the 'father of Australian boxing', coached many fine fighters, including Albert Griffiths who won an unofficial version of the world featherweight title in 1889. The staging in Sydney in 1908 of the world heavyweight championship match between Tommy Burns and Jack Johnson encouraged the rapid growth of the sport and led to the construction of many stadiums. > *Les Darcy* was the leading fighter of this era, but died in the US in 1917 while preparing for a world title fight.

During the 1930s depression boxing was a popular form of entertainment and a chance for some to earn a living; Australia had many world-ranked fighters in this period. After World War 2, Dave Sands and Ron Richards came close to winning world titles, but the honour of Australia's first official world crown went to Jimmy Carruthers, bantamweight champion in 1952. Despite this, the sport went through one of its periodic downturns in the late 1950s, but revived as a television event in the mid-1960s. The victories of Lionel Rose (bantamweight, 1968) and Johnny Famechon (featherweight, 1969), followed in both cases by successful title defences, mark the pinnacle of Australian boxing. After some lean years in the 1970s and early 1980s, only Rocky Mattioli (middleweight, 1977) stood out. Lester Ellis and Barry Michael signalled a further revival with junior lightweight titles in 1985 and 1986, but it was > *Jeff Fenech* who stamped himself as possibly Australia's greatest boxer. At the Seoul Olympic Games in 1988, Grahame Cheney equalled Australia's best Olympic result with a silver medal in the light-welterweight division.

box jellies > *jellyfishes*

Boyd, Benjamin (?1803–51), entrepreneur, b. Scotland. Boyd arrived in Australia in 1842, becoming a banker, squatter, and shipping and whaling magnate. He owned vast sheep runs in southern NSW and in Vic., and built Boydtown (1843) at Twofold Bay in NSW as a whaling station and port. In 1847 he began to import Pacific islanders as station labour, but met so much opposition that he had to give it up. Boyd's ventures failed, the town was abandoned (only one building and a ruined church remain), and he vanished in the Solomon Islands in 1851.

Boyd, Martin > *Boyd family*; *literature and writing*

Boyd, Robin > *architecture*; *Boyd family*; *design*

Boyd family, pre-eminent in Australian art and letters for more than a century. **Arthur Merric** (1862–1940), b. NZ, arrived in Australia in 1866; he and his wife Emmie Minna were talented landscape painters. Their second son, **(William) Merric** (1888–1959) b. Melbourne, is generally recognised as Australia's first artist potter, noted particularly for his incorporation of distinctive Australian motifs. His brother **(Theodore) Penleigh** (1890–1923), b. England, was educated in Melbourne where he became a noted landscape painter and etcher. Another brother, **Martin à'Beckett** (1893–1972), b. Switzerland, was also educated in Melbourne and trained as an architect but turned to writing in the 1920s. His quartet of novels (1952–62) *The Cardboard Crown, A Difficult Young Man, Outbreak of Love* and *When the Blackbirds Sing* were based on his family background and reflect the conflicting loyalties of European immigrants in the Antipodes. Merric's son **Arthur Merric Bloomfield** (1920–), b. Murrumbeena, Vic. is a leading painter, sculptor and potter. He exhibited with the Contemporary Art Society in Melbourne during and after World War 2, and for a time worked as a potter with his brother-in-law John Perceval. His dramatic, luminous 'Half-Caste Bride' series, first exhibited in 1958, led him away from landscape painting to more figurative work. His brother **Guy Martin à'Beckett** (1923–), b. Melbourne, is a sculptor who has produced major mural sculptures for civic buildings in Vic., NSW and the ACT. Merric's third son, **David Fielding Gough** (1924–), b. Melbourne, studied music but took up full-time painting in the 1950s. Penleigh's son **Robin Gerald Penleigh** (1919–71) was an eminent architect and one of the most articulate critics of the Australian aesthetic ethos; his twelve books include the classic *The Australian Ugliness* (1960), a scathing attack on Australians' love of 'featurism' and lack of visual sensibility.

Boyer, Sir Richard James Fildes (1891–1961), broadcasting administrator, b. Taree, NSW. After military service in World War 1, Boyer became a prominent Qld pastoralist. He was appointed to the ABC in 1940 and served as chairman 1945–61, during which time he helped to expand the organisation and ensure its independence. He strongly promoted educational and cultural activities, especially after the introduction of television in 1956. The annual Boyer Lectures, in which a discourse by a distinguished Australian is broadcast on the ABC, commemorate his contribution to the formative years of the organisation.

Brabham, Jack (Sir John) (1926–), racing driver, b. Hurstville, NSW. Having won the national title in midget-car speedway racing in 1951, Brabham moved to road racing in 1952 and in the following year went to England in the hope of competing in Formula One racing. Driving Cooper machines and using cool tactics, he won the World Drivers' Championship in 1959; in the deciding race, he had to push his car across the line after it had run out of fuel. He was world champion also in 1960 and again in 1966, when he was the first to win the title in a car of his own name: a Repco Brabham, designed, built and driven by himself.

Brack, (Cecil) John (1920–), painter, b. Melbourne. Brack was head of the Vic. National Gallery Art School 1962–8, when he resigned to paint full-time. His paintings of social comment and urban satire are distinguished by purity of line, linear perspective, flat surfaces and often idiosyncratic use of colour. His exhibitions have frequently dealt with one intently observed subject, from clinically arrayed medical equipment to luridly coloured ballroom-dancing.

Braddon, Russell (1921–), author, b. Sydney. Braddon graduated from Sydney University. Soon afterwards he spent four years as a Japanese prisoner of war in Changi, the subject of *The Naked Island* (1952), which was produced as a play in 1962. He has lived in England since 1949, writing novels with an Australian background such as *Out of the Storm* (1956) and *The Year of the Angry Rabbit* (1964), documentaries, and biographies including *Cheshire VC* (1954), *Nancy Wake* (1956) and *Joan Sutherland* (1962).

Bradfield, John Job Crew (1867–1943), civil engineer, b. Sandgate, Qld. Perhaps best known for designing the Sydney Harbour Bridge (for the NSW Public Works Department), Bradfield was also consulting engineer for the Story and Indooroopilly bridges in Brisbane and helped to design and plan the

University of Qld St Lucia campus. Deeply interested in water conservation and irrigation, he contributed to the design of the Cataract and Burrinjuck dams in NSW and in 1938 proposed a far-reaching scheme – the Bradfield Plan – to direct certain northern Qld rivers to water dry inland areas, although later assessment of the problems involved make it unlikely that this plan will ever be realised. In Sydney, the road across the Harbour Bridge was named in Bradfield's honour.

Bradman, Sir Donald George (1908–), cricketer, b. Cootamundra, NSW. Bradman is still one of Australia's sporting heroes, some 60 years after he first played in Sheffield Shield cricket. In first-class games, Bradman totalled 28 067 runs: in 37 Tests against England 1928–48, he averaged 89 runs with nineteen centuries, of which two exceeded 300 and six 200, although he failed by four runs to win a Test average of 100; his record of 1448 runs in one season was unbeaten until 1971. While not popular among all his fellow players or critics, Bradman always drew great crowds; in 1989 a museum of Bradman memorabilia was opened in Bowral, NSW, where his career began in country cricket.

Brady, E. J. (Edwin James) (1869–1952), author and editor, b. Carcoar, NSW. Brady was a balladist of sea and bush, a roamer, a journalist, and much else from canvasser to soldier; his best sea ballads rank with those of Rudyard Kipling and Henry Newbolt. His fifteen books include *The Ways of Many Waters* (1899), *Sea Rovers* (1911) and *Australia Unlimited* (1918); he also wrote children's books. Brady's entertaining autobiography, 'Life's Highway', was published in *Southerly* (1952–5). Settling at Mallacoota in Vic., which he dubbed an 'Australian Arcadia', Brady wrote prodigiously for 40 years until his death.

Brady, Matthew (1799–1826), bushranger, b. England. Tas.'s most audacious bushranger, Brady escaped from Port Macquarie in 1824. He answered Governor Arthur's offers of rewards for his capture with posters in Hobart offering rum in return for the capture of Arthur. At his trial, after capture by John Batman in April 1826, he faced more than 300 charges, including many of having murdered stockmen and settlers.

Bragg, Sir William Henry (1862–1942), physicist, b. England. Bragg won the Nobel

Prize for physics in 1915 with his son, William Lawrence (who at 25 was the youngest-ever Nobel Laureate), for having founded the science of X-ray analysis of crystal structure. Bragg's academic career began in 1885 with his appointment as professor of mathematics and physics at the University of Adelaide, where research on the ionisation of gases earned him a fellowship of the Royal Society in 1907. He was subsequently Cavendish professor of mathematics at Leeds University (1908) and professor of physics at University College, London (1915).

Brampton Island > *Cumberland Islands*

Brassicaceae > *mustard family*

Bray, J. J. (John Jefferson) (1912–), lawyer and poet, b. Adelaide. Bray lectured in law at the University of Adelaide in 1941 and 1966 and was chancellor 1968–83. As chief justice of the SA Supreme Court 1967–78, his judgments were distinguished by their intellectual honesty. Bray published three volumes of poetry in the 1960s and 1970s.

bream This category includes some of the sea fish most prized in Australia for both sporting and commercial purposes, among them the black bream or yellow-fin bream, *Acanthopagrus australis*, of the eastern coast and the bluenose, *A. butcheri*, of the south and west coasts. They are deep-bodied fish, mainly of temperate waters, although their habitat extends into the tropics. Bream often spawn inshore or in estuaries, moving their feeding grounds at other times to deeper, offshore waters. The rounded molar teeth are used for crushing snails and shells.

Brennan, Christopher John (1870–1932), poet, b. Sydney. Brennan is considered by some as Australia's greatest poet. A graduate of Sydney University, Brennan was both an ebullient wit and a brilliant intellectual; his poems are short, philosophical and scholarly, but often inaccessible. Several volumes were published, most notably *Poems (1913)* in 1914. He was associate professor of German and comparative literature at Sydney University 1920–5, but was dismissed following a much-publicised affair and alleged intemperance and degeneracy.

'Brent of Bin Bin' > *Franklin, Miles*

Brereton, John le Gay (1871–1933), academic and author, b. Sydney. Brereton was the son of a doctor and poet who arrived in Australia in 1859 and published several volumes of verse. As professor of English literature at Sydney University 1921–33, Brereton was a notable Elizabethan scholar and minor mystic poet. He had an important influence on Australian literature through his friendship with, and encouragement of, writers such as Henry Lawson and Christopher Brennan.

brewing industry Brewing is one of Australia's oldest industries, the first brewery being established in NSW in 1804. By the end of the 19th century dozens of small breweries were operating, but gradually the city-based companies – with their large markets and 'tied house' structures – came to predominate. In NSW, by the 1960s Tooth & Co. and Tooheys Ltd shared the market between them; in Vic. a merger of six businesses in 1907 to create Carlton & United Breweries resulted in CUB having a monopoly of State beer production by 1930. The pattern was repeated in other States, with Castlemaine Perkins dominant in Qld, Swan Brewery in WA, Cascade in Tas. and the SA Brewing Co. in that State.

Recent developments have seen further consolidation and take-overs: Elders-IXL now owns CUB (which itself had previously acquired Tooth & Co.) and the Bond Corporation owns Swan Brewery and the merged Castlemaine Tooheys. As well, what was once a regional industry – when each State tended to drink its own beer – is now a national one, in which the five dominant companies compete against each other for a share of the diminishing beer market. As the domestic market has declined Australian brewers have turned overseas, exporting or licensing production of popular brands such as Fosters, or purchasing breweries, as Elders-IXL has done in Britain and the Bond Corporation in the US.

Bribie Island Qld A large sandy island at the north end of Moreton Bay, Bribie extends north–south for about 30km and is separated from the mainland by the narrow Pumicestone Channel. It is a major tourist resort, offering facilities for swimming, surfing and water skiing; the main town is Bongaree.

Bridgetown WA (pop. 1478) On the Blackwood River some 265km from Perth, Bridgetown is a service centre for the surrounding rural area; its main economic activities are grazing and the production of tin and timber. It is noted for its annual marathon and Australia's longest motor-powered dinghy race, the Blackwood Classic 250.

brigalow > *wattle*

Bright Vic. (pop. 1673) This tourist centre in the Ovens valley lies about 312km northeast of Melbourne, near Mt Buffalo. Timber and tobacco are grown in the area but the principal economic activity is tourism, as Bright is a gateway to the Vic. alps and in particular the splendid Mt Buffalo National Park. It was a goldfield in the 1850s and its settlement history is reflected in a number of well-preserved historic buildings.

Brisbane Qld The capital city of Qld and Australia's third-largest city, Brisbane is a relaxed tropical town which long approximated more a provincial than a State capital. It accommodates only about 42% of the State's population (a much smaller proportion than other mainland capitals) and its development as a metropolis – while rapid – is relatively recent. Lying largely along the meanders of the Brisbane River, it is subject to periodic flooding. Because swamps and the coastal inlet of Moreton Bay block development to the east, and the Taylor Range impedes expansion to the west, growth has been northwest, southwest and southeast in the form of an inverted Y. The climate is subtropical, mean temperatures ranging from 9.7°C to 30°C, with high humidity and a mean annual rainfall of 1090mm which falls mainly from December to March. Air pollution is a growing problem in the city, as the result of its topography and prevailing wind direction.

Brisbane is named after Sir Thomas Brisbane, NSW governor when the area was settled; it was first occupied by Europeans in 1825, as a convict establishment, and was known as the Moreton Bay District. There was conflict with Aborigines, but few details are known. Gold rushes in northern Qld in the 1870s made Brisbane a sizeable city by the 1890s, with outlying settlements almost to the present boundaries; then, during a period of consolidation which lasted until World War 2, all of what is now Greater Brisbane was brought under the same municipal authority. For much of World War 2, Brisbane was a military garrison and the headquarters of the American general Douglas MacArthur. The city expanded rapidly from the 1970s, hosting the 1982 Commonwealth Games and six years later staging Expo 88.

At the census of 1986 the Brisbane Statistical Division had a population of 1 149 401, which showed a growth rate of 11.75% over the five years between censuses – higher than that of any capital except Canberra (12.71%). Brisbane did not gain many immigrants during the postwar immigration boom, but there has been a large influx since the 1970s, almost half of them from NZ. Of the State capitals, Brisbane has the second-lowest number (after Hobart) of overseas-born residents.

Business activity in Brisbane is dominated by the primary industries, both pastoral and extractive, which are the basis of the Qld economy. Tourism, especially since the Commonwealth Games and Expo 88, is of major economic importance, with the immensely popular resort of the Gold Coast only about 60km from the city. Manufacturing is concerned largely with the processing of foods, although the State government has established 'industrial parks' to encourage the production of capital and high-technology goods. Because of Brisbane's riverside location and the fact that most bridges have been built near the city centre, crossing the river has presented increasing transport problems; the Gateway Bridge, opened in 1986 downstream from the city, has alleviated this problem to some extent by allowing north–south traffic to bypass Brisbane.

Brisbane, Sir Thomas Makdougall (1773–1860), colonial administrator, b. Scotland. After army service 1789–1805 and 1810–18, Brisbane had returned to astronomical work (for which he is particularly noted) when he was appointed to succeed Governor Macquarie in NSW. During his term (1821–5), NSW saw important developments: the 1823 constitution, press freedom, currency stabilisation (including an attempt to use Spanish dollars), exploration, some limitation of land grants and the segregation of the worst types of convicts to Port Macquarie, Moreton Bay and Norfolk Island. Brisbane built and equipped Parramatta observatory, but was not forceful enough to control the turbulent factions of the times, or his disloyal subordinates. He was recalled in 1824.

Brisbane Water NSW This is a sheltered and shallow inlet on the northern side of Broken Bay, about 40km north of Sydney.

Early settlers in the district engaged in farming, timber-getting and lime-burning, and ship-building was pioneered here as early as 1824. Today the towns of > *Gosford* (at the head of the bay), Woy Woy and Ettalong (on the western shore) are popular holiday resorts, and there is also development of residential areas for commuters to Sydney. Brisbane Water National Park occupies much of the land between Mooney Creek and the inlet's western shore.

brittlestars > *starfishes*

broadcasting Australians have been eager consumers of broadcasting services since the first regular radio broadcasts began in 1923. The vastness of the country was most easily beaten by such media and Australians took to broadcasting forms with alacrity. Following the introduction of radio, television and colour television transmission, the speed with which these new media penetrated the market was remarkable by international standards, and each time exceeded original estimates. By 1989, there were an estimated 25.3 million radio receivers to service a population of 16.4 million. Just over 70% of Australians lived in houses with at least four radios, 98% of cars had radios, and Australians listened to about 22 hours of radio a week; at the same time, 98% of Australian homes had a colour television set, another 1% had a black-and-white set, and more than one-third of all homes had two or more sets. Australians watch an average of 20 hours of television a week.

The broadcasting industry is divided into three sectors: commercial, public and national. The national service comprises the > *ABC* and the > *SBS*. In the private sector in 1989, there were 50 commercial television stations and three remote commercial channels; and 140 commercial radio stations and 74 public radio stations, with several more public broadcasting organisations holding licences but not operative at the time. Out of total advertising revenue in 1987 of $3881 million, television received 34.3% and radio 9.2%.

Radio The federal government assumed control of broadcasting regulation in 1905 with the passing of the Wireless Telegraphy Act; the Marconi company set up a two-way radio station at Queenscliff in Vic. in the same year. Numerous experimental and demonstration transmissions followed and amateur (ham) radio stations were set up in Vic., Sydney and

Perth during the early 1920s. The first international radio telegraphy transmission occurred in 1918, when Prime Minister W.M. Hughes took part in a test broadcast from Wales picked up by the Amalgamated Wireless (Australasia) Ltd (AWA) equipment in Wahroonga, Sydney. The first public demonstration of broadcast music took place in Sydney in 1919.

AWA, which at first was interested mainly in building and equipping radio stations, announced in 1922 its agreement with the Commonwealth to set up a regular broadcasting service based on the 'sealed set' system, in which listeners paid a licence fee to the government and a subscription to the broadcaster. Regular transmission began the following year, with 2SB in Sydney being the first to broadcast (on 23 November); three other stations followed but the sealed-set system was abandoned within a year. In July 1924 the Postmaster-General's Department announced new regulations that divided transmitters into two classes; 'A' stations were financed through licence fees, and 'B' stations supported themselves from advertising. This was the basis of the dual system that underpinned Australian broadcasting until the introduction of public broadcasting in the mid-1970s. Radio 2UE in Sydney was the first 'B' station and began transmission in January 1925.

Acceptance of radio was rapid: by mid-1925, 38 000 licences had been issued; by July 1929, the number had grown to 310 000. The cost of broadcasting in larger States and remote areas was high, however, and initially city-dwellers were much better served by the new medium, although from 1925 till the mid-1930s country areas were intermittently serviced by mobile studios. In 1929 the Scullin Labor government nationalised 'A' stations and set up an Australia-wide broadcasting service. The ABC made its first broadcast in July 1932; it was initially funded from licence fees, but these were insufficient to cover costs and it was subsequently funded from consolidated revenue (although licence fees remained until 1974). Radio was not profitable at first, but it was popular and its programming varied. The early experimental broadcasts contained mainly music, formal speeches or readings, but sport was soon incorporated: the first simulated Test cricket broadcast was heard on 5CL (Adelaide) in 1925 and by 1930 commentaries on football matches were broadcast in all capital cities. Plays, quiz shows, variety programs and talent quests were the popular fare of commercial radio in the mid-1930s, while the ABC favoured 'talk shows' and formal debates.

In the postwar years, the invention of the transistor made radio even more attractive to listeners and advertisers. Large advertising companies set up production arms, such as the Colgate Unit which made favourites such as 'Pick a Box', 'Calling the Stars' and 'Can You Top This?'. Local content was high, in 1947 less than 5% of programs being imported. Dramatised musicals and 'drop dramas' were introduced by Hector Crawford in 1945 and proved very popular, but were usurped by television and by the mid-1960s most of the independent radio production houses had closed.

In the early years, few commercial stations had independent news services. During World War 2, for example, commercial radio was censored by the government and three stations were put off air for mentioning the sinking of HMAS *Sydney*. After the war, stations put greater emphasis on independent news services and this trend increased after the introduction of television because radio had the advantage of immediacy. In the 1970s radio used its technical advantage again with the introduction of talk-back radio.

National radio networking began informally in 1930 to help offset production costs; the Macquarie Network, formed in 1938, was the largest single radio producer in the British Commonwealth after the war. Radio markets remained persistently parochial, however, despite attempts in the mid-1980s to network 'talk-back' programs; the future of networking was made brighter by legislative changes in 1988 and the advent of satellite technology. Other technological changes also affected commercial radio in the 1980s. Following the introduction of frequency-modulation (FM) licences in 1980, FM stations rapidly diverted their share of audiences and revenue from AM stations. In 1987, the federal government announced further opening up of the FM band, allowing ten existing AM metropolitan stations to convert to FM, and granting 20 new FM licences. These changes are likely to have a continuing effect on commercial radio ownership and programming formats during the 1990s.

The dual system of radio broadcasting was broken in 1973 with the introduction of public radio. By 1989, nearly 90 public radio licences had been granted in three categories: educational, special-interest and community.

Television Regular experimental television transmissions date from May 1934, in Brisbane, but such broadcasts were stopped by government decree at the outbreak of World War 2. In 1949, the Chifley government announced plans to establish a national television system, but with the government's defeat in the same year the proposal was put aside. A 1953 royal commission recommended the gradual introduction of television under a dual system similar to that applying to radio and the first commercial licence hearings began in January 1955. Sydney's TCN–9 was the first operative television channel, introducing four hours of programs on 16 September 1956.

Initially, two commercial licences were granted in both Melbourne and Sydney to complement the ABC channel in each city. Television had reached the other State capitals by 1960 and Canberra and twelve large regional centres by 1964. In 1965, an extra commercial licence was granted in each capital except Hobart, despite proprietors' fears that the market could not support the move. By 1968, another 20 smaller country centres had commercial television stations; not part of the networks, they bought programs selectively. Colour transmission began in 1975, using the European phase-alternation line (PAL) system.

In general, television was accepted more rapidly than anyone had anticipated. By October 1957, 7% of Australian homes had television sets and the appetite of the population for the new medium appeared insatiable; by the end of 1959, TCN-9 was transmitting 80 hours of programming each week, well above its original estimate. The demand for programs put pressure on the new media managements. They imported the bulk of material, and only the news services and a few showcase programs – mainly low-budget but popular variety shows like GTV-9's 'In Melbourne Tonight' and ATN–7's 'Revue' series in Sydney – were produced locally. The police drama 'Homicide', the first local drama series, began in the 1960s but expense dictated that most local programs were simple, cheap 'chat' and variety shows.

The amount and quality of local content has always been a contentious issue. The Australian Broadcasting Control Board, forerunner to the > *Australian Broadcasting Tribunal* (ABT), tried to formulate policy on Australian content no fewer than eight times between 1960 and 1976. In 1973, it introduced a points system that placed emphasis on quality rather than quantity and every channel had to conform to a quota of minimum points: each commercial television licensee had to show a minimum of

104 hours of 'first-run' Australian drama in prime time; other locally made programs were given points weighted for their program type, broadcast times and 'first-run' status. Audience acceptance of local drama was slow, but helped by the imposed content standards home-grown products gradually won favour in the late 1960s and 1970s with shows such as 'Cop Shop', 'Number 96' and the ubiquitous 'Skippy'.

Channels always regarded their news services as flagships. The immense success of the Nine Network's '60 Minutes' (which began in 1979), however, focused attention on news and current affairs programs as audience-winners and these shows proliferated in the 1980s. Access to a 24-hour overseas satellite news service also boosted the number of hours devoted to news and current affairs, as channels sought to maximise the use of expensive news material coming in by satellite. Before 1982, all channels were dependent on a single overseas news source, Visnews, which from 1975 supplied news footage by satellite under a pool arrangement. This link was broken when the Nine Network negotiated an exclusive 24-hour link with the US network CBS and the other networks quickly followed suit. Similar exclusive agreements were negotiated with American drama producers.

Children's television programming has been no less controversial than the local content of programs. The ABT has an advisory committee on children's programs, set up in 1978 after an ABT inquiry found considerable community concern about the standard of children's television. The committees devised a special classification for high-quality programs for children aged 5–13, and licensees must set aside the hour from 4 p.m. each week night for such programs. The government-funded Australian Children's Television Foundation was established to commission scripts and raise private finance for the production of high-quality, local children's drama. >> *media ownership and control*

Broken Bay NSW Broken Bay forms the estuary of the Hawkesbury River about 25km north of Sydney; it is a drowned valley, with steep, rugged shores which struck James Cook as 'some broken land like a bay'. It has three distinct branches: Brisbane Water in the north, Pittwater in the south, and the Hawkesbury mouth in the west. Parts of the western and northern shore are declared national parks and it has long been a holiday area, but there is also considerable urban development in what has become both a commuter zone for Sydney and a retirement place.

Broken Hill NSW (pop. 24 460) A fading union town which lies on the world's richest deposit of lead-silver-zinc ores, Broken Hill is 1125km northwest of Sydney in the arid outback of the State. Following mineral discoveries from the mid-1870s, much of the area was taken over in 1885 by the original BHP Co. and the district boomed. After several major industrial disputes, all local unions amalgamated in 1925 as the Barrier Industrial Council which among other achievements negotiated the city's 'lead bonus', a unique profit-sharing scheme for miners. Assured water supply allowed the 'greening' of the city and helped to reduce the health hazards formerly caused by dust. Known ore reserves are expected to last only for 10–20 years and the closure of the main South Mine in 1972 initiated local job losses which are likely to be compounded by the 1988 merger between the two remaining underground mining companies.

Broken Hill Proprietary Ltd > *BHP*

brolga The brolga, *Grus rubicunda*, is a long-legged bird of generally light-grey plumage and standing about 1.5m, having a green and red head, a longish, sharp beak and a long neck; it is the only true crane in Australia. Its alternative name, native companion, is alleged to have been given because originally it was often seen near Aboriginal camps. Brolgas are found in wetlands, where their food includes fish, frogs and insects. The brolga's elaborate dances – typical of all cranes, especially when mating – are the subject of many traditional Aboriginal dances.

Brookes, Sir Norman Everard (1877–1968), tennis player and businessman, b. Melbourne. A great left-handed tennis player, Brookes was the first Australian to break into international tennis, when he won at Wimbledon in 1905. He played in the Davis Cup between 1905 and 1921, captaining six winning teams, and was president of the LTAA 1926–55, during which time he was a very influential administrator of the game. His business interests included Australian Paper Manufacturers Ltd and the North British Insurance Co.

Broome WA (pop. 5778) On the north shore of Roebuck Bay, some 2300km northwest of

Perth, Broome has been known particularly as a pearling centre since the 1890s. It was developed initially as a port for the Kimberley region; it was also an important telegraph station and nearby Cable Beach is named after an underwater cable that reached Broome from Java in 1889. Today its main industry is meat-processing, based on beef cattle grazed in the nearby inland.

Broughton, William Grant (1788–1853), Anglican prelate, b. England. Broughton succeeded Thomas Hobbes Scott as archdeacon of NSW in 1828, and was appointed bishop of Australia in 1836. While sincere and well loved, Broughton was anti-democratic and opposed non-denominational state schooling; he feared that Irish Catholic immigrants would dominate the colony and fought to uphold the Anglicans' early established position of privilege and social prestige. He was responsible for the founding of the King's School at Parramatta in 1832.

Brown, Bryan (1948–   ), actor, b. Sydney. After working in theatre in England, Brown returned to Australia in 1975, becoming one of the stalwarts of the revived Australian film industry. Notable for his appearances in *Newsfront* (1978), *Breaker Morant* (1980), and the television mini-series 'A Town Like Alice' (1980) and 'The Shiralee' (1987), Brown is a dependable actor who appears more comfortable in home-grown products than in US-produced exotica such as *Taipan* (1985) and *Gorillas in the Mist* (1988).

Brown, Carter [Alan Geoffrey Yates] (1923–85), novelist, b. London. Arriving in Australia in 1948, Yates began writing pulp fiction under various pseudonyms, settling on Carter Brown in 1950. His innumerable mystery stories written under that name were particularly popular in the US; their hard-boiled heroes inhabit a Mickey Spillane world of hard knocks, hard drinking and hard dames (who are usually blonde and, when not corpses, have hearts of gold). His work has fallen on hard times in today's non-sexist but more explicitly violent climate.

Brown, Robert (1773–1858), pioneer botanist, b. Scotland. Brown sailed with Matthew Flinders aboard the *Investigator* 1801–03, collecting plants at more than 30 locations along the Australian coast and inshore islands. Brown stayed in Australia until 1805, collecting plants in the Sydney region (assisted by the botanical artist Ferdinand Bauer) and later in Tas.; he was the first to record some 2000 Australian plant species. Volume 1 of his *Prodromus Florae Novae Hollandiae et Insulae Van Diemen* was published in 1810, but poor sales forced him to abandon work on the second volume. On his return to England in 1805 he became librarian to Joseph Banks and, later, keeper of botany at the British Museum.

Browne, Thomas Alexander > *Boldrewood, Rolf*

Bruce, Mary Grant (1878–1958), children's novelist, b. Sale, Vic. In her early 20s, Bruce became editor of the children's page of the *Leader*, a weekly supplement to the Melbourne *Age*. There the first of her immensely successful Billabong stories, *A Little Bush Maid*, was serialised in 1905–07; some 37 other children's novels followed, most of which were centred on the fictional station Billabong, and celebrated such traditional bush values as honesty and mateship. In her time, Bruce was one of Australia's best-known writers and her books have sold an estimated two million copies.

Bruce, Stanley Melbourne (1883–1967), politician, b. Melbourne. Bruce entered the House of Representatives in 1918, replacing W.M. Hughes as prime minister in 1923. Although he lost both government and his own seat in 1929 as the result of his mishandling of industrial arbitration, his joint ministry with the Country Party under Earle Page achieved much in the prosperous pre-depression years. Bruce's ability lay in seeing the need for overall planning: as well as establishing the Council for Scientific and Industrial Research (1926), he planned a comprehensive system of national insurance and rationalised the financial relationship of Commonwealth and States in 1927. As high commissioner in London 1933–45, his shrewd financial mind, important contacts and supreme confidence achieved much for Australia. He later served as independent chairman of the World Food Council of the Food and Agricultural Organisation, and was the first chancellor of the Australian National University 1951–61. Created 1st Viscount Bruce of Melbourne in 1947, he was the first Australian to be granted a viscountcy.

Bruny Island Tas. Off the southeast coast between D'Entrecasteaux Channel and Storm Bay, there are actually two islands, North and South Bruny, linked by a very narrow isthmus 6km long; activities include fruit growing, timber-getting, dairying and sheep grazing. The island was named by Admiral Bruny d'Entrecasteaux in 1792, but had been discovered by Abel Tasman 150 years before.

brush turkey > *mound-building birds*

Bryant, William (?–1791), convict, b. England. Bryant and his wife Mary (1765–?) escaped from Sydney in March 1791 with their two children and seven other convicts – Bryant was in charge of the colony's fishing boats. They stole a six-oared boat (the governor's cutter) which they navigated 5240km to Timor in ten weeks. All survived to this point, but Bryant, the children and three convicts died either there or on the voyage to England, where Mary and the others were leniently treated and then released, largely through the efforts of James Boswell. One, John Butcher, joined the NSW Corps and settled in Australia.

Bryozoa An ancient phylum of colonial – usually marine – invertebrates commonly found attached to objects in shallow water, Bryozoa often appear as a dense mass or like branched clumps of moss – hence their name, which means 'moss animals'; they are a dominant element in Australian coastal communities. Colonies grow very rapidly and secrete a calcareous exoskeleton; some species cause fouling on the bottom of small boats. The relatively few species of Bryozoa found in freshwater are almost cosmopolitan in distribution, occuring in both stagnant and fast-moving water; some have been known to block water pipes.

bubble shells > *gastropods*

Buccaneer Archipelago WA This is a group of islands off the northwest coast in Yampi Sound; it includes Cockatoo Island, with its large iron-ore deposits, and Koolan Island. A reef-strewn, hazardous area for shipping, it was named by Phillip Parker King in 1821 after the buccaneer, William Dampier.

Buchanan, Nat(haniel) (1826–1901), pastoralist and explorer, b. Ireland. Buchanan was responsible for pioneering stock routes and opening up land for settlement in northern Australia. He explored the tributaries of the Fitzroy River and the region of Bowen Downs near Longreach in Qld, and discovered Buchanan Creek and part of the Barkly Tableland. In 1883 he was the first to take cattle into the Kimberleys, WA, overlanding stock for the Ord River station. In 1896, aged 70, he led an unsuccessful expedition in search of a stock route from northern Qld to WA.

Buckland Tableland Qld An extensive plateau in central western Qld, this tableland stands some 600m above sea-level. A number of major inland rivers rise there, including the Warrego, the Barcoo and the Maranoa (which joins the Balonne, ultimately becoming part of the Darling River system).

Buckley, William (1780–1856), convict, b. England. Buckley escaped from David Collins' abortive settlement at Port Phillip in 1803 and lived with Aborigines in the Barwon area until 1835, when he was found by a group of settlers associated with John Batman. For a time he acted as an interpreter for whites and Aborigines, but with no great success. He lived subsequently in Tas., where he was later granted a government pension.

budgerigar > *parrots*

buffaloes > *cattle industry*

bugs True bugs are insects of the order Hemiptera and are characterised by a distinctive, piercing and sucking proboscis and by incomplete metamorphosis. Although some are predacious, most suck plant juices and some are serious crop pests. The Australian fauna contains more than 4000 described species, and two major suborders are recognised: Heteroptera and Homoptera.

The Heteroptera have leathery forewings and include species which are aquatic and/or predacious. The shield and stink bugs of the superfamily Pentatomoidea include many large and showy species, all of which secrete an unpleasant, defensive fluid. The introduced green vegetable bug is a serious pest of crops, especially of citrus; other notable pests include the cotton harlequin and bronze orange bugs, and among the plant bugs – of the family Miridae, with more than 500 species – there are many crop pest species. The water striders (family Gerridae), with long slender legs, skate on the surface of water; some species are found on the open ocean. The giant water bugs (family Belostomatidae), are up to 7cm long and have raptorial forelegs.

In the suborder Homoptera, both pairs of wings are membranous, and all homopherous insects feed on plant sap. Many groups in this suborder are tended by ants, which offer protection in exchange for sugary exudates from the feeding bugs. Species of the primitive family Peloridiidae, found in southeastern Australia, Lord Howe Island, NZ and southern South America, feed on mosses and liverworts in cool rainforest. The superfamily Cicadelloidea, with more than 500 species, includes the leaf-hoppers and the tree-hoppers (which often have dorsal, thorn-like extensions on the thorax); and the superfamily Fulgoroidea, with more than 400 species, contains the frog-hoppers; both superfamilies include serious plant pests, some of which transmit plant viruses while feeding. Lerp insects or jumping plant lice, which are among the 100 species of the family Psyllidae, between moults often secrete a gummy covering known as 'lerp'. 'Whitefly', of the family Aleyrodidae, secrete a white, waxy covering and are often pests in greenhouses. Aphids belong to the family Aphididae (with about 100 species in Australia), are soft-bodied and often secrete wax; many species have a complex life cycle, involving both sexual and parthenogenetic reproduction, variously producing both wingless sedentary and winged dispersal forms. The woolly apple aphid and the grape phylloxera are among the many aphid pest species, and parasitic hymenoptera have been used for the biological control of some species. Female scale insects and mealy bugs, which are among the 500-plus Australian species of the superfamily Coccoidea, are wingless and are fixed to plants by their mouthparts. Many scale insects are pests of citrus. >> *beetles*

building and construction industry

Australia's oldest industry, building began in the first days of European settlement. It is also one of the country's most important industries, including as it does everything from the construction of suburban homes to massive civil engineering projects.

Building has always been seen as a prime indicator of Australia's economic health, the number of houses, offices or other works being constructed showing the degree of confidence in the overall economy. The ramifications of the industry are immense, particularly in the generation of wealth and employment: for every one of the 500 000 jobs in the industry itself, many more are provided in associated areas such as manufacturing, banking, architecture and real estate. In the period 1986–7, residential and non-residential buildings to the value of $17 490.4 million were under construction, of which $15 584.1 million represented operations completed. Additionally, public- and private-sector engineering construction amounting to $47 140.9 million was either commenced, under way or completed. Surprisingly, for such a large industry, its structure is very fragmented, the majority of building firms being small; the few larger construction companies prefer contract labour to wage labour, partly because of the numerous trade-union problems that have bedevilled the industry owing to its transient and cyclical nature.

Although Australian building design and construction have mainly followed European and US patterns there has been some local innovation, such as the fibrous-plaster sheet and cavity-wall construction. The government has established a division of building research as part of the CSIRO and also a National Building Technology Centre, and there are numerous industry-based organisations such as the Housing Industry Association and the Australian Institute of Building.

building societies Australian building societies date from about 1845, when the first were formed in the manner of English institutions that had arisen in the preceding decade. They played an important part in the land boom of the 1880s and the financial collapse that followed. While building societies were generally established with the express purpose of providing long-term loans for housing purchases, this function was to a large extent taken over by private banks in the early 20th century. Their popularity was revived in the 1960s and 1970s, partly because they were not subject to the restrictions (such as low limits on interest rates) placed on savings banks after 1960. Deregulation of the Australian financial system after 1983 again reduced this competitive advantage, however, and by the end of the decade an increasing number of building societies were converting themselves into banks to maintain their hold on the market. >> *banks and banking*

bulbul > *birds, introduced*

Bulletin, the This weekly magazine was founded in 1880 by Sydney journalist John Haynes and > *J.F. Archibald* (then a cadet reporter). In its first 30 years it became Australia's most widely read and influential journal of politics and literature. The *Bulletin* was put on its feet by W.H. Traill, proprietor 1881–7 (and editor in 1882 while its founders served a jail sentence for libel). The brilliant editorship of Archibald gave the paper its predominance, ably helped by A.G. Stephens's literary criticism on the famous Red Page after 1896. During this time the Australian short story was at its peak and innumerable writers and cartoonists, including Henry Lawson and Norman Lindsay, were encouraged, published and paid. In politics the *Bulletin* pursued protectionism, the White Australia policy, secular education, federation and republicanism. From the 1920s its dominance faded and it became increasingly conservative. After a number of ownership changes, it was sold to Australian Consolidated Press in 1960; it was principally a news magazine in the 1970s and turned more to 'lifestyle' journalism in the 1980s. >> *magazines and periodicals*

bullrout A member of the spiny scorpion-fish family, the bullrout, *Notesthes robusta*, is particularly poisonous because some of its spines have venom-glands. Marbled brown and black, with spines on snout, head and fins, it can grow to 30cm long; it is found in the estuaries of northern NSW and Qld, and often also in the lower reaches of freshwater streams.

Bunbury WA (pop. 23 031) The third-largest city in WA, Bunbury is the main port and commercial centre for the State's southwest and a popular resort. It was named after Lt. Henry Bunbury, who first explored the area in 1836. Traditionally a timber port, it is also an outlet for mineral sands and the produce of a rich farming district.

Bundaberg Qld (pop. 33 368) An important provincial centre on the Burnett River, 374km north of Brisbane, Bundaberg is best known as a producer of rum and sugar; the latter industry was established from 1875 on large plantations using imported Kanaka labour. Sugar is by far the most important crop, although others include peanuts, dairy products, tobacco and tropical fruit. Sugar-harvesting equipment is made locally and exported.

Bungle Bungle Ranges WA This ancient and remote range in the Kimberley region of northwest WA is a dramatic landscape steeped in Aboriginal history and mythology. It is composed of sculpturally eroded sandstone (rising to 450m above the surrounding plain) amid pristine grasslands which were recommended by the 1980 World Conservation Strategy as in need of protection. The region has since attracted increasing attention from Australian conservationists and was proposed as a national park in 1984.

Bunny, Rupert Charles Wulsten (1864–1947), painter, b. St Kilda, Vic. Bunny spent most his life in France, influenced by the romantic tradition, the French light and the Provençal landscape. His early dramatic and large-scale salon works gave way to more simplified landscapes, although his colouring remained distinctively high-keyed; his mythological scenes and idealised paintings of everyday life ignored – in both content and method – the Impressionism of the Paris salons. He exhibited regularly, and his works were purchased for French public galleries. He returned to Australia in 1933 and the National Gallery of Vic. held an extensive retrospective exhibition of his work in 1945. In recent years, Bunny's work has commanded prices of more than \$1 million.

Bunya Range Qld Northeast of Dalby, in southeastern Qld, these mountains – part of the Great Dividing Range – are famous for their forests of bunya pine but also include kauri and hoop-pine, and some 11 600ha are reserved as a national park. Vegetation combines rainforest, open hardwood forest and low scrub. Aborigines used to make long treks to the mountains to gather the edible seeds of the bunya pine; thus the mountains were an important tribal meeting place.

Burchett, Wilfred (1911–83), journalist and author, b. Melbourne. Burchett left Australia in 1936 and spent most of his writing life overseas. He contributed from Asia and the Pacific during World War 2, including the first Allied account of the Hiroshima atomic-bomb aftermath, and later reported extensively from eastern-bloc countries for conservative British papers. He was refused entry to Australia by successive governments 1956–72 because of his alleged communist sympathies. An outspoken and often controversial idealist, he published more than 20 books including his autobiography *At the Barricades* (1981).

Burdekin River Qld A major coastal river, the Burdekin rises in the Seaview Range and flows southwest for over 700km, receiving several tributaries. The Burdekin Falls dam has been constructed where the river turns north towards an estuary near Ayr. Beef production is important on the upper reaches while sugar cane is grown extensively on the delta together with rice, maize, tobacco and vegetables. The river was discovered by Ludwig Leichhardt in 1845.

Burke, Brian Thomas (1947–), politician, b. Perth. Labor premier of WA from 1983, Burke resigned in December 1987 to become Australia's ambassador to Ireland. His government was marked by an almost total lack of factionalism and a strong alliance with business; a newspaper and television journalist before his election to parliament in 1973, Burke was renowned for his ability to handle the media.

Burke, Robert O'Hara (1821–61), explorer, b. Ireland. Burke arrived in Australia in 1853. He was a police inspector on the Vic. goldfields when he was appointed to lead the Great Northern Exploration Expedition, aimed at a south–north continental crossing from Melbourne to the Gulf of Carpentaria; the lavishly equipped party left with much pomp in August 1861. Leaving the heavy stores to follow from Menindee, Burke established a base camp on Cooper Creek and set off with Gray, Wills and King on a rapid dash to the Gulf, reaching tidal waters in February. On the disastrous return journey Burke, Wills and Gray died; King was saved by Aborigines. In the subsequent inquiry, Burke was described as having more zeal than prudence; it seems clear that his hasty unscientific temperament made him a tragic choice for work calling for these qualities as much as for the courage he certainly had in plenty.

Burketown Qld (pop. 232) Purportedly the prototype for Nevil Shute's long-lived novel *A Town Like Alice*, Burketown is a small cattle centre 32km inland of the Gulf of Carpentaria, on the Albert River.

Burnet, Sir (Frank) Macfarlane (1899–1985), medical scientist, b. Traralgon, Vic. An outstanding medical scientist and researcher, Burnet was director of the Walter and Eliza Hall Institute at the University of Melbourne 1944–65. He shared the Nobel Prize for medicine in 1960 for his work on the immune system (immunological tolerance) in the human body. His early studies of the viruses that infect bacterial cells later proved crucial in the genetic-engineering revolution; he also pioneered the use of fertile hens' eggs for virus multiplication, a method still used in the production of vaccines. Burnet took an increasing interest in social issues after his retirement in 1965 and the sixteen books he wrote in this period deal mainly with the relationship between science and society.

Burnett River Qld This river rises in the Burnett Range in southeast Qld, and drains grazing lands before reaching the coast in dairy and sugar-cane country near Bundaberg. It was discovered by the surveyor, J.C. Burnett, in 1847, and is one of only two rivers inhabited by the Qld lungfish.

Burnie–Somerset Tas. (pop. 20 665) The State's fourth-largest city and a large service centre for the northwest, Bumie–Somerset expanded rapidly after 1938 when paper mills were established by Associated Pulp and Paper Mills Ltd. The port, on Emu Bay, processes and exports minerals from Rosebery and Mt Lyell; other activities include the manufacture of dairy products, bricks and titanium oxide pigments.

Burning Mountain NSW At the head of the Hunter Valley, near Wingen, this mountain contains a burning seam of coal. The seam, which emits sulphurous smoke, is estimated to be 450m below the surface and has been burning for at least 1000 years, was probably ignited by a lightning strike.

Burns, Sir James (1846–1923), businessman, b. Scotland. Burns immigrated to Qld in 1862 and became a storekeeper and shipping agent in Townsville. In 1877 he moved to Sydney to set up new headquarters with the intention of establishing a regular shipping line between Sydney and Townsville. In 1883 his several businesses merged to become Burns, Philp & Co., his partner Robert Philp having previously been in charge of the Qld enterprise. Burns Philp expanded to become one of Australia's major companies, its extensive shipping services being combined with pastoral development and other business ventures. From 1908 until his death, Burns was a member of the NSW parliament.

Burnum Burnum [Harry Penrith] (1936–), Aboriginal advocate, b. Wallaga Lake, NSW. Burnum Burnum is a flamboyant figure perhaps best known for having stood under England's Dover cliffs on Australia Day 1988 to claim Britain for the Aborigines. A much-publicised campaigner for Aboriginal rights, he has been a central figure in protest activities such as the establishment of a 'tent embassy' in the grounds of Parliament House in Canberra in 1972 and was instrumental in the recovery and ceremonial cremation of the bones of Truganini in 1976. His acceptance of a Bicentennial grant in 1988 to write a travel guide to Aboriginal Australia was the subject of some controversy within the Aboriginal community.

Burrows, Don(ald Vernon) (1928–), jazz musician, b. Sydney. Burrows played clarinet with the ABC's Sydney Studio Orchestra from the age of 15. In 1961 he established the Don Burrows Quartet, which has since played regularly throughout Australia and has represented the nation at major international jazz festivals. Burrows also established jazz studies at the NSW Conservatorium of Music and became the program's chairman in 1980.

Busby, John (1765–1857), engineer, b. England. Busby arrived in Australia in 1824 to supervise coal development at Newcastle and to devise a water supply for Sydney. A 3660m tunnel, known as Busby's Bore and measuring 1.5m by 1.8m, was cut (1827–37) from swamps (now Centennial Park) to the site of Hyde Park. His second son, **James** (1801–71), viticulturist, b. Scotland, was an early authority and influence on viticulture in NSW, touring Europe to collect cuttings and writing with style and great polish on the subject. He was the first British Resident in NZ 1833–40, and settled there.

bushfires Several factors make Australia prone to regular bushfires. On the one hand, recurring periods of extreme heat – often following rainy periods of lush growth – tend to dry out plant litter which accumulates in combustible quantities; in addition, the hard sclerophyllous leaves of many native plants (such as the oil-bearing eucalypts) cause them to burn explosively. Once alight, fires are often fanned by hot northerly winds from the interior.

Human activity is, however, a principal factor in Australian bushfires and has been so since prehistoric times when the Aborigines lit fires to flush out game and to stimulate new growth of grasses to attract animals. With the arrival of Europeans, fire became even more common. There are many records of major bushfires from the early years of European settlement. On 'Black Thursday' in February 1851, enormous fires in Vic. reached their peak and swept much of the colony from the north and east of Melbourne virtually to the SA border. There were also devastating fires throughout southeastern Australia in 1899–1900, 1919, 1926, 1939, 1964–5, 1968–9 and 1972 – in many cases associated with severe drought years. The most recent major outbreaks – again the culmination of a prolonged drought – were the Ash Wednesday fires of February 1983 in SA and Vic., which took more than 70 lives and destroyed entire towns. As well as causing loss of life and property, bushfires have repeatedly destroyed invaluable grazing lands and native forests.

The prevention and control of bushfires is a major preoccupation of State and local governments. Most rural communities have volunteer fire brigades, and bushfire warnings are posted along highways throughout the summer months; fire trails have been constructed along forest ridges to allow access in remote areas. Controlled burning during the cooler winter months to reduce plant litter has long been common in many fire-prone regions. The practice has been criticised by conservation groups, however, as unseasonal fires can seriously disrupt the natural lifecycles of both plants and ground-dwelling wildlife; in addition, much native flora is adapted to the rapid fires characteristic of the summer but is less able to withstand the slower 'cool burns'.

Although techniques such as backburning, the establishment of firebreaks, and the use of fire-retardants are useful in some cases, major fires associated with hot winds are often uncontrollable. As many fires are started by human carelessness (such as 'burning-off' or camp fires) open fires are usually banned during periods of high fire risk. Disturbingly, some of the fatal fires of Ash Wednesday were the result of arson.

bushfly The first record of the bushfly, *Musca vetustissima,* is perhaps the earliest reference to Australian fauna, as both François Pelsaert (in 1629) and William Dampier (in 1688) noted that they were plagued by the flies in their ships off the WA coast. Bushflies are attracted to the human face, seeking moisture from sweat and from the eyes and lips, and this has given rise to the 'great Australian salute' – the waving of flies from the face. The flies breed primarily in dung, under warm conditions; they are cold-sensitive, and die off in southern Australia during winter, but re-invade annually in the spring on hot, dry northwesterly winds. The introduction of cattle to the continent greatly increased the amount of available dung, and consequently the number of bushflies; in order to reduce their numbers, African dung beetles, used to handling the moist droppings of large grazing animals, were introduced to Australia during the 1960s to dispose of cattle dung. This has dramatically reduced the number of breeding sites and has contributed to a marked drop in fly populations in recent years.

bushranging Bushrangers – the antipodean counterpart of Europe's 19th-century highwaymen – are an enduring part of Australian folklore and their exploits have been immortalised in song, verse and fiction. Over the years, they have generally been admired and abhorred in relatively equal measure: on the one hand they have been lionised for personifying the anti-authority and larrikin aspects of the Australian character; on the other hand, their deeds were seen by many as sordid and their lives in the main as 'nasty and brutish' as well as short.

There were four phases and types of bushranging activity, which extended over the first century of European settlement. The first period lasted from 1789 until the 1840s: the earliest bushrangers were escaped convicts, nicknamed 'bolters', the worst of them based in Van Diemen's Land where the penal settlements of Port Arthur and Macquarie Harbour received the most hardened criminals. Among these were John Whitehead (active 1810–15), with a gang of 28; the Aborigines Musquito and Tegg, the latter turning to bushranging after he tracked down Musquito but did not receive the promised reward; brazen > *Matthew Brady*; and the redoubtable > *Martin Cash*, who was noted for his courtesy, his top hat, and his eventual pardon and respectable end (including brief custodianship of the Hobart Botanic Gardens). NSW also had its share of ex-convict bushrangers, including the negro 'Black Caesar' (active 1790–6); > *John Donahoe* and his accomplice Darkey Underwood, who later led his own gang; and William Westwoo (1840–2).

An 1830 Act which allowed search and arrest by citizens and summary hanging without the right of appeal, and the end of mainland transportation in 1842, combined to bring about a decade of relative peace. There was a resurgence of bushranging in the 1850s, however, especially in Vic. where the gold rushes drew many ex-convicts from Van Diemen's Land. Notable Vic. bushrangers of this period included Burgess (1852), who set himself up as a Melbourne dandy on the proceeds of stolen gold before being captured, and later became a notorious criminal in NZ; Captain Melville (1852); and Garrett, who robbed a Melbourne bank of £14 000 in 1854. Reflecting the influx of immigrants during this decade, there was even a Chinese bushranger – San Poo – in NSW.

The period 1860–80 was the heyday of bushranging in NSW, by then involving the Australian-born sons of ex-convicts or poor settlers who found it more congenial to rob than to work for a living. They roamed mainly in well-organised gangs, with the connivance – willing and unwilling – of the local people, who in general retained a contempt for the law. Legendary NSW bushrangers of this period were > *Frank Gardiner*, > *Ben Hall*, 'Mad Dan' Morgan (active 1862–5), and > *Captain Thunderbolt*. Legislation introduced in 1865 allowed armed outlaws to be shot on sight, which brought another decade of comparative calm before a final outburst of activity in 1878–80. Of particular note in this brief twilight of bushranging was > *Captain Moonlite*, who had begun his career of crime in Vic. in 1869 and took up bushranging in NSW in 1879 on his release from an eleven-year gaol sentence. Most notorious of all, however, was the > *Kelly gang*, whose exploits 1878–80 had their roots not only in the convict past but also in the transplanted hatred of the Irish Catholic for the English Protestant.

business Australian business, like the national economy, has been subject to cyclical boom and bust since the early 19th century. Its history has been punctuated by three depressions (in the 1840s, 1890s and 1930s) and a period of frequent recession and inflation 1975–85, each of which was triggered by conditions overseas and exacerbated by Australia's continuing reliance on both foreign finance and primary-industry exports.

Many of Australia's business leaders have been entrepreneurs, a legacy of the enterprising and often opportunistic spirit which characterised the colonial era. The traders and merchants of the early 19th century were followed by speculators and developers who made (and often lost) much capital out of the prospering society; they were in turn succeeded by several generations of industrialists, many of whom effectively underwrote the rapid growth of Australian industry from the early 20th century. By the 1970s and 1980s, in step with the increasingly international and paper-based nature of commerce in the late 20th century, a new breed of stock-market traders and 'corporate raiders' had emerged. All these players had in common their dependence on contemporary economic conditions and usually only the cautious or determined survived.

Historical development The early 19th century was a period of great prosperity in the infant colonies, principally because of the tremendous growth of the local wool industry to service the British market. By 1850, Australia was supplying well over half of the British woollen mills; local manufacturing industries also sprang up to supply products that could not be imported or were geared to the wool boom. Sydney in particular produced some remarkable mercantile entrepreneurs during this period, such as merchant and manufacturer > *Simeon Lord*, trader and ship-builder Joseph Underwood, and speculator Samuel Terry (known to his contemporaries as 'the Botany Bay Rothschild'). A depression in 1842, caused by a downturn in the English textile industry, eradicated much of the wealth accumulated up to that time. Within a decade, however, the gold rushes enabled many land-owners and merchants to rebuild their fortunes, often to even greater heights.

The wealth produced by gold, and the recovery of the pastoral industries, engendered a boom which lasted from 1860 until 1890: banking, commerce, manufacturing, and transport and communications burgeoned in response to the needs of the rapidly expanding population. Some of Australia's great companies (such as > *BHP*) and dynasties (such as the Darling and Baillieu families) were founded during this period. In 1890, however, a financial crisis in London stopped the flow of capital to the colonies and investment and construction ceased. Few businesses survived into the 20th century and those that did were in many cases incidental to the dynasties behind them, notable exceptions being BHP and the Colonial Sugar Refinery.

From the turn of the century, Australia was dominated by a generation of true entrepreneurs who saw as their destiny the creation of the nation's industry; most acquired great personal wealth in the process. This period saw the establishment of several major businesses, including the leading retailers G.J. Coles and Myer. Some survivors of the 1890s depression also flourished – such as BHP and the collection of companies which became known as the Collins House group, all of which were founded in Melbourne on the great base-metals wealth of Broken Hill in NSW. Central to development of the mineral industry were W.L. Baillieu and W.S. Robinson, who helped finance the development of Broken Hill and founded a number of mining companies including the Zinc Corporation (forerunner to Conzinc Riotinto Australia) and Western Mining Corporation. The Darling family, which controlled BHP Ltd, established Australia's iron and steel industry: the man most responsible for its success was Essington Lewis, who joined BHP in 1907 and helped make its steel works one of the most efficient in the world as well as instigating its expansion into coal mining and shipping.

A range of new industries was established in the first half of the 20th century, from the immortal Arnott Biscuit Co. to the shipping and trading empire of Burns, Philp & Co. From the 1920s, the US supplanted Britain as Australia's main source of finance: the inflow of US money and the immense cash flows generated by the mining industry (especially Broken Hill) meant that by 1939 secondary industry was sufficiently developed and diverse to respond to the need for war materials and equipment. A decade of industrial rebirth witnessed the rise of new and expansive industrialists such as > *Reginald Ansett*.

The period 1945–70 was one of stable prosperity for Australian business: immigration produced a steady increase in local demand; the dominant US multinationals provided almost limitless capital; and steady growth in world commodity markets meant continuous wealth for mining and agricultural industries. The resulting climate of optimism in the late 1960s produced Australia's greatest stockmarket flowering – the so-called 'Poseidon boom' of 1968–70, which saw many major fortunes won and as quickly lost. This was followed by an equally rapid property boom and collapse in 1974.

The 1970s and beyond The period 1975–85 was a volatile one for Australian business, as the result of rising oil prices, fluctuating commodities markets, political uncertainty, and severe recessions (in 1974–5 and 1982). Deregulation of the financial system by the incoming Labor government in 1983 exposed Australian markets to world forces just as commodity prices dived: Australia's terms of trade fell 10% and the value of the Australian dollar dropped accordingly.

In the early 1980s, several aggressive entrepreneurs – notably > *Robert Holmes à Court*, > *Alan Bond*, > *John Elliott*, > *Christopher Skase*, Ron Brierley and John Spalvins – came to dominate the public face of Australian business. While each had slightly different interests and strategies, they had one important technique in common – they borrowed freely to allow them to take over other businesses, used the tax-deductibility of interest on their debt to increase cash flow, and then made profits from the sale of assets while repaying the debt. They also shared the advantage of one of the most sustained 'bull' markets in Australia's history – five years of continuously rising share prices. Only John Elliott emerged completely unscathed from the stockmarket crash of October 1987, by which time his Elders-IXL empire had an industrial base that did not rely on share prices for its wealth. It was invariably financial corporations and merchant banks – such as Rothwell's, Ariadne and Equiticorp – which were the great casualties of the 1980s crash, as was the case with Mineral Securities, Mainline Corporation and Cambridge Credit in the 1970s.

The business failures of 1988–90 produced a new distaste for debt and risk and thus a more conservative approach to business and investment. As Australia entered the 1990s, the new heroes of business were again industrialists and manufacturers, rather than the 'paper tigers' of a decade before. >> *banks and banking*; *economy*

Busselton WA (pop. 7784) A popular holiday centre on Geographe Bay, 238km south of Perth, Busselton was once the regional port. Industries include timber production (from the local jarrah forests), vineyards, fishing, beef production and dairying. It was named after the Bussells, a pioneering family who settled in the area in the 1830s.

bustard Also known as the plains turkey, the Australian species of bustard, *Ardeotis australis*, is a wary, ground-dwelling bird found throughout the mainland – particularly inland – and with relatives in Europe and Asia. Reaching

1.2m tall and weighing up to 14kg, it has black-and-yellow head and eye stripes, brown wings with blue-and-white flash, dark-mottled light-buff breast, and light underparts. It is now protected, the population having been greatly reduced by both shooting and attacks by foxes. The male breeding display is spectacular, and includes a peculiar low, roaring call.

butcher-birds > *magpies, currawongs and butcher-birds*

Butement, William Alan Stewart (1904–), scientist, b. NZ. Designer of a proximity fuse (1943) which enabled guided weapons to target German flying bombs, Japanese Kamikaze bombers and tanks during World War 2, Butement also developed the first beamed radar as well as equipment for mobile communications. In 1946 he set up the Woomera rocket range, becoming its first chief superintendent, then took up the post of chief scientist of the Australian Department of Supply (1949–67).

buttercup family The Ranunculaceae or buttercup family is a large worldwide group of flowering plants, which are most diverse in the northern hemisphere. Only four genera are native to Australia, the largest being *Ranunculus* itself, which has about 35 native species most of which are moisture-loving alpine or subalpine plants. Most beautiful, with large white flowers, is the anemone buttercup, *R. anemoneus*, which is restricted to a limited area around Mt Kosciusko in NSW. The genus *Anemone* is represented by a single species in Tas., and *Caltha* by one species in Tas. and one in the Australian Alps. The genus *Clematis* has six native species, all climbing plants of forest areas except for the Tas. endemic, *C. gentianoides*, which is a herbaceous perennial; the common climbing species, traveller's joy and old man's beard, bear masses of pure white flowers followed by balls of plumed fruitlets.

butterflies and moths Insects of this large order, Lepidoptera, are characterised by four large wings, all covered with dense layers of overlapping scales and often brightly coloured. In Australia there are an estimated 20 000 species, of which only 380 are butterflies (day-flying, with clubbed antennae), the remainder being roughly classed as 'moths' (usually night-flying, being attracted to light and with unclubbed antennae). The mouthparts of adults are modified into an elongate tube for taking nectar, while caterpillars have strong chewing mandibles for ingesting leaves and other plant matter. Some of the greatest pests of crops, clothing and stored products are Lepidoptera, many of which were accidentally introduced from overseas; one deliberate introduction, however, the *Cactoblastis* moth, helped to eradicate prickly pear cactus from much of Australia. Only a few of the more prominent Lepidoptera families are treated here.

Moths The swift or ghost moths (family Hepialidae) are often large insects whose larvae feed internally in wood or on the roots of grasses. There are numerous families of tiny moths, 'microlepidoptera', which include many leaf-miners, clothes moths and leaf-rolling caterpillars, as well as a large group adapted to feeding on dry gum leaves. The giant, wood-boring larvae of the family Cossidae include species regarded as > *witchetty grubs*; the bag-moth caterpillars (Psychidae) spin a silken bag into which are incorporated fragments of materials such as sand, bark or twigs, and they are often seen dragging their cases up walls or trees. The family Noctuidae, mostly medium-sized, brown insects such as the > *Bogong moth*, includes many crop pests whose cater-pillars are known as cutworms. The hawk moths (Sphingidae) have cigar-shaped abdomens and small hindwings, and are strong fliers, able to hover while taking nectar from flowers; the family Saturniidae includes several large spe-cies, in particular the spectacular Hercules moth from northern Qld, *Coscinocera hercules*, which has a wingspan of 25cm. The emperor gum moth, *Antheraea eucalypti*, of the endemic Australian family Antheridae, has large eyespots on its wings; its spiny cater-pillars are often seen feeding on gum leaves.

Butterflies Because butterflies fly by day and are often brightly coloured, they are much better known than moths even though they constitute only a minor part of the Lepidoptera fauna. The skippers (Hesperiidae) are small, yellow-and-brown butterflies with a rapid, jerky flight. The swallowtails (Papillionidae) include various black-coloured species having a distinct tail on the hindwing, as well as the spectacular birdwings; these are most diverse in Southeast Asia and NG but have only a single Australian representative, the Richmond birdwing, *Ornithoptera priamus*, which ranges as far south as northern NSW. The family Nymphalidae includes such species as the painted lady, the crows, and the monarch or wanderer butterfly, which has spread here naturally from North America. The whites (Pieridae) include the cabbage butterfly, an introduced pest. The family Lycaenidae – the blues, coppers and hairstreaks – produce larvae which live in ant nests and sometimes feed on ant larvae.

butterfly cod A marine fish occurring throughout the Indo-Pacific region, the butterfly cod, *Pterois volitans*, is brilliantly coloured and bears venomous fin spines. The dorsal and pectoral fins have deeply incised membranes, which combine with the fish's slow, graceful swimming motion to create a striking effect.

butterfly fishes > *coral fishes*

Button Plan > *motor-vehicle industry*

Buvelot, (Abram) Louis (1814–88), painter, b. Switzerland. Buvelot arrived in Australia in 1865, after living for eighteen years in Brazil, and worked in Melbourne as a photographer and art teacher. He was arguably the most important of a group of immigrant artists who greatly influenced Australian painting in the 1870s. The first painter to depict familiar views – principally softly lit farming scenes – in preference to simply 'picturesque' land-scapes, he was a seminal inspiration to younger artists such as Tom Roberts and Frederick McCubbin, around whom developed the so-called Heidelberg School.

buzzards > *eagles and hawks*

Byron Bay NSW (pop. 3730) A former coastal port, sheltered by Cape Byron, Byron Bay lies 839km north of Sydney. Whaling and food-processing industries have given way to tourism, with excellent surfing and the rain-forest hinterland being the major attractions. The area, notably nearby Nimbin, has been a centre of the alternative culture since the 1960s. Cape Byron is the most easterly point in mainland Australia, named by Cook in 1770 after Commander Byron, grandfather of the poet and commander of a round-the-world survey ship a few years earlier. The lighthouse, con-structed in 1901, towers 113m above sea-level.

C

Caboolture Qld (pop. 8195) This town on the Caboolture River lies 49km north of Brisbane and is a commercial and residential centre for the Sunshine Coast. Also the main centre for a productive rural hinterland based on dairying and cropping (particularly fruit), Caboolture has been developed substantially in recent years.

caddis flies These are moth-like insects of the order Trichoptera, with hairy wings and long antennae; the larvae, which are an important food source for many freshwater fish, are aquatic, feeding mostly on plant and particulate matter. Many larvae construct elaborate, portable cases from various materials such as sand, twigs or leaf fragments, held together with a viscous secretion; some spin silken nets to entrap passing food particles, while others are free-living and carnivorous. The Australian fauna comprises some 500 species, with the greatest diversity in upland and southern waters; adults are generally nocturnal, and often congregate in great numbers around lights near rivers. The remarkable *Philanisus plebeius*, the world's only known marine caddis fly, is found on the rocky coasts of eastern Australia and NZ, where it constructs its case of fragments of the coral algae on which it feeds.

Cadell, Francis (1822–79), Murray River pioneer, b. Scotland. Cadell arrived in Australia in 1852 and a year later won a government-sponsored race (but not the reward) for the first steamboat to navigate the Murray River, in the *Lady Augusta*. He was subsequently director of a riverboat company which plied the Murray until 1858, and then operated as a river trader until 1861. His name was given to Cadell in SA, an irrigation area on the left bank of the Murray.

Cain family, prominent in Vic. politics. **John** (1882–1957), politician, b. Blackwood,

Vic., was a greengrocer before entering the Vic. parliament as a Labor member in 1917; he was premier for three terms (1943, 1945–7 and 1952–5). A moderate man, Cain was noted for his political integrity. Much the same can be said of his son, **John** (1931–), a solicitor who entered the Vic. parliament in 1976 and was elected premier in 1982, a position he still held in 1990 after winning two further elections. Often deemed colourless, Cain is an able politician; economic mismanagement by his government, however, caused a great swing against the ALP in Vic. in the 1990 federal election.

Cairns Qld (pop. 54 862) Situated on Trinity Bay 2000km north of Brisbane, Cairns is the commercial capital of far north Qld and one of Australia's leading tourist centres. Cairns once relied heavily on the sugar industry, which developed in the 1880s, but now services the agricultural, pastoral and mining industries of the Atherton Tableland, and the fishing industry of the Gulf of Carpentaria and Cape York to the north; it is also a supply and service point for industries in the NT, West Irian and PNG. Its international airport opened in 1984, boosting the tourism that earns the region an estimated $200 million a year; other recent developments include the construction of an international cruise terminal and a marina, and a regional campus of Townsville's James Cook University. The site was discovered by James Cook in 1770 and was proclaimed a new settlement in 1876 by William Cairns, governor of Qld, in whose honour it was subsequently named.

Cairns, Jim (James Ford) (1914–), politician, b. Carlton, Vic. Cairns was recognised as the driving force of the Labor left wing in the 1960s and 1970s, during which time he led the Vic. moratorium movement against the Vietnam War and the anti-conscription campaign. Appointed a minister in the Whitlam government in 1972, he later became deputy prime minister and treasurer. His period in office was marred by the controversy surrounding his relationship with his secretary, Juni Morosi, and subsequently by his apparent misleading of parliament concerning his involvement in the government's unorthodox attempt to borrow considerable sums from Arab sources in 1974–5. This led to his dismissal by Whitlam in 1975; since his resignation from parliament in 1977, he has worked with the alternative culture.

calamaries > *cephalopods*

Call to Australia party This reactionary political grouping, formed in the 1980s, is successor to the Family Action Movement; it chiefly represents the Festival of Light (formed 1973), a socio-religious movement committed to conservative family and community values and strongly opposed to homosexuality, pornography and abortion. The Call to Australia party is led by the Rev. Fred Nile, director of the Festival of Light.

Callide Valley Qld Lying west of the Calliope Range, this valley produces cotton, sorghum and wheat but is better known for its major coal deposits, discovered in 1890. Since 1944 mining has been by open cut; some coal is used in the Calcap power station, and some is railed to Gladstone for export.

callop > *fishes, freshwater and marine*

Caloundra Qld (pop. 16 215) This resort on the Sunshine Coast, 96km north of Brisbane, is known for its surf, fishing and splendid views of the coast and hinterland. The name is thought to be derived from an Aboriginal word meaning 'beautiful'.

Calwell, Arthur Augustus (1896–1973), politician, b. Melbourne. One of the last of the old-time Labor-machine politicians, Calwell led the ALP 1960–7, but the opportunity to become prime minister was lost in the 1961 election when Labor was defeated by the narrowest of margins. As minister for information and immigration 1945–9, Calwell initiated large-scale non-British immigration but rigidly maintained the White Australia policy. He was at the forefront of the movement against the Vietnam War, during which period he survived

an assassination attempt; Calwell retired from politics in 1972.

Cambridge, Ada (1844–1926), author, b. England. Cambridge, the wife of clergyman George Goss, arrived in Vic. in 1870 and published several volumes between 1875 and 1913. She also wrote a number of novels, several of which rose above the generally mediocre romance fiction of her time and reflected not only a social conscience but also an unusually realistic and satirical view of colonial society. Her autobiography, *Thirty Years in Australia* (1903), is a useful period source.

Cambridge Gulf WA A deep inlet on the northern coast of WA, the gulf is divided into West Arm (on which is situated Wyndham, the main port for East Kimberley) and East Arm, into which the Ord River runs. The gulf was named in 1819 by Phillip Parker King after the Duke of Cambridge.

Camden NSW (pop. 10 065) With nearby Campbelltown designated the Macarthur regional growth centre in 1975, Camden lies 60km southwest of Sydney. Known particularly for its breeding of thoroughbred horses, it is surrounded by a mixed-farming district which includes dairying, pigs, poultry, beef, fruit, agriculture and coal-mining. John Macarthur pioneered the breeding of merino sheep on two properties he was granted in the area in 1805; he named one of them Camden Park in honour of Lord Camden, then secretary of state for the colonies, who authorised the land grants.

camels Camels played a very important part in the opening up of the arid interior of Australia between the 1860s and 1920s. The first camels imported were Arabian, later replaced with more sturdy Indian and Afghan breeds. The > *Afghans* used camels mainly as pack animals, carrying carefully arranged loads of up to 400kg of mining goods and poles for the Overland Telegraph. They also carried supplies to stations and return loads of wool to ports or, more often, railheads. A network of camel tracks quickly became established, as did camps on the outskirts of towns. As most camel drivers were Muslims, another religion and way of life was introduced to the outback. By the 1930s motor lorries carried all the goods, with only a few camels used by boundary riders for mustering or pulling government drilling rigs. Many were turned loose in the desert, where their descendants roam in numbers which at times reach pest proportions. Camels have been exported from Australia in recent years.

Campaspe River Vic. Rising near Mt Macedon in the Great Dividing Range, some 80km northwest of Melbourne, the Campaspe flows through agricultural country to join the Murray near Echuca, providing water both for irrigation and for urban use in rural districts. It was discovered and named by Thomas Mitchell in 1836.

Campbell, Archibald James (1853–1929), ornithologist, b. Fitzroy, Vic. One of the early serious students of Australian bird life, Campbell travelled across much of the continent and contributed many papers to scientific journals. His *Nests and Eggs of Australian Birds*, published in 1900, has remained a standard reference. He was active in the Australasian Ornithologists' Union, and in 1905 helped to found the Bird Observers' Club of Vic. A number of subspecies of birds are named after him.

Campbell, David Watt Ian (1915–79), farmer and poet, b. Ellerslie, NSW. Campbell was educated at the King's School, Parramatta, and at Cambridge, and during World War 2 served in the RAAF with distinction. Always a bushman, as a poet he is as distinctively Australian as 'Banjo' Paterson, but more intellectual and wide-ranging. From *Speak with the Sun* (1949), his poetry matured to the perceptive modernism of *The Branch of Dodona* (1970) and the lyricism of *The Man in the Honeysuckle* (1979). He also wrote short stories. He became poetry editor of the *Australian* in 1964 and edited several volumes of Australian poetry.

Campbelltown NSW (pop. 121 297) This city lies some 52km southeast of Sydney and is within the metropolitan area. Named by Lachlan Macquarie in 1820 after his wife's family home, it was settled as early as 1811 and still has some fine early buildings in the colonial Georgian style; wheat was one of the region's first crops. Together with Camden to the south, Campbelltown was nominated as a self-contained urban area in 1975.

Camperdown Vic. (pop. 3458) This town lies 193km southwest of Melbourne amid the rich farmlands of the Western District. A busy commercial and service centre for the surrounding region, it has processing industries such as a dairy factory and an abattoir. Lying at the foot of the extinct volcano Mt Leura, it also has several lakes nearby which are noted for their trout and salmon. The town was settled in 1850 and there are several fine 19th-century buildings in the area, among the most notable of which is the mansion Purrumbete.

Canberra Capital city of the Commonwealth, and Australia's seventh-largest city, Canberra is the only city of the ACT and the nation's largest inland centre. It is the seat of the federal government and home of the High Court of Australia as well as Australia's national university, library and art gallery. Because of the city's geographical isolation, most of these institutions – especially the government – have been accused of being remote from the real life of Australia.

Located some 248km from Sydney and 483km from Meloune, and bounded in the west by the Brindabella Range, Canberra lies in undulating country, mainly in the valleys of the Molonglo River and its tributaries. It is centred around the artificial lake, Burley Griffin. Its inland site and relatively high altitude cause it to experience large diurnal differences of temperature as well as large seasonal variations – minimums ranging from –0.3°C to 12.9°C and maximums from 11.1°C to 27.9°C; the average rainfall is 639mm, distributed throughout the year.

It is believed that the name Canberra derives from an Aboriginal word meaning 'meeting place', and if this is so then it is the only Australian capital with an Aboriginal name. It certainly owes its location to colonial rivalries between NSW and Vic., each of which was determined that the other should neither be nor be near the national capital. The ACT was ceded by NSW as the new seat of government in 1911, but there was little construction until after World War 1 and it was not until 1927 that the federal parliament moved from Melbourne to Canberra. The economic depression of the 1930s again slowed development, but since World War 2 Canberra has been Australia's fastest-growing city.

At the census of 1986 the Canberra Statistical Division had a population of 248 441, which showed a growth-rate of 12.71% over the five years between censuses. In 1947 its population was only 15 156: it has grown in tandem with the expansion of government and bureaucracy, and most of its residents are directly or indirectly government-employed; there are very few blue-collar workers. Manufacturing employs less than 4% of the workforce, but building (again, largely for the government) employs considerably more. One of the products of that industry, the new Parliament House (opened in 1988), has been criticised for its cost and opulence but has also been praised by many as fine architecture. Canberra's plan for decentralised employment and service centres has recently been less successful than it was until the 1970s, and this has led to some traffic congestion; perhaps ironically, the decentralisation, when it was successful, led to the capital being described as 'a city in search of a soul'. >> *Australian Capital Territory*

cane toad Also known as the giant or Qld toad, the cane toad, *Bufo marinus,* was introduced to north Qld in 1935 from Hawaii (where it had previously been imported from South America) in the hope of controlling beetle pests in the sugar-cane fields. Freed from any natural controlling agents, the toad population quickly multiplied, spreading rapidly down the Qld coast to northern NSW and westwards to the NT; it proved to be of only minor value in controlling cane pests, and began to eat native fauna as well. The animal's warty skin has numerous poison glands which kill any potential native predator, as well as domestic cats and dogs. The incidence of cane toads is such that often large numbers of them are found squashed on north Qld roads. Although regarded as a noxious pest, the cane toad is sometimes treated with roguish affection; it gives its name to an 'underground' political newspaper in Qld, and is the subject of a humorous, award-winning documentary.

Canning Basin > *Great Sandy Desert*

canoeing This sport is practised in two forms: in kayaks, with a double-ended paddle, and in canoes, which use a single-bladed paddle. Clubs were formed in Australia in the 1930s, but not until 1951 did the Australian Canoe Federation, established in 1949, conduct the first national championships. There are nearly 8000 registered participants in the sport in Australia. Australian canoeists first competed in the Olympic Games in 1956, winning a bronze medal in the 10 000m double kayak event. Drawing on competitors with surf experience, Australia has since then become a

leading contender; John Jacoby was world marathon champion in 1985, 1986 and 1987. In the 1988 Olympic Games in Seoul, every crew entered reached the final in its event, winning one silver and one bronze medal.

Cape Barren goose > *geese*

Cape Barren Island > *Furneaux Islands*

Cape Catastrophe SA This rugged headland on the western side of the mouth of Spencer Gulf was named by Matthew Flinders in 1802 during the voyage of the *Investigator*, when the men of a shore party were drowned while returning to the ship.

Cape Everard > *Point Hicks*

Cape Howe This low headland is the coastal border point between Vic. and NSW, established by Act of parliament in 1842 when the Port Phillip District was created, and adopted by Vic. when it became a separate colony in 1851. The easternmost section of the boundary is a straight line from the cape 'to the nearest source of the River Murray'.

Cape Leeuwin WA A rocky peninsula in the extreme southwest, Cape Leeuwin (named for a Dutch ship that passed the point in 1622) marks the dividing point between the Indian and Southern Oceans. A lighthouse built in 1895 is now a meteorological station and is listed by the National Trust for preservation. Coastline and forest lands in the north and east of the cape are reserved as a national park.

Cape Melville Qld A rugged coastal headland east of Princess Charlotte Bay on Cape York Peninsula, Cape Melville is the northern extremity of the range of that name. Heaps of great granite blocks scattered on the land and extending into the sea are a remarkable feature of the cape, which was the scene of a shipping disaster in March 1899 when two converging cyclones destroyed five large vessels and an estimated 50 smaller craft, and about 300 men were killed.

caper family Capers are the flower buds of the scrambling shrub *Capparis spinosa*, which is widely distributed in Australia, Asia and the Pacific and is closely related to the true Mediterranean caper. It belongs to the genus *Capparis*, of which seventeen species are native to Australia; most are large climbers or small trees. The wild orange or native pomegranate, *C. mitchellii*, is a small tree of the semi-arid inland; its large, tough-skinned fruit, when ripe, is a favourite food of the Aborigines. Related to *Capparis* is the warrior bush, *Apophyllum anomalum*, a remarkable large shrub with a thick trunk and a tangle of wiry leafless branches; it is confined to western NSW and adjacent regions of Qld. The herbaceous genus *Cleome* has six native species, all of which are rather weedy tropical plants.

Cape York Peninsula Qld Cape York is the most northerly point of mainland Australia, named by James Cook in 1770. The peninsula forms a rough triangle about 800km from apex to base, the latter generally taken to be a line drawn from Cairns to Normanton. Dutch navigators in 1606 were the first to reach the west coast; the first settlement was not made until 1863, at Port Albany. Discovery of rich alluvial gold deposits on the Palmer River led to the development of Cooktown in 1873; today this is still a centre for some gold and tin mining, for pearl fishing and some tourism. The first hills of the Great Dividing Range lie along the east coast of the peninsula; in the west are vast alluvial lowlands crossed by rivers (including the Mitchell and the Gilbert) flowing to the Gulf of Carpentaria. Much of the northern land is rugged, inhospitable and uninhabited, although major industrial development took place with the discovery in 1955, at Weipa on the northwest coast, of enormous reserves of high-grade bauxite; the main rural activity is beef-cattle grazing. The peninsula contains several national parks incorporating a range of vegetation from rainforest to dry plains, and including some outstanding Aboriginal cave paintings.

Capricorn–Bunker Islands Qld At the southern end of the Great Barrier Reef, off Gladstone, these low sandy islands (composed mainly of coral detritus) are part of the Capricornia section of the Great Barrier Reef Marine Park. They include Heron Island, noted for its biological station and tourist resort, and afforded the highest degree of protection for its marine life; and One Tree Island, which is a scientific research zone.

Captains Flat NSW This former mining district southeast of Canberra yielded various minerals – including gold and zinc – during the period 1874– 1962. Largely abandoned for nearly two decades, the area is now developing as a residential area for commuters to Canberra.

car manufacture > *motor-vehicle industry*

Carey, Peter (1943–   ), novelist, b. Bacchus Marsh, Vic. Carey is an advertising man whose short stories have been collected in two volumes, *The Fat Man in History* (1974) and *War Crimes* (1979). He has also published three novels, *Bliss* (1981), *Illywhacker* (1985) and *Oscar and Lucinda* (1988), the last of which won the UK's prestigious Booker McConnell prize for fiction in that year. Carey's work is characterised by the impingement of the surreal on the real, coupled with a sardonic humour, which often results in a nightmarish quality.

Carnarvon WA (pop. 6847) This town and former port at the mouth of the Gascoyne River, some 904km north of Perth, is the centre for an extensive pastoral and agricultural hinterland. Whaling ceased in the 1960s but fishing, prawning and (most recently) oyster farming are important to the local economy. The coast is fringed with sand-dunes and lagoons, including Lake Macleod to the north, which is mined for both salt and potash. A space-tracking station was established in 1964, but like the nearby telecommunications station has since ceased operation.

Carnarvon Range Qld A spur of the Great Dividing Range in south-central Qld, Carnarvon Range is the watershed between the headwaters of the Dawson River system and the Maranoa and Warrego rivers. It is noted for its striking sandstone hills and valleys, cliffs, deep gorges and pinnacles, and a number of Aboriginal rock paintings; part of the range is reserved as a national park. Ludwig Leichhardt was the first to explore the area, in 1844.

carp > *fishes, introduced*

carrot family The Apiaceae or Umbelliferae family is a group of mainly herbaceous flowering plants that includes vegetables such as carrots, parsnips and celery, and herbs such as parsley, dill, fennel, caraway and coriander. In Australia it is represented by 150 or so native species in 22 genera, of which half are endemic. Well-known members include the flannel-flower, genus *Actinotus*, remarkable for its daisy-like flower heads with rings of felted bracts; the common flannel-flower, *A. helianthi*, of NSW and Qld is often abundant on coastal sands. The genus *Trachymene* has about 40 species, mostly inland plants and some of which are poisonous to stock. *T. caerulea* is the blue laceflower of WA, with sky-blue flower heads and sometimes grown as a garden flower. Also from WA is the southern cross, *Xanthosia rotundifolia*, its small flowers backed by four large white bracts in cross formation; the genus, of about 20 species, is spread across southern Australia. A number of the genera are confined to alpine and high mountain areas, including the native caraways, *Oreomyrrhis*.

Carruthers, Jimmy (James William)
> *boxing*

Carter, Herbert James (1858–1940),
entomologist, b. England. After migrating to Australia and establishing himself as a teacher, Carter became interested in the Coleoptera, an order that includes beetles and weevils, and was the author of some 65 papers on that subject. He served as president of the Linnaean Society of NSW and was co-editor of the first *Australian Encyclopaedia*, supervising the preparation of scientific articles. His popular book *Gulliver in the Bush* (1933) is an account of collecting trips in Australia.

cartoons Australia has a long and illustrious – if irreverent – tradition of cartooning. While the work of local artists was initially beholden to overseas styles and techniques – most notably of Britain's *Punch* magazine – by the late 19th century a distinctively sardonic flavour had emerged in Australian cartoons, with particular strength in the areas of caricature and political satire.

The advent of the > *Bulletin* heralded the first prolific period of cartoon and caricature, the years immediately before and after Federation providing plentiful targets for the witty pen. Major *Bulletin* contributors included Phil May 1885–8; 'Hop' (Livingston Hopkins), for 30 years from 1883; David Souter and George Washington Lambert from the 1890s; Norman Lindsay and his sister Ruby after 1900; and the supreme cartoonist, David Low, 1911–19.

Smith's Weekly rivalled the *Bulletin*'s comic output 1910–50, providing a showcase for outstanding graphic humorists and caricaturists such as Stan Cross (creator of the 'Dad and

Dave' comic strip) and George Finey. The 1920s and 1930s were particularly fertile decades, witnessing the birth of J.C. Bancks's legendary street urchin 'Ginger Meggs' in Sydney's *Sunday Sun* in 1921 and Pat Sullivan's 'Felix the Cat', both of which achieved world notoriety and continue to enjoy periodic revivals. In the same period, characters such as 'Fatty Finn' by Syd Nicholls, 'Ben Bowyang' by Alex McCrae and 'Saltbush Bill' by Eric Jolliffe further developed the larrikin theme which for many years was central to Australian cartooning.

Since the 1970s there has been a revival of political and 'editorial' cartooning and a corresponding decline of the joke-based cartoon strips which once filled whole pages of the daily newspapers. Idiosyncratic but enduring work of this genre has issued from the pens of George Molnar, Bruce Petty, Patrick Cook, Les Tanner, Ron Tandberg and John Spooner; in the 1980s, they were joined by a new breed of whimsical social commentators with simple but distinctive graphic styles, including Martin Matthews, Michael Leunig (creator, inter alia, of the poignant 'Mr Curly'), Mary Leunig and Victoria Roberts.

Casey > *Antarctic Territory*

Casey, Richard Gardiner (Baron Casey
of Berwick) (1890–1976), politician, b. Brisbane. An engineer by training, Casey was appointed a liaison officer in London in 1924 and subsequently helped negotiate the legislation governing relations between Britain and its dominions, including Australia. He entered federal parliament in 1931 and held portfolios in the Lyons and Menzies governments; in 1940 he was appointed Australia's first official diplomatic representative, in Washington. After various further diplomatic postings, including a term as governor of Bengal in India 1944–6, he was elected to federal parliament as a Liberal 1949–60; as minister for external affairs 1951–60, he was influential in developing Australia's relations with both Asia and the US. He was governor-general of Australia 1965–9.

Cash, Martin (?1808–77), bushranger, b.
Ireland. Known as the 'gentleman bushranger', Cash was originally transported to NSW in 1828 for housebreaking. After serving his sentence in NSW he went to Tas., where he was convicted again in 1840. His escape was followed by years of bushranging, and he was

sentenced to hang for murdering a constable in 1843. This sentence was commuted to life imprisonment on Norfolk Island, but Cash was pardoned in 1853 and released as a 'model prisoner'. He died on his Glenorchy farm more than 20 years later. *The Bushranger of Van Diemen's Land* (1870), his colourful auto-biography, reaffirmed his notoriety.

Cash, Pat(rick Hart) > *tennis*

Casino NSW (pop. 10 800) This town on the Richmond River, 885km northwest of Sydney and 228km southeast of Brisbane, is a local road, rail and air link. It also serves as an industrial and service centre for the surround-ing region, of which the main activities are forestry and timber, beef production, and some dairying. The site (then a pastoral property) was named by the first white settlers, in 1840, after the Italian town of Cassino.

casinos > *gambling*

Cassia > *legumes*

cassowary A large, flightless bird of rain-forests in northeastern Qld and in NG, the cassowary, *Casuarius casuarius*, is related to the emu; its croaking and booming grunts re-call the emu's cries. It stands over 1.2m high, is mainly blue-black, and has vestigial wings but no real tail. The head has a large red-brown crest, said to function as a crash-helmet as the bird runs through thick forest; the featherless neck is bright blue, with bright-red nape and front decorations. The cassowary's nest is a bed of plant litter at the foot of a forest tree; in this, three to five light-green eggs are laid between July and September. If cornered, the bird may deliver a powerful kick: it has a blade-like inner toe, and is known to have killed at least two humans in this way. In an age of diminishing species, as long as large tracts of rainforest are preserved the casso-wary's future in Australia is assured.

Castle Hill rising On 4 March 1804, some 300 armed Irish convicts led by William Johnston and Philip Cunningham set out to march from Castle Hill to Sydney, armed with pikes and rifles and vowing vengeance on their Protestant overlords. Betrayed by a fellow convict, they were met after only 16km by Major George Johnston. The leaders were cap-tured under a flag of truce: Johnston's troops charged, killing more than twelve convicts. Nine were hanged, many flogged, and others sent by Governor King to Coal River (now Newcastle).

Castlemaine Vic. (pop. 7656) This manu-facturing, market and service town in central Vic., some 117km northwest of Melbourne, was a prosperous gold-mining town at the height of the Vic. gold rushes from 1851. Farming development and early secondary industry saved it from becoming another of that industry's ghost towns, and today Castlemaine is a regional centre for a dairying and sheep region; its historical links, colonial architecture and impressive art gallery, as well as its attractive rural surrounds, have made this a popular tourist destination.

Castlereagh River NSW The Castlereagh River rises in the Warrumbungle Range, and after flowing through Coonabarabran turns south and then north and west to join the Macquarie and eventually the Barwon–Darling system. It was discovered in 1818 by George Evans, a member of the expedition through the region led by John Oxley.

casuarinas The flowering-plant family Casuarinaceae is centred on Australia and consists of trees and shrubs with needle-like branchlets bearing regular whorls of minute scale-leaves. They are commonly called 'she-oak' (or just 'oak'), a reference to the large rays in the wood which resemble those of the true oaks of the northern hemisphere. Casua-rinas have highly reduced floral structures, similar to those found in other plant groups adapted to wind-pollination. The male flowers occur in profuse long catkins terminating the branchlets, often colouring the whole plant yellow-brown to red-brown; female flowers are in short clusters arising from thicker branches, appearing as a mass of deep-red stigmas. In fruit these become woody cylindrical 'cones' which at maturity shrink apart to release small winged nutlets – the true fruits – which are dispersed by the wind.

Traditionally a single genus, *Casuarina*, was recognised but four distinct genera are now acknowledged. Casuarinas in the narrow sense comprise five species in Australia and a number of others in NG and the Malay archipelago. The native species are all import-ant trees and include the tall river oak, *C. cunninghamiana*, of freshwater streams from

Cape York to Arnhem Land and southern NSW; the coarser swamp oak, *C. glauca*, of eastern seashores and saline swamps; the belah, *C. cristata*, of sandy inland soils; and the beach she-oak, *C. equisetifolia*, of tropical seashores. The newly recognised genus *Allocasuarina* accounts for 53 of the native species and is endemic to Australia; it consists of shrubs and mostly smaller trees, adapted to nutrient-deficient soils. Notable tree species include the eastern forest oak, *A. torulosa*; black she-oak, *A. littoralis*; drooping she-oak, *A. verticillata*; WA she-oak, *A. fraseriana*; and the large desert oak, *A. decaisneana*, of central Australia. The third genus is *Gymnostoma*, confined to the Malay region, PNG and the Pacific except for a single species found on Thornton Peak in far northern Qld. A fourth genus occurs in the Philippines, Borneo and NG.

She-oaks have many uses, providing timber (notably from trees such as the forest oak and WA she-oak), stabilising riverbanks (particularly river oaks), browsed by livestock, and used as ornamental plants. There is also growing overseas interest in she-oak plantations as a fast-growing source of timber and fuel.

cataractbird > *cavebird*

catbird > *bower-birds*

catfish > *fishes, freshwater and marine*

Catholic Church With more than 3.5 million members, the Catholic Church is Australia's second-largest religious denomination; it also shows the most rapid increase (estimated at well over 500 000 since 1947), largely through European immigration. The majority of Catholics are now of Italian rather than Irish origin, but the mass is celebrated in 20 languages, indicating the ethnic diversity of members.

The first mass was held in 1803 by an Irish priest who was an emancipated convict; the > *Castle Hill rising* led to withdrawal of this privilege, and only clandestine celebrations were possible until the arrival of the Rev. John Joseph Therry and the Rev. P. Connolly in 1820. The first bishop was > *John Bede Polding*, who arrived in Sydney in 1835. The church's early years were characterised by the struggle for freedom to worship, the Catholic Irish accounting for about 30% of the NSW population in 1828; this coloured the subse-

quent role played by the church – generally anti-English and for the working class, which in turn led it to support the ALP in its early days. > *Daniel Mannix* was the clergy's most outspoken and controversial figure 1912–62, aggressively opposing conscription during World War 1 and a strong Labor supporter. From 1950 the lay Catholic Social Studies Movement led by B.A. Santamaria joined Mannix in his active opposition to the influence of communism and was instrumental in the formation of the > *DLP*. The movement had evolved out of 'Catholic Action', formed in the 1930s with the aim of joint action between the church hierarchy and lay groups.

Today, as well as running a comprehensive education system (now supported largely by public funds), the Catholic Church is active in all areas of social welfare and charity work (the latter notably through the St Vincent de Paul Society) and is committed to financial and spiritual assistance for developing countries (especially in Asia). The church was less active politically by the 1980s, but religio-ethical issues such as IVF and abortion continue to attract its comment and concern. >> *religion*

cattle industry There are some 21.4 million head of cattle in Australia, of which 2.6 million form the basis of the > *dairy industry* and 18.8 million are grazed for meat. Of the latter, almost half are in Qld, a quarter in NSW and the remainder distributed throughout the other States, Tas. having a mere 2%. Because of tight world markets, the total number grazed has declined considerably from a peak of 33.4 million in 1976. The decline has been more marked in southern Australia, where beef cattle production is moderately intensive and where farmers often also have the option of sheep or crop production instead. Beef produced in northern Australia is mainly for export, while the temperate regions produce for both overseas and domestic markets.

Historical development Some cattle were brought to Australia aboard the First Fleet, but not until 1804 did large consignments begin to arrive. Beef was produced entirely for the local market, and by 1843 production greatly exceeded demand; the industry survived by boiling down the slaughtered beasts for tallow which, with the hides, was exported. In 1847 the canning of meat for export was introduced by Henry and William Dangar at a plant near Newcastle, NSW; the export of frozen meat commenced in 1880, following experiments in refrigeration by T.S. Mort and E.D. Nicolle. In 1932 a satisfactory method was evolved of chilling meat, rather than freezing it; this is the current method used, although some beasts are exported 'on the hoof'. The quantity of beef exported varies considerably from year to year, ranging from 600 000t to 850 000t; the principal markets in the 1980s were the US, Japan and Canada, although this situation may be jeopardised by the recent discovery of pesticide residues in some Australian meat.

The dominant breeds of beef cattle are Shorthorns – especially in the north – and Herefords, with Poll Shorthorns and Poll Herefords growing in popularity; other British breeds include the Aberdeen Angus and the Devon. Since 1933 there has been an increasing tendency to cross Brahman cattle with British breeds to produce beasts that can withstand the heat of northern regions and are tick-resistant: breeds so produced include the Santa Gertrudis (first bred in the USA) and the Braford, Brangus and Droughtmaster (all bred in Australia). Another Australian breed is the Murray Grey, evolved from crossing the Aberdeen Angus and Shorthorn and found mainly in temperate areas of good rainfall. More recently introduced varieties include the Simmental (Swiss), the Charolais (French) and the Red Lincoln (British).

Buffaloes Water buffaloes were introduced to the NT in the 1820s and 1830s. Often left to range freely as settlements were abandoned, from them came the feral herds that have roamed low-lying, high-rainfall regions of the NT and northern Qld throughout the 20th century. Their destructive wallowing habits, which cause substantial damage to wetlands and waterways, and the infestation of cattle by buffalo flies, have made them the target of stringent measures to reduce their population. Large numbers are slaughtered annually for their meat, which is processed at two abattoirs in the NT; there is a small but growing local market for buffalo meat and other products such as specialty cheeses made from buffalo milk.

cavebird Known also as the rock warbler or cataractbird, the small brown cavebird, *Origmella solitaria*, is found only in the sandstone country around Sydney and the Jenolan limestone region. It makes its nest under rock overhangs and in caves, and sometimes even behind waterfalls; it rarely alights on trees, preferring to rest on sandstone outcrops. The cavebird is unusual in having no near relatives.

caves Caves exist in many parts of Australia and probably none of the underground systems has been fully explored. Caves form in many ways: the most complex and the largest, of limestone and dolomite, appear in carbonate rocks, since these are more readily water-soluble than most. Formation may extend over millions of years, and can be dated by fossils observed in limestone formations. Certain caves, of the type known as 'vadose seepage', are vertically formed by trickling rain or soil water creating shafts; particularly deep examples of this type are found near Bungonia Gorge in NSW, and at Mini-Martin Cave (220m) and Ice Tube Cave (345m) in Tas. Vadose flow caves, on the other hand, are created by eroding streams whose origin is in water-filled rock cavities; an example of this is Tas.'s Exit Cave, to which Mini-Martin drops and which, with 16km of passages, is Australia's longest. Most caves are complex, with various sections formed in different ways; the rocks in which caves in this country are found vary in age from 100 000 to 6 million years. Many are richly decorated with the mineral formations of stalactites and stalagmites, with cave pearls (dust or rock nucleus with calcite or aragonite cover) and cave coral.

Many sea caves appear in the cliffs along the southern Australian coast, where wave action has eroded joints or weaker rocks; there are well-known sea caves at Port Campbell, Vic. Other caves are created by volcanic action, or by atmospheric weathering; the latter form shallow shelters in rock such as granite or sandstone, and when decorated with rock paintings are important as sites of Aboriginal occupation. Numerous examples of these are found in Arnhem Land, in central Qld and on the Nullarbor Plain. Aborigines have used caves since the last ice age; stone implements have been found in deposits calculated to date back 24 000 years. Arnhem Land and Kakadu National Park are particularly rich in Aboriginal cave sites, as is Carnarvon Gorge in Qld.

Notable among Australian caves are Jenolan in NSW, Mammoth in WA and Koonalda in SA. Jenolan comprises a series of spectacular limestone caves in the Blue Mountains, west of Sydney. Discovered probably in the 1830s in the course of a search for a bushranger, in 1865 they were declared a reserve. First seen by candle or torchlight, they were equipped in

1894 with electric lighting to illuminate the 'columns and canopies and cornices, shining white or tinted rose-pink and amber ... frozen cascades and gleaming terraces; all the mechanical work of quiet waters'. The Temple of Baal, in the River Cave, is 60m long, 18m wide and 27m high, and Cathedral Cave is 76m high and 42m across its floor. Mammoth Cave, discovered in 1894, is a vast cavern in the Leeuwin-Naturaliste ridge area; it is one of many limestone caves in this region, which is on the register of the national estate. Since early this century there have been important finds of fossil bones and fragments beneath the cave floor. Koonalda Cave in SA lies 76m beneath the Nullarbor Plain, some 70km east of the WA border. Visited by several expeditions 1957–67, it yielded evidence of flint-quarrying in the inner cave, and patterned markings (yet unexplained) in the form of concentric circles, lattice and herringbone on the limestone walls of the connecting passage; both quarry and rock paintings have been assessed as 20 000 years old. These caves were declared a protected area in 1968.

Cawley, Evonne Fay (1951–), tennis player, b. Barellan, NSW. The first Aboriginal tennis player to have the chance to develop a natural talent, Cawley (then Evonne Goolagong) was guided by coaches Vic and Eva Edwards. She won 37 junior titles – including the Australian Under 19 in 1970 – and senior State titles in 1970 and 1971; in the latter year she defeated Margaret Court to win at Wimbledon. Years of hard work and determination enhanced her naturally fluent style. Cawley repeated her Wimbledon victory in 1981, to become one of the most popular Australian champions in any field of sport.

Cayley, N. W. (Neville William) (1886–1950), ornithological artist, b. Yamba, NSW. Cayley's career was established with the publication of his immensely popular *What Bird Is That?* (1931), which contained a coloured illustration of every known Australian bird and was continuously in print for 50 years. His most important work is represented in succeeding books on birds and wildlife and in his illustration of the work of other authors.

Cazaly, Roy (1896–1963), footballer, b. Melbourne. Cazaly played Australian Rules football in Vic. for St Kilda and South Melbourne, and later became a successful coach. He was a keen student of physical fitness, and his study of breathing techniques enabled him to become one of the finest exponents of the high mark: 'Up there, Cazaly!' was a popular catchcry of St Kilda supporters, and has since entered popular football idiom. In 1979 it was revived as the title of a popular song that has become synonymous with Australian Rules football.

Cazneaux, Harold (1878–1953), photographer, b. NZ. A pioneer photographer, 'Caz' held Australia's first one-man show (1909): it was both a critical and a popular success, and lifted photography to the status of art. Official photographer for Sydney Ure Smith's prestigious *Art in Australia* publications, he produced memorable portraits of artists, actors and musicians, and illustrated many books. His dramatically lit black-and-white photographs capture 'Old Sydney' at its most evocative; the Harbour Bridge studies are unequalled.

cedar This is the common name of two rainforest trees of Australia's east coast, which belong to the > *mahogany family* and are unrelated to coniferous cedars. The red cedar, *Toona Australis*, is one of the few deciduous trees of southern rainforests; it is common from far north Qld south to Milton in the Illawarra district of NSW, with closely related species extending to tropical Asia. Accessible stands of red cedar were eagerly exploited by early white settlers because the pink-reddish timber is soft, easily worked and very durable; the industry spread rapidly along the NSW and south Qld coasts and mature trees were rare by the late 19th century. White cedar, *Melia azedarach*, is another deciduous member of the mahogany family, with a pale, durable timber; it occurs in both eastern and northern rainforests of Australia and is widespread in tropical Asia.

census > *population*

centipedes and millipedes Both these arthropod groups are elongated and segmented, with numerous legs. Centipedes, of the class Chilopoda, are flattened and fast-moving, and have a single pair of legs on each segment. They are active predators, and the first pair of legs is often modified into a claw-like poison-fang. There are more than 150 species of centipede in Australia. The millipedes, which belong to the class Diplopoda and of which

Australia has more than 180 species, are cylindrical and have two pairs of legs associated with each segment. Slow-moving, they are often found in leaf litter and under logs, where they feed on plant debris.

Central Mount Stuart NT This flat-topped mountain, reaching 845m above sea-level, rises some 300m above the surrounding country about 160km north of Alice Springs. It was discovered in 1860 by John McDouall Stuart, who named it after the explorer Charles Sturt; the name was published as 'Central Mount Stuart', however, and has remained so despite suggestions that it should revert to 'Sturt'.

cephalopods This is a class of the phylum mollusca in which the 'foot' has become modified into a number of sucker-bearing tentacles and movement is achieved by jet propulsion. Best known of the cephalopods are > *octopuses*, squids and cuttlefish. Oceanic floating and planktonic specimens with an external shell include the relatively large (15–18cm) *Nautilus alumnus*, which has a beautiful, whorled shell of cream mottled with red-brown, and the smaller, white ram's horn shell, *Spirula spirula*; both are sometimes washed ashore in eastern Australia. (The brittle paper nautilus is not a true shell, but the egg-case of an octopus of the family Argonautidae.) Gould's squid, *Nototodarus gouldi*, is a rapidly swimming Pacific squid whose slender, internal bone-like shell is also often found on eastern Australian beaches, as is the broad, flat, oval cuttle-bone of the cuttlefish, *Solitosepia liliana*. Calamaries are small, rapidly moving squids, often netted in great schools; they are an increasingly popular seafood in Australia.

ceramics > *pottery and ceramics*

cereals and grains Australia's cereal and grain crops account for 25% of the gross value of agriculture and 12% of the country's exports. The most widely grown is > *wheat*, followed by barley (4 868 000t in 1985–6), grain sorghum, oats and maize. Others include rye, triticale (a wheat-rye hybrid), canary seed and millets, and grain legumes such as lupins, peas and beans. Much of the grain produced is used for livestock feed, although wheat, oats, rice, barley and maize are important in human foods: wheat for flour; oatmeal in breakfast foods; barley in beer, spirits, vinegar, and malt extract; maize for cornflour and sweeteners.

Cereal crops are grown widely in all mainland States; exceptions are maize and sorghum, which are almost entirely confined to Qld and northern NSW, and > *rice*, most of which is grown in NSW. The market for grains for human consumption is fairly stable, but crops for stock feed are vulnerable to the state of the livestock industries.

Cerutty, Percy Wells (1895–1975), athletics coach, b. Melbourne. Cerutty rose from obscurity to become the world's most controversial and eccentric athletics coach of the 1950s and 1960s. A serious health breakdown in 1939 had led him to devise a diet and fitness regimen that included runs of up to 160km. He established himself as a coach at Portsea, where his mixture of gruelling sandhill running and a strict dietary creed drew many aspiring champions, most of whom found his personality entrancing but his training ultimately too demanding. The most successful of them was Herb Elliott, who in attributing his success to Cerutty described him as 'a mixture of Svengali and Salvador Dali'.

Cessnock NSW (pop. 41 700) The main urban centre in the Hunter Valley, the city of Cessnock lies 180km north of Sydney; it incorporates more than 20 urban settlements, the largest being Cessnock itself, Kurri Kurri and Weston, and Bellbird. It has been an important coal-mining area since the 1880s, when Sir Edgeworth David found the Greta seam (1886); the settlement was named by an early Scottish settler, after a castle in Ayrshire. Wine production is the other major activity in the district, the first vineyard being that at Pokolbin (established in 1856); further industries include farming, timber-milling, and aluminium smelting at Kurri Kurri.

chafers > *beetles*

Chaffey brothers, pioneers of irrigation. **George** (1848–1932) and **William** (1856–1926), both b. Canada, were working in California, where George had tapped underground water for irrigation, when they met Alfred Deakin, who was investigating overseas methods of water conservation and irrigation. At Deakin's suggestion and on the strength of an agreement with the Vic. government that land would be granted to them in return for their establishing scientific irrigation, the brothers came to Australia and set up an irrigation and land company in Mildura, Vic. They pumped water from the Murray River through an extensive system of channels to the mallee country, using a triple-expansion marine engine (which remained in operation until 1959). Their success encouraged them to establish a companion settlement at Renmark, SA, but owing to financial and transport problems and the 1890s depression, Chaffey Brothers Ltd went into liquidation in 1895. George returned to California, but William remained to become a prominent citizen of Mildura.

Challis, John Henry (1809–80), philanthropist, b. England. Challis arrived in Sydney in 1829 and became an extremely successful merchant, retiring a wealthy man in 1855. He returned to England but maintained an interest in the University of Sydney, donating a stained-glass window for its Great Hall in 1856 and bequeathing to the university his estate of £200 000.

Chamberlain case The cause célèbre of Australia in the 1980s, this legal case centred on Lindy (Alice Lynne) and Michael Leigh Chamberlain, charged with the murder of their infant daughter, Azaria, near Ayers Rock, NT. In August 1980, Azaria disappeared while the Chamberlains were camping at Ayers Rock with their three children. The Chamberlains alleged that the two-month-old baby was taken by a dingo, but after nearly two years of rumour and legal investigation the mother was charged with murder and the father with being an accessory after the fact ; there were, however, no eyewitnesses, no body, no confession and no apparent motive. Lindy Chamberlain was sentenced to life imprisonment and Michael Chamberlain to eighteen months, although he was released immediately on a good-behaviour bond. Public debate over the case continued, including accusations of 'trial by the media'; much of the Crown's evidence was discredited as more witnesses and evidence were produced, and Lindy Chamberlain was released after having served three years of her sentence. In 1987, following two court appeals and a lengthy public inquiry, the Chamberlains were legally pardoned; in 1990, financial compensation by the Crown was still being negotiated.

Chambers Pillar NT This sandstone monolith, 34m high and 6m wide, stands between the Stuart Highway and the Adelaide–Alice Springs railway, 16km north of the Finke River. It was discovered and named by John McDouall Stuart in 1860. The surrounding area became a national reserve in 1970.

Channel Country Qld A region of southwestern Qld, this country is so named because of the shallow stream beds cut into the flood plains of the Mulligan, Georgina and Diamantina rivers and Cooper Creek, all of which flow towards Lake Eyre. After floods, the rich alluvium supports lush grasslands, used to fatten cattle. From the 1880s the NT 'Cattle King', Sidney Kidman, often drove his herds into the region to take advantage of the ephemeral grazing.

Chappell family, three brothers notable as cricketers. These brothers, all b. Adelaide, came from a cricketing family, their grandfather, Vic Richardson, having captained Australia in the 1930s. They dominated Australian Test cricket in the 1970s and 1980s and were key figures in the breakaway World Series cricket in 1977. **Ian Michael** (1943–) began his Test career in 1964 and in the course of 75 Tests made fourteen centuries. He was an aggressive, courageous batsman, and these qualities were reflected in his captaincy (from 1971) when he moulded an aggressive team that defeated all rivals. **Gregory Stephen** (1948–) made a century in his Test debut in 1970, and in 87 subsequent Tests scored 7110 runs including 24 centuries. Greg was an elegant, classical batsman but his game was affected by the burdens of captaincy, which he twice relinquished. **Trevor** (1952–) played three Tests in 1981, but is best remembered for having bowled underarm in February of that year (on instructions from the captain, his brother Greg) for the last ball of the limited-over final against NZ.

Charlesworth, Ric(hard Ian) > *hockey*

Charleville Qld (pop. 3588) The outback town of Charleville lies on the Warrego River 777km west of Brisbane, at the heart of a productive grazing region. The town site was surveyed in 1868 and was reached by railway in the 1880s; it was a stopping-point for Cobb & Co. coaches, was on the route of the first regular service by the original Qantas airline, and is still a base for the Royal Flying Doctor service.

Charlton, Boy (Andrew Murray) (1907–75), swimmer, b. North Sydney. Charlton became a popular idol and a national hero in the 1920s because of his prowess in distance swimming. Although he preferred surfing to swimming, he became a champion with minimal training and in 1923 set a new world record of 11 min. 5.2 sec. for the 880yds freestyle, taking 19 sec. off the old time. The next year he lowered this time to 10 min. 51.8 sec. and at the 1924 Olympic Games won the 1500m, setting a new world and Olympic record of 20 min. 6.6 sec. He was unplaced in the 400m and 1500m at the 1932 Olympics, but won his last race – the 880yds event at the 1935 NSW championships – before retiring to become a grazier. He was responsible for reviving interest in competitive swimming in Australia.

Charlton, Eddie (Edward Francis)
> billiards and snooker

Charters Towers Qld (pop. 7208) A city 135km inland from Mt Isa and about 1400km north of Brisbane, Charters Towers was Qld's richest goldfield 1872–1909, during which period the population reached 30 000, and gold worth £30 million was extracted from its reefs. It is now the main centre for its surrounding district, where the principal activities are beef production, dairying, and the production of crops such as fruit (notably grapes). Charters Towers has retained much of its early architecture, including notable public buildings as well as fine examples of the breezy but ornate Qld vernacular style.

chats Small, brightly coloured birds living mostly in semi-arid country, Australian chats form an endemic family, Ephthianuridae, and are unrelated to those outside the continent. The common white-fronted chat is found throughout southern Australia; the yellow, crimson or orange species are restricted to inland areas. In all species the male plumage is more brightly coloured than the female. Chats build cup-shaped nests of grass in tussocks or low bushes, and are among those birds that practise injury-feigning – fluttering as though helpless on the ground – to distract intruders. A bird probably related to this group is the desert chat or gibber-bird, discovered only in 1911, and confined to desert areas of the interior.

Chauncy, Nan(cen Beryl) (1900-70), author, b. England. Chauncy arrived in Tas. in 1912, and it subsequently provided the setting for her dozen or so children's books, which are credited with having established realistic fiction for children in Australia. Chauncy won the Children's Book of the Year award three times – for *Tiger in the Bush* (1957), *Devil's Hill* (1958), and *Tangara* (1960) – and her books have been translated into many languages. The quinquennial award of Australia's Children's Book Council is named in her honour.

Chauvel, Charles Edward (1897–1959), film producer and director, b. Warwick, Qld. In partnership with his wife Elsa, Chauvel made many silent films. In 1933 their first sound film, *In the Wake of the Bounty*, launched Errol Flynn's career. Other notable films included *Forty Thousand Horsemen* (1940), *The Rats of Tobruk* (1944) and *Jedda* (1955), the last-named being the final gasp of a dying industry, which had to wait until the 1970s for a rebirth. The Chauvels also made the television series 'Walkabout' for the ABC.

Chauvel, Sir Henry George (1865–1945), soldier, b. Tabulam, NSW. A career soldier, Chauvel fought with the Australian Commonwealth Horse in the Boer War and during World War 1 was commander of the 1st Light Horse Brigade in Egypt and Gallipoli (1914–15). In 1917 he commanded the Desert Mounted Corps, which included British, Indian and French cavalry as well as Anzacs. During the British advance into Palestine, he led the corps to spectacular victories at Beersheba and Damascus. Chauvel was chief-of-staff of the Australian Military Forces 1923–30.

cheese > dairy industry

chemical and plastics industries Australia produces many of the chemicals it needs, including sulphuric and phosphoric acids for chemical fertilisers and synthetics, alkalis such as caustic soda (used in alumina production) and soda ash (a component of glass), and the widely used petrochemicals. The chemical industry was established in the 1860s with plants to make sulphuric and nitric acids for the fertilisers needed by farmers. World War 2 fostered the production of even more complex chemicals, gearing the industry up for rapid growth, which occurred at twice the rate experienced by industry generally in the 1950s and 1960s; huge sums were spent on research and development. Its success has had spin-offs

in the construction and engineering industries – from which it has bought much new capital equipment – and in mining, which has benefited from the demand for petroleum, sulphur, phosphate and other raw materials. Increasing concern about the environment has led to the development of a wider range of biodegradable chemicals.

The chemical industry is closely linked to the plastics industry, whose products are made from petrochemicals, and between them they account for about 10% of the value of production in Australia's manufacturing sector. Sales of plastics and related products were worth more than $3 billion in 1989, plastics being used for everything from food packaging to household products and work tools. During the 1980s the plastics industry grew rapidly, and both the number of manufacturers and the range of products were rationalised. More modest but steady growth is predicted for the 1990s.

Chenopodiaceae > *saltbush family*

Chevalier, Nicholas (1828–1902), artist, b. Russia. Chevalier studied painting, lithography and architecture in Europe before arriving in Melbourne in 1855, where he became cartoonist for the Melbourne *Punch* (1856–61) and travelled in the colony with his friend Eugène von Guérard. Handsome and urbane, he achieved considerable success but his heavily romanticised landscapes convey little of the nature of Australia's scenery. After settling in London in 1871, he was London adviser to the National Gallery of NSW for 20 years.

Chifley, Ben (Joseph Benedict) (1885–1951), politician, b. Bathurst, NSW. Of an Irish-Catholic background, Chifley worked for NSW railways, representing his union at arbitration (joining the 1917 strike, for which he was dismissed) and becoming increasingly concerned with Labor ideals. Elected to federal parliament 1928–31, he was minister of defence under J.H. Scullin but lost his seat to the faction led by Jack Lang. He served on a royal commission on banking in 1935, recommending nationalisation of the Australian banking system (a longstanding aim). Re-elected to parliament in 1940 (representing Macquarie), he became federal treasurer when Labor won government in 1941, and succeeded John Curtin as prime minister 1945–9. He

immediately launched a full-scale realisation of the welfare and nationalisation aims of the ALP, which he succeeded in uniting. Obstinate single-mindedness lay behind Chifley's homely, gentle exterior; an outstanding administrator, politician and planner, he continues to be lionised by many Labor adherents. The famous gravelly voice could produce fluent, compelling argument from a throat described by a specialist as resembling worn-out leather.

Childe, (Vere) Gordon (1892–1957), archaeologist and author, b. Sydney. A graduate of Sydney and Oxford universities, Childe was professor of prehistoric archaeology at Edinburgh University 1927–46, and director of the Institute of Archaeology at London University 1947–57. He was a pioneer in the study of prehistoric culture in Europe and the Middle East, and his research established the guidelines for much contemporary analytical archaeology. An ardent socialist and pacifist (which views are believed to have militated against his appointment to Australian universities), he published about 20 books including the long-standing reference *The Dawn of European Civilisation* (1925).

children's books Although Australia was referred to in children's books from the 1790s (originally by Maria Edgeworth in *Lazy Lawrence*), it was not until 1841 that the first children's book was written and published in Australia. Titled *A Mother's Offering to Her Children: by a Lady Long Resident in New South Wales*, it was an instructional story in dialogue. By the late 19th century, in keeping with general trends in literature, children's books began to present an Australian point of view – most notably in Ethel Turner's *Seven Little Australians* (1894); a realistic yet humorous story of middle-class family life, it was immediately successful and is still enjoyed by children today. Pursuing the tradition established by such writers as Louisa M. Alcott in the US, Turner subsequently published 27 novels all characterised by sympathy with the viewpoint of children.

Other significant children's writers and illustrators of the early 20th century include > *Mary Grant Bruce*, > *May Gibbs* and > *Ida Rentoul Outhwaite*. Bruce's 'Billabong' series, set in rural Australia and celebrating 'bush' types and virtues, has lasting popularity. Gibbs also used the bush for her inspiration, with fanciful illustrations of imaginary bush creatures accompanying her simply written stories; *Gumnut Babies* (1916) was followed by a string of similar tales, the best known of which is *Snugglepot and Cuddlepie* (1918). Outhwaite's books are memorable particularly for their delicate, if sentimental, drawings, which were shown to best advantage in the three lavish publications *Elves and Fairies* (1916), *The Enchanted Forest* (1921) and *The Fairyland of Ida Rentoul Outhwaite* (1926).

Arguably the outstanding children's novel of the early 20th century was *The Magic Pudding* (1918), written and illustrated by Norman Lindsay; droll, vigorous and sometimes vulgar, the story of three villainous friends and their efforts to save their magic pudding is enriched by Lindsay's idiosyncratic illustrations and remains irresistible.

In the years following World War 2, a distinctively Australian children's literature developed with the work of such discrete authors as Hesba Brinsmead, > *Nan Chauncy,* Joan Phipson, > *Ivan Southall,* > *Colin Thiele* and Patricia Wrightson. Many also achieved popularity overseas, most notably Southall in his realistic novels about ordinary people in exceptional circumstances.

In the last 20 years, both the content and production standards of children's books in Australia have become increasingly sophisticated, in part reflecting a greater emphasis on children's real interests. They are also, accordingly, increasingly international, and illustrated books in particular have won wide acclaim overseas. Outstanding authors include Allan Baillie, Simon French, Paul Jennings, Victor Kelleher and Robin Klein; their productivity and popularity are matched by the brilliant work of artists such as Jeannie Baker, Graeme Base, Robert Ingpen, Craig Smith and Julie Vivas.

Chinese in Australia > *ethnic groups; immigration; racial conflict*

Chipp, Don > *Australian Democrats*

Chisholm, A.H. (Alexander Hugh)

(1890–1977) naturalist and editor, b. Maryborough, Vic. From the 1920s, Chisholm was successively editor of the Melbourne *Argus,* the *Australasian,* and the Sydney *Sunday Pictorial.* Largely self-educated from voracious reading and 'idling in green places', he edited several natural-history journals and wrote his autobiography, an affectionate memoir of C.J. Dennis, and some ten other books, including *Mateship with Birds* (1922) and *Bird Wonders of Australia* (1934). He was also editor-in-chief of the second edition of the multi-volume *Australian Encyclopaedia* (1958).

Chisholm, Caroline (1808–77), philanthropist, b. England. Caroline Chisholm arrived in Australia from Madras in 1838, with her husband. Horrified by the squalid conditions and neglect of immigrants, she met their ships, opened a reception home for females, found them employment and personally escorted immigrants into the country. In London 1846–54 she organised the Family Colonisation Loan Society, subsequently returning to Australia 1854–66.

chitons Of the class Amphineura, these are flat, rock-clinging molluscs with a tough carapace of eight plates held together by ligaments and surrounded by a ring of leathery tissue; the separated plates are sometimes washed ashore as attractive blue or green 'butterfly shells'. Perhaps the commonest species in eastern Australia is the snakeskin chiton, *Sypharochiton pelliserpentis,* grey-green, about 3cm long and often seen in clefts of rock platforms at about low-tide level. The larger, olive-green *Ischnoradsia australis* is sometimes seen in rock pools and under stones.

chough > *mudlarks and allies*

Christmas bush > *Cunoniaceae; mint family; mistletoes; pittosporum family*

Christmas Island An Australian territory in the Indian Ocean, Christmas Island lies about 350km south of Java. Although volcanic in origin, it has large outcrops of coralline limestone and phosphate, the latter being mined as the island's primary industry. Christmas Island was discovered in 1615 by Richard Rowe and appeared on Dutch charts shortly thereafter. It was annexed by Britain in 1888, and transferred to Australia in 1958.

Churchill Fellowships This scheme is administered by the Winston Churchill Memorial Trust, which was established in 1965 from public donation. The fellowships are awarded annually to Australians over 18 years, financing overseas study by promising young workers, or by older people of proven achievement in any

field (from primary industry to education or the arts). Fellowships are also available to indigenous residents of territories other than the ACT, for study or work within Australia.

Church of England > *Anglican Church*; *religion*

cicadas This insect group forms a very audible part of the Australian summer fauna. The male has large, sound-producing 'tymbals' and air-filled, resonating chambers at the side of the abdomen, and each species produces a characteristic shrill courtship call. Hatching from eggs, cicada nymphs burrow into the soil and there feed on sap from roots; after one or more years they crawl into trees, at which point the adults emerge, leaving the nymphal cuticles attached to a trunk or branch. Australia has a very rich cicada fauna of more than 250 species: the endemic family Tettigarctidae, or hairy cicadas, contains a few members restricted to cool, montane forests in Tas. and southeastern Australia; the family Cicadidae comprises the majority of species. Perhaps the most unusual member of the family is the green bladder cicada, *Cystosoma saundersii*, in which the male has a large, inflated – mostly air-filled – abdomen.

Cilento family, eminent in various fields. **Sir Raphael West** (1893–1985), b. Jamestown, SA, was a doctor and leading administrator in the field of tropical medicine, especially in Qld and NG. He served as UN director for refugees and displaced persons 1946–51 and was also keenly involved in heritage conservation in Qld. His wife, **(Lady) Phyllis Dorothy** (1894–1987), b. Sydney, was also a doctor. A medical journalist and early nutritionist, she published a number of books on family health. Their daughter **(Elizabeth) Diane** (1932–), b. Brisbane, is an international stage and film actress as well as an author and scriptwriter. She is an active campaigner for nature conservation in northern Qld, where she lives.

cinema > *film industry*

circuses The official beginning of the circus in Australia was in 1847, when Launceston publican Robert Radford established his successful Royal Amphitheatre. Two of his performers, equestrians James Ashton and John Jones, who later adopted the more flamboyant pseudonym St Leon, established their own

troupes in the early 1850s and toured eastern Australia with 'king of the ring' Henry Burton. The gold rushes attracted visits by overseas circuses and inspired smaller local troupes to join the itinerant population, setting up calico tents and advertising their 'extraordinary feats' with extravagant praise. The celebrated Italian Chiarini Circus visited Australia three times in the 1870s and 1880s, eclipsing local circus talent. In the 1890s the FitzGerald Brothers' huge travelling show dominated Australian circus entertainment: they travelled to Europe to hire the most dazzling acts from the top international shows and catered to the demands of their audiences for ever more daring tricks. When the brothers died in 1906, the Wirth Brothers' Circus – which had been touring abroad for seven years – became the country's premier troupe, with its own train, a well-established touring route, and international stars.

By the 1950s the introduction of television and the ready availability of other forms of entertainment had greatly affected the popularity of all circuses. Wirth's closed in 1963, and Bullen Brothers (started after World War 2) closed too, in 1968; Ashton's, Sole Brothers' and Perry's circuses continue to tour, but on a greatly reduced scale. Today, only visiting performers such as the Great Moscow Circus attract huge audiences and conjure up the splendour of past circuses. Modern shows such as the idiosyncratic Circus Oz and the children's Flying Fruitfly Circus – both specialising in acrobatic feats – have largely replaced traditional ring circus, but carry on the spirit of the old-time travelling troupes.

Citizen Military Force > *defence forces*

citizenship Official Australian citizenship dates from the passage of the Australian Citizenship Act 1948. Before that time, Australian residents were by law British citizens and in fact Australian citizens remained British subjects until this legal provision was repealed in 1987. Citizenship is automatic for those born in Australia, except in certain cases (such as the children of diplomats) where one parent is neither an Australian citizen nor a permanent resident. Others deemed to be Australian citizens include people born outside Australia of an Australian parent (if the birth is registered at an Australian consulate within eighteen years), British subjects resident for five years or more prior to 1949, or those whose fathers or husbands qualified as citizens in 1949. Citizenship is otherwise acquired by application and the procedure of 'naturalisation' which dates back to the early 19th century. All adult immigrants who have some knowledge of English can seek citizenship after one year's residence in the preceding two years, or two years' residence over the previous five years. The legal qualifications for citizenship – whether British or Australian – have been altered periodically since the 19th century, largely reflecting > *immigration* policy; the most notable change was the gradual abandonment of discrimination based on racial origin. Applications and procedures for citizenship are administered by the federal Department of Immigration and Ethnic Affairs.

citrus family A characteristic of all members of the flowering-plant family Rutaceae is the presence in leaves, bark, flowers and fruit of cavities filled with aromatic oils; nearly all members of the family – which includes citrus fruits – are trees or shrubs.

Australia has about 40 native genera of this family, more than half of which are endemic (most belonging to the > *boronias*). Many are trees and shrubs of rainforests, the most important such genus being *Flindersia*, with sixteen species in eastern and central Australia as well as NG and New Caledonia. Some members of this genus, notably the native teak or crow's ash, *F. australis*, and the maple, *F. brayleana*, yield valuable timber. Cudgerie, *F. schottiana*, is a very large tree occurring in wet rainforest from NSW to NG; the leopardwood, *F. maculosa*, is a decorative small tree restricted to the semi-arid inland plains of Qld and NSW. While there are no Australian representatives of the genus *Citrus*, close relatives include the desert lime, *Eremocitrus glauca*, a suckering spiny shrub with small greenish-yellow sharp-tasting fruits, and the five species of the prickly genus *Microcitrus* of eastern rainforests. >> *fruit-growing*

civil engineering This field covers the construction of roads, bridges, dams, harbours, canals and drainage systems. The first 'civil engineers' in Australia were the British marine officers who arrived with the First Fleet in 1788, and Australia's first bridge was constructed over the Tank Stream in the year of arrival, near what is now Bridge Street in Sydney. Very little of permanent worth was constructed, however, and Lachlan Macquarie

found the colony in a 'wretched state' when he took up the post of governor in 1809. Macquarie immediately set about implementing an immense scheme of public works, the cost of which provoked protests from the British government. New towns such as Liverpool, Windsor and Bathurst were his creations, as were the roads west over the Blue Mountains, south to the Cookbundoon Range, and north to Port Macquarie. While Macquarie was the father in Australia of what we call civil engineering today, much of the practical work was carried out by Francis Greenway, designer and builder of some of the colony's best churches and government establishments. Prepared to turn his hand to anything, Greenway was instrumental in training the artisans needed for civil engineering works. Greenway, like all those who laboured for him, had arrived in Australia as a convict and an immense debt is owed for the roads and bridges built by what was in fact, if not in theory, a slave labour force. By 1826, the Tank Stream had become too polluted to be used for Sydney's water supply and John Busby began construction of a tunnel to carry water from the Waterloo swamp to Hyde Park. Using convict labour, it was completed in 1837.

The best-known of the early civil engineers, > *David Lennox*, arrived in Australia in 1832. He was a prolific builder of roads and bridges, both in Sydney and in Melbourne. In a country as large, dry and inhospitable as Australia most major civil engineering projects involve vast financial and labour resources, often beyond the means of such a small population. Nevertheless, large essential projects have been successfully undertaken, notably the > *Snowy Mountains Scheme*, which is perhaps Australia's greatest civil engineering achievement. Other massive projects include the Ord River Scheme in the Kimberley area of WA, the hydro-electric network of Tas., and one of Australia's few internationally recognised landmarks, the > *Sydney Harbour Bridge*.

clams > *bivalves*

Clare SA (pop. 2591) This town about 135km north of Adelaide is the heart of the Clare Valley, a region noted particularly for its wines. It was named by the first settler, E. Gleeson, in 1842, after his native County Clare in Ireland; Jesuit priests established a church and seminary nearby in 1851 and planted the area's first vines. The Clare region also produces sheep, wool, fruit, honey, barley and wheat.

Clarence River NSW A major river of northern NSW, the Clarence drains a large catchment south of the Border Ranges; important tributaries include the Mann, Nymboida and Guy Fawkes rivers. The land of the lower reaches has been cleared for dairying and agriculture, but that of most of the headwaters remains densely forested. Grafton, on the lower flood plain, was once a major river port. The Clarence joins the Tasman Sea between Yamba and Iluka.

Clark, (Charles) Manning (Hope) (1915–), historian, b. Melbourne. From 1949 to 1975 Clark was foundation professor of Australian history at the Australian National University, Canberra, and his two published collections of documents on Australian history (1950-5 and 1957) have become standard references. His numerous ensuing publications – especially the six-volume work *A History of Australia* (1962-87) – have gained him many followers, although his apocalyptic style and occasional historical lapses have also provoked criticism.

Clark, Colin Grant (1905–), economist, b. England. Clark arrived in Qld in 1938 to take up advisory and administrative positions in the field of labour, industry and finance. He is noted for his views on population – particularly his rejection of the theory of 'population explosion' – and for his support of Catholic opposition to birth control. He has published numerous books including (with John Crawford) *The National Income of Australia* (1938), which was a landmark in Australian writing on economics. In 1978 he became an honorary research consultant to the University of Qld.

Clark, John James (1838–1915), architect, b. England. As government architect in Vic., aged just 19, Clark designed the elegant Treasury building (1857–62); the Royal Mint (1872), Old Melbourne Gaol (n.d.) and Melbourne City Baths (1903) were among his other grand and diverse designs. His Treasury building in Brisbane (1885–1928) is regarded as one of the finest Australian buildings in the Italian Renaissance style.

Clarke, Marcus (Andrew Hislop) (1846–81), journalist and author, b. England.

Clarke arrived in Australia in 1863. As a journalist he wrote numerous satirical newspaper sketches, lively historical essays, and some poor verse. He is best known for his convict novel *His Natural Life*, published as a serial 1870–2 in the *Australian Journal* and in revised book form in 1874 (retitled *For the Term of His Natural Life* in 1882). A lively, witty figure of the Melbourne scene, he was a co-founder of the literary Yorick Club.

Clarke, Ron(ald William) (1937–), athlete, b. Melbourne. A distance runner of enormous talent, Clarke achieved success in breaking records rather than in winning Olympic medals. An outstanding junior, he was chosen to carry the torch into the main stadium at the 1956 Melbourne Olympic Games. He dropped out of competition for a time, but Herb Elliot's influence in 1960 inspired him to prepare for the 1962 Commonwealth Games, where he came second in the 3-mile (4800m) event. Between 1963 and 1967 he broke seventeen world records, at one time holding the record for every event from 3200m to 20 000m, but his inability to master race tactics meant that he was outrun at the 1964 and 1968 Olympics, despite heroic efforts. He retired from competitive running in 1969.

Clarke, William Branwhite (1798–1878), geologist, b. England. Although a clergyman for most of his life, Clarke is best known for his geological work. He discovered gold at Hartley Vale and in the Bathurst district, NSW, in the 1840s, and suggested its existence in Vic., which ultimately led to the discovery of the Ballarat fields. Commissioned by the government to make geological surveys of NSW, he produced major reports on the coalfields and discovered the existence of tin. He was secretary (1841–5) and a trustee (1853–73) of the Australian Museum, and a founder of the Royal Society of NSW. He became a Fellow of the Royal Society in 1876.

Cleary, Jon Stephen (1917–), author, b. Sydney. After army service during World War 2, Cleary took up full-time writing and his first novel, *You Can't See Round Corners,* was published in 1948. A prolific and immensely popular author of atmospheric adventure fiction, Cleary has enjoyed worldwide success with such novels as *The Sundowners* (1952), *The High Commissioner* (1966) and *Helga's*

Web (1970). His best-known character is the Sydney detective, Scobie Malone.

Cleland, Sir John Burton (1878–1971), medical scientist and naturalist, b. Adelaide. Cleland is best known for his botanical studies; his collection of 30 000 plants, presented to the SA Herbarium, included 60 new species. His early work in microbiology included important discoveries regarding the tropical diseases dengue and encephalitis. He was subsequently government pathologist and bacteriologist in WA (1906–09), a microbiologist with the NSW Department of Public Health from 1913, and professor of pathology at the University of Adelaide 1920–48. After his retirement in 1948, Cleland devoted himself to the cause of wildlife conservation.

clematis > *buttercup family*

climate For a continent of such great size, Australia has a relatively small range of climates, largely owing to the fact that much of the country lies in the subtropical latitudes. It is, on the other hand, noted for its uncomfortable extremes of weather, the most consistent themes being prevalent heat and cyclical drought and flood. Also notwithstanding its immense internal distances, Australia has an extensive meteorological service which was well established within little more than 100 years of European settlement. Another century on, this network draws on a sophisticated range of technologies which provide increasingly accurate information on climate, weather and atmospheric systems. While Australia's small latitudinal extent (33°) and generally low relief (mountain barriers acting as major climatic divides) together produce a smaller range of climatic types than is found in other continents, it does have number of distinct climatic regimes. The country being in effect a vast island continent, there is a substantial difference between the 'continental' climates of the interior (with large annual and daily temperature ranges, and very variable rainfall) and the 'maritime' climates of most of the coastal regions (which experience relatively small ranges of temperature, and much more consistent rainfall). The greatest contrasts arise because of variations in latitude, however, there being a clear distinction between the climates north and south of the subtropical anticyclone belt.

Rainfall and temperature With an average annual rainfall of only 420mm, and very vari-able occurrence of rain over much of the country, Australia is the second-driest continent in the world (after Antarctica). Temperatures are generally high, but vary greatly according to latitude: summer (January) averages range from 29°C in the north to 18°C in the more temperate south, the winter (July) averages being 24°C and 10°C respectively.

In the tropical and subtropical north, the winds are predominantly easterly and the airstreams moving across the continent from the Pacific Ocean and the Coral Sea are usually quite humid. The wettest area in Australia is accordingly found along the Qld coastal ranges between Cairns and Townsville, where the prevailing moist easterly flow is forced to rise and thus creates frequent clouds and rain. Tully, with a median annual rainfall of over 4000mm, is the country's wettest spot; it is in this area that Australia's tropical rainforests are (or were) located.

In most of northern and northeastern Australia, the maximum rainfall occurs in the warm season. The main reason for this is the southward movement of the subtropical anticyclones in summer, with the result that the moist easterlies to their north extend across a much greater area of the continent and bring more extensive rain; at the same time, monsoonal westerlies push down across Arnhem Land and Cape York Peninsula, bringing frequent tropical thunderstorms to these areas. Another major contributing factor is the occurrence of tropical cyclones, which form only in regions where the sea-surface temperature exceeds 27.5°C and are thus almost exclusively a warm-season phenomenon. Such storms emanate from the Coral and Timor Seas and the Gulf of Carpentaria, and when they approach or cross the Australian coastline, large areas are exposed to very heavy rainfall and extensive flooding often occurs.

In many parts of southern Australia, by contrast, the maximum rainfall occurs in winter and spring. At these times, the subtropical anticyclones have retreated northwards to the centre of the continent and the southern regions experience mid-latitude westerly air streams. Cold fronts within these westerlies move across the regions about twice a week, bringing extensive cloud and rain (and winter snowfalls on the higher peaks). Some areas, such as Tas. and southern Vic., remain south of the anticyclonic belt almost all the year and thus experience little seasonal variation in rainfall; other areas – notably southern WA, southern

SA and northwestern Vic. – are under the influence of the anticyclonic belt during summer and do have their maximum in winter.

Lying between the temperate south and the tropical north, a large area of inland Australia is under anticyclonic control all year and therefore arid: the driest region is in northeastern SA, where the median rainfall is below 100mm. The generally clear skies of the inland produce great daytime heat in summer – temperatures in excess of 50°C have been recorded at many stations, the highest being 53.1°C at Cloncurry in Qld in 1889. The relatively low temperatures observed in these areas in winter, however, mean that the highest annual average temperatures in the country – some 27°C – occur along the northern coast. Temperatures are generally lower in the south, with annual averages of around 10°C in much of Tas. and 6°C in higher alpine areas; the lowest temperature ever recorded in Australia is –22.2°C, at Charlotte Pass in the Snowy Mountains, NSW.

Climatic patterns Research has shown that a major cause of Australia's erratic weather is the so-called 'ENSO' effect (an acronym for El Nino Southern Oscillation). This is a complex global phenomenon of the oceans and the atmosphere – in effect a see-sawing of atmospheric pressure between the southeastern Pacific Ocean and the 'maritime continent' of Indonesia and the Philippines – every three to five years, which disrupts the usual climatic rhythm. Climatologists attribute the disastrous weather extremes of the 1980s to this fluctuating cycle. In 1982–3, the normal interplay of climatic forces altered substantially, with the result that the rainfall due to Australia fell instead over the central Pacific: Australia experienced its worst drought in 200 years, severe storms hit California and French Polynesia, and worldwide damage was estimated in billions of dollars. A reversal of these events occurred in 1988–9, with much of northern and eastern Australia being inundated.

Throughout its existence Australia has experienced significant climatic changes, the last ice age ending only about 10 000 years ago. The possibility of rapid global warming due to the > *greenhouse effect* is now, however, a matter of widespread concern, annual mean temperatures being predicted to increase by 2–4°C by the year 2040. An accompanying southward shift in the anticyclonic belt would also substantially alter the pattern of rainfall over Australia, reduce the winter snow-cover in alpine areas, and bring tropical cyclones much further south than at present. While policies and programs are being devised by governments to deal with the potential effects of these climatic shifts, many scientists remain sceptical about the urgency of the problem and attribute the phenomenon to longer-term climatic cycles.

Meteorology Australia was settled at a time of growing international interest in the development of uniform and systematic meteorological observations. The first records of weather in the colonies were made by William Dawes, from the observatory he set up soon after the arrival of the First Fleet; valuable observations were also made by early maritime and land explorers. Official weather stations were gradually established and the resulting network allowed daily weather maps to be published in the newspapers from 1879. Notable pioneers in the field were Charles Todd, who efficaciously combined his official roles as postmaster-general, astronomer and meteorologist in SA from 1855 to gather and disseminate weather observations; and Clement Wragge, government meteorologist in Qld 1887–93, whose contributions included the development of long-range forecasting and the tradition of naming cyclones (Wragge dubbing them in honour of some of his less favourite politicians).

The Commonwealth Bureau of Meteorology was established in 1906 and despite limited resources for many years its achievements were many – including the creation of outpost observation stations and the introduction of radio forecasting in 1924. The strategic usefulness of meteorology during World War 2 subsequently encouraged great expansion of funding, personnel and training. Technological developments in meteorology were also rapid after the war, including the use of radar for wind measurements from the late 1940s, televised weather forecasts from 1956, satellite transmission from the 1960s, and computerised storage and analysis of information from the 1970s. By 2000, further advances in these areas – particularly in the application of radar, satellites and computers – will allow increasingly accurate weather forecasts and warnings, and better understanding of climatic patterns and atmospheric systems and conditions.

Cloncurry Qld (pop. 2297) This pastoral and copper-mining town lies on the Cloncurry River, 124km from Mt Isa and some 1650km northwest of Brisbane. It developed quickly after the discovery of rich copper fields in 1867 but has relied periodically on pastoralism when copper prices have fallen (notably after World War 1). Other minerals in the area include silver-lead, zinc, iron ore and gold.

clothing and footwear industry This industry has a long but comparatively unstable history in Australian manufacturing, being particularly vulnerable to economic recession and overseas competition; it has frequently been at the centre of debate over tariff protection.

Simeon Lord started a textile factory at Botany Bay in 1815, and by 1820 colonial tanneries were making leather for harnesses and shoes. As textile mills were established, clothing manufacture was extended. The gold rushes interrupted growth in both NSW and Vic., but after Vic. introduced import tariffs in the 1860s its clothing and footwear industry developed more rapidly; in the 1980s Melbourne was the leading production centre.

As it is labour-intensive, supplies a comparatively limited market and faces intense competition from Asian markets, the industry has struggled to survive, especially since the 1970s; some Australian companies have set up factories in Southeast Asia, from there to export goods back to Australia, and this exacerbates the problem. Although tariff protection has been continuously in force since the 1950s, imports have increased rapidly, accounting for 28% of the domestic market 1983–4. Clothing and footwear production has been seriously affected both by structural and technological change and by the recession in manufacturing industry generally since the mid-1970s, and the federal government – despite lobbying by importers, consumers and Asian trading partners – has continued to support the industry. Notable features are the high proportion in the workforce of women and of immigrants (in 1979, 84% and 52% respectively of all the workers) and the concentration of the industry in inner-suburban areas, where few other employment opportunities exist.

clubmosses > *ferns and fern allies*

Clune, Frank (Francis Patrick) (1893 – 1971), adventurer and author, b. Sydney. Clune progressed to being the most popular Australian author of his day, after having been a newspaper boy, world roamer, Gallipoli veteran, vaudevillian and mousetrap salesman. He abandoned accountancy following the publication of *Try Anything Once* (1933), an account of his earlier travels which he wrote while recuperating from ulcers; he subsequently produced more than 60 books. Beginning with *Dig* (1937), an undetermined and rarely acknowledged number of racy, often unreliable books were written by P. R. ('Inky') Stephensen from material provided by Clune.

Clunes Vic. (pop. 817) Site of Vic.'s first recorded gold discovery, in 1850 on a local property, Clunes lies in the heart of the Vic. goldfields some 40km north of Ballarat and 150km northwest of Melbourne. News of the find was suppressed until 1851, when its publication engendered the State's first major gold rush. With neighbouring Talbot, Clunes was made a shire in 1965; while little more than a hamlet, it is still graced by some fine early buildings.

Clunies Ross family, administrators of the Cocos Islands and later noted in science. First to be known as 'King of the Cocos' was **John**, a Scottish sea-captain who settled in the Cocos (Keeling) Islands in 1827, bringing labourers to develop and improve the native coconut crop. He and his descendants increased plantations, imported machinery, built mills and workshops, and established a stable community. John's son, **John George**, who devised the simple legal code adopted in the settlements, was formally appointed superintendent when the islands were declared part of the British dominions in 1857. It was his son, **George**, who in 1886 was granted a perpetual lease on the islands by Queen Victoria; George also launched a settlement on Christmas Island (Indian Ocean) and shared in the establishment of the prosperous Christmas Island Phosphate Co. Most notable in this century was **Sir Ian** (1899–1959), scientist, b. Bathurst, NSW. He held appointments at the University of Sydney and at the CSIR, and was president of the Australian Institute of International Affairs 1941–5. He became first chairman of the CSIRO (the reconstituted CSIR) in 1949 and was instrumental in developing its work for the wool industry. Public recognition of his outstanding work included the establishment in 1959 of the Ian Clunies Ross memorial foundation to further scientific research and technology throughout Australia.

Clyde Co. This agricultural company was established in Vic. in 1836. Presided over by Tas. settlers Patrick Wood and Philip Russell, and formed in association with five Glasgow merchants, the company acquired land near Geelong and stocked it with sheep and cattle. George Russell managed it throughout the economically difficult 1840s; it was dissolved, with considerable profit, in the 1850s.

Clyde River NSW In the southeast of the State, the Clyde River drains mostly forested country on the eastern edge of the southern tablelands, and empties into Batemans Bay. The river was once the main outlet for gold taken on the Braidwood and Araluen diggings.

Cnidaria Of this phylum of aquatic, mainly marine animals Australia has a great range, in three classes: > *hydrozoa*, including freshwater polyps, 'hydroid zoophytes' and bluebottles; Scyphozoa, roughly coinciding with > *jelly-fishes*; and Actinozoa, which includes the > *sea-anemones* and > *corals*. The Cnidaria are more or less radially symmetrical, of jelly-like consistency and with no blood or excretory system, the body cavity having only one opening. Most genera within these classes have some form of mechanism with which to paralyse and convey prey to the central mouth – some stings being harmful to humans – and there is a general tendency towards stages in the life cycle involving a stationary polyp stage, familiar from sea-anemones and coral polyps, and a more mobile medusa stage of swimming by expansion and contraction of a cup-shaped body, familiar from the jellyfishes.

coaches and coaching The first regular coach service in Australia was established by William Highland in 1814, to run from Sydney to Parramatta, Richmond and Windsor. Other small coach firms followed, using coaches manufactured in England and often quite unsuited to Australian conditions. By 1850, there were coach services from Sydney to Berrima, Goulburn and Yass, and an irregular service to Melbourne. The history of coaching in Australia is really, however, the story of one firm – Cobb & Co. Established in 1853 by Freeman Cobb and three fellow-Americans, Cobb & Co. introduced robust American-built coaches with leather springs, which made for a more comfortable journey. The firm's first service was from Melbourne to Port Melbourne, but was soon extended to the newly discovered

goldfields around Ballarat and Bendigo. Cobb sold the firm in 1859, but his name continued in use. Competition from the railways caused another American, James Rutherford, to move the headquarters of the firm to Bathurst, NSW, in 1862. The Cobb & Co. network soon straddled the eastern colonies, constantly extending inland as the railways encroached on its coastal routes and helping to open up remote areas. The last Cobb & Co. service ran in 1924 on the Yeulba–Surat route in Queensland. It is said that in 75 years of service Cobb & Co. had only four fatal accidents. Given fire, flood, bushrangers, and the state of the roads, this claim, if true, is a remarkable comment on the quality of the service.

coal Coal is Australia's single most valuable export by a long margin, and economically recoverable reserves are estimated to be 34Gt of black coal and 43Gt of brown coal. Although by no means the world's biggest producer, Australia is the major exporting nation, supplying 92 million t of raw black coal worth $5327 million to overseas markets in 1986, over 40% of it to Japan. Large quantities of steaming and coking coal were also exported, most of it going to fuel the Japanese steel industry.

Coal is found and mined in all Australian States except the NT. The industry's history dates from 1791, when coal was discovered in the Newcastle area of NSW; development swiftly followed, and it was coal that powered Australia in the first century after European settlement. The richest mines of high-quality bituminous coal are found in NSW and Qld, the major known reserves being located in the Sydney Basin and Bowen Basin of those States respectively.

The main mining areas in NSW are found in an arc around Sydney – from Wollongong in the south to Newcastle and the lower Hunter Valley in the north – and in a band from Lithgow to Mudgee; both underground and open-cut methods are used. In Qld, the main deposits are in the Galilee and Bowen Basins, in the central-east of the State. Major mines, which are mostly open-cut, include Blair Athol, Oaky Creek, Kianga-Moura and Newlands. The bulk of Qld coal is exported through Gladstone and purpose-built ports, such as Hay Point.

The dominant company in NSW and Qld coal-mining is BHP, which as well as owning mines uses about 15% of Australian-consumed black coal for its iron and steel production.

Other major companies in the industry include MIM Holdings Ltd, Conzinc Riotinto of Australia Ltd, British Petroleum and Coal and Allied Industries Ltd.

Medium-quality sub-bituminous coal is mined in WA, SA and Tas. Production is on a relatively small scale, the major part being used for local electricity generation. Brown coal (lignite) is mined only in Vic., mainly in the Latrobe Valley by open-cut methods. Because of its low energy value and high water content it is not practical or economic to transport brown coal long distances and most is used by the State Electricity Commission for electricity generation on site, a small percentage being made into briquettes for industry and domestic consumption.

Both federal and State governments play an important role in the control and development of the industry. A Joint Coal Board was established in 1946 between the Commonwealth and NSW to regulate production and, importantly, to oversee the health and safety of workers in an industry notorious for its dangers. A Queensland Coal Board with similar responsibilities was established in 1947. General government policy is co-ordinated through the Australian Minerals and Energy Council, established in 1976, to provide a forum for State energy ministers.

coastal features > *geology and major landforms*

Coastwatchers The Coastwatchers were civilian volunteer intelligence personnel, originally formed in 1919 to observe potential attackers off the Australian coast. They achieved most fame and note for their work behind Japanese lines in PNG and the Pacific Islands from 1942, with great feats of courage and severe losses.

Cobar NSW (pop. 4287) The State's principal copper producer, Cobar lies 706km northwest of Sydney. Copper was first detected in the region in the 1860s and mining has since continued periodically, although development has been greatest since the 1960s. The surrounding region is largely pastoral although further mineral deposits – notably lead, zinc and silver – are also mined.

Cobb & Co. > *coaches and coaching*

Cobourg Peninsula NT A narrow peninsula at the northwestern tip of Arnhem Land, it extends for about 100km, flanked by the Arafura Sea and Van Diemen Gulf. The most westerly point is Cape Don. At Port Essington and Raffles Bay, on the deeply indented northern shore, settlements were established early last century, but proved unsuccessful. The peninsula is now a wildlife sanctuary and flora reserve.

Coburn, John (1925–), artist, b. Ingham, Qld. Coburn's outstanding public work is the set of tapestry curtains commissioned for the Sydney Opera House. They were woven at Aubusson in France – famous since the 15th century for its tapestries and carpets – where he supervised production of a number of his tapestry designs. Coburn lived in France 1969–72, after which time he returned to become head of the National Art School in Sydney, 1972–4.

cockatiel > *parrots*

Cockatoo Island NSW Lying just within the mouth of the Parramatta River, this 16 ha sandstone island was originally a prison. In 1851 work began to establish it as a dockyard, and although remaining also a prison for some years – it accommodated a women's reformatory as late as 1910 – it has since become a major Australian centre for shipbuilding and refitting. A naval dockyard 1913–21 and then transferred to the Commonwealth Shipping Board, since 1933 it has been leased to and operated by Vickers Cockatoo Dockyard Pty Ltd. The island was a base for building and refitting during both world wars, and now also services submarines.

Cockatoo Island WA Owned by Dampier Mining Co. Ltd, a subsidiary of BHP Ltd, Cockatoo Island is in Yampi Sound off the Kimberley coast in northwest WA. It is a source of rich iron-ore deposits; mining operations began in 1951, but reserves cannot be completely exploited since it is uneconomic to mine below sea-level.

cockatoos > *parrots*

Cockburn Sound WA A large natural harbour south of Fremantle, Cockburn Sound extends north–south for about 15km; it is bounded on the south and east by the mainland and on the west by Garden Island, which is linked to the mainland by a causeway. Since the 1950s it has been developed as a major part of Fremantle's outer harbour, serving the Kwinana oil refinery and major shipping; in 1978 the naval base, HMAS *Stirling*, was established there. The sound was named after a British admiral Sir George Cockburn.

cockroaches Primitive insects of the order Blattodea, with flattened bodies, chewing mouthparts and spiny legs, most cockroaches prefer to conceal themselves under bark, stones or logs, and tend to be nocturnal. Apart from such introduced cosmopolitan species as the Oriental, American and German cockroaches, – those commonly found in houses and other man-made structures – Australia has a rich native fauna of more than 450 species, many of which are very colourful. They range from the tiny foliage-dwellers of the genus *Ellipsidion* to the much larger and aptly named burrower *Macropanesthia rhinocerus*, of tropical Qld.

Cocos (Keeling) Islands Believed to have been discovered in 1609 by Captain William Keeling of the East India Company, this Australian territory in the Indian Ocean is made up of 27 islands in two separate atolls. The southern atoll is composed of a horseshoe-shaped chain enclosing a central lagoon, but the northern one is a single island, North Keeling; in no place is the land more than 6m above sea-level. Of the group, only Home Island and West Island are inhabited; the others are visited to harvest the coconuts they bear. The islands were originally settled in 1826 by an Englishman, Alexander Hare, followed in 1827 by John Clunies Ross (> *Clunies Ross family*), who proceeded – with the help of Malay workers, brought mainly from Java – to improve the indigenous coconut trees and establish the islands' sole industry, copra production. While paternalistic, the regime established by the Clunies Ross family was by the 1940s deemed to be 'a monument to good government'.

This small, self-contained territory has in the past twice assumed international importance: as a cable station in World Wars 1 and 2, and – with construction of an airport on West Island – as a link in the Australia–South Africa air route. In 1955 the islands became a territory of the Commonwealth of Australia, although administrative costs for Home Island were borne by the Clunies Ross family until the 1970s. Following a UN report on the islands in 1974, a number of changes were implemented in the

areas of health, finance and administration. John Clunies Ross relinquished his inherited rights of ownership to the Australian government in 1978, for an estimated \$6.25 million. The islands' first elected local council was instituted in 1979.

cods In Australia, these are marine fishes of the family Moridae (related to the North Atlantic cod), all of which have a fleshy filament on the chin. The bearded or red cod, *Pseudophycis barbatus,* is an important commercial fish in Tas. >> *butterfly cods*; *Murray cod*; *rock-cods*

Coe, Kelvin (1946–), dancer, b. Melbourne. Coe won a silver medal at the 1973 International Ballet Competition in Moscow and was subsequently invited to appear as a guest artist with the Bolshoi Ballet. He has been an outstanding member of the Australian Ballet and makes regular guest appearances with the company. Graeme Murphy created the ballet *Homelands* for Coe, who danced it with the Sydney Dance Company in New York in 1985 and later appeared in Murphy's *Beyond Twelve* (1987).

Coffs Harbour NSW (pop. 18 074) A timber port and popular seaside resort often dubbed the capital of the mid-north coast, Coffs Harbour lies 580km north of Sydney. It has recently undergone substantial industrial, retail and tourist development. The local area produces bananas, vegetables, dairy products and fish.

Colac Vic. (pop. 10 545) On the shore of Lake Colac 150km southwest of Melbourne, this city is the centre for the Western District's grazing and farming activities. It also has engineering, timber, masonry and brick-making industries. Colac developed on a coach route from Melbourne (now followed by the Princes Highway) in the mid-19th century and later became a rail centre; it still has some fine colonial buildings.

Coleoptera > *beetles*

Coles family, five brothers who founded G. J. Coles and Co., a retail firm now part of the giant Coles-Myer corporation. **Sir George James** (1885–1977), b. Jung, Vic., opened the original store in Collingwood, Vic., in 1914; modelled on the 'five and dime' stores of

F.W. Woolworth in the US, it carried the motto 'Nothing over a shilling'. His brothers **Sir Arthur William** (1892–1982), **Sir Kenneth Frank** (1896–1985) and **Sir Edgar Barton** (1899–1981) joined the firm in 1919 and **Sir Norman Cameron** (1907–89) in 1924; the brothers were all notable in Australian civic affairs and Sir Arthur served in the Vic. parliament 1940–6. G.J. Coles & Co. expanded interstate in the 1920s and eventually became one of Australia's largest retail chains, by the 1970s incorporating supermarkets and discount stores. It merged with Myer in the 1980s.

colleges of advanced education > *education*

Collie WA (pop. 7829) Servicing the State's only coalfield, Collie lies inland of Bunbury some 200km southeast of Perth. The surrounding jarrah forests are being cleared increasingly for sheep grazing but still conceal the open cuts and waste-heaps of the underground mines. The town and nearby river were named after Alexander Collie, an explorer and administrator of Albany 1831–3. The Collie River was dammed from the 1930s and provides irrigation as well as town and farm water supplies in the region.

Collins, David (1756–1810), colonial administrator, b. England. Collins, a military officer, was notable in three capacities in early Australian settlement: as judge-advocate in NSW (1788–96); as founder of Hobart Town and lt-governor of Van Diemen's Land 1804-10; and as historian for his work *An Account of the English Colony in New South Wales* (1798). In 1803 he was sent to establish a new settlement at Port Phillip, but considered it unsuitable and obtained permission to move to Van Diemen's Land. His administration there faced many difficulties, not least among them being repeated shortages of food, the arrival of Norfolk Island settlers, and the appearance in Hobart of the importunate William Bligh, whose demands for support Collins rejected.

Collins, Tom > *Furphy, Joseph*

Colombo Plan > *foreign aid*

colonial administration Until Federation in 1901, all six of the present Australian States were separate colonies. By 1856, all except Qld (not yet separated from NSW) and WA

had achieved a form of self-government, but this was won only gradually and the degree to which it was representative is questionable. That responsible government was not achieved for more than 50 years after European settlement reflects partly the political climate of the day but also the socio-economic development of the colonies. British governments of the 19th century, although not enamoured of democracy, had learnt from the American Revolution that some degree of self-government was necessary if colonies of settlement were to remain loyal to the Crown. Self-government was obviously not applicable to colonies such as NSW and Tas. (called Van Diemen's Land until 1855) while they were still predominantly penal settlements, as were Qld (then the Moreton Bay District of NSW) until the 1840s and WA 1849-68. Similarly, until SA and Vic. had a sufficient European population and were economically self-supporting the question of self-government did not arise there either.

NSW was ruled 1788–1823 by governors with despotic powers, subject only to intervention by the British government. The 1808 Rum Rebellion, by which the NSW Corps overthrew Governor Bligh, did not alter the form of administration, it simply usurped the governor's authority. From 1823 NSW had a nominated (not elected) legislative council to assist the governor; similar forms of administration existed in Tas. after its separation from NSW in 1825, and in SA from its settlement by Europeans in 1836; WA fell into the same pattern in 1832, having been ruled by a governor from settlement in 1829 (the 1826 Albany settlement was at first governed from NSW). In NSW and Tas. the fight for self-government was fought mainly by large land-holders and its aim – eventually achieved – was government *by* large land-holders. In 1841 NSW achieved a legislative council, one-third of which was nominated and two-thirds elected on a property-based franchise. Vic. (then still the Port Phillip District of NSW) elected five members to that council but soon demanded self-government. In 1850, largely as a result of agitation by Vic., it was separated from NSW and with SA and Tas. was granted a legislative council on the NSW model. WA, by then a penal colony with only a small European population, was not considered ready for a partly elected government and did not follow the NSW model until 1870.

The power of these partly elected legislative councils was still in many respects subject to the governors, and because of a limited franchise they represented only a select few of the colonists. The growing number of free settlers and native-born continued to agitate for a more representative form of government, and eventually succeeded. Legislative councils continued to exist – in some cases still nominated (theoretically so until 1978 in NSW), in others elected on a limited franchise – but were relegated to the role of upper houses, although still with considerable powers. Lower houses came into being in NSW, Tas., Vic. and SA by 1856, with similar systems becoming established in Qld on its separation from NSW in 1859, and in WA in 1890. (The lower houses were called legislative assemblies in NSW, Vic., Qld and WA, and houses of assembly in Tas. and SA.) The franchise varied from colony to colony: SA introduced adult (over 21) male suffrage in 1856 – the first government in the world to do so – and by 1900 all the other colonies had followed suit. The secret ballot was introduced in Vic. and SA in 1856, in NSW and Tas. in 1858, in Qld in 1859 and in WA in 1877; and plural voting was progressively abolished (in NSW and SA in 1893, Vic. in 1899, Tas. in 1900, Qld in 1905, and WA in 1907).

By 1890, accordingly, representative government of a kind existed throughout Australia. Britain's Australian colonies remained just that, however: the Colonial Laws Validity Act, passed by the British parliament in 1865, stated that future British statutes would apply in the Australian colonies only if the British parliament so dictated and that Acts passed in the colonies were valid so long as they were not 'repugnant' to British law. This Act applied in Australia until 1942, when the Australian government, albeit reluctantly, ratified the Statute of Westminster (passed by the British parliament in 1931) which stipulated that Britain could no longer legislate for the dominions unless they so requested. In 1986, Australia did so request and the British, federal and State parliaments passed legislation exempting the States (as opposed to the Commonwealth) from the Act. The question of when Australia ceased to be a British colony is thus open to debate. >> *government*; *law and legal system*; *States, origins and boundaries*

comb-jellies This is a popular name for members of the phylum Ctenophora, one of the great community of plankton. Also known as sea gooseberries, they are usually clear, globular animals, 1–2cm long, drifting in the surface waters of the sea, although there is some swimming power in the 'combs' – eight rows of movable, thread-like cilia; there are also two tentacles in pouches on opposite sides of the body. *Neis cordigera*, a larger specimen (10cm), sometimes produces spectra in the waters of Sydney Harbour, and phosphorescence by night.

Committee for Economic Development (CEDA) An influential independent organisation comprising both business leaders and academics, CEDA has played an important role in all major economic debates in Australia since it was formed in 1960. Its stated aim is to encourage a better understanding of 'the problems of the economy and the ways in which they can be managed': it combines business and academic approaches in its research, the results of which are published in occasional papers and through seminars and conferences.

Commonwealth Day > *holidays and national days*

Commonwealth Games The formation of an Empire sports movement was proposed by J. Astley Cooper in 1891. The idea was supported enthusiastically in Australia, but the subsequent revival of the Olympic Games overshadowed Empire sport. The first official British Empire Games were held in Hamilton, Canada, in 1930. Australian venues have been Sydney in 1938, where Decima Norman won five gold medals; Perth in 1962, by which time the meeting was known as the Commonwealth Games; and Brisbane in 1982. Australia has generally performed well, both in mainstream sports and in those where competitors are usually outclassed at Olympic Games. Outstanding individual achievements have been recorded by Dave Power (athletics, 1958), Murray Rose (swimming, 1962), Raelene Boyle (athletics, 1970 and 1974), Michael Wenden (swimming, 1974), Tracey Wickham (swimming, 1978), Robert de Castella (marathon, 1982 and 1986) and Lisa Martin (swimming, 1988).

Commonwealth Scientific and Industrial Research Organisation > *CSIRO*; *science and technology*

Commonwealth–State relations > *Constitution*; *federalism*

communications technology Communications technology has undergone revolutionary change since World War 2 as systems developed for military use were modified to meet peace-time needs. The marriage of communications technologies with the techniques of electronic data-processing has assisted this transformation, and changes to the regulatory control of telecommunications in most industrialised countries have enabled computer suppliers to enter the market for communications equipment, and telecommunications carriers to sell computers. The integration of the two fields has been assisted by services such as videotex, electronic mail and information retrieval that draw on both the computing and communications technologies. Computers are now electromechanical systems, thus reducing maintenance, making fault-finding easier and reducing installation and operating costs. Electronic systems also allow new services to be introduced, making the telephone network, for example, resemble a giant computer in its capacity to be reprogrammed, and revolutionising basic services such as banking.

Transmission media and techniques have moved beyond copper and aluminium to coaxial cable, which has much more band width, and can thus carry television images. Telecom Australia's coaxial cable network links all major cities and transmits a mixture of voice and data traffic, some at very high speeds using digital techniques. From the late 1980s, that network was supplemented by fibre-optic links, which transmit information by light waves; fibre-optic submarine cables linking Australia to other countries will come into operation in the early 1990s. Telecom's long-distance voice and data networks make extensive use of conventional and digital microwave transmission – a development of wartime radar. Radio signals received and transmitted by satellite are also used for distributing television traffic and for some data services by both Aussat and Telecom, as well as for overseas communications through the Overseas Telecommunications Commission.

Widespread use of computers in government, commerce and business has sharply increased the amount of data traffic on telecommunications networks. Specialised networks for data transmitted at very high speed link the major population centres, and the 'Auspak' message-switching network is used for lower-speed applications such as inform-ation retrieval from data bases or through videotex services. The telex network, which carries traffic between teleprinters within Australia and through international switchboards to overseas countries is being challenged by facsimile transmission (fax), which uses the public telephone network. Facsimile machines employing digital techniques of data compression are able to transmit at higher speeds and lower costs over long distances. >> *post and telecommunications*; *science and technology*

communism There are several small communist parties and sects in Australia. Of the parties that retain some trade-union influence, the Communist Party of Australia (Marxist-Leninist) split from the Communist Party of Australia (CPA) in 1963 in support of Maoism, and the Moscow-oriented Socialist Party of Australia (SPA) was formed in 1971 – a breakaway prompted by the CPA's denunciation of the 1968 Soviet invasion of Czechoslovakia; a third organisation, the Democratic Socialist Party, was never part of the CPA but began as a Trotskyist group, the Socialist Workers Party. The CPA itself, with some 1300 members in 1984 and half that number by the end of the decade, has had a chequered career. Formed in 1920 and 'Stalinised' in the 1930s, it gained control in major unions and during World War 2 boasted some 24 000 members. It survived attempts by R. G. Menzies to ban it in 1950, following Soviet policies until it moved more towards democratic socialism from the late 1960s. Its influence continued to decline and the party had dissolved itself by 1990.

computers > *communications technology*; *electronics industry*; *science and technology*

conciliation and arbitration In Australia, both federal and State legislation makes it compulsory for unresolved disputes between trade unions and employers to be settled by independent tribunals; more than 85% of the Australian workforce is affected by such decisions. Although recourse to the system is mandatory, there is a general reluctance to enforce the legislation as this has generally proved counter-productive in the past. When the principle of conciliation and arbitration was adopted at the turn of the century, in the aftermath of the great strikes of the 1890s, it was envisaged that the tribunals would deal principally with strikes and lockouts. The system was soon, however, extended to 'paper disputes' involving written logs of claims covering many aspects of employment. Today the Conciliation and Arbitration Commission also plays a leading role in national economic issues.

In the 19th century there was general disagreement among the colonies as to the most appropriate method of resolving industrial disputes. NZ adopted a system of compulsory arbitration in 1894 and its success encouraged WA and NSW to follow suit by the end of the century. All States except Vic. have since adopted the system; the Vic. process is in fact similar, but uses wages boards rather than tribunals. A federal system was instituted in 1904 with the Conciliation and Arbitration Act, which established the Commonwealth Arbitration Commission. This body has been reconstituted periodically since that time: in 1956 it was separated into the Conciliation and Arbitration Commission and the Industrial Court of Australia, and from 1976 the Industrial Court became the Industrial Division of the Federal Court. As an increasing number of trade unions have organised themselves on a national basis, a growing proportion of disputes are now affected by federal awards.

Conciliation of industrial disputes under the guidance of a tribunal member is usually successful. If it fails, the dispute is adjudicated by the tribunal and the resulting settlement is formalised as an award that is legally enforceable. Award provisions prescribe minimum employer obligations and employee entitlements, and override any inconsistent terms in individual contracts: an agreement between employer and employee that wages will be below the award rate is not binding, for example, whereas an agreement for employment terms that are better than the award provision (such as over-award wages, or shorter hours) is enforceable unless an award stipulates maximum as well as minimum terms. Industrial tribunals also set standards and guidelines for dealing uniformly with some common disputes, especially those that have economy-wide effects. The national wage decisions of the federal tribunal – to which governments as well as unions and employers make submissions – are the best-known example, and there are occasional test cases on other matters such as hours, leave, termination of employment, and superannuation.

Because of limitations on federal legislation in the Constitution, as interpreted by the High Court, the powers of the federal industrial tribunal have been narrower than those of the State bodies. The federal system has nevertheless predominated, and its influence is likely to increase as a result of decisions of the High Court in the 1980s which have given more liberal interpretations of federal power. >> *industrial disputes*; *trade unions*; *wage determination*

Condamine River Qld In the southeast of the State, the Condamine rises on the western slopes of the Great Dividing Range. About 700km long, the river flows northwest through the Darling Downs, then turns west and southwest to become the Balonne River which in turn becomes part of the Darling-Murray system; thus the Condamine waters flow more than 3000km to the sea. The river was named by Allan Cunningham for T. de la Condamine, an aide to Governor Darling.

Conder, Charles Edward (1868–1909), painter, b. England. Conder came to Australia in 1884. A poetic painter, he was influenced by the art of Girolamo Nerli and was later a member of the Heidelberg School. He contributed 46 works and designed the catalogue cover for the famous 9 x 5 Exhibition, held in Melbourne in 1889. He returned to Europe in 1890, soon establishing himself as an artist and associating with a fashionable coterie including Henri de Toulouse-Lautrec, Oscar Wilde and painter William Rothenstein. Symbolism and Art Nouveau replaced his Australian Impressionism, and his delicate watercolours on silk fans won him wide acclaim.

cone shells > *gastropods*

Congregational Church > *Uniting Church*

conifers These cone-bearing trees and shrubs are generally regarded as representing an earlier stage of evolution than the flowering plants that now dominate the world's vegetation. Australia has a number of interesting conifer genera, some of which are endemic; the major conifer family, Pinaceae, is virtually restricted to the northern hemisphere, although many of its species (most notably *Pinus radiata*) have been introduced to Australia for timber or ornament.

The worldwide cypress family, Cupressaceae, contains the largest genus of native conifers, *Callitris*, consisting of fourteen species endemic to Australia and two to New Caledonia. Chief among these is the white cypress-pine, *C. glaucophylla,* which dominates the vegetation in parts of NSW and central Qld, yielding a useful, termite-resistant timber. The small genus *Actinostrobus* is endemic to the far southwest of Australia; and two further genera are endemic to Tas., the most important being *Athrotaxis*, which comprises the King Billy pine, *A. selaginoides*, and pencil pine, *A. cupressoides* – both slow-growing mountain tress yielding fine close-grained timber.

The family Araucariaceae consists of two genera only, both of which are represented in Australia. The genus *Araucaria* of tall and straight-stemmed trees includes the hoop pine, *A. cunninghamii*, which is widespread in rainforest along coastal ranges of Qld and NSW; the bunya pine, *A. bidwillii*, which is restricted in the wild to the Brisbane region and the mountains of northern Qld; and the endemic Norfolk Island pine, *A. heterophylla*, which has been widely planted as an ornamental. The genus *Agathis* includes three native species of kauri, the best known being the huge Queesland kauri, *A. robusta*.

The family Podocarpaceae, like the Araucariaceae, is characteristic of the early Tertiary forests of Gondwana. Most widespread is the plum-pine genus, *Podocarpus*, several species of which occur in rainforests or high mountains of the east coast and Tas.; two shrub species occur in sandy open forest in NSW and southwest WA. The mountain plum-pine, *P. lawrencei*, is a gnarled small tree or prostrate shrub of NSW and Tas.; the taller coastal brown pine, *P. elatus*, of Qld and NSW, has edible purple-black seed-stalks. The Tas. huon pine, *Lagarostrobos franklinii*, is restricted to river gorges of the rugged southwest: it lives to 2000 years or more and yields an exceptionally fine-grained tough timber, now scarce owing to past exploitation.

conscription During World War 1, compulsory military service was rejected narrowly in two referendums, 1916 and 1917, both proposed by W. M. Hughes. A growing disillusionment with the progress and aims of the war had dampened earlier enthusiasm, and the referendum campaigns, especially the second, saw unparalleled bitterness and division. During World War 2, compulsory military training was introduced soon after war began. In the initial stages, only volunteer troops of the AIF were sent to overseas theatres, but conscripts were later dispatched to fight in PNG and a defined sector of the southwest Pacific. There was no conscription during the Korean War,

but in 1965 it was reintroduced on a ballot basis for 20-year-old men. In 1966 conscripts were sent to fight in Vietnam, a situation that resulted in draft evasion and widespread social and political protest. Conscription was ended by the Whitlam government in 1972 and there has been no compulsory military service in Australia since then.

conservation > *environment and conservation; fauna; flora; heritage conservation*

Constitution Australia's Commonwealth Constitution was drafted by parliamentary and legal representatives at conferences held in 1891 and 1897-8. Once approved by referendum, the Constitution was passed by the British parliament on 9 July 1900 and came into force on 1 January 1901. With the benefit of earlier experiments in federation (especially in the US) and the heritage of British parliamentary development, the drafters of the Constitution produced a masterly compromise well suited to conditions in the newly united country.
Legislative and executive power The main subject of the Constitution is the national system of government, although it upholds the continued operation of the State constitutions, legislatures and laws. The Constitution sets out the structure and powers of the national government and judicature; it is left to the parliament itself to prescribe the actual number of parliamentarians, the qualifications for election, and the voting system.

The legislative powers of the two houses of parliament are equal for most purposes: legislation can be introduced in either house and must be approved by both. There are two major exceptions to this rule. The first is the provision for a joint sitting of both houses in the event of a parliamentary deadlock and double dissolution: there have been six double dissolutions since Federation (in 1914, 1951, 1974, 1975, 1983 and 1987), but only one joint sitting (in 1974). The other exception concerns financial legislation, whereby while the House of Representatives has the sole right to introduce most appropriation and taxation bills, the Senate does have the power to reject them.

The actual processes of national government owe much to conventions that supplement the Constitution, which does not in fact refer to the government, to the Opposition, or even to the prime minister. The custom of government being formed by the majority party in the lower house, for example, derives primarily from the control of that house over financial legislation; equally, Australia's traditional system of parliamentary government rests mainly on the constitutional requirement that ministers be members of parliament.

Conventions are also important in controlling the extensive powers conferred on the governor-general – to summon and dissolve parliament, assent to legislation, appoint and dismiss ministers, exercise the Commonwealth's executive power, establish government departments, be commander-in-chief of the armed forces, and appoint judges. The governor-general traditionally relies on the advice of government ministers, usually through the federal Executive Council, although a noted exception occurred in 1975 when the governor-general exercised his discretionary powers and dismissed the prime minister (> *constitutional crisis 1975*).

Commonwealth and State powers Another major subject of the Constitution is the division of authority between the Commonwealth and the States. The specified legislative powers of the federal parliament include the regulation of commerce, communications, and interstate industrial disputes; and areas where national or uniform laws are desirable, such as defence, external affairs, immigration, and marriage and divorce. The law-making powers of the State parliaments are not defined and they may legislate in any area not specifically ascribed to the Commonwealth. If federal and State laws conflict, the former prevail.

The Commonwealth has greatly expanded its responsibilities since Federation and now exerts a substantial influence in areas once thought to be the responsibility primarily of the States – such as health, education, housing, transport, environment, and urban development. This has mainly arisen as the result of interpretations of the Constitution made by the High Court: under its external-affairs powers, for example, the Commonwealth can regulate internal matters while fulfilling international treaty obligations (as has occurred in relation to both the construction of dams and logging in areas on the World Heritage List). Rulings by the High Court have also enabled the Commonwealth to regulate nationally on such matters as aviation and trade practices, although earlier attempts to confer such powers on the federal governement were defeated at referendum. The High Court has also accepted that the Commonwealth may use its constitutional power of imposing conditions on

financial grants to the States, thus influencing State policies and budgets.

Equity The Constitution includes explicit provisions to ensure that the federal system operates fairly. It stipulates, for example, that the Commonwealth must not discriminate against the States when imposing taxes or regulating commerce, that interstate commerce must be free, and that one State must not discriminate against the residents of another. There are also a number of more general provisos, such as the requirement that the Commonwealth must allow the free exercise of religion and must pay fair compensation when property is compulsorily acquired. Otherwise, the Constitution includes very few guarantees of individual or human rights: it does not precisely state, for example, that all adults have the right to vote for the federal parliament, that voting will be secret, or that every vote will have equal value.

Altering the Constitution The Constitution also defines the procedures for its own amendment. A proposal to amend the Constitution must be initiated by the federal parliament and approved at a referendum by a majority of electors both nationally and in a majority of States. In practice this has proved very difficult and only eight of 42 referendum proposals have been approved. Constitutional reform has, nonetheless, been a mattter of repeated concern: among the bodies that have made proposals for extensive amendment of the Constitution are the royal commission on the Constitution in 1929, a parliamentary committee on constitutional review in 1959, and a constitutional convention appointed by the Whitlam government and which held six sessions 1973–85. A commission set up in 1988 proposed amendments to virtually every aspect of the Constitution: expansion of Commonwealth legislative powers, greater financial independence for the States, limitation of the powers of the governor-general, more accurate description of the principles of parliamentary government, introduction of human rights guarantees, modernisation of the electoral process, reform of the national judicial system, and repeal of outmoded provisions. >> *federalism; Federation; govern ment; law and legal system; referendums*

constitutional crisis 1975 This series of events, centred on the dismissal in 1975 of the Whitlam Labor government by the governor-general Sir John Kerr, polarised the Australian community and engendered longstanding debate about the most appropriate methods of interpreting the > *Constitution*. The Whitlam government was re-elected in 1974 after a double dissolution of parliament: it did not have a majority in the Senate and its strength was further reduced in 1975 when – in breach of parliamentary convention – both the NSW and Qld parliaments decided not to appoint the Labor nominee to the Senate vacancy caused in each case by the departure of a Labor senator. During 1975 a deadlock developed between the two houses when the Senate deferred the government's supply bills, which included fundamental budgetary legislation – a further break with convention, in this case that the Senate will grant the government the necessary funds for its operation. Rather than requesting another double dissolution, Whitlam advised the governor-general to call a half-Senate election: also flying in the face of convention by invoking the reserve powers accorded to him under the Constitution, the governor-general instead withdrew Whitlam's commission as prime minister (on the grounds that his government could not guarantee supply) and appointed Opposition leader Malcolm Fraser as caretaker prime minister. The supply bills were then passed by the Senate, and an election for both Houses, held on 13 December under the deadlock provisions of the Constitution, brought the Fraser government to power.

consumer credit Hire purchase and, more recently, credit cards have been the basis of consumer credit in Australia. The growth of banks, building societies, credit unions and finance companies has been closely tied to the rise of consumer debt throughout the 20th century, which in Australia exceeded $25 billion in 1989. Today credit is increasingly easy to acquire and competition between the providers is fierce: with the promise of instant gratification often being irresistible, there is increasing concern at the level of debt carried by Australian households (an average of $1300 per person). Since the 1970s there has been increasing legislation to protect the rights of consumers and increasing debate over the ethical and social responsibilities of the institutions offering products on credit.

Hire purchase was introduced in Australia in the 1860s. The first period of major growth occurred after 1918, however, with the advent of mass-produced motor cars: although radios, home appliances and televisions were gradu-

ally added to the list, cars have always been the main consumer-credit item.

Hire-purchase finance in Australia reached a peak of £29 million in 1938, declined during World War 2, and then went through its most rapid period of growth in the 1950s to reach about £500 million by 1960. Finance institutions grew dramatically during this period and banks responded by buying up many of the major companies so as to keep control of the market. The use of hire purchase was much more restrained during the 1960s as a credit squeeze in 1962 discouraged lending and banks increased the provision of personal loans.

In 1974 the first credit cards – Bankcard – were issued by Australian banks in a joint venture whereby they shared administration costs and charged identical interest rates. Bankcard revolutionised consumer credit for several reasons: it was uniform for all banks, it provided interest-free funds for 55 days, and above all it was convenient as customers could borrow for goods without applying for a loan each time. Although its interest rate, at 18% a year, was higher than other forms of credit, the convenience factor made Bankcard extremely popular. While interest rates rose generally during the 1970s, the Bankcard rate remained the same and there was a boom in consumer credit.

During the 1980s, the increasing internationalisation of business and banking, together with more tourism, made major international credit cards such as MasterCard and Visa more popular. A wide range of credit cards is now available and the electronic transfer of funds has made cashless shopping even more widespread. While legislation covering consumer credit has been in force since the 1930s, more specific Acts have been introduced in most States since the 1970s and consumers are generally better informed about their rights and obligations. >> *retail trade*

consumer price index (CPI) The most common measure of the rate of inflation and changes in the cost of living, the CPI documents the retail prices of a range of basic goods and services, from food and clothing to housing and education. Current prices are expressed as a percentage of prices in the base year, and inflation is calculated as the percentage change each year. The CPI is prepared by the Australian Bureau of Statistics and since 1960 has been published quarterly for the seven State capitals and Canberra (separately and combined). While the index is commonly used as a basis for wage negotiations, it is generally considered inadequate as a barometer of economic conditions.

consumer protection 'Let the buyer beware' expresses the traditional attitude of common law to consumers. In the last 30 years, however, increasingly effective protections and remedies have been provided for consumers through legislation and through organisations established by both the government and independent interests. The principal aim of consumer-protection legislation is to ensure that buyers of goods and services know exactly what their rights and obligations are before they enter a transaction, which is particularly important in the difficult area of > *consumer credit*.

The federal and State governments – through their consumer-protection offices – receive and investigate consumer complaints and prosecute fraudulent or unfair traders; they also publish information on consumer protection and are responsible for safety standards. The principal legislative mechanisms are the Commonwealth Trade Practices Act 1974 and State Acts covering credit contracts and fair trading. The credit Acts, for example, require that consumers be given clear written details of a financial commitment before the contract is made, and regulate credit advertising. Consumer legislation has also given courts wide powers to set aside unjust consumer contracts and order appropriate remedies for aggrieved consumers.

Independent organisations also provide important services for consumers. The first such body was the Australian Consumers' Association, a non-profit organisation founded in 1959 to provide independent advice on goods and services in the marketplace. Based on the British consumer magazine *Which?*, its publication *Choice* (first published in 1960) continues to offer forthright information and product-testing for consumers as well as lobbying for legislative change in the field of consumer affairs.

continental drift This theory holds that the earth's continents have slowly changed their relative positions. The present configuration is believed to be the result of the division, 200 million years ago, of a single landmass, Pangaea; this split to create two 'supercontinents' – Laurasia in the north and > *Gondwana* in the south. The latter in its turn gradually frag-

mented to form the continents of the southern hemisphere.

convicts and transportation Exile to overseas prison settlements was devised by Britain in the early 18th century as a punitive measure for more than 200 crimes from petty thieving to crimes of violence, and including political offences. The achievement of American independence in 1776 prevented further transportation there, and after a period of crowding in gaols and old boat hulks the suggestion of using newly discovered Botany Bay was seized on; the first consignment of convicts was dispatched to the Australian colonies under Arthur Phillip in the First Fleet in 1787. Contract payment per head to ships' masters led to appalling conditions on the convict voyages until 1802, when more control was established. Transportation continued to NSW (which then included Moreton Bay and Port Phillip) until 1840; to Tas. until 1852; and SA used some convict labour. An estimated 165 000 convicts were transported, the majority between 1820 and 1840; in 1836, of Britain's 14 000 convicted felons 4400 were transported. While a few were minor offenders, political exiles and spirited rogues, the majority were the recidivist poor of Britain's urban, industrialising society. Much debate has ensued about both the real motives for the British government's adoption of the transportation system and the character of the convicts.

Abolition of transportation was primarily stimulated from Britain, notably by the Protestant archbishop of Dublin, who pointed out that neither its deterrent nor its reforming functions were demonstrable. Opposition developed in the colonies themselves from the increasing numbers of free settlers, who resented the stigma of a penal colony and feared the labour competition. The squatters found common ground in wishing to prolong it, for their prosperity depended on cheap labour under the > *assignment system*; they yielded only when it was clear that transportation and self-government were incompatible. A committee on transportation (1837–8) revealed the sordid horrors of the system: a revised scheme of sending probationary prisoners was tried in the 1840s, but failed. Attempts to re-introduce transportation engendered near-rebellion in Sydney and Melbourne in 1849, and the convicts had to be sent to Moreton Bay. The eastern colonies officially ended transportation in 1852, but the system persisted in WA until 1868.

Coober Pedy SA (pop. 2103) This singular opal-mining town in the arid heart of the State, some 930km northwest of Adelaide, was established after 1915 when opals were first discovered. Most of the white population live underground to escape the extreme summer heat and winter cold; this gave rise to the Aboriginal name of *kupa piti*, meaning 'white man's burrow'. Opals are gouged from shallow shafts, the fields extending for some 40km around the settlement.

Cook, James (1728–79), navigator and explorer, b. England. 'I am one who has ambition not only to go further than any one has done before but as far as it is possible for a man to go.' Cook, one of the great men of all time, was apprenticed to Whitby coal shippers before joining the navy as an able seaman in 1755. In the Seven Years War in Europe, and in America, his abilities as leader, cartographer, observer and surveyor (especially of the St Lawrence River and Newfoundland after the war) led to promotion, and in 1768, in command of the *Endeavour*, he was sent by the Admiralty and the Royal Society to the Pacific primarily to observe the 'passage of the planet Venus over the Disk of the Sun on 3rd June [1769]' along with Charles Green, Joseph Banks and Daniel Solander. Cook also had sealed orders: 'whereas there is reason to imagine a Continent or land of great extent ... to proceed southwards in order to make discovery of the Continent above mentioned'. Cook was sceptical of the continent's existence, but having spent over six months charting the NZ coast he decided to return home via Van Diemen's Land, NG and the Cape of Good Hope. The prevailing winds carried him north of his intended route and on 19 April land was sighted and named Point Hicks. On 28 April Cook landed at Botany Bay, at first named Sting Ray Harbour. He did not consider this to be the 'great south land' he was sent to look for; he summed up its potentialities as barren in its natural state but capable of producing roots, grain and fruit, and of pasturing cattle. He observed the Aborigines with sympathy, not with the contempt expressed by previous explorers. He proceeded northwards, charting the east coast and landing three more times: the *Endeavour* was careened at Endeavour Bay (site of Cooktown). In August he reached and named Possession Island, and for King George claimed as NSW all the land north of 38°S.

In 1771 Cook, commanding *Resolution* and with *Adventure* under Tobias Furneaux, made another voyage in search of *terra australis incognita*. Sailing in high latitudes to regions of perpetual snow and ice, in 1773 he became the first man in history to enter the Antarctic Circle and observe the ice barrier. The remainder of that year was spent in exhaustive exploration of the South Pacific, proving that no other 'great south land' existed.

Cook's third voyage in 1777–9 was to seek a northern passage between the Pacific and the Atlantic; in this he was unsuccessful, but on the journey north to Bering Strait he discovered the Hawaiian islands. Returning to Hawaii early in 1779, in the course of a dispute with the natives Cook was killed. This lean, self-contained man, apparently without strong religious beliefs but with a passionate curiosity and dedication to work, left charts of the Pacific and its lands which remain valid today. That he discovered what was to become the focal area of a new continent was incidental – even accidental.

Cook, Sir Joseph (1860–1947), politician, b. England. Cook arrived in Australia in 1885 to pursue his trade of coal-mining but quickly entered Labor politics in NSW. He left the ALP over its caucus system, joined the Liberal Party, and subsequently rose through its ranks to succeed the party's NSW leader Sir George Reid. As leader of the Free Trade Party from 1908, he combined with the Liberal Party to form a Fusion government in 1909; he subsequently became leader of the Liberal Party, and prime minister in 1913. His government (elected with a majority of one) was defeated in 1914; Cook served in the National government 1917–20 before his retirement a year later.

Cook, William Delafield (1936–), artist, b. Melbourne. An expatriate since the 1970s, Cook renders his meticulous, photo-realist paintings and drawings with a refined classicism. An indefatigable traveller (in Europe, England, Japan and South America), he returns regularly to paint in Australia. Recent works evoke the timelessness of Arnhem Land and Kakadu.

Cooktown Qld (pop. 1300) This township at the mouth of the Endeavour River, 2120km north of Brisbane, was named in honour of James Cook whose ship was careened there in

1770. It was established in 1873 as a port for Palmer River goldfields; until the 1890s its population exceeded 20 000 (including many Chinese) but numbers fell rapidly after the gold-rush era. Cyclones in 1907, 1919 and 1949 discouraged permanent residents, but since the 1970s an upsurge in tourism has encourged an increase in both population and development.

coolabah > *eucalypts*

Coolgardie WA (pop. 989) A former gold-mining town 550km east of Perth, Coolgardie has its origins in a tent town that sprang up following the discovery of gold by Arthur Bayley ('Bayley's Reward') in 1892. In spite of acute water shortage, which caused disease and virtual evacuation in summer, the population of Coolgardie grew to 15 000 during its prosperous years, with a further 10 000 living in nearby camps. Kambalda, within the shire of Coolgardie, is the site of the State's first nickel mine and smelter. As with other former gold-fields, Coolgardie is a popular tourist destination; mining revived in the 1980s in response to high gold prices.

Cooma NSW (pop. 7406) A tourist centre on the southern tablelands, 440km southwest of Sydney, Cooma experienced its most rapid growth during construction of the Snowy Mountains hydro-electric scheme from the 1950s. The project attracted many immigrant workers, numbers of whom stayed on and gave the highland town a distinctively cosmopolitan air. Cooma is the headquarters of the scheme's controlling authority, as well as a base for visitors (skiers, walkers and fishing enthusiasts) to the Snowy Mountains.

Coombs, H. C. (Herbert Cole) (1906–), economist, b. Kalamunda, WA. Educated in Perth and at the London School of Economics, Coombs rose swiftly through the ranks of the Australian treasury before joining the Commonwealth Bank board in 1942. He became governor of that bank in 1949 and chairman in 1951, and inaugural chairman of the Reserve Bank in 1959. He retired from that position in 1968 to become first chairman of the Council for Aboriginal Affairs and the Australian Council for the Arts (now the Australia Council). As adviser to prime ministers William McMahon and Gough Whitlam in the 1970s, he was outspoken on both economic

and environmental issues. His publications include *Other People's Money* (1971).

Coonalpyn Downs > *Ninety Mile Desert*

Coonawarra SA This small vineyard district lies near Penola, about 60km north of Mt Gambier. Vines were first planted on its rich red soils in the 1890s, and although its overall contribution to wine production is small it has developed a very high reputation for red wines.

Cooper Creek Qld/SA Discovered in 1845 by Charles Sturt, who named it Cooper's Creek (the possessive is no longer used), this river is formed by the confluence of the Thomson and Barcoo rivers and runs across southwest Qld into northeast SA, towards Lake Eyre. It is one of the main streams of the Channel Country, flowing irregularly through usually arid land; its bed is often dry, and even when flowing its waters are divided among many shallow channels – only in extremely wet years will it actually reach the lake. Burke and Wills perished on its banks in 1861.

Coorong, the SA A narrow coastal lagoon which is both shallow and saline, the Coorong stretches over 125km behind the dunes of the Younghusband Peninsula – this and other similar formations resulting from past changes in the sea-level. At its west end, the Murray River cuts through to join the sea. The Coorong National Park, including both the lagoon and the peninsula, covers most of the area and contains a rich diversity of waterfowl.

coots > *rails and crakes*

Copland, Sir Douglas Berry (1894–1971), economist, b. NZ. Copland was the first vice-chancellor of the Australian National University (1948–52) and served on many NZ and Australian government committees, including the Brigden Committee on tariffs. He is best known for his work as economic adviser to governments during and after the 1930s depression; he was chairman of a committee formed in 1931 to advise State premiers on means of alleviating the subsequent economic problems, which resulted in the Premiers' Plan for government economy. In addition to holding directorships in many companies, he was Commonwealth Prices Commissioner 1939–49, and economic consultant to the prime minister 1941–5.

copper In 1986 Australian mine production of copper was 248 496t, about 2.9% of the world's output, the main producer being Chile.

Copper has been mined in all States and Territories, but today the main mines are Mt Isa in Qld, Mt Lyell in Tas., Cobar and Woodlawn in NSW, and Tennant Creek in the NT; the main refineries are at Mt Isa, Townsville, Rockhampton and Port Kembla. Owing to a lower output from the Warrego mine in the NT and the cessation of production at the Mt Gunson (SA) and Teutonic Bore (WA) mines, production of copper has been dropping in recent years. Once the mammoth Olympic Dam prospect in SA begins producing, however, this situation will change: discovered by Western Mining Corporation in 1975 on the Roxby Downs station near Andamooka, the prospect will be one of the world's largest copper-uranium-gold mines. An annual production of about 30 000t of refined copper is planned, but much is dependent on an adequate world price being maintained. Australia is an associate member of the Council of Copper Exporting Countries, an organisation aimed at regulating the international industry in order to achieve stable prices.

copperhead > *snakes*

copyright Copyright is a complex and often controversial area that has long been the focus of international agreements (and disagreements). While the principle of protecting the right of creators to exploit their product as they see fit is undisputed, it is commonly believed that prohibitions on the importation of copyright works have influenced both the price and availability of much material – particularly books and records – in Australia. Those opposed to this view consider that there are other factors involved and that the removal of copyright restrictions would not necessarily improve either the price or the availability of such goods.

In Australia, the Copyright Act 1968 forbids the copying of original literary, dramatic, musical and artistic works, sound recordings, films, TV and radio broadcasts, and computer software. Protection lasts 50 years after the death of the author of the copyright work, or in some cases 50 years after first publication. Australia is also a signatory to the two major international copyright agreements – the Berne Convention and the Universal Copyright Convention – through which works of Australian authors obtain virtually worldwide protection against copying, and authors from other countries are similarly protected in Australia.

Australian copyright law closely followed that of Britain and the US, although Australia was a world leader in areas such as photocopying by educational institutions and the home taping of records and broadcasts. Australia has not yet extended copyright protection to performers, however, or recognised the right of authors to object to alteration of their works once they have been sold. Obtaining the right balance between the interests of copyright owners to exploit their property and public access to copyright works is a continuing challenge for copyright law.

Proposals to modify the legislation are made periodically, and extensive amendments to the Copyright Act were made most recently in 1980 and 1986. A further review of the Act was initiated by the federal attorney-general in 1989; among the proposed amendments was the loss of copyright protection in Australia for titles first published overseas, if the book is not made available in Australia within a specified time.

coral fishes Beautifully coloured fishes of the family Chaetodontidae, generally found among coral reefs in Australian waters, these are also known as butterfly fishes. Many have a prominent black spot near the tail and a dark line through the eye, which apparently causes predators to attack the tail instead of the head. There are about 60 Australian species, some found as far south as Sydney and Wollongong. Angel fishes are a closely related group.

corals This is a popular name for a group of mainly colonial marine polyps of the phylum Cnidaria. Hard or stony corals secrete a calcium-carbonate base that accumulates to create great reefs; the living coral forms only a surface veneer, however, since the polyps can survive only in shallow water where sunlight reaches the algae that live within the coral and provide them with nutrients.

There are three main types of reef structure: coastal, fringing reefs, along the shore; barrier reefs that follow the edge of the continental shelf, of which Australia's > *Great Barrier Reef* is the best known example; and coral atolls around sunken volcanic islands. Reefs either grow or decline in accordance with varying sea-level and earth movement. In Australia, apart from the Barrier Reef, various examples are found across the tropical north and as far south as Carnarvon, WA.

Australia has a very rich coral fauna. The Alcyonarian or soft corals have eight branched tentacles: some are quite soft and yielding – as in the convoluted but cushion-like *Sacrophyton* – though with calcareous spicules within the tissues; others have more firm-to-massive skeletons in the colonies and, unlike the true or stony corals, retain their colouring after the death of the polyps.

The Scleractinian or stony corals have numerous tentacles, often in multiples of six, and the characteristic hard skeleton of the colony's home is coloured by symbiotic algae in life but is pure white when cleaned or bleached. Common stony corals include solitary corals resembling anemones with a calcareous skeleton, such as the mushroom coral of the genus *Fungia*, the fan-shaped crisp coral, genus *Flabellum* (found in waters as far south as Tas.), and the conical *Conocyathus* of Sydney Harbour. Others are star-corals, of the genera *Goniastraea* and *Favia*; and brain-corals, genera *Meandrina* and *Coeloria*. >> *fossils*

Coral Sea Islands Territory

This territory comprises scattered, uninhabited islands lying off the northeast Australian coast in an area covering about a million sq. km. It was proclaimed by Australia in 1969 and 1973, and is administered from Norfolk Island. In 1982, under the National Parks and Wildlife Conservation Act, two marine reserves – Coringa-Herald and Lihou Reef – were established to protect an extensive and as yet little-known marine environment.

corella > *parrots*

Corio Bay

Vic. This is the western section of Port Phillip Bay. The city of Geelong, with extensive port facilities, occupies much of the shore and a number of large industrial organisations are established in the environs, including the Shell oil refinery, the International Harvester Co., the Ford Motor Works and at Point Henry, in the southeast, the Alcoa aluminium smelting works. Pollution of the bay is a major problem.

cormorants In Australia these are primarily inhabitants of either coastal or inland lakes, swamps and streams. They are large, web-footed birds standing from some 60cm to over 90cm; they have long necks and beaks, are good swimmers and divers, and are sometimes harried by fishermen, although their diet consists primarily of non-commercial fish. They are characteristically a dark blue-black, but some have white breasts and some yellow beaks. A typical sight is that of a cormorant perched on a rock or a tree-branch, preening, or ready to dive for prey. The largest of them is the black cormorant, *Phalacrocorax carbo,* and the names of the others are fairly descriptive: the little black cormorant, *P. sulcirostris*; the black-faced cormorant, *P. fuscescens*; yellow-faced cormorant, *P. varius*, typically seen in quiet, mangrove-fringed lagoons; and the little pied cormorant, *P. melanoleucos*. All species build large, untidy, communal nests, often in swampland trees. In Australia the cormorant is known by the alternative name 'shag', in contrast to British usage where the two names apply to different species.

Corner Inlet

Vic. A shallow, sandy, almost entirely enclosed bay on the south coast, Corner Inlet is bounded by Wilsons Promontory in the south and east and the Yanakie isthmus in the west, with Snake and Little Snake Islands standing sentinel at the entrance. On the northern shore there are several beach resorts. The inlet was discovered by George Bass in 1798.

Cornforth, Sir John Warcup

(1917–), research chemist, b. Sydney. Cornforth shared the 1975 Nobel Prize in chemistry for his work on the stereochemistry of enzymes – the catalysts for life's basic processes – developing methods to work out the vital spatial arrangements of molecules. Deaf from the age of 17, Cornforth won an exhibition to Oxford University in 1939 and since then has lived in England, becoming the Royal Society research professor of molecular sciences at the University of Sussex in 1975. He was knighted in 1977.

cotton Cotton was grown only sporadically in Australia until the 1960s, since when improved technology and irrigation – and greatly increased investment – have caused prodigious growth of the industry. It now meets all domestic demand for raw cotton, and the substantial surplus (some 92% in 1984–5) is exported, mainly to Japan, Taiwan and South Korea.

Cotton was first grown commercially in Qld, in 1852, when world prices rose in response to reduced American production during the Civil War. Governments encouraged growers with periodic bounties from that time, but it was not until irrigated cultivation was developed in NSW in the early 1960s that commercial production could be sustained.

More than 75% of the national crop is still grown in NSW, principally around the Namoi and Macquarie rivers; the rest comes from central and southeastern Qld, especially the fertile Callide and Balonne valleys and the Darling Downs. Its high field value seems to assure continued growth, although like other agricultural industries cotton faces long-term problems of land degradation, notably of erosion.

Cotton, John (1801–49), squatter, b. England. Cotton arrived in Australia in 1843 with his family and took up the Doogallook sheep and cattle run, near the Goulburn River in Vic.; by 1846, the station extended over 160sq.km. Cotton was an amateur artist, naturalist and scientist, and a prolific writer, his published letters and diary extracts providing an intriguing account of colonial life.

Counihan, Noel Jack (1913–86), artist, b. Melbourne. A leading social-realist painter, Counihan's powerful works aligned him closely with the causes of immigrants, workers and trade unions. He worked as an illustrator, cartoonist and press artist in the 1930s and 1950s, and exhibited extensively in Europe, including eastern-bloc countries.

country music This rustic style of music first appeared in Australia in the late 1920s with Australian pressings of US hillbilly and country-and-western music for Columbia Records. The idiom was readily accepted by rural-dwellers, as it reflected their interests and lifestyle more strongly than other contemporary popular music. Australian country music came about with the advent of the legendary Tex Morton, a New Zealander (whose other talents included hypnotism and sharp-shooting) who started recording in Sydney in 1936 and toured extensively. Australia's first country band was the Roughriders, who with Sister Dorrie (the first female country singer) gained recognition after 1940. They were soon followed by Buddy Williams, Sydney-born but country-raised; Smoky Dawson, star of a radio drama broadcast nationally on 69 radio stations; and Shirley Thoms, who made her first recordings at the age of 16. Slim Dusty, arguably the king of Australian country music, recorded Gordon Parsons's laconic song 'Pub with No Beer' in 1958; it was an immediate hit in

Australia and overseas, despite the fact that this was the height of rock'n'roll's popularity. At times country music fuses with traditional folk music, but more often it retains its 'cowboy' image; bush bands and bluegrass bands often span both genres. Country music has undergone a revival since the 1970s and now reaches a much wider audience. An annual country-music festival has been staged at Tamworth, NSW, since the 1970s. >> *folk music*

Country Party > *National Party*

coursing > *greyhound racing and coursing*

Court, Sir Charles Walter Michael (1911–), politician, b. England. A chartered accountant, Court entered the WA parliament in 1953 and became leader of the State Liberal Party in 1972; he was premier of WA 1974–82. Court's right-wing views and pro-development philosophy often brought him into conflict with unions, conservationists and, on occasions, the federal government. He oversaw development of iron ore in the Pilbara, of natural gas on the North West Shelf, and of aluminium in the Darling Range. Former tennis champion Margaret Court is his daughter-in-law.

Court, Margaret (1942–) tennis player, b. Albury, NSW. In 1970 Court became the first Australian woman to win the Grand Slam – the Australian, French, Wimbledon and US women's singles titles in the one year. She is the greatest winner of major women's tournaments in tennis history, with three Wimbledon singles titles (1963, 1965, 1970), five American (1962, 1965, 1969–71), four French (1964, 1969, 1970, 1973) and eleven Australian, including (as Margaret Smith) seven consecutive wins from 1960, when she became, at 17, the youngest-ever champion.

courts and tribunals > *administrative law; law and legal system*

Cowen, Sir Zelman (1919–), academic and lawyer, b. Melbourne. Elected Rhodes Scholar for Vic. in 1940, Cowen was dean of the faculty of law, University of Melbourne 1951–67, and vice-chancellor of the University of New England 1967–70 and the University of Queensland 1970–7. A brilliant jurist of international stature, Cowen served as governor-general 1977–82 and helped to recover some of the public's respect for the office, undermined by the constitutional crisis of 1975.

Cowpastures This name, long used for an area now centred on Camden, some 60km southwest of Sydney, was given because of the herd of cattle found in the region in 1795. The animals were descended from four cows and two bulls which had escaped from the herd of South African cattle brought to Sydney Cove by Governor Phillip in 1788. The cattle exceeded 3000 head by 1806 and were protected for some years before being dispersed, domesticated or killed.

Cowra NSW (pop. 11 562) A growing market, service and manufacturing centre for sheep and wheat country, Cowra lies on the Lachlan River some 319km southwest of Sydney. Research stations for agriculture and soil conservation are based in the area, which is noted for the 'Cowra breakout' – the escape of Japanese prisoners from a nearby camp in 1944; a commemorative Japanese garden and cultural centre was opened in 1979.

cowries > *gastropods*

Cox, Paul (1940–), film director and screenwriter, b. Holland. After a career as a photographer, Cox turned to making documentaries. His first feature film was *Illuminations* (1976), which was followed by *Kostas* (1979), *Lonely Hearts* (1982), *Man of Flowers* (1983) and *Cactus* (1987). Cox specialises in small-scale, claustrophobic films that closely examine human relationships; his films have occasionally been criticised for being self-consciously 'arty' and too European for Australian tastes.

Cox, William (1764–1837), pioneer road-builder, b. England. Cox arrived in Australia in 1800 as paymaster in the NSW Corps. He soon acquired land and was appointed by Governor Macquarie to supervise construction of the first road over the Blue Mountains, which was completed and allowed the first mountain crossing in 1813. His major feat was to organise the building of 162km of road (with more than a dozen bridges) from Penrith to Bathurst; this was undertaken by some 30 men (including 20 convicts) between July 1814 and January 1815, with no loss of life or disciplinary problems.

crabs This is an almost entirely marine group of crustaceans of the order Decapoda (animals having five pairs of walking legs). True crabs are distinct from other decapods in having a short abdomen that fits into a groove below the carapace. In Australia there are almost 700 known species, contained in 23 families.

In almost all cases the lifecycle comprises several stages as small, shrimp-like, free-floating larvae, the final, pre-adult stage being more crab-like. In exceptional forms – known as direct development – maturation takes place within the egg and the young appear as miniature adults. True crabs fall generally into three groups.

The Dromiacea, which include examples of direct development, are the sponge crabs, probably the most primitive existing specimens, carrying a mass of living sponge or other organism above the body, held by the two back pairs of legs. Found either in the tidal regions or offshore, two species are represented in Australia.

The Oxystomata are identified by a triangular mouthframe and include the box crab, family Calappidae, with large, flat pincers, and the dawn crab, of the same family but with spines projecting from the sides of the shell and flattened limbs for burrowing and swimming. Both are tropical species.

The third group, Brachygnatha, contains by far the majority of species, characterised by a square mouthframe and classed in two further categories: oxyrhynchans, with generally a triangular shell and including particularly the spider crabs; and brachyrhynchans, which in fact make up most of the world crab population and of which there are two main types – cancroid, with oval bodies, and grapsoid, with squarish bodies. The family Xanthidae contains many colourful tropical species, but also the largest of all Australian crabs, *Pseudocarcinus gigas*, the giant Tas. crab, sometimes over 35cm in body width and weighing 14kg. The swimming crabs of the family Portunidae have paddle-shaped extremities on the back pair of legs, and the Grapsidae includes most of the common shore crabs. In the family Ocypodidae are several groups with long eye-stalks and distinctive chelae – among them is the fiddler crab of the genus *Uca*, with a disproportionately large nipper used in both courtship and aggression. The Mictyridae family contains the soldier crabs, which when disturbed disappear abruptly beneath the sand. The widely distributed Potamidae family includes the six Australian species of the freshwater genus *Paratelphusa*, most common of which is the burrow-dwelling *P. transversa*, about 5cm wide, found in the banks of creeks, dams and swamps.

Crab fishing is based chiefly on two portunid species: mud or mangrove crabs, *Scylla serrata*, and sand or blue swimming crabs, *Portunis pelagicus*, both table delicacies. Mud crabs occur around the coast from Broome, WA, to Bermagui, NSW, in mudflats and tidal estuaries; sand crabs are found around the entire continent and also in Tas. Minor fisheries harvest Qld spanner crabs, *Ranina ranina*, and the Tas. giant crab. In recent years crab fishing has been restricted and habitats protected in reserves or sanctuaries because of overfishing and habitat damage caused by agricultural and industrial development. >> *hermit crabs*

Cradle Mountain–Lake St Clair

Tas. Cradle Mountain (1545m), so called from its resemblance to a miner's cradle, lies in the northern section of a national park 64km south-west of Devonport. The glacial Lake St Clair, in the southern section, is 737m above sea-level and reaches a depth of 160m. The park – since extended – was first proclaimed in 1922, largely from interest created by Gustav Weindorfer, an Austrian immigrant settler. It is a watershed for rivers flowing to the north, west and south coasts and contains, among other peaks, Tas.'s highest mountain, Mt Ossa (1617m). The terrain is rugged; vegetation is predominantly temperate rainforest and includes, on Cradle Mountain, one of the few native deciduous trees, the endemic beech. Running through the park is the 80km 'overland track', from Cynthia Bay in the south to Cradle Valley in the north.

craft Some high-quality and distinctively Australian crafts were produced during the colonial era – such as fine pottery and silverware and elegant furniture – but generally shared the fate of other local art forms in being passed over in favour of imported products. The basis of today's craft traditions was established in the early 20th century. Inspired by the British Arts and Crafts Movement of the 1890s, the NSW Society of Arts and Crafts was founded in 1906 and the Arts and Crafts Society of Vic. in 1908. They actively encouraged crafts, which became an accepted recreational diversion (especially by the middle classes) as well as a creative outlet. In keeping with the spirit of the time, Australian motifs were incorporated, most notably by artists such as Robert Prenzel, whose beautiful wood carvings featured native flora and fauna, and potters Merric Boyd in Vic. and Grace Seacombe in NSW.

Craft work remained comparatively specialised until the 1960s and 1970s, when there was a remarkable burgeoning of community interest and involvement in a whole range of craft activities. State Craft Councils were established in the 1960s, followed by the Crafts Council of Australia in 1971, giving the artist-craftspeople a new voice, new authority, learning opportunities, a national network and eventually an audience and a marketplace. Today's craftworkers use clay, fibre, glass, metals, leather and wood to produce pieces frequently inspired by the Australian landscape and culture, owing much of their physical quality and beauty to local materials but often drawing on the aesthetic traditions of Europe and Asia. Pottery and ceramics is the most widely practised and taught craft, and Australia has produced many exponents of international stature. Textile arts have recently flourished and the Vic. Tapestry Workshop (established in 1976) has led a resurgence in weaving. Major corporate commissions have taken Australian tapestry into company boardrooms and weaving has become established in the mainstream of contemporary crafts. Jewellery-making, too, is reaching new standards, with specialist galleries providing a venue for the work. The hand-crafting of furniture is another dynamic area, with styles ranging from high-tech and classical to bush basic; local timbers are being used with increasing thoughtfulness and originality.

Major craft centres in all States now provide exhibition space and public galleries are actively involved in collecting and exhibiting work. International ties in all craft areas have been strengthened and a number of Australians are exhibiting their work overseas as well as travelling abroad to study. In 1988, the Craft Council of Australia organised and hosted the World Crafts Council Conference in Sydney, with delegates from more than 45 countries. >> *pottery and ceramics*

crakes > *rails and crakes*

Cranbourne

Vic. (pop. 14 005) This former dairying town 47km southeast of Melbourne is now on the metropolitan fringe and has recently experienced rapid growth as a regional centre. Dairying is still an important local industry, with quarrying, building, and machinery manufacture. The area was first settled in 1852 and the town proclaimed in 1861.

crane > *brolga*

Crawford, Hector William (1913–), musical conductor and broadcasting producer, b. Melbourne.

In 1938 Crawford inaugurated the enormously successful 'Music for the People', a series of free, open-air concerts in Melbourne, which ran for more than 40 years. In 1945, with his sister Dorothy, he founded Crawford Productions to produce radio and television programs; the Crawfords were instrumental in the development of Australia's broadcasting industry and in fostering the talents of many Australian writers, actors, producers and directors. The company's productions have included radio classics such as the police drama 'D 24' (1950s) and enduring television series such as 'Homicide' (1960) and 'The Sullivans' (1976–7). Crawford's wife Glenda Raymond was a successful singer in the 1950s and 1960s, and was involved in Crawford Productions for many years.

Crawford, Sir John Grenfell (1910– 84), economist, b. Hurstville, NSW.

Crawford first gained prominence in 1938 when, as a lecturer in rural economics at Sydney University, he was co-author, with Colin Clark, of *The National Income of Australia*, a landmark in Australian national accounting. He served for many years as a government administrator and academic, but is best known for his work on two advisory committees: the Vernon Committee of Economic Inquiry (1963–5) and the Crawford Committee on Structural Adjustment (1977–9); the latter, of which he was chairman, recommended the reduction of tariff protection for Australian manufacturing industries as one of a range of measures to improve their competitiveness.

crayfishes and allies These are aquatic (mainly marine) crustaceans, those with large pincers traditionally being known as lobsters.

Marine crayfishes Unlike certain freshwater crayfish and some prawns and shrimps, marine crayfishes in Australia do not have large pincers. Most, including the main commercial species, have somewhat cylindrical bodies and considerable power to curve and straighten them, using the broad, flat tail as a powerful swimming tool; these form the family Palinuridae. The main commercial species are the southern crayfish or rock lobster, occurring from Tas. to WA, and the eastern crayfish, important all along the eastern coast; in WA the species *Panulirus longipes* is important for the export of lobster tails. The family Scyllaridae includes the Moreton Bay bug from Australian tropical regions, *Thenus orientalis*, and the Balmain bug, *Ibacus peronii*, from southern Australia; both are found in muddy, shallow waters.

Freshwater crayfishes Found throughout Australia, these include forms with well-developed pincers, all of the family Parastacidae. The spiny Tas. genus *Astacopsis* inhabits clear mountain streams, while the rest of Australia has many species of the smooth-bodied *Cherax*, including the yabbie. The marron of WA is *C. tenuimanus*, and can grow to 40cm. Species of this genus may appear as pests in irrigation channels by burrowing in the banks, as does the large Murray River lobster, *Euastacus armatus*. In periods of drought, all Australian freshwater crayfishes can evade the dry conditions by burrowing in the beds of streams, lakes and dams.

Crean family, prominent in politics and industrial relations.

Frank (1916–), politician, b. Hamilton, Vic., was formerly an accountant; he served two terms in the Vic. parliament before becoming federal member for Melbourne Ports 1951–77. During the Whitlam administration he was treasurer (1972–4), minister for overseas trade (1975) and deputy prime minister (1975). His son **Simon** (1949–), lawyer and trade unionist, was president of the ACTU 1985–9. Often mooted as a future leader of the ALP, he was elected to federal parliament in 1990 and was immediately appointed a minister.

cricket Cricket was first played in Sydney in 1803.

At that time the game was still in an evolutionary stage, but it spread rapidly and was encouraged by governments because it exhibited qualities of respectability that many contemporary sports lacked. The Melbourne Cricket Club was formed in 1838 and the first intercolonial match was played on the club's ground in 1856; in 1892 the donation of a trophy by the Earl of Sheffield saw the institution of intercolonial – and later interstate – games as the Sheffield Shield competition. The early English touring teams, the first of which came in 1861, were private ventures in which matches were played by teams of fifteen or 22.

In 1876–7 the first Test match was played between England and Australia at the Melbourne Cricket Ground; it was won by Australia, and the first Test century was made by Charles Bannerman, with a score of 165. The first official Australian tour took place in 1878 (a privately organised Aboriginal team had toured England in 1868), and in 1882, led by the bowling of 'the Demon' > *Frederick Spofforth*, Australia secured the Ashes. This symbol – originally of the destruction of English cricket – has been the prize for all subsequent Anglo-Australian contests.

International competition has gradually been expanded to include India, Pakistan, NZ, South Africa (until 1968–9), West Indies and Sri Lanka. Among memorable series was the 1932–3 English tour of Australia, which gave rise to bitter controversy over what was termed England's 'bodyline bowling', by which the seemingly invincible > *Donald Bradman* was the subject of allegedly intimidatory bowling, several Australian batsman were injured, and Anglo–Australian cricket relations were threatened. In their 1948 tour of England the Australians remained unbeaten, Ray Lindwall and Keith Miller providing a formidable opening bowling combination; during the 1960–1 West Indies tour Brisbane witnessed the first tied Test (the Australians playing under Richie Benaud) and Melbourne established a world attendance record with a crowd of 90 800 at the MCG.

Australia re-emerged as a cricketing power in the 1970s under the captaincy of Ian Chappell (> *Chappell family*) and with the opening-bowling combination of > *Dennis Lillee* and Jeff Thomson; in the Centenary Test in Melbourne in 1977 England was defeated by 45 runs – the same margin as in the original match. Immediately after this, however, traditional cricket was torn apart as the majority of leading players left to play in the World Series, which had been established by Kerry Packer with the aim of securing exclusive television rights to the game and was supported by players in an effort to seek better remuneration. Australia's success in the 1980s was limited, although it won the World Cup in India in 1987. In the intervening years Bradman's record in Test run-making was overtaken first by Greg Chappell and then by > *Allan Border*. In 1989 Border led the Test team in a record-breaking victory, when the Australians regained the Ashes on English soil for the first time in more than 50 years.

Although the game has changed rapidly in recent years, with greater emphasis on limited-over matches and with full professionalism at Test level, it remains enormously popular and has gained many new adherents as a result of the changes. There are over 550 000 registered male players in Australia, and in addition, many men and women play indoor cricket. Women's cricket has been officially organised at club and State level since the 1930s; although only 5000 players are registered, this number should rise steeply as the game receives greater publicity and promotion in schools. In 1982 the Australian women's team won the World Cup; notable performers were Denise Alderman and Sharon Tredrea, and the high standard of the Australian players was praised by the English umpires.

crickets > *grasshoppers, locusts and crickets*

crime and criminal law Each State and Territory has jurisdiction over crimes committed within its borders: in Qld, WA and Tas., all criminal offences are codified in statutes; Vic., NSW, SA, the NT and the ACT are common-law jurisdictions, the basis of their criminal law being court decisions as well as statute law. Although the constitutional powers of the Commonwealth do not include criminal jurisdiction, the federal government does have incidental powers that allow it to legislate on a wide range of criminal matters: the importation of prohibited drugs, for example, is regulated by the Commonwealth Customs Act.

The study of crime and criminal behaviour in Australia is mainly undertaken by the Australian Institute of Criminology (AIC), a statutory body established in 1971. It includes representatives from each of the States, and from relevant institutions such as university law schools. The AIC has published a large body of research on crime in Australia, from conference papers to monographs; its periodical, *Trends and issues in crime and criminal justice*, covers a wide range of issues such as community–police relations and Aboriginal criminal justice.

Patterns of crime The incidence of crime in Australia is difficult to assess: much crime is not reported, goes undetected, and even where reported is difficult to prosecute because of lack of evidence. Surveys carried out by the AIC, however, do show that the annual murder rate is generally lower than two per 100 000 and varies little from year to year, with only the NT having a consistently high rate. Serious assaults are reported to the police at a frequency of 59 per 100 000. Rape, which includes a wide range of sexual offences, has increased considerably in recent years and currently accounts for about 10% of all violent crimes, occurring at an annual rate of about twelve per 100 000. The incidence of robbery has increased from 23 per 100 000 in the early 1970s to 43 per 100 000 in the mid-1980s; breaking and entering also increased in the same period, more than doubling from 880 per 100 000 to 1746.

It is noteworthy that offences against property (such as larceny, motor-vehicle theft, and fraud) outnumber violent crimes by a ratio of 40 to 1. At the same time, far fewer property offences result in criminal charges being laid than is the case with violent crime: according to AIC statistics, 65–80% of reported violent crimes in 1986–7 resulted in prosecutions, compared with figures of 25% for robbery offences and about 10% for motor-vehicle theft and break-enter-and-steal offences.

Patterns of crime have been changing in recent years. Largely as the result of increasing drug use and attempts to deal with the drug problem by enacting more and more draconian legislation, many violent crimes and break-and-enter offences are now drug-related. Another noticeable trend has been the increased incidence of both 'white-collar' crime (such as computer crime, embezzlement, tax avoidance, and insider trading) and corporate crime (ranging from restrictive trade practices to failure to comply with health, safety and environmental-protection laws). >> *law and legal system*; *police*; *prisons and prison systems*

Croatians in Australia > *ethnic groups*

crocodiles In the 1980s the estuarine or salt-water crocodile, *Crocodilus porosus*, became an object of great public interest; this was due to several factors: an increase in crocodile numbers as a result of conservation measures, the opening of the far north to tourism, the success of the 1986 film *Crocodile Dundee*, and a number of well-publicised attacks on humans.

The estuarine crocodile ranges in distribution from India to the western Pacific. In Australia it is found both in estuaries and upstream in large coastal rivers in an area extending from Broome, WA, to Rockhampton, Qld; as one of its common names implies, it is a sea-going animal, and can be found in the open ocean travelling between islands. Crocodiles feed mainly on small aquatic animals such as fish, crabs and water rats, but sometimes turn to larger prey such as cattle, horses or humans, which they seize and drown before eating; their stomachs often contain large stones, which act as ballast. The estuarine crocodile can reach a length of 7m; on land, its usual lumbering amble can speed up to a fast run, with the tail raised. The female lays 40–80 eggs in a leaf-mould nesting mound that she tends, and the sex of individuals is determined by the temperature of the incubation mound, not by sex chromosomes. After hatching, the young stay with their mother, and can be heard to emit shrill, squeaky sounds.

Estuarine crocodiles have in the past been hunted extensively for their skins, and populations were seriously depleted across much of northern Australia, but since WA and the NT granted them complete protection in 1971, and Qld followed suit in 1974, there has been a dramatic recovery in numbers. As an alternative to hunting, several successful crocodile farms have been established in Qld and the NT for meat production; a number are operated by Aboriginal people.

The smaller freshwater or Johnston's crocodile, *C. johnstoni*, is found only in billabongs and lagoons of monsoonal rivers, ranging from the Gulf of Carpentaria to Broome, WA. This shy species is harmless to humans, feeds only on small prey, and rarely exceeds 3m in length.

Crowley, Grace Adela (1890–1979), painter b. Cobbadah, NSW. Having studied in Sydney (under Julian Ashton) and later in Paris, Crowley returned to Australia in 1930. Joining forces with Roy de Maistre, Roland Wakelin, Grace Cossington Smith and others, she became an influential member of the modern-art movement in Sydney which introduced new French trends to local artists. Her work combines her painterly talents with the influence of cubism and constructivism. With Rah Fizelle, she helped establish an art school in Sydney.

Crown land > *land ownership*

crown-of-thorns starfish A starfish characterised by an abundance of strong, sharp spines, the crown-of-thorns, *Acanthaster planci*, is found on coral reefs throughout the Indo-Pacific region; it feeds on coral polyps. Since the early 1960s it has developed huge populations throughout its range, and has destroyed large areas of living coral; there has been considerable concern about the long-term effects of these outbreaks on the Great Barrier Reef and on other oceanic reefs. Although corals are able to regenerate if undisturbed, continual predation by the starfish may permanently damage reefs or even kill them.

Several theories have been produced to account for the apparently sudden massive invasion by the starfish. These include a decline in the numbers of its major natural predator, the triton shell, brought about through overcollecting of these shells; pollution of the seas with pesticide runoff, affecting population balance; an increase in the survival rate of larval starfish; and the proposition that such outbreaks are natural, cyclical phenomena which occur at irregular intervals, but which have not previously been witnessed by scientists. None of these theories is entirely satisfactory. Considering the scale of the problem, control measures appear to be futile, although labour-intensive methods such as hand-removal and injecting individual starfish with poison have been successful on tourist reefs.

crows and ravens These sturdy black birds of the genus *Corvus* are closely related, and in Australia comprise three species of ravens (Australian, forest and little ravens) and two species of crows (Australian and little crows). Although superficially similar, these five species differ in size, plumage, call and behaviour, but all utter the harsh croak of the crow family and eat mainly insects, including blowflies on sheep. The raven is reputed also to prey on lambs – although research indicates that it usually attacks sick animals, rarely healthy ones – and sometimes to raid orchards.

crucifers > *mustard family*

crustaceans This large phylum comprises animals with a hard exoskeleton and jointed legs; most are aquatic in marine and freshwater habitats, although some are terrestrial in moist leaf litter. >> *amphipods*; *crabs*; *crayfishes and allies*; *hermit crabs*; *mountain shrimp*; *prawns and shrimp*; *water-fleas*; *wood-lice and sea-lice*

CSIRO Australia's Commonwealth Scientific and Industrial Research Organisation is one of the largest and most diverse research insti-

tutions in the world. About one-third of the staff of over 7000 are scientists, working in 100 laboratories and field stations throughout Australia; collectively they provide expertise in almost every scientific discipline.

The organisation began life in 1926 as the Council for Scientific and Industrial Research (CSIR), its main concern being research for agriculture and primary industry. In 1936 CSIR began catering to secondary industry with the establishment of aeronautics, industrial-chemistry and standards laboratories. These played an important role in the rapid wartime development of Australian industry. CSIR ceased defence-related work in 1949, when it was reconstituted as CSIRO and diversified to carry out strategic research for all industries. Early research is still paying dividends, particularly in the fields of agriculture, mining and timber production. CSIRO is credited with saving the wool industry from the 1950s onslaught of man-made fibres: research transformed wool into a modern, high-fashion material that could be shrink-proofed, moth-proofed and permanently pressed. Similar contributions are reflected in many industries. The CSIRO invention in 1952 of atomic absorption spectroscopy became one of the most widely used methods of analysing trace elements; manufacture of equipment in Melbourne laid the ground for a thriving scientific instruments industry, earning more than $100 million in exports annually.

Since the late 1970s CSIRO has shifted the balance of its efforts, with more research being carried out for the manufacturing, information and communications industries. A greater emphasis has been placed on the commercial development of successful research and on improved links with industry. In 1984 Sirotech Ltd was established – a commercial company that has signed major agreements with Australian and international companies. Some of the technologies already bearing commercial results are a new $13 million zirconia plant, advanced ceramic materials, new mineral-processing technologies, logic chips, a pulsed-arc welder, space antennas and fertiliser test kits. CSIRO research sponsored by Australian companies is valued at more than $16 million.

CSIRO is now facing the most turbulent period in its history. In December 1986 the organisation began operating under a ten-member board chaired by the former NSW premier, Neville Wran. The board restructured the organisation into six institutes comprising 35 divisions (including three research units). In

1988–9 the federal budget cut CSIRO's funds by approximately 8.9% in real terms, the fifth successive such reduction, and in a bid to develop a more entrepreneurial spirit a target was set of obtaining 30% of funds from external sources by 1992. The government's justification for these changes is to increase industry involvement in research and development; critics of the cutbacks take a more pessimistic view, however, and believe that they will have unacceptably destructive effects on Australian scientific research and development.

Ctenophora > *comb-jellies*

cuckoos More than a dozen species of these birds are found in Australia. They are often migratory or semi-migratory, and range in size from the large swamp cuckoo of northern Australia, *Centropus phasianinus* – sometimes called swamp pheasant or coucal, and the only one that does not lay its eggs in other birds' nests – to the dainty bronze cuckoos, which have green-bronze backs and brown-and-white striped breasts, and which lay bronze-brown eggs like those of the host. A medium-sized species is the fan-tailed cuckoo of Australia and NG, *Cacomantis pyrrhophanus*. In this species the mature bird has a slate-grey back and a rich, orange-buff breast, and lays a single, purple-flecked egg in the domed nest of the small scrub-wren or in the nests of other small birds; the host's young are often heaved from the nest by the young cuckoos. Cuckoos are mainly insectivorous, and their cries tend towards trilling. Many have the wave-like flight seen in jungle birds, and erect the tail on landing as if using a parachute-brake.

cuckoo-shrikes and trillers There are eight species in Australia and Tas. of this group of perching birds of the family Campephagidae. Most are insectivorous, but they also eat native fruits and often combine to form feeding parties. The most familiar species is the black-faced cuckoo-shrike, which has a black band across its eyes. Trillers are named and best known for their rapid series of melodious chattering, and include the migratory cicada-bird, whose trilling is similar to that of a cicada.

Culotta, Nino [John Patrick O'Grady] (1907–81), author, b. Sydney. O'Grady began writing short stories and plays when employed as a commercial traveller. He mined his rich experience – then and subsequently as a pharmacist, builder's labourer and fisherman – for *They're a Weird Mob* (1957), a hugely popular comic novel purportedly written by an Italian immigrant confused by Australian speech and habits. Two later Culotta books and sixteen under his own name were less successful.

Cumberland Islands Qld This group of about 100 granitic islands lies within the Great Barrier Reef and forms the eastern boundary of Whitsunday Passage and Hillsborough Channel, extending over some 60km from Hayman Island in the north to Snare Peak in the South. Most of the islands are covered with rainforest and have fringing coral reefs; the largest is Whitsunday, a national park of 19 900ha, on which Whitsunday Peak rises to 440m. Some have been developed as tourist resorts, such as Brampton, Daydream, Lindeman, Hayman and South Molle; Hook Island, in the north, which is also a national park, has a submarine observatory.

cumbungi This is the common name of Aboriginal origin for plants of the genus *Typha*, family Typhaceae, otherwise known as reedmaces, bulrushes or flags. They are semi-aquatic plants with flattened, ribbon-like leaves and erect flowering spikes divided into a male upper portion and a female lower portion; the latter matures to a dense brown fruiting cylinder that finally disintegrates into a vast number of tiny wind-borne 'seeds'. Two common native species are *T. orientalis* and *T. domingensis*, difficult to tell apart and both extending well beyond Australia. Cumbungi is common on the edges of water-bodies or swamps and is often regarded as a troublesome weed of farm dams. Aborigines made use of the young rhizomes as food, and made twine from the leaves.

Cummings, Bart (James Bartholomew) > *horse-racing*

cunjevoi This is a name of Aboriginal origin, commonly used for two quite unrelated organisms, a marine animal and a rainforest plant. It is doubtful that east-coast Aborigines used the same name for both, so presumably there has been subsequent confusion. The animal is the > *sea-squirt, Pyura praeputialis*, common on ocean rocks in the intertidal zone. The plant is *Alocasia macrorrhizos*, a lily of the arum family; also known as cunjevoi lily or spoon lily, it is a large-leafed herb with a solitary, finger-like flower spike half enclosed in a green bract.

Cunningham brothers, botanists and explorers, b. England. **Allan** (1791–1839) was appointed in 1814 to collect plants in Brazil and then NSW. He arrived at Sydney in 1816 and joined John Oxley's 1817 expedition to the interior before accompanying Phillip Parker King on his coastal surveys 1817–22. An inveterate traveller and collector, he subsequently (1823–8) undertook notable explorations of his own, discovering the Liverpool Plains and Darling Downs and a route back to the coast at Moreton Bay. He was the first to record many Australian plants, a number of which were named after him. He refused the post of NSW government botanist in 1831, in favour of his brother **Richard** (1793–1835), who accordingly arrived in Sydney in 1833. Richard made several collecting trips before disappearing during Thomas Mitchell's expedition to the Darling River in 1835. Allan then agreed to replace him as government botanist; attached to the Sydney Botanic Garden, his work was largely confined to tending the extensive vegetable garden and he resigned in protest in 1837.

Cunoniaceae A family of trees and shrubs found mainly in cooler rainforests, this group is believed to have originated in the ancient southern landmass Gondwana. The mountains of northern Qld have the highest concentration of tree species, of which there are six genera. A well-known representative is the NSW Christmas bush, *Ceratopetalum gummiferum*, found in coastal eucalypt forests and bearing masses of bright-red fruiting calyxes in December. In the same genus is coachwood, *C. apetalum*, a larger rainforest tree yielding a valued timber (now in scarce supply). The endemic Tas. genus *Anodopetalum*, the single species of which forms dense thickets in the southwest, is commonly known as 'horizontal' for the angled growth of its trunk. The > *blackwattle* of the Sydney area is also the sole member of its genus; a similar plant, the low shrub *Acrophyllum australe*, is known only from a small population in sandstone gorges of the Blue Mountains.

currawongs > *magpies, currawongs and butcher-birds*

currency Since 1966 Australia's basic unit of currency has been the dollar, consisting of 100 cents. This decimal system replaced the 'sterling' pounds, shillings and pence inherited from Britain in 1826 (with 12 pence to a shilling and 20 shillings to a pound).

In the early days of settlement a cash shortage developed and in 1813 Governor Macquarie ordered that Spanish dollars be used. The centres were stamped out of these to make the so-called 'holey dollars', and the small excised pieces ('dumps') became 15-pence coins. English currency was issued after 1817 by the Bank of NSW and most of the Spanish dollars were out of circulation by the 1830s. With the discovery of gold in the 1850s gold dust was commonly used as legal tender but, more important, gold coins began to be produced; mints were gradually established in all the colonies. After Federation in 1901, local gold coins circulated in tandem with silver and bronze currency from Britain. In 1910, the issue of notes was taken over by the Commonwealth Treasury. In July 1944 a conference at Bretton Woods in the US established a new world order for currencies in the postwar period; this fixed international exchange rates to the US dollar, which in turn was tied to gold. In 1972, however, the US government broke with the gold standard and the Bretton Woods regime collapsed accordingly; in Australia the dollar was fixed against a 'basket' or range of currencies expressed through a figure called the Trade Weighted Index, which averages the value of the dollar against the currencies of Australia's major trading partners. In December 1983 the Australian government floated the Australian dollar, hence allowing its value to be determined by supply and demand on foreign-exchange markets. The Reserve Bank of Australia occasionally intervenes to smooth out the more extreme effects of this process. >> *banks and banking*

currency lads and lasses This term was widely used in the early days of settlement in NSW to distinguish the Australian-born from immigrants. In some areas the word 'currency' was applied only to children of convicts, but generally it was used in reference to all native-born youth as distinct from 'sterling' (the British-born). The terms were popular in the 1820s, but had fallen into disuse by the middle of the century.

Curtin, John Joseph (1885–1945), politician, b. Creswick, Vic. Son of an Irish-Catholic police sergeant, Curtin was a trade-union organiser and editor of the anti-conscription *Westra-*

lian Worker in Perth, where he settled in 1916. He entered federal parliament in 1928, succeeding J. H. Scullin in 1935 as leader of the ALP and soon restoring unity within its ranks. He moved the no-confidence vote which brought down the Fadden government in 1941, thus becoming (almost reluctantly) a wartime Labor prime minister, 1941–5. In that capacity, he accomplished the reorientation towards the US alliance made necessary by the Japanese advance, and also the acceptance of conscription for home and NG defence, although battling with his party die-hards on its extension to service in Dutch NG. He died in office.

cuscuses > *possums*

Cussen, Sir Leo Finn Bernard (1859–1933), lawyer, b. Portland, Vic. Cussen practised as a barrister in Vic. and was rare in being appointed to the Vic. Supreme Court (1906) without first having become a QC. He remained on the court until his death and was noted particularly for his scholarly judgments, which continue to be highly regarded by members of the legal profession. He was also responsible for the preparation of two important statutory consolidations: the first, enshrined in the Imperial Acts Application Act 1922, documented for the first time which of the statutes inherited from Britain had local application in Australia; the second was the general consolidation of the Vic. statutes, in 1928.

customs and excise > *tariffs*

Cuthbert, Betty (1938–), athlete, b. Merrylands, NSW. With her distinctive, high-stepping stride, Betty Cuthbert was the 'Golden Girl' of the 1956 Melbourne Olympic Games, winning gold medals in the 100m, 200m and 4x100m relay. In the following six years she achieved few world-class times, yet determined to repeat her success. Advised by long-time coach June Ferguson to switch to the 400m event, Cuthbert broke the world record for this distance and, overcoming injury, won the event at the 1964 Tokyo Olympics. Her fighting spirit was once again evident when she was diagnosed as having multiple sclerosis; she has since become an active campaigner to raise funds and to increase public awareness of this disease.

cuttlefish > *cephalopods*

cycads The fossil ancestors of this group of primitive cone-bearing plants date back about 200 million years. Living cycads, which occur in the families Cycadaceae and Zamiaceae, are few in number and geographically restricted: Australia has about 26 native species out of a world total of around 90; cycads are also well represented in tropical America and southern Africa. They are mostly palm-like in appearance, with long pinnate fronds, the male and female cones occurring on different plants. The foliage of all cycads is poisonous to livestock and the large starchy seeds are poisonous to humans.

Australia has three endemic genera – *Macrozamia*, *Lepidozamia* and *Bowenia* – of the family Zamiaceae, and one non-endemic genus, *Cycas*, belonging to the Cycadaceae. *Macrozamia* is the largest genus, with fourteen species of which most are native to NSW or southern Qld; the burrawang, *M. communis*, is unusually abundant in eucalypt forests of coastal NSW. *Lepidozamia* consists of two species, one in north Qld rainforests and the other in wet eucalypt forests of southern Qld and northern NSW: these are among the tallest of all cycads, exceeding 10m in height. *Bowenia* consists of two endemic Qld species of curious fern-like cycads with underground tuberous stems and long-stalked, bipinnate leaves. The genus *Cycas*, which occurs also in southern Asia and the Pacific, has about eight Australian species scattered across the tropical north. They differ from other cycads in that the female cones have long stalked scales, each bearing several seeds.

cycling The first bicycle appeared in Australia in 1869; the generally flat terrain and mild climate led to its rapid adoption as a method of transport and as a vehicle for sport, especially after the invention of the pneumatic tyre in the early 1880s. One of the world's first six-day cycling events was staged in Australia in 1881, followed by the Austral Wheel Race (1887) and the Warrnambool–Melbourne (1895). At that time bicycle racing was dominated by professionals and there was a strong gambling element; allegations of rigging in 1901 considerably damaged the standing of the sport.

Since then, amateur and professional cycling groups have co-existed, and many champions have emerged. Olympic gold medallists since the 1930s include Duncan Gray, Russell Mockridge, Lionel Cox, Ian Browne, Tony Marchant, and the 4000m pursuit team (1984).

Professional cyclists have included Bob Spears, > *Hubert Opperman*, Sid Patterson, Gordon Johnson, Danny Clark and Phil Anderson.

After declining in the 1970s, cycling has undergone a resurgence. Victory at the 1984 Olympic Games by the Australians paved the way for further success at the Seoul Olympics in 1988: Martin Vinnicombe and Dean Woods won silver medals, Gary Niewand and the pursuit team won bronze medals, and Julie Speight finished fifth in the women's sprint.

cyclones > *climate*

Cyperaceae > *sedge family*

cypress > *conifers*

D

dabchicks > *grebes*

Daintree region Qld This is a wilderness region of northeastern Qld, covering 120 000ha and including a river, coral reef and rainforest. The river rises in the Coast Range, runs for some 108km through tropical forest and agricultural land, and reaches the sea at Port Douglas. The region contains a wealth of native fauna and flora, including thirteen of the nineteen primitive plant families known in the world, and species of trees and shrubs found only in these forests. The rarest living mammal, the tube-nosed bat, inhabits this region only, and other unique creatures are the golden-tipped bat, Bennett's tree kangaroo and four species of possum. An intense campaign has centred on Daintree, reflecting world concern to preserve remaining rainforest. In 1984 the Australian Heritage Commission recommended that the area be recognised as a World Heritage region, but the survival of the various sections of Daintree depends upon maintaining a balanced environment. Conservationists have fought to prevent logging, real-estate subdivision and road-building; a road was constructed through the region, but public debate continues.

dairy industry Dairying is concentrated in the temperate southeast of Australia, principally Vic., NSW and Tas. but also in southeastern Qld and on the south coast of WA; the Atherton Tableland in Qld is the only tropical centre. There were more than 2.7 million dairy cows in 1986, nearly half of the herd comprising Friesians; the other main breeds are Jerseys and Illawarra Shorthorns, with much smaller numbers of Guernseys, Ayrshires and zebus (the last being favoured in the tropical north). Dairy cattle are fed almost entirely on improved pastures or fodder crops.

The Australian dairy industry is relatively small, although milk production accounts for about 10% of the value of rural output. More than one-third of the milk is made into butter; cheese production and liquid milk each account for a further 27%, the balance being used to manufacture milk powder, casein and condensed milk.

Although dairy cows were imported in 1788, the limited availability of good pastures restricted development of the industry for many years, even on the coast. The pattern of small, family-run farms was established early. Refrigeration and other technological innovations, as well as transport developments, encouraged expansion of the industry from the late 19th century, and further growth occurred after World War 2. Since the late 1950s, government intervention (including price-fixing and the imposition of production quotas) and market forces have together compelled rationalisation of the industry. The number of dairy cattle has gradually decreased since that time, although improved farm management practices dramatically increased productivity in the same period.

The 1980s and beyond Despite improved yields in the 1980s, dairy farmers continue to face severe problems: a recent world butter glut, combined with the increased popularity of margarine, has greatly reduced the demand for butter; high establishment and production costs are not being matched by increased prices; local products, particularly cheese, face intense competition from imports; and cheese factories have pollution problems in disposing of their wastes. Many small farms have been forced out of business in recent years and others are finding the cost of land prohibitive.

Like other rural industries, the profitability of dairying is closely tied to world commodity prices and will thus continue to be governed by international trade. Changing consumer preferences will also continue to affect the industry: increased consumption of cheese in Australia since the 1960s has already sparked great growth in this area, with cheese manufacture more than doubling 1970–86. Creative diversification was a hallmark of the 1980s, with spectacular growth in the production of high-quality speciality cheeses by 'boutique' dairies on King Island and mainland Vic., and in NSW and WA.

daisy family In Australia the Asteraceae, one of the world's largest flowering-plant families, are most diverse in arid and semi-arid inland areas but also well represented in the Australian Alps and the mountains of Tas. The most distinctive characteristic of members of the daisy family is the dense head of small flowers (florets) which resembles a single large flower. In the group broadly classified as everlastings, which is well represented in Australia, the typical flattened outer rays are lacking but the head is surrounded by a circle of papery bracts. Variations in flower-head structure roughly correspond with the dozen or more tribes into which Australia's 120 native daisy genera are divided, all of which also occur outside Australia.

Most daisy genera are herbaceous but there are also many shrubs and small–medium trees. Australia has only about 50 native species in the genus *Senecio*, one of the world's largest plant genera. Striking inland species include showy groundsel, *S. magnificus*, and the beautiful fleshy groundsel; *S. gregorii*, of central Australian sand ridges. Some introduced species such as ragwort, *S. jacobaea*, are noxious weeds which are poisonous to livestock. A related group is the blanket-leaf genus *Bedfordia*, comprising two tree species (of Tas. and southeastern mountains) which can reach to 20m in height. The genus *Olearia*, which also occurs in NZ and NG, includes about 80 native species, most of which are shrubs: conspicuous especially in higher mountain areas, many have showy flower heads with pure-white rays. Related herbaceous genera include the alpine *Celmisia* or snow daisies, of few but showy species which sometimes carpet the treeless high country; *Brachycome*, the 75 species of which occur in diverse habitats; and the abundant inland group *Calotis* or burr-daisies, which are very similar to *Brachycome* but bear prickly, barbed seed heads.

Everlastings and their relatives constitute one of the largest daisy tribes in Australia. The best-known and largest genus is *Helichrysum*, with around 100 native species including the most typical everlastings, such as golden everlasting, *H. bracteatum*, which occurs in all States and includes both annual and perennial forms. A large group of *Helichrysum* species are shrubs, some of which grow to 4m and are often difficult to distinguish from the closely related genus *Cassinia*, consisting entirely of shrubs with aromatic foliage. One purely herbaceous genus of everlastings is *Helipterum* or sunrays, with about 60 native species. Two species endemic to WA, *H. manglesii* and *H. roseum*, have heads with beautiful pink bracts; the alpine sunray, *H. albicans*, is one of the most striking wildflowers of the alpine summits. Other genera of everlastings include *Ammobium, Waitzia* and *Myriocephalus*, the last of which includes the distinctive poached-egg daisy of inland sandhills.

The daisy family also includes a large number of introduced weeds (most notably thistles), and familiar vegetables and crop plants such as lettuce, artichoke and the > *oilseeds* sunflower and safflower.

Dakin, William John (1883–1950), zoologist, b. England. After graduating in zoology from the University of Liverpool, in 1913 Dakin was the first professor of biology appointed at the new University of WA; later, following a period at Liverpool University, he occupied the chair of zoology at the University of Sydney 1929–48. An authority on marine life, he was known worldwide for his research on plankton, fishes and oceanography; he was government adviser on whaling and fisheries and was chiefly responsible for the establishment of the CSIR (now CSIRO) Fisheries Division. As well as publishing numerous scientific papers, he had a regular series of ABC radio talks, 'Science in the News'.

Dalby Qld (pop. 8338) A commercial and service centre for the rich grain and grazing region of the Darling Downs, Dalby lies 240km west of Brisbane. Its development dates from pastoral settlement in the area in the 1840s and the establishment of a rail link with Ipswich in 1868. Nearby is the scenic Bunya Range National Park, noted for its diverse flora (from grassland to rainforest) and fauna (particularly its birdlife).

Dalrymple, Alexander (1737–1808), hydrographer, b. Scotland. Dalrymple served with both the East India Company and the British Admiralty, and was famous for the improvements he made to British charts. Intensely interested in exploration, he was convinced of the existence of the 'great south land' postulated by early Dutch and French cartographers, bringing to British notice evidence that the voyage of the Spaniard Luis Vaez de Torres proved there was indeed a passage south of NG. Subsequently, James Cook earned Dalrymple's lasting enmity by proving that no great southern continent – as described by the latter – existed. Dalrymple is honoured in several Australian place names, including Port Dalrymple, Tas.

Daly River NT Formed by the combined waters of the King, Katherine and Flora rivers, this major waterway of the northwest flows some 320km to an estuary on Anson Bay, at the east end of Joseph Bonaparte Gulf. Along the gulf coast are the Daly River Wildlife Sanctuary and the Daly River Aboriginal Reserve. With a long dry season and unreliable rainfall, the region has proved difficult to settle; it is chiefly occupied by large cattle stations, although sorghum is grown for fodder, and peanuts and tobacco are produced in the river valley.

Dampier, William (1651–1715), adventurer, b. England. Dampier became a buccaneer in the West Indies. Later, in the pirate ship *Cygnet*, he visited the Philippines and Timor, and sighted northwest Australia in 1688 at Buccaneer Archipelago. His withering description of the barren land, the flies and the natives, 'the miserablest people on earth', was published in the highly popular *New Voyage Round the World* (1697). The book brought him fame, and command of the *Roebuck* (1699) with orders to explore New Holland further. He reached Shark Bay, WA, after an 11 200km voyage from Brazil. A leaking boat and scurvy caused him to return, after carrying out exploratory work northeast from Shark Bay and in waters off the northern shores of New Guinea. Dampier was an adventurer and fine seaman, but a poor leader.

Dampier Archipelago WA A group of islands off the northwest coast of WA, near Roebourne, the archipelago extends for approximately 64km east–west. It was first visited by William Dampier in 1699, and named for him by Phillip Parker King. The islands' scientific importance rests in the diverse forms of fauna and flora they support.

Port facilities for the export of Hamersley iron ore have been developed at the mainland town of Dampier.

Dampier Land WA A low-lying peninsula of red sand and gravels and poor scrub (known as pindan country), Dampier Land lies west of the Kimberley between Roebuck Bay and King Sound. Most of the land is occupied by an Aboriginal reserve, with mission stations at Lombardina and Beagle Bay.

dams and reservoirs Australia has more than 320 large dams – a 'large dam' being defined as one more than 15m high from lowest foundation to highest point. Storages are designed variously for water conservation, irrigation, hydro-electricity, water supply and sewerage, and flood control. The first major dam to be constructed was Yan Yean, completed in 1857 to provide water for Melbourne; the Cataract Dam, to supply Sydney and Wollongong, was built in 1907. From that time, and particularly since World War 2, many major dams have been constructed to use to best advantage the country's relatively sparse rainfall. Australia's largest earth and rockfill dam is the Dartmouth, in northern Vic., but in addition to the major works there are numerous small dams and impounds on agricultural properties for watering livestock and other purposes.

In an arid continent such as Australia, dams traditionally have been regarded with favour. However, conservationists increasingly criticise continual dam building, deploring the loss of rivers and drowning of landscapes. Hydro-electric projects in Tas. have been at the centre of much controversy. >> *water and water resources*

damselflies > *dragonflies and damselflies*

dance > *ballet and dance*

Dandenong Ranges Vic. This relatively low range lies at the eastern boundary of metropolitan Melbourne. The rich volcanic soils support orchards, market gardens and lush vegetation, and the region is noted for its rhododendron and azalea gardens. Reserves include Ferntree Gully National Park, densely forested and with verdant fern gullies, and Sherbrooke Forest, where patience may be rewarded with a lyrebird display. Other tourist attractions include the William Ricketts Sanctuary, displaying this artist's sculptures of Aboriginal people, and the 20km ride along the narrow-gauge railway on the stream train *Puffing Billy*. Silvan dam, part of Melbourne's water supply system, is in the eastern part of the range; on the southwest slopes, the industrial city of Dandenong combines traditional cattle-marketing for Gippsland producers with development of car, rubber, canning and glass factories, and is now part of the Melbourne metropolitan area.

Darcy, Les (James Leslie) (1895–1917), boxer, b. Stradbroke, NSW. Darcy was a blacksmith's apprentice before he took up boxing in 1911. Arguably Australia's greatest boxing hero, he took part in some 50 fights in the next five years and lost only four. He was variously Australian lightweight, middleweight and heavyweight champion. He died in the US, after contracting pneumonia.

Dargie, Sir William Alexander (1912–   ), painter, b. Melbourne. A traditional portraitist of great merit, Dargie has won the prestigious Archibald Prize eight times. He has painted portraits of many noted Australians, including the scientist Sir Macfarlane Burnet and artists such as Sir Lionel Lindsay and Albert Namatjira; major overseas commissions have included portraits of Queen Elizabeth II and others of the British royal family, and members of the British aristocracy. Dargie served as official war artist 1941–6, and was director of the Vic. National Gallery art school 1946–53.

Dark, Eleanor (1901–86), novelist, b. Sydney. After contributing short stories and verse to magazines such as the *Bulletin*, Dark wrote her first novel, *Slow Dawning*, in 1932. Her most notable work is the landmark historical trilogy, *The Timeless Land* (1941), *Storm of Time* (1948) and *No Barrier* (1954), which covered the development of European settlement in Australia from 1788 to the crossing of the Blue Mountains in 1814. Dark was one of Australia's best-selling serious novelists in the 1940s and 1950s; her work received little attention for many years but is now regaining popularity and critical recognition.

Darling, Sir James Ralph (1899–   ), educator, b. England. After teaching at Merchant Taylors' School and Charterhouse in England, Darling was appointed headmaster of Geelong Grammar School in Vic. in 1929; he

subsequently exercised great influence over Australian secondary and tertiary education until his retirement in 1961, most notably as secretary and chairman of the Headmasters' Conference of Australia. He was also chairman of numerous public bodies, including the ABC 1961–7. His autobiography, *Richly Rewarding*, was published in 1978.

Darling Downs A distinctive region of southeast Qld lying west of the Great Dividing Range at a height of 350–600m, the Darling Downs includes the southeast–northwest course of the Condamine River, which is fed by short streams from the Main Range and the Bunya Range. In the west the region is bounded by poorer sandstone country, in the south by the granite belt and in the north also by the Great Dividing Range, here a low plateau. Originally a sheep-raising district, the fertile soils now support extensive grain-growing, chiefly wheat but including barley, maize, oats and oilseeds; irrigated land in the west produces cotton. Dairy and beef cattle also important, and oil, natural gas and coal are natural resources. Discovered in 1827 by Allan Cunningham (who named the region after Sir Ralph Darling, governor of NSW), the region was first settled by pastoralist Patrick Leslie in 1840. Toowoomba is the main market and industrial centre.

Darling Range WA The southwestern edge of the great inland plateau, rising abruptly to present a rather even skyline of 240–300m elevation east of the coastal plains around metropolitan Perth, the range extends about 300km north–south; the highest point is Mt Cooke (580m). Short rivers dissect the forested scarp; on a number of them dams have been constructed to provide water for urban purposes and irrigation, including the goldfields water-supply scheme. Widespread bauxite deposits are worked at Jarrahdale and Hotham Valley. The range was named in 1827 by James Stirling after the governor of NSW.

Darling River NSW Uniting the waters of a number of rivers, the Darling system drains an immense area of about 650 000sq.km in NSW and southern Qld. The Darling itself flows for some 1900km from the confluence of the Barwon and Culgoa rivers to join the Murray at Wentworth. Above the Barwon-Culgoa confluence are its major tributaries, rising on the western slopes of the Great Dividing Range:

the Maranoa and the Condamine/Balonne (via the Culgoa) in Qld, and the Macintyre/Dumaresq, Gwydir, Namoi, Castlereagh, Macquarie and Bogan (via the Barwon) in NSW. Below Bourke it is fed by the intermittent flow of the Warrego and the Paroo. Much of the Darling's meandering course, with many anabranches, is through extensive saltbush pastures with less than 25cm mean annual rainfall; numerous distributaries set off, only to end in dry, sandy channels. Water conservation and irrigation are of prime importance in this arid region, and weirs and dams dot the Darling and its tributaries; the Menindee Lakes are used to store water for stock and domestic purposes. Charles Sturt and Hamilton Hume first reached the Darling, in 1828, near the present town of Bourke. The basin was settled by pastoralists, and some of Australia's finest merino wool is produced in the region.

darter A large, aquatic bird with a long, slender neck, the darter, *Anhinga novaehollandiae,* inhabits rivers and swamplands throughout Australia; it is closely related to the cormorants. Swimming underwater, the darter impales fish on its sharp bill; when only the body is submerged the visible head and neck resemble an emerging snake, which is the source of an alternative name, snakebird. Darters breed in small colonies, nesting in swampland trees.

Darwin NT Capital of the NT and Australia's northernmost city, Darwin is one of the most rapidly growing cities of the nation but still the smallest capital. Until quite recently still a relaxed, tropical frontier town, Darwin was almost completely rebuilt after its destruction by Cyclone Tracy in 1974 and is now a truly modern metropolis. Occupying a flat peninsula at the northeast entry to Port Darwin, the city has a humid tropical climate, with average temperatures ranging from 20°C to 30°C, and an annual rainfall of more than 1500mm. Its wet season, from November to March, regularly brings tropical cyclones, which have destroyed its fabric five times (1878, 1882, 1897, 1937 and 1974).

The land around the harbour was named in honour of Charles Darwin in 1839. The original settlement, surveyed by George Goyder in 1869, was called Palmerston after a British prime minister; it was renamed Darwin in 1911, when the Commonwealth took over administration of the NT. Darwin was intended as a port for

trade with Asia, but neither trade nor agriculture prospered and for a time the settlement existed mainly as an Overland Telegraph link to overseas. A gold rush to Pine Creek in 1872, and the discovery of pearlshell in 1884, helped to sustain growth and in the 1930s Darwin became the principal point of entry and exit for air services to and from Australia. During World War 2 Darwin was bombed by Japanese forces and the civilian population was evacuated, but the war also led to a better transport system and the setting up of a military garrison; after the war, pastoral and mineral developments led to renewed expansion. Like World War 2, Cyclone Tracy was not an unmitigated disaster for Darwin: the destruction was massive, but has led to a better-planned system of continued growth since 1974.

At the census of 1986 the Darwin Statistical Division had a population of 72 937, which showed a growth rate of 11.08% over the five years between censuses. The city is characterised by its cultural diversity, with large numbers of Aborigines, Chinese, Greeks and Italians. Service industries and the public sector – including defence establishments – provide employment for most of Darwin's workforce, with tourism the major growth industry and the NT government a part-proprietor of tourist-based enterprises. Prawning, other fisheries and the production of cultured pearls are important, and Darwin is the main port for export of the NT's production of beef, uranium, zinc and lead. Darwin suffers traffic congestion, largely because its central business district is located on a peninsula; this problem seems likely to worsen as the city continues to grow and new southern suburbs are developed.

David, Sir (Tannatt William) Edgeworth (1858–1934), geologist, b. Wales. David came to Australia in 1882. As a surveyor with the NSW Department of Mines, he investigated the coal deposits of the Hunter Valley, which included tracing the rich Greta seams. He was professor of geology and physical geography at Sydney University 1891–1924, carrying out fundamental geological research; his definitive work, *The Geology of the Commonwealth of Australia* (1950) was completed after his death by W. R. Browne. A member of the Shackleton Antarctic expedition 1907–9, he led the ascent of Mt Erebus, and with two companions made the epic journey to the South Magnetic Pole.

Davies, David (1864–1939), painter, b. Ballarat, Vic. A student of Vic.'s National Gallery art school in the late 1880s, Davies was a romantic landscape painter who adopted *plein-air* techniques and was associated with the Heidelberg School. After studies in Paris and a sojourn in Cornwall, he returned to Melbourne 1893–7 but later went again to the UK and eventually settled in France, where he continued to paint until the 1930s. His only major exhibition in Australia was in 1926, but his work is highly prized (and valued) in Australia today.

Davies family, prominent in Tas. newspaper publishing and politics. **John** (1813–72), b. England, was transported for fraud in 1831 and after his release in 1837 was variously a hotel-keeper, reporter and policeman. In 1852, with Auber George Jones, he founded the *Hobarton Guardian*, of which he became sole proprietor when it was merged with the *Hobarton Mercury* in 1854. His sons **John George** (1846–1913) and **Charles Ellis** (1847–1921), both b. Hobart, took over the *Mercury* in 1871; both also served in the Tas. parliament, John being Speaker 1903–13 and knighted in the latter year. Davies Brothers Ltd, publisher of the Hobart *Mercury* and the *Sunday Tasmanian*, was under family control until it became a wholly owned subsidiary of News Ltd in 1987.

Davis > *Antarctic Territory*

Davis, Arthur Hoey > *Rudd, Steele*

Davis, Judy (1955–), actress, b. Perth. A sensitive actress of brooding mien, Davis first received public and critical acclaim in *My Brilliant Career* (1979). Other films include *Winter of Our Dreams* (1981), *Heatwave* (1982) and *High Tide* (1987). For her leading role in British director David Lean's *A Passage to India* (1984), she was nominated for a US Academy Award. Also a stage actress of note, her major roles have included those of Lulu and Hedda Gabler.

Davis Cup > *tennis*

Davison, Frank Dalby (1893–1970) author, b. Glenferrie, Vic. In his youth Davison travelled widely in the US and West Indies. After service during World War 1, he returned to Australia and his novels and short stories began to be published in the 1920s. Among the first was the perennially popular *Man-Shy* (first serialised 1923–5); like most of his stories, it is closely observed and written in almost lyrical prose, with a country background.

Dawe, Bruce (1930–), poet, b. Geelong, Vic. Dawe is a prolific poet – the tough-minded, satirical celebrant of Australian sub-urbia. After various aimless jobs, he completed his schooling and briefly attended the University of Melbourne. He spent nine years in the RAAF, during which he married, published two volumes of verse and completed his first degree. He turned academic and teacher in Qld, becoming widely enjoyed for his succinct, wittily colloquial poems, his ironic yet essentially serious and tender affirmation of human existence.

Dawson, Peter Smith (1882–1961), singer, b. Adelaide. In 1902 Dawson left for London, where he made his first appearance at Covent Garden in 1909 and became principal baritone for music publisher Chappell's ballad concerts in 1910. A prolific and popular singer with a range that extended from grand opera to the music hall, Dawson made some 3500 record-ings, many under pseudonyms. He also com-posed songs under the name J. P. McCall.

Dawson River Qld A major tributary of the Fitzroy River, the Dawson rises in the Carnarvon Range; it flows through an area of brigalow scrub, although much of this has been cleared for cattle rearing. A system of weirs has been constructed to supply the Dawson Valley irrigation area, which produces wheat, sorghum and cotton. The river was discovered by Ludwig Leichhardt in 1844.

Daydream Island > *Cumberland Islands*

Daylesford Vic. (pop. 3111) A former gold-mining town some 110km northwest of Melbourne, Daylesford is best known for its mineral springs, and like nearby Hepburn Springs it has become a popular spa and tourist resort.

Deakin, Alfred (1856–1919), politician, b. Collingwood, Vic. Prime minister of Australia three times 1903–10, Deakin was the out-standing political leader of the first years of the Commonwealth. Training in law and journa-lism preceded his entering the Vic. legislative assembly in 1879, where he soon achieved eminence through his powerful advocacy and personality. He was distinguished by his outspoken defence of Australian interests in Pacific affairs at the 1887 London colonial conference, and his great work in the Federation movement was one of negotiation, persuasion, diplomacy and advocacy; he played a major role in seeing the Federation Bill accepted in London. His posthumously published *The Federal Story*, edited by H. Brookes (1944), is a brilliantly analytical (if sometimes biased) account of the personalities involved. As attorney-general in the first federal parliament, he succeeded Sir Edmund Barton as prime minister 1903–4. The emerging Labor party supported him in his second and most constructive ministry, 1905–8, which laid foundations for pensions, defence, protection and the broad bases of Australian life for 30 years. Labor's support being withdrawn in 1908, Deakin formed, with former political opponents, the anti-Labor Fusion Party for his third term in office, 1909–10. He retired in 1913, having consistently refused all honours.

death adder > *snakes*

Debenham, Frank (1883–1965), geographer, b. Bowral, NSW. Debenham served as geologist with Scott's Antarctic expedition (1910–13); he later moved to England, where he lectured in surveying (1919) and later became professor of geography (1930–49) at Cambridge University. He was founding director of the Scott Polar Research Institute and published many notable works on geography and cartography. In 1948 he was awarded the Victoria Medal for his contribution to geographical education and polar exploration.

de Castella, Robert > *athletics*

deer Deer were first brought to Australia in the early 19th century, and there are now six species of feral animals – fallow, rusa, red, sambar, chital and hog. A further four types live in captivity: Wapiti, whitetail and Pere David's in NSW, and muntjae in SA. Of the feral deer, four species are commonly farmed (fallow, rusa, chital and red), mainly for venison but also for antler velvet, which is used in Asian medicines. About 40 000 animals graze on several hundred deer farms, and almost all venison produced is consumed locally, mainly in restaurants; however, two-thirds of Australia's venison demand is imported.

defence Australia, like most small countries in a world of superpowers, relies on an alliance for its ultimate defence. For the first 150 years of settlement, this alliance was with Britain; since World War 2, it has been with the US.

Prior to Federation in 1901 the defence of the colonies was undertaken by the British government, although individual colonies established small militias, particularly after 1870 when all British troops were withdrawn. At the 1887 colonial conference in London, the colonies were authorised to operate auxiliary naval squadrons, which were later consolidated into an Australian navy. Under the Defence Act 1903, the higher organisation of military forces rested with a federal minister for defence, a defence council that advised on policy and co-ordination, and naval and military boards that administered these two branches of the service; an air board was added after World War 1. This structure lasted until World War 2, when the government established separate ministries for each armed service.

The two world wars Between 1901 and 1941, Australian defence policy was linked completely to Britain's, the Royal Navy being Australia's first line of defence. During World War 1, Australian contingents operated generally as an integral part of British forces, usually under direct British command. Australia willingly provided troops for the Middle East and the Western Front, and having done so was initially prepared to have them fight where Britain wanted. As the war dragged on, this attitude was questioned and attempts to introduce > *conscription* caused bitter divisions in Australian society. From a population of fewer than 5 million, however, some 417 000 Australians enlisted voluntarily to fight for the British Empire. At the end of the war, Australia was still linked militarily to Britain: it used British ships, guns and organisational methods, and its own tiny permanent forces provided protection for but one tentacle of Britain's vast Asian domain, the military centre of which was Singapore (expanded into a major base in the 1920s).

At the outbreak of World War 2, Australia repeated the pattern of World War 1 and sent a second AIF to the Middle East; pilots were seconded to the RAF, and RAAF squadrons were later sent to the European theatre. Although Japan had been bellicose since 1932 (when it invaded Manchuria and then China), it was thought unlikely to take on the British

Empire: this assumption was proved wrong when, in the few months following the attack on Pearl Harbor in December 1941, Japan invaded not only the British colonies in Asia but also those of the Dutch, as well as the US-protected Philippines. The British battleships *Prince of Wales* and *Repulse*, sent by Churchill to provide 'a vague menace', were both sunk on 10 December 1941. In 1942, the 'impregnable' Singapore base proved to be a chimera: 130 000 British troops were captured at its fall, including 15 000 Australians. For the first time, Australia had an enemy on its doorstep; so did Britain half a world away, and it was in no position to offer Australia protection. The South-West Pacific Command was set up under US general Douglas MacArthur and, in tandem but under overall American command, Australian and US forces slowly pushed the Japanese northwards. This association represented the entry of the US as Australia's umbrella and major ally, a position it has held ever since.

Postwar defence The prewar colonial structure in Asia was re-established after World War 2, but it soon became obvious that the days of European empires in Asia were over. It was equally obvious that Australia could no longer rely on Britain for protection; in fact, Britain was becoming reliant increasingly on Australia to help protect its Asian interests. Initially, the only postwar overseas deployment of Australian troops was as part of the British Commonwealth Occupation Force (BCOF) in Japan, but in 1948 the ANZAM agreement was signed between Britain, NZ and Australia, which was directed against a communist-led insurrection in Malaya. During this 'emergency', which extended from 1948 to 1960, Australia sent troops and aircraft. At the outbreak of the > *Korean War*, Australia was one of the first countries to rally under the UN flag, initially sending forces from BCOF. In 1951, at the height of that war, Australia signed the > *ANZUS treaty* with the US and NZ, which declared that the three countries would combine in the event of an attack against any one of them; this agreement heralded the nation's emotional and practical break with Britain. At the time some were surprised that Britain was not invited to participate; this was not so with the British themselves, however, as they were already extended beyond their means and beginning to relinquish the role of world policeman to the US.

In 1954, the South-East Asia Treaty Organisation (> *SEATO*) was established after the collapse of the French regime in Indochina. Australia saw SEATO as an organisation through which it could apply a policy of 'forward defence', but during the > *Vietnam War* of 1962–72 this approach was proved to be fruitless. Australia had meanwhile (1963–5) been involved in the Indonesian confrontation with Malaysia, through its commitment to the British Commonwealth Strategic Reserve. In 1971, following Britain's decision to withdraw from its Southeast Asian bases, a military treaty, the Five Power Defence Arrangement (FPDA), was signed between Britain, Australia, NZ, Malaysia and Singapore. Initially, Australia provided about half of the ground forces, all air defence capability and a naval force.

The FPDA is still active and provides Australia's major overseas defence commitment through its Mirage squadron and Orion surveillance aircraft stationed at Butterworth, near Penang in Malaysia. Australia also has co-operative defence arrangements with other Asian countries, including Thailand, the Philippines and Brunei, which generally involve joint exercises and a high degree of participation with the US. Australia also has a close relationship with PNG, providing specialist advice and training, and with the island nations of the South Pacific. Through the Pacific Patrol Boat Project, boats are supplied to PNG, Vanuatu, Western Samoa, Fiji, the Solomon Islands and the Cook Islands.

Australian defence policy is aimed at the development of an independent defence capability, based more on 'continental' than 'forward' defence. Great value is placed on developing defence relationships with neighbouring countries, however, and the ANZUS treaty is still of primary importance, although some doubts have been expressed about possible US action should Australia ever become embroiled in a confrontation with Indonesia, which is friendly to the US. When Indonesia invaded and annexed the former Portuguese colony of East Timor in 1975, Australia wisely avoided a military confrontation in view of its limited strike capability and the certain lack of support from the US; such docile acceptance of Indonesia's action did, however, cause some controversy at the time.

At present there are no external threats to Australia's security, although there is a feeling that PNG might present a future problem in the form of a military coup. Because of its close relationship with PNG, and billion-dollar investment there, Australia could not stand by in such an event, particularly if a government unfriendly to Australian interests took control. It could therefore be forced into a 'police' action of a type practised elsewhere by Britain and the US; the role that Indonesia might play in such an event is a moot point and one of some concern to defence planners.

Defence administration In 1972, the Whitlam government restructured not only defence policy but also the machinery of defence. As was the case earlier this century, a single cabinet minister – the minister for defence – controls the armed forces, which are generally known collectively as the defence force; a junior minister handles defence science and personnel. The government is advised by the chief of the defence force and the secretary of the Department of Defence, and by a Council of Defence in matters of control and administration. Three main committees take part in forward planning, budget estimates and defence policy, the most important of these being the Chiefs of Staff Committee, which contains a member from each branch of the armed forces and provides general advice to the chief of the defence force. Expenditure on defence in 1987 was $7578 million, of which over $2000 million was spent on new equipment.

A Defence Logistics Organisation (DLO) was created in 1984, partly in response to the complexity of modern defence requirements. It provides a structure for co-ordinating all facets of the defence force, both within Australia and overseas, through international agreements concerning the purchase of equipment and supply of spare parts. With the high costs involved it is important to justify acquisitions, particularly as year by year a greater percentage of the defence budget has to be spent on major new equipment. A computer development program undertaken by the DLO will support management and operational needs of the defence force beyond the year 2000.

Other arms of the defence infrastructure include the Defence Science and Technology Organisation (DSTO), the Natural Disasters Organisation (NDO), and the Office of Defence Production (ODP). The DSTO is the second-largest research organisation in Australia: its seven main laboratories around Australia conduct research into the entire gamut of defence and defence-related needs, from aeronautics and weapons systems to food science. The NDO provides armed forces for State and Territory anti-disaster organisations when requested, and operates a counter-disaster col-lege at Mt Macedon, Vic. The ODP manages the government-owned factories and dockyards related to the defence force, such as the Aerospace Technologies of Australia at Fishermans Bend in Vic. and the Garden Island Dockyard in NSW.

In March 1987, a government White Paper on the defence of Australia defined self-reliance as being a crucial part of defence policy. To this end, involvement by Australian industry is seen as vital if the defence force is to be independent of overseas sources. At the present time, over 90% of defence expenditure on repair and maintenance is incurred in Australia and some 30% of the contract value of imported armaments is offset to local industry. In 1988, six new submarines worth $3900 million were being built in SA, with an offset value of over 70%; a new mine-hunter was being built in Newcastle, NSW; 38 Black Hawk helicopters were being assembled at Bankstown, NSW; and a contract had been signed for 67 Pilatus PC9 trainer aircraft, 65 of which will be constructed in Australia. >> *defence forces; foreign policy; World War 1; World War 2*

defence forces The three main arms of Australia's defence force are the Royal Australian Navy, the Australian Army and the Royal Australian Air Force.

Royal Australian Navy (RAN) Australian naval defence was in the hands of the Royal Navy until the colonial conference in London in 1887. This authorised the various colonies to operate an auxiliary naval squadron, with ships lent by Britain but staffed by Australians. Three ships of the Australian auxiliary fought in the China War of 1900, raising protests from the colonies about the use of Australian vessels and men in a war in which they had no interest. Following Federation, a naval board was instituted in 1905 with the purpose of consolidating the colonial fleet. The Australian navy came into being in 1910, much of its organisation planned by Captain (later Vice-Admiral Sir) William Creswell, an RN officer after whom the present-day naval college is named. In 1911, King George V granted the navy the title 'Royal'.

At the start of World War 1, the RAN fleet consisted of one battle cruiser, the *Australia*, twelve smaller cruisers and destroyers, and two submarines. Officers were still from the Royal Navy, the naval college having been established only in 1913. During the war, the cruiser

Sydney sank the German raider *Emden* off the Cocos Islands, and both submarines were lost: the *AE1* disappearing off the coast of New Britain, and the *AE2* being scuttled while trying to force the Straits of Marmara prior to the Gallipoli Campaign. Postwar, the RAN's strength was reduced dramatically, partly as a result of the Washington Conference of 1921–2 during which limits were imposed on the size of the British, US and Japanese naval fleets. The RAN's largest ship, the *Australia*, was scrapped. Overall, Australian defence policy between the wars was interlinked with Britain, which in the case of naval power in Asia revolved around the RN base in Singapore. The RAN was simply an adjunct to this, its only role being to protect coastal shipping lanes. At the outbreak of World War 2 the RAN had only sixteen vessels in commission, but a concentrated effort of building started which produced warships up to the size of destroyers and corvettes. RAN ships served in nearly all theatres of the war, from Tobruk to Borneo, losing three cruisers, three destroyers, and numerous smaller vessels. Nevertheless, by 1945 the RAN had 317 ships in commission.

Postwar an aircraft carrier, the *Sydney*, was acquired, and a Fleet Air Arm was established in 1948. Nine RAN warships, including the *Sydney*, saw action during the Korean War, and four destroyers were sent to support US ships during the Vietnam War. In February 1964, Australia's worst peacetime naval accident occurred when the RAN's second carrier and flagship, the *Melbourne*, collided with the destroyer *Voyager* off Jervis Bay, NSW, cutting it in two with the loss of 82 lives. Amazingly, the *Melbourne* was involved in a similar accident in June 1969 in the South China Sea, when she cut the US destroyer *Frank E. Evans* in two, with the loss of 74 US sailors. In neither case was blame attributed to the *Melbourne*.

Ships of the RAN include three guided missile destroyers, four guided missile frigates (with two on order), five destroyer escorts, six submarines (with six on order), and various supply, hydrographic research and patrol vessels. The RAN has no aircraft carriers and the Fleet Air Arm operates mainly helicopters. The RAN's basic duties are antisubmarine surveillance and coastal patrol. Total personnel strength of the RAN in 1987 was 15 803 (14 345 men and 1458 women).

Australian Army British army regiments – along with naval personnel and marines – protected the colonies from the time of the First Fleet up to 1870, when British troops were withdrawn. Prior to this, all the colonies had raised small detachments of volunteer militia, which in 1877–83 were co-ordinated into a parallel force, based on the reports of Major-General Sir William Jervois and Lieutenant Peter Scratchley. Immediately after Federation the government took control of the various State forces, and through the Defence Act of 1903 the Australian army was formed under the command of Major-General Sir Edward Hutton. Numbers and effectiveness had been stimulated by the Sudan campaign in 1885, to which NSW had sent an infantry battalion and battery of field artillery, and by the Boer War. In 1909 an Act for compulsory military training was passed. In 1910 a report by Lord Kitchener led to the division of Australia into 215 areas for land-defence purposes and to the extension of compulsory training for what was basically a citizens militia.

The first regular force of any size, the Australian Imperial Force (AIF), was formed in 1914 after the outbreak of World War 1. Between the two world wars, the army again reverted to a mainly citizens militia although retaining the structure and organisation of the AIF. This situation continued into World War 2 and at the outbreak of the war Australian army strength was 82 800, of which 80 000 were from the militia; limited conscription was introduced. World War 2 saw the development of Australia's first regular army, which was maintained after the war, partly as a response to a constant series of crises in Asia, including the Korean War, the Malayan insurgency, the Indonesian confrontation and the Vietnam War. The regular army was supplemented by the Citizen Military Force (CMF). During this period, training was angled more towards jungle warfare and away from the desert warfare for which Australians had been famous in the two world wars.

In 1972, the most radical changes to the army's structure since Federation were announced: the geographical commands were replaced by three functional commands – land, training and logistics – based on seven military districts covering the whole of Australia; as well, the CMF – now called the Army Reserve – was made a volunteer force and conscription was abolished. Although a small army by world standards, the Australian army – like the British – is a highly professional force unencumbered by conscripts and able to respond quickly to any emergency. Total personnel strength in 1987 was 32 311 (30 016 men and 2295 women).

Royal Australian Air Force (RAAF) The RAAF was created in 1921, based on the Australian Flying Corps that was formed early in World War 1 and saw action on the Western Front and in the Middle East. The foundation strength of the RAAF was 130 airmen and 20 officers, flying 128 aircraft that were a gift from the British government. The first squadron was formed in 1922 and was based at Laverton, Vic. The depression of the early 1930s inhibited expansion, but by 1938 the expansion of the German air force and Japanese aggression in China were causing concern; under pressure from Britain, elaborate plans were implemented to double the size of the RAAF. Owing to a shortage of aircraft, the Commonwealth Aircraft Corporation was formed, which manufactured the Wirraway, a plane based on the American NA33. During World War 2, RAAF pilots flew in most theatres of operation, many flying in RAF bomber squadrons over Germany.

After the war, a dramatic cutback in resources left the RAAF with only three active fighter squadrons, one of which fought in Korea flying Meteors, a jet that proved to be no match for Russian-built MiGs. RAAF squadrons were stationed in Malaya during the communist insurgency of the 1950s, flying Sabre fighters and Canberra bombers. During the 1960s, the RAAF's main fighter plane was the French-designed Mirage, which was supplemented by Caribou and Hercules transport aircraft and army-support squadrons of Iriquois and Chinook helicopters, all of which were used during the Vietnam War.

The RAAF is organised into two groups, Operational Command, which supplies combat-ready forces, and Support Command, which provides training and maintenance. The strike-reconnaissance force of the RAAF is equipped with F-111 fighter-bombers, which replaced Canberras and Sabres, and F/A-18 Hornets, multi-role fighters that are replacing the ageing Mirages. Other aircraft include Orion P-3Cs for maritime surveillance, and various transport and training planes. New helicopters on order include the Black Hawk and Sikorsky, both being assembled in Australia. Total personnel strength of the RAAF in 1987 was 22 647 (20 161 men and 2846 women).

Defence force colleges Australia has four main institutions for the training of officers for the armed services. The Royal Military College was suggested originally by Lord Kitchener in 1910 and was established at Duntroon, a sheep station in the ACT, in 1911. The Royal Australian Naval College, HMAS *Creswell*, started operation in Geelong in 1913 and two years later moved to its present site at Jervis Bay. The Royal Australian Air Force Academy was established at Point Cook, Vic., in 1947, with flying training being undertaken at Pearce, WA.

In 1974, the Commonwealth government announced its intention to establish a single tertiary educational institution for all defence forces. The Australian Defence Force Academy, located in Canberra, was opened in 1986 with the University of NSW responsible for its academic integrity. Degrees are offered in arts, science and engineering up to PhD level. Entry is by selection and all undergraduates are officer cadets of their respective services. The number of officer cadets was about 1100 in 1989, and ADFA will supply about 40% of all defence-force officers. Each service also has a staff college for the training of officers for command and higher appointments: the army at Queenscliff, Vic., the navy at Balmoral, NSW, and the airforce at Fairbairn, ACT.

de Maistre, Roy [Leroy Leveson Laurent Joseph de Mestre] (1894–1968), artist, b. Bowral, NSW. An exponent of cubism and post-Impressionism, de Maistre – with Roland Wakelin and Grace Cossington Smith – was responsible for helping to introduce these styles to NSW artists. A former student of the Sydney Conservatorium, his thematic preoccupations were music, colour and (in later life) religion; a major commission was *Stations of the Cross* for Westminster Cathedral. He settled permanently in London in 1930, and exhibited in London, Paris, Sydney and New York.

Democratic Labor Party > *DLP*

Deniliquin NSW (pop. 8000) This market and service centre for the Riverina district lies on the Edward River (an anabranch of the Murray) 750km southwest of Sydney. The surrounding region is noted for its sheep, wool, wheat and dairying, as well as crops (grown mainly under irrigation); the pioneering merino stud farms developed by the Falkiner family lie to the north of the town; a local museum features the history of their Peppin strain of merino sheep.

Dennis, C. J. (Clarence Michael James)
(1876–1938), journalist and poet, b. Auburn, SA. Dennis had various occupations, from barman to journalist, during which he wrote his famous humorous, slang-filled light verse of the Melbourne larrikin redeemed by the 'love of a pure woman'. He was hailed in his time as the first poet to capture the Australian national spirit, most notably in the idiosyncratic characters and humour of *The Songs of a Sentimental Bloke* (1915); and its sequel written especially for the AIF, *The Moods of Ginger Mick* (1916).

D'Entrecasteaux, Joseph-Antoine Raymond de Bruny
(1739–93), navigator and hydrographer, b. France. D'Entrecasteaux was in charge of an expedition sent 1791–3 to look for the explorer La Pérouse, and to carry out scientific research. The expedition charted the southwest coast of Tas. and much of the coast east to Nuyts Archipelago. Later it also accomplished much Pacific investigation.

D'Entrecasteaux Channel
Tas. This 56km channel separates Bruny Island from the southeastern Tas. mainland and is the centre of the Australian scallop industry. It is named for Admiral Bruny d'Entrecasteaux, whose survey determined that the body of water was a channel – not, as previously thought, a bay.

depressions and recessions, economic
> *business; economy*

Derby
WA (pop. 3258) Situated on King Sound northeast of Broome and 2370km northeast of Perth, Derby is a major centre for mineral exploration in the Kimberley region and an administrative centre for the State's northwest. Although developed as a port, Derby experiences extreme tidal ranges which have frequently stranded ships.

Derwent River
Tas. The Derwent flows 190km southeast from Lake St Clair in central Tas. and empties into Storm Bay some 19km north of Hobart. In its upper reaches it is joined by a number of streams including the Nive, Dee, Ouse, Clyde and Florentine, the first two of which – like the Derwent itself – have been developed for hydro-electricity. The lower course of the river, a fault-lined depression filled with sediments and carved into terraces by river action, is a rich farming area centred on New Norfolk and producing apples, pears and hops.

design
Australian design has long embodied a fusion of overseas ideas and influences. Although local materials and motifs were used from the 19th century, imported styles – and goods themselves – were generally deemed superior and adopted indiscriminately until well into the 20th century. The nation's aesthetic ethos was immortalised by architect and critic Robin Boyd as late as 1960 in his *The Australian Ugliness* and in his castigation of Australians' 'savage urge to decorate'. In the last 20 years, however, Australian design has come of age and its styles and products – from clothing to homewares and furniture – are competing most successfully in world markets.

During the 19th century, Australian design was by and large a copy of English (sometimes European) styles and fashions. The nationalism of the 1890s awakened some to the possibility of a distinctly Australian culture, but those who could afford to do so still imported British fashion, furniture, textiles and interior style. In the early 20th century, European Art Nouveau was followed by Moderne and Art Deco, although antipodean imagery was gradually incorporated.

By the 1940s a few maverick Australians had begun to produce original and distinctive designs: furniture by Grant Featherstone in Melbourne and Douglas Snelling and Roger McClay in Sydney, for example, used modern techniques and materials to produce streamlined shapes. In the 1950s the inventive mettle, heralded much earlier by creations such as the Coolgardie food safe, was realised in such problem-solving classics as the Hills rotary clothes-hoist and Victa lawn-mower. The affluence of the 1960s and attendant consumer demand saw more products designed and produced for specific Australian conditions, a trend that continued into the 1970s; improved industrial design made mass production viable. Professionals such as > *Gordon Andrews*, working in diverse design fields from graphics to household utensils, continued and refined the tradition of solving technical problems with aesthetically pleasing solutions.

The 1980s witnessed increasing sophistication and commercial development in all fields of design – interiors, fashion, decorative arts, architecture, theatre design, and exhibitions. The independent Design Institute of Australia (founded 1958) and the Design Committee of the Australia Council have been instrumental in fostering design excellence and education. The wit and ingenuity of Ken Cato's graphics, the elegant designs of Richard Carlson (creator of the Decor BYO wine cooler), the environmentally sympathetic architectural solutions of Glen Murcutt, the garden design of Andrew Pfeiffer, the technical wizardry of Paul Schremmer's communications and safety equipment, and the innovative work of young designers in all fields demonstrate the value of good design in everyday life. In concept, technical innovation and expertise, and aesthetic quality, the best of Australian design is now international. >> *architecture*; *craft*; *fashion industry*

Devil's Marbles NT In the Devil's Marbles conservation reserve, 96km south of Tennant Creek, is this collection of granite boulders – some extremely large – scattered in groups about a shallow valley. Originally granite blocks created by the basic rock splitting along joint planes, in the arid climatic conditions they have weathered to become roughly spherical, varying in diameter from 30cm to about 6m, and in some cases poised apparently precariously one upon another. The Marbles figure in legends of the local Aborigines.

Devonport Tas. (pop. 22 645) The State's fourth-largest city, Devonport lies on the Mersey River 288km northwest of Hobart; it was formed by the joining of two settlements, Formby and Torquay, in 1890. It is a busy industrial town, the shipment point for exports from the Mersey valley (notably fruit, dairy products and paper) and the terminal for the Tas.–Vic. ferry.

Diamantina River Qld/SA An intermittent river with headwaters in the Selwyn Range southeast of Cloncurry, the Diamantina flows for over 800km southwest towards Lake Eyre through the Channel Country and across the SA border, where its lower course is called the Warburton. Traversing a region of little and unreliable rainfall, its waters reach Lake Eyre only in exceptionally wet seasons.

diamond birds > *pardalotes*

diamonds > *gems and gemstones*

Dickerson, Robert Henry (1924–), artist, b. Hurstville, NSW. A leading Australian painter since the 1960s, Dickerson had no formal art training and spent four years as a professional boxer before joining the RAAF

during World War 2. A figurative painter who was associated with Melbourne's Antipodean Group from 1959, he has concentrated on the melancholy and loneliness of daily – principally urban – life. His stylistically simple paintings are peopled by two-dimensional figures.

dingo Believed to have been introduced to the Australian mainland (never in Tas.) by Aborigines less than 5000 years ago, the dingo or warrigal, *Canis familiaris dingo*, is now widely distributed; in central Australia the majority of animals are pure-bred, while in the east they have interbred with domestic dogs. Generally yellowish in colour, with white toes and tail-tip, the dingo is usually a solitary animal, although loosely knit groups exist and may gather to hunt large prey or in the breeding season; the familiar howl is used both as a means of contact and as an advertisement of territorial rights. An opportunistic hunter of virtually anything edible, from the earliest days of white settlement the dingo was a predator upon livestock – chiefly sheep. Methods of control have included poisoning, trapping, shooting, bounty payments and exclusion fencing, the last-named employed on both Qld–NSW and NSW–SA borders, and within the States of Qld, SA and WA.

diplomatic representation > *embassies and high commissions*

Diptera > *flies*

Dirk Hartog Island WA This elongated finger of land, 77km long and less than 10km wide, lies at the south of the entrance to Shark Bay. It is the westernmost point of Australia, and is named after the Dutch explorer who was the first European to set foot on the continent. He recorded his landing (in 1616) by leaving a pewter plate on the northern tip of the island, which was later named Point Inscription.

disarmament and arms control The movement for nuclear disarmament was a minor and peripheral phenomenon in Australian politics before the 1980s. In 1984, however, it demonstrated a new level of public support and political importance when the newly formed > *Nuclear Disarmament Party* received 7.2% of the national vote in the Senate elections. The Hawke government responded to this situation by appointing one of the People for Nuclear Disarmament convenors, Richard Butler, as

Australia's first special ambassador for disarmament to the UN. Since then, Australia has emerged as an active and independent member of various UN bodies on disarmament. Its stated purpose has been to reduce the world's nuclear armaments with the ultimate objective of eliminating them, but emphasis on the short-term goal has meant a continuation of its concentration on arms control rather than on disarmament. This ambivalence is shown in its call on the one hand for nuclear-free zones and a comprehensive test-ban treaty, while on the other hand maintaining > *US bases in Australia* under the justification of establishing an important deterrent to global nuclear war.

discovery, voyages of From the time of the ancient Greeks, Europeans conjectured that there existed a southern continent, which appeared fancifully on their maps. The first incontrovertible recorded sightings of Australia were made by the Dutch vessel *Duyfken*, under Willem Jansz, in 1606, although it is quite probable that Asians and Pacific islanders had some prior knowledge of the north coast.

Portuguese and Spanish voyages From the 16th century, navigational aids pioneered by the Portuguese gradually made possible a serious search for sea routes to the eastern Spice Islands, the Moluccas. The Portuguese reached the Moluccas in 1509, followed in 1521 by the Spaniard Ferdinand Magellan, who made a remarkable voyage around Cape Horn into the Pacific. Australia was completely missed by these early navigators, as the prevailing winds and currents concentrated their routes to the north; however, a series of French maps, 1536–67, clearly based on Portuguese originals and bearing remarkable correlations with the Australian coast (called Jave la Grande), are generally accepted as evidence that the Portuguese did first sight the Australian continent, probably during the 1520s.

NG was discovered by the Spanish in 1526–7, but they lost interest in that region after colonising the Philippines. Pedro Fernandez de Quiros reached the New Hebrides in 1606 by sailing west from Peru, but more significant was the voyage made by his companions, Luis Vaez de Torres and Diego de Prado, who continued westwards and were driven south of NG through the Torres Strait by adverse weather conditions. The significance of this course was not appreciated for two centuries, during which time it was assumed that NG and Australia were part of one landmass.

The Dutch in the Pacific By the early 17th century, Dutch and English mercantile interests were also seeking trade and new lands. Thus it was that the *Duyfken,* sent from Batavia for this purpose, made the first proven landfall on the Australian coast, on the western shore of Cape York: the land was found to be 'for the greater part desert, with wild cruel black savages', and the crew was 'constrained to return finding no good to be done there' and without observing Torres Strait.

The next discoveries were accidental but inevitable, following the development of a new route running due east 3200km from the Cape of Good Hope before turning north to Java. A series of landfalls was made along the west coast of Australia 1616–28, the first by Dirk Hartog, who in 1616 left an inscribed pewter plate on the island named after him. Sightings were made by the Dutch vessels *Zeewolf* and *Mauritius* in 1617, and by Frederik de Houtman, who landed on the Houtman Abrolhos islands in 1619. In 1622 the *Leeuwin* (master unknown) discovered the southwest tip of the continent.

These accidental discoveries were followed by a serious exploratory voyage by the Dutch to follow up that of the *Duyfken*. In 1623 Jan Carstensz sailed along the southern NG coast, again missing Torres Strait but adding to knowledge of the Cape York coastline; his companion, Willem van Coolsteerdt, found the northeastern tip of Arnhem Land (named for his ship) on his way back to Java. In 1627 Pieter Nuyts and François Thyssen followed the southern coast eastwards for some 1500km, and an accidental discovery by Gerrit de Witt in 1628 sketched in more of the northwest coast. There were a number of other sporadic sightings along the west coast, and on a journey to Java François Pelsaert finally esablished the already suspected continuity of the coastline as far as North West Cape. Gerrit Pool and Pieter Pieterzoon, sent to the Carpentaria region in 1637, failed to establish whether this western region (New Holland) was separated from the eastern land discovered by Jansz and Carstensz.

The Dutch East India Company commissioned > *Abel Tasman* to explore further 1642–3. Travelling south from Mauritius, Tasman was turned back by bad weather at 50° south; sailing eastwards across the Great Australian Bight he reached the west coast of Tas. which he named after Anthony van Diemen, the Dutch governor-general in Batavia. Rounding the south Tas. coast, Tasman again travelled east, sighting NZ and continuing to Fiji before returning to Java via the north coast of NG. To the Dutch the results were disappointing, and in 1644 Tasman was sent to ascertain whether the two parts of the 'south land' were linked or were separated by sea. He failed to do so; once again, Torres Strait eluded the explorer.

From this time, further sightings were more or less incidental and charting by Dutch navigators such as Willem de Vlamingh (who found Hartog's plate in 1696 and who named the Swan River) only seemed to verify the barren, unprofitable character of the new land.

English discoveries The first English sighting of Australia was along the northwest coast, in 1622, when the East India Company vessel *Tryal* was wrecked off the Monte Bello Islands. In 1688 and 1689 the buccaneer > *William Dampier* also visited the northwest coast and confirmed the earlier impression of the Dutch that this was an unrewarding country.

Almost a hundred years later, in 1768, > *James Cook* was sent to Tahiti to observe the passage of the planet Venus across the face of the sun and thence to proceed westwards to explore the South Pacific. In April 1770, having charted the coastline of NZ, he sailed west towards Tasman's Van Diemen's Land, but was edged northwards by the swell and so made the first recorded sighting of the east coast of Australia. With superb skill and seamanship he sailed north from the first landfall at Point Hicks in Vic., landing at Botany Bay. Once more heading north, he charted the coast to Cape York, landing at Possession Island where in the name of George III he claimed possession of the whole eastern coast, which he called New South Wales. He then proceeded along the NG coast, having proved the existence of a strait between that island and Australia.

Refining the charts By 1788 the remaining problem was to discover whether the three known segments – NSW, Van Diemen's Land and the western part of the continent (New Holland) – formed one landmass. By 1798 > *Matthew Flinders* and George Bass had established the probability of a strait between Australia and Van Diemen's Land, their work being further elucidated by James Grant in 1800. The French navigator Nicolas Baudin discovered part of the southern coast west of Port Phillip in 1802, during which journey he met Flinders returning eastwards on his great circumnavigation of the continent, which had charted the rest of the southern shore.

In four voyages 1817–21, Phillip Parker King greatly refined the charts (made mainly by Tasman) of the northwest coast, and when John Wickham and John Lort Stokes, in the *Beagle*, surveyed the Darwin–Victoria River stretch in 1839, the discovery of Australia might be said to be complete. However, because Flinders saw no great river mouths on his circumnavigation of the continent, there persisted a firm belief in the possibility of a vast inland sea which was not disproved until the great period of land exploration was complete.

Discovery Bay Vic./SA This is a wide indentation stretching for almost 80km from Cape Bridgewater (Vic.) to Port MacDonnell (SA). Sand-dunes dominate the shoreline, and behind them lie shallow lagoons; near the SA border is the estuary of the Glenelg River. Discovery Bay Coastal Park, covering beach, dunes, lagoons and swamps, stretches from Portland to the SA border. First seen by James Grant in 1800, the bay was named by Thomas Mitchell in 1836, when he followed the Glenelg to its mouth.

diving > *swimming and diving*

divorce > *family law*

Dixon, Sir Owen (1886–1972), lawyer, b. Melbourne. As a barrister from 1910, Dixon came to dominate the Bar and loved advocacy. Appointed acting justice of the Vic. Supreme Court in 1926, he joined the High Court in 1929 and became chief justice in 1952. Arguably the greatest judicial lawyer of his time, Dixon was awarded many honours, including the rarely awarded Order of Merit (1963) a year before he retired. His *Jesting Pilate and Other Papers and Addresses* (1965) is regarded as a legal classic.

Dixson family, noted business leaders and philanthropists. **Sir Hugh** (1841–1926), b. Sydney, an astute businessman, was chairman of the British Australasian Tobacco Co. Ltd but is best remembered as a benefactor of the Baptist Church. His eldest son, **Sir William** (1870–1952) was a company director and an avid and scholarly collector of Australiana, including manuscripts, rare books, maps and other material. In 1919 he gave to the NSW government an outstanding collection of pictures relating to Australia and the South Pacific which was later housed in the Dixson wing of the State Library, 1929. He also gave 1500 Australian and NG anthropological items to the Australian Museum, and bequeathed his entire estate to the NSW Library.

DLP Formed as a result of a split in the Labor Party 1956–7, the Democratic Labor Party (DLP) was a conservative, anti-communist party inspired by the actions of B. A. Santamaria's Catholic Social Studies Movement (> *National Civic Council*). At the height of its power in 1970 the DLP held five Senate seats, but lost them all in 1974. Its influence waned after the Whitlam Labor government was elected in 1972, and it was disbanded in 1978. A spent force, the DLP's main historical importance is that it kept Labor out of government throughout the 1950s and 1960s. >> *political parties*

Dobell, Sir William (1899–1970), artist, b. Newcastle, NSW. One of the outstanding figures in Australian art, Dobell was acclaimed above all for his forceful and penetrating portraiture. Having studied and worked in London from 1929, he returned to Sydney in 1939. In 1943, his Archibald Prize painting of fellow artist Joshua Smith, alleged to be a caricature, led to a lawsuit which Dobell won; he was awarded the Archibald Prize again in 1948 and 1959. He painted NG subjects 1949–54, returning to portraiture 1950–9. He bequeathed his estate to the promotion of art in NSW and the Dobell art foundation was established soon after his death.

Dobson, Rosemary de Brissac (1920–), poet, b. Sydney. Dobson is a granddaughter of the English essayist Austin Dobson. She was an editor for the publisher Angus & Robertson when her first collection, *In a Convex Mirror* (1944), established her as a poet of cool elegance. The triumph of art over time, as manifest in the paintings of the Renaissance masters, inspires many of her poems; others reflect her love of Greek themes. In poet A. D. Hope's phrase, her work possesses a 'passionate serenity'.

Dods, Sir Lorimer Fenton (1900–81), paediatrician, b. Sydney. A pioneer of specialised health care for children, Dods was instrumental in the growth and success of paediatrics in Australian medicine. In 1949 he was ap-

pointed to Australia's first chair of child health, at Sydney University, a position he held until 1960. He was an active campaigner for funds to establish the Children's Medical Research Foundation at Sydney's Royal Alexandra Hospital for Children, which opened in 1960 with Dods as honorary director; he was its chairman 1966–80. The importance of his work is underlined by the subsequent establishment of university departments of child health throughout Australia.

dogs As might be expected in a wealthy western nation with an inherited dog-loving tradition, Australia has a great diversity of domesticated dogs. Several distinct local breeds have been developed. In the early days of settlement, greyhounds were crossed with Scottish deerhounds to produce the 'kangaroo-dog', used as protection against both kangaroos and dingoes. A number of cattle-dogs were bred to tend stock: the kelpie, derived from border collies (widely held theories attributing some dingo blood are not substantiated), takes its name from one of the breed's early champions; the kelpie is smooth-haired, with a sharp nose and sharp ears. Two breeds of small terriers have also been developed: the Australian or Sydney silky, a toy dog with a long, steely blue coat, and the Australian terrier, a short-coated sporting dog; both these breeds have become popular overseas.

dolphin fishes The two species of dolphin fishes, *Coryphaena hippurus* and *C. equisetis*, are not to be confused with the mammalian dolphins; they are large, fast-swimming oceanic fishes, mainly blue, yellow and green, and are widely distributed in the warmer waters of the world, including those of Australia. The dolphin fish reaches lengths of up to 2m; it has a fin running the length of the back, and old male specimens have a blunt, whale-like head. It is popular with game fishermen, and the flesh is excellent eating.

dolphins > *whales and dolphins*

Donahoe, John (1806–30), bushranger, b. Ireland. Transported for life in 1825 and escaping in 1828, Donahoe lived as a bush 'dandy', robbing mainly the rich. An intensive hunt ended at Campbelltown when Donahoe was shot. The song 'A Wild Colonial Boy', based on his exploits, was banned by police of the time.

Done, Ken (1940–), graphic artist, b. Sydney. Done is possibly the most important (and certainly the best-known) Australian graphic artist of the 1980s; his brightly coloured, whimsical freehand illustrations have captured the mood and imagination of a generation. His signature designs – inspired by Sydney sun, sea and surf – adorn everything from postcards to bed-linen and are sold worldwide.

dories This is a group of fishes belonging to the family Zeidae, having deep, laterally compressed oval bodies. There are eight species in Australian waters, including the mirror and silver dories and the John Dory, which has prominent, ragged fins and an unusually extensible mouth; it approaches its prey stealthily, apparently camouflaged as a straggling, vertical piece of seaweed. It is dark brown – though it may flush or pale – with a lighter belly and the well-marked 'thumb-print of St Peter', with lighter aureole, on its side; it is netted commercially and fished for sport, and is one of the finest table fishes.

dotterel > *waders*

doves > *pigeons and doves*

Downer family, prominent in Australian law and politics. **Sir John William** (1843–1915), b. Adelaide, became a QC in 1878. He was a member of the SA parliament 1878–1901 and premier 1885–7 and 1892–3. As a delegate to the constitutional conventions of the 1890s, he argued for a federal upper house that would preserve the States' rights; he was also an early opponent of appeals to the Privy Council. Elected as an SA senator at the first federal election, he resigned in 1903 to spend more time as a barrister and was a member of the SA legislative council from 1905 until his death. A Canberra suburb is named in his honour. His son **Sir Alexander Russell** (1910–81), b. Adelaide, became a barrister in 1934 but turned to politics after World War 2. He entered federal parliament as a Liberal in 1949 and was minister for immigration 1958–63; he was Australian high commissioner in London 1964–72.

Downing, Richard Ivan (1915–75), economist, b. Melbourne. Downing was a leading and influential advocate of economic reform in Australia. He held the chair of economic research at the University of Melbourne 1954–75, was editor of the *Australian Economic Record* for 20 years, and pioneered research into poverty in Australia. Also actively involved in Australian cultural life, Downing was chairman of the ABC 1973–5.

dragonflies and damselflies True dragonflies, of the suborder Anisoptera, are relatively stout insects with broad-based wings held outstretched at rest. Damselflies, suborder Zygoptera, are more delicate and have narrow-based wings, which are folded above the body at rest. Dragonflies are strong fliers and catch prey on the wing; when mating, the male grasps the female's neck with claspers on the tip of his abdomen, and the pair fly in tandem. Eggs are laid in water, and the immature stages are found in various freshwater habitats; the larvae catch prey by shooting out a strong, extensible 'mask' derived from the lower lip. The Australian fauna comprises about 300 species, many of them endemic; one archaic species, *Hemiphlebia mirabilis*, representative of a family unique to Australia, is endangered by destruction of its habitat by human activity.

drama > *theatre*

Dreyfus, George (1928–), composer, b. Germany. Arriving in Australia in 1939, Dreyfus studied at the Melbourne University Conservatorium, later becoming a bassoonist with the Melbourne Symphony Orchestra. A prolific composer with a wide range, his work includes a sextet for didjeridu and wind instruments; an opera, *Garni Sands* (1972); *Symphonie Concertante* (1977); and numerous film and television scores, including the immensely popular theme for the ABC television series 'Rush'. His autobiography, *The Last Frivolous Book*, was published in 1984.

dried-fruits industry Australia's dried-fruits industry was established in 1887 in the Murray Valley, and production is still centred on the irrigated region of the Murray and its NSW and Vic. tributaries. Vine fruits – sultanas, raisins and currants – constitute by far the greater part of the industry's products, but some tree fruits (apricots, peaches, pears and nectarines) are also dried, and the prune industry is based almost entirely on dried d'Agen plums. Australia is a major producer of dried vine fruits; average annual production of currants and raisins is about 4800t, and of sultanas 67 000t, but as sultana and raisin grapes are also used for wine-making, the area cultivated for dried fruits varies considerably.

All vine fruits are sun-dried, currants in January, sultanas in February and raisins last; raisins and sultanas are dipped in or sprayed with potash and emulsive oil before drying, and pesticides and fungicides are widely used.

Australia has significant internal dried-grape sales; the local industry has recently suffered owing to competition from subsidised imports from Greece and to a lesser extent from the US. >> *wine industry*

drongo, speckled This bird, *Dicrunis bracteatus*, is the only Australian representative of the Old World drongo family. Roaming throughout the tropics and sometimes along the eastern coast as far south as Vic., it is glossy and black, with metallic green colouration; it has a harsh call, is active and noisy – perhaps the reason for its use as a term of derision in Australian slang – and is also a mimic of other bird calls.

droughts Drought has been one of the major hindrances to the development of Australia: its immediate effects are stock and crop losses, bushfires and dust storms; in the long term it may lead to the abandonment of settlement and an increase in desert areas. The most serious drought in Australia's history was from 1895 to 1903 when almost the entire continent was affected, the worst hit areas being coastal Qld, inland NSW, and SA and central Australia. In the west of NSW there were more than 36 drought months in succession at many stations.

Drought is a relative concept, but is generally considered to exist when a region receives less than 10% of its average monthly rainfall over a long period. Inappropriate land use in arid regions can exacerbate its effects: in particular, the destruction of the natural drought-resistant plant cover by overgrazing or ploughing reduces the water-holding capacity of soil. Some States have accordingly attempted to restrict land use in arid zones.

In Australia, State agricultural departments can declare areas drought-stricken upon the advice of pasture protection boards and local councils, and stricken primary producers are often granted rebates and concessions on the transport of water, fodder and stock.

Periods of drought in Australia have been linked with changes in ocean currents and winds in the eastern Pacific, and warming of the earth's atmosphere will also have major effects. >> *climates*; *water and water resources*

droving The droving or 'overlanding' of sheep and cattle has been an important factor in the Australian pastoral industry. The earliest overlanders, John Gardiner and Joseph Hawdon, linked the Monaro Plain and Murray Valley with Port Phillip in 1837; in 1838 an overland route to Adelaide was found first by Hawdon and Charles Bonney and then by Charles Sturt, who claimed that his overlanding trip to Adelaide was more difficult than his explorations. With the opening up of the western Qld pastures, overlanding began to the north, notably with the famous trek by the Jardine family from Rockhampton to Cape York in 1864. The greatest overlanding exploits were carried out in the 1880s by Nat Buchanan and the Durack family, moving cattle from NSW to the Kimberley and Arnhem Land. The most famous stock routes were the Murranji Track through Qld to the NT, the Birdsville Track from Qld to SA, and the Canning Stock Route in WA. Droving is still used for short journeys, on dirt roads or when stock must be moved because of drought or flood, but since the 1970s almost all major stock movements have been by road or rail.

drugs and drug use Although mood-affecting drugs have been available for thousands of years, their use (particularly by youth) has been increasingly widespread and of increasing community concern since the mid-20th century. By the 1980s, in Australia as elsewhere, public attention had focused on two major drug issues: the serious health risks associated with chronic drug use – highlighted by the spread of AIDS and hepatitis among intravenous drug-users – and the dramatically increased incidence of drug-related crime, from domestic violence to large-scale drug trafficking.

A national campaign against the misuse of drugs was launched by the federal government in 1985. It identified three main areas of concern – the use of illegal drugs such as heroin and cocaine; the illicit use of legal drugs such as tranquillisers and narcotics; and the licit use of legal drugs such as alcohol, tobacco, and prescription or proprietary drugs. While statistics are not entirely reliable in this area, the Department of Community Services and Health estimates that in 1984 there were 20 232 drug-related deaths in Australia: just over 80% of these were attributed to tobacco, 15.7% to alcohol (of which more than half were due to motor-vehicle accidents involving alcohol), 0.6% were related to opiates such as heroin, and the remainder were caused by other drugs.

The popularity of illegal drugs follows fashion and availability. The most commonly used drugs in the 1980s were marijuana, heroin and other opium derivatives, cocaine and its derivatives, tranquillisers, amphetamines and hallucinogenic drugs. Although tranquillisers and narcotic drugs such as pethidine and morphine are legally available, their addictive properties make them a target for misuse: they are used extensively by people who are addicted to other drugs, and are often traded illegally or obtained with forged prescriptions.

Debate over the legalisation of marijuana was joined in the 1980s by pressure to legalise heroin. Similar arguments have been put forward by proponents of legalisation, who claim that the criminal activity associated with drug supply is worse than the health costs of the drug itself. The increase in the number of AIDS patients has added weight to the argument, as the sharing of hypodermic syringes by heroin addicts is seen as a prime way that the disease can spread beyond the current high-risk groups. Several new illegal drugs that made an appearance 1980s caused a flurry of media activity, despite their limited distribution. A cheap derivative of cocaine called 'crack', which can be smoked, attracted a great deal of comment because it was feared that it would be attractive to younger users, and another of the so-called 'designer drugs' – a variation of amphetamine called Ecstasy – gained notoriety as a party drug.

Legally obtained pharmaceutical drugs are being recognised increasingly as having the potential to cause health problems. Benzodiazepines, for example, which have largely replaced barbiturates in the treatment of anxiety, depression and insomnia as a result of the large number of deaths caused from barbiturate overdose, can be addictive even in therapeutic doses. Excessive amounts of analgesics, the most commonly used class of drugs in Australia, can also damage health: it has been estimated that in 1980–4 there were 100 new cases a year of analgesic nephropathy (kidney damage), and that 16% of cases of severe renal disease in 1984 were due to analgesic abuse. Another recently recognised health problem associated with substance abuse is 'sniffing' –

the inhalation of volatile products such as glue or petrol. This is particularly a problem among 14–19 year olds and is a serious health problem in Aboriginal communities.

Drug laws and drug offences Australia is a signatory to a number of international conventions which make the manufacture, importation and use of a range of addictive substances illegal. Responsibility for drug-law enforcement is shared by the federal, State and NT police forces and the Australian Customs Service; each force has a drug squad with jurisdiction over the relevant State or Territory laws, and all forces collaborate to provide Australia-wide coverage.

Australian drug laws incorporate the penalties and controls of the relevant international agreements: these range from fines to gaol sentences, depending on the type of drug, the amount seized, and whether the drug was for personal use or to be sold. The drug-offence rate appears to have increased between 1975 and 1984. In NSW, for example, there were 83.6 offences per 100 000 of population in 1975 compared with 343.8 per 100 000 in 1984. In the same period, SA had the greatest rate of increase (812%) and the ACT the lowest (55%); the national average increase was 369%.

drummer fishes Of the family Kyphosidae, these include fishes of southeastern Australia with a particularly oval body; although the back fin is continuous, the front is differentiated as a fan of 10–12 strong spines. Other species, known as buffalo bream, are found in the tropics; all have mouths adapted to eating seaweed, their primary source of food.

Drummond, James (1783–1863) botanist, b. Scotland. A curator of the botanic gardens in Cork, Ireland, from 1809, Drummond settled in Australia, near Perth, in 1829. He created Perth's first botanic garden, at Stirling Square, and was a constant collector and cultivator of native plant species – many specimens of which he sold overseas to supplement his income. Drummond recorded much of the rich flora of southwest WA and more than 100 endemic species were named in his honour.

Drysdale, Sir (George) Russell (1912–81), painter, b. England. A strikingly original interpreter of the Australian landscape from the 1940s, Drysdale won international acclaim for his work. He portrayed the harshness of the

Australian environment boldly but with compassion; his work was characterised by the pervasive use of reds and golds, and by his lean, almost surrealist figures. His outback travels in the late 1950s were reflected in his later preoccupations with both the Aboriginal people and northern Australia. His work is represented overseas in London's Tate Gallery and the New York Museum of Modern Art.

Drysdale River WA The Drysdale River rises near Mt Hann in the northeast of the Kimberley Plateau and flows over 400km to Napier Broome Bay on the north coast. The river's pattern is of alternate flood and intermittent flow. The Drysdale River National Park lies along the middle section of the valley and includes much rugged – and often inaccessible – country.

Dubbo NSW (pop. 31 050) This busy city lies on the Macquarie River, 412km northwest of Sydney. It is the regional and transport centre for a large area of central NSW, with a range of secondary industries servicing the predominantly pastoral region which is noted for the production of timber, wool, flour and meat. First settled in the 1840s, Dubbo soon developed as a stopping-place for drovers travelling between northern NSW and Vic.; it subsequently developed as the chief road, rail and air junction for central NSW. Dubbo has experienced dramatic growth in the last 30 years and the highest growth rate (18.5%) of all the State's provincial capitals.

ducks Widespread in Australia in suitable aquatic habitats, ducks usually construct reedy nests in swamps or on islands, although sometimes in tree-holes; as elsewhere, they are seasonal migrants to some extent. They are frequently shot as game, and sometimes as pests of rice fields, but some rare varieties are protected.

The very widespread black duck, *Anas superciliosa*, is a dark-flecked, brown bird with touches of green on the wings. Also widespread beyond Australia, or closely related to ducks elsewhere in the world, are the rather similar grey teal, *A. gibberifrons*, the chestnut teal, *A. castanea* (with metallic-green head and neck) and the blue-winged shoveller, *A. rhynchotis*, which has a whitish face and shows blue as well as green on the wing. Of the two handsome sheldrakes or shelducks the shy or mountain species, *Tadorna tadornoides*, has a green head

and neck and a white collar, while the Burdekin shelduck, *Tadorna radjah*, is predominantly white. Distinctively Australia genera include the rare, light-brown, freckled or monkey duck, *Sticonetta naevosa*, of southern Australia; the very prominently billed pink-eared zebra or pink-eyed duck, *Malacorhynchus membranaceus*, sometimes seen in small groups sifting mud for insects in a shallow, inland lake or swamp-pool; and the musk duck, *Biziura lobata*, distinctive in its secretion of a strong, musk-like odour in a sac hanging from its lower jaw. The whistling tree-duck, *Dendrocygna arcuata*, tends more towards the tropics, extending into southeast Asia; it is often seen flocking in inland lagoons and commonly roosting – rather than nesting – in trees. Its whistling or piping call is distinctive, though not by any means unique among ducks.

The hunting of ducks is drawing increasing criticism from animal-welfare groups in Australia, resulting in annual confrontations between shooters and conservationists when the duck season opens. >> *geese*

Duffy family, distinguished in law and politics. **Sir Charles Gavan** (1816–1903), b. Ireland, an ardent Irish nationalist who was tried but acquitted on a charge of treason in 1848, was elected to the British parliament 1852–5. Elected to the Vic. parliament on his arrival in Australia in 1856, he was responsible for the largely unsuccessful Duffy Land Act of 1862 which favoured free selection and abolition of property qualification for the lower house. He was premier of Vic. 1871–2 and retired in 1880 (having meanwhile declined a seat in the British parliament). He published a number of books on Irish history as well as of his experiences in Australia in *My Life in Two Hemispheres* (1898). His son **John Gavan** (1844–1917), b. Ireland, was a member of the Vic. parliament 1874–1904, serving as president of the Board of Land and Works in 1880 and postmaster-general 1890–2 and 1894–9. John's brother **Sir Frank Gavan** (1852–1936), b. Ireland, was founding editor of the *Australian Law Times* 1879–83 and editor of the *Victorian Law Reports* from 1907. A brilliant advocate, he was a High Court judge 1913–30 and its chief justice 1930–6. Another brother, **Charles Gavan** (1855–1932), b. Ireland, held various parliamentary clerical positions 1901–20 and was assistant secretary to the federal convention in 1897. Sir Frank's son **Sir Charles Gavan** (1882–1961), b. Melbourne, became a barrister in 1908 and practised and lectured in law after World War 1. He became a justice of the Supreme Court in 1933.

dugong The name Sirenia, the order to which the dugong (or sea-cow) belongs, derives from the identification of this mammal as the origin of the belief in the mythical mermaid, or siren. The Australian species, *Dugong australis*, is a slow-breeding, vegetarian, aquatic animal 2.5 to 3m long and weighing 400–550kg, with a whale-like tail, hide and blubber but more mobile front flippers (which allow the female, floating on her side, to hold the young to her nipple, just above the water). The dugong frequents bays and estuaries rather than the open sea; formerly occurring as far south as Sydney, it has been hunted to extinction except around the Great Barrier Reef, in the region extending along the Qld coast and round to Broome in WA, and in southeastern Asia. In the Cape York area, hunting the dugong from bark canoes, outriggers or platforms was a main means of support for Aborigines, who used an ingenious harpoon with a detachable tip. A period of commercial hunting by Europeans for medicinal-oil purposes caused heavy slaughter in the late 19th century, and dugongs are now totally protected in Australia, except for subsistence hunting by Aborigines.

Dumaresq family, distinguished in various fields. Three Dumaresq brothers came to Australia in 1825 with Governor Darling, who had married their sister. All became big landowners, respected for their enlightened treatment of convict labour. **Henry** (1792–1838) was a pioneer of the New England district and later commissioner of the Australian Agricultural Co.; **William John** (1793–1868) became a member of the NSW legislative council, 1843–8 and 1851–6; **Edward** (1802–1906) was head of the Surveyor General's Department in Tas. and later a police magistrate. William's grandson **John Saumarez** (1873–1922), b. Sydney, joined the navy in 1886. He was distinguished for his introduction of many technological improvements, including several instruments to his own designs. He was commodore of the Australian fleet from 1919 and was made a rear admiral in 1921.

Dunk Island Qld A small, forested, granitic island fringed with coral, Dunk lies about 5km off the coast, near Tully. With an area of about 5sq.km, it is fertile and well-watered, and was made famous by the writings of E. J. Banfield, notably in *Confessions of a Beachcomber* (1908). It is now a tourist resort, and despite major development as recently as 1978, retains much of the tranquil, unspoiled nature Banfield knew.

Dunlop, Brian James (1938–), painter, b. Sydney. One of Australia's foremost realist painters, Dunlop is renowned especially for his coolly elegant interiors. A single, isolated figure near a window to the outside world has been a recurrent leitmotif. Time spent in Greece and Italy 1963–8 and 1983 has influenced his colour and painstaking composition. A fine draughtsman and talented portraitist, in 1985 he was commissioned by the National Gallery of Vic. to paint Queen Elizabeth II.

Dunstan, Don(ald Allan) (1926–), politician, b. Fiji. A solicitor, Dunstan entered the SA parliament as a Labor member in 1953 and was premier 1967–8 and 1970–9. A notable reformer, particularly in the field of civil and human rights, Dunstan was perhaps ahead of his time, being an unusually civilised figure in the traditionally craggy world of Australian politics. He resigned as premier in 1979 owing to ill health, but served as chairman of the Vic. Tourism Commission 1982–6.

Duntroon > *defence forces*

Dupain, Max(well Spencer) (1911–), photographer, b. Sydney. One of Australia's foremost photographers, Dupain combines technical mastery and flawless composition; his innovative use of light and shade is particularly effective in the architectural photography in which he specialises. His career has spanned six decades and he is highly regarded by professional peers and collectors alike.

Durack, Fanny (1892–1956), swimmer, b. Sydney. Durack was Australia's first great swimming champion, holding every national record for women's swimming in the period 1912–20. In the 1912 Olympic Games she won the inaugural women's championship – the 100m – thus also becoming the nation's first female gold medallist.

Durack family, pioneers of north and north-west Australia. Of Irish origin, the Duracks were responsible for opening up vast areas of Qld and the Kimberley district of WA. **Jeremiah Darby** (1819–73) and his brother **Michael** (1808–53) founded the dynasty in Australia. In 1882 Michael's sons **Patrick** (1834–98) and **Michael** (1845–95), along with other family members, took stock from the Durack properties and overlanded them to the Ord River, WA, on an epic journey that took more than two years. When the Ord River scheme was implemented in the 1970s, some of the Duracks' land was inundated, before which one of the family's early homesteads, the historic Argyle Downs station, was relocated. **Michael Patrick** (1865–1950) was a member of the WA legislative assembly 1917–24, and his daughter **Dame Mary** (1913–), is a well-known author; her best-known work, *Kings in Grass Castles* (1959), chronicles the family's pioneering endeavours. Her sister **Elizabeth** (1916–) is an established artist, much of whose work depicts the Kimberley landscape.

Durack River WA A seasonally flowing river rising south of Bluff Face Range in the north-central Kimberleys, the Durack runs 240km north to Cambridge Gulf through grassed, open woodland and a number of rough gorges. Large cattle-grazing properties represent the main rural activity. The river was named after the Durack family, pioneer pastoralists of this region.

Dusty, Slim > *country music*

Dutton, Geoffrey Piers Henry (1922–), author and editor, b. Kapunda, SA. An important figure in the Australian literary world, Dutton launched the literary magazines *Australian Letters* and *Australian Book Review* (with Max Harris), was Australian editor for Penguin Books 1961–5, and founded the publishing firm Sun Books (with Brian Stonier) in 1965. He has also published seven verse collections, four novels, and numerous works of art and literary criticism, most notably *The Literature of Australia* (1964). He has been editor of the *Bulletin* quarterly literary supplement and the *Australian*'s literary pages.

Dyson, Will(iam) (1880–1938), artist, b. Ballarat, Vic. A world-famed cartoonist in London 1910–25 and 1930–8, Dyson first worked in Australia as an illustrator with the *Lone Hand* and the *Bulletin*. Also an acclaimed dry-point artist, he was noted above all for his incisive satirical cartooning. He married Ruby Lindsay in 1909 and his poems *In Memory of a Wife* (1919) contain beautiful lyric verse. The fine drawings published in *Australia at War* (1919) resulted from his service as a war artist. His brother **Edward George** (1865–1931) was best known for his mining ballads and humorous stories. Another brother, **Ambrose Arthur** (1876–1913) was a promising illustrator and cartoonist, but died young.

E

eagles and hawks These birds of prey of the family Accipitridae have strong, hooked beaks and talons for catching live creatures. There are 25 known species in Australia, spread among six groups – eagles, falcons, goshawks, kites, ospreys and harriers. Traditionally considered predatory pests, they are themselves in fact of great benefit in controlling many pest species; there is increasing public awareness of their important ecological role and all are now protected by law.

Of the five species of Australian eagles, the wedge-tailed *Aquila audax* is best known and is one of the largest eagles in the world, with a wing-span of up to 2.75m and a distinctive, diamond-shaped tail. Although feeding mostly on small marsupials and rabbits, it is unjustifiably accused of taking lambs and has been shot for that reason, yet it is of immense value in controlling rabbit populations. The white-breasted sea eagle is found along the Australian coast, its diet consisting of fish.

Of the smaller hawks, common species include the cosmopolitan peregrine falcon, which may fly at 240–90kmh in its aerial pursuit of small birds; it nests on a cliff-ledge or in a high tree-hollow, preferably in rugged timber country. Falcons also include the Australian or nankeen kestrel, *Falco cenchroides*, a small (36cm) brownish species common throughout the continent. Among the goshawks, the common brown goshawk relies on ambush rather than giving chase but the other two Australian members of this group are exceedingly swift in pursuit of their bird and insect prey. There are eight species of kite in Australia, which frequent either grasslands or woodlands; the closely related black-breasted buzzard is a large brownish bird found in the interior, feeding on reptiles and small mammals. The cosmopolitan osprey or fish-hawk is common along the coast. The two harrier species found in Australia are fairly widespread; like buzz-ards, they prefer grasslands or other low vegetation where they prey on reptiles and small mammals.

Earle, Augustus (1793–1838), painter, b. England. Earle's prolonged travels took him to the Mediterranean, to North and South America and to India before he visited Hobart and Sydney in the 1820s. There he completed some fine portraits and landscapes, a number of them later published in *Australian Scrap Book* (1830) and *Views in New South Wales and Van Diemen's Land* (1830). He also spent time in NZ. With Charles Darwin, Earle was appointed draughtsman on HMS *Beagle* in 1831, but resigned because of ill health and returned to London, where he died in 1838.

earthquakes Australia is relatively free of such major earthquakes as are experienced by neighbouring Pacific 'Ring of Fire' countries – Indonesia, PNG, the Solomon Islands, Vanuatu and NZ. Although minor crustal readjustments in Australian fault zones are enough to cause earth tremors, most of these are barely perceptible: the strongest earthquakes have been recorded in WA – at Port Hedland in 1977 (Richter magnitude 7.5) and Meckering in 1968 (6.9), the latter causing considerable damage. The most recent serious earthquakes occurred in the NT in January 1988 (the largest of which registered 7.0) and at Newcastle in NSW in December 1989 (5.5). Occasional tremors also occur in eastern SA and along the ranges of the Great Divide from Qld to Tas. Seismographic recording stations are maintained by the CSIRO and by various universities.

earthworms Terrestrial or freshwater segmented worms of the phylum Annelida, whose cuticle bears short bristles, earthworms feed by ingesting soil, absorbing nutrients from it, and then discharging it; they thus play an important role in soil aeration. Australia has more than 100 species, the most famous of which is the giant earthworm, *Megascolides australis*, found only in Gippsland, Vic. and considered to be the world's largest, reaching a length of 3.7m and having a diameter of 2.5cm. The dark-coloured squirter worm *Didymogaster sylvaticus*, found in eastern Australian rainforests, ejects its body fluid through pores when disturbed. Masses of undulating specimens of *Tubifex*, a peculiar aquatic earthworm, are commonly found in muddy or polluted water. A number of cosmopolitan earthworm species have been introduced to Australia with the importation of soil.

earwigs Scavenging insects of the order Dermaptera, distinctive for rear pincers (that are probably defensive), earwigs are usually found under the bark of trees or beneath debris on the ground. There are some 60 known species in Australia, the largest of which is *Titanolabis colossea*, up to 5cm long and with formidable forceps, found on the eastern coast and tablelands.

Eccles, Sir John Carew (1903–), neuro-physiologist, b. Melbourne. Eccles taught at Oxford University 1927–37, was professor of physiology at the University of Otago, NZ, 1943–50 and was appointed professor at the John Curtin School of Medical Research in Canberra in 1951. Co-winner of the 1963 Nobel Prize for medicine, he contributed much to knowledge of the central nervous system, particularly of the chemical transmission of nerve impulses. He also undertook extensive research on the cerebellum, the part of the brain that regulates bodily equilibrium and muscular co-ordination. He has lived and worked overseas since 1966, first in the US and later Europe; he has published widely on neurophysiology, the human mind, and the relationship between science and philosophy.

echidna > *monotremes*

echinoderms These are spiny-skinned sea creatures of the phylum Echinodermata, of which the common element is the reinforcing of the skin by limy plates – a characteristic most obvious in the > *sea-urchins*, > *starfishes* and > *sea-lilies*. Australia's echinoderms are many and varied, with more than 900 known species. >> *sea-cucumbers*

Echuca Vic. (pop. 8409) Situated at the confluence of the Murray and Campaspe rivers some 206km north of Melbourne, Echuca is a busy city and service centre for the surrounding pastoral and agricultural region and has a substantial tourist industry based chiefly on its river-trade history. Echuca was the greatest inland port for several decades after it was linked to Melbourne by rail in 1864. By the 1850s, Henry Hopwood had already established a small settlement around his punt and pontoon bridge across the Murray; thereafter, river steamers brought wool, wheat and timber from the outback to Echuca for consignment to Melbourne. Railway extensions into inland areas killed the river trade from the 1880s and the town dwindled until irrigation from the Goulburn River brought it new life as a market centre for local produce; today this includes wool, beef and a variety of crops, upon which the city's manufacturing industries are based. Tourism has been particularly important since the old port was restored in 1974; the wharf, built high to cope with the vagaries of the river, is now the port's main feature.

economy Wool – and later gold – launched the Australian colonies on a path of rapid (if sometimes faltering) economic growth. Despite industrialisation from the mid-19th century, the economy has remained specialised and heavily dependent on the export of farming and mineral products: while they have proved profitable, this dependency has also created long-term problems because trade in such commodities is greatly affected by fluctuating world markets. Although Australia has experienced periods of great growth and its standard of living has generally remained high, economic instability has been a fact of life since the 1970s, resulting in enforced economic restraint and lowered employment opportunities and living standards. It is now generally recognised as essential that the nation's heavily protected but uncompetitive manufacturing industries be rationalised and modernised, and that the range of traded and tradeable goods, particularly in the service sector, be expanded.

The first 100 years The task of overseeing a penal colony did not combine easily with the development of agricultural self-sufficiency or the promotion of economic development. There were several reasons for this: the erratic growth of the convict population, which led to sharp fluctuations in demand; climatic irregularities; the infertile soil of the coastal region around

Sydney to which settlement was initially confined; inadequate equipment, and deficient farming knowledge. For at least the first 30 years of white settlement Australia appeared destined to remain an economic backwater, relying heavily on imports to supply it with a great range of material needs but lacking adequate means to pay for them.

Despite these early difficulties, the colonies were in fact ideally placed to enjoy sustained and rapid economic growth once a suitable export staple was discovered and settlement was allowed to move beyond the Blue Mountains. Southeastern Australia possessed an abundance of natural resources, being especially favoured with fertile, open grasslands that could be converted to farming and pastoral use; and in some areas, it was later discovered, the land yielded rich mineral resources.

From the 1830s, wool emerged as Australia's most important export staple. With low labour requirements and a high value per unit of weight, which helped to overcome the cost disadvantages imposed by high domestic and international transport charges, wool – unlike wheat – did not have to wait until the railway boom of the 1860s to become a competitive export. Furthermore, it was a durable substance; by contrast, exports of meat, fruit and dairy products remained restricted until the development of refrigerated shipping in the 1880s. The pastoral industry was fortunate in that Britain (in the throes of the Industrial Revolution) was for the most part an eager customer for its fine wool, and it had the additional advantage of being a prime attraction for British investors.

During the 1850s wool's pre-eminence was challenged by the discovery of > gold, which added greatly to export earnings and had a powerful influence on population growth by attracting a large number of immigrants; it also helped to diversify the economy by providing employment in associated industries including agriculture, construction and retailing. The pastoral industry was only temporarily eclipsed, however, and wool remained by far the most important influence on the nature and scale of Australia's economic development throughout the 19th century and well into the 20th.

One of the most significant effects of the primacy of pastoralism was its hindering of diversification through industrialisation: the pastoral industry was remarkably efficient, and as a result tended to restrict the growth of the rudimentary manufacturing sector. The efficiency of the woollen industry, which allowed

relatively high wages to be paid to farm labourers, was also detrimental to the growth of domestic manufacturing by reducing its competitiveness. The problem was compounded by the fact that there were very few firms in Australia that processed pastoral products: for the most part wool was processed by overseas mills, and boiling-down works and leather-making establishments were the main local beneficiaries of pastoralism. At the same time, reliant as it was on shipping and commercial activities, wool growing played a major role in urbanisation and in the concentration of the urban population in the capital cities, all of which were ports as well as commercial centres. In so doing, it did indirectly provide some stimulus to a range of naturally sheltered manufacturing industries – contrary to the usual pattern, in Australia urbanisation thus preceded and encouraged industrialisation, rather than the reverse.

A key feature of the Australian economy in the 19th century was the high degree of specialisation – the economy's fate being largely determined by the performance of the primary sector, especially of the wool industry – and its heavy dependence on export markets. The domestic market was very small (even by 1900 the population was not much more than three million) and rapid economic growth was therefore possible only if foreign markets were tapped. Also notable were the reliance on Britain as a source of export demand, population (through migration) and capital resources, and (after responsible government was achieved in the 1850s) the relatively large contribution of the public sector to total expenditure. Colonial governments shouldered the main responsibility for providing the infrastructure upon which the private sector depended: the public provision of a transport network – particularly the building of railways – was especially important; governments were also instrumental in determining the conditions under which land could be leased, bought and used. During the second half of the century Australia enjoyed perhaps the highest level of personal income in the world – though in a world devoid of social services, economic life was necessarily precarious once an individual ceased to have paid employment.

One of the lessons of the 19th century was that economic specialisation and dependence can bestow great benefits, especially if the demand for and price of a country's limited range of staple products are maintained at high levels, and if supply can expand sufficiently quickly to meet – but not exceed – demand. These conditions are, however, unlikely to persist. The risks entailed in overspecialisation were dramatically demonstrated in the closing decade of the century, when Australia experienced a severe economic depression, persistent droughts and a financial crisis, which together caused a sharp and prolonged decline in material living standards and greatly weakened the labour movement. The popular notion that Australia was a 'working man's paradise' quickly evaporated.

The 20th century The high risks associated with overspecialisation were evident again in the worldwide depression of the 1930s. Being heavily involved in international trade but unable to influence the course of events, Australia was bound to suffer disproportionately from the disturbances felt in both commodity and capital markets. Its difficulties were intensified by the fact that the export base remained so narrow: the main exports were wool (which generated about 50% of export earnings), wheat (which had increased greatly in significance since the 1890s) and minerals, but wool was particularly sensitive to a decline in income and there was a chronic oversupply of wheat in the 1920s. Australia was made all the more vulnerable by having allowed a massive build-up of foreign debt during and after World War 1, mostly to finance defence requirements, land settlement schemes and urban infrastructure. The threat of default on overseas loans was a dominant concern of governments during the first few years of the depression; so too were the broader problems of reducing imports to restore the balance of payments and ensuring adequate funds to preserve international solvency. Another major concern, according to the economic pundits of the time, was the restoration of balanced budgets, which was tackled in the conventional manner by attempting to reduce expenditure and increase revenue – measures that dampened the recovery process.

The 1930s depression was the worst phase in a long period of relatively poor economic performance stretching back to World War 1. One positive feature of these years, however, was the rise of heavy industry in Australia, most notably the manufacture of iron and steel and the construction of motor-vehicle bodies. These industries differed from existing manufacturing firms in their much larger plant size, their concentration on supplying the national rather than the local or regional market, their greater capital-intensity and economic efficiency, and the sophistication of their production techniques. Even so, manufacturers continued to be hampered by high labour costs, and remained critically dependent on tariffs and other forms of government protection; also, they continued to be inward-looking, tied to the domestic market and dependent on imported technology. These were to prove enduring features and help to explain why Australia's path to industrial maturity was so protracted.

With the onset of World War 2, the Australian economy quickly moved from a situation in which resources were for the most part underemployed to one in which excess demand was the norm. The result was persistent inflationary forces. The war years saw a great increase in the economic presence of governments, in a financial as well as a regulatory sense. Where governments had previously been preaching the need for expenditure restraint, they now increased spending on a dramatic scale: expenditure rose much more quickly than revenue, resulting in large budget deficits. Economic power was increasingly concentrated in the hands of the federal government and its agencies, an important example being the introduction in 1942 of uniform taxation by which the federal government became the sole levier of income tax. An attempt was also made to better co-ordinate economic policy by granting the Commonwealth Bank the powers of a truly central bank and by making the federal Treasury responsible for providing advice on macroeconomic policy. Economic life was closely regulated, controls being imposed on such things as wages, profits, interest rates, prices, rent and consumer purchases.

The juxtaposition of depression and war created insistent demands for social reform – for improvements in social welfare, for high levels of employment and thus for an end to economic insecurity. These demands were in turn part of a profound shift in community views on what governments could and should do in the economic and social spheres. Symbolic of this change was a White Paper issued in 1945 in which the federal government pledged to maintain full employment after the war; it aimed to do this by regulating the level of aggregate demand.

World War 2 gave way to a remarkable period in Australia's economic history: a boom that lasted until 1973 and was characterised by high economic growth, average unemployment rates of less than 2% of the labour force, continuous increases in real wages and real household incomes, and a tendency toward excess demand. The latter gave rise to sustained inflationary pressures and (especially in the 1950s) periodic balance-of-payments problems. The boom years saw the rise of the modern consumer society in Australia: ownership of cars, electrical appliances and other consumer durables increased rapidly; so too did home-ownership, which leapt from about 50% of households in 1945 to around 70% by the early 1960s. Accompanying these developments was a sharp rise in household indebtedness because of increasing reliance on mortgage and hire-purchase finance.

These decades of widespread and sustained increases in affluence were bound to cause a change in community aspirations and expectations. A new confidence emerged, the future seeming to offer continuing prosperity and the possibility that nearly everyone would share in it. The standards used for judging economic performance tended to be revised forever upwards, with emphasis on faster growth rates and more rapid improvements in material living standards.

The 1970s and beyond These changing expectations help to explain the onset of economic difficulties in the 1970s, for from the late 1960s they contributed to three linked developments: a marked increase in industrial militancy, an acceleration in wage increases and rising inflation. These problems were to become particularly serious in 1974, when a recession occurred that marked the beginning of a relatively long period of economic instability characterised by faltering economic growth, the coexistence of relatively high inflation and unemployment, and balance-of-payments difficulties.

With the economy in difficulties, attitudes about the appropriate role of governments began to change: political rhetoric began to be dominated by the need to reduce the size of the public sector, to act consistently and predictably, and to establish a more competitive framework within which resources could be allocated more efficiently and the economy restructured to make the most of its comparative advantage. The instability of the 1970s was in part a reflection of similar problems in the international economy and a legacy of the inflationary pressures unleashed by events such as US borrowing to fund the Vietnam War, the rise of OPEC oil prices in 1973 and the commodity boom of the early 1970s. Australia's

inflationary difficulties were compounded by the big-spending policies of the Whitlam government. In the midst of these developments, a severe credit squeeze occurred in 1973, tariffs were cut by 25% in the same year, and a wages 'explosion' occurred in 1974. The inevitable result was sharply reduced profits, which led in turn to a marked reduction in investment.

Australia's difficulties in the 1970s and 1980s were a reflection also of long-term trends, and hence raised concerns for the future. The manufacturing sector, which remained urban-based and urban-oriented and which continued to rely too heavily on government protection, was placed in great difficulties by the rise of the newly industrialised countries of east and southeast Asia. Australia also suffered because the export base remained narrow: although the relative values had changed, exports continued to be dominated by pastoral products, cereals and mining commodities – industries which were, in contrast to manufacturing, highly efficient and internationally competitive but subject to adverse historical forces. Such forces included a slowing in population growth, the tendency for affluent societies to devote their increased income to the purchase of things other than basic foodstuffs, a move towards self-sufficiency by those countries traditionally reliant on Australian exports, and increasing competition from substitute products. >> *banks and banking; business*

Eddy, Cecil Ernest (1900–56), nuclear physicist, b. Albury, NSW. A world authority on nuclear radiation, Eddy conducted research in X-rays, spectroscopic analysis and beta-ray absorption, the last under the noted NZ physicist Ernest Rutherford while on a Rockefeller Foundation scholarship. In 1935 he was appointed director of the new Commonwealth X-ray and Radium Laboratory. Eddy represented Australia on many international bodies, serving as chairman of the UN scientific committee on the effects of atomic radiation.

Eden NSW (pop. 3248) This small town lies on the coast 512km south of Sydney and has a range of industries based on local produce, most notably fish and dairy products, and (most controversially) woodchips. Eden developed first as a whaling station, which operated for nearly a century from 1828. Early settlers included Benjamin Boyd, although the most vigorous – if shortlived – development occurred during the rush to the nearby Kiandra goldfields in 1860.

Edgley, Michael (1943–), entertainment entrepreneur, b. Perth. Edgley took over the family entrepreneurial business (started by his father Eric, formerly an English comedian) in the 1960s. In 1968 he brought the Moscow Circus to Australia and by the 1970s he had built Edgley International into a multimillion-dollar enterprise that organised Australian tours by leading international companies such as the Bolshoi Ballet and the Georgian Dancers; he subsequently produced the enormously successful films *The Man from Snowy River* (1982) and *Phar Lap* (1983).

education The provision of education in Australia is primarily in the charge of the States; the federal government's responsibility lies in the ACT and in Aboriginal and migrant education, and it also provides financial assistance for the State governments and for students. This division of responsibility has presented a number of problems over the years because procedures and requirements vary widely between States, but education ministers now meet biannually in an attempt to resolve their differences. In 1989 a common core curriculum to Year 10 was adopted by all States in an attempt to simplify pupil transfer between school systems.

Schooling is provided by both government and non-government schools and is compulsory between the ages of 5–6 and 15–16. In remote areas of NSW, SA, WA, Qld and the NT it is furnished by correspondence, or by schools of the air (first established in the NT in 1951) using two-way radios. Post-secondary education is available in universities and in colleges of technical and further education (TAFE). Most universities are autonomous and funded by the Commonwealth, whereas TAFE institutions are part of the State education systems; in 1989, Australia's first private university was established in Qld by businessman Alan Bond. Continuing or adult education is catered for by Councils of Adult Education, TAFE institutions, private and community organisations, and on-campus facilities offered by some universities.

Historical development Education was not provided in the first years of settlement, but schools began to be set up during the 1790s for the children of settlers and convicts. From early in the 19th century the government provided grants for schools established by the Anglican church; from 1836 Catholic, Methodist and Presbyterian schools were also subsidised.

Each colony evolved a dual system of denominational and national schools, the latter committed to broad Christian but non-denominational principles of teaching.

From the mid-century growing liberalism, dissatisfaction with poor teaching standards, and interdenominational strife led to a series of State Acts creating central education authorities. Except in SA, church schools continued to be subsidised until the early 1870s, when a free, compulsory and secular education system was established. The resulting arrangement of free government schools and unfunded, fee-paying, non-government schooling continued for the next 90 years.

Although the States retained responsibility after Federation, the federal government has played an increasing role in education provision and in policy determinations since the 1960s. It has funded initiatives to provide more and better libraries and science laboratories, to improve teacher in-service training and to meet the needs of special groups such as Aborigines, migrants, and children in country areas; today it provides most of the funding for post-school education. In 1974 the longstanding debate over government funding was shelved with the introduction of per-capita grants to religious and independent schools, which vary from 20% of fees for the wealthiest schools to over 75% for the most needy (these often being Catholic schools). Capital grants have also been provided, which become the property of the relevant school or system; it is noteworthy that in Australia these funds are disbursed without requiring free pupil places or public access, as occurs in the UK and elsewhere.

Primary and secondary schooling More than 3.1 million children attend Australia's schools and preschools. In the past decade the number has risen by 24%, largely owing to increased retention rates at the secondary level. Primary schooling extends over five or six years, and about 90% of primary students attend government schools. Each State maintains relatively close control over a predetermined curriculum with specific requirements for instruction in areas such as numeracy, literacy, physical and health education, art and music.

At secondary level about 30% of pupils attend non-government schools. There is a great deal of variation in curriculum and school management, with some States allowing schools a significant degree of autonomy concerning the subjects taught, compulsory studies and parental input. At the end of the 1980s, two-thirds of all students (more girls than boys) completed the final year of secondary school, Year 12, in which achievement is measured by external examinations or school-based assessment. Selection for entry to tertiary study is based on the level of achievement in these examinations, although most universities have less stringent requirements for mature-age applicants.

The supply of teachers for government schools is organised centrally within each State, although moves are now being made to decentralise this system and elicit greater parental involvement (particularly in the selection of principals). As a result of strong union pressure, teachers in all schools are required to have teaching as well as academic qualifications. Although the majority of teachers, especially in primary schools, are women, on a national basis fewer than a quarter of school principals are, and plans to increase the proportion of women in this role have been adopted in all States except Tas.

Technical education Technical training began in > *mechanics institutes* in the early 19th century. Technical schools and colleges began to be established from the 1880s, and enrolments increased dramatically in the 1920s. After World War 2 the growth of manufacturing industries boosted the demand for skilled workers, and technical education in Australia came under increasing public scrutiny. Beginning with the Martin Report in 1964, a series of national investigations deplored the low level of skills training in Australia and noted the virtual absence of women and Aboriginal students in this sector. A system of TAFE colleges (now numbering about 1000) was set up in 1974 to provide more advanced and better integrated studies.

A wide range of trade and technical studies is provided by TAFE institutions as well as by specialist colleges. Apprenticeship training, usually in conjunction with employment, begins at about age fifteen.

Post-secondary education Tertiary education was provided from the late 19th century onwards through a binary system of teachers colleges or colleges of advanced education and universities. After World War 2, university enrolments increased substantially and a wider range of courses was offered. By the 1960s there was a recognised need for a greater range of institutions and for higher academic standards, and the number of universities expanded as Commonwealth funding was sharply

increased. Considerable overlap remained between the college and university systems, however, with degrees being awarded in both but transfer from one to the other being difficult. In 1989 this structure was reorganised and most colleges were amalgamated into the nineteen existing universities; TAFE remained a separate system. Other changes included the introduction of full-scale degree studies for courses requiring substantial on-the-job training (such as nursing, physiotherapy and chiropractic). Distance education contracts were awarded to a small number of institutions with the proviso that they include additional courses such as postgraduate medical and paramedical training, and expanded business studies. More student places were provided following an increase of more than 37% in the numbers of students in the previous decade. By the end of the 1980s there were some 180 000 full-time university students – overall, more women than men, although some faculties (particularly engineering) remained largely male. Increasing emphasis was being placed on the development of skills that would contribute to Australia's economic growth, particularly in the area of science and technology.

All States except WA charged fees for post-secondary studies until 1974, when all tertiary education became free, but in 1988 the federal government established an administrative levy and a year later introduced fees equal to 20% of the cost of tertiary study. Although TAFE remained free, the move met with strenuous opposition from many educators as well as from students, and was seen as militating against the principle of lifelong learning for low-income groups.

Educational research There are a number of educational research organisations in Australia; among the largest is the Australian Council for Educational Research (ACER), which has affiliated institutes in each State. Educational research is funded by the government, but by comparison with other OECD countries the commitment has been a relatively small proportion of national income. Efforts to increase the contribution of the private sector have so far met with little success. In 1989 a White Paper established guidelines for specific areas of research, with major increases in funding for science.

Aborigines in education Relative to the rest of the Australian community, Aborigines have low education-participation rates and low educational qualifications. In the NT, the majority of Aborigines live outside the town centres, and children are educated in mission or government schools or outstations. The National Aboriginal Education Committee advises the federal government on issues affecting both Aborigines and Torres Strait Islanders, and recommends appropriate methods of meeting their needs. Recent initiatives include the construction of better school facilities in Aboriginal and Torres Strait Islander communities, the establishment of residential schools in Alice Springs and Darwin, NT, the provision of bilingual school programs incorporating a range of Aboriginal languages, and the provision of bridging courses and other programs to encourage greater participation in tertiary education.

Migrant education By the 1980s, students from non-English-speaking backgrounds accounted for more than 20% of all school enrolments. While progressive waves of immigration have placed particular demands on the system, the education level of the Australian population as a whole has gained slightly from immigrant intakes, as people arriving since 1982 have been more likely than the Australian-born to have degrees or higher qualifications. Since 1970 the federal government has provided funds for the teaching of English as a second language, and in 1987 a report on national language policy recommended that all Australian children learn at least two languages, including English.

Education issues The education system has in recent decades been presented with a number of challenges that seem likely to persist well into the 1990s. These include the small proportion of students taking science, low school-retention rates, the disadvantage faced by some minority groups in the community, and criticism of education standards and assessment methods.

Science is now recognised as being of vital importance in post-industrial societies such as Australia. The overall number of students taking science subjects in schools and universities needs to be increased and greater participation by females to be encouraged, especially at the most senior levels. These concerns led to a national review of science-teacher education in 1988–9. While school-retention rates have recently improved, this has largely been a response to teenage unemployment and fewer than two-thirds of all students complete the twelve available years of schooling. Attempts to improve retention rates have included youth > *training programs* and reduced unemploy-

ment benefits for those under 18 years, to dissuade them from leaving school. The issue of equal opportunity in education – particularly for historically disadvantaged groups, such as women and those with physical and mental disabilities – began to receive attention from the mid-1970s, and universal access to all forms of education and training is now a requirement under > *equal-opportunity legislation*. Efforts are also being made to encourage girls to study a wider range of subjects than has traditionally been the case, in order to improve their employment opportunities. During the 1980s trials were undertaken to integrate children with mental or physical disabilities into local (mostly government) schools; the number of teacher aides was expanded, as were special education facilities and teacher education in this field.

Improving the standard of numeracy and literacy, and determining the most reliable assessment method, have been the subject of regular debate since the 1960s. The value of rigid academic examinations for the increasing numbers of secondary students continues to be questioned, in terms of their validity both as a measure of student competence for further studies and as an educational practice. Each State has gradually reduced the number of compulsory examinations for transfer between levels at Years 10, 11 and 12, and by 1985 most retained only a final, externally monitored examination at the end of schooling. The demand for a qualification on leaving has declined as more students remain in school longer, and the range of subjects examined has been broadened to include studies more relevant to modern life and work, such as industrial relations. At the same time, a sharp rise in youth unemployment and the presence in schools of large numbers of young people who were not there by choice led to frequent allegations that education standards were declining. Concern to ensure that literacy and numeracy standards are being maintained prompted the development by the ACER of national testing programs for ages 7, 10 and 14: preliminary results suggest that there is no evidence of declining standards, but this program has yet to be adopted nationwide.

These problems are unlikely to be resolved in the short term. The rapid developments in technology since the 1980s are demanding new skills, while the competition for jobs continues to place pressure on students to obtain higher and higher qualifications. In addition, there is likely to be renewed demand for greater access to university and other post-secondary training by those sections of the population disadvantaged by the introduction of fees in 1989. TAFE seems certain to be expanded in view of the problems of unemployed youth, many of whom will be unqualified and financially unable to enter further studies in the early 1990s. Education faces the challenge of both catering for and engaging the interest of a very large number of disaffected young people.

Edward River NSW This is the largest anabranch of the Murray River. It issues from the Murray about 48km upstream of Echuca, flows north through Deniliquin and then continues northwest before rejoining the Murray downstream of Swan Hill, beyond the Murray-Murrumbidgee confluence. The Edward has its own anabranches, most notably the Wakool, and also receives Billabong Creek-Yanco anabranch from the Murrumbidgee. Stevens Weir, 15km south of Deniliquin, provides irrigation water for an extensive area of the Riverina used for rice-growing, fodder crops and pastures.

eels These are elongate fishes of the order Anguilliformes, of which Australia has about 60 species, found in both fresh and sea waters. Marine eels – many of them brightly coloured – occur around rocks and coral reefs, chiefly in tropical waters; an example is the thick moray or reef eel, which has fang-like teeth – sometimes used to bite man – and very variable colours and markings. The banded snake eel frequents temperate waters. The eels that occur in Australia spawn in the Coral Sea, and in the larval stage are carried southwards by the current. Reaching the continental shelf, they metamorphose into transparent 'glass eels'; migrating to fresh water, they shelter in estuaries, where the juvenile form is developed before journeying upstream and, after a number of years, returning as adults to the spawning grounds.

egg production > *poultry industries*

egrets > *bitterns, egrets and herons*

Eighty Mile Beach WA A barren stretch of dunes and salty marshes on the shore of the Indian Ocean, this is the coastal edge of the Canning Basin and an extension of the desolate Great Sandy Desert. It was formerly known as Ninety Mile Beach; the name was changed in 1946 to avoid confusion with Ninety Mile Beach in Gippsland, Vic. Running parallel to the coast is the Great Northern Highway.

Elcho Island > *Galiwinku*

Elder, Sir Thomas (1818–97), pastoralist and philanthropist, b. Scotland. Elder arrived in Australia in 1840 to join his brother Alexander's wool and agricultural agency, which was joined by Robert Smith in 1863 to form Elder, Smith. In 1963 the firm amalgamated with Goldsbrough Mort to become the biggest wool-broking firm in Australia, with wide ancillary interests. Sir Thomas held extensive SA pastoral runs and introduced camels to Australia. He financed exploration in search of new grazing lands, and gave money for Adelaide's university and botanic gardens as well as a chair of music in the Elder Conservatorium of Music (founded 1898).

Eldershaw, Flora > *Eldershaw, M. Barnard*

Eldershaw, M. Barnard This was the pseudonym of **Marjorie Faith Barnard** (1897–1988), author and librarian, b. Sydney, and **Flora Sydney Patricia Eldershaw** (1897–1956), teacher and author, b. Sydney. Barnard and Eldershaw met at Sydney University and in 1929 published the first of their five joint novels, the acclaimed family saga *A House is Built*. They subsequently collaborated on three histories, and many short stories and critical essays. Barnard, the more prolific writer, independently wrote children's stories, several histories, and significant assessments of Miles Franklin and Patrick White.

elections Although the Australian colonies inherited Britain's electoral practices in tandem with the Westminster system of government, there have been major and innovative changes to these processes since the 19th century. Australia led the world in many aspects of electoral reform, most notably in introducing the secret ballot (in all self-governing States from the 1850s, although initially abhorred by a NSW colonial secretary as 'not only unconstitutional, but un-British'), in adopting adult male suffrage (in SA from 1856) and giving women the vote (again inaugurated by SA, in 1894); it also initiated compulsory voting in 1915 and discarded the British tradition of 'first past the post' voting in favour of preferential systems from 1919. It was, on the other hand, deplorably slow in granting the vote to Aborigines, who were not enfranchised until 1967. Since the 1970s, the minimum age for voters in federal and State parliaments has been 18.

Voting systems The Australian Constitution is deliberately vague on the details of voting methods and in fact nowhere asserts specifically that the people possess the right to vote. As the all-important machinery of elections and voting is thus determined by parliament, a government with a majority in both houses can – in theory at least – alter the Commonwealth Electoral Act virtually at will. Two electoral systems are used in Australia: preferential voting, and proportional representation.

The preferential ('alternate ballot') system is used in the House of Representatives and most of the State lower houses. Voters are required to mark each square on the ballot paper in order of preference and a candidate must achieve an absolute majority (50% plus one vote) over all other candidates. If no candidate obtains an absolute majority of first-preference votes, the candidate with the fewest votes is eliminated and his or her second preferences are distributed to those remaining until one candidate receives an absolute majority. The preferential system is based on single-member, geographically defined electorates and thus does not mean that parties win seats in proportion to votes received. In a two-party contest, for example, a party receiving 51% of the vote in every constituency wins every seat in parliament, while the second party (with 49% of the overall vote) wins none: this 'exaggerated majority' can occur even when all electorates are equal in enrolment.

The proportional-representation system – which operates in the Senate, both Tas. houses of parliament, and the NSW, SA and WA upper houses – solves the problem of exaggerated majorities. Based on multi-member electorates and a quota system for vote counting (with a candidate's 'surplus' votes being transferable), it ensures that seats are allocated in better proportion to votes received.

Recent electoral reform In the early 1970s the Whitlam government reduced the voting age from 21 to 18 years but failed in its attempts to introduce broader electoral reforms. Since 1983, the Hawke government has achieved major reform of federal electoral procedures. Among the more important of these are the establishment of an independent Electoral Commission, with wider powers than its predecessors; major changes to the procedures for redistributing electoral boundaries; enlargement of the Senate to 76 members and the House of Representatives to 148; the public funding of registered political parties and stricter requirements for disclosures of donations to candidates and parties; and various initiatives aimed at reducing the number of informal votes at federal elections, particularly for the Senate. Although it is ALP policy to make the indication of preferences optional, and this has been practised in NSW since the 1970s, no attempt has yet been made to introduce such a system for House of Representatives elections. >> *gerrymander; government*

electrical energy The electricity industry in Australia is a major player on the stage of the national economy. The largest of the country's energy industries in terms of both employment and capital investment, it accounts for 3% of gross domestic product and 1.4% of jobs; the industry has a good record in providing a reliable electricity supply and in creating new generating capacity to meet growing demand. In the 20 years to 1986 installations more than doubled, to a 34 000 000kW capacity. In the late 1980s, however, a slowing in demand necessitated major reassessments of the industry; with recognised overcapacity in the generating system, there has been increasing pressure on authorities to improve efficiency and to take account of environmental concerns.

Demand On an international scale Australians are big users of electricity, ranking eighth in 1984 in terms of consumption per capita. Electricity at present provides 16.7% of total energy consumed – a contribution increased from a level of 12% ten years ago, mainly at the expense of oil. Rapid growth in demand was a feature of the industry until the mid-1970s, with annual rates averaging 8%; since then annual growth has been about 5%, in part due to large electricity-intensive industries such as aluminium smelting. Growth in demand to 2000 is expected to drop to between 2.0% and 3.8%, as a result of which the outlook in 1989 was for a decreased rate of capacity expansion, plans being for an increase of 4300MW by 1996.

Administration Some 92% of the country's electricity is supplied by public authorities, prime responsibility resting with the States. Each State commission is responsible for generation, bulk transmission and planning. Some electricity is supplied in bulk for distribution by local authorities and to large private companies; in Tas., seventeen companies with bulk supply contracts use 66% of all electricity consumed. The two largest systems, those of Vic. and NSW, together account for about 60% of total Australian consumption; although the country does not have an integrated national grid, these two States have been interconnected since 1960 by the > *Snowy Mountains Scheme*. A similar link between Vic. and SA, due to be completed in 1990, offers further opportunities to co-ordinate planning of capacity increments.

The federal government's prime responsibility is administration of the Snowy Mountains Scheme, although it also plays a role in co-ordinating co-operation and monitoring industry borrowings.

Generation In the past decade, electricity generation has increased by 63% and installed capacity by 66%, and there has been an associated investment rise. Capital expenditure grew from $468 million in the mid-1970s to $2734 million in 1986–7, leading to a marked increase in borrowings.

Steam-powered stations fuelled by coal, natural gas or fuel oil are the source of 86.5% of electricity generated in Australia. Hydro-electric generation, although it has dropped from a peak in the mid-1970s of 22%, still accounts for 12.3%; gas-turbine and diesel generating plants account for most of the small remainder. Methods of generation reflect the respective endowments of suitable energy resources in the States: black coal in NSW and Qld, brown coal in Vic., and sub-bituminous coal in SA and WA; the last two also rely heavily on natural gas, as does the NT. Tas. alone uses hydro-electricity to supply base load.

In areas remote from the major State grids, generation costs anywhere from three to 20 times that in metropolitan areas. Recently, the federal and State governments have promoted the development of more sophisticated renewable power-supply systems, which could meet some of the requirements of remote homesteads and communities. Wind, wave and thermal heat generation projects are under way: a wind farm comprising six 60kW wind turbines at Esperance, WA, and a geothermal power plant at Mulka Station, SA. There are also plans to construct a 120kW geothermal plant at Birdsville and a wave-generating plant in Bass Strait.

Under pressure to improve efficiency, electricity bodies are looking at ways of increasing private generation. One initiative by the State Electricity Commission of Vic. in 1987 was the introduction of incentives for co-generation – the utilisation of waste heat from industrial processes to generate electricity. The SEC estimates that co-generation power could equal the output of the 400MW Loy Yang power station within a decade.

Hydro-electricity Because of its low rainfall and lack of high mountains, Australia is not well endowed with hydro-electric resources. About half of the potential is in Tas. and the other half along the Great Dividing Range. Despite this, hydropower has had a long history in Australia and large-scale installations such as the Snowy Mountains, Kiewa and Tas. schemes comprise more than one-quarter of the country's generating capacity. In the mainland States, hydro-electric stations are mainly used to supply peak loads because of their ability to start up and shut down easily. In Tas., the mountainous terrain and high rainfall of the western part of the State together with the central lakes provide many opportunities for hydro-electric development: the Hydro-electric Commission has installed 25 power stations, twelve major storage reservoirs and more than 30 dams with a total system capacity of 1816MW.

Economics and politics Until the mid-1970s, economies of scale helped reduce the cost of producing electricity and its price for the consumer. Since then, however, fuel, labour and interest charges have risen significantly: borrowings tripled in the following decade as new power-station construction surged ahead, putting severe strains on the finances of authorities. The industry rose to sudden prominence as the subject of political controversy in the 1980s. There were price rises, blackouts during 1981 in Vic. and NSW caused by temporary shortages of capacity, and arguments over the prices to be charged to aluminium smelters. More important, there was strong opposition on environmental grounds to proposed hydro-electric schemes in Tas., especially the flooding of the lower reaches of the Franklin River; in 1983 the federal government intervened to stop construction there by nominating the area for World Heritage listing. Similar public protest was instrumental in 1989 in preventing construction of a high-voltage power line through the suburbs of Melbourne. The developing concern – both in Australia and overseas – about the environmental consequences (such as the greenhouse effect) of continued use of fossil fuels has yet to have a major impact on authorities. It is an issue they will have to tackle along with fiscal restraint and more efficient use of generating capacity. >> *energy resources*

electronics industry An examination of the history of the Australian electronics industry reveals few examples of sustained local operations by indigenous companies. Notable exceptions include the development and production of electronic defence systems, which have achieved a measure of success, and the local manufacture of first black-and-white and later colour television sets. In general, however, good basic research in the field of electronics – by organisations such as the CSIRO and Telecom, as well as universities and to a lesser degree private companies – has rarely been converted into products because of a lack of both government support and a sufficiently large and sophisticated market. A reduction in import tariffs on electronic components in the mid-1970s is generally held responsible for the closure of a number of consumer-goods assembly plants.

More recently, and despite a steady 30% annual growth rate in the installation of computers in Australia, attempts to establish microchip and computer-hardware manufacturing have also failed and their supply is dominated by transnational companies that either assemble from imported parts or import their products completely. Research into electronics continues at a high level, however, in areas such as microelectronic circuitry and the development of new transmission and switching devices in telecommunications. Joint ventures between university research organisations and government bodies such as the CSIRO or locally owned companies such as Amalgamated Wireless (Australasia) Ltd, offer hope for the development of a number of projects in the near future. >> *communications technology*; *post and telecommunications*; *science and technology*

Elizabeth SA (pop. 30 687) This city was specifically planned and built by the SA Housing Trust in the 1950s as an independent residential and industrial town. Situated some 27km north of Adelaide, it was later subsumed within the metropolitan area and many residents commute to Adelaide factories, Salisbury,

and the coastal salt and chemical works. It was named after Queen Elizabeth II, and has traditionally had a high proportion of British-born residents.

Elizabethan Theatre Trust, Australian This autonomous government organisation was established in 1954 – largely through the agency of economist H.C. Coombs and ABC general manager Charles Moses – as an entrepreneur for the performing arts in Australia. Although its achievements included founding the Australian Opera and Australian Ballet, it was often criticised for its amateurism and for its preoccupation with popular entertainment. Its role was largely usurped with the establishment of the Australia Council in 1968. Today it is a relatively ineffectual body, which collects tax-deductible donations and allocates them to regional organisations and companies under its aegis.

Elkin, Adolphus Peter (1891–1979), anthropologist, b. Maitland, NSW. Responsible for the first methodical survey of Aboriginal society and traditions, which he carried out in SA and WA 1927–31, Elkin was a noted student and documenter of Aboriginal culture. His research produced many articles and books, notably *The Australian Aborigines: How to Understand Them* (1938) and *Aboriginal Men of High Degree* (1946). He was professor of anthropology at the University of Sydney 1934–56 and a founding member of the Australian Institute of Aboriginal Studies.

Ella family, prominent in rugby union football. Twins **Mark** and **Glen** (1959–) and their brother **Gary** (1960–), all b. Sydney, first won the public's attention when they played in the 1977 Australian schoolboys team. They subsequently played at Randwick, whose team won six premierships while the brothers played for the club. Mark first played for Australia in 1980 and was joined by his brothers in 1982, in the centre and as fullback respectively. Mark captained Australia in 1983 both at home and on tour, but in 1984 he relinquished the captaincy; in that year he became the first player to score a try in each Test, as the Australian team scored the 'grand slam' of victories over England, Ireland, Scotland and Wales.

Elliott, Herbert James (1938–), athlete, b. Perth. At the Rome World Championships in 1987, Herb Elliott was voted the greatest-ever

1500m runner. From the age of 14 Elliott was only defeated once over 1500m or a mile; when he retired in 1961 at the age of 22, he had outclassed all competition without ever being truly stretched to the limit. At the Rome Olympic Games in 1960 he won the 1500m by more than 18m. Elliott had abandoned running after a promising junior career, but returned to training under Percy Cerutty's strenuous regimen; although not without its conflicts, this partnership saw Elliott develop an unsurpassed mental toughness and composure that allowed him to break the 4 min. mile seventeen times from 1959.

Elliott, John Dorman (1941–), business entrepreneur, b. Melbourne. Trained as a management consultant, Elliott is chairman and chief executive of one of Australia's largest conglomerates, Elders-IXL, formed by the merging of many formerly independent companies including a jam-maker (Henry Jones IXL), a brewery (Carlton & United Breweries) and a pastoral trading house (Elder Smith Goldsbrough Mort). The company has numerous overseas interests, notably Courage Breweries of the UK. Elliott is also chairman of Elders Resources, a company with broad-based mining and oil interests, and in 1988 became president of the Australian Liberal Party.

Elliott, Sumner Locke (1917–), author, b. Sydney. Elliott was the son of journalist Henry Logan Elliott and writer Sumner Locke, whose untimely death left his upbringing to aunts after prolonged dispute over his custody. He became an actor and playwright, basing *Rusty Bugles* (1948) on his army experience in the NT during World War 2; resoundingly successful, it was initially censored and for some time the centre of fierce controversy because of its allegedly blasphemous language. Elliott went to live in the US in 1948, wrote for television and the stage, became a successful novelist, and eventually took out American citizenship. His autobiographical novel *Careful He Might Hear You* (1963) won the Miles Franklin Award and has been filmed; his novel of 1930s Sydney, *Water Under the Bridge* (1977) was produced as a television series in 1980.

emancipists This historical term technically applies to convicts fully or conditionally pardoned for conduct or service, but was also applied (until about 1840) to time-expired convicts and also to a major pressure group campaigning vigorously under W.C. Wentworth for emancipists' equality, trial by jury, and elected government. They were opposed by the 'exclusivist' faction of free settlers under Macarthur, who feared their numerical superiority and considered them socially undesirable. Most governors, except Darling, favoured the emancipists – Macquarie to the extent of appointing them to high office. In 1821, 1367 emancipists signed a petition to the Crown pointing out that they comprised 7556 adults compared with 1558 free settlers, possessed three times as much land, had contributed greatly to the colony's development and held official positions, yet were being denied equal legal rights. A few attained wealth and position, notably merchant and manufacturer Simeon Lord, surgeon William Redfern, architect Francis Greenway, merchant and shipowner Henry Kable, and clergyman Henry Fulton. The first emancipist was J. Irving, surgeon, freed in 1790.

embassies and high commissions Australia has diplomatic representation – in the form of more than 150 embassies, high commissions, and consulates – throughout the world. The main emphasis of embassies and high commissions is maintaining Australia's relations with other governments, fostering international co-operation, and promoting Australia's image and interests (particularly trade); consular services are for the protection and welfare of Australian citizens and their overseas interests, and deal primarily with such issues as deaths overseas, arrests in foreign countries and assistance in times of political danger or natural disaster. Diplomatic representatives are responsible to the Department of Foreign Affairs and Trade, which also appoints missions to such bodies as the EEC (Brussels), the UN (New York) and UNESCO (Paris). >> *foreign policy*

emblems and flags While Australia has no official floral or faunal emblems, those commonly accepted are the golden wattle, the red kangaroo and the emu. The design of the national flag – the Union Jack in the top left corner, a seven-pointed white star (symbolising federation), and the five stars of the southern cross – dates from a competition held in 1901; it attracted 32 823 entries, and five entrants who had submitted similar designs shared first prize. Although the winning design was approved by King Edward VII in 1903, the flag was not formally adopted until 1953 (with the pasage of the Flags Act); the RAN, RAAF and merchant marines have flags that are variations on the national flag. Leading up to the Australian bicentenary in 1988 there were unofficial moves to find a new national flag, the main motivation being to eliminate the Union Jack. The idea – and the winning design in a new competition – met with public and political uninterest.

States and Territories Each of the States and Territories has its own official emblems (floral and in most cases faunal) and flag. The NSW emblems are the waratah, the platypus and the kookaburra; its flag (dating from 1876) comprises a golden lion on a red cross of St George, within a white circle. The Tas. floral emblem is the Tas. blue gum; its flag (also dating from 1876) is a red lion on a white background. The Qld floral emblem is the Cooktown orchid, and its faunal emblem the koala; its flag (adopted 1876) is a blue Maltese cross with a central imperial crown, on a white background. The Vic. emblems are the common heath, Leadbeater's possum and the helmeted honeyeater; its flag (adopted 1856) comprises the five stars of the southern cross surmounted by a crown (this being added in 1872). SA's emblems are Sturt's desert pea, the hairy-nosed wombat and the piping shrike; its flag (1904) also depicts the piping shrike, on a yellow background. The WA emblems are the kangaroo paw, the numbat and the black swan (adopted as the colonial emblem in 1829); its flag also features the black swan, on a yellow background. The NT emblem is Sturt's desert rose; its flag (adopted on self-government in 1978) depicts the floral emblem and the five stars of the southern cross in black, white and yellow. The ACT floral emblem is the bluebell.

Emerald Qld (pop. 5982) On the Nogoa River some 900km northwest of Brisbane, Emerald is the hub of Qld's central highlands. Its cattle industry is long established and the development of irrigation in the 1970s enabled the cultivation of grain and oilseeds (including cotton). The new Gregory coalfields are to the north, and gemstones are also exploited.

emeralds > *gems and gemstones*

Empire Games > *Commonwealth Games*

employers' associations There are numerous organisations of employers in Australia acting as lobby groups to government, providing industrial relations services and representing trade or professional interests. The two most important broad-based associations are the Confederation of Australian Industry (CAI), established in 1977, which represents over 50 000 firms and organisations spread across primary, secondary and tertiary industries, and the Business Council of Australia (BCA), established in 1983, which represents the 80 largest Australian companies and acts mainly as a lobbying organisation. Another association is the Australian Federation of Employers (AFE), established in 1986 as a right-wing alternative to the CAI and the BCA; its small membership is mainly rural-based.

employment and unemployment Like most other countries, Australia has experienced persistent unemployment for much of its history. Although from the 1950s to the mid-1970s unemployment was only 1–3% and Australians had come to believe that anyone who wanted a job could find one, that period was in fact an aberration. The only other times of full employment in Australia's history occurred briefly during the gold rushes of the 1850s and again during the building boom of the 1880s.

In the 1930s depression unemployment reached an all-time high of more than 20%; at the outbreak of World War 2 the figure was still relatively high, at around 10%. After the war the government adopted 'full employment' as an explicit policy, which worked reasonably well until the early 1970s; by the 1960s, however, it was accepted by economists that some level of unemployment was inevitable and 'full employment' was redefined accordingly.

In the 1970s both the labour market and the labour force underwent a revolution. Unemployment rose rapidly, reaching 6.2% in 1978. The main factors were a dramatic increase in the size of the labour force between 1971 and 1981 (a growth rate of 15.2%, compared with about 2% per annum during the previous three decades), largely as the result of increased participation by women; a reduction in the number of job vacancies as the result of the 1973 oil crisis; and a huge increase (81.9%) in part-time or casual work, while full-time employment increased by only 7.5%. Wages rose substantially at the same time, which in turn caused labour costs to rise and forced widespread retrenchments, especially in manufacturing industries. Unemployment was, and still is, highest in the 15–19 age group.

After 1983 the increase in unemployment slowed and then reversed. This was largely due to the improved competitiveness of Australian industry, which resulted both from devaluing the Australian dollar and from the Prices and Incomes Accord between unions and the federal government, the latter keeping wage growth below the rate of inflation. A million new jobs were created 1983–8, and the rate of unemployment fell from a peak of more than 10% in 1983 to less than 8% in 1988. It is, however, clear that the 'normal' situation of some level of unemployment has been restored. The effects of recent technological and structural change continue to be reflected not only in changed work patterns but also in the lowered expectations of those actively seeking work.

emu The emu, *Dromaius novaehollandiae*, is Australia's largest bird, and of living birds is second in size only to the ostrich; with the cassowary it forms the group of Australian ratites, or flightless birds, standing some 1.5m high, weighing up to 55kg, and bearing fawn-brown feathers. Vestigial wings, hardly visible on casual inspection, are held close to the body. The flesh on head and neck is bluish, the bill is short and black and the legs are powerful, with large, three-toed feet; the emu is capable of running at up to 48kmh. It formerly inhabited the whole of Australia, but is now extinct in Tas., King Island and Kangaroo Island. It is seen mostly in open inland country, but since it destroys fences, competes for pasture, and damages wheat (though it also eats pests such as caterpillars and grasshoppers) it has been eliminated in some areas and is restricted to residual woodland refuges; it generally persists in large numbers, however, especially where some protection is granted.

The male bird makes a platform-like nest of trampled herbage and it is he who incubates the eggs, stretching his long neck along the ground to escape detection if danger is sensed. There may be seven to ten greenish-black eggs, each weighing about 0.5kg and laid between April and November; the chicks hatch after two months' incubation, and have brown and white stripes along their backs and sides. In early settlements emu eggs were often a source of food, and oil extracted from the birds' bodies was used for burning in lamps or for lubrication.

emu-wren > *wrens*

Encounter Bay SA A shallow inlet in the southeast of the Henrieu Peninsula, immediately west of the mouth of the Murray River, the bay takes its name from the historic encounter in April 1802 of Matthew Flinders and Nicolas Baudin. Formerly a whaling and sealing centre, it is now a recreation area, Victor Harbor being the major town.

Endeavour River Qld A river that flows to the coast at Cooktown on Cape York Peninsula, the Endeavour rises in the coastal range only 30km from the sea. James Cook named it when his ship was beached near its mouth after running aground on a reef in June 1770.

energy resources Australia is richly endowed with energy resources, having vast reserves of > *coal*, natural gas and > *uranium*. Since the oil crises of the 1970s, energy policy has been dominated by the desire to secure a reliable oil supply at reasonable prices. Fuel substitution, energy conservation, and research and development have been encouraged to reduce the relative importance of petroleum in the total energy mix.

The oil industry underpins most aspects of economic activity and everyday life. While crude oil and condensate represent less than 1% of Australia's demonstrated economic energy resources, they account for 39% of total energy demand and some 66% of this is used in the transport sector. Until the development of the Bass Strait fields in the 1960s, Australian refineries were almost entirely dependent on imported oil; the need for imports has since declined to relatively low levels, but production from the older fields is now falling. Following renewed exploration and new discoveries in the 1980s, estimates of production by 1988 showed a substantial improvement, with more than 200 exploration wells onshore and offshore.

Alternative fuels Alternatives to fuels based on crude oil have the potential to make a major contribution to Australia's future energy security, particularly in the vulnerable area of transport. Alternative fuels can be categorised into two broad types: those readily available using established technology, such as liquefied petroleum gas (LPG), natural gas for vehicles, and alcohol fuels; and those with longer-term possibilities, such as synthetic liquid fuels. LPG production, occurring naturally in petroleum reserves, is currently about 2.7 million a year. One of the cleanest fuels available, its use has expanded rapidly, supplying 21% of the transport sector with an alternative to gasoline.

The major synthetic liquid fuels plant in Australia is the brown-coal liquefaction pilot plant in the Latrobe Valley, Vic., financed by the Japanese government. Australia has large uncommitted reserves of natural gas, oil shale, black coal and brown coal suitable for the production of alternative fuels. The technology for their use is well advanced, but the economic viability has not been established. Government support for research is provided through the National Energy Research Development and Demonstration Program, which has committed $33.4 million since 1978.

In contrast to known oil resources, Australia has sufficient natural gas to meet demand for many decades to come: it currently provides 16% of total energy demand – ranking third after oil and coal. Its appearance in the southern and eastern States led to rapidly increasing demand during the 1960s and 1970s, to the extent that it has replaced oil and coal in most of the industrial and commercial sectors, and demand is predicted to grow at around 2.2% a year. In 1989 Australia became a major exporter of liquid natural gas (LNG) from the North West Shelf project. This is the largest single resource project ever undertaken in the country, with total investment expected to reach $12 billion.

Renewable energy The most promising renewable energy technologies are solar; they include domestic water heaters, passive solar household design, and photovoltaics for small-scale electricity production in remote areas. Some 300 000 (5%) Australian households already use such water heaters; in WA the figure is one in four, while in the NT it is a staggering 75%. It would appear that, in the foreseeable future, areas remote from major State electricity grids offer the best prospects for using many of the known renewable energy technologies; these include wind turbines, ocean energy conversion systems and geothermal systems. >> *electrical energy*; *oil and natural gas*

Entrance, the NSW (pop. 16 967) This resort area at the entrance to the Tuggerah lakes, 108km north of Sydney, comprises a group of towns including the Entrance, Bateau Bay, Berkeley Vale, part of Chittaway Point, Killarney Vale, Long Jetty, Toowoon Bay and Tumbi Umbi. It is named for the natural passage from the lakes through sand dunes to the sea.

environment and conservation Until very recently the earth was seen has having unlimited capacity to support human activity. Particularly since World War 2, however, it has been greatly strained by population increases, by the enormous expansion of human productivity and technology, and by careless consumption on the part of affluent societies. In Australia, as elsewhere in the world, environmental problems such as land degradation, contamination of water and air, and human-induced atmospheric changes are now of real concern.

Before Australia was colonised by the British it was inhabited by an estimated 300 000 Aborigines, semi-nomadic hunter-gatherers who had lived in respectful harmony with the land for more than 30 000 years. Two centuries of white settlement have had a dramatic effect on the continent, which was viewed by the new immigrants as a virgin territory to be developed at will. The European population grew apace in the first 60 years of settlement, reaching about a million by the 1850s and continuing to expand rapidly throughout the 19th century.

Australia was settled at a time of rapid mechanisation in agriculture, and its open and relatively flat expanses lent themselves to attempts at intensive farming. Deforestation, the introduction of exotic plants and animals and inappropriate farming techniques combined to ravage the land on a massive scale, and as much as 60% of Australian soils now require urgent treatment for erosion, compaction, acidification and salinity. Hunting and the destruction of habitats also played havoc with the wildlife population: at least eighteen native species of birds and mammals and 78 species of plants have been exterminated in the last 200 years, and many more are in danger of extinction.

Since World War 2, the rapid increase of population and the growth of sprawling urban areas have made constant demands on Australia's natural resources. Until quite recently, development for settlements, industry and transport was based on the assumption that the land could accommodate both unlimited use and endless abuse from the uncontrolled discharge of waste products: air and noise pollution and the contamination of waterways have been serious problems since the 1960s, and the increasing production of toxic wastes poses problems for the future. Although Australia's problems in these areas are not as serious as those of other western nations because of its low population densities, many of its natural resources and ecosystems are unarguably threatened by intensive urban development and the demands of tourism – beach erosion, for example, is already widespread and the > *greenhouse effect* is thought likely to compound the problem.

Public and political action In Australia, responses to environmental problems have been similar to those elsewhere in the world. The environmental movement is centred on the twin notions of preserving the nation's natural and cultural heritage, and conservation – which includes proper management – of ecosystems such as those of flora, fauna, water and soil. The Australian conservation movement is a loose amalgam of many diverse groups emphasising particular aspects of environmental quality and forming and re-forming around specific issues; they vary in their success at eliciting a response from the public and action from the government. The first major national organisation concerned with the state of the environment was the Australian Conservation Foundation (ACF), formed in 1966 to bring nature conservation into the public arena; by the 1980s it had become a powerful lobby group for all kinds of environmental issues. The ACF was followed by a number of other lobby groups such as the Tas. Wilderness Society, which was active in the 1970s and 1980s and instrumental in preventing the proposed damming of the Franklin River in that State in the early 1980s.

The government's response to environmental issues also has largely followed those in Europe and the US. Prior to World War 2 the only relevant legislation was in the form of State regulations regarding human health and the use of natural resources, the latter largely aimed at encouraging development. By the end of the 1950s, in response to outstanding environmental problems, most States had passed laws concerning nature conservation; in the 1960s, increased awareness of > *pollution* problems led to further legislation protecting air and water quality, the use of pesticides and the disposal of toxic wastes.

The 1970s was the great decade of the environment. In keeping with the spirit of the times, a major electoral plank of the incoming Whitlam government in 1972 was to improve the 'quality of life' of Australians: its recognition of the need for federal involvement in environmental protection was reflected in such initiatives as passage of the Australian Heritage Commission Act 1975, which set up a commission to develop a register of the national estate and required federal authorities to take account of environmental factors in all their programs. In the next few years, the federal and most State governments passed legislation on national parks; environmental planning (including the requirement for Environment Effects Statements for major developments); air, water and noise pollution; wildlife protection, and other aspects of > *heritage conservation*. Statutory bodies and government agencies were set up to implement these laws, centres for environmental research were established by most universities, and environmental education entered the curriculum in some secondary schools.

The 1980s and beyond In the 1980s environmental protection became an integral part of State land-use planning procedures, typically under the control of departments of planning and environment. Many university centres for environmental studies became teaching departments concerned with training professionals in the fields of environmental planning and management. The conservation debate moved into a new phase – whether to permit development at all in particularly sensitive areas – and public debate focused on a number of development proposals. In the case of the Lake Pedder hydro-electric scheme in Tas. and of the road through the Daintree rainforest area in Qld, the developers prevailed. The forces of conservation succeeded, on the other hand, in banning oil drilling on the Great Barrier Reef and sand mining on Fraser Island in Qld, in stopping the Gordon-below-Franklin hydro-electric scheme in Tas., and in having the north Qld rainforest declared a World Heritage area. Some compromise between conservation and development either has been reached or is still being sought on uranium mining adjacent to Kakadu National Park in the NT, woodchipping at Eden in NSW and East Gippsland in Vic., forestry in the Lemonthyme and Southern forests in Tas., and the continued development of Uluru National Park as a tourist attraction in the NT.

In 1983 the Australian government produced a national conservation 'strategy' in response to the World Conservation Strategy developed in 1980, and some States have followed suit. These documents provide a theoretical basis for making decisions in areas of conflict, the most important element of which is the notion of sustainable development – which means that societies must take account of ecological factors to ensure that development provides continuing benefits. At the end of the 1980s, however, the federal government still had no explicit powers concerning environment and conservation matters and was forced either to rely on constitutional provisions concerning external affairs or to fall back on its international responsibilities concerning heritage protection. As a result, decision making in conservation disputes continued to be largely ad hoc and often based on expediency. There is increasing pressure for appropriate national legislation to be introduced, ensuring that federal planning and policy on environmental matters is both coherent and credible. After the 1989 Tas. elections, which resulted in four Independent 'green' candidates holding the balance of power in that State's parliament, it was clear that environmental issues will remain in the political arena at least in the short term. >> *energy resources*; *forests and forestry*; *heritage conservation*; *national parks*; *national trusts*; *pollution*; *soils and soil conservation*; *urban planning*; *water and water resources*

epacrids This family of wiry flowering plants is generally viewed as the antipodean counterpart of the related northern-hemisphere family Ericaceae, which includes heaths and rhododendrons. Epacridaceae are small-leafed shrubs or trees with smallish, tubular or bell-shaped flowers; 90% of the world's epacrid species are endemic to Australia and most of these are restricted to higher-rainfall regions in the south, where they are prominent in heathy vegetation on boggy soil. A common genus of the Australian Alps is the endemic *Epacris*, which also occurs in lower mountain and coastal areas of southeastern Australia: it has some 35 species, among the most familiar of which is the showy pink heath, *E. impressa*, the floral emblem of Vic. There are 27 further native genera in about 350 species – the largest is *Leucopogon* or whitebeards, which like most epacrids is endemic to eastern or southwestern Australia although a few species extend to semi-arid regions.

epidemics Outbreaks of pervasive diseases have been remarkably few and light in Australia, particularly considering the problems of controlling hygiene during times of rapid development (such as the gold rushes) and the frequent import of infections to a population with low immunity. Australia's vast distances

and relatively scattered population have spared many areas from epidemics because contact has been too irregular to maintain infection, but the fact of being an island (once an informal barrier to disease) is less effective in an era of fast and extensive international travel: in 1989 the federal government introduced AIDS-testing for immigrants to Australia and there was increasing pressure to extend this to other potentially invasive diseases as well.

In the early days of settlement, the incidence of disease was linked to waves of immigration and to the state of the economy. While there were periodic outbreaks of influenza, smallpox and measles, and scarlet fever killed many small children in the 1840s and 1870s, Europeans were in fact more likely to die of prosaic infections such as bronchitis, gastro-enteritis, dysentery or venereal disease; relatively few died during the pandemics of measles in 1867, smallpox 1881–2, Asiatic flu 1890–1 and bubonic plague in 1900. The incidence of disease fell at the end of the 19th century, probably because of improvements in sewerage and water supply as well as improved economic conditions. The influenza pandemic of 1919–20 was relatively light, having been checked by > *quarantine*. Similarly, children's diseases such as poliomyelitis, whooping cough, diphtheria and measles – which were widespread in the late 19th century – are now rare as a result of improved treatment and the availability of vaccines.

As in the 19th century, public concern today tends to focus on controversial diseases such as AIDS or exotic disorders such as legionnaires' disease or the viral infection Lassa fever, but the most commonly notified infectious diseases are still venereal infections: herpes, non-specific urethritis, gonorrhea and syphilis. The next most troublesome are hepatitis and infections caused by the bacteria salmonella, but influenza (which was widespread in Australia in 1988 and 1989) is still capable of causing serious illness.

equal-opportunity legislation Specific legislation to ensure equality of opportunity in Australian society – and to outlaw discrimination (intentional or unintentional) on such grounds as race or sex – has been introduced by the federal government and by the governments of Vic., NSW, SA and WA since the 1970s. Such legislation falls into two broad categories, 'complaints-based' and 'affirmative action'.

Complaints-based legislation – such as the federal Racial Discrimination Act 1975 and Sex Discrimination Act 1984 – provides an avenue for remedy where discrimination has occurred. The main emphasis is on the confidential conciliation of grievances; where this is ineffective or inappropriate, complaints may be heard by a tribunal or board. The various federal and State Acts specify the grounds on which discrimination is illegal: these are sex, marital status, pregnancy, race, colour, religious or political beliefs, and physical or intellectual impairments; the NSW Anti-Discrimination Act 1977 also includes homosexuality, the SA Equal Opportunity Act 1984, sexuality. The Vic. Equal Opportunity Act 1984, which has the widest coverage, has been extended recently to cover the presence of disease-causing organisms, which makes discrimination illegal on the basis of AIDS or imputed AIDS.

'Affirmative-action' legislation differs from complaints-based legislation by requiring employers to eliminate discriminatory practices by developing positive policies and programs to achieve equality of opportunity. The federal Affirmative Action (Equal Employment Opportunity for Women) Act 1986, for example, is an attempt to improve the position of women in the labour market, as Australia has traditionally had a highly sex-segregated workforce which contributes in part to the lower wages received by women. The NSW and WA equal-opportunity legislation and the Commonwealth Public Service Act also require active strategies to achieve equal employment opportunity for designated groups. There has been some opposition to affirmative-action legislation in Australia, based largely on misconceptions of provisions in the US counterpart. The Australian legislation differs in important respects from that in the US, however, involving neither externally imposed quotas nor positive or reverse discrimination but rather upholding the principle that all employees should have an equal chance to demonstrate merit.

There is considerable debate about the effectiveness of equal-opportunity legislation. On the one hand, complaints-based laws have been criticised because they tackle discrimination on a case-by-case basis; on the other, the effectiveness of affirmative-action legislation is limited by sociological factors outside employer organisations. The legislation has, however, opened the issues to public discussion and provides a formal base for following the Australian precept of 'a fair go for all'.

equestrian sports Equestrian sports have flourished in Australia, particularly in rural areas, where graziers and bush-battlers alike compete at annual shows. Despite the absence of overseas competition, occasioned by Australia's isolation and by its quarantine ban on importing animals from overseas, a high standard has been achieved. Ironically, it was the quarantine regulations that brought these sports on to the international stage: as it was not possible to hold the equestrian events in Melbourne at the 1956 Olympic Games, they were held in Stockholm, and there Australia made its Olympic debut, using borrowed mounts and finishing a creditable fourth. As a result, local competitions are now conducted to Olympic specifications.

In Rome in 1960, the Australian team worked for twelve months under Austrian coach Franz Maringer; they won the three-day event, in which captain Bill Roycroft became a national hero for continuing to ride after a fall in which he was heavily concussed. Laurie Morgan took out the individual gold medal for the event. Roycroft competed in five further Olympics, and was a member of the bronze-winning team in 1976; Australia was not successful at Seoul in 1988. Equestrian sports continue to be popular in Australia, with 22 000 registered participants. Polo was introduced in the late 19th century and competitions were instituted from the 1890s. The standard of play was relatively low until quite recently, although Robert Skene was prominent in international competitions in the 1930s and Sinclair Hill in the 1970s; the game has benefited more recently from the patronage of Sydney businessman Kerry Packer.

Ern Malley hoax This celebrated hoax was an experiment carried out in 1944 by writers > *James McAuley* and > *Harold Stewart*, in which they submitted to Max Harris, editor of the magazine *Angry Penguins*, poems by a fictitious, deceased insurance agent. The sixteen poems, together titled 'The Darkening Ecliptic', were in fact concocted from a random selection of words and phrases: the intention of McAuley and Stewart (divulged only later) to illustrate the undiscriminating contemporary response to avant-garde poetry was well realised when several literary pundits acclaimed the verse highly. Harris was fined for publishing indecent material; revelation of the hoax engendered longstanding controversy within Australian literary circles and did little for the cause of modernism.

Ernabella SA An Aboriginal community in the remote Musgrave Ranges, Ernabella was founded as a Presbyterian mission in 1937. Administrative responsibility was transferred to the local Pitjantjatara community in the late 1970s.

erosion > *environment and conservation*; *soils and soil conservation*

Escape Cliffs NT On Adam Bay, near the mouth of the Adelaide River, this was the site of an attempted settlement by SA after it was given jurisidiction over the NT in 1863. The place received its name at the time of the *Beagle* voyage of 1839 when a shore party, confronted by Aborigines threatening them from the clifftop, escaped by dancing and singing, so causing their attackers to break into laughter.

Esk rivers Tas. Although the North Esk and South Esk both rise near Ben Nevis in the Ben Lomond massif, they follow distinctly different courses. The North Esk flows almost due west; the South Esk runs east and then south, skirting the Ben Lomond plateau before turning north-west to join the North Esk at Launceston, where the two form the River Tamar. The South Esk has several important tributaries, the combined waters being harnessed by the Trevallyn Dam, near Launceston, which is part of the Great Lake hydro-electricity scheme.

Esperance WA (pop. 6440) This deepwater port on the south coast of WA, 725km south-east of Perth, was named after his ship by the French navigator Bruny D'Entrecasteaux in 1792. The site was a whaling settlement until the town boomed during the 1890s as a port for the goldfields; after 1949, when trace elements added to the soil transformed it into fertile land, the region developed rapidly as grazing and crop land; tourism and fishing are now of increasing importance.

Esson, (Thomas) Louis (Buvelot) (1878–1943), playwright, b. Scotland. Having arrived in Australia in his childhood, Esson travelled extensively 1915–20 and was encouraged by Irish poet W.B. Yeats and dramatist J.M. Synge to write Australian plays; of these the best are the one-act *Dead Timber* (1911) and *The Drovers* (1920). He started the nationalist theatre company, the Pioneer Players, in Melbourne 1921–2 with Vance Palmer and Stewart Macky, and his writing generally concentrated on realistic Australian themes.

Etheridge, Robert (1846–1920), palaeontologist, b. England. Etheridge worked initially with the Vic. and NSW geological surveys, and in 1895 became curator of palaeontology at the Australian Museum in Sydney. He published many scientific papers, was co-author of *The Geology and Palaeontology of Queensland and New Guinea* (1892), and later in his career undertook research into Aboriginal culture. A Queensland goldfield and a peak near Mt Kosciusko bear his name, and several species of animals also were named in his honour.

ethnic groups The concept of ethnicity has been developed over the past 30 years, mainly by American sociologists. UNESCO, moving away from the older and discredited term 'race', approved the description 'ethnic group' for any identifiable community with linguistic, religious or other cultural attributes. In the 19th century, such classifications were based on now out-moded racial theories that credited people of different origins with ineradicable characteristics: there seems to be no major difference in degrees of assimilation between people of different races (differing appearances), though some cultures (beliefs and forms of behaviour) are more resistant to change than others.

The boundaries of ethnic groups in immigrant situations are often fluid. In popular Australian usage the term 'ethnic' is reserved for those recently immigrated from a non-English-speaking country and their locally born children. Official sources have recently adopted the terminology 'non-English-speaking background' (NESB) to identify this category. Aborigines, Australians of British and Irish origins, and many of long-established German, Scandinavian or other European descent, are not normally described as belonging to an ethnic group. Very few of Australia's 880 000 English immigrants regard themselves as members of an 'English ethnic group'; in the 19th century, however, there were major cultural differences among people from Britain and they could reasonably be regarded as forming distinct ethnic groups: Irish-descended Catholics are still seen as an ethnic group by many Protestant Australians, although this is much less common than in the recent past. These conventions are followed in the naming of many organisations and services: there are Ethnic Affairs Commissions in four States, an Ethnic Communities' Council in each State and Territory, and the federal Department of Immigration has included Ethnic Affairs in its title since 1976.

Ethnic groups in Australia The 1986 census indicates the strength of ethnic groups in Australia by providing numbers for those using a language other than English, for birthplace, for religion and for ancestry. This was the first census to give such a range of indicators of ethnicity; it does not, however, give definitive numbers for the membership of each ethnic group, which is theoretically impossible on any of the currently used definitions except for Aborigines and Torres Strait Islanders. In fact, three-quarters of Australians do not think of themselves as belonging to an ethnic group. In 1986 many census respondents declined to give an ancestry (8%), or said they were Australians (20%) or of English origin (40%). Another 4 million Australians identify in some way with an ethnic group, even if they do not take part in organised activities, speak another language, or associate in any way with an ethnic minority. Two million were born in a non-English-speaking country and speak its language.

Confining discussion to NESB Australians, there are more than 100 identifiable ethnic groups in Australia and at least 4000 organisations, clubs and religious centres with a distinct ethnic character. Although the numbers cannot be given with any certainty, the 1986 census suggests that the largest ethnic groups in Australia (in order of size) are Italians, Germans, Greeks, Dutch, Chinese, Croatians, Poles, Jews, Lebanese, Maltese and Vietnamese. Other communities with a variety of origins or sub-cultures include Spanish-speakers, French-speakers, Turks, Macedonians, Filipinos, and many small but highly organised groups from eastern Europe such as Hungarians or Ukrainians. These groups are at different stages of assimilation and have varied characters and histories; most Chinese do not directly originate in China; most Germans are long established and very assimilated; Jews came from many countries and do not have a common language; Italians speak a variety of dialects.

The persistence of distinct ethnic groups in Australia has caused critics to talk of 'warring tribes' and to favour a return to assimilationist public policy. The settlement experience of Australia has, however, been quite benign compared with that of most other countries. Many ethnic groups will undoubtedly exist as social entities well into the next century, while others will gradually assimilate and disappear. There is little evidence that the great ethnic diversity of Australia since the 1950s has caused any important social problems; similarly, there is no evidence for the popular view that Asians assimilate less readily than Europeans. The major threat to harmony in the future does, however, lie in racist attitudes towards ethnic groups and individuals originating in Asia.

Italians Italian is spoken by more than 400 000 Australians and Italians have been established as a recognisable community since the gold rush of the 1850s. In the 19th century most Italians came from northern Italy or Switzerland; by the 1920s many were coming from Sicily and Calabria, which are still the major areas of origin of the Italian-born. The peak of Italian immigration was in the 1950s and 1960s, as the result of an agreement with the Italian government in 1951. The largest numbers settled in Melbourne, especially in the northern suburbs (such as Carlton, Brunswick and Coburg); in Sydney the Italian centre was Leichhardt. From the 1920s many Italians came to rural areas and their descendants are numerous in north Qld, the Murrumbidgee Irrigation Area and along the Murray. There has been considerable settlement in WA since the 1890s.

Germans Germans became established in SA almost from its beginning, with the arrival of Silesian Lutheran farmers in November 1838. In the same year, German missionaries became the first free settlers of Qld. Many thousands in SA and Qld are descendants of German pioneers, especially in the Barossa Valley, SA, and the Lockyer Valley, Qld. Germans were also numerous in Vic. during the gold rushes. Hostility in World War 1 led to the renaming of many SA townships, to internment, and to the banning of the German language in Lutheran schools. German immigration was most numerous in the 1950s under an agreement with the West German government from 1952. Germans are widely scattered throughout Australia and German-speakers include many from Austria, Switzerland and eastern Europe.

Greeks Greek is the third most commonly spoken language in Australia, being used by 277 000 in 1986. Many Greeks came from Cyprus and North Africa, though the early pioneers in the 19th century were mainly from islands such as Kythera; most early settlers were single men. By the 1890s there were enough Greeks to create the Orthodox communities of Sydney and Melbourne which are now almost a century old. Greek immigration increased in the 1920s but peaked in the 1960s under an agreement signed in 1952. The largest numbers went to Melbourne, especially to inner suburbs like Richmond and Northcote; many also settled in Sydney, around Newtown, and in Adelaide, around Thebarton. The Greeks have a vigorous press and school system and are among the most successful in maintaining their culture, religion and language. Many Greeks have entered the business and professional classes.

Dutch The Dutch connection with Australia goes back to the explorations of the 17th century but there was little Dutch settlement until the 1950s. The Dutch were considered especially likely to assimilate and an agreement was signed with the Netherlands government in 1951 for assisted passages to Australia. The Dutch have maintained a low profile until recently and have largely adopted the English language even at home. They settled in outer suburbs and rural areas to a greater extent than many other immigrants. With the decline in Dutch immigration and the return of many to the Netherlands, the Dutch are now an ageing community.

Chinese The Chinese have been the most controversial immigrants in Australian history and were excluded from settlement altogether after the introduction of the Immigration Restriction Act in 1901. The 19th-century Chinese, who came from the Guangzhou region of south China and spoke Cantonese, were almost all men: many arrived during the gold rushes and settled in mining centres such as Ballarat, Bendigo and Beechworth in Vic. and the Palmer River in Qld; there were also large Chinese populations in Cairns and in Darwin (where they outnumbered Europeans in the late 19th century). Most of these communities died away by the 1950s, after which the Chinese population was centred mainly in Sydney and Melbourne. Their numbers grew again rapidly in the 1970s and by 1986 there were 139 000 Chinese-speakers in Australia, mainly from Southeast Asia. Despite the persistence of 'Chinatowns' as social centres, Chinese are now widely distributed throughout the suburbs of Sydney, Melbourne, Perth and Brisbane.

Croatians In Australia the largest of the various ethnic groups which make up the Yugoslav population is the Croatians. Croatians from the coasts and islands of Dalmatia began arriving in Australia in the 19th century, most settling in WA, Broken Hill in NSW, and in north Qld. Most of these immigrants were men and worked as miners, labourers and cane-cutters; some played an important role in founding the WA wine industry, while others became orchardists and market gardeners. More than 20 000 Croatians arrived as 'displaced persons' after 1947 and they are still important in the leadership of Croatian organisations. Many more Croatians arrived in the 1960s and an immigration agreement was signed with the Yugoslav government in 1970.

Poles Although Polish immigrants date back as far as the 1830s (including the explorer Paul Edmund de Strzelecki), the largest numbers have arrived as refugees from communism in the mid-20th century; new arrivals in the 1980s helped replenish the rapidly ageing Polish community in Australia. Poles have been especially anxious to maintain their language, which is used by 68 000 Australians. Poles are found mainly in Melbourne, Sydney, Adelaide and Perth and are predominantly industrial workers, although there is a considerable professional class within the Polish community. Many of the Polish-born are Jewish and associate with Jewish rather than Catholic Poles.

Jews The Jewish people differ from other ethnic groups in not having a recent homeland. There were more than 69 000 Australian Jews in 1986, the highest number since records began to be kept in 1828: just under one-half were born in Australia, the rest being from a wide range of countries, especially Poland, the UK, the USSR, Hungary, Germany, Israel, South Africa, Austria and Czechoslovakia. There were at least eight Jewish convicts on the First Fleet and the first Jewish organisation, the Chevra Kadisha, was set up in Sydney in 1817. The Jewish community has been regularly replenished by new immigrants, most of them escaping from persecution in Europe. Jews in Australia were not subject to the restrictions common elsewhere and have included two governors-general and the World War 1 commander, Sir John Monash.

Lebanese The Lebanese make up the largest section of the Arabic-speaking people of Australia. The majority are Catholic or Orthodox Christians, although Muslim immigration has risen rapidly since the start of the Lebanese civil war in 1976. Early immigrants (often called Syrians) were mainly hawkers and shopkeepers in rural areas, but later settlers began to concentrate in Sydney, which is still the main Lebanese centre. Although some Lebanese have been established since the early years of this century, most arrived to escape warfare in the 1970s.

Maltese The first immigrants from Malta arrived in 1883 and for the next generation Maltese were found mainly in the Qld canefields. As British subjects they were often favoured by immigration policy, but like other southern Europeans their entry was restricted in the 1920s. The largest numbers arrived in the 1950s and 1960s and went to the western industrial suburbs of Melbourne (especially Sunshine) and Sydney (especially Holroyd). The Maltese are mostly industrial and transport workers but have a middle class drawn to a large extent from Maltese expelled from Egypt in 1956.

Vietnamese The Vietnamese differ from other ethnic groups in Australia, in having no history of settlement before 1975. They are an entirely refugee population, numbering about 70 000 (with a further 40 000 or so also derived from Vietnam but of Chinese origin). Vietnamese have concentrated in Cabramatta, NSW, and Richmond and Springvale in Vic. Attempts were made to settle refugees in other areas such as Hobart, Whyalla in SA, or Albury–Wodonga and a substantial number went to Adelaide. Vietnamese, who have suffered a high level of unemployment, have also been the target of much of the racial prejudice directed against Asians in the 1980s.

Ethnic organisations and services The federal government provides general and welfare services for immigrants and ethnic communities through the Department of Immigration, Local Government and Ethnic Affairs (DILGEA), the Advisory Council on Multicultural Affairs and the Office of Multicultural Affairs. Settlement services in every State and Territory also provide support and counselling for individuals and groups. The Special Broadcasting Service (> *SBS*) was set up by the federal government in 1977 to provide multilingual broadcasting services: these include the ethnic radio stations 2EA in Sydney and 3EA in Melbourne, and a television network serving all capital cities except Darwin and some regional centres. A telephone interpreting service, established in 1973, also operates in all capital cities and some provincial centres; migrant resource centres have been established in many areas with large immigrant populations, to help develop appropriate community resources. More than 200 ethnic organisations receive support from the federal government to deliver welfare services; many more receive State grants for

cultural activity, the production of newsletters or the organisation of festivals. Only the Greek Orthodox and Jewish communities maintain school systems, mainly in Melbourne, and these are funded on the same basis as other religious schools. Courses in interpreting and translation expanded substantially during the 1980s.

Government support for ethnic organisations is modest and conforms to principles already established for aiding welfare, cultural and educational services by other voluntary organisations. Such support, which was rationalised by the Galbally report on post-arrival services in 1978, marks a departure from the policy of assimilation practised until the early 1970s. >> *immigration*; *multiculturalism*; *racial conflict*; *White Australia Policy*

eucalypts The most abundant and significant group of Australian trees, the genus *Eucalyptus* belongs to the > *myrtle family* but is believed to have emerged as a distinct group at an early stage of its evolution. Estimates of the number of eucalypt species range from 500 to 700; they occur throughout Australia and a few extend into NG and southern Indonesia. Eucalypts dominate most forest vegetation in Australia, the major exception being rainforests, of which they penetrate only the margins. In the arid interior they give way to wattles and other shrubs, except in areas of moist soils such as stream channels and the bases of cliffs. In semi-arid regions they are represented mostly by low-growing mallee forms, which have multiple trunks arising from an underground woody root-stock (lignotuber) which sends up new stems after fire. Mallee eucalypts dominate sandy or stony areas of southern Australia.

The classification of eucalypts into subgroups has long presented problems, largely because of their continuing evolution, geographical separation, and hybridisation. They are therefore commonly classified according to their bark types. The smooth-barked species, which shed a layer of outer bark annually, are those popularly termed 'gums'. Other broad but convenient groupings include the stringybarks, in which the whole trunk is clothed in rough, long-fibred bark; the ironbarks, with furrowed corky bark darkened by tannins; and the bloodwoods, with crumbling tessellated scales. In some species generally referred to as half-barks – including boxes, peppermints and bloodwoods – the lower trunk is rough-barked but the limbs smooth.

The most widespread eucalypt is the river red gum, *E. camaldulensis*, a smooth-barked species found virtually throughout the mainland along river channels; it yields a valued deep-red timber; the closely related forest red gum, *E. toroticornis*, ranges from southern NG to eastern Vic. In a different group are the Sydney blue gum, *E. saligna*, and the flooded gum, *E. grandis*, of the subtropical east coast; and the giant karri, *E. diversicolor*, and the jarrah, *E. marginata*, of southwest WA. Two isolated members of the bloodwood group occur in the same corner of WA: the marri, *E. calophylla*, and the famous red-flowering gum, *E. ficifolia*, much planted as an ornamental; also restricted to the southwest is the wandoo, *E. wandoo*, a tall tree reaching 30m. The red bloodwood, *E. gummifera*, is a common tree of the temperate east coast; the inland bloodwood, *E. terminalis*, is widespread in the central and northern inland and around the northern coast. The largely tropical, paper-fruited bloodwood group includes the ghost gum, *E. papuana*, which extends to central Australia, and the carbeen, *E. tessellaris*, of eastern Qld. Smooth-barked bloodwoods include the lemon-scented gum, *E. citriodora*.

Stringybarks are a group of eastern species that yield tough timbers; their thick bark was used by Aborigines for canoes and waterproof shelters, and by white settlers for the roofs and walls of dwellings. The tall, slender ashes (usually half-barked) belong to the same broad subgroup as stringybarks and yield a springy, pale timber used for furniture and tool handles; the world's tallest flowering plant is the mountain ash, *E. regnans*, of southern Vic. and Tas., which attains heights of 100m or more. The related messmate, *E. obliqua*, is another very large timber tree of the cool southeast, as is the narrow-leaved peppermint, *E. radiata*. The snow gum, *E. niphophila* (or *E. pauciflora*), is a small tree found at altitudes of up to 1800m in the Australian Alps. Another eastern group, the scribbly gums, are white-barked small trees whose characteristic 'scribbles' are produced by the burrowing larvae of a small moth.

Ironbarks and boxes are very widespread, although predominantly tropical. Significant species include the silver-leaved ironbark, *E. melanophloia*, of Qld and northern NSW and the mugga ironbark, *E. sideroxylon*, of drier parts of southern Qld, NSW and Vic. The yellow box, *E. melliodora*, of the temperate east is famous for the yield and quality of its honey. Another well-known member of the box group is the coolabah, *E. microtheca*, which extends across central and northern

Australia along riverbanks and heavy-soil floodplains. Virtually confined to cooler southeastern regions is a group of closely related species centred around the Tas. blue gum, *E. globulus*, a large handsome tree with the longest adult leaves (to 70cm) of any eucalypt; these include the ribbon gum, *E. viminalis*, named for the pendulous curls of shed bark that hang from its branches. The long-lived tallow-wood, *E. microcorys*, of wet forests in northern NSW and southern Qld, grows to over 70m tall and provides one of the most valuable native hardwoods. >> *flora*; *forests and forestry*

euphorbia family The Euphorbiaceae is a worldwide flowering-plant family, most diverse in tropical rainforests. The large genus *Euphorbia* accounts for some 2000 of the family's 5000 species, of which 85 occur in Australia. This group, which is characterised by a highly specialised inflorescence structure and a caustic white latex, includes such diverse plants as cactus-like succulents and the scarlet-flowered poinsettia; Australian species are mainly the small herbs of inland areas known as caustic-weed, of which some are succulents and most poisonous to livestock. Another 35 tree and shrub genera, most represented by few species, occur mainly in eastern rainforests or scrubs of the monsoonal north. More distinctively Australian is a group of nine endemic shrub and herb genera, the Stenolobeae, which have adopted the sclerophyll growth habit typical of nutrient-deficient soils; one of these, *Ricinocarpos*, consists of shrubs with showy white flowers that have earned them the name 'wedding-bush'.

Eureka Stockade This legendary armed riot near Ballarat, Vic., in which a number of disaffected goldminers armed themselves behind a stockade of wooden slabs and raised a new Australian flag (showing the Southern Cross against a blue ground), took place on 3 December 1854. The rebels were overrun by troops in 15 minutes: about 24 miners and six soldiers were killed, many were wounded and some 120 prisoners were taken. Others escaped, including the leader, Peter Lalor. Thirteen miners – including Raffaello Carboni, who later wrote a vigorous account of the insurrection – were tried for high treason, but public opinion swung behind the miners and no convictions were obtained.

Causes of the Eureka rebellion included resentment against the licensing system for goldminers and the harsh way it was administered, as well as a general demand for voting rights by the miners. Underlying these grievances was the influence of the Chartists, and perhaps also Irish antagonism towards British rule. Subsequent legislation gave miners cheaper licences, better goldfields administration, and the franchise. The incident, claimed as the birth of Australian democracy, has long been enlarged and sentimentalised.

euro > *kangaroos, wallabies and allies*

Evatt family, prominent in Australian law and politics. **H.V. (Herbert Vere)** (1894–1965), b. Maitland, NSW, entered the NSW parliament in 1925 and was a High Court justice 1930–40. In federal parliament 1940–60, he was influential in the moves leading to Labor's period of office 1941–9, during which he served as attorney-general and minister for external affairs. He played a leading role in the formation of the UN and was president of its General Assembly 1948–9. Evatt was leader of the ALP 1951–60, but his outspoken campaign against R.G. Menzies' moves to ban the Communist Party in 1951 and his appearance for members of his staff accused in the > *Petrov affair* in 1954 brought suspicion of his left-wing views and at least influenced the 1955 split in the Labor Party. Evatt retired from politics in 1960 to take up the office of chief justice in NSW; he wrote a number of books on Australian history and politics and was himself the subject of several books including *Evatt, the Enigma* by Allan Dalziel (1967). His brother **Clive Raleigh** (1900–84), was a member of the NSW parliament 1939–59, holding several ministerial posts. Clive's daughter, **Elizabeth Andreas** (1933–), b. Sydney, became a barrister in 1955 and practised law in England from 1958. She was chief judge of the Australian Family Court 1975–87 and has been president of the Australian Law Reform Commission since 1987. Her cousin, **Phillip George** (1922–), b. Sydney, became a barrister in 1951 and a QC in 1973. He was a judge in the Federal Court 1977–87.

Everingham, Paul Anthony Edward (1943–), politician, b. Innisfail, Qld. A solicitor, Everingham was elected to the NT parliament in 1974 and became the Territory's Country-Liberal Party leader in 1977. After the NT achieved self-government in 1980, he was attorney-general and chief minister until he resigned in 1983 to enter federal politics. The high hopes held of his federal career were not fulfilled; having aligned himself briefly with the Liberal Party, he resigned from parliament in 1986.

exhibitions, international Inspired by the grand exhibitions held in England and Europe, the Australian colonies held a number of inter-colonial exhibitions in the 1860s and 1870s specialising in industrial products. The first international exhibition opened in Sydney in 1879, in the elaborate, specially designed Garden Palace. The Great Exhibitions of 1880 and 1888 held in the Melbourne Exhibition Building in Carlton Gardens, and similar displays in Adelaide (1881 and 1887–8), Launceston (1891–2), Hobart (1894–5) and Brisbane (1897), introduced the most up-to-date technology from abroad and were a showcase for all things Australian – from scientific developments to farm equipment and carved emu eggs. Although such comprehensive displays became less popular after 1900, Australia continued to be represented at overseas exhibitions such as the New York World Fair 1939 and the International 'Expos' in Canada and Japan in the 1960s and 1970s. Brisbane's Expo 88 was one of the most successful components of the Australian bicentennial year, its blend of culture and space-age technology from around the world attracting more than 4 million visitors. Specialist trade exhibitions are also held regularly in capital cities, and Australian displays are held overseas.

Exmouth Gulf WA A large, shallow inlet between North West Cape and the WA mainland, the gulf is 45km across at the entrance and extends approximately 88km southwards. A former pearling centre, it now supports commercial prawn fisheries and a solar salt project. It was named by Phillip Parker King in 1818. A military base, Learmonth Camp, was established on its western shore during World War 2, and also on North West Cape is the restricted area occupied by the US naval communications centre.

exploration by land Land exploration began immediately the colony of NSW was founded in 1788. From the time of Arthur Phillip's tentative forays to the complete aerial surveys of modern times, the frontiers were pushed back gradually from the southeast and southwest corners towards the arid centre and tropical north. The pattern of exploration thus resembles that of population density today, fanning out from the fertile fringes to the thinly peopled, least productive and last-explored areas; it is also the reverse of the pattern of discovery, which started from the north and west.

Exploration was motivated mainly by practical needs – first for more cropland to feed the isolated colony, then for pastures for the increasing herds. The first explorers were naval or military men, but later the majority were trained surveyors; official expeditions were supplemented first by shipwrecked sailors and escaped convicts, subsequently by privately financed searchers for fresh pastures, and by the overlanders. Gold prospectors also – and geologists looking for other minerals (including oil) – have filled in many blank corners.

Personal rewards varied, and tended to be in proportion to the value of the land discovered: > *Thomas Mitchell* was knighted for discovering the grasslands of western Qld and the fertile 'Australia Felix' of western Vic., journeys accomplished with skill enough but no undue hardship, whereas > *Ernest Giles*, whose desert exploits were epics of endurance, died a poor Coolgardie clerk. There was a spirit of adventure and a wish to serve, but there was also ambition, desire for recognition, and bitter personal rivalry between Sturt and Mitchell, Strzelecki and McMillan, Warburton and Giles. Interstate rivalry, both for honour and for practical gain, inspired the south–north expedition of Burke and Wills in 1861 and the desert crossings of the 1870s.

Phase 1: to 1815 Initial exploratory journeys, most notably by Phillip, Watkin Tench and William Dawes, were in search of waterways and agricultural land close to Sydney. The Blue Mountains seemed an impassable barrier, for the early attempts to cross them followed the valleys and led only to precipitous sandstone scarps. But the need for new land increased, aggravated by drought, and in 1813 a renewed attack by William Lawson, Gregory Blaxland (> *Blaxland brothers*) and William Wentworth (> *Wentworth family*) succeeded by keeping to the watersheds. Governor Macquarie wasted no time in following up George Evans' discovery of the first west-flowing stream (the Lachlan, in 1815); a road was built and the settlement of the western slopes began. In Tas., exploration remained confined to the estuaries of the Derwent and the Tamar.

Phase 2: 1815–27 The prospects of limitless expansion beyond the Blue Mountains faded in 1827 with John Oxley's report that the west-flowing Macquarie and Lachlan rivers ended in marshes – the edge, he suggested, of an inland sea. This belief influenced exploration for several decades. In 1824 the Murray was discovered by > *Hamilton Hume* and > *William Hovell*, who continued on to Port Phillip and the south coast. Land routes were also being pioneered to the north and in 1827 Allan Cunningham led an expedition to the Darling Downs. In Tas. the Van Diemen's Land Co. was opening up the northwest, and the Tamar and Derwent settlements had been linked by land.

Phase 3: 1828–40 The southeast corner was now becoming known in broad outline from Melbourne to Brisbane, including large areas west of the Great Dividing Range. The ultimate course of the west-flowing rivers remained a mystery until in 1828 > *Charles Sturt*, giant among explorers, followed up his discovery of the Darling by sailing down the Murrumbidgee to the Murray River and then the Murray–Darling confluence. He continued on to dune-fringed Lake Alexandrina, its junction with the sea hitherto hidden from the coastal explorers, who had looked for a major river mouth. Sturt's discoveries were largely confirmed by Mitchell, who traced the Darling further and crossed the Murray to the fertile Western District of Vic.

By 1835 enterprising Tas. squatters had crossed Bass Strait to settle on its shores; squatters and overlanders arrived literally in Mitchell's tracks, and the frontier was pushed back to stretch from Adelaide to Brisbane. In 1836 a group of pioneers made the first epic cattle trek from the Murray to Port Phillip. The urgency, excitement and rivalry of the period is captured in Paul Strzelecki's 'I'm off to the Snowies this minute ...'; he traversed the range, naming the highest mountain Kosciusko and following > *Angus McMillan* down into eastern Vic., which he named Gipps Land. In WA, meanwhile, George Grey explored the northwest coast and hinterland and discovered the colony's major river mouths.

Phase 4: 1840–50 Attention now turned to the centre and the north. > *Edward Eyre*, commissioned to find an overland route between SA and WA, was consumed with curiosity about the heart of the continent. Turned back from this objective by Lake Torrens (thought to be part of a great horseshoe lake barring the routes north), he went westwards and crossed to King George Sound, but in 2000km found no running water. Sturt, also obsessed by the centre but believing it contained a sea, spent seventeen months 1844–5 on a burning march and an enforced encampment beside the only water in hundreds of kilometres; he was halted by the Simpson Desert. In the same year, > *Ludwig Leichhardt* achieved an east–west continental crossing from Qld to Arnhem Land and discovered the rivers flowing to the Gulf of Carpentaria. In 1846, Mitchell (whose obsession was with a great, northwest-flowing river) persuaded himself that the wandering channels of the Barcoo were 'the river leading to India: the grand goal'. The following year Leichhardt vanished on an attempted Qld–WA crossing.

Phase 5: 1850–70 The pace of exploration slackened somewhat after the mid-century. The discovery of gold, while encouraging prospecting journeys, also drew away many potential explorers – as did the Crimean War. Moreover, there was plenty of good land, and what remained unknown was likely to be less valuable. Britain, still hoping for a new Ganges, sponsored exploration in the northwest and the rich Kimberley grasslands were found by Augustus Gregory (> *Gregory brothers*), who then reversed Leichhardt's 1844 journey (with considerably more efficiency) and finally resolved the problem of the river systems leading to Lake Eyre; the lakes themselves were outlined. Crossing the interior now became a race between SA and Vic. and was achieved in 1860 by the two vastly contrasting expeditions of > *Robert O'Hara Burke* and > *John McDouall Stuart*. The former, ending in disaster, was the first to reach tidal waters in the gulf, more by luck than good management, while Stuart, after three dogged attempts, made the much longer Adelaide–Arnhem Land crossing 1861 through the real centre. Relief expeditions for Burke and Wills and for Leichhardt accomplished more than the original journeys: William Landsborough, for instance, reported so favourably on western Qld that an influx of squatters followed. Pastoralists were also penetrating the southwest corner of WA and the best Tas. farmlands.

Phase 6: 1871–1939 The largest remaining blank was the western central desert. Hopes were no longer held for a sea or a great river in the interior: the best that was expected was poor grazing on the margins of a desert. The Overland Telegraph provided a useful base and supply line for a number of east–west desert crossings in the 1870s, notably those of > *John Forrest*, Ernest Giles and > *Peter Warburton*. Minor unknown areas, most notably in WA and north Qld, were meanwhile opened up by smaller official expeditions and also frequently by questing pastoralists whose overlanding feats were as great as many exploratory expeditions.

An aerial survey of the Simpson Desert was made in 1929, and many of the remaining details were charted by Donald McKay in the 1930s. This was followed in 1939 by the last great land exploration, when > *C.T. Madigan*, using camels, traversed the Simpson's northern fringes from the southwest and emerged near the point at which Sturt, almost a century before, had been beaten back across the stony desert that bears his name.

Although the continent was well mapped by mid-century, some of its wilder regions – southwestern Tas., parts of the eastern ranges and northern jungles, and much of the central desert – were not traversed by white Australians until relatively recent times, and there are still pockets in those areas that remain inaccessible, even to the well-equipped adventurer of the late 20th century.

ex-service organisations There have been numerous organisations created for the benefit of Australia's ex-service personnel, the first being formed in 1885 by the members of the NSW Contingent, which fought in the Sudan War. The largest of the organisations is the Returned Services League of Australia (RSL), which was formed in 1916 as a federation of smaller State organisations. By 1919 it was sufficiently powerful to gain, and retain, the government's attention – in fact, the RSL has always exerted proportionately more influence than equivalent overseas bodies such as the American or British Legions. The original aim of the RSL was to safeguard the rights and pensions of returned service personnel, a role in which it has been extremely successful. In many parts of Australia the local RSL club is a social focus, particularly in NSW where poker machines have provided a substantial income which has subsidised superior facilities. The declining number of older members has led to a slow change in the traditionally conservative stance of the RSL, but despite its valuable social and community work it is still seen as a reactionary body, particularly on such subjects as Asian immigration.

Smaller ex-service organisations include the Australian Legion of Ex-servicemen and Women, the Vietnam Veterans' Organisation, and Legacy, which is dedicated to the welfare of the dependants of deceased ex-service personnel who served overseas. >> *war veterans, repatriation of*

Eyre, Edward John (1815–1901), explorer, b. England. Eyre immigrated to Australia in 1833, soon afterwards overlanding cattle to Port Phillip and Adelaide and settling in SA. He made important exploratory journeys to seek new grazing lands in 1839, but was rebuffed by the seemingly impassable barrier of salt pans to the north and the sterile Eyre peninsula to the west. In 1841, commissioned originally to find a land route to Perth but personally drawn by curiosity about the interior, he again travelled northwards; he was forced by the bogs round Lake Torrens to turn west, and so achieved the remarkable journey to Albany, during which his companion, Baxter, was killed by two of the party's three Aborigines; the third, Wylie, loyally stayed with him. After a period as protector of Aborigines in SA, Eyre became lt-governor of NZ and then held administrative posts in the West Indies. His allegedly brutal suppression of a rebellion while Jamaican governor in 1864 led to prolonged inquiry, a royal commission and civil suits; he was exonerated, however.

Eyre Peninsula SA A large triangular area between the Great Australian Bight and Spencer Gulf, defined at its base by the Gawler Ranges, the peninsula extends south about 280km to its tip at Cape Catastrophe. Wheat and sheep are raised on its sandy soils; other industries include fish-canning at Port Lincoln in the south, iron-mining in the Middleback Range and shipbuilding at Whyalla, near the head of Spencer Gulf. A third major port is Port Augusta. Two national parks have been established in the extreme south: Coffin Bay, a peninsula on the west, and Lincoln, which includes Cape Catastrophe and offshore islands. The peninsula was noted by Matthew Flinders in 1802; the first major land exploration was by Edward Eyre in 1839, after whom it was subsequently named.

F

Fabaceae > *legumes*

Fairfax family, one of Australia's major publishing and business dynasties. **John** (1805–77), b. England, arrived in Australia in 1838 and with Charles Kemp bought the *Sydney Herald* in 1841. The paper's name was changed to the *Sydney Morning Herald* in 1842; Fairfax bought out Kemp in 1853 and for almost 100 years his descendants retained full ownership and management of the company. His son **James Reading** (1834–1919), b. England, became a partner in the firm in 1856 and took control of both the *Sydney Morning Herald* and the *Sydney Mail* in 1863. He introduced many technological improvements, notably the use of telegraphy by journalists, and was prominent in many business and sporting organisations. His two sons **Geoffrey Evan** (1861–1930) and **Sir James Oswald** (1863–1928) retained control of the firm throughout their lifetimes; other notable directors include the latter's son **Sir Warwick Oswald** (1901–87), who was chairman of the firm 1930–77, and his son **James Oswald** (1933–   ). John Fairfax and Sons Ltd became a public company in 1956 and the family's shareholding was reduced to just over 50%; the company subsequently acquired a wide range of media interests (> *media ownership and control*). Sir Warwick's son **Warwick Geoffrey Oswald** (1960–   ), b. Sydney, repurchased John Fairfax Ltd in 1987 and became sole proprietor; the substantial debt incurred by the take-over, however, necessitated the closure or sale of many of the firm's longstanding assets.

Fairweather, Ian (1890–1974), painter, b. Scotland. Fairweather studied art at London's distinguished Slade School but was influenced above all by an itinerant existence in exotic places and an empathy for Chinese culture (he lived six years in China). His paintings are typically abstract and monochromatic, with calligraphic marks. Fairweather first visited Australia in 1933; he lived as a recluse in a bush hut on Bribie Island, north of Brisbane, from 1952 until his death.

fairy wrens > *wrens*

falcons > *eagles and hawks*

Falkiner family, well-known pastoralists and merino-breeders for more than a century. **Franc Sadlier** (1833–1909), b. Ireland, migrated to Australia in 1853. In 1878 he bought Boonoke, a 30 000ha station in NSW, where he developed a stud whose rams were famed for their size, sturdiness and high-quality wool. He bought five more stations, put one of his sons in charge of each and formed the longstanding pastoral company F.S. Falkiner & Sons Ltd in the 1890s. After his death his eldest son, **Franc Brereton Sadlier** (1867–1929), b. Ararat, Vic., succeeded him as managing director but resigned to become an independent sheep farmer and a member of the House of Representatives. Franc Jr's elder son, **George Brereton Sadlier** (1907–61), b. Melbourne, further developed his father's Haddon Rig stud and bought other properties. Franc Jnr was succeeded as head of the family company by his brother **Otway Rothwell** (1874–1961), under whose management, it is said, 75% of Australian pedigree merinos were related to Falkiner stock. The family's pastoral properties were sold to Cleckheaton Ltd in 1971.

Famechon, Johnny > *boxing*

family law Family law in Australia is a dynamic field, reflecting the fact that its subject matter – the family – is constantly changing. Today it encompasses not only laws on marriage and divorce but also a growing body of legislation on related matters ranging from de facto marriages to domestic violence.

Most law concerning the family is Commonwealth law, principally the Marriage Act 1961 and the Family Law Act 1975. The States and Territories do have some responsibilities in the area, however: WA and Qld have their own laws concerning maintenance and custody of illegitimate children; financial and property disputes between de facto spouses are dealt with under State legislation; and people seeking help about family violence tend to do so through State rather than federal legal channels. Family law is administered by the federal Family Court (established in 1975) and in State and Territory magistrates' courts, except in WA which has its own Family Law Court.

Both attitudes to and patterns of marriage and divorce have undergone many changes in recent years. While there has been a general increase in the Australian marriage rate throughout the 20th century, the divorce rate peaked in the late 1970s after the introduction of the Family Law Act which made the dissolution of marriages both simpler and less expensive. By the late 1980s, the duration of marriages that ended in divorce was still decreasing (from 10.6 years in 1986 to 10.2 years in 1987), and statistics indicate that 16% of Australian children are likely to experience the divorce of their parents before the age of 16. While there are no absolutely reliable figures on de facto marriages, they are estimated to have increased tenfold between 1971 and 1982 and by 1986 more than 6% of all heterosexual couples were living together unmarried.

Marriage and divorce laws A couple may be married legally if they are both unmarried and at least 18 years of age; with the permission of their parents or custodians, a boy may marry at sixteen and a girl at fourteen. A couple may divorce after they have lived apart for twelve months, except where the marriage has lasted less than two years or where reconciliation looks likely. Once a divorce is granted by the court, it takes the form of a temporary decree for one month, after which the dissolution of the marriage becomes final. The rules governing divorce changed dramatically with the passage of the Family Law Act, which removed the concept of fault (such as adultery or desertion by one of the partners) and substituted the sole grounds of irretrievable breakdown of the marriage. It also introduced new arrangements concerning the division of property and the custody of children.

In the event of a divorce, the Family Court has wide discretionary powers to divide property and order maintenance: equal division between the parties is usually taken as a starting point, unless the marriage has been particularly short or has produced no children, but the figure may be adjusted if one spouse is in greater financial need than the other. Since 1989, many child-maintenance payments have been calculated automatically using prescribed formulae and information collected by an agency. Children's welfare and rights are paramount in deciding who will have custody of them; technically there is no legal preference for the mother. Where custody of a child is disputed, the court usually orders a report to be prepared by a welfare officer, which brings together all the relevant information.

Other aspects of family law Although de facto relationships are now legally recognised, they are not yet treated in the same way as legal marriages. NSW and Vic. courts have greater powers to divide the property of separating de facto spouses than is the case in other States and Territories, where the law is often uncertain; NSW courts are also empowered to order one spouse to pay maintenance to the other.

Courts have also recently been given greater powers to intervene in the event of domestic violence. A wife, for example, may apply to the court to have her husband excluded from the family home if this is deemed necessary for her safety or that of her children.

Farm Cove A bay on the south shore of Port Jackson, NSW, just east of Bennelong Point, site of the Sydney Opera House. In 1788, the colony's first stock were grazed there and the first crops sown. Today the Sydney Botanic Gardens include the foreshores at the head of the bay.

Farrer, William James (1845–1906), agricultural scientist, b. England. Arriving in Australia in 1870, Farrer was a tutor and later a surveyor before acquiring in 1886 his own property, Lambrigg, near present-day Canberra. Here he began experiments in wheat-breeding to produce wheats suitable for Australian conditions and resistant to disease, particularly rust; within two decades, improved varieties such as Federation, Bobs and Canberra had enabled commercial wheat production to expand into previously dry pastoral areas in southwest and southeast Australia. Farrer's work laid the foundations of the modern industry, paving the way for Australia's development as a major producer and exporter of wheat.

fashion industry Until the 1960s, Australian fashion was almost invariably either a direct copy or a pale imitation of overseas looks. Since that time, however, names such as Prue Acton, Trent Nathan, Carla Zampatti, Adele Palmer and Weiss have produced classic designs with an Australian accent, and have created a fashion industry with an international profile and huge export potential. Country Road, with its well-bred, town-and-country look, and Jenny Kee, with her brilliantly coloured, idiosyncratic knitwear and party clothes, are two of the diverse but dynamic talents of today. The Australian Wool Corporation (through advertising, promotion and parades) and the growing number of fashion magazines have helped to build the industry's reputation. Perhaps one of Australia's most original contributions has been the work clothing designed for the outback – the Driza-bone oilskin riding coat, the moleskin shearers' trousers and elastic-sided riding boots – most of which is synonymous with the legendary R.M. Williams, the original bushman's outfitter; this multimillion-dollar business now exports to over 25 countries. Another fashion with a strong Australian identity is swimwear – especially Speedo bathers, the 'all-Aussie-cozzie' first released in the 1920s and now sold worldwide.

fauna Australia has long been justifiably renowned as a land of zoological curiosities, although much of its fauna is in fact shared by NG and many closely related creatures are found in South America. The uniqueness of Australian wildlife is largely the result of the continent's long period of separation from the rest of the world – at least 40 million years – during which time its original fauna evolved in isolation.

Australia was originally part of the ancient southern-hemisphere landmass > *Gondwana*, which began to split up and drift apart 85–100 million years ago. Different faunal elements became isolated on each of the three resulting continents – Australia, South America and Africa – and as Australia drifted north alone it became a 'Noah's Ark' for groups such as > *monotremes* and > *marsupials*, which evolved free from contact with (and competition from) terrestrial placental mammals. As it neared the Asian continent about 20 million years ago new groups of animals began to immigrate, but

there remained a clear distinction between 'Australasian' and 'Oriental' faunas – marked by > *Wallace's line*. As the other Gondwanan continents underwent similar forms of faunal exchange with northern-hemisphere landmasses, their ancient wildlife elements often became extinct and the singular nature of Australia's fauna was further emphasised. Marine animals, being able to disperse relatively freely across continental shelves and sometimes through the oceans (especially at the immature planktonic stage), are less restricted in distribution than terrestrial and freshwater life. Australia's northern waters are part of a large marine region that roughly encompasses the tropical and subtropical Indian and Pacific Oceans, which accommodates a very diverse range of species, many of which are widely distributed; the cooler waters of southern Australia have fewer species and many are of more limited distribution.

Australia's fauna, like its flora, evolved and diversified mainly in response to changing climatic conditions. Rainforest associated with cooler climates covered much of the continent until about 30 million years ago, when a period of increasing aridity set in. Unable to adapt to the drier environment, many creatures became confined to the remnant patches of rainforest; others became acclimatised and remained relatively widespread. More recent climatic fluctuations brought on by the ice ages of the Cainozoic era also affected the fauna: as the ice caps expanded and sea-levels fell, the Australian mainland was connected to Tas. and NG by broad land bridges and extensive faunal interchange took place. The native fauna of Australia thus comprises three main elements: those that are uniquely Australian; those of Gondwanan origin and having similarities with the wildlife of other southern continents; and those of relatively recent Oriental origin. It includes some 250 species of mammal (of which more than half are marsupials); some 700 birds; well over 500 > *reptiles* and amphibians, including 145 species of snake; more than 22 000 fishes, only about 150 of which are freshwater species; 65 000 known insect species; and 1500 > *spiders*.

Of the fauna unique to Australia, perhaps the most extraordinary group is the > *monotremes* – the echidnas and platypuses – which are found nowhere else in the world, even in fossil form. Distinctive birds include lyre-birds, scrub-birds, Cape Barren geese, and fairy wrens. There are various unique invertebrate groups, the primitive mountain shrimp of Tas. being perhaps of greatest interest.

Australia has a rich fauna showing links with other Gondwana continents, in particular South America. In Australia, such creatures are often found in the cooler regions, especially Tas., the southern mainland, and along the eastern ranges. Vertebrates showing Gondwana affinities include marsupials, the emu and cassowary, geckoes, side-necked tortoises, most frogs, and a number of fishes including the lungfish and barramundi. Many insects and other invertebrates also display affinities with those of other southern landmasses.

Animals of relatively recent Oriental origin (sometimes referred to as the Asian Tertiary element) arrived in Australia within the last 30 million years or so, as the Australian continental plate drifted closer to Asia. They include flying or wind-borne creatures such as > *bats*, birds and insects; and many rodents, lizards, snakes and invertebrates, a number of which immigrated on 'rafts' of floating vegetation. Many of these groups are concentrated in northern Australia, reflecting their tropical origins.

Wildlife conservation While long-term climatic changes caused the extinction of many wildlife species in Australia and will continue to do so, human activities have wrought irreparable damage in a much shorter space of time. As with Australia's natural vegetation, estimates of wildlife species lost as the result of human occupation of the continent vary widely, but it is believed that nearly 20 species have been lost since European settlement. The main causes are the destruction or disruption of habitats through vegetation clearance and fires, and the introduction of competitors and predators. The greatest losses have occurred in the woodlands and grasslands of the east and southwest of the continent, cleared for grazing and wheat production: mammals that have become extinct in these regions include wallabies, bandicoots and several species of hopping mouse.

While some species thought to be extinct have reappeared – such as the rare Leadbeater's possum rediscovered in forested central Vic. in 1961, and arguably the > *thylacine*, alleged to have been sighted in Tas. in recent years – a further 30–40 species are considered under threat. These include a number of marsupials, from kangaroos and wombats to the unique numbat, and many birds of both the mainland and offshore islands. All native fauna is pro-

tected under federal law and the State governments also have special legislation covering endangered species. >> *animals, introduced*; *birds, native*; *environment and conservation*; *fishes, freshwater and marine*; *fossils*; *insects*

Fawkner, John Pascoe (1792–1869), co-founder of Melbourne, b. England. Fawkner came with his mother and convict father to the abortive Port Phillip settlement of 1803 and later to Tas., where his enterprises included a nursery, a bakery, a newspaper and a farm. He was transported to Newcastle 1816–17 for helping convicts to escape. In 1835 his party in turn established a Port Phillip settlement (though Fawkner was delayed in Launceston over debts) on the site previously selected by Batman. A member of the legislative council 1851–69, he became the 'grand old man' of Vic. politics: aggressive and reactionary, but with ideals.

featherstars > *sea-lilies and featherstars*

feathertail glider > *possums*

Federal Court > *law and legal system*

federalism When the Commonwealth of Australia was instituted in 1901, it adopted the federalist model of government established in the US in 1788, rather than the unitarist system in operation in the UK. Although the six colonial governments were effectively the progenitors of the Commonwealth, they were in many respects reluctant parents. The new Australian nation was described as 'one indissoluble Federal Commonwealth' but was still in fact very much a weak colonial confederation; since then, the power of the Commonwealth has grown to such an extent that one writer described the status of the States in 1975 as 'little more than noisome beggars or, at best, administrative agencies' of the national government. While relations between the federal and State governments have often been tense – to the extent that WA made an unsuccessful attempt to secede from the federation in 1933 – federalism is deeply entrenched in the fabric of Australian politics and is unlikely to be abandoned in the foreseeable future.

Commonwealth-State relations After > *Federation* the colonies were retitled States and transferred some of their powers (such as foreign affairs and defence) to the new federal parliament; at the same time, they retained powers in such important areas as education, housing, roads and public health, and their governmental structures were largely untouched.

The framers of the Constitution were keen to keep the federal parliament as weak as possible, but were to be disappointed. The federal government has continually increased its political authority throughout this century, most notably by assuming financial dominance over the States. From its inception, the Commonwealth controlled customs duties and tariffs, at that time the most fruitful sources of revenue. Following the establishment of the Australian Loan Council in 1927, it obtained a large degree of control over borrowing by the States; and in 1942, to meet wartime needs, it acquired a monopoly over the collection of income tax.

Its control of the nation's purse strings gives the federal government considerable power over policy in areas theoretically controlled by the States. There have been periodic moves to restore taxation powers to the States (the most recent in 1989), but this seems unlikely to take place as it is generally recognised that double taxation would be no vote-winner.

The 1980s and beyond The federal government's centralist initiatives have been secured more by judicial interpretation than by changes to the Constitution via referendums. Until recently, High Court rulings in this regard tended to favour States' rights, but two decisions in the 1980s accorded primacy to the Commonwealth: in 1983, the High Court ruled that federal powers in foreign affairs entitled the federal government to prohibit construction by the Tas. government of a dam that would have flooded the Franklin River; later, federal anti-discrimination legislation was enforced in Qld against the wishes of its government. These decisions occasioned much public controversy and have been seen as pivotal for Commonwealth-State relations. Supporters of States' rights argue that the Commonwealth has taken by stealth powers not accorded it under the Constitution, while those who consider the States no longer relevant (but impossible to abolish under the Constitution) see the High Court rulings as a significant step towards a more organic form of federalism. By the late 1980s there was some relaxing of the Commonwealth's centralist tendencies, particularly in the area of financial relations, and this is likely to be sharpened by continuing difficulties in the federal economy. >> *Constitution*; *government*

Federation The formation of an 'indissoluble Federal Commonwealth' of Australia was not easily achieved. Federation was mooted – but not legislated for – in 1850, when the Australian Colonies Government Act was passed, and for a time Fiji and NZ were envisaged as members. Jealousy between the colonies and divergent economic interests precluded progress until the 1880s, when fear of French and German activities in the Pacific region led to the formation in 1886 of the Federal Council of Australasia. This continued to meet until 1899, with WA, Fiji, Qld, Tas. and Vic. participating, but SA attended only for two years and NSW not at all. Another powerful influence was fear of non-white immigration resulting in lowered standards and wages, and the need for uniform legislation.

Henry Parkes, a proponent of federalism from the late 1860s, lent his political skill first to instigating the ministers' conference in Melbourne (1890) and then to presiding over the ensuing Australasian Federal Convention in Sydney (1891); he thus became identified as the father of Federation. More credit, though, was due to Sir Samuel Griffith and Edmund Barton, who at different stages were its chief architects, and to Alfred Deakin, its unswerving advocate throughout the difficult period 1891–1900. The work of the 1891 convention was to draw in bold outline the shape of the proposed constitution of a Commonwealth of Australasia – the name proposed by Parkes. The main debating points were tariffs, financial residues and the relative power of the proposed two houses. There followed a period of stagnation on the issue: Parkes retired from politics in 1891; an economic depression brought financial crises in the early 1890s, engrossing the colonial parliaments; and NZ and Fiji dropped entirely from the stage.

The popular agitation for unity soon became irresistible, however, sponsored by organisations such as the Australian Natives' Association and the growing nationalist movements. A second federal convention, called by Sir George Reid, met first in Adelaide in March 1897, then in Sydney and Melbourne. This time Qld, split by the Kanaka problem, stayed away. The principles of the 1891 draft were filled out and amended and the delegates went home to put it to a referendum. Reid, by raising the agreed minimum in favour from 50 000 to 80 000, ensured its defeat in NSW. Amendments were made in 1898 that finally brought acceptance by an average of 59% of those voting. WA, after a threatened separatist movement by the gold miners, yielded to a referendum. One amendment sought to satisfy the bedevilling NSW– Vic. rivalry by providing for a federal capital within NSW but not less than 100 miles from Sydney. The draft was approved in London after an amendment, at the instigation of Joseph Chamberlain, extending the right of appeal to the Privy Council, which lasted in full until 1967 and in part until the passage of the Australia Act in 1986. On 17 September 1900 Queen Victoria proclaimed that the Commonwealth of Australia would come into being on 1 January 1901. >> *federalism*

Federation Peak

Federation Peak Tas. A distinctive mountain (1233m) at the eastern end of the Arthur Range, Federation Peak stands in the South West National Park and is a favourite destination for wilderness bushwalkers in southern Tas.

Felton Bequest Alfred Felton (1831–1904) was a wealthy Melbourne dealer, druggist and investor, and a frugal-living bachelor, interested in art. His estate was worth £378 000; half was left to charities and half to the National Gallery of Vic. While the bequest has been the largest single factor in establishing the pre-eminence of the Vic. National Gallery collection, its purchasing power has been seriously eroded by inflation and by rapidly increasing prices for major works in the art market.

Female Factory This building in Parramatta, NSW, housed female convicts 1804–48; spinning and weaving were carried out there. It was above the gaol until a separate three-storey building was provided: designed by Francis Greenway, this was also used for weaving, subsequently becoming a lunatic asylum and paupers' hospital.

Fenech, Jeff (1964–), boxer, b. Sydney. The 'Marrickville mauler' personifies the classic boxing story of the battler making good. Sent to a boys' home on an assault charge at 12 years of age, Fenech was rescued from a life of street-fighting by policeman Pat Jarvis, who introduced him to the Newtown Police Boys' Club and trainer Johnny Lewis. Fenech applied himself to boxing with enormous energy, conviction and natural talent. In 1984 he turned professional and within three years he had won world titles in the bantamweight, super-bantamweight and featherweight divisions. His ferocious punching power marks him as one of the best boxers of all time.

feral animals > *animals, introduced*

ferns and fern allies Australia has about 400 species of these ancient spore-bearing plants. They are mainly concentrated in the wet rainforests of northeast Qld although many also occur in NSW, Vic. and Tas. rainforests. Some tropical species are also found in the northern monsoonal zone. Ferns are generally classified in the broad group of pteridophytes, which include the oldest land plants with distinct conducting tissue and first appeared about 350 million years ago. This classification includes subgroups such as fork-ferns and clubmosses, which are commonly described as fern allies.

The true ferns include a large and relatively advanced group of families and genera ('leptosporangiate ferns') and several more primitive families ('eusporangiate ferns'). The most primitive are the closely related families Marattiaceae and Angiopteridaceae – each represented in Australia by one species – of which the living forms are similar to fossils more than 200 million years old. They are the potato fern, *Marattia salicina*, and the giant fern, *Angiopteris evecta*, both massive specimens that survive in sheltered spots in tropical and subtropical rainforests. At the other extreme is the family Ophioglossaceae, a group of small tuberous-rooted ferns mostly reduced to a single frond and lacking any but recent fossil records. All three of its genera, *Ophioglossum* or adder's-tongues, *Botrychium* or moonworts, and *Helminthostachys*, occur in Australia. There are four native *Ophioglossum* species, three of which are tiny plants of grasslands and the fourth a rainforest epiphyte with a solitary ribbon-like leaf.

In Australia, as elsewhere, the leptosporangiate ferns account for the great majority of species. Outstanding genera include the tree-ferns *Cyathea* and *Dicksonia*, which reach heights of up to 15m and are long-lived; they are restricted to wetter rainforest and eucalypt forests in the east. The filmy ferns, family Hymenophyllaceae, are delicate creeping plants seldom more than 10cm high and many are moss-like in appearance; the 30-odd species are restricted to permanently moist, shaded habitats. The climbing ferns, of the genus *Lygodium* include four native species of twining climbers, mostly tropical. Staghorn and elkhorn ferns, genus *Platycerium,* are a spectacular group of epiphytes represented by four native species. The large genus *Blechnum* or water ferns consists of about eighteen native species with fishbone-like leaves. The family Gleicheniaceae includes the distinctive genera *Gleichenia, Dicranopteris* and *Sticherus*, the wiry stems of which form dense tangles in moist sandstone country. The most widespread of all ferns is the ubiquitous bracken, *Pteridium esculentum*, of forested country; its amazingly extensive networks of deep, starch-filled rhizomes ensure rapid regeneration and it often forms a dense cover to a height of 1.5m.

Fern allies The two extant genera of the subdivision Psilotopsida – considered to be the most primitive of all pteridophytes – are represented in Australia: the most widespread is the fork-fern, *Psilotum*. There are about seventeen species of clubmoss, forming the genus *Lycopodium* in the subdivision Lycopsida: they include the spectacular tassel fern, pendant epiphytes of tropical rainforests; and the endemic single-species genus of pigmy clubmoss, *Phylloglossum*, a minute tuberous-rooted plant of peaty ground.

ferries > *public transport; river transport*

Festival of Light > *Call to Australia party*

festivals Although Australia's earliest festivals were usually related to traditional seasonal events such as harvest and blossom time, cultural and general festivals have become established in all capital cities and some country towns, particularly since World War 2. Film festivals are held regularly in many cities, those of longest standing being the annual Melbourne and Sydney festivals which screen an eclectic range of local and overseas films, from the newest experimental works to period classics.

The Festival of Sydney, held annually in January since 1977, combines fun and culture during a month of outdoor concerts (ranging from ballet to rock-and-roll), children's films, art exhibitions, a regatta and fireworks. Qld, well endowed with purely fun festivals often centred on the State's natural resources and largely tourist-oriented, has joined the move towards cultural celebrations with events such as the Warana Festival of Arts, held in Brisbane each year since 1961. Melbourne's Moomba Festival, held annually since March 1955, is a self-styled 'people's festival' of sport, carnival and arts that remains immensely popular despite

recent criticisms that it is too 'lowbrow'. Another noted event in that city is the Lygon Street Festa, an Italian street carnival and arts festival in the suburb of Carlton which has been held annually since the late 1970s and attracts some 500 000 visitors over three days. The Melbourne Spoleto Festival is a cultural celebration based on an Italian model and has been held since 1985. The Adelaide Festival of Arts, inaugurated in 1947 and held biennially since the early 1960s, has become the benchmark for Australian cultural festivals, staging some of the best and most innovative theatre, music and performances by Australian and international artists. The associated Writers' Festival is increasingly important as a venue for local and overseas writers, readers and publishers. Also in SA, Hahndorf's annual Schuetzenfest (shooting festival) commemorates the State's early settlers, and German wine festivals are also popular and well-attended. The Festival of Perth, annual since 1953, is an arts festival of high standard that presents opera, dance, theatre and art exhibitions. Like Qld, the NT has a tradition of light-hearted festivals; the best-known of these are the Henley-on-Todd regatta, a mock yacht race on the dry bed of the Todd River, and the Alice Springs Camel Cup. More recently, a number of regular arts festivals have been inaugurated in Darwin and Alice Springs, several of which focus on Aboriginal culture. Held over ten days and the largest festival in the ACT, the Canberra Festival is a week-long celebration of music, theatre, wine and food. The major Tas. festival is the annual Tas. Fiesta, which coincides with the Sydney–Hobart and Melbourne–Hobart yacht races in December–January and features both sporting and cultural events across the State.

Ficus > *figs*

figbirds > *orioles and figbirds*

figs Trees and shrubs of the large genus *Ficus*, which belongs to the mulberry family, occur throughout tropical and subtropical regions of the world. They are all characterised by an inflorescence in the form of a hollow receptacle (the fig) with numerous small flowers on the inside, many of which are edible. Australia has about 40 native fig species, most concentrated in northern Qld. The majority are trees belonging to the strangler-fig subgenus, members of which start life as seedlings on tree crotches or rockfaces, sending roots to the soil below that eventually fuse into a trunk. Well-known examples are the Port Jackson or rusty fig, *F. rubiginosa*, the Moreton Bay fig, *F. macrophylla*, and the central Australian fig, *F. platypoda*. Another subgenus includes the distinctive sand-paper figs, with extraordinarily rough leaves; the species *F. coronata*, the only fig found as far south as Vic., produces one of the most palatable Australian figs.

film industry Australia was early to join the film-making nations. Apart from the biblical epic *Soldiers of the Cross*, a mixture of live action and stills made by the Salvation Army in 1900, Australia can claim to have produced one of the world's first feature films – Charles Tait's *The Story of the Kelly Gang* (1905), which ran for some 45 minutes (only fragments have survived). Documentary film-making has an even longer history, dating back to 1896 when two French cameramen recorded the Melbourne Cup. This auspicious start to the industry was upheld by the quality – if not the quantity – of early features and documentaries, but owing largely to competition from imported films (especially from the US) production waned from the 1920s until the industry was to some extent revived in the 1970s.

Historical development Tait's pioneering historical action-adventure helped promote a stream of rough-and-ready bushranger films that were shown, along with stagily filmed theatrical productions, in the rudimentary cinemas that existed before World War 1. The demand for Australian films declined, however, as cinema distribution and exhibition were monopolised by management groups (at first locally owned, later controlled by overseas interests). Production of cinema newsreels began in 1911 and remained the mainstay of the local industry for several decades. The production of feature films continued, although often with difficulty, and in the last decade of the silent-film era (1918–28) their form and content improved. The most celebrated director of the time was > *Raymond Longford*, best known for his version of the C. J. Dennis verse narrative *The Sentimental Bloke* (1919). Other notable film-makers of the 1920s were Franklyn Barrett, who made arguably the best film of the period, *A Girl in the Bush* (1920), and the prolific Beaumont Smith. Photographer > *Frank Hurley* made a range of outstanding documentaries from 1913 onwards.

The first successful Australian sound film was Frank W. Thring's *Diggers* (1931), adapted from a stage show by Pat Hannah. Thring established a thriving studio in Melbourne, an enterprise eclipsed by > *Ken Hall* at Cinesound in Sydney. Hall took the lead in establishing Australian film-making in the Hollywood vein and throughout the 1930s and early 1940s he directed and produced a stream of features that found favour with local audiences and were distributed overseas. The best of them were *It Isn't Done* (1937), *Mr Chedworth Steps Out* (1939), *The Silence of Dean Maitland* (1934), *The Squatter's Daughter* (1933), *Tall Timbers* (1937) and *Smithy* (1946). A more accomplished film-maker was > *Charles Chauvel*, whose production career began with the silent *The Moth of Moonbi* (1926) and extended to the first Australian colour feature film, *Jedda*, in 1955. After World War 2, few truly Australian feature films were made for almost a quarter of a century, although the sparse rate of production was augmented by Australian-based films made by US and British interests. Some notable documentaries were made during this period by Stanley Hawes and John Heyers, but even cinema newsreels began to decline after the war and were superseded by television news in the 1960s.

The 1970s and beyond It took long-advocated, but never seriously attempted, government intervention to revive the production of feature films. In 1970, the federal government set up the Australian Film Development Corporation (re-established in 1975, with additional powers, as the Australian Film Commission). As well as taking responsibility for the government's own film-making arm, Film Australia, it began funding film production and an immediate flow of local features resulted; throughout the 1970s, State bodies with similar functions added to the growing volume of local production. A singular catalyst in this period of growth was > *Phillip Adams*, who both championed the cause of the local industry and produced a range of films including such diverse classics as *The Adventures of Barry McKenzie* (1972) and *We of the Never Never* (1982).

Technical quality improved steadily, reinforced by expertise acquired in the television industry from the 1950s and by the federally funded Australian Film and Television School, founded in 1973. The 1970s produced a number of major films that had both commercial and critical success, with the emergence of new and important directors such as > *Peter Weir*, > *Fred Schepisi*, Phillip Noyce, > *Bruce Beresford* and > *Gillian Armstrong*. Films such as Weir's *Picnic at Hanging Rock* (1975), Beresford's *The Getting of Wisdom* (1977) and Armstrong's *My Brilliant Career* (1979) – all based on Australian novels – were internationally acclaimed and gave a much-needed shot in the arm to the industry. The optimism generated by the resurrection of Australian feature films was relatively short-lived, however, and the new vitality of the industry was sapped by the loss to the US of talents such as Weir, Beresford and Schepisi. By the end of the decade, the contribution of the private sector to local film-making was dwindling and the number of productions dropped accordingly.

In 1981 the Fraser government introduced a system of tax incentives to encourage commercial investment in locally produced films, a policy that has been maintained since but with progressively lower levels of tax-deductibility – partly in response to abuses of the system which yielded a number of low-quality films. Greater sophistication of technique and a more worldly orientation of content characterised much of the 1980s. The international box-office success of George Miller's *Mad Max* science-fiction adventures (1979, 1981, 1985) was followed by the quite startling world triumph of Peter Faiman's *Crocodile Dundee* (1986), a satirical adventure starring television comedian > *Paul Hogan*. Other major films of the decade include Beresford's *Breaker Morant* (1980), Weir's *Gallipoli* (1981) and Ray Lawrence's *Bliss* (1985). Directorial talents to come to the fore included > *Paul Cox* and John Duigan (whose earlier works were eclipsed by *The Year My Voice Broke* in 1987). A slowing-down in production, in tandem with a further change in government funding (to a Film Finance Corporation, or 'film bank') marked the latter part of the decade.

Finch, Peter Ingle (1916–77), actor, b. England. In the 1930s, Finch worked in Australian radio and cinema, and at the Independent Theatre in Sydney. He was invited to London by Laurence Olivier, where he won acclaim for his part in the play *Daphne Laureola* (1949). His later career was as an intelligent and dependable screen actor, of limited range. Major films include *The Nun's Story* (1959), *The Man with the Green Carnation* (1960) and *Far from the Madding Crowd* (1967); arguably his best performance was as the homosexual doctor in *Sunday, Bloody Sunday* (1971). Finch was awarded a posthumous US Academy Award for his uncharacteristic performance in *Network* (1976).

finches Indigenous finches of Australia belong to the family Ploceidae, the weaver finches, as distinct from the European birds (> *birds, introduced*) of the family Fringillidae, although some of these have become acclimatised. They are small, often brightly coloured seed-eaters with stout, blunt bills; there are over 20 species. Most construct a dome- or bottle-shaped nest of materials such as woven grass or bark, and usually in thick grass or low bushes. The mostly black-and-white zebra finch is widespread in desert conditions, usually moving in flocks. Other striking birds include the banded finch, red-mowed finch, diamond firetail and beautiful firetail. Among the most beautifully coloured are the gouldian finch of the tropical north – in green, yellow and blue, the male sometimes with a scarlet head – and the crimson finches of northwest and northeast Australia.

Finke River A seasonal river that rises in the Macdonnell Ranges, the Finke follows a course of over 600km southeast towards Lake Eyre, although its waters seldom reach the lake. The Finke Gorge National Park in the Krichauff Ranges south of Hermannsburg is notable for its relict fauna and flora, including the palm *Livistonia mariae*, found only in Palm Valley. The presence of permanent waterholes along the river's course is the source of its Aboriginal name, *Larapinta*, meaning 'creek with permanent water'. It was discovered by J. McDouall Stuart in 1860 and named after his financial backer, William Finke.

fireflies > *beetles*

First Fleet This was the name given, after its arrival, to the eleven sailing ships that took the first convicts to Botany Bay 1787–8. Ships, stores and crews were assembled during the 1786–7 winter: preparations were disorganised until Arthur Phillip took charge and his superb leadership undoubtedly accounted for the success of the hazardous voyage of over 24 000km in about 250 days. It was accomplished with only 32 deaths from illness out of about 1475 people on board, credit for this largely being due to the surgeon, John White. The total tonnage (3892 tons) was less than a modest steamer, and that of the individual ships was less than an average ferryboat today. The fleet sailed from Portsmouth, calling at Tenerife.

Water shortage led to rationing and sickness between there and Rio de Janeiro, where the fleet loaded food and water as well as tropical plants and seeds, and rum. At Cape Town further livestock were added to those brought from England, and more plants and seeds. The voyage is documented in many journals and letters by officers, seamen, and at least one convict. Ships were: *Sirius*, Royal Navy Convoy; *Supply*, Royal Navy armed tender; transport ships: *Alexander, Lady Penrhyn, Charlotte, Scarborough, Friendship, Prince of Wales*; store ships: *Fishburn, Golden Grove, Borrowdale*.

Firth-Smith, John (1943–), painter b. Melbourne. Firth-Smith's huge-scale marine abstracts, with their freely applied paint and broad planes of colour, explore the essence of Sydney Harbour, the docks and the sea – recurring themes in his work for over two decades. He has exhibited in Tokyo, London and Paris, and is well represented in State galleries and corporate collections.

Fisher, Andrew (1862–1928), politician, b. Scotland. After immigrating to Qld in 1885, Fisher worked as a coal-miner and a union leader before entering the legislative assembly as a Labor member (1893) and then becoming a member of the House of Representatives at the first federal election in 1901. Elected leader of the Labor Party in 1907, he was prime minister and treasurer 1908–9 and 1910–13; his many achievements include the establishment of the Commonwealth Bank and the introduction of maternity allowances and invalid pensions. Returning briefly to office in 1914, he retired in favour of W.M. Hughes in the following year, subsequently serving as Australian high commissioner in London (1916–25).

fishes, freshwater and marine Despite its relative paucity of rivers, Australia has about 150 species of freshwater fishes, although some entire families of later-evolved Old World species are not represented. Noteworthy Australian species are treated separately, either individually or as groups; others are described briefly below. Australia also has a rich fauna of marine fishes, occurring in almost every habitat; in particular, the coral reefs host many species remarkable for shape and colour. Most of the commercial species, however, are found in the deeper and cooler waters of the southern margin of the continent, and much of the offshore fauna is similar in

general composition to that found around other southern continents. The important marine fishes are treated separately under either individual or group headings.

The freshwater herring, *Potamalosa richmondia*, is found in coastal rivers of NSW and Vic. and spawns in salt water in winter; the almost transparent smelt, three species of *Retropinna*, may be seen in schools in many streams in southeastern Australia, its food including mosquito larvae. The Tas. troutlet, *Lovettia seallii*, is netted in the upper Derwent River in autumn, and canned for commercial use; the Australian grayling, *Prototroctes maraena*, is a brown-and-yellow fish with a grey side-stripe: it is good to eat, but apparently in retreat before the larger, introduced trout. The native or mountain trout, a small, scaleless fish measuring about 15–18cm and lacking a fin in the centre of the back, is a representative of the widespread genus *Galaxias*, which is found mainly in fresh water. The eastern Australian freshwater catfish, tandan or dew-fish, *Tandanus tandanus*, is distinguished by whiskers or barbels and a long, fringing fin uniting the rear dorsal, tail and anal fins. The small-headed pipe-fish, *Oxleyana parviceps*, is a relative of the sea-horse and has a somewhat similar snout, and the river garfish of eastern Australia, *Reporhamphus ardelio*, has a beak-like lower jaw.

The small, silvery hardyheads of the genus *Atherinosoma* appear in the western half of southern Australia and have an orange, yellow or black side-stripe that becomes more vivid if the fish is excited; these fishes are related to mullets, and some species can move between fresh and salt water. Most inland hardyheads belong to the genus *Craterocephalus*, of which some have a body-line at eye-level. The freshwater mullet of eastern Australia, *Trachystoma petardi*, is cultivated in farm dams and commonly reaches a length of 30cm.

The bass or perch, *Percalates colonorum*, silvery-olive above and yellow-grey below, is a good angling fish with a fairly deep body, large scales and a continuous dorsal fin, the front part fan-like and slightly spined; the fish is widespread in eastern coastal streams and has been introduced into WA. The widespread silver perch or bidyan, *Bidyanus bidyanus* is also a good food fish. The Macquarie perch or silvereye, *Macquaria australasica*, and the commercially important callop or yellowbelly, *Plectroplites ambiguus*, each have a rather stumpy tail without the slight swallow-tail element.

The nursery fish or humphead, *Kurtus gulliveri*, is purplish-silver with some black markings and has an unusual, deep-bodied diamond-shape, with a single, deep dorsal fin and a long anal fin; the male has a forehead hump housing a bony cavity in which the female lays the eggs and where they are incubated in conditions of water circulation and aeration not easy to secure in the muddy tropical waters that the fish inhabit. The small slippery or river black-fish, *Gadopsis marmoratus*, is unique to streams of Tas. and southeastern Australia; it has a long dorsal fin, deeper to the rear, a long anal fin, and a vestigial ventral fin under the gills.

There are many genera of gudgeon, of varying size and in habitats varying from streams to billabongs; they include the cave-living blind gudgeon, *Milyeringa veritas*. Gobies are similar to gudgeons, but their ventral fins are fused to form a sucker-like anchor; they are found in a wide range of habitats – for example, the Tasman goby is mainly a salt-water species, in contrast to the isolated spring goby of the Lake Eyre area in central Australia.

Many salt-water fishes are recorded as entering freshwater rivers. Among them are the cartilaginous sharks and sawfish, and many bony fishes both large and small such as barramundi, mullet, threadfin and eels, the lesser jewfish or mulloway, the deep-bodied and sometimes spectacularly marked small batfish, the slender bramah or beach salmon, and adults or young of several gobies. It is possible that the relative lack of freshwater species in Australia has brought into fresh water several genera that elsewhere are marine.

fishes, introduced Australia's freshwater streams and lakes contain introduced species of both sporting and food fish. These include the rainbow trout from North America, *Salmo gairdneri,* and the European brown trout, *S. trutta* – the former is said to prefer swifter streams but to be able also to withstand higher water temperatures. Established trout hatcheries rear fish for release into mountain streams for sport fishing, or for commercial sale; introduced trout have tipped the ecological balance against some smaller indigenous fish in the higher and cooler streams of southeastern Australia and Tas. The introduction of the Atlantic salmon, *S. salar*, has been particularly successful in Tas., which markets both chilled and smoked fish. The English perch or redfin, *Perca fluviatilis*, gives moderate sport and food from many lakes and streams in southern Australia. Carp, of the genera *Cyprinus* and *Carassius,* also have been introduced into many rivers, but they are little used for food; they are now considered to be pest species, and have contributed to the reduction of Murray cod populations. The well-known top-minnow, *Gambusia affinis*, has locally been useful as a consumer of mosquito larvae; another exotic, the snake-head, *Channa striata*, has been introduced as a food fish by the Chinese.

fishing Nearly 250 000 Australians are members of angling clubs, but annual sales of fishing tackle indicate the existence of over a million amateur anglers in any one year.

Fishing as a sport originated in the search for food by both black and white Australians, and then (as now) Australia's extensive coastline offered opportunities in a wide variety of locations. Areas north of Brisbane provide sub-tropical fish; more southern seas produce different species in cooler waters, although there is a considerable overlap. Coastal fishing can be either in surf, in estuaries, from rocks or – for deep-sea fishing – from boats; since World War 2, the widespread availability of small portable craft has made many previously inaccessible areas open to a greater number of anglers. In eastern Australia especially, inland rivers and lakes provide excellent fishing for native species and for European and North American trout introduced into Australian waters in the early 20th century. The Game Fishing Association controls this aspect of the sport which, since the discovery of black marlin off the Qld coast near Cairns, has become a major international tourist attraction. However, pollution of oceans and waterways, and the destruction caused by the European carp, which fouls the water by rooting among water plants, are becoming a threat to the continued enjoyment of fishing.

fishing industry Despite a 36 000km coastline and the 3000 varieties of fish found in its waters, Australia does not have a large fishing industry. This is partly because of the narrow continental shelf and relatively warm surrounding oceans, which lack the vast shoals of fish of a single species found in colder, shallower waters. Nevertheless, the industry is of major commercial importance: although the annual catch is small by weight (about 150 000t in 1986), it is of a high value in cash terms – about $592 million in that year – owing to the large proportion of crustaceans (principally lobsters and prawns) and molluscs (abalone and scallops) for which there is a ready and growing export market, particularly in Asia. In 1986, Australia exported 22 645t of crustaceans and molluscs, worth over $414 million – a remarkable figure, and nearly double that of exports of sheep meat or fruit and nuts.

The Australian industry had a bad start when William Bryant, the convicted smuggler appointed by Arthur Phillip as the First Fleet's master fisherman, absconded to Timor in the governor's cutter in 1791, taking with him what little fishing expertise there was in the colony. In general, ignorance of local conditions and patterns of fish migration meant the industry did not flourish. Bad luck struck again over a century later when Harold Dannevig, a Norwegian appointed as first director of fisheries by the Commonwealth, was lost at sea in 1914 along with the research vessel, *Endeavour*. In the same year, however, the NSW government imported three North Sea trawlers, soon supplementing them with local boats when a measure of professionalism began to appear in the industry.

As elsewhere in the world, the Australian fishing industry is divided into estuarine, coastal, pelagic (surface) and demersal (deep-sea) fishing. The major fishing areas are the northeast, southeast and southwest coasts. The main estuarine species caught are barramundi, mullet, bream and Australian salmon; major pelagic species are mackerel, tuna, barracouta, pilchards and anchovies. Demersal species include flathead, morwong, redfish, gemfish, orange roughy, trevally, inshore snapper and whiting. School and gummy sharks are also caught in Bass Strait.

Since the adoption of a 200-nautical-mile Australian Fishing Zone (AFZ) in 1979, vast areas – including the entire Gulf of Carpentaria – have been brought under Australian supervision and foreign fishing boats are required to hold licences and pay access fees. This has helped reduce fears of future overfishing, which plagued the industry in earlier times.

Most of Australia's fin fish are marketed and consumed locally. In the case of tuna, barracouta and Australian salmon, there is a sizeable canning industry. The best-quality rock lobsters, prawns, abalone, sea-urchin roe, and some fresh-chilled tuna are exported, often by air freight. The freshwater industry is small and centred mainly on the Murray–Darling system, the major catches being Murray cod, perch and catfish.

The east-coast oyster industry (> *oysters and oyster culture*) is based in NSW, the prized Sydney rock oyster being cultivated from Qld to the Vic. border. Smaller quantities of scallops and mussels are also harvested, mainly in the eastern states but with some production in WA.

The potential of Australia's fisheries is immense given the vast export markets available, but its development has been haphazard and fragmented owing to a lack of co-ordination between first the colonies and then the Commonwealth and States, which led to over-exploitation of fish populations. Since the establishment of the AFZ and the enactment of much associated fisheries control legislation in the 1980s, the situation has improved.

Fisk, Sir Ernest Thomas (1886–1965), radio pioneer and businessman, b. England. Initially a radio operator and Australian agent for the English wireless-telegraph firm Marconi, Fisk established Amalgamated Wireless (Australasia) Ltd in 1913; he became managing director in 1917 and was chairman from 1932. Fisk was the first to establish direct radio links between Britain and Australia, pioneered broadcasting and radio-telephone throughout the British empire, and was a noted advocate of professionalism in the infant industry; he also encouraged local manufacture of radio equipment.

Fitton, Doris > *theatre*

FitzGerald, R. D. (Robert David) (1902–87), poet, b. Sydney. A land surveyor by training, FitzGerald worked with the Department of the Interior until his retirement in 1965. His poetry, of which the first published volume was *The Greater Apollo: Seven Metaphysical Songs* (1927) and the last, *Product* (1977), is relatively obscure and has never received a wide readership. Critical controversy has dogged his reputation: some have seen his verse as unlyrical and contrived; others have seen him as a major poet and an important influence in freeing Australian verse from the parochial and pedestrian.

Fitzpatrick, Brian Charles (1905–65), journalist and historian, b. Cudgee, Vic. Fitzpatrick was a regular contributor to *Smith's Weekly* in the 1940s, published the *Australian Democrat* journal 1947–51, and edited the *Labor Newsletter* from 1958 until his death. His several social and economic histories of

Australia reflected his entrenched views as a radical socialist: these include *British Imperialism and Australia* (1939), *A Short History of the Labor Movement* (1940) and *The Australian Commonwealth* (1956), all of which have contributed significantly to Australian historical study.

Fitzroy River Qld This is the main stream of the second-largest river system of Qld's east coast. It is formed by the confluence of the Dawson and Mackenzie rivers, and flows for some 480km to the sea at Keppel Bay, being navigable for deep-water ships upstream as far as Rockhampton. The river was named after Sir Charles Fitz Roy, a governor of NSW.

Fitzroy River WA The Fitzroy River rises in the Durack Range in the eastern Kimberleys and follows a course of more than 550km to King Sound, in the far northwest. En route it crosses King Leopold Range and passes the spectacular limestone cliffs of Geikie Gorge upstream from Fitzroy Crossing; this is part of the Geikie Gorge National Park, established chiefly to preserve the cliffs and the fauna of the gorge pool and immediate environs. The river was named after Captain Robert Fitzroy, a former commander of the *Beagle*.

Five Towns Also known as the 'Macquarie towns', the settlements of Windsor, Richmond, Wilberforce, Castlereagh and Pitt Town lie near the Hawkesbury River just northwest of Sydney. On land high enough to provide protection in times of flood, they were chosen by Governor Macquarie in 1810 as a potential refuge, at a time when the colony's chief source of produce was the Hawkesbury valley.

Five Power Defence Arrangement > *defence*

Flack, Edwin > *athletics*; *Olympic Games*

flag, Australian > *emblems and flags*

flame tree > *sterculia family*

flatworms > *helminths*

fleas These laterally compressed, wingless external parasites of mammals and birds are of the order Siphonaptera. Some 80 species are known in Australia, about ten of them introduced by man, including species commonly

associated with cats, dogs, rats, and poultry. Some are carriers of disease. Most endemic species are found on marsupials and native rodents. The European rabbit flea has been deliberately introduced to assist in the transmission of myxomatosis and so reduce the feral rabbit population.

flies Flies are often the most numerically abundant insect group and are found in an extraordinary range of habitats. Australia has more than 7000 known species, but considerably more await description. Many blood-taking groups act as vectors of pathogens, and thus are of paramount medical and veterinary concern. In true or two-winged flies of the order Diptera only the forewings are functional, the hindwings having been modified into clublike appendages that act as balancing organs during flight. The immature stages of higher flies are legless maggots, and their ability to develop rapidly enables them to take advantage of temporary nutrient-rich environments such as rotting fruit, excrement or carrion. A representative few of the approximately 90 fly families, classified into three suborders, are considered here.

The insect of the suborder Nematocera has a many-segmented antenna and often a complex venation. The cranefly family (Tipulidae) is one of the largest, with more than 700 Australian species; craneflies have long, delicate legs and are commonly found in forests. Midges (Chironomidae) have aquatic larvae and are important in freshwater food chains; adults are often seen at dusk in aerial mating swarms along rivers. In addition to the > *mosquitoes* there are several bloodsucking families in the Nematocera, including the tiny 'sandflies' or biting midges (Ceratopogonidae), the blackflies (Simuliidae) and some mothflies (Psychodidae). Larvae of the fungus gnats (Mycetophilidae) usually feed on fungi, but this family also includes > *glow-worms*. The unusual family Perissommatidae, discovered in 1957, is found only in cool uplands in eastern Australia and Chile; these flies are small and fragile, and their larvae live in rotting fungi.

Flies of the suborder Brachycera usually have a short, three-segmented antenna and a reduced venation. The march flies (Tabanidae) are ferocious, biting pests and are particularly abundant near creeks and swamps, where their aquatic larvae develop. Robberflies (Asilidae) are often seen sitting on perches from which they swoop down to capture prey on the wing.

The suborder Cyclorrhapha contains a wide range of families. Hoverflies (Syrphidae) have remarkable flying ability and are able, as their name implies, to hover in front of flowers. Some fruit flies (Tephritidae) are serious agricultural pests, especially the imported Mediterranean 'medfly', *Ceratitus capitata*, and the native Qld species, *Dacus tryoni*; interstate transportation of produce in Australia is often subject to quarantine to stop the spread of these pests. Ferment-flies, *Drosophila*, are often seen around rotting fruit and are used as experimental animals in genetical studies. As larvae, flies of the family Tachinidae are all parasites within bodies of other insects and thus aid the control of pest species; > *botflies* are parasites within the bodies of mammals. A group of families including the Muscidae (houseflies and the closely related > *bushfly*) and Calliphoridae (> *blowflies*) have rapidly developing larvae that are able to utilise temporary habitats such as excrement and carrion.

Flinders, Matthew (1774–1814), explorer,

b. England. Flinders was one of the greatest explorers. He became a friend of George Bass when both accompanied Governor Hunter to NSW in 1794, and together they examined the coasts south of Sydney in the tiny *Tom Thumb*. Convinced that there was a strait between Van Diemen's Land and NSW, they cirumnavigated Van Diemen's Land in the *Norfolk*, 1798. Returning to England, Flinders published his valuable observations, dedicated to Sir Joseph Banks.

Sailing again, in the *Investigator*, he reached Cape Leeuwin in 1801; from that point he charted the south coast, much of which was previously unknown. After refitting the *Investigator* in Sydney he sailed north, eventually circumnavigating the continent 1802–3. On his return journey to England he called at Mauritius, unaware that Britain and France were at war, and was subsequently detained there for six and a half years in spite of having documents promising his safe passage with no molestation from the French. He was finally released and reached London in 1810, broken in health but able to complete *A Voyage to Terra Australis*, published just before his death. His grandson was Flinders Petrie, the great Egyptologist.

Flindersia > *citrus family*

Flinders Group Qld This is made up of six

islands (Blackwood, Clack, Denham, Flinders, Maclear and Stanley) lying off Bathurst Head at the eastern end of Princess Charlotte Bay, in north Qld; the largest is Flinders Island, containing rocky Flinders Peak (320m). All are fringed with coral reefs; vegetation is eucalypt forest, and mangroves on the shores. The group has been important in Aboriginal life; there are numerous prehistoric art sites and, on Flinders Island, evidence of a long period of occupation. The islands are part of Cape Melville National Park.

Flinders Island Tas. This is the largest of

the > *Furneaux Islands* in eastern Bass Strait, named by Governor Philip King after Matthew Flinders; in its early days it was a sealing centre, and briefly (1830–47) a reserve for Tas. Aborigines. In the west the land is mountainous, the greatest height being Strzelecki Peaks, 778m. Industry centres on beef cattle, wool, fat lambs, dairying and fishing; muttonbirding is declining in importance. Strzelecki National Park occupies part of the island's southwest, and in 1980 a sanctuary was established to protect Cape Barren geese.

Flinders Ranges SA This chain of moun-

tains, of Precambrian origin, extends for some 500km from Crystal Brook (near Port Pirie) north to the arid Lake Eyre region. It was sighted in 1802 by Matthew Flinders and named in his honour by George Gawler in 1839. Graziers moved into the region by the 1860s but retreated from the barren interior with the inevitable recurrence of drought conditions; sheep, wheat and fruit are the region's main farm products today. Copper and other minerals were mined periodically in the area, most notably 1860–90; coal is still extracted, by open cut, at Leigh Creek. The ranges are of considerable scientific significance: they bear some of the world's most primitive fossils and are noted for the diversity of native mammals – including the rare yellow-footed rock wallaby – as well as numerous bird and reptile species. Several national parks have been declared in the area: the largest are the Flinders Ranges National Park, which covers some 78 500ha and is centred on rugged > *Wilpena Pound*, and the arid wilderness region of Gammon Ranges National Park (nearly 99 440ha). The stark beauty of the region has long attracted walkers, artists and photographers, and has been captured most notably in the paintings of Sir Hans Heysen.

Flinders River Qld The longest river in

Qld, the Flinders rises on the western slopes of the Great Dividing Range and follows a course of 840km to an estuary at the southeast corner of the Gulf of Carpentaria. With rainfall concentrated in the summer months, the river floods in the wet season and may cease to flow in the dry; its major tributaries are the Cloncurry and the Saxby. Grazing country supports sheep in the upper basin and chiefly beef cattle on grasslands of the lower section. It was discovered in 1841 by Captain J. Stokes of the *Beagle*, and named after Matthew Flinders.

Flintoff-King, Debbie > *athletics*

floods Because of its relatively low relief and its geographical position in the tropical-cyclone belt, much of Australia is subject to floods. Along the eastern coast and ranges, the relatively short rivers that drain the rugged Great Divide rise rapidly with the onset of heavy rains, often flooding the settled coastal plains with little warning. By contrast, the long rivers on the lesser gradients of the western slopes have much larger catchments and are more predictable, although floods on these rivers often persist longer, cover wide areas, and may take months to reach the river outlets far removed from the flood source: Darling River flooding is usually associated with summer monsoonal rain in Qld catchments, while the Murray River floods as a result of spring rain and snow-melt on the Australian Alps. Flooding of the arid interior often results in the periodic filling of saline lakes. Although often destructive from a human viewpoint, floods are essential for the plant and animal life of arid lands. Plants grow rapidly and flower in response to floodwater, and algal blooms in the nutrient-rich waters allow waterfowl and fish to breed in large numbers.

Flood warning and forecasting is well developed in Australia, but the unpredictability of weather can cause flash floods, especially along the eastern coast. Most local councils have adopted zoning that prohibits construction on floodplains, instead reserving the land for recreation. Construction of dams and levees, acquisition of flood-prone land, and erosion control are other methods of flood mitigation in settled areas. Some types of land use in river basins, especially deforestation and poor agricultural practices, have increased the intensity of flooding in some areas. >> *climate*; *water and water resources*

flora The first Europeans to visit Australia were impressed by what they perceived to be its 'unique' flora. In reality many plant families in Australia occur elsewhere in the world and large plant families from elsewhere occur in Australia. Only about twelve small vascular plant families are endemic, three of which are confined to rainforests and the rest to arid areas or poor soils; the number of endemic genera is correspondingly higher (numbering over 530), with similar distribution. The great majority of native species are, on the other hand, endemic and it is this feature that gives the Australian flora its uniqueness.

Geological evidence supports the theory that the similarities between the floras of southern hemisphere countries stems from their common origin in the ancient southern continent > *Gondwana*. When the Australian part of Gondwana migrated northwards it took with it an assortment of ancient floral elements, the basis of our present native flora, which then diversified in geographical isolation and under changing climatic conditions. There is evidence to suggest that genera with greatest affinities in the northern hemisphere, such as *Ranunculus* (> *buttercup family*), may have entered Australia along the high mountain chains or even by long-distance dispersal; more recently there has been some dispersal of plants between Australia and regions to the north. It is not surprising that early botanists thought the leathery leaves of many Australian species and the reduced, pointed leaves and reduced size (scleromorphy) of others was strongly linked to the arid environment; it was, however, later realised that plants with these features also developed in heath communities in areas of high rainfall but on low nutrient soils. Nowhere is the development of scleromorphic communities more evident than in southwest WA, where about 40% of all known Australian *Acacia* species (> *wattle*) occur and about one-third of the world's protea species are found. The vegetation of Australia can broadly be divided into seven major types: rainforest, communities dominated by > *eucalypts*, by wattles, by > *casuarinas* and by native conifers; shrublands dominated by plants adapted to saline conditions; grasslands. Heath communities, aquatic communities, coastal plants and alpine communities are also significant.

> *Rainforests* occur in relatively small areas in high-rainfall regions of the north coast and along the eastern coast from Cape York to Tas. The richest type, lowland tropical rainforest, is found in northeast Qld on fertile soils and contains an extraordinarily diverse assortment

of plants, many of them relicts from the original Gondwana flora (such as members of the > *laurel family*) as well as the most primitive members of more widespread groups such as the myrtle and protea families. The endemic species huon pine and celery-top pine are common components of cool temperate rainforests in Tas., which probably come closest to giving some idea of conditions in Gondwana before it broke up.

Despite its large number of endemic species, the vascular flora of Australia is dominated by two large genera, *Eucalyptus* and *Acacia*. Eucalypt forests and woodlands can be divided into communities that occur mostly in the northwest and northeast and those more or less restricted to the southwest and southeast. The southwest communities exhibit a high degree of endemism, probably due to a long period of geographic isolation. Commonly two or three species form a mosaic with other associations across the continent; the river red gum is the most widespread of all eucalypts, being scattered over most of Australia except southwest WA and the Nullarbor Plain. While some species are restricted to forest or woodland, at least some occur in both and assume quite different forms depending on where they are found.

The genus *Acacia* is widespread (occurring also in Africa and tropical America) but most Australian species belong to one section of the genus where the leaves are reduced to flattened petioles called phyllodes. Although wattles tend to replace eucalypts in arid and semi-arid areas they are also an important component in plant communities of higher rainfall areas. Although there are some 900 known wattle species in Australia, vast areas are dominated by a few species, such as brigalow in Qld and to a lesser extent in NSW, mulga in arid and semi-arid regions, and gidgee.

In the drier parts of Australia, casuarinas such as the belah or black oak, the desert oak and bull oak dominate woodland areas. The tallest desert oak, a species renowned for its extremely hard wood, may reach a height of 20m. Unlike many northern-hemisphere countries, Australia does not have large areas dominated by conifers. The white cypress pine is, however, widespread from southern Qld to Vic. and often forms extensive pure stands on infertile soils. Shrublands often devoid of trees and dominated by salt-tolerant species mainly belonging to the > *saltbush family* occur on saline soils with a high clay content. These shrublands are more or less confined to the southern half of Australia, covering extensive areas of the Nullarbor Plain, northeastern SA, southwest Qld and the western plains of NSW. The dominant species frequently form the greater part of the understorey of adjoining woodland. In some areas grazing stock have removed the perennial species and they have been replaced by serious annual weeds such as galvanised burr. The saltmarsh areas on the coast are similarly often dominated by saltbushes.

Natural > *grasses and grasslands* occur in areas where the development of trees and shrubs is in some way inhibited, often owing simply to insufficient annual rainfall. Grass communities in Australia are generally either northern summer-growing species or temperate species that grow most vigorously during the cooler months. On destabilised sand dunes in arid areas, perennial grasses may provide brief cover after good rain.

Heathlands are usually less than 1m tall and have most commonly developed in high-rainfall areas on the coast. They often have a very rich flora and are commonly dominated by epacrids, banksias, species of *Leptospermum* and casuarinas.

More or less superimposed over the land flora are rich plant communities associated with waterlogged soils. This aquatic and semi-aquatic vegetation encompasses free-floating plants, submerged plants, and plants rooted in mud (either submerged or with the stems emergent); smaller plants forming sedgelands; and plants forming scrubs or thickets (such as > *melaleucas* along the Gulf of Carpentaria).

The flora of the littoral, apart from salt-tolerant shrublands dominated by saltbushes, includes the important seagrass communities that may consist of one dominant species covering several hundred square kilometres. > *Mangroves* are also an important component, particularly in tropical areas where this formation reaches its greatest complexity in estuaries or on protected coastlines on rich alluvium.

Alpine communities occur above the treeline in Tas., Vic. and NSW areas characterised by low temperatures and cold, often gale-force, winds with up to half the annual precipitation falling as snow. Many shrubs have a prostrate growth habit and some species form characteristic cushions. Bogs are often dominated by the moss *Sphagnum* and fens by sedges such as *Carex*.

Flora conservation Human activities have had their effect on Australia's natural vegetation for at least 30 000 years, with deliberate firing of large areas by the Aborigines and their systematic tilling of the land with digging sticks in the search for edible roots, bulbs and corms. The vegetation patterns we see today have been greatly altered in the past 200 years with the introduction of plants (either deliberately or accidentally) of which many have now become serious weeds. Large areas of native vegetation have also been replaced with pastures for grazing and extensive areas cleared for crops and urban settlements. Some native plants that have been removed from their natural environment are now showing themselves to have great weed potential.

Some 97 vascular plant species in Australia are now presumed to be extinct, many known only from the original collections housed in herbariums. It is estimated that a rather alarming 17% (more than 3300 species) of Australia's vascular plant flora is rare or threatened and almost 1000 species considered to be either endangered or vulnerable. Since the 1970s the federal and State governments have played an increasing part in nature conservation through departments of the environment as well as specialised agencies such as the National Parks and Wildlife Service. Many significant areas have been set aside in national parks and reserves, and schemes such as the National Tree Program are intended to encourage both individuals and communities to conserve, plant and regenerate tree cover throughout Australia. >> *botany and botanists*; *environment and conservation*; *food plants, native*; *forests and forestry*; *fossils*

Florey, Howard Walter, (Baron Florey of Adelaide and Marston) (1898–1968), medical scientist, b. Adelaide. Florey shared the 1945 Nobel Prize for medicine with Dr Ernest Chain for his part in developing the world's first antibiotic drug – penicillin – from the mould *Penicillium notatum* discovered by Sir Alexander Fleming in 1928; this work made possible the mass production of penicillin in the latter part of World War 2. Florey was professor of pathology at Universities of Sheffield (1931–5) and Oxford (1935–62), was appointed a life peer in 1965 and chancellor of the Australian National University in 1966. Melbourne's Howard Florey Institute of Experimental Physiology and Medicine was named in his honour.

flower-growing > *nursery trade*

flukes These parasitic flatworms belong to the class Trematoda and are somewhat similar to the carnivorous, free-living planarian worms but have the sucker characteristic of parasitic worms. As a family they are mainly fish parasites, with a simple cycle comprising aquatic eggs, aquatic free-swimming larvae that during a short life must find a suitable host, and the adult phase attached to the host and obtaining sustenance from it.

The well-known liver-fluke of sheep, *Fasciola hepatica*, is larger than most and more complex in its cycle. The adult form may be seen in the liver like a white, slowly moving leaf; enormous numbers of eggs are excreted, but only those reaching water have even a chance of continuing the cycle: the larvae are motile and swim in search of a particular water-snail, in which they develop further before then emerging to encyst on wet grass. When subsequently ingested by browsing sheep, the cyst cover is dissolved by the sheep's gastric juices and the free larvae travel up the bile duct to develop to adult form in the liver. The human blood fluke, *Schistosoma*, which is responsible for the debilitating tropical disease bilharzia, is fortunately absent from Australia. >> *helminths*

flycatchers This is a group of small, perching, insectivorous birds of the family Mascicapidae, typified by broad beaks surrounded with bristles and long tails that can be spread to resemble fans. The restless flycatcher, *Myiagra inquieta*, is often seen capturing spiders in the corners of windows; its occasional nickname, scissor-grinder, comes from the repeated grinding sound that follows its single, harsh call.

The willy wagtail, *Rhipidura leucophrys*, is familiar in most parts of Australia in town and country, and may often be seen sallying forth from a perch to catch an insect with well-judged aerobatics. It is at times nocturnal, and has a pleasant, repetitive call; like other flycatchers, it makes a well-finished, cup-like nest which is often completed with cobwebs and lichen.

The jacky winter, *Microeca leucophaea*, is also a familiar bird of town and country in much of Australia, sitting on a favourite perch repeatedly calling 'jacky-jacky' or 'peter-peter' and so accounting for two of its many popular names, which include post-sitter and stump-bird. It takes flight to catch insects in the air or seize them on the ground.

Flying Doctor Service > *aerial medical services*

flying fishes Of this family, Exocoetidae, found throughout the world, more than twelve species occur in Australian waters. Flying fishes have enlarged pectoral fins that, after swimming rapidly and gaining speed near the water surface, they use in gliding – not flying – above the waves; this is probably a means of escaping pursuit by predators. Glides lasting up to 13 seconds have been recorded, and a speed of 60km per hour observed. At night the fish are often attracted by ships' lights, and have been known to land on decks 6m above the sea. The largest Australian specimens measure about 0.5m long.

flying foxes > *bats*

Flynn, Errol Leslie (1909–59), actor and author, b. Hobart. While working in PNG as a trader Flynn met film director Charles Chauvel, which led to his first film appearance, in Chauvel's *In the Wake of the Bounty* (1933). From there he went on to Hollywood, where he found fame in films such as *Captain Blood* (1935), *The Adventures of Robin Hood* (1938) and *The Sea Hawk* (1940); his later career was blighted by alcohol and satyriasis. Although an actor of limited ability, Flynn had immense charm, humour and good looks; he was also a talented writer, his published works including *Beam Ends* (1937) and the autobiography *My Wicked, Wicked Ways* (1959).

Flynn, John (1880–1951), missionary, b. Moliagul, Vic. A teacher in Vic. 1898–1902, Flynn was ordained as a Presbyterian minister in 1911 and subsequently served in SA. He was commissioned to report on the NT and central Australia for the General Assembly of the Presbyterian Church in 1912, and as a result of his findings on their needs a 'special home mission' for the area was established, with Flynn as its organiser; he supervised the Australian Inland Mission for 39 years. Flynn's most notable achievement in this capacity was the setting up of the Royal Flying Doctor Service (> *aerial medical services*). A legendary outback figure known popularly as 'Flynn of the Inland', Flynn was moderator-general of the Presbyterian Church 1939–42.

fodder crops As Australia suffers from unreliable rainfall and periodic drought, as well as low winter temperatures in some regions, fodder is required as a regular pasture supplement. The main forms of fodder used in Australia are hay (the dried leaves and stems of a wide range of plants), grains, and silage (compressed and fermented plant material).

Hay is the most common fodder crop, and rows of hay bales probably the most familiar sight of rural Australia. Hay is dried naturally or by artificial means, the latter producing feed with higher nutritional value but at a higher cost. A number of different plants are used, including grasses, cereals and clovers. Oats are the most important source, accounting for about three-quarters of all crops sown for hay. Lucerne was long the most important of all the grasses and pasture plants used for hay, but production has been more than halved since 1977 because of aphid infestations; countermeasures such as biological controls and the development of new, more resistant lucerne varieties are now proving successful.

Oats, wheat and barley are the main cereals used for grain fodder and in some regions are a staple livestock food. Silage is produced from both crops (including vegetables) and pasture plants. After cutting, the plant material is stored in silos or pits, compressed to exclude air, and then subjected to fermentation to reduce spoilage. Lupins have also recently become a major fodder crop, particularly in WA, and production exceeded that for silage by the late 1980s. >> *pasture plants*

Foley, Gary (1950–   ), Aboriginal advocate, b. Grafton, NSW. An activist who achieved prominence as part of the Aboriginal political movement of the late 1960s and early 1970s, Foley was central in the formation and expression of Aboriginal ideology and new tactics. He has since held a number of public positions, including adviser to the Muirhead royal commission on Aboriginal deaths in custody during the late 1980s.

folk and traditional music Australia's folk-music tradition is largely Celtic and Anglo-Saxon in origin and includes the ballads and bush songs that both preserve the legends of the 19th century and chronicle much of the country's early history. Transportation, the discovery of gold and the spread of pastoralism each makes its own contribution to folk-music style and lyrics, although anti-authoritarianism, humour and a grudging acceptance of fate are surprisingly consistent characteristics. Following the publication of numerous anthologies of early ballads from the 1950s onwards, folk music has enjoyed regular revivals. Paradoxically, it is now most popular in the cities, rural Australians generally having turned to American-style > *country music*.

The earliest folk-songs owed something to the rollicking sea shanties and rural ballads of Britain, but the music halls and street ballads of the urban poor were also a strong influence. The multinational goldfields' population, covering all classes and education levels, introduced new musical influences and instruments; many popular music-hall songs were adapted for local circumstances and passed thus into the oral tradition. In the latter half of the 19th century, pastoralism and a large itinerant population spawned distinctive bush songs such as 'The Ryebuck Shearer' and 'Click Go the Shears', characterised by their sardonic humour and their celebration of pioneering life and lives.

The bush ethos was embraced – and refined – by the literary balladists of the nationalistic 1890s, notably > *Adam Lindsay Gordon* and > *'Banjo' Paterson*. Paterson's *The Old Bush Songs* (1905) was the first anthology of Australian folk-songs and took the music to a much wider, and primarily urban, audience.

A.L. Lloyd (in the 1930s) and Percy Jones (1950s) were among the first anthologists to publish folk-music scores as well as the lyrics. By the 1950s, inspired by an American folk revival, a number of researchers, academics and writers began collecting and analysing Australian traditional music; they also recorded longstanding folksingers such as Duke Tritton, Sally Sloane and Joe Cashmere. A wealth of material was published in the 1960s that made folk music, lyrics and history readily available.

In the 1970s and 1980s, there was a periodic revival of interest in folk music and new songs were composed in the folk tradition. From 1974, Warren Fahey's Larrikin record company (like the Wattle label 20 years earlier) perpetuated a substantial body of traditional Australian songs and its success encouraged a number of other companies to follow suit. 'Bush bands' such as the Bushwackers and Redgum continue to attract large audiences. Eric Bogle, whose best-known song is 'And the Band Played Waltzing Matilda' (1972), and Ted Egan are among contemporary songwriters indebted to the bush tradition.

food As unaware of as they were uninterested in native foods, Australia's first white settlers relied on imported rations for the first five years of life in the colonies and only gradually developed a system of farming to provide dietary staples. Today the manufacture of food and drink is Australia's largest secondary industry, in both employment and financial terms. Like much of the manufacturing sector the structure of the food industry has undergone great changes since the 1960s, with many Australian-owned companies being taken over by multinationals and many small factories being absorbed by larger operations. There have also been moves by foreign parent companies to take up full ownership of their Australian subsidiaries.

The range of foods available in Australia has increased enormously in 200 years, the continent's range of climates allowing many fruits and vegetables to be available much of the year round. The Australian 'table' firmly followed the British model until World War 2, with traditional family meals based on meat and (commonly three) vegetables. The nation's diet has changed dramatically since the 1950s, however, due to the influences of immigration, changing family and work patterns, and more recently increased awareness of the links between diet and health. Postwar immigration introduced the principally Anglo-Celtic population to a range of new cuisines, first from Europe (notably Italian and Greek) and then from Asia (Turkish, Lebanese, Chinese, Indonesian, Vietnamese, Indian, Malay and Thai). This influx had an unparalleled influence on Australian diet and eating patterns, as an attendant profusion of restaurants and foods became accessible. Less salubrious but in many cases no less welcome was the advent of 'fast foods'. This industry has boomed in the last 20 years with the increasing number of single-parent and dual-career families: in the 1980s, the average Australian ate four or five takeaway meals a week and the nation spent about $1.5 billion a year on convenience foods, from the hamburgers, fried chicken and pizzas sold by American-owned food chains to the indigenous 'Chiko Roll' and meat pie.

The most recent source of change in the nation's eating habits has been increasing awareness of good nutrition and the links between diet and disease, particularly the association of fats with cholesterol levels and heart disease. During the 1980s, Australian consumption of red meat, dairy produce, eggs, oils and fats continued to drop and that of white meat, fruit and vegetables increased accordingly: in the ten years 1977–87, for example, annual per-capita consumption of beef and veal fell by 43% (from 61.9kg to 39.1kg) but chicken sales increased by 50%; by 1989, annual seafood consumption had reached 7.6kg per head, a gain of nearly 17% on 1980–1.

Increased mindfulness of the importance of diet to good health has been accompanied by a growing concern about the contamination of food with artificial substances ranging from flavourings and colourings to the residues of agricultural chemicals. A 1986 survey by the National Health and Medical Research Council found illegal levels of metals and metallic elements in wines and various foods, as well as carcinogens and pesticides. Organically grown fruit, vegetables and grains – once the preserve of health 'fanatics' – are increasingly available on supermarket shelves, as are products free of artificial additives, salt, sugar and animal fats. Health concerns have also fuelled the controversy over food irradiation, a process promoted by the food industry because it kills pests and helps preserve food by controlling the growth of mould and microbes. Consumer organisations have fought the use of irradiation by the Australian food industry, and in 1988 a federal parliamentary committee recommended against its introduction until possible adverse effects had been throughly analysed. The industry carries out its own research and development, with substantial input from the CSIRO's Division of Food Research.

food plants, native Aborigines have long exploited a range of Australian plants for food. In recent years the culinary potential of native plants has also been recognised by the white community and 'bush tucker' is now on the menu of many restaurants and food stores.

Tubers (or rhizomes) and seeds are a potential food staple and were used thus by Aborigines throughout the continent. Edible and nutritious tubers include > yams and some species of the morning glory, *Ipomoea*, > sedges (including the nalgoo or bush onion, *Cyperus bulbosus*), and many ground-dwelling orchids. In some southern areas the rhizomes of ferns, saw sedges and > cumbungi were among the few plentiful sources of starch available to Aborigines, although parts of Vic. and SA yield the abundant sweet tubers of the dandelion-like murnong or yam daisy, *Microseris scapigera*, which supported large populations.

The seeds of many native grasses are also edible and seasonal harvesting of many cereal grasses was – and still is – practised by inland Aborigines, especially in the arid centre of the continent; particularly productive is the native millet, *Panicum decompositum*. Other plants yielding edible seed include parakeelya, the bunya pine, some species of wattle, and the kurrajong (> *sterculia family*). Some may be eaten whole, but most are ground for flour or pastes; the essence of distilled wattle seeds is also used as a flavouring. The spore case of the nardoo fern, *Marsilea*, is a source of starch but little nutriment. The sweet young leaf bases and flower buds of certain plants, notably palms and grass-trees, can be eatern raw or cooked.

Many native trees and shrubs have edible fruits and berries, although large-scale commercial development is unlikely. Plants of the sandy coastal heaths of non-tropical Australia – notably some epacrids and the geebungs (the latter a genus in the protea family) – yield only small fruits that are laborious to gather. The wet forests of the east and north have a relative abundance of larger and often extremely palatable fruits, however, the most attractive of which are fleshy-fruited genera of the > *myrtle family* such as the lillypilly; the large-fruited lady apple, *Syzygium suborbiculare*, of the tropical north; and the midgenberry, *Austromyrtus dulcis*, a shrub of the southern Qld coast with. profuse, sweet grey fruits. Other groups bearing palatable fruit include the > *madder family*, > *euphorbia family*, native cherries, some > *figs*, the lily genus *Dianella*, and the pittosporum genus *Billardiera*. The large blue-black fruits of the small rainforest tree Davidson's plum, *Davidsonia pruriens*, are receiving increasing attention and while sour make fine preserves. In the arid inland, two prominent species are the quandong (> *sandalwood family*), which bears red globular fruits; and the nitre bush, *Nitraria billardiera*, of the > *twinleaf family*, which has masses of salty but juicy yellow to red berries.

football > *Australian Rules football*; *rugby*; *soccer*

footracing Professional footracing developed as an organised sport in the 1870s; the handicap system was instituted, and large crowds – especially in Sydney – watched and bet on races which carried large stakes. The centre of athletic events then moved to Vic., where the inaugural Stawell Gift was run in 1878; with the Bendigo Thousand, first run in 1946, it is one of the world's leading professional races.

Arthur Postle and Jack Donaldson dominated the sport in the early years of the century, and in the 1930s, 1932 dual Olympic sprint champion Eddie Tolan won the world professional crown in Australia.

Although professional running is dominated by sprints, middle- and long-distance races are also staged. Australian Harold Downes was the first professional to run the mile (1600m) in less than four minutes, in 1963, and in the 1960s Bill Emmerton set many long-distance and endurance records. The annual Sydney–Melbourne Ultra marathon in 1983 produced a national folk hero in the person of 61-year-old potato farmer Cliff Young, who shuffled the 875km to victory.

footwear industry > *clothing and footwear industry*

Forbes NSW (pop. 10 910) Situated some 380km west of Sydney, on the fertile river flats of the Lachlan River, Forbes is in a rich agricultural area. Major produce of the region includes livestock lucerne, wheat, fruit and vegetables. A gold-rush town of the 1860s, Forbes survived as a local service and market area and now has a range of operations including saleyards, mills and an abattoir.

Forbes, Sir Francis (1784–1841), lawyer, b. Bermuda. Forbes helped draft the New South Wales Act 1823, which established the colony's first court system and legislative council. He arrived in Sydney in 1824 to take up the position of NSW chief justice, a post he held until 1836; he was particularly noted for the introduction in 1824 of the system of trial by jury and the use of emancipist jurors. From 1828 he came into conflict with Governor Darling, by vetoing his proposed censorship of the press – which Forbes deemed 'repugnant to the laws of England' – and over the assignment and ticket-of-leave systems for convicts.

Forde, Francis Michael (1890–1983), politician, b. Mitchell, Qld. Forde was elected as a Labor member of the Qld parliament in 1917 but resigned in 1922 to enter federal politics. He remained there until 1946 and although he held various portfolios during that time he is best remembered for his exceedingly brief term as prime minister, 6–13 July 1945, between the death of John Curtin and the assumption of office by Ben Chifley.

foreign aid In 1987–8 Australia spent $1008 million in a diverse foreign-aid program covering some 90 countries and involving educational, project and food aid as well as direct budget support. This figure represents about 0.4% of the gross national product, and although the UN target for contributors is 0.7% of GNP Australia's percentage contribution has been getting smaller in recent years.

Australia's foreign aid is intended to assist the development of needy countries and to reinforce Australia's present and future political and economic interests. With these ends in mind, the bulk of Australia's aid goes to neighbouring countries in the southern Pacific and Southeast Asian regions. The two basic programs – country and global – are administered by the Australian International Development Assistance Bureau (AIDAB). The first provides direct aid to specific countries and had a budget of $669 million in 1987–8. The global program, with an expenditure of some $271 million, is directed to the development of third-world countries in general and for the relief of refugees and victims of disasters; Ethiopia, Mozambique and Egypt received $29 million in food aid through this program in 1986–7.

Australia's first major foreign-aid program was developed through the Colombo Plan. This program, established at a meeting of Commonwealth foreign ministers in Colombo in 1950, was the first step towards economic cooperation and development in South and Southeast Asia. The plan was initiated by the then Australian minister for external affairs, Sir Percy Spender, who proposed the provision of economic and technical assistance to the Commonwealth countries and dependent territories of the region on a bilateral basis.

The initial membership of the consultative committee was Australia, Canada, Ceylon, India, Pakistan, NZ and the UK, but the program soon developed to extend beyond the limits originally planned. The US and Japan joined in 1954, and by the end of that year most countries of Southeast Asia had become members. Programs under the plan are aimed at agricultural development, land settlement, irrigation and rural electrification, and improvements in transport, communication and health. Though the Colombo Plan still exists, its basic aims have been achieved and, from Australia's viewpoint, its practical applications have been subsumed within Australia's overall aid program.

PNG receives the largest amount of Australian aid, $301 million in 1987–8, a figure representing nearly one-quarter of that nation's total budget receipts. To date most of the aid has been in the form of direct cash grants, but future emphasis will be more on project aid, education and training. The continuing cash subsidisation of PNG has been the cause of some controversy, resulting from allegations that much of the subsidy has been misspent. The island nations of the southern Pacific received $68 million in 1987–8, mainly in the form of project aid.

Aid to Southeast Asia takes the form of specific project aid, Indonesia being the largest recipient (receiving $44 million in 1987–8), followed by the Philippines and Thailand. Australia also supports regional development programs such as the ASEAN-Australia Economic Co-operation Program.

Australia is also a major contributor to international aid organisations, particularly those controlled by the UN, such as UNICEF and the UN Works and Relief Agency; this assistance is mainly in the form of food and housing materials. International financial organisations such as the World Bank and the Asian Development Bank are also supported. In addition, it is government policy to support voluntary agencies – such as Community Aid Abroad, founded in 1953 as 'Food for Peace' and renamed in 1962 – undertaking development projects, and to provide subsidies to businesses supplying necessary goods and services to some third-world nations.

While the benefits of foreign aid are manifold, it has been suggested that it merely redistributes income from the poor in rich countries to the rich in poor countries. It is now generally accepted that the emphasis should be on encouraging economic growth in the receiving countries through practical assistance rather than direct cash grants.

foreign investment As a young and sparsely populated country, Australia had only a limited supply of domestic capital. During the first 150 years of European settlement almost all major developments were financed by foreign investment, and more often than not this inflow of funds continued to be encouraged by the government. The rise of multinational companies after World War 2 and their increasing involvement in the development of Australia's natural resources made foreign investment a controversial issue in the 1960s and 1970s; by

the 1980s, public concern was also being expressed about the extent of overseas stakes in Australian real estate.

Historical development Overseas investment in Australia could be said to have begun with the arrival of wealthy settlers; from the 1850s it involved the use of overseas capital to finance public works and farming and mining developments. The first phase of large-scale foreign investment, however, was during the boom of the 1880s, when Australian companies started listing on the London stock exchange and British financiers lent substantial sums to the colonial governments for public works. During this period, about half of all capital investment in Australia was funded from overseas.

Foreign investment never again reached that level, despite a further surge by Britain and the US after World War 1. Foreign capital financed 25% of Australian investment by the 1920s, and half as much again by 1950. In this period US companies dominated Australia's oil and manufacturing industries; foreign technology also made a substantial contribution to postwar industrial expansion.

The government's welcoming attitude towards foreign investment began to change from the early 1960s, reflected in the well-publicised comment in 1963 by the deputy prime minister and leader of the Country Party, John McEwen, that 'We live comfortably by selling a bit of the farm every year'. Foreign investment henceforth became a public issue, being seen by many as a threat to Australian autonomy and a deterrent to local inventiveness. Legislation was introduced in 1972 enabling the federal government to block take-overs of Australian companies by overseas interests, but this power was rarely invoked. In 1976 the Foreign Investment Review Board (FIRB) was set up to examine all foreign investment proposals, but in practice overseas investment has continued to increase since that time owing both to the continuing activities of multinational companies and to increased interest in Australian stocks and shares.

The most rapid growth in foreign investment in Australia's history has in fact occurred in the last decade. The level of investment 1980–6 tripled to $139 billion, mainly because of a massive increase in foreign debt. In the same period, a wave of take-overs by Australian entrepreneurs and large infrastructure borrowings by the States helped to increase Australia's indebtedness from $15 billion to $90 billion, with severe repercussions for the nation's balance of payments because of high interest repayments. Asian (particularly Japanese) investment has increased markedly in the last decade, most notably in the areas of real estate and property development.

Multinational corporations have played a central and at times controversial role in the development of the Australian economy. For 200 years English companies had been involved in Australia's commerce, but the real growth of multinationals in Australia occurred after World War 2 with the investments of large American companies, whose interests extended throughout the world. The oil and petroleum industry of Australia was developed mainly by US multinationals, and until the relatively recent advent of similar Japanese corporations, Americans dominated the Australian motor industry and other manufacturing industries.

foreign policy Until the mid-20th century, Australia's international relations reflected its economic, cultural and political dependence on Britain. This was evidenced in most aspects of its dealings with other countries, from immigration to trade and defence. From World War 2 to the 1970s the focus shifted to the US, with an attendant growth of economic and political ties. It was only in the 1980s, 200 years after white settlement, that Australia began to develop a more independent course in world affairs and one more appropriate to its geographic position, with increasing attention to the Asia-Pacific region.

Historical development Australia's emergence as a nation in 1901 did not involve any dramatic wrench from its colonial past. In fact, it continued to share strong political, cultural and sentimental ties with Britain and felt no need to establish an independent foreign policy. The fact that Asia was still largely dominated by European powers meant that Asian international relations were often seen as an extension of those of Europe, where Australia's allegiance to Britain was beyond dispute. Furthermore, Australia saw itself as an isolated and vulnerable British outpost on the periphery of Asia and believed that its security against either hostile European powers or potential Asian threats lay in the defence provided by Britain. Immigration policy continued to favour British settlers and exclude Asians until well into the 20th century.

Between Federation and World War 2, nevertheless, it became increasingly apparent

that Australian and British interests were not always identical and throughout the period there were recurring complaints from Australia concerning the lack of adequate consultation by the British. As early as 1902 the Anglo-Japanese agreement caused considerable consternation among Australia's leaders, raising questions as to the reliability of British assistance in times of crisis; similarly, the Japanese invasion of Manchuria in northeast China in 1931 created different problems for and responses from Australia and Britain. Australia's trade with Japan and the US also created serious problems for Australia and led to the ill-conceived trade diversion policy of 1936, which amounted to the declaration of a short-lived trade war with those two nations.

The increasing complexity and tensions in matters of foreign policy led Australia in 1935 to establish a separate department of external affairs. By 1939, nonetheless, Australia's ties with Britain were still so close that the prime minister, Robert Menzies, expressed the sentiments of a nation when he announced that 'Great Britain has declared war on her [Germany] and ... as a result, Australia is also at war'. That war saw the realisation of one of Australia's greatest fears – attack from Japan; it also shattered Australia's assumption that Britain would always come to its rescue in times of threat. The advent of US support in 1942 did not alter the basis of Australian foreign policy: Australia was still a vulnerable western outpost in a hostile world, but simply had a new and powerful ally.

While minister for external affairs 1941–9, > H.V. Evatt was arguably the first to devise a foreign policy based on Australian self-reliance. From the 1950s, successive governments presided over a great expansion of Australia's immigrant intake and changing patterns of trade; Australia also took some minor initiatives in the field of foreign aid and played a major role in the administration and development of PNG. For four decades after the war, however, the emphasis of Australian foreign policy was overwhelmingly geared to defence. The liberal terms of the peace treaty with Japan made Australia fearful of a Japanese resurgence; the communist victory in China in 1949 and the outbreak of the Korean War in the following year fuelled the longstanding fear of rampant communism; and the decolonisation of the Asian region generated a disturbing level of political change and uncertainty. Australia took two major steps to save itself from these perceived threats. The first was a consistent effort to bolster the status quo against the winds of change: the government lamented the French retreat from Indochina and the British decision to withdraw from east of Suez, it defended the right of the Dutch to maintain their control of West Irian, and it encouraged substantial and increased US presence in the region. Then, having signed the > *ANZUS treaty* in 1951 and the > *SEATO* agreement in 1954, the Australian government undertook a policy of forward defence: over the next two decades it dispatched troops to fight the communists in Korea, Malaya and Vietnam; it supported right-wing dictatorships in South Vietnam, China and the Philippines; it denounced the ultimately victorious communist forces in Vietnam and China and also the Indonesian government as it moved to the left in the 1960s; furthermore, it failed to establish any warm relationship with the ideologically uncommitted governments of India and of Cambodia under Prince Sihanouk. Australia thus emerged as the champion of western interests and of the conservative old order of Asia.

The defeat of the US in the Vietnam War marked a watershed in Australia's foreign policy. Nixon's 'Guam Doctrine' of 1969 – in which it was made clear that nations under threat would in future have to provide for their own defence – indicated that Australia could no longer assume that the US would automatically come to its aid in times of crisis. With no alternative powerful ally in the offing, in 1972 the Whitlam government set about a substantial reassessment of Australian foreign policy, which has been maintained by succeeding governments.

The 1980s and beyond Following the Whitlam initiatives, Australia has adopted a more independent and realistic view of the US alliance; it has played down the military, ideological and racist emphases of the past; and it has played an increasingly active role in the economic and diplomatic issues of the Pacific rim. It is paradoxical that at the very time when Japan, China, the USSR and Vietnam have shown their greatest strength and influence, Australia has shown itself to feel less threatened than at any other stage during the past 50 years and free to pursue a distinctive role in the political, economic and diplomatic life of its own geographic region. This is a difficult task, but Australia at last appears to have no option but to tackle it. >> *defence*; *immigration*; *trade*

foreign trade > *trade*

forests and forestry Forest cover in Australia extends over some 35.2 million ha, much of it dominated by one or more species of eucalypt. The higher-rainfall areas were once covered by forests, which formed a belt up to 400km wide along the eastern and southern parts of Australia, extended over much of Tas. and a wedge-shaped area in the southwest of WA, and spanned a belt of varying width along the northern extremities of the continent. Further inland, in the lower-rainfall regions, there is a discontinuous belt of some 65 million ha of lower, more open woodland, which is often dominated by non-eucalypt species such as mulga and is used principally for grazing.

Three-quarters of Australia's forests are owned by the State concerned; in Vic., WA and the NT, a single agency manages all public forests and land; elsewhere, separate management services exist for forests, national parks and public lands. Some 14% of all native forest is held as national parks or other reserves concerned with nature conservation, access for recreation and education, or water production: with very few (and minor) exceptions, wood production is not permitted in these areas. A further 36% is designated State forest and is used for wood production, conservation of flora and fauna, water production, recreation, or some combination of these. A further 25% is public land which is usually managed by the State forest services; several uses are permitted in such forests, often including wood production. The balance of the native forest is privately owned: although small, these tracts are important for other reasons, generally occurring as remnant forests on individual farms where they provide beauty, shade and shelter, and make a particular contribution to flora and fauna conservation in areas where the original vegetation has been cleared and the land is subject to problems such as salinity and soil erosion.

Much debate has taken place in the last 20 years over the appropriate balance between the two broad forms of forest tenure in Australia – those that permit wood production and those that do not. Export woodchipping operations in native forests have provoked particular criticism from the conservation movement because of their scale, the use of clear-felling techniques, the predominance of the Japanese market, and the politics of licensing. The area of national parks has been increased substantially in the same period, with a corresponding decrease in the areas available for wood production; further and substantial additions are likely to be made as the result of the nomination of the tropical rainforests in north Qld and the Lemonthyme and Southern forests in Tas. to the World Heritage list.

Native forests Eucalypt forests and woodlands are perhaps the most distinctive feature of the Australian landscape, its characteristic blue-green hue being produced by the evaporation of volatile oils from eucalypt leaves. The eucalypts include valuable timber species such as mountain ash and alpine ash from Vic. and Tas.; blackbutt, spotted gum, and various blue gums and ironbarks from NSW and Qld; and jarrah and karri from WA. Substantial areas of remnant > *rainforests* have survived in the highest rainfall areas, especially in north Qld. They accommodate a great variety of plant groups, some of which probably migrated from the tropical islands north of Australia, but many of which reflect an earlier and much more widespread rainforest that had its origins in > *Gondwana*. Rainforest species include valuable cabinet and specialty woods such as Qld maple and walnut, black bean, and red cedar (which was much sought after by early timber-getters and virtually cut out by the 20th century); they also include some of the few native softwoods, such as hoop, bunya and kauri pines. The rainforests of southern Australia are much more limited in both extent and the range of genera. They are mainly dominated by the myrtle beech, which was represented elsewhere in Gondwana along with a few other northern rainforest genera. In Tas. there are also small areas of native softwoods (such as huon, celery-top and King William pines) which have links with genera in other parts of Gondwana. Another extensive and distinctive group is the cypress pine, found in the drier inland periphery of the eastern and northern forests. Although slow-growing, it has remarkable capacity to withstand drought and fire and to yield a wood that is naturally preserved against termites, one of the major pests of timber in dry and medium rainfall areas.

Plantation forests Australia's plantation forests extend over about 904 000ha, some 69% being in public ownership. Although not large in relation to the total area of forest, plantations supplied about 32% of the industrial wood used in 1987 and that proportion will rise to more than 50% by the year 2000 as the large areas planted in the 1960s come into full production. Over 68% is planted to *Pinus radiata*, introduced from southern California; exotics such as *Pinus caribaea* and *Pinus elliottii* are used in the subtropical and tropical regions. Pine plantations supply wood that is suitable for pulp, newsprint, fibreboard, plywood and sawn timber and is relatively fast-grown and cheap. In some regions, the extensive use of these exotic species is a source of friction between industry and local interest groups: many other species – both native and exotic – have been tried in plantations, but none matches those most in use in terms of return on investment, growth rates, and versatility. The area of eucalypt plantations is quite small because native forests provide a plentiful supply of wood, but may increase in the future.

The timber industry The contribution of Australian forests to the supply of industrial and domestic wood is substantial, amounting to the equivalent of 19 million cu.m per year in log volume. The forest-products industry obtains over 80% of its raw material from Australian forests, the remainder being imported (chiefly from NZ, the US, Scandinavia and Southeast Asia) as intermediate or final products. The industry is diverse in character and location. Pulp and paper plants tend to be very large and are therefore few in number, the largest being at Maryvale in Vic., Burnie and Boyer in Tas., and Albury in NSW. Sawmills, plymills and board mills using exotic pine are intermediate in size and are located at regional plantation centres. Sawmills using native timbers vary widely in scale according to the location, the size of the resource and the market being supplied. The overwhelming majority of initial processing takes in rural areas and the contribution of the industry to the rural infrastructure is very important. The domestic supply of wood for fuel has become more important in rural areas following the rise in oil prices, but it tends to be supplied by small local contractors.

Other forest commodities include honey and native flowers, oils and seeds; forests are also used for grazing. Some forest activities are, on the other hand, non-commercial: entry fees are rarely charged for recreational use; water production, another unpriced good, is likely to become increasingly important in southern Australia because of the limited area of high-rainfall catchments and the growing demands of an increasing population.

Controversy over the use of public forests has caused two significant changes in forest policy and management. First, it has led to much tighter controls over harvesting and other timber operations, especially in those native forests where such activities are permitted. All States are now implementing codes of forest practice that stipulate measures to minimise environmental damage: the setting aside of buffer strips along waterways to maintain water quality, and of wildlife corridors and nature reserves to preserve particular ecosystems, has among other things led to a substantial reduction in the actual area of public forest that can be harvested. In Vic., for example, it is estimated that only about 30% of the area designated as being available for wood production will actually be harvested. These measures are likely to attract continuing debate, because some conservationists want wood production in native forest banned entirely, much to the consternation of both the timber industry and dependent rural communities.

The second change is the increasing involvement of the federal government in forest matters that have traditionally been solely under State control, owing in part to pressure from the conservation movement. The Australian Heritage Act 1975 makes provision for areas of aesthetic, historic, scientific, social or other special significance to be listed on the register of the national estate; and the World Heritage Properties Conservation Act of 1983 gives the Commonwealth control over proposed or declared World Heritage areas. The Heritage Act does not, however, give the federal government specific conservation controls except where these relate to established areas of federal authority such as overseas trade: it thus provides a clear basis for federal control over woodchip exports but does not provide for direct control of sawlog or pulpwood harvesting for domestic consumption. Contests between the Commonwealth and individual States have thus arisen over the use of public lands, which have been likened to a game played according to two different sets of rules and umpires – providing great entertainment but little enlightenment.

The 1980s and beyond At the end of the 1980s the conservation movement and the forest industry continued to vie for the use of public land for their particular purposes. The Commonwealth has recently announced the establishment of a Resources Assessment Commission to advise and arbitrate on these issues, but its role is not yet clear. The debates are, however, widening in scope to encompass the use of private forest and land, the issues of land degradation and revegetation, woodlands and shrublands under grazing leases, coastal vegetation, and the impact of the greenhouse effect. While the outcomes may be unclear, the controversies are likely to remain a feature of Australian life and politics into the next century. >> *environment and conservation*; *flora*; *soils and soil conservation*

Forrest brothers, prominent in WA exploration, government and pastoral development. The elder, **Sir John** (1847–1918), b. Bunbury, WA, was trained as a surveyor. He made his first exploratory journey to follow up a report of possible Leichhardt remains in 1869, and later made two well-organised west–east crossings of WA. In 1870 he reversed Eyre's route; later, in 1874, he explored the headwaters of the Murchison River and then the Musgrave Ranges. He was the first premier of WA, 1890–1901, and was concerned with the goldfields water supply scheme as well as railway and port construction. He had turbulent relations with the miners and, it has been suggested, introduced women's suffrage as a counterweight to their vote. During the Federation negotiations, he fought for and obtained the promise of the trans-continental railway, and tariff benefits for WA as a price for joining the Commonwealth. He represented Swan in federal parliament 1901–18, holding several cabinet posts. He was created 1st Baron Forrest of Bunbury in 1918, the first Australian-born peer. His brother **Alexander** (1849–1901), b. Bunbury, acted as his second in command on his 1870 and 1874 journeys, and in 1879 discovered the pastures of the northwest of WA between the Fitzroy River and Leopold Ranges, Ord River and Victoria River.

Forster, Johann Reinhold (1729–98), botanist, b. Poland. Forster accompanied James Cook on his second Pacific voyage (1772–5), as official naturalist; his son **George** (Johann Georg) (1759–94) was illustrator to the expedition. Although quarrelsome and uncooperative, the Forsters were respected for their scientific contribution, discovering a number of new plants and naming a number of the genera prominent in Australia's flora. The results of their botanical observations were published in *Characteres Generum Plantarum* (1776) and their account of the voyage in *A Voyage Round the World* (1777).

Forster–Tuncurry NSW (pop. 11 239) These twin resort towns lie 333km north of Sydney, on Wallis Lake in the Great Lakes district. On opposite sides of the lake, the towns were linked only by ferry from the 1870s until a bridge was built in 1959. They are one of the State's chief sources of seafoods.

Fortescue River WA Rising in the Ophthalmia Range, this river runs north and then northwest for over 600km, skirting the northern side of the Hamersley Range and flowing to a swampy estuary on the Indian Ocean shore, about 80km south of Dampier Archipelago. The Hamersley Range National Park lies near the middle section of its course, south of Wittenoom, and includes spectacular mountain scenery.

Forth River Tas. This river rises near Mt Pelion West in Cradle Mountain-Lake St Clair National Park and flows northwards to the coastal plain and an estuary on Bass Strait. On the Forth River, which falls steeply from the highlands, there are five of the seven power stations of the Mersey-Forth hydro-electric power development; the forests above the Lemonthyme power station were recently given World Heritage listing.

fossils As elsewhere in the world, Australia's fossil record provides key evidence for the evolution of the continent, its climates and life forms. Australia has some of the oldest fossils in the world – in the form of algae and soft-bodied invertebrates that originated in the warm seas of the Precambrian era and have been dated back at least 3000 million years. Fossil evidence from succeeding eras has verified Australia's prehistoric links with the other southern continents of Antarctica, Africa, India and South America; its separation from the giant Gondwanan landmass; and the subsequent evolution, in isolation, of its unique flora and fauna. Finally – but not as yet indisputably – the fossil record has provided the basis for theories about the history of human occupation of the continent.

Australia has fossils from each of the geological ages: the Precambrian era (to c600 million years ago); the Palaeozoic or Primary (to c.220 million years ago, and including the Cambrian, Ordovician, Silurian, Devonian, Carboniferous and Permian periods); the Mesozoic or Secondary (to c.60 million years ago and including the Triassic, Jurassic and

Cretaceous periods); and the Cainozoic (to the present day, including the Tertiary and Quaternary periods).

Invertebrates The Precambrian sandstones of Ediacara, SA, contain the world's best-preserved deposit of early multi-celled invertebrates. These soft-bodied animals – preserved as faint impressions – are similar to jellyfish, worms and soft corals as well as organisms with no living relatives. The beginning of the Cambrian saw the evolution of hard-bodied invertebrate groups that radiated in warm seas around the world. These groups, which include the brachiopods, echinoderms such as sea-lilies, corals, bryozoans, molluscs, the extinct sponge-like archaeocyathids, graptolites and trilobites, are found in many Australian Palaeozoic deposits. The major limestone deposits of Australia have their origins in the reefs of shallow ancient seas, perhaps similar to the Great Barrier Reef, formed in the Devonian period. The end of the Permian period saw the worldwide extinction of such groups as the trilobites and graptolites, and the Mesozoic marine deposits of Australia are dominated by molluscs (including various bivalves, gastropods and ammonites, a group similar to the chambered nautilus), corals, and single-celled organisms with calcareous shells. After another major extinction at the end of the Mesozoic, a rather modern marine fauna arose during the Cainozoic.

Fossils of terrestrial invertebrates in Australia include major deposits of insects, which became increasingly widespread during the Permian and Triassic periods. Found in fine clay deposits in the Sydney Basin and near Ipswich in Qld, these specimens – which are mostly known from wings – include representatives of extinct insect orders.

The plant record The first record of Australian land plants is from the Carboniferous period, named for the large coal deposits that formed during that time in northern-hemisphere swamps. Most of Gondwana was closer to the South Pole at that time, under conditions unsuitable for the development of coal swamps, but extensive coal beds formed in the southern hemisphere during the subsequent Permian period, including major deposits in the Sydney Basin, NSW, and the Bowen Basin, Qld. The large distinctive leaves of the extinct seed-fern *Glossopteris* are common only in Permian deposits of Gondwanan landmasses, evidence that these southern continents were joined but separate from the northern hemisphere.

Tall forests were widespread by the Carboniferous period and plant fossils from the Triassic, Jurassic and Cretaceous periods indicate the presence of seed-ferns, cycads, ferns, conifers, and relatives of the gingko. Flowering plants did not become dominant in Australia until the late Cretaceous period but were abundant by the Cainozoic, when much of Australia was covered with rainforest that contained familiar groups such as the southern beech, myrtles, proteas, casuarinas and podocarps. Leaf fossils from Tas. indicate the presence of a rainforest type now found only in northeastern Qld and montane NG. Fossil eucalypt leaves appear in rocks from the mid-Tertiary and the genus became dominant late in the period with increasing continental aridity. Climatic changes in the Quaternary ice ages forced shifts in vegetation composition, reflected in the pollen profiles accumulated in bogs and lakes. The pollen record also indicates changes in floristic composition resulting from the extensive burning undertaken by Aborigines from this time.

Vertebrates Australia is not the richest continent for vertebrate palaeontology, because potential fossil-bearing strata are poorly exposed or covered by deeply weathered soils. The earliest deposits are from the Devonian period, when shallow seas still covered much of eastern Australia and the present WA coastline: they comprise lungfishes, lobe-finned fishes (ancestors of terrestrial vertebrates), sharks and the heavily armoured primitive antiarchs. One of the world's richest sources of fish fossils from this period is the Gogo formation in WA, where the fauna is so well preserved that even internal anatomy can be studied. Vertebrates are poorly represented in Carboniferous deposits, but Permian coal measures from Newcastle, NSW, have yielded both fish and amphibians.

At the beginning of the Mesozoic era reptiles rose to dominance on land, and fossil reptiles and amphibians from the Triassic period occur in deposits near Hobart, Tas., and the Sydney Basin. Palaeontologists are particularly eager to compare Australia's Triassic vertebrates with those of other Gondwana continents, to find what similarity existed among the faunas before the landmass began to split up in the late Jurassic. The first dinosaurs also appeared at the beginning of the Mesozoic and reached their greatest numbers in the Jurassic period: part of the skeleton of a large sauropod dinosaur, *Rhoetosaurus*, estimated to be more than 15m long, is known from Jurassic deposits in central Qld. Dinosaur fauna from the Cretaceous period is known from excavations in parts of Qld, Vic. and NSW: it includes the *Austrosaurus*, a large sauropod reaching a length of 17m; *Muttaburrasaurus*, a duckbilled dinosaur; *Minmi*, an armoured ankylosaur; *Rapator*, a carnivorous dinosaur that reached a length of 8m; and the remains of flying reptiles. The recently discovered Dinosaur Cave, near the Otway Range in Vic., contains a rich fossil fauna. Perhaps the most spectacular fossil ever discovered in Australia was an almost complete 13m skeleton of the carnivorous marine reptile *Kronosaurus queenslandicus*, which, unfortunately, is displayed overseas. Opalised dinosaurs and aquatic plesiosaurs are known from Lightning Ridge, NSW, as is the opalised jaw of Australia's earliest mammal, thought to be a monotreme. Important Mesozoic freshwater-fish deposits have yielded a variety of primitive bony fishes, lungfishes and sharks, and include Triassic deposits in the Sydney Basin (especially the rich Somersby quarry) and the Bowen Basin, Qld, the Jurassic Talbragar beds near Gulgong, NSW, and the Cretaceous Koonwarra deposits of southern Vic.

Mammals The separation of Australia from the other Gondwana continents during the early Tertiary (about 45 million years ago) and its subsequent drift northwards allowed its fauna to evolve in isolation. Unfortunately there are few mammal fossils in Australia's early Tertiary deposits, the oldest known marsupial remains being 30–40 million years old, in Tas. *Wynyardia*, a possum-like member of an extinct marsupial family, is known from deposits in northern Tas., which are 10–25 million years old. Deposits from the same period in central Australia indicate a much moister climate and the fossil evidence includes freshwater dolphins, flamingoes, crocodiles, lungfishes, and platypus in the freshwater lakes that dotted the region. There were also representatives of most modern marsupial families, as well as those of two extinct families, the Diprotodontidae and Thylacoleontidae. The diprotodon was a grazing animal about the size of a small rhinoceros and is often found in late Tertiary deposits. The carnivorous thylacoleo or 'marsupial lion' was the size of a small leopard and had specialised shearing pre-molars; its remains are often found in cave deposits. Gigantic flightless birds called mihirungs, which stood up to 3m high and are thus the largest birds that ever lived, are also known from these deposits; as is the giant goanna, *Megalania*, which attained a length of 6m, making it larger than the Komodo dragon. A variety of macropod fossils is present, including the extinct short-faced kangaroo *Sthenurus*. Perhaps Australia's most spectacular fossil find is the recently discovered Riversleigh deposit (about 15 million years old) in northwestern Qld: this deposit of freshwater limestone contains enormous numbers of fossilised creatures from a rich vertebrate community that included giant pythons, the carnivorous kangaroo *Ekaltadeta*, thylacoleo, thylacines, horned turtles, diprotodons, mihirungs and platypus, as well as numerous bats and other fauna. More recent deposits from Lake Callabonna in SA, the Darling Downs in Qld, and Wellington Cave in NSW indicate that large marsupials such as diprotodons, giant wombats and giant kangaroos were present as late as 20 000 years ago. >> *archaeology*; *geology and major landforms*

Fox, Emanuel Phillips (1865–1915),

painter, b. Melbourne. Having studied art in Paris 1887–92, Fox returned to Melbourne and helped found the Melbourne Art School in 1893. A contemporary of Rupert Bunny and Frederick McCubbin, he was a masterful painter of colour and light in the Impressionist tradition and an influential figure in the Melbourne art world before his departure for London in 1901. There he completed a painting of James Cook's landfall in Australia, commissioned by the Vic. National Gallery. Although he lived in Europe from 1901 until his death – becoming an accepted member of the French art establishment – he returned to Australia for exhibitions of his work in 1908 and 1913.

foxes > *animals, introduced*

foxglove family The Scrophulariaceae family of flowering plants – which includes foxgloves, snapdragons and veronicas – is most diverse in the northern hemisphere but some 120 species are native to Australia. The veronica tribe has a few species in Australia, notably in the genus *Parahebe* which includes the widespread southeastern *P. perfoliata*, a herbaceous perennial commonly known as diggers' speedwell for the old belief that its presence signified gold-bearing country. About 22 other genera are native to Australia, nearly all of which are herbaceous. Conspicuous in alpine grasslands and herbfields are the colourful eyebrights, semi-parasitic species of the temperate genus *Euphrasia*. A number of small herbaceous genera are common on muddy banks and alluvium of the inland, including *Morgania, Limosella, Peplidium* and *Glossostigma*.

Frankland River WA A river in the southwest of the State, the Frankland drains good agricultural land and flows to the sea at Nornalup Inlet, 96km west of Albany; stands of kauri are found in the wooded sections of the lower reaches. Rocky Gully, on the upper Frankland, was a soldier settlement community following World War 2. The river was named after a surveyor-general of Tas.

Franklin, Sir John (1786–1847), explorer

and colonial administrator, b. England. Franklin accompanied Matthew Flinders on his circumnavigation of Australia 1802–03 and later made two polar expeditions (1819–23 and 1825–7). His appointment as governor of Tas. in 1837 was not a success: economic difficulties, anti-transportation movements, a recalcitrant council and subordinates, and a vast influx of convicts were problems beyond the competence of this brilliant, liberal man, and he was recalled to England in 1843. His second wife, **Jane** (1791–1875), b. England, made a great impact on Tas. during her husband's governorship, with her wide journeyings, concern for convict welfare, and scientific and educational interests. She founded Hobart's first museum.

Franklin, (Stella Maria) Miles (1879–

1954), novelist, b. Tumut, NSW. Franklin's first published work, *My Brilliant Career* (1901), was a combination of fiction and autobiography; like much of her writing, it was set in the Murrumbidgee area of her childhood. There was a long interval before her next novel was published, while she worked as a journalist in Sydney and then lived in the US, England and Europe. She published *Old Blastus of Bandicoot* (1931) two years before her return to Australia; this was followed by arguably her best work, the historical saga *All That Swagger* (1936). Franklin also wrote several books under the pen-name 'Brent of Bin Bin', including *Up the Country* (1928), *Back to Bool Bool* (1931), and *Cockatoos* (1954); this identity was long denied by Franklin and was only proved finally in 1966 with the issue of her personal papers, earlier bequeathed to the Mitchell Library in Sydney with a stipulated ten-year period before publication.

Franklin River Tas. The Franklin River rises near Mt Hugel in the southwest of the State and flows through rugged country – much of which is contained in the Franklin-Lower Gordon Wild Rivers National Park – to join the Gordon River. This region is listed by the World Heritage Commission as a wilderness area. In 1981–3 a major controversy arose over a decision to dam the Gordon River below the confluence of the two, which would have flooded limestone gorges on the Franklin, an estimated 40% of the State's huon pine forest, and archaeological sites that mark the most southerly point of human occupation, during the last ice age. The plan was subsequently abandoned.

Fraser, Dawn (1937–), swimmer, b. Sydney. Hand-picked by coach Harry Gallagher in 1953, Fraser began her domination of world swimming at the 1956 Melbourne Olympics where she won the 100m freestyle and was a member of the victorious 4x100m relay team. She repeated her 100m victory in Rome in 1960 and Tokyo in 1964, despite constant clashes with officials that eventually led to her suspension from competitive swimming. In 1983 she was voted by her Australian sporting peers as the nation's greatest Olympian. Fraser set 40 world records during her career and was the first woman to break the minute barrier for the 100m freestyle. She was elected to the NSW parliament in 1988.

Fraser, (John) Malcolm (1930–), politician, b. Melbourne. A grazier, Fraser entered federal politics as a Liberal in 1955. Ambitious, and hardened by having to wait eleven years on the back bench before receiving his first portfolio in 1966, he was instrumental in the downfall of John Gorton in 1971. Elected leader of the Liberal Party in 1975, he was equally determined in bringing down the Whitlam Labor administration (> *constitutional crisis 1975*), becoming prime minister in that year. Two further election victories followed (1977 and 1980) before he was defeated by Bob Hawke in 1983. Fraser was an able politician but a dour figure; his run of election victories was due in part to a lacklustre Opposition and the electorate's fear of a return to the turbulence of the preceding Labor regime. Since resigning from parliament in 1983 he has remained active in affairs of state, notably in anti-apartheid activities as co-chairman of the Commonwealth Group of Eminent Persons.

Fraser, Neale > *tennis*

Fraser Island Qld Also known as Great Sandy Island, this is a long, low, dune-fringed island off the southeast Qld coast, east of Maryborough; its varied landscape includes extensive rainforests and numerous freshwater lakes. Concern over environmental disturbance caused by mining led the federal government to ban the export of mineral sands from the island in 1977. In 1989 most of the northern third was preserved as Great Sandy National Park, but conservation groups are still lobbying to have the entire island reserved and placed on the World Heritage list. There are numerous wrecks along the island shore. In 1836, Captain James Fraser and other survivors from his ship *Stirling Castle* landed on the island; all except Fraser's wife, Eliza, were killed by local Aborigines.

Frater, Jock William (1890–1947), painter, b. Scotland. Frater arrived in Australia in 1910. Together with George Bell and Arnold Shore, he was recognised as a pioneer of modernism in Vic. His apprenticeship and work as a stained-glass artist and his appreciation of the post-Impressionists influenced his technique. He advocated the principles of Cézanne, and his portraits and landscapes break from tradition in their freshness and spontaneity.

freedom of information (FOI) Public access to government information has traditionally been restricted, largely in the alleged interest of national security. Federal legislation for freedom of information was introduced in 1982, followed by similar legislation in Vic., and, most recently, NSW. While such laws theoretically allow universal right to access to documents held by government representatives and agencies, the government may in fact refuse such access in certain cases. Such exemptions are applied to protect the 'public interest', aspects of the workings of government – such as cabinet decision-making, intergovernment relations, and law enforcement – and the privacy and business interests of individuals.

freedom of the press Despite a history of intermittent censorship, Australia today has a relatively free press. The Constitution contains no explicit guarantees in this regard, however, and many clauses in both federal and State law can be used as a means of restriction. Responsibility for press law is divided between the

Commonwealth and the States. Federal powers cover security matters and self-regulation is practised through the D-notice system whereby publication of nominated matters of national security is restricted voluntarily. The States have jurisdiction over newspaper registration, blasphemy, obscenity, sedition and libel.

The earliest papers were subject to official control. The *Sydney Gazette* was censored regularly and publishers in various colonies fell foul of the authorities, including Andrew Bent in Tas., William Wentworth and Robert Wardell in Sydney, and Robert Thomas in Adelaide. In the mid-1820s, Governor Darling's attempts to curb the press were thwarted by Chief Justice Forbes, but his law requiring pledges against publishing libel, sedition and blasphemy was used occasionally until 1901. Several prosecutions for seditious libel were launched in the 19th century and the various colonies tried to combat the many vigorous scandal sheets with laws against obscene libel.

After Federation, the Commonwealth invoked its powers of censorship on several occasions, especially in war-time. From 1915, military censorship powers were used extensively for domestic political reasons; and during World War 2, censorship led to bans on nine communist papers in 1940 and considerable censorship of other papers until 1944, when several leading papers retaliated by printing black spaces in protest against censorship of non-military items. Since that time the main restriction on press freedom has been the various State libel laws, although there have also been attempts to prevent publication of material on foreign affairs and defence through court injunctions. Closure of magistrates' courts to the press increased during the 1970s and 1980s.

freemasonry Although this all-male secret society claims to have its origins in the masons' guilds of medieval Britain, the modern movement dates back only to the 18th century. Its expressed aims are to serve the community and inculcate in members a sense of religious duty, although today masonic lodges function chiefly as charitable organisations. While the secrecy, symbolism and rituals of freemasonry have had enduring appeal, they have often been perceived as sinister and the fraternity has been banned in some countries. It is widespread in Australia, where it dates from the 1790s and was well established by the mid-19th century. Membership has declined markedly since the 1950s, although there are lodges in all States.

free selection This was a system by means of which people could choose Crown land and pay for it over a period of time. It was introduced in Tas. (1859), Vic. and Qld (1860), NSW (1861), SA (1869) and WA (1872); selectors were mainly either from the urban working class, both native-born and immigrant, or were farm hands or former gold-miners. They generally failed to make a living, lacking the capital and skill to combat flood, fire, drought and infertile soil. Failure to maintain the three-year payment for the land and the use of bribery or the employment of 'dummies' at sales led to many selections being taken over by > *squatters*. The squalid rural slums of earth-floored 'humpies' are the scene of writings by Henry Lawson, Barbara Baynton and Steele Rudd. The system had modest success in SA and Vic., failed almost completely in NSW and Qld, and was little used in Tas. and WA. >> *land settlement*

free settlers > *colonial administration*; *convicts and transportation*; *land settlement*

Fremantle WA (pop. 22 709) At the mouth of the Swan River, and the State's chief port, the city of Fremantle lies 17km southwest of Perth and is now part of the metropolitan area. It has undergone great urban development since the 1970s, largely in response to industrial growth at nearby Kwinana, and further expansion occurred prior to the America's Cup yacht-race series in 1986–7. Captain Charles Fremantle arrived with orders to claim the west coast in 1829, followed shortly by Captain James Stirling and a small group of settlers; the settlement was chiefly a whaling centre and fishing port until the 1850s. An artificial harbour was built in the 1890s, turning the town henceforth into an important port; it receives petroleum products, caustic soda, fertilisers, iron and steel, and is the export terminal for grain, alumina, petroleum products and mineral sands.

French, Leonard (1928–), artist, b. Melbourne. A leading contemporary artist in the 1960s and 1970s, French is noted especially for his grand geometric abstractions in a variety of mediums – murals, tapestry and stained glass. Often based on heroic and religious themes, his work is distinguished by its use of vibrant, jewel-like colours and Byzantine effects. The huge stained-glass ceiling of the Great Hall of the National Gallery of Vic., commissioned in 1963, is justly famous; he also produced a vast, circular glass mandala for Blackwood Hall at Monash University, Vic. (1969).

Frenchmans Cap Tas. A striking, white quartzite peak (1445m), this lies in the rugged country of the Franklin–Lower Gordon Wild Rivers National Park, east of Macquarie Harbour. The mountain contains a group of glacial lakes, and on the eastern side includes a steep, 300m face. Although recorded as early as 1826, the origin of the name is unknown.

Freycinet Peninsula Tas. On the east of Great Oyster Bay, this peninsula is dominated by Mt Freycinet (614m) and is linked to the mainland by twin sand spits. The deeply indented shoreline – with sandy beaches and precipitous, red granite cliffs about 300m high – is of scientific interest as an example of a coastline drowned with the melting of the ice following the Pleistocene epoch. The peninsula has been a national park since 1916.

friarbird > *honeyeaters*

Friend, Donald Stuart Leslie (1915–89), painter, b. Sydney. A figurative artist of international repute, Friend was a brilliant draughtsman whose highly decorative and often sensual paintings reflected his sojourns in tropical places – including the Torres Strait Islands, Nigeria and Sri Lanka. In Australia he became an important member of the progressive Sydney artists of the 1950s, but is probably best known for the highly decorative work he completed in Bali, where he lived 1967–80. He suffered a stroke soon after his return to Australia but continued to draw and paint; a major retrospective exhibition of his work was staged by the Art Gallery of NSW in 1990.

frigatebirds > *sea-birds*

frogmouths The tawny frogmouth, *Padargus strigoides*, is the most common of the four Australian species of frogmouths, nocturnal birds with generally grey plumage, a long head and a very wide mouth. In daylight the frogmouth usually roosts on a tree branch, its colouring and its ability to stiffen when disturbed providing effective camouflage; it nests on a small platform of twigs in a tree fork or stump. It feeds on flying insects (including those attracted to street lights) caught in the open mouth, but at least one species has been found to consume mice, spiders, ground insects, and even berries. One large species, *P. papuensis*, extends from northern Qld into NG.

frogs Australia has some 200 species of frogs representing four families; they include some of the world's most unusual specimens, which have developed bizarre adaptations to life in arid habitats. Frogs are more often heard than seen, for the mating 'croak' of the male is amplified by a distensible throat pouch that acts as a resonating chamber. Individual frog species can often be recognised by their calls.

The southern frog of the family Myobatrachidae, in which there are about 100 species, is found in many habitats, ranging from coastal forests to the arid interior. The development of the tadpole varies from the typical, free-swimming form to one of growth entirely within the egg; for example, in the marsupial frog, *Assa darlingtoni*, all development takes place in special brood-pouches on the back of the male. One of the most remarkable of all is the recently discovered gastric-brooding frog, *Rheobatrachus*, of which the female broods her young in her own stomach for several weeks; during this time all gastric secretion stops, and she eats no food. The two known species of this frog appear to have very restricted distributions in the ranges of Qld, and one of them is threatened by logging. The central Australian water-holding frog, *Cyclorana platycephalus*, survives drought by burrowing deep into the earth and storing water both within its body and in a sealed chamber, in which it lies until the next rain; desert Aborigines used to dig these animals up to obtain water during severe drought. After heavy rains the frogs emerge to breed, and the tadpoles develop rapidly in temporary pools. Several species, such as the crucifix frog, *Notaden bennetti*, secrete a foul-smelling poison from their skin. The brightly coloured yellow-and-black corroboree frog, *Pseudophryne corroboree*, is found in alpine bogs of southeastern Australia.

Among the tree frogs of the family Hylidae, which contains about 50 species, there are terrestrial as well as arboreal groups; these frogs have circular toe-discs for climbing. The green tree frog, *Litorea caerulea*, is one of the largest and is widespread across much of northern and eastern Australia; the smaller, brown tree frog, *L. rubella*, is also common. The northern dwarf species, *L. bicolor*, is only about 2.5cm long and is sometimes found in the leaf axils of palms.

The tiny, narrow-mouthed frogs belonging to the family Microhylidae are confined to northern Australia; they deposit their eggs on land but in moist places, and the tadpoles grow and metamorphose before they hatch. Of the so-called 'true frogs', family Ranidae, in Australia there is only one species, *Rana papua*, and these are found in northeastern Qld.

fruit flies > *flies*; *insect pests*

fruit-growing Fruits grown in Australia, of which almost all are introduced species, range from those of the tropics, such as papaws, to temperate-zone berries and pome fruits. In 1987 fruit production covered 164 000ha of which 57 000 were devoted to grapes, 18 000 to tropical and other fruits, and 89 000 to orchard fruits; the last are now more usually described in terms of thousands of trees, because of the varying productivity of soils. Grapes constitute about 30% of all fruit produced, but the proportions used as fresh fruit and for the production of dried fruit and wine vary from year to year. Citrus trees provide nearly half of the remaining annual yield, apples 20%, bananas, pineapples and pears about 10% each, peaches 4% and apricots 2%.

Historical development Fruit-growing was established early in the colonies. Apples and oranges – as well as exotica such as figs and grapes – were introduced aboard the First Fleet in 1788 and by the early 1820s some 484ha of orchards and gardens surrounded Sydney. Improvements in irrigation, and in storage and preservation technology, encouraged great expansion of the industry from the 1880s.

Citrus fruits are largely produced in irrigated areas along the Murrumbidgee and Murray rivers, but are also found on the eastern coast and in the Darling Range of WA. Oranges make up more than 80% of the crop, lemons and limes together about 6%, and mandarins and grapefruit each 5%. Of the oranges, some 90% is for the domestic market, and of this two-thirds is processed as juice.

Apples are grown in every State, with a total of about 6.35 million trees in 1987. Some 33% of the crop is processed, but since Britain joined the EEC less than 10% of the crop is exported; there has also been a decrease in the number of growers. One of the best known varieties, the Granny Smith, was developed in Sydney, from Tas. seed, by Maria Ann Smith in 1868. Pear trees totalled 1.55 million in 1987; nearly three-quarters of them were in

Vic., which has a canning industry centred on the city of Shepparton. Although the canning market is declining, there is an increase in the export of pear pulp and juice, and also of the fermented juice, or 'perry'.

Bananas are produced in frost-free, high-rainfall areas, the greater proportion in NSW, and almost the entire crop is for domestic consumption. Pineapples come chiefly from coastal Qld, both southern and tropical areas; in the tropics the growing cycle is shorter. Consumption is of both fresh and canned fruit.

Stone fruits form about 10% of orchard crops. The major varieties grown are peaches and apricots; others are plums, cherries and nectarines. Production is concentrated in Vic., SA and NSW, and much of the crop is dried, canned, or made into jam; fresh fruit is distributed via city markets.

The chief berry fruits are strawberries, raspberries, blackcurrants, loganberries and gooseberries; apart from strawberries, most are grown in high-altitude areas. Berry fruits are used fresh, canned or dried (currants), and for jams and juices.

Other fruits as yet account for only a small fraction of the market. Tropical fruits – including mangoes, papaws and guavas – are grown mainly in Qld, although there is also some production in northern NSW, WA and the NT. With increasing consumer interest in exotic fruits, cultivation of avocadoes and mangoes has expanded enormously since the 1970s and new tropical crops such as rambutans and lychees are also being produced commercially. >> *dried-fruits industry*; *nuts and nut-growing*; *wine industry*

Fulbright Scholarships This Australian/American post-graduate scholarship, named in honour of a US senator, aims to further understanding between the two countries and to provide an educational and professional exchange. Students in all fields are eligible; the national competition, held annually, is administered by the Australian/American Educational Foundation. Sir Zelman Cowen, former governor-general of Australia, and Nick Greiner, premier of NSW, are among former Fulbright scholars.

fungi This very large group of organisms was traditionally classified as a plant group but is now regarded as comprising a kingdom distinct from both plants and animals. Fungi take a great variety of forms in addition to the familiar mushrooms and toadstools, ranging from microscopic yeasts and mildews to giant bracket fungi with a diameter of 60cm or more. Like animals, fungi are unable to synthesise their own carbohydrates from water and carbon dioxide and must grow on organic matter, either live or dead. They play an essential role in the breakdown of dead organic matter, thus releasing nutrients back into the soil; the soil itself contains vast numbers of diverse fungi, some of which are harmful parasites and others beneficial agents that transfer nutrients from dead organic matter. Many plant and animal diseases are caused by a parasitic fungus that attacks only one species: the rust fungi of Australia's wheatlands are one such group.

There are an estimated 250 000 species of fungi throughout the world, of which at least 30 000 occur in Australia. Some are specific to certain plant groups and this determines their geographic distribution: an interesting example is the beech orange fungus, *Cyttaria*, sole genus of the family Cyttariaceae, which parasitises only *Nothofagus* trees and is thus largely confined to Australia, NZ and South America. Apart from this, Australia has representatives of most of the world's families of fungi and a large proportion of the genera; most groups have been so inadequately studied, however, that the correspondence between Australian and non-Australian species has not as yet been established. The fruiting bodies of fungi, where these are large and visible, provide the means by which fungal families and genera are most easily recognised. Mushrooms, toadstools and bracket fungi comprise the order Agaricales, with gilled or pored fruiting bodies; various other orders with obvious fruiting bodies include the Gasteromycetes (puffballs, earthstars and stinkhorns); the colourful branched coral fungi; and Discomycetes or cup fungi, which include a native truffle, *Stephensia arenivaga*, of central Australia.

A number of fungi, such as the oyster mushroom, are specifically cultivated for food and many of those found in the wild are edible. Some, on the other hand, are poisonous and their toxins unaffected by cooking; any species, particularly toadstools and mushrooms that are harvested from the wild, should therefore be scientifically identified before being eaten.

funnelweb spiders > *spiders*

Furneaux Islands Tas. This island group at the eastern end of Bass Strait includes > *Flinders Island* (the largest), Cape Barren, Babel, Clarke, and a number of smaller islands. Cape Barren is home to the increasingly rare Cape Barren goose, as well as muttonbirds; Babel is one of the major areas for muttonbirding, although this is now restricted to a brief annual season. Clarke Island grazes sheep and cattle. The group was named in 1773 by James Cook in honour of Tobias Furneaux, captain of Cook's companion ship on his second voyage.

Furphy, Joseph (1843–1912), author, b. Yarra Glen, Vic. The son of immigrant Irish parents, Furphy began contributing pieces to the *Bulletin* in 1889 and adopted the pen-name 'Tom Collins' (a fictional minor official in the Riverina district of NSW) from 1893. His unique novel *Such is Life* (1903) is a kaleidoscopic study of country life in diary form, including description, serio-comic anecdote, pun and quotation, political and social comment, essay and satire. Two sections, pruned at the suggestion of A.G. Stephens, appeared as *Rigby's Romance* (1921) and *The Buln Buln and the Brolga* (1948). After working on a poor selection and as a bullock teamster, he worked in his brother's foundry at Shepparton, Vic., before joining his sons in a similar business in Fremantle, WA, in 1905.

G

Gabo Island Vic. This small granitic island lies about 8km southwest of Cape Howe, the eastern tip of Vic. Its importance lies in its lighthouse, since it is here that ships make the turn from the south to the east coast, and vice versa.

Gair, Vincent Clair (1902–80), politician, b. Rockhampton, Qld. Joining the ALP in 1919, Gair entered the Qld parliament in 1932, becoming premier in 1952. Expelled from the ALP in 1957 in the aftermath of the party's earlier schism, he continued as premier and formed the Qld Labor Party but lost power to the Country Liberal coalition in the same year. Merging his splinter party with the DLP, Gair entered federal parliament as a Qld senator in 1965. In 1974 the Whitlam government, hoping to win an additional Senate seat, made Gair ambassador to Ireland; the plan misfired owing to obstruction by the Qld government, and Gair was recalled from this post by the Fraser government in 1976.

galah > *parrots*

Galiwinku NT Originally the name of the main settlement on Elcho Island, which lies off Arnhem Land, Galiwinku now refers to the whole island and its resident Aboriginal community. Formerly a Methodist mission, the community is now autonomous and permission is required for entry by non-Aborigines; the main economic activities are vegetable-growing and timber production. The island is officially part of Arnhem Land.

Gallipoli > *World War1*

gambling Australians are reputed to be the world's greatest gamblers, being prepared to place a bet on virtually anything that runs, rolls or spins, or which can be dealt or thrown. The control of gambling rests with the State governments, a privilege that is guarded carefully as the revenue generated through a tax on turnover is substantial: in 1985–6, for example, NSW's gambling tax amounted to $532 million, 9.5% of the government's total tax receipts; in Vic. the figure was $312 million (9.1%). Australians are legally permitted to gamble on horses, dogs, various forms of numbers games such as lotteries and pools and, in NSW and the ACT, slot machines.

Betting on the racing of horses and dogs has been a national passion since colonial days and was the continuation of an Irish tradition. Wagers are placed either through bookmakers on the course or through a Totalisator Agency Board (TAB) run by the government. The TAB system was introduced in Vic. and WA in 1961 and soon after in other States, partly as a way of eliminating the illegal (and untaxed) SP bookmaker. The TAB is now also an agency for betting on other sporting events such as cricket, football and motor racing.

Half of all Australians buy a lottery ticket of some kind every week. The idea is an ancient one but was popularised in Australia by George Adams, who established a lottery at Tattersall's Hotel in Sydney in 1881. Driven from NSW, Adams set up his business in Tas.; in 1954, Tattersall's transferred to Vic., where it still holds the lottery franchise and provides immense revenue for the government, which takes 31% of turnover, a figure of $179.8 million in 1985–6. All other States run or franchise lotteries, the most famous being the Sydney Opera House Lottery established by the NSW government in 1958 to help pay for the construction of that edifice. Instant ('scratch-card') lotteries have proliferated in recent years.

Slot machines – called 'poker machines' in Australia and known more appositely as 'one-armed bandits' – were legalised in NSW in 1956 for use in non-proprietary clubs. They were introduced in the ACT in 1976 but have been resisted by all other States to date, with the exception of Qld, where electronic blackjack is permitted in casinos. In NSW in 1985–6, poker machines provided the government with $179.7 million in tax revenue, a figure nearly equal to that for race-betting taxes ($182.5 million) and surpassing that for the State's lotteries ($165.3 million).

Casinos Legal casino gaming took a long time to arrive in Australia, possibly because of the deep-seated puritanism that came to mark the predominantly Protestant society and which associated casinos with European moral laxity or American vice. Illegal casinos flourished nevertheless – and still do – in the major cities, particularly Sydney, where during the administration of Sir Robert Askin (1965–75) they were given de facto if not de jure recognition. The first legal casino was opened in Hobart in 1973; today they exist in all States (Qld and the NT having two each) except NSW and Vic. All offer the full complement of international casino games including roulette, baccarat, craps, blackjack, and the so-called wheels of fortune; a local curiosity is a streamlined version of 'two-up'. Australian casinos have generally adopted US methods of control and atmosphere rather than the more civilised French standard.

gang-gang > *parrots*

gannets > *sea-birds*

Garden Island NSW This former island was joined to the southern shore of Port Jackson by land reclamation and the eventual construction of the Captain Cook Graving Dock, in 1942. The island first appears in the log of HMS *Sirius* in 1788, when it was to be 'cleared for a garden'. Subsequently on occasion a quarantine station, in 1866 it became a naval depot; administered variously by imperial, federal and NSW governments, it was finally acquired by the Commonwealth in 1945 and has since been extensively modified.

Garden Island WA A small, sandy island that forms the western side of Cockburn Sound, it extends north–south for 10.5km but is nowhere more than 2km wide. The first WA settlers stayed on Garden Island in May 1829 when rough seas prevented them from reaching the mainland, and the colony was first proclaimed there. Since 1978 the site of a naval installation (HMAS *Stirling*) and also containing holiday resorts, it is linked by a causeway to the mainland.

Gardiner, Frank (Francis) (1830–95), bushranger, b. Boro Creek, NSW. Son of a Scottish immigrant, Christie, and a servant girl, Clarke, Gardiner used both those names but mainly the one he adopted from an employer, Gardiner. Two convictions for horse-stealing were followed by a period (1859–62) as leader of a gang based in the Weddin Ranges, whose activities culminated in the hold-up in 1862 of the Forbes gold escort at Eugowra – the subject of the famous painting by Tom Roberts, *Bailed Up*. Gardiner was living as a storekeeper in Qld when finally captured in 1864. He was released in 1872 on condition that he leave the colony – an incident causing the downfall of Henry Parkes – and he died in the US.

Gardner, Wayne (1959–), motorcycle racer, b. Wollongong, NSW. In 1981 Gardner, having twice won the Castrol six-hour race, went to the UK and secured a place on the British Honda team. By 1986 he was recognised as the number two rider in the world and had gained substantial sponsorship contracts. In 1987 he established himself as first in the field, becoming the first Australian to win the world 500cc motorcycle championship; he won seven of the fifteen grand prix races, setting ten lap records. Gardner's victory at the inaugural Australian Grand Prix at Phillip Island, Vic., in 1989 was a fitting and enormously popular result.

Garran family, noted in journalism, politics and law. **Andrew** (1825–1901), b. England, arrived in Adelaide in 1851; after working as a journalist he joined the *Sydney Morning Herald* as assistant editor in 1856 and was editor 1873–85. He was a member of the NSW parliament 1887–92. His son **Sir Robert Randolph** (1867–1957), b. Sydney, became a barrister. As secretary to Edmund Barton in the 1890s, he was an active proponent of Federation and collaborated with John Quick on the monumental *Annotated Constitution of the Australian Commonwealth* (1901). After Federation he was one of the first Commonwealth public servants, as secretary to the attorney-general's department, and was solicitor-general from 1916. He played an active part in Canberra's cultural life from 1927 and was closely involved in the establishment of the Australian National University.

gas industry > *oil and natural gas*

Gascoyne River WA The Gascoyne is a sporadic 800km stream that rises near the Collier Range in the centre of the State and flows largely west to reach the Indian Ocean at Carnarvon; its main tributary is the Lyons River. Irrigation from the stream bed supports a limited area of crops in the river's lower reaches, particularly bananas and vegetables; also near the coast, the surrounding plains carry merino sheep.

gastropods Gastropods are a class of the phylum Mollusca; adults are characterised by a single shell or valve (they are also called univalves), which is usually in a spiral form. Aspects of some representative Australian species are discussed below; others are considered individually.

True limpets, of the family Patellidae, have a 'foot' specialised for applying suction to rocks and include the common or colourful limpet of southeastern Australia, usually having alternate light and dark rays of yellow, orange, brown or black on the outside of the shell, which is silvery inside. The families Bullidae and Hydatinidae (bubble shells) differ from most other gastropods in being hermaphroditic (that is, the individual has both male and female sex organs); both the shells and the animals inside are commonly very beautiful. Top shells, of the family Trochidae, vary widely in both shape and colour. The shell of the trochus, *Trochus niloticus*, is of some commercial importance; formerly used extensively in the manufacture of buttons, it has now largely been replaced by plastics. It is found off the coral reefs of Qld. The turban shells of the family Turbinidae vary in appearance from those with flattened whorls, as in the widespread heavy turban shell, to the high-coned bell tent shell of NSW. The australwinks, of the periwinkle family Littorinidae, include the common blue species *Melarapha unifasciata*, clustering in rock crevices near high-water mark, and the mangrove australwink, *M. scabra*, found on the stems and leaves of mangroves.

Australia has a great variety of marine gastropods whose shells are prized by collectors. The waters around the Great Barrier Reef are particularly rich in examples of many families: they include the cones, which if not handled carefully can inject poison with their sharp radula, the mitre shells, the tritons, the beautifully patterned cowries and the large baler shells. >> *abalone*; *snails and slugs*

GATT > *trade*

Gawler SA (pop. 11 354) This prosperous town 40km northeast of Adelaide lies at the foot of the Mt Lofty Ranges (on a site chosen by William Light) and at the edge of the Barossa Valley. In the second half of the 19th century an important industrial town, Gawler is now the centre of thriving farmlands producing wine grapes, wool, wheat and dairy products.

Gawler Ranges SA These ranges lie south of Lake Gairdner, extending about 160km east–west across the base of the Eyre Peninsula. Vegetation is shrub steppe, suitable for grazing but with a low carrying capacity; the highest point is Nukey Bluff (472m). Columnar formation of porphyry at Yardea and the Yantanabie Historic Reserve (an Aboriginal quarry) are both listed on the register of the national estate. The ranges were first seen by Edward Eyre in 1839.

Gaze, Andrew (1965–), basketball player, b. Melbourne. Two metres tall and weighing 90kg, Gaze was almost literally born into basketball – his father, Lindsay, being formerly a prominent player and later an outstanding coach of both national and club teams. He has represented Australia on more than 100 occasions, including the 1984 and 1988 Olympic Games; at Seoul he showed himself to be among the best scorers in the world when he held second place in the Games points tally. Gaze has played college basketball in the US, representing Seton Hall.

geckoes > *lizards*

Geelong Vic. (pop. 125 833) The largest provincial city in Vic., some 72km southwest of Melbourne on Corio Bay, Geelong grew as the port and social and market centre for the rich Western District – which role is still reflected in its institutions (notably the leading private school Geelong Grammar, founded in 1855), grand residences, and substantial wool stores and warehouses. In the 20th century its former gentility has been overshadowed by industrial development – most conspicuously oil refineries, but including car manufacture, glass and salt works, and aluminium smelting – that has spread the town along the sides of the bay and accounted for its rapid population growth and large immigrant community. The city has retained its educational function, with new institutions including nearby Deakin University (established in 1977), and has undergone substantial refurbishment in the last 20 years.

geese Australian geese include several distinctive species. The magpie goose, *Anseranas semipalmata*, is a large bird with black head, neck and wings, and a white breast. It was eradicated from NSW in the early 1900s as a result of its wetland habitats being drained, and also of poison, and is now common only in northern and northeastern Australia. It has been reported as damaging rice-fields, but normally searches for food in shallow natural swamp-pools. The Cape Barren goose, *Cereopsis novaehollandiae*, is found in coastal southern Australian and offshore islands, where it breeds; it is largely vegetarian, its food including saltmarsh grasses and sedges. It had become rare as a result of hunting, but is now protected and numbers are increasing. The two pygmy geese are *Nettapus coromvandelianus* and *N. pulchellus*, extending from Southeast Asia into northeastern Australia; both are seen on inland streams and lakes, and have predominantly green and white plumage. The maned goose, *Chenonetta jubata*, a grass-eater of inland streams and timbered swamp-margins in much of Australia, is mainly black-flecked white with a brown head and 'mane', and nests in tree-holes, often far from water. >> *ducks*

Geeveston Tas. (pop. 1400) Just west of the Huon estuary, some 60km southwest of Hobart, this traditional apple-growing area has expanded its interests in recent years to include forestry and associated industries – notably paper and pulp production – as well as tourism.

Gellibrand, Joseph Tice (1786–1837), lawyer and explorer, b. England. Appointed the first attorney-general in Tas. in 1823, Gellibrand clashed with Governor Arthur and was dismissed in 1826. In the 1830s, as a member of the Port Phillip Association, he undertook explorations but was killed by Aborigines on his second journey into the Port Phillip hinterland in 1837. His grandson, **Sir John** (1872–1945), b. Ouse, Tas., was an oustanding AIF officer during World War 1, having served in the British Army before returning to Tas. to farm in 1912.

gemfish > *barracouta*

gems and gemstones Australia has an abundance of gems and gemstones, being the world's largest producer of opals and, since 1986, of industrial diamonds. Sapphire, emerald, ruby, nephrite jade, amethyst and numerous other gemstones are also found, but in smaller quantities.

The national product represents over 90% of the world's opal, worth $67.4 million in 1986–7. It is found in numerous places, but the highest quality stone is at Coober Pedy and Mintabie in SA and at Lightning Ridge in NSW, the source of the highly prized black opal. Once Australia's most valuable gemstone export, opal now pales into relative insignificance when compared with diamonds.

Small quantities of diamonds have been found in Australia since the latter half of the 19th century, but in 1979 a major source was discovered at the Lake Argyle prospect near Kununurra in WA. In 1986, the first year of full-scale mining, 29 210 764 carats were extracted, a figure surpassing the annual production of any other country, including South Africa. Although only about 6% of these diamonds were of gem quality (more than half being industrial grades), the value of Australian diamond production leapt from a negligible figure in 1984 to $284 million in 1986–7. The success of the Argyle prospect has led to renewed interest in diamond exploration, and promising prospects have been found in WA and in the New England district of NSW.

Sapphire production, which is centred in NSW and Qld, has increased in recent years and was worth $16.4 million in 1986–7. The only shadow over the Australian gem industry is cast by the commercial development of synthetic stones, particularly opals and diamonds.

General Motors Holden's Ltd > *GMH*

genetic engineering > *biotechnology*

Geographe Bay WA This is a wide indentation on the extreme southwest coast of WA. It extends from Cape Naturaliste, the low-lying, swampy shore curving south and then north towards Bunbury. The town of Busselton lies at the head of the bay, which supports a fishing industry. Nicolas Baudin in 1801 named the bay and the cape after his two ships.

geological surveys Geological surveys underpinned the discovery and development of Australia's great mineral resources. All Australian States have geological surveys, the federal organisation concerned being the Bureau of Mineral Resources, Geology and Geophysics.

The scope of the surveys covers provision of detailed geological maps showing the nature of underlying bedrock; reports on mineralisation, groundwater potential, sources of sand, road metal and building stone; advice on geological data associated with engineering works such as the construction of roads, dams and large buildings; and marine geology and geophysics, for the study of offshore conditions and processes.

Geological surveys were first made in the early 19th century, and were intensified after substantial mineral deposits were revealed in SA during the 1840s. Often initially undertaken by amateurs, surveys became increasingly professional from the mid-19th century although financial resources were limited. The greatest expansion took place after World War 2, the Bureau of Mineral Resources being set up in 1946.

geology and major landforms Australia is the lowest and flattest of the world's continents. Almost two-thirds of its land surface is a plateau that averages 300–600m above sea-level and only its highest peaks exceed 2000m, giving them the status of foothills relative to the ranges on most other continents. Unlike the landforms of Europe and the US, which developed in the last 20 000 years, Australia's geological history dates back to the Precambrian era and the evolution of its present landscape began in the Permian period. Sedimentary deposition by shallow ancient seas, and exposure to long periods of erosion, have been the major factors in the development of this landscape, which has experienced insignificant geological activity and glaciation relative to other major continents.

Geological history Precambrian rock (more than 600 million years old) is exposed across much of Australia, the oldest constituting the metamorphosed shield areas of the Pilbara and Yilgarn areas in WA, which both bear important mineral deposits. Younger Precambrian rocks are found at Rum Jungle and in the Macdonnell Ranges, NT, the Barrier Range (incorporating mineral-rich Broken Hill) in NSW, and in western Qld; the enormous sedimentary iron-ore deposits of the Hamersley Range in WA and the Gawler Ranges in SA also date from this time. The presence of tillites (scoured rock fragments) in SA suggest glaciation during the late Precambrian era.

During the Cambrian period at the beginning of the Paleozoic era (570 million–220 million years ago), seas invaded much of eastern Australia, depositing marine sediments such as limestone and shales; the presence of black shales indicate that much of the region was still under deep water during the Ordovician. A major period of mountain building occurred in Tas. in the Cambrian and Ordovician periods, and sedimentary deposits in central Australia were uplifted and folded during the early Silurian. Shallower marine conditions prevailed in eastern Australia, favouring the growth of coral reefs which are the source of limestone deposits from which developed many of the spectacular caves of Qld and NSW. Marine deposition continued in the Devonian, during which age a period of mountain-building compressed and folded the thick sedimentary deposits of eastern Australia and an enormous reef deposit was formed south of the Kimberleys in WA. A major episode of mountain-building in eastern Australia during the early Carboniferous led to increased deposits of sandstone and conglomerate sediments, and the intrusion of large granitic batholiths (as at Bathurst in NSW). From the middle Carboniferous to the early Permian, Australia was located at a much higher latitude and there is evidence of cooling and glaciation across much of the continent at this time. Permian deposits include the sandstones and conglomerates – interspersed with coal measures – which formed in the Sydney Basin, NSW, and the Bowen Basin in Qld, and elsewhere along their coasts. A further period of mountain-building in NSW and Qld, which produced the large granitic batholith of New England, occurred at the end of the Paleozoic era.

At the beginning of the Mesozoic era (220 million–60 million years ago), sedimentation continued in swamps and deltas along the eastern coast, including deposition of both the Hawkesbury sandstone in NSW and the sandstone aquifer that underlies much of the Great Artesian Basin in Qld; much of southeastern Qld experienced volcanic activity during this time. Sedimentation continued in parts of eastern Australia during the Jurassic, and the Walloon coal measures were laid down in Qld; in Tas., large sheets of volcanic dolerite were intruded and the jointed columns of this formation today caps many of the island's highest peaks. During the Cretaceous, much of Australia was covered by seas which deposited extensive flat marine limestones and shales in most of the artesian basins of the interior.

The opening of the Tertiary period, which marked the beginning of the Cainozoic era (60 million years to the present), saw continued marine deposition across much of southern Australia: the spectacular sea cliffs of western Vic. and the Nullarbor Plain of SA and WA date from this time, as do the Latrobe Valley coal measures in Vic., which were deposited by freshwater swamps. Eastern Australia was the site of much volcanic activity during the Tertiary period, resulting in the basaltic caps which are found on many peaks of the eastern uplands: the Glasshouse Mountains in Qld; the extinct Tweed volcano of the Border Ranges, the Warrumbungle and Nandewar ranges and Mt Canobolas in NSW; and Mt Macedon in Vic. In the Quaternary period, volcanic activity continued in the Atherton Tableland and Mt Gambier region. Glaciation was limited relative to that experienced in the northern hemisphere, but much of Tas. and the Kosciusko region of NSW were covered with ice caps; as the ice melted, rising seas flooded many eastern rivers, producing deep harbours. There was a general uplift during this period, which produced many of the eastern plateau areas and revived the rivers.

Major landforms Australia has three major physiographic provinces: the Great Western Plateau, covering most of the west and north of the continent and composed primarily of resistant Precambrian rock; the Eastern Highlands, which extend from Qld to Tas. and generally comprise folded and uplifted Palaeozoic sediments; and the Central Lowlands, which extend across western Qld, NSW and Vic., and into SA, and are covered by flat-lying sediments.

The Great Western Plateau encompasses the folded and deformed Yilgarn and Pilbara shields of WA, the roots of ancient mountains. Other ranges of the Great Western Plateau are upfaulted blocks (such as the Hamersley and Ophthalmia ranges in WA) or flat-topped dissected tablelands (such as the Kimberley plateau in WA, Arnhem Land in the NT, and the Barkly Tableland of the NT and Qld). The Macdonnell and Musgrave ranges of central Australia, and the Flinders and Mt Lofty ranges of SA, are composed of folded and uplifted Precambrian strata.

The Eastern Highlands comprise folded Palaeozoic sediments. South of the elevated Atherton Tableland, most of the low ranges of central Qld are separated by broad lowlands and river valleys. The volcanic Border Ranges and granitic New England plateau of southeastern Qld and northern NSW form an elevated escarpment as far south as the Hunter Valley;

their deeply entrenched eastern rivers descend rapidly to the coastal plain, often forming deep gorges. Further south is a large expanse of flatlying sandstone that was uplifted to form the Blue Mountains and Budawang Range. The Australian Alps and associated highlands rise from the southern tablelands of NSW and continue to western Vic. as the Grampians and also south to Wilson's Promontory. Most of western Tas. is composed of folded limestone and shales; ancient intruded sheets of volcanic dolerite form the jointed columns and wall-like tiers on many of the island's highest peaks. The mountains of highland Tas. and the Australian Alps were cold enough to maintain glaciers during the Quaternary ice ages and their landscapes are marked by features of ice-scouring, such as glacial lakes and valleys.

The Central Lowlands occupy much of the interior and are underlain by limestones and shales, many of which were deposited by Cretaceous seas. The artesian basins of this region reflect the presence of aquifers within these strata: the area is drained by the Murray–Darling system from the east, but in the more arid regions most of the watercourses terminate in intermittent saline lakes. In general the drainage is flat and poorly developed, leading to widespread flooding after heavy rains.

Coastal features The extensive Australian coastline (more than 36 000km long) shows the combined effects of ancient sedimentary deposition and long-term erosion. Outcrops of resistant rock often form prominant headlands or capes, with adjacent sandy beaches where the rock was more easily eroded. More common, however, are long stretches of featureless cliffs, such as the massive limestone bluffs that front the Great Australian Bight for hundreds of kilometres along the southern edge of the Nullarbor Plain. Low-lying coasts are often covered by sand beaches, the sand being deposited by offshore currents in combination with wave action. Dunes formed by onshore sea breezes are common along many coastal areas, continuing to advance inland unless stabilised by vegetation. Currents often deposit sandbars near the mouths of rivers and have initiated the formation of coastal lakes and lagoons such as the Coorong in SA, the Gippsland Lakes in Vic. and Lake Macquarie in NSW.

The great sand islands of southeastern Qld – such as Fraser, Moreton and Stradbroke – are among the largest such formations in the world. Evidence of erosion during periods of lower sea-levels is seen in drowned river valleys such as Port Jackson (Sydney Harbour), which over millions of years was transformed into a complex of bays and headlands. Where rivers empty into protected shallow bays in warm regions, tidal > *mangroves* have been formed – mostly in the tropical north. Also a tropical phenomenon are coral reefs, which flourish in the shallow warm seas along the northeast and northwest coast. >> *fossils*; *geological surveys*; *soils and soil conservation*; *water and water resources*

George Town

Tas. (pop. 6938) Located on Bass Strait at the mouth of the Tamar River, 250km north of Hobart, George Town has been the chief residential area for the Bell Bay aluminium works since the 1970s and has more recently undergone urban and industrial expansion. It was originally intended to be the northern capital of Tas. but was soon overtaken by Launceston.

Georgina River

NT/Qld From its source on the Barkly Tableland, the 1300km Georgina flows southeast through Qld's arid extreme west, then joins the Hamilton to become Eyre Creek and continue through the Channel Country towards SA and Lake Eyre. The river is generally dry – its waters rarely reach the lake – but can cause extensive flooding in the wet season.

Geraldton

WA (pop. 21 726) Proclaimed a city in 1988, Geraldton is the second-largest port in WA; it lies 424km north of Perth, on Champion Bay, and serves a large rural and mining area as well as a substantial crayfish industry that supplies the US and Japanese markets. Main industries include fish processing, tourism, and the manufacture of superphosphate for the farming hinterland; in the last 20 years it has developed as a commercial and service centre for the hinterland.

geranium family

These worldwide flowering plants belong to the Geraniaceae family, which has 700–800 species divided into eleven genera. Australia has ten species of the genus *Geranium*, which consists mainly of annual and perennial herbaceous plants with attractive five-petalled flowers. The garden geraniums are hybrids derived from South African species of the genus *Pelargonium*, with a shrubby or scrambling growth habit and large, brightly coloured flowers; some species and hybrids are grown primarily for their scented foliage. Australia, with seven small-flowered herbaceous species, is one of the few landmasses outside southern Africa where this genus occurs. The third genus represented in Australia is *Erodium*, of which there are three native species comprising pink or bluish-flowered small herbs commonly called crowsfoot.

Germans in Australia > *ethnic groups*

gerrymander

The geographical weighting of votes through manipulation of electoral zonings has a long history in Australia, particularly in the State electoral systems. The practice has been most overt in Qld, WA and – until a redistribution in 1969 – SA, where city electorates for many years typically had three times as many voters as country seats. In WA the gerrymander has survived despite repeated attempts at its abolition by the State government; as a result, each of Perth's 30 seats holds roughly twice as many voters as one of the State's 27 country electorates. In Qld, the system was renamed by its opponents the 'Bjelkemander', after the premier who long benefited from it (> *Sir Joh Bjelke-Petersen*), his National Party being able to form a government 1983–7 with only 39% of the vote. >> *elections*

giant clams > *bivalves*

gibber-bird > *chats*

Gibbs, (Cecilia) May

(1877–1969), author and illustrator, b. England. After moving to Sydney c.1914, Gibbs created Australia's first truly indigenous fairytales with her whimsical bush creatures, the gumnut babies. Books such as *The Gumnut Babies* (1916), *Bib and Bub* (1925) and the classic *Snugglepot and Cuddlepie* (1918) are all still in print and continue to capture the imagination of children and adults alike.

Gibbs, Sir Harry Talbot

(1917–), lawyer and academic, b. Sydney. Gibbs became a barrister in 1939 and after distinguished service during World War 2 he lectured in law at the University of Qld. He became a QC in 1957 and was a judge of the Qld Supreme Court 1961–7. He was subsequently a judge of the Federal Court of Bankruptcy and the ACT Supreme Court 1967–70, a High Court justice 1970–81 and chief justice 1981–7.

Giblin family, prominent in politics and economics. **William Robert** (1840–87) was parliamentary member for Hobart and Tas. premier 1879–84, and later served as chief justice of the State. His son, **Lyndhurst Falkiner** (1872–1951), was nationally known as an economist, especially during the 1930s when he served on the 1931 committee that formulated the short-lived 'premiers' plan' to combat the depression. As chairman of an advisory committee on financial and economic policy 1939–47 he helped curb wartime inflation.

Gibson, Mel (1956–), actor, b. US. Although American-born, Gibson was brought up in Australia and graduated from NIDA in 1977. A good-looking actor of limited range, he achieved international stardom with *Mad Max* (1979) and its sequels; his other films include *Gallipoli* (1981), *The Year of Living Dangerously* (1982), *The Bounty* (1984) and *Mrs Soffel* (1984).

Gibson, Sir Robert (1863–1934), businessman, b. Scotland. Gibson immigrated to Melbourne at the age of 27 and established a manufacturing business (1897) and a foundry (1907). During World War 1 he served on the Coal Board, and later he was chairman of a royal commission on federal economics. In addition to many important directorships, he was chairman of the Commonwealth Bank 1926–34 and president of the Vic. Chamber of Manufactures 1922–5.

Gibson Desert WA This is a vast area of laterite plains lying between the Great Sandy Desert in the north and the Great Victoria Desert in the south; with shrub steppe and mulga scrub the main vegetation, it is now the Gibson Desert Nature Reserve, covering about 1.74 million ha. The desert was crossed by Ernest Giles in 1874, and named after an expedition member who died during the journey.

Gilbert River Qld From its source in the Gilbert Range, a spur of the Gregory Range, the Gilbert River flows for some 500km northwest through a region of high rainfall which is concentrated in summer, giving rise to contrasting floods and dry periods. Its main tributary is the Einasleigh, which joins the Gilbert about 160km from its estuary on the southeast coast of the Gulf of Carpentaria. The chief rural industry is beef cattle.

Giles, (William) Ernest (Powell) (1835–97), explorer, b. England. Giles arrived in Australia in 1851. He failed at the diggings and became a clerk in Melbourne, but hated town life and turned to exploration (financed by pastoralists seeking new land). In 1872 he found Lake Amadeus; in 1874 he penetrated to the Gibson Desert, named after his companion; and in 1875–6, backed by Sir Thomas Elder and using camels, he crossed from SA to WA, well north of Eyre's route, and returned by a route 644km further north again – the only explorer to cross the worst of the Western Desert both ways. Giles received little official recognition; he died when working, again as a clerk, at Coolgardie.

Gill, S.T. (Samuel Thomas) (1818–80), artist, b. England. Gill arrived in Australia in 1839 with his father, a minister. His prolific lithographed sketches, first of SA but notably of the Vic. goldfields, won him contemporary fame and a prosperity which did not, however, last until his death. His lithographs provide a lively, often humorous, historically invaluable record of the gold-rush period and its excesses.

Gilmore, Dame Mary Jean (1865–1962), poet and journalist, b. Cottawalla, NSW. Gilmore was an important poet whose large output, although varying in quality, was dominated by a simple sincerity and devotion to humanity. After teaching, she joined the unsuccessful utopian New Australia settlement and returned to Australia in 1902. She subsequently became a journalist specialising in socialist causes, editing the women's page of the labour newspaper *Australian Worker* 1908–31. Her first, lively volume of poetry was published in 1910; she subsequently produced six further volumes, the last when she was 89.

Gilroy, Sir Norman Thomas (1896–1977), Catholic prelate, b. Glebe, NSW. A wireless operator during World War 1, Gilroy worked as a post-office engineer before training for the Catholic priesthood. He was ordained in 1923 and appointed bishop of Port Augusta in 1934. As archbishop of Sydney 1940–71, he was a conservative influence and unlike his outspoken Melbourne counterpart Archbishop Mannix he opposed church involvement in political activities, especially the Catholic Social Studies Movement. In 1946 he became the first Australian-born cardinal.

Gippsland Vic. This region in southeastern Vic. extends from Westernport Bay (southeast of Melbourne) for about 400km northeastwards to the NSW border. Its diverse landscapes range from forested hills in the north (the foothills of the Australian Alps), a Tertiary sedimentary basin in the west (which includes the coal deposits of the > *Latrobe Valley*), and a varying coastline of low sandy expanses (notably the Ninety Mile Beach which separates the > *Gippsland Lakes* from Bass Strait) and granitic headlands such as > *Wilsons Promontory* in the southwest. The region was discovered by Angus McMillan in 1839 but his chosen name, 'Caledonia Australis', failed in favour of that given by Paul Strzelecki in 1840, after the NSW governor. Beef and sheep were raised on roughly cleared pastures from the 1850s, followed by intensive dairying and market-gardening. These activities persist today but the prime industry of the region is coalmining in the Latrobe Valley (since the 1920s) and more recently offshore production of oil and natural gas. The region's main towns are Bairnsdale, Sale, Moe, Traralgon and Morwell, the last three being industrial, residential and service centres for the coal industry.

Gippsland Lakes Vic. This group of shallow coastal lagoons, separated from Bass Strait by a broad sandy barrier known as the Ninety Mile Beach, together form the largest navigable inland waterway in Australia. The main lakes – Wellington, Victoria and King, which were created by wave action within the lagoon system – cover an area of 340sq.km and have a shoreline of 320km. The lakes complex is fed by five large rivers – the Latrobe, Avon, Nicholson, Tambo and Mitchell – and is characterised by flat coastal plains and wetlands. When the lakes were discovered by Angus McMillan in 1839–40, their natural sea entrance was further east; creation of the present artificial entrance, at the township of > *Lakes Entrance*, in 1889 has allowed more sea water to enter the lakes and thus increased salinity to the extent that the region's natural vegetation and wildlife have altered dramatically and in some cases been lost; pollution and erosion in the catchment area is also of increasing concern to local authorities. The lakes have long been a popular holiday destination, noted particularly for fishing, and in recent years they have also attracted a growing number of permanent residents.

Gladstone Qld (pop. 22 033) The State's premier port city, lying on Port Curtis about 540km north of Brisbane, Gladstone underwent dramatic urban expansion in the 1980s as the result of a sustained industrial boom since 1960. Settlement dates from 1847, when William Gladstone, then secretary of state for the colonies, proposed to colonise the area with ex-convicts; while the plan was countermanded, settlement nevertheless occurred and the town developed as a regional centre for the rural hinterland. Recent industrial developments include a diesel electric railway bringing coal from central Qld for export to Japan, an alumina refinery smelter, a power station that supplies 60% of the State's needs, and large cement works; tourism has also gathered pace, and a marina complex was constructed recently to service the yachts, fishing boats and cruisers which are the stuff of local recreation.

Glanville-Hicks, Peggy (1912–), music composer and critic, b. Melbourne. After studying at the Royal College of Music in London, Glanville-Hicks started composing; she later moved to the US, where she was a notable figure in the contemporary music field and music critic of the New York *Herald Tribune* 1948–58. Represented at the International Society for Contemporary Music festivals in 1938 and 1948, her compositions include *Choral Suite* (1938), the ballet *The Masque of the Wild Man* (1959), and the operas, *Nausicaa* (1961) and *Sappho* (1966).

Glasshouse Mountains Qld This is a group of eleven peaks rising dramatically from the coastal plain about 70km north of Brisbane; the highest is Mt Beerwah (555m). The mountains are volcanic plugs – the cores of volcanoes long extinct – composed of rhyolite and trachyte. They were named in 1770 by James Cook, but whether this was because the smooth rocks reflected the sun, like glass, or because they resembled glass furnaces, is uncertain. Four of the mountains are declared national parks.

glass manufacture Australia's first glassblowing factory was started by the merchant Simeon Lord in 1813 in Sydney, but the venture was not successful. In 1872 the Melbourne Glass Bottle Works was set up as a subsidiary of a pharmaceutical firm; this company expanded Australia-wide and became Australian Glass Manufacturers Co. Ltd in 1915 and subsequently Australian Consolidated Industries

(ACI) in 1939; it is today Australia's major glass manufacturer. Recently there has been a revival in stained, blown and kiln-formed glass as an art form.

glasswort > *saltbush family*

Gleeson, James Timothy (1915–), painter, b. Sydney. Recognised as Australia's first surrealist painter, Gleeson was early influenced by Salvador Dali and has continued to paint in this style since his first exhibition in 1939. He has made a valuable contribution to Australian art as a critic, lecturer and curator.

Glenelg River Vic. This river rises in the Grampians and flows southwest for some 470km to an estuary on Discovery Bay. Its upper reaches are dammed at the Rocklands reservoir and this is the chief storage for the Wimmera–Mallee supply system, serving both domestic and livestock needs. The Lower Glenelg National Park includes the 65km, wide rocky gorge, where the river passes between cliffs up to 46m high. The river was discovered by Thomas Mitchell in 1836 and named after Lord Glenelg, secretary of state for the colonies.

Glenrowan Vic. (pop. 216) This small town 220km northeast of Melbourne is best known as the site of the last siege of the bushranging > *Kelly gang*, in 1880. It is at the centre of a grazing and agricultural district, but the town's economy depends largely on tourism centred on the Kelly episode.

gliders > *possums*

gliding > *sky sports*

Glover, John (1767–1849), painter, b. England. After a successful career as an artist in England, working first with watercolours and later with oils, Glover joined his sons in Australia in 1830. He bought land in Tas. in exchange for paintings, and from his 2800ha station near Ben Lomond he produced a large number of landscape paintings, many of which were exhibited in London in 1835. Distinguished by his appreciation of Australian colour, landforms and light, he was also one of the few early painters who portrayed Aboriginal society and traditions.

glow-worms These light-producing larvae of the fungus-gnat genus *Arachnocampa* of

Australia and NZ should not be confused with fireflies, which are beetles. The larvae, found in caves, rock overhangs and even moist, shaded road-cuts, possess luminescent organs at the tips of their translucent abdomens; the light serves to attract insect prey, which become entangled in mucilaginous webs secreted by the larvae. The light is extinguished if the animals are disturbed.

GMH General Motors Holden's Ltd was formed in 1931 by the merger of an Australian subsidiary of the US company General Motors with Holden's Motor Body Builders Ltd. The latter was an Adelaide firm of which the managing director was E.W. (later Sir Edward) Holden, who with his father had established the business in 1917. GMH initially assembled British and US vehicles, but during World War 2 produced all types of armaments including aircraft engines and guns. Following the federal government's proposal for an Australian-made car, the GMH design was accepted in 1945 and the first car was produced in 1948: it was immediately and enormously successful, and the millionth Holden came off the assembly line in 1962. In the 1950s GMH held 50% of the new-vehicle market, but in the face of Japanese competition this share had dropped to 17% by 1987 and the company had a long run of profitless years. Following a drastic restructuring in 1988, GMH has been turned round and is now second only to Ford in the local market.

goanna > *lizards*

gobies > *fishes, freshwater and marine*

gold The discovery of payable gold in Australia in the 1850s had far-reaching economic, social and political effects on the young country. Although production declined after 1910 and new discoveries have been few, interest in gold-mining has revived since 1980 as the result of the freezing of gold prices in the late 1960s, more recent price increases, and modern cost-effective mining methods. Between 20 and 30 mines a year were opened or commissioned in the 1980s and retreatment has commenced at many old centres. Australia is now the third-ranking gold producer in the world: gold has been the fastest-growing export since 1981 and by the late 1980s was one of the few bright spots in the bearish mineral industry. WA accounts for about 70% of annual production.

The gold rushes The first record of gold is in the 1823 notebook of a road surveyor working near Fish Creek, NSW. The next sightings – by explorer Paul Strzelecki in 1839 and the Rev. Clarke in 1841 – were suppressed: when Clarke showed specimens of his find to Governor Gipps and several members of the NSW legislative council in 1844, Gipps is reported to have said, 'Put it away or we'll all have our throats cut'. The Californian gold rush of 1839 and the resulting exodus of men from the Australian colonies soon, however, caused the government to reverse this policy.

The first official discoverer of gold was > *Edward Hargraves*, who used his panning experience from the Californian diggings to find gold near Bathurst in February 1851. Coupled with finds by his associates this started a gold rush, for which he was handsomely rewarded by the government. By the end of 1851 more than 5000 men had taken out gold-mining licences in NSW.

Vic. employers – alarmed by the diminishing labour force and by a current depression – offered a reward for payable gold found within 320km of Melbourne. This was won by James Esmond for his find at Clunes in July 1851; his success was soon repeated at Castlemaine, Ballarat and Bendigo in 1851, and in the Ovens Valley fields in 1852. The Vic. fields were more compact, more rapidly discovered and much richer than those of NSW; there, however, new finds were made at Araluen (near the coast) in 1851, near Tamworth and further north on the Gwydir River in 1852, at Kiandra on the Snowy River in 1859, at Lambing Flat near Young in 1860, and at Grenfell (then Emu Creek) in 1866.

SA had only minor rushes, to Echunga in 1852 and Gawler in 1869. In Qld there were minor finds near Rockhampton from 1858, the first sustained rush being to Gympie in 1867; Mt Morgan, the 'mountain of gold', was developed from finds in 1882, and Charters Towers in 1872 – the year that saw a major but short-lived rush to the Palmer River area. In the NT, gold was found in the course of constructing the Overland Telegraph, and a disastrous rush to the alternately searing and steaming Pine Creek region cost many their health and savings. In the 1890s the main focus shifted to WA: the Kimberley field (discovered in 1885) had dwindled, but sporadic gold was being found in a 3000km belt south to Norseman. From 1892 prospectors poured into Coolgardie and nearby Hannon's Find – the beginnings of Kalgoorlie.

Until September 1852, migration in search of gold was between the colonies only. Then came the overseas influx – 95 000 in 1852 alone, of whom at least 80 000 stayed inVic.; Europeans predominated, but there were also Americans and (from 1856) Chinese. The early goldfields were a scene of frantic activity by blue-shirted workers in a lunar landscape of shafts, holes and heaps, shanties and tents – waterlogged in winter, saharan in summer. There was considerable order, honesty and discipline among the diggers, nevertheless, in contrast to the hysterical urban scene where many squandered their finds. Violence did occur on the fields as the result of grievances over licences (which led to the > *Eureka Stockade* incident in 1854), from anti-Chinese feeling, and from disputes over claims (as in the Tipperary riots near Maryborough in 1855).

Surface gold was exhausted very soon. Deeper 'leads' in old, buried alluvium were still accessible for some years, but the chance of finding them was rare and it was back-breaking work to sink and line the shafts, and extract and wash the ore. For a time it was also possible to crush gold-bearing rock with primitive stamping and washing equipment, but as the surface reefs gave out deeper mining was required and this in turn demanded capital: innumerable companies were formed that depended on small investors and employed labour. The digger's day was over – many made little; a number, a working wage; a few, a fortune.

The effects of the gold rushes Through uncovering great wealth and trebling the population of the colonies in just ten years, the gold rushes hastened constitutional development, encouraged diversification in the economy and led to a growing dominance of urban over rural settlements. Such was the rate of economic growth that the period 1860–90 is often described as the 'long boom', increased immigration ensuring a continued demand for goods and services. It was in Vic. that the wider effects of the gold rushes were first and perhaps most remarkably demonstrated, since between 1851 and 1861 its population rose from 97 000 to 539 000 – the increase being more than the total population of the colonies in 1850 and ushering in great social change.

The political impact of gold was widespread. Resentment at the digger's licence widened to include demands for suffrage so that diggers could be represented on the legislative council, then dominated by hostile squatters. As easy pickings disappeared, a drought and depression in 1864 turned ex-diggers' attention to the land only to find it, too, locked in the hands of the squatters, and access to small selections was included in their demands. Gold also hastened the end of transportation, since a penal colony with gold for the getting was ludicrous. In WA it was the vote of the miners – largely those from the eastern States – that pushed the colony into Federation. The longstanding > *White Australia Policy* was partly rooted in the animosity between European and Chinese miners at the diggings, which led the Vic. parliament to restrict Chinese immigration as early as the 1850s. >> *economy*; *mining industry*; *racial conflict*

Gold Coast Qld (pop. 84 001) Australia's most developed, commercialised and popular resort centre, which includes the famous Surfers Paradise beach, the Gold Coast is a city extending for 32km of sandy coastline from Southport to Coolangatta on the NSW border. Coolangatta is a 'twin town' with the NSW port of Tweed Heads, which is also part of the Gold Coast conurbation. The area's first hotel, at Southport, was built in 1876; the city has grown most quickly and continuously since building regulations were eased in 1952, which led to continuing high-rise development that has caused overshadowing of the beaches and environmental problems such as accelerated erosion. Today the Gold Coast depends almost entirely on tourists, with the population trebling in summer, but its permanent population continues to grow with the influx of many southerners.

Golden Mile This is the name given to the incredibly rich gold-bearing reef about 8km south of > *Kalgoorlie*, WA. Extending for about 3km by 2km, it was first discovered in 1893 by Patrick Hannon and initiated a rush to the area. The greatest concentrations of gold are in the deep-lying telluride ores, which require expensive methods of extraction and processing but yielded up to 100 000kg of gold in less than a century.

Goldfields and Agricultural Water Supply WA This vast pipeline system developed from the engineering masterpiece of 1896–1903, the goldfields water supply scheme. Now linked with the Perth and Southern Town water supplies, it also serves more than 90 towns in the wheat-sheep belts of WA and 2.7 million ha of farmland as well as the south-western nickel mines.

In the 1880s, water for WA's eastern goldfields – centred on Coolgardie and Kalgoorlie – was condensed from brackish lakes and groundwater, and typhoid outbreaks were common. The government announced a proposal to pipe water to the area from the Darling Range in 1895 and construction of the Mundaring weir began two years later. The scheme met with much opposition from affected landholders, a contributing cause of the suicide of its chief engineer, > *Charles Yelverton O'Connor*.

The project, completed in 1903, comprised 550km of 75cm pipes and eight steam-driven pumping stations which raised the water to a second reservoir from where gravity led it to the goldfields. The capacity of the Mundaring weir was about 21 000ML, which has since been increased nearly fourfold. >> *water and water resources*

Goldsbrough, Richard (1821–86), woolbroker, b. England. Goldsbrough immigrated to Melbourne in 1847, eventually – through his company Goldsborough, Mort & Co. Ltd – becoming the city's leading woolbroker. He helped to establish efficient woolbroking systems in Australia, encouraged the marketing of Australian wool overseas and developed the financial arrangements that made possible Australia's great pastoral expansion 1860–90.

Goldstein, Vida Jane Mary (1869–1949), feminist and suffragist, b. Portland, Vic. Initiated by her mother into working for women's suffrage, Goldstein became head of the United Council for Women's Suffrage in Melbourne in 1899. In 1902 she attended the first international women's suffrage conference in the US, and a year later formed the Melbourne Women's Political Association; she was supported by the association when she became one of the first four Australian women to stand for federal parliament in 1903. Goldstein stood twice for the House of Representatives and three times for the Senate 1903–17, but never won a seat. In 1911 she travelled to England to support the British suffragists. An outspoken pacifist during World War 1, she formed the Women's Peace Army in 1915 and in 1919 represented Australia at an international peace conference in Zurich. She withdrew from public life on her return to Australia and devoted the rest of her life to Christian Science. The Vic. federal seat of Goldstein is named after her.

golf Australia is remarkably well endowed with golf courses, but with more than 300 000 men and 130 000 women registered as members of golf clubs and an additional demand from many hundreds of thousands of casual players, driving ranges are now being introduced to ease the pressure. At the same time, a number of Japanese consortiums are investigating the possibility of purchasing existing courses or constructing new ones to meet the demand from their own golfers.

Golf was first played in Tas. by Scotsman Alexander Reid in the early 1820s, but the first course was established on Melbourne's Flagstaff Hill in 1847. Interest in the game spread through the colonies but for some time it remained a minority sport, usually pursued by Scottish settlers; it became established in the 1880s, and the leading clubs were granted the 'Royal' prefix. Women began to take up the game during the 1890s.

The first player to achieve national prominence was Ivo Whitton, five times winner of the Australian Open between 1912 and 1931. The first to achieve international recognition was Jim Ferrier, who in the 1930s won five Australian amateur championships and two opens; he turned professional in 1940 and in 1947 became the first Australian to win the US Open. Prominent players on the local and international circuit in the 1950s included Ossie Pickworth, Norman Von Nida, Kel Nagle and > Peter Thomson, the last-named winning the British Open five times and, with Nagle, the Canada Cup in 1954 and 1959. In the 1960s and 1970s Bruce Devlin, Bruce Crampton and David Graham competed successfully on the US circuit, and in so doing achieved millionaire status. Jan Stephenson's victory in the US Women's Open in 1983 was seen as a great breakthrough for women's golf in Australia. In the 1980s > Greg Norman, recognised as one of the world's greatest players, became a national sporting idol, with victories in more than 50 major tournaments.

Gondwana This is the name given to the southern-hemisphere supercontinent that began to split up and drift apart some 150 million years ago. The fragments formed present-day Australia, Antarctica, South America, Africa, the Indian peninsula, Madagascar and NZ; in a reconstruction of Gondwanaland, South America is joined to the Atlantic coast of Africa and part of Antarctica fits into the Great Australian Bight.

It is at present believed that Africa and South America separated from each other about 110 million years ago, the Atlantic Ocean appearing between them. Africa parted from Antarctica about 90 million years ago, NZ about 80 million years ago, India and Australia respectively about 65 and 45 million years ago. After its separation Australia moved northwards, taking NG with it. Evidence for unity of the present-day continents is seen in similar geological formations and common fossil flora and fauna in the regions where they are believed to have been joined. These conclusions result from the development of the > continental drift theory, according to which Gondwanaland, 200 million years ago, was itself part of a single landmass, Pangaea. >> fauna; flora; fossils

goodenias The Goodeniaceae family of flowering plants is confined to Australia, where eleven of its seventeen genera of shrubs, herbs and climbers are endemic. The mostly blue or yellow flowers are distinctive, usually with the lower petals spread out like a hand or fan. Goodenia is the largest genus, with 170 or so native species throughout Australia, the yellow flowers of some herbaceous species being seasonally conspicuous on inland plains. The genus Scaevola has about 80 Australian species and is also the genus most widespread beyond Australia, chiefly on tropical seashores. The 66 Dampiera species, on the other hand, are strictly endemic. The most brilliantly coloured flowers are found in the endemic (chiefly western) genus Lechenaultia; the blue-flowered L. biloba being one of WA's best-known wildflowers.

Goolagong, Evonne Fay > Cawley, Evonne

Goolwa SA (pop. 2359) A rural centre and resort town about 90km south of Adelaide, Goolwa is 12km from the mouth of the Murray River near Lake Alexandrina. A key port in riverboat days, the area has a strong tradition of shipbuilding, trade and fishing. The first (horse-drawn) public SA railway took produce from Goolwa to Victor Harbor (1856).

Goossens, Sir (Aynsley) Eugene (1893–1962), musical conductor and composer, b. England. A member of a well-known Anglo-Belgian musical family, Goossens was appointed resident conductor of the Sydney Symphony Orchestra in 1946 and director of the NSW Conservatorium of Music in 1947. An important figure in raising Australian orchestral standards, Goossens resigned his posts and left Australia in 1956 following a scandal concerning an attempt he made to import prohibited personal items. He composed more than 70 works, including two symphonies, two operas and an oratorio.

Gordon, Adam Lindsay (1833–70), poet, b. Azores.

Of English parentage, Gordon was sent to SA in 1853 after a reckless youth; he became a police trooper, then a horse-breaker and steeplechase rider. Proud, shy and melancholy, he shot himself after financial downfall and his daughter's death, just as his second and successful book was about to appear: *Bush Ballads and Galloping Rhymes* (1870). Although generally regarded as mediocre, his verse was spirited and seen as typifying the new, adventurous country; it was exceedingly popular, as the result not only of its appeal to the burgeoning 'bush' ethos of the day but also of Gordon's life of reckless derring-do and dramatic death.

Gordon River

Tas. In the mountainous southwest of the State, the 200km Gordon River rises in King William Range, flows south and then turns northwest to Macquarie Harbour. Its chief tributaries are the Franklin, Denison and Olga rivers. Construction of a dam on the Gordon above its junction with the Serpentine has created Lake Gordon, with an area of 272sq.km. A plan to further dam the Gordon below its junction with the Franklin created bitter controversy in the early 1980s; the region is a spectacular wilderness, much of it reserved as national parks – notably the Franklin-Lower Gordon Wild Rivers National Park – and a large part listed as a wilderness area by the World Heritage Commission. Federal intervention and a High Court decision prevented the proposed dam construction.

Gorham, Kathleen (1932–83), dancer, b. Sydney.

Having joined the Borovansky Ballet in 1947, Gorham danced leading roles with the English Ballet Rambert 1947–9, the Ballet de Paris in France in 1949, the Sadler's Wells Theatre Ballet in London 1951–2, and the prestigious Grand Ballet du Marquis de Cuevas in Paris in 1953. Returning to Australia in 1954, she danced again with the Borovansky Ballet and was the first prima ballerina with the newly founded Australian Ballet 1962–6. Gorham was renowned for her strongly drama-

tic style and expressive talent, used to great advantage in Robert Helpmann's ballets *The Display* (1964) and *Yugen* (1965). She retired in 1966 and became a teacher.

Gorton, Sir John Grey (1911–), politician, b. Melbourne.

A grazier, Gorton was elected as a federal Liberal senator in 1949. After holding various ministries under R.G. Menzies and Harold Holt, following the latter's death in 1968 he was the first senator ever to be elected prime minister. He subsequently entered the House of Representatives, but was forced by dissension in his own party to resign as prime minister in 1971. Gorton was always outspoken, his informal lifestyle and crumpled features (the result of injury sustained during his RAAF service during World War 2) making him a generally popular figure except in the hierarchy of his own party.

Gosford

NSW (pop. 109 278) The main centre of the beautiful > *Brisbane Water* area, the city of Gosford is 85km north of Sydney. The city incorporates the resort and commuter town of Woy Woy, as well as Umina, Blackwell, Booker Bay, Ettalong and Pearl Beach. The region has long been a popular holiday and retirement centre but more recently has also become a commuter base for Sydney workers and has experienced substantial urban growth. As well as administrative and service functions, it has a variety of manufacturing industries. The attractive local sandstone is valued for building and ornamental construction.

goshawks > *eagles and hawks*

Goulburn

NSW (pop. 21 552) A cathedral city and the transport, service and market centre for the northeast region of the southern tablelands, Goulburn lies 208km south of Sydney. From the 1830s it was a garrison and convict town; it still has a maximum security jail and a police academy. Goulburn is a general centre for education, professional services, wool and stock sales, and meatworks, and a major railway depot and junction on the Sydney–Melbourne route; manufactures include textiles and footwear. Its annual lilac festival attracts many tourists. The city was named after Henry Goulburn, under-secretary for the colonies 1812–21.

Goulburn River

Vic. Rising on the northern slopes of the Great Dividing Range, the Goulburn flows some 550km to the Murray

River above Echuca. Much of its flow is now diverted by the Eildon reservoir, the Goulburn weir and the Warenga Basin, and this has created salinity problems. Eildon is the main storage for the Goulburn Valley irrigation scheme, one of Australia's major irrigation projects. Seymour and Shepparton are the chief towns of the Goulburn Valley, which supports fruit- and grain-growing, beef cattle and dairying. At the headwaters of the river is Fraser National Park.

Gould, John (1804–81), ornithologist, b. England. Trained as a taxidermist and married to Elizabeth Coxen, a skilled artist, Gould saw business possibilities in illustrated bird books. Having already produced volumes on Himalayan and European birds, he set sail for Australia in 1838 and spent nearly two years on the continent collecting specimens, assisted by John Gilbert. Upon return to England he published (with the help of his wife) his famous *Birds of Australia*, comprising 681 plates and appearing in 36 parts. He later produced the three-volume *Mammals of Australia* (1845–63), and *Handbook to the Birds of Australia* (1865). Although he spent little time in Australia, he is regarded as the 'father' of Australian bird-study; the Gould Leagues perpetuate his name.

Gould, Nat(haniel) (1857–1919), journalist and novelist, b. England. Short, tubby, jovial and the possessor of a luxuriant moustache, Gould left business for journalism and spent eleven years in Australia from 1884. He became a racing tipster for the Sydney *Referee*, and before returning to England wrote the first nine of his 130 – mainly sporting – novels, including *The Double Event* (1891). Sales of his books, some 40 of which were set in Australia, have been estimated in tens of millions.

Gould, Shane > *swimming and diving*

Gould, William Buelow (1801–53), convict artist, b. England. Transported for theft in 1827 and sent to Port Arthur (1833) for continual drunkenness, Gould was finally freed in 1835. Circumstances notwithstanding, he completed many beautiful, small still-life paintings and botanical studies, some fine portraits (including Aborigines, commissioned by George Robinson) and historically important sketches of Macquarie Harbour, made during his imprisonment there.

Gould Leagues This group of organisations was established to promote the knowledge and protection of wildlife, especially to schoolchildren. Named after ornithologist > *John Gould*, the first organisation was formed in 1908, based on the similar Audubon Societies of the US and originally known as the Gould League of Bird Lovers. The name was later shortened to reflect an interest in all wildlife. The leagues, now established in several States, have been active in producing literature, magazines and films, and were major conservation groups before the advent in the 1970s of organisations such as the Australian Conservation Foundation and the Tas. Wilderness Society.

Gove Peninsula NT The northeastern peninsula of > *Arnhem Land*, Gove is part of the traditional territory of the Yirrkala people and was the centre of a key land-rights case in the late 1960s and early 1970s. The peninsula has been under Aboriginal control since 1976 and the region's substantial bauxite deposits are being developed by arrangement with the local community. Nhulunby, constructed by the mining company Nabalco, is the main settlement for the industry and contains an alumina reduction plant. Most Aborigines now reside at the former Methodist mission, established in 1953. >> *land rights, Aboriginal*

government Australia is a parliamentary democracy based on the UK model, but unlike the Westminster system in Australia the primacy of parliament is limited by the > *Constitution*; in addition, as evidenced by the > *constitutional crisis 1975*, the authority of the House of Representatives can in practice be constrained by the Senate. The retention of the British monarch as nominal head of the Australian government has been a matter of public debate since the 19th century; however, while the notion of an Australian republic has reasonable support, the nation's sentimental attachment to the monarchy makes it an unlikely vote-winner for some years to come.

The right to govern, in both the national and State parliaments, is held by the political party (or coalition of parties) with the most representatives in the lower house, as determined by periodic > *elections*. The three-tiered system of government – federal, State and local – is a complex and cumbersome one, and on a per-capita basis Australia is often said to be the most overgoverned nation in the world.

Historical development Early legislative, executive and judicial authority was wielded by the governor alone, under orders from the secretary of state in London. Doubts about the legitimacy of this warrant were expressed by – among others – the noted English jurist, Jeremy Bentham. The governor's rule was challenged effectively, if illegally, first by officers of the NSW Corps and later by factions such as exclusivists, emancipists and squatters.

Proper political institutions were established only slowly. The NSW Judicature Act of 1823 created an advisory, nominated legislative council and a smaller executive council. A colonial secretary and a number of administrators were also sent from London, which often resulted in serious conflicts with the governors.

The legislative council was enlarged and given greater power in 1828. A further advance towards self-government was made in 1842 through an Act that made the council two-thirds elective, although the high property qualifications required of members vested most of this power in the hands of the squatters rather than the increasing urban population. The Australian Colonies Government Act of 1850 established legislative councils for the separate self-governing colonies, which were maintained until > *Federation*. Constitutions were approved for NSW, Vic., Tas. and SA by 1855, for Qld in 1859 and for WA in 1890.

The legislature Since 1901 Australia has had a federal system of government, with a Commonwealth and six State parliaments each described by a written and in some respects inflexible constitution; the ACT and NT have representative councils. In the federal and State parliaments the leader of the majority party automatically becomes respectively prime minister or premier, and in practice controls the operation of parliament.

The Australian national parliament officially includes the sovereign (represented by the governor-general) as well as the two houses. The lower house, or House of Representatives, comprises 148 members elected at least every three years: members come from single constituencies and voting (since 1918) is by the preferential method. The upper house, or Senate, is composed of twelve members from each State and two from each of the Territories; for Senate elections each State or Territory forms a multimember constituency, and voting is by proportional representation. State senators are elected for six years and those from the ACT and NT for three years. The Senate's dual role – representing the interests of the States and reviewing legislation – is constrained to a large degree by party politics; there is also continuing debate about the extent to which the Senate is representative, as each State and Territory has the same number of senators regardless of population size.

The State parliamentary system follows this modified Westminster model, but with some differences. All States have a governor as the sovereign's representative and (except for Qld, which abolished its upper house in 1922) two houses of parliament. The lower house is called the legislative assembly in NSW, Vic. and WA, and the house of assembly in Tas. and SA (Qld's single house remains the legislative assembly also); all upper houses are called legislative councils. Members of the lower house are elected for four years, except in Qld. The term for members of the legislative council is usually twice that for those of the lower house, except in NSW where it is three times as long; voting is by proportional representation in NSW and SA.

The State Constitutions, which all date from the colonial period, are relatively straightforward definitive and procedural documents. Unlike the federal Constitution they can be amended by the relevant parliament, although some sections (such as those dealing with the abolition of upper houses) may be changed only with popular consent through referendums. The Constitutions generally require that money bills originate in the lower house, and prevent their amendments by the legislative council; NSW and SA have deadlock provisions, but even so the powers of upper houses remain controversial.

In the NT and ACT, the head of the majority party in parliament is designated chief minister rather than premier, and the sovereign's representative (appointed by the governor-general) is called an administrator. Members of the single house of parliament – the legislative assembly – are elected for four years. > *Local government* falls within State jurisdiction. There are some 850 municipal and shire councils.

The executive Although the executive power of Australian governments is technically vested in the British monarch, represented by the governor-general or governors, in practice this authority is exercised by a cabinet of leading members of the majority party in the lower house. (Like the office of prime minister, cabinet is not formally recognised in the Constitution.) The prime minister and premiers select ministers and allocate portfolios except in the case of the ALP, where caucus elects the ministry. In federal parliament, cabinet consists of 'senior' ministers only – a practice introduced by R.G. Menzies in the 1950s and continued by all succeeding governments except that of Gough Whitlam; at the State level, all ministers are cabinet members. Cabinet is the linchpin of the executive and makes the major policy and administrative decisions, although it is not as powerful as its British counterpart. The federal and State Constitutions contain rules on the proportion of ministers to be chosen from each house.

Ministers are responsible for 'the business of government': they run the government departments and must answer to both parliament and the public for the conduct of such affairs. In practice, ministerial control over the public service is less than perfect, as demonstrated by various royal commissions during the 1980s. The size and role of the bureaucracy has varied widely: the seven original Commonwealth departments had grown to 37 by 1972 but were cut to 30 in 1987; the latter change also saw the introduction of junior ministers. The > *public service* comprises all government departments and organisations. >> *colonial administration*; *federalism*; *law and legal system*; *local government*; *political parties*

governors > *government*; Appendix

governors-general > *government*; Appendix

Goyder's Line This line of demarcation, established in SA in 1865 by the surveyor George Goyder, separates the drought-prone arid region from potential agricultural land. The line starts near the base of Yorke Peninsula and runs north into the Flinders Ranges, turning east near Mt Remarkable and running south parallel to the eastern edge of the Mt Lofty Ranges. It follows the southern limit of saltbush, and approximately bounds the zone of 250mm annual rainfall, considered suitable for agriculture. About 80% of SA lies in the arid zone north of the line.

Grafton NSW (pop. 16 647) Grafton is the main centre for the Clarence River area, 670km north of Sydney, and an important road and rail junction. The city, which has many jacaranda-lined avenues, has been severely flooded several times; North Grafton has been protected by a levee bank since 1972, and one for South Grafton is being constructed. The area's estab-

lished activities include brewing, timber-milling and farming (cattle, pork and dairy products); along the lower river, sugar, fishing and processing, prawn farming and fruit growing form the bulk of industrial activity, with tourism centring on the Yamba area. New developments include building-products manufacture, woodchip exports, and horse-breeding.

grain > *cereals and grains*; *fodder crops*; *wheat*

Grainger, Percy Aldridge (1882–1961), pianist and composer, b. Brighton, Vic. After studying piano and composition in Germany, Grainger toured the world as a concert pianist, but his interest shifted gradually to the study of folk music and innovative musical forms. He became a US citizen in 1918 and lived most of his life in that country, being head of the music department at New York University 1932–3. Although a serious composer of experimental music, Grainger is perhaps best known for his popular works such as *Country Gardens* and *Handel in the Strand*. The current revival of interest in his work is in part due to a prurient curiosity about Grainger's relationship with his possessive mother and his eccentric sexual practices.

Gramineae > *grasses and grasslands*

Grampian Ranges Vic. The Grampians comprise three sandstone ranges forming a north–south arc some 145km long, lying about 250km southwest of Melbourne. The highest is the Mt William Range (1167m), at the eastern end of the system; the others are the Serra Range, terminating in the noted tourist feature Halls Gap, and the arching Mt Difficult Range to the north. The Grampian Ranges were first explored in 1836, by Thomas Mitchell, who named them after a Scottish mountain range. The rugged Grampians landscape, now listed on the register of the national estate, has long been a popular tourist destination noted for its seasonal wildflower displays and diverse flora and fauna. The region is an important catchment: it receives 750mm average annual rainfall and is the source of the Glenelg River, the waters of which are impounded in the Rocklands reservoir to supply the arid Mallee-Wimmera region further inland.

Granites, the NT This rocky outcrop rises from the spinifex and desert plains of the

> *Tanami Desert*, about 500km northwest of Alice Springs. It was the scene of the last great Australian gold rush, in 1932; hundreds of aspiring miners battled through the trackless, waterless wastes to no avail and many were soon destitute. Mining commenced in the 1980s, however, with anticipated production of some 300 000t of ore a year.

grape family The flowering-plant family Vitaceae is mainly tropical, the deciduous grape genus *Vitis* (which includes wine grapes) of temperate regions representing an evolutionary offshoot. Nearly all members of the family are climbers, for which they bear tendrils or adhesive pads; the small flowers are greenish and the fruit is a dark fleshy berry. Australia has five native genera, with a total of about 40 species. The delicate vine *Clematicissus* is the only endemic genus, its single species confined to a small area of WA. *Cissus* is the largest genus, with around 20 native species most of which are rainforest climbers although the native grape, *C. hypoglauca*, extends as far south as eastern Vic. The kangaroo vine, *C. antarctica*, is popular as an indoor plant but grows into a giant liana in the wild. The other native genera are *Tetrastigma, Cayratia* and *Ampelocissus*, species of the last two being characteristic of monsoonal woodlands in far northern Australia.

grapes, cultivated > *dried-fruits industry*; *wine industry*

grasses and grasslands Grasses belong to the family Poaceae (or Gramineae), of which there are at least 10 000 species in some 670 genera. One of the largest flowering-plant families in the world, grasses are also arguably the most important plant group in terms of both natural ecosystems and human economy: they occur (often in abundance) in nearly all other vegetation types, and their nutritious seeds (cereal grains) have long been exploited as a source of food and fodder.

Major grass types Australia has a rich grass flora, with some 900 native species (mostly endemic) in about 150 genera. While the distinctive mound-forming grasses of inland plains are often termed 'spinifexes', they are unrelated to the three native species of the true *Spinifex* genus. These are the common beach grasses of coastal sands, the creeping stems of which bind and thus stabilise sand dunes; their foliage is silvery and the seeds are in spidery globular heads (a familiar sight as they are bowled across the sand by winds). Couch is the common name for almost any small creeping grass. The cosmopolitan salt couch, *Sporobolus virginicus*, is common in coastal saltmarshes and damp sands; the common couch, *Cynodon dactylon*, also cosmopolitan, is frequent in less saline although usually sandy ground from the coast to the far inland. The common reed, *Phragmites australis*, grows in shallow fresh water throughout temperate Australia; in the tropics its place is taken by the tropical reed, *P. karka*. Blady grass, *Imperata cylindrica*, dominates the understorey in wetter forest country of eastern and northern Australia, wherever there is sufficient light; one of the few native grasses with a deeply buried rhizome, it produces spaced vertical shoots with distinctive ribbon-like leaves and is one of the first plants to resprout after bushfires. Kangaroo grass, *Themeda australis*, is one of the most widespread native grasses, distinctive for its brownish tufted seedheads: it often forms mats on exposed coastal headlands, or grows to a metre or more in fertile inland valleys. *Poa* is strictly a temperate genus of which about 35 species are native to Australia, the majority alpine or subalpine and known as snow grasses; they are the chief tussock grasses of these regions. The genus *Stipa* includes more than 60 native species, also entirely temperate. Known as speargrasses for their long pointed seedheads, they range over many habitats and vary greatly in size: some species are the dominant grasses on certain soil types and provide good grazing, although the seeds cause problems in sheep fleeces and may penetrate their flesh. In warmer areas, the 50 or so native species of *Aristida* are another major group of speargrasses, although their distinct three-pronged seedheads have earned them the additional names three-awn and wire-grass. Another important speargrass genus is *Heteropogon*, especially in subcoastal tropical woodlands and grasslands. The common species is bunch speargrass, *H. contortus*, so-called for its tangled masses of needle-sharp seedheads; in Qld it often forms a continuous understorey to scattered trees. The endemic Mitchell grass genus *Astrebla* consists of four species of perennial tussock grasses occurring in the central and northern inland, usually on river flood-plains. The love-grass genus, *Eragrostis*, is among the most diverse in both growth habit and distribution of its 50-odd native species. In arid regions is found the largest species, swamp canegrass, *E. australasica*, a bamboo-like plant with waxy blue stems which grows in mud. Very different is woollybutt or neverfail, *E. eriopoda*, a dominant but smallish grass over large areas of the inland on sandy soils; the bases of its stems are thickened, with a knot of woolly-haired bracts.

The most significant endemic grass genera are *Triodia* and *Plectrachne*, the so-called spinifexes or porcupine grasses that dominate hummock grasslands. With respectively about 40 and sixteen species, they are both most diverse in WA. Most of their species form dense mounds 1–2m high and have rigid, needle-like leaves; many exude a sticky aromatic resin used by Aborigines as an adhesive. Other large and important genera are *Panicum*, panics or millets; *Digitaria*, umbrella grass or summer grass; *Brachiaria*, armgrasses; *Sorghum*, sorghums; *Eriachne*, wanderrie grasses; and *Danthonia*, wallaby grasses. Bamboos are represented by only three native species, in the genus *Bambusa* of far northern Qld and the NT.

Grasslands In Australia's arid and semi-arid regions, and the limited alpine areas, grasses dominate to the extent that they form 'grasslands'.

Hummock grassland is dominated by grasses of the genus *Triodia*; covering very large areas of infertile sandy or stony ground in the centre and northwest, it forms a distinctive landscape of little value for stock grazing but providing shelter for a diverse fauna. The other major inland type of grassland, Mitchell grass plain, provides nutritious grazing and has suffered severely from grazing pressure; occupying a zone of slightly higher rainfall and fertile soils, mainly to the north and east of the hummock-grassland areas, it is dominated by several species of *Astrebla* or Mitchell grass as well as other genera. Mulga woodland, dominated by the small tree *Acacia aneura*, occupies more fertile soils of the far inland. This vegetation zone has abundant and diverse grasses providing valuable fodder for both native and introduced animals. In the more southern arid regions, such as the Nullarbor Plain, saltbushes and other shrubs often dominate treeless areas, but grasses are invariably an important component.

Tropical grasslands, of which native sorghum species are a major component, occur further to the north and northeast, covering a broad belt paralleling the coasts. Often carrying scattered trees, they are characterised by their height (1–3m) and extreme seasonality – dense and lush in the wet season and dead and brown in the dry.

In the cool, moist tablelands and valleys of the southeast (including Tas.), grasses often form the chief ground layer in eucalypt forests and dominate the valleys and frost-hollows. The most common species are tussock grasses of the genus *Poa*, which become predominant and more diverse in subalpine and alpine regions. >> *pasture plants*

grasshoppers, locusts and crickets Distinctive features of these insects of the order Orthoptera – a large order of which there are more than 1400 known species from Australia – are leathery forewings, membranous hindwings, hind legs developed for jumping, and organs of stridulation. Crickets form two families: Gryllotalpidae, the mole crickets, with front legs adapted for digging, and Gryllidae, the field crickets, one of which is the black field cricket, *Gryllus servillei*, often seen in gardens.

The nocturnal, greenish, long-horned grasshoppers of the family Tettigoniidae have long, hair-like antennae and are often found in trees and shrubs; the males stridulate by rubbing their wings together, and are often heard on warm, summer nights.

Short-horned grasshoppers have short antennae with fewer segments, and are usually active during the day; many are strong fliers, with long wings. Among these are the four Australian species of locusts, the best known of which is the plague locust, *Chorotoicetes terminifera*, spreading in great swarms as a serious pest of crops and pastures in years when the locust population has greatly multiplied and their local supply of food has been consumed. Scientific study of the movements and habits of these insects has made possible a considerable degree of control through careful surveillance of breeding areas; measures generally employed are sprays and poison baits, the latter being spread through swarms in the pre-adult, flightless stage, and eagerly consumed by the 'hoppers'. In recent years, however, baits have been largely superseded by aerial sprays.

grass-trees These distinctive plants of the genus *Xanthorrhoea* are a uniquely Australian group that comprises 28 species. Long-lived shrubs with rosettes of narrow grass-like leaves emanating from a short trunk or underground stem, they bear small white flowers densely packed on to a long cylindrical spike at the end of a bare stalk – the whole forming an erect spear-like structure. The combination of a 'spear' and fire-blackened trunk in some species gave rise to the plant's common name of 'blackboy'. Traditionally classified as a member of the family Liliaceae, *Xanthorrhoea* is now generally treated as a unique family, the Xanthorrhoeaceae, endemic to Australia. Grass-trees are confined largely to the eastern, southern and western coastal regions, often conspicuous in the vegetation in areas of poor sandy or stony soil. They are highly fire-resistant and among the first plants to sprout green foliage after a fierce bushfire; the scorched trunks exude a fragrant red resin formerly used in varnishes and in the manufacture of picric acid.

grass-wrens > *wrens*

Gray, Robin Trevor (1940–   ), politician, b. Melbourne. In Tas. from 1965, Gray was an agricultural consultant and lecturer, and farmers' advocate. He entered the Tas. parliament as a Liberal in 1976 and became leader of the Opposition in 1981. Premier of Tas. 1982–9, Gray was the first Liberal leader to win two successive elections in that State (the second in 1986) and under him the party also governed in its own right for the first time. As minister for forests 1984–6, Gray supported forest clearance and the timber industry in the face of growing opposition from conservationists; he lost government to the combined forces of Labor and Independent 'green' candidates in 1989.

grayling > *fishes, freshwater and marine*

Great Artesian Basin > *water and water resources*

Great Australian Bight WA/SA This vast indentation of the coasts of WA and SA extends for over 1100km from Cape Pasley, east of Esperance, to West Point, the tip of Eyre Peninsula. Much of the shoreline is composed of cliffs of up to 70m; part of it borders the Nullarbor Plain, also known as Bunda Plateau. There are settlements at Eyre and Eucla in WA, and at Ceduna in SA, southeast of which is Streaky Bay, the bight's only safe anchorage in an area notorious for its storms and rough seas. On the coast also are two national parks: Cape Arid, containing Cape Pasley, and Nullarbor, near the head of the bight.

Great Barrier Reef This spectacular string of reefs and islands extends for more than 2000km along Australia's east coast, from near the mouth of the Fly River in the Gulf of Papua south to a point east of Gladstone. The entire region is listed on the register of the national estate and is included on the World Heritage list. The reef follows the line of the ancient coast of Australia; three distinct sections – north, central and south – can be identified, according to depth, and overall there is a further distinction between outer and inner reefs.

The outer reefs of the system lie at the edge of the continental shelf – in the north at a depth generally less than 30m and in a series of curves 200–1000m wide, separated by narrow channels and rising from a steep submarine scarp; an almost unbroken line of breakers results. There are only four passages through the reef between the mainland and the Coral Sea, the only one navigable by large ships being > *Hydrographers Passage*. The outer edges of these reefs are living corals, crested with a ridge of sand, shells and coral detritus sloping westward into inner sheltered waters. South of Cairns the reefs become more scattered and in the central section (30–60m deep) appear to be degenerating, being subject to varying hydrological forces. In the southern section, at depths beyond 60m, the reefs tend to occur in clusters – such as the Swain and Capricorn groups between which there is a deep indentation creating the Capricorn Channel, the main southern passage through the barrier. Between shelf edge and shoreline rise innumerable inner reefs, many in crescent shapes formed by prevailing weather conditions and many also bearing mangrove-covered flats. Some have become small islands with a covering of sand or coral shingle, and sometimes vegetation; most larger islands are continental in origin – some steep, others low-lying and generally thickly vegetated, and many themselves fringed with coral.

Reef development is governed chiefly by fluctuating sea-levels. Some corals live and grow only in warm, shallow sea water and as the sea rises the lower coral dies; the remaining skeletons form a massive stony foundation on which new coral grows. As the sea-level has risen since the Pleistocene epoch (with intermittent periods of fall or inertia), drowned topographical features have provided bases for colonising polyps, thus forming inner reefs. The reef's marine life is the most diverse and complex in the world, and a riot of colour. The nature of coral growth creates a number of pools, lagoons and grottoes which are warm and teeming with plankton. Seaweeds, sponges, molluscs, soft coral, marine algae and fish are abundant; there are an estimated 10 000 species of sponges alone, 350 of corals, 4000 of molluscs and more than 1200 of fish. The land vegetation, by contrast, is very limited. Naturalist J. Beete Jukes was the first to examine the reef scientifically, in 1843. Many have followed, and in 1922 a committee was formed to support and conduct such investigations. Research stations have been established on Heron Island (now operated by the University of Qld), Lizard Island (by the Australian Museum) and Orpheus (by James Cook University). Among many programs, the Australian Institute of Marine Science was opened in Townsville in 1973 expressly for reef research. In recent years, invasion of the reef by the voracious crown-of-thorns starfish has caused concern – in the 1960s they destroyed an estimated 80% of the reef around Green Island, subsequently moving southwards.

The Great Barrier Reef is Australia's preeminent tourist attraction and a number of continental islands (and two coral cays, Green and Heron) have been developed as resorts. Many more are national parks, such as Dunk, Hinchinbrook and most of the Whitsunday group. In 1976 the Great Barrier Reef Marine Park Authority was established to take ultimate responsibility for the entire reef region; the marine park itself, which does not include the islands, has three sections: Cairns (34 000sq. km), Capricornia (12 000sq.km) and Cormorant (2000sq.km).

Great Dividing Range The mountain groups contained under this name – a misnomer, since many are not high, nor is it recognisable as a single range – extend from Cape York Peninsula in north Qld, south along the east coast to Vic. and then west through that State. The width of the range varies from 160km to over 300km, and the distance from the coast from 1km to 250km; its sections bear many names – alps, plateaus, tablelands, ranges or just mountains; some of the best known are the Atherton Tableland and McPherson Range, Qld; the New England Plateau, Warrumbungle Range and Blue Mountains, NSW; the Australian Alps (NSW–Vic.), in which is Australia's highest peak, Mt Kosciusko (2230m); and the tilted, jagged peaks of the Grampians in western Vic. In the east the mountains generally rise steeply; the western slopes are more gently inclined: both provide the source for many rivers of eastern Australia.

Great Lake Tas. This is the largest natural freshwater lake in Australia, lying in a shallow basin on the Tas. central plateau near the Great Western Tiers. Its waters have been increased by construction of the Miena dam – itself raised three times since 1922 – at the outlet to the Shannon River. Water from Lake Augusta and Arthurs Lake is diverted to Great Lake, which is a source for Poatina and Trevallyn power stations and the Cressy-Longford irrigation scheme. It is a region of summer pasture and tourism; trout were introduced in 1864, and the lake is now a major fishing resort.

Great Sandy Desert WA The most northerly of WA's three great deserts and one of the least explored and most inhospitable regions on the continent, this is composed mainly of sandhills, with a section of stony desert; virtually the only vegetation is porcupine spinifex. It lies between the Kimberleys and the Gibson Desert; the first crossing was made in 1873 by P.E. Warburton. The dunes in this and the other deserts form longitudinal ridges in an anticlockwise swirl believed to be effected by the influence of the earth's rotation on wind direction. The desert is traversed by the Canning Stock Route, and underlying it is the Canning Basin, which covers 474 000sq.km but in which the incidence of water is as yet little known.

Great Victoria Desert WA/SA A vast area north of the Nullarbor Plain, consisting of sand plains, sandhills and desert loam, this is the southernmost of the three great western deserts (to the north are the Gibson and Great Sandy deserts). Vegetation is variously spinifex, myall and mallee. In the north the desert extends into the Central Australia Aboriginal Reserve, and the Great Victoria Desert Nature Reserve takes in part of the Nullarbor Plain and Forrest Lakes area; the Un-named Conservation Park, one of two SA biosphere reserves, covers 2 132 600ha and is one of the world's largest parks. The desert was first crossed in 1875 by Ernest Giles.

Great Western Tiers Tas. On the northeast edge of the Tas. central plateau, the basaltic cliffs of the tiers rise to more than 1220m above sea-level, towering above the midlands and the north coastal plain. The formation is caused by faulting. The sharp drop from the Great Western Tiers has been used to advantage in both the Great Lake–Esk River and Mersey–Forth hydro-electric schemes.

grebes These aquatic birds belonging to the family Podicipidae chiefly inhabit swamps, lakes and billabongs, but sometimes appear on ocean inlets; expert divers, they feed on small fish, which they catch by swimming underwater, and aquatic insects. There are three species in Australia: the two smaller ones, also known as dabchicks, are the hoary-headed grebe (endemic to Australia) and black-throated grebe; the largest is the crested grebe. These birds have elaborate mating dances, and usually construct nests from piles of floating vegetation.

Greeks in Australia > *ethnic groups*

Green, H. M. (Henry Mackenzie) (1881–1962), journalist and critic, b. Sydney. After graduating in arts and law, Green worked on Sydney newspapers before becoming a librarian and lecturer at the University of Sydney. He broadcast on Australian literature for the ABC and wrote criticism, short stories and poetry. The scholarly two-volume *A History of Australian Literature* (1961), his literary monument, was republished in 1987 after revision by his widow, the poet Dorothy Green.

green bans So-called green bans began in the early 1970s when the NSW Builders' Labourers Federation, under Jack Mundey, placed work bans on a number of Sydney development projects considered to be environmentally or socially destructive. Starting with the preservation of Kelly's Bush in Hunter's Hill, green bans were extended to preserve the historical atmosphere of The Rocks, retain low-cost housing in Woolloomooloo and preserve city parkland; green bans were also initiated in Melbourne. The bans increased public awareness of the need for conservation and led to the establishment of the Commission of Inquiry into the National Estate. These actions were seen as a major innovation in both the conservation and union movements, which brought worldwide attention to Jack Mundey and his philosophy.

greenhouse effect The greenhouse effect, like > *ozone depletion*, is seen by many as a major threat to animal life, natural ecosystems and farming throughout the world. The term describes the progressive warming of the earth's atmosphere as the result of the build-up of gases – principally carbon dioxide, methane, chlorofluorocarbons (CFCs) and nitrous oxide – which are emitted as a by-product of many human activities. The rising temperatures are likely to effect changes in the world's climate and sea-levels, the most notable being the potential melting of the polar ice caps, which could cause inundation of coastal lands – the major population centres of many countries, including Australia.

In Australia, as elsewhere, the greenhouse effect has helped to focus public attention on the extent to which human activities are straining the world's natural order. The burning of fossil fuels such as oil and coal, the clearing of forests for settlement and agriculture, and the domestic use of artificial gases (for purposes such as refrigeration, air conditioning, and aerosol sprays) have increased dramatically in the past 100 years. Although Australia only contributes about 1.5% of the world's greenhouse gases, on a per-capita basis its emissions are the highest in the world (0.96kg a head in the late 1980s, compared with 0.89kg in the US and 0.81 in the EEC).

In Australia the potential effects of the greenhouse process include a southward movement of climatic zones, and rising sea-levels; in addition, the inundation of many Pacific islands would create a large homeless population seeking refuge in nearby countries, such as Australia, whose resources may already be strained. The climatic changes may affect agriculture directly by reducing productivity, and indirectly by increasing the incidence of parasitic pests that thrive in warm conditions. The range and number of many indigenous animal species may be reduced as their breeding patterns are affected or they are forced to seek new habitats.

As described below, governments and groups around the world are now working to stem the possible effects of a global warming. At the same time, by 1990 many scientists were expressing doubts about the 'greenhouse' theory and the reasons for such environmental changes were increasingly in dispute.

Proposed remedies Australia is a signatory to several international agreements, including the Montreal Protocol and the Hague Declaration, dedicated to protecting the atmosphere by reducing emissions of greenhouse gases. The initial target of halving emissions by 1995 has already, however, been recognised as inadequate, and the goal is now to phase them out completely by that date. In 1988 the federal government allocated more than $7 million for research into the problem, and established a national committee to advise on policy and remedial actions. Work by the CSIRO includes development of a climatic model for Australia, to help predict the types, levels and impacts of change.

Environmental groups such as the Australian Conservation Foundation are contributing to public education campaigns that stress individual responsibility; they are also pressuring government and industry for more extreme controls on the production of harmful gases and for reduced production, consumption and export of fossil fuels. Although the problem is now at the forefront of the community's consciousness and is increasingly being forced into the political arena, it remains to be seen whether the Australian community as a whole will accept curtailment of its consumer way of life. >> *climate*; *environment and conservation*

Green Island Qld A small coral island of the Great Barrier Reef, 27km northeast of Cairns, Green Island is well known for its submarine observatory and has been developed as a tourist resort. Composed of sand and coral debris and fringed with reefs, the greater part of the island – together with all the surrounding reefs – is reserved as a marine park.

Greenway, Francis Howard (1777–1837), architect, b. England. Greenway was transported to Australia for forging a contract in connection with the building firm he ran with his brothers. He was commended by Arthur Phillip to Governor Macquarie, who pardoned him and appointed him Sydney's civil architect in 1816. He designed more than 40 buildings, outstanding for their simple elegance: these include St Matthews, Windsor (1817), and St James, Sydney (1820); Hyde Park Barracks (1817), and the castellated stables of Government House, now the NSW conservatorium of music. Working mainly within the Georgian style, Greenway added individual elements, revealing a sensitive talent. He clashed with many, including the civil engineer G. Druitt, who supervised construction of many of his buildings. After his dismissal by Governor Brisbane following the Bigge Report,

he lapsed into obscurity and died in some poverty without, he said, adequate rewards for his work.

Greer, Germaine (1939–   ), author and academic, b. Melbourne. Expatriate since the 1960s, Greer became a leading light of the international feminist movement after the publication of *The Female Eunuch* (1971), which examined female stereotyping. Her other publications include *The Obstacle Race* (1979), which documented the historical impediments to achievement by women painters; *The Revolting Garden* (1979, earlier published in the English satirical magazine *Private Eye* under the pseudonym 'Rose Blight'); *Sex and Destiny* (1984); a collection of her essays and journalism, *The Madwoman's Underclothes* (1986); and an autobiographical exploration, *Daddy, We Hardly Knew You* (1988). In the US 1979–82, she was director of the Tulsa Center for the Study of Women's Literature.

Gregg, Sir Norman McAlister (1892–1966), ophthalmologist, b. Burwood, NSW. The announcement in 1941 of Gregg's discovery that rubella (German measles) in a pregnant woman could cause blindness or deformity in her child was a major medical landmark. His interest in child medicine led him to help set up the Children's Medical Research Foundation at Sydney's Royal Alexandra Hospital for Children, of which he later became president. He also helped establish the Ophthalmic Research Institute of Australia.

Gregory brothers, colonial explorers. **Sir Augustus Charles** (1819–1905), b. England, was brought to WA by his parents in 1829. An explorer and surveyor, in 1846 and 1848 he led official expeditions inland and north from Perth to the Gascoyne River. His major northern Australian expedition (1855–6) was financed by the British government at the instigation of the Royal Geographical Society. Following up the Victoria River, Gregory was repulsed by desert and crossed the continent reversing Ludwig Leichhardt's 1884 route in a third of the time. In 1858, when sent to look for Leichhardt's lost expedition, he confirmed that Mitchell's 'Victoria River' was indeed a headwater of Cooper Creek, and proceeding south to Adelaide he solved the puzzle of the SA salt lakes. His brother, **Francis Thomas** (1821––88), also contributed to exploration, notably in the northwest of WA in 1861.

Gregory River Qld A large, monsoonal river perennially maintained by springs at its source in the Barkly Tableland, the Gregory flows for over 200km to meet the Nicholson River and thence to an estuary in the southeast of the Gulf of Carpentaria, near Burketown. The main rural industry of the region is beef-cattle grazing.

Greiner, Nick (Nicholas Frank) (1947–), politician, b. Hungary. After a career in business, Greiner entered the NSW parliament as a Liberal in 1980 and became leader of the NSW Liberal Party in 1983. Elected premier in 1988, he promised a cleansing of the Augean stables of NSW politics; he is generally characterised as a technocrat and able administrator modelled somewhat on US lines.

grevilleas The tree and shrub genus *Grevillea* is the largest genus in the > *protea family*. Almost all of its 250 species are endemic, most being widespread across the continent but particularly numerous in heathlands or open forest of the eastern and southwestern coasts. They are generally diverse in appearance, with flowers ranging from spikes to globular clusters; like most members of their family, many are extremely resistant to fire. Among the best known grevilleas are the silky oak, *G. robusta*, and white oak, *G. pinnatifida*, both common rainforest species. Representatives in the arid and semi-arid inland include the beefwood, *G. striata*, a stout tree growing to 12m and bearing cream flowers in profusion.

Grey, Sir George (1812–98), explorer and administrator, b. Portugal. Grey came to Australia in 1837 to explore the northwest coast for a great river outlet, but the expedition was cut short when he was wounded by Aborigines. In 1839 he landed further south at Shark Bay, lost first his stores and then his whaleboats, and made a forced overland march to Perth. He was governor of SA 1841–5 and rescued the bankrupt colony with stringent economic measures. He took a great interest in Aboriginal welfare and culture; as NZ governor (1845–53, 1861–8) and prime minister (1877–9), and as governor of Cape Colony (1854–61), he concerned himself primarily with the administration of native affairs. He represented NZ at Australia's 1891 federal convention.

greyhound coursing and racing The coursing of greyhounds using live hares was first practised at Narracoorte, SA, in 1867. The sport quickly became established in country areas and on the fringes of major cities. As the use of live hares was opposed, it declined, and was finally banned in 1953 to be replaced by greyhound track racing, which uses a mechanical lure and was introduced into NSW and Vic. from the US in 1927 by Frederick Swindell. Opposition from other racing interests and from some church groups led to bans on night racing and gambling, but after protracted legal battles mechanical hare racing became legal in NSW in 1937 and in Vic. in 1956. Only 7% of trainers are professional, the remainder being part-timers involved both for pleasure and for the chance to make a profit. In recent years, despite improved facilities, crowd numbers and betting turnover have declined. The most important race, the Australian Cup, held at Olympic Park in Melbourne, carries over $100 000 in stakes.

Grey Range Qld This range is a line of low hills forming the divide between the Bulloo River and the Cooper Creek system of intermittent streams flowing towards Lake Eyre in SA. It lies in the eastern section of the Channel Country, continuing then across the northwest corner of NSW. Beef-cattle grazing is the chief rural industry, although gold and opals have been mined in some areas since the 1870s.

Griffin, Walter Burley (1876–1937), architect, b. US. Griffin arrived in Australia in 1913 after winning, in collaboration with his future wife Marion Mahony, the international competition for a plan for the new federal capital. Griffin's plan, while modified, set the basic pattern for Canberra although, continually frustrated by official opposition, he discontinued his association with it from 1920. He was equally influential in private practice: Newman College, University of Melbourne (1916), the Capitol Theatre in Melbourne (1924), with its brilliant use of interior plaster work, and the town plan of Griffith, NSW, are diverse examples of his innovative approach. In domestic architecture he aimed to design houses for urban living with space, privacy and unobtrusive building: this is best seen at Castlecrag in Sydney, where he bought land and developed a small community of low houses that merged naturally into the bushland. The Griffins left Australia in 1936 to design university buildings in Lucknow in India.

Griffith NSW (pop. 13 630) The town of Griffith was planned as a model settlement by Canberra's architect, Walter Burley Griffin. Some 616km southwest of Sydney, it is the commercial and processing centre for the Murrumbidgee Irrigation Area, Australia's richest food-producing region. Crops include rice, wine grapes, oranges and other fruit, wheat and vegetables; local industries include eighteen wineries (producing 80% of the State's wines), rice mills, brickworks, an abattoir, and machinery and engineering manufacturers. It is a multicultural community in which Italians predominate.

Griffith, Sir Samuel Walker (1845–1920), lawyer and politician, b. Wales. Griffith arrived in Australia in 1854 as a Congregational minister and entered the Qld parliament in 1872; he was attorney-general 1874–8 and premier 1883–8 and 1890–3. An active politician, his achievements included a bill for free, secular and compulsory education (1875), legislation to end blackbirding (1890), and drafting of Qld's criminal law; he was chief justice of Qld 1893–1903 and lt–governor (1899–1903). A supporter of Federation, Griffith was the main drafter of the Constitution bill and represented Qld at federal conventions. Chief justice of the High Court 1903–19, he was noted for his impartiality and high judicial standards.

Grimwade, Sir (Wilfrid) Russell (1879–1955), industrial chemist and philanthropist, b. Caulfield, Vic. Grimwade was notable particularly in the fields of chemistry, biochemistry and conservation. He was responsible for having the Yorkshire home of James Cook's parents, now known as 'Captain Cook's Cottage', carried to Australia and reassembled in the Fitzroy Gardens, Melbourne, in 1932.

Groote Eylandt NT An island in the Gulf of Carpentaria which has the same rock structures as Arnhem Land, Groote Eylandt contains Australia's largest reserves of manganese, which are mined by open cut and shipped out at Milner Bay. A wide variety of tropical fruit – including citrus – is grown, and cattle are reared on planted lucerne. The island measures approximately 60km north–south by 50km east–west, and is part of the Arnhem Land Aboriginal Reserve. The name was given by Abel Tasman in 1644.

gropers In Australia this name is applied to tropical fish of several different families. The large blue and red gropers of the genus *Achoerodus* vary widely in colour, reach a length of over 1m and weigh over 18kg; they are bulky fish with very thick lips. The rather sharp-snouted pigfishes, such as *Verreo bellis*, are mainly pink with several dark, interrupted lines along the sides. The oval-bodied macaw fish, *Lienardella fasciata*, is a fish of coral reefs, gorgeously cross-striped in green, blue and scarlet, with teeth partly fused into a bony ridge. The Qld groper, *Promicsops lanceolatus*, is Australia's largest fish and can reach 280kg in weight; it lurks in submarine caverns and is considered to be dangerous. The deep-water fish hapuka, *Polyprion oxygeneios*, also referred to as the NZ groper, is excellent eating and is fished commercially in deeper parts of the eastern continental shelf.

Grose, Francis (1754–1814), army officer and colonial administrator, b. England. Appointed in 1789 to form and command a special army corps, which became known as the NSW Corps, Grose arrived in Sydney in February 1792, having meanwhile also been appointed lieut.-governor of the colony. When Governor Phillip left at the end of that year, Grose took charge; his short period of control (December 1792–December 1794) was controversial. He improved the staggering economy, but at the cost of disregarding Phillip's principles: he granted land, allowed the employment of convicts, who were paid in rum, and permitted trading by officers. Jovial, worldly and popular, his efforts were beneficial in the short term but sowed the seeds of much of the subsequent dissipation and trouble in the colony.

Grounds, Sir Roy Burman (1905–81), architect, b. Melbourne. Grounds was a pioneer of modern architecture in Australia: his early work with Geoffrey Mewton (in the 1930s) tempered functionalism with Australian elements such as verandahs, shutters, and wide eaves. His later buildings were geometrical and generally austere: the internal detailing and severe lines of Clendon flats (1940) in Toorak, Vic., were widely imitated, but the domed Academy of Sciences building in Canberra (1959) remains unique. Amongst his best-known – and most controversial – buildings is the fortress-like Victorian Arts Centre complex (1969–84).

groundwater > *water and water resources*

Group Settlement Scheme Devised in 1921 by WA premier Sir James Mitchell, this plan was to bring out British immigrants and settle them in the southwest of the State in loosely associated groups that would share the initial bush-clearing of a planned 6000 holdings. It failed largely through lack of technical knowledge in coping with the difficult climate and terrain. There were some 10 000 group settlers and a maximum of 2442 holdings, many later abandoned or amalgamated.

Gruner, Elioth (1882–1939), painter, b. NZ. A landscape painter of exceptional talent and sensitivity, Gruner studied under Julian Ashton in Sydney. His works characteristically capture the serenity and calm of early morning light; he painted *en plein air*, frequently camping outdoors for long periods. He achieved popular acclaim in his day, and won the highly regarded Wynne Prize for landscape painting seven times 1916–37.

gudgeons > *fishes, freshwater and marine*

Guilfoyle, William Robert (1840–1912), botanist, b. England. In 1853 Guilfoyle immigrated with his family to Sydney, where his father ran a nursery. He took part in botanical collecting expeditions and spent some time farming near the Tweed River before succeeding Ferdinand von Mueller in 1873 as director of the Melbourne botanic gardens. He held this position until 1909, during which time he greatly extended the gardens and was largely responsible for the landscaping as it exists today, for which work he achieved international acclaim. His publications included *Australian Plants* (1911).

guinea flowers This is the common name, alluding to the golden-yellow disc-like flowers, of shrubs and scramblers in the genus *Hibbertia*, family Dilleniaceae. The group comprises about 150 species, of which the majority are Australian endemics. They are comparatively primitive plants, with flowers adapted to pollination primarily by beetles. A well-known eastern species is the twining guinea flower, *H. scandens*, with perhaps the largest flowers of the genus. A shrub of coastal dunes and karri and jarrah forests of southwestern Australia, *H. cuneiformis*, grows to 2m or more.

Gulf of Carpentaria A large inlet on the northern Australian coast, its shore divided between NT and Qld, the gulf is 480km across its mouth – between Cape York and Arnhem Land – and extends over 600km southwards; its waters are nowhere more than 65m deep. This was probably the first Australian landfall made by Europeans (the Dutch, in 1605–06) and was named in 1623 after Pierre Carpentier, governor-general of the Dutch East Indies. The chief ports now service mining operations: bauxite (Weipa), aluminium (Gove) and manganese (on Groote Eylandt); extensive prawn-fishing is centred at Karumba and Groote Eylandt. Islands include the Sir Edward Pellew and Wellesley groups; Groote Eylandt is an Aboriginal reserve.

gulls > *sea-birds*

Gulpilil, David (1953–), actor and dancer, b. Arnhem Land, NT. An Aborigine, Gulpilil was a noted traditional dancer before appearing in his first film, Nicholas Roeg's *Walkabout* (1971). Subsequent films include *Storm Boy* (1976), *The Last Wave* (1977) and *The Right Stuff* (1983). Gulpilil has also appeared in many television series, including 'Homicide' and 'Rush', and in stage plays.

gums > *eucalypts*

Gundagai NSW (pop. 2124) On the Hume Highway, 400km from Sydney, Gundagai is most familiar to many Australians as the subject of a 19th-century droving ballad, 'Nine Miles from Gundagai', by Jack Moses; a pioneer monument of a dog on a tuckerbox, which commemorates the song, lies 8km from the town. The original town was built (after 1838) on low-lying flats, despite the warnings of local Aborigines, and a disastrous flood that occurred in 1852 led the town to be relocated on higher ground. It is now the centre for a rich pastoral and agricultural district.

Gunn, Jeannie (Mrs Aeneas) (1870–1961), author and social worker, b. Melbourne. The wife of a station manager in the NT, Gunn wrote the minor classic of outback life *We of the Never Never* (1908), which has sold more than half a million copies. Her only other book is *The Little Black Princess* (1905). She was later a social worker in Melbourne.

Gunnedah NSW (pop. 9144) This rural town lies on the Namoi River 476km northwest of Sydney and is a processing and market centre for the Liverpool Plains region. It has its origins in a river crossing and drovers' meeting-place in the 19th century. Gunnedah is the administrative headquarters for the nearby Keepit dam, and as well as a livestock market has various industries such as an abattoir, flour mill, brick factory and sawmill.

gurnards These bony fishes of the family Triglidae are common in eastern Australian waters. All are distinguished by an armamented head, limb-like lower rays of the pectoral fins, and a brilliantly coloured upper pectoral fin. Species of tropical Qld waters include the red gurnard, *Chelidonichthys kumu*.

Gwydir River NSW Rising near Uralla on the New England plateau, the Gwydir flows west through Moree to join the Barwon–Darling system near Collarenebri. The Copeton dam, on the upper reaches, stores water for irrigation livestock and domestic purposes, and sheep grazing is the major industry along the river's course. It was named after a British peer by Allan Cunningham, in 1827.

Gympie Qld (pop. 10 772) A city in the Mary River valley, 160km north of Brisbane, Gympie is the main service centre for the surrounding rural land. The main local products are tropical fruits, timber, beef, and dairy products. Development began when James Nash discovered gold in 1867; a rush to the alluvial diggings was followed by 50 years of reef-mining, by which time dairying and agriculture were also well established.

H

Haasts Bluff NT This mountain stands at the western end of the Macdonnell Ranges, within the Haasts Bluff Aboriginal Reserve. It was discovered by Ernest Giles in 1872 and named after a well-known NZ geologist-explorer. Giles described the bluff and its 'singular and grotesque' neighbours: 'The middle line of hills is the most strange looking ... all have a circular curve, all are coloured red, and in perspective appear like a gigantic flat stairway ...'

Hackett, Sir John Winthrop (1848–1916), journalist and benefactor, b. Ireland. Trained in law, Hackett immigrated to Australia in 1875 and eventually settled in WA, where he helped establish and eventually became editor (from 1887) of the *West Australian* newspaper. Hackett advanced progressive government and women's suffrage, and served in the WA parliament from 1904 until his death; he also promoted cultural and educational institutions and was a major benefactor (and first chancellor) of the University of WA. A Canberra suburb bears his name.

Haddon, Robert (1866–1929), architect, b. England. Haddon immigrated to Australia in 1891 and practised and taught architecture in Melbourne from 1900. He pioneered and ardently promoted the integration of design and craftsmanship in architecture, which was later expressed in the local 'Federation' style. His distinctive buildings, such as Anselm in Caulfield (1906), and his book *Australian Domestic Architecture* (1908), mark him as one of the design pioneers of the early 20th century. His work is commemorated in Vic. by a travelling scholarship for architecture students.

hakeas > *protea family*

Hall, Ben(jamin) (1838–65), bushranger, b. Breeza, NSW. Hall was said to have been driven to bushranging by the desertion of his wife when he was (possibly wrongly) accused of being an accomplice of Frank Gardiner. In the Forbes region 1862–5 he led a gang that seemed immune to police action – robbing homesteads, banks and stage coaches to the widespread admiration of all but the victims and the police. Hall killed no one, but was not able to prevent his gang from doing so. He was shot, after betrayal, while camped near Forbes.

Hall, Ken(neth George) (1901–), film producer and director, b. Sydney. A pioneer of Australian cinema, Hall entered the industry as a theatre publicist in the 1920s. His company Cinesound Productions – under the aegis of Greater Union Theatres – made some of the most popular feature films of the 1930s and 1940s, including *On Our Selection* (1932), *The Silence of Dean Maitland* (1934) and *Dad and Dave Come to Town* (1938); the last of his seventeen feature films was *Smithy* (1946), based on the life of aviator Charles Kingsford Smith. He was chief executive of Television Corporation 1957–66 and published an autobiography, *Directed by Ken G. Hall*, in 1977.

Hall, (Lindsay) Bernard (1859–1935), painter, b. England. Having trained as an artist in London, Antwerp and Munich, Hall painted and exhibited successfully for ten years in London before coming to Australia (1892) to become director of the Vic. National Gallery. He held this position for 43 years, during which time he was an influential teacher at the gallery school and was competent and conscientious as first purchaser for the Felton Bequest.

Halls Creek WA (pop. 1182) A centre for the grazing and mining industries of the east

Kimberley region, Halls Creek lies about 2850km northeast of Perth. It was the site of the State's first gold discovery, in 1885, but soon diminished from a tent town of several thousand inhabitants to a small outback settlement. It was rebuilt 15km from the original site to ensure a better water supply.

Hamer, Dick (Sir Rupert James)

(1916–), politician, b. Melbourne. A solicitor, Hamer entered the Vic. parliament as a Liberal in 1958 and held various portfolios in the lengthy administration of Sir Henry Bolte. He became premier in 1972 after Bolte's retirement. A believer more in consensus government than was his aggressive predecessor, he was a respected figure; discord within the Liberal Party led to his resignation as premier in 1981.

Hamersley Range

WA A plateau lying southeast of the Fortescue River, this is WA's highest mountain range and includes Mt Meharry (1251m) and Mt Bruce (1235m). Horizontal Precambrian sediments, brilliantly coloured in reds and purples, are gashed by the deep gorges of the Fortescue and Ashburton rivers and their tributaries; this is in the northern section – there are few south-flowing streams and the southern escarpment is comparatively unbroken, standing about 300m above the surrounding land. Vegetation on the hills is chiefly spinifex and mulga; even in dry periods, deep pools and rich green vegetation contrast strongly with the brown savannah of the plateau surface. In the central section is Hamersley Range National Park – Australia's second-largest national park – which includes Mt Bruce; a notable feature is the blooming of the wildflowers after winter rain. To the west and southeast respectively of the park are the vast iron-ore reserves at Mt Tom Price and Mt Newman, which underpin Australia's iron and steel industry and much of its primary export wealth.

Hamilton

Vic. (pop. 9969) A prosperous city and market centre for the Western District, Hamilton grew around an inn at the crossing of the Grange Burn (a river named by Thomas Mitchell in 1836) and was known as the Grange until renamed Hamilton in 1851. As well as processing and manufacturing industries, the city is noted for its botanic gardens and zoo and its fine art gallery.

Hammond, Dame Joan Hood

(1912–), opera singer, b. NZ. Trained as a violinist, Hammond turned to singing after an arm injury. She made her operatic debut in Vienna in 1939; after World War 2, she sang in all the major opera houses of the world, enjoying a remarkable career until illness forced her retirement from the stage in 1965. She subsequently taught and was for a time head of vocal studies at the Vic. College of the Arts. Also a notable sportswoman, she held many junior swimming, golf and squash titles in the 1930s.

Hancock, Lang(ley George)

(1909–), mining entrepreneur, b. Perth. A pastoralist, Hancock uncovered and developed the blue asbestos at Wittenoom, WA, from the 1930s. He is best known, however, for detecting the immense deposits of iron ore in the Hamersley Range of the Pilbara region of WA in the 1950s, using the then-novel method of aerial prospecting. These and numerous subsequent discoveries in the region during the 1960s – for all of which Hancock negotiated substantial mining royalties – led to Australia becoming a major world exporter of iron ore. One of Australia's wealthiest men, Hancock has supported many controversial right-wing causes.

Hancock, Sir (William) Keith

(1898–), historian, b. Melbourne. An economic historian of high international repute, Hancock was professor of history successively at the universities of Adelaide and Birmingham 1926–41 and of economic history at Oxford 1944–9. He edited the civil series of the UK war histories 1941–3. Hancock joined the Australian National University in 1957 and helped found its research school of social sciences. A prolific author, his publications range from the classic cultural history *Australia* (1930) to biographies, books on the historian's craft such as *Perspectives in History* (1982), and two volumes of autobiography (1954, 1976).

hang-gliding > *sky sports*

Hanson, Raymond

(1913–76), music composer and teacher, b. Sydney. Hanson studied at the NSW Conservatorium of Music and joined its teaching staff in 1948; he lectured on composition until his death and had enormous influence on the development of Australian music. His own composition was strongly influenced by the writings on harmony of the German composer Paul Hindemith; his trumpet concerto in B Flat was one of the first recorded Australian compositions to be released internationally.

Hansard The official transcripts of Australia's parliamentary debates are named after Luke Hansard, whose family published British parliamentary proceedings from 1774 until the late 1800s. All States and the federal parliament have their own Hansards, which are recorded by shorthand reporters. Transcripts are essentially verbatim, but may be corrected for grammar and repetition and do not include remarks that the Speaker orders to be struck from the record.

hapuka > *gropers*

Hardy, Frank (Francis Joseph) (1917–), author, b. Southern Cross, Vic. Hardy left school at the age of thirteen and tried many, mostly menial, jobs. He became a communist, worked for the Australian army magazine *Salt*, and later joined the Realist Writers' Group. His semi-fictional novel, *Power Without Glory* (1950), based on the life of businessman John Wren, inspired an unsuccessful prosecution for criminal libel. Hardy has persisted with novels although his metier is the short story, as exemplified in *Legends from Benson's Valley* (1963) and *The Yarns of Billy Borker* (1965).

Hargrave, Lawrence (1850–1915), aviation pioneer, b. England. An engineering draftsman and later astronomical observer at Sydney Observatory, Hargrave arrived in Australia in 1866. From 1883 he devoted himself to research; he invented a rotary engine propelled by means of compressed air (forerunner of the internal combustion engine used in many early aeroplanes), and discovered the superiority of curved wing surfaces over flat surfaces in producing lift. His experiments with box kites revealed important principles that could be applied in the development of powered flight.

Hargraves, Edward Hammond (1816–91), gold prospector, b. England. After gaining experience in the Californian goldfields 1849–51, Hargraves prospected in the Bathurst-Orange region of NSW with John Lister and the Tom brothers. In 1851 he panned gold at Summer Hill Creek, later the site of the Ophir goldfield. He was officially recognised (and handsomely rewarded) by the NSW government as the first discoverer of payable gold in Australia, although this claim was later disputed. Subsequent gold searches by him for the WA and Tas. governments proved unsuccessful.

Harpur, Charles (1813–68), poet, b. Windsor, NSW. The son of former convicts, Harpur is considered the first important Australian poet: although strongly influenced by English poets (mainly Wordsworth and Milton), his subjects were the Australia environment, its vastness and ever-changing light. *The Poetical Works of Charles Harpur* (1984) is the most complete collection of his poetry. His best work was blank narrative verse, but he also wrote verse drama, lyrical, satirical and political verse, and prose criticism. He worked variously as clerk, farmer and gold commissioner.

Harris, Alexander (1805–74), author, b. London. Harris was in Australia 1825–40: under the pseudonym 'An Emigrant Mechanic', he wrote extensively about the colony in *Settlers and Convicts* (1847) and *Testimony to the Truth* (1848) – both autobiographical – and a novel, *The Emigrant Family* (1849). The last was one of the major novels of its time and all his works contained invaluable comment on colonial life. His authorship was disputed until clarified by a Canadian grandson, who published *The Secrets of Alexander Harris* (1961).

Harris, John (1754–1838), surgeon and magistrate, b. Ireland. Harris arrived in Australia in 1790 with the NSW Corps; he was made a magistrate in 1800, and officer in charge of the port of Sydney in 1801. His attempts to put an end to the liquor trade made him many enemies and he was the victim of two trumped-up courts-martial; he also ran foul of Governor Bligh, George Johnston and John Macarthur. After retiring from the NSW Corps in 1814, Harris developed his estates, helped found the Bank of NSW and served as surgeon in John Oxley's expedition.

Harris, Max(well Henley) (1921–), editor and publisher, b. Adelaide. Harris founded and co-edited the literary journals, *Angry Penguins* (1940–6), *Australian Letters* (1957–68) and *Australian Book Review* (1961–74). He also established the publishing firm of

Reed Harris and the Mary Martin bookshop chain. A noted belletrist and social commentator, Harris has been a controversial figure throughout his career; his publications include *The Angry Eye* (1973) and *The Unknown Great Australian* (1983).

Harrison, James (1816?–93), journalist and inventor, b. Scotland. Harrison arrived in Sydney in 1837 but soon moved to Port Phillip, where Fawkner commissioned him to found the weekly *Geelong Advertiser*. Harrison bought the paper in 1842 and thenceforth published it daily; he was the first journalistic advocate of protectionism, espousing what was then an unpopular cause as early as 1852. Harrison undertook ingenious but expensive experimentation with refrigeration, establishing Australia's first ice-plant in the early 1850s, patenting several refrigerator designs and noted as a pioneer of ship refrigeration. These ventures were commercially unsuccessful and Harrison was forced to sell the *Advertiser* in 1862.

Harrower, Elizabeth (1928–   ), novelist, b. Sydney. Harrower spent her childhood in Newcastle, NSW, the 'Ballowra' of *The Long Prospect* (1958), which is sometimes ranked next to Patrick White's *Voss* in postwar Australian fiction. She studied psychology, worked as a clerk and in publishing, and lived in London 1951–9, writing stories and novels. *The Watch Tower*, the last of her four subtle novels exploring the ambivalence of life's motivating forces, was published in 1966.

Hart, Pro (Kevin Charles) (1928–   ), painter, b. Broken Hill, NSW. One of the well-known 'Brushmen of the Bush', Hart is a colourful character whose prolific output has brought national fame, popular success and considerable wealth. His vibrant paintings mostly depict the barren Broken Hill region, where he has lived all his life. His own gallery houses one of Australia's largest private art collections.

Hartigan, Patrick Joseph (1879–52), priest and poet, b. Yass, NSW. Hartigan was ordained a Catholic priest in 1903 and served at Narrandera, NSW, 1917–44. There, under the pen-name John O'Brien, he began writing poetry and his first – and highly successful – collection of bush ballads, *Around the Boree Log* was published in 1921. Simple but lively, his verse depicts the Catholic Irish-Australian

settlers he knew so well. Another volume of verse, *The Parish of St Mel's*, was published in 1954.

Hartnett, Sir Laurence John (1898–1986), engineer, b. England. Hartnett immigrated to Australia and was managing director of GMH 1934–47, during which time he was instrumental in the later development of the Australian-made Holden car. He was subsequently involved in two projects to manufacture cars in Australia, but both failed. His autobiography, *Big Wheels and Little Wheels*, was published in 1964 (updated in 1974 and 1981).

Hartog, Dirk (or Dirck) An early 17th-century Dutch sea captain of whom no personal details are known, Hartog was the first recorded European to land in WA. He left an inscribed pewter plate (now in Amsterdam) nailed to a post at the north end of Dirk Hartog Island, later named Cape Inscription. Translated, it begins: '1616. On the 25th October there arrived here the ship *den Eendraght* of Amsterdam'. The plate was found in 1697 by Willem de Vlamingh, and is Australia's earliest European relic.

Hartz Mountains Tas. A heavily glaciated range southwest of Hobart, this range lies between the Arve and Picton rivers and extends north–south for approximately 45km; the northern section is part of a national park of the same name. The highest point is Hartz Peak, 1254m, and most of the region is alpine moorland.

Harvester judgment This judgment, made in 1907 by Mr Justice Higgins, president of the Commonwealth Court of Conciliation and Arbitration, established the concept of a 'basic wage'. In that year H.V. McKay, of the Sunshine Harvester Works, applied for exemption from excise duty on the grounds that the wages paid to his employees were 'fair and reasonable'. Justice Higgins found that to satisfy the normal needs of the average employee, married with three children, 'living in a civilised community', the minimum wage should be 7s a day for a six-day working week. >> *wage determination*

Harvey River WA With a course of only 60km, the Harvey River rises east of the Darling Range and flows to an estuary at Peel Inlet on the west coast. Production in this district includes potatoes, sheep and cattle, fruit, dairying and timber. The first WA irrigation scheme began in 1916 with the construction of the Harvey dam; this was later enlarged, and the supply further augmented with the addition in 1948 of the Stirling dam and in 1963 of the Logue Brook dam. Irrigation was established first for production of citrus fruit, but subsequently for improved pastures for dairy cattle.

Hasluck family, noted in politics and literature. **Sir Paul Meernaa Caedwalla** (1905–), b. Fremantle, WA, was a journalist and academic before entering federal parliament as a Liberal in 1949. An effective minister, he held the portfolios of Territories (1951–63), defence (1963) and external affairs (1964–9); he was governor-general 1969–74. One of the rare intellectuals in Australian politics, he published several books including *Black Australians* (1942) and *Native Welfare in Australia* (1953). His wife **Dame Alexandra Margaret Martin** (1908–), b. Perth, is a noted writer of short stories, history and biography: her publications include a biography of colonial botanist Georgiana Molloy, *Portrait with Background* (1955), and an autobiography, *Portrait in a Mirror* (1981). Their son **Nicholas** (1942–), b. Canberra, is a lawyer and a prolific writer of poetry, short stories and novels; in the last field, his *The Bellarmine Jug* (1984) won the *Age* Book of the Year Award in that year.

Hastings River NSW Discovered on John Oxley's expedition of 1818, the Hastings drains a large basin of forested, high-rainfall country on the eastern escarpment of the New England plateau. The upper river flows through Werrikimbe National Park – a wilderness park – cutting a deep gorge near Mt Werrikimbe. Rural industries include timber (in the upper valley) and dairying, with fodder crops grown on the lower slopes and alluvial flats; major centres are Wauchope and Port Macquarie, the latter being a popular holiday and tourist resort.

Hawke, Bob (Robert James Lee) (1929–), politician, b. Bordertown, SA. Son of a Congregational minister, Hawke was educated at the University of WA and won a Rhodes Scholarship in 1952. In 1958 he became a research officer and industrial advocate at the ACTU, becoming its president in 1970. A successful mediator in industrial dis-

putes, Hawke soon gained a reputation as an expert negotiator of compromise settlements. Elected to federal parliament in 1980, he became leader of the ALP in February 1983, leading it to electoral victory and becoming prime minister a month later; three further victories followed, in 1985, 1987 (making Hawke the longest-serving Labor prime minister), and 1990. A consensus politician, Hawke has led an effective middle-of-the-road administration. Criticised in some quarters for his public displays of temperament and for his friendship with the rich and famous, he nevertheless remains a successful populist leader.

Hawker, Harry George (1889–1921), aviator, b. Moorabbin, Vic. A daring test pilot, Hawker joined the Sopwith Aviation Company in 1911, where he helped design the Sopwith Tabloid biplane and set a British flight endurance record. After war service with the Royal Navy Air Service, he attempted a trans-Atlantic flight in 1919 but crashed at sea. In 1920, he established a company to make motorcycles, which later grew into the giant Hawker-Siddeley aircraft company. He was killed in 1921 when his Goshawk plane crashed at Hendon, England.

Hawkesbury River NSW The Hawkesbury, a large river that flows west and north of metropolitan Sydney, undergoes a series of name changes along its course owing to the separate discovery of the various sections, then believed to be separate rivers. After rising as the Wollondilly on the southern tablelands it passes through gorges in the Blue Mountains (where it is known as the Warragamba and has been dammed for Sydney's water supply); it is next called the Nepean, and only after the entry of the Grose does it become the Hawkesbury, flowing west, north and west again, beyond the entry of the Colo, to the wide estuary in Broken Bay. The Hawkesbury system in all is some 480km long. The Hawkesbury River section was discovered by Arthur Phillip in 1789 and the district was settled in 1794; farming, chiefly wheat and maize, was early established, and Australia's first irrigation project was developed there in 1828. After the 1870s production was mainly of fruit and vegetables, and the region has also developed as a popular recreation area. On the north bank, above the river mouth, is Dharug National Park, named after the former Aboriginal inhabitants.

hawks > *eagles and hawks*

Hay, William Gosse (1875–1945), author, b. Adelaide. From 1901, Hay wrote six historical novels and a book of essays. Most have been critically dismissed as melodramatic and of negligible literary merit, although *The Escape of the Notorious Sir William Heans* (1919) is a useful study of the convict system.

Hayden, Bill (William George) (1933–), politician, b. Brisbane. A former policeman, Hayden entered federal parliament as a Labor member in 1961. From 1972 he was minister for social security in the Whitlam government, overseeing the introduction of much reformist legislation (including Medibank, the national health insurance scheme). In 1975 he became treasurer, but the Opposition blocked the federal budget in that year and Labor lost office in the ensuing election. Hayden was Opposition leader from 1978 until he was replaced by Bob Hawke, who was considered to be electorally more popular, in 1983. In 1988 Hayden resigned as minister for foreign affairs to become governor-general, a surprising move in the light of his earlier avowed republicanism.

Hayes, Colin > *horse-racing*

Hayman Island > *Cumberland Islands*

Hazzard, Shirley (1931–) novelist, b. Sydney. Settling in New York in 1952, Hazzard worked for the UN 1952–62. She is the author of numerous short stories and several novels, all characterised by their coolly elegant prose and preoccupation with the psychology of human relations. Some of her early short stories, most originally published in the *New Yorker*, were collected in *The Cliffs of Fall* (1963). Of her four novels the most ambitious and successful is *The Transit of Venus* (1980), which won the US National Book Critics' Circle Award and established her as a major novelist.

Heagney, Muriel (1885–1974), b. Brisbane, union organiser. Born into a devoutly Labor family, Heagney devoted her life to the Labor movement and the pursuit of equal opportunity and equal pay for women. Variously a clerk, waitress, school-teacher and union organiser, in 1933 she stood unsuccessfully as an ALP candidate in Qld. Her book *Are Women Taking Men's Jobs?* was published in 1935; in 1937 she founded the Council of Action for Equal Pay and single-handedly prepared and presented a submission on equal pay to the Arbitration Court.

health and health services The standard of health in Australia is very high and has improved greatly since the first years of European settlement. Whereas early health problems were those associated with poor hygiene, cramped living conditions, and malnutrition, the health targets endorsed by Australia's health ministers in 1988 reflect a quite different set of issues. The five areas deemed to require urgent action were the control of blood pressure, which has been linked to an increased risk of heart attack and stroke; improved nutrition to deal with widespread obesity in the community; injury prevention, particularly in relation to road accidents; and the prevention of lung, skin, breast and cervical cancers. In general, these aims reflect the prevalence of 'lifestyle-related' diseases in the community. It is, however, noteworthy that while white urban Australians have a health profile similar to countries such as the US, the nation's 227 000 Aborigines and Torres Straight Islanders remain subject to serious health problems associated with poor nutrition – more commonly seen in developing countries.

Mortality and life expectancy In 1986, life expectancy at birth for all females in Australia was 79 years and for males 73 years, a dramatic increase from the 1870 figures of 50 years and 48 years respectively. Similar improvements can be seen in the infant mortality rate, which has declined from 103.6 per thousand live births at the turn of the century to 8.8 per thousand in 1986. Despite this impressive decline, Australia still ranks eighteenth in the world for infant mortality (Japan having the lowest rate, of 6 per thousand).

These figures belie, however, the poor rates of life expectancy and infant mortality among Australia's Aborigines. Complete statistics are not readily available, but by the 1980s average life expectancy was estimated at 55; the Australian Institute of Health in 1988 gave a figure of 61 years for males and 65 years for females in the Kimberley region of WA, and 51 years for males and 59 years for females in country NSW. Available statistics on infant mortality indicate infant death rates of 33 deaths per thousand in the Kimberleys and 21–25 deaths per thousand in country NSW.

Causes of death in Australia reflect changes in both lifestyle and medical technology over the years. In the early years of the colony the main causes of death were infectious diseases such as gastroenteritis, dysentery, diarrhoea, bronchitis, sexually transmitted diseases, and eye and skin infections. These more common ailments were interspersed with periodic outbreaks of smallpox, plague, influenza, measles and scarlet fever (> *epidemics*). The death rate from infectious diseases began to drop as improvements were made in the areas of housing, water supply, waste disposal and food supply and there was a movement of the population to the more salubrious rural areas.

By the mid-1980s the main causes of death among Australians were diseases of the circulatory system (causing heart attacks and strokes), cancers (mostly of the stomach, bowel, lungs and breast), injuries (mostly from motor-vehicle accidents), poisonings, and diseases of the respiratory system other than cancer. In 1986, 73% of deaths were due to diseases of the circulatory system and cancer.

The development of medical services The first doctors in the Australian colonies were naval surgeons; limited medical treatments were available and patients were cared for in their own homes, if possible, as the early hospitals were relatively crude and unhygienic. The first hospital was constructed in Sydney, in March 1788 on the west side of Sydney Cove; it comprised two long thatched-roof sheds that accommodated 200 patients. Another hospital was built in the nearby Rocks area in 1796, but this was replaced by the forerunner of the present Sydney hospital in 1810.

The early doctors were rather haphazardly trained. William Redfern, for example, was given a certificate of competence in 1808 after practising on Norfolk Island for six years with no evidence of any previous qualifications; he was then put in charge of training medical students at Sydney Hospital, some of whom began their apprenticeships as young as 14. It was not until 1839 that legislation was passed that set up a medical board to examine the qualifications of people wishing to practise. The first medical school in Australia was established at the University of Melbourne in 1862, but doctors continued to travel to Britain for further medical education well into the 20th century. In fact, medical schools in Australia continued to be accredited by the General Medical Council in Britain until 1985, when Australia established its own Medical Council.

Nursing standards in the early years were similarly rough. The first nurses in the hospitals were male convicts, ex-patients or elderly women, none of whom was given any training. The first trained nurses were nuns, who arrived in 1838; they worked initially at the women's penitentiary in Parramatta and later opened a hospital in Potts Point. St Vincent's Hospital in Sydney, now comprising a public teaching hospital with a medical research institute, a private hospital and a medical centre, was opened in 1858 by the Sisters of Charity. Professional training for nurses began in the 1860s at the Lying-in Hospital in Carlton, Vic., which later became the Royal Women's Hospital. The training was initially one month, but this was extended to six months in 1885 and twelve in 1888; as the nurses began to gain more qualifications, male nursing positions were abolished.

Medical treatments became more effective with the introduction of new drugs and the recognition of the importance of sterile procedures. As medical knowledge became more detailed doctors began to specialise, the first such group appearing in 1925 when the College of Surgeons was established to set standards for surgical care. The number of specialist colleges has increased significantly since that time, to cover the fields of pathology, radiology, psychiatry, obstetrics and gynaecology, and various medical subgroups. All doctors wishing to practise as specialists are required to undertake postgraduate training and meet the registration requirements of the college in their field. In 1989, moves began to make general practice a specialty by introducing requirements for the vocational training of family doctors. The training for nurses has also become more detailed, with a move away from hospital-based training to tertiary qualifications obtained from colleges of advanced education and universities.

As the main causes of ill health in Australia have changed, so there has been a change in attitude towards health care. There is an increasing emphasis on preventing disease as well as curing it, and the range of health professionals has widened to include dieticians, physiotherapists, occupational therapists, psychologists and other counsellors. In addition, there has been a growth in the popularity of alternative therapies such as naturopathy, homoeopathy, chiropractic and acupuncture, although these have yet to be recognised by government funding bodies.

Health services Health care in Australia is financed at four levels – by federal and State budgets, by private health insurance, and by direct patient contribution. The federal government is responsible for the formation of national health policies, and for the implementation of national health services including the universal health-insurance scheme Medicare, the Pharmaceutical Benefits Scheme, regulations on the importation and marketing of new drugs, the distribution of funds for medical research money, the collection of national medical statistics, and > *quarantine* services. Each State is responsible for the provision of hospital and community health services within its boundaries, as well as community health issues such as housing, waste disposal, and hygiene.

Health care in Australia is largely paid for on a fee-for-service basis, with patients paying a doctor or hospital for services provided and then claiming a proportion of their health costs from a health-insurance scheme. Some services – such as outpatient departments in hospitals and medical centres for people with special health needs – are provided free of charge by salaried doctors. In addition, all doctors have the option to 'bulk-bill', which means they are paid a fee directly by Medicare without a patient contribution.

Medicare is a publicly funded health-insurance scheme that covers all Australians. The first such system in Australia, Medibank, was introduced in July 1975 but was changed and modified by successive federal governments until replaced by Medicare in 1984. Medicare reimburses a patient for 85% of a government-set fee for doctors' services and provides 100% coverage for public patients treated in public hospitals. Patients may elect to take out private insurance to cover them for treatment by a doctor of their choice in a public or private hospital, but since the introduction of Medicare only 47% of the population has chosen to do so. Medicare is financed by the federal government from a 1.25% levy on income tax and from general revenue; it has been estimated, however, that the levy would need to be in the order of 3–4% to cover the actual cost of the system. The federal government administers the reimbursement of doctors' fees through the Health Insurance Commission; hospital services and some community health services are administered by the State governments, with block grants provided by the Commonwealth every five years.

Total health expenditure in 1985–6 was $18 172 million (some 7.8% of the gross domestic product) and represented an outlay of $1161 per person. The federal contribution amounted to $6970 million, which was largely paid out through the Medicare program and included the grants made to the States for hospital services. State and local governments contributed $6296 million, while a further $4906 million was derived from the private sector – including money spent in private hospitals, on health professionals not covered by Medicare (such as dentists), and half of the expenditure on pharmaceuticals.

The federal government is responsible for the regulation of pharmaceutical drugs in Australia: before drugs may be marketed, the company is required to produce evidence of effectiveness, low toxicity, and good standards of manufacture. The subsidised Pharmaceutical Benefits Scheme is intended to provide needed drugs to all sectors of the community at a minimum cost. A number of such systems have been instituted since the first was introduced in the late 1940s, but the scheme operating in 1988 provided a wide range of drugs for a cost of about $11 for most patients, $2 for social-security beneficiaries, and free of charge to pensioners. The cost of the scheme has been a major concern for successive federal governments, as newer and more expensive drugs have appeared on the market. The 1985–6 expenditure on drugs under the scheme was $860 million, an increase of about 13% a year on the 1982–3 expenditure of $605 million.

The cost of all health services will inevitably rise, because of the increasing proportion of elderly people in the community, the increased unit-cost of health services, and increased expectation of medical treatments. The increased interest in preventive health measures is a reflection of both the general high standard of health in Australia and the growing concern about a possible 'blow-out' in health costs. The link between smoking and a number of respiratory illnesses and cancers has, for example, led to intense efforts at a number of levels to persuade people to give up the habit. Doctors are encouraged to counsel their patients to this end, public education programs have been developed, legislation has been introduced to restrict cigarette advertising, a tax has been levied on cigarette sales in some States, and smoking is prohibited increasingly on public transport and in the workplace. Similar wide-ranging preventive measures have been adopted to promote better health practices among specific groups (such as youth and women) and to reduce the risk factors known to be associated with prevalent diseases (such as heart and alcohol-related disorders). In the absence of either a cure or a vaccine for > *AIDS*, efforts to restrict its spread throughout the Australian community have also been directed at public education. >> *medical research*; *quarantine*; *social services*

Heard and McDonald islands These Antarctic islands, which lie in the Southern Ocean north of the Antarctic Circle and some 4100km southwest of Fremantle in WA, were transferred from British to Australian control in 1947, becoming subject to the laws of the ACT in 1953. The rocky islets of the McDonald group and the larger Heard Island are all volcanic, rising from the submarine Kerguelen ridge. Heard Island, which is about 43km long and 21km wide, comprises the central rock mass Big Ben, which was volcanically active early this century, of which the highest point is Mawson Peak (2745m). First sighted in 1833 by a British sealer, the island is named after the American captain who discovered it 20 years later; in the latter half of the 19th century, and briefly in the early 20th, the island was occupied by sealers. It was visited by Douglas Mawson in 1929, and a scientific research station was set up by ANARE in 1947, closing in 1955 with the establishment of Mawson base in Antarctica; since that time it has been maintained as a base camp and is visited regularly by Australian expeditions. The McDonald group, which lies to the west of Heard Island, was discovered in 1854; no recorded landing was made until 1971, when two Australian scientists were dropped by helicopter on the largest of the group – McDonald Island – and discovered that it abounded with birdlife.

Hearn, William Edward (1826–88), academic and politician, b. Ireland. Hearn arrived in Vic. in 1854 as one of four original professors at the University of Melbourne and subsequently acquired a world reputation in economics and law. In 1873 he became the first dean of the university's law faculty and was prominent in university politics and public affairs, serving as a member of the Vic. parliament.

Heidelberg School This is the name commonly applied to the group of artists who painted outdoors in the Heidelberg district of Melbourne in the late 1880s and 1890s, and who provided the impetus for the first school of truly 'Australian' painting. The founding members of the group were Tom Roberts, Frederick McCubbin, Arthur Streeton and Charles Conder; the first three studied together at the Vic. National Gallery School in the 1870s and were greatly influenced by immigrant artists such as Conder, Julian Ashton and Louis Buvelot in the 1880s. Ashton's naturalistic, *plein-air* paintings were an inspiration to the young painters, who set up an artists' camp at Box Hill in Vic. in 1885, followed by others at Mentone and Eaglemont. The mood of their painting was Impressionist – small, fleeting impressions of changing light and atmosphere, to which the lyrical quality of the undulating outer-Melbourne landscape was well suited. They staged an exhibition of their work in 1889, dubbed the 9×5 Exhibition for the uniform proportions of the cigar-box lids on which they presented their 182 oil sketches. Although the original members went their separate ways in the early 1890s, the 'Heidelberg era' has long been perceived as laying the foundations for the golden age of nationalism in Australian painting.

Heinze, Sir Bernard Thomas (1894–1982), music conductor and teacher, b. Shepparton, Vic. An important figure in the development of Australian music, Heinze was appointed Ormond professor of music at the University of Melbourne in 1925. He was musical adviser to the ABC from its establishment in 1929, in which capacity he was largely responsible for the creation of the State symphony orchestras. Heinze was a principal conductor of the Vic. Symphony Orchestra 1933–56 and director of the NSW Conservatorium of Music 1956–66; he was also a guest conductor with numerous leading international orchestras.

helminths This is a widely accepted term for worm-like creatures that are often parasitic on animal hosts, frequently of a particular species. Flatworms, usually flat on back and belly, thin laterally, and lacking a body cavity, include the > *flukes* or trematodes and the tapeworms or cestodes. Numerous tapeworms may be found causing small, spherical cysts in rabbit meat, or in the flesh of the jewfish. The dog tapeworm causes hydatid disease, and the pig parasite sometimes causes serious illness to humans who have eaten infected pork that has been inadequately cooked.

Roundworms, or nematodes, are almost universal – free-living forms in soil, swamps, lakes, rivers and the sea, as well as parasitic species. They include the mosquito-borne filarial worm, *Wuchereria bancrofti*, and the hookworm. The former, present in Qld where it was discovered by Joseph Bancroft, develops in the mosquito after ingestion of the larval form in blood from human hosts. Hookworms are present in coastal northeastern Australia, and may cause some debility.

Helpmann, Sir Robert Murray (1909–86), dancer and actor, b. Mt Gambier, SA. A man of many parts, Helpmann shared his prolific talents among ballet, theatre and cinema. He began his career as a dancer, studying with Anna Pavlova during her 1926 Australian tour and making his professional debut in Sydney in 1927; he joined the Vic-Wells Ballet in London in 1933. His acting debut was as Oberon in *A Midsummer Night's Dream* at the Old Vic in 1937. He appeared in a number of films including *The Red Shoes* (1948), which he also choreographed, and *The Tales of Hoffmann* (1951). He was joint artistic director of the Australian Ballet 1965–76, and was knighted in 1968.

Hemiptera > *bugs*

Henderson, Moya Patricia (1941–), composer, b. Quirindi, NSW. Foremost among Australian women composers, Henderson studied in Cologne on a German exchange scholarship 1974–6. Since returning to Australia in 1977, she has composed numerous choral, vocal and instrumental works, of which some, such as 'Min Min Light', have been inspired by Aboriginal legends.

Henty family, important in the early settlement of Tas. and Vic. As farmers and bankers in England, they had Australian connections through merino breeding, and saw the colony as being able to 'do more for our family than England ever will'. **Thomas** (1775–1839) and his seven sons immigrated 1829–37, first to WA, where their grant proved useless land; next to Tas., where Thomas and several sons remained; then to Portland Bay, Vic., where **Edward** (1810–78) became in 1834 the first permanent settler, preceding the 'discovery' of western Vic. in 1835 by Thomas Mitchell.

Herbert, (Alfred Francis) Xavier (1901–84), author, b. Port Hedland, WA. Herbert qualified as a pharmacist but soon turned to writing and the first of his many short stories was published in 1926. He then went roaming in the NT, the setting for both his passionately indignant novel *Capricornia* (1938) and the prodigiously long but lesser *Poor Fellow My Country* (1975). Herbert's writing, often exaggerated, portrays underlying truth rather than reality. His aptly titled autobiography, *Disturbing Element* (1963), epitomises his provocative, emphatic character.

Herbert River Qld A river that rises on the Atherton Tableland, the Herbert flows for 240km southeast to the Hinchinbrook Channel, near Ingham. The upper reaches are partly rugged forest, partly cattle-grazing land; the middle region is dense rainforest; and the lowlands have been cleared for intensive cultivation, chiefly of sugar cane. At the Wallaman Falls on one of the Herbert's tributaries, Stony Creek, the river drops 305m.

herbicides > *biocides*; *weeds*

heritage conservation Although Australia's first national trust was formed in 1945 (in NSW), the systematic identification and protection of historic sites and relics has been carried out only since the 1970s. Heritage conservation now extends to landscapes and physical features, Aboriginal culture, and artefacts ranging from private gardens to shipwrecks and industrial structures and memorabilia. Increasing attention is being paid to appropriate management and interpretation of this legacy.

In 1974 Australia became a signatory to the International Convention for the Protection of the World Cultural and National Heritage, which came into force in 1975. A major impetus to heritage conservation was given by a 1974 report, commissioned by the federal government, that clearly defined Australia's national estate and recommended conservation measures on a cost-benefit basis. The Australian Heritage Commission was established in 1975 to develop policies and programs for the protection of the nation's cultural heritage, and since then more than 8000 places – from Aboriginal rock-art sites to historic towns – have been entered in the register of the national estate. Legislation protecting the nation's cultural and scientific heritage now exists in most States; government programs include physical works, advisory services, grants and loans for restoration projects, and controls over development in significant areas.

While much has been achieved, heritage conservation remains a difficult and often controversial area. The problems are complex and mostly arise from the conflicting claims of conservation and development. Difficult decisions must be made, particularly about which sites merit preservation and whether this is financially justified in the long term; statutory standards for works on registered sites are often prohibitively expensive for property owners to implement. At the same time, the economic benefits of preserving our cultural heritage – particularly in attracting tourists – have often encouraged substandard re-creations of the past, the worst of which have been described as 'historical disasters'; uncontrolled public access has in many cases caused irreparable damage to fragile sites. Attempts to reconcile conservation and development have led to many unsuccessful compromises, perhaps the most visible of these being 'facadism', where a modern structure is erected behind the shell of an historic building. In the 1980s the conflicting claims of conservation and development became a cause célèbre when several resource-rich sites (including Kakadu National Park) were added to the World Heritage list. >> *architecture*; *environment and conservation*; *museums*; *national trusts*

Herman, Sali (1898–), painter, b. Switzerland. Herman arrived in Australia in 1937. He first studied in Melbourne under George Bell, later becoming noted for his atmospheric, crowded urban paintings of Sydney. He was an official war artist 1945–6 and a winner of the Wynne Prize three times and the Sulman Prize twice.

hermit crabs This is a group of marine crustaceans adapted to using discarded gastropod shells as protection for their own soft hindparts, which are spirally twisted to fit the interior of shells. Australian species vary from the large (23cm) scaly-legged hermit crab and the stridulating hermit crab – named for its habit of rubbing together its ridged claws – to small burrow-inhabiting species such as the miner crab, seen in estuaries in southeastern Australia.

Heron Island > *Capricorn–Bunker Islands*

herons > *bitterns, egrets and herons*

Herring, Sir Edmund Francis (1892– 1982), lawyer and soldier, b. Maryborough, Vic. Herring served with distinction in World War 1 and became a barrister in 1920. An outstanding military leader during World War 2, he was chief justice of the Vic. Supreme Court 1944–64, a period of considerable expansion of that court. He established a law reform committee in 1944 and was lt-governor of Vic. 1945–72.

herrings The family Clupeidae, to which herrings belong, includes a number of closely related fishes such as pilchards and sprats. In Australia they are mainly inshore and estuarine fishes of tropical regions. Among representative species are the large-scaled, silvery oxeye herring, *Megalops cyprinoides*, the giant herring, *Elops australis*, the long, lean and voracious wolf herring, *Chirocentrus vorax*, and a number of shoal herrings similar to those of Europe, such as *Maugeclupea novaehollandiae*, which like pilchards are often found in more temperate waters. Commercial fishing of herrings in Australia is limited.

Hervey Bay Qld (pop. 14 410) This city and the large inlet after which it is named lie 289km north of Brisbane. Hervey Bay is a large conurbation that services the local fishing, timber and agricultural industries (notably sugar and fruit production); tourism is the city's main industry, however, and the bay is lined with beach resorts, including Pialba and Torquay, which attract thousands of holidaymakers throughout the year.

Hester, Joy (1920–60), artist, b. Elsternwick, Vic. Hester was a member of the avant-garde Melbourne coterie that included Sidney Nolan, Arthur Boyd and patrons John and Sunday Reed. Married first to Albert Tucker and later to Gray Smith, Hester was a fine draughtswoman and original artist whose talent and powerful imagery was not publicly recognised until after her death.

Heysen, Sir Hans (1877–1968), painter, b. Germany. Heysen arrived in Australia in 1884 and grew up in SA. A landscape artist especially adept at watercolour, he was known for his lyrical, light-filled depictions of the massive gum trees and vivid rocks of the Flinders Ranges and the landscape near Hahndorf in the Adelaide Hills, where he lived

for more than 50 years. Heysen won the Wynne Prize for landscape painting nine times.

Hibberd, Jack (John Charles) (1940–), playwright, b. Warracknabeal, Vic. A prolific playwright, Hibberd practised medicine until the 1973 success of *Dimboola* (1974), his best-known play, enabled him to turn to the stage full-time. *A Stretch of the Imagination* (1973) is, however, considered by many to be his best work. Hibberd has been influenced by a range of theatrical forms and dramatists, including Harold Pinter and Bertold Brecht; he is noted for portraying 'ocker' stereotypes and mingling fun with gravity in popular works ranging from the musical *Marvellous Melbourne* (1977), to celebrations of national legends in *A Toast to Melba* (1976), *The Les Darcy Show* (1976) and *Captain Midnight VC* (1972).

hibiscus This genus of striking trees and shrubs, which belongs to the > *mallow family*, is represented in Australia by 35 species. Most are tropical or subtropical, although some species extend to the arid inland. Among the most common is the native rosella or cottonwood, *H. heterophyllus*, which grows to about 10m and has white or yellow flowers with the group's characteristic dark petal bases. The mangrove hibiscus, *H. tiliaceous*, is a small spreading tree of the eastern coast, also yellow-flowered. Some members of this group are weak shrubs, such as the pink-flowered *H. sturtii* of the arid inland. The bark fibre of several species was used by Aborigines for fishing nets and lines, and the roots and leaves for food.

Hicks, Sir (Cedric) Stanton (1892–1976) physiologist, b. NZ. During World War 1, Hicks developed a drug that helped to control meningitis among army troops. After research work in pharmacology at Cambridge University, he was professor of human physiology and pharmacology at Adelaide University 1926–58. He worked with the SA government as an adviser on nutrition during and after the 1930s depression and it is in this field that he became particularly noted; during World War 2 he instituted major improvements to army food and helped to establish the first catering corps. He published widely on science and nutrition, including the books *Food Facts* (1958) and *Who Called the Cook a Bastard?* (1971).

Higgins, Henry Bournes (1851–1929), politician and lawyer, b. Ireland. Higgins

arrived in Australia in 1870 with his family and graduated in law from the University of Melbourne in 1875. A member of the Vic. parliament 1894–1900, he then entered federal politics and was attorney-general in the short-lived government of J.C. Watson in 1904. A High Court judge from 1906 and president of the Commonwealth Court of Conciliation and Arbitration 1907–21, his lasting achievements included the > *Harvester judgment*, which introduced the principle of a fair minimum wage.

High Court of Australia > *law and legal system*

Higinbotham, George (1826–92), lawyer and politician, b. Ireland. Higinbotham arrived in Vic. in 1854 and was editor of the Melbourne *Argus* 1856–9. He was elected to the Vic. parliament in 1861 and was attorney-general 1863–8; a political radical, he advocated colonial independence and the curbing of the governor's powers as well as supporting female franchise. Appointed to the Supreme Court in 1860, he became chief justice in 1886 and as such continued his support of responsible government, most notably in his dissenting judgment in *Toy v. Musgrove*. He completed Vic.'s statute law in 1890, accepting no payment for this task and later refusing public honours because they originated in Britain.

Hilder, Jesse Jewhurst (1881–1916), artist, b. Toowoomba, Qld. Although plagued by ill health, Hilder, who worked as a bank clerk 1898–1909, persisted with his art. He achieved some recognition for his delicate, high-keyed paintings – usually small-scale landscapes in watercolour – which reflected his great love of the French landscape-painter Corot.

Hill, Alfred Francis (1870–1960), music composer and conductor, b. Melbourne. Brought up in NZ, Hill was a musical prodigy who performed with the NZ Opera orchestra from 1884. While still a youth he studied in Leipzig for five years, returning to NZ in 1891 to become director of the Wellington Orchestral Society. Hill was later principal conductor for J.C. Williamson in Australia, and from 1915 taught at the NSW Conservatorium of Music; in 1935 he opened his own music school in Sydney. A prolific composer, much of his work was influenced by Maori chants and legends, including an opera *Tapu* and the well-known song, 'Waiata Poi'.

Hinchinbrook Island Qld An island of forests and spectacular mountains, Hinchinbrook lies off the Qld coast east of Ingham. The highest of the several rocky peaks is Mt Bowen (1117m); the slopes of the island are clothed in thick tropical vegetation, and mangrove forests border the drowned valley, Hinchinbrook Channel, which separates it from the mainland. Hinchinbrook is about 35km long, and 24km wide at its broadest point; it was declared a national park in 1932.

Hinton, Howard (1867–1948), art collector, b. England. Hinton arrived in Australia in 1892. A businessman, patron of the arts, and keen art collector, during the 1930s and 1940s he purchased – and later donated to the Armidale Teachers College, NSW – more than 1000 paintings, 700 art books and some sculpture. This, the Howard Hinton Art Collection, formed the basis of the New England Regional Art Museum; it is widely representative of many of the most important Australian painters of both the 19th and 20th centuries.

historical records > *archives*

Hoad, Lew(is Allan) (1934–), tennis player, b. Sydney. A national hero of amateur tennis in the 1950s, Hoad was noted for his powerful play and top-spin backhands. He had a long rivalry with Ken Rosewall from their first appearance together in 1946. Hoad played in Davis Cup matches 1952–6 and won at Wimbledon in 1957; he subsequently turned professional (reputedly for the largest sum of money ever offered to an amateur) and retired to Spain in 1967 to run a tennis coaching centre.

Hobart Tas. The capital of Tas. and Australia's ninth-largest city, Hobart is the smallest capital city in the Commonwealth and houses an uncommonly small proportion (40%) of the State's population; it is also Australia's second-oldest city and has the largest concentration of early colonial buildings. Dominated by Mt Wellington (1271m), Hobart extends along both shores of the Derwent River estuary, for 25km on the western shore and 15km on the eastern. With cool to mild winters and mild to warm summers, the city

has an average annual precipitation ranging from 1150mm in the west to 500mm in the east; there are occasional snowfalls in winter on the higher suburbs.

Hobart is named after Robert Hobart, 4th Earl of Buckinghamshire, the British colonial secretary at the time of its founding. Originally there were two settlements on the Derwent, one founded by John Bowen at Risdon Cove in 1803 (where settlers first used firearms against Tas. Aborigines) and the other a penal settlement founded by David Collins at Sullivans Cove in 1804. Later that year the Risdon settlement moved to join Collins, and in 1812 Hobarton, as it was then called, was declared the capital. By 1852, just before transportation ended, Hobart seemed likely to compete with Sydney as a commercial centre, but the Vic. goldrushes led to stagnation and thereafter growth was slow. The construction of bridges at various points over the Derwent, and industries based on hydro-electric development, have led to Hobart's subsequent expansion, mainly as a service and commercial centre.

At the census of 1986 the Hobart Statistical Division had a population of 175 082, which showed a growth rate of 3.99% over the five years between censuses, the lowest of any Australian capital. Hobart is also characterised by very high concentrations of single-parent families and the highest youth unemployment rate of any capital city. Despite being mainly a service centre, Hobart is the principal manufacturing city of Tas., with an electrolytic zinc plant at Risdon and Australia's largest newsprint-manufacturing plant at Boyer. Wholesaling and retailing, the public service (including the Hydro-electric Commission) and the tourist industry are the main employers. Tourists are attracted by the Wrest Point Casino – Australia's first such institution – and the city's fine colonial architecture (although the latter is in need of protection from the industrial pollution of that section of the Derwent River).

hockey Hockey was introduced to Australia at the turn of the century, developing initially in WA and SA with strong bases in universities across the country. Men's and women's competitions were established almost concurrently; overseas tours were undertaken to various parts of the British Empire, and the Australian Hockey Association was formed in 1925. In the interwar years the sport was dominated by the Pearce family of WA.

Hockey received the greatest boost when Australia first entered Olympic competition at the Melbourne Games in 1956. Subsequently, the men's team finished third in 1964, second in 1968 and 1976, and after having won the 1986 World Cup, were favourites in Seoul in 1988. However, Ric Charlesworth, playing in his fourth Olympic event, retired without achieving the elusive gold medal. Women's hockey was included as an Olympic event for the first time in 1984 and the 1988 team won Australia's first medal of the Seoul Games with a 2-nil win over its South Korean hosts; after a shaky start to the series, the team had defeated arch-rivals Holland 3–2 in the semifinal.

Today there are 70 000 men and 112 000 women registered as hockey players in Australia.

Hoddle, Robert

Hoddle, Robert (1794–1881), colonial surveyor, b. England. In 1823 Hoddle was appointed assistant government surveyor in NSW under John Oxley, whom he assisted in the survey and establishment of Brisbane (1824). Appointed senior surveyor in Port Phillip (1837), he was responsible for Melbourne's formal grid layout although his subordinate Robert Russell claimed the credit and controversy remains. Hoddle was auctioneer at the first sale of Crown Land (1837) and was first surveyor-general after Vic. separated from NSW in 1851. His foresight and imagination ensured the wide boulevards that are still one of Melbourne's major attributes.

Hogan, Paul

Hogan, Paul (1939–), actor and comedian, b. Sydney. A rigger on the Sydney Harbour Bridge, Hogan entered television after appearing in a talent quest in 1972. With a dry, laconic style, Hogan enjoyed remarkable success with his television programs and advertisements in Australia and overseas in the 1970s. Having come to represent the archetypal 'Aussie', he also promoted Australian beer and tourism in the US and UK during the 1980s. He played the eponymous antihero in the film *Crocodile Dundee* (1985) – which he also co-wrote – a spectacular commercial success in the US as well as Australia. A sequel, *Crocodile Dundee II*, was released in 1988.

Holden, Sir Edward Wheewall > GMH

Holden, Sir Edward Wheewall > *GMH*

holidays and national days

holidays and national days In addition to traditional, worldwide public holidays (such as Christmas Day), Australia has several national

public holidays and a number of less rigorously observed commemorative days throughout the year. Some are moveable feasts, to the extent that they are celebrated on the Monday closest to the official holiday date, which has led Australia to be characterised as 'the land of the long weekend'.

Australia Day commemorates the landing of the First Fleet in NSW, on 26 January 1788. This day was officially designated a public holiday in 1838 (and was for some time known as 'Foundation Day'); it is generally observed on the first Monday after 26 January.

Anzac Day was inaugurated to commemorate the landing of the Anzac troops at Gallipoli on 25 April 1915. It was later extended to honour all who have died in military conflicts in which Australia has been involved, including the most recent, the Vietnam War.

The Queen's (or King's) Birthday, the official celebration of the birthday of the British monarch, has been observed since the first years of white settlement. Since the reign of King George V, whose birthday was on 3 June, it has generally been observed on the second Monday in June.

Commonwealth Day, which is observed by most member nations of the Commonwealth, is celebrated on 11 June, the official birthday of Queen Elizabeth II. This holiday was called Empire Day and observed on 24 May (Queen Victoria's birthday) from its inception in 1905 until 1958, whence it was called British Commonwealth Day; its current name and date were adopted in 1966.

Other noteworthy Australian holidays include Remembrance Day, on 11 November; and Labour Day, which commemorates the achievement of an eight-hour working day by trade unions in the 19th century and is observed in all States but on varying dates. Melbourne Cup Day, on the first Tuesday in November, while not designated a public holiday outside Melbourne effectively brings the nation to a standstill at least for the duration of that horse race.

Holmes à Court, (Michael) Robert

Holmes à Court, (Michael) Robert (1937–), business entrepreneur, b. South Africa. A lawyer, Holmes à Court was reputed to be Australia's richest man until the stockmarket crash of October 1987. A master of company take-overs, he built up a vast conglomerate under the umbrella of his Bell Group, which included interests in transport, entertainment, mining, oil, publishing and television; he was forced to relinquish many of his interests after 1987. He is also a notable collector of Australian art, and a horse-breeder.

Holothuroidea > *sea-cucumbers*

Holt, Harold Edward (1908–67) politician, b. Sydney. Holt's parliamentary career began in 1935 and included several cabinet positions before he succeeded Sir Robert Menzies as prime minister in 1966. He inherited and fostered the US alliance; particularly notable was the increased commitment of Australian troops in the Vietnam War. Although returned to office in the 1966 election he faced increasing political difficulties, but was still in office when in December 1967 he was drowned while swimming near Portsea, Vic.

Holtermann, Bernard Otto (1838–85), gold-miner and photographic patron, b. Germany. Holtermann arrived in Australia in 1858. At Hill End (NSW) in 1872 the 'Holtermann Nugget' (actually a piece of reef gold) was found in a mine owned by Holtermann and Louis Beyers. Having thereby amassed considerable wealth, Holtermann later settled in Sydney and in the 1870s commissioned a unique series of photographs of the goldfields of NSW and Vic. One of the largest assignments during the period of wet-plate photography, the photographs were taken by noted early photographers such as Beaufoy Merlin and later Charles Bayliss and provide an invaluable chronicle of goldfields life.

honeyeaters There are about a dozen genera, comprising 70 species, of the family Meliphagidae in Australia and these extend also into the southwest Pacific and Southeast Asia. They are sprightly, mainly green-brown birds (although some species are brightly coloured) differing considerably in body size, beak size and shape, habitat, habits and calls; however, the forked and bristly brush-tongue – used for brushing out nectar – is a distinctive feature of all species.

The most familiar honeyeaters have biggish, down-curved beaks and a bold and agile manner; most species have either a white or a yellow feather patch on the side of the head, a brightly coloured piece of bare skin above the eye, or a fleshy wattle. All eat nectar, and for some it is the staple food so that they tend to be migratory, like the apiarist, but insects are probably the more important form of food of the whole group.

Among the typical green-yellowish birds, often having a pale streak below the eye, is the white-plumed honeyeater, *Meliphaga penicillata*, common across much of Australia; spinebills, of the genus *Acanthorhynchus*, have rather large heads and downward-curved beaks. The crescent honeyeater of the genus *Meliornis* inhabits coastal areas of Australia, including Tas. The soldier-birds, miner-birds and bell-birds, genus *Manorina*, occur in most parts of Australia, ranging widely in search of a varied diet of nectar, insects and berries; the characteristic, ringing call of the bellbird or bell-miner is often heard in the wet forests of eastern Australia. The friarbird, of the genus *Philemon*, earns its popular name by reason of its bare head; it is often either grey or black, with the line of the large beak continuing the curve of the head. Wattlebirds, species of *Anthochaera,* are large birds with fleshy red or yellow wattles on the lower cheeks.

honours and awards In Australia, honours and awards are conferred by the British monarch on the recommendation of the federal and State governments. An honour is an appointment to an order or chivalry; an award is usually defined as a decoration for civil or military distinction. Honours and awards fall into two categories, Imperial (of British origin) and Australian; they are announced at the New Year, on Australia Day and on the Queen's official birthday. In the 1970s, in keeping with its republican philosophy, the Whitlam Labor government refused to nominate Australians for Imperial honours and instead instituted the Order of Australia. Imperial honours were reinstated by the succeeding Liberal government, under Malcolm Fraser, but again discontinued by the Hawke Labor government in the 1980s.

The major Australian honours were established in 1975 and comprise the Order of Australia, the Australian Bravery Awards and the National Medal. The Order of Australia is modelled on the Imperial orders of chivalry and consists of Companions (AC), Officers (AO), Members (AM) and Medals (OAM); knighthoods and damehoods were abolished by the Hawke government in 1986. The Australian Bravery Awards consist of the Cross of Valour (CV), the Star of Courage (SC), the Bravery Medal (BM) and the Commendation for Brave Conduct. The National Medal is awarded for long service in the defence, police, fire and ambulance services. The main Imperial orders are the Garter, Bath, St Michael and St George and the Order of the British Empire. The highest class of most orders confers a knighthood and the lower classes confer a rank such as commander, companion or member. The George Cross was created in 1940 and is primarily an award for acts of great heroism by civilians.

Military awards Decorations for gallantry – of British origin – include the Victoria Cross (VC), the George Cross (GC), and various awards related to specific branches of the armed forces, such as the Distinguished Flying Cross (DFC) and Military Cross (MC). The most famous, the Victoria Cross, was created in 1856 for conspicuous bravery in the face of the enemy. It was originally fashioned from the metal of cannons captured at Sebastopol during the Crimean War. Ninety-four Australians have received it, 28 of them posthumously.

hookworms > *helminths*

Hope, A.D. (Alec Derwent) (1907–), poet and academic, b. Cooma, NSW. Educated at the universities of Sydney and Oxford, Hope was professor of English at the Australian National University, Canberra, 1951–68. He is a leading Australian poet, writing brilliant and often sharply witty verse which has been collected in several volumes since the first, *The Wandering Islands*, was published in 1955. Also a witty and influential literary critic, Hope has fought occasionally controversial battles against what he considers the second-rate; a collection of his essays and reviews was published as *Native Companions* (1974).

Hopkins, John Raymond (1927–), music conductor and teacher, b. England. Principal conductor of the NZ Symphony Orchestra 1957–63, Hopkins was director of music for the ABC 1963–73, during which time he was an ardent supporter of Australian music through commissions and performance. He also formed a national training orchestra and established a series of 'Prom' concerts in Sydney and Melbourne. In 1973, he was appointed dean of the school of music at the Vic. College of the Arts. He has been director of the NSW Conservatorium since 1986.

Hopkins, Livingston (1846–1927), cartoonist, b. USA. 'Hop' was already a success-ful cartoonist and illustrator in New York when invited to join the Sydney *Bulletin* in 1882, where he worked for over 30 years. A veteran of the American Civil War, his politically trenchant cartoons brought him national fame. He was involved in the Sydney art world as an etcher and watercolourist, and helped to establish an artists' camp at Balmoral, NSW, with Julian Ashton.

Hopman, Harry (Henry Christian) (1906–85), tennis player, b. Sydney. An outstanding player in his own right, Hopman made his name as captain of the Australian Davis Cup team 1938–9 and 1950–69; his captaincy led Australia to sixteen victories. A wily tactician and a strict disciplinarian whose fines, curfews and dictatorial style often drew criticism from both players and public, he is well remembered for his training of Lew Hoad and Ken Rosewall, who as 18-year-olds won the Davis Cup for Australia in 1953. Hopman was president of the Lawn Tennis Association of Vic. 1964–9, and an Australian selector 1962–9, and published two books, *Aces and Places* (1957) and *Better Tennis for Boys and Girls* (1972). He moved to the US in 1970.

Hordern family, distinguished in Australian commerce and pastoralism. **Anthony** (1789–1869), b. England, arrived in Australia in 1824; his wife Ann established a family drapery business in Sydney, which continued both there and in Melbourne. Their twin sons **John** (1819–64) and **Anthony** (1819–76), and a third son **Lebbeus** (1826–81), all continued in drapery and commerce; the first started the longstanding Sydney department store Hordern Bros in 1844, and the other two founded the family's largest business, Anthony Hordern and Sons, in 1844. Other notable family members include **Samuel** (1849–1900), who initiated the family's pastoral interests and became a leading breeder of both cattle and horses at his Bowral and Picton properties. His eldest son **Samuel** (1876–1956) was head of the family business 1909–26, at the end of which period Anthony Hordern and Sons became a public company. Anthony II's son **Anthony** (1842–86) sponsored railway and immigration projects in WA; his cousin **Lebbeus** (1891–1928), a son of Samuel II, was a pioneer of Australian commercial aviation.

Horne, Donald (Richmond) (1921–), journalist and author, b. Muswellbrook, NSW.

255

Editor of numerous magazines during his career, including the *Bulletin* 1961–62 and 1967–72, Horne achieved prominence with the publication of *The Lucky Country* (1964), an examination of the materialism, philistinism and provincialism of Australian society at the time. Other works of social comment include *Death of the Lucky Country* (1976), *Time of Hope* (1980) and *Winner Take All*? (1981); many consider his best work to be his autobiography, *The Education of Young Donald* (1967). A lecturer in politics at the University of NSW 1973–7, Horne has been a vocal political commentator; he became chairman of the Australia Council in 1985.

horse-racing Horse-racing occupies a unique place in Australian life. Since the first formal meeting in 1810 and the formation of the Sydney Turf Club in 1825, racing and gambling have indulged a passion shared by all levels of society and every region in the country. With 500 clubs and 423 venues, Australia has the highest concentration of racing in the world; in 1987–8 prize money of over $146 million was offered, and in Vic. alone nearly $1.25 billion was invested on the TAB. The industry as a whole provides employment for over 30 000, enjoyment for millions, and misery and ruin for not a few.

Racing early spread through all the colonies and in 1841 the Australian St Leger, the nation's oldest classic race, was first run, although the > *Melbourne Cup* has become Australia's premier race.

The Australian Jockey Club, formed in 1842, instituted a scale of weight-for-age in 1860, in consideration of which all horses are adjudged to have their birthdays on 1 August. The Australian rules of racing were codified in 1912, and since 1970–1 Australia has followed the international practice of grading all races. Steeplechases and hurdles remain popular in Vic. and SA and each State features classic races, while the Spring Carnival in Melbourne and the Autumn Carnival in Sydney are the major features of the racing calendar.

Each era has produced its champions. Great horses from the past include The Barb, Archer, Poseidon, Gloaming, Carbine, Ajax, Peter Pan and > *Phar Lap*. The rise in stake money in recent times makes it impossible to compare the achievements of horses on the basis of their winnings, but the first horse to top the $1 million mark was Kingston Town in 1981, while Beau Zam and Our Poetic Prince have

gone on to win more than $2 million. The major races – the Melbourne Cup and the Golden Slipper Stakes – each carry prize money of over $2 million.

Successful trainers in the early period were John Higgerson and James Scobie; the modern era has been dominated by Tommy Smith, who in 1985 won the Sydney trainers' premiership for a record 33rd time; Bart Cummings, who in 1973–4 became the first trainer to exceed $1 million in a season and in 1977 achieved a record sixth Melbourne Cup; and Colin Hayes, who won his first Melbourne Cup in 1980. Famous jockeys include Bobby Lewis, James Pike, Myles Connell, D.H. (Darby) Munro, Scobie Breasley, George Moore, Roy Higgins and Darren Gauci. After a long struggle, women won the right to ride as jockeys in 1979.

Despite falling attendances at tracks and a number of corruption scandals in the mid-1980s, racing remains buoyant and an integral part of Australian life.

Horsham Vic. (pop. 12 174) A city on the Wimmera River, generally regarded as the region's capital, Horsham lies about 300km northwest of Melbourne. It is a market, road, service and tourist centre, with some industry based on agriculture, including machinery and textiles. It is boosted by its position on the Western Highway between Melbourne and Adelaide, and has a noted agricultural college and wheat-research institute.

horticulture > *agriculture*; *fruit-growing*; *nursery trade*; *vegetable-growing*

Hoskins family, pioneers of the Australian steel industry. **Charles Henry** (1851–1926), b. England, arrived in Australia in 1854. With his brother **George John** (1848–1926), he developed a firm specialising in the fabrication of steel and cast-iron pipes. The company expanded in both Sydney and Brisbane, supplying most State governments and a number of water authorities, and in 1907 took over an existing steelworks at Lithgow. Hoskins Iron and Steel was established in 1920 and two years later acquired land at Port Kembla; further expansion included iron-ore and limestone quarries, coal mines and coke ovens. Under Charles's son **Sir Cecil Harold** (1889–1971), b. Petersham, NSW, the Lithgow works were dismantled and Australian Iron and Steel Ltd was formed at Port Kembla in 1928, with Sir Cecil and his brother as joint managing directors. In 1935 the firm merged with BHP Ltd. The family name is commemorated in the giant Hoskins Kembla Works at Port Kembla.

hospitals > *health and health services*

Hotham, Sir Charles (1806–55), colonial administrator, b. England. Hotham was lt-governor of Vic. 1853–5. He succeeded Charles La Trobe after naval and diplomatic service, and was faced with serious unemployment, ubiquitous financial problems, and goldfields unrest; his enforcement of gold-licensing laws culminated in the > *Eureka Stockade* incident. While not unsympathetic to the miners' grievances, he blamed foreign subversive elements, and hand-led the situation with naval discipline.

Houses of Representatives > *government*

housing Owning their own home has long been the ambition of most Australians, and governments have fostered the principle since the 19th century. In 1986, nearly 70% of Australian households owned or were in the process of buying their dwellings and more than three-quarters of all occupied homes were separate houses, typically on allotments of 0.1ha or more. By this time, however, the commitment to home ownership was hardly appropriate to the nation's demographic and economic circumstances: on the one hand, nearly half of all households comprised only one or two people and some 24% of the population moved house each year; on the other hand, an increasing number of Australians were finding the cost of renting or buying a home prohibitive. The relatively low provision of welfare housing in Australia – accounting for little more than 5% of dwellings in 1986 – is generally attributed to the longstanding government policies favouring home-owners.

Historical development The low building density of most Australian towns and the predominance of home ownership were initiated by the land-grant and auction policies and subdivision practices from the early 19th century. This was particularly the case in non-metropolitan and rural areas: larger conurbations typically developed high-density cores and spreading, lower-density suburbs along the transport routes. The rapid growth of cities was rarely matched by the provision of services, with the result that overcrowding and poor housing conditions were common in cities such

as Melbourne and Sydney by the end of the century. Low wages or persistent unemployment for many workers, and inadequate social services, created a large clientele for low-cost housing which was generally found in the dilapidating high-density city centres or on the outer fringes of urban settlements.

A housing-reform movement was active from the early 20th century: the SA Housing Trust (1936) and the NSW Housing Commission (1941) were established to provide accommodation for workers, and the Vic. Housing Commission was formed in 1937 for the explicit purpose of abolishing slums and 'reclaiming' housing conditions; similar housing authorities followed in the other States. These concerns were also taken up by the federal Labor governments of the 1940s, the 1945 Commonwealth-State Housing Agreement authorising low-interest loans to the States for public-sector rental housing. Amendments to this agreement in the 1950s shifted its focus to home-ownership, however, as did banking reforms that required savings banks to direct finance to home-buyers at interest rates which were, in effect, subsidised by low returns to depositors. Between 1952 and 1974, investment in housing averaged about 5% of gross domestic product (the previous peak being about 2% in the late 1930s); by 1966, some 69% of Sydney households and 73% in Melbourne were occupied by their owners, compared with figures of 40% and 46% respectively in 1947. The housing boom was fostered by rising real wages and spreading car ownership, the latter encouraging expansion to cheaper land away from the public-transport network.

Whereas the early years of the postwar housing boom mainly saw the development of detached houses on 'green' allotments, inner-suburban flats and apartments became increasingly common in the 1960s. By 1965 flats accounted for nearly half of new dwellings being constructed in Sydney and Melbourne, the demand being generated by both the entry of the postwar 'baby boom' generation into the workforce and the high number of immigrants from southern Europe. These tenants gradually abandoned the inner areas and the boom accordingly shifted to new 'green fields' subdivisions and development of detached houses. By the early 1970s, there was considerable speculative investment in land on the urban fringe in the expectation of continuing demand. As the 'baby boomers' passed through the market, however, the demand began to decline and the progressive deregulation of the Australian financial system led to rising interest rates which threatened – and in many cases bankrupted – speculators and developers. Bank and government incentives to home buyers, including the pegging of mortgage-interest rates, led to a boom in house prices in Sydney, Melbourne and Adelaide. Prices continued to rise consistently until 1977, after which the increases were more uneven – very high in Sydney, less so in the other cities, and falling relative to inflation in rural areas. In the capital cities the greatest price rises were in the more convenient established suburbs, which were increasingly subject to gentrification.

The 1980s and beyond The events of the 1970s had serious consequences for housing in – and arguably beyond – the 1980s. First, purchasing a home became less and less affordable: by 1974 mortgage repayments on an average-priced house in Melbourne had reached 40% of male average earnings (and more in Sydney), compared with a figure of 25% in the 1950s and 1960s; rising mortgage-interest rates exacerbated the problem. Second, households on average incomes were increasingly obliged to rent rather than buy their homes; those still able to purchase were generally relegated to the lowest-priced areas, typically in the least convenient locations with the poorest services. Third, housing became an increasing source of wealth redistribution as the extreme differences in price rises gave different groups differing levels of capital gains and home-owners reaped much greater gains than were available to renters.

In response to these problems, the State governments attempted to reduce the land component of house prices by adopting policies of urban consolidation – encouraging higher-density housing in established suburbs to make use of existing infrastructure. Planning schemes were amended to allow smaller allotment sizes and to encourage the development of town and row houses or dual occupancy (the provision of two or more dwellings on an existing allotment). The result hoped for is a greater range of dwelling types and sizes, more appropriate to Australia's increasing household diversity than is the historical uniformity of most of its suburbs and towns.

A number of housing issues remain unresolved, however, most notably the growing number of Australians to whom adequate housing is still unavailable and the continuing deterioration of many urban areas. There is likely to be persistent and growing pressure on governments and planners to meet these challenges in the 1990s. >> *architecture*; *land settlement*; *urban planning*

Houtman Abrolhos WA These three groups of uninhabited islands – Pelsaert, Easter and Wallabi – lie about 80km off the coast, due west of Geraldton, and together stretch for some 80km. The islands have a history of shipwrecks, including that of François Pelsaert in the *Batavia* in 1629. The Portuguese name 'Abrolhos' (an elision of the term meaning 'watch out!') was given in 1598 by the Dutch captain Frederik de Houtman; other famous shipwrecks in the area included those of the *Zeewyk* (1727) and the *Ocean Queen* (1840). In the past the islands were quarried for both guano and phosphate but they are now a wildlife sanctuary; tourists are prohibited, but the islands are a fishing centre, notably for crayfish.

Hovell, William Hilton (1786–1875), explorer, b. England. Hovell immigrated to NSW in 1813, and settled to farm after serving on trading ships for the merchant Simeon Lord. In 1824 he accompanied Hamilton Hume on an exploratory journey that led to the discovery of the Murray River and finished at Port Phillip Bay. Later there was a bitter dispute regarding their mistake in thinking that they had reached Westernport, Hume (the native-born) believing that Hovell (the immigrant) was at fault.

Howard, John Winston (1939–), politician, b. Earlwood, NSW. Howard practised as a solicitor until he entered federal parliament as a Liberal member in 1974. He became a minister in the Fraser government in 1975 and was treasurer 1977–83. From March 1983 he was shadow treasurer, and in September 1985 he replaced Andrew Peacock as federal leader of the Liberal Party. Although generally deemed to be a colourless figure and having failed to unseat Labor in the 1987 election, Howard retained the party leadership until 1989 when he was in turn replaced by Peacock.

Howe, Michael (1787–1818), bushranger, b. England. Howe was transported to Tas. for highway robbery in 1811, and escaped to become the notorious, audacious and brutal bushranger 'Black Howe' 1814–18, making this a period of terror for settlers and travellers.

He was killed near the Shannon River, having been decoyed there after a year in hiding. *Michael Howe, the Last and Worst of the Bushrangers of Van Diemen's Land* by Thomas Wells, published by Andrew Bent (1818), was the first Australian work of general literature, of which only three known copies survive.

Howitt, Alfred William (1830–1908), explorer and anthropologist, b. England. Howitt arrived in Australia in 1852 with his father **William** (1792–1879), a prolific writer whose publications about colonial life included the popular 'guidebook novel' *Land, Labour and Gold* (1855). In addition to his achievements as an explorer, Alfred became a noted prospector, geologist, naturalist (making important contributions on eucalypts) and anthropologist, collaborating with Rev. Lorimer Fison to write *Tribes of South East Australia* (London, 1904), a standard work. He also led an expedition sent to trace Burke and Wills in 1861.

Hudson, Sir William (1896–1978), hydro-electrical engineer, b. NZ. After working on major hydro-electric schemes in NZ, NSW and Scotland, Hudson returned to Sydney in 1938 to join the Metropolitan Water Sewerage and Drainage Board, eventually becoming its chief engineer. He was appointed commissioner of the Snowy Mountains Hydro-electric Authority in 1949 and his engineering skill and management ability in directing this, one of the world's largest undertakings of its kind, constitute his most notable achievement.

Hughes, Richard (1906–84), journalist, b. Melbourne. One of the great foreign correspondents, Hughes began as a junior reporter on the Melbourne *Star*. In 1940 he became Tokyo correspondent for the Sydney *Telegraph*, later covering the North African campaign for that paper. Postwar, he became Asia correspondent for the London *Sunday Times*, the *Economist* and, in 1973, the *Times*. Establishing his reputation with his coverage of the Chinese revolution and the Korean War, Hughes's knowledge and understanding of Asian affairs were legendary, resulting in fictionalised appearances in novels by Ian Fleming and John le Carré.

Hughes, Robert (1938–), art critic and author, b. Sydney. Hughes has contributed art criticism to a number of papers and magazines, including the Sydney weekly, *Nation*, and later (in London) the *Observer*. He has also presented television programs, including the series 'The Shock of the New' (1980) for the BBC. Art critic of *Time* magazine since 1970, he is also author of the seminal *The Art of Australia* (1966), *Heaven and Hell in Western Art* (1968) and *The Fatal Shore* (1987), a best-selling history of Australia's convict origins. Hughes's reputation is based on his literacy, clarity of vision and extensive knowledge.

Hughes, William Morris (1862–1952), politician, b. England. One of the most controversial politicians in Australia's history, 'Billy' Hughes arrived in Australia in 1884, becoming secretary of the wharf labourers' union in 1890. Elected to the first federal parliament as a Labor member in 1901, he became prime minister upon Andrew Fisher's retirement in 1915. His tenacious advocacy of > *conscription* led to his expulsion from the Labor Party in 1916, but he managed to remain prime minister with support from the Liberal Party; in 1917 he formed the National Party from a coalition of Liberals and errant Labor members.

At the Versailles peace conference in 1919, Hughes fought pugnaciously for Australian interests. He was re-elected in 1919 and 1922, but lost the prime-ministership to S. M. Bruce in 1923 following dissension in the coalition. Allying himself temporarily with the Labor Party, he brought about the downfall of Bruce, which led to his expulsion from the Nationalists. He then joined the right-wing United Australia Party, and in the leadership contest following the death of Joe Lyons in 1939 was narrowly defeated by R. G. Menzies. When the UAP withdrew from the Advisory War Council in 1944, Hughes chose to remain and was expelled from his party yet again. In 1945 he joined the UAP's successor, the Liberal Party, remaining with it until his death. Popularly known as 'the Little Digger', Hughes was admired and despised in equal measure.

human rights In Australia, discussion about human rights focuses mainly on civil and political rights, such as freedom of expression and religion. The concept of human rights is in fact much wider than this, extending to economic, social and cultural rights such as fair working conditions, social security and education, and freedom from discrimination. International activity in all these fields has been high, especially since World War 2. An international bill of rights dates from 1948 and further international agreements on civil, political, economic, social and cultural rights were introduced in the 1970s.

The Australian Constitution contains few explicit safeguards concerning human rights. In recent years there has been criticism of inequities in a number of areas, most notably the treatment of Aborigines and of women in Australian society; other recognised shortcomings in the field of human rights include the delays occurring in the criminal trial system; electoral law in Qld; and the categorical social-security system, which does not confer enforceable rights and allows some people to fall into 'gaps' between the categories. Discrimination on grounds of race, sex and marital status has been the subject of legislation by the Commonwealth and Vic., NSW, SA and WA. The federal Human Rights and Equal Opportunity Commission (established in 1981 as the Human Rights Commission) and State equivalents receive and attempt to conciliate complaints in the field of human rights; remedies through tribunals and courts are also available if conciliation fails.

Although human rights described are thus to some extent embodied in law, Australia – with the UK and NZ – is one of the few countries without a specific bill of rights. Attempts were made to introduce such legislation in 1973, 1983 and 1986, and a referendum containing some proposals relating to human rights was held in 1988, but all were unsuccessful.
>> *equal-opportunity legislation*

Hume, Hamilton (1797–1873), explorer, b. Parramatta, NSW. Son of a convict superintendent, Hume was a member of several exploration expeditions 1814–21 in the Berrima, Goulburn and Yass districts and on the NSW south coast. His major contribution was to lead an expedition 1824, accompanied by William Hovell, originally intended to reach Spencer Gulf, but turning south to reach the western shore of Port Phillip (mistakenly identified as Westernport), discovering en route the Murray. Hume accompanied Charles Sturt to the Darling in 1828, and later squatted in the Yass plains, which he had explored in 1821. His name is commemorated in the Hume Highway and the Hume reservoir.

Humphries, (John) Barry (1934–), writer and self-styled 'music-hall artiste', b. Melbourne. A satirist of immense talent, Humphries has dissected Australian society with a range of memorable characters, which include the lugubrious Sandy Stone, the bibulous Australian statesperson-at-large Dr Sir Leslie Colin Patterson, and – most famous of all – the 'housewife megastar', Dame Edna Everage. Through the voices of his characters, Humphries has single-handedly preserved the rapidly disappearing colloquialisms of Australian speech; he also created the cartoon strip 'The Adventures of Barry McKenzie' (1963–74) and compiled unorthodox anthologies such as *Bizarre* (1967), *Innocent Austral Verse* (1968) and *Treasury of Australian Kitsch* (1980).

Humpty Doo NT (pop. 1265 in 1981) A town on the flood-plains of the Adelaide River, 65km southeast of Darwin, Humpty Doo is best known as the site of an abortive attempt at large-scale rice-growing 1954–60. In spite of early experimental success, it failed through a combination of technical mistakes (such as insufficient land levelling), climatic hazards, and pests including wild buffalo, rats and geese. An agricultural research station was maintained there until the 1980s.

Hunt, Geoff(rey Brian) (1948–), squash player, b. Melbourne. Hunt is considered to be the best male squash player Australia has produced, dominating world tournaments in the 1960s and 1970s. In 1965, at 17, he became the youngest-ever player to win the Australian championship. He indicated his world class with victories in the world amateur championships of 1967 and 1969, and won the British Open (the unofficial championship) eight times 1969–81. He consolidated his position with victory in the inaugural World Open championship in 1976, a title he retained the following year. In 1981 he was ranked the leading player in the world for the seventh consecutive year. He retired in 1982.

Hunt, John Horbury (1838–1904), architect, b. Canada. Boston-trained, Hunt arrived in Sydney in 1863. He was a brilliant, unconventional architect whose handsome and robust buildings (characteristically in brick) eschewed Victorian eclecticism and frivolous ornamentation. Christ Church Cathedral in Newcastle, NSW (1885–95) and the brick mansion Booloominbah in Armidale, NSW (1887) are fine examples. His timber-shingled houses of the 1880s and 1890s, although romantic and idiosyncratic, did not influence Australian architectural style.

Hunter, Henry (1832–92), architect, b. England. Hunter arrived in Australia in 1848. He commenced practice in Hobart in 1855 and his prodigious output, especially of churches (he designed 31 in Hobart alone) dominated mid-Victorian architecture in Tas. Hobart's Museum (1862), Town Hall (1864–6) and St Mary's Cathedral (c. 1862) were among his designs, which generally favoured Gothic Revival.

Hunter Valley NSW The broad, flat Hunter Valley on the mid-north coast of NSW is formed by the Hunter River, which rises in the Mt Royal Range and after receiving the Goulburn River from the west and the Wollombi from sandstone country to the south forms rich alluvial flats near Singleton and flows to the sea at Newcastle. The river was discovered in 1797 and named after the governor, John Hunter. The valley was settled in the early 1800s and became a prosperous agricultural and grazing district; coal mining began in the Newcastle area and expanded to Maitland and Cessnock early this century. The subsequent establishment in 1915 of BHP steelworks contributed to Newcastle's development as a heavy industrial base centred on steel production and manufacturing; power generation is important on and south of Lake Macquarie and in the northwest near Singleton, and coal exports have increased since World War 2. Although much of the lower Hunter has become industrialised with chemical industries and aluminium smelters, the upper reaches constitute a productive agricultural district famed particularly for its vineyards but also for dairying, sheep raising and stud farming. Flooding on the Hunter has been a perennial problem, now to some extent controlled since the construction of the Glenbawn dam, near Aberdeen, and the Lostock dam on the Paterson River, both of which also supply water for irrigation, but other problems such as air and water pollution and unregulated development are demanding attention.

huntsman spiders > *spiders*

Huon River Tas. Rising on the southern slopes of Mt Wedge, the Huon River flows through dense upland forest for much of its 160km course; east of the Huon Gorge it is joined by its two largest tributaries, the Picton and the Weld, and in the lower reaches it runs south through orchard country to an estuary on D'Entrecasteaux Channel. The Huon valley is the State's most important fruit-growing region, producing apples chiefly but including pears, hops and other small fruits. The main townships are Huonville, Geeveston and Cygnet (on a bay of the estuary). The Huon was discovered in 1792 by Bruny D'Entrecasteaux and named after his second-in-command, Huon de Kermadec. In the early 1800s timber-getters worked the area to exploit the valuable softwood, huon pine; today the region's eucalypts are the basis of a sawmilling industry for use as woodchips, and there is a pulp mill at Port Huon.

Hurley, Frank (James Francis) (1885–1962), photographer, b. Sydney. Hurley's distinguished career lasted over 60 years. He went on six expeditions to Antarctica, including the first Australasian expedition (1911–13) led by Douglas Mawson, and is renowned for the powerful images and technical excellence of his AIF photos during both world wars. He also made a number of documentaries based on his travels in the Antarctic, NG and the Torres Strait Islands. As cameraman for Cinesound Productions in the 1930s, he worked on a number of feature films including Ken Hall's *The Squatter's Daughter* (1933). Thirteen books of his photographic studies of Australia were published.

Hutt River Province WA (pop. approx 30) This is a 7474ha property 450km north of Perth, whose owner Leonard Casley 'seceded' from the Commonwealth of Australia in 1970. A farmer angered by a quota the WA government imposed on his wheat production – which he described as 'unrealistic, uneconomic and illegal' – Casley declared his independence, named the property Hutt River Province, and dubbed himself its administrator. He later upgraded the province to a principality and gave himself the title of 'Prince Leonard'. The principality is not recognised by the State or federal governments and has been developed as a tourist attraction.

hydatids > *helminths*

hydro-electricity > *electrical energy; Snowy Mountains Scheme*

Hydrographers Passage Qld This deep-water passage through the Great Barrier Reef was discovered only in the early 1980s, during a survey of the Whitsunday area by the RAN vessel HMAS *Flinders*. Providing the first navigable route for large ships wishing to pass through the reef between the mainland and the Coral Sea, it is some 80 nautical miles long and bears four lighthouses. Until Hydrographers Passage was surveyed and marked, large vessels travelling between north Qld ports (such as Mackay) and Asia were forced to make extensive detours.

hydrographic surveys > *maps and mapping*

hydrozoa This is a class of aquatic, mainly marine, animals of the phylum Cnidaria, some species of which occur in Australian waters. Species of the simple freshwater genus *Hydra* are small green-to-brown polyps using tentacles to search for prey on aquatic plants. There are naked marine forms such as *Tubularia*, in which the polyp looks like a group of separate flowers – hence the name zoophyte, meaning animal plant – and there are the rough, branching stems and many polyps of *Pennaria*, common on rocks and wharves. Among hydrozoans in which the free-swimming (medusa) stage is dominant are the harmless by-the-wind sailor, genus *Velella* – which has a buoyant sac like a Brazil nut – and the noxious bluebottle or Portuguese man-of-war, *Physalia physalis*, with a rounder, blue air-sac and tentacles; both are often blown into surfing bays and on to beaches in southeastern Australia. The bluebottle has long, trailing tentacles with stinging cells which can immobilise small prey and cause throbbing pain in humans.

Hymenoptera A large order of insects with well-developed mouthparts and a characteristic arrangement of veins, this includes two major suborders: the plant-feeding Symphyta (> *sawflies and wood-wasps*), characterised by a broad abdomen, and the mostly parasitic Apocrita, which has a slender or petioliate abdomen. The Apocrita is divided into the Aculeata (> *ants*; *bees and bee-keeping*; *wasps*) and remaining parasitoid groups, sometimes referred to as the Parasitica, which are discussed below.

Parasitoids feed on their living hosts, ultimately killing them; this is a slow form of predation rather than true parasitism. Females do not make nests, but lay their eggs on free-living hosts – usually the larval or pupal stage of other insects – through needle-like ovipositors. The closely related families Ichneumonidae and Braconidae show enormous diversity, and many are parasitoids of lepidopterous larvae and pupae. Members of the superfamily Chalcidoidea may be less than 1mm in length and sometimes parasitise insect eggs. Many Parasitica are important in limiting populations of insect-pest species by means of biological control; species of the egg parasite of the genus *Trichogramma* have been used in this way.

Some Parasitica have become secondarily plant-feeding; these include the gall-making family Cynididae, and the strange fig wasps of the family Agaonidae, which live within the fruits of native figs.

I

ibises and spoonbills These large, long-legged birds of the family Threskiornithidae are usually found in aquatic habitats. Australia has three species of ibis, all characterised by a long, curved, probing bill and a knob-like head: the common straw-necked ibis has recently become a member of the avifauna of Sydney parks (together with pigeons and gulls), and uses its long bill to probe waste-bins for food; the other species are the white and the glossy ibis. The two Australian spoonbills, black-billed and yellow-billed, use their distinctively shaped bills to sweep shallow water for aquatic organisms; they nest colonially, usually in a structure composed of sticks and twigs.

Idriess, Ion Llewellyn, (1889–1979), novelist and biographer, b. Sydney. Idriess spent 25 nomadic years as a sailor, soldier, buffalo hunter, and miner. He turned a diary kept while marooned off the Qld coast into the semi-fictional *Madman's Island* (1927), the first of more than 40 books. For some 30 years after *Lasseter's Last Ride* (1931), this racy descriptive writer remained a household name and Australian best-seller.

Illawarra district NSW A coastal region of NSW south of metropolitan Sydney, extending from Bald Hill, near Stanwell Park, to the Shoalhaven River, this district is bounded on the west by the Illawarra escarpment and the Cambewarra Range. Much of the coastal plain in the northern section is occupied by the industrial city of Wollongong whose large steel mills are supplied with coal extracted chiefly by tunnelling into the escarpment. Immediately south of Wollongong is Lake Illawarra. Port Kembla serves as the chief port for the region; others are Kiama and Shellharbour. In the early years of the 19th century cedar-getting was an important industry, but little forested land now remains, except on the steeper slopes. Cattle were pastured as early as 1815; this was followed by grain and potato growing, and dairying. Coal mining began in 1849 at Mt Keira. A notable pastoral development is the Australian Illawarra Shorthorn, one of the few registered breeds developed in Australia. In this district, discovered by Bass and Flinders in 1796, there is evidence of occupation by Aborigines as long as 20 000 years ago; the name is of Aboriginal origin.

immigration The growth of Australia's population to its present total of more than 16 million is the direct result of immigration over the past two centuries. The majority of Australians cannot trace their local ancestry further back than the 1880s, and today one in five residents was born overseas and a further one in five is the child of one or two immigrant parents.

Immigrants since 1788 have fallen into four major categories: convicts, assisted immigrants, unassisted immigrants, and refugees; smaller numbers came as indentured labourers or entered illegally. The predominant sources of immigrants have been the UK and Europe – the US and Canada were the main destinations of the vast number of European emigrants in the 19th century and most of those who came to Australia, on the other side of the world, did so because it went out of its way to bring them (with financial assistance or other strong incentives). Immigration policy has always aimed at attracting settlers who would remain in Australia to build up its population and develop its resources, and immigration programs have encouraged family migration ever since the wives and children of convicts were allowed to join them in the 1830s. Today there are no restrictions on immigrants on the basis of race or nationality, but selection takes employability and skills into account; no immigrants except refugees are assisted by the government. Australia remains one of the most sparsely populated states in the world and arguments for 'zero population growth' and reduced immigration will undoubtedly continue to meet with strong resistance from government, business and the source countries of potential immigrants.

The convicts NSW was established to receive convicts: its earliest settlers were either transportees or the soldiers and marines sent to guard them – overwhelmingly men, although the transportation of women was not discontinued until 1840. Officers were given land grants to enable them to settle and to employ convicts on assignment, thus beginning the process of tying land to both settlement and immigrant employment which continued in varying forms until the 1920s.

Assisted immigration The male preponderance and criminal background of the convicts raised official doubts about their suitability as the backbone of a stable society. Some free immigrants were brought out to the colonies during the convict period (to NSW from 1793 and to Van Diemen's Land from 1815), often as workers whose passage was paid by land-owning settlers. The failure of the 1829 Swan River settlement in WA, where land-owners imported workers from southern England, inspired the alternative scheme adopted in founding the colony of SA in 1836 – the Wakefield system, which used the proceeds of land sales to pay the fares of immigrants in the expectation that they would become rural labourers. This was the first of many programs of assisted passages, whereby the colonies paid the fares of immigrants recruited through the Colonial Land and Emigration Commission in London; eventually the colonies took over recruiting and the commission was abolished in 1872. Until as late as the 1950s, with the exception of Germans and Scandinavians in Qld, government assistance was available only to British immigrants. Passages were paid on the assumption that the immigrants would settle in the colonies and the schemes aimed to attract women and families, rather than single men. Nearly 700 000 assisted immigrants arrived between the start of the schemes in 1831 and the end of the century; after 1901, control over immigration passed to the new federal government although the States continued to recruit until 1921.

The major periods of assisted immigration were 1835–56, 1875–90, 1905–14, 1921–9 and 1947–82, after which the practice was discontinued except in the case of refugees. Assisted passages had the advantage that the Australian authorities could control the type of immigrant and could cut off assistance when economic conditions deteriorated. There was always some discontent with the quality of immigrants, the first of whom were mainly paupers or unemployed rural labourers; as free immigrants they were not obliged to go on the land and many remained in the capital cities.

Unassisted immigration Most non-British immigrants were unassisted by the government until the mid-20th century. The largest number arrived during the gold rush of the 1850s and included many Europeans, Americans and Chinese; commonly single males, they usually borrowed their fares from relatives already in Australia. Many unassisted immigrants came from southern Europe in the 1920s after access to the US was restricted, but their entry to Australia was also limited with the onset of the depression in 1930. Owing partly to a desire to augment the population after World War 2, immigration from Europe – most notably from Malta, Italy, Greece and Yugoslavia – was increased in the 1950s and 1960s; in some cases assistance was provided, as the result of agreements with the various governments.

Unofficial immigrants Smaller numbers of immigrants entered Australia as indentured labour or without official approval. Binding immigrant workers to contracts was widespread in the British Empire in the 18th and 19th centuries and once the convict system was abandoned it became appealing to employers in the Australian colonies, especially in the case of Asian and Pacific Island labourers (> *blackbirding*). Opposition to the use of indentured labour grew from trade unionists and from those favouring a 'white Australia', and official policy since 1901 has opposed the practice. ('Displaced persons' were bound to work for two years after arrival, but at full union rates.) Many skilled workers are still brought out on short contracts, but proposals to introduce a system like the European 'guest workers' were rejected as recently as 1988, in the FitzGerald report on immigration policy.

Another controversial category of immigrants is those who arrive without permission to settle. In the 19th century these were mainly sailors jumping ship, which was illegal under British maritime law; more recently about 50 000 immigrants have settled without permission, most having entered on a short-term visa and remaining after its expiry.

Refugees While the early German Lutheran settlers in SA in 1838 might be described as refugees, the official category was invented by the League of Nations to deal with upheavals in Europe in the 1920s following World War 1 and was revived by the UN for the even greater disturbances after 1945. The first important group of refugees to come to Australia were Jews escaping Hitler, who were admitted under the Evian agreement of 1938; most came between 1947 and 1952 as 'displaced persons' from eastern Europe. Between 1945 and 1985 more than 430 000 refugees entered Australia: the largest numbers came from Vietnam, Poland, Hungary, Yugoslavia, Latvia, Czechoslovakia, Lebanon, Ukraine and Cambodia; but more than 14 000 Russians came from China after the civil war there in 1949, and 6000 refugees were admitted from East Timor in the 1970s. The great majority of refugees have been from communist states, but small numbers have also come from Latin America; very few have come from the two largest refugee concentrations in the world, in eastern Africa and around Afghanistan. Refugee settlement has always involved voluntary effort, mainly by religious groups such as the World Council of Churches, and this has been formalised under the Community Refugee Settlement Scheme which was begun in 1979. Although émigrés from states such as Lebanon or Chile were not refugees according to the narrow UN definition, many qualified for admission under Australia's Special Humanitarian Program. Refugee settlement has been controversial since the 1930s, especially with the admission of large numbers of Asians after 1975. It is commonly, but mistakenly, believed that refugees receive generous official assistance; there is in fact a high level of unemployment among those recently arrived from Indochina, Lebanon and Poland.

Immigration policy There have been non-British immigrants since 1788, but until the 1950s they were restricted by official policy – which was aimed at creating a British society in Australia. It was also official policy to maintain a balance between English, Scottish and Irish immigrants which reflected the proportions in the UK. Legislation to restrict non-European immigrants – particularly the Chinese – was passed in Vic. and SA in the 1850s and NSW in the 1860s but did not become completely effective until the federal Immigration Restriction Act of 1901 (> *White Australia Policy*). Europeans were also sometimes restricted: the dictation text for aspiring immigrants was occasionally used to exclude 'undesirable' applicants from Europe, and southern Europeans were subject to immigration quotas during the 1920s and 1930s. Largely in response to the influx of displaced persons after World War 2, a campaign to 'Bring out a Briton' was launched as late as 1957.

Preference for British immigrants was gradually abandoned from the 1960s, particularly when Britain began imposing restrictions on Australian immigrants in 1968. The requirement for all British immigrants to obtain resident visas on the same basis as other applicants, which was introduced in the early 1970s, was the most fundamental departure from Australian immigration policy since 1788. The second major change was the official ending in 1973 of the White Australia Policy, and since then the proportion of Asians in the immigrant intake has risen to more than 35%. In 1986 there were 536 000 Asians resident in Australia (although this included some from countries not previously regarded as subject to the White Australia Policy, such as Turkey and Cyprus), the largest numbers coming from Vietnam (83 000), China and Hong Kong (65 000), Lebanon (56 000), Malaysia (48 000), India (48 000), Philippines (34 000) and Sri Lanka (22 000). English-speaking immigration continued at a high level, however, the British being supplemented by growing numbers of New Zealanders, the only nationality allowed unrestricted entry.

The 1980s and beyond These moves away from the British, towards Europeans in the 1950s and 1960s and towards Asians in the 1970s and 1980s, were achieved with little social tension. Immigration became increasingly controversial from the early 1980s, however: heated public debate was sparked in 1984 by historian Geoffrey Blainey, who questioned the desirability of a continuing large Asian intake although he did not favour a return to a White Australia; small racist groups became active, especially in Perth and Sydney; and opinion polls showed that a substantial number of Australians (though not necessarily a majority) were opposed to Asian immigration. The major political parties continued to reject the White Australia Policy, to which they had all subscribed before 1965.

By the late 1980s there was increasing insistence that Australia no longer needed mass immigration, which was seen by many of its critics as both threatening the employment chances of native-born Australians and placing increasing pressure on the already strained capacity of the land. Public debate centred around Asian and refugee settlement, while official and expert analysis was more concerned with the economic rationale. Government, business and the immigrant communities all wanted a high immigration intake, although often for different reasons: government stressed its international obligations, especially towards refugees; business wanted larger markets and a more skilled labour force; and immigrant groups favoured family reunion. In 1988 the FitzGerald committee recommended an annual intake of about 140 000, with an emphasis on skill, and this was accepted by the Hawke government with some modifications. The Opposition questioned the level of Asian intake and the official policy of > *multiculturalism*, but did not support a reduction in the number of immigrants. There was also considerable discussion about whether immigrants should maintain their own culture and languages. These arguments cut across normal party lines.

The FitzGerald report predicted that refugee pressures would decline, but this seems optimistic. Mass population movements from Asia have grown and will continue to be relevant to Australia. While Britain and Europe have become less important sources of immigrants as their living standards have risen and their populations stabilised, the growth of the Pacific Rim economies has meant increasing movement within the region, which will undoubtedly affect Australia. >> *ethnic groups*; *population*; *racial conflict*

income tax > *economy*; *taxation*

industrial design > *design*

industrial disputes Australia has had a long and often turbulent history of industrial disputes. In the late 1980s, however, the number of working days lost in disputes averaged about 1.5 million a year, an insignificant figure in comparison with those of notably bad years such as 1917 (4.689 million), 1929 (4.461 million) and 1974 (6.292 million). Reasons for the improvement are numerous, and include the lack of strong inflationary pressure (a major cause of the large 1974 figure); the presence of a Labor government, and its close relationship with the ACTU as regards wage restraint; an increasingly sophisticated – and perhaps benign – workforce with a collective memory of previous wage and price spirals; and the existence of an elaborate system of > *conciliation and arbitration*.

Strikes were rare in Australia before the middle of the 19th century, principally because a large proportion of the workforce consisted of convicts. With the end of transportation and the establishment of unions, strikes became more frequent, the most dramatic being the so-called Maritime Strike of 1890 – beginning in the merchant navy, it soon involved other large sections of the labour force, including miners and transport workers. More than 50 000 unionists were 'out' over a two- to eight-week period, and services in the eastern colonies were almost paralysed; troops were called out to control rioters in Sydney and Melbourne. This was the first co-ordinated attempt by trade unions to assert themselves; they demanded recognition by employers and the establishment of industry agreements between workers and management, particularly in relation to the hiring of union labour. The unions' demands were resisted by employers and were ultimately defeated, but the battle left a bitter memory. Two important indirect results of this strike – and of the shearers' strikes in Qld in 1891 and 1894, which were fought on the same issue – were the formation of the ALP and the passage of legislation that introduced a national system of conciliation and arbitration.

Contrary to much popular opinion, Australia is not a notably 'strike-happy' nation. There have been bad periods this century, particularly towards the end of each world war (when strikers gave expression to a pent-up desire for shorter working hours and an increase in real wages after years of restraint); and in the early 1970s, a period of worldwide inflation that was reflected in Australia by a far higher percentage than usual of disputes related to wage increases. There are, however, certain industries – notably mining and construction – that are notoriously strike-prone, partly because of the fractured nature of their organisation. In the mining industry, the coal-mining sector has by far the worst record of strikes, historically because of wages and conditions and today because of a drastic restructuring of the industry. The mining industry throughout the world has a high level of strikes, and it is noteworthy that Japan, which is often seen by Australians as a model of good industrial relations, now has no such industry; when it had one, Japan's record with regard to industrial disputes was poor.

Although the protracted pilots' dispute of 1989 stemmed from their demands for higher pay, today most disputes in Australia involve workers' reactions to managerial policy or their demands for better conditions and shorter hours, rather than for wage increases. If the working days lost in the mining industry – which on average account for 30–50% of all working days lost – are excluded, Australia's record in industrial disputation is fairly good.

industrial relations > *conciliation and arbitration*; *industrial disputes*

Industries Assistance Commission

(IAC) This statutory authority was established by the Commonwealth in 1973 to replace the Tariff Board, whose function was restricted to the manufacturing industry. The IAC's duty is to advise government on the nature and extent of possible assistance for industries in the rural, mining, manufacturing and service sectors in order to increase efficiency and encourage competition; to this end it holds public inquiries and prepares and publishes reports on proposed assistance or on matters related to assistance. The IAC is only an advisory body, however, and the government is not obliged to accept its recommendations.

information industries > *service industries*

Ingamells, Rex (Reginald Charles)

(1913–55), poet, b. Ororoo, SA. Ingamelis was a competent and often elegant poet whose verse was published in a number of volumes in the 30 years following the appearance of his first anthology, *Gumtops* (1935). He is perhaps better known as the founder of the radical nationalist literary movement, the Jindyworobaks, in the 1930s.

Innamincka SA (pop. 15) This outback ghost-town lies about 1100km northeast of Adelaide, where the sporadic Cooper and Strzelecki creeks separate. It originated as a police base and intercolonial customs post in the 1880s, but the settlement was gradually abandoned from the early 20th century. It is the grave site of the ill-fated explorers Burke and Wills. The town has been revived somewhat since the 1970s, largely in response to the development of tourism and a gas industry (at nearby Gidgealpa) in the region; the establishment of a regional reserve of some 13 800 sq. km was announced by the SA government in 1986.

Innisfail Qld (pop. 8113) This town lies 1632km north of Brisbane at the junction of the North and South Johnstone rivers, at the heart of a flourishing rural region. The original settlement, established when sugar cane was planted there in 1880, was known as Geraldton until 1910; its name was changed chiefly because of persisting confusion with the WA town of the same name. The region's main products are bananas and other tropical fruit, cattle and timber (notably red cedar, black walnut, silky oak and Queensland maple). Game fishing is increasing in importance as a recreational activity.

insecticides > *biocides*; *insect pests*

insect pests Insects affect almost all human activity, but the most serious pests are those associated with the production and storage of food. Measures to control insects are costly, both in monetary terms and in terms of environmental impact. Since World War 2, synthetic organic insecticides have been increasingly used to control pest populations, but as they become incorporated into food chains they affect other organisms, including humans. As well, insecticides often kill off natural enemies of pests, resulting in larger pest populations. There is growing scientific and public concern about the indiscriminate use of pesticides, and efforts are being made to develop more environmentally sound methods of controlling pests. A developing trend in agriculture is integrated pest management (IPM), where the ecology and life cycles of pests are studied to determine the most effective period in which to apply control measures; with this knowledge insecticide application can be minimised. Biological control, the use of a natural predator to control specific pests, has been effective in a number of cases.

Many major insect pests in Australia were accidentally introduced, usually in association with the crops they affect. There are, however, a number of native species that also affect wood, pastures and human health. Pests of stock such as sheep and cattle include > *blow-flies*, > *botflies*, various biting flies, and external parasites such as > *lice* and > *ticks and mites* (the tick is in fact an arachnid, not an insect). Pastures are affected by outbreaks of locusts (> *grasshoppers, locusts and crickets*), various burrowing scarab beetles, and some caterpillars such as those of the > *Bogong moth*. Orchard pests include the codling moths, *Cydia,* that burrow into pome fruit such as apples; the light-brown apple moth *Epiphyas*; fruit flies, and the banana weevil borer *Cosmopolites sordidus*. The many pests of vegetables include the cabbage butterfly *Pieris rapae*, budworm caterpillars *Heliothus*, the sorghum midge *Contarinia*, and the African black beetle *Heteronychus* on sugar cane and maize. Many plant-sucking > *bugs*, such as leafhoppers and aphids, transmit plant viruses. Stored products such as grain and flour are affected by a wide variety of tiny > *beetles* and moths. Cotton is affected by the boll weevil and budworm moths.

Native > *termites* are major pests of both standing trees and construction timber. The sirex wasp (> *sawflies and wood-wasps*) threatens exotic pine plantations in eastern Australia and there is concern that bark beetles may also become established there. Human household pests include cockroaches, silverfish and various ants. Fleas from domestic cats and dogs, and human body lice, can cause irritation, but the once common bedbug *Cimex* is now rare. Houseflies and bushflies are often merely annoying, but the wide range of biting flies, including > *mosquitoes*, can often transmit disease.

insects Insects represent the most diverse group of living things; there are about one million described species, and considerably more await description. They are found in a wide range of terrestrial and freshwater habitats, and a few species have become marine. Their fecundity, adaptability, short generation period, dispersal ability, and complex life histories that allow survival under unfavourable conditions have made insects one of the most successful groups of organisms. They have a major influence on human activity; they are an important link in terrestrial and freshwater foodchains, and they are pollinators of many food crops. However, they also often come in conflict with humans both in destroying crops, stored products and wood, and – in medical and veterinary areas – as parasites and vectors of pathogens (> *insect pests*).

Adult insects have three major body sections: head, thorax and abdomen. The thorax bears the organs of locomotion: three pairs of legs and, in most forms, two pairs of wings which are often secondarily modified; insects are among the few groups of animals to successfully develop and use wings. Two major types of development from the egg stage are recognised. With incomplete metamorphosis, the egg hatches into a nymph which often appears like the adult and feeds on food similar to it; the nymph undergoes a series of moults, the final moult producing the winged, sexually mature adult. In complete metamorphosis, the egg hatches into a grub or caterpillar-like larva which feeds until it is ready to pupate; in the pupal stage the larval body is completely reorganised, ultimately appearing as the adult. Complete metamorphosis is characteristic of the most advanced insect orders, and has enabled the larva to occupy a completely different habitat from that of the adult.

About 80 000 species of insects are known from Australia, but several times that number are yet to be described. Many large families are known only in outline, the common or prominent species alone having been named. With modern mass-collection techniques and with more attention being paid to smaller insects (those less than 1cm long), the enormous size of the undescribed fauna has become evident.

The Australian fauna may be divided into three major ecological-biogeographical groups. The cool-temperate species, found in Tas., southeastern and southwestern Australia and the mountain ranges of the eastern coast, often belong to families with an ancient Gondwana distribution, having links with the faunas of NZ and southern South America. The endemic Australian species are often adapted to arid lands and eucalypt-dominated habitats. Much of the tropical fauna, especially that of the monsoonal north and the tropical rainforests of the eastern coast, is closely related to the Oriental and Papuan insect faunas and appears to be more recently derived, the result of dispersal from the Orient during the northwards drift of the Australian continental plate in the Tertiary period.

insurance Insurance in Australia has largely followed the British model. In the last 20 years, however, the insurance industry has become increasingly international so that the majority of Australian companies are subsidiaries of large global organisations. In addition, most banks now include insurance in their services and eventually the industry is likely to be taken over completely by large finance conglomerates.

The first insurance companies were established in the 1830s, with marine insurance offices (based on similar institutions in England) providing cover for the colonies' fishing and trading interests. The first 'mutual life' insurance company (whereby the firm is owned by policyholders rather than shareholders) was formed in 1849 and this system of life insurance has predominated since that time. All aspects of the industry are governed by federal legislation and there is increasing emphasis on consumer protection through mechanisms such as the Trade Practices Act 1974 and the Insurance (Agents and Brokers) Act 1984. >> *health and health services; superannuation*

intelligence services Australia's main intelligence organisation, the Australian Security Intelligence Organisation (> *ASIO*), was established in 1949 by the Chifley government but only formalised in legislation in 1956. An internal counter-espionage agency, ASIO has the express aim of obtaining and evaluating information relevant to Australia's security. Its external counterpart is the Australian Secret Intelligence Service (ASIS), which operates secretly in selected countries and is responsible to the minister for foreign affairs. Other agencies are the Defence Signals Directorate (DSD), which collects foreign intelligence through electronic interception; the Joint Intelligence Organisation (JIO), which is the main agency for assessing intelligence on behalf of the defence forces; and the Office of National Assessments, which acts as a filter for information supplied by the active field agencies ASIO, ASIS and DSD.

Much concern has been expressed about the activities of ASIO, particularly during the Vietnam War, and two royal commissions (1974 and 1983 – both chaired by Mr Justice Hope) have examined and been critical of Australia's intelligence services in general, noting poor organisation and co-ordination, and lack of effective control. An office of inspector-general of intelligence and security was instituted in 1986, to ensure that the intelligence agencies acted within the law and respected civil rights.

International Cultural Corporation of Australia This non-profit public company was established by the Australian government in 1980 to arrange and manage international exhibitions of artistic, cultural and historical significance. It brings exhibitions to Australia and arranges for Australian shows to travel overseas, funded largely through corporate sponsorship. Among the exhibitions it has stage-managed are the spectacularly popular 'Entombed Warriors' (terracotta figures from China) in 1983, a Picasso retrospective in 1984, and masterpieces from the Hermitage Museum in Leningrad in 1988.

international relations > *defence; embassies and high commissions; foreign policy; trade*

Inverell NSW (pop. 9693) A regional service centre on the western edge of the Great Dividing Range, Inverell lies on the rich New England plateau about 680km north of Sydney. As well as producing wheat, cotton, fat lambs, and beer, the area is an important mining centre – the world's largest sapphire producer and also important for tin and diamonds. It was originally settled in the 1840s and was proclaimed a municipality in 1872.

Investigator Strait SA This stretch of water lies between Yorke Peninsula and Kangaroo Island. It is the western entrance to St Vincent Gulf, and was named by Matthew Flinders in 1802 after his ship, the *Investigator*.

Ipswich Qld (pop. 74 842) A city on the Bremer River, 40km west of Brisbane and on the western boundary of the metropolitan area, Ipswich dates from 1827 when a convict settlement called Limestone Hills was established to work nearby limestone deposits for Brisbane buildings. It was renamed in 1843 (after the English city in Suffolk), and developed quickly thanks to huge coal deposits. Industries include large railway workshops, brickworks, light engineering, butter, earthenware and hardboard factories, and more recently the manufacture of furniture and plywood, and sapphire-cutting. As well as being an important industrial nucleus, Ipswich is also the centre of the West Moreton coalfield, which produced more than 3 million t of black coal in 1985–6.

Iridaceae > *iris family*

iris family Members of the Iridaceae family of flowering plants have grass-like leaves and mostly colourful flowers. Although most diverse in Africa and the Americas, the few Australian genera include some conspicuous wildflowers. Best known is the near-endemic native iris or purple flag, *Patersonia*, the seventeen native species of which are scattered around the temperate coast but concentrated in the southwest. They have tufts of stiff leaves and large mauve-purple (occasionally yellow) three-petalled flowers that emerge in succession from a flower head sheathed in hard brown or blackish bracts. The genus *Orthrosanthus* has four species of softer-leaved plants with taller, branched flower spikes and small blue or yellow flowers; all are southwestern except one species that extends to SA and west Vic. The genus *Diplarrena* has two species, their attractive iris-like white flowers having yellow and purple markings; both occur in Tas., *D. moraea* also extending to southern Vic. and south-eastern NSW. Also in Tas. is *Isophysis*, an endemic single-species genus with no obvious relatives. The other native genus is the south-eastern *Libertia*, which comprises two species of rush-like plants with small starry white flowers. Other irises also occur in Australia as naturalised aliens, mostly abundantly in the coastal sands of the southwest: the majority are South African and include freesias, gladioli and ixias; Cape tulips of the genus *Homeria* are notorious livestock poisons.

iron and steel industry With exports worth $1700 million in 1987, Australia is the world's second-largest exporter of iron ore. The principal production centre is the Pilbara region of WA, one of the continent's most ancient rock formations and a veritable treasure trove of minerals; the main steel-making centres are Port Kembla and Newcastle in NSW, and Whyalla in SA. Despite intermittent challenges Australia's largest company, > *BHP*, has virtually monopolised the industry since the 1930s.

While Australia ranks fourth in iron-ore production capacity (after the USSR, China and Brazil), there has been a downturn in steel-making since the late 1970s owing to the combined effects of high costs and fluctuating market prices, and reduced domestic demand for steel because of a slump in local manufacturing. As a result, by the late 1980s Australia ranked a lowly 22nd among the world's steel producers, from a peak of fourteenth in the early 1970s.

Iron ore Iron-bearing formations in the Middleback Range in SA were identified by the explorer Edward John Eyre in 1840 and leased by BHP in 1897 to provide flux for its blast furnaces at Port Pirie. Between 1915 and the 1970s, this region provided most of the iron ore used for steel-making in Australia, although mining was also carried out at Cockatoo Island (from 1951) and Koolyanobbing (from 1960) in WA. As only limited reserves of cheap iron ore were known, exports were banned by the federal government 1938–60.

Following the discovery of the massive Pilbara deposits (mainly haematite) by > *Lang Hancock* and Stan Hilditch from the late 1950s, the export ban was relaxed in 1960 and finally lifted in 1963. An assured Japanese market for iron ore fostered the construction of railways, ports and infrastructure – financed largely by US and UK interests – and mining began at Mt Goldsworthy and Mt Tom Price in 1966, Mt Newman in 1969 and Robe River in 1972. Smaller ore bodies in other States – such as Frances Creek in the NT and Savage River in Tas. – were also mined from the 1960s. By the 1980s, iron-ore mining had largely been returned to Australian hands.

Steel-making The steel-making industry in Australia had fitful beginnings. Pig iron was first produced by the Fitz Roy Iron Mining Company in 1851, at Mittagong in NSW, but the firm failed in 1877. The only successful venture of the 19th century was the Eskbank Iron Works Company established by James Rutherford at Lithgow, NSW, in 1875, although it was forced to rely on re-rolling scrap iron until the 1880s. Bought by William Sandford in 1894, the company produced Australia's first steel in 1900 and was taken over by the nation's first major steel-maker, G. & C. Hoskins (> *Hoskins family*), in 1907.

Having determined the economy of shipping ore from the Middleback Range to the NSW seaboard, BHP commenced steel-making in Newcastle in 1915 and by 1935 it was able to take over the Port Kembla plant of the Hoskins brothers, Australian Iron and Steel Ltd; defence requirements during World War 2 stepped up production and the Port Kembla plant was expanded substantially in 1955. The robust steel industry attracted interstate interest and the renewal of ore leases began to be made conditional on the establishment of local plants: this resulted in the development of furnaces and mills at Whyalla from the 1940s and Kwinana from the 1960s, and Geelong in Vic. from 1976. BHP staved off periodic challenges from overseas interests largely by continually updating its technology and maintaining cash flows in difficult times by exporting up to 40% of its production.

The 1980s and beyond By the end of the 1980s, iron ore was still Australia's second most valuable mineral export. While some uneconomic iron mines (such as Koolyanobbing and Cockatoo Island) have been closed down, new ore bodies – such as Deepdale and Yandicoogina in the Pilbara – are being developed, and production at existing centres (such as Shay Gap and Newman) is being expanded.

BHP continues to defend its near monopoly of steel-making. Concern at dramatic sharp cutbacks during the economic downturn of the early 1980s – including reduction of the BHP workforce by one-third, which had substantial socio-economic effects on the centres affected – led the federal government to introduce a five-year Steel Industry Plan in 1983. This effectively guaranteed BHP at least a four-fifths share of the domestic steel market in return for continuing investment in the industry. >> *mining industry*

ironbarks > *eucalypts*

iron ore > *iron and steel industry*

irrigation > *dams and reservoirs; soils and soil conservation; water and water resources*

Isaacs, Sir Isaac Alfred (1855–1948), lawyer, b. Melbourne. Isaacs graduated in law in 1880 and subsequently became a barrister and QC. A member of the Vic. parliament 1892–1901, he helped draft the Constitution at the federal convention of 1897–8 and was elected to federal parliament 1901–06. A justice of the High Court from 1906 and chief justice from 1930, he was the first Australian-born governor-general 1931–6 despite strenuous opposition to the appointment from King George V. He earned wide respect in this posi-tion and retained a strong interest in constitutional law after his retirement, continuing his longstanding support for the expansion of federal powers.

Isoptera > *termites*

Italians in Australia > *ethnic groups*

IVF The technique of in-vitro fertilisation (IVF), whereby eggs are fertilised outside a woman's body and subsequently transplanted into the womb, was developed almost simultaneously by two English medical scientists and a research team in the department of obstetrics and gynaecology at Monash University, Vic., led by Dr Carl Wood. Australia's first births by this method occurred in 1980, in Melbourne, and the procedure has subsequently produced thousands of births. The team led by Wood also pioneered the technique of freezing excess embryos that have been produced by IVF. Like other aspects of > *biotechnology*, IVF has engendered widespread debate in the community and is vociferously opposed by groups such as the Right to Life movement, and many Catholics and feminists. The legal and ethical issues are the subject of continuing scrutiny by both the government and medical bodies such as the Fertility Society of Australia; codes of practice have been devised, which in Vic. were enshrined in legislation in 1984. >> *medical research*

J

jabiru The jabiru, *Xenorhynchus asiaticus*, is Australia's only member of the stork family. Also known as the black-necked stork or policeman bird, it is a swamp-dweller found across the northern tropics and down the eastern coast, sometimes as far south as Sydney. It is a handsome figure: the body white and green, the legs red, and the bill long and black; it feeds on aquatic animals, though also eating carrion, and builds a very large nest, up to 2m broad, usually in a tree. It is generally supposed to be a voiceless bird.

Jack, Kenneth William David (1924–), painter and printmaker, b. Caulfield, Vic. One of Australia's most consistent, prolific and respected watercolourists and printmakers, Jack's best known works are country townscapes conveying the isolation and character of old Australian gold settlements and ghost-towns. Books he has illustrated include *The Melbourne Book* (1948) and *The Charm of Hobart* (1949).

Jackson, Marjorie > *athletics*

James, Clive (1939–), author and critic, b. Sydney. James's trenchant wit and incisive writing style – which owes a debt to the US writers H.L. Mencken and Raymond Chandler – brought him immediate success as television critic for the London *Observer* 1972–82; he has subsequently interspersed this role with appearances in the same medium as interviewer and commentator. As a serious literary journalist, James is the author of *The Metropolitan Critic* (1974) and *At the Pillar of Hercules* (1979); he has also written eccentric 'epic' poems and two novels, *Brilliant Creatures* (1983) and *The Remake* (1987). His best work is probably the autobiographical *Unreliable Memoirs* (1980); this was followed by the less successful *Falling Towards England* (1985).

jarrah > *eucalypts*

jazz Jazz music was well established in Australia by the 1920s, but the improvisational jazz style was set in motion in the late 1930s when beat musicians first encountered the Race label recordings imported from the US, which were largely a white interpretation of the black American musical tradition. By the 1950s jazz had become a respectable middle-class entertainment, distanced from its political and social origins. Frank Coughlan, a trombone and trumpet player who appeared on the first professional jazz record made in Australia (1925), remained one of the most notable jazz musicians for a further two decades. Enduring names of Australian jazz include > *Graeme Bell* and the Port Jackson Jazz Band from the 1940s; Ray Price from the 1950s; and > *Don Burrows*, Don Banks, Dick Hughes and Frank Traynor from the 1960s. More recently there has been a shift back to original values in Australian jazz, notably by performers from the women's movement. Although there were female jazz musicians as early as the 1920s, they first came to public prominence during World War 2 – in most cases taking the place of enlisted men – and many formed their own bands. They were invariably replaced as bandsmen returned at the war's end, but by the 1970s were again finding a degree of acceptance. NZ-born Judy Bailey remains one of the finest pianists and composers in the genre and more recently Kate Ceberano, an exceptional jazz vocalist, has developed a dedicated following.

jellyfishes This is the popular name for certain aquatic, mainly marine cnidarians of the class Scyphozoa. The most common genus of Australian coastal waters is *Aurelia*, with its umbrella-shaped form about 10cm across, numerous fringing tentacles and four purple, horseshoe markings in the jelly. Large jelly-fishes of southeastern waters include *Cyanea annaskala*, which is milky white-mauve, pink or brown, measures 60cm across, has tentacles up to 4m long and is probably responsible for severely stinging surfers when it is blown close inshore, and also *Catostylus*, which is sometimes common in the harbours and also stings sharply on occasions.

Among the jellyfishes most dangerous to humans are the oblong-bodied box jellies – sea-wasps or cubomedusans. They include the SA *Carybdea rastonii*, with 15cm stinging tentacles that cause sharp pain and illness but are not fatal, and the deadly Qld *Chironex fleckeri*, known to have killed over 40 people in the north; its sting results in severe pain and temporary paralysis. This deadly specimen is clear and almost colourless – only very slightly blue; it measures some 15cm across the box or bell, and trails tentacles up to 2m long.

Jenolan Caves > *caves*

Jervis Bay NSW Site of the RAN college 1915–30 and again since 1957, this broad inlet lies about 170km south of Sydney and its southernmost headland is administered by the > *ACT*. A fine natural harbour and a popular holiday resort, it is also noted for its diverse floral ecosystems (ranging from heaths to lush rainforest) and incorporates a nature reserve of 4500ha. It also contains many significant sites attesting to longstanding Aboriginal occupancy – from shell middens to rock art – and some 87ha around Summer-cloud Bay and Shelleys Point have been transferred to the control of the local Aboriginal community. Jervis Bay was intended as the principal port for Canberra, but this – like many proposals for the area over the years – did not come to fruition. More recently it has been proposed for development as Australia's principal eastern naval base, but this has been strenuously opposed by local residents and conservationists.

Jews in Australia > *ethnic groups*

Jindyworobaks This literary group was founded in Adelaide in 1938, by poets > *Rex Ingamells* and Ian Mudie, to encourage more distinctive 'Australianism' in Australian writing; the name, adapted from an Aboriginal word meaning 'to join', was chosen for both its symbolism and its distinctiveness. The Jindy-worobaks published a manifesto of their aims in 1938 and thenceforth published an anthology of poetry each year until 1953, by which time the movement had gone into decline. Notable members included > *Max Harris* and author Nancy Cato.

John Dory > *dories*

Johnston, George Henry (1912–70), novelist, b. Melbourne. Gravitating from art student to journalist, Johnston won attention as a correspondent during World War 2. From 1954 he and his second wife Charmian Clift spent ten years in Greece, both writing full-time. Johnston churned out pot-boilers such as *Shane Martin*, but proved his true stature with the trilogy, *My Brother Jack* (1964), *Clean Straw for Nothing* (1969) and *A Cartload of Clay* (1971); the first two won Miles Franklin Awards.

Jolley, Elizabeth (1923–), novelist, b. England. Jolley arrived in WA in 1959 with her father (a Quaker) and her Viennese mother. She has published three short-story collections and five novels since first appearing in print in 1975: in each, her distinctive, slyly comic gaze focuses disturbingly on the 'morality of the single person against the crowd'. *Mr Scobie's Riddle* (1982) and *My Father's Moon* (1989) won the *Age* Book of the Year award, and *The Well* (1986) the Miles Franklin Award. Jolley has also written several plays for radio.

Jones, Alan > *motor sports*

Jones, Barry Owen (1932–), politician and author, b. Geelong, Vic. Trained as a solicitor and a teacher, Jones won fame and money on television quiz shows in the 1960s with his prodigious general knowledge. Labor MLA in Vic. 1972–7, he entered federal parliament in 1977 and was minister for science 1983–90; his eccentricities and outspokenness did not make him popular with colleagues. His publications include *Age of Apocalypse* (1975) and *Sleepers, Wake!* (1982). He played an important part in the 1970s revival of the local film industry.

Jones family, best known for its role in Australian retailing since the 1830s. The family's first store was opened in 1838 at the corner of George and Barrack Streets, Sydney, by **David** (1793–1873), b. Wales. His eldest son, **Sir Philip Sydney** (1836–1918), was a prominent surgeon, notable for his study of tuberculosis and its methods of treatment. It was David's grandson, **Sir Charles Lloyd** (1878–1958), who was the architect of the family firm's expansion, opening stores in most States and many country centres. His work was continued by his son, **David Lloyd** (1931–61), who on his death was succeeded by his brother, **Charles Lloyd** (1932–   ). Today the firm is controlled by the Adelaide Steamship Co., a large and diversified corporation which has nevertheless maintained 'DJ's' reputation as Australia's highest-quality department store chain.

Jones, Inigo (1872–1954), meteorologist, b. England. Famous for his long-range weather forecasts based on astronomical observation and study of weather cycles, Jones accurately predicted many periods of drought and subsequent or otherwise specific rainfall, which earned him a large following among primary producers. Supported in his earlier work by the Qld government and the Colonial Sugar Refining Co., in 1942 the Long-Range Weather Forecasting Trust was established near Brisbane to enable him to pursue his research. After his death, his work was continued by Lennox Walker.

Jones, Marilyn Fay (1940–   ), dancer, b. Newcastle, NSW. A ballet dancer of international repute from the late 1950s, Jones began her career with the Royal Ballet in London in 1957. She has partnered such luminaries as Rudolph Nureyev and Robert Helpmann, and performed with the famed Ballet du Marquis de Cuevas in Paris (1961). She was subsequently prima ballerina with the Borovansky Ballet and with the Australian Ballet 1966–71. In 1979 Jones was appointed artistic director of the Australian Ballet and in 1982 she opened a ballet school in Sydney with her husband and fellow dancer Garth Welch.

Jorgensen, Jorgen (1780–1841), adventurer and author, b. Denmark. Jorgensen visited Australia as a sailor on survey and whaling ships 1801–5. He engineered an Icelandic revolution, acting as self-appointed protector for two months in 1809. He was transported to Tas. in 1826 for petty crime in Britain, induced by gambling. Pardoned in 1833 after he had undertaken useful exploration, he turned to writing and studied the Aborigines. He wrote plays, an Aboriginal dictionary and an autobiography.

Joseph Bonaparte Gulf NT/WA A wide indentation on the coast of the Timor Sea, the gulf lies between Cape Londonderry (WA) and Cape Scott (NT), which are about 290km apart. On its shores are a number of swampy river estuaries, the major ones being those of the Ord and Victoria rivers. It was named in 1803 by the French explorer, Nicolas Baudin, after the eldest brother of Napoleon Bonaparte.

Joyce, Eileen (1912–   ), pianist, b. Zeehan, Tas. Joyce was brought up in WA, where a public subscription enabled her to travel to Germany to study at the Leipzig Conservatorium, after which she made her London debut in 1931. She toured Australia for the first time in 1936, and again in 1948. She was much loved for her public concerts during the London blitz, and a film version of her early life, *Wherever She Goes*, was made in 1950. Resident in England, she has played the piano for many film soundtracks.

Judaism > *religion*

Julius, Sir George Alfred (1873–1946), engineer, b. England. Julius invented the automatic totalisator, a machine first used at Auckland in 1913 and subsequently at racecourses all over the world. After positions in the railways and as a consultant, he was appointed the first chairman of the Council for Scientific and Industrial Research (1926–46) and gave research priority to agricultural production; despite opposition, he also pressed for more research relevant to secondary industry.

K

Kakadu National Park NT A tract of some 1.7 million ha east of Darwin, including the lands of the South and West Alligator rivers and extending to the western escarpment of Arnhem Land, Kakadu was one of the first two Australian regions to be placed on the World Heritage list. Consisting of tidal flats, estuaries and lagoons, grasslands and paperbark country, it is dominated by the sandstone escarpment of the Arnhem Land plateau which stretches for more than 600km and in places is 450m high. It is believed to have been Aboriginal land for at least 30 000 years; it holds one of the greatest collections of cave paintings, including possibly the world's oldest known examples of rock art. The region takes its name from the original inhabitants, the Gagudju, and is now owned by the Aborigines and leased to the Australian National Parks and Wildlife Service. The diverse fauna includes a great variety of wildfowl and also the water buffalo (introduced last century). The reserve was created in three stages, each stage taking in a large parcel of land. There are large > *uranium* deposits in the region and the three major deposits have been excluded from the reserved area. Mineral exploration and development in Kakadu remains a controversial issue.

Kalgoorlie WA (pop. 19 848) This regional centre, generally linked with nearby Boulder, lies 595km east of Perth at the heart of the State's southeastern mining region; it developed as Hannan's Find in 1893, when diggers rushed east from Coolgardie to work the rich alluvial and reef deposits of gold; it was later named Kalgurli (an Aboriginal word for a local bush). Kalgoorlie escaped the ghost-town fate of most of the State's eastern goldfields, because of the rich deep ores of the > *Golden Mile* 5km to the south, for which it became the residential centre; by 1900 it was a wages town and small prospectors had moved on. The > *Goldfields*

and Agricultural Water Supply scheme, connected in 1903, piped desperately needed water 563km from Mundaring. Kalgoorlie is in a harsh environment which has been exacerbated by the denudation of woodlands for fuel; gold-boom buildings, many of them classified by the National Trust, line the wide streets. The town is reviving and expanding as the centre for the developing nickel fields nearby, with a recently built smelter and rail links north to nickel mines and south to Kambalda and Esperance. Gold is still mined and there has been an upsurge of exploration in the district as gold prices have risen.

Kambalda WA (pop. 3519) This mining town 616km east of Perth, founded as a goldfield in the 1890s, was revived dramatically when nickel was discovered in the 1960s. It is principally a residential and service centre for mining in the region, the products of which are transported – to Kwinana and Kalgoorlie – for processing. While the mining of nickel declined in the 1980s as the result of falling prices, a number of gold mines were reopened in the same period.

Kanakas > *blackbirding*

Kangaroo Island SA Lying south of St Vincent Gulf, this is Australia's third-largest offshore island, after Tas. and Melville Island. It measures 145km by 55km at its widest point, and geologically speaking is an extension of the Flinders-Mt Lofty ranges; its steep cliffs have witnessed many shipwrecks. Before regular settlement it was the haunt of whalers and sealers; the economy is now based on pine plantations, sheep and cattle, fishing, gypsum mining and tourism, and the western end is reserved as Flinders Chase National Park. It was named in 1802 by Matthew Flinders, whose crew killed some of its large, fearless kangaroos to obtain fresh meat. In 1836 the first colonists in SA camped at Nepean Bay, on the northeast coast, until the site of Adelaide was chosen for settlement.

kangaroo paws There are twelve species of these grassy-leaved plants, all of which are endemic to southwest WA. Belonging to the herbaceous family Haemodoraceae, they derive their name from the claw-like formation of the shaggy-haired tubular flowers in most species. Best known is WA's floral emblem, the red and green kangaroo paw, *Anigozanthos manglesii*, which is common in sandy ground from near Albany north to Shark Bay.

kangaroos, wallabies and allies The kangaroo has long been the worldwide symbol of Australia and has many heraldic, commercial and cultural representations in Australian life; of the family Macropodidae, to which it belongs, there are about 50 Australian species. Macropods are found in almost all habitats, from subalpine moors to coastal heath, from deserts to rainforests; some have even become arboreal. Most species occur on the Australian continent, although some are native to NG and the Bismarck Archipelago.

As their family name implies, macropod marsupials have large hind legs, used for hopping; characteristic also of most species is a heavy, thick tail, which acts as a counter-balance during locomotion and as a prop when the animal stands upright. Some kangaroos and wallabies display an unusual reproductive feature known as embryonic diapause, in which a viable embryo may be retained in the female reproductive tract, developing only after an older offspring has left the pouch or – in the case of desert species – following an increase in the food supply resulting from heavy rainfall; reproductive diapause allows these species to rapidly take advantage of favourable conditions.

The musky rat-kangaroo of northern Qld, *Hypsiprymnodon moschatus,* is a small macropod with a scaly tail and only moderately enlarged hindlegs; small rat-kangaroos display features that relate them to their possum-like ancestors. Most species make grass nests; Lesueur's rat-kangaroo, *Bettongia lesueuri,* is the only burrowing macropod, and it may construct large underground warrens. Other species include the short-nosed rat-kangaroos of the genus *Bettongia,* the rufous *Aepyprymnus rufescens,* and the potoroos, genus *Potorus.*

True kangaroos, members of the subfamily Macropodinae, are very diverse. The small hare wallabies (genera *Lagostrophus* and *Lagorchestes*) are mostly confined to semi-arid habitats in southern Australia; tree kangaroos – *Dendrolagus,* having two species in northeast Qld and five in NG – have shortened hindlimbs and very long tails as an adaptation for climbing and living in trees. The pademelon (genus *Thyogale*) from eastern Australia and quokka (genus *Setonix*) from WA are each about the size of a large cat. Rock wallabies of the *Petrogale* genus have granulated footpads for gripping rocks in the steep mountains and gorges of their habitats, and the nail-tailed wallaby, *Onychogalea,* has a small, horny spine near the tip of its tail. The genus *Macropus* contains most of the larger species, such as the grey or forester kangaroos, *M. giganteum,* the wallaroos (a group that includes the euro), *M. robustus,* and the red kangaroos, *M. rufus,* while the genus *Wallabia* contains a number of smaller wallabies.

Some macropods are either endangered or have become extinct through habitat destruction and predation by foxes. On the other hand, a number of the larger species are regarded as pests by graziers in that they compete with livestock for grass. Given the absence of large predators, populations are able to increase rapidly. In the arid and semi-arid regions of eastern Australia, wild kangaroos – primarily the red kangaroo – are hunted commercially both for their skins and for use as pet food, and this has resulted in a perennial controversy, generating much heated debate. There are many points of conflict: the method of killing (spotlighting or shooting), the extent to which species are threatened, and the question of whether the 'national symbol' should be so poorly treated. Animal protection groups continue to lobby foreign countries to ban the import of kangaroo skins, but others have argued that kangaroos are a renewable resource that should be harvested, especially given the great reproductive capacity of some species. Some researchers have suggested replacing sheep with kangaroos in the semi-arid lands, especially since kangaroos (with their soft feet) cause less damage to soil and vegetation and are better adapted to these habitats. Advocates of this policy note that kangaroos, as well as yielding skins, have a highly nutritious meat of low cholesterol content, which could be marketed for human consumption.

Karmel, Peter Henry (1922–), educator and academic, b. Melbourne. Educated at Melbourne and Cambridge universities, Karmel was appointed professor of economics at the

University of Adelaide in 1950. Over the last thirty years he has chaired many committees concerned with Australian secondary and tertiary education, and is regarded by many as the country's most influential educationalist. Among his numerous academic posts was that of vice-chancellor of the ANU (1982–7), and he also is a former chairman of the Australia Council (1974–7).

Karratha WA (pop. 9533) Established in 1969 as the residential and service centre for the mining operations of the Pilbara region, Karratha lies 1467km northeast of Perth; it also now services the North West Shelf gas project and is the administrative centre for the Roebourne Shire. Nearby Roebourne (pop. 1269) was the first town in the northwest; originally based on the pastoral industry, it now survives on tourism.

karri > *eucalypts*

Katherine NT (pop. 6100) A tourist town and service centre for a beef, mining and horticultural district, Katherine lies 303km south of Darwin where the Stuart Highway crosses the Katherine River. Its meatworks process beef and buffalo for worldwide export, and its new dairy is Australia's third-largest. Local horticulture developed from riverside vegetable farms set up to feed troops in World War 2, which later formed the basis for CSIRO experiments in tropical crops (notably sorghum, peanuts and cotton) as well as fodder crops and improved pastures. Local tourism has long centred largely on the spectacular 16.8km-long Katherine Gorge (some 32km from the town) and scenic Cutta Cutta Caves, which house rare bats; in 1989 the gorge was returned to the control of local Aborigines. Katherine was named after a daughter of a patron of explorer John McDouall Stuart, who found the river in 1862.

Katoomba NSW (pop. 15 627) With Wentworth Falls forming the administrative and tourist centre of the Blue Mountains, Katoomba is 107km west of Sydney. The city developed from coal-mining in the 19th century, and with the advent of the railway from Sydney in the 1870s it was soon attracting Sydney visitors seeking to escape the summer heat. The coal mine failed but Katoomba continued to develop as a base for visitors to the area's magnificent mountain scenery. Today it has become virtually a dormitory suburb of Sydney.

Keating, Paul John (1944–), politician, b. Sydney. Keating was an industrial advocate before entering federal parliament as a Labor member in 1969. Briefly minister for northern Australia (1975) in the Whitlam government, he became treasurer when the Hawke government was elected in 1983. He has remained in that position since, overseeing many controversial changes in the operation of the Australian economy, including the so-called Prices and Incomes Accord between the federal government and the ACTU, substantial reforms to the taxation system, and general deregulation of the economy. Widely considered to be an outstanding treasurer, Keating is a conspicuous, if caustic, politician who since the mid-1980s has been mooted consistently as a future federal leader of the ALP.

Kellerman, Annette Maria Sarah > *swimming and diving*

Kelly gang, legendary Vic. bushrangers of the 1870s. The gang, which was led by **Ned (Edward)** (1855–80), b. Beveridge, Vic., included his younger brother Dan and two associates, Joe Byrne and Steve Hart. Kelly was the son of Irish ex-convict 'Red' Kelly and Ellen Quinn; he grew up among the rural poor in the Wangaratta-Beechworth area of Vic., which in the light of ensuing events came to be known as 'Kelly country'. Cattle thieving was rife and there were continual clashes with the police: Kelly asserted persecution of his family, and it is possible that neither the first police charge against him (of assault) nor the second (of receiving a stolen horse) was wholly justified. In 1878, a dubious incident during which Dan Kelly 'resisted arrest' led to the imprisonment of Ellen Kelly for her alleged part in the attempted murder of the policeman concerned. Ned and Dan went into hiding: superb bushmen, they were helped by the local, closely knit (largely Irish) community to elude the police for eighteen months, the intensive hunt involving humiliating fiascos for the force. Audacious bank robberies, first at Euroa in December 1878 and then at Glenrowan, NSW, in December 1879 (when the gang imprisoned two local policemen), increased both the prestige of the Kellys and the reward money. In June 1880, at Glenrowan, a former friend of Byrne turned informer and was shot by Byrne and Dan Kelly. Ned planned to ambush the trainload of police sent from Melbourne as the result of this incident, and held the townsfolk of Glenrowan hostage in the hotel. The police were warned and Dan Kelly, Byrne and Hart were killed during the ensuing hotel battle. Ned was wounded, escaped briefly, but returned the next morning and – despite his 40kg home-made armour – was shot and captured. Tried for murder, he was hanged in Melbourne on 11 November 1880. The Kelly gang rapidly entered Australian folklore and has been studied and celebrated in book and film, poetry and painting. These give the full range of opinions about the gang – from murderous outlaws to wronged heroes who personified Australian 'mateship' and the deep-seated Irish-English and selector-squatter hatreds of 19th-century Australia.

kelpies > *dogs*

Kemp, Roger (1908–87) artist, b. Bendigo, Vic. Kemp began painting in 1935 but supported himself by factory work until 1966, after which he became a full-time professional artist. Often described as an 'artist's artist', his influence on Australian painters can be seen most clearly in the work of Leonard French and Jan Senbergs. During the 1960s he came to the notice of the wider Australian public, winning several major prizes. His style changed very little over the years, his works being mostly large, abstract and often strangely troubling in their intensity.

Kempsey NSW (pop. 9335) This town, which lies about 458km north of Sydney, is the commercial centre of the Macleay valley. It is built on a river levee and the lower parts are fairly frequently flooded. The region is noted for Akubra hats, dairy and beef cattle, maize, potatoes, fishing and prawning, timber and tourism.

Kendall, Henry Clarence (1839–82), poet, b. Ulladulla, NSW. Kendall's first volume of poetry was published in 1862; informed by his childhood in coastal NSW, his best works – while generally unfashionable throughout the 20th century and often considered derivative – were lyrical descriptions of the green sea-washed plains and forests of those regions. Beset by financial and family problems from the late 1860s, he owed his recovery from alcoholism to the charitable support of friends; his third and final volume of poetry, *Songs from the Mountains*, was published in 1880.

Keneally, Thomas Michael (1935–), novelist, b. Sydney. After abandoning study for the priesthood, and working as a school-teacher, Keneally published his first novel, *The Place at Whitton*, in 1964. Success came with *Bring Larks and Heroes* (1967), and since then he has become one of Australia's major novelists and has won numerous awards, including the UK's Booker McConnell fiction prize in 1982 for *Schindler's Ark*; other novels include *The Chant of Jimmie Blacksmith* (1972), *Gossip from the Forest* (1975), *Confederates* (1979) and *The Playmaker* (1988). Keneally's subject range is unusually wide and he enjoys the position of being a serious writer who is also popular, both in Australia and overseas.

Kennedy, Edmund Besley Court (1818–48), surveyor and explorer, b. Channel Islands. Kennedy arrived in Australia in 1840. He was second in command to Thomas Mitchell on his 1845 expedition, and in the following year dispelled the hopes that they had found a great northwest-flowing river. Killed by Aborigines in 1848 when he had nearly completed a journey through Cape York Peninsula, his fate was reported by his loyal and remarkable Aboriginal companion, Jacky Jacky.

Kennedy, Graham Cyril (1934–), television presenter and actor, b. Melbourne. Kennedy began his television career as the compere of a variety program, 'In Melbourne Tonight' (1957–69). Quick of wit but occasionally salacious, he has survived numerous vicissitudes to remain an Australian institution; he presented an idiosyncratic late-night news program, 'Coast to Coast', 1988–9. Kennedy is also a competent film actor, notably in *Don's Party* (1976), *The Odd Angry Shot* (1979), and *Travelling North* (1987).

Kenny, Elizabeth (1886–1952), poliomyelitis therapist, b. Warialda, NSW. Working as a bush nurse in Qld after 1910, Kenny encountered an unfamiliar illness which was diagnosed by telegraph as infantile paralysis. She developed a method of treatment involving hot baths, passive movement and the discarding of braces; this was at odds with conventional medicine and she was derided by doctors who found her technical explanations of the cause of paralysis ill-informed. She had some remarkable success, however, established several clinics in Australia, and also introduced her method to the US. Although a 1938 royal commission on the treatment of poliomyelitis brought a judgment against Kenny's method, it was subsequently vindicated by the National Foundation for Infantile Paralysis and some current rehabilitation methods have drawn on her work.

Keppel islands Qld Situated at the northern end of Keppel Bay, northeast of Rockhampton, this group comprises Great Keppel, North Keppel, and a number of smaller islands. Great Keppel is a major tourist resort; of the other islands, eleven together make up a national park, the largest being North Keppel. The terrain is generally hilly, and the islands are fringed with reefs. Captain Cook discovered them in 1770 and named them after a naval officer who was later first lord of the Admiralty.

Kerr, Sir John Robert (1914–), lawyer, b. Sydney. A barrister, Kerr was appointed chief justice of NSW in 1972 and governor-general of Australia in 1974. Following the blocking of supply by a Senate hostile to the Labor administration, he dismissed the Whitlam government on 11 November 1975 using powers he considered to be vested in him under section 64 of the Constitution (> *constitutional crisis 1975*). Though much criticised at the time, Kerr's action – in effect if not in manner and method – has since been seen by some as justified, given Whitlam's refusal to call an election to break the parliamentary deadlock. Having retired as governor-general in 1977, he published an apologia, *Matters for Judgment*, in 1978.

kestrel > *eagles and hawks*

Kiama NSW (pop. 9184) A former cedar port 120km south of Sydney, Kiama is now a popular retirement and tourist centre (and increasingly a residential base for Wollongong workers). Local attractions include a blowhole, 19th-century lighthouse and nature trails. The harbour was discovered as early as 1797 by George Bass and was used by cedar-cutters from 1815; today dairying and mixed farming are the principal regional activities.

Kidman, Sir Sidney (1857–1935), pastoralist, b. Adelaide. Later known as the 'Cattle King', Kidman left home at 13. After working on stations near Broken Hill and Menindee, NSW, he began an extensive trade in horses and cattle. In 1880 he bought his first property, Owen Springs, in central Australia, and from there went on to become one of the largest landowners in the country's history; estimates

of the eventual extent of his holdings vary from 120 000 to 170 000sq.km, which allowed him to move stock according to grazing conditions and water supplies.

Kiewa River Vic. Rising near Mt Bogong in the Australian Alps, the Kiewa flows northwards for 185km to enter the Murray River near Albury–Wodonga. The upper sections lie in heavily timbered country, and are snow-covered in winter. The combination of high rainfall and steep slopes has been used to advantage in Vic.'s largest hydro-electric scheme, which takes water from a catchment of 303sq.km. The main storage is Rocky Valley dam, on the Bogong High Plains.

Kimberley(s), the WA This vast rugged region in the far north of the State – a statistical division of some 356 500sq.km – is bounded by the sea to the north and west, the Fitzroy River valley to the south, and the Ord River valley to the east. A remote, almost empty land averaging a height of 610m and dipping northwest to a drowned coast, it is bounded by steep, faulted faces on the southwest (King Leopold Range), the northeast (Durack Range) and southeast (Antrim plateau). Its Precambrian sandstones are cut deeply by rivers radiating from Mt Hann (776m), all with mangrove-lined estuaries edged by cliffs. Following Alexander Forrest's 1879 exploration, sheep farmers came from the south of WA to the Fitzroy River region, and cattlemen overlanded from Qld and NSW to East Kimberley; famous treks lasting years were made by the MacDonald brothers, the Durack and Buchanan families, and others. Gold brought a brief rush to Halls Creek in 1885 and led to the building of > *Wyndham* as a port. Beef cattle and sheep are still grazed on huge stations, but droving has been replaced by road trains. Ord River irrigation has prompted more intensive rural production, but vast distance from markets stifles expansion. Iron-ore mining takes place on Koolan Island, and diamond mining at Argyle; bauxite deposits are to be developed around Admiralty Gulf. Spectacular scenery, and improved access through newly opened roads, have boosted tourism in recent years; the region has several Aboriginal sites of outstanding significance, notably the rock art of Windjana Gorge National Park.

King, Ingeborg Victoria (1918–), sculptor, b. Germany. A sculptor of formidable talent, King is particularly known for her monolithic abstract works in industrial metals (aluminium, iron, and bronzed and stainless steel). Apprenticed in Germany to a wood-carver, she studied sculpture in Berlin, London and Glasgow in the late 1930s and the 1940s, working in a range of classical materials. She arrived in Australia in 1951. *Forward Surge* (1975) a huge, curved steel sculpture commissioned for the Vic. Arts Centre plaza, epitomises the clarity, balance and power of her best work.

King, Philip Gidley (1758–1808), naval officer and colonial administrator, b. England. As NSW governor 1800–07, King succeeded Hunter and preceded Bligh. He had previously been aide to Arthur Phillip aboard the First Fleet. In February 1788 he was sent with 23 persons to found the Norfolk Island settlement; by 1793 the settlement contained 1000 people and had an export surplus of grain. King's illegitimate son was the first child born there. Following his return to England on leave, King obtained, with Sir Joseph Banks's influence, a 'dormant commission' to act as substitute and eventual successor to Hunter. Able and conscientious, his period of control yet failed to curb the officers' trading monopoly; he encouraged exploration, emancipation of convicts, and the development of whaling. His son **Phillip Parker** (1791–1856), b. Norfolk Island, contributed notably to charting of the Australian coast in four voyages 1817–22, particularly in the northwest.

Kingaroy Qld (pop. 6362) Located 255km north of Brisbane in the south Burnett district, Kingaroy is noted particularly as Australia's largest peanut-producing region. Its tall silos and butter factory reflect its function as the centre for dairying to the east and for the grains and vegetables grown on the rich, red soils to the west.

kingfishers These distinctive birds have short wings and strong beaks and feed mostly on fish, reptiles and insects; they frequently nest in tree-holes, termite nests and riverbanks. Australia has ten species, divided between two families. True kingfishers are members of the *Alcedinidae*: one of them is the azure kingfisher, *Alcyone azurea*, which is found along streams in northern Australia and down the eastern coast as far as Tas. The eight species of forest kingfishers, family *Dacelonidae*, are often found well away from water: the most famous of these is the kookaburra or laughing jackass, *Dacelo gigas*, well known for its mocking call. It is the world's largest kingfisher, and although originally found only in eastern mainland Australia, it has since been introduced to Tas. and WA. A second species – the blue-winged kookaburra, *D. leachi* – is found in northern Australia and in NG. The kookaburra's food includes insects, young birds and small reptiles; it moves in close family groups, usually with only one pair breeding.

kingfishes This name is applied to a number of marine fishes conspicuous by reason of size, appearance or food value, but most commonly to the yellowtail kingfish, *Seriola lalandi*. This is a gamefish, related to the trevally and occurring in waters extending from south Qld around the southern coast. It may reach a length of over 2m and a weight of 68kg.

King George Sound WA This magnificent harbour is one of the finest anchorages on the Australian coast. Named after George III by surveyor George Vancouver in 1791, it has two inner arms: Oyster Harbour and Princess Royal Harbour, on which is the town of Albany. The sound was formerly WA's major port and a coaling station for ocean steamers, and on the western shore, at Frenchman's Bay, Australia's only whaling station operated until 1978. In World War 1 it was the assembly point for troopships bound for Gallipoli, and in World War 2 it was a US naval base. On the peninsula at the west of the sound is the Torndirrup National Park.

King Island Tas. With land generally undulating and measuring approximately 64km by 26km, King Island lies at the western end of Bass Strait and is a municipality of Tas.; it was named after NSW Governor Philip Gidley King. The main town is Currie, but chief port development is at Grassy, where scheelite deposits provide Australia's main source of tungsten ore. Major rural activities are sheep, beef cattle and dairying; in recent years King Island has become famous for its high-quality dairy products. In the early 19th century the island was known worldwide for the numerous seals and sea elephants, which in consequence were hunted almost to extinction. The violent storms typical of the region causing many shipwrecks on the coast, King Island once was known as the 'graveyard of Bass Strait'.

King Leopold Range WA This range is in fact the rugged southwestern scarp of the Kimberley plateau; it extends about 225km southeast from Collier Bay. The Fitzroy, Margaret and Lennard rivers cut through the range, of which the highest point is Mt Ord (936m). The region was explored in 1879 by Alexander Forrest, who named the range after the Belgian king, Leopold II.

Kings Cross NSW This precinct in the suburb of Darlinghurst, 2km from the centre of Sydney and named for its location at the junction of five main city roads, has long been renowned as the city's 'red light' district and more recently as a centre for illicit drugs and gambling. It has a diverse and cosmopolitan population, and a plethora of entertainment venues and restaurants, all of which attract an abundance of tourists. Despite its colour and vitality, the sleazy reality of life 'at the Cross' is reflected in a large street-based population, shopfront pornography, and the pre-eminence of the drug trade.

Kingsford Smith, Sir Charles Edward (1897–1935), aviator, b. Hamilton, Qld. One of the great aviation pioneers, Kingsford Smith flew in the Royal Flying Corps in World War 1, winning the Military Cross. In 1927 he and Charles Ulm set a record for a round-Australia flight, and the following year they made the first trans-Pacific flight in a Fokker tri-motor, the *Southern Cross*. Numerous other record-breaking flights followed. In 1930, Kingsford Smith established the first Australian National Airways, which foundered after the loss of the *Southern Cloud*. In November 1935, his plane, the *Lady Southern Cross*, disappeared after taking off from Allahabad in India while on a flight from England to Australia; it is believed to have crashed off the coast of Burma. In an era when aviation was still novel and romantic, 'Smithy', like Lindbergh in the US, achieved near-legendary status in his own lifetime.

Kingsley, Henry (1830–76), novelist, b. England. Kingsley was the younger brother of the novelist Charles Kingsley. Having wandered in southeastern Australia 1853–7 as a digger, police trooper and station hand, he wrote *The Recollections of Geoffry Hamlyn* (1859), then hailed as one of the best of Australia's pastoral chronicles. While its critical popularity waned in the 20th century, the novel is still generally considered a landmark in Australian fiction and

the model for later classics such as *His Natural Life* by Marcus Clarke. Kingsley published many more novels, mostly historical sagas, of which only *The Hillyars and the Burtons* (1865) was considered of note.

Kingston Tas. (pop. 10 932) This commuter town and regional centre lies on the Derwent estuary 13km south of Hobart; the region was settled from 1804. A busy industrial, commercial and administrative town, Kingston is also a popular holiday centre and offers a range of recreational pursuits including fishing. It is the site of Australia's Antarctic Division headquarters, and industries include fish processing, manufacturing and engineering.

Kirby, Sir Richard Clarence (1904–), lawyer, b. Charters Towers, Qld. Kirby graduated in law from the University of Sydney in 1927 and became a barrister in 1933. He was appointed to the NSW District Court in 1944 and to the Commonwealth Arbitration Court in 1947, remaining a vigorous proponent of Australia's industrial-arbitration and wage-determination systems throughout his career. Following a case in which the functions of the Arbitration Court were held unconstitutional, he was appointed chief judge of a reconstituted body, the Court of Conciliation and Arbitration, in 1956; he was also president of the Commonwealth Conciliation and Arbitration Commission 1956–73.

kites > *eagles and hawks*

Klippel, Robert Edward (1920–), sculptor, b. Sydney. An innovative sculptor, Klippel is one of Australia's greatest contemporary artists in this field. His earliest 'assemblages' (dating from London in the 1940s), which combined organic and man-made items, attracted the attention of the French surrealist André Breton, who arranged a Paris exhibition in 1949. Klippel lived and taught in the US 1957–63; his idiosyncratic machine and junk-metal sculptures are critically acclaimed both there and in Australia. His most recent work uses weathered wooden machinery parts with faded colours, and ranges from the small-scale to the monumental.

Knopfelmacher, Frank (1923–), social scientist, b. Czechoslovakia. An outspoken right-wing intellectual who arrived in Australia in 1955, Knopfelmacher is notable for his strong views on communism (which he vehemently opposes) and is an articulate critic of multiculturalism, arguing that Australia's cultural homogeneity is its greatest national asset. As lecturer and later reader in psychology at the University of Melbourne 1955–88, he was influential during the formative stage of several generations of intellectuals of varying political persuasions.

Knox, James Robert (1914–83), Catholic prelate, b. Perth. Educated at New Norcia, WA, Knox was ordained a Catholic priest in Rome in 1941. Eventually one of the highest-ranking Australians in the Catholic priesthood, he led a distinguished religious career, serving in senior positions in Italy, Japan, Africa and India. He was archbishop of Melbourne 1967–74; made a cardinal in 1973, he returned a year later to the Vatican to assume the post of a prefect in the church's governing office, the Roman Curia. He was buried in St Patrick's Cathedral, Melbourne.

koala This remarkable arboreal marsupial, well known for its 'teddy-bear' look, has large furry ears, a black leathery nose and strong claws. The koala, *Phascolarctos cinereus*, feeds exclusively on the leaves of certain eucalypts, an adult consuming some 500g daily; the harsh tannins and oils of the leaves are neutralised and digested in its stomach and remarkably long intestine. In addition to providing nutrition, the leaves contain water sufficient for the animal's needs – hence its name, said to be an Aboriginal word meaning 'it does not drink', although in fact it can and does drink on occasion. The koala has a home range of some fourteen or fifteen trees, but individuals usually appear to favour a particular one. Although koalas are classified in the superfamily Vombatoidea, which includes wombats, the two are not closely related; the koala's rudimentary tail and two-teated pouch do, however, resemble those of the wombat and suggest a terrestrial – perhaps burrowing – phase. Koalas are large and heavily built, adult males being known to reach 12–13kg in weight and the females 8kg. They breed during spring and summer, the gestation period of about 35 days producing a single offspring of only about 0.5kg in weight.

Originally abundant in mainland eucalypt forests from northern Qld to southeastern SA, from the turn of the century until about 1930 koalas were hunted ruthlessly for their skins, especially in their southern Qld stronghold.

Increasing public revulsion against this slaughter, together with a collapse in the market as the result of a US ban on imports, saved the remaining populations, which were subsequently declared to be totally protected by law. Although numbers have recovered somewhat koalas are nevertheless still absent from much of their former range, where habitat destruction and fragmentation prevents recolonisation. Additionally, some populations are suffering from a fatal form of ophthalmia caused by parasites.

Kokoda Trail > *World War 2*

Konrads family swimming champions, b. Latvia. The Konrads family arrived in Australia in 1949; **John** (1942–) and **Ilsa** (1944–) were taught to swim in the pool at a migrant camp near Wagga, because it was feared they might drown in nearby waterholes. On moving to Sydney they were given lessons by Don Talbot, who quickly recognised their ability. John liked Talbot's strict methods and trained relentlessly; a reserve at the 1956 Olympic Games, he set fourteen world records in quick succession and became the first male to hold simultaneously every world record from 200m to 1500m. He crowned his achievement with a gold medal in the 1500m at Rome in 1960. Ilsa broke her first world record at 13, and defeated Dawn Fraser and Lorraine Crapp in the 440yd freestyle at the 1958 Empire and Commonwealth Games. Both John and Ilsa later embarked on successful business and professional careers.

kookaburra > *kingfishers*

Koolan Island WA > *Yampi Sound*

Koonalda > *caves*

Koorie >> *Aboriginal culture and society*

Korean War (June 1950–July 1953) Following the invasion of South Korea by communist North Korea, a force to repel the aggressor was formed from sixteen nations and placed under the flag of the UN. Four days after the start of hostilities, Australian naval and air squadrons were put at the disposal of US command, and ground forces followed in July. After Chinese forces entered the war in November, Australian forces made distinguished rearguard actions at Pakchon and Kapyong. An armistice was signed in July 1953, leaving both sides holding much the same territory as when war started; Australia's total war casualties were 339 killed and about 1300 wounded. At home, the Menzies government's anti-communist moves were strengthened; other effects of the war included vast wool profits and high export earnings (which resulted in serious inflation) and intensified mineral prospecting]. >> *defence*; *foreign policy*

Kramer, Dame Leonie Judith (1924–), academic, b. Melbourne. Educated at the universities of Melbourne and Oxford, Kramer was appointed professor of Australian literature at the University of Sydney in 1968. She has been a member of many committees on educational and community affairs and was chairwoman of the ABC 1982–3, when her outspoken views on the need for higher broadcasting standards aroused some controversy. Editor of *The Oxford History of Australian Literature* (1981) and various anthologies, her other publications include extensive examinations of the work of Henry Handel Richardson, namely *Henry Handel Richardson and Some of Her Sources* (1954), *A Companion to Australia Felix* (1962) and *Myself When Laura* (1966).

krill These small shrimp-like crustaceans of the order Euphausiacea form enormous shoals in Antarctic waters; they are important as food for many fish, whales and sea-birds, and although recognised as a rich source of human food are greatly under-utilised. Many fishing nations are starting to exploit this protein resource, and krill is sometimes sold in Australian fish shops; there is, however, concern that overfishing could affect Antarctic wildlife, especially whales.

Kununurra WA (pop. 3137) This town in the east Kimberley region, 3216km northeast of Perth, is the service and residential centre for the Ord River irrigation scheme, to which its fortunes are tied. Much depends on the success of crops such as oilseeds, rice and sorghum, and on the outcome of proposals for a sugar industry, although the town has recently received a boost from development of the Argyle diamond mine 200km away.

Ku-ring-gai NSW This is the name of both a municipality and a national park about 20km north of Sydney. The municipality covers several outer suburbs of Sydney's North Shore; the park – Ku-ring-gai Chase – is a forested sandstone plateau extending to Broken Bay and including the deeply indented shores of Pittwater and Cowan Creek. Declared in 1894, it protects large Aboriginal rock engravings (the Dharuk Aborigines were its original inhabitants) and is noted for a rich display of flora from late winter to spring.

kurrajong > *sterculia family*

Kurri Kurri–Weston NSW (pop. 13 411) These adjoining towns are part of the city of Cessnock, 172km north of Sydney, and a residential centre for miners from the northern coalfields. Aluminium smelting is now a major local industry, and the area also has saw-milling, clothing manufacture, fruit-growing and dairying.

Kwinana WA (pop. 11 798) The State's main heavy industry is based at Kwinana beach, 19km south of Perth on Cockburn Sound. Formerly a quiet holiday resort, Kwinana developed dramatically from the 1950s with construction of a port and oil refinery; industries now include alumina and nickel refining, the production of chemicals, electricity generation, and a host of engineering works. The foothills to the east contain five residential suburbs – Medina, Calista, Orelia, Parmelia and Leda – named after ships that carried the first settlers to the locality in 1829. The town was named after the *Kwinana*, a coastal freighter beached in the 1920s.

L

Labiatae > *mint family*

Labor Party > *ALP*

Labour Day > *holidays and national days*

Laby, Thomas Howell (1880–1946) physicist, b. Creswick, Vic. After publishing the first results of Australian research into radioactivity (1904), Laby won an exhibition to the Cavendish Laboratory at Cambridge. Subsequently professor of natural philosophy at the University of Melbourne (1915–44), he promoted the introduction of radium treatment for cancer; he also helped establish the Commonwealth Radium Laboratory in 1936, and the Vic. Anti-Cancer Council. During World War 2, he co-ordinated the development of optical components and other military instruments.

lacewings and antlions Of the order Neuroptera, these are insects with long, membranous wings that bear a fine network of veins; most are predacious, both as larvae and as adults. Australia has one of the richest Neuroptera faunas in the world, comprising more than 700 species and including several unique and primitive families. The endemic family Nymphidae includes the common large, orange-brown lacewing, *Nymphes myrmeleonides*; the green lacewings of the family Chrysopidae feed voraciously on aphids and scale insects, and lay their eggs singly, on stalks. The Mantispidae, with their spined, raptorial forelegs, strongly resemble mantids. The antlions (family Myrmeleontidae) are very diverse in Australia. Antlion larvae lie in wait for ant prey at the base of conical pits in dry sand; as adults, they superficially resemble dragonflies. Members of the family Nemopteridae have long, trailing hindwings, and are found primarily in arid regions.

Lachlan River NSW Chief tributary of the Murrumbidgee River, the Lachlan flows for some 1500km from its headwaters in the Great Dividing Range, southwest of Goulburn, to its junction with the Murrumbidgee northwest of Balranald, thus becoming part of the Murray-Darling system. Upstream from Cowra is the Wyangala dam and on the middle and lower reaches a number of weirs have been built; these combine to mitigate flooding in years of heavy rainfall and to provide water for livestock, domestic use and some irrigation. Mountain regions of the upper reaches support forestry and sheep grazing; the course is then through crop and grazing lands to the more arid, woolgrowing plains. The river was explored by John Oxley in 1817, and was named after Lachlan Macquarie.

ladybirds > *beetles*

Lake Albacutya Vic. In an area of little and irregular rainfall northwest of the Wimmera town of Jeparit, Lake Albacutya is frequently dry; in wet seasons it receives water from the Wimmera River, through Lake Hindmarsh and Outlet Creek. The lake's name is from an Aboriginal word meaning 'place of bitter quandongs'.

Lake Alexandrina SA A wide (38km), shallow lake into which the Murray River flows before it enters the sea, Alexandrina is connected in the southeast to the smaller Lake Albert by the narrow Albert Passage at Narrung. Milang, on the western shore, now a dairy and vegetable-growing centre for Adelaide, was an important port until the decline of the river trade. In 1940, five barrages were built to join the islands across the mouth of the Murray and so prevent salt-water intrusion when the river is low. Charles Sturt named the lake, in 1830, in honour of the princess who became Queen Victoria.

Lake Amadeus NT This is a dazzling stretch of salty mud flats (about 120km long) lying between the Macdonnell (to the north) and Musgrave ranges and surrounded by many sandhills. It was discovered by Ernest Giles in 1872 and named for the Spanish King Amadeo; Giles, turned back by the waterless desert to the west, described the area as 'the bottomless bed of an infernal lake'. In 1964 drilling revealed the existence of natural gas and oil in the underlying sedimentary rock north of the lake, and gas is piped 1500km north to Darwin.

Lake Bathurst NSW This is a small, shallow lake about 32km south of Goulburn. Although having a maximum depth of only 3m and an average of 1.2m, it dries less frequently than nearby Lake George. It was discovered by Hamilton Hume and James Meehan in 1818.

Lake Callabonna SA A salt lake near Lake Frome, Callabonna is one of a chain of lakes to the east and north of the Flinders Ranges. It is famous for its fossil deposits, particularly for the number of complete skeletons of the diprotodon, the largest of Australian marsupials. Occasionally its southern section is filled, and becomes a breeding ground for colonies of birds.

Lake Cargelligo NSW This is the name of both a town and the lake beside which it stands, about 5km from the Lachlan River and some 150km west of Forbes. The town is a rail and service centre for a fertile agricultural district producing wheat, fat lambs, wool, and fruit and vegetables. The lake, which is a wildlife sanctuary, is also a recreation area and part of the Lachlan water conservation scheme. The district was explored by John Oxley in 1817; gold was discovered in the 1870s and a brief rush ensued. Lake Cargelligo has an historical museum exhibiting machinery and implements of the agricultural industries developed in this period.

Lake Corangamite Vic. In the Western District, between Colac and Camperdown, this is the largest natural lake in the State. Although about 50km from the sea, it is salty; it is also very shallow, having an average depth of only 2m but a circumference of nearly 160km. In contrast to other Western District lakes it lies not in a volcanic crater but in a depression in the plain; before the construction of a channel

to the Barwon River (1956) as an outlet for excess water, in periods of heavy rainfall the surrounding farmlands would be flooded as the level of the lake rose. The name Corangamite comes from an Aboriginal word meaning 'bitter water'.

Lake Disappointment WA This is a salt lake lying across the Tropic of Capricorn in the west of the Gibson Desert. It has an area of about 160sq.km and is frequently dry and sometimes marshy; it was named in 1897 by explorer F. H. Hann, who had hoped to find fresh water there. The Canning Stock Route skirts the northern shore.

Lake Echo Tas. At the head of the Dee River (a tributary of the Derwent), Lake Echo lies in the central plateau region and extends about 11km north–south. Its waters, with capacity increased by construction of a dam and by diversion from the Ouse River, are used in power generation; Lake Echo power station is an integral part of the highlands hydro-electric system.

Lake Eucumbene NSW A major dam in the Snowy Mountains hydro-electric scheme, Eucumbene was the first storage in the scheme to be completed, in 1958. It receives water from the upper sections of the Murrumbidgee and Snowy rivers, and from it water can be tunnelled to the Tumut and Murray–Snowy sections of the scheme. Stocked with rainbow trout, the lake is now a major tourist and fishing centre. The nearby town of Adaminaby, which then lay 9km northeast of its present location, was partially flooded by construction of the dam and was subsequently relocated.

Lake Eyre SA Lying in an area of extreme aridity, the result of a combination of low rainfall and a high rate of evaporation, this lake is divided into two distinct sections connected by a channel: the larger, northern part is 145km long and up to 64km wide, and the southern section is 64km by, at the most, 29km. It is one of the great salt lakes in the north of the State – rarely containing water, but consisting of salty mud partly covered with a thick crust of salt; the lowest part lies some 16m below sea-level. The main rivers whose waters in exceptional seasons reach Lake Eyre are Cooper Creek and the Warburton. Discovered by Edward Eyre in 1840, it was later named after him by G. W. Goyder. In 1964 the British driver

Donald Campbell used the vast, featureless surface to set a land speed record of 648.6kmh.

Lake Frome SA This is a pear-shaped salt flat in an arid region to the east of the Flinders Ranges, extending 96km north–south and reaching some 48km at the widest east–west point. It receives water only after heavy rain in the northern ranges, from which streams drain, or from the overflow of Lake Callabonna, lying to the north. First seen in 1840 by Edward Eyre, who supposed it to be part of a horseshoe-shaped continuation of Lake Torrens, it was later named for SA surveyor-general, E. C. Frome.

Lake Gairdner SA This is the largest of the salt lakes west of Lake Torrens and just north of the Gawler Ranges. Over 150km long and about 40km wide, it lies in an arid region where rainfall is little and irregular, so that the lake is usually dry. It was discovered almost simultaneously in 1857 by exploring parties under Stephen Hack and P. E. Warburton, and named in honour of a senior member of the British colonial office.

Lake George NSW Various theories have been formulated to explain the periodic drying up of this lake, which lies in the Lake George Range just north of Canberra; the phenomenon is believed to result from the fine balance between rainfall and evaporation. When filled it is 26km long, about 9km wide and up to 8m deep; when dry it is rich pastureland, and a study of drilling cores taken from the lake bed has provided scientists with the longest continuous record of continental hydrological changes. The lake's English name was given in 1820 in honour of George IV; to the Aborigines, it was Werriwa.

Lake Hindmarsh Vic. In the Wimmera region, this lake lies about 40km northwest of Warracknabeal; it is fed by the Wimmera River. Its size varies according to rainfall: it can cover 130sq.km and it can be completely dry; in wet seasons its overflow fills Lake Albacutya, via Outlet Creek. Discovered by Edward Eyre in 1838 and named after the governor of SA, the lake contains islands notable as pelican rookeries.

Lake Illawarra NSW The suburbs of Wollongong border the northern shore of this coastal lagoon in the Illawarra region. It is almost completely cut off from the sea by a sand-dune barrier, and is a popular recreation area, with fishing and boating facilities. The waters of the lake are used in the Tallawarra power station, situated on the west shore. It was discovered in 1796 by Bass and Flinders in the *Tom Thumb*, and was called by them Tom Thumb's Lagoon – a name now given to a small lagoon to the north.

Lake Macquarie NSW This is a coastal stretch of water immediately south of the city of Newcastle, which extends around the lake's northern shore. About 24km long, the lake has a narrow tidal outlet to the sea; it was formed by the gradual creation of sand bars, driven by wind and weather to enclose what was once a broad inlet. Tourist resorts in the district offer boating, fishing and swimming, and surfing and surf-fishing on the adjacent beaches; industrial activity includes coal-mining and mineral processing, with important power stations at Vales Point and Wangi Wangi. The region was once the home of the Awabakal Aborigines, but with white settlement their numbers rapidly diminished.

Lake Pedder Tas. The natural Lake Pedder was a small glacial lake on the Serpentine River – a tributary of the Gordon – in the rugged southwest region of Tas. The present lake (242sq.km) was formed by the construction of three dams – the Serpentine in the northwest and the Scotts Peak and Edgar in the southeast – that are major components of the Gordon River hydro-electric scheme. The destruction of Lake Pedder – set in wilderness country and noted especially for a fine, white, sandy beach – caused bitter controversy and sustained opposition by conservationists; the new lake, however, has become a popular resort for fishing and water sports. It occupies the northeast corner of the South West National Park.

Lakes Entrance Vic. (pop. 4104) This fishing and resort town, about 319km east of Melbourne, developed at the artificial entrance dug from the > *Gippsland Lakes* to the sea in 1889. The channel is maintained by tidal action at a minimum depth of 6–9m, but an offshore bar less than 3m below the surface at low tide prevents ships entering or leaving when waves break on it in stormy weather. Lakes Entrance is the main centre for the Gippsland Lakes and, like the rest of the region, is increasingly popular for permanent residency. The spread of urban development in the area has caused some concern to authorities because infrastructure and land capability are limited, and there is a need to prevent development encroaching on the surrounding rural region.

Lake St Clair > *Cradle Mountain–Lake St Clair*

Lake Wellington Vic. This is the innermost and least saline of the > *Gippsland Lakes*. It is shallow – less than 4m deep – and is a popular holiday resort and tourist area. It receives the waters of the Latrobe and Avon rivers, and is connected to adjacent Lake Victoria by McLennans Strait.

Lalor, Peter (1827–1889), Eureka rebel and later politician, b. Ireland. Lalor arrived in Australia in 1852. He was working on the Ballarat diggings when his quiet yet authoritative manner led to his selection to lead – albeit reluctantly – the rebellious miners at the > *Eureka Stockade*. He organised the stockade, and in the action received a wound leading to the loss of an arm. He went into hiding until acquittal of other leaders made it safe to emerge. Elected to the Vic. parliament 1855–71 and 1875–87, he served in various posts including that of Speaker (1880–7).

Lambert, George Washington Thomas (1873–1930), artist, b. Russia. Born of Anglo-American parents, Lambert arrived in Australia in 1887 and contributed cartoons and illustrations to the Sydney *Bulletin* 1895–1901. He was awarded the 1899 Wynne Prize for his painting *Across the Black Soil Plains* and left for Paris on a travelling scholarship in 1901. Attentive to detail and sensitive to the futility of war, he produced some memorable work as a war artist in Palestine and Gallipoli before returning to Australia in 1921. A raffish socialite generally considered to be a conservative artist, he was nevertheless a supporter of the Sydney circle of modernists (known as the Contemporary Group) that gave great impetus to modern art in Australia. Lambert's two sons were born in England: **Maurice** (1901–64) became a noted sculptor, and **Constant** (1905–51) was a distinguished composer and conductor

Lamiaceae > *mint family*

Lamington Plateau Qld A rugged, basalt-capped plateau in the extreme southeast of the State, Lamington stands immediately north of the McPherson Range; from it flow the headwaters of the Coomera and Albert rivers and the Logan River tributaries. There are stands of Antarctic beech in the temperate forests of 20 200ha Lamington National Park, 1200m above sea-level, and the central plateau is cut by several gorges displaying many waterfalls. To the west of the park lies the township of Lamington.

lampreys Although they superficially resemble eels, lampreys are grouped separately in the class Agnatha; together with hagfishes, they are the only living relatives of the jawless fishes, the most primitive vertebrates. They have no bony skeleton and no scales; they spawn in fresh water, but in many cases part of the lifecycle is spent in the sea. The adult form exhibits two types of behaviour: non-parasitic, in which the animal remains in fresh water, and breeds and dies soon after metamorphosis; and parasitic, in which the adult feeds, in either sea or fresh water, by extracting blood and flesh from other fishes by means of a rasp-like oral disc which is its mouthpart. Two Australian species are *Geotria australis* and *Mordacia mordax*, both parasitic and both up to 60cm long. A third form, *M. praecox*, is non-parasitic.

Lanceley, Colin (1938–), artist, b. NZ. Lanceley arrived in Australia in 1940 and came to prominence in the early 1960s as one of a trio of 'imitation realists' with two startling but successful exhibitions of junk 'assemblages' and paintings. He travelled to Europe on a scholarship (1964), then settled in England where he established a reputation exhibiting with the prestigious Marlborough Gallery and also teaching. His works, with their vivid colour, surrealistic forms, and objects integrated to create an extra dimension, reveal a highly personal artistic vision. He returned to live in Sydney in 1981.

land ownership The ownership of land in Australia remains subject to British common law and all title to the land is thus theoretically vested in the Crown. In practice there are three broad types of land tenure – Crown leases, freehold and leasehold.

The transfer of title to land is generally governed by the Torrens system, which was originated in SA in 1858 by politician Sir Robert Torrens (> *Torrens family*). This system aims to give simple and secure rights to land, that can be transferred easily and relatively cheaply through a single deed of title; it is effected through a public official, the registrar of titles. After its successful introduction in the Australian colonies, the system was subsequently adopted in NZ, some US states, Canada and, eventually, Britain. Although some private land in Australia is still covered by common-law provisions rather than the Torrens system, all titles are gradually being converted.

Crown leases Crown leases are still an important feature of landholding throughout Australia, and approximately 80% of all land (mainly rural) alienated by the Crown is held through Crown leasehold. In the ACT, virtually all urban and rural land is held under Crown leases.

The variety of Crown leases largely reflects the many changes of policy that have occurred in the last 200 years, particularly in relation to the holding of grazing land. The length of leases may vary from very short to 999 years or perpetuity, and rents vary similarly from a peppercorn or 5 cents per annum to full commercial rents. The conditions included in such leases permit the Crown to control the use of the land — such as specifying maximum stock numbers or regulating tree-felling — or to require improvements such as clearing and development or the sinking of water bores. Except in Qld and Tas., Crown leases are registered under the Torrens system; some include a right for the lessee to purchase the title to the leased land, either outright or over a period of years.

Although Crown leasehold grants relatively secure tenure, it usually only confers rights over the land surface or the air space above it; the leases are invariably subject to any grants made by the Crown for minerals exploration or development on or under the land. >> *land rights, Aboriginal; land settlement*

land rights, Aboriginal

The rights of indigenous people to the land they inhabited were recognised to some extent or even wholly in most of the European colonies founded in the 18th and 19th centuries, but not in Australia. Apparently, the British were unable or unwilling to see that the Aborigines' relationship with the land was of a kind that could be defined and enforced by the introduced English law; no particularly satisfying explanation of their attitude has ever been given.

Dissenters from the prevailing view could be found, but they were few and uninfluential until the 1960s, before which time the best done for the Aboriginal people was to set aside reserves for their 'use and benefit' and to preserve certain hunting and gathering rights for them when granting leases to pastoralists. Most of the reserves were small, however, often they were distant from the traditional territories of the Aborigines who lived on them, and they were controlled by missionaries or government officials. Aborigines had no legally enforceable rights to the land reserved for them: while the hunting and gathering provision in pastoral leases may have been enforceable, in practice Aborigines lacked the knowledge and resources necessary for a resort to law, and the officials who were supposed to protect their interests usually failed to do so.

The Gove case and beyond The turning-point in the history of Aboriginal land rights was the Gove case, decided in 1971, whereby the Aborigines of Yirrkala on the Gove Peninsula in the NT sued over the federal government's grant of mining leases on land reserved to them. Two issues raised in this complex case are of special interest. First, it was argued for the Aboriginal plaintiffs that English and international law included a doctrine of communal native title which should be accepted as forming part of Australian law and thus as being available to protect the plaintiffs' interests. Secondly, it was argued that the relationship to land of the Yirrkala people was sufficiently similar to property rights (as already understood in Australian law) for it to be similarly protected against violation. The case was lost but the presiding judge did comment that the evidence showed the Aborigines to have 'a subtle and elaborate system highly adapted to the country ... which provided a stable order of society and was remarkably free from the vagaries of personal whim'.

The fact that the Gove case was heard at all gave added impetus to the campaign for Aboriginal land rights that had arisen in the 1960s. After 1972, the federal Labor government prepared comprehensive land-rights legislation for the NT (then still controlled from Canberra), a revised version of which was passed by the succeeding government.

Land-rights legislation The Aboriginal Land Rights (Northern Territory) Act 1976 is one of the world's outstanding laws on indigenous rights. It turned over the reserves (about 18% of the NT) to Aboriginal ownership and allowed for vacant Crown land (about 30% of the NT) to be claimed by its traditional owners; to date, such claims have enjoyed a high rate of success.

Land in town areas and land held by non-Aborigines may not be claimed.

SA had led the way in transferring government-administered reserves to Aboriginal ownership with its Aboriginal Lands Trust Act 1966. Vic. and NSW followed suit, in 1970 and 1973 respectively, but in their case the reserves were minuscule. None of these laws allowed claims to be made, nor did they recognise traditional Aboriginal relationships to land. Further legislation in SA in 1981 and 1986 transferred large areas in remote parts of the State to their traditional Aboriginal owners; legislation in NSW in 1983 allowed claims to vacant Crown land that was not needed or likely to be needed for public purposes, and established a fund for land purchase. The Qld and WA governments have shown a strong tendency to oppose land rights for Aborigines; at the end of the 1980s, however, Qld was making deeds of grant of reserve land to Aboriginal communities and WA was making long-term land leases available. Since the 1960s, the federal government has provided money for the purchase of land for Aborigines in all parts of Australia.

The 1980s and beyond The net result of all these measures is that about 11% of Australia is held by Aboriginal groups or communities, or is held for them by Aboriginal-controlled corporations. Aboriginal land rights do not, however, pass unchallenged: the NT government has opposed many claims; the NSW legislation is under threat; and the federal government's plan for national land-rights legislation collapsed in 1985, largely owing to opposition from mining companies and some of the States. Among Aborigines themselves, debate continues over the legal form that should be given to their land rights. In addition, many of them feel that much more land should be made available and that they should be compensated for land that cannot be returned. >> *Aboriginal culture and society; land ownership; missions and reserves*

land settlement From the moment in 1770 when James Cook took possession of the continent on behalf of the British government, all land was the property of the Crown. The early governors were profligate with the Crown's land: they gave it away to emancipated convicts, free settlers, marines and military officers, the area granted being determined by the status of the grantee. From 1792 officers of the NSW Corps benefited especially from this system, and Governor Macquarie's attempts to compel grantees to occupy and improve their grants gave rise to great hostility. The result of the free-grants system was that big pastoralists bought or squeezed out smaller land-holders and large tracts of the best land were held by a very few.

Sale of land, as opposed to grants, began in NSW and Tas. in 1825. From 1831 the colonisation theories of E.G. Wakefield had their impact on Australia, their aim being to slow the spread of settlement and finance the immigration of free labour by selling the land at a fairly high price. From 1829, too, the occupation of land beyond the Nineteen Counties was prohibited. This was to no avail, as squatters crossed the Blue Mountains to the west and also spread to the north and south; in 1836 Governor Bourke surrendered and allowed them grazing rights in return for a licence fee of £10 per year. SA and WA were meanwhile settled under modified versions of the Wakefield system.

In 1846 the British government passed the Sale of Waste Lands Act, which gave squatters the right to lease the land they grazed and to purchase part of it. Squatters took advantage of this by using their right of purchase for 'peacocking' (buying those tracts of land watered by rivers and creeks, thus rendering the remainder of the land useless except to themselves) and by buying out the land rights of pastoralists less successful than themselves. These practices were largely confined to the eastern colonies, but by the 1850s – when the goldrushes brought many free immigrants to Australia – little land was available to them.

From 1856 all the colonies except WA and Qld exercised self-government, and colonial politicians turned their attention to the problems of land settlement. An answer was seen in free selection – the right of would-be landowners to purchase, on the payment of a deposit, any Crown land, whether leased by a squatter or not. Acts to this effect were passed in Tas. (1858), NSW (1861), Vic. (1862), Qld (1868), and SA and WA (1872). Overall, free selection was a failure: many selectors were hard-working (though some were incompetent, dishonest or both) but in almost all cases they were hampered by lack of capital and by the implacable hostility of the squatters; the latter used peacocking, 'dummy' selectors and sometimes force to keep their land. Quite a few selectors survived, but a major result of the land Acts was to allow former lease-holding squatters to become big freeholders.

By the 1890s, with a growing population and the increasing importance of agricultural exports, administrators once again sought to achieve fuller use of land by implementing closer settlement. Land taxes, seen as a way of inducing large land-holders to sell parts of their holdings, were introduced in most States between 1884 and 1915, as was a Commonwealth tax between 1910 and 1952. Little subdivision resulted, since many pastoral families simply redistributed the land within the family to avoid the tax. More success was achieved with the compulsory repurchase of land which was adopted in the eastern States between 1903 and 1911, whereby more than 10 500 new farms were created. Similar temporary successes with closer settlement were won again after World Wars 1 and 2 in the various > *soldier settlement schemes*, but all these gains were offset over time by the failure of smaller farms and their purchase by neighbours, and by periodic rationalisations of the agricultural economy (especially in the 1970s and 1980s).

By the late 1980s, of the 485 million ha in Australia in agricultural use, only 48 million ha were under crops or pasture, the vast remainder being unimproved and used for grazing. The total number of holdings continues to fall, and many larger establishments are in the hands of corporations, some of them overseas-owned. >> *free selection*; *land ownership*; *squatters*

Landy, John Michael (1930–   ), athlete, b. Melbourne. Landy was the first athlete to train under the rigorous program devised by Percy Cerutty. Although the first four-minute mile was run by Roger Bannister in early 1954, later in that year Landy reduced Bannister's time by 1.7 sec., setting a record that stood for four years. Also in 1954 he broke the world record in the 1500m, with a time of 3min. 41.8sec. His clash with Bannister at the 1954 Empire Games was billed the 'mile of the century'; running with an injured foot, Landy was defeated but had refrained from mentioning the injury before the race, an action typical of many that earned him admiration for his modesty, integrity and sportsmanship. He was a popular choice to take the Olympic oath at the Melbourne Games in 1956, in which (despite injuries) he ran a creditable third in the 1500m.

Lane, William (1861–1917), social reformer, b. England. Lane arrived in Australia in 1885 and became a journalist in Brisbane. First writing in the *Courier*, then in *Boomerang* (which he edited and part-owned 1887–92) and the *Worker*, he spread socialist doctrines and was a major figure, with labour leader W.G. Spence, behind the great strikes of 1890–1, but as labour moved into political power he was disillusioned by the inevitable party manoeuvres. He organised the New Australia Settlement Association; pioneers left Sydney in 1893 to found a > *New Australia* in Paraguay. Lane lived mainly in NZ after 1900, becoming increasingly conservative and imperialistic in outlook.

Lang, Jack (John Thomas) (1876–1975), politician, b. Sydney. From a poor background, Lang entered the NSW parliament as a Labor member in 1913, serving as premier 1925–7 and 1930–2. A man of the people and a great reformer, his first premiership was notable for a sweeping social program. His second term, during the worldwide economic depression, ended in his dismissal by the governor, Sir Phillip Game, after Lang refused to honour overseas and federal interest payments due by NSW, stating the principle of 'wages before dividends'. Attacked by the right-wing > *New Guard* and by conservative members of his own party, notably J. H. Scullin, Lang was expelled from the Labor Party in 1943 but served terms in the NSW (1943–6) and federal (1946–9) parliaments as an Independent.

Lang, John Dunmore (1799–1878), Presbyterian minister and politician, b. Scotland. Lang arrived in Australia in 1823, with the express aim of establishing the Presbyterian Church in the colonies. Founder of the Scots Church in Sydney in 1826, he was its minister until 1876 although officially deposed by the church synod 1842–63. Lang was energetically – and often vitriolically – involved in public affairs from the outset. His most important work was the development of family immigration schemes from the 1830s; he opposed bitterly the Anglican domination of education, and as strongly proposed a republican, independent Australia and the separation of the States. He was a member of the NSW parliament 1843–7, 1850–1, 1854–6 and 1859–69.

language > *Australian English*

lantana > weeds

lanternfishes This group of fishes inhabiting oceanic depths up to 1000m belongs to the largest of the deep-sea fish families, Myctophidae. All have light-producing organs (photophores) along their bodies, often forming distinctive patterns. They are small, but occur in very large numbers; migrating to upper waters during the night hours to feed on plankton, they are themselves a valuable source of food for other ocean fishes, marine mammals and birds, a factor which must be considered before their commercial value is exploited, as has been suggested. More than 90 species of lanternfish have been found in Australian waters.

La Pérouse, Jean-François de Galaup, Comte de (1741–88), navigator, b. France. A naval commander, La Pérouse, after five years of Pacific exploration and charting, reached Botany Bay on 24 January 1788 with his two ships only a few days after the arrival of the First Fleet. He remained there for six weeks, establishing a camp in the area that now bears his name.

larks and pipits There are three groups in Australia of these small, perching birds, which typically nest on the ground and sing in flight; all belong to different families. The fieldlark, of the genus *Mirafra*, is found in many open parts of the mainland, including croplands. A plain-coloured bird, it feeds mainly on grass-seeds and has a melodious song on the wing, not unlike that of the skylark; it also mimics the calls of other birds. The pipit or groundlark, genus *Anthus*, found throughout Australia and Tas., is more usually a ground-running bird, taking only brief flights; it has a short but pleasant song. The two songlarks of the third group are species of the genus *Cinclorhamphus*, specific to Australia and found throughout the continent; they are the brown and the rufous songlarks. The males of both groups are strong singers in flight.

Lasseter's Reef One of the great fables of Australian mining lore, this reef was a rich gold deposit supposedly discovered in 1897 by H. B. Lasseter in the Petermann Range on the WA–NT border. Becoming lost after his discovery, Lasseter was rescued by an Afghan camel driver. In 1930 he returned to search for the reef, but died in the attempt. Numerous other expeditions have been mounted, many inspired by Ion Idriess's colourful work, *Lasseter's Last Ride* (1931), which helped to popularise the legend.

Latham, Sir John Greig (1877–1964), lawyer and politician, b. Ascot Vale, Vic. Latham graduated in law in 1902 and became a QC in 1922. After working with the intelligence service during World War 1, he represented Australia at the Versailles peace conference in 1919. He entered federal parliament in 1922 and subsequently held several Nationalist portfolios including the attorney-generalship. As chief justice 1935–52, his most significant contributions were in constitutional law and court administration.

Latrobe Tas. (pop. 2578) This small town 264km north of Hobart is the service centre for a large agricultural district on the Mersey River. Limestone quarries at nearby Railton produce more than 275 000t a year, used for cement production. The surrounding region produces mainly fruit, vegetables and grains.

La Trobe, Charles Joseph (1801–75), colonial administrator, b. England. La Trobe had taught, travelled, and written reports on West Indian education before he was appointed to the emerging settlement at Port Phillip in 1839. He was superintendent of the Port Phillip District 1839–51, becoming first lt-governor of Vic. 1851–4, making his one of the longest periods of administration in Australia at that time. With considerable diplomacy and skill, he saw Vic. through the early squatter phase, the attainment of separate statehood and the early years of the gold rush.

La Trobe Library > *libraries*

Latrobe Valley Vic. Centred on the Latrobe River in central Gippsland, about 150km east of Melbourne, the Latrobe Valley is noted particularly as the site of one of the world's largest deposits of brown coal; its main population centres are > *Moe*, > *Morwell* and > *Traralgon*. The Latrobe River rises on the southern slopes of the Great Dividing Range and flows generally eastward before emptying into the Gippsland Lakes. While dairying and pastoralism are the region's longstanding industries, the central part of the Latrobe Valley is devoted to coal extraction, electricity generation, and briquette manufacture – all of which began in the 1920s and rapidly overtook farming as the region's mainstay. Less beneficial results of the industry have included serious air pollution and scarring of the landscape by open-cut mining.

Launceston Tas. (pop. 66 286) Tas.'s second-largest city, Launceston lies 200km north of Hobart at the junction of the North and South Esk rivers, which together form the 65km tidal estuary of the Tamar. Launceston is the State's chief freight centre and services a fertile hinterland that supports the production of fruit (particularly apples and wine grapes) and vegetables, wool and wheat; industries include food and timber processing, textile manufacture and tourism. The region was first settled in 1806 and named after the Cornish birthplace of Governor King. It flourished henceforth as a port and the colony's northern capital, this role being augmented by mineral discoveries (notably tin) from the 1870s. Despite its importance, Launceston has escaped the worst excesses of metropolitan life, due in part to its pleasant hilly surrounds and numerous parks and gardens. It has a number of fine colonial buildings as well as many outstanding natural attractions including nearby Cataract Gorge.

Lauraceae > *laurel family*

laurel family The Lauraceae family consists chiefly of rainforest trees and is well represented throughout tropical Australia. About 100 species occur in Australia, including familiar representatives such as the bay tree, *Laurus nobilis*, source of bay leaves; camphor laurel, *Cinnamomum camphora*; and avocado, *Persea americana*. All have aromatic leaves and bark and fatty-fleshed fruits; in many species these are an important food source for birds, especially native pigeons, for which reason they are commonly called 'pigeonberries'. The genus *Cassytha* is hardly recognisable as belonging to the same family. Its fourteen native species consist of leafless twining parasites that form dense masses over shrubs and small trees, known as devil's twine or dodder laurel.

Laver, Rod(ney George) (1938–   ), tennis player, b. Langdale, Qld. Among the greatest players of all time, the 'Rockhampton Rocket' overcame the possible disadvantage of slight stature by concentrated development of his left (playing) arm, at the suggestion of coach Charlie Holls; the result was the devastating top-spin that characterised his game. Winning the first of his Australian-record four Wimbledon crowns in 1961, in 1962 he went on to achieve his first Grand Slam (the Australian, French, British and US titles in one year). He turned professional in the following year, and when in 1969 professionals were admitted to major world championship, he repeated this performance, becoming the first man to win two Grand Slams. Over a 20-year period, Laver won 47 major tournaments.

law and legal system The Commonwealth of Australia was established on 1 January 1901 from the former British colonies of NSW, Vic., Qld, Tas., WA and SA, which became States in the new structure. The legislative powers of the Commonwealth, set out in the > *Constitution*, are vested in the federal parliament, which consists of a House of Representatives and a Senate, with the British monarch as titular head. Many of the Commonwealth's legislative powers are held concurrently with the State parliaments, whose powers are defined in their own Constitution Acts; in the event of a State law being inconsistent with a Commonwealth law, the latter prevails.

When the Australian colonies were settled in the late 18th century, the settlers brought British law – both case law and statutes – with them. In time, the establishment of colonial courts and legislatures and later the federal parliament and High Court of Australia reduced the influence of the decisions of British courts on Australian law. Even today, however, in the absence of local authority which an Australian court would be obliged to follow, decisions of England's Court of Appeal and the House of Lords are frequently relied upon. British statute law (with some exceptions) ceased to be admitted in NSW, Vic., Qld and Tas. from 1828, WA in 1829, and in SA in 1836; thereafter, the only British statutes employed were those which explicitly applied to the colonies or could be inferred to do so. In 1986, following the passage of the Australia Acts (which abolished the last colonial ties with Britain) the British parliament ceased to have power to pass such statutes, and State parliaments acquired the power to amend or repeal them.

Law courts Australia has both State and federal courts, each arranged in a hierarchical structure. State courts exercise jurisdiction under some federal Acts as well as State law; the jurisdiction of the federal courts is conferred by federal Acts.

At the bottom of the State hierarchies are the magistrates' courts (in some States called local courts). These courts have general jurisdiction over persons charged with less serious criminal offences (such as infringements of traffic laws), together with authority to commit persons for trial for indictable offences (those tried before a jury). In committal proceedings the magistrate must decide whether the evidence against the charged person is sufficient to warrant placing that person on trial. Magistrates' courts also have jurisdiction in civil matters where relatively small amounts of money are involved.

Most States have an intermediate level of courts -- usually called district courts – which have criminal and civil jurisdiction over more serious offences. These courts are presided over by judges, and juries are empanelled for some cases. In NSW, for example, charges relating to indictable offences (apart from murder and other serious offences formerly punishable by death) are heard in the district court; in civil matters, the district court has jurisdiction where the amount claimed is not more than $100 000 or is more than that amount if each party consents. District courts also hear appeals from magistrates' courts.

All States have supreme courts which have wider jurisdiction, in both criminal and civil matters, than those described above: they generally hear charges involving the most serious indictable offences and exercise civil jurisdiction without any monetary limits, and also have jurisdiction which is not exercisable by other courts (over admiralty and probate matters, for example). Original jurisdiction (the hearing of cases for the first time) is exercised by a single judge, whereas appeals are normally heard by a full court of three judges (in NSW called the court of appeal).

Australia's federal courts are of comparatively recent origin. The Family Court, which was established in 1976, hears applications for dissolution of marriage and is empowered to make orders in relation to maintenance, matrimonial property and custody of children. The Federal Court (established in 1977) exercises jurisdiction under several federal Acts, in matters such as industrial proceedings, bankruptcy, and restrictive trade practices; it also hears appeals against some decisions of State courts exercising federal jurisdiction.

At the apex of Australia's judicial system is the High Court, which consists of a chief justice and six justices (formerly appointed for life but since 1977 appointed to the age of 70). Most of the cases heard by the High Court are appeals but it also has original jurisdiction, most notably over interpretation of the federal Constitution; decisions of the High Court are binding on all other Australian courts.

Legislation was introduced in 1987 which allowed cases formerly triable only in a federal court or the courts of a particular State to be heard in any State or federal court; a court may, however, decline to hear cases which are brought before it. As a result it is less likely that aspects of a legal dispute will have to be litigated in separate courts.

Judicial process Civil proceedings are commonly initiated by a writ of summons commanding the defendant to enter an appearance (that is, to deliver a memorandum in the prescribed form to an officer of the court). Pleadings may then be exchanged to clarify the issues of fact in dispute: the plaintiff makes a statement of claim, which summarises the relevant facts including the particulars of the injury or damage suffered; the defendant then replies with a defence, after which the plaintiff also has the opportunity to reply. On completion of pleadings, the case is set down for trial. In most States, civil actions are heard by a judge sitting without a jury. The hearing begins with an address by the counsel representing the plaintiff, who then calls the first witness; the counsel for the defendant may then cross-examine the witness, who may also be re-examined by the plaintiff's counsel. This procedure continues until the end of the case for the plaintiff. Once the case for the plaintiff has been presented the process is repeated on behalf of the defendant, after which each counsel gives a final address. Then, if there is a jury, the judge sums up the case: the judge must direct the jury on any relevant questions of law and the jury must make findings on the facts presented, although the judge may give the jury guidance on the evidence; the jury (usually numbering four in civil proceedings) then retires to consider its verdict. When the jury has given its verdict – or, in the absence of a jury, when the judge has given the finding – the court's ruling is announced, which often includes the allocation of costs. In civil proceedings, the plaintiff must prove the case on the balance of probabilities.

Less serious criminal offences are tried summarily (before a magistrate or justice of the peace), whereas more serious offences are tried before a jury. If the defendant pleads guilty, statements are read and character witnesses are called to help determine the appropriate penalty; if the defendant pleads not guilty, a jury of twelve is empanelled. The process of calling and examining witnesses is the same as for civil actions; the defendant may give evidence, although in cross-examination testimony as to the defendant's bad character or prior convictions is usually inadmissible. In most States a defendant who does not wish to give evidence may make an unsworn statement from the dock, which is not open to cross-examination. In most States the verdict of a criminal jury must be unanimous, although some allow for a decision of fewer than twelve jurors to be treated as the verdict of the whole jury. The standard of proof in criminal cases is proof beyond reasonable doubt. If the verdict is 'not guilty', the defendant is released from custody immediately unless there are other charges to be heard; if the verdict is 'guilty', character evidence may be presented on behalf of the defendant and any prior convictions are read out before the judge pronounces sentence.

Legal profession In Australia lawyers may practise as both barristers and solicitors, except in NSW and Qld where they may practise as a barrister or solicitor only; even where the profession is not legally divided, however, there is likely to be a de facto division. The preparation of a case for trial is primarily the responsibility of a solicitor, who briefs a barrister to argue it in court. Admission to practise law is usually by means of a university degree in law, supplemented by an apprenticeship period (called articles) with a firm of legal practitioners or the completion of a legal-skills course.

Legal aid The greater part of the public funds allocated for legal aid goes to private legal practitioners who act for clients who have been means-tested and found eligible for assistance. The system is administered by Legal Aid Commissions, which exist in all States except Tas. and include representatives of government, law societies and community groups. In Tas., which has a funded Law Society scheme, this function is performed by lawyers employed in the Australian Legal Aid Office. Legal assistance may also be obtained from community legal centres and Aboriginal legal services, which are also publicly funded and operate in all States.

Law reform The Australian Law Reform Commission and State commissions or committees have primary responsibility for law reform. These organisations have both full-time and part-time members – usually judges, practising barristers or solicitors, or academic lawyers – who recommend statutory changes to the law after consultation with experts and with the groups most affected by the proposed reforms. As the national body, the Australian Law Reform Commission (first appointed in 1975) serves as a clearing-house for all the State law-reform agencies: it publishes information on the reports of these agencies from 1910 to the present in its *Law Reform Digest* and quarterly bulletin *Reform*. >> *administrative law; colonial administration; family law; government; royal commissions*

Lawler, Ray(mond Evenor) (1921–),

playwright, b. Melbourne. An interest in amateur acting led Lawler to the Melbourne Theatre Company in the late 1940s. There, his play *Summer of the Seventeenth Doll* (1955) proved to be a landmark in Australian theatre, dissecting in a naturalistic manner both a complex relationship and numerous accepted Australian attitudes. Less successful were the two sequels, *Kid Stakes* (1975) and *Other Times* (1976), which completed the 'Doll' trilogy. Other plays include *The Piccadilly Bushman* (1959) and *The Man Who Shot the Albatross* (1970).

lawn bowls > *bowls*

law reform > *law and legal system*

Lawrence, Marjorie Florence (1908–79), singer, b. Deans Marsh, Vic. Winning the *Sun* aria competition in 1928, Lawrence studied in Paris and New York before making her operatic debut in Monte Carlo in 1932, which was followed by a spectacular Brunnhilde at the Metropolitan Opera, New York, in 1935. Stricken by polio in 1941, she continued to perform on stage in a wheelchair. After retiring, she taught singing at a number of US universities. A film of her life, *Interrupted Melody*, was made in 1955.

Lawson, Henry Archibald (1867–1922), author, b. Grenfell, NSW. Lawson was born in a goldfields tent, of a Norwegian father (Niels Larsen) and an Australian mother who was a powerful influence on him after his parents' separation (1883); his early boyhood was wretched, on a poor bush farm and later in Sydney. His first stories were for the *Bulletin*, from 1888. His short stories of the 1890s, of a very high standard and immensely popular, reflect the bush life of the period: harsh, often melancholy, but with dry country humour and rough comradeship. Lawson's ballads, which do not match those of Banjo Paterson, share the melancholy background and unfortunate

characters of his stories; his verse, which was rebellious and often rumbustious, was more popular but like the ballads is now considered of little more than historical value. Lawson's mother, **Louisa** (1848–1920), b. Mudgee, NSW, was a woman of great physical strength and spiritual vigour, who supported her five children by domestic labour. In 1887, she bought the radical monthly *Republican* before starting *Dawn*, Australia's first feminist journal, in 1888. *Dawn* elevated women's affairs to serious public attention, enhanced the climate for female suffrage, and employed female printers. It closed down in 1905 and Lawson ended her days in the Gladesville Hospital for the Insane.

lead and zinc Australia is a major producer of lead and zinc, which commonly occur together in ore deposits along with silver and copper. In 1986, Australia produced (in ore and concentrates) 448 000t of lead – of which it is the world's largest exporter – and 712 000t of zinc. The long-established base-metal mines at Mt Isa in Qld and Broken Hill in NSW together produce about three-quarters of Australia's lead and zinc. Both metals are also mined in substantial quantities at Rosebery and Que River in northwest Tas. and Woodlawn and Cobar in NSW. Major smelters are at Port Pirie in SA, Risdon in Tas. and Cockle Creek in NSW. Most lead from Mt Isa is shipped as lead bullion to the Northfleet refinery in the UK; Mount Isa Mines Ltd (MIM) is developing the nearby Hilton mine, which will offset declining production at Mt Isa itself.

While lead and zinc are currently in strong demand, this demand is very much linked to the motor-vehicle industry, which uses some 60% of production. Future problems facing the industry are increased competition from light-weight aluminium and plastics, and the world-wide move towards lead-free petrol. >> *mining industry*

leaf insects > *stick and leaf insects*

League of Rights The Australian League of Rights is an extreme right-wing organisation founded in Vic. in 1946 and organised on a national basis since the 1960s; its credo in-cludes patriotism and loyalty to the monarchy, anti-communism, and opposition to govern-ment limits on personal freedom. It has been subject to persistent allegations of racism, particularly of anti-semitism, and of infiltrating the Liberal and National (Country) parties, which have provoked the suggestion that its activities should be officially investigated.

leatherjackets These are fish of the family Monacanthidae, which has a rich fauna of some 60 species in Australian waters. As their common name implies they have a tough, leathery skin – this is covered with numerous denticles – and they are often beautifully coloured. A strong spine above the head can be erected to prevent the leatherjacket from being swallowed by a larger fish. If the skin is removed these fish make excellent eating, and they are sold commercially. Well-known forms include the jenny, and the Chinaman, fan-bellied, pygmy and Captain Cook's leather-jackets; those of tropical waters include the harlequin and jumping leatherjackets.

Lebanese in Australia > *ethnic groups*

leeches These worm-like animals, with suckers either at both nose and tail or at the tail only, are placed in the class Hirundinea within the phylum Annelida. Leeches of different species are adapted to either salt or fresh water, and some to damp, terrestrial habitats. The leech of bloodsucking species is able to inject a local anaesthetic to avoid disturbing its victim, and also to put an anti-coagulant into the ingested blood, to assist assimilation.

Largest and most common of Australian leeches is the jawed scrub leech, *Limnobdella australis*, a freshwater and terrestrial species with black and yellow stripes along its back; it measures 2–10cm in length. Formerly used for medicinal bleeding, even today it occasionally serves this purpose. In wet weather, or when traversing damp gullies, bushwalkers may find these leeches clinging to their skin. Other species are sometimes found on both fresh-water and marine fishes.

Leeton NSW (pop. 6421) Like Griffith, Leeton was planned specifically to service the Murrumbidgee irrigation areas; lying 615km southwest of Sydney, it was developed from the 1920s to Walter Burley Griffin's design. It remains the chief administrative and proces-sing centre for that region, which produces fruit, rice, beef and lamb; Leeton's industries include fruit-canning, cheese-making and rice-milling. The nearby town of Yanco has a large abattoir and an agricultural research centre; the former home of Samuel McCaughey, who pioneered irrigation in the region, is now an agricultural high school.

legal aid > *law and legal system*

legislative assemblies > *colonial administration*; *government*

legislative councils > *colonial administration*; *government*

legumes The Fabaceae (or Leguminosae) family is one of the world's largest and most important flowering-plant families, comprising at least 18 000 species in about 700 genera. The common features of all legumes are the 'pod' fruit containing a single row of seeds – as in peas and beans – and nodules on the roots containing nitrogen-fixing bacteria by which they build up supplies of this vital plant nutrient in the soil. More than 2000 legumes are native to Australia, occurring in 150 genera.

Mimosas, which form the legume subfamily Mimosoideae, account for almost half of all species and about 900 of these belong to the genus *Acacia* (> *wattle*). Of the other nine genera in this subfamily none has more than nine species, the largest being the rainforest tree genus *Archidendron*. Mimosas also include a number of introduced weeds, the most troublesome being species of the genera *Mimosa* and *Prosopis* (or mesquite), both American in origin.

The subfamily Caesalpinioideae is most widely represented by the large genus *Cassia*, which includes shrubs, trees and herbaceous plants. Many are shrubby species that are a distinctive feature of the sandy inland. The other well-known genus of this subfamily is *Bauhinia*; it includes five species of small, often gnarled and stout-trunked trees of northern Australia, with attractive white or reddish flowers, now often placed in genus *Lysiphyllum*.

The pea-flowered subfamily Faboideae is extremely diverse, in Australia as well as elsewhere. The Australian genera fall into about eighteen tribes, two of which – the Mirbelieae and the Bossiaeae – are a major endemic element of the Australian flora and account for a large majority of native pea-flower species. These are mainly shrubs of higher-rainfall regions, although also represented in more arid parts; they have adopted the sclerophyll growth form of plants in nutrient-deficient soils, with mostly small and woody-textured leaves. Like the acacias, they all have hard, long-lived seeds that germinate after bushfires; most have seeds with a fatty appendage that attracts ants, which carry away seeds and bury them in their nests, further assisting dispersal and germination. There are only a few native species of the bean tribe Phaseoleae, but these include two important endemic genera *Kennedia* and *Hardenbergia*. The first has fifteen species, most WA endemics, but also includes the more widespread running postman, *K. prostrata*, and dusky coral-pea, *K. rubicunda*. The cosmopolitan tribe Galegeae includes the spectacular Sturt's desert pea, *Clianthus formosus*, of the arid inland, which is the floral emblem of SA. The large and near-endemic genus *Swainsona*, a close relative, comprises herbaceous plants with showy flowers that are conspicuous in arid and semi-arid plains; some species, the Darling peas, are poisonous to livestock. Several tribes of mainly tropical trees and climbers are regarded as somewhat primitive legumes, including that containing the Qld black bean, *Castanospermum australe*, a valued timber tree of eastern riverine rainforest that bears spectacular orange flowers and huge fleshy seeds. Significant genera in other cosmopolitan tribes are *Indigofera*, the native indigos; *Desmodium*, the tick-trefoils; *Crotalaria*, the rattlepods; and *Tephrosia*.

Leichhardt, (Friedrich Wilhelm) Ludwig (1813–48?), explorer, b. Prussia. The strangest character in Australian exploration, Leichhardt arrived in 1842 after three years of European wandering. He soon found Australian patrons, and in 1843 walked the 768km from Sydney to Moreton Bay. The following year he led a privately financed expedition north from Brisbane, west across the ranges to the Gulf of Carpentaria, thence over the Roper River and on to the coast at Port Essington. Although a great feat, it was a badly organised journey with grave miscalculations and sidetracking. On his return to Sydney Leichhardt was lionised, and inspired to attempt an east–west continental crossing in 1847, but the half-starved explorers returned after eight months. He set off once more in 1848 from a station near Roma, Qld, and was never heard of again. The latest of many expeditions to solve the mystery failed in 1938.

Leichhardt tree > *madder family*

Leigh Creek SA (pop. 1967) This small town lies 570km north of Adelaide in the

State's arid inland. It is notable chiefly as a coalfield, which has been mined sporadically since 1899; the open-cut mine eventually encroached on the original settlement and the town was moved 13km south in 1981.

Lennox, David (1788–1873), civil engineer, b. Scotland. Trained as a stonemason, Lennox worked on bridge building in Britain before immigrating to Australia in 1832. Thomas Mitchell, the surveyor-general, appointed him inspector of bridges, a post that also involved design and construction. In 1834 he built what is perhaps his best-known extant bridge, over Prospect Creek at Lansdowne, Sydney. He was appointed superintendent of bridges at Port Phillip in 1844 and built the original Princes Bridge over the Yarra in Melbourne; opened in 1850, it was demolished in 1886. Lennox was also a prolific builder of roads, often under difficult circumstances owing to the lack of skilled artisans in the colony.

Lepidoptera > *butterflies and moths*

Leptospermum > *myrtle family*

lerp insects > *bugs*

Le Souef, (William Henry) Dudley (1857–1923), zoologist, b. Melbourne. Traveller, lecturer, and author of many articles contributed to zoological journals, in 1902 Dudley Le Souef succeeded his father, A. A. C. Le Souef, as director of the Melbourne Zoo. He also had a long association – including a term as president – with the Royal Australian Ornithological Union. Two of his brothers also were directors of zoological gardens: Ernest in Perth and Albert at Taronga Park in Sydney.

Lewin, John William (1770–1819), artist, b. England. Lewin arrived in Sydney in 1800. Although he painted miniatures and portraits and taught art, his major work comprises engravings of the butterflies, moths and birds of NSW. Among his many – often unsuccessful – enterprises, he produced Australia's first engravings (1803–04) which were published in London in 1805. His next work, *Birds of New Holland with their Natural History*, was published in London in 1808 and was subsequently reissued several times; the 1813 volume was the first illustrated book published in Australia, and a facsimile edition was produced in 1978. Many of Lewin's paintings are in the Mitchell Library, Sydney, and the National Gallery in Canberra.

Lewis, Essington (1881–1961), industrialist, b. Burra, SA. After joining BHP Ltd in 1904, Lewis helped develop the company's ore deposits at Iron Knob and later its steelworks in Newcastle. Becoming chief general manager in 1938, he was instrumental in bringing about a spectacular increase in BHP's steel production. During World War 2, Lewis was chairman of the Defence Board of Business Administration and director-general of munitions and of aircraft production; he returned to BHP after the war, becoming chairman of directors. Lewis is often seen as the father of the Australian steel industry; his wartime work also made a vital contribution to Australia's defence capacity.

Lewis, Mortimer William (1796–1879), architect and surveyor, b. England. Lewis arrived in Sydney in 1829, becoming assistant to surveyor-general Thomas Mitchell 1830–5, after which he was appointed government architect. Over the next fifteen years he became Australia's leading protagonist of Greek Revival architecture – of which the courthouse at Darlinghurst, NSW (1836), is an impressive example – and proved himself also adept at Gothic Revival. His output was prolific, but he remained a meticulous draughtsman and paid great attention to structural detail. A dispute over funds for Sydney's first museum resulted in an inquiry and Lewis's resignation in 1849.

Lexcen, Ben [Robert Miller] (1936–88), nautical designer, b. Boggabri, NSW. Having developed a successful business in sail design, Lexcen gradually moved into designing and building yachts, one of these being Alan Bond's radical 12m *Australia* which, captained by John Bertrand, won the America's Cup in 1983. Its winged keel was at first a well-kept secret and subsequently the subject of legal challenges.

Liardet, Wilbraham Frederick Evelyn (1799–1878), painter, b. England. Liardet, a former cavalry officer, arrived in Australia in 1839 with his wife and children and settled soon after on the shore of Port Phillip Bay. After a colourful career as innkeeper and sea-mail contractor, he painted a series of views of early Melbourne (of which 38 remain) and compiled an entertaining account of the colonial era. *Liardet's Water-colours of Early*

Melbourne was published in 1972 by the Library Council of Vic.

Liberal Party The present form of the Liberal Party of Australia was created in 1945 by > *Sir Robert Menzies*. Since then it has remained Australia's major conservative party and the one with the longest consecutive period in federal government, from 1949 to 1972.

An earlier Liberal Party (which generally espoused the liberal values of the British party of the same name) was formed in 1909 by the amalgamation of the two main non-Labor groupings, the Protectionists and Free Traders; it was led first by Alfred Deakin (prime minister 1909–10) and later by Joseph Cook (prime minister 1913–14). This party was both re-formed and renamed periodically over the next 30 years, the most consistent factors during this period being its strongly conservative bias and its continuing dependence on support from the Country Party (> *National Party*) in order to win government.

During World War 1 a split in the ALP over conscription led former Labor prime minister W. M. Hughes and his supporters to combine with the Liberals as the Nationalist Party. It retained government 1917–29, with Hughes as prime minister 1917–23, followed by S. M. Bruce who governed in coalition with the Country Party. Having resigned from the Scullin Labor government in 1931, J. A. Lyons combined with the Nationalists to form the United Australia Party (UAP), which was in government 1932–9, ruling with the assistance of the Country Party 1938–9 but relegated to junior partner in a brief caretaker government led by Earle Page after Lyons' death. Menzies succeeded Lyons as leader of the UAP in 1939 and subsequently became prime minister, but the party was by then disunited and Menzies resigned in 1941; during the coalition's brief term in office in 1941, it was again led by the Country Party, under Arthur Fadden.

Unlike its predecessors, the Liberal Party created by Menzies in 1945 from the remnants of the UAP and other conservative groupings was strongly organised on a national basis. It remained conservative (although 'wet' in contemporary terms), committed to economic growth based on private enterprise and maintaining a consistent appeal to middle-class voters. The Liberals retained government under Menzies until his retirement in 1966: this period, seen by many as the party's golden years, was one of rapid growth and economic buoyancy, with

consistently low unemployment. In the absence of Menzies' strong leadership the party became less unified, although it retained office under > *Harold Holt* 1966–8 and > *John Gorton* 1968–71; under > *William McMahon*, however, it lost the 1972 election to a revitalised ALP led by Gough Whitlam.

With the fall of the Whitlam government in 1975, a new Menzies era seemed imminent: the Liberals' new leader, > *Malcolm Fraser*, shared with Menzies a firm (often ruthless) leadership style and general conservatism, especially in the area of economic policy. He led the party to electoral victory in 1975, 1977 and 1980 but was defeated by Labor in 1983 and immediately relinquished the party leadership. By that year the Liberals held office only in Tas. and the party's political doldrums were reflected in a period of ideological and leadership instability, with > *Andrew Peacock* and > *John Howard* alternating as federal leader of the party 1983–9. While the Liberals regained government in NSW in 1988, they lost Tas. in 1989 and (with Peacock as leader) failed to unseat Labor in the 1990 federal election. On Peacock's subsequent resignation as leader, the Liberals began to reassemble their forces and tend the wounds left by years of factionalism. A relative newcomer, John Hewson, was elected to the party leadership. >> *political parties*

libraries Long a vital part of Australian educational and cultural life, libraries are no longer simply repositories for books but increasingly 'resource centres' that use computer technology to catalogue, store and disseminate information. As the rapid retrieval of up-to-date material becomes increasingly essential for government, business, research and even personal needs, compact discs, video tapes and videotext systems will be the stuff of such institutions in the future.

Graduate and post-graduate courses exist for the training of librarians and teacher–librarians in most States. The Australian Library and Information Association (originally the Australian Institute of Librarians, formed in 1937 and based in Sydney) is the main professional organisation and is actively involved in professional development for librarians.

Historical development Only a few private libraries (the first of which was listed in 1821) existed for the first 50 years of European settlement. The earliest public institution was a small subscription library and reading room established in Sydney in 1827. 'Artisan libraries' developed in association with the growth of mechanics institutes from the 1830s, but by the end of the century these schools had lost much of their cultural function and their libraries were in a state of decay.

The modern era in library development began in the 1930s, following the publication in 1935 of the results of a professional survey (the Munn–Pitt Report) which severely criticised the backwardness of Australian libraries. This stimulated the development of a lobby group known as the Free Library Movement, which helped to achieve legislation establishing free libraries in all States (except SA) by 1951; in many cases they were based on the former artisan libraries. The degree of State subsidisation varies and many local libraries are funded largely by local rates.

Public libraries in Australia have been reviewed periodically since the 1960s and have periodically been found wanting, largely because deficient funding makes it difficult for them to meet the demand for services and facilities. Many local libraries have accordingly combined their resources to create regional services, or provide joint services with local schools. A 1976 inquiry strongly recommended that public libraries receive federal funding, but this seems unlikely to eventuate in the short term. There is, however, growing recognition of the need to both maintain existing collections and make the best possible use of current technology to meet the needs of an increasingly information-based society.

School libraries have undergone a transformation since the late 1960s and early 1970s, when consistent lobbying resulted in a massive and much-needed injection of federal funding. As a result most are relatively well housed and well equipped, although the level of funding continues to fluctuate. The computerised Australian Schools Cataloguing Information Service, a major State-federal government initiative, was set up in 1984.

National Library of Australia The National Library of Australia in Canberra was developed from the Commonwealth Parliamentary Library (1901) but became a separate institution in 1960; it has been housed in its present marble-clad building since 1968. It now holds more than 6 million records of Australian and overseas library holdings and maintains a national collection in all subject fields: this includes more than 4 million volumes (including microfilm); 39 300 paintings, pictures and prints; and a vast holding of photographs, manuscripts,

maps, films and tapes. The National Library has been in the forefront of computerisation, devising (in conjunction with the CSIRO) computerised services for literature searching in the early 1970s. It set up the Australian Information Network (> *Ausinet*) in the late 1970s and launched the Australian Bibliographic Network, a national on-line cataloguing system, in 1981.

The National Library has been the beneficiary of many notable collections, including the Petherick and Ferguson collections of Australiana, the Cook manuscripts, the Cumpston collection on public health, the Mathews ornithological collection, the > *Rex Nan Kivell* collection of volumes and prints, the David Nicholl Smith collection of 18th-century English literature, and the Braga collection of Portuguese material relating to Asia.

State libraries Until the introduction of community libraries in the mid-20th century, the State public libraries were the main resource for borrowing books. Today, with in excess of 7 million volumes, they are the main reference libraries and provide extensive loan services to country areas. Like other public libraries, the State libraries do not receive federal funding and have laboured under the burden of conserving historically valuable collections, maintaining old and often inadequate buildings, and keeping pace with technological innovation.

The State Library of Vic., established in 1853, was the first government public library in Australia. It incorporates the La Trobe Library, which specialises in Australiana and includes the J. K. Moir Australian collection, the M. V. Anderson chess collection and the Brodie shipping collection. Plans for desperately needed building extension and refurbishment were approved by the State government in 1988.

The State Library of NSW, which opened in 1869, has since 1988 been housed in a new eleven-storey building with an auditorium, family-history centre, and technology access centre. It contains the Mitchell Library, endowed by > *David Scott Mitchell* and including the nation's pre-eminent collection of Australiana; and the W. Dixson Gallery of historic pictures and publications.

The other State libraries also date from the 19th century and have valuable historical collections, notably Qld's Oxley Memorial Library of Australian and Qld material, and WA's J. S. Battye Library of WA history. The Tas. Library was founded in 1870, SA in 1884, Qld in 1896 and WA in 1899. The NT Reference Library opened in 1980.

University and college libraries With the help of federal funding since the 1950s, university libraries have grown rapidly. The second-largest library in Australia (after the National Library) is the Fisher Library at the University of Sydney – named after a Sydney merchant of the late 19th century who left a £30 000 endowment for the purpose – which holds more than 3 million volumes. Similarly, the Baillieu Trust has greatly enhanced the University of Melbourne library, which has more than a million books. The library of the Australian National University in Canberra is noted for its outstanding Asian collections. Other considerable university libraries are those at the University of Adelaide, the University of WA, the University of Qld, and Monash University (Vic.). Many TAFE colleges, again supported by Commonwealth funds, are building important library collections.

Specialist libraries Australia has a wide range of specialist libraries, from parliamentary archives to the collections of corporations, government departments and research institutions. They include the unique scientific and technical collection of the CSIRO, State archives, the collections held by historical societies, the Australian War Memorial Library, and the Patent Office Library. >> *archives*; *museums*

lice These small, flattened wingless insects include the chewing lice of the order Mallophaga and the sucking lice, order Anoplura; most species of lice are specific to one species of host – bird or mammal. Chewing lice are generally parasitic on birds, eating feathers and scales of skin, though some species parasitise mammals and live on hair; sucking lice have a distinctive piercing and extractive mouthpiece and are parasites of mammals. Eggs (those of the human head louse being known as nits) are cemented to hair or feathers and shortly hatch to reveal a nymph. Australian native species are predominantly chewing lice, parasitising not only birds but also many marsupials; one of the few native sucking lice occurs on the water-rat. Many species have been introduced, including those parasitic on poultry, cattle, pigs and sheep, and also on man (crab-lice).

lichens This worldwide group of lower plants typically consists of a tough, encrusting or branched body formed from a fungus, within which dwell single-celled algae. Lichens grow on stone, soil, bark and dead wood, in more humid climates adhering to twigs and leaves;

colours range from greenish-white through blue-grey to yellow, orange, red and black. Australia has around 200 genera of lichen, many of the species being endemic. Familiar genera include *Usnea*, forming long pale wisps from tree branches; *Cladonia*, also branched but forming more compact clusters; *Parmelia*, leaf-like forms with finely divided lobes, common on rocks and damp soil; and *Caloplaca*, fine crusty mats, often orange or yellow in colour.

Light, William (1786–1839), founder of Adelaide, b. Malaya. After extensive war service and travel, Light took up the position of SA surveyor-general in 1836, with full authority to choose the location of the first settlement. Having anchored at Port Adelaide, he selected and surveyed a site for the township and stuck by his decision in the face of bitter opposition from Governor Hindmarsh. Light's imaginative layout was ahead of its time and his choice of site has been well vindicated; he was allowed neither sufficient time nor men to complete the total survey in accordance with his own high standards, however, and resigned in June 1838.

Lightning Ridge NSW (pop. 1292) This small outback town 770km northwest of Sydney is best known as an opal-mining centre. The region's prized black opals were first discovered in the 1880s, although commercial mining did not begin until the 20th century. Today it is a popular destination for both fossickers and outback tourists, and has been developed accordingly.

lignum This is the common name of *Muehlenbeckia cunninghamii*, a common cany-stemmed shrub of inland watercourses and swamps, which often forms dense tangled masses of near-leafless stems 2–3m high. In the early 19th century it was classified in the genus *Polygonum*, which became corrupted to 'lignum'. The genus *Muehlenbeckia* includes another ten or so Australian species, most smaller shrubs or twining climbers; one is the Macquarie grape of Tas., a vigorous climber with heart-shaped leaves and edible fruit receptacles that were used in cooking by early settlers.

Liliaceae > *lilies*

lilies While the term 'lily' strictly refers to species of the genus *Lilium* in family Liliaceae, it is most commonly used to describe any monocotyledonous plant with broad-petalled flowers. The Australian native spoon lily or > *cunjevoi*, for example, is a member of the unrelated arum family. There is, however, a large group of plant families related to the Liliaceae, some fifteen of which occur in Australia.

The Anthericaceae family accounts for the largest number of Australian lilies. Its largest native genus is *Thysanotus*, which comprises 49 species of fringe-lilies all but three of which endemic, mostly to southern WA; all have attractive pink to purple flowers with broad, fringed petals. Other genera are *Sowerbaea*, rush-lilies, with dense heads of perfumed mauve flowers; *Tricoryne*, with starry yellow flowers that twist tightly after closing; and *Borya*, a genus of mostly prickly plants of bare rock slopes (mainly in WA), which turn orange as they become dormant but revive after rain. The Asphodelaceae family is represented in Australia by native species of the genus *Bulbine*, the succulent yellowed-flowered native leeks of grasslands and arid plains. Asteliaceae is a primitive southern-hemisphere family represented in Australia by the genera *Astelia*, *Milligania* and *Neoastelia*, the last two endemic to Tas. and NSW respectively. Also in this family are the shrubby *Cordyline* species, the palm-lilies of rainforests, which are popular indoor plants. The Phormiaceae are represented mainly by *Dianella*, the blue-flowered flax-lilies of moist eastern forests. Meriting a family of its own – Doryanthaceae – is the unique genus *Doryanthes*, with two species of massive sword-leaved plants with tall red inflorescences: the gymea lily of the Newcastle–Sydney–Wollongong district of NSW, and the gigantic lily of southeast Qld and far northeast NSW. Blandfordiaceae also consists of a single genus, *Blandfordia*, which comprises the four species of colourful Christmas bells. The large Dasypogonaceae family comprises ten harsh-leaved endemic (mainly western) genera (several of which are sometimes grouped with > *grass-trees* in the family Xanthorrhoeaceae). The genus *Lomandra* has 50 species, found in most parts of Australia and sometimes collectively called mat-rushes; *Kingia* has one species, the remarkable black gin of southwest WA, resembling a tall grass-tree but with a circle of knob-like flower-heads instead of the long spear; *Calectasia* has three species in WA, SA and Vic. known as tinsel-lilies for their iridescent, papery bluish flowers. The family Amarylli-

daceae, which includes the familiar narcissi and hippeastrums, is represented in Australia by the genera *Crinum, Proiphys* and *Calostemma*, only the last being endemic. Five *Crinum* species are native, including the Darling lily, *C. flaccidum* of the southern inland.

Lillee, Dennis Keith (1949–   ), cricketer, b. Perth. Lillee is one of Australia's great fast-bowlers. From the time of his debut in 1970–1 he took 355 wickets in 70 Test matches with an average of 23.92. This total would have been considerably higher but for more than one season missed through injury and from playing World Series cricket, in which he took 67 wickets. Lillee worked hard to develop a classical, flowing action, matched with fire and aggression; his greatest moments came in tandem with Jeff Thompson, in one of cricket's great fast-bowling partnerships. Later in his career he developed greater guile, while bowling with reduced pace. Throughout his career Lillee was a central figure – though sometimes a controversial one – in the world of first-class cricket.

lillypilly > *myrtle family*

limestone Reserves of limestone in Australia are extremely large, the industry dating back to the early days of the NSW colony when shells were gathered in the Broken Bay estuary for burning into lime at Millers Point, Sydney. In 1986–7 Australia produced 12.3 million t of limestone, worth $72 million, the bulk being used in cement production. Substantial limestone deposits are found in all States, but NSW is the largest producer (3.4 million t in 1986–7).

limpets > *gastropods*

Lindeman Island > *Cumberland Islands*

Lindrum family > *billiards and snooker*

Lindsay family, renowned artists and writers. The family was founded in Australia by Irishman Dr R. C. Lindsay and his wife Jane, who brought up their ten children in Creswick, Vic. **Percy (Percival Charles)** (1870–1952), was notable particularly as a landscape painter; he was a prominent member of Melbourne's radical intelligentsia in the 1890s and pursued a bohemian life in Sydney from 1918. **Sir Lionel Arthur** (1874–1961), was a cartoonist for the Sydney *Evening News* 1903–26, a fine watercolourist, and internationally renowned for his superb wood engravings and etchings. He was also an outspoken art critic and author of several books, including a provocative discourse on modernism, *Addled Art* (1942). **Norman Alfred William** (1879–1969) is probably the most famous family member. In 1901 he joined the *Bulletin* as an artist and writer; he was strongly satirical in both fields and an enormously influential (if arrogant) Sydney literary figure in the 1920s. His children's story *The Magic Pudding* (1918), which he also illustrated, is an enduring classic. His many novels include *Saturdee* (1933) and *Halfway to Anywhere* (1947), whose sexual frankness and easily identifiable character sketches earned them censorship in Australia, as did his novels of adult social relationships. His paintings, drawings and etchings, frequently of voluptuous women and erotic nymphs and satyrs, earned him the relentless disapproval of the 'wowsers' he despised. **Ruby** (1887–1919) was a talented illustrator and cartoonist who contributed to leading magazines such as the *Lone Hand*; she married cartoonist Will Dyson in 1909. **Sir Daryl** (1890–1976) was a bank clerk and jackeroo before serving in the AIF during World War 1. He subsequently became a painter and was an innovative director of the National Gallery of Vic. 1942–55; he was also an influential art adviser. His wife **(Lady) Joan**, née Weigall (1896–1984), was a painter and writer best known for her haunting novel *Picnic at Hanging Rock* (1967). **Jack** (1900–90), son of Norman, was a distinguished classics scholar and prolific author who lived in England from 1926.

Lindwall, Ray > *cricket*

Lismore NSW (pop. 24 896) Situated on Wilsons River, 785km north of Sydney, Lismore is the commercial and administrative capital of the State's north coast. It developed originally (from the 1840s) as a timber port, particularly for cedar, and there are still remnants of the 'Big Scrub' rainforests on its outskirts. Forest logging was still important until the early 1980s, when production ceased after protracted disputes between the industry and conservationists. The region's principal activities are dairying and the production of sugar and tropical fruits; industries in Lismore include the processing of local produce as well as heavy industries such as engineering and steelmaking.

Lister, William Lister (1859–1943), painter, b. Sydney. Lister was educated in England, France and Scotland 1867–80; while trained as an engineer, his great love was painting. After four years at sea and four in London, he returned to Australia in 1888 to embark upon a successful career as an academic painter, best known for grand seascapes and coastal views. He won the Wynne Prize seven times between 1898 and 1925.

literary awards The first Australian literary award took the form of two cows, presented to the poet Michael Massey Robinson in 1818. Today, in addition to grants made by the Literature Board of the Australia Council, some 80 prizes are available to Australian writers: most are annual awards, ranging from a few dollars to several thousand, and between them they cover all literary categories. Rich major prizes include annual awards by the premiers of NSW and Vic., and biennial awards by the SA government; the WA government also makes three biennial awards to local writers. The Vic. Fellowship of Australian Writers administers eighteen prizes on behalf of various sponsors and the National Book Council administers two privately funded annual awards. Other prestigious prizes are the Miles Franklin Award, the *Age* Book of the Year, the *Australian* Vogel National Literary Award, the Patrick White Award, the Children's Book of the Year Awards, the Braille Book of the Year, the Australian Book Publishers' Association Book Design Awards and the Australian Literature Society Gold Medal.

literature and writing Australian writing, like that of all countries evolving from colonial origins, is often judged on two levels: for its significance in the development of a national culture, and for its contribution to the mainstream of world literature. In each realm there has been considerable achievement, but as yet only a few creative writers have at once met both criteria: in prose Christina Stead, Patrick White and Thomas Keneally; in poetry, A. D. Hope and Peter Porter.

The Commonwealth Literary Fund (established in 1908 and expanded greatly in 1939) was Australia's main government funding body for literature until 1973, when its operations were taken over and augmented by the Literature Board of the Arts Council. The board, which provides seeding assistance to writers, publishers and journals, is the envy of writers in many other countries, as is the > *public lending right scheme* instituted in 1975. The main literary journals are *Southerly* (founded 1939), devoted largely to Australian writing; *Meanjin* (1940), which looks both within and beyond Australia and has developed a lasting reputation for its reviews; *Overland* (1954), concerned with both literary and social topics and of self-styled 'temper democratic, bias Australian'; *Quadrant* (1956), distinguished particularly for its poetry and criticism; and *Scripsi* (1981).

Colonial writing The earliest white arrivals, voluntary and involuntary, found a harsh environment in which the struggle to survive filled their lives. Some were nevertheless able to record their experiences and impressions: of these, naval officer Watkin Tench's journals are outstanding in their detached observations and vivid evocation; the worm's eye view of the convicts (most notably James Hardy Vaux) always found a ready market in England, but had little lasting merit. Convict songs and stories did, however, provide the roots from which indigenous Australian ballads developed. Published verse first took the form of sycophantic public odes by Michael Massey Robinson, from 1810.

As exploration widened the horizons, many descriptive works were produced. The explorers, often being men of imagination, sometimes created in their journals works of enduring merit; this was true of Charles Sturt, and to a lesser extent Edward Eyre and Ernest Giles. The first works of fiction based on the Australian environment flowed from the annalist tradition, with factual accounts thinly disguised. Many were 'guidebook novels', produced with the specific purpose of encouraging immigrants from England; among the authors were Charles Rowcroft and Alexander Harris, who represented the opposing viewpoints of romantic and realist. Henry Savery's *Quintus Servinton* (Hobart, 1831), the first novel published in Australia, was the story of a convict; as was the more skilful *The Adventures of Ralph Rashleigh* (not published until 1929, but written c. 1845–6), which is generally attributed to James Tucker. The first real poet was > *Charles Harpur*, publishing from 1833 and taking his subjects and inspiration from the Australian scene but treating them in a post-Augustan lyrical manner. From 1859 he was followed by *Henry Kendall*, who wrote mainly about the soft coastal scenery of southern NSW.

The mid-19th century was a period of expansion to the frontiers. Henry Kingsley wrote the first major work of fiction, *The Recollections of Geoffrey Hamlyn* (1859), about the adventures of pioneering life. The turbulent times were also reflected in the popular swinging verse of > *Adam Lindsay Gordon*, and in Rolf Boldrewood's *Robbery Under Arms* (1888); transportation, although by then a thing of the past, provided material for one of the great Australian novels, Marcus Clarke's *His Natural Life* (1874). At the same time, a more settled, leisurely life was developing, which was depicted in particular by female novelists, notably > *Ada Cambridge* who used formula romantic fiction laced with occasional sharp realism. A counterblast was provided by the down-to-earth humour of > *Steele Rudd*'s tales of the squalid life of a small Qld farmer.

Towards a national identity The last decades of the 19th century brought a break away from the English heritage and a struggle for national identity. Undoubtedly the most important catalyst of nationalism, in both the literary and political fields, was the weekly magazine the *Bulletin* (founded 1880), whose republican editor J. F. Archibald encouraged his writers and artists to take their inspiration from 'the bush'. Much of their work has been forgotten, but the writings of > *Henry Lawson*, > *Banjo Paterson*, > *Joseph Furphy* and > *Miles Franklin* were important milestones. Ballads of the bush, of the sea, of mines and of the city proliferated – all important as popular folk-expressions of the day. A. G. Stephens, literary editor of the *Bulletin* after 1896, did much to encourage the writing of Furphy, Rudd and Franklin as well as poets. In the latter field several important figures emerged, including > *Christopher Brennan*, > *John Shaw Neilson*, > *Bernard O'Dowd* and > *Mary Gilmore*, the last two writing with an underlying social purpose. In Europe, meanwhile, > *Henry Handel Richardson* was beginning a career of powerful writing that gave her an international reputation.

After 1920 there was an increasing expatriation of Australian writers: among those who, perhaps in order to write more freely, lived outside Australia from this time were > *Christina Stead* and Martin Boyd (> *Boyd family*). The dominant literary group in the 1920s was the circle of Sydney writers and artists around Norman Lindsay; their creed was hedonism and it gave rise to exotic works of prose, art and poetry. Writers who found impetus in this atmosphere but went on from its limited field to develop individual styles include the poets > *Kenneth Slessor*, > *R. D. FitzGerald*, and

> *James McAuley*. Two brief rebellious literary movements took place in Adelaide in the 1940s, one (the > *Jindyworobaks*) advocating Australian themes in poetry, the other a surrealist school.

There was, after 1920, an ever-increasing output of novels, which can be grouped variously: there are pioneering sagas, of which Miles Franklin (*All That Swagger*, 1936) wrote the finest example, with a useful counterbalance in Brian Penton's tale of the harsher realities of Qld pioneering (*The Landtakers*, 1934); historical novels are best represented by > *Eleanor Dark*. Others continued the Lawson and Furphy tradition of outback harshness: and in a powerful novel of the cattle country of the far northwest (*Coonardoo*, 1929) > *Katharine Susannah Prichard* introduced black–white sexual relationships; it was > *Xavier Herbert*, however, who exposed this particular aspect of contemporary Australia in its rawest form, in *Capricornia* (1938). The preponderantly urban element in the population was also reflected increasingly in the literature from early this century. Louis Stone (*Jonah*, 1911) wrote the first important work with a town setting, in the Sydney slums; later, the 1930s depression was recorded by M. Barnard Eldershaw in *Tomorrow and Tomorrow* (1947), by > *Kylie Tennant* in *Tiburon* (1935) and by Christina Stead in *Seven Poor Men of Sydney* (1934). George Johnston's semi-autobiographical *My Brother Jack* (1964) was set in working-class Melbourne between the two world wars.

Postwar writing A remarkable upsurge of modernism in the arts occurred after World War 2. In literature, it was perhaps stronger in poetry than in fiction and two major poets emerged at about this time: > *A.D. Hope* (from 1955, though much earlier in journals), writing astringent, often sexual, often humorous verse, rich in allusion; and > *Judith Wright* (from 1946), whose work is universal in both emotional appeal and metaphysical approach. Gwen Harwood has proved to be Wright's most passionate successor, and > *Les Murray* has taken up the rural verities of his *Bulletin* forebears: *Ethnic Radio* (1977) displays his diverting powers at their most inventive. The diverse poetries of > *Bruce Dawe*, Judith Rodriguez and John Tranter display the present imaginative range. Fiction-writing also gathered pace and new force. Expatriate since the mid-1930s, > *Patrick White* returned to Australia after the war and remains the nation's most challenging and versatile novelist. The writings of Martin Boyd were increasingly influenced by his residence in Italy from the 1950s, although he continued to use Australian settings.

There was a further wave of emigration by writers during the 1950s and 1960s. Although it was still possible in 1962 for A. A. Phillips to castigate his fellow writers for their 'cultural cringe' to Europe, Australian literature began to show signs of nascent maturity from the end of that decade. An eclectic range of themes, styles and settings has been used by the ebullient > *Thomas Keneally*; Frank Moorhouse, on the other hand, has maintained a consistently semi-factual approach, from *The Americans Baby* (1972) through to *Forty-Seventeen* (1988). One of the most disconcerting of the postwar novelists is Peter Mathers, whose *Trap* (1966) and *The Wort Papers* (1972) were followed by a long silence. From the 1950s European–Aboriginal relationships were examined increasingly; an important turning point was Randolph Stow's *To the Islands* (1958), which explored the theme of white guilt. Aboriginal writers also began to emerge at this time, including the poet > *Oodgeroo Noonuccal* and the novelist Mudrooroo Narogin.

Short-story writers have tended to forsake the disciplined brevity of the *Bulletin*. The genre revived in the 1950s and 1960s, notable work coming from Gavin Casey (writing about the WA goldfields) and Dal Stivens (specialising in the 'tall story'). Glenda Adams, Helen Garner and > *David Malouf* are outstanding among the more recent voices: Garner's *The Children's Bach* (1984) and Malouf's *An Imaginary Life* (1978) brought the novella to a new kind of formal perfection. Distinguished non-fiction has also been a hallmark of the postwar period: > *Manning Clark*'s six-volume *History of Australia* (1962–87) is a major literary achievement, as are the autobiographies of Jack Lindsay (a trilogy of 1950, 1960 and 1962), > *Hal Porter* (1963, 1966 and 1973) and > *Bernard Smith* (1984).

The current period is tricky to assess. By the 1980s, however, Australian writing was less concerned with parochial self-assertion: the increasing confidence of the nation in its own identity, an ability to laugh at itself, and the watering down of old ethnic prejudices are all finding expression. The large-scale, sweeping narrative, as practised by Stead and White, came to new fruition in > *Peter Carey*'s *Oscar and Lucinda* (1988); and the anarchic comedies of > *Elizabeth Jolley* overpower most other contemporary novels. Account must also be taken of several immigrant writers working in their native languages, most notably Dimitris Tsaloumas (Greek), Rose Cappiello (Italian) and Walter Adamson (German). >> *children's books*; *publishing and bookselling*; *theatre*

Lithgow NSW (pop. 12 369) A mining and manufacturing city about 130km west of Sydney, Lithgow developed thus from the 1870s – made possible largely by the zigzag railway, an engineering masterpiece (completed 1866–9) which linked the settlement with Sydney by allowing trains to descend the sheer western slopes of the Blue Mountains. Early industries included a pottery, iron-making and a meat-works. Today the city houses the federal government's small-arms factory (established in 1913), a power station (with a second under construction at Mt Piper) and various factories.

Little Desert Vic. This semi-arid region in the Wimmera extends from the SA border to the vicinity of Dimboola and includes, just southwest of that town, the Little Desert National Park – noted especially for the unique mallee fowl. The area was named in the 1870s, when the soil was found to be unsuitable for crops, but recent research indicates that if supplemented with trace elements and nitrogenous fertilisers it could be suitable for beef cattle grazing and woolgrowing.

Liverpool Plains NSW Chiefly a wheat-producing area, these plains lie north of the volcanic Liverpool and Warrumbungle ranges; the major town is Gunnedah, where large silos have been built. Discovered by John Oxley in 1818 and settled in the 1820s, the fertile plains also support crops, including sorghum and soya beans, and livestock farming includes sheep, cattle and pigs. In 1833 the Australian Agricultural Co. – Australia's oldest pastoral company – obtained an extensive land grant and developed large-scale holdings, now subdivided and part of the sheep–wheat belt.

liverworts > *mosses and liverworts*

Lizard Island Qld This is a high granitic island about 30km northeast of Cape Flattery, on Cape York Peninsula. The island is a national park; it includes a major marine research station and a small tourist resort – said to be the only one on the outer reef – where facilities include big-game fishing. It was named in 1770 by James Cook, who on landing there 'saw no other animals but lizards'.

lizards Australia has a diverse lizard fauna of more than 450 species, particularly rich in the arid regions of the continent where lizards are dominant predators in desert ecosystems. Probably originating in the Orient, the Australian fauna is related to groups predominant in tropical regions of the Old World.

Together with snakes, lizards make up the order Squamata. Features by which they can be distinguished from snakes (since some lizards have lost their legs, and appear snake-like) include external ears and ear-openings, which are absent in snakes, and rows of short teeth in contrast to the snake's strong, socketed teeth. Most lizards lay eggs and show little interest in their offspring, and most feed on a variety of small prey. Five families are represented in Australia.

The geckoes – about 65 species, of the family Gekkonidae – have prominent, bulging eyes that lack eyelids: they clean their eyes by licking them. They have padded, adhesive digits that enable them to cling to objects and even to move or rest on ceilings; some have developed the ability to shed and subsequently regenerate the tail – a device designed to confuse predators. Common species include the leaf-tailed or fat-tailed gecko, *Phyllurus cornutus*, and the house gecko, *Gehyra variegata*.

Legless lizards, slow-worms and snake lizards, belonging to the family Pygopididae, are known only from mainland Australia and NG; they lack forelegs, and their hindlegs are reduced to tiny flaps. Although snake-like in appearance, they are derived from geckoes and, like them, lack eyelids.

Dragon lizards of the family Agamidae are among the best known species. They are insectivorous, in many cases have a rough, strikingly ornamented skin, and when alarmed, tend to run rapidly on their hindlegs. As a warning display the spectacular frill-necked lizard from northern Australia, *Chamlydosaurus kingii*, is able to expand the loose skin around its neck into an umbrella-like ruff with internal cartilaginous supports (it is so featured on the 2-cent coin). This family also includes the semi-aquatic eastern water dragon, *Physignathus lesueurii*, which reaches the length of 1m, and the multicoloured thorny devil of central Australia, *Moloch horridus*.

The goanna or monitor lizard belongs to the family Varanidae and should not be confused with New World iguana, although the name is a corruption of that word. It has a long, forked, snake-like tongue that is flicked in and out;

most species feed on insects and small reptiles, but larger animals will take birds, mammals and carrion. The largest living Australian lizard is the central Australian desert perentie, *Varanus giganteus*, which may grow to 2.5m; fossil Australian monitors, however, are known to have measured as much as 6m and to have weighed an estimated 600kg – more than twice the size of the largest extant monitor, the Komodo dragon. Some species are arboreal, one of them being the common lace monitor of eastern Australia, *V. varius*.

The family Scincidae, the skinks, constitutes the most diverse group of lizards in Australia, inhabiting a variety of regions from subalpine moors to deserts or tropical rainforests. Most are small and have smooth, silky scales; some burrowing species have lost their legs, and appear snake-like. Although most species lay eggs, a number bear live young and even show some parental care. Well-known species include the common blue-tongue, *Tiliqua scincoides*, often found in suburban gardens; the land mullet, *Egernia bungana*, and the shingle-back lizard, *Trachydosaurus rugosus*.

Loan Council In order to prevent competition in the money market between Commonwealth and States, the Loan Council was established in 1924 to co-ordinate their borrowing powers both in Australia and overseas; in 1927, following an amendment to the Constitution, the council was made permanent. At its meetings, which coincide with premiers' conferences, each State has one vote and the Commonwealth has two votes plus a casting vote, which effectively gives the Commonwealth dominance. Changes were made to these arrangements in 1982, since when major State electricity authorities have been permitted to borrow independently of the council for a trial period.

lobsters > *crayfishes and allies*

local government This, the third tier of government in Australia, consists of local authorities (which include municipal councils and rural shire or district councils) that are responsible to the minister for local government of the State in which they are located. Such authorities lack Commonwealth constitutional status; a referendum in 1988 on the question of achieving this was unsuccessful.

Each local authority administers a specified geographical area and is responsible for the financing, provision, operation and maintenance of basic community facilities, provided for the benefit of property owners and residents. Basic concerns include road making and maintenance, garbage collection, building regulations and general control of property, but recently local government has also undertaken wider responsibility in the provision of social services such as recreation facilities, care of the aged, and community health. This has led to conflict in local affairs and to much strain between this and the other levels of government. Australia's 835 municipal councils – composed of about 10 000 councillors – derive their income from local taxes, fees, fines, public enterprise ventures, borrowings, and financial grants from their own State and the federal government. Each municipality or shire is administered by elected community representatives, assisted by paid employees; local government accounts for about 9.2% of the total Australian public-sector workforce. Some local authorities have been criticised for their lack of modern management techniques and their inexpertness in management. >> *government*

Lockyer, Edmund (1784–1860), explorer, b. England. Lockyer arrived in Australia in 1825 as an army officer, and was sent by Governor Brisbane to explore the Brisbane River in 1825 and to forestall possible French annexation of WA (New Holland) in 1826. He landed at King George Sound on 25 December 1826, formally declaring the territory a British possession.

Lockyer Valley Qld Rising on the eastern slopes of the Great Dividing Range, near Toowoomba, Lockyer Creek is a tributary of the Brisbane River. The rich, alluvial soil of the valley supports market gardens, fodder crops and dairying, with irrigation from underground water. Gatton is the main centre of population, and the site of an agricultural research station. In 1970, in response to increased demand for irrigation, the Atkinson dam was completed, built across the outlet of Atkinson Lagoon, adjoining the river and creating a lake of 567ha.

locusts > *grasshoppers, locusts and crickets*

Loddon River Vic. Flowing for more than 320km northwards from the central uplands, southeast of Daylesford, the Loddon joins the Murray at Swan Hill. It is variable in volume but is dammed in several places, storages including Cairn Curran, Tullaroop and Laanecoorie.

The Loddon was discovered in 1836 by Thomas Mitchell and named after a river in Berkshire, England.

logrunners > *babblers and allies*

Long, Sydney (1871–1955), artist, b. Goulburn, NSW. Influenced by the contemporary Art Nouveau style, Long's work depicted fauns, nymphs and other mythical creatures frolicking in romanticised Australian landscapes, which caused some controversy. He studied under Julian Ashton, then spent fifteen years in London before returning to Australia where he became especially well known for his fine etchings. He was a prominent member of various art societies and a trustee of the Art Gallery of NSW 1933–49.

Longford, Raymond Hollis [John Walter Longford] (1878–1959), film director, b. Melbourne. Often in association with actress Lottie Lyell, Longford was a prolific early Australian film-maker who directed more than 30 silent films including the original versions of *The Silence of Dean Maitland* (1914), *The Sentimental Bloke* (1919) and *On Our Selection* (1920). He left the film industry in the 1930s and his last years were spent working as a night watchman in Sydney.

Longreach Qld (pop. 3159) On the banks of the Thomson River 1170km northwest of Brisbane, Longreach is a centre for the surrounding pastoral district. It developed around a drovers' camp site in the 1860s, with vast properties being established in the following decade; nearby Starlight's Lookout is believed to be the starting point of Harry Redford's epic journey to Adelaide with 1000 stolen head of cattle, commemorated in the novel *Robbery Under Arms*.

Longstaff, Sir John (1862–1941), painter, b. Clunes, Vic. Longstaff's reputation rests on his prolific talents as a portraitist and historical painter in the grand, classical manner. He studied in Paris and was acquainted with some of the leading figures of the avant garde, but remained a traditionalist. His sitters included members of fashionable London and Australian society, British royalty, military leaders during World War 1, and Australian artists and writers; he won the Archibald Prize for portraiture in 1925, 1928, 1929, 1931 and 1935. The massive historical painting, *Arrival of Burke, Wills and King at Cooper's Creek* (1907), is his best-known work.

Loranthaceae > *mistletoe family*

Lord, Simeon (1770–1840), merchant and manufacturer, b. England. An important figure in the commercial life of the young NSW colony, Lord arrived as a convict in 1790. By 1800 he was a free man and beginning to trade in numerous commodities, acting also as public auctioneer. Clashing with William Bligh, Lord played an active part in the Rum Rebellion. Although the favour shown him by Lachlan Macquarie was the cause of much jealousy and controversy, his business interests expanded into the manufacture of woollens and glassware; he was made a magistrate and a trustee of the Sydney–Hawkesbury turnpike in 1810. Lord's six sons all became prominent figures in NSW in the latter half of the 19th century.

Lord Howe Island NSW In the Tasman Sea, 700km northeast of Sydney, this island forms a crescent about 11km north–south and 2.5km at its widest point. The west coast lagoon is fringed with the most southerly known coral reef, its existence explained by the warm offshore current. In the south are two precipitous mountains: Mt Gower (865m) and Mt Lidgbird (763m). The island was discovered by Lidgbird Ball in 1788, and named after the British admiral Lord Howe; it was first settled in 1834. The Lord Howe Island Board now manages the affairs of the islanders, who vote with a Sydney electorate, and tourism is the main source of income. There are two national parks, and the island has World Heritage listing.

lorikeets > *parrots*

lotteries > *gambling*

lotusbird > *waders*

Low, Sir David Alexander Cecil (1891–1963), political cartoonist, b. NZ. Becoming a staff cartoonist on the Sydney *Bulletin* at the age of 20, Low made his name with a series of caricatures of politician W. M. Hughes. Moving to England in 1919, Low worked for numerous newspapers including the *Daily Herald*, the *Manchester Guardian* and the *Evening Standard*, where he created his most famous character, Colonel Blimp, in 1932. One of the most significant cartoonists of the century, Low's simple and clear draughtsmanship belied the strong influence his work had on the political events of his times.

lowan > *mound-building birds*

LPG > *energy resources*

lungfish The Qld lungfish, *Neoceratodus forsteri*, large-scaled, green-backed and white-bellied, has a bulky body running to a deep, pointed tail and measuring up to 1.8m. Like lungfish in other continents it has gills, but it also has a swim-bladder modified into a lung by development of the breathing apparatus of veins and arteries. With this adaptation, the lungfish is better able to survive at times when the river it inhabits is reduced to stagnant pools, but if left entirely without water it soon dies; its flipper-like fins do not enable it to move on land. It eats waterweed and small animals, and its eggs and young resemble frogspawn and tadpoles. It was a source of food for Aborigines and for early white settlers, but is now strictly protected because of its great scientific interest. It is often referred to as a 'living fossil', which means that related orders of fish remain only as fossils in the Permian rocks formed over 200 million years ago. The fish's original range was restricted to the Burnett and Mary rivers of north Qld, but it has now been introduced to a number of rivers in the south of that State. The lungfish exists today in only three living genera (in Australia, Africa and South America), relics of an ancient Gondwana distribution.

Lutheran Church > *religion*

Lycett, Joseph (1774–1825?), artist, b. England. Lycett was transported to NSW in 1814 for forgery. His prolific artistic output included commissions of country mansions, botanical sketches, and topographical drawings for Governor Macquarie; he received a full pardon in 1821 and returned to England the following year. His *Views in Australia and Van Diemen's Land* was published in thirteen parts (1824–5), but his 'faithful depictions' owe more to the ordered English landscape than to the reality of colonial Australia.

Lyle, Sir Thomas Ranken (1860–1944), physicist, b. Ireland. Appointed professor of natural philosophy at the University of

Melbourne in 1889, Lyle undertook research that made an important contribution to the development of electromagnetism and X-rays. He took the first radiograph in Australia (1896) and later demonstrated the use of X-rays during surgery. Elected a Fellow of the Royal Society in 1912, he was appointed chairman of the Vic. Electricity Commission in 1919.

Lyons, Joe (Joseph Aloysius) (1879–1939), politician, b. Circular Head, Tas. Lyons entered the Tas. parliament as a Labor member in 1909 and gained a reputation as a very efficient treasurer; he was subsequently premier 1923–9. He then entered federal politics, serving under J. H. Scullin before resigning from the Labor Party in 1931 over financial policy, doubts about the reinstatement of treasurer E. G. Theodore and a revulsion against factionalism. He formed the United Australia Party in alliance with the Opposition, and on Labor's defeat in 1931 he became prime minister. Lyons' popularity was due not only to his patent sincerity, but also in some measure to his lack of brilliance and hence identification by and with the 'man in the street'. He died in office. His widow, **Dame Enid Muriel** (1897–1981), b. Leesville, Tas., entered federal politics in 1943; she was appointed to cabinet in 1949 – the first woman to achieve this station – and remained there until her retirement from politics in 1951. She subsequently held various public positions, was a newspaper columnist, and published three books including two volumes of personal and political reminiscences.

lyrebirds Two species of these birds are unique to Australia: the superb lyrebird, *Menura superba*, found in wet sclerophyll forest from southeastern Qld to Vic., and the smaller and less spectacular Prince Albert lyrebird, *M. alberti*, of the subtropical rainforests in the Border Ranges of northeastern NSW and southeastern Qld. The male superb lyrebird is about 40cm long, with a long tail of some 60cm which during his remarkable courtship display and 'dance' is brought right up over the back and spread fanwise over the whole body; the dance is performed on mounds of forest litter about 90cm in diameter. The female, which lacks the male ornamentation, builds a large, domed nest, lined with feathers from her breast, in which to lay her one grey-brown egg. Lyrebirds' food includes insects and snails found by raking over leaves and twigs or by attacking logs; the birds normally roost in tree-branches. The lyrebird's mimicry of other birds, especially in the male, is almost as remarkable as its plumage and display. The superb lyrebird is often commonly occurring throughout its range, and is even found in some suburban bush reserves.

M

Maatsuyker islands Tas. The most southerly lighthouse in Australia stands at the southwest tip of Maatsuyker Island, one of this group of small islands and rocks lying off Red Point on the south coast of Tas. A region of wild seas and desolate landscape, it includes De Witt Island, known locally as the Big Witch, and Mewstone, most southerly of the group; the larger islands are breeding grounds for a great number of sea-birds.

Macalister River Vic. This coastal Gippsland stream rises in the Great Dividing Range southeast of Mt Buller and flows for some 170km through hilly country before joining the Thomson River. Glenmaggie reservoir is the chief storage in an irrigation system that supplies pastoral country around Maffra and Sale. The Macalister was discovered by Augus McMillan in 1839.

Macarthur family, eminent pastoralists and agriculturists also involved in early NSW politics. **John** (1767–1834) b. England, had exceptional influence on the political and economic development of NSW to 1820. He arrived in 1790 with the NSW Corps and in 1793 was granted promotion and about 40ha at Parramatta. He named it Elizabeth Farm, and played a leading role in the establishment of the NSW wool industry, crossing Bengal and Irish sheep and later importing merinos. He introduced the first animal-drawn iron plough to the colony in 1795, by which time he had become one of its most substantial farmers and stock owners, but his vision of the colony was of landed pastoralist families; he resented the efforts of Governors Bligh and Macquarie to establish smaller agricultural communities and, especially, the increasing favours given to emancipists. His complaints to London led to the removal of Governor Hunter; he quarrelled with Hunter's successor, Philip Gidley King,

who sent him to London in 1801 to be court-martialled for duelling. Macarthur was permitted to resign from the army, and returned in triumph in 1805 with sheep from George III's own flock and the promise of c. 4000ha of his own selection, as well as provision of convict labour. He established Camden Park, but soon quarrelled with the new governor, William Bligh, who arrested him on a trivial charge in December 1807; the trial was chaotic and the tables were turned when Major George Johnston responded to Macarthur's appeal to arrest Bligh and take command in the so-called Rum Rebellion. Again Macarthur went to England (1809) and appeared as a witness at Johnston's trial, remaining in exile until 1817. He had taken his sons with him, and during this time they travelled and were educated in Europe, learning especially about wine production, an occupation which one son, **William** (1800–82), later pursued. Macarthur, while superficially supporting Macquarie, covertly set about undermining him by gaining the ear of J. T. Bigge and by using his London contacts to vilify him. Increasingly weighed down by illness, his choleric personality becoming more unpleasant, Macarthur continued to harass Governors Brisbane and Darling, but with less and less potency, until in 1832 he lost his reason altogether. **Elizabeth** (1766–1850), his courageous and energetic wife, played an important part in John's success as a farmer as well as in the social life of the colony. She developed her husband's property and greatly improved the livestock. **Hannibal Hawkins** (1788–1861), John's nephew, assisted John as a trading partner and helped Elizabeth during her husband's long absences from the colony. Later he was actively involved in community affairs, in both Parramatta and Sydney. **James** (1798–1867), John's fourth son, became an important public figure. He long supported conservative and exclusivist movements, and through a 'useful' marriage saved the family estates when Hannibal was bankrupted in the depression of the 1840s.

Macassans Sailors from Macassar in the Celebes (today Sulawesi) frequented the north coast of Australia from 1700 onwards, to fish for sea-cucumbers (bêche-de-mer). A fleet of possibly 50–60 boats (*praus*) usually arrived in December, and returned to Macassar in about April to sell the dried animals. Many traces of Macassan pottery, stone fireplaces and camps have been excavated. The Macassans made contact – in most cases friendly – with the Aborigines, who adopted some of their words and depicted them in legends and art. Fishing licences and customs duties introduced in 1882 discouraged the sailors, however, and the last *prau* came in 1906.

McAuley, James Phillip (1917–76), poet and critic, b. Sydney. After service in PNG during World War 2, McAuley published many articles on that society in the 1940s and 1950s. Editor of the literary journal *Quadrant* 1956–63, he also taught and was eventually professor of English at the University of Tas. McAuley's first volume of poetry was published in 1946. Like A. D. Hope and Harold Stewart, he drew on both ancient and 18th-century verse forms; his best verse was lyrical, and deepened by his search for metaphysical values. Scholarly but conservative, his essays and criticism – including the collection *The End of Modernity* (1959) – are held in high regard.

McBride, William Griffith (1927–), gynaecologist, b. Sydney. In a research paper delivered in 1961, McBride verified the link between the drug thalidomide and birth deformities, for which he won international acclaim. With the proceeds of an ensuing award from a French institution in 1971, McBride established Foundation 41, a centre to research the first 41 weeks of human life. In 1988 he was forced to resign as the centre's medical director after a judicial inquiry found him guilty of scientific fraud over his research into the anti-nausea drug Debendox; he subsequently launched court action in order to clear his name. In 1989 McBride was the subject of an inquiry by the Australian Medical Board for improper medical practices.

McCabe, Stan(ley Joseph) > *cricket*

MacCallum, Sir Peter (1885–1974), pathologist, b. Scotland. MacCallum, professor of pathology at Melbourne University from 1924, encouraged the Vic. government to establish a cancer centre in 1949, and gave it his lifelong support and advice. The clinic, which in 1950 was named after him, has pioneered many significant advances in treatment and research. In 1989, however, funding problems forced the clinic to curtail a number of its services.

McCaughey family, pastoral dynasty of NSW and Qld. **Sir Samuel** (1835–1919) immigrated to Australia in 1856 and became a partner in his uncle's property Coonong, in NSW, in 1860. He introduced many technical improvements, including mechanical shearing, and was a noted wool-producer. A pioneer of irrigation and water conservation, he created one of the earliest artesian-water systems and constructed a dam and pumping station on his property Yanco, beside the Murrumbidgee River, which he acquired in 1899. He retained substantial land-holdings in NSW and Qld until the early 20th century and was a generous benefactor of the universities of Sydney and Qld as well as schools and welfare organisations. His nephew **Samuel** (1892–1955) inherited the family property Coree, near Jerilderie in NSW, in 1899; he established a pastoral company in the 1930s and became a noted sheep-breeder. He and his brother David were benefactors of the McCaughey Institute, a pastoral research centre established at Coree in the 1950s. Sir Samuel's nephew, **Sir (David) Roy** (1898–1971), bought Coonong from his uncle in 1919 and also became a noted pastoralist; he was chairman of the Commonwealth Wool Producers' Co. 1950–5.

McColl, Hugh (1819–85), pioneer of irrigation, b. Scotland. McColl arrived in Australia in 1852 and subsequently worked in Bendigo, Vic. In 1874 he became secretary of a company which proposed to divert water from the Goulburn River westward to a canal running from Portland to the Murray River, but the scheme proved economically unviable. After being elected to the Vic. parliament in 1880, McColl actively promoted irrigation and was instrumental in the passage of the Water and Irrigation Act of 1886.

McCrae family, notable for literary and artistic talent. **Georgiana Huntly** (1804–90) artist and diarist, b. England, arrived in Australia in 1841 with her husband (Andrew Murison McCrae) and family; she was trained as a miniaturist and a landscape painter. Although restricted by family life (the couple had eight children), her diary (1841–6) is a fascinating account of the Vic. colonial era; it was eventually published, with her illustrations, as *Georgiana's Journal* (1934). Her son **George Gordon** (1833–1927), b. Scotland, was a leading literary figure and patron, and a poet (though little known today). His son **Hugh Raymond** (1876–1958), author, b. Melbourne, was a lifelong friend of Norman Lindsay (who illustrated some of his poems) and joined the *Bulletin* coterie in Sydney from 1904. A prolific writer, critic and sometime illustrator, he is best remembered for his lyrical poetry; published volumes included *Satyrs and Sunlight* (1909), a bacchanalian departure from the ballads of the period, and *Forests of Pan* (1944).

McCubbin, Frederick (1855–1917),

painter, b. Melbourne. McCubbin is celebrated for his haunting, often melancholy depictions of the Australian bush and pioneer settlers, stylistically influenced by Impressionism but still academically composed and tonally restrained. A fine figure draughtsman, he was drawing master at the National Gallery School in Melbourne 1886–1917. With Louis Abrahams and Tom Roberts he set up at Box Hill (1885) the first of the artists' camps that eventually led to what became known as the Heidelberg School. After his only trip to Europe (1907), his work became smaller in scale, brighter, and more purely Impressionist.

McCulloch, Colleen Margaretta

(1937–), novelist, b. Wellington, NSW. A neurophysiologist by training, McCulloch wrote her first novel, *Tim,* in 1974. It was a modest prelude to *The Thorn Birds* (1977), a bodice-ripper on the grand scale, dealing with an Irish–Australian family's problems with romance, sex, religion, natural disasters and death over several generations; initially published in the US, it has sold some 20 million copies. Her other novels are *An Indecent Obsession* (1981) and *The Ladies of Missalonghi* (1987).

McDonald Island > *Heard and McDonald islands*

Macdonnell Ranges NT These parallel

ridges of red quartzite and sandstone extend for about 200km west and northeast of Alice Springs; their highest point is Mt Zeil (1511m). The ranges are the source of the Finke and Todd rivers; the mountains' rate of uplift was

sufficiently slow for the rivers to keep pace, and they have cut transversely through the ranges in deep and spectacular canyons – notably > *Standley Chasm*, and Glen Helen and Ormiston gorges. The rich flora of the gorges is in stark contrast to the barren surrounding hills. The Macdonnell Ranges were discovered by John McDouall Stuart in 1860 and named by him after the SA governor.

McEwen, Sir John (1900–80), politician,

b. Chiltern, Vic. Leader of the Country Party and deputy prime minister 1958–71, McEwen was prime minister of Australia December 1967–January 1968, the interval between the death of Harold Holt and the Liberals' selection of John Gorton as their new leader. As minister for trade 1956–71, McEwen worked energetically in this expanding field, negotiating several important international agreements.

McGilvray, Alan (1910–), cricket com-

mentator, b. Sydney. McGilvray represented the voice of Australian cricket broadcasting for over 50 years. A talented all-round cricketer who captained NSW, his career as commentator began in 1935 when he was approached by the ABC to provide brief post-match summaries. Always noted for his clear diction – the legacy of elocution lessons to overcome a childhood stammer – McGilvray subsequently took part in the studio broadcast of the 1938 Ashes series, in which a team of commentators translated brief cables into a remarkably authentic representation of play, with appropriate sound effects. A fine tribute was paid to him when, on 1 February 1980, the scoreboard at the Melbourne Cricket Ground read 'McGilvray 100' – the occasion being his hundredth Australia–England Test broadcast.

McInnes, Colin (1914–76), novelist, b.

England. Son of the novelist Angela Thirkell, McInnes was educated in Australia but returned to the UK in 1930. He is particularly noted for the so-called 'London' trilogy of novels, the centrepiece of which is *Absolute Beginners* (1959), a vivid examination of British youth in the 1950s. He published two novels with Australian settings, *June in her Spring* (1952) and *All Day Saturday* (1966), both inferior works. A collection of his journalistic pieces was published as *England, Half English* (1966).

Macintyre River NSW A tributary of the

Darling River system, the Macintyre rises near

Glen Innes on the western slopes of the granitic New England plateau. Glen Innes and Inverell – the major towns along the river – are centres for wheat-growing and for production of beef cattle, fat lambs and merinos. A major tributary of the Macintyre is the Severn, on which is the Pindari dam; where it meets the Dumaresq River, the Macintyre becomes part of the border between NSW and Qld, then flows through open plains and subsequently is known as the Barwon.

Mackaness, George (1882–1968), historian and editor, b. Sydney. Head of the department of English at Sydney Teachers' College 1924–46, Mackaness was a prolific anthologist and editor, notably in the series *Australian Historical Monographs* (1935–62), which covered some of the lesser known byways of Australian history. His most important works are biographies of William Bligh (1931), Joseph Banks (1936) and Arthur Phillip (1937); in 1934, he also edited the extremely popular poetry anthology *The Wide Brown Land*. A longstanding bibliophile, Mackaness described this aspect of his life in *Bibliomania: An Australian Book Collector's Essays* (1965).

Mackay Qld (pop. 38 603) Australia's sugar capital, Mackay straddles both banks of the Pioneer River (4.8km from its mouth) some 975km north of Brisbane. It was discovered by John MacKay in 1860 and sugar-growing was well established in the area within a decade. Mackay now produces one-third of the nation's sugar and has eight sugar-processing mills as well as one of the world's largest storage sheds, which is located at the city's man-made deepwater harbour (built in 1939). Local industries include dairying, tropical fruit, timber, pigs and beef cattle; meat is shipped from the Mackay port, as is coal (from central Qld) and grain from the Clermont district. Tourism is of growing importance, with beach and island resorts nearby and the splendid rainforest of Eungella National Park 80km to the west.

McKay, Heather (1942–), squash player, b. Queanbeyan, NSW. McKay did not lose a match – and rarely a game – after dropping just one on her first trip to Britain in 1962, the year in which she became the first overseas player to win the British Women's Open – in effect, the world championship. She subsequently won that title a further fifteen times, in 1976 overwhelming her opponent in a mere nine

minutes. Always a fair player, McKay worked relentlessly to maintain physical fitness and improve her stroke play. In 1976, at the close of her career, she won the inaugural Women's World Open championship, and emerged from retirement to win it once again in 1979.

McKay, Hugh Victor (1865–1926), inventor and manufacturer, b. Raywood, Vic. Designer and manufacturer of the Sunshine Harvester, a machine which stripped, threshed and winnowed grain (patented 1885), McKay also built machines for cultivation and sowing, and in his large factory at Braybrook (now Sunshine) insisted on an 'open shop'. McKay's submission to the Arbitration Court in 1907 regarding wage rates resulted in the > *Harvester judgment*.

McKell, Sir William John (1891–1986) politician, b. Pambula, NSW. McKell was the second Australian-born governor-general (1947–53). Following association with the Boilermakers' Union, he entered the NSW parliament in 1917 and rose in Labor politics to become premier 1941–7, stabilising the State Labor Party after the period under Jack Lang. His moderate style laid the foundation for subsequent Labor governments.

Mackellar, (Isobel Marian) Dorothea (1885–1968), poet and novelist, b. Sydney. Mackellar was educated privately and at Sydney University. At the age of 19 she wrote 'Core of My Heart', published by the London *Spectator* in 1908 and revised as 'My Country' in *The Closed Door* (1911); the second verse, beginning 'I love a sunburnt country', is possibly the most quoted fragment in Australian poetry. Mackellar published four volumes of poetry and three novels up to about 1926.

Mackennal, Sir (Edgar) Bertram (1863–1931), sculptor, b. Melbourne. The most successful Australian visual artist of his era, Mackennal was the first Australian to be made a full member of the Royal Academy (London) and the first Australian artist to be knighted (1921). He trained in England and France, and although he lived most of his life in England, he successfully maintained links with Australia. In Paris he was introduced by fellow artist John Peter Russell to the avant-garde French sculptor Auguste Rodin, but Mackennal remained a traditional classical realist. The hauntingly beautiful bronze, *Circe*, exhibited at the Paris Salon in 1893, established his career.

Mackenzie, Stuart > *rowing and sculling*

mackerels These fishes combine with tunas to make up the family Scombridae; 23 of approximately 44 world species are known in Australian waters. Mackerel species include the butterfly mackerel, *Gasterochisma melampus*, with a blunt head and large scales unlike any other scombroid. There are also four species of the Spanish mackerel (known in Qld as king-fish), of the genus *Scomberomorus*, the largest of which can reach 60kg; the smaller *S. com-mersoni* is one of the most important species of the Qld fishing industry. Tuna – the only known 'warm-blooded' fish – belongs to the genus *Thonna*, the seven species of which are Australia's most valuable commercial fish; they are exported in large quantities to Japan, although harvesting of the southern bluefin tuna, *T. maccoyi*, is now restricted because of overfishing. Other members of the mackerel family include the wahoo, *Acanthocybium solandri*, a tropical species distinguished by its slender shape and long snout; the largest recorded specimen caught in Australian waters weighed more than 56kg.

McKern, Leo (Reginald) (1920–), actor, b. Sydney. Trained as an engineer, McKern took up amateur acting during World War 2. He went to London in 1946 and subsequently made his reputation acting with such companies as the Old Vic and the Royal Shakespeare Company. He is also a film actor, particularly noted for his performance as the devious Thomas Cromwell in *A Man for All Seasons* (1966). Other films include *Ryan's Daughter* (1970) and *Travelling North* (1987), for which he won an AFI Best Actor Award. He is perhaps best known for his role as the avuncular barrister in the television series 'Rumpole of the Bailey'.

Mackerras, Sir (Alan) Charles (1925–), music conductor, b. US. Mackerras arrived, with his Australian parents, in NSW in 1927 and later studied at the NSW Conservatorium of Music. He was principal oboist with the Sydney Symphony Orchestra 1944–6, staff conductor of the Sadler's Wells Opera 1949–53, principal conductor of the BBC Concert Orchestra 1954–65 and the Hamburg State Opera 1966–9, and musical director of the English National Opera 1970–9. He has made many commercial recordings, notably of Janáček operas and a Handel series. He has been musical director of the Welsh National Opera since 1986.

McKillop, Mary Helen (1842–1909), Catholic nun, b. Melbourne. After working as a governess, McKillop established a school at Penola, SA, in the 1860s. Taking the name Mother Mary of the Cross, she also founded in SA the Congregation of the Sisters of St Joseph of the Most Sacred Heart of Jesus, an order dedicated to the welfare and education of the poor. After numerous vicissitudes, including a period of excommunication after a disagreement with the local diocesan authority, she was confirmed in 1873 as founder of the order by Pope Pius IX. In 1973, formal moves were initiated to have her canonised as Australia's first saint.

Macleay family, eminent in Australian natural history, pastoralism and politics. **Alexander** (1767–1848), b. Scotland, was a very able colonial secretary in NSW 1825–37 under Governors Darling and Bourke; he quarrelled bitterly with the latter, mainly over exclusivist/emancipist disputes. In NSW he added to his already substantial entomological collection and developed an outstanding ornamental garden at Elizabeth Bay House, built for him in 1832 by John Verge. He was a noted supporter of exploration, botany, agriculture and culture in the young colony. His eldest son, **William Sharp** (1792–1865), b. England, arrived in Australia in 1838; he, too, was an outstanding naturalist and expanded both the Elizabeth Bay House garden and his father's natural-history collection. Another of Alexander's sons, **Sir George** (1809–91), b. England, accompanied Charles Sturt's expedition to the mouth of the Murray River in 1829; he was a NSW politician 1851–9. Alexander's nephew **William John** (1820–91), b. Scotland, was a Murrumbidgee squatter who further developed the Macleay entomological collection, adding to it from an NG expedition of 1875. He also published a catalogue of Australian fishes (1881). He donated (and endowed) the Macleay natural-history collection to the University of Sydney in 1890 and also made generous bequests to the NSW Linnean Society.

Macleay River NSW The Macleay rises on the New England Plateau as the Guyra River. It cascades over the escarpment into an extensive area of wild gorge country, as do its major tributaries, creating spectacular waterfalls (such as those on the Wollomombi River, the highest in Australia) as they descend into the gorges. After leaving the ranges, the Macleay forms broad flood-plains, where the chief rural industry is dairying, and flows past Kempsey – the major town of the Macleay basin – to join the sea at Trial Bay. The river was named after Alexander Macleay.

McMahon, Sir William (1908–88), politician, b. Sydney. Liberal prime minister for 20 months between the deposing of John Gorton in 1971 and the ALP's victory in the 1972 election, McMahon had earlier been an able treasurer (1966–9) and administrator, as minister for labour (1958–66) presiding over extensive changes designed to make the public service more efficient. After the 1972 electoral defeat, he remained a backbencher until his resignation from parliament in 1982.

McMillan, Angus (1810–65), explorer, b. Scotland. McMillan immigrated to Australia in 1838. In 1839 he explored southward from the Monaro plains in NSW and thereby discovered the Gippsland region of Vic. In the following two years he made several forays through southeastern Vic., discovering the river system which empties into the Gippsland Lakes and eventually reaching the Vic. south coast at Port Albert. He remained in Vic. to export cattle to Tas.

MacNamara, Dame (Annie) Jean (1899–1968), physician, b. Beechworth, Vic. A world authority on poliomyelitis, Dame Jean was instrumental in establishing the Yooralla Hospital for crippled children, in Melbourne in 1927; she was an honorary medical adviser there until 1951. She was also an early advocate of the introduction of myxomatosis into Australia for the control of rabbits, a solution not adopted until the 1950s. She was created DBE in 1935.

Maconochie, Alexander (1787–1860), geographer and penal reformer, b. Scotland. A founder of London's Royal Geographical Society in 1828 and first professor of geography at the University of London 1833–6, Maconochie was appointed secretary to Sir John Franklin in Tas. in 1836. Believing that punishment and inhuman treatment of prisoners debased both the victim and society, he prepared a report on the convict system which advocated the rehabilitation of prisoners and

was an effective indictment of the Tas. system. Thereby invoking Franklin's wrath, Maconochie was dismissed from his post in 1839 but in charge of Norfolk Island convicts 1840–4 he put his theories into practice with some success. Recalled to England in 1844, he continued his campaign for penal reform.

Macquarie, Lachlan (1762–1824), colonial administrator, b. Scotland. After army service in America and India, Macquarie came to Australia in 1809 as commander of his regiment. He was appointed governor of NSW in 1810. During his period of office he reduced the use of rum as currency (introducing old Spanish dollars for this purpose), tried to improve the moral life of the colony by stern sabbatarian rules, set up the Bank of NSW and educational institutions, and encouraged exploration beyond the Blue Mountains. He envisaged a land of close settlement with small agricultural holdings, and opposed large estates for wool-growing. Under him the first fine buildings were erected, many designed by Francis Greenway. Macquarie was particularly noted for his humanitarian attitudes towards convicts and in general he believed in encouraging emancipists. Thus he made enemies, notably of Samuel Marsden, the Macarthur family and the Bent brothers, which resulted in the commissioning of J. T. Bigge to report on the conditions in the colony. Macquarie resigned in 1821, leaving the colony in 1822; he was not permitted to publish any justification after the predominantly hostile Bigge Report came out. To many he was as much a father of Australia as was his arch-enemy Macarthur. His second wife **Elizabeth Henrietta** (1778–1835), b. Scotland, accompanied Macquarie to NSW in 1809. She took an active interest in the affairs of the colony, particularly its nascent architecture and the welfare of both Aborigines and female convicts.

Macquarie Island This narrow, windswept, subantarctic island, some 34km long, lies about 800km southeast of Tas., from which it is administered. It consists mostly of a plateau, the edge falling steeply to sea or beach; there are no trees but many lakes, and low vegetation on the slopes and the flat coastal regions. Discovered in 1810 and named after Lachlan Macquarie, it became a base for sealers: by the mid-1830s the fur seal population had been hunted to extinction, and only in 1956 were they observed to have returned to breed. On the island's southeast tip is one of the world's largest penguin rookeries. Several scientific expeditions have visited and explored the island, and the Australian National Antarctic Research Expedition has maintained a permanent base since 1948. The island has been a wildlife sanctuary since 1933 and a Tas. State reserve since 1972.

Macquarie River NSW A headwater of the Darling River system, the Macquarie rises on the western slopes of the Great Dividing Range, cutting northwest through the sheep and wheat lands of the plateau and the towns of Bathurst and Dubbo. It becomes increasingly seasonal in flow along its course; north of Warren it flows into the Macquarie Marshes and beyond them meets the Castlereagh River, which in turn joins the Barwon. The marshes – now a sanctuary – abound with waterfowl; confronted with them in 1818, John Oxley thought them to be the shore of a shallow inland sea. The Burrendong dam near Wellington, a major storage, regulates the river flow to avoid flooding. Discovered by George Evans in 1813, the river was named after Lachlan Macquarie.

madder family The large flowering-plant family Rubiaceae occurs worldwide but is most diverse in the tropics, where it consists mainly of trees and shrubs; it is the source of both coffee and quinine. Australia has native representatives of many widespread genera, both tropical and temperate, and a few endemic genera. Across northern Australia a common large tree fringing permanent streams is the Leichhardt tree, *Nauclea orientalis*, with large leaves and globular pincushion-like heads of small flowers. The fifteen or so native *Gardenia* species, shrubs or small trees with fragrant white flowers and woody globular fruits, are common in northern rainforest and monsoonal woodland. There are five species of the remarkable ant-house plant, swollen-stemmed epiphytes of the genera *Myrmecodia* and *Hydnophytum* with ant-inhabited internal passages, which are all confined to far northern Qld. Temperate herbaceous genera include *Nertera*, which is closely allied to the shrub genus *Coprosma*, of which Australia has eight native species.

Madigan, C. T. (Cecil Thomas) (1889–1947), geologist and explorer, b. Renmark, SA. A member of Douglas Mawson's Antarctic expedition 1912–14, Madigan then served with distinction in World War 1 and joined the Sudan

civil service 1920–2. While lecturing in geology at Adelaide University from 1923, Madigan undertook geological exploration in central Australia and made an aerial survey of the region in 1929. Further expeditions in the 1930s included a crossing of the Simpson Desert (using camels) in 1939. He described his inland journeys in *Central Australia* (1936) and *Crossing the Dead Heart* (1946).

magazines and periodicals The publication of magazines and periodicals in Australia has had a chequered history, specialist and 'serious' journals in particular suffering from the combined effects of a relatively small population and the vagaries of public taste. By 1989, however, more than 1600 magazines were published regularly in Australia. While many cover special interests (ranging from surfing to pig-farming or holistic medicine) and have limited circulation, there are some 30 major magazines: reflecting the affluence and materialism of the previous decade, there were about ten 'lifestyle' monthlies, about half this number each of general-interest, home-maker and business publications, and only two (weeklies) devoted to news reviews.

Historical development Illiteracy, and the lack of both printing presses and experienced publishers, hindered the establishment of a magazine tradition. Periodical publication began in 1821, with the short-lived *Australian Magazine*, a monthly dedicated to 'useful knowledge, religious principles and moral habits'. Most magazines in the mid-19th century modelled themselves on their English counterparts. The first genuinely literary magazine was the *Hobart Town Magazine*, published in 1834, which contained essays, short stories and poems. James Tegg's *Literary News*, published in Sydney from 1837, also specialised in literary material and was the first Australian magazine to carry illustrations.

Illustrated magazines became more common in the late 1840s. The difficulties of magazine production eased during the 1850s as technical problems were overcome and the discovery of gold provided potentially larger audiences. A number of news magazines were produced, such as the *Illustrated Sydney News* (1853) and Melbourne *Punch* (1855), and in 1856 the Melbourne *Age* began the first regular weekly companion to a daily paper with the *Leader*, a highly successful publication that contained news summaries as well as features and rural information. Similar supplements were the

Argus's Australasian (1864) and the Melbourne *Herald's Weekly Times* (1869). The relative success of the news magazines during the 1860s, and their improved presentation (the *Illustrated Sydney News* pioneering the use of colour) led to the partial eclipse of purely literary magazines. A notable exception was the long-lived *Australian Journal*, published weekly 1865–9 and monthly 1869–1962, which specialised in Australian writing and content and published many important writers including Marcus Clarke and Rolf Boldrewood.

By the end of the 1870s, the magazine market was improving but still variable. The buoyant 1880s saw a magazine boom, however; there was also a significant change in the tone of publications, heralded by the arrival of the explicitly nationalistic > *Bulletin* in 1880. Outspoken and serious-minded, a number of periodicals – from Louisa Lawson's feminist *Dawn* (1888) to the socialist *Tocsin* (founded 1897, later the *Labor Call* and *Labor*) – concentrated on specific social and political causes.

The *Bulletin's* aggressive nationalism helped improve the climate for Australian writers by the early 20th century. A new batch of literary and satirical magazines began, including the *Bookfellow* (1899), *Steele Rudd's Magazine* (1904), the *Gadfly* (1906) and *Art in Australia* (1916). Women's magazines also began to be published at the end of the century, the *Australian Home Journal* (1894) being followed by *New Idea* in 1902. Field magazines prospered during World War 1 and their short items and humorous drawings were carried over into the general market after the war in magazines such as *Smith's Weekly* (1919). In the 1930s, despite the poor economic climate, a flush of new titles was published: *Walkabout* and *Wild Life*, the > *Australian Women's Weekly*, *People*, *Man* and *Man Junior* all reflected the increasing segmentation of the popular market. The more serious reader was catered for by political and social journals like the stalwart *Bulletin* and the *Australian Quarterly* (1929); and with the arrival of new literary magazines such as *Southerly* (1939) and *Meanjin* (1940).

Following World War 2, illustrated general-interest magazines such as the *Australasian Post* (1946, born of the longstanding *Australasian*) retained their wide popularity and a number of new women's magazines were founded. At the same time, the complacent conservatism of the 1950s spawned a reaction in the form of literary and issues-oriented journals such as *Overland* (1954) and later *Quadrant*

(1965), as well as a handful of radical socialist journals such as *Dissent* (1961) and the *Australian Left Review* (1966). The 1970s were characterised above all by the plethora of more sophisticated magazines such as *Cleo* (1972) and *Cosmopolitan* (1973) for women and *Dolly* (1970) for adolescents; *Australian Playboy* (1979) perpetuated the tradition of 'girlie' magazines, with an overlay of serious features.

The 1980s and beyond There were great changes in the magazine industry during the 1980s. Increased competition and higher costs caused revamping of many established journals, the most notable being the format change of the country's highest-circulation magazine, the *Women's Weekly*, into a glossy monthly, and incorporation of the US publication *Newsweek* into the *Bulletin*. Other characteristics of the decade were the burgeoning of financial periodicals *Australian Business* and *Business Review Weekly* (both 1980), the advent of Australian issues of overseas magazines, such as *Time* (1986) and *Harper's Bazaar* (1988), and the plethora of 'lifestyle', fashion and decorating journals. Also noteworthy was the series of takeovers which saw the Fairfax group eclipsed as a magazine publisher and the market dominated by Rupert Murdoch's Southdown Press and the Packer family's Australian Consolidated Press. >> *cartoons and cartooning*; *newspapers*

Magnetic Island Qld Magnetic Island, lying in Halifax Bay 8km from Townsville, is a thickly wooded and mountainous tourist resort, rising to 497m and with an area of 49sq.km; coral reefs enclose some of the bays and Magnetic Island National Park displays hoop pine and eucalypt forest, supporting many native animals. The island was named Magnetical Isle by James Cook in 1770, in the belief – unconfirmed – that magnetic ore in the hills had affected the *Endeavour's* compass.

magpie goose > *geese*

magpie-lark > *mudlarks and allies*

magpies, currawongs and butcherbirds There are about ten Australian and NG species of this family, the Cracticidae. They are crow-like birds with long straight beaks slightly down-curved at the end; they are pied, or predominantly black or grey, and their bowl-shaped nests of sticks and twigs are built in trees. They feed mainly on insects. Although found in a variety of habitats, the most familiar species frequent open forests and suburban gardens. They form close family groups, and fully grown young are often seen still demanding food from their parents. The Australian magpies, of the genus *Gymnorhina*, are not related to the European birds of the same name. The pied butcher-bird, *Cracticus nigrogularis*, is a smaller creature, with a white abdomen and rump, and a tuneful song; related species have a more regional distribution. The pied currawong, *Strepera graculina*, is a common visitor to gardens, but a most unwelcome one in orchards. The call of the currawong (reproduced in its name) and the curious rolling, twanging melody of the white-backed and black-backed magpies are among the bird calls most prized by and nostalgic to Australians.

mahogany family The Meliaceae family of flowering plants consists chiefly of rainforest trees of tropical and warm-temperate regions of the world. Among them are some of the world's most valued cabinet timbers, including true mahoganies and the American cigar-box cedars. In Australia about 35 species are native, comprising eleven genera of which the best known are red and white > *cedar*. The largest number of species (fourteen) belongs to *Dysoxylum*, which includes the east-coast rosewood, *D. fraserianum*, a prized cabinet timber. Only two genera are endemic, *Synoum* and *Owenia*, the latter including species of the inland plains and monsoonal north as well as eastern rainforests; *O. acidula* is the emu apple of the plains, a shapely small tree with decorative but hard red-brown fruits that are eaten by emus.

Maiden, Joseph Henry (1859–1925), botanist, b. England. Arriving in Sydney in 1880, Maiden became curator of the Sydney Technological Museum and his *Useful Native Plants of Australia* was published in 1889. He was an outstanding director of the Sydney Botanic Gardens 1896–1924, during which time he energetically initiated both taxonomic research (chiefly on eucalypts) and public instruction programs. He wrote the multi-volume illustrated works *Forest Flora of New South Wales* and *A Critical Revision of the Genus Eucalyptus* – although these were uncompleted by the time of his death – as well as innumerable shorter works and scientific papers (some co-authored by Ernst Betche). Maiden was influential in scientific circles, holding office in several learned societies and receiving various awards.

Maitland NSW (pop. 43 247) A city about 200km north of Sydney, Maitland is the main centre for the dairying and crop lands of the lower Hunter Valley. It is situated where the Hunter River emerges on to a wide flood-plain, with the result that the busy commercial centre and some suburbs have been isolated repeatedly by flooding; flood-control works have reduced this threat, as has the relocation of residential areas on to higher land. Textiles are a major part of the city's economic life, but it has a wide range of light industries including steel fabrication, brickworks and the servicing of heavy machinery as well as farm-based industries. Settled from about 1813, Maitland is one of the State's oldest towns and has many noteworthy historic buildings. Tourism is of growing importance to the city and it has also developed recently as a commuter base for Newcastle workers.

Mallacoota Inlet Vic. Situated in far eastern Gippsland some 560km east of Melbourne, this deep inlet is in fact a drowned river valley and was formed about 6000 years ago. The small fishing and holiday township of Mallacoota, and nearby Gipsy Point, are bases for visitors to the area; the coastal and mountain landscapes have been set aside in several national parks – most notably Croajingolong, which covers some 86 000ha.

mallee This is the common name of Aboriginal origin for the unusual growth form of some 150 species of > *eucalypts*. All develop large underground lignotubers from which issue a multitude of stems, the base of each plant often extending over several metres. Mallee eucalypts are widespread in the southern inland – in northwest Vic., southwest NSW, southern SA and to a lesser degree in southeast WA – where they form a distinctive scrub which dominates the landscape; typical species include the red mallee, *E. oleosa*, and the congoo mallee, *E. dumosa*. Mallee scrublands generally provide a rich habitat for some rare wildlife species, such as the pygmy possum and mallee fowl. Large tracts of mallee had been cleared for agriculture by the early 20th century, which subsequently caused serious soil erosion; most areas are now protected in national parks or reserves.

mallee fowl > *mound-building birds*

Mallee region The distinctive > *mallee* eucalypt scrub has given its name to a region of northwestern Vic. covering about 44 000sq.km between the Wimmera and Murray rivers. The low variable rainfall averages 250–300mm, but the soils are rich despite lacking nitrogen and phosphate. The region has been transformed by water brought to the southern half from the Glenelg River through 16 000km of channels that feed farm dams. Dry farming for wheat, with rotation to avoid leaving bare ground, is supplemented by irrigated fodder crops and stock-farming, with lucerne and lupins on the sand-hills. Former wheat-farming practices caused extensive wind erosion of the thin soils, however. Substantial sections of the Mallee are preserved in the Wyperfeld and Big Desert national parks.

mallow family The Malvaceae family of flowering plants includes cotton, *Gossypium hirsutum*, and the genus > *Hibiscus*. It is represented in Australia by about 150 native species in eighteen genera, the greatest concentration of species being in the drier subtropical and tropical regions. Soft-wooded native shrubs and subshrubs of the genera *Sida* and *Abutilon* occur on stony inland hills and on both sandy and heavy-soil plains. Most members of the genus *Hibiscus* are endemic, ranging from small trees of eastern rainforests to prostrate perennial herbs of the far inland. The cotton genus *Gossypium* has nine endemic species in the inland and far north, including the widespread desert rose, *G. sturtianum*, the floral emblem of the NT. The family also includes a number of endemic genera such as *Alyogyne*, several species of which are shrubs with large, striking mauve or bluish flowers; most are confined to WA. *Howittia* has a single species – a scrambling pink-flowered shrub restricted to moist valley forests in NSW and Vic. *Lawrencia* consists of twelve species of small-flowered shrubs concentrated in southern coastal and inland areas, often in saline environments.

Malouf, David (1934–) poet and novelist, b. Brisbane. Of Lebanese and English parents, Malouf taught in England for nine years before joining the University of Sydney in 1968. *Bicycle and Other Poems* (1970) was followed by three other collections of poetry and five novels, including the prize-winning *An Imaginary Life* (1978) and *Fly Away Peter* (1982), and *Harland's Half Acre* (1984). He divides his time between Australia and Tuscany.

Maltese in Australia > *ethnic groups*

Malvaceae > *mallow family*

Mammoth Cave > *caves*

Mandurah WA (pop 18 016) A service centre and holiday town at the narrow mouth of the Peel Inlet, Mandurah lies 75km south of Perth. Its main industries are fishing, alumina-processing and tourism. Development dates from 1829, when it was the site of an abortive settlement scheme by pioneer Thomas Peel.

manganese Australia is a major producer and exporter of manganese, a metallic element used extensively in the iron and steel industry. In 1986, Australian output was 1649 million t of manganese ore, about 6.8% of world production. All Australian ore comes from a BHP-owned mine on Groote Eylandt in the Gulf of Carpentaria; the bulk is exported and the remainder shipped to the BHP smelter at Bell Bay, Tas., for refining into manganese alloys. Australia has an estimated 436 million t of economically recoverable reserves, which indicates a bright future given the growth of the steel industry in Asia.

mangroves These specialised trees and shrubs are adapted to growth in the intertidal zone of seashores and estuaries, and characteristically form a fringe of vegetation between deeper water and dry land. They are unique among woody plants in being able to survive in salt water, having evolved a variety of physiological mechanisms as well as adaptations for growth in the absence of oxygen for their root systems.

Mangroves are most abundant and diverse in the tropics, diminishing rapidly across temperate zones to disappear entirely by about 40° latitude. Mangrove communities are composed of several unrelated plant families, fifteen of which (in some 30 species) are represented in Australia. The major world family is the Rhizophoraceae, which is allied to the myrtle family. Australia has three native genera, *Rhizophora, Bruguiera* and *Ceriops*, totalling eleven species which are confined to the tropical and subtropical coasts where they occupy the deep-water zones of mangrove belts. The family Avicenniaceae (allied to verbenas) has the one genus, *Avicennia* or grey mangroves: of the two wide-ranging species one comprises the southernmost mangrove stands in Australia, scattered along the south coast in places such as Westernport Bay in Vic. and Spencer Gulf in SA. *Avicennia* dominates mangrove stands on the temperate east coast, although it is frequently accompanied by the smaller river mangrove, *Aegiceras*, the sole mangrove genus of the family Myrsinaceae (mainly rainforest trees and shrubs). Mangroves are particularly diverse on Australia's far northern coast (although still dominated by Rhizophoraceae and *Avicennia*), with fourteen plant families represented in about 20 species.

Mangroves have adopted a variety of mechanisms for dealing with saline conditions, some species apparently filtering out the salt in their roots, others excreting it through leaf glands, and a third group diverting it into particular tissues. Supporting and root-aerating mechanisms also vary – many tropical mangroves display striking stilt-roots or buttresses, or upward-pointing root-prongs (pneumatophores) that emerge from the mud. Another feature of many mangroves is fleshy viviparous seeds that float in the currents and take root almost the moment they are left stranded by the falling tide.

The ecology of mangroves is complex and fascinating. They are most prolific on shores where wave action is not too severe and where freshwater streams deposit large quantities of silt and organic matter – notably the deltas of large tropical rivers. Distribution of the species shows interesting zonation patterns, those most tolerant of waves and salt occurring at the outer edge and those requiring relatively fresh water at the inner. Mangroves provide a hospitable environment for a wide range of other organisms, especially animals. Nutrition is abundant, the long food chains starting with organisms that feed on leaf-litter from the mangroves themselves and ending with the larger predatory fish and birds. It is now recognised that commercial fisheries depend on the continued existence of mangrove stands, which serve as nurseries for many fish species.

Manifold, John Streeter (1915–   ), poet and editor, b. Melbourne. After a period as an editor-translator in Germany, Manifold served with British army intelligence in World War 2. Returning to Australia in 1949, he established the left-wing Realist Writers group, wrote poetry, and made invaluable collections and recordings of bush songs and ballads. He is editor of *Bandicoot Ballads* (1953) and *The Penguin Australian Song Book* (1964); his *Collected Verse* was published in 1978.

Manning River NSW This river rises in the Mount Royal Range about 250km northeast of Sydney and flows some 225km to the sea at Harrington Inlet. The heavily timbered upper reaches are a source of fine eucalypt hardwoods; the river has many tributaries, and drains a large area of the eastern highlands. The lower reaches pass through fertile agricultural land; industries include butter, milk, vegetables and maize, and dairy farms are established on four islands in the stream and near the mouth – Jones, Oxley, Mitchell and Dumaresq. Gloucester, Taree and Wingham are the chief towns of the district.

Mannix, Daniel (1864–1963), Catholic prelate, b. Ireland. Mannix arrived in Australia in 1912 and was Catholic archbishop of Melbourne 1917–63. In his long career, this outspoken churchman had a profound influence on Irish Catholics throughout Australia as the result of his vehemently expressed views: against conscription during World War 1, against capitalism, and against communism (the last promoting the rise of the lay Catholic Action and Catholic Social Studies movements which contributed to the 1955 split in the ALP). He also campaigned vigorously for government aid to Catholic schools.

Mannum SA (pop. 2056) This small town lies on the Murray River about 84km east of Adelaide; it is best known as a major river port from the mid-19th century, and although later bypassed by the railways it revived to become the main service centre for downstream dairy lands. The first Murray River paddlesteamer – the *Mary Ann* – was built at Mannum in 1852 and launched there a year later. Today local industries include tourism, dairying, cereal and sheep farming, and the manufacture of agricultural machinery.

mantids Predatory insects of the order Mantodea, mantids have spined, raptorial forelegs adapted for grasping prey (usually other insects) that they have first struck with a very rapid movement of the forelimbs. The characteristic position of the forelimbs in repose has given rise to the name 'praying mantis'. Mantids are derived from cockroaches, and both orders share the habit of laying eggs in a frothy mass known as an ootheca; females have been known to consume their mates during copulation. More than 120 species are known from Australia, some of which are cryptically coloured to blend with their backgrounds. The most common Australian mantid, *Orthodera* *ministralis*, is green with a purple spot on the inside of the foreleg. Some small species appear to mimic ants – whether as a means of predation, or as protection from predators that would avoid the ants, is unknown.

manufacturing industries Although Australia's secondary industries experienced great growth for more than 20 years after World War 2, the manufacturing sector today is in straitened circumstances. While it is the nation's third-largest employer, supplying jobs in 1985 for 1.01 million people or 18% of the workforce, it produces only 18% of the gross domestic product; the 1% of the workforce employed in the mining sector, on the other hand, produces 5% of GDP. A contrast with earlier years is also salutary: in 1960–1, manufacturing employed 28% of the workforce and produced 29% of GDP.

Historical development In the early days of settlement, the only manufactured articles were the necessities of life such as food, candles and basic tools. As the pastoral economy developed so did concomitant manufacturing industries – flour milling, brewing, ship-building and metal-working – but often to the displeasure of Britain, which saw Australia (like India and Canada) as a market for its own manufactured products. The gold discoveries of the 1850s provided the greatest spur to the development of manufacturing, providing as it did much-needed capital and a large influx of immigrants, many of them skilled. Between 1860 and 1890 all the colonies except SA and Tas. enjoyed boom times, reflected in the manufacturing sector by railway construction, mining and agricultural machinery building, and food processing. Factory employment rose from 11 000 in 1851 to 149 000 in 1891, with a doubling of the manufacturing contribution to GDP over the same period.

Recovery from the depression of the 1890s was rapid, with Federation in 1901 leading to the elimination of internal customs barriers and a limited expansion of external tariff protection, which gave a boost to what was still a small-scale but vibrant manufacturing industry. World War 1 saw the development of a local steel industry, and the immediate postwar years were followed by expansionary fiscal policies made possible by high world prices for wool and wheat. Manufacturing, along with Australia, prospered on both the sheep's back and an increasingly high tariff wall, the latter being seen as essential if Australia was to be self-sufficient. The 1920s saw a dramatic increase in both Australian manufacturing and government recourse to tariffs as a cure-all for industrial ills. The Tariff Board was established in 1921, and although the Brigden Committee of 1927 recommended circumspection in the matter of tariffs its advice was ignored. In effect, excessive tariff protection was perpetuating and feather-bedding basically inefficient manufacturing industries.

Increased tariffs did not protect Australian manufacturing from the effects of the depression in the early 1930s, but may have helped secondary industry lead the country's overall employment recovery in the years before World War 2. By 1939, Australia had major industries in the areas of iron and steel, building products, engineering, electrical goods, clothing, printing and motor assembly. All prospered during the war years, a period that prepared the ground for Australian manufacturing's halcyon phase of 1945–70. During this period Australia experienced sustained growth in all sectors of the economy, with large-scale immigration coupled with capital inflow and new mineral and oil discoveries leading to a maturation of Australia's industrial base. Dramatic expansion took place – particularly in the motor-vehicle, chemical, electrical goods, heavy engineering, construction and metal-fabricating industries.

There was, however, another country undergoing an even more dramatic manufacturing expansion at the time, a country then known mainly for its tinny radios and not taken seriously at all in Australia. The impact of Japan on Australian manufacturing was very gradual, and in fact barely noticed by local industry and its mainly Anglo-American parents in the initial phase. The oil crisis of 1973–4, which led to a worldwide recession resulting in lower growth rates, massive inflation and dramatic wage rises in all sectors of the Australian economy, caused the first significant breach in the Australian manufacturing boom. Despite the imposition of swingeing import restrictions (which negated the basically beneficial impact of certain pre-crisis tariff reductions), Japan entered through the breach, often dumping its manufactured goods if such an expedient was necessary to establish a foothold in a foreign market. As Australia's manufacturing sector shrank, the resources sector expanded and took with it much of Australia's limited investment capital.

The 1980s and beyond The decline of manufacturing in the 1970s continued into the 1980s, with no sign of a reversal except in resource-related industries such as chemicals and aluminium, or service-related industries such as paper-making and publishing. The time-honoured Australian solution of throwing up tariff barriers was, however, increasingly recognised as ineffective, and government policy – as illustrated by the Button Plan (> *motor-vehicle industry*) – moved towards reducing tariff protection and concentrating more on a positive approach incorporating modernisation, rationalisation, research, marketing, and taxation reform.

One major problem is that the bulk of the immense capital inflow into Australia in the 1980s went to mining, services and real estate, and very little to manufacturing. The limited overseas capital that has been invested in manufacturing – usually through corporate purchase – has often been treated with great suspicion: with the motor-vehicle industry already completely in US and Japanese hands, and with many large Australian companies purchasable at bargain prices by world standards, the prospect of further multinational control of Australian manufacturing remains a matter of concern. In 1988, Australian control or equity was lost in Cadbury Schweppes, Thorn EMI, Taubmans and Bushells; many other well-known Australian manufacturers are also owned or controlled by overseas interests, including Arnott's (30% by Campbell's Soup, US), BTR Nylex (63% by BTR Pty Ltd, UK), Commonwealth Industrial Gas (87% by BOC Pty Ltd, UK) and Leighton (50% by Hochtief, West Germany). Concern about losing control of the manufacturing base led the Liberal Party to reverse its policy of abolishing the Foreign Investment Review Board.

The need to expand the traded – and tradeable – goods sector of Australia's export economy is crucial, but the problems are immense: Australian manufacturing plant has been allowed to run down over decades; the quality of locally manufactured goods is often poor; and above all there are few, if any, goods manufactured in Australia that cannot be made better and cheaper elsewhere. In the face of the manufacturing capacity of Asia, in the late 1980s the prospects for Australian manufacturing were bleak. > *economy; tariffs*

maps and mapping The cartographic history of Australia began with the fanciful notions of 16th-century European mapmakers, who postulated the existence of a great southern continent (in part to 'balance' the large land-mass of the northern hemisphere) and included it on maps, calling it variously 'Terra Australis', 'Notasia', 'Maletur' and 'Jave la Grande'. The earliest factual maps are representations of the northwestern Australian coast based on the explorations of Dutch explorers such as Abel Tasman, who ventured southwards from Java. The first authoritative map was produced by James Cook as a result of his *Endeavour* voyage along the eastern Australian coast.

The terrestrial mapping of Australia began soon after settlement. Exploratory expeditions usually included officers with cartographic and navigational experience, and the resulting sketch maps and narrative detail helped to piece together the topography of the coastal areas. Most colonies established the position of surveyor-general to promote inland exploration, and some incumbents, such as John Oxley and Thomas Mitchell in NSW, themselves undertook expeditions. By the end of the 19th century the colonies had all government surveys working to produce maps for land settlement, townships, property boundaries, roads and railways, and some trigonometrical surveys were initiated. After Federation a national program was started under the three armed forces, and the National Mapping Council was established in 1945 to co-ordinate the activities of the Commonwealth and State agencies.

Cartography has become increasingly sophisticated, aerial photography largely replacing many of the older ground-based survey techniques. Modern methods that utilise LANDSAT satellite imagery and other remote sensing techniques have produced a new generation of maps, useful in studying vegetation, geology, pollution, human activity and resource potential.

Hydrographic surveys The mapping of the coastal waters was a major focus of early exploratory voyages, beginning with Matthew Flinders's survey 1801–02. Accurate coastal charts for safe navigation by commercial and naval vessels were of the utmost necessity in an era when all major transport was marine. Among other early surveys were those of Phillip Parker King along the eastern and northern coasts 1817–22, the French expeditions of Louis de Freycinet, Isadore Duperrey and Jules Dumont d'Urville, and Royal Navy surveys under J. C. Wickham, J. L. Stokes, F. P. Blackwood and Owen Stanley. Having made these initial exploratory surveys, the Admiralty negotiated agreements with individual Australian colonies to share the cost of detailed coastal surveys, and in 1908 the Australian government agreed to contribute half the cost of hydrographic work conducted by the Admiralty in Australian waters. The Royal Australian Navy Hydrographic Service was established in 1921 and has been especially active in northern waters, including PNG. Australia now has several computerised surveying vessels that use modern sonar and position-fixing equipment. The RAN Hydrographic Service also publishes tide tables and notices to mariners. >> *discovery, voyages of*; *exploration by land*; *geological surveys*

Maralinga SA This corner of the Nullarbor Plain, 850km northeast of Adelaide, is noted as the site of British nuclear tests 1952–7. In response to public concern about the likely effects of the tests on the region's Aboriginal population, a royal commission was held in 1985: it found, inter alia, that inadequate consultation was held within the federal government before permission was granted to hold the tests, that the Aboriginal owners of the land had been denied reasonable access to the region – which is still prohibited to the public – and that there was residual radioactive contamination (by plutonium) of the land; it assigned responsibility for cleaning up the area the British government. The name Maralinga, appropriately enough, derives from an Aboriginal word meaning 'thunder'.

Marble Bar WA (pop. 332) Putatively Australia's hottest town, Marble Bar lies 1495km north of Perth in the east Pilbara region; it is distinguished not only for its searing summer temperatures, which regularly reach 40°C, but also for having experienced the nation's most protracted heatwave: in 1923–4, when the temperature exceeded 37.8°C for 170 days in a row. Marble Bar is the main centre for the sparsely populated region's pastoral and mining industries; it grew originally (from the 1880s) as a tent town centred on nearby gold deposits. The town, which was declared in 1893, derived its name from the mineralised ridge (in fact composed of jasper) that crosses the Coongan River 3km away.

Mareeba Qld (pop. 6614) This town of the Atherton Tableland, situated on the Barron River some 1779km north of Brisbane, derives its name from the Aboriginal term for 'meeting of the waters'. Tobacco-growing is the main local activity although other crops include rice,

grains, fruits and vegetables, most grown under irrigation; grazing, forestry and mining (at nearby Chillagoe), are also of some importance. Regional tourism is well established, based on the Barron Falls, the limestone caves at Chillagoe, and the town's annual rodeo.

marine borers A group of marine molluscs and crustaceans that attack and destroy wood, marine borers are a pest of wooden wharves and boats. The best known of the molluscs is the bivalve family Teredinidae, commonly called shipworms or pileworms, which are equipped with enzymes to digest the cellulose in standing wooden structures. Notable among crustaceans are the isopods of the genus *Limnoria* which, preferring wood infested with marine fungi, create long tunnels just below the wood surface and feed on the fungi within their galleries. Control of borers is difficult, although treatment with creosote extends the life of timber structures, as do mechanical barriers such as plastic or copper sheathing. Some tree species, such as the Australian turpentine, are naturally resistant to marine borers and so are often used for marine piles.

marine worms The large diversity of worm-like animals grouped as marine worms belong in four phyla: Annelida, Platyhelminthes, Nemertea and Enteropneusto.

Segmented or annelid worms of the phylum Annelida include lug-worms, somewhat resembling earthworms and occurring in wet beach sands, and bristle-worms, which have bristles on each segment. One of these is the surf bait worm, the formidably jawed beach-dweller often sought for bait by surf fishermen, who use a pair of pliers to catch the worm behind the head when it appears above the sand. Some bristle-worms, such as the beautiful feather-duster worm, live in tubes fixed to rocks. Flatworms of the phylum Platyhelminthes are free-living relatives of the parasitic > *flukes* and include the pests of oyster beds, the genus *Leptoplana*, and the colourfully banded magic carpet worm, named for its graceful, gliding motion and seen in the Great Barrier Reef region. Ribbon worms, of the phylum Nemertea, are like long, narrow flatworms but with a narrow sticky proboscis that is protruded and retracted in the search for food, almost like a lassoo. Acorn worms, that belong to the phylum Enteropneusto, are transitional between invertebrates and vertebrates. They are often brilliant yellow in colour, and are common along the Australian coast.

Maritime Strike > *industrial disputes*

marlins > *swordfishes and marlins*

Maroochydore Qld (pop. 20 365 with Mooloolaba) This beach resort lies 112km north of Brisbane, on the Sunshine Coast; in the south it merges with the towns of Mooloolaba and Alexandra Headland. The name is thought to derive from an Aboriginal word meaning 'water where the black swan lives'.

Marree SA (pop. n/a) This small settlement 644km north of Adelaide lies amid thinly peopled pastoral desert country. It is noted mainly for its position at the southern end of the Birdsville Track, for its historical role as a camel-drivers' depot and intercolonial customs post, and (until 1980) as the point where the original central Australian railway changed from narrow to standard gauge.

marriage > *family law*

Marsden, Samuel (1764–1838), Anglican priest, b. England. Marsden arrived in NSW in 1794 as assistant to the Rev. Richard Johnson and for 30 years was a colourful, controversial and influential personality in the colony. As a priest he was vitriolic but deeply sincere in his beliefs; as a magistrate, he was brutal in his sentences, earning criticism and hatred for the floggings he ordered; as a farmer, he pioneered sheep-breeding on a level comparable to that of John Macarthur. In politics, Marsden supported Bligh in 1808 (although in England at the time) blaming Macarthur, whom he hated. He quarrelled with Macquarie, especially over his emancipist policy, and with the ensuing governors, Darling and Brisbane. His influence waned with the decline of the exclusivist faction.

Marshall, Alan (1902–84), author, b. Noorat, Vic. Permanently crippled by poliomyelitis, Marshall moved to Melbourne when he was 16. He contributed whimsical sketches and columns to newspapers and magazines from 1935, after closure of the Melbourne shoe factory in which he was employed as accountant. *Tell Us About the Turkey, Jo* (1946), his first short-story collection, established his mastery of the bush yarn; he achieved dramatic success,

however, with the autobiographical *I Can Jump Puddles* (1955), which has sold more than 3 million copies and was particularly acclaimed in eastern Europe; it was made into a film in Czechoslovakia (1970) and a television series in Australia (1981).

Marshall, Jock (Alan John) (1911–67), zoologist and author, b. Sydney. A colourful and energetic man, Marshall participated in exploring expeditions in Australia, Vanuatu and NG, and later served in the AIF in NG, despite having lost an arm in a shooting accident at the age of 16. After obtaining degrees in England, he was appointed foundation professor of zoology and comparative physiology at Monash University, Melbourne. He wrote many scientific papers and several books, including *The Men and Birds of Paradise* (1938), and *The Great Extermination* (1966); in the latter he emerged as a champion of conservation with a scathing criticism of wildlife exploitation in Australia. His popular work *Journey Among Men* (1962) was written in conjunction with artist Russell Drysdale, and is an account of a journey through the outback.

marsupial mice Although marsupial mice resemble small rodents, they are in fact carnivorous marsupials belonging to the same family (Dasyuridae) as tiger cats and the Tasmanian devil. They have voracious appetites, consuming large numbers of invertebrates and even small vertebrates; most species are nocturnal, and generally construct underground nests. In Australia, about 37 species fall into four main groups: the broad-footed marsupial mice, genera *Antechinus* and *Phascogale*; the planigales, genus *Planigale*; the narrow-footed marsupial mice or dunnarts, *Sminthopsis*; and the kultarr or jerboa marsupial, *Antechinomys*, which has a very long tail and resembles the true jerboa (a rodent). Although rarely visible, marsupial mice exist in a variety of habitats, and are often abundant; some species are, however, threatened by habitat destruction and by predation of foxes and feral cats.

marsupial mole The small, blind, burrowing marsupial mole, *Notoryctes typhlops*, is found in sand-ridge deserts from central Australia to the northwest. It has a stocky body and stout limbs adapted for digging; two of the foreclaws are spade-like and extremely large, and the nose has a horny shield for pushing aside sand. Its eyes are degenerate and functionless and there are no external ears – only small holes under the fur, yet hearing is apparently acute. The fur varies from cream to reddish-gold. Very little is known of its habits but it prefers deep, sandy soil, spending most of its time underground and apparently feeding primarily on insect larvae. Although it is seldom seen, this bizarre little animal is apparently widespread and not rare; only its cryptic lifestyle prevents it from being commonly encountered.

marsupials In contrast to the placental mammals, a group in which the young (attached to a placenta) undergo most development within the female, pouched mammals of the order Marsupiala produce young at a very early stage of development; special adaptations enable the offspring to crawl unaided to the mother's pouch, in which they are suckled until able to survive in the outside world. There are marsupials in the Americas (including the opossums), NG and the Molucca Islands, and fossil remains are found in Europe; it is postulated that these animals came to Australia via Gondwana, and that after Australia became separated from that continent they were able to flourish in isolation, with no competition from placental mammalian carnivores and herbivores (> *fauna*). From ancestral roots, common descent is shown by a characteristic flanged lower jaw not found in placentals, but the evolution of marsupials has been remarkably varied, often showing concurrence in form and habits with the evolution of placental mammals elsewhere in the world.

There are in all nineteen marsupial families, of which sixteen are native to the Australian region and divide naturally into four broad groups. The carnivorous and insectivorous order Dasyurida includes > *marsupial mice,* > *native and tiger cats,* the > *Tasmanian devil* and the > *thylacine.* The order Myrmecobiidae comprises a single species of specialised feeders, the > *numbat;* as does the order Notoryctemorpha, of which the > *marsupial mole* is the sole member. The order Peramelina has two families of mixed feeders, including the > *bandicoots.* The ten families of the order Diprotodonta, by contrast, are mostly vegetarian: they include > *possums,* > *koalas,* > *wombats,* and > *kangaroos, wallabies and allies.*

Martens, Conrad (1801–78), painter, b. England. Martens was a notable colonial artist, who arrived in Australia in 1835 after serving as a topographic artist on the survey vessel *Beagle*. The first colonial landscape painter to make a substantial living from his art – largely through commissions – he produced many fine watercolours of Sydney Harbour and (although fewer in number) of rural NSW and Qld. He turned his hand to lithography in the 1840s, publishing an edition of Sydney views in 1843, and later to astronomy.

Martin, Sir James (1820–86), lawyer and politician, b. Ireland. Martin arrived in Australia with his family in 1821 and was a noted journalist and essayist in his youth. He graduated in law in 1845, was editor of the newspaper *Atlas* 1845–7 and a year later began his long career in NSW politics. Premier three times (1863–5, 1866–8 and 1870–2) and a distinguished chief justice 1873–86, he was one of the key personalities in the turbulent politics of NSW in the later part of the 19th century. Martin Place in Sydney is named after him.

martins > *swallows and martins*

Maryborough Qld (pop. 20 177) This city, port and industrial centre lies on the Mary River 269km north of Brisbane. It was settled in the 1840s and became a port for local produce (notably timber, sugar and other crops) from the 1860s. Today industries include sawmilling, sugar refining, tourism, grazing and engineering.

Mary Kathleen Qld This former mining town near Mt Isa, 1810km northwest of Brisbane, was for a time at the centre of public controversy over uranium mining. A substantial deposit of uranium ore was found in 1954 and a model township, mine and treatment plant followed; the settlement was named after the wife of Norman McConachy, one of the ore discoverers. Mining continued sporadically until operations finally ceased in 1982; a year later the whole town was auctioned and the site has now been overgrown and little sign remains of the settlement.

Masson, Sir David Orme (1858–1937) chemist, b. England. Masson was a gifted teacher and administrator for 36 years at the University of Melbourne, finally becoming dean of the science faculty. He founded two chemical societies, became foundation president of the Australian Chemical Institute in 1917 and president of the National Research Council in 1922. He chaired the committee that planned and in 1926 saw the establishment of the Council for Scientific and Industrial Research, and a long involvement with Antarctic research began with his assistance in the organisation of Douglas Mawson's expedition (1911).

Mawson > *Antarctic Territory*

Mawson, Sir Douglas (1882–1958), explorer and geologist, b. England. Mawson came with his family to Australia in 1886. Graduating from Sydney University, in 1905 he was appointed lecturer at Adelaide University, later becoming professor of geology. As a member of Ernest Shackleton's Antarctic expedition of 1907, Mawson took part in the first ascent of Mt Erebus and the first journey to reach the south magnetic pole. He led the Australian Antarctic Expedition of 1911–14 which mapped 1500km of coast and explored inland in places to 500km, during which Mawson achieved perhaps the greatest feat of endurance in Antarctic exploration – his return alone to base camp after the death of two companions. His subsequent publication, *The Home of the Blizzard* (1915), is a classic of polar literature. Two journeys to Antarctica led by Mawson 1929–31 conducted marine and aerial surveys; he was instrumental in the establishment of the Australian National Antarctic Research Expedition (1947) and of the Antarctic Division of the Department of External Affairs (1948). Australia's chief Antarctic base now bears his name.

May, Phil(ip Williams) (1864–1903), cartoonist, b. England. Invited to Australia to join the Sydney *Bulletin* in 1885, May in just three years produced more than 900 drawings, many dealing with the critical political issues of the day. His insight into character, and his deft draughtsmanship and powerful portraiture established him as one of the finest black-and-white artists in Australian history. After returning to England in 1895, he worked for *Punch* and other periodicals and many volumes of his work were published.

Meale, Richard Graham (1932–), composer, b. Sydney. Arguably Australia's major contemporary composer, Meale was trained at the NSW Conservatorium of Music and the University of California. A prolific and eclectic musician, in his work Meale has ranged from the extremes of avant-garde to the traditional. He was also the first of local com-

posers to be influenced by oriental music, notably in *Images (Naguata)* (1966) and *Clouds Now and Then* (1969). His opera, *Voss* (1987), based on the novel by Patrick White, with a libretto by David Malouf, has been both a popular and a critical success.

mechanics institutes Also known as artisans' schools or schools of art, these organisations – originating in Britain in the 1820s – were established in Australia soon after to help educate working men and to teach trade skills. They subsequently assumed wider educational importance for the community, offering library facilities and lectures on a broad range of topics. Buildings known as mechanics institutes were erected in many Australian towns and some are still extant, although most were converted for recreational use early in the 20th century. Sydney Technical College and the Royal Melbourne Institute of Technology both began as working men's colleges established under the aegis of mechanics institutes.

media ownership and control Australia has arguably the most concentrated media ownership of all free-enterprise economies. Federal law has regulated ownership of broadcast outlets since 1942 and indirectly affects newspaper ownership.

Broadcast media In 1987 and 1988, changes to the Broadcasting Act caused substantial shifts in television ownership patterns. The original law restricted control by a single owner to two television stations; no owner could control more than eight radio licences, of which no more than four could be in metropolitan areas or in a single State. The changes eliminated the two-station rule and substituted the concept of 'audience reach': no single owner of television stations is allowed more than 60% of the national audience; the allowable number of radio licences was increased to sixteen, but no more than half of these may be in a single service area. New provisions prohibit television owners from having more than a 5% interest in any daily English-language paper in the same capital city as their television interests, prohibit radio owners from controlling daily papers in the same market, and prevent either group owning another broadcast outlet in the same market. Further amendments (to be introduced progressively in the 1990s) aim to give regional viewers access to three commercial television stations by expanding the size of delineated 'approved markets', in each of which owners may hold only one licence. Clauses preventing foreign ownership of Australian broadcasting licences remain in force.

A flurry of ownership changes following the amendments resulted in three main television networks by early 1989: Seven (owned by Universal Telecasters), Nine (Bond Media) and Ten (Northern Star Ltd); by the end of that year, however, liquidity problems had caused all but Nine to be sold yet again. A further seven companies hold most of the remaining commercial television and radio licences.

Newspapers Newspaper ownership is highly concentrated. The take-over of the Herald & Weekly Times group by > *Rupert Murdoch*'s News Ltd in early 1987 consolidated this trend, which began after World War 2. In 1910, Australia's seventeen metropolitan daily newspapers – which served a population of 4.5 million – were all individually owned. By 1960 the Herald & Weekly Times controlled 47.5% of the nation's metropolitan daily circulation and the Fairfax group (> *Fairfax family*) another 26%, these figures remaining relatively constant until the late 1980s. By mid-1988, however, two of the nineteen metropolitan dailies had closed, ten had changed hands (three of them twice), and only seven were with their original owners; News Ltd controlled nine, accounting for 61.6% of total circulation, and Fairfax three (18%).

Concentration of ownership has also characterised country and suburban newspapers. In 1947, most of them were owned by small independents and the largest chain comprised eight papers; by the end of the 1980s, however, the majority of country and suburban papers were in the hands of the two major companies, with News Ltd controlling nearly 53% of the circulation of weekly papers. >> *broadcasting*; *freedom of the press*; *newspapers*

medical research Medical research began in Australia largely as the work of individual doctors and scientists who sought answers to the common health problems of the day. Today most research is carried out in universities, teaching hospitals and medical institutes: by the mid-1980s more than $200 million was spent on medical research each year, nearly three-quarters of which was provided by the federal government in the form of direct grants to specialist organisations such as the National Heart Foundation or funds allocated to hospitals and universities. As with science gen-

erally, the level of private-sector support for medical research in Australia is low by world standards and in fact decreased by more than 3% between 1975 and 1985. In 1987, Australia's pharmaceutical industry spent some $32 million – or 2.9% of turnover – on medical research; in the UK, by comparison, the industry provided about 66% of all funding for medical research in that country, or 20% of the value of its sales.

Historical development The first medical researcher was probably John White, the principal surgeon of the First Fleet. His search for treatments for the common illnesses of scurvy and dysentery led to the remedial use of various native plants including eucalypts, grass-trees and sarsaparilla. The spread of settlement into the tropical north brought a need for research into tropical medicine. Important work was done in this field by Joseph Bancroft and his son Thomas (> *Bancroft family*) in the late 19th and early 20th centuries, and by the Australian Institute of Tropical Medicine, which was set up in Townsville in 1909. The country's earliest official research unit was the NSW Bureau of Microbiology, established in 1908. Its first director, Frank Tidswell, working with J. Ashburton Thompson, was responsible for demonstrating that bubonic plague was transmitted via rat fleas; another notable researcher with the organisation was > *J. B. Cleland*.

Research into infectious diseases dominated Australian medical research until after World War 2, when effective antibiotics and better living conditions reduced mortality from those causes. Despite meagre funding and the emigration of many scientists in the 'brain drain' that characterised the first half of the 20th century, Australia's major research institutions were all established by the 1940s; the first was the > *Walter and Eliza Hall Institute* in Melbourne, founded in 1916. Since World War 2, the emphasis of medical research has shifted to contemporary ills (such as mental disease, cancer, and diseases of the circulatory system) and new medical technology such as microsurgery, ultrasonics and > *biotechnology*.

Research organisations and funding The National Health and Medical Research Council is the principal federal government body involved in medical research, both advising the government and administering funds; its budget in 1989 was $72.7 million. Most of the council's funds are allocated as project grants for individual investigators in universities, hospitals and centres of advanced education; not all recommended projects are funded, however, owing to a shortage of funds. The five major medical research institutes – the Walter and Eliza Hall Institute, the Howard Florey Institute, the Baker Medical Research Institute, and the Garvan Institute (all in Melbourne), and the Murdoch Institute in Sydney – receive 18.8% of the funds allocated by the council. Its remaining funds are distributed as program grants, fellowships, training awards, and special awards for research into particular health issues.

Medical research in Australia covers all health areas, although government funds are allocated according to the quality of the proposed project and community needs. Considerable financial support is now being given by the State and federal governments for research into > AIDS, which is being undertaken in a variety of disciplines: pharmacologists are testing new drugs to combat the disease, epidemiologists are studying its spread from one risk group to another, health educators are developing and testing prevention programs, and virologists are studying the structure and reproduction of HIV, the virus responsible.

As in other western countries the Australian government is concerned to encourage more commercial investment in medical research and is encouraging research groups to find business sponsorship for their projects. These increasingly are being assessed according to their potential for commercial development and many universities have formed companies to sell the results of their research. Despite constant battles for funding, Australia continues to make major contributions to international medical investigations. The Walter and Eliza Hall Institute, for example, has done pioneering research into malaria and is currently developing a genetically engineered malaria vaccine. Australia was also a world leader in the development of in-vitro fertilisation (> IVF), which led to the export of IVF techniques to countries such as the US. >> biotechnology; health and health services; science and technology

Medicare > health and health services; social services

Melaleuca > myrtle family

Melba, Dame Nellie [Helen Porter Mitchell] (1861–1931), b. Richmond, Vic. Melba began her professional singing career in 1884 and left for London in 1886; she was trained in Paris by the renowned teacher Madame Marchesi, and in 1887 made a successful opera debut in Brussels. Two years later she received acclaim in London for her role as Juliet in Romeo and Juliet (1889) and from that point enjoyed a long and successful association with Covent Garden. Throughout her career she sang in Europe and the US as well as in London, and made many appearances in Australia, which she first toured 1902–03. In 1913 she donated the proceeds from one of her Melbourne appearances to build the Melba Hall at the Conservatorium of Music at the University. She made her final Covent Garden appearance in 1926.

Melbourne Vic. The capital of Vic. and Australia's second-largest city, Melbourne is today also second to Sydney as a commercial and industrial capital but remains the principal centre for banking and mining finance. Like Sydney, it faces problems in the areas of housing, unemployment and traffic congestion. Melbourne is centred on the Yarra River, with suburbs extending eastward around Port Phillip Bay to Westernport, northwest beyond Werribee and northeast to the Plenty valley and Dandenong Ranges. The climate is generally temperate, with mean temperatures ranging from 14.9°C to 26.5°C, and an average annual rainfall of 657mm distributed evenly over the year. Contrary to its reputation, Melbourne is not especially prone to rain, wet days averaging about 120 per year.

Melbourne derives its name from William Lamb, 2nd Viscount Melbourne, a British prime minister of the Victorian era. In 1835 John Batman and John Fawkner, both from Tas., established British settlements in what became the Port Phillip District, and the Aborigines were gradually dispersed; the government in Sydney recognised the settlements were there to stay, and dispatched William Lonsdale to Port Phillip as resident magistrate. During the 1840s Melbourne grew steadily, but the gold rushes of the 1850s trebled its population in three years, and from then until the 1890s it was Australia's largest city, remaining the financial capital until the 1970s. From Federation in 1901 until 1927 Melbourne was the seat of the federal government and temporarily official capital of Australia. After World War 2 it expanded rapidly as a result of immigration and industrial development, but the recession of the 1970s hit the Vic. capital badly, largely because manufacturing there relied heavily on the clothing and motor-vehicle industries.

At the census of 1986 the Melbourne Statistical Division had a population of 2 832 893, which showed a growth rate of 4.04% over the five years between censuses. A relatively large proportion of the population is of Greek or Italian descent. As elsewhere, the inner suburbs have declined in population, with lower-paid workers and the unemployed pushed by the more affluent into the outer suburbs with little access to the urban amenities. Melbourne's manufacturing sector still produces about 28% of Australia's manufactured goods, but declines in this sector have slowed the city's growth rate. Newer, large-scale industrial centres have grown up in the outer suburbs, especially in the vicinity of Westernport Bay. Motor vehicles in Melbourne, as elsewhere, constitute the main means of transport (though Melbourne is the only Australian city to have retained trams as a major part of its transport system), and there are growing problems of congestion and pollution. There are also problems for the unemployed, and others who cannot afford motor vehicles: in the 1960s and 1970s the State government constructed cheap high-rise housing near the city, but this proved unpopular and the emphasis is now on low- and medium-rise accommodation.

Melbourne Cup Racing was established in Melbourne in 1838, but in the early years bickering between rival clubs threatened its survival. Stability was established with the formation in 1864 of the Victoria Racing Club, which inherited the Melbourne Cup from the Victoria Turf Club. The first Cup was run in 1861: at that meeting only four races were on the program, which contained many other entertainments for the 4000 spectators; Archer, at 6/1, completed the 2-mile course with the slowest ever time of 3.52 min. From these humble beginnings, the event on the first Tuesday in November has become one of the world's great races, and a national institution: a public holiday is declared in Melbourne, and across the nation Australians stop to listen to or watch the race. Despite attempts by other clubs to match its prize money, the Melbourne Cup remains Australia's pre-eminent racing event. Great winners include Carbine (1890), Phar Lap (1930), Peter Pan (1932, 1934), Rain Lover (1968, 1969) and Think Big (1974, 1975). >> *horse-racing*

Meldrum (Duncan) Max (1875–1955), painter, b. Scotland. A controversial but influential figure in Australian art (especially between the two world wars), Meldrum ex- pounded his own theory of 'tonal realism' (limited colour range, minimal drawing, realistic rendition) to a wide and receptive audience. He was a successful portraitist, although his obsession with scientific theory had a stultifying effect on his later work.

Meliaceae > *mahogany family*

Melville Island NT A large island of low wooded hills and mangrove swamp, Melville Island lies off northwest Arnhem Land, forming the western shore of Van Diemen Gulf. It is an Aboriginal reserve. Sighted by Tasman in 1644, surveyed by Phillip Parker King in 1818 and named after the First Lord of the Admiralty, it saw the establishment of an illfated convict settlement on Apsley Strait at Fort Dundas, 1824–9. This is now the site of a Roman Catholic mission, Garden Point. The Tiwi Aborigines were the original inhabitants of the island, which is no longer Crown land as ownership passed to the Tiwi Land Council (composed of tribal elders) in 1978. There is some pearling and trepang-fishing off the coast, and timber-getting and sawmilling have been established at the government settlement at Milikapiti. The Aborigines know the island as Yermalner.

Menzies, Sir Robert Gordon (1894– 1978), politician, b. Jeparit, Vic. Australia's longest-serving prime minister, Menzies was a barrister before being elected to the Vic. parliament in 1928. Entering federal parliament in 1934 as a member of the United Australia Party, he became prime minister in 1939 but resigned in 1941 because of dissatisfaction with his leadership. By 1945 he had nevertheless formed a new > *Liberal Party* which he led to victory in 1949, remaining prime minister until his retirement in 1966. His period in office was one of major economic growth and stability, notable for the encouragement of foreign investment, a large immigration program, the establishment of numerous social services and the introduction of tertiary education grants. Although a man of ready wit and charm, Menzies was ruthless with his opponents and emasculated the Labor Party during his term of office. An emotional attachment to Britain was tempered with a realistic appraisal of the US role in Australia's future security. Domestic success was not always matched internationally: he took little interest in Asia, supported the white minority regimes in southern Africa, and was instrumental in the failure of the UK mission to Egyptian president G.A. Nasser over the Suez Canal nationalisation in 1956. A conservative with some unusually progressive social views, Menzies is remembered with respect, if not always with affection.

Meredith, Louisa Anne (1812–95), author and artist, b. England. Meredith, who married her cousin in 1839, had already published articles and verse before arriving in Australia in 1840. *Notes and Sketches of New South Wales* (1844) and *My Home in Tasmania* (1852), which record her early years in the colonies in an amusing, acutely observant (sometimes caustic) manner, were enormously popular in Britain and Australia. She published nineteen major books in all, was a talented artist who illustrated many other books, and an early and effective and conservationist. Her husband **Charles** (1811–80), b. England, was the son of early Tas. settler George Meredith. Encouraged by his wife, he became a member of the Tas. parliament and introduced important legislation for the protection of Tas. wildlife.

merinos > *sheep*; *wool*

Mersey River Tas. Rising in the north of the State on the central plateau west of Great Lake, the Mersey flows north, east and north again for some 160km before entering Bass Strait at Devonport. It has numerous meltwater tributaries and has cut deep gorges in its passage through the plateau – some nearly 600m deep. There are interesting limestone caves upstream from Mole Creek, and the D'Alton Falls on the Mersey are contained in Cradle Mountain-Lake St Clair National Park. On the upper course, two reservoirs supply the Rowallan and Fisher power stations.

Messenger, Dally (Herbert Henry) > *rugby*

messmate > *eucalypts*

meteorites Meteorites are fragments of small planetary bodies that have fallen to earth; most large ones are composed of iron-nickel alloys. The largest examples in Australia are two pieces weighing 12t and 8t; found on the Nullabor Plain, WA, they originally formed a single mass. Meteorite craters are evidence of past tremendous impacts in which the meteorites disinte-

grated; the three major craters in Australia are at Wolf Creek in the Kimberley, WA (the largest, 853m in diameter), and at Henbury (210m) and Box Hole (174m) near Alice Springs, NT. Other remnants of rock falls from outer space are tektites, small, glassy stones often found on desert surfaces in southern and central Australia, where they are called 'australites'. They are believed to originate as molten particles thrown into orbit by meteor impact, which upon re-entering the atmosphere fall to the ground. Large or well-formed australites were valued by the Aborigines as magical objects.

meteorology > *climate*

Methodist Church > *religion*; *Uniting Church*

mice > *marsupial mice*; *rats and mice*

Michell, Keith (1928–   ), actor, b. Adelaide. After training as an artist, Michell joined the Old Vic Theatre School in London in 1949. A versatile actor, he has performed in productions ranging from classical theatre to Broadway musicals, most notably in *Irma La Douce* (1958) and *Man of La Mancha* (1968), but is perhaps best known for his role in the BBC series 'The Six Wives of Henry VIII' (1970). He was artistic director of the Chichester Festival Theatre 1974–7.

Middleback Range SA This series of hills, west of Spencer Gulf and about 260km northwest of Adelaide, is noted for deposits of high-grade haematite iron ore that has been mined since early this century and was Australia's major source of iron ore before developments in the Hamersley Range of WA. The highest point of the range is Mt Middleback (380m); mining is centred at Iron Prince; the ore is shipped to Whyalla from the township of Iron Knob, which like the Iron Monarch mine lies some 30km north of the Middleback Range.

midges > *flies*

Miklouho-Maclay, Nicolai Nicolaievitch (1846–88), scientist and explorer, b. Russia. Known for his anthropological and ethnological studies of Melanesians, in 1871 Miklouho-Maclay set up a base at Astrolabe Bay, NG, and later undertook many other expeditions to the Philippines, Celebes (now Sulawesi) and Moluccas, and to Malaya. He campaigned vigorously against the white exploitation of natives and was responsible for the establishment of a marine studies laboratory at Watsons Bay, Sydney, in 1881. Part of his specimen collection is in the Macleay Museum at the University of Sydney.

Mildura Vic. (pop. 20 512) This city on the Murray River, some 557km northwest of Melbourne, is the centre for the Mallee agricultural lands. Formerly an important riverboat town, Mildura was also the site of one of Australia's first major irrigation projects, developed by the > *Chaffey brothers*. Fruit-growing – still the region's principal activity – was established soon afterwards and Mildura produces 80% of the nation's dried fruits; it is also the State's principal wine-producing region.

Milingimbi Island NT Close to the northern coast of Arnhem Land, Milingimbi forms the west shore of Castlereagh Bay. In 1923 a Methodist mission was established on the island; population is small (564), but the Uniting Church is still represented there. The original island-dwellers were the Djinang Aborigines.

military awards > *honours and awards*

Miller, Godfrey (1893–1964), artist, b. NZ. After studying art at London's Slade School, Miller settled in Sydney in 1948 and was an influential art-teacher for some years. A figurative painter whose affection for ancient Egyptian and Chinese art was reflected in the classical subject-matter of his work, he was at the same time a metaphysical artist noted for his innovative use of form and colour. Painstaking in their execution, his paintings were exhibited throughout the 1950s in London and Australia, and a large retrospective exhibition was staged in Sydney in 1965.

Miller, Keith > *cricket*

Millicent SA (pop. 8640) The regional centre for the State's rural southeast, Millicent lies 409km southeast of Adelaide. The region's main activities are farming, fishing, and forestry based on pine plantations at Snuggery and Mt Burr; the town's industries include two paper mills. Nearby features include Canunda National Park, an important fauna habitat, and the Wyrie peat swamp which has yielded the immaculately preserved remains of prehistoric Aboriginal tools.

millipedes > *centipedes and millipedes*

mimosas > *legumes; wattle*

mineral sands and rare earths Australia is the largest producer and exporter of beach-sand minerals, supplying about 47% of the world's rutile, 19% of ilmenite, 61% of zircon and 60% of monazite, a rare-earth phosphate. This pre-eminence has been eroded in recent years, however, because of low prices, higher mining costs and increased international competition.

Until the 1970s mining was confined mainly to Qld and NSW, but WA is now becoming the leading producer because of both declining grades and concern about the effects of mining along the eastern seaboard; the controversial Fraser Island mining venture, begun in 1975 despite conservationists' objections, was the subject of a government inquiry that resulted in 1976 in a ban on the export of Fraser Island sands. Two of Australia's richest deposits are in the Capel-Bunbury and Eneabba areas of WA. It is expected that any new developments in the industry, including processing, will occur in the west even though WA deposits are more expensive to mine, being 'dry mined' (using heavy earth-moving equipment) rather than 'wet mined' (using dredges) as on the east coast. With diminishing world supplies of natural rutile, two synthetic rutile plants have been built in WA.

Monazite, which contains many rare-earth elements and thorium, is recovered as a by-product of titanium (itself derived from rutile and ilmenite) and zirconium concentrates. As Australia is the world's largest producer of monazite, consideration is being given to the establishment of local separation plants.

miner-birds > *honeyeaters*

mining industry Mining has been central to the Australian economy since the 19th century, as both a catalyst to national development and a major source of export income. Australia is nearly self-sufficient in minerals and is a leading world supplier of mineral commodities from aluminium to zircons, mining exports being valued at more than $13 000 million in 1985. This position has been achieved despite remoteness from traditional markets, high transport costs, and physical limitations to exploration in an arid continent.

While Australia's mineral earnings continue to grow, the industry has slowed since the

1970s, largely because mine profitability is so closely tied to both the fluctuating exchange rate and equally unstable commodity prices. The inevitable depletion of Australia's mineral reserves has intensified exploration, but the search for new and economic mineral provinces requires increasingly sophisticated and capital-intensive techniques, and searches have been halted periodically until some measure of reward for the risks involved has been restored.

Historical development Mining and mineral processing began with the quarrying of sandstone and the burning of shells from Aboriginal middens (to produce lime for mortar) at the initial Sydney Cove settlement. Coal was discovered at Newcastle, NSW, in 1791 and was being exported by 1800.

Iron ore was the first metalliferous mineral detected in Australia and pig iron was produced from a trial furnace in 1848: one of the resulting wrought-iron spades was used to turn the first sod for the Sydney–Parramatta railway. There were a number of early discoveries in SA, with a silver-lead mine operating at Glen Osmond from 1841; copper mining commenced a year later at Kapunda, followed by discoveries at Burra, Moonta and Wallaroo which soon made SA a significant exporter of minerals.

The discovery of > *gold* profoundly affected the development of the colonies from the 1850s: the search for minerals encouraged exploration of the hinterland and an influx of immigrants; towns, roads, railways and ports were established to service the mines and miners; industries sprang up to supply the burgeoning population; and finance organisations were set up to meet the demand for capital formation. Further metal ores were discovered in the 1870s and 1880s – tin and copper in NSW and Tas., gold and copper at Mt Morgan in Qld, and the mountain of silver-lead-zinc ores at Broken Hill, NSW. The interaction of management and workers in the coal- and metal-mining industries changed the pattern of industrial relations in the colonies and is still an important socioeconomic force. These industries spawned some of the earliest craft associations and Broken Hill was a union town by 1884. Increasingly protracted strikes in 1889, 1890 and 1892 left simmering discontent which was fuelled by health problems associated with the industry: fierce confrontations during World War 1 culminated in an eighteen-month strike in 1919–20, which produced better working conditions and a more conciliatory approach to industrial relations generally.

In 1907 mineral production in Australia reached $56 million, its highest point for another 30 years. The first decades of the new century were marked by the commencement of the steel industry in NSW (at Lithgow from 1900 and Newcastle from 1915), the discovery of lead, zinc and copper deposits at Mt Isa, Qld, in 1923, and the first sand-mining operations (at Byron Bay, NSW, in 1934). During World War 2, many minerals (including magnesium and scheelite) were mined for strategic purposes; uranium exploration and the manufacture of yellowcake were initiated from 1947. Mineral production intensified after the war, with substantial assistance from overseas (particularly US) sources. Major discoveries in the 1960s, most notably nickel in WA, led to a mineral boom which nearly quadrupled the value of production between 1960 and 1970. By 1980, mineral production was worth some $7400 million and the value of exports exceeded that of pastoral and agricultural commodities.

The 1980s and beyond New tools for the scientific exploration and evaluation of minerals, such as geochemical searches and satellite scanning of sites, are altering the balance in favour of economic discoveries. Mines opened in the 1980s – particularly for gold, bauxite and diamonds – are likely to ensure the growth of mineral exports for some time to come. Prior to World War 2, Australia's main markets were Europe and the UK, but this situation has since changed markedly and Asia was buying 63% of all mineral exports by 1985. Japan has been the major market since the 1960s, although the rapid industrialisation of other Asian nations such as South Korea, China and India may alter this balance in the future.

The mining industry has faced new problems in recent years. First, it no longer has carte blanche for exploration and development: many companies are feeling the pinch of protracted negotiations for the use of land granted to Aboriginal communities since the 1970s (particularly in the NT and Qld), and of increasingly rigorous controls on extraction and processing activities owing to their damaging effects on the environment. Second, the disturbingly high incidence of mining-related diseases such as silicosis and mesothelioma has focused attention on the very real health hazards associated with the industry. Restrictions on the industry to reduce health dangers and environmental damage, and high industrial costs (for exploration, freight, and taxes and royalties) are in some cases proving prohibitive.

mint family The Lamiaceae (or Labiatae) family of flowering plants has many aromatic herbaceous members in the northern hemisphere, including culinary herbs such as the mints, thymes, marjoram, sage, bergamot and basil. In the southern hemisphere it has a number of more shrubby genera, some species even attaining small-tree size. Australia has 20 genera with a total of around 200 species. The largest is the mint-bush genus *Prostanthera*, of around 80 species concentrated mainly in the south and east. These are mostly small to medium-sized shrubs, the bruised foliage giving off a variety of aromas and their massed bell-shaped flowers often showy. The Vic. Christmas bush, *P. lasianthos*, which can grow to a 10m tree and bears profuse near-white flowers in summer, extends through the mountain forests of the four eastern states. The closely related genus *Westringia* has about 25 species of mostly lower shrubs, including the native rosemary, *W. fruticosa*, of exposed seashores in NSW. Unrelated is the genus *Plectranthus* (also diverse in Africa) with about fifteen native species of attractive subshrubs occurring mostly on rocky outcrops. Cosmopolitan genera represented in Australia by a few native species include *Mentha* (the mint genus), *Teucrium, Ajuga, Scutellaria, Ocimum* and *Salvia*.

Missionaries Plain NT A sandy area between the Macdonnell and James ranges, this plain is crossed by the Finke River. It was suggested by George Goyder, SA surveyor-general, as a suitable area for Aboriginal mission work, and takes its name from the Hermannsburg Lutheran Mission established there in 1877.

missions and reserves Religious missions were part of the baggage of 19th-century colonialism and in Australia were commonly under the indirect control of governments through their leasing of mission land to the churches. While missions were generally established for the specific purpose of converting and educating Aborigines, most of the early reserves were created as a means of segregating Aboriginal communities from the white settlers, ostensibly for their mutual protection.

By the mid-19th century, various religious groups including Methodists and Lutherans had founded Aboriginal missions in all the eastern colonies. In keeping with government policies of 'protection' for Aborigines, these were intended to provide shelter and some physical security as well as spiritual education; they achieved few converts, however, and in uprooting Aborigines from their traditional lands deprived them of their fundamental source of physical, social and spiritual sustenance. Mission leases were frequently revoked by the colonial governments in favour of settlers, and most had closed or were abandoned by the end of the 19th century.

Also as part of the government's protection policies, reserves were established throughout the 19th century to accommodate Aboriginal communities. Invariably in remote and isolated regions, often far from the residents' traditional lands, they became an effective means of incarcerating a rapidly dwindling but burdensome population. There, as in the missions, the life and opportunities of Aborigines were rigorously controlled, with a resulting loss of both individual and community autonomy. With the expansion of white settlement into outlying areas, part-Aborigines were commonly removed from their families and dispatched to missions or reserves. The development of reserves during this period was generally ad hoc and they were often declared around existing Aboriginal settlements on the urban fringe to ensure continuing division between the black and white communities.

By the early 20th century there was increasing public concern at the conditions being experienced by the Aboriginal people. New and much larger reserves of traditional lands began to be set aside in outback SA, WA and the NT from the 1920s onwards, including the vast Arnhem Land reserve which was created in 1931. This encouraged a further period of missionary expansion, again most notably by the Methodists. The remoteness of the reserves remained a barrier to improved conditions for Aborigines until the concerted political activity of the 1960s. The government policy of assimilation proposed from the 1930s onwards was gradually replaced by one of self-determination and economic independence for Aborigines, and since the 1970s most of the original missions and reserves have been transferred to the control of Aboriginal communities. While the majority live in towns and cities, many have chosen to return to the self-governing reserves and a more traditional way of life. >> *Aboriginal culture and society; Australian Inland Mission; land rights, Aboriginal*

mistletoe bird Belonging to a group known as flower-peckers, the mistletoe bird, *Dicaeum* *hirundinaceum*, dwells in the treetops throughout most of the mainland, feeding largely on the berries of native mistletoe and thereby helping in their dissemination. The glossy-feathered male is blue-black with a bright-red breast and a red patch under the tail; the female's colouring is duller. Mistletoe birds construct remarkable nests woven of white plant-down and cobwebs, and suspended from a branch.

mistletoes The Loranthaceae family of flowering-plants is most diverse in the tropics and southern hemisphere. All its members are parasitic on other plants, robbing them of water and nutrients. Australia has 70 species in twelve genera, the majority of which are true (twining) mistletoes. The most widespread genera are *Amyema* and *Lysiana*, with 36 and eight native species respectively. They occur in most vegetation types and on a wide range of host trees, though many *Amyema* species are restricted to eucalypts or acacias. Mistletoes spread by sticky seeds contained in fleshy fruits that attract birds: the mistletoe bird, *Dicaeum hirundinaceum*, depends on mistletoe fruits for its diet. Two endemic genera are terrestrial plants, forming underground connections to the roots of host plants: *Nuytsia*, the sole species of which is the WA Christmas bush, produces masses of bright-orange blossom in early summer and is WA's most spectacular flowering tree; the shrubby *Atkinsonia*, also a single-species genus, is endemic to the Blue Mountains of NSW.

A related family of mistletoes is the Viscaceae, to which the European mistletoe, *Viscum album*, belongs. It is represented in Australia by fourteen species in three genera. Some of its species may parasitise other mistletoes of family Loranthaceae – that is, they are parasites on parasites.

Mitchell, David Scott (1836–1907), bibliophile and benefactor, b. Sydney. Of independent means, Mitchell qualified as a barrister but had no interest in law, politics or business. The study of English literature dominated his life until c.1886, when – probably influenced by publisher and bookseller George Robertson, an ardent collector of Australiana – he set out to acquire as many documents and memorabilia as possible that related to Australia. The resulting collection – which included, inter alia, more than 60 000 volumes – was bequeathed on his death to the Public Library of NSW and con-

stitutes the base from which the Mitchell Library grew. He also made a financial bequest of £70 000 for construction of the library building.

Mitchell, Dame Roma Flinders (1913–), lawyer, b. Adelaide. Mitchell graduated in law from the University of Adelaide; she was Australia's first female QC (1962) and Supreme Court judge (1965), and has specialised in family and criminal law. A judge of the SA Supreme Court 1965–83, she was also chairman of the Commonwealth Human Rights Commission 1981–6 and has led a number of public and cultural organisations.

Mitchell, Sir Thomas Livingstone (1792–1855), surveyor and explorer, b. Scotland. Surveyor-general for NSW 1825–55, Mitchell had the enormous task of planning roads, towns and bridges. He also led four exploratory expeditions, the first three (1831, 1835 and 1836) along the Murray–Darling system; during the last of these he made the important discovery of the fertile Western District of Vic. and 'the Major's Route' was immediately followed by overlanders and squatters. His final expedition (1845), aiming to cross the continent to Port Essington and confirm his theory of a great northwest-flowing river, ended at Cooper Creek (or Barcoo), which he named Victoria before turning back. Never popular, he conflicted openly with Governor Darling and made jealous attacks on other explorers. He was nevertheless a gifted man of letters who made large natural-history collections, and several native species of plants and animals bear his name.

Mitchell Library > *libraries*

Mitchell River Qld Rising northwest of Cairns in the Great Dividing Range, the river flows for some 560km across Cape York Peninsula, mainly through scrub-covered cattle country, to an estuary on the Gulf of Carpentaria, receiving many tributaries along its course. The Mitchell and Alice River National Park lies in the triangle formed by the meeting of these rivers, and beyond this the Mitchell flows to the gulf through Aboriginal land, in which is the Mitchell River community (Kowanyama).

mites > *ticks and mites*

Mittagong NSW (pop. 4828) This pleasant town, which lies in the southern highlands about 125km south of Sydney, is a tourist and commercial centre for the surrounding dairying and mixed-farming region. For 30 years from the 1840s it was the location of Australia's first iron smelter, based on local ores, limestone and coal.

Mitta Mitta River Vic. Discovered by William Hovell and Hamilton Hume in 1824, the Mitta Mitta rises in the Great Dividing Range beyond Omeo and flows slightly west of north to join the Murray just above the Hume reservoir. The upper valley is heavily timbered; the river plains provide rich agricultural and pastoral land, with crops such as tobacco and hops. Across a gorge in the upper valley is the Dartmouth dam (1973), the largest reservoir in Vic. and part of the Murray River water conservation scheme. The river's name is Aboriginal, said to mean either 'where reeds grow', 'little waters' or 'thunder'.

'Mo' > *Rene, Roy; theatre*

Moe Vic. (pop. 18 376) A city 135km southeast of Melbourne, Moe is a service centre for the dairying and timber area of south Gippsland as well as a growing residential centre for workers in the Latrobe Valley coalfields. It has absorbed many former residents of the nearby industrial town of Yallourn (built by the SEC in 1921), which was virtually demolished to make way for extensions to the open-cut mine.

Molle Islands > *Cumberland Islands*

Molloy, Georgiana (1805–43), amateur botanist, b. England. Molloy immigrated to Australia in 1830 with her husband John Molloy. Through her meticulous and carefully documented botanical fieldwork, she became a leading expert in WA wildflowers and contributed substantially to research into new plant species and their curative powers.

molluscs Molluscs form a phylum of the invertebrates second in number only to the arthropods. Molluscs are soft-bodied but most secrete calcareous material to form a protective shell: this is usually external, but in some (such as the cuttlefish) the shell is internal and others have shells only in the larval stages (such as octopuses and many slugs). The size of molluscs varies from enormous squids and giant clams to snails less than 1mm long, but the greater proportion, elsewhere and in Australia, are small.

Australia has some 10 000 of the 80 000 species known in the world. >> *bivalves; cephalopods; chitons; gastropods; tusk shells*

Monash, Sir John (1865–1931), engineer and soldier, b. Melbourne. Of Jewish parentage, Monash graduated in arts (1887) and civil engineering (1891) from the University of Melbourne; from 1904, he was in private practice and designed a number of civil engineering projects. Monash served with distinction during World War 1 at Gallipoli and in France, where he succeeded General Sir William Birdwood as commander of the Australian Army Corps. His plans were in part responsible for the success of the 1918 offensive to break the Hindenburg Line. After the war, as general manager of the SEC of Vic., Monash planned and oversaw the development of the vast brown-coal resources in the Latrobe Valley. Monash University in Vic. was named in his honour.

Moncrieff, Gladys (1892–1976), singer, b. Bundaberg, Qld. Commencing her career in vaudeville, Moncrieff joined J. C. Williamson's in 1911, where she sang in light opera and musical comedy, finding fame in 1921 as Teresa in *The Maid of the Mountains*, a role she made uniquely her own and which she played some 3000 times over a period of 30 years. Other notable successes were in *Rio Rita* and *The Merry Widow*. Australia's most popular musical-comedy star, 'Our Glad' (as she was known throughout Australia) retired in 1959 after a career spanning 50 years.

monitor > *lizards*

monotremes Australia and NG are the only areas in which there are representatives of this unusual, egg-laying order of mammals. The monotremes represent an early mammalian lineage that branched off from the main stock more than 80 million years ago; the only fossils of this group are from Australia: an opalised jaw from the Cretaceous, found at Lightning Ridge, NSW, and a fossil platypus of the more recent Miocene period, from SA. In addition to their egg-laying habit, monotremes differ from all other mammals in lacking nipples – the young are nourished by licking milk secreted from the mother's body. Only three species are known: the platypus, and two species of echidna.

The platypus, or duckbilled platypus, *Ornithorhynchus anatinus*, is found in coastal streams of Tas. and from northern Qld to eastern

SA, from cold, subalpine forests to tropical lowlands. To feed, the animal uses its broad, sensitive, flattened bill to locate invertebrate prey on stream beds by means of a unique sensing device that detects changes in electrical fields. Platypuses prefer quiet pools, and make their nests under the roots of trees along stream banks; usually two eggs are laid, and incubated by the female. The adult male has a sharp, hollow spur on each ankle, equipped with a poison gland. Although common in places, the platypus is particularly vulnerable to land disturbance and to the effect of chemical runoff from agricultural land.

The two species of echidna are the short-beaked *Tachyglossus aculeatus*, occurring in many habitats across Australia and in lowland NG, and the long-beaked *Zaglossus*, now found only in NG. As its other common name – spiny anteater – implies, the short-beaked echidna has a covering of strong, hollow spines and feeds on ants and termites, which adhere to the sticky saliva on its long tongue. Echidnas normally rest in hollow logs or under piles of debris; females dig burrows to rear their young, and usually only a single egg is laid. The spiny coat provides an excellent defence – echidnas have few major predators; the Australian species is common, and is in no apparent danger of extinction. >> *fauna*

Monte Bello Islands WA A small, coral and limestone group just north of Barrow Island, these uninhabited islets were first noted in 1622 by survivors of the British ship *Tryal*, wrecked on rocks at the north end of the Monte Bello reef. In his voyage of 1801–2 Nicolas Baudin named the islands after the Duke of Montebello, one of Napoleon's marshals. In 1952 the islands were the site of the first British atomic explosion.

Moomba > *festivals*

Moonlite, Captain [Andrew George Scott] (1842–79), bushranger, b. Ireland. A parson's son and the most intriguing bushranger of all, Scott was also a superb confidence trickster; while a lay preacher at Mt Egerton, Vic., he succeeded in holding up the bank manager, who was believed by no one when he identified Scott as the 'Captain Moonlite' who had robbed him. After a gaol sentence for passing a false cheque in Sydney and the now-discovered bank robbery, Scott had a brief phase of preaching and then took to bushranging 1879–80,

which culminated in a brutal station hold-up, his capture and hanging.

Moore, Charles (1820–1905), botanist, b. Scotland. Moore arrived in Australia in 1848 to take up the position of director of the Sydney Botanic Gardens. He pursued his task with vigour and tenacity until his retirement in 1896, creating the gardens very much in their existing form. He collected plant seeds in NZ, the New Hebrides and New Caledonia in 1855, and on Lord Howe Island in 1869; he also travelled extensively in NSW, collecting and describing a number of plants. One of his few published works is *Handbook of the Flora of New South Wales* (1893), co-written by Ernst Betche.

Moorehead, Alan McCrae (1910–83), journalist and author, b. Melbourne. After five years with the Melbourne *Herald,* Moorehead left for London in 1936. In World War 2 he made his name as the *Daily Express* correspondent during the North African campaign, his experiences of which were published in three volumes as *African Trilogy* (1944). An exceptional reporter and popular historian, Moorehead published biographies of Churchill (1955 and 1960) and Montgomery (1946), and the best-selling historical narratives *Gallipoli* (1956), *The White Nile* (1960), *The Blue Nile* (1962) and *The Fatal Impact* (1966).

Mootwingie NSW This national park of some 68 910ha lies in the Bynguano Range in the State's arid west, beyond Broken Hill and some 1200km northeast of Sydney. It is noted particularly for its abundance of prehistoric Aboriginal sites and relics – including rock art, camp-sites and stone tools – and is listed on the register of the national estate.

mopoke > *owls*

Moran, Patrick Francis (1830–1911), Catholic prelate, b. Ireland. Moran arrived in Australia in 1884 to take up the position of Catholic archbishop of Sydney; he became the first Australian cardinal, in 1885, and identified himself wholly with his adopted country. His sympathy with the labour movement aroused some controversy within the church. He published an extensive *History of the Catholic Church in Australasia* in 1895.

Morant, 'Breaker' (Henry Harbord) (1865–1902), soldier and poet, b. England.

Morant arrived in Australia in 1884, in which year (as Edwin Henry Murant) he is believed to have married Daisy Bates; the union lasted a short time only. In the 1890s, under the pen-name 'The Breaker' he contributed mediocre bush verse to the Sydney *Bulletin*. He fought with the Australian force during the Boer War and in 1901 (with three other officers) was court-martialled and convicted for disobeying orders by killing prisoners. Morant's execution on 27 February 1902 aroused much public controversy and was deemed by many to have been politically motivated. A legendary figure who symbolised the wildest days of the Australian bush, Morant has been widely portrayed and assessed in paintings, books and the 1980 film *Breaker Morant*.

Moree NSW (pop. 10 215) This town on the Gwydir River, 679km northwest of Sydney, is the service centre for a region that produces cattle and sheep, cotton, wheat, oilseeds and pecan nuts. A mineral-rich artesian bore (opened in 1895) is now used principally for medicinal spa baths rather than irrigation.

Moreton Bay bug > *crayfishes and allies*

Morgan SA (pop. 430) This small town on a major bend of the Murray River, 164km northeast of Adelaide, is noted chiefly as a former river port and railhead, and the starting point for the 360km pipeline to Whyalla, which supplies water to the industrial cities of Spencer Gulf and to towns and farmlands to the north.

morning glory Australia has about 100 native species of twining plants of the family Convolvulaceae. Divided among seventeen genera, of which *Ipomoea* is the largest with around 40 native species, they are restricted largely to the northern half of Australia and far inland. Goatsfoot morning-glory, *I. pes-caprae,* creeps over beach sands throughout the tropics and extends south as far as the NSW central coast; it has distinctive broadly notched leaves and large pink flowers. Bindweeds, which form the genus *Convolvulus*, include the widespread pink-flowered native *C. erubescens* and the introduced *C. arvensis*, a troublesome crop weed. Several introduced *Ipomoea* species are also familiar weeds in the south, most notably the blue morning-glory, *I. indica*, which smothers trees and shrubs in moister urban bushland; the introduced coastal morning-glory, *I. cairica*, is also is a common prostrate plant of dunes and estuary shores.

Mornington Peninsula Vic. Lying between Port Phillip and Westernport bays, this hilly peninsula has long been a major holiday and recreation area for Melbourne's population; farming is also important, and includes dairying, fruit and vegetable growing, cattle and sheep grazing, and poultry farming. The varied coastline provides sheltered bays on Port Phillip and ocean beaches on the Bass Strait shore; there has been considerable industrial development on the shore of Westernport Bay, contributing to increased urbanisation. Flinders Naval Base (HMAS *Cerberus*) is on the southeast coast, and west of the base are two reserves, Nepean State Park and Cape Schanck Coastal Park.

Morrison, George Ernest ('Chinese') (1862–1920), journalist and adventurer, b. Geelong, Vic. Having failed his medical degree, Morrison became a journalist with the Melbourne *Age* and travelled in Australia and NG. He was treated for a wound in Scotland, where he stayed to graduate in medicine in 1887. A fearless and insatiable traveller, he alternated between exploring and writing about exotic places and practising medicine in the US, West Indies, Spain, Morocco and Ballarat. After the publication of his *An Australian in China* (1895), he was appointed Far East correspondent for the *Times* and wielded powerful political influence with the new Chinese government. The Morrison Papers (held in the Mitchell Library, Sydney) are an unrivalled source on modern Chinese political and social history.

Morwell Vic. (pop. 16 887) Situated at the centre of the Latrobe Valley, 150km southeast of Melbourne, Morwell has been transformed from a small dairying centre into one of the closely linked series of industrial towns engendered by the region's brown-coal mines and associated electricity industries. The town's principal industries are briquette manufacture, and pulp and paper production. A joint Australian–Japanese pilot plant converts brown coal to refinery grade oils.

morwongs A group of sea fishes of the family Cheilodactylidae, morwongs are found mainly in temperate offshore waters. They are deepbodied fish with continuous dorsal fins and feed on animals such as crabs, shrimps, worms and sea urchins. There are nine species in Australian waters; with the exception of the dusky morwong, all are excellent table fish. The jackass and rubberlip, trawled in considerable numbers offshore, are commercially important in NSW and are sold as sea bream.

Moses, Sir Charles Joseph Alfred

(1900–88), broadcaster and administrator, b. England. A graduate of Sandhurst military college and sometime fruit-grower and car salesman, Moses arrived in Australia in 1922. Having started in radio as an ice-hockey commentator, he joined the ABC in 1932. As general manager 1935–65, he oversaw the development of the ABC's independent news service, symphony orchestras, school and rural broadcasts, and the introduction of television. An urbane and cultured man, Moses remained an ardent sports enthusiast.

mosquitoes Slender flies characterised by scales on the major wing veins and an elongate proboscis, mosquitoes are members of the family Culcidae. There are about 250 known species in Australia. Although both sexes suck plant juices, blood is also taken by females in order to provide nutrients for egg maturation. The immature stages develop in various fresh and brackish water habitats; the larvae, or 'wrigglers', feed on algae and other particulate matter – in some species, they prey on other mosquito larvae. Most species feed on warm-blooded mammals and birds, but some take blood from reptiles and amphibians.

Mosquitoes are important vectors of disease: although malaria and filariasis are no longer a problem in Australia, there are occasional incidences of mosquito-borne Murray Valley encephalitis, dengue fever and epidemic polyarthritis. Several endemic *Anopheles* species are capable of transmitting malaria, the introduced *Aedes aegypti* carries dengue fever, and the endemic *Culex annulirostris* is responsible for outbreaks of Murray Valley encephalitis. Dirofilariasis – or heartworm in dogs – is carried by mosquitoes, which are also important in transmitting myxomatosis among rabbits. Control of mosquitoes concentrates on eliminating their breeding sites in standing water, and on spraying.

moss animals > *Bryozoa*

mosses and liverworts These low-growing flowerless green plants, which comprise one of the major subdivisions of the plant kingdom, are conveniently referred to as the bryophytes.

They form the three groups Bryopsida (mosses), Hepaticopsida (liverworts) and Anthocerotopsida (hornworts). Bryophytes are more primitively constructed than ferns, gymnosperms and flowering plants, but advanced in relation to the green algae from which they apparently evolved: they lack a vascular system and proper roots, and like algae are dependent on contact with water for completion of their sexual cycle. They have nonetheless succeeded in diversifying and penetrating most of the world's land-plant environments, although they are most diverse in moist sheltered environments. Mosses are the most ubiquitous group, although many of the plants popularly termed 'moss' are in fact liverworts, lichens, algae, or even small flowering plants.

Australia has about 2000 bryophyte species, more than half of them mosses; genera of mosses number about 220, of liverworts possibly 100, and of hornworts only two. The most easily recognised moss genus is *Sphagnum*, which forms pale green masses in bogs, especially in cooler regions; they are highly absorbent, and important both environmentally and commercially. In alpine and subalpine areas, sphagnum bogs constitute a vast reservoir that feeds a regulated flow of water into all the stream heads. A distinctively Australasian genus is *Dawsonia*; its most conspicuous species, *D. superba*, restricted to moist eastern forests, has shoots to 30cm tall. Numerous mosses are confined to high mountain or rainforest environments, often epiphytic on tree-trunks, twigs or even leaves; there are also many smaller-growing mosses in harsher environments including man-made structures in towns and cities, and some appear to have been introduced following white settlement.

Liverworts are generally more fleshy or membranous than mosses and are usually prostrate. They divide into two types: thallose forms consist of a flattened body (thallus), commonly forked although in some genera its margins are deeply lobed; leafy forms have two or four rows of membranous leaves that are often so small and crowded that they appear as a solid band. The largest, fleshiest liverwort is *Marchantia*, with a contorted bright-green thallus bearing spore bodies on umbrella-shaped organs. Similar but smaller is *Lunularia*, ubiquitous in damp gardens and greenhouses, rarely sporing but reproducing by means of bud-like organs (*gemmae*) on the thallus surface. In many drier areas, species of the bluish-green *Riccia* are common on compacted soil surfaces. Most leafy liverworts are delicate plants of moist, sheltered environments such as stream banks and rainforests, but a few genera have adapted to drier rockfaces and exposed tree trunks.

moths > *butterflies and moths*

motor sports Motor sports in Australia began at the turn of this century, although races were staged on roads and cycling or horse-racing tracks until car circuits were constructed; the first of these was developed at Aspendale (now Sandown) in Vic., in 1906.

Motorcycle racing Motorcycle clubs were formed early in the 20th century, and the Auto Cycle Council of Australia was established in 1928. A separate committee controls speedway racing, an Australian innovation developed by Johnny Hoskins in Maitland, NSW, in the 1920s and subsequently taken up in Britain. Other major forms of racing are road, dirt track, motocross (scrambles) and reliability trials. In the 1950s Australia produced world champions in Bert Kavanagh, Keith Campbell, Tom Phillis, Ken Carruthers, Barry Smith, Gregg Hansford, Jack Findlay and John Dodds, but it was the victory of > *Wayne Gardner* in the 500cc championship in 1987 and his popular win in the inaugural Australian motorcycle Grand Prix at Phillip Island in 1989 that finally established the sport. Other world-class 500cc riders are Kevin Magee and Peter Doohan.

Car racing Motor racing, which now has 38 000 registered participants, is controlled by the Confederation of Australian Motor Sport, but it began on an informal basis using ordinary touring vehicles. The first race was held on grass at Sandown, Vic., in 1904 and the first reliability trial, the Buchanan Cup, in 1905; adventurous – and barely legal – inter-city races remained popular for years. In the 1920s highly banked circuits, the most famous of which was at Maroubra, NSW, became the focus for the racing of high-powered, imported machines.

The first Australian Grand Prix (AGP) was held at Phillip Island in 1928; this makes it the world's third-oldest continuously contested event. Nevertheless, the sport did not win mass appeal but existed precariously, often as an appendage to centenary celebrations or tourist proposals and never with a permanent home; on the other hand, the Redex reliability trials, held from 1953, and the 500-mile (now 1000km) event instituted at Bathurst in 1963 – where nine-times winner Peter Brock became 'king of the mountain' – seemed to capture the public imagination. The AGP developed further in 1963 with the formation of the Tasman series, which attracted the world's leading drivers and cars; successful Australian competitors were > *Jack Brabham*, three times world champion, and Alan Jones, champion in 1980. In 1985 the AGP finally reached maturity when it found a permanent home in Adelaide, and a place on the world Formula One circuit; overnight it became one of Australia's premier sporting events.

motor-vehicle industry The Australian motor-vehicle industry traditionally follows a 'boom and bust' cycle, a bad year following a good one with startling regularity. While this is an essential industry (employing around 33 000 people directly and many more indirectly) and makes a major contribution to the balance of trade, it has been beset by problems since its inception, the main one being the existence of too many manufacturers producing too many models for too small a market. Moreover, it is not an industry for the faint-hearted: all attempts to produce a genuinely home-grown vehicle in the 1920s and 1930s ended in commercial failure, and more recently some of the giants of the industry (including Chrysler, Volkswagen and the British Motor Corporation) have ceased operation.

Today the industry is divided between five overseas-controlled companies. The US companies are > *GMH* and Ford, the latter being the most successful Australian car manufacturer in recent years with its popular six-cylinder Falcon. The Japanese companies are Toyota (and its local assembly operation, AMI-Toyota), Mitsubishi and Nissan; Australian interests have minority equity in both AMI-Toyota and Mitsubishi Australia. Between them the five companies share a strongly fluctuating market that swung, for example, from a high of 674 830 new registrations in 1984–5 to a low of 468 801 in 1986–7. Responsibility for the dramatically low 1986–7 figure has been attributed to increased taxation, including the fringe-benefits tax, which led to fewer 'fleet' purchases, and a luxury-car tax. Although 1988–9 promised to be a boom year for car sales, such an unreliable market makes both industry rationalisation and increased exports necessary if car manufacturing in Australia is to prosper. With the exception of Ford and Toyota, all the companies have recently experienced years of running at a loss.

The commercial realities of the industry have already encouraged rationalisation and intercompany co-operation: GMH and Nissan, for example, market the same car under the brand names Pulsar and the Astra respectively; GMH sells two rebadged Toyota cars under its own brand name and supplies its Commodore to Toyota to sell as the Lexcen; Mitsubishi sells castings to Ford and GMH supplies Nissan and Toyota with sheet metal; and there are plans for Nissan and Ford to produce a car jointly. As far as exports are concerned, there is a small but growing overseas market, mainly for engines and components rather than for complete vehicles. GMH, for example, sells four-cylinder engines to its parent company's overseas assembly plants, a success somewhat counterbalanced by the necessity for it to import six-cylinder engines from Nissan in Japan.

The 1980s and beyond Much of the current rationalisation in the industry has been inspired by the 1984 Button Plan (named after the then-minister for industry and commerce, John Button), which has called for fewer car models on the market and the elimination, through model and component sharing, of the wasteful duplication of resources. Import duties on motor vehicles have always been high in Australia, resulting in a feather-bedded local industry, and an essential part of the plan is the gradual lowering of protection in the hope that this will make the industry more efficient. In 1987, a 'local content plan' was introduced, whereby in simple terms a vehicle is considered to be an Australian product if it has 85% local content; the plan is complex, however, and allows the averaging of content across models and 'export credits' to be take into consideration.

If year-by-year fluctuations are excluded, the future of the industry appears assured, given Australia's ready access to raw materials, a skilled workforce and the vast infrastructure already in place. Unless a much larger export business is generated, however, it is unlikely that the industry can continue to support five competing manufacturers.

mound-building birds This group of large, ground-dwelling birds of the family Megapodiidae are known for their habit of building nest-mounds in which they deposit their eggs to be hatched by the heat of decaying vegetation or of the sun. The mound is constructed by the male, and after the female has deposited her eggs the pair tend it by covering or uncovering it with earth and debris to ensure that a constant interior temperature of about 35°C is maintained for proper incubation; after hatching, the young fend for themselves without parental care. Food consists of insects, seeds and berries, which are often scratched out of the ground.

Australia has three species of this family: the scrubfowl, *Megapodius freycinet*, found along the tropical north and in NG; the brush turkey, *Alectura lathami*, a striking, black bird with a bare red-and-yellow head, occurring in eastern rainforests from Cape York to the Illawarra district, NSW; and the mallee fowl or lowan, *Loipoa ocellata*, of the mallee districts of southern Australia. The mallee fowl has become rare as a result of habitat destruction, hunting, and predation by foxes, but members are now increasing somewhat in protected areas of mallee country.

mountaineering and rock-climbing Australia possesses no mountains of a height to provide opportunities for true mountain-climbing; Australian mountaineers must go to NZ or to the Himalayas for such projects. On the other hand, the extreme age of the Australian continent has resulted in unique and challenging rock formations, and the sport of rock-climbing developed after World War 2, when sites were examined and courses planned; John Ewbank perfected a rating scale of 1–28, with any site above 18 being regarded as difficult. New areas for rock-climbing are constantly being opened up, and older sites are being tackled anew from more difficult aspects. Notable rock-climbing sites include the Glasshouse Mountains in Qld, the Blue Mountains and Warrumbungle Range in NSW, the Grampian Ranges and Mt Arapiles in Vic., the Flinders Ranges in SA, the Stirling and Pororongorup ranges in WA, and Mt Wellington and the Freycinet National Park in Tas.

mountain shrimp This extremely primitive crustacean, *Anaspides tasmaniae*, is considered to be a living fossil and is found only in mountain streams and lakes of southwest Tas. It differs from the true shrimp in lacking a carapace – that is, the exterior body segments are not fused. Brown in colour and 5cm long, the mountain shrimp is an omnivorous feeder.

Mt Arapiles Vic. This striking sandstone outcrop rises 230m from the Wimmera plains in western Vic. The area has a rich flora and fauna, protected in a forest reserve, and is a noted rock-climbing venue. In 1852 a cave on the mountain served as a hide-out for the notorious bushranger, Captain Melville.

Mt Barrow Tas. This peak (1415m) lies east of Launceston and is the source of tributaries of the St Patrick's River, which flows into the South Esk. A telecommunications tower is located on its summit. It is known as the habitat of *Richea scoparia*, a yellow wildflower restricted to this mountain-top and Ben Lomond.

Mt Bartle Frere Qld > *Bellenden Ker Range*

Mt Beauty Vic. (pop. 1564) This town lies in the valley of the Kiewa River at the foot of Mt Bogong, about 345km northeast of Melbourne. The area was originally a cattle centre for the Bogong High Plains, and grazing, dairying and agriculture are still the chief local activities. The town was established by the SEC in 1947 as a base during construction of the Kiewa hydro-electric scheme, and has since developed as a service and tourist centre for the region.

Mt Bimberi ACT Also known as Bimberi Peak, this is the highest point (1910m) in the Bimberi Range, which extends south of the Brindabella Range, southwest of Canberra, in an area of dense forest.

Mt Buffalo Vic. The Mt Buffalo region has been a national reserve since 1898. Since enlarged, it now extends over 31 000ha and consists of a plateau flanked by steep-sided granite tors of which the highest is The Horn (Mt Buffalo, 1720m). A place of spectacular scenery, it has been developed as a skiing resort, and is a popular area for bushwalking in summer. Several streams rising on the plateau become tributaries of the Ovens River. Mt Buffalo itself was named in 1824 by Hamilton Hume and William Hovell because of its distinctive shape when seen from a distance.

Mt Canobolas NSW This is an extinct volcano, 1397m high, about 14km southwest of Orange. The crater is timber-covered and the slopes are planted with pines. With twin peaks known as Old Man Canobolas and Young Man Canobolas, the name is thought to come from the Aboriginal *coonabooloo*, meaning 'two shoulders'.

Mt Conner NT This is the most easterly of the 'Three Great Tors' of conglomerate rising above the desert plain north of the Musgrave Ranges; the others are Mt Olga and Ayers Rock. Conner differs from these two in being flat-topped, oval in shape, and bounded by sheer cliffs 120m high, below which steep, scree-covered slopes fall for another 120m. The mountain is about 3km long and 1.2km wide, and was discovered and named after an SA politician by W. C. Gosse in 1873.

Mt Feathertop Vic. In the southern part of the Australian Alps, near the headwaters of the Ovens and Kiewa rivers, this is the second-highest peak in Vic. (1924m), with broad alpine meadows covered by deep snow in winter and brilliant wildflowers in spring.

Mt Field Tas. The twin peaks of this mountain lie 82km north of Hobart at the heart of a 16 000ha national park; the highest point is Mt Field West (1434m). This is a region of rugged and spectacular landscapes ranging from alpine moors to glacial lakes and precipitous gorges; it is also one of the State's principal snowfields.

Mountford, C.P. (Charles Pearcy) (1890–1977), anthropologist and author, b. Hallett, SA. A noted student and exponent of Aboriginal culture, Mountford travelled extensively in central Australia from the 1940s. He wrote a number of books on Aboriginal art, music and mythology over the next 30 years, many of which were illustrated with his masterly photographs. His publications included the classic *Brown Men and Red Sand* (1948); *The Art, Myth and Symbolism of Arnhem Land* (1956); and *The Dreamtime Book* (1973), which was a compendium of three earlier collections of Aboriginal myths, illustrated by Ainslie Roberts.

Mt Gambier SA (pop. 20 813) This city, the third-largest in the State, lies about 460km southeast of Adelaide on the side of an extinct volcano. The rich volcanic soils support agriculture, sheep farming, dairying and extensive pine plantations, for all of which activities Mt Gambier is the commercial, industrial and service centre. It is also an important base for tourists in the region, the most renowned nearby attraction being the group of four crater lakes including > *Blue Lake*. Mt Gambier was established in the 1850s as a pastoral settlement but has undergone most rapid growth in the last 40 years with the development of supporting industries for regional produce. It is noted for its white (local) stone buildings, many of which have been classified by the National Trust.

Mt Goldsworthy WA Discovered in 1879 by Alexander Forrest and named after the then colonial secretary, Mt Goldsworthy is about 117km east of Port Hedland. In the 1960s production of iron ore began with an open-cut mine that has since reduced the mountain, formerly 132m, to a pit. The nearby town of Goldsworthy was built solely to accommodate workers at the mine, from which the ore is shipped to Finucane Island, Port Hedland, for export.

Mt Hotham Vic. Near the Bogong High Plains in the Australian Alps, this is one of Vic.'s highest mountains (1861m) and a popular holiday area for skiing, bushwalking and trout fishing in the appropriate seasons. Tributaries of the Ovens and Kiewa rivers rise in this region, which was first explored in 1854 by Ferdinand von Mueller and named in honour of Lt-Governor Sir Charles Hotham.

Mt Isa Qld (pop. 23 348) This near-legendary mining city is on the Leichhardt River 1867km northwest of Brisbane, in the Selwyn Range. It lies in harsh, remote hills surrounded by spinifex country, and the establishment of infrastructure and facilities was achieved largely with UK and US assistance. The town was first developed for the area's silver, lead and zinc ores, from the 1920s; the minerals were discovered accidentally, it is said, by prospector John Miles as he rested his horse near the Leichhardt River. All leases were acquired by Mt Isa Mines Ltd (MIM) in 1925. The production of silver-lead-zinc has alternated with copper mining since the 1940s, according to demand; ore is railed 970km by narrow-gauge rail to Townsville. There has been great expansion in mining and processing since the 1950s, although prosperous periods have been interspersed with economic uncertainty as well as periodic industrial problems – most notably in 1964–5 where a prolonged wages dispute led to the introduction of martial law.

Mt Keira–Mt Kembla NSW These adjacent peaks, dominating the skyline above Wollongong, are part of the eastern escarpment that rises west of the Illawarra district; beneath the sandstone walls are major seams of coal.

Mt Keira was the first mine to operate in the area, in 1849; in 1902, Mt Kembla was the site of Australia's worst mining disaster, when an explosion killed 95 men. The two now operate as a single mine, having been linked by a tunnel.

Mt Kosciusko NSW Kosciusko, in the Snowy Mountains, is Australia's highest peak (2228m). It was named in 1840 by Paul Strzelecki from a fancied resemblance to the tomb of Polish patriot Tadeusz Kosciuszko (although it is possible that Strzelecki in fact climbed what is now Mt Townsend). Rising above the rolling plateau, it is a great snowfield in winter – a major centre for winter sports – and in summer a place for bushwalking and trout fishing. The alpine country and forested slopes are included in Kosciusko National Park, the largest in NSW (629 708ha), extending from the ACT to the Vic. border. The region is geologically very interesting, since the presence of moraines, glaciated rock and glacial lakes – such as Blue Lake, Albina and Cootapatamba – presents rare evidence of glaciation on mainland Australia during the last ice age.

Mt Lofty Ranges SA A southern extension of the Flinders Ranges but with a softer and more humid landscape, these mountains lie between the Murray River plain (to the east) and the coastal Adelaide plain. They are divided at the Barossa Valley; in the north the highest peak is Mt Bryan (932m) and in the south, where urban Adelaide reaches almost to the foothills, it is Mt Lofty (727m), which was named by Matthew Flinders in 1802. The ranges' significance for water catchment and farming in a generally arid State is disproportionately high: this closely settled intensively cultivated landscape supplies Adelaide with food and water, and provides recreation areas. The ranges were severely damaged in the Ash Wednesday bushfires of 1983.

Mt Macedon Vic. A volcanic mountain about 64km northwest of Melbourne, Mt Macedon is notable for fine Victorian homes and gardens, one of which was formerly the State governor's summer residence; the area is now part of Melbourne's commuter zone. The 1014m mountain was first climbed in 1836 by Thomas Mitchell and named apparently in honour of Philip of Macedon. The entire area suffered severely in the Ash Wednesday bushfires of 1983.

Mt Morgan Qld (pop. 2866) This mining centre lies beside the vestiges of a former mountain, its 800m-diameter crater having been created by open-cut mining for gold, silver and copper. Mining began in the 1880s, and in its prime the town had a population of 15 000; mining still takes place, but the area relies mainly on tourism.

Mt Royal Range NSW Branching from the Great Dividing Range at Ben Hall's Gap, about 64km southeast of Tamworth, this range continues south for some 80km, forming a divide between the Hunter and Manning rivers. The catchment area in the region of Mt Royal and Barrington Tops (at 1586m, the range's highest point) is reserved as State forest. The waters of Glenbawn dam edge the foothills of the range.

Mt Stromlo Observatory > *astronomy*

Mt Superbus Qld In the Great Dividing Range, this is the highest point in southeast Qld, rising to 1380m. It lies where the McPherson Range diverges from the Main Range, near the headwaters of the upper tributaries of the Condamine River.

Mt Wellington Tas. Dominating the western skyline of Hobart and only 20km from the centre of the city, Mt Wellington (1270m) commands a striking view of the city and the Derwent River valley. A notable feature of the mountain – which is snow-covered in winter and whose catchment provides a large proportion of Hobart's water supply – is a columnar rock formation below the summit known as the Organ Pipes. Although the mountain was sighted first by William Bligh in 1788, its name dates only from 1824, given to honour the victor of Waterloo.

mudbrick building Soon after the First Fleet landed in 1788, convicts were patching together primitive houses with earth walls, using thin pieces of pliable timber (commonly branches of blackwattle) fixed to or between framing timbers and thickly plastered, usually with mud. These so-called wattle-and-daub constructions frequently were washed away in heavy rains, but later variations with stronger posts and protective rendering were more durable. Pisé or rammed-earth walls provided good insulation and were more permanent, ideal where timber was scarce and mud easily excavated. Adobe or mudbrick construction, a

principle brought to Kalgoorlie by miners from the California goldfields, uses sun-dried blocks of clay mortared with mud; 19th-century examples can still be seen. Adobe or mudbrick houses became fashionable for a time after World War 2 when other building materials were scarce, but once the shortage was over many people returned to more conventional materials. The Vic. designer Alistair Knox was a leading promoter of mudbrick construction, notably in Eltham, Vic., where the method became something of a regional speciality. Since the 1970s, mudbrick has been adopted by many alternative communities in northern NSW and Qld; many architects are now adopting this form of construction because of its stylistic simplicity and environmental soundness.

Mudgee NSW (pop 7000) This rural centre lies 260km northwest of Sydney in a district noted for the production of wine, wool, beef, wheat, coal, butter and honey. Settled in the 1820s, Mudgee grew with the gold rushes of the 1850s and retains many fine historic buildings. The boyhood home of Henry Lawson was in nearby Eurunderee and the district colours much of his writing.

Mudie, James (1779–1852), pioneer, b. Scotland. A Royal Marine officer, dismissed in 1810, Mudie arrived in Australia in 1822 and built a prosperous, productive farm on his generous grant of land in the Hunter River area. His brutal, inhumane treatment of convicts brought him into conflict with Governor Bourke, and in 1837 he published *The Felonry of NSW* to expose, he said, the incumbent colonial government's convict sympathies. Widely unpopular in the colony, in 1842 he returned to England.

mudlarks and allies Mudlarks are a group of perching birds forming the family Grallinidae, all distinguished by their construction of mud nests; three of the four known species are unique to Australia. The magpie lark or peewee, *Grallina cyanoleuca*, is a small black-and-white bird with long legs and smallish beak; its alternative name stems from its call on being disturbed, heard particularly when the bird is taking off or landing. The chough, *Corcorax melanorhamphos*, is a crow-like bird of inland eastern Australia, particularly of the Murray-basin forests; it is black, with small, white wing-patches, and has a longish, slightly down-curved beak, eating insects and some forest or orchard fruit. *Struthidea cinerea*, the apostle-bird (so-called for its habit of flocking in groups of about a dozen), is also known as the grey jumper: in ascending a tree, it hops from branch to branch as if on a staircase. It is a common and easily tamed species of inland east and north Australia, making cup-shaped, mud nests in groups of trees, and lining the nest with fine grass.

Mueller, Baron Sir Ferdinand Jakob Heinrich von

(1825–96), botanist and explorer, b. Germany. Arguably Australia's foremost 19th-century botanist, Mueller came to Australia in 1847 and was appointed the first Vic. government botanist in 1853. In this capacity he travelled extensively in Vic. as well as northern Australia (1855), WA (1867 and 1877) and Tas. (1869), collecting and identifying hundreds of new plant species. As director of the Melbourne Botanic Gardens from 1857, he was an indefatigable worker, amassing 350 000 plant specimens and contributing much knowledge about eucalypts and acacias. His rigorously scientific approach to his work at the Botanic Gardens was criticised by a public demanding more fashionable 'pleasure gardens', however, and he was dismissed in 1873. Mueller published hundreds of scientific papers and numerous books, including the seven-volume *Flora Australiensis* (1863–78, in collaboration with George Bentham). He was also influential in the formation of the Vic. Royal Society and the University of Melbourne.

mulga > *grasses and grasslands; wattle*

mullets These fishes of the family Mulgilidae, of which there are seventeen Australian species, are found in coastal waters but migrate northwards in enormous numbers to spawn in estuaries and coastal lakes. They have peculiar, small mouths with either very small teeth or none at all, and are bottom-feeders, chiefly on microscopic organic material and detritus. Several species are commercially important as excellent table fish, notably the sea mullet, *Mugil cephalus*, fished in very large numbers particularly during the migration period. Other species include the silver or fantail mullet, the yelloweye, the flat-tail and the sand mullet.

mulloway Also known as the jewfish, the mulloway is a large and commercially important marine fish, taken in large numbers around the Australian coast, especially of NSW. Of the

several species, the largest can attain a length of 2m and weigh some 67kg; the larger specimens are caught in offshore waters. The name is of Aboriginal origin.

multiculturalism The term multiculturalism, coined in Canada in the late 1960s, was in official use in Australia by 1973. It has been developed since in the government publication *Multiculturalism for All Australians* (1982) and by the Office of Multicultural Affairs, set up within the prime minister's department in 1987. Multiculturalism as a public policy recognises that Australians are drawn from many backgrounds, that special approaches and services are needed for those of differing language or religion, and that social cohesion is attained by tolerating differences within an agreed legal and constitutional framework. This was accepted by the Whitlam, Fraser and Hawke governments but questioned by the then Liberal leader John Howard in the 1980s and by the FitzGerald Report on immigration policy in mid-1988. Conservative critics argue that multiculturalism is divisive and denies Australia's British inheritance: despite this, national and State governments have adopted a wide range of multicultural services and institutions with the support of all major parties. >> *ethnic groups*; *immigration*

multinational corporations > *foreign investment*

Mundey, Jack > *green bans*

Murchison River WA A sporadically flowing watercourse fed mainly by winter rains, the Murchison River flows for over 700km from its headwaters in the Robinson Range to Gantheaume Bay on the Indian Ocean, midway between Geraldton and Shark Bay. It was discovered by George Grey in 1839. The Kalbarri National Park (186 000ha), near the mouth of the river, includes a spectacular sandstone gorge, which extends for some 80km.

Murdoch, Sir Walter Logie Forbes

(1874–1970), essayist and academic, b. Scotland. Murdoch was a teacher and headmaster before becoming lecturer in English at Melbourne University in 1904. A regular contributor to the *Argus* 1899–1938, he was the first professor of English at the University of WA 1912–39 and later chancellor (1943–7). The many published selections of Murdoch's essays reflect his light, deceptively simple and often whimsical style.

Murdoch family, pre-eminent in Australian journalism and media industries. **Sir Keith Arthur** (1886–1952), b. Melbourne, established a powerful presence in Australian journalism. He was a controversial World War 1 correspondent, an opinionated editor of the Melbourne *Herald* (from 1921) and a founder of the news agency Australian Associated Press. From the late 1920s he was chairman of the Herald & Weekly Times and acquired newspaper holdings in Adelaide through his shareholding in News Ltd. Though a conservative in politics, he was an enthusiastic supporter of modern art. His wife, **Dame Elisabeth Joy** (1909–), b. Toorak, Vic., is a noted charity worker and patron of the arts. Their son **(Keith) Rupert** (1931–), b. Melbourne, graduated from Oxford University and worked as a journalist in London before inheriting his father's newspaper interests. He began to expand News Ltd from the 1960s, also founding the *Australian* (1964) and purchasing two London newspapers (1969); by the 1980s the corporation had extensive holdings in Australia, the UK and US including newspaper, magazine and book publishing as well as broadcasting and satellite networks; Murdoch took US citizenship to allow expansion of his US interests. He is a controversial figure owing to his dominance of information industries, tough dealing with labour unions, and marketing of unashamedly populist journalism. >> *media ownership and control*

Murphy, Graeme (1950–), dancer and choreographer, b. Melbourne. One of the most innovative choreographers of modern dance, Murphy was trained as a classical ballet dancer. In 1969 he joined the Australian Ballet (for whom he later choreographed a number of ballets) and in 1972 he moved to the distinguished Sadler's Wells Ballet in London. As artistic director of the Sydney Dance Company since 1976, Murphy has established a contemporary dance group of world renown: it has performed in Italy (1980), New York (1981, 1985), London (1981) and China (1985).

Murphy, Lionel Keith (1922–86), lawyer and politician, b. Sydney. Admitted to the NSW bar in 1947, Murphy became a QC in 1960 and entered federal parliament in 1962. A Labor senator 1962–75, Murphy was attorney-general in the Whitlam government 1972–5, during which period he was responsible for the introduction of major legislative reforms in the areas of family law, trade practices, legal aid and racial discrimination. As a High Court judge from 1975, he was noted for his unorthodox and sometimes controversial judgments, which continued to reflect his reforming zeal and concern for human rights. Shortly before his death he was accused and acquitted of conspiring to pervert the course of justice on behalf of solicitor Morgan Ryan.

Murray, Les(lie Allan) (1938–), poet and editor, b. Nabiac, NSW. Murray's rural upbringing has much influenced his poetry, which was first published in Sydney University literary magazines. Since the late 1960s he has been a full-time writer, with some ten volumes of poetry to his credit, all distinguished by both their energy and their ingenuity of expression and imagery; *The People's Otherworld* (1983) won the Australian Literature Society's Gold Medal in 1984. Murray is also a noted book reviewer and anthologist, his *New Oxford Book of Australian Verse* (1983) notably reflecting his idiosyncratic and uncluttered approach to the genre.

Murray Bridge SA (pop. 11 893) This town lies on the Murray River 80km southeast of Adelaide, where the river is crossed by the main Melbourne–Adelaide road and railway. It became a noted river port once the railway bridge was constructed at the town in 1886. Tailem Bend, 20km away (pop. 1542) overlooks irrigated dairy pastureland on the reclaimed flood-plain.

Murray cod, The sporting and commercial king of Australian freshwater fishes, the Murray cod, *Maccullochella macquariensis*, can reach a length of 1.8m and weigh 80kg on its diet of shrimps, mussels, crayfishes, frogs and other aquatic animals of the Murray-Darling basin. It is a large, brown-spotted, olive-green fish with a rounded tail and a continuous dorsal fin (the front part spined), very deep- and broad-bodied in large specimens. It seems to be losing ground to the introduced perch and carp, and perhaps also because of alterations in the river ecology through human interference, effects of which include siltation, agricultural chemical run-off, and lower water temperatures resulting from reservoir construction.

Murray Islands Qld This group of three coral islets in Torres Strait lies some 185km northeast of Cape York, at the beginning of the Great Barrier Reef. They form the northernmost territory of Qld. Of the three – Maer (Mer, usually known as Murray), Dower (Dauar) and Wyer (Weier) – only Murray is inhabited, and is known for its numerous and extensive rock fish-traps.

Murray River Australia's principal river, some 2600km in length, the Murray forms much of the NSW–Vic. border. It receives a number of important tributaries, the largest being the Darling; the Murray–Darling system (> *Darling River*) drains more than 1 000 000sq.km in NSW, Vic., SA and Qld. From its source in the Great Dividing Range in northeast Vic. the Murray flows steeply, falling almost 1500m in about 200km, and passes through hilly country almost to Albury-Wodonga. A number of major Vic. tributaries – the Mitta Mitta, Kiewa, Ovens, Goulburn, Campaspe and Loddon – join the river on its westward course through a region of riverine flood-plains cut by numerous distributaries, anabranches and billabongs, usually lined with large river red gums. Beyond Swan Hill the Murray flows through semi-arid country and at Wentworth is joined by the Darling River before continuing west to SA, turning suddenly at Morgan to flow south to enter the shallow Lake Alexandrina (formed by large sand bars) and reach its narrow mouth in Encounter Bay.

The Murray was discovered by Hamilton Hume and William Hovell in 1824 and charted by Charles Sturt in 1829. From the 1850s until the development of railways, riverboats were the principal means of communication and transport. There are a number of water-control and irrigation schemes on the Murray and its tributaries, the entire drainage constituting Australia's richest agricultural area. Salinity and pollution (through agricultural run-off) remain of serious concern, particularly as the Murray not only feeds agricultural lands but also underpins the water supply of urban areas including Adelaide. >> *water and water resources*

Murray-Smith, Stephen (1922–88), academic and editor, b. Melbourne. After service with the AIF in World War 2, Murray-Smith taught in London and Prague 1948–51. He edited *Realist Writer* (1952–54) and founded the literary magazine *Overland* in 1954. A reader in education at the University of Melbourne, he edited a range of works including *The Tracks We Travel* (1953) and *Classic Australian Short Stories* (1974), and wrote *Right Words* (1987). Murray-Smith was chairman of the National Book Council 1981–3.

Murrumbidgee River NSW The second-longest river in the State, the Murrumbidgee rises in the Great Dividing Range north of Kiandra and follows a course of 2170km to become ultimately part of the Murray–Darling system. It receives a number of tributaries from the southern tablelands, including the Molonglo, Cotter, Tumut, Bredbo and Yass rivers, before passing through Gundagai; the major tributary, the Lachlan, joins the Murrumbidgee in semi-arid country further west, before it merges with the Murray. Downstream from Wagga Wagga is the Murrumbidgee Irrigation Area, a rich agricultural district producing fruits, vegetables, grapes, cotton and other crops; Griffith and Leeton, the main towns of the MIA, process much of the region's produce. There are a number of dams on the tributaries of the Murrumbidgee, and water from the Snowy Mountains Scheme supplies dams and irrigation systems. The upper reaches of the Murrumbidgee were discovered in the early 1820s, but major exploration was by Charles Sturt 1829–30. The river's name is from an Aboriginal word meaning 'big water'.

museums Most of Australia's major public museums date from the early and middle 19th century: in keeping with the spirit of the time, they were generally housed in grandiose buildings and exhibited an eclectic range of art, artefacts and natural-history curiosities. Since World War 2 – in step with growing popular interest in local, regional and national history – there has been a substantial increase in the number of museums throughout Australia, many of which are specialist in focus and adopt the modern 'interactive' approach to their exhibitions. In the last decade or so there has has also been much greater community interest in Aboriginal prehistory and culture, with an attendant increase in number of museums in this field.

The State collections The major State museums have retained their natural-history emphasis, but some now incorporate art galleries and science museums; most have significant collections focusing on State history and regional activities.

The Australian Museum in Sydney, which dates back to 1827, is noted for its ethnographic, natural-history, geological and other science collections, and for its longstanding research and educational activities. The Tas. Museum and Art Gallery, established in Hobart in 1829, houses a substantial collection of material relating to the State's colonial history. The Museum of Vic. in Melbourne was created in 1983 by amalgamation of the National Museum of Vic. (established 1854) and the Science Museum (1870); it has a valued scientific collection and was the first Australian museum to establish a planetarium, a children's exhibition space, and a specialised unit for the acquisition and display of Aboriginal artefacts. The SA Museum in Adelaide was constituted in its present form in 1956 but derives from an 1850s institution; it is particularly noted for its anthropological and archaeological exhibits. The Qld Museum in Brisbane has its origins in a collection established in 1862, which was rehoused in the Qld Cultural Centre in 1986; originally specialising in marine and geological exhibits, it now has a substantial historic and technological collection. The WA Museum in Perth was established in 1892 when the museum of the Swan River Mechanics Institute (1860) and the Geological Museum in Fremantle (1881) were combined; it has a major collection of maritime relics and is noted for its conservation work in this field. The Museum and Art Gallery of the NT in Darwin, founded in 1964, was destroyed during the 1974 cyclone but rehoused in a new building in 1981; it has an important collection of Aboriginal and Pacific Island cultural relics. In Canberra, the > *Australian War Memorial* will be joined by the National Museum of Australia in 1990; its particular focus will be Australian history and prehistory and the natural environment.

Other museums There are hundreds of other museums around Australia – in universities, country and coastal towns, and historic buildings, and housed aboard trains and ships. The Macleay and Nicholson museums at the University of Sydney began as private collections in the 19th century: the Macleay Museum houses an eclectic range of natural-history specimens, ancient art and artefacts, and an invaluable collection of early Australian photographs; the Nicholson Museum is particularly noted for its classical relics. While many science and technology collections also date back to the 19th century, methods of display and interpretation have become much more sophisticated; in the 1980s, Sydney's Museum of Applied Arts and Sciences was reconstituted in four separate venues including the old observatory building on Observatory Hill and the Powerhouse Museum at Darling Harbour. Also of long standing are the transport museums which exist in most States – devoted to planes

and aviation technology, early trams and trains, horse-drawn vehicles and vintage cars. Open-air museums, on the other hand, are largely a postwar phenomenon: among the best known are the recreated settlements of Sovereign Hill in Vic. and Old Sydney Town in NSW; some of the more recent 'facsimile' museums have, however, been criticised for their lack of historical authenticity. Maritime and industrial museums are also a relatively recent development: noted examples including the Maritime Museum housed in the historic barque *Polly Woodside* in Melbourne and the National Maritime Museum at Darling Harbour in Sydney.

Museum standards Although facilities and standards of display have generally improved in recent decades, in 1975 a national inquiry into Australia's museums and collections documented many serious problems, from inadequate space for storage and display to the deterioration of collections as the result of unsuitable atmospheric controls – which were in most cases compounded by insufficient funds. The report also identified broader concerns such as the need to rationalise acquisition policies and improve the research and educative role of museums. In the 1980s a number of major new museums were opened and others were substantially refurbished; by the end of the decade, however, the fundamental problems identified in 1975 were still unresolved. >> *art galleries*; *libraries*

Musgrave Ranges SA/NT These ranges extend from the far northwest of SA into the NT and are the source of several streams that drain either northeast to Lake Amadeus or southeast towards Lake Eyre. The ranges stretch for some 150km east–west and 15km north–south; their highest point is Mt Woodroffe (1513m). Much of the region is set aside within Aboriginal reserves and includes – in the east – the former Ernabella mission.

mushrooms > *fungi*

music and musical composition 'High-art' music in Australia reflected British tastes until quite recently. Particularly since the 1960s, cross-cultural influences have widened the horizons of local performers and composers to embrace not only European and US traditions but also those of Asia and the Pacific region. Such exchanges have on the one hand enriched local composition, and on the other helped to blur the distinction between 'serious' and 'popular' music.

Historical development British musical forms and preferences were transported to the founding colony, in the fashion of the time, as trappings of the drawingroom. The need for social establishment in a mainly convict population, reinforced by recurring waves of British middle-class immigration, resulted in socially useful music-making that was conservative in every sense of the word. By the early 19th century, communal and choral singing, piano-centred entertainment and ensemble-playing were the principal domestic amusements; concerts, performed by amateurs in public halls and by military bands in the open air, were regular events in all the major towns and were soon adopted elsewhere.

With the sudden influx of population in the 1850s, many towns became cities with a middle class determined to consolidate its position and display its wealth and status. Music became rapidly institutionalised as the need for professionalism became apparent. Choral music became the province of philharmonic societies, which specialised in oratorio. Liedertafel, all-male singing clubs introduced by German immigrants in SA, provided concerts of a less demanding order, but a highly fashionable social life developed around them. Music societies flourished in cities and country towns alike until well into the 20th century and only lapsed as technological changes made other forms of music available. Passive listening, frequently lacking the score-reading ability that had been hitherto widespread, replaced the active and educated musical life of earlier generations.

Late in the 19th century music became part of academic life, with departments of music being established first at Adelaide University (1885) and then at the University of Melbourne (1891). Conservatoriums followed in most other States by the early 20th century. Departments of music devoted to research are a much more recent phenomenon and it was only with their advent that composers at last had job opportunities as teachers of the craft. This, together with government funding of composition and performance, has made it possible for a few Australian composers to survive without recourse to other earnings.

Musical performance Australian singers – in both the concert hall and the opera house – have long had an international reputation. In relation to population Australia has produced a disproportionate number of outstanding voices, most notably > *Nellie Melba* (from the late 1880s), > *Peter Dawson* (from 1909), > *Florence Austral* (from the 1920s), > *Marjorie Lawrence* (from the 1930s); John Shaw, > *Donald Smith* and > *Joan Sutherland* (from the 1950s); Donald Shanks (from the 1960s), and Neil Warren-Smith (from the 1970s). Instrumental music lagged behind vocal forms for most of Australia's history, with the notable exception of the piano. The pianist Ernest Hutchinson, who achieved an international reputation in the late 19th century, was followed by the prodigal and prodigious expatriate > *Percy Grainger* (from the 1890s), > *Eileen Joyce* (from the 1950s) and more recently > *Roger Woodward*.

It was not until Melbourne's Centennial Exhibition of 1888 that the first professional orchestra – the Vic. Orchestra – came into existence. This group failed in 1891, but a year later George Marshall-Hall, first Ormond professor of music at the University of Melbourne, founded his own orchestra and sustained its highly successful career until 1911. It was succeeded by Alberto Zelman Jnr's Melbourne Symphony Orchestra, which began as an amateur body in 1906 and continued under Zelman's baton until his death in 1927; in Sydney a similar function was served by Henri Verbrugghen's orchestra between 1915 and 1922. In the 1920s the conductor > *Bernard Heinze*, an organisational visionary, set in motion the establishment of six State orchestras with the ABC as impresario. The resulting concert network permitted broadcast performances to be heard nationally, a factor that rapidly altered public perceptions of musical standards and acted as a form of public education. Today State orchestras are becoming self-managing, although the ABC concert network – linked to radio and television – remains in place. On a smaller scale, Musica Viva (founded 1946) is an important entrepreneur for chamber music groups: in 1987 it presented 1500 concerts throughout Australia and overseas.

Musical composition Until the 1960s, Australian composition was regarded as inferior to music created in Britain. The colonial stigma was compounded by the low esteem in which the English held their own music for most of the period of Australia's existence – looking instead to Europe in general, and to Germany and Italy in particular. The result was a plethora of unperformed Australian works from composers, curiously undaunted by being silenced but whose compositions are only now being heard. This is particularly true in the case of opera, as small-scale works – being cheaper to perform – found a readier audience. Today Australian composition is increasingly in demand as composers turn towards more easily communicable styles than were the vogue earlier this century.

Australian composition was established by Isaac Nathan in the mid-19th century and George Marshall-Hall towards its end. Both were immigrants, however, as were their successors in the early decades of the 20th century: > *Alfred Hill*, Fritz Hart and Florence Ewart. Furthermore, the first generation of native-born composers of any note were expatriate for much of their careers: Arthur Benjamin, > *Peggy Glanville-Hicks* (recently returned to Australia) and May Brahe.

After World War 2, the work of > *Margaret Sutherland* gradually won wide recognition and she remained the doyenne of Australian composers until her death in 1984. During the same period the expatriates Percy Grainger (the first Australian composer to achieve an international reputation and still active in the immediate postwar years) and the much younger > *Malcolm Williamson* were creating an awareness of Australian music both at home and abroad. Since the 1960s, as with other creative fields, local composition has been strengthened by international exchange. The presence of overseas-born composers, such as George Dreyfus and > *Felix Werder*, has also been influential, particularly in the development of less conventional musical forms. Among the first of the modern composers to introduce a distinctively 'Australian' flavour was > *Peter Sculthorpe*, in his *Sun Music* series of the 1960s. Prominent among resident composers is > *Richard Meale*: the performance of his work *Voss* by the Australian Opera in 1986 was a landmark in the acceptance of local opera. Other contemporary composers include > *Moya Henderson*, Nigel Butterley and Colin Brumby, whose work ranges from vocal to orchestral; and a younger generation of increasingly eclectic composers such as Brian Howard, Ann Carr-Boyd and Barry Conyngham. >> *folk and traditional music*; *jazz*; *opera*; *rock and pop music*

mussels > *bivalves*; *fishing industry*

mustard family This large family of herbaceous plants, the Brassicaceae or crucifers, occurs worldwide and includes common vegetables such as cabbage, cauliflower, cress, radish and turnip as well as garden flowers such as stock and alyssum. Most are annuals with small four-petalled flowers and commonly contain oils with acrid sulphurous compounds that give a sharp flavour to the leaves and seeds. Australia has about 90 native species in 20 genera: few are of any economic consequence but some are notable wildflowers of the inland plains or alpine areas; a number of introduced species are common weeds of roadsides and cultivation, commonly known as 'wild mustards'.

Muswellbrook NSW (pop. 9988) This coal-mining town in the upper Hunter Valley is also the regional centre for the surrounding farmlands. The town was officially known as Muscle Brook from its inception in 1833 until 1949. The area's thick coal seams are mined by open cut and in mechanised tunnels; there is a large power station (and State mine) at nearby Liddell, and a second is under construction at Bayswater. The region is also noted for pastoralism, dairying and, more recently, wine production; local secondary industries include clothing manufacture and cement and brick production.

muttonbird Also known as the short-tailed shearwater, the muttonbird, *Puffinus tenuirostris*, is a migratory oceanic bird of an inconspicuous brown colour, which travels from Japan to breed in burrows on islands of southeastern Australia, especially in Bass Strait. It was an important food of some Aboriginal groups, who reached the islands at considerable risk to collect young birds from their burrows – the nearly fledged young are abandoned by their parents and left in the burrows to mature. The birds' large reserves of fat and oil have made them subject to considerable commercial exploitation.

myall > *wattle*

Myall Lakes These lagoons extend over about 10 000ha and are situated about 240km north of Sydney. Most of the area is a national park, which covers some 27 500ha and incorporates some spectacular coastal scenery as well as forested sand dunes; it also forms an important habitat for a range of marsupials and other wildlife.

Myer family, prominent in Australian retailing. **Sidney Baevski** (1878–1934), b. Russia, having opened his first store in Bendigo in partnership with his brother, Elcon, established the famous Myer Emporium in Bourke Street, Melbourne, in 1911. He was noted for his unusual promotional ideas, good treatment of staff, and civic philanthropy. These traditions were carried on by his nephew, **Sir Norman Baevski** (1898–1956), who led a dramatic expansion of the business after World War 2; and by his son, **Kenneth Baillieu** (1921–), who extended the company's reach into the suburbs, opening Australia's first integrated regional shopping centre – at Chadstone, Vic. – in 1961. Later expansion included the purchase of Farmers Stores, Sydney, and Boans Stores, WA, and the development of the Target discount chain. Momentum was lost in the early 1980s, however, and the Myer Emporium Ltd was merged with G. J. Coles to form Coles-Myer, Australia's largest retailer.

Myrtaceae > *myrtle family*

myrtle family The Myrtaceae family of flowering plants is centred in the southern hemisphere and is represented in Australia by some 1300 native species, including the > *eucalypts* as well as many other distinctively 'Australian' genera. All are trees or shrubs and are usually classified in two subfamilies – the Myrtoideae and the Leptospermoideae. The Myrtoideae comprise mostly rainforest trees; these include the lillypilly genus *Acmena*, of which there are about fifteen species, all bearing masses of white-purple fruits.

The Leptospermoideae, which are much more diverse in appearance and growth habits, include some of Australia's most distinctive genera. Among these is the teatree genus *Leptospermum*, which has about 80 species, mostly shrubs: they are particularly diverse along the southeastern coast, where familiar species include the tall and slender yellow teatree, *L. flavescens*, and its near relative the lemon-scented teatree, *L. petersonii*. Also in this subfamily is the endemic genus *Syncarpia*: its two species include the important timber-bearing turpentine tree, *S. glomulifera*, which is found in wet eucalypt forests and reaches a height of 60m. Other distinctive Leptospermoideae include the bottlebrush genus *Callistemon*, also endemic and comprising some 30 species (most confined to NSW); it is aptly named for its cylindrical spikes of crimson flowers, borne at the end of the branches. The most familiar species is the common bottlebrush, *C. citrinus*, of Vic., NSW and southern Qld; the Albany bottlebrush, *C. speciosus*, is one of the two species endemic to WA. Closely related to bottlebrushes is the genus *Melaleuca*, sometimes called paperbarks, which comprises about 200 species of shrubs and small trees; flowers range from white to red and are often carried on spikes. Smaller endemic genera in this subfamily include *Thryptomene*, a group of some 32 species of twiggy shrubs with small but profuse pale flowers; and Morrison flowers or *Verticordia*, some 60 species of brightly coloured shrubs found mainly in WA.

myxomatosis > *rabbits*

N

Nabarlek > *uranium*

Namatjira, Albert (1902–59), painter, b. NT. An Aborigine of the Aranda tribe, Namatjira was trained (from 1936) by the artist Rex Battarbee to paint in watercolours. He first exhibited his realistic landscapes of central Australia in 1938 in Melbourne, and was widely acclaimed; subsequent exhibitions of his work were held in several States during the 1940s and 1950s and his work is represented in most State galleries. Made an Australian citizen in 1957 (ten years before this right was officially granted to the Aboriginal people), he was increasingly divided by the irreconcilable claims of Aboriginal and European culture. Arrested and gaoled for distributing alcohol to his Aboriginal kin in 1958, he was released after two months and returned to Hermannsburg (his birthplace) where he remained until shortly before his death from a heart attack. A major retrospective exhibition, held in Alice Springs in 1984, revived interest in and critical appreciation of Namatjira's work.

Nambour Qld (pop. 9579) This town lies east of the timbered Blackall Range and 112km north of Brisbane; it serves an area noted for producing sugar and tropical fruits and the town has sugar and timber mills. It was settled in the 1860s by miners from the Gympie gold rush and is named after a red-flowering teatree that grows in the area.

Nandewar Range NSW This range forms the divide between the Namoi and Gwydir rivers, branching west from the New England Plateau. At the western end of the range, the spectacular volcanic plugs around Mt Kaputar (1523m) are part of a national park of that name. From there, the town of Narrabri lies directly to the west.

Nan Kivell, Sir Rex de Charembac (1899–1977), art dealer and collector, b. NZ. While director of the Redfern Gallery in London from 1922, Nan Kivell acquired an outstanding personal collection of historical material on Australia and the Pacific region – some 16 000 items including paintings and prints, books and photographs. The collection was acquired by the federal government in 1959 and now resides in the National Library of Australia in Canberra.

nannygai Also called redfish, the nannygai, *Centroberyx affinis*, occurs in offshore waters around the southern Australian coast. Distinguished by a large eye, a deeply forked tail and a deep-pink colour, it can measure some 40cm and weigh about 1.5kg; the major fishing area is in waters south of Sydney. The name, which has been variously spelt, appears to derive from an Aboriginal language.

Naracoorte SA (pop. 4636) Naracoorte lies 352km southeast of Adelaide, and is a service centre for the dairy and sheep pastures of the State's southeast; it is also the base for visitors to nearby fossil caves as well as the extensive wetlands of the Bool Lagoon Game Reserve.

nardoo This is the common name (of Aboriginal origin) for the unique *Marsilea* genus of aquatic ferns. Found in warmer climates around the world, the genus is represented in Australia by seven native species, five of them endemic. Most common in inland regions, when inundated they produce floating leaves which are replaced by smaller, erect leaves when the water recedes. During the dryland phase they produce spores in specialised woody, pod-like organs called sporocarps – actually modified leaves – which dry out during droughts but swell and open when wet and release water-borne spores. The common nardoo of the inland, *M. drummondii*, was at times used as food by Aborigines, who ground the sporocarps into a paste and baked it.

national anthems As a British colony, Australia inherited the British national anthem, 'God Save the King/Queen', from the first day of white settlement. Discontent with this legacy was documented as early as the 1820s, notably by the multifaceted republican J. D. Lang who devised both an anthem and a hymn to Australia and published them in his *Aurora Australis* (1826). The British anthem persisted nevertheless until 1974, when the 19th-century song 'Advance Australia Fair' received a majority vote at a national poll (held by the incumbent Labor government) for a replacement; 'Advance Australia Fair' was accordingly adopted for non-royal occasions by that government. In 1976 the succeeding Fraser government gave the choice of either the British anthem or 'Advance Australia Fair' for non-military and non-royal occasions; these guidelines were in turn overridden in 1984 by the Hawke Labor government, which ruled that 'Advance Australia Fair' would be played as the national anthem except when the British monarch was present. Perhaps surprisingly, the best known Australian song – 'Waltzing Matilda', popular since the late 19th century and the ballad most closely associated with Australia and Australians – received only 28% of the vote at a national poll conducted in 1977, compared with 43% for 'Advance Australia Fair'.

National Civic Council (NCC) A rightwing, anti-communist organisation of Catholic laity formed in 1957, the NCC evolved out of the trade-union pressure group, the Catholic Social Studies Movement, which because of its methods and secrecy had caused concern to many Catholic bishops in the 1940s and 1950s. Most of the NCC's original support came from Vic., where it was closely connected with the DLP; until its demise in the 1970s, the DLP remained the NCC's major conduit for exerting influence. While still claiming a substantial membership in the 1980s, times have moved on and most of the NCC's conservative aims and policies have been bypassed or rejected by history.

National Companies and Securities Commission (NCSC) This organisation was established by the federal government in 1979 to act as the controlling body for the Australian stock market. It has broad powers to act as judge, jury and law-enforcer in regard to Australia's 700 000 companies, working in conjunction with the Corporate Affairs Commission of each State and acting under the direction of the respective attorneys-general and the federal minister for business and consumer affairs. The NCSC has on occasions been criticised as ineffective, and as being too secretive in making its decisions.

National Country Party > *National Party*

national estate > *environment and conservation*; *heritage conservation*

national income and expenditure Published quarterly since 1945, the national accounts represent Australia's 'housekeeping budget'. On one side is the national disposable income – all wages, salaries and supplements, net operating profits and indirect taxes, less subsidies from the domestic production account, and payments overseas – and on the other, all expenditures on domestic products; the balance represents the nation's savings. Since World War 2, Australia's gross domestic product (GDP) has risen from about $4.4 billion (at 1989 values) to more than $275 billion. About half of that amount stems from wages and salaries, and the other half from company profits and indirect taxes.

nationalism Despite sporadic outbursts of republican fervour from the early 19th century onwards, Australian nationalism is still relatively feeble. Similarly, and despite the great growth of debate about Australian identity since the 1960s, a consensus on the 'national character' remains elusive after more than 200 years of white settlement. It has been observed that, in the absence of a unifying war of independence like that undertaken by America, Australia has remained a land never wholly won – either emotionally or culturally – by its people; this not only prolonged Australians' feelings of special inferiority because of their country's convict origins, but also perpetuated confusing triple loyalties – to Britain. and Empire, to colony and State, and to the emergent Australian commonwealth.

From the earliest years of settlement, the presence of Irish convicts and immigrants with anti-British prejudices fostered local nationalism. Most immigrants were English, however, and remained loyal to the British Empire. The colonies' mainly British population and continuing dependence on Britain underpinned Australia's involvement in the Sudan expedition (1885), the Boer War (1899-1902), and two world wars in the 20th century; in 1947, 65% of Australians still preferred British to Australian nationality. Despite Britain's entry into the EEC in 1973, the modern preponderance of non-British immigrants, and the growth of economic and political ties with the US, Australians persist in their allegiance to an absentee monarch.

Colonial loyalty was expressed as early as 1804 in the journal of Maurice Margarot, a transported English Jacobin; 'Let Government behave as kindly as they please to the Colony of NSWales, it must and will in the course of a few years become independent . . .' Like many others he envisaged Australia as a future America and was confident of its republican destiny, and was thus as much an Australian as a colonial nationalist. The > *Eureka Stockade* incident in Vic. inspired calls for Vic. independence in the form of nationhood, but as in the other colonies the achievement of democratic self-government in the 1850s to a large extent removed the spur to 'cut the painter'. Intercolonial rivalry persisted, and the reluctant and limited federation of 1901 left State nationalism dominant: as late as 1933 most citizens of WA voted to leave the Federation; and today Melbourne's Moomba parade draws larger crowds than do national celebrations such Anzac Day and Australia Day.

Australian loyalty was rarely called upon in the 19th century. The rare exceptions included the Australasian Anti-Transportation League (1851-3) and the cricket Tests against England from 1877. The cheeky Sydney *Bulletin* and the Heidelberg painters in Vic. have long been presented as early champions of Australian nationalism, but in both cases the American influence was paramount: the *Bulletin* preached radical republican nationalism in the American manner, and the 'bush' paintings of Tom Roberts, Arthur Streeton and Frederick McCubbin (in particular) owed much to the iconography of the Wild West and the influence of American art critic Sydney Dickinson. Federation did not bring nationhood, Australia's participation in World War 1 reflecting the population's loyalty to Britain as much as to Australia.

Overt Australian nationalism remained largely the province of the ALP for some time

to come and indeed has intruded rarely, even among those who cheer loudest at sporting events. While Australian cultural and political independence has strengthened since the 1960s, it must now be reconciled with new factors such as multiculturalism and hardening Aboriginal nationalism. >> *federalism*; *foreign policy*; *republicanism*.

Nationalist Party > *Liberal Party*

national parks and reserves Australia's national parks are established and controlled by the State governments or, in the case of those in the Territories, by the federal government. Australia was one of the first nations to create a public park – Kings Park in Perth, in 1872 – and the Royal National Park in Sydney, established in 1879, was the world's first public parkland to be designated a 'national' park.

As with > *heritage conservation* generally, it is only in the last 20 years that significant sites have been identified and acquired on a systematic basis. Today some 28.2 million ha – about 3.7% of Australia's land surface – are reserved as national parks or for other conservation purposes. As their names suggest, national parks are set aside principally for public recreation whereas many reserves (or conservation parks) are created to protect significant or endangered features and access to them is limited or prohibited. A wide range of locations and features are thus protected: prehistoric rock art, sacred or ceremonial Aboriginal sites, wilderness areas, marine and terrestrial habitats, and sites of historic or scientific interest. In many cases, there has been a conflict of interests between conservation and economics: conspicuous among these is continuing dissension over the right to investigate and extract minerals in reserved areas (most notably in the NT), to log or clear protected forests (in all eastern States, but with greatest impact in > *Tas.*), and to graze cattle in protected areas (most notably in the Vic. alps).

Major parks and reserves National parks or reserves exist – to a greater or lesser degree – in all States and Territories.

In Qld, about 1.9% of the State is thus protected, the first declared national parks being at Witches Falls on Tamborine Mountain (1908). Other noteworthy reserved areas include most (98%) of the Great Barrier Reef, the rainforests of the Lamington plateau, Fraser Island, the volcanic lakes Eacham and Barrine, and Lakefield National Park on Cape York Peninsula.

In NSW there are several hundred national parks and other reserved areas. These encompass regions such as the Snowy Mountains, the Blue Mountains and other highland formations such as the Warrumbungle Range and Barrington Tops, Ku-ring-gai near Sydney, coastal features such as the Myall Lakes, parts of Lord Howe Island, and some offshore marine areas.

Vic. also has extensive areas set aside in national parks and reserves. These include coastal sites and landscapes, such as Croajingolong near Mallacoota, the Big Desert wilderness reserve, marine reserves in Port Phillip Bay and off south Gippsland, and inland landscapes such as the Little Desert and Wyperfeld.

Tas. was one of the first States to declare national parks, at Mt Field and Freycinet. Many are in the alpine centre of the State or in the rugged wilderness regions of the west and southwest: the South-West National Park encompasses several areas that were the centre of much controversy in the 1980s over proposed hydro-electric and forestry developments.

SA had only one national park until the 1950s. Since that time nearly 100 reserves have been declared, many of which protect the State's unique desert regions such as the Nullarbor Plain and the Simpson Desert. Others encompass noted regions such as the Mt Lofty Ranges, and coastal environments such as the lagoons of the Coorong.

In WA there are a number of national parks and reserves protecting remote mountain regions such as the Kimberley and Hamersley ranges, although mining is permitted in both cases. Coastal and marine landscapes are also protected, notably in the Fitzgerald River and D'Entrecasteaux parks; representative arid regions such as the Nullarbor and Gibson deserts are also reserved.

While the NT has fewer national parks than other States and the ACT, it contains two of the nation's best-known and most idiosyncratic reserves – > *Kakadu* and Uluru (> *Ayers Rock*). Wildlife and marine reserves are also important, including the Cobourg Peninsula marine park. The rugged inland scenery of the Macdonnell Ranges and Katherine Gorge are also protected.

Much of the ACT is set aside for nature conservation, the largest such reserve being Namadgi which covers about 40% of the Territory. Much smaller but also of significance is nearby Tidbinbilla, noted as a fauna habitat.

>> *botanic gardens*; *environment and conservation*; *zoos*

National Party First called the Country Party (from 1920), then the National Country Party (from 1975), the National Party adopted its present name in 1982: a conservative party, it has traditionally represented Australia's rural voters. The third-largest party in Australian federal politics, the Nationals have long wielded influence disproportionate to the size of the party because of their ability to hold the balance of power in the federal parliament.

The origins of the National Party lie in the feelings of social and economic isolation shared by farmers and rural residents in a predominantly urban and industrial nation. These groups first found political expression in the WA parliament, where they sought tariff protection and opposed a compulsory minimum wage. Federal representation (in eleven seats) was achieved in 1919, with the support and financial backing of graziers who opposed controls imposed by the Nationalist government and the introduction of preferential voting. (Paradoxically, since that time many seats have been won by the National Party on the second preferences of both Labor and Liberal voters.)

Unlike the two major parties, the National Party has until quite recently maintained stable leadership and support. It has been a partner in every non-Labor government since its first coalition with the Nationalist Party in 1923, except for two brief periods in the 1930s. While it has produced only three (interim) prime ministers, the party has invariably received the position of deputy prime minister when in government and that of deputy leader of the Opposition when out of office. Its leaders have been W. J. McWilliams (1920–1), > *Earle Page* (1921–39), Archie Cameron (1939–40), > *Arthur Fadden* (1940–58), > *John McEwen* (1958–71), > *Doug Anthony* (1971–84), > *Ian Sinclair* (1984–9), and Charles Blunt (1989–90). Undoubtedly the most publicised National parliamentarian was the truculent conservative, > *Sir Joh Bjelke-Petersen*, leader of the Qld Party 1968–87. His unsuccessful bid to enter federal parliament in 1987 led to considerable cooling of relations between the Nationals and the Liberal Party, which had hitherto remained relatively cordial.

In the last 20 years, largely in response to the declining proportion of rural voters and the loss of rural seats through redistribution, the

National Party has worked to broaden its electoral base. At the State level this change was particularly successful in Qld, where the party was the senior partner in the coalition government 1957–83 and thence governed alone until it was defeated by Labor in 1989. The party has also been important in NSW, but less so in Vic., SA and WA; it has been virtually non-existent in Tas. since the 1920s. The election of solicitor Charles Blunt as leader of the federal party in 1989 reflected the Nationals' move towards the middle ground of politics and the party's increasing distance from its historical rural base. The swing against the party in the 1990 federal election raised questions about its future role. >> *political parties*

national trusts Based on the British model, Australia's several national trusts have played a vital role in alerting governments and the public to the need for conservation of both natural and artificial environments of aesthetic, historic, social, scientific or other special value. NSW formed the first trust in Australia, in 1945, and was followed by SA (1955), Vic. (1956), WA (1959), Tas. (1960), Qld (1963), and ACT and NT (both 1975). The Australian Council of National Trusts was formed in 1965 to represent the trusts at national and international level and to act as a co-ordinating body. Despite having no legal force, the trusts have been influential in introducing important legislation to help protect the national heritage, assessing and classifying buildings – and, more recently, aspects of the natural environment – deemed worthy of preservation, and compiling a register of such features. The federal government's Heritage Commission now carries out this work officially with the register of the national estate (although the trusts continue their own valuable listings).

Through donation, bequest and purchase, the trusts now own a diverse and distinguished range of properties (more than 200 in all); many of them are open for public inspection, including in Vic. the barque *Polly Woodside* (1885); in NSW, Old Government House, the country's oldest remaining public building (1799); in Qld, Charters Towers' gold-boom Royal Stock Exchange (1878); in SA, mining buildings and cottages at Moonta (1860s–70s); and in Tas. the colonial Georgian mansion Clarendon (1838). Volunteers are central to the trust's activities, although professional, full-time staff are increasingly being employed for specialist work. Research, conservation and restoration activities, education (through publications, lectures and seminars), and fund-raising to support the work are the main trust undertakings. Members are also represented on advisory bodies to State and Commonwealth governments, and command respect for their considerable expertise.

The trusts – especially in NSW and Vic. in the 1960s and 1970s – were instrumental in arresting some of the worst destructive excesses of so-called progress, although many battles were lost. Recently they have been criticised for becoming too conservative, unwilling to confront government and big business. With a national membership in the 1980s exceeding 80 000, however, the trusts have the potential to be a potent force if and when they so choose. >> *heritage conservation*

native and tiger cats These animals, members of the family Dasyuridae, are nocturnal, carnivorous marsupials that feed on insects, small lizards, birds and mammals. Many species have declined in range because of habitat destruction, competition with foxes and feral cats, and an epidemic which seems to have substantially reduced populations of carnivorous marsupials around the turn of the century.

The arboreal tiger cat or spotted-tailed quoll, *Dasyurus maculatus*, is about the size of a domestic cat and is found in rainforest and eucalypt forest from Qld to Tas. The eastern quoll or eastern native cat, *D. viverrinus*, was once widespread across much of southeastern Australia, but is now rare on the mainland (probably owing to the epidemic mentioned above); only in Tas. is it found in any numbers. This species frequently hunts on the ground.

Related species include the western quoll, *D. geoffroii*, restricted to southern WA, and the northern quoll, *D. hallucatus*, which is common in northern tropical Australia.

native companion > *brolga*

native police Aboriginal troops used for police work in NSW and Vic. for several decades from the 1830s, the native police were created largely because of the proven skills of early black trackers. The first such force was organised in Vic. in the 1830s: under Henry Dana it functioned as a mounted patrol 1842–52. The longest-running native force was formed in NSW in 1848, to handle continuing trouble between Aborigines and white settlers.

It was used mainly in the north of the colony, which at that time included Qld, and was eventually absorbed into the Qld force after that colony became self-governing. This, the last native police force, was disbanded by 1900 although black trackers continued to be used in outback areas of eastern and central Australia until the 1970s.

natural gas > *oil and natural gas*

nautilus > *cephalopods*

navy, Australian > *defence forces*

Neilson, John Shaw (1872–1942), poet, b. Penola, SA. Of humble Scottish parentage, Neilson had a bush boyhood and little formal education, and worked in various labouring jobs. First published in the *Bulletin* in 1896, he befriended its editor A. G. Stephens, who did much to mould and publicise his work. His graceful, lyrical poems, first collected in 1919, are deceptively simple in structure; their insight, imagery and intellectuality are strangely at odds with the harsh realities of his life.

nematodes > *helminths*

Nerli, Girolamo Pieri (1860–1926), painter, b. Italy. A flamboyant character, son of an Italian nobleman and an English mother, Nerli was trained in Florence. He arrived in Sydney in 1885 and painted and taught art in both Australia and NZ until his return to Italy in about 1900. An advocate of *plein air* painting and Impressionist in approach, he is particularly noted for his street and beach scenes. In Sydney he befriended Julian Ashton and Charles Conder, and was especially influential in the latter's own painting.

netball Netball, originally known as women's basketball, has 400 000 registered players (compared with 110 000 in the early 1970s) and 542 leagues, making it the most popular women's competitive sport in Australia. It is played from school and junior level through to a growing Masters competition. In the 1970s, sponsorship has seen the development of full-time coaching and administration.

The All-Australian Women's Basket Ball Association was formed in the 1920s, and although there are variations between netball and basketball in player numbers, court dimensions and rules, the sport retained its original name until 1970; regular interstate competition began in 1926. In 1963 Australia won the title at the inaugural world championships, and this dominance continued with victories in the 1979 and 1983 world championships. Regular competitions are now being played against the West Indies.

nettles These herbaceous plants or scrambling shrubs of the genus *Urtica*, family Urticaceae, are scattered through most temperate regions of the world. Two nettle species are common in Australia: the native scrub nettle, *U. incisa*, a perennial of eastern forests with long arching stems; and the introduced stinging nettle, *U. urens*, an erect annual of waste ground. >> *stinging-trees*

Neuroptera > *lacewings and antlions*

New Australia This attempted utopian socialist settlement was founded by 240 Australians on an 18 000ha grant from the Paraguayan government. It was established in 1893 on the banks of a tributary of the River Plate, 24km from Asuncion, by William Lane who, after the arrival of new recruits in 1894, led a group of 58 dissidents to found Cosme, 32km away, on more communistic lines. Both ventures failed. Cosme had 131 people in 1897 but only fifteen in 1921, and their descendants are now assimilated.

Newcastle NSW (pop. 255 787) The largest city in Australia outside the State capitals, Newcastle lies at the mouth of the Hunter River 167km north of Sydney; it is a major port and a huge centre for heavy industry – notably the BHP steelworks – and commerce. Newcastle was developed for coal-mining as early as the 1820s and this remained its chief function for nearly a century, until BHP opened a steelworks in 1915; this has grown into a massive complex on a 120ha site. Newcastle is also one of Australia's largest seaports in terms of freight handled, exporting coal from the northern NSW fields as well as other commodities such as wool, wheat and frozen meat. The city's other industries include the processing of minerals, engineering works, and the manufacture of clothing, glass, chemicals (particularly fertilisers), and bricks and pottery. As the principal administrative and cultural centre for much of northern NSW, Newcastle is well served with educational institutions (including a university and a number of tertiary colleges) and has an impressive cultural centre. It has, however, suffered periodically from fluctuations in the industries on which it depends – most recently in the 1980s – and unemployment is a serious problem.

New England region

NSW A section of the Great Dividing Range extending north–south roughly from the Qld border to the Hastings and Liverpool ranges, this is mainly rolling, pastoral country generally over 1000m and covering about 27 000sq.km, although the New England New State Movement would view it as somewhat larger than this. The plateau has a gentle western dip and a precipitous eastern scarp; of the peaks rising above it, the highest are Round Mountain (1615m), Point Lookout (1600m), Mt Bajimba (1524m) and Ben Lomond (1520m). A number of rivers rise here; in the west they flow to inland plains, while the eastern edge has many incised gorges and waterfalls, such as Wollomombi.

The southern part of the plateau was discovered by John Oxley in 1818 and settlement followed in the 1830s (the name was first used in 1836). Mining was important in the latter part of last century; the main rural activities today are grazing, agriculture, and fruit and vegetable growing, the chief urban centres being Armidale, Glen Innes, Inverell and Walcha. Armidale also is the site of the University of New England, and some 85km to the east is New England National Park, one of seven parks widely distributed along the plateau.

New Guard

An extreme right-wing organisation in NSW 1931–5, the New Guard was run on military lines by Eric Campbell, a Sydney solicitor, avowedly to fight extreme socialism and communism. Probably the movement's greatest claim to fame was its pre-empting of the official ribbon-cutting at the opening of the Sydney Harbour Bridge in 1932: violently opposed to the Labor government of Jack Lang, the New Guard staged a protest whereby one of its officers, Francis de Groot, rode up and cut the ceremonial ribbon with his sword before Premier Lang could do so. Although the New Guard's membership had reached an estimated 10 000 by 1932, the movement declined rapidly after Lang's dismissal in that year and was defunct by 1935.

New Holland

Nova Hollandia was the name given to the western part of the Australian continent by Dutch navigators in the 17th century; it was at that time unknown whether the landmass discovered by explorers such as Dirk Hartog (in fact the western part of the continent) was separate from the land encountered by others such as Jan Carstenz (southeastern Australia). James Cook set out specifically to find the eastern coast of New Holland in 1770, and named it New South Wales. It was not confirmed until the voyages of Matthew Flinders that NSW and New Holland formed one landmass, but that Van Diemen's Land was an island.

New Norcia

WA (pop. c. 200). This Benedictine community and diocesan centre is in the Moore Valley about 130km south of Perth. Named after the Italian birthplace of St Benedict, it was founded in 1846 by Spanish Benedictines and a monastery constructed the following year; it became the centre of an Aboriginal community and was made an abbey in 1867. Its Salvado College is a secondary boarding school.

New Norfolk

Tas. (pop. 6152) This historic town lies 37km northeast of Hobart and is the main service centre for the hop and apple farms of the lower Derwent River as well as the residential centre for the major newsprint works at neighbouring Boyer. The area was named when about 1000 free settlers were transferred there from Norfolk Island in 1807–08. Noted for its scenic surrounds and fine colonial buildings, the whole town has been classified by the National Trust.

New South Wales (NSW)

The fourth-largest Australian State (excluding the NT) in terms of area, but by far the largest in terms of population, NSW is the most highly industrialised State as well as being a significant source of agricultural and mineral products. With an area of 801 600sq.km (10.4% of Australia's total) and a coastline of some 1900km, NSW is made up of four main zones – the coastal lowlands, the tablelands, the western slopes and the western plains. The climate is generally temperate, with the northwest experiencing the highest temperatures and the southeast the lowest; rainfall varies from up to 2000mm per year in northern parts of the coastal lowlands to 200mm in the northwest of the State. The coastal lowlands vary in width from 80km in the north to less than 1km in parts of the south, but indentations such as the

Hunter Valley take the lowlands up to 160km westwards; the rainfall is reliable and well-distributed, and the rivers short, flowing generally eastward, with considerable discharges. The tablelands average 750m in height, reaching 1200m in the New England ranges and 2230m at Mt Kosciusko in the south, Australia's highest point; the rivers flowing both eastwards and westwards rise in the tablelands, which have a generally high rainfall. The western slopes usually have adequate rain, whereas the falls in the western plains are low and erratic; in both regions the rivers are slow and long, losing considerable water by evaporation and seepage before entering the Murray-Darling river system. The State's three major industrial cities, > *Sydney*, > *Newcastle* and > *Wollongong*, are all on the coast, as are the conurbations of Maitland and Lismore; other important urban centres are Tamworth and Goulburn on the tablelands; Wagga Wagga, Albury, Orange and Dubbo on the western slopes; and Broken Hill on the western plains.

Historical development The Aboriginal inhabitants of NSW were probably more numerous at the time of European settlement than has been thought, as it seems likely that many of them died from European diseases such as smallpox, contracted from other Aborigines who had been in contact with Europeans. From Governor Phillip's bitter struggle for survival developed the pastoral settlement, dominated by the squatters once the Blue Mountains had been crossed and the interior settled after 1815, although politics were controlled by personalities rather than policies or parties for several decades. Manufacturing developed slowly, and NSW supported free trade against the protectionism espoused by Vic; it was luke-warm about Federation. The depression of the 1890s was less severe in NSW than in other colonies, but the State suffered serious trouble in the depression of the 1930s. The State has at times experienced considerable industrial unrest, notably in the coal and transport industries, but it has also had a record (recently eclipsed by SA) of enlightened social legislation. In the 20th century urban rather than pastoral interests have dominated and, particularly since World War 2, immigration has led to huge increases in population in the Newcastle-Sydney-Wollongong region; this region, however, suffered in the recession of the 1970s and 1980s, especially in the manufacturing sector.

Population and economy The population of NSW at the 1986 census was 5 401 881, which showed a growth rate of only 0.03% over the five years between censuses. The growth rates of Vic., SA and Tas. were even lower, however, and NSW – with 34.7% of Australia's population – seems unlikely to be overtaken as the most populous State in the foreseeable future. The present figure gives a population density of 6.74 per sq.km, third after those of Vic. and Tas., but some 75% of the population lives in the Newcastle-Sydney-Wollongong region, with the rest of the State only sparsely occupied. About 80% of the population is Australian-born.

Despite its decline in recent years, manufacturing remains a major sector of the NSW economy, employing some 365 000 people and producing about 37% of the Australian total. Agriculture, yielding mainly dairy products on the coast and wool, wheat and beef inland, but with cotton, woodchips and bananas also important, contributes almost 26% of the Australian total. Almost 20% of Australia's annual mineral output comes from NSW, with coal (49%) being the most important. As elsewhere, retail trade is a major employer, and tourism is growing in importance, its annual earnings having grown by 274% since 1978–9.

Government and politics NSW was in the forefront of the fight to win self-government from Britain, but when this was achieved in 1855–6 it meant in practice government largely by squatters and urban property-owners. Until the early 20th century, government was by factions – political parties not yet having come into existence – and early premiers, from Stuart Donaldson (whose administration survived only for a day, 6 June 1856) onwards, almost invariably headed short-lived ministries. By the 1870s the factional alliances tended to be longer-lasting and two figures, > *John Robertson* and > *Henry Parkes*, stand out as premiers, neither of them notable for subservience to the squattocracy. By the 1890s a strong labour movement had developed, at first partly rurally based, and almost from the time of Federation NSW can be seen as a predominantly Labor State. The first Labor Premier, James McGowan, was succeeded by William Holman, who became a Nationalist following the Labor split over conscription in World War 1. The premiership of > *Jack Lang*, with its controversial solutions to economic depression, led to the conservatives holding office 1932–41, but there followed an unbroken 24 years of Labor rule which was ended by the election in 1965 of the Liberal government of > *Sir*

Robert Askin. While Askin retained power for some ten years, his successors were less adept and in 1976 > *Neville Wran* led Labor back to power for a further decade. His successor, Barrie Unsworth, was less successful and in 1988 the Liberals under Nick Greiner regained office. With its industrial heart in the Newcastle-Sydney-Wollongong complex, NSW does nevertheless remain basically a Labor State.

New South Wales Corps This infantry regiment was specially recruited for garrison duties in the infant colony of NSW, the first detachment arriving with the Second Fleet in 1790 under Captain Nicholas Nepean and the second in 1792 under Major Francis Grose. A further company of the corps, composed of former First Fleet marines, was commanded by Major George Johnston. Except for a large number of enlisted men who transferred to Governor Macquarie's 73rd Regiment, the corps returned to England in 1810, having played a very important – if not always creditable – role in the colony's early days (> *Rum Rebellion*). Many officers received land grants, becoming the first free settlers; they engaged in lucrative trading and, with time on their hands, also engaged in duels and feuds. There were also constant disputes with successive governors. On the other hand, early explorations, land settlement, trade development and surveying owed much to the NSW Corps.

newspapers Australia has one of the highest per-capita newspaper readerships in the world. The characteristics of Australian newspaper publishing are general editorial competence – which rarely reaches either the sustained heights of professionalism or the sensationalist lows seen in Europe and the US – political conservatism, relatively low prices and concentrated ownership (> *media ownership and control*).
Historical development Australia's first paper was the *Sydney Gazette and New South Wales Advertiser* (founded 1803) which, like its later fellows, was privately owned but subject to considerable government intervention. By the mid-1820s, however, the change from a predominantly penal colony to a basically free society demanded a different style of press. By 1848 there were at least eleven daily papers, all of them aggressively independent and partisan. After the discovery of gold, the industry expanded even more, particularly in country

areas, although the first rural paper, the *Tasmanian*, had begun in Launceston as early as 1825. Among the new country newspapers were the *Geelong Advertiser* (1840) and *Warrnambool Standard* (1870) in Vic.; and the *Maitland Mercury* (1843) and *Illawarra Mercury* (1855) in NSW. By 1913 there were 249 country papers in NSW and 99 in Qld.

Most 19th-century newspapers devoted much space to local news, crime and rural matters. They had small staffs and copied material from the overseas press; although overseas coverage was extensive, it was usually published intermittently in special supplements whenever ships brought the latest news from Europe. A characteristic of the Australian press in its first 100 years was the number of its individual (and individualistic) proprietor-editors, who paid little attention to neutrality and produced papers that were gutsy, partisan and often intemperate. By the second half of the 19th century, a number of these papers – notably the populist Melbourne *Age* (1854) and Sydney *Daily Telegraph* (1879) and the conservative *Sydney Morning Herald* (1842) and *Brisbane Courier* (1864, now the *Courier-Mail*) – wielded considerable influence.

The 20th century brought both physical and temperamental changes to the newspaper industry. In 1910 the Sydney *Sun* became the first daily to put news on the front page, and in 1922 the *Sun News-Pictorial* in Melbourne was launched as the country's first picture-tabloid daily. Some established papers followed suit and converted to the tabloid format, including the *Daily Telegraph* (1927) and the Melbourne *Argus* (1937). Today many dailies, most regional papers and all suburban papers are tabloids; the remaining broadsheet dailies are all morning papers, with the exception of the Melbourne *Herald*. Free suburban papers were first published in the 1920s.

As newspaper ownership moved to the second generation, the major metropolitan papers became generally more conservative editorially (although some Labor-oriented papers survived until World War 2). Their presentation was not conservative, however, and there was a general trend towards larger headlines, more white space, shorter paragraphs, more illustrations and a less discursive style. In the 1930s, the move to more entertaining newspapers included the introduction of comic strips, more light features, and special supplements (the last being discontinued during World War 2 because of paper rationing). In 1935, the Australian

Associated Press (AAP) was formed by several newspaper proprietors to supply overseas news.

In the years immediately after World War 2, circulation figures reached unprecedented levels. The Melbourne *Argus* used colour printing from the early 1950s and competition became even fiercer. The metropolitan papers became increasingly concentrated in a few hands (notably the Herald & Weekly Times group, the Fairfax group and News Ltd), a cause of growing concern after the closure of four dailies (including the Melbourne *Argus* in 1957). A more personalised style of journalism, with increasing use of by-lines, began to emerge in the 1950s although this trend did not peak until two decades later. The conservative, competitive tone of the 1950s decade continued in the 1960s although a few newspapers, most notably the Melbourne *Age*, started to break the tradition with hard-hitting investigative journalism that better reflected the growing restlessness of the community. Of the various national daily papers founded from the 1960s, the *Australian Financial Review* (daily from 1963) and the *Australian* (1964) are the only survivors.

The introduction of new printing technology was the main preoccupation of the 1970s, although aggressive promotional campaigns re-emerged to counter declining overall circulations. The *Dubbo Liberal* in NSW was the first Australian paper to be produced with computerised ('cold-metal') setting. The Fairfax Sydney papers were the first major papers to employ the new technology, in 1976, and although the perceived threats to employment caused a number of strikes by printers and journalists the disruption was much less than that experienced overseas (especially England). Newspaper profitability slumped over the decade, resulting from the large expenditure needed for the new equipment combined with a general decline in circulation and a national economic downturn. Evening newspapers were particularly affected by decreasing circulation, a worldwide phenomenon caused in part by the advent of television.

The 1980s and beyond In the 1980s, unease about the concentration of ownership flared again following News Ltd's unsuccessful attempt to take over the Herald & Weekly Times in 1979. Australia's only inquiry into newspaper ownership, the Norris Inquiry, was set up in Vic. and recommended some ownership controls so that diversity of opinion could be maintained. No appropriate mechanisms were introduced, however, and News Ltd finally succeeded in acquiring the Herald & Weekly Times group in 1987. Newspaper circulations continued to fall, relative to population increase, during the 1980s. To counter this decline, many papers introduced 'lifestyle' supplements and some, such as the Adelaide *News*, sought new distribution outlets including supermarkets. The size of papers increased, however, their enormous advertising supplements enlarging the *Age* and *Sydney Morning Herald* to more than 200 pages on Saturdays.

By the end of the decade, circulation decreases had not been stemmed but on the surface the scene looked healthy. As well as the two national dailies, there were fifteen metropolitan dailies and ten metropolitan weeklies, 39 regional dailies, and more than 400 provincial and suburban papers. The metropolitan dailies had a combined circulation of about 3.3 million and were read regularly by about 70% of the population. The future of the Australian newspaper industry is unclear. Economies of scale through mergers will be possible for News Ltd, but the Fairfax group will take some time to recover from the expensive flurry of take-over activity in 1987–8. The publication of several new Sunday papers in the eastern capitals will put further pressure on the weaker publisher, which may result in more ownership changes. >> *freedom of the press*; *magazines and periodicals*; *press, foreign-language*; *printing industry*

Nicholls, Sir Doug(las Ralph) (1906–88), pastor and Aboriginal advocate, b. Cummeragunja, NSW. A leading athlete and footballer in Vic. during his youth, Nicholls became a pastor of the Church of Christ Aboriginal mission in Melbourne in 1947. An active campaigner for Aboriginal rights in the seminal 1960s, he played a vital role in bringing together Vic. Aborigines and was founding director of the Aboriginal Advancement League 1969–74. The first Aborigine to be appointed MBE (1962) and to receive a knighthood (1972), he was also the nation's first Aboriginal governor, in SA 1976–7.

nickel Australia is the third-largest producer of nickel, after Canada and the USSR, producing 77 000t of refined nickel in 1986, some 10% of world production. The biggest producer is Western Mining Corporation, which has major nickel-sulphide mines at Kambalda and Mt Windarra in WA, and refineries at Kwinana and Kalgoorlie. Nickel-laterite ore is mined at Greenvale, Qld, and treated at the Yabulu refinery to produce nickel oxide for export. Nickel was the mineral behind the spectacular share-market boom of 1969–70, when companies like Poseidon – then half-owner of the Mt Windarra mine, and whose share price reached $280 in 1970 – became household words.

nightjars Australia has three species of these nocturnal birds: the tropical, long-tailed night-jar of northern Qld, *Caprimulgus macrurus*, and the spotted and white-throated nightjars of the genus *Eurostopodus*, which extend throughout the southern part – chiefly in the interior – of Australia. They are noted for the swift flight by means of which they capture insects on the wing, and for their peculiar calls; the long-tailed species makes a 'chopping' sound, so that it has been sometimes called axebird or carpenterbird, and the white-throated nightjar, with a trilling call, is in some places known as the laughing owl. In daylight these birds often rest on open ground, where they also build their nests.

nightshade family This large worldwide family of flowering plants, which is at its most diverse in Central and South America, includes herbaceous plants, climbers and shrubs; it includes food plants such as the potato, drug-yielding plants such as *Nicotiana* (tobacco) and some notorious > *poisonous plants*. The huge nightshade genus *Solanum*, which accounts for about three-fifths of all species, is represented in Australia by 94 native species. Many are sprawling subshrubs of inland areas, with needle-like spines and purple flowers; some are poisonous to grazing stock. The spineless kangaroo apple, *S. aviculare,* is a large rain-forest shrub with sprays of orange fruits said to be an Aboriginal food. Also important is the tobacco genus *Nicotiana*, for which Australia (with sixteen native species) is the second centre of diversity after South America; most contain nicotine, some in appreciable quantities. The Anthocercideae tribe is virtually endemic, consisting of seven genera and 29 species with greatest concentration in WA. The *Duboisia* is significant for its drug content: the two small eastern trees *D. myoporoides* (corkwood) and *D. leichhardtii* have been exploited for the medicinal drugs scopolamine and hyoscyamine; the nicotine-bearing pituri

shrub, *D. hopwoodii*, was chewed by Aborigines as a stimulant.

Niland, D'Arcy Francis (1919–67) novelist, b. Glen Innes, NSW. Niland was a peripatetic shearer, rouseabout, boxer and circus-hand before turning to writing. An excellent craftsman without pretension to the first rank, he wrote six novels including the best-selling *The Shiralee* (1955); he also wrote ballads, radio and television plays, and hundreds of short stories. Niland collaborated with his wife, novelist Ruth Park, in a joint autobiography *The Drums Go Bang!* (1956).

9 × 5 Exhibition > *Heidelberg School*

Nineteen Counties This was the name applied to geographical units identified in 1829 following instructions that NSW be divided into counties, hundreds and parishes, but with revision of boundaries and official proclamation in 1835. They were Cumberland, Camden, St Vincent, Argyle, Northumberland, Gloucester, Durham, Hunter, Cook, Westmoreland, Murray, King, Georgiana, Bathurst, Roxburgh, Phillip, Brisbane, Bligh and Wellington. Forming a semicircular area of 240–320km radius, centred on Sydney, they were declared by Governor Darling as the limit of legal settlement although already by that time overreached by the squatters.

Ninety Mile Beach Vic. This wide expanse of sand stretches from Port Albert east to Lakes Entrance, on the Gippsland coast. It consists partly of an extensive sandspit, created by the prevailing southwesterly current of Bass Strait, which encloses a number of lakes fed by south- and east-flowing rivers. The section of beach from Seaspray to Lakes Entrance contains the Gippsland Lakes Coastal Park and the area is a popular resort for fishing and camping.

Ninety Mile Desert SA This name is loosely given to the region of mallee country between the Coorong and the Vic. border. Legislation by both SA and Vic. governments instituted a program whereby trace elements were added to the soil, transforming substantial areas into agricultural land (as was done with similar areas of the Big and Little Deserts in Vic.); that portion now under cultivation is known as Coonalpyn Downs. Other sections of the Ninety Mile Desert are reserved as conservation parks, including both mallee country and swamplands.

Noarlunga SA (pop. 75 000) One of SA's main conurbations, the city of Noarlunga lies about 30km south of Adelaide. It is a major residential, industrial and service centre, with abattoirs and wine-making based on farming in the Mt Lofty Ranges to the southeast. At nearby Hallett Cove is the Port Stanvac oil refinery, on the only available deepwater anchorage within reach of the city markets.

Nolan, Sir Sidney Robert (1917–), painter, b. Melbourne. One of the most widely known Australian artists – and with his contemporary Albert Tucker generally credited with bringing to the attention of the world the painterly potential of Australia – Nolan has lived mainly overseas since 1950. One of the group of literary and artistic rebels in Melbourne in the 1930s and 1940s, and associated with the Angry Penguins, his early work was aggressively abstract. After war service 1942–5, he began a series of paintings based on 19th-century Australian history, including the famous Ned Kelly narrative (1948) and his equally distinctive portrayal of the Burke and Wills expedition (1950). Later subjects ranged from the Australian outback to classical mythology, his work remaining highly individual and deceptively 'primitive'. Nolan has donated many paintings from his huge body of work to the Australian people – including the monumental 'Paradise Garden' series that graces the Vic. Arts Centre. A major retrospective exhibition, which toured nationally, was held in 1988.

Noonuccal, Oodgeroo (1920–), poet, b. Stradbroke Island, Qld. Noonuccal is a part-Aboriginal poet and the first of the modern protest writers of her race. As Kath Walker, she published *We Are Going*, the first of her three volumes of poetry, in 1964. A formidable Aboriginal activist, she has described her poetry as 'sloganistic, civil rightish, plain and simple', which greatly underrates her remarkable talent. *Stradbroke Dreamtime* (1972) mingles old Aboriginal folk tales and new stories in traditional form.

Noosa Qld (pop. 11 296) This popular tourist resort lies near the mouth of the Noosa River about 140km north of Brisbane; the shire incorporates the nearby town of Tewantin. A region of coastal lagoons and coloured sands, Noosa has undergone dramatic urban and tourist development since the late 1970s. Development dates from cedar-cutting and its export to Brisbane in the 1870s; the local rainforest is protected in Cooloola National Park.

Norfolk Island (pop. 2367) This small and hilly island, of about 40sq.km, lies in the Pacific Ocean about 1670km northeast of Sydney and has been a federal Territory since 1914. It is best known for its role as a convict settlement 1788–1814 and 1825–56, which was notorious for the brutality of its administration. It was made a Crown colony in 1856, and was a dependency of NSW from 1897 until it became a Territory. Since 1979 the island has exercised limited self-government through a nine-member legislative assembly and three-member executive council. The island's economy is based chiefly on tourism and its historic sites and structures have been well preserved. Some 460ha have been set aside as a national park, which encompasses subtropical rainforest, stands of the indigenous Norfolk Island pine, and many representatives of the island's noted birdlife.

Norman, Greg(ory John) (1955–), golfer, b. Mt Isa, Qld. Norman became a professional golfer in 1976 and within a decade was the world's leading professional player. In 1986 alone he won nine tournaments, including the British Open, and is also distinguished by becoming the first professional golfer to win $1 million in one year.

Norseman WA (pop. 1775) A gold-mining town 730km east of Perth, Norseman is near the Dundas goldfields (discovered in 1892); the Central Norseman mine, Australia's richest quartz reef, was reopened in the 1970s and is now a major production centre. The first major settlement at the western edge of the Nullarbor Plain, Norseman is a tourist base and affords some fine views as well as fossicking sites.

Northern Territory (NT) Encompassing much of central Australia, the federal NT is larger by far in area than the ACT but has a population of less than two-thirds of the latter; among the States, only WA and Qld are bigger in area than the NT. Politically, it is the only division of Australia where the Aboriginal vote is substantial enough to capture the attention of federal politicians, but since gaining self-government in 1978 the NT has elected only conservative (Country-Liberal Party) governments. With an area of 1 346 200sq.km (17.5% of Australia's total) and a coastline of 6200km, the NT can be divided into three main regions – the northern coastal plains, plateaus and offshore islands; the central plateaus and basins; and the southern mountains and basins. The northern region, often known as 'the top end', includes > *Arnhem Land*, the northern parts of the Barkly Tableland, the Gulf Country, Groote Eylandt in the > *Gulf of Carpentaria*, and Bathurst and Melville islands in the northwest. The centre ranges from grassland to scrub and desert and includes most of the Barkly Tableland as well as the Tanami Desert; it serves as a watershed between the north-flowing rivers – intermittent except in their lower reaches – and the south-flowing, virtually non-existent except after the very irregular rains. The southern region includes the Macdonnell and Petermann ranges, Lake Amadeus, Mt Olga, > *Ayers Rock* and part of the Simpson Desert. Most of the NT lies north of the Tropic of Capricorn and its northern parts receive high monsoonal rainfalls during the wet season (November to March), more than 1600mm per year in places; the south has irregular rain, in some areas less than 120mm per year. Average temperatures range from 20°C to 28°C and extremes from –7.2°C to 47.2°C. > *Darwin* (the capital) and > *Alice Springs* are the main centres, with Nhulunbuy, Katherine and Tennant Creek also important.

Historical development It has been estimated that there were about 35 000 Aborigines in the NT before European settlement, and their tribal cultures were more numerous and diverse than those in the rest of Australia. The usual battles between the Aborigines and the settlers took place, but Aboriginal culture has survived in the north to a greater extent than elsewhere. The first attempts at British settlement, made on the north coast to forestall possible French interest and to develop Asian trade, were failures. Further exploration aroused interest in the region, however, and in 1862 SA gained jurisdiction over it; an SA settlement at Escape Cliffs (1864–7) failed, but another was successfully established at Palmerston (now Darwin) in 1868. Development was slow despite a brief gold rush in the 1870s, but pastoralists from SA gradually moved into the south of the NT. Chinese were important immigrants, but the Japanese declined an invitation

to send settlers. In 1911 the Commonwealth took over government of the NT from SA, and from 1926 to 1931 it was divided into two territories, Central Australia and Northern Australia. Even after reunification, the NT was largely neglected until the bombing of Darwin by the Japanese during World War 2 led to hasty road construction and a strengthening of the garrison. After the war the pastoral development of the NT speeded up, and until well into the 1960s this was the Territory's economic mainstay; since then, it has been overtaken by mining and tourism.

Population and economy The population of the NT at the 1986 census was 154 848, which represented a growth-rate of 21% over the five years between censuses – higher than that of any other State. The present figure gives a population density of 0.12 per sq.km, lower than that of any other State or the ACT. The NT has the highest Asian population of any division of Australia, and also the greatest number of Aborigines and Torres Strait Islanders, the population of the last two groups at the 1986 census (34 739) constituting 22% of that of the Territory as a whole.

More than 34% of the NT is controlled by Aborigines and used traditionally, pastorally and/or as national parks. Beef production, based increasingly on tropical breeds, is the dominant form of land use. The main mining activities centre on bauxite from the Gove Peninsula, manganese from Groote Eylandt, and uranium from Nabarlek and Ranger, with Jabiluka still to be developed; gold is also produced, and a pipeline carrying natural gas from the Amadeus Basin to a power station in Darwin was opened in 1987. Tourism is largely centred on Alice Springs and the Uluru National Park area, but the north, with Darwin and its casino, is also popular. Secondary industry is negligible.

Government and politics The boundaries of the NT were drawn by neighbouring colonies with the aim of excluding land they saw little advantage in owning. When SA took over government of the territory from NSW in 1862, speculation rather than development was the order of the day, except in the south, and by 1911 major debts had been accumulated by the NT administration; these SA was relieved to pass over to the federal government. Until World War 2 Commonwealth administrators governed the NT, with no elected representatives even as advisers, but after that war there was established a partly elected and partly appointed legislative council, and this system, with some variations, continued until 1974. In that year a fully elected legislative assembly came into being, although still subject to the federal government's veto. Finally, in 1978 the NT was granted self-government, although the Commonwealth retains responsibility for uranium mining, Aboriginal matters and some aspects of national parks. The NT is represented in Canberra by two senators and one member of the House of Representatives; perhaps partly for that reason, successive governments since the 1970s have given Aborigines greater rights in the NT than they have yet achieved elsewhere. The question of full statehood for the NT is raised fairly frequently, but it is difficult to see what useful purpose it would serve while the NT government remains dependent on the Commonwealth for some 90% of its revenue.

North West Cape > *US bases in Australia*

North West Shelf WA This is the name given to the continental shelf off the northwest (Pilbara) coast of WA, where in the early 1970s three large natural-gas fields – North Rankin, Goodwyn and the Angel – were discovered, lying some 130km offshore at a depth of about 125m. In 1980 it was decided to proceed with the development and a consortium of oil companies – BP, Standard Oil, Shell, BHP and Woodside – launched what was at that time the most costly single developmental scheme in Australia's history. >> *oil and natural gas*

Norton family, prominent in journalism and newspaper publishing. **John** (1858–1916), b. England, arrived in Sydney in 1884 and became a propagandist for the emerging labour movement. He took over the new weekly *Truth* in 1896, developing its abusive, ebullient style and publishing editions in other capital cities after 1900. He also established *Sportsman* in 1900 but wielded greatest influence through the immensely popular and reformist *Truth*. His son **Ezra** (1897–1967), b. Sydney, was initially cut out of his father's will but gained control of *Truth* by court action in 1922. He expanded the empire to include the Sydney *Daily Mirror* (1941) and *Sunday Mirror* (1958), before selling his interests in 1958.

Nossal, Sir Gustav Joseph Victor

(1931–), medical scientist, b. Austria. Nossal graduated from the universities of Sydney and Melbourne in the 1950s and subsequently worked as a researcher at the Walter and Eliza Hall Institute in Melbourne. His discoveries in the field of immunology, particularly in relation to the formation of antibodies and immunological tolerance, were of major significance and underpin today's knowledge of the immune response. Keen to see the development of vaccines for cancers and third-world diseases, Nossal has worked closely with the World Health Organisation since his appointment as director of the Walter and Eliza Hall Institute in 1965. His directorship has overseen increasing involvement by the institute in commercial development of its scientific research.

Nothofagus Regarded as the southern counterpart of the true beeches (*Fagus*), trees of this genus of the beech and oak family Fagaceae occur only in Australia, NZ, NG, New Caledonia and temperate South America, where they dominate forest vegetation in cool regions with very high rainfall. Evidence from pollen deposits indicates that *Nothofagus* forests covered much of eastern Australia during the Tertiary period, but they are now widespread only in Tas. There the common species is myrtle beech, *N. cunninghamii*, the dominant and largest tree of temperate rainforests which also occurs in limited areas of Vic. It is evergreen, in contrast with the other Tas. endemic species, the deciduous beech or tanglefoot, *N. gunnii*, a small subalpine tree or shrub with foliage turning gold in autumn. The third Australian species is the Antarctic beech, *N. moorei*, endemic to the higher mountains of northeastern NSW and the Qld border. Also a tall evergreen tree, larger-leaved than the myrtle beech, it forms majestic forests on plateaus such as Barrington Tops. The NG and New Caledonian species form a distinct group, known from fossils to have formerly been common in Australia.

Nowra-Bomaderry NSW (pop. 19 553) The administrative and commercial centre of the Shoalhaven district, Nowra lies 159km south of Sydney on the south bank of the Shoalhaven River; the small town of Bomaderry is situated on the opposite bank. Proclaimed a city in 1979, the area has a thriving tourist trade and attracts an estimated 1.7 million visitors each year to the 100 beaches along its coast. Dairying, timber and fishing are the chief local activities, with associated industries including a large paper mill and a dairy factory; other secondary industries include the manufacture of agricultural machinery, the production of boats and surfboards, and a flour mill. The district was explored first by James Meehan, in 1802, and was settled by cedar-cutters a few years later. Pioneer pastoralists included Alexander Berry, whose name was given to the nearby township of Berry. Picturesque Kangaroo Valley, just inland, was also settled in the 1820s. The RAN aircraft base, *HMAS Albatross*, is located at Nowra and incorporates a naval aviation museum.

nuclear disarmament > *disarmament and arms control*

Nuclear Disarmament Party (NDP)
This political party was formed in 1984 and won a WA senate seat in the federal election of that year; it captured particular attention through the publicity accorded one of its founders, the rock singer Peter Garrett. Discord occurred within the party in 1985, largely because of alleged infiltration by the Socialist Workers Party; several members subsequently formed an alternative political grouping, the Nuclear Free Australia Party, and some others joined the Australian Democrats.

Nullarbor Plain SA/WA This renowned expanse of arid land stretches for some 725km from southwest SA into WA, bordering the Great Australian Bight and extending for about 400km inland. It is in fact a vast slab of ancient limestone, thought to be the world's largest flat surface; the land rises gently inland to about 180m, from a cliffed coastline. The name, coined from Latin by E. Alfred Delisser in 1860, means 'no tree'. It is indeed sparsely vegetated, bearing wattle and eucalypt scrub near the coast but accommodating only hardy saltbush and other grasslands further inland. The uncertain winter rainfall generally seeps underground and leaves negligible surface water; in percolating through the limestone it has created innumerable tunnels and > *caves*, among the most notable of which are Koonalda and the 5km-long Mullamullang. Settlement is limited to sheep stations on the very margins of the region, which rely on subartesian water.

numbat This striking marsupial, *Myrmecobius fasciatus*, has a distinctive striped coat

and is an active ground-dweller, usually nesting in hollow logs. It has 50 tiny teeth and feeds almost entirely on termites, which it gathers on the sticky saliva of its long tubular tongue. Although once widespread across much of southern Australia, it is now an endangered species, confined almost entirely to parts of the southwest. Alternatively but not commonly known as the banded anteater, it is the State emblem of WA.

Nurrungar > *US bases in Australia*

nursery trade The commercial cultivation of flowers and ornamental plants in Australia developed apace from the 1850s. A strong industry has grown to supply the local market, with an estimated value of about $1000 million a year. It is extremely subject to the vagaries of fashion and public taste, and small specialised nurseries are becoming increasingly common. While native plants have been persistently popular in the 20th century, the last decade or so has seen renewed interest in old-fashioned and cottage gardens blending both local and introduced species; sales of ancillary products such as decorative pots and statuary have also become more important. As elsewhere in the world, the associated profession of landscape design expanded rapidly after World War 2 and courses are available throughout Australia; noted institutions include the Ryde School of Horticulture in NSW and the Vic. College of Agriculture and Horticulture in Melbourne. This aspect of the industry has been boosted by a growing trend for local councils to require landscaping plans for new buildings and developments, and for plantings in commercial and office premises to be subcontracted to professionals.

nuts and nut-growing Several varieties of nut – including hazelnuts, pistachios, pecans, walnuts and almonds – are grown commercially in Australia, but the market is generally small. Excluding peanuts (> *oilseeds*), historically by far the most important of these has been the introduced almond, which is grown principally in SA and Vic. Since the 1970s, however, cultivation of the native macadamia has expanded dramatically and annual production was valued at about $5 million by the late 1980s; the main growing centres are the coastal areas of northern NSW and southern Qld. Production of pecan nuts and pistachios is also increasing, the latter being grown from

NSW around southern Australia to WA. The culinary potential of indigenous nuts such as quandongs, candlenuts and bunya nuts – all of which are traditional Aboriginal foods – is now attracting increasing attention > *food plants, native*

O

oats > *cereals and grains*; *fodder crops*

'O'Brien, John' > *Hartigan, Patrick Joseph*

O'Brien, Justin (Maurice) (1917–), painter, b. Sydney. O'Brien was art master at Cranbrook School in Sydney 1945–67; his work has been exhibited in Australia and Europe since the 1950s. His elegant, highly detailed figurative paintings are influenced by the Byzantine tradition and the golden light and ambience of Rome, where he has lived since 1967.

Ocean Grove–Barwon Heads Vic. (pop. 8680) This pair of seaside towns at the mouth of the Barwon River, 97km southwest of Melbourne, are popular beach resorts for residents of both Melbourne and Geelong. Ocean Grove was founded by American Methodists in 1887 and was given the name of a settlement in the US. The area is noted for fishing as well as the 3km of surf beach and the more sheltered estuary waters; development has occurred particularly since the 1960s.

O'Connor, Charles Yelverton (1843–1902), engineer, b. Ireland. In 1891 O'Connor arrived in Australia to become chief engineer of WA. He established Fremantle harbour 1892–1900 and was also chief engineer and general manager of the railways. His major work was the planning and construction of the > *Goldfields and Agricultural Water Supply*, a scheme that despite its excellence and lasting value – O'Connor's concern extended to its effects on land use – was attacked in many quarters. The strain of criticism superimposed upon the responsibility entailed is believed to have caused his suicide, the year before the pipeline was completed.

O'Connor, Richard Edward (1851–1912), politician and lawyer, b. Sydney. A leading architect of the Constitution, O'Connor served on the drafting committee of the federal convention 1897–8. He was subsequently solicitor-general and minister of justice before becoming a senator in the first federal parliament. Appointed one of the first High Court judges, in 1903, he remained on the bench until his death; he was also foundation president of the Commonwealth Court of Conciliation and Arbitration in 1905.

octopuses Octopods, forming an order of cephalopod molluscs, represent the extreme example of molluscs with evolutionary development of the 'foot' into eight tentacles around a 'head' or body, and no external shell at all. They have a somewhat parrot-like 'beak' and can give a painfully venomous bite. Some species are known to prey on other molluscs by injecting poison through holes drilled in the shells. The blue-ringed octopus, *Hapalochlaena maculosa*, is often seen in temperate Australian rock pools; its poison has caused human deaths and there is no known antidote. A similar species inhabits northern waters.

O'Dowd, Bernard Patrick (1866–1953), b. Beaufort, Vic. O'Dowd was a leading intellectual and socialist poet of Vic. in the 1890s, writing ardently radical political verse and pamphlets, idealistic yet socialistically militant on the future of Australia. He worked variously as a lawyer, parliamentary draughtsman and librarian.

Ogilvie, Will(iam Henry) (1869–1963), poet. b. Scotland. Attracted by the romance of the bush, Ogilvie lived in Australia 1889–1901 and worked as a station hand. He was a prolific contributor to the *Bulletin* during this period, celebrating outback life in lively yet lyrical verses and ballads. These were collected in three volumes, the most popular of which was *Fair Girls and Grey Horses* (1898).

O'Grady, John Patrick > *Culotta, Nino*

O'Harris, Pixie (1903–   ), artist and author, b. Wales. O'Harris arrived in Australia with her family in the 1920s. She has written and illustrated more than 20 children's books since her first, *The Pixie O'Harris Fairy Book*, was published in 1925. Her murals decorate many hospitals, museums and schools.

oil and natural gas The discovery of commercial quantities of petroleum hydrocarbons – oil and gas – in Australia in the 1960s made an axiom of author Donald Horne's descriptive title *The Lucky Country*. Until that time the only thing retarding Australian agricultural and mineral self-sufficiency was oil, and grave doubts had been expressed as to whether sufficient resources would ever be found.

Within 20 years, Australia was about 70% self-sufficient in oil and totally self-sufficient in natural gas (with vast reserves available for export). As well, on the basis of recent finds, the nation's future supply of oil and associated gases seems reasonably assured. Although Australia's major oil and gas field, Bass Strait, is declining in production, the prospects for further discoveries are good, particularly in sedimentary basins off the northwest coast. The Bureau of Mineral Resources, Geology and Geophysics estimates that there is a 50% chance of finding another 1800 million barrels of oil in Australia, a figure greater than today's demonstrated economically recoverable reserves of 1522 million barrels.

Historical development In the 19th and early 20th centuries, shows of oil and gas were often reported from wells drilled for water. Although such finds were frequently in the three areas that later proved to be in or adjacent to major oil discoveries – Roma in Qld, the Kimberley district of WA and the Lakes Entrance district of Vic. – initial high hopes were regularly dashed as the discoveries proved to be uneconomic. In 1953, an exploration company made brief headline news when it struck oil with its first well at Rough Range near North West Cape, WA, but the discovery was a one-day wonder. Gas shows at Roma in the Surat-Bowen basins in 1960 again created great excitement, and indeed Australia's first commercially viable oil discovery – the Moonie field – was made in this basin in 1961.

The Surat-Bowen discoveries put oil exploration on a sound professional basis for the first time, with the importation of experts and technological knowledge from the US. In fact, it was an American geologist, Lewis Weeks, who pointed BHP in the right direction by advising the company to 'get its feet wet' and explore offshore, which led to the discovery of Australia's largest oilfield in the Gippsland Basin of Bass Strait. In 1965 BHP, in association with Esso, discovered the Barracouta gas field off the southeast coast of Vic., soon to be followed by the contiguous Marlin gas field and the Kingfish and Halibut oilfields. Gas production began from these fields in 1969, and oil production in 1970. Since then numerous other Bass Strait fields have been discovered, but as offshore drilling is costly much development has been dependent on the price of crude oil and the rate of tax extracted from the industry. In 1988, average daily production from the thirteen platforms in Bass Strait accounted for 57% of Australian oil and met all of Vic.'s gas consumption demands.

The two other major oil and gas fields are in the Cooper-Eromanga basins of northeast SA and southwest Qld, and the Carnarvon Basin of WA. Commercial gas fields were discovered in the Cooper Basin in the mid-1960s, the largest of which is Moomba, supplying about 40% of Australia's natural gas through underground pipelines to Sydney, Adelaide and Canberra. Oil was later discovered in the Qld section of the basins and is piped, via Moonie, to Brisbane for refining. The first major discovery of oil in the Carnarvon Basin was made at Barrow Island, off the northwest coast, in 1964, and for some years in the 1970s this field produced about 10% of Australia's oil. The Carnarvon Basin also contains the North West Shelf gas fields, developed by a consortium of six companies led by BHP and Woodside Petroleum, which has invested $11 billion in the enterprise. The North West Shelf liquid natural gas (LNG) project was Australia's largest natural resources venture in 1989; it was already supplying gas to the WA market and liquefied natural gas for export to Japan, with planned future shipments of 6 million t of LNG annually to Japan's power and gas utilities.

The 1980s and beyond The most recent commercial oil strike was in the Timor Sea, some 600km west of Darwin, in 1983. The Jabiru and nearby Challis fields were the most significant offshore finds of the 1980s and future prospects in this area appear good, given a reasonably high international oil price. In 1989 Jabiru produced about 45 000 barrels a day, most of it for direct export. Smaller commercial oil and gas fields are found in the Perth and Canning basins of WA and in the Amadeus Basin of the NT.

In the 1980s the industry moved from a position of strict control of pricing and exports by the federal government to one of virtual deregulation. Since January 1988, the refining sector has no longer been obliged to absorb particular quantities of Australian crude oil; the government no longer fixes an import parity price (which was a way of pricing domestic oil based on the price of the imported product) and the industry is free to export crude oil without government interference. Opening up the market is intended to give companies an incentive to increase exploration and development.

The industry is still, however, affected by substantial 'secondary' taxes, such as excise and royalty taxes or resource rent taxes. The tax structure is complex, and is based on the location of the petroleum resource, the date of discovery and the date of first production – 'old' oil (discovered before 18 September 1975) attracting a higher rate of excise than 'new' oil. There is also a Commonwealth royalty levied on most offshore oil, which is shared on a 40:60 basis between the Commonwealth and the relevant State. >> *energy resources*

oilseeds A number of oil-bearing plants and seeds are of commercial importance in Australia, the best known and most valuable of which are peanuts. Others include sunflower, safflower and soybean – all of which have grown in importance in the last 20 years owing to the increased demand for unsaturated oils and for margarine – and to a much lesser extent rapeseed, linseed and the jojoba bean. Cottonseed oil is also an important by-product of the > *cotton* industry. About 500 000ha were sown to oilseed crops in the mid-1980s, mostly in Qld and NSW; the main products are seeds, oil from the seeds, and processing residues which are used for both human and livestock consumption.

The main peanut-growing regions are Kingaroy and the Atherton tableland in Qld, with smaller amounts being produced in NSW, around the Ord River in WA, and in the NT. The main emphasis of production is peanuts and commodities such as peanut butter, confectionery and livestock feed, with peanut oil a lesser by-product. The gross value of peanut production in 1985–6 was \$38 million, the industry providing mainly for the domestic market although any surplus is exported.

Sunflower and safflower are cultivated principally for their oils, which are the basis of

margarine and are also used as cooking oils. Oilseeds are also being developed as a possible alternative fuel for diesel engines. Jojoba has a variety of applications and is used in the pharmaceutical industry.

oil shale Australia has vast reserves of oil shale, a fine-grained sedimentary rock that yields oil when heated in a closed retort; it was mined from colonial times until 1952, mainly in the coal-mining areas of NSW. The industry died when cheap and plentiful local and imported oil became available, but a resurgence of interest occurred after the dramatic rise in crude-oil prices in 1973. Interest again waned when oil prices gradually fell and the cost of extraction from shale was considered. Nevertheless, Australia's major reserves in the Toolebuc formation of the Carpentaria and Eromanga basins in Queensland are an important future energy resource.

Olgas, the NT The brilliant red monoliths that form the group known as Mt Olga – or, commonly, the Olgas – lie in the southwest of the NT, and with Ayers Rock and Mt Conner are contained in Uluru National Park; the region is particularly sacred to the Aborigines, who call it Kata Tjuta – 'many heads'. Described by explorer Ernest Giles in 1872 as 'monstrous pink haystacks', the conglomerate rocks have weathered to rounded, dome-shaped segments; the highest monolith stands 450m above the surrounding land (1069m above sea-level), and clustered about it are 30 lesser rocks, all separated by narrow ravines; together the giant domes cover some 65sq.km, rising sheer above the desert plains. At the request of Ferdinand von Mueller, Giles named the mountain to honour the Queen of Württemberg.

Oliphant, Sir Mark (Marcus Laurence Elwin) (1901–), physicist, b. Adelaide. In 1927 Oliphant began research at Cavendish Laboratory, Cambridge, and subsequently held academic posts in Britain, where he directed advanced microwave radar research and was one of the first scientists to work on atomic energy (1941); he was among those who campaigned for the peaceful use of atomic energy and against the policy of secrecy surrounding development of the atomic bomb. He returned to Australia in 1950 as research director in physical sciences at the new Australian National University; he was governor of SA 1971–6.

Olsen, John (1928–), painter, b. Newcastle, NSW. Olsen is a leading contemporary artist of abstract work, much of which is yet firmly based on the colour and form of the Australian landscape. He originated the Sydney 9, a Sydney coterie similar to Melbourne's Antipodean Group. The large-scale mural *Five Bells* (1973) in the Sydney Opera House is one of his best-known works.

Olympic Games Australia is one of only three nations to have been represented at every Olympic Games meeting of the modern era (from 1896). Representation was rather haphazard at the earliest Games, but the successes of Edwin Flack (athletics), Freddy Lane (swimming), > *Frank Beaurepaire*, > *Snowy Baker* and > *Fanny Durack* alerted Australians to their significance.

In the interwar years Australia continued to send Olympic teams, although at times there was strong pressure to withdraw in favour of exclusive participation in the Empire Games (> *Commonwealth Games*), which were staged for the first time in 1930. > *Boy Charlton* (swimming), Dick Eve (diving), Nick Winter (athletics), Bobby Pearce (rowing), Clare Dennis (swimming) and Duncan Gray (cycling) all won gold medals to continue Australia's sound Olympic showing.

The Games survived World War 2 despite predictions that international sporting competition was doomed. John Winter (high jump) and Mervyn Wood (rowing) won gold medals in 1948; as did John Davies (swimming), Russell Mockridge and Lionel Cox (cycling), and Marjorie Jackson and > *Shirley Strickland* (athletics) in 1952. Considerable local and international attention was given to Melbourne's preparations for the 1956 Games, which it had been awarded in 1949; several times it seemed that mismanagement would see the opportunity withdrawn, but despite these troubles the Melbourne Games were a great success. Australia won thirteen gold medals and competitors such as > *Betty Cuthbert* and Shirley Strickland (athletics), Lorraine Crapp, > *Dawn Fraser*, Jon Henricks, Murray Rose, Ian Browne and Tony Marchant (swimming) became the pride of the nation. Australia's achievement in 1956 can be attributed to the advantage of competing at home for the first time, and to the efforts of coaches who had developed promising young swimmers and athletes.

In the next few Olympics Australian performance began to lag as other nations stepped up their coaching and provision of facilities. Winning performances were recorded by John Devitt, Dawn Fraser, John Konrads (> *Konrads family*) and David Thiele (swimming), > *Herb Elliott*, and Laurie Morgan and the equestrian team in 1960; by Kevin Berry, Dawn Fraser, Ian O'Brien and Robert Windle (swimming), Betty Cuthbert (athletics) and the yachting crew in 1964; by Maureen Caird and Ralph Doubell (athletics), and Lyn McClements and Michael Wenden (swimming) in 1968; and by Brad Cooper, Shane Gould, Gail Neal and Beverley Whitfield (swimming) and two yachting crews in 1972. All were creditable performances, especially considering the meagre government assistance provided, but the failure to win a gold medal in 1976 produced a public outcry, the result of which was the establishment of the Australian Institute of Sport in 1981 and a more realistic assessment of Olympic performances.

Reassessment was further encouraged with the winning of gold by Michelle Ford and the 4×100m medley relay team in the 1980 Moscow Games (which were marred for Australian participants by conflict over a boycott); by Dean Lukin (weightlifting), Glynnis Nunn (athletics), Jon Sieben (swimming) and the cyclists in 1984; and by Duncan Armstrong (swimming), Debbie Flintoff-King (athletics) and the women's hockey team in 1988.

O'Malley, King (?1854–1953), politician, b. ? Canada. O'Malley immigrated to Australia in the late 1880s, entered the SA parliament in 1896 and was elected to the first federal parliament in 1901. A controversial radical whose tendency to buffoonery and flamboyant personal style earned him enemies, O'Malley also gained attention for his genuinely held beliefs; he was the chief force behind both the development of the Commonwealth Bank and the acquisition of the site for a national capital. He stood unsuccessfully for parliament in 1917 and 1919, and thereafter retired.

ombudsman This office was introduced to Australia in the 1970s, based on the Swedish model; there is now a federal ombudsman and one for each State and Territory. The ombudsman receives and investigates complaints about government decisions, and determines whether the decisions are legal, reasonable and properly made. The ombudsman has no power to change a decision but recommends remedies to the affected agency and may inform the parliament if this is deemed necessary. The institution of ombudsman has proved to be a cheap, quick and informal means of resolving disputes with government agencies, and relative to population it is used more in Australia than in any other country. Its success has encouraged the establishment of similar offices to deal with complaints in the private sector. >> *administrative law*

Oodnadatta SA (pop. 200) This small outback settlement lies amid arid gibber-plain country some 1100km northwest of Adelaide; historically, its importance was as a cameldrivers' depot and later as the chief railhead for central Australia. It was bypassed by the new central Australian railway in 1980, and its main function today is as a centre for the outlying pastoral region and the site of substantial State power stations fuelled by coal from Leigh Creek. Despite its remote location, Oodnadatta has some noteworthy historic buildings.

opals > *gems and gemstones*

opera Like theatre and classical music, the popularity of live opera in Australia has waxed and waned in step with changing fashions and economic circumstances, and competition from radio, film and television. It has enjoyed a resurgence since the 1970s, although imported operas continue to enjoy much greater attention than the creations of local composers. Sometimes attributed to the nation's pride in physical prowess, Australia has produced a surprising number of world-class opera singers, including the legendary > *Nellie Melba*, > *Florence Austral*, John Brownlee and the pre-eminent diva > *Joan Sutherland*. Several Australian conductors have also made outstanding contributions to opera, most notably > *Richard Bonynge*, > *Sir Charles Mackerras* and, more recently, Stuart Challender.

Opera was performed in the colonies early in the 19th century; Italian works dominated for some years from the 1840s, although lighter works such as French comic opera and English operetta enjoyed periodic ascendancy. Entrepreneurs such as George Coppin (from the 1850s), William Saurin Lyster (from the 1860s), and J. C. Williamson and George Musgrove (from the 1880s) introduced a wide range of works to colonial audiences and in some cases gave important encouragement to local singers. Although operas were written by local composers from the 1840s, one of the few to be

performed professionally was Isaac Nathan's *Don John of Austria* (1846). The > *Tait family* succeeded to the J. C. Williamson empire in 1920 and the group was Australia's leading opera impresario until the 1960s. In the 1930s, the severe depression and the advent of soundtrack films adversely affected audience attendance; fewer tours from overseas did, however, help encourage the growth of local opera companies in the 1940s and 1950s. The Elizabethan Theatre Trust formed the first truly national company, which made several successful tours from 1956 but suffered financial losses which in turn caused a lowering of production and performance standards.

The Australian Opera, established with both government and private support in 1970, is now the largest performing-arts organisation in Australia. Faced with the huge costs of maintaining a professional company and staging large-scale works, combined with the relatively small Australian audience, it relies heavily on government subsidy (which in the late 1980s accounted for more than a quarter of the company's budget). State – and in some cases regional – opera companies now exist in most States, the most successful of which (in both critical and commercial terms) is the Vic. State Opera. In the face of high ticket prices, the televising of live productions has recently helped to bring opera to a much wider audience. >> *music and musical composition*

Ophthalmia Range WA Mt Newman (1128m) is the highest point of these low mountains, which extend for about 100km near the eastern end of the Hamersley Range. Iron ore is mined in the range, at Mt Whaleback. The somewhat unusual name derives from an attack of ophthalmia suffered by the discoverer of the mountains, Ernest Giles, in 1876.

Opperman, Sir Hubert (Ferdinand) (1904–   ), cyclist and politician, b. Rochester, Vic. Opperman achieved national prominence in the Australian road-racing championships during the 1920s, and his success led him to try his luck on the European circuit. In his first year in France, 'Oppy' finished 17th in the Tour de France – a remarkable feat, as he was competing solo against teams of up to ten – and in 1928 he won the Bol d'Or. Two years later he cemented his fame by winning the Paris–Brest–Paris marathon of 1168km, and returning to Australia set a series of remarkable endurance and city-to-city records. He entered federal parliament 1949–67, and after a successful political career was appointed Australian high commissioner in Malta, 1967–72.

Orange NSW (pop. 28 935) This prosperous city lies about 265km west of Sydney and just northeast of the extinct volcano Mt Canobolas, in an agricultural region known particularly for fruit-growing. It began as a village in the late 1820s and grew with the 1850s gold rush. The city is now a regional market and service centre, with fruit-processing, meat, wool and brick works, and a cordial factory. The birthplace of poet A. B. Paterson, Orange is also a tourist centre noted for its many parks and trees (particularly ornamental cherries, in homage to its principal products) as well as the beauty of the surrounding landscape.

Orban, Desiderius (1884–1986), painter, b. Hungary. A romantic figurative painter, Orban exhibited widely in Europe before settling in Australia in 1939. Entrée to Gertrude Stein's Paris salon (frequented by Picasso, Matisse and others) was influential on his painting and eventually – through the Orban School in Sydney, established 1941 – on the work of several generations of Australian artists.

Orchidaceae > *orchids*

orchids This large family of herbaceous flowering plants, the Orchidaceae, is represented in Australia by some 550 species. Their appearance and growth habits vary widely and most Qld species are rainforest epiphytes. Although best known – and widely cultivated – for their eye-catching blooms, many in fact have minute flowers. In Australia orchids are mainly found along the coast, in both temperate and tropical regions although they are at their most prolific and diverse in the warm moist environment of rainforests. Noteworthy species include the Cooktown orchid, *Dendrobium bigibbum*, the floral emblem of Qld; many members of the genus *Dendrobium* are rainforest epiphytes, including the rock lily, *D. speciosum*. Terrestrial orchids include the rare subalpine species *Prasophyllum alpinum*; others are found in the semi-arid inland, including the custard orchid, *Thelymitra villosa*.

Ord River WA This river, the centre of Australia's most costly irrigation scheme, rises in the East Kimberley plateau and flows north to Cambridge Gulf. The Ord River project was

initiated in 1963 to permit development of large-scale agriculture – chiefly, at first, cotton growing – and completed in 1967. The second stage, 1970–2, created the country's largest freshwater lake, Lake Argyle, a storage that could irrigate 60 000ha in WA and NT and provided potential for a hydro-electric power station. Research has been carried out since the 1940s to determine which tropical crops would be suitable for production in this scheme. Cotton proved unsuccessful owing to difficulty of insect-pest control and the termination of the cotton bounty; others tried are oilseeds such as peanuts and sunflower, sorghum, millet and rice, and sugar cane has been suggested. Further difficulties include problems with soil fertilisation and the remoteness of the region from major markets.

O'Reilly, Bill (William Joseph) (1905–) cricketer, b. Wingello, NSW. Known as 'Tiger' for his fierce competitiveness, O'Reilly was the best and most individual spin-bowler in the world during his Test career 1931–46. Unusually tall (190.5cm) for a spin-bowler, O'Reilly was noted for his long run-up, flailing arms, unusual pace, and the vicious spin he conferred on the ball; he took 144 Test wickets for an average of 22.59 runs. On retirement, O'Reilly entered journalism, writing elegant and informed commentaries and in later years adopting a divertingly irascible manner of criticising aspects of the modern game that did not meet with his approval.

orioles and figbirds These closely related birds belong to the family Oriolidae. There are two species of orioles in eastern Australian forests – the green and yellow – both feeding on forest fruits and insects and building cup-shaped nests among the leaves. At times the green oriole becomes a clever mimic of other bird-calls. The figbird is found in wet forests along the eastern coast and into NG; it is a perching bird, the male yellowish-green with a black head and the female brown with white underparts. As the name implies, it feeds mostly on native figs, although also on other forest fruits. Its nest is slight and built of twigs, usually in a fork of a horizontal branch, towards the outer edge.

Orthodox churches > *religion*

Orthoptera > *grasshoppers, locusts and crickets*

O'Shane, Pat(ricia) (1941–), lawyer and Aboriginal advocate, b. Mossman, Qld. A former school-teacher, O'Shane studied law at the University of Sydney and in 1978 became Australia's first Aboriginal barrister. Appointed head of the NSW Ministry of Aboriginal Affairs in 1981, she oversaw the passage of land-rights legislation in that State in 1983. She became a magistrate in 1987.

ospreys > *eagles and hawks*

Otway Range Vic. Forming a coastal range in southern Vic., these hills extend northeast from Cape Otway for about 80km, some rising above 600m. Much of the forest area is reserved, although some settlements have been established, among them Beech Forest and Lavers Hill. This is a region of unusually high rainfall: in places the annual average can be as much as 2000mm, which can result in serious landslides; it is also subject to severe bushfires, and was devastated in the fires of 1851, 1919, 1939 and 1983. The Barwon and Gellibrand rivers rise on the northwest-facing slopes of the range, and several small streams on the seaward side drain to estuaries on Bass Strait.

Ovens River Vic. This river of northeastern Vic. rises in the Australian Alps, on the north slopes of Mt Hotham. It is a tributary of the Murray, its course running generally northwest for some 200km to join that river west of Corowa, meanwhile receiving its own major tributary rivers, the Buffalo and the King. Rural activity in the Ovens valley today includes dairying and wool-growing; in the latter part of the 19th century and early this century, gold-mining was important. Major towns of the region are Beechworth, Wangaratta and Myrtleford. The river was named after John Ovens, an army officer under Governor Brisbane, and some-time explorer.

overlanding > *droving*

Overland Telegraph Constructed between 1870 and 1872, this overhead telegraph line connected Adelaide to Darwin and then – via an underwater cable to Java – linked Australia with the outside world. The line had a total length of over 3000km and its construction was a monumental achievement given the terrain it traversed, much of it following the route of explorer J. M. Stuart. Beset by drought, flood, problems of supply, and the threat of a com-peting proposal by Qld, the line was completed in August 1872, the first telegrams having been transmitted in June with the aid of a pony-express link between Daly Waters and Tennant Creek. The cost of the project was £480 000, borne entirely by SA and an enormous sum for a State with a European population of barely 200 000. >> *post and telecommunications*

owls There are twelve Australian species of owl, divided between two families: the brown owls of the family Strigidae and the whitish barn owls, family Tytonidae. All are adapted for a nocturnal and carnivorous life, helpful to humans in preying on insects and rodents – for which purpose they use their large, sensitive eyes, powerful beaks and claws, noiseless flight and perhaps, at times, cries calculated to 'freeze' the prey. The 'screaming woman' cry of the eastern Australian bush belongs to the many-voiced barking owl, *Ninox connivens*, while the call 'mo-poke' or 'boo-book' is that of the common mopoke or boobook owl, *N. boobook*. The largest Australian specimen is the powerful owl, *N. strenua*, found only in wild forests. The barn owl, *Tyto alba*, occurs almost worldwide, and frequently nests in barns or abandoned buildings.

Oxley, John Joseph William Molesworth (1785–1828), explorer, b. England. Oxley was appointed surveyor-general in NSW in 1812. With George Evans and Allan Cunningham, in 1817 he explored the Lachlan River and in 1818 the Macquarie. Turning east from the Macquarie marshes, Oxley crossed the mountains and followed the Hastings valley to the bay he named Port Macquarie. In 1819 he explored the coastal region of southern NSW, and in 1823 the Moreton Bay area of Qld. Oxley contributed much, not only to exploration, but also to settlement of the Bowral area and the early development of banking, learned societies and libraries in the colony.

oyster-catchers > *waders*

oysters and oyster culture Australia has about ten species of native oyster, which are harvested in all States, but the delicate Sydney rock oyster, *Crassostrea commercialis*, is commercially the most important. An emerging rival in recent years is the larger, introduced Pacific oyster, *C. gigas*.

Oysters have been a traditional food of Aborigines in coastal areas since prehistoric times and shell middens are common along the eastern seaboard. After European settlement, oysters were not only collected for food but were burnt to yield lime for mortar, with the result that their populations had decreased markedly by the mid-19th century. Oyster farming began near Sydney in 1870, although initially with limited success.

The Sydney rock oyster occurs in estuaries from eastern Vic. through NSW to the Brisbane area in Qld, although its greatest concentration is around Sydney and NSW provides 90% of the annual oyster harvest. The Pacific oyster was introduced to Tas. and WA from Japan in 1947 but flourished only in Tas., whence it was introduced to SA in the late 1960s. Cultivation problems due to the high salt content of SA coastal waters led to commercial production being confined to the Coffin Bay region of that State. The Port Lincoln oyster, *Ostrea angasi*, which compares favourably with the prized flat oyster of Europe (now threatened by pollution and disease) is being farmed in SA and Vic. and is considered to have good export potential. >> *bivalves*; *fishing industry*

ozone depletion In 1984 two British scientists noted a 'hole' in the ozone layer – the thin mantle of gases in the stratosphere that absorbs up to 99% of the sun's harmful ultraviolet rays. By 1987 it was recognised that the ozone layer was rapidly being destroyed by pollutant gases such as chlorofluorocarbons (CFCs) and halons, which are continually being released into the lower and middle atmosphere. This problem is closely associated with the > *greenhouse effect*, because some gases contribute both to the general warming of the atmosphere and to depletion of the stratospheric ozone.

Diminution of the ozone layer is considered to be a threat to human life and productivity: it will increase the incidence of skin cancer, reduce immunity to diseases and infections, and decrease yields of essentials such as food and timber. It is also likely to compound the greenhouse effect, because it may destroy life forms such as plants and ocean plankton which absorb carbon dioxide – a major greenhouse gas.

Australia is a signatory to several international agreements committed to phasing out the use of CFCs and other contributory gases. By the late 1980s, however, environmental groups were pressing for more rigorous protective legislation, more control of CFC production, and the development of benign substitutes wherever possible.

P

Packer family, noted press dynasty and long-standing patrons of Australian sport. **Robert Clyde** (1879–1934), b. Hobart, was a journalist in Tas., Qld and Sydney before launching the racy Sydney magazine *Smith's Weekly* (with Joynton Smith and Claude McKay) in 1919. In the 1920s he started the *Daily Guardian* and *Sunday Guardian*, which prospered with a mix of sport, crime and political scandal. Packer organised the first Miss Australia Quest as a circulation booster in 1926. His son **Sir (Douglas) Frank (Hewson)** (1906–74), b. Sydney, entered journalism in 1923. He founded the > *Australian Women's Weekly* in 1933 and was managing director of Consolidated Press from 1936. Notoriously gruff and tough, Sir Frank built the company into the Australian Consolidated Press empire with a string of magazines, suburban and country newspapers, and (until 1972) the Sydney *Daily Telegraph* and *Sunday Telegraph*. His substantial broadcasting interests included large radio shareholdings and chairmanship of the Channel Nine companies in Sydney and Melbourne. An avid sportsman, he headed two unsuccessful America's Cup challenges (1962 and 1970) and was a leading racehorse owner. Sir Frank's first son, **(Robert) Clyde** (1935–), b. Sydney, held various managerial posts in the family companies 1959–72 and was a member of the NSW parliament 1964–72. He has since lived in the US. Clyde's brother **Kerry Francis Bullmore** (1937–), b. Sydney, joined the family empire in 1955 and has been chairman since 1974. He is credited with having changed the face of cricket when he introduced the World Series of one-day matches (and non-traditional garb) in the mid-1970s. Packer sold his television interests in 1987 to allow acquisition of the Fairfax group's magazine holdings. Magazines and the *Canberra Times* are the main media interests of Consolidated Press, which has diversified into pastoral and manufacturing activities.

pademelon > *kangaroos, wallabies and allies*

Page, Sir Earle Christmas Grafton
(1880–1961), politician, b. Grafton, NSW. A former medical practitioner, on entering federal politics in 1919 Page helped to form the Australian Country Party which he led 1921–39. As a corner party, it supported the Bruce government 1923–9, and with Page as treasurer this is often called the Bruce–Page government. After its defeat in 1929, Page held ministerial posts under first Joe Lyons and then R.G. Menzies until 1956. He was also the first chancellor of the University of New England.

painting, Australian Painting has played an important role in the creation of an Australian consciousness. Although for much of its history taste and artistic styles have been more or less dictated by Europe and, since World War 2, by the US, from the beginning Australia's unique environment and cultural experience have informed the vision of its artists and created a distinctive pictorial language.
Early colonial period The first European artists in Australia were employed in the service of science: topographical draughtsmen, such as William Westall, recorded the coastal profile of the continent; natural-history artists, like > *Sydney Parkinson* and the unidentified 'Port Jackson Painter', concentrated on the exotic flora and fauna of the new land and on the habits and customs of the indigenous inhabitants. As the first colonies of NSW and Van Diemen's Land became more independent economically and culturally, there was a corresponding increase in demand for pictures reflecting both the aspirations and the taste of the emergent society. Although there was a steady demand for portraits, in this period only > *Augustus Earle* in Sydney and Thomas Bock, Benjamin Duterrau and > *Thomas Wainewright* in Tas. raised local art above the mediocre or naive. Landscape was

the absorbing interest of the majority of artists: the topographic tradition of the early artists was continued by artists like > *Joseph Lycett*, whose *Views of Australia* celebrated the success of individual settlers and the general progress of the colony.

The search for the 'picturesque' and the 'romantic' in the antipodean landscape, evident already in the earliest extant oil painting (Thomas Watling's *A View of Sydney Cove*, 1794), shaped the vision of the two most important painters of this period. > *John Glover*, already established as a landscape artist in England, arrived in Tas. in 1831 and spent the rest of his life painting romantic English scenes for nostalgic fellow settlers and Tas. landscapes for the curious at home. > *Conrad Martens*, based in Sydney from 1835, was above all concerned to capture the effect of light and atmosphere in the Australian landscape.

Development of a national school With the discovery of gold in the early 1850s, Vic. became rich overnight. Melbourne soon became the most important cultural and artistic centre, with an influx of artists and the rapid establishment of art societies, art schools and public galleries. The colonists were beginning to see their experiences as uniquely Australian and the artists of this time made a significant contribution to the fashioning of a national identity: > *S.T. Gill* recorded with verve scenes on the goldfields and in the cities and > *William Strutt* commemorated historical and typical events of colonial life. In landscape painting, too, the subject-matter was valued for its Australianness: > *Nicholas Chevalier* and > *Eugène von Guérard* painted the untamed wilderness and the vast sheep runs of the squatters, while > *Louis Buvelot* captured the domestic landscape. It was directly from the *plein air* tradition introduced by Buvelot that the so-called > *Heidelberg School* developed, with the aim of painting the bush landscape from nature; particularly under > *Frederick McCubbin* and > *Tom Roberts*, this concept was expanded to include 'the national life of Australia'. A similar nationalistic feeling was finding contemporary literary expression in the *Bulletin*, which also gave an outlet for black-and-white > *cartoons*.

In the early 20th century many Australian artists were working overseas, where > *John Peter Russell*, > *Rupert Bunny*, > *Hugh Ramsay* and > *E. Phillips Fox* especially gained recognition. In Australia, with the decline of the Heidelberg School, a number of styles were adopted: some, like the Art Nouveau of Sydney

Long, were relatively short-lived; others, such as the romantic-realist landscapes of > *Hans Heysen*, established a long tradition.

Modernism Although the full impact of modernism did not take effect in Australia till the 1930s, some students of the Neopolitan-trained Dattilo Rubbo – > *Roland Wakelin*, > *Grace Cossington Smith* and > *Roy de Maistre* – developed an interest in neo-Impressionist and post-Impressionist painting in Sydney, which led to an exhibition of 'Synchromies' in 1919. In Melbourne, Arnold Shore and William Frater also became interested in post-Impressionism; in opposition to the strict dogma of tonal naturalism held by the teacher-painter Max Meldrum they established, with George Bell, a school to teach 'the principles of modern art'. Cubism and constructivism made little impact till the 1930s, when > *Grace Crowley* and Rah Fizelle opened a studio-school emphasising geometric form and dynamic symmetry. In defiance of the art establishment – which was deeply conservative, academic and institutionalised – the Contemporary Art Society was set up, first in Melbourne and later in other States, as the mouthpiece of the avant garde. Of profound influence was the exhibition of French and British Modern Masters, which opened in Melbourne in 1939 and gave many artists the first chance to see modern painting. The work of Salvador Dali stimulated an interest in surrealism, notably on the part of > *James Gleeson* and Eric Thake, but the realist-expressionist works were to have the most lasting impact, reflected in the formation of the > *Antipodean Group* in Melbourne in the 1950s and the gathering of a social-realist group around > *Noel Counihan* and > *Josl Bergner*.

After World War 2, painting in Sydney acquired a neo-romantic elegance – the eclectic, predominantly figurative Sydney group included Paul Haefliger, Jean Bellette, > *Donald Friend*, Michael Kmit and > *Justin O'Brien*. In the 1950s there was a more general move towards non-figurative and semi-figurative art under the influence of > *John Passmore*, Godfrey Miller and > *Ian Fairweather*. Conflict between the figurative and non-figurative painters was provoked by the exhibition and manifesto produced by the Antipodean Group in 1959. The leading abstract Impressionist was > *John Olsen*; other outstanding abstract artists at this time were > *Roger Kemp*, Donald Laycock and John Coburn. Throughout the postwar period artists like > *William Dobell*, > *Russell Drysdale* and > *Fred Williams* pursued their personal visions outside the bounds of any group. As the 1960s advanced, progressive art became more and more responsive to avant-garde movements in the US, particularly the various manifestations of colour painting such as hard edge, optical, and colour field. The Annandale imitation realists – Ross Crothall, > *Colin Lanceley* and Michael Brown – experimented with assemblage, and pop art and minimalism both attracted some adherents.

Contemporary art The 1970s were marked by a growing internationalism and the proliferation of a variety of post-object, post-minimal and post-modern styles. Painters already established in the 1960s, such as Roger Kemp, > *John Brack*, Fred Williams and John Olsen, worked outside the major movements but continued their own development and produced some of their best work in the 1970s. Emerging artists such as Jan Senbergs, Lesley Dumbrell, > *John Firth-Smith* and Fred Cress found the road more difficult, and acceptance slow in coming. Perhaps the major figure to emerge from the late 1970s was > *Peter Booth*, whose menacing neo-expressionist works were to provide a stimulus for the new generation of artists that appeared in the following decade. In keeping with the socio-political values which characterised the decade there was a growth of art collectives and co-operative exhibitive exhibitions, most commonly by feminist artists.

The 1980s saw a refreshing new repertoire of imagery and a renewed commitment to painting and to formalised sculpture. Neo-expressionism – inspired by Booth and stimulated by developments in Europe – was an important movement in the first half of the decade but plurality remained the dominant note, making it difficult to characterise the Australian school in this period. One of the notable features of the 1980s was the major role played by women artists within the context of Australian art rather than being primarily political as they had been the decade before. The opening of Australian National Gallery in Canberra in 1982 and the marked increase in Australian art-history publishing reflected a growing interest in Australian art in general and gave impetus to the artists' own self-concept. >> *art, Aboriginal*; *art awards*; *craft*; *photography*; *sculpture*

Palmer, (Edward) Vance and Nettie (Janet Gertrude), noted literary partnership. **Vance** (1885–1959), b. Bundaberg, Qld, came from a literary family. After early world travels, he finally settled in Australia with his

wife in 1915. He was a prolific writer of novels, short stories, poems and plays, all of which revealed great craftsmanship and expressed both his humanism and robust realism. An ardent nationalist and influential figure in literary circles, he helped to establish Australian drama through the Pioneer Players 1922–6 and published a series of books (1940–54) on leading Australian figures. His wife **Nettie** (1885–1964), b. Bendigo, Vic., graduated from Melbourne University in 1909 and married Palmer in 1914. Also an extremely productive writer she published, inter alia, two volumes of poetry, a collection of essays, and two striking personal reminiscences. Her many studies of Australian writers include *Henry Handel Richardson* (1950), which was instrumental in drawing popular attention to Richardson and her work.

palm family The Arecaceae family of flowering plants contains the largest monocotyledonous plants, although many of the world's 2800 or so palm species are small-medium rainforest shrubs or climbers. Australia has about 50 native palm species, divided among eighteen genera and confined almost exclusively to the tropical north.

All but two of the 18–20 species of fan palms belong to the largest and most widespread genus, *Livistona*. The common cabbage-tree palm of the temperate east coast, *L. australis*, grows to 30m and is the only palm extending to Vic. (in far east Gippsland). The diminutive sand palm of the NT, *L. humilis*, grows abundantly in the Darwin region and Arnhem Land; the small and isolated population of *L. mariae* is found only in Palm Valley in the Macdonnell Ranges, NT.

Feather palms include the prickly climbing *Calamus* (which yields rattan) of which there are eight native Qld species. The tallest feather palms are the two species of the endemic genus *Archontophoenix* of eastern coastal rainforests; one species is essentially tropical, the other temperate (extending to southern NSW). The smallest are the six short and slender-stemmed species of the walking-stick palms, *Linospadix*, most of which are endemic to northern Qld. Four feather-palm species belong to three endemic genera on Lord Howe Island off northern NSW: the Kentia palm, *Howea forsteriana*, is the most popular indoor palm of Europe and the US and trade in its seeds is a major source of the island's income.

The tropical coconut palm, *Cocos nucifera* – a source of copra, coconut-oil and coir – occurs wild on some northern Qld beaches but commercial plantings have had little success. This has also been the case with the date palms, *Phoenix dactylifera*, but African oil palms, *Elaeis guineensis*, have recently been established in far northern Qld.

Palm islands Qld These islands lie east of Ingham, between the Great Barrier Reef and Qld's central east coast. On the largest, Great Palm Island, is a government community for Aborigines established in 1918 and comprising both original inhabitants and descendants of mainland peoples. The second-largest, Orpheus, coral-reefed and thickly forested, is a national park and tourist resort. The name was bestowed by James Cook in 1770, in reference to the islands' cabbage palms.

Palm Valley NT > *Finke River*

Pandanus This genus of palm-like plants of the family Pandanaceae are sometimes called 'screwpines' for the spiral arrangement of their sword-like leaves. Australia has about fifteen native species, which are mainly confined to the tropical north except for the east-coast seashore species *P. tectorius*, which extends south almost to Taree in NSW. The tropical species are predominantly small trees of poorly drained ground, although a few northern Qld species are rainforest dwellers. *P. aquaticus*, centred on the NT, is a characteristic plant around edges of permanent water bodies, while in the same locality *P. basedowii* is unusual in growing on dry sandstone cliff ledges. The compound fruiting heads ripen to bright orange or red; the fruit flesh is usually too astringent for human consumption, although the seeds are extremely palatable either raw or roasted.

Pandorea A genus of lianas in the plant family Bignoniaceae, *Pandorea* is endemic to Australia except for one species which extends to NG and the nearer Pacific islands. This, *P. pandorana*, is also the most widespread species within Australia, although its shrubby narrow-leaved inland forms are often treated as the separate species *P. doratoxylon*. The climbing forms of eastern forests are known as wonga vines, while the inland plants are called spearwood for their straight cane-like branches which were used as spear-shafts by Aborigines. All species have attractive bell-shaped flowers in clusters, variously coloured and usually with contrasting markings in the throat. The three

other *Pandorea* species are rainforest lianas of Qld and NSW: *P. jasminoides*, a popular garden plant known as the bower climber, has pale-pink flowers with a purple throat.

paper industry Australia's flourishing paper-making industry commenced in the mid-19th century, in both Sydney and Melbourne. It initially involved the manufacture of paper from rags, waste paper and imported pulp, and it was not until 1929 that paper was first made successfully from eucalypt pulp. Major developments took place in the 1920s and 1930s with the formation of Australian Paper Manufacturers (APM) and Associated Pulp and Paper Manufacturers (APPM), which are Australia's largest producers. APM, which has mills in every State, chiefly produces heavy industrial paper and packaging; APPM – a subsidiary of the mining company, North Broken Hill – controls the fine-paper market, with mills at Burnie and Wesley Vale in Tas. Other companies are Smorgon Consolidated Ltd, a producer of industrial and packaging papers; Australian Newsprint Mills, a subsidiary of the Herald & Weekly Times group with a mill at Boyer in Tas.; and the US-owned Kimberley-Clark and Anglo-American Bowater-Scott, the major producers of domestic tissue and lavatory paper.

The Australian industry manufactures about 70% of the country's paper needs; imports consist mainly of high-quality paper and half the newsprint requirement (mostly from NZ). In 1986–7 imports were worth $1013.5 million, a high figure when balanced against the very small export market of $103.6 million in the same period. Australian paper is expensive by world standards, owing to a small market, which militates against the economies of large-scale production. To protect the local industry, import duties are levied on all paper products except newsprint.

Papunya > *art, Aboriginal*

parakeelya This is the common name of Aboriginal origin for succulent plants of the genus *Calandrinia* in the family Portulacaceae. There are some 40 native Australian species, mostly found inland although some inhabit wetter coastal areas. Several of the far inland species contribute much-needed colour to the arid vegetation, their profuse carmine-pink flowers (up to 4cm wide) carried close to the ground. The small succulent leaves are valuable animal fodder, and like the tiny but profuse seeds were baked and eaten by Aborigines.

parakeets > *parrots*

parasitic plants Among plants, parasitism has evolved independently in a number of unrelated groups, principally of flowering plants. Some parasitic plants depend on the host only for water and inorganic nutrients, while others have lost all photosynthetic capacity and must get carbohydrates from the host's sap; in both types this is achieved mostly through a specialised absorptive organ, the haustorium, which invades the host's conducting tissues.

Australia has representatives of a number of plant genera which are wholly or partly parasitic. Some families indeed consist entirely of parasites, most conspicuous of which are the > *mistletoes* and the > *sandalwood family*. Another common group of photosynthetic parasites are the leafless twiners of the genus *Cassytha*, in the otherwise non-parasitic > *laurel family*, which are known as devil's-twine or dodder laurel. A superficially similar genus is that of the true dodders, *Cuscuta*, although they belong to the unrelated Convolvulaceae family; mostly introduced in Australia, these are destructive crop weeds. A number of genera of the large > *foxglove family* are parasitic, including the eyebrights, witchweeds and broomrapes (the last two considered serious pest weeds). Two remarkable tropical families of parasites, Rafflesiaceae and Balanophoraceae, are represented in Australia: the first by the two WA *Pilostyles* species which are visible as multiple tiny globular flowers on the stems of certain shrub legumes; and the second by the remarkable *Balanophora fungosa* of Qld rainforests, which consists of a buried tuber with a cluster of club-shaped inflorescences terminating in a spherical head of about one million minute female flowers. Many Australian orchids (notably the genera *Gastrodia*, *Dipodium* and *Galeola*) lack chlorophyll and appear to behave as parasites although they do not make direct contact with the host plants but draw nutrients from them through their threadlike fungi; elusive underground orchids of the genus *Rhizanthella*, endemic to WA and NSW, also seem to be parasites of this kind.

pardalotes These are very small, insectivorous birds, also known as diamond birds. They are brightly coloured and spotted, hence their name, from the Greek *pardalotos*, meaning

'spotted like a leopard'. There are six or seven species of the genus *Pardalotus* found through Australia and Tas.: the most common is the spotted pardalote; others include the black-headed and striated pardalotes, and a species peculiar to Tas. known as the forty-spotted pardalote. The birds choose cavities in ground or trees to built nests of grass and bark.

Parer, Damien (1912–44), photographer, b. Melbourne. Educated for the priesthood, Parer found his vocation in photography, working with film-maker Charles Chauvel in the early 1930s and later with leading photographer Max Dupain. His war photographs and documentaries from the Middle East and the Pacific were compelling and also outspoken in their championing of the common soldier; his *Jungle Warfare on the Kokoda Front* (1942) won an Oscar in 1943. A man of legendary courage for the risks taken in the interests of his work, Parer was killed filming the American forces landing on Peleliu in September 1944.

Park, Ruth (?1923–), novelist and children's author, b. NZ. Arriving in Australia in 1942, Park married the writer D'Arcy Niland and her first novel *The Harp in the South* (1947) was inspired by their early life in the Sydney slums. Seven other adult novels followed, including the best-selling *Swords and Crowns and Rings* (1977), but Park is probably best known as a writer of children's stories, including *Playing Beatie Bow* and *When the Wind Changed* (both 1980). She also created the long-lived 'Muddle-Headed Wombat' series for the ABC.

Parkes, Sir Henry (1815–96), politician, b. England. Parkes arrived penniless in Australia in 1839. Variously a labourer, journalist and (unsuccessful) businessman, he had a brilliant political instinct, a massively impressive physical appearance, and clever if undistinguished oratory which brought him to gradual dominance of the confused NSW political scene from his election to parliament in 1854. He was premier five times 1872–91 and worked enthusiastically for Federation, although this was tempered by political expedience; thus, although instigating both, he prevented NSW from joining the federal council in 1883, or passing the draft constitution of 1891. Parkes was closely identified with the development of education, supported free trade and increased European immigration and land selection, while curbing the Chinese influx. He wrote poor verse himself, but encouraged both Charles Harpur and Henry Kendall. He died in some poverty.

Parkes NSW (pop. 8739) Lying 364km west of Sydney in a grazing and grain-producing region, Parkes is an important market, service and manufacturing centre. Situated on the Melbourne–Brisbane highway and the east–west rail line, it is also developing as a transport centre of national significance. Parkes was an important gold-mining centre from the 1860s; originally called Bushman's Lead, it was renamed in 1873 in honour of the premier of NSW, Sir Henry Parkes. A radio-telescope 64m high was constructed near the town in 1961 and attracts an estimated 60 000 visitors a year.

Parkinson, Sydney (1745–71), artist, b. Scotland. A talented botanical artist, Parkinson was contracted by Joseph Banks to accompany James Cook on his *Endeavour* voyage in 1768. A conscientious worker, before he died on the return journey he had completed at least 1300 drawings. Parkinson's botanical sketches and studies, which include many exquisite water-colours, are held in the British Museum; his few drawings of Aborigines and of Australian fauna – while valuable as the earliest such portrayals by an English artist – have less artistic merit. His account of the voyage was published posthumously in 1773.

parliament > *Constitution*; *government*

Parramatta NSW A city 24km west of Sydney and now part of the metropolitan area, Parramatta was Australia's second settlement and today is officially Sydney's second business centre. Explored by Governor Phillip in 1788, it was first named Rose Hill after a British treasury official; the original town was laid out in 1790, and the name changed to the present one (of Aboriginal origin) the next year. From the 1790s it developed mainly as Sydney's farmlands although the town continued to grow and was settled by notable pioneers such as John Macarthur; it has many significant buildings dating from this period, including Experiment and Elizabeth Farms. Parramatta is thriving owing to the westward spread of Sydney's population, the recent expansion of its CBD, and the locational advantage of being at the crossroads of western

Sydney's main transport routes. Its large new industrial estates are abandoning traditional manufacturing and distribution in favour of high technology, combining offices, factories and warehouses under the same roof. Parramatta is also a centre for diverse light manufacturing, commercial offices, and a strong retail sector.

parrot-fishes The teeth of these fishes of the family Scaridae are fused to form a parrot-like beak, which breaks off pieces of coral, and grinding plates to crush this to release the polyps and enclosed organisms before it is swallowed. There are about 24 species, many of them brightly coloured; they are hermaphroditic, varying in colour as they grow and change from female to male. Occurring in tropical waters, they are sometimes found as far south as Sydney in the warmer months. Wrasses also are called parrot-fishes in Australia, and a temperate relative is the rainbowfish.

parrots Australian members of the psittacine order vary in size from cockatoos some 60cm long to tiny, sparrow-sized parrots; there are over 50 species, representing about one-fifth of the world fauna. The Australian fauna includes rosellas, lorikeets, cockatoos and parakeets. Parrots are often brightly coloured, have strong, hooked bills and claws with a firm grasp; they have two toes in front and one behind. They range extensively throughout the contrasting habitats of the continent, from rainforest to semi-desert. Most nest in tree-hollows, some in cliff-cavities; two to four white eggs are laid.

The rosellas, which form the genus *Platycerus*, are brightly coloured, long-tailed parrots living mainly in forests and eating seeds and berries, although some are known to raid orchards. They include the eastern rosella, with a red head and a green body, the wings and tail edged with blue; the western and northern rosellas, and the pale-headed rosella of eastern Qld. There are also several ring-necked parrots which are mainly green, with yellow collars. The name rosella is said to derive from 'Rosehiller', Rose Hill being the former name of Parramatta, NSW, where the eastern rosella was first observed.

Lorikeets are nectar-eating parrots, generally small, short-tailed and mainly bright green; they feed boldly and greedily, darting swiftly from blossom to blossom, their movement through the forests following the flowering of the trees. The tongue is often hair-covered, to assist in extracting nectar. The largest and very beautiful member of this group is the rainbow lorikeet, *Trichoglossus haemotodus*. Somewhat similar to the lorikeets are the fig-parrots, *Psittaculirostris diophthalma*; they are very small, generally green with red-and-blue faces and yellow on the flanks; they eat the fruit of figs and other trees deep in the Qld rainforests.

Cockatoos, which constitute the genera *Cacatua*, *Callocephalon* and *Calyptorhynchus*, are prominent members of the parrot fauna. The grey-backed, pink-headed and pink-bellied galah – an Aboriginal name – or pink cockatoo is common throughout Australia; the sulphur-crested white cockatoo occurs in the northern and eastern mainland and in Tas. The gang-gang or red-headed cockatoo of the southeast mountains has a beautiful red head, and the pale corella is found in arid Australia. Darker-coloured species include the glossy black cockatoo, found in thick forests, and the palm cockatoo of northeastern Qld and NG. Other large birds are the magnificent parrots, and the superb and yellow-breasted regent parrots.

Parakeets, or grass parrots, are small, greenish, long-tailed birds, flocking in open woodland or interior grasslands and typified by the well-known and colourful budgerigar, *Melopsittacus undulatus*, found throughout the mainland with the exception of the rainforests. Others important in this group are the blue-winged parrot of southeastern Australia; the mulga parrot and its relatives, including the blue-bonnets; and the rare paradise parrot, *Psephotus pulcherrimus*. The dainty, crested cockatiel of the genus *Nymphicus*, with a grey body and yellow-and-orange cheeks, is also a grass-eater. A separate category might also be allotted to the ground parrot, sole member of the genus *Pezoporus*, which dwells much closer to the ground in isolated heaths of the southeast, and the rare, central Australian night parrot.

The smuggling of Australian parrots – both rare and common species – is a major problem; they are in great demand by overseas collectors and people are frequently apprehended trying to smuggle cases of drugged birds out of the country. In an attempt to counteract this there have been proposals to allow common 'pest' species, such as galahs or sulphur-crested cockatoos, to be exported.

Partridge, Eric Honeywood (1894– 1979), author and lexicographer, b. NZ. Partridge arrived in Australia in 1907 and served in the AIF in World War 1. In London in 1927 he founded Scholartis Press, which published his first lexicographic work, *Songs and Slang of the British Army 1914– 1918* (1930). A tireless researcher, he published numerous works on the English language but is particularly noted for his witty examinations of colloquial usage. His best-known works are *A Dictionary of Slang and Unconventional English* (1937), *A Dictionary of Cliches* (1940) and *Usage and Abusage* (1942), the last-named ranking with similar works by H.W. Fowler and Sir Ernest Gowers.

Passiflora > *passionflowers*

passionflowers This genus (*Passiflora*) of the family Passifloraceae includes several edible plants, most notably the edible passionfruit, *P. edulis*, and the giant-fruited granadilla, *P. quadrangularis*. These and most other species are indigenous to South America but Australia has three native species – all restricted to the east coast in rainforest margins and moist eucalypt forest and on seashores. Two are endemic: the orange-flowered *P. cinnibarina* ranges from Tas. to northern NSW, and *P. herbertiana* from southern NSW to southern Qld. The third species, *P. aurantia*, extends from northern NSW to northern Qld and beyond.

Passmore, John (1904–84), painter, b. Sydney. Passmore was a pupil of Julian Ashton and subsequently spent seventeen years in Europe (1933–50), where he absorbed the influence of such pre-eminent modernists as Cézanne and Picasso. In 1956 he was a dominant figure in the critical Sydney exhibition 'Direction 1', which confirmed the importance of abstract art in that city. Sydney Harbour, the sun and the sea are recurrent themes in his abstract expressionist work.

pasture plants Australia's native > *grasses and grasslands* have long provided grazing for the nation's livestock, to the extent that some species – notably the tall kangaroo grasses – have virtually disappeared in some regions. Pastures are also important in maintaining soil fertility and stabilising catchment areas, so that erosion and weed infestations have often resulted where they have been replaced with sown species. The principal natural pastures include hummock and tussock grasslands, mulga and saltbush in arid regions; mallee, spear-grasses and wallaby grasses in temperate and better-watered areas; and heathlands and sedges along the coast. Introduced pasture plants now cover some 27 million ha. Many are sown or naturalised grasses: these include buffel grass and green panic, which have largely replaced the former brigalow grasslands of northeastern Australia; other important species include lucerne, rye grasses, cocksfoot, guinea grass, paspalum and kikuyu. Legumes are of increasing significance in many areas, however, largely owing to their ability to flourish in nitrogen-deficient soils; among the main varieties used are species of clover, stylo and medic.

patents The granting of patents by the government protects inventions by according the creator a monopoly over the manufacture, use and sale of the product; the invention may be an actual product or simply a manufacturing method. In Australia such protection is obtained by registration under the federal Patents Act 1952, which is preceded by an elaborate process of examination within the Patents Office and publication of the proposed patent to allow rival manufacturers to object. A patent lasts for sixteen years in most cases, after which the invention becomes public property. While the system is both slow and expensive, it is particularly useful for protecting inventions that can be readily copied. >> *trademarks*

Paterson, A. B. 'Banjo' (Andrew Barton) (1864–1941), poet, b. Narrambla, NSW. Paterson's boyhood near Yass gave him a lifelong love of the country. He began training as a solicitor, turned to journalism, and was a correspondent in the Boer War and in China and the Philippines. First published in the *Bulletin* (1889), his verse – largely bush ballads – is generally considered to be peerless. His racing evocative rhythms captured the atmosphere and action of 'the bush' and were in marked contrast with the depressing realism of Henry Lawson's verse. 'The Man from Snowy River' (1895) is his most famous composition.

Paterson's curse > *weeds*

Peacock, Andrew Sharp (1939–), politician, b. Melbourne. A lawyer, Peacock entered federal parliament as a Liberal in 1966. He held various ministries in the McMahon and Fraser governments, including foreign affairs 1975–80, and unsuccessfully challenged Malcolm Fraser (then prime minister) for the Liberal party leadership in 1981. His political

fortunes have fluctuated since that time and he is seen by many as a lightweight, owing in part to his modish personal style. Elected leader of the Liberals in 1983, he was deposed by John Howard in 1985 but resumed the leadership in 1989. After the Liberals failed to oust Labor in the 1990 election, Peacock resigned as party leader and relinquished any further claim to the position.

peanuts > *oilseeds*

Pearl, Cyril Alston (1906–87), journalist and biographer, b. Fitzroy, Vic. Successively editor of Sydney's *Sunday Telegraph*, *A.M.* and *Sunday Mirror* 1939–61, Pearl revealed his sharp perception of human frailty in his historical studies *The Girl with the Swansdown Seat* (1955) and *Wild Men of Sydney* (1958). After 1961, he turned to full-time writing and became a television commentater; his subsequent and prolific output included *Morrison of Peking* (1967), *Brilliant Dan Deniehy* (1972) and *The Three Lives of Gavan Duffy* (1979).

pearls and pearling Pearl-fishing was one of the more romantic, if hazardous, industries of 19th-century Australia. Once the province of divers, who sought natural pearls from mother-of-pearl (the shell of the pearl oyster) and trochus shells, the pearling industry today is based on the artificial culture of pearls. In Australia it is centred in WA and, to a much lesser extent, the NT and northern Qld.

Commercial pearl-fishing began in WA in the 1860s and about 350 luggers were operating from Broome by the early 20th century. Diving was dangerous and the death rate – commonly from 'the bends' but also from treacherous weather, including cyclones – was high. The shell beds were largely depleted by the 1930s, however, and the industry only began to revive in the 1950s.

Today pearling in Australia is commonly undertaken jointly with Japanese companies. Young pearl oysters of the genus *Pinctada* are collected by divers and a nucleus (made from an American freshwater mussel) is inserted in the shell, after which the oysters are housed in 'pearl farms' while the pearl develops. Harvesting usually takes place about two years later and most of the yield is exploited. By the late 1980s the WA industry alone was worth about \$40 million each year; in the light of continuing expansion in that State, and the prospect of new leases being made available in the Gulf of Carpentaria, the value of the industry is certain to rise substantially.

pelicans Australia's only member of the pelican family, *Pelecanus conspicillatus*, is the largest species in the world and is found throughout the continent (including Tas.) and NG, chiefly in lakes and rivers but also on the coast. Plumage is white, with black increasing towards the rear in body and wings; it is web-footed, and feeds on fish and shellfish in both fresh and salt water. Though in the past killed by fishermen, it is now protected in many of its breeding places in coastal or inland swamps, and is holding its own; tiny Walker's Island in the Gulf of Carpentaria has probably the world's biggest pelican rookery. The Australian pelican was first observed in 1697 by Dutch navigator Willem de Vlamingh, on the Swan River in WA.

Pelsaert, François (or Francisco) (?1590–1630), official of the Dutch East India Co., b. Belgium. Pelsaert commanded the ship *Batavia*, wrecked in 1629 on the Abrolhos Islands. With a small group of the survivors, he made the 3200km journey to Batavia in a month, in an open boat. Landing frequently on the Australian coast, the men were appalled by the lack of water and vegetation, and by the flies. Returning with help, Pelsaert had to quell a mutiny and he marooned two of the culprits on shore, to become the first of Australia's involuntary white settlers. Explorer Abel Tasman was instructed to look for them in 1644, but found no trace.

Pemulwuy (?1756–1802), legendary Aboriginal leader, b. ? NSW. A member of the original inhabitants of the Botany Bay region near Sydney, Pemulwuy led a series of raids against the early British settlers between 1790 and 1802. After a major confrontation at the Parramatta settlement in 1797, followed by periodic attacks attributed to Pemulwuy, a reward was offered for his capture or death in 1801. He was shot and beheaded in a police ambush in 1802; he was succeeded by his son Tedbury, who was captured and imprisoned in 1805.

penguins There are some seventeen recognised species of these marine birds, whose very small wings are used not for flying but as an effective aid in swimming. Although they are confined mostly to the cold Antarctic and sub-antarctic oceans, some species wander north as far as Tas. and Australia's southern coasts. Only one species, however, the fairy penguin, *Eudyptula minor*, is a resident breeder in Australian waters. It extends as far north as the Qld-NSW border in the east and the Houtman Abrolhos in the west, usually nesting in rock cavities or burrows. The colony on Phillip Island, Vic. is a major tourist attraction.

Penrith NSW A city on the Sydney metropolitan fringe, some 53km west of the capital, Penrith lies near the Nepean River. Long the centre of a dairying and mixed-farming region, it has retained a rural character despite rapid growth that has made it the cultural, commercial, educational and recreational focus of Sydney's outer western region; proposed developments for the 1990s include a university and performing-arts centre. Penrith was settled in 1815 after the barrier of the Blue Mountains was overcome in that year.

Perceval, John de Burgh (1923–), artist, b. Bruce Rock, WA. A contemporary of Sidney Nolan and Albert Tucker, Perceval was one of the avant-garde artists associated with the Angry Penguins. His naive expressionist paintings, with their lavishly applied paint, range from social comment to ebullient landscapes and domestic scenes. From 1944 to the 1950s he worked as potter and ceramic sculptor at Murrumbeena, Vic., with the Boyd family (he married Mary Boyd). His ceramic work includes the celebrated 'angels', exhibited in 1958.

perches The freshwater and marine fishes known in Australia as perches bear no resemblance to the true perches of the northern hemisphere. In the case of marine species, the name perch is often applied to many different fishes; among them are several members of the family Scorpaenidae, which includes the > *butterfly cod* and > *gurnards*, as well as unrelated species in the family Serranidae such as the hapuka. Some freshwater perches found in the Murray–Darling river system also belong to the latter family: these include the Macquarie perch, *Macquaria australasica*, and the golden perch, *Plectroplites ambigus* (which is also known as the callop or yellowbelly). Like other freshwater perches – notably the grunters, which belong to the family Theraponidae – these species have been severely affected by damage to their habitat and the Macquarie perch is considered to be an endangered species. Of the true perches, the European freshwater perch, *Perca fluviatilis*, has been introduced to Australia; it is commonly known as the redfin.

perentie > *lizards*

periodicals > *magazines and periodicals*

peripatus This strange, worm-like arthropod of the phylum Onychophora is found in wet forest litter, generally on the southern continents that once constituted Gondwana. It is an ancient group, first occurring as fossils in the Cambrian period, and is considered to represent an evolutionary link between worms and insects; most are viviparous but several species (including two in Vic.) lay large eggs. There are more than 40 Australian species, and as elsewhere in their range these are rare but quite widely distributed, particularly in eastern Australia.

Perkin, (Edwin) Graham (1929–75), journalist and editor, b. Hopetoun, Vic. Perkin joined the Melbourne *Age* as a cadet in 1949 and fourteen years later became news editor. As editor 1966–75, Perkin is credited with changing the *Age* during that period from a stuffy parochial newspaper to one of the world's top ten papers. A campaigning journalist and fine writer, he was appointed *Age* editor-in-chief two years before his death; he was also chairman of Australian Associated Press 1970–2.

Perkins, Charles Nelson (1936–), administrator and Aboriginal advocate, b. Alice Springs, NT. A professional soccer player in the 1950s, in 1965 Perkins became the first Aboriginal university graduate. As a student, his work for Aboriginal rights included a well-publicised 'freedom ride' through NSW outback towns alleged to be racist. He joined the federal Department of Aboriginal Affairs (DAA) in 1979 and was chairman of the Aboriginal Development Commission from 1980. As head of the DAA from 1984 he was always outspoken, largely in support of Aboriginal rights but also on wider aspects of government policy such as Asian immigration to Australia. He was dismissed from the DAA in 1988 after allegations of maladministration, although an auditor-general's report subsequently cleared his name.

Perth WA The capital of WA, Perth is Australia's fourth-largest city and also its most isolated capital; its population density is very low, but since employment is to be found mainly in or near the city centre this has led to long-distance commuting and traffic congestion. Perth is located on the estuaries of the Swan and Canning rivers, and bounded on the west by the Darling Range; southward it has extended past > *Fremantle* to Rockingham, and northward to Burns Beach. Its climate is moderate, with average temperatures ranging from 9.2°C to 17.6°C, though the average maximum for January is 30.3°C; the average annual rainfall is 879mm, falling mainly in winter.

Named after a city in Scotland, Perth was founded in 1829 by Captain James Stirling. Major battles took place in the hinterland between Aborigines and the British settlers, and WA's agricultural development was at first very slow. Because of a labour shortage, convict labour was used 1850–68, by the end of which period Perth had slowly grown to a moderate size. In the 1890s gold was found in the Kimberley and Pilbara regions, and rapid development of both colony and capital followed. Perth's municipal area was expanded by amalgamations from 1904, and the city grew steadily through the 1920s and 1930s. After World War 2 mineral development in WA – based on iron ore, bauxite, natural gas, gold, nickel and diamonds – together with massive immigration more than tripled Perth's population by the 1980s.

At the census of 1986 the Perth Statistical Division had a population of 994 472, which showed a growth rate of 10.63% over the five years between censuses, during which period Perth had outstripped Adelaide to become Australia's fourth city. Residential areas have spread in four main directions from the city centre, with the greatest expansion to the north but major growth in lower-income residences to the southeast where there is ready access to the industrialised regions of the south. Perth is predominantly an administrative and service centre rather than an industrial base, but because of isolation many consumer goods are manufactured locally. Large-scale industries include the processing of iron ore, nickel, bauxite and petroleum; they are located largely in the Kwinana region, where pollution is a growing problem. Government involvement was successful in moving heavy industries to outer regions, but less so in attempts to decentralise commercial and light-industrial enterprises: the corridor plan of 1985 envisioned a growth of employment in regional centres with a corresponding drop in inner-city congestion, but this has failed to take place.

pests and weeds > *insect pests; weeds*

petrels > *sea-birds*

petroleum > *energy resources; oil and natural gas*

Petrov affair On 3 April 1954, Vladimir Petrov, third secretary of the Soviet embassy in Canberra, asked for asylum, claiming that he had been in charge of Soviet non-military espionage in Australia. On 20 April his wife also asked for asylum at Darwin airport, after being freed from Soviet armed guards escorting her back to the USSR. A royal commission was formed to investigate Petrov's allegations. Its findings were unsurprising, confirming that the USSR had indeed used its embassy as a cover for espionage; domestic repercussions were great, however, as two of the witnesses called before the commission and named as helpful to Soviet ends were on the staff of Labor leader H.V. Evatt. Evatt claimed that the evidence against them had been fabricated as part of a conspiracy to injure the > *ALP* in the 1954 federal election. The resulting controversy helped precipitate the 1955 ALP split that led to the formation of the > *DLP*.

phalangers > *possums*

Phar Lap The racehorse Phar Lap occupies a unique place in the pantheon of Australian sport. The NZ-bred chestnut gelding, standing 17½ hands, after an indifferent start to his career became the favourite of Australian racing crowds. Phar Lap's strapper, Tommy Woodcock, was responsible for nurturing him through a gruelling program that saw him win fourteen successive class races, including the 1930 Melbourne Cup at odds of 11/8 on, carrying 62.6kg. In March 1932 he was taken to the US, where he won his first start – the Agua Caliente Handicap, in Mexico – in brilliant style and seemed destined to reproduce his best Australian form. Four days later, on 4 April, he was dead. Rumours circulated that he was a victim of a Mafia plot, or more general American hostility, but the actual cause of his death has never been established. Phar Lap recorded 37 wins from 51 starts; today his stuffed and mounted skin stands on display at

the State Museum of Victoria. His heart, which proved to be larger than average, is preserved at the National Museum of Australia in Canberra.

pharmaceutical industry Historically Australia has done little in the field of drug research and development, and although of necessity this situation improved somewhat during and after World War 2, Australia is still very dependent on overseas supplies. During the first century of European settlement nearly all drugs were imported, although some wholesalers began manufacturing in the 1870s. Today, because the Australian market is small and modern research is increasingly expensive and specialised, most basic research is done at the headquarters of the multinational companies that dominate the industry. Australia's main work – much of it done by universities – is in investigating the safety, use and effects of drugs developed overseas.

The manufacturing side of the industry is established principally in Sydney and Melbourne, the major part being in Sydney. Its work chiefly involves making up imported active ingredients into tablets, mixtures, ointments and other medicines, although cortisone, penicillin and some older pharmaceutical products are made locally. Expenditure on pharmaceutical drugs in Australia in 1987 was estimated to be $1402 million, about two-thirds of which was accounted for by drugs requiring a prescription. The most commonly used medications are analgesics.

Phascogale > *marsupial mice*

pheasants > *quails and pheasants*

Phillip, Arthur (1738–1814), colonial administrator, b. England. Son of a German father and English mother, Phillip became the paramount character in the colony's first perilous years and the one to whom it owed its survival. Appointed in 1786 to command the First Fleet, from the outset Phillip concerned himself energetically and persistently with the voyage preparations, with superb organisation and attention to detail. On reaching Botany Bay, he quickly dismissed it for the settlement. Within a few days he had explored the magnificent Port Jackson inlet and selected Sydney Cove where, on 7 February 1788, before his assembled charges, official proclamations were read. Phillip had almost absolute power, controlling law, finance, trade and defence – indeed every aspect of life in the settlement. Difficulties multiplied: the convicts were largely shiftless, lazy and debauched; the guards were jealous, homesick and unco-operative, the soil was unyielding and food supplies were dwindling. Phillip put his own rations into the common pool when starvation level was almost reached. Meanwhile he had commissioned a fine town, personally explored by land and water, and tried hard to establish good relations with the Aborigines. Envisaging a colony based on free settlers, he began land grants to ex-convicts and marines, and assigned convicts as labourers. His requests to be relieved as his health broke were finally granted, and he returned home in 1793.

Phillip Island Vic. Situated at the entrance to Westernport Bay, Phillip Island is known chiefly as a holiday and tourist resort and is linked to the mainland by a bridge at San Remo. Wildlife abounds on the island; there are koala reserves near Cowes (the main township) and penguins, seals and muttonbirds on the south coast, including the world-famous 'penguin parade'. Sailing, fishing, surfing and water-skiing are other attractions, as is motor racing: the Australian Grand Prix was held there 1928–35, and the Motorcycle Grand Prix in 1989 and 1990. Discovered by George Bass in 1798, it was originally called Snapper Island; the name was later changed to honour Arthur Phillip.

Phillips, A.A. (Arthur Angell) (1900–86), critic, b. Melbourne. After studying at Melbourne and Oxford universities, Phillips taught for 46 years at Wesley College in Melbourne. 'The Cultural Cringe', an article he contributed in 1950 to the literary journal *Meanjin,* linked the phrase indelibly to his name. Apart from literary journalism and several anthologies, including *Coast to Coast* (1968), his chief works are *The Australian Tradition* (1958) and a critical study, *Henry Lawson* (1970).

photography The first photograph in Australia was taken by a Frenchman in Sydney in 1841, but photography really began with the gold rushes from 1850 on – when equipment, techniques, and keen amateur and professional photographers arrived in quantity. By 1855 Sydney boasted 20 studios and Melbourne ten; many photographers went 'up-country' in search of subjects, and the goldfields and diggers (especially the newly wealthy) were recorded

assiduously. The French government sent the urbane Antoine Fauchery in 1857 to document life in the Antipodes, which he did memorably in many superb and lively photographs. The energetic Beaufoy Merlin, largely sponsored by > *Bernard Holtermann,* left a remarkable record of rural Vic. and NSW, most notably gold-mining towns such as Gulgong and Hill End; when he died in 1873, his assistant Charles Bayliss carried on his work, specialising in expansive, technically refined panoramas. Despite the rudimentary techniques (portable dark-room tents, fragile glass plates) and primitive conditions, especially in the bush, the era produced a rich photographic legacy: among the exceptional talents were Charles Nettleton, John Lindt and Nicholas Caire, who helped immortalise 'Marvellous Melbourne'; Charles Gabriel with his evocative photographs of Gundagai, NSW; Charles Kerry's portraits of pioneers and early skiers at Kiandra, NSW, at the end of the 19th century; and Baldwin Spencer's outstanding images of the NT Aborigines. Women were active as both amateur and commercial photographers from the mid-19th century, including professionals such as Letitia Davidson who worked in both Melbourne and Hobart during the 1860s.

Early in the 20th century, > *Harold Cazneaux* gave photography new status as an art. He contributed immense talent and energy to promoting photography in Australia and left an impressive body of images of the Australian people, life and environment. The documentary tradition established the 19th century was continued by photographers such as > *Damien Parer,* who left a poignant record of the World War 2 battlefields; and the indefatigable > *Frank Hurley,* who photographed both world wars, Antarctic expeditions and the Australian landscape with equal dedication and skill.

After World War 2 the introduction of more sophisticated equipment, the growth of magazine publishing and the demands of the advertising industry were a great stimulus to commercial photography. Leaders in this field since that time have included > *Max Dupain,* unequalled for architectural photography; David Moore, master of both human and abstract images; Laurence le Guay, a fashion photographer now noted for his travel assignments; Wolfgang Sievers, a brilliant technical photographer; Athol Shmith and Helmut Newton, both internationally acclaimed fashion photographers; and scenic photographers Robin Smith and Dougglas Baglin. Paul Cox, John Cato, Rennie Ellis,

Richard Woldendorp and Angie Heinl are noteworthy among today's numerous commercial and art photographers. The first national organisation of photographers was the Australian Photographic Society, formed in 1962. The Australian Centre for Photography in Sydney, opened in 1973, has since been an important showcase for local and overseas work; and an increasing number of art galleries are acknowledging the importance of historic and contemporary photography by establishing special collections and appointing photography curators.

physical features > *geology and major landforms*

physical fitness > *sport and recreation*

Pichi Richi Pass SA This 16km-long gorge is a natural corridor through the south Flinders Ranges, between Port Augusta and Quorn. It was a pioneer transport route through the ranges from the coastal plains, and formerly also the way of the Port Augusta–Alice Springs railway. (A section of the old narrow-gauge track has been restored, with steam trains operating as a tourist attraction.) The area was explored in 1843; the name of the pass derives from 'pituri', a native shrub belonging to the nightshade family.

pigeons and doves Excluding introduced species, among which are the turtle-dove and the domestic pigeon, Australia has more than 20 species of these birds, forming three families. In the Columbidae there are two rainforest species: the beautiful purple-to-green-backed whiteheaded pigeon, *Columba norfolciensis*, and the brown pigeon, *Macropygia phasianella*, which has a conspicuous tail. In the family Turturidae the widely distributed forest bronzewing, *Phaps chalcoptera*, lives in open woodland and is hunted for food; it has several close relatives, including the brush bronze-wing, *P. elegans*. The wonga pigeon, *Leucosarcia melanoleuca*, named from its monotonous call, 'wonk-wonk-wonk', is the largest ground-bird and inhabits rainforests from Cape York to Vic.; the small, attractive green-winged pigeon, *Chalcophaps chrysochlora,* extends into Southeast Asia. Fruit-pigeons, of the family Treronidae and brilliantly coloured, appear in eight species in northern and eastern Australia, among them being the spectacular topknot pigeon, *Lopholaimus antarcticus*. The purple-breasted pigeon, or wompoo, *Megaloprepia magnifica*, and the

nutmeg pigeon, *Mystristicivora spilorrhoa*, live largely in forests, being fruit- and berry-eaters.

At the time of Australia's early settlement, various kinds of pigeons were to be seen in large numbers – sometimes in enormous flocks. In many species, numbers are now drastically reduced; NSW in 1953 proclaimed four species of fruit-pigeons to be 'rare fauna', in which case to kill any of these birds is to incur serious penalties, including possible imprisonment.

pigfaces These succulent plants of the family Aizoaceae, which are most diverse in southern Africa, bear fleshy fruits with sepals of unequal size deemed to give the detached fruit a resemblance to a pig's head. Pigfaces of the genus *Carpobrotus* are widespread in southern Australia: four of the six species present are regarded as native, while the others are naturalised South African species. All are prostrate plants with fleshy three-edged leaves and colourful many-petalled flowers, found mostly on sand dunes or edges of cliffs, though one species, *C. rossii*, extends into southern inland areas. The fruits are edible and very sweet when ripe. The closely related native genera *Disphyma* and *Sarcozona*, of similar appearance, are widespread in both inland and drier coastal areas across southern Australia.

pigs While pigs were brought to Australia in the First Fleet and pedigreed animals were imported in the 1820s, the industry has remained a relatively small one. Whereas pig farming was traditionally a farming sideline, the trend is now to specialisation in pig–dairy farms, pig–wheat farms and specialist piggeries, in all of which production is scientifically based. Research in genetic engineering has brought breakthroughs in breeding, and a new vaccine has been developed against swine dysentery. Feral pigs, estimated to number about five million in Australia, are a serious agricultural pest and cost rural industry millions of dollars a year through spreading disease and damaging both crops and land.

Piguenit, William Charles (1836–1914), painter, b. Hobart. A conservative but accomplished landscape artist, Piguenit is considered the first Australian-born professional painter. His formal, meticulous compositions and acute observations capture the sombre, remote scenery of the Tas. wilderness and the mountain country of NSW, which were his frequent subjects.

pikes All Australian pikes have pointed heads and very large teeth, but the name is applied to several distinct fishes which differ in types of fins and scales. Australian waters hold several species of the genus *Sphyraena*, in which the scales are well-developed and the ventral fins are below the pectorals. The tropical species may reach 2.5m and weigh 55kg; the barracuda, *S. barracuda*, is a gamefish in north Qld, the record weight being 22kg. The snook, a sea pike of the genus *Australuzza*, is an important commercial species; a very slender fish with very small scales, it can grow to 1m. An indigene of southern regions is the long-finned sea pike or jack, *Dinolestes lewini*, a fine eating fish generally about 50cm in length.

Pilbara region WA The rolling countryside of this minerals-rich region lies 1200km northeast of Perth; as a statistical division, it covers some 440 000sq.km. The Pilbara is best known as the abundant source of rich iron-ore deposits – most notably in the Hamersley Range – which have been mined since the 1960s; it is also the source of tin, lead, nickel and manganese, as well as the offshore oil and gas yielded by the North West Shelf. The Pilbara is a region of little and very variable rainfall, and much of the terrain is inhospitable. Pastoral leases were established in the region from the 1860s; although a goldfield was declared in the region in 1888, this was short-lived and the area was sparsely settled and devoted chiefly to grazing until large-scale mining progressed in the 1960s. Economic development was rapid from that time, as ports, towns and railways were established to service the mining industry. Its very ancient rock formations yield some marvellous scenery and much of this is protected in national parks, including those of Hamersley and Millstream-Chichester; there are also many important prehistoric sites, including Aboriginal rock engravings and paintings. Like other outlying regions, the Pilbara is now an important tourist centre.

Pimelea This is a genus of native shrubs and herbaceous plants found in most parts of Australia but elsewhere only in NZ. The approximately 100 native species are characterised by tough, flexible bark (usable as twine), smallish leaves, and small four-petalled flowers which in many species are tightly clustered in globular heads. In eastern states the common name is riceflower (the small elliptic petals resembling rice grains), while in WA some species are known under the Aboriginal names banjine or bunjong. The common riceflower of the east is the widespread *P. linifolia*, a low shrub with massed white flower-heads.

Pine Gap > *US bases in Australia*

Pinnacles, the WA The Pinnacle Desert lies near the coast, south of Cervantes, about 200km north of Perth. The 'pinnacles' are formed from limestone, about 0.5–2m high and standing 2–10m apart. In 1968, the desert was made part of Nambung National Park.

Pioneer River Qld On Qld's central east coast, this river rises in Connors Range and runs some 80km to the sea near Mackay, flowing east from the forested and largely inaccessible Eungella Range National Park. The lower valley, and that of its tributary, Cattle Creek, form an alluvial plain between the Clarke and Connors ranges, and are important sugar-cane areas, also producing tropical fruits and grazing beef and dairy cattle. The river was discovered in 1869 by John Mackay.

pipis > *bivalves*

pipits > *larks and pipits*

pitcher-plants These bizarre insectivorous plants have leaves modified into pitcher-like structures in which insects are trapped and drowned.Worldwide there are five genera in three families, the largest being the Asiatic *Nepenthes*. Australia has two native pitcher-plants, confined to opposite corners of the continent. *Nepenthes mirabilis*, a scrambling climber of heathy scrub, is native to far north Qld; its pitchers, often colourfully marked, are up to 15cm long. Confined to southern WA between Albany and Denmark is the remarkable Albany pitcher-plant, *Cephalotus follicularis*, the only member of the endemic family Cephalotaceae; its pitchers are similar to those of *Nepenthes*, including a 'lid' which may serve to exclude rainwater.

Pittosporaceae > *pittosporum family*

pittosporum family The best-known member of the Australian flowering-plant family Pittosporaceae is the tree and shrub genus *Pittosporum*, which extends through the Pacific to Asia and Africa. Australia has about nine native *Pittosporum* species, most restricted to eastern forests. The common pittosporum of Sydney and Melbourne, *P. undulatum*, is a small to medium-sized tree now more common in gardens than in its native forest. The most wide-ranging species is the berrigan or native willow, *P. phylliraeoides*, a narrow-leaved small tree with decorative orange fruits. The endemic genus *Bursaria*, which has six species, consists of smaller-leaved trees and shrubs with massed tiny white flowers. The native blackthorn or SA Christmas bush, *B. spinosa*, is a common thorny shrub of southern and eastern coastal regions including Tas. The nine other genera, mostly endemic, include *Billardiera*, with 25 species (mostly climbers), and the similar *Sollya*, with three species including the WA bluebell.

plains turkey > *bustards*

plains wanderer > *quails and pheasants*

planigales > *marsupial mice*

plastics industry > *chemical and plastics industries*

platypus > *monotremes*

Playford family, prominent in SA politics. **Thomas** (1837–1915), b. England, arrived in SA with his family in 1844. He entered the SA parliament as a Liberal in 1868 and was subsequently premier twice (1887–9 and 1892–3); he also served in the first and second federal parliaments before his retirement in 1906. His grandson **Sir Thomas** (1896–1981), b. Norton's Summit, SA, entered the SA parliament as a Liberal in 1933. He was premier for the record term 1938–65, during which period he virtually dominated SA political life. Noted for his political conservatism and encouragement of economic growth in SA, Playford is generally credited with the great development of power and industry in that State following the 1930s depression. His hold on government was maintained largely by a gerrymander, which was accordingly dubbed 'playmander'. His government was defeated in 1965 and he retired three years later.

Poaceae > *grasses and grasslands*

Poeppel's Corner This is the meeting point, in the Simpson Desert, of the NT/Qld border. and that of SA; it was marked by SA surveyor Augustus Poeppel in 1883. The position of 'Poeppel's Peg', a coolabah stump with which he marked the spot, was later discovered by W.H. Cornish to be about 300m too far west, and was corrected.

poinsettia > *euphorbia family*

Point Hicks Vic. A promontory at the eastern end of the Vic. coast, this is generally considered to mark the first sighting by James Cook of eastern Australia, in 1770, commemorated by an obelisk at the point. Named by Cook after his lieutenant, Zachary Hicks, it later became Cape Everard (1865), but the Vic. government restored the original name in 1970 to mark the bicentenary of Cook's arrival. (An alternative view is held that the landfall would more probably have been Ram Head, a little further east.)

poisonous plants A number of Australian native plants are poisonous to livestock and in some cases to humans. The Aborigines accumulated millennia of experience as to which fruits, buds, seeds and tubers are safe to eat, and white settlers were able to profit from this knowledge.

Some toxic compounds responsible for poisoning are fairly simple, such as nitrites and nitrates, but most are complex organic compounds of which the most numerous and diverse are the alkaloids. The best known alkaloid is nicotine, found not only in the tobacco plant but in some of its Australian relatives in the genus *Nicotiana* and other members of the > *nightshade family*. Notable poisonous genera are the native *Duboisia* (also used as a drug source) and *Solanum* species. Another group of powerful toxic compounds are the glycosides: cyanogenetic forms (which release deadly hydrocyanic acid on chewing or digestion), occur in many grasses and in the native emu bush *Eremophila*; another type of glycoside, liver toxin, is found in the seeds of > *cycads*, making this otherwise nutritious food source highly dangerous.

An unusual toxic compound contained in some Australian leguminous trees and shrubs is fluoroacetate – the active ingredient of the rabbit-control poison '1080' – which occurs in many species of the poison-pea genus *Gastrolobium* and in the Georgina gidgee, *Acacia georginae*, both notorious livestock poisons. Saponins, another group of moderately toxic compounds, are found in the Qld blackbean, *Casatanospermum australe*, the large seeds of which have proved poisonous to humans and pigs.

A number of poisonous plants contain active principles which have proved difficult to classify. Some are very complex protein-like molecules, such as the abrin in the native crabs-eye bean, one small seed of which is sufficient to kill a human. The most virulent compound in the poison glands of the native > *stinging-trees* has defied identification, as has the toxin in the Darling peas, *Swainsona*, which slowly poison stock in some inland areas.

Polding, John Bede (1794–1877), Catholic

prelate, b. England. Polding arrived in Australia in 1835 as the colonies' first Catholic bishop. In 1842 he was created metropolitan of Australia and archbishop of Sydney, thereby drawing protest from the Anglican Church (which considered it was owed precedence). Polding travelled widely – building on the pioneer work of John Joseph Therry and William Ullathorne to build up his church, bring out priests and organise education, for which purposes he returned frequently to Europe.

Poles in Australia > *ethnic groups*

police In 1987 there were about 36 930 police in Australia. Each State and the NT has its own police force; there is also a national force, the Australian Federal Police (AFP), which provides police for the ACT and is responsible for enforcing federal laws. The structure of each force is generally similar, with a chief commissioner or commissioner at its head and a hierarchy of ranks ranging from chief superintendent down to constable; police powers are generally set out in statutes, which vary between States. The State and Territory forces often work in association with the federal police in matters of national extent or significance, particularly drug-trafficking, white-collar and organised crime, and criminological research.

With the spread of population in the 20th century, the States have generally been divided into regions and districts which are each the responsibility of a police division; specialist departments for activities such as traffic control or fraud are organised centrally. Today police work incorporates general community assistance – such as attending domestic disputes and other emergencies, and supervising Neighbourhood Watch schemes – as well as crime prevention. In response to the growth of violent crime, most police forces also provide a number of support services such as counselling victims.

Historical development The organisation and operation of the police today derives largely from systems established by law in the 19th century. NSW was settled during a period of change in policing philosophy and practices in England, and its first legislation in the field – the Sydney Police Act 1833 – followed the model developed a few years earlier in Britain. Military police were used in the early years of the penal colony, only gradually being replaced by civilian (generally convict) forces. By the 1840s there were both an urban police force and mounted troops who patrolled the remoter parts of the colony to counter the prevailing lawlessness and disorder – manifested in bushrangers, escaped convicts, and goldfields violence. NSW began to recruit police officers from England after 1830, as did Vic. when it became a separate colony in 1851. The first inspector-general of police, J. McClerie, was appointed following the introduction of the Police Act 1862, which set up the police system that still generally operates in NSW today.

The first police magistrate was appointed in Tas. in 1815 and the main duties of the civil and military force for the first 20 years were convict administration. Police districts were created by the first Police Act in 1834, but it was not until the late 1850s that the first police department was formed. Legislation passed in 1865 established a dual system of municipal and colonial policing which continued until the system was centralised in 1898.

By the time of its separation from NSW, Vic. had an urban police force and several outlying police stations; their ranks were rapidly depleted, however, with the general exodus that followed the discovery of gold in the colony. In 1852 a select parliamentary committee was set up to inquire into the police department; the first relevant legislation was passed in 1853, in which year 54 policemen from London arrived in Vic. to provide the basis of the colony's first civilian force.

In WA a preliminary police force was established after the colony was founded in 1829 and constables were appointed for the various districts with the commencement of transportation in 1850. There were two forces, of native police and convict police, which were combined as an 'enrolled force' in 1853. The Police Ordinance of 1861 established the hierarchy of the force, which was greatly increased after the discovery of gold in 1892.

As with Vic., Qld's police were part of the NSW force until it became a separate colony in 1859, although there was a police magistrate in Moreton Bay from 1842 and a force of > *native police* was set up in 1848 to protect the settlers in the southeast of the colony. In 1859 two special forces were established – the Brisbane force and the Water Police. With the passage of a police Act in 1863, the NSW legislation became defunct and the four Qld police groups were brought together in one organisation. The native police force was disbanded in 1899, following a royal commission.

SA was policed by marines until 1837, when a small civilian force was established. A regular police force was created in 1839, which carried out both civil and military duties. Outback patrols in the far north of SA (and the NT from the 1860s) were mounted on camels.

Policing in the NT was controlled by NSW until 1863, when general administration of the region was transferred to SA. NT police then became part of the SA mounted police force until 1911, when administration was again transferred (this time to the Commonwealth) and a small NT police force was established. The present system was introduced by the Police Administration Act 1984.

The Australian Federal Police Federal policing began with the establishment of a Commonwealth force in 1917. An Investigation Branch was created in 1919 (its functions taken over by > *ASIO* in 1949), and with the passage of the Commonwealth Police Act 1957 a new Commonwealth police force was formed in 1960. Attempts were made from 1975 to combine the Commonwealth, ACT and NT forces, which was finally effected by the Australian Federal Police Act of 1979. The AFP has offices in all capital cities and provincial centres; members of the force have wide-ranging responsibilities, from the investigation of major crimes (particularly drug-trafficking, organised crime, and large-scale fraud) to intelligence work and anti-terrorist activities. By 1988, about one-third of all AFP recruits had some tertiary qualifications and there was a continuing increase in the number of applicants aged over 30.

The 1980s and beyond In the late 1980s, Australia's annual expenditure on police services was estimated to be more than $1800 million. There are regular calls for even greater resources to be devoted to policing in the light of the growing number of crimes reported, but a 1988 study by the Australian Institute of Criminology suggested that more efficient use

could be made of existing resources and that new organisational methods be considered. Violent and drug-related crimes are making ever-increasing inroads on police time and resources, the number of recorded drug offences having increased from about 1700 in 1971 to more than 23 000 by the mid-1980s.

By the 1980s the police were also facing new problems of credibility. Alleged corruption within the forces, usually linked with organised crime, has long been a matter of public concern in several States; in Qld the accusations were confirmed by the findings of a royal commission appointed in 1987 to investigate possible misconduct and illegal activities on the part of the Qld force; as a result of this inquiry, a independent investigation into alleged corruption in NSW was also established in 1988. >> *crime and criminal law; prisons and prison systems*

political parties Australia has a strong party political system similar to those in Britain and NZ. While effectively a three-party system since the 1920s, it has periodically sustained minority parties – most notably the > *DLP* in the 1950s and 1960s, and more recently the > *Australian Democrats* – which have wielded some electoral influence at the federal level. In Tas. in 1989, the electoral success of four independent candidates linked by their conservationist platform reflects the growing importance – and power – of 'green' politics.

Conservative political groupings developed first during the colonial period and by Federation were well entrenched, although not united. Initially divided on the issue of tariffs, the free-trade and protectionist groups contained rural and urban factions as well as Whig and Tory tendencies; colonial governments frequently relied on the support of a coalition of these groups, called 'ministerialists'. The rise of the > *ALP* in the 1890s forced the conservative factions to adopt a more or less stable party structure, and from 1910 two parties (Labor and Liberal) dominated State and federal politics: between them they captured 90% of the vote in all elections until 1990, when the figure was reduced somewhat owing to public disenchantment with both groups. In the 1920s the Country Party emerged to join the > *Liberal Party* in battles with the ALP, but despite longstanding coalition between the Liberal and Country parties at the federal and some State levels, relations have remained tense and important policy differences exist.

The ALP has found it difficult to win office in some States and in federal politics; it was out of office federally 1949–72, and has only recently established its capacity to win successive elections at both levels of government. In the past 80 years it has governed for fourteen years in Vic., 24 nationally, 27 in SA, 38 in WA, 39 in Qld (all prior to 1957, although Labor resumed power in late 1989), 48 in NSW and 52 in Tas.

The organisational structure of the parties reflects their differing ideologies and bases of support. The ALP has an elaborate State branch structure, which controls both preselection and policy. A national conference and national executive set policy at the federal level, and the increasing power of the executive has been seen in successful interventions in the affairs of several State branches in the past 20 years. The trade unions affiliated with the ALP elect a significant proportion of delegates to State conferences, giving their leaders access to policy making and to executive positions. In addition, the ALP has an organised system of factional groupings ranging from left to centre and to right. These groups openly debate their different views on major policy and endeavour to control access to party preselection; their prominence is widely held to be the chief reason for the decline of branch involvement in the Labor Party since the 1970s. The Liberals and their rural allies, the National Party, also have extensive organisations but these have neither the role in general policy nor the regular influence over members of parliament that is typical in the ALP. The major business interests that support the conservative parties do not have direct affiliation, but exercise their influence informally. Lack of direct influence has tended to make the conservative party branches prone to local brawling and maverick behaviour, further limiting the influence their parliamentary leadership is willing to grant them. >> *communism*; *government*

pollution The long-standing and widespread pollution of Australia's environment has been a cause of growing public concern in the last 20 years. The urban air is polluted by emissions from motor vehicles and industry as well as by the burning of domestic fires; land, beaches and waterways are contaminated by human effluent and by domestic and industrial waste ranging from litter to chemicals, organic and inorganic sludges, and tainted liquids. Rural areas also suffer – from the discharges of industries such as tanning and food-processing,

pulp and paper manufacturing, and mining. Land clearance, construction, and farming and forestry operations continue to contribute to erosion, resulting in sediment-laden run-off that pollutes streams and lakes; many pesticides persist in the soil and are passed along the food chain.

Government action – or inaction – occurs largely on a State basis, although the Australian Environment Council – established by agreement between Commonwealth, State and Territory governments in 1972 as a forum for national discussion and action – developed the country's unleaded-petrol strategy and national vehicle-emission guidelines. It also set up national guidelines for dealing with hazardous waste, and developed a scheme for requiring the assessment of all new chemicals in order to determine their environmental health impact. State measures include public education programs to encourage responsible practices such as recycling and power conservation; legal changes, to force industry to minimise waste and to dispose carefully of what cannot be avoided; the banning of dangerous substances such as ozone-depleting chlorofluorocarbons, and more carefully planned urban development. >> *environment and conservation*; *water and water resources*

pop music > *rock and pop music*

population The resident population of Australia passed 16 million in June 1986, with a total of 16 250 000 by mid-1987. The estimated population on the first day of white settlement in 1788 was some 1030 Europeans and at least 300 000 Aborigines.

The population is highly urbanised and concentrated strikingly within 350km of the coast, in a belt from Port Pirie in SA, to Rockhampton in Qld with patches in southwest WA and in Qld northward to Cairns. This pattern is attributable largely to the colonies' early dependence on shipping and therefore ports, and to the curbs on settlement and intensive farming presented by the inhospitably arid interior of the continent.

'Musters' of population were taken from 1788 on, the first regular census being in 1828, in NSW. The first Australia-wide census (held in all colonies, and later States, on a specific date) was in 1881, followed in 1891 and 1901. A regular national census has been organised by the Commonwealth Statistician since 1911, with a census of population and housing held every five years since 1961. Aborigines have only been included in official census statistics since 1967. The Commonwealth Bureau of Census and Statistics was formed in 1906 and co-operates with the relevant State authorities to avoid duplication and ensure uniformity of data as far as possible; Tas. statistics are collected by the Commonwealth.

Distribution and structure At the 1986 census, 62.1% of the Australian population was living in NSW, Vic. and ACT. The ACT had the highest population density, 107.9 persons per sq. km, followed by Vic. (18.3) and NSW (6.9); at the other end of the scale, WA had only 0.6 and the NT 0.1 per sq. km. Between 1921 and 1947, 71.1% of the population increase was in capital cities and this proportion increased to 81.0% between 1947 and 1981. Between the censuses of 1976 and 1981, however, the proportion of the population in rural areas increased from 13.9% to 14.2%. The proportion of State populations living in the capital cities of Sydney, Melbourne, Brisbane and Adelaide has fallen marginally since 1976; there has also been a trend towards the rapid growth of smaller coastal towns in Qld, NSW and Vic. The ranking order of population numbers in 1901 – NSW, Vic., Qld, SA, WA and Tas. – remained the same until 1982, when the WA population exceeded that of SA.

Although the population was heavily male-dominated in the early days of settlement, attempts were made to balance the ratio by encouraging families and single women to immigrate; in 1881, the ratio was 121 males males for every 100 females. Male-dominated immigration after World War 2 affected this ratio, but by the 1950s and 1960s it remained at about 102 males to 100 females. By 1981, the female population marginally exceeded the male population. Census figures also reveal clearly that Australia's is an ageing population. Largely as the result of increased life expectancy and lower birth rates, the proportion of the population aged 65 and over increased from 2.2% in 1881 to 9.7% in 1981; similarly, the median age was 20.8 years in 1881, 29.6 years by 1981, and is predicted to rise to approximately 34 years by 2001. It is noteworthy that even in the 1980s the life expectancy of the Aboriginal population (55 years) is still substantially lower than that of the total Australian population (73 years for males and 79 years for females).

For the first 80 years of European settlement the non-Aboriginal population was predominantly British-born, but by the 1870s the majority of the population was born in Australia. In 1986, those born in Australia accounted for 77.6% of the population; the largest overseas-born group comprises those born in the UK and Ireland (7.2%), followed by Italians (about 1.7%).

Historical change Following the arrival of officers and convicts aboard the First Fleet in 1788, the white population fell in the first difficult years but reached about 3000 in the early 1790s. Increases fluctuating between 2.5% and 4% prevailed until about 1850; high birth rates were accompanied by high but decreasing mortality, and considerable natural increases were complemented by immigration (mainly from Britain). With the sharp increase in population – more cosmopolitan in composition – associated with the gold rushes of the 1850s, the population exceeded a million before 1860. Thereafter the rates of increase were lower but, in relation to the larger total, absolute increases were commonly larger. Birth rates declined gradually, with sharp decreases during the 1890s and 1930s depressions, but death rates declined from about fourteen per 1000 in 1870 to about nine in recent decades and natural increase has generally remained well over 1% per annum, accounting for some 55% of total increase. Population growth slowed in the 1970s as both immigration and natural increase declined, but this trend reversed slightly in the 1980s with natural increase stabilising and immigration increasing. >> *health and health services; immigration*

porcupine-fishes and toadoes Of the families Diodontidae and Tetraodontidae respectively, these make up a group of fishes of which the skins are usually covered with spines; about ten species occur in Australian waters. Some species are served in specialised Japanese cuisine, but the flesh of others is often highly poisonous; all share the ability to inflate their bodies until they become almost globular. Common names for these fishes include toad-fish, puffer-fish, blow-fish and globe-fish – all, as with porcupine-fish, reflecting their habit or appearance. They are found in all Australian waters; a small species found near Sydney, *Torquigenes hamiltoni*, has caused death in both humans and animals.

Porongorup Range WA A small, granitic range running roughly northwest–southeast, it rises sharply from the plain about 40km north of Albany. It is noted for the karri forests on the lower slopes, and in spring for the striking display of wildflowers among the granite boulders on the heights. Porongorup National Park contains more than 20 peaks over 600m high.

Port Arthur Tas. This name refers both to an inlet on the Tasman Peninsula, 100km southeast of Hobart, and the penal settlement on its western shore 1830–77. The latter, now a mellow, much-visited ruin, has been variously painted as a place of unlimited brutality and of enlightened reform in the treatment of its total of 30 000 convicts.

Port Augusta SA (pop. 15 291) This busy industrial city at the head of Spencer Gulf, 317km north of Adelaide, developed from 1854 as a port to serve the surrounding pastoral and wheat lands. Transport is still the economic base of Port Augusta, which is the terminus for both the central Australian and transcontinental railways and the headquarters of the Flying Doctor Service; workshops and housing are at nearby Stirling. It has not, however, functioned as a port since the 1970s. There is a US space-tracking station at Island Lagoon, 22km away.

Port Davey Tas. This large inlet 120km southwest of Hobart on the southwest coast is a fiord formation, glaciated in the last ice age. It has two main arms running at right angles to each other: Payne Bay, into which the Davey River runs; and Bathurst Harbour, which receives the Old River and is reached from the main bay by a narrow channel. The area is mountainous and beautiful, but now uninhabited; it was once the haunt of Tas. Aborigines, until they were removed by the government in 1833.

Port Douglas Qld (pop. 1333) This former goldfields port 179km north of Brisbane is now a fishing and tourist resort which has undergone substantial development since the 1970s. Surveyed in 1877, the town boomed in the 1880s supported by gold, silver and tin mining, cedar-cutting and sugar-cane growing. Its population peaked at 12 000 in that decade but declined with the introduction of the Cairns–Mareeba railway in the 1890s.

Porter, Hal (1911–84), author, b. Melbourne. A prolific and versatile writer, Porter has a mannered, baroque style intended to achieve 'incandescence'. Until turning to full-time writing in 1963, he followed many occupations but was principally a teacher and librarian. Best known for his autobiographical trilogy, *The Watcher on the Cast-iron Balcony* (1963), *The Paper Chase* (1966), and *The Extra* (1975), in all he published three novels, seven short-story collections, three poetry volumes and three plays.

Porter, Peter (1929–), poet, b. Brisbane. After a short career in journalism, Porter left for England in 1951 and has lived there since. A freelance writer and reviewer who has worked for numerous magazines and the BBC, Porter is the author of nine volumes of poetry, two collaborations with the painter Arthur Boyd, and a number of radio plays. His poetry is noted for its elegant wit and incisive use of aphorisms; *Collected Poems* (1983) confirmed his status as a major poet.

Port Essington NT An inlet penetrating 40km from the north coast of Cobourg Peninsula, about 200km northeast of Darwin, Port Essington was surveyed in 1818 by Phillip Parker King, who later advocated its settlement. In 1838 an attempt was made to establish a base, Victoria, on the southwest shore, but this was abandoned in 1849. Hopes of developing Victoria as a commercial centre finally faded when the site of Darwin was selected in 1869, but during its brief life it was a useful base for exploration and natural-history research.

Port Hacking NSW This is a small, indented inlet opening out to Bate Bay and lying 27km south of Sydney, whose suburbs extend to its northern shore. On the south shore is the Royal National Park. Aboriginal shell middens have been found in the area, which was discovered by Henry Hacking, an early seaman explorer. It is now a popular water-sport centre for southern metropolitan Sydney.

Port Hedland WA (pop. 13 069) Situated on a tidal island reached by a causeway, about 1660km north of Perth, Port Hedland grew as an outlet first for the pastoral industry and later for the Pilbara mining industries. Iron ore from Mt Goldsworthy and Mt Newman, and solar-evaporated salt, are the main export cargoes. The satellite towns of South Hedland and Finucane Island have been established to cater for the rapid expansion of Port Hedland in the last 20 years; recent developments include an international airport and the Wedgefield industrial estate a few kilometres inland.

Port Jackson NSW Named but not entered by James Cook in 1770, and described in 1788 by Arthur Phillip as 'the finest harbour in the world', Port Jackson extends westwards to the Parramatta River and northwest to the Lane Cove River, and includes Sydney Harbour and Middle Harbour. The steep sandstone cliffs of North and South Heads were once islands, the formation of sandbars joining them to the mainland. The indented shores are the walls of a drowned river valley, providing deep-water anchorage at all times; in 1975 all State-owned foreshore land was declared Sydney Harbour National Park. In this setting Sydney is a major world port, handling some 3000 ships a year and moving 35 million t of cargo. >> *Sydney*

Portland Vic. (pop. 10 934) This town and port is situated on the sheltered side of Portland Bay, 362km west of Melbourne; it is the chief deep-water port for western Vic. and south-eastern SA. It was named by Lt James Grant in 1800 (after the Duke of Portland), although undoubtedly already known to Bass Strait whalers and sealers. The Henty brothers established Vic.'s first permanent settlement there in 1834 and the town has several noteworthy historic buildings including nearby Cape Nelson lighthouse. Industries include a giant aluminium smelter, a particle-board factory and phosphate and meat-processing works.

Port Lincoln SA (pop. 11 552) Situated 650km west of Adelaide, Port Lincoln lies on Boston Bay – which is several times larger than Sydney Harbour. It is the chief shipping centre for the peninsula's pastoral and agricultural produce, and Australia's largest commercial fishing fleet moors at the new Lincoln Cove commercial–residential marina. With such facilities, and with its splendid surrounds and pleasant climate, Port Lincoln is increasingly popular as a tourist resort.

Port Macquarie NSW (pop. 22 884) This fishing and tourist centre lies 421km north of Sydney at the mouth of the Hastings River. Found by John Oxley in 1818, it was used as a prison from the 1820s but received free settlers from 1830. It is now a regional centre as well as a resort and has some manufacturing industry. A handsome church designed by Francis Greenway in 1824 is among the town's significant historic sites.

Port Phillip Association Registered in June 1835 in Launceston, Tas., with fifteen members led by John Batman, this organisation was formed to establish a settlement in the Port Phillip area. Its claim to legal ownership of the land was not recognised, although eventually some adjustment was made in the purchase price of land in view of the expenses originally incurred by its members. The association was dissolved by 1842.

Port Phillip Bay Vic. The State's capital, Melbourne, and the provincial city of Geelong both lie on this wide enclosed inlet on the south coast of Vic. Port Phillip Bay extends nearly 60km north–south and 67km east–west, terminating in a narrow sea entrance afforded by the > *Bellarine Peninsula* (Point Nepean) in the southwest and the > *Mornington Peninsula* (Point Lonsdale) in the southeast; at this entrance, a treacherous tidal race known as the Rip – the downfall of many vessels in the past – makes pilotage mandatory. The bay was discovered by Lt John Murray in 1802 and in the same year it was explored by Matthew Flinders; it was the site of a short-lived settlement under David Collins in 1803 but was not settled permanently until 1835, in which year John Batman – under the aegis of the Port Phillip Association – concluded a spurious treaty with the local Aborigines. The central and northern parts of the bay's 225km shoreline are chiefly residential and industrial suburbs of the Melbourne metropolitan area, and its farther reaches are the city's prime holiday area. The longstanding use of the bay shoreline and hinterland has created serious problems of pollution and erosion, which are now being tackled by State and local authorities.

Port Pirie SA (pop. 13 960) This city 224km north of Adelaide, on Spencer Gulf, is the State's second port. It was created by dredging a swamp-lined inlet for wheat export in the 1870s, but owes its development to the establishment in 1889 of lead-smelting and the export of ores by BHP. Other local industries are mostly based on the processing of produce from the hinterland – notably wheat, timber, livestock and dairying – as well as fishing.

ports and harbours > *ships and shipping*

Port Stephens NSW This inlet is the estuary of the Karuah River, 35km northeast of

Newcastle. Sighted and named by James Cook in 1770, from about 1816 it was a centre for cedar-cutting and exporting, and from 1826 was the headquarters of the Australian Agricultural Co. The inlet is a drowned valley, with potential for development as a major port, but proposals in this direction remained unfulfilled; commercial activity centred round fishing, prawning and oyster culture, and only in the early 1970s did Port Stephens develop as a popular tourist resort. Port Stephens lighthouse, with the keeper's house, is classified by the National Trust.

Portuguese man-of-war > hydrozoa

Possession Island Qld On this small island at the entrance to Endeavour Strait, west of Cape York, James Cook formally claimed possession of the eastern Australian coast, from lat. 38°S to lat. 10°30'S, in the name of King George III; the date was 22 August 1770. An inscribed obelisk on the island (a national park) commemorates the proclamation.

possums Also known as phalangers, these arboreal marsupials of the family Phalangeridae commonly take a mixed diet of insects, nectar, blossom and pollen. James Cook, in 1770, noted their resemblance to the American opossums, but in omitting the initial 'o' gave rise to the Australian usage. Possums range from small, mouse-like animals to quite large gliding and brush-tailed forms; there are 42 species in Australia.

The honey possum, *Tarsipes spenserae*, is found in coastal WA; it has a prehensile tail, a proboscis-like snout, a slender, extensible tongue with bristles to help in gathering sticky food from flowers, and flanges on the lips that form channels through which nectar or honey can be drawn. Striped possums, *Dactylopsila*, found in NG and northeastern Qld, have a long fourth finger particularly suitable for extracting insects from hard wood; Leadbeater's possum is an uncommon species from southeastern Vic., living in tree-hollows. The pygmy or feathertail glider, *Acrobates pygmaeus*, is found in the eucalypt-forest zone from SA to northern Qld. It has a feather-like tail, which aids its gliding 'flight', and membranes between front and back legs; it eats nectar from the ever-blossoming eucalypts and builds a globular nest of leaves in a high tree-hollow. The lesser gliding possums, *Petaurus*, are distributed in the coastal bush of eastern Australia;

among them are the attractive sugar glider, *P. breviceps*, eating insects and blossoms and nesting in tree-hollows, and the squirrel and yellow-bellied gliders. The greater glider, a consumer of blossoms and leaves, is on record as having covered 540m in six successive glides.

Pygmy possums, *Cercartetus*, are nocturnal, climbing in search of insects and honey and using their prehensile tails to advantage, especially in descending; these possums hibernate during the coldest months. Ring-tailed possums, genus *Pseudocheirus*, also have very prehensile tails; they are quarrelsome animals, widely distributed throughout coastal Australia. The brush-tailed ring-tail takes very long leaps between trees, using its bushy tail as a rudder; it occurs in rainforest and swampforest in northern Qld. It was the brush-tailed possum's tail and general appearance that led naturalists of 1789 to describe the specimen from Sydney Cove as vulpine (fox-like). These possums are much sought after for their fur; they were formerly protected, but the restriction was lifted in 1931–2 to provide a source of employment during the depression and this resulted in the export of over a million skins from NSW. The species has a wide distribution in mainland and insular Australia from Melville and Bathurst islands to Kangaroo Island; it shows remarkable adaptability, living in tree-hollows, rockholes, rabbit warrens or burrows in creek banks, and is common in Australian cities. Mainly a leaf-eater, it damages single-stand plantations – such as of pine – and as an introduced animal has harmed forests in NZ.

The wyulda or scaly-tailed possum is a species adapted to dry and rocky conditions in north WA. Cuscuses of the genus *Phalanger* are very large possums with a range extending from Timor and Sulawesi through NG to the Solomons and Cape York; the two Australian species are the grey cuscus of Cape York and NG and the spotted cuscus, which is brown with creamy patches on the back. The ground-dwelling mountain pygmy possum, *Burramys parvus*, was formerly considered to be extinct but has been found in isolated patches of the Vic. alps and the Snowy Mountains, NSW; it was first described from fossil evidence, the living animals only being discovered in 1966.

postage stamps Postage stamps were first issued in Australia in the mid-19th century, a decade after their inauguration in Britain. Each colony produced its own stamps until

Federation and thereafter State stamps had national validity until 1913 when the first Australian issue was made available by the federal government. The first Commonwealth stamps featured a kangaroo superimposed on a map of Australia; this departure from the British tradition of portraying the reigning monarch engendered substantial debate and from 1914 a series of George V stamps was issued concurrently. These early series were long-lived, the kangaroo series surviving until 1945 and George V until 1937. From 1938 Australian themes appeared more frequently, with depictions of the koala, merino, kookaburra, platypus and lyrebird. The first commemorative stamp was issued in 1927 to mark the opening of Parliament House in Canberra. Three recurring commemorative stamps mark Australia Day, the Queen's Birthday and Christmas, with occasional issues for such events as coronations and royal weddings, the Melbourne Cup and the Olympic Games; public figures from Winston Churchill to Nellie Melba have also featured periodically. In recent years, Australia Post has broadened the range of stamp subjects to cover Australian folklore, history, flora and fauna, and the natural and man-made landscapes.

Stamp collecting began in Australia in the 1860s and has continued to flourish since that time. There are about 300 philatelic clubs throughout the country, with an estimated minimum of 400 000 serious collectors.

post and telecommunications Today, legendary Australian institutions such as the School of the Air and the 'bush telegraph' are almost a thing of the past, as facsimile machines, computer networks and satellite receivers make instant communication an affordable reality even in the most far-flung corners of the outback. In 1975, the federal Postmaster-General's Department was split into Telecom Australia and Australia Post, in recognition that the two services faced different challenges. Since that time, increasingly sophisticated technology has allowed rapid expansion in both areas, but particularly in telecommunications. The processing and transmission of information are now an extremely marketable commodity, and by the late 1980s the government's monopoly over these facilities, and its capacity to provide efficient and economic services, were increasingly in question.
Historical development By the 1850s, most Australian towns of any size boasted a post

office; domestic mail was carried by coach or rail from the 1850s, at which time a regular steamship service to the UK was also introduced. Post offices soon moved beyond the physical delivery of letters and parcels: telegraphy was widespread by the 1860s and the following decade witnessed one of the supreme achievements of telecommunications – completion of the 3000km > *Overland Telegraph* line. As a result, by the early 1870s Australia had a telegraph link with Asia and Europe, via a line that was attached to submarine cable at Darwin before traversing inland Australia to connect the major cities. Australia was equally quick to adopt telephones, with exchanges being established in the capital cities as early as the 1870s. Henry Sutton, from Ballarat in Vic., was an early telephone inventor whose machines were efficient enough to prevent patents being registered in Australia by Alexander Graham Bell when he visited the colonies in the 1880s.

After Federation, the postal and telephone services hitherto administered individually by the colonies were amalgamated in the federal Postmaster-General's Department (PMG). Motor vehicles were brought into use for mail delivery after 1910, and aircraft by the early 1930s; overseas airmail was introduced in 1934. The PMG also had responsibility for radio broadcasting: the first services, in the early 1920s, were made to fixed-frequency receiving sets which were soon replaced by equipment that could accept signals from a number of stations.

Wireless telegraphy, which enabled direct telephone calls to be made overseas, was in the hands of a private company until the government was alerted to the strategic importance of international communications during World War 2. The Overseas Telecommunications Commission (OTC) was accordingly formed in 1946, with responsibility for Australia's international telecommunications system. By the late 1960s, OTC operated gateway earth stations which sent and received television signals overseas, either by submarine cable or through the international satellite consortium Intelsat (of which OTC was a founding member).

Technological developments were rapid after the war, including the automation (eventually computerisation) of telephone exchanges and the expansion of postal services. By the 1970s, in step with developments in telecommunications technologies and the increasing number of private telephones, some traditional postal services such as the telegram began to be used less and less. The steady growth in conventional post was supplemented by Australia Post's entry into bulk mailing for businesses, courier services, facsimile transmission services and electronic mail.

The 1980s and beyond The growth of postal services in recent decades was dwarfed by a telecommunications explosion which made Telecom Australia one of the country's largest and most profitable enterprises by the 1980s. At the core of this technological revolution were the vastly increased capacity provided by fibre-optic cable and the use of electronics in the switching and transmission of voice and data traffic. By the end of the 1980s, more than 90% of households had a telephone service, many of them with electronic handsets.

The major question mark over the future of postal and telecommunications services is their continuing monopolisation by the public sector. Telecom in particular has been the target of criticism from large-scale users, which culminated in public inquiries in 1982 and 1987 that both focused on the issue of public versus private ownership. Among the institutions that stand to benefit from a more competitive environment is Aussat, the national satellite operator formed in 1981. Set up (after protracted decision-making) as a separate government entity, it is prohibited by law from competing with Telecom over specified services and from providing telecommunications facilities for potential Telecom competitors.

The report of the 1987 review of telecommunications policy was released in 1988. While rejecting demands for outright privatisation of telecommunications services in Australia (following the recent privatisation of British Telecom), it proposed radical restructuring of the regulations governing Telecom, OTC and Aussat to permit greater competition. The debate over deregulation was still unresolved by the end of the decade. >> *broadcasting*; *communications technology*

potoroos > *kangaroos, wallabies and allies*

pottery and ceramics The production of pottery and ceramics still relies on traditional techniques, although steam, electricity and, more recently, electronics have brought great changes to the production processes. The emphasis is now mainly on creating artworks rather than functional items, although handmade domestic wares have enjoyed fairly consistent popularity throughout the 20th century.

Few of Australia's early commercial potteries survive today: many adapted to and thus survived the fluctuations of public taste, but few were able to withstand competition first from imports and later from substitute materials such as metals, PVC and plastics. A notable exception is the Epsom Potteries in Bendigo, Vic., founded in 1857, which still makes a wide range of household pottery.

Historical development Invariably in association with brick-making, pottery was one of the first colonial industries and pipes and domestic ware were produced at Brickfield Hill in Sydney soon after 1800. Among the earliest firms to concentrate on the domestic market was the Irrawang pottery in the Hunter Valley, NSW, founded by James King in 1833: he imported English potters as well as moulds and glazing materials, and his range of products included fine salt-glazed stoneware. Like many other manufactories of the period, the pottery closed in 1855 as workers downed tools to leave for the goldfields. The search for gold often revealed good pottery clays, as was the case in the Bendigo area of Vic. The Epsom pottery was started there in 1857 by G.D. Guthrie, who used the fine red local clay to produce the familiar brown 'Bendigo' stonewares as well as more delicate household ceramics. Pioneering work was also done at the Lithgow Valley Pottery and Pipeworks (established in the 1870s), particularly by English potter James Silcock in the late 1880s. The Lithgow pottery closed by 1896, owing in part to competition from imported porcelains with the abolition of tariff protection in the early 1890s, but its wares are a popular collector's item today.

Like other crafts, pottery developed a stronger artistic tradition from the early 20th century. Influential at this time was Merric Boyd, who built one of the first pottery 'studios' (in Murrumbeena, Vic., in 1911) and encouraged the use of Australian motifs. Local materials have been used increasingly creatively, influenced by the work of potters such as Ivan McMeekin, whose Sturt Pottery at Mittagong, NSW, in the 1950s used the region's fine clay to produce a characteristic blue-toned stoneware. More recently, Eileen Keys has created a distinctive range of rugged pottery using WA minerals and clays.

Since the 1970s, Australian potters have been influenced by a range of traditions (particularly Asian styles and techniques) and concerns, but continue to draw on local colours and textures. Important work has been done by Peter Rushforth, who is increasingly affected by Japanese idioms but draws his inspiration from the Australian landscape; the influential teacher Milton Moon, who has helped foster wider interest in professional pottery; and by Marea Gazzard, whose large sculptural ceramics are based on environmental themes. Pottery has become one of Australia's most popular craft hobbies, and classes and exhibitions are well attended. >> *craft*

poultry industries Until the mid-20th century, the production of poultry meat and eggs was largely a backyard operation based in the 'chook sheds' of Australia's suburbs and country towns. From these humble beginnings, in the last 20 years poultry-farming has developed into a highly efficient and also capital-intensive business, with the production of meat and eggs effectively separate industries. Although small-scale enterprises still account for up to one-quarter of annual production, the poultry industries are now generally concentrated in the hands of a few large companies.

Poultry is now Australia's second most popular meat and annual consumption was about 23kg per head in 1984–5. Largely in response to this change in the nation's dietary habits, the production of poultry meat has increased dramatically since the 1960s and annual output was valued at about $1000 million by the 1980s. The industry is mainly based in large hatcheries and most aspects of production – from incubation to feeding and watering – are highly automated; the demand for specialised meats, such as quail, is still met mainly by small producers. About 85% of all poultry meat is marketed fresh, in pre-packaged form. While there is some indication that consumers are beginning to prefer the products of 'free-range' farming, it remains to be seen whether this will affect the structure and operation of the industry in the long term.

Egg production is a similarly large-scale and specialised activity, industry rationalisation having reduced the number of farms from about 11 000 in the late 1960s to 2600 by the late 1970s. The industry has benefited less from changing dietary habits and the production of eggs exceeded demand by the early 1980s, with the result that the industry introduced a five-year plan to reduce output.

poverty Australian poverty was only seriously evaluated for the first time in the 1970s. A survey of poverty in Melbourne was conducted by Professor Ronald Henderson in 1966 and introduced the notion of a 'poverty line', which – while debated by many social and economic commentators – has subsequently been adopted in wage and welfare reckonings. In its final months of office in 1972, the McMahon government appointed Henderson chairman of a national inquiry into poverty, the size and scope of which was increased by the succeeding Whitlam government. Henderson drew the poverty line at 56.5% of average earnings and found that 10.2% of Australian households fell below it and a further 7.7% were less than 20% above it. The inquiry's four reports made 119 recommendations to alleviate poverty in Australia, but only one – an increase in family allowance – was acted upon. The inquiry found poverty to be greatest among fatherless families, single aged people, the unemployed, and those who were sick or invalid. By the end of the 1980s the proportion of Australians living below the poverty line had grown by 50%, the most affected groups being Aborigines, children in low-income families, and women. While the debate about defining – and tackling – poverty is unresolved, the figures successfully counter the longstanding myth of universal affluence in Australia. >> *social services*

prawns and shrimps These two groups are closely related decapod crustaceans. Since the first European settlement in Australia prawns have been harvested with fine seine-nets in coastal lagoons, and before that were trapped by Aborigines. It was long known that they migrated seaward on moonless, summer nights, and since they were often casually caught by trawlers working offshore, it was reasoned that deliberate offshore trawling might be productive.

The main group of commercially caught prawns belong to the family Penaeidae. In specimens of this family the first three pairs of legs have claws – quite short, and placed under the mouth to convey food into it. The principal commercial species are the king prawn, the school prawn and the green-tailed or greasy-back, all from NSW and Qld, and the banana or white prawn, which is found in the tropical waters of WA and Qld.

Freshwater shrimps – various members of the Atyidae family, including the common shrimp of the Murray–Darling system – have weak pincer development of the two front pairs of legs. The mantis shrimp, a stomatopod, is distinguished by its long, mobile eyes and large, mantid-like forelimbs. Commonly found on coral reefs, overall there are about 40 species in Australian waters. >> *fishing industry*

preferential voting > *elections*; *government*

prehistory > *Aboriginal culture and society*; *archaeology*

premiers > *government*; Appendix

Presbyterian Church > *religion*; *Uniting Church*

press > *freedom of the press*; *media control and ownership*; *newspapers*; *press, foreign-language*

press, foreign-language Since the first paper for non-English-speakers – the *German Australian Post* – was published in SA in 1848, the fortunes of Australia's foreign-language press have fluctuated. Many have been short-lived, although the oldest extant paper, the monthly *Le Courrier Australien*, was first published in 1892. Federal legislation 1934–56 required at least one-quarter of all newspaper material to be in English; the majority of foreign-language papers were founded since that time, owing partly to greatly increased postwar immigration. In 1988 there were 100 ethnic publication in 33 languages, with an unofficial total circulation of one million each week; most are published weekly or monthly, only the Chinese, Greek and Vietnamese communities producing daily papers. Because the ethnic press relies heavily on continuing waves of first-generation immigrants, its health will continue to be tied closely to immigration policy. Papers such as the Italian *La Fiamma* have, however, tried to overcome this dependence with special pages for young second-generation Australians.

Preston, Margaret Rose (1875–1963), artist, b. Adelaide. From the 1920s Preston, a painter and printmaker, developed a uniquely Australian style inspired by native flora and Aboriginal culture; her prints, particularly the dramatic woodcuts, heralded a new era in print-making. Simplified, flattened shapes and bold planes of colour characterise her work. An inveterate traveller and an art lecturer and critic, she championed the cause of a distinctive Australian culture at a time when many artists were still clinging to European traditions.

Price, Sir Archibald Grenfell (1892–1977), geographer and historian, b. Adelaide. An academic, Price was also chairman of the Commonwealth Literary Fund advisory board 1952–72, deputy chairman of the Australian Humanities Research Council 1955–64, and chairman of the National Library of Australia Council 1960–71. Among his many publications are *Founders and Pioneers of South Australia* (1928) and *The Winning of Australian Antarctica* (1962). He was a Fellow of the Royal Geographical Society, and was knighted in 1963.

Prichard, Katharine Susannah (1883–1969), author, b. Fiji. The daughter of an Australian journalist, Prichard learned her trade through journalism, working freelance in Australia, London and US; she lived mainly in WA after establishing a literary reputation with *The Pioneers* (1915). Her best works have Australian themes and strong tones of social protest; they cover the karri timber industry, cattle stations and circus life. The prevalent theme of tragedy is especially poignant in *Coonardoo* (1929). She also wrote short stories, poetry and plays, and an autobiography, *Child of the Hurricane* (1963).

prickly pear The common name for cacti of the genus *Opuntia*, these plants are endemic to the Americas but are notorious pests in a number of countries including Australia. Small trees with succulent spring stems, they were introduced into Australia as ornamentals in the 19th century and about a dozen species became naturalised. By 1925, the species *O. stricta* had infested some 26 million ha of grazing land in inland southeast Qld and adjacent areas of NSW. One of the plant's natural insect predators, the South American moth *Cactoblastus cactorum*, was released in large numbers into infested areas 1927–30 and by 1934 the stands of prickly pear had been largely destroyed, although scattered plants survived and persist up to the present day. Other species, notably the tiger pear *O. aurantiaca* – a prostrate plant with savage spines which lacerate stock – have been controlled by the release of sap-sucking cochineal insects of the genus *Dactylopius*. Government agencies in Qld and NSW still conduct programs to combat continuing up-surges in prickly pear.

primary industry > *agriculture*; *cattle industry*; *cereals and grains*; *cotton*; *dairy industry*; *economy*; *fishing industry*; *forests* *and forestry; fruit-growing; mining industry; nuts and nut-growing; sheep; sugar industry; wheat; wine industry*

prime ministers > *government*; Appendix

printing industry Australians have an insatiable appetite for the printed word, being among the largest per-capita book, newspaper and periodical purchasers in the world. Consequently, printing, publishing and their associated industries together constitute the fourth-largest segment of Australian manufacturing industries, employing 102 095 people in 2972 establishments in 1984–5. About 75% of printing firms are engaged in general commercial work, 20% in the production of newspapers and magazines and 5% in packaging printing.

A printing press was brought out with the First Fleet but was apparently not used until 1796, when George Hughes printed some instructions for Governor Hunter. Hughes was followed as government printer by George Howe, who produced Australia's first book in 1802: *New South Wales Standing Orders, Part I.* Howe also printed Australia's first newspaper, the *Sydney Gazette and New South Wales Advertiser*, in 1803.

From a humble beginning on a single-sheet letterpress, the industry already has passed through one major evolution – mechanical typesetting and printing – and is now abreast of a second, based on electronic composition and printing. Mechanical typesetting has been superseded by computerised setting, and the various photographic processes which in the main replaced letterpress printing are in turn about to be replaced by the laser printer. There is already available a 'one-stop', one-person machine that incorporates facilities for the entire printing process, from scanning type and graphics to binding the finished product.

Because of relatively high local labour and material costs, much Australian book printing – and some magazine printing – is done overseas, particularly in Asia, even though the federal government offers a subsidy for books printed in Australia. With the advent of new, cheaper technology it is possible that some of this business will return to Australia, but perhaps not to the traditional industry. In an era of desktop publishing virtually everyone can be a jobbing typesetter and graphic designer, and it is only a matter of time before any person with the appropriate equipment can be a printer as well. >> *paper industry*

prisons and prison systems The sentencing of prisoners and the control of prisons in Australia is a State responsibility. Each State and the NT has its own prison system; in the ACT there is provision for short-term remand custody, probation and parole, but adult prisoners are held in NSW institutions. There are 89 prisons and correction centres throughout Australia and the total prison population was just over 11 000 in 1987.

The national daily rate of imprisonment is about 80 per 100 000 population, which is reasonably low by world standards (the highest rate being 400, in South Africa). The figures vary widely across Australia, however, NSW having the largest number of prisoners but the NT having by far the highest rate of imprisonment per 100 000 population. In the late 1980s the main offences of Australia's prison population were crimes against property (32%), crimes against the person (27%), robbery and/or extortion (14%), and drug-related crimes (12%).

In a 1987 discussion paper, the Australian Law Reform Commission identified the problems of the Australian prison system as overcrowding, poor conditions (which in many cases fail to meet internationally recognised standards), a lack of treatment programs for prisoners, and a failure to protect prisoners' civil rights. As the construction and maintenance of prisons is extremely expensive (expenditure per prisoner being some $45 000 in 1987–8), non-custodial alternatives such as probation, parole, periodic detention and community-service orders are being increasingly adopted. While there is continuing pressure to keep the number of prisoners as low as possible, the increasing rate of imprisonment since the mid-1980s makes it unlikely that a solution to these problems will be found in the short term.

Prison systems Prison systems and facilities, like the rates of imprisonment, differ between States. The minimum age for imprisonment is 17 in Vic., Qld, Tas. and the NT; and 18 in NSW, WA, SA and the ACT. Separate provisions and institutions exist for juvenile offenders, although in all States younger people convicted of particularly serious offences may be held in adult prisons. Recently, the term prison has been largely replaced by 'correctional institution'.

Australian prisons have traditionally been housed in old buildings in or near the major cities. In the last 20 years, there have been moves in all States to both decentralise the prison population and create open or partly open institutions with lower security and some training facilities. In 1976, in the light of extensive criticisms of the NSW prison system by the Nagle Royal Commission, the high-security Katingal prison (described as a 'human zoo') was closed down; the present government has announced its intention to reopen Katingal, but the high costs involved have delayed the scheme.

Prisons generally operate through a classification system for prisoners, based on factors such as their security rating, health, and education needs. Prisoners may be transferred between institutions for legal or welfare reasons. Long-stay prisoners are subject to decreasing degrees of security as their terms progress; penalties for serious infringements of prison rules, on the other hand, may include increased sentences.

Prison conditions and problems With the exception of Tas., overcrowding is a serious problem in most Australian prisons. While it is generally agreed that 85% occupancy is the maximum allowing a prison to operate efficiently, many Australian prisons are more than 100% full. This invariably creates degrading conditions and leads to increased stress for both prisoners and staff, often militating against attempts at prisoner rehabilitation. There is increasing concern that unconvicted prisoners account for some 15% of the total prison population and Vic., SA and the ACT now have separate remand centres for people awaiting court hearings.

Also of continuing concern is the high rate of imprisonment for Aborigines, who comprise more than 30% of Australia's prison population. The high number of Aborigines who have died while held in custody was investigated by a royal commission in 1987–8; an interim report was released in 1988 but the commission's complete findings are not expected until the end of 1990. The increased number of female prisoners during the 1980s (nearly doubling to just under 5% of the total prison population) is also a matter of growing concern; it is also causing logistical problems for prison administrators over accommodation requirements, particularly for women with dependent children.

Proctor, Thea (1879–1966), painter, b. Armidale, NSW. Proctor lived in England 1903–21 where she was a pupil and close friend of George Lambert. She exhibited regularly in England and Europe, her work in-

cluding elegant designs for silk fans. After returning to Australia she promoted print-making, and although personally conservative she helped to found (in 1926) the Contemporary Group (which included Margaret Preston and Roy de Maistre), and championed their cause.

proportional representation > *elections*; *government*

Proserpine Qld (pop. 2762) This sugar centre lies on the lower Proserpine River about 1090km north of Brisbane. It was named after the Roman fertility goddess Proserpina, reflecting the highly productive lands of the district. The town is also a base for tourists to the Cumberland Islands.

protea family This large family of trees and shrubs is found mostly in the southern hemisphere and is thought to have originated on the ancient southern landmass Gondwana. In Australia there are 45 genera and about 900 species: although some genera – such as > *banksias*, > *grevilleas*, *Isopogon* and *Petrophile* – are widespread across the continent, the greatest concentration of species occurs in the shrublands of WA and rainforests of northern Qld. Most are small wiry shrubs and have small flowers, but foliage and fruit vary widely; species growing in shrubland or heathland, which are often subject to fires, regenerate from lignotubers or have woody fruits which require heat to release the seeds. Banksias, grevilleas and hakeas produce abundant nectar and some are pollinated by native birds and marsupials as well as insects. The wood has distinctive, broad vascular rays that give a decorative oak-like grain, and the timber of species such as the silky oak, *Grevillea robusta*, is highly valued. The family includes several species of macadamia, two of which – *M. integrifolia* and *M. tetraphylla* – are Australia's only native commercial food trees.

Prout, John Skinner (1806–76) painter, b. England. While in Australia 1840–8, Prout held a series of successful lectures in Sydney and later in Hobart, where he helped to arrange the first Australian exhibition of paintings (1845). He published several folios of lithographic vignettes of the colonies, and also books about his experiences.

Ptilotus This group of shrubs is the largest Australian genus of the worldwide amaranth family; all but one of its 100 or so species are endemic. Found chiefly in arid areas, they are mostly herbaceous plants with dense spikes or heads of narrow flowers clothed in long hairs, earning them such names as pussytails, lambtails, foxtails and bottlewashers (in WA they are called by the Aboriginal name mulla mulla). Colours vary from white and green to pink or purple, and in good seasons these plants contribute an attractive element to the wildflower displays of the arid centre.

public health > *health and health services*

public lending right scheme (PLR)

Introduced by the Whitlam government in 1974, the PLR scheme makes payments to Australian authors and publishers for the use of their books in public libraries. In 1987–8, the rate of payment was 80 cents a copy for authors, illustrators or other creators and 20 cents for publishers. The total annual payment by the Commonwealth government amounts to more than $2 million.

public service The public service constitutes the administrative or bureaucratic arm of government, its duty being to put into effect the policies and laws made by parliament. In the 1820s a framework of departmental government – upon which the Australian public service has since been built – was constructed by Governor Darling, who introduced local taxation to provide a police force, a town water supply and a postal service. However, appointments were still by political patronage until almost the end of the 19th century, when the Vic. Public Service Act 1883 was followed by legislation in other States.

Strictly speaking, the term 'public servant' refers only to those persons employed under the Public Service Acts of the Commonwealth and the States, and excludes such groups as school-teachers, academics and the police. Moreover, extraordinarily rapid growth of tertiary-sector and government employment since 1947 has made the use of 'public servant' somewhat outmoded and 'public-sector employee' is now probably more accurate. There are approximately 1.7 million such employees in Australia, accounting for about 30% of the total workforce, and while Canberra may be the public-service capital of Australia over 70% of public-sector workers are employed by State and local authorities. Entry into the career grades of the public service has traditionally been by way of

competitive examination at the conclusion of secondary education, although since the 1960s there has been a trend to lateral recruitment with an emphasis on the employment of university and college graduates. Simultaneously, and largely as a consequence of a series of inquiries into the Commonwealth and State public services in the 1970s, there has been a conscious attempt to raise the academic qualifications of public servants.

Since 1972 a new element has been injected into governmental employment, whereby federal and State ministers hire personal advisers who hold office at the whim of the relevant minister. This intrusion encountered resistance from senior career-grade officers, who feared diminished access to 'their' ministers. By law, a minister of the Crown is the head of each public service department and (theoretically at least) is responsible to parliament for its actions. In practice a senior public servant is appointed as an apolitical 'permanent head', with the primary duty of advising the minister. Public servants traditionally enjoy greater security of tenure than most private-sector employees, though the extent of this security is often exaggerated.

A major contribution by the public service to the working of a representative democracy such as Australia is that it provides a continuity of professional and technical expertise regardless of which political party is in government. There is persistent controversy in Australian politics over the extent to which public servants should make policy as opposed to their implementing policies crafted by politicians. The dilemma is not easily resolved, involving as it does conflicting objectives of efficiency and democracy. Administrative reform was a political priority in the 1980s, and the federal Labor government has been innovative in this area. The Public Service Reform Act 1984 and the Administrative Arrangement Act 1987 have, among other things, transformed the public service board into a commission and replaced the first and second divisions of the public service with a senior executive service. The declared objective of the various reforms is increased efficiency and accountability.

Public-sector unionism in Australia dates from the late 19th century and now occupies an important place in the trade-union movement; in the late 1970s federal public servants discarded their non-militant heritage and embarked on a series of industrial actions concerning tenure, salaries and professional issues. >> *government*

public transport All large Australian cities have well-integrated networks of public transport based on buses and electric trains; Melbourne also has trams, and Sydney a ferry service. The pre-eminence of the car in the last 40 years has meant that most of Australia's public transport systems are under-utilised and run at a substantial loss, necessitating heavy government subsidy. (In 1986 the loss on government and municipal bus services in NSW was $82 million and this deficit pattern was repeated in every State and Territory.) They are, however, reasonably efficient, comparing more than favourably with those in the US though generally inferior to European systems. A serious problem with most suburban train networks in Australian cities is their spoke layout, which offers no direct cross-town access. In 1984 Melbourne completed an underground city loop line which has helped alleviate this problem.

Trams were once the main form of inner-urban transport in all Australian capital cities and numerous country towns; early models were horse-drawn or steam-driven, or powered by cable traction. Electric trams were introduced early this century and proved to be an efficient, relatively pollution-free method of moving people; they were withdrawn in the 1950s and 1960s in favour of buses, as they caused congestion in narrow city streets and impeded traffic flow. Melbourne, with its wide streets and grid pattern, is the only city to retain a tram network, which has 329km of track; Adelaide has retained one tramway 11km long, from the city to Glenelg. An oil crisis like that of the early 1970s could see a renewed interest in trams, although a more likely solution to inner-city transport needs is a high-speed overhead monorail of the kind linking the centre of Sydney to Darling Harbour.

As trams are to Melbourne, so ferries are to Sydney. Historically, ferry transport was important in the development of all Australian capital cities except Adelaide, but today Sydney is the only city retaining an extensive ferry network. As well as being picturesque and a great tourist drawcard, Sydney ferries are an integrated and valuable part of the transport network, particularly the hydrofoils running from Circular Quay to Manly. Perth, Brisbane, Hobart and Devonport all retain small ferry services, and passenger ferries also operate in NSW coastal waterways such as Pittwater and Brisbane Water. >> *railways*

publishing and bookselling Perhaps because of their long isolation from the rest of the English-speaking world, Australians are avid readers and book-buyers. For the first 150 years of settlement the demand for books was met mainly by imports, the greatest growth in local book production and sales having occurred since World War 2. In the 1950s, 85% of books sold in Australia were produced overseas; by the late 1980s, however, locally published books accounted for about half of all sales and imports from the UK and US were rapidly diminishing.

By the late 1980s there were 200 book publishers in Australia and an average of 3000 titles were published each year. In 1986 the retail value of locally published books was $900 million and approximately 6% were exported. Most publishers distribute their own titles and many act as agents for other publishers' books.

Historical development There was no recognisable book trade in Australia until the second decade of the 19th century. Although there was a printing press aboard the First Fleet, it was mainly reserved for administrative use and the settlers generally brought books with them or ordered titles from Britain. The first non-government books – a volume of verse and the biography of a bushranger – were published in 1819. The first Sydney bookseller is thought to have been Robert Howe (son of the first colonial printer, George Howe), who in the 1820s combined bookselling with stationery sales and printing. He was soon followed by Charles Platt in Adelaide and Samuel Tegg in Launceston; in Melbourne, the enterprising John Pascoe Fawkner combined bookselling with the sale of pigs and beer.

The seeds of several great Australian publishing houses were sown in the 1850s. In 1852, three men arrived in Melbourne who made a lasting impression on the book trade and who established a long tradition of combining bookselling with publishing. Edward William Cole was the founder (1879) of Cole's Book Arcade, a flourishing Melbourne institution until the early 20th century; he was also the creator of *Cole's Funny Books*, a landmark in Australian publishing. Scottish-born George Robertson (1825–98) opened a bookshop in Melbourne in 1853 and went on to publish more than 600 books in the next 30 years; the firm of Robertson & Mullen (named for Robertson's assistant and later partner, Samuel Mullen) was also a longstanding Melbourne institution. The firm of Rigby, a major Australian publisher in the 20th century, had its roots in a bookshop opened in Adelaide by newly arrived William Rigby in 1859. In Sydney, David Angus and a second George Robertson (1869–1933) formed Angus & Robertson in 1886, one of the most prominent names in the history of Australian publishing and bookselling. By the end of the 19th century, a range of local books – both fiction and non-fiction – was being published locally. The first works with a marked Australian flavour were published by the Sydney George Robertson, A.C. Rowlandson and the publishing arm of the *Bulletin* in the 1890s, the heyday of radical nationalism.

British books continued to dominate the market in the first decades of the 20th century, although several more Australian publishers appeared: Lothian, which was founded in Melbourne in 1888 but published its first title in 1905; Sydney-based Horwitz, from 1921; the first of the university presses, Melbourne University Press, in 1922; and the bookseller/publisher Cheshire's, in Melbourne, from 1925. The magnum opus of the 1920s was the first encyclopaedia of Australia, published by Angus & Robertson. From the 1930s, a great stimulus was given to local publishing by the introduction of sales and import taxes that substantially raised the price of imported books. At the same time, many major Australian writers (such as Katharine Susannah Prichard, Vance Palmer and Christina Stead) were being published overseas rather than by Australian companies.

From World War 2, the rapid growth of both population and education and increasing national self-consciousness gave a further boost to local production and the sale of local books. A number of new publishers appeared, including Ure Smith (1939) and Jacaranda Press (1952), and established companies such as Rigby greatly expanded their publishing programs; the first Australian paperback imprint, Sun Books, was established in 1963 by Brian Stonier, Geoffrey Dutton and Max Harris. From the 1950s, many British and US publishers including Collins, Penguin, Macmillan, and Allen & Unwin established full-scale Australian branches to safeguard their slice of the market.

The 1970s and beyond Bookselling in Australia changed dramatically in 1972 when resale price maintenance on books was abolished. This brought orderly marketing to an end, with widespread price-cutting on new titles and many books being subject to discount and remainder selling. The new bookselling and publishing environment which resulted was claimed on the one hand to have made the Australian book trade more progressive and aggressive, and on the other to have adversely affected independent booksellers to the detriment of book-buyers. Today most books are sold through bookshops and book chains, the other main outlets being newsagents and department stores; the balance is accounted for by book clubs, mail-order, and non-book outlets. While many Australian titles are still published by the local subsidiaries of UK and US companies, locally owned publishers led the way in the upsurge in Australian publishing which occurred from the late 1960s onwards. The postwar growth of established firms was accompanied by the rise of smaller entrepreneurial companies such as McPhee Gribble and Fremantle Arts Centre Press, which both continued to maintain their independence and high standards in the face of increasing 'rationalisation' of the industry, although McPhee Gribble was taken over by Penguin in 1989. As elsewhere in the world, take-overs are now a fact of publishing life in Australia, stalwarts such as Angus & Robertson now being owned by media conglomerates.

The trend towards conglomerate publishing and bookselling will undoubtedly continue: the ultimate goal of the 'global book' released simultaneously throughout the world would solve at least partially the sometimes complicated territorial > *copyright* problems. Technological advances – rather than making books obsolete, as was suggested with the advent of computers – will considerably accelerate this process and maintain the central position of books in the wide spectrum of communication media.

Trade organisation and assistance Trade associations include the Australian Book Publishers Association, the Australian Booksellers Association and the National Book Council (which is concerned mainly with the promotion of books and reading). Writing and publishing are supported by the federal government through direct grants to writers, as well as a book bounty which helps reduce printing costs for books printed in Australia. Both schemes continue to be controversial, however: as elsewhere in the world, the principle of governments subsidising creative writers and artists is a matter of continuing public debate; and in practice the book bounty has failed to make local printing competitive, with the result that the majority of books continue to be printed much more cheaply in Southeast Asia. Other forms of assistance include the > *public lending right scheme* whereby authors and publishers are paid for books held in public libraries, and payment of a fee to authors for photocopying of their books in libraries and educational institutions. >> *literature and writing*; *printing industry*

Pugh, Clifton Ernest (1924–), painter, b. Melbourne. An artist and conservationist, Pugh is renowned for his love of the Australian bush and native animals and his forceful depiction of them in his stylised, figurative oil paintings. He is an incisive portraitist (three times winner of the Archibald Prize), whose sitters have included prominent artists, academics and controversial politicians. An influential arts lobbyist, Pugh was chairman of the Arts Advisory Committee (1971) and was instrumental in the formation of the Australia Council. His illustrations for the books such as *Death of a Wombat* (1972) and *Dingo King* (1977) are widely acclaimed.

pythons > *snakes*

Q

Qantas > *aviation*

quails and pheasants There are three species of true quails in Australia; the stubble-quail of Tas. and southern Australia, the brown or swamp quail, occurring from the Molucca islands south to Tas., and the king quail, ranging throughout eastern Australia and north to China. They are ground-frequenting birds, usually among tall grasses, and some lay a large number of eggs. Quails are often sought by hunters, but as avid consumers of weed-seeds and insects they are beneficial to the farmer. The quail-like plains wanderer, *Pedionomus torquatus*, is found in open country of southern Australia, but unlike the quail it is relatively solitary in its habits; subject to the attentions of hunters, foxes and feral cats, it is becoming less common. Pheasants, which like quails are of the family Phasianidae, were introduced to Australia from Asia and have become feral in some places; the ring-necked pheasant, for example, is established on Rottnest Island and King Island, and in Tas.

quandong > *sandalwood family*

quarantine Although quarantine was used as a matter of course in the Australian colonies from the early 19th century, and a co-ordinated system was suggested in the 1880s, a national guarantine service was not established until the 20th century. This development was largely in response to a ten-year plague which reached Australia in 1900 and moved the newly united States to co-ordinate their hitherto separate quarantine activities. Responsibility was accordingly transferred to a federal quarantine service (based in the Department of Trade and Customs) in 1909, although there was an impractical overlap between the administrative responsibilities of the States and the Commonwealth for some years. An international influenza epidemic at the end of World War 1, and widespread hookworm infestations in Qld in 1918, encouraged the establishment of the Commonwealth Department of Health in 1921; it has retained responsibility for human quarantine since that time. The principal measure is surveillance at ports of entry to detect people with notifiable infections; an isolation unit exists at Melbourne's Fairfield Infectious Diseases Hospital for the treatment of patients. The importation of animals, plants, soil, cultural organisms and some foods is strictly regulated in an attempt to keep Australia free of agricultural pests and diseases. >> *health and health services*

quaternary industries > *service industries*

Queanbeyan NSW (pop. 24 060) This city lies on the Queanbeyan River, about 306km south of Sydney and 8km west of Canberra, and is the market and service centre for the central region of the State's southern tablelands. It continues to grow in importance as a commuter base for Canberra workers and its industries include the production of building materials for the capital.

Queensland (Qld) The second-largest Australian State (after WA) in terms of area and the third-largest in terms of population, Qld is also the most idiosyncratic State, the least urbanised, and in recent years one of the most important producers of minerals. Its economy has altered dramatically in the last 20 years, from a predominantly pastoral and agricultural base to one underpinned by wealth generated by minerals and associated manufacturing, and tourism focused on its tropical climate and coastal splendour. With an area of 1 727 500sq.km (22.4% of Australia's total) and a coastline of 7400km, Qld is made up of three main zones – the eastern coast, the Great

Dividing Range, and the western plains. The eastern coast – offshore from which is the > *Great Barrier Reef* – is well watered, in the north by tropical monsoons in summer, and has a wealth of farming land and beaches. The Great Dividing Range runs from the north across the State's southern border, in Qld being narrowest at each end; in the (northern) Bellenden Ker Range is Mt Bartle Frere (1611m), the State's highest point; other notable places include the > *Atherton Tableland* (also in the north) and Mt Superbus and the > *Darling Downs* (in the south). The western plains do not have a reliable rainfall and depend on groundwater from the Great Artesian Basin; in the southwest is the arid Channel Country. There are two major river systems in Qld: the fast-flowing eastern rivers draining from the Great Divide to the Pacific Ocean, and the intermittent west-flowing streams draining variously to the Gulf of Carpentaria, Lake Eyre or the Darling River. The State has more large provincial centres than does any other: on the coast are > *Townsville*, > *Cairns*, Mackay, Rockhampton, > *Gladstone*, > *Brisbane* (the capital) and Bundaberg; west of the mountains are Toowoomba, Mt Isa, Dalby, Roma and Warwick.

Historical development Until the 19th century, about 30% of Australia's Aborigines probably lived in Qld and European settlement progressed by means of a northward-moving frontier war in which some 20 000 Aborigines and 1000 Europeans died. A convict settlement was established at Moreton Bay in 1824, and although officially not permitted until 1842 movement north by squatters began almost immediately. Pastoralists prevailed west of the Great Dividing Range initially, but along the coast sugar plantations developed (using Pacific islander labour) and quickly became crucial to the colony's economy. After self-government was granted in 1859, pastoral interests for a time remained politically dominant, but mineral finds brought about changes to the population mix, and after Federation the abolition of > *blackbirding* led to the breaking up of many large sugar estates and an increase in the number of small farmers along the coast. Agriculture, in one form or another, nevertheless remained the State's mainstay and numerous regional centres were established, providing the base for Qld's future political development. Its agricultural base allowed Qld to ride out the economic depressions of the 1890s and 1930s more comfortably than did

the other States, but from the 1960s this was gradually displaced by further large mining developments and manufacturing based on the mineral and food industries. Qld is now the major coal-producing State and an important tourist destination.

Population and economy The population of Qld at the 1986 census was 2 587 315, which showed a growth rate of 0.1% over the five years between censuses, second only to that of WA and much higher than those of the other States. The present figure gives a population density of 1.5 per sq. km, a little higher than that of SA; the population is much more widely distributed than is the case in other States, with 54% living in centres other than the State capital. About 15% of the population is overseas-born.

The western plains of Qld are, as they have been almost since European settlement began, important producers of wool and beef, with tropical breeds of cattle grazed in the northern sections. On the Darling Downs and elsewhere wheat, sorghum, barley and maize are produced, and the brigalow district of the State's central east is noted for pasture plants. Sugar, Qld's most important crop, is produced on the coast and about 70% is exported to increasingly uncertain world markets. Peanuts and fruit are also grown extensively, and fisheries – especially prawn fisheries on the gulf – are important. Coal, largely for export, is the major mineral produced, from mines at West Moreton, Collinsville, Blair Athol, Clermont and the Bowen Basin. Gold, silver, lead, copper, nickel and zinc are also mined and crude oil and natural gas produced. Since the 1960s secondary industry has come almost to equal agriculture in output, and this has led to growth of urban centres in coastal regions. Tourism, and retirement investment, are also important sources of revenue.

Government and politics Pastoralists, either conservative or liberal in outlook, controlled the governments of Qld after it first separated from NSW in 1859. Political parties as such did not operate until 1911, when the first and only Liberal government was elected. The Labor Party had its origins in the north and west of the State, not in Brisbane, and when it gained office in 1915 under R.J. Ryan it was a farmers' party as much as – or more than – a traditional Labor Party. As such, in regional and rural Qld it was able to govern continuously 1915–28 and 1933–57; in the interlude 1929–32, the Country and Progressive National Party (a precursor of the Country Party) held office.

During its term Labor tried to strengthen its electoral base against the growing power of Brisbane by increasing the existent gerrymander in favour of rural votes. The split in the Labor Party of the 1950s deprived Qld Labor of its rural base and resulted in the Country Party (now the National Party) winning office in 1957, at first in coalition with the Liberals. > *Sir Joh Bjelke-Petersen*, who became premier in 1968 and dispensed with his Liberal coalition partners in 1983, governed until deposed by his own party in 1987. His rule was characterised by uncritical support for major commercial developments and opposition to the labour movement, Aboriginal rights, feminism and even the theory of evolution. His successor, Michael Ahern, set up a public inquiry which led to the exposure in 1989 of widespread and long-established corruption in Qld; this was a key factor in the ALP's electoral victory in the same year, which brought to an end the 32-year reign of the National Party in Qld.

Queenstown Tas. (pop. 3593) This mining town lies in the Queen River valley, 256km northwest of Hobart. It owes its existence – and survival today – to copper found at nearby Mt Lyell in 1883, after which Queenstown developed rapidly as a residential centre for workers in mining and associated industries. The surrounding hills were cleared of their forest cover by pollution from the refineries and were subject to serious erosion. Large-scale underground mining is planned by the Mt Lyell Co., but economic copper reserves are expected to last only until the mid-1990s.

Quick, Sir John (1852–1932), politician and author, b. England. Quick arrived in Australia in 1854; he was a journalist before graduating in law in 1882. A member of the Vic. parliament 1880–9, he was a key figure in the Federation movement and co-authored, with Sir Robert Garran, the monumental *Annotated Constitution of the Australian Commonwealth* (1901). He was chairman of the first Tariff Commission (1905–7), postmaster-general 1909–10, and a successful deputy president of the Commonwealth Court of Conciliation and Arbitration 1922–30. A keen bibliographer of Australian writing, he initiated the mammoth chronological survey *Australia Literature from its Beginnings to 1935* (1940).

Quiros, Pedro Fernandez de (1563–1615), navigator, b. Portugal. A navigator of great skill and even greater religious zeal, Quiros was dedicated to saving souls in the undiscovered lands of the South Seas. In 1605 he sailed in search of the 'great south land'; a year later his ship separated from the rest of the fleet which, thence led by Luis Vaez de Torres, discovered the strait between Australia and NG.

quokka > *kangaroos, wallabies and allies*

quolls > *native and tiger cats*

R

RAAF > *defence forces*

rabbits Feral rabbits have been the scourge of Australian farmlands for more than a century. Domestic rabbits were brought to Australia with the First Fleet in 1788, but widespread infestation dates from Thomas Austin's importation to Vic., in 1859, of a dozen wild rabbits. Intended for sport on his property Barwon Park, they were released to breed and did so in unforeseen numbers. Within 30 years authorities had realised their awesome potential for damage to agriculture, and thousands of kilometres of barrier fences were erected, notably on the borders of Vic. and SA, NSW and SA, and NSW and Qld. The fences were of little avail, however, often coming too late and being discouragingly difficult and costly to maintain.

Now officially vermin, rabbits occupy approximately 4 000 000sq.km of southern Australia. They devour pastureland, destroying the choicest grasses first, and have few predators. The pox-like disease myxomatosis, introduced after World War 2 to control their numbers, had a 99% mortality rate when it first became epidemic, but this has now dropped to about 40% as less virulent strains have developed and rabbits have become more resistant to the disease. It has been estimated, however, that since its introduction myxomatosis has saved the nation at least $100 million, as reduction of the rabbit population has resulted in a great increase in wool and meat production. Present methods of control include shooting and trapping, poisoning, fumigation, warren destruction and biological control.

racial conflict Racial conflict occurs when groups perceived to be physically and culturally distinct enter into competition over a scarce resource, such as land. Racist thought, which justifies and explains this conflict, invokes ideas of superiority and inferiority, the destiny of peoples, and immutable, genetically determined, moral and intellectual characteristics.

For much of the 20th century, Australians rejoiced in the belief that – unlike the US or South Africa – their country was peacefully settled and free from racial conflict. In reality, racial conflict has long characterised relations with Aborigines and some immigrant groups, although this has been less the case in the main centres of population, the urban areas.
Aborigines Theories of race were not fully developed in 1788. The Aboriginal way of life was little understood by the British settlers, however, and their failure to cultivate the land, establish permanent settlements and respond to missionary activity characterised them as a people who could not be civilised. The dispossession of the Aborigines was achieved largely through violence. The conflict was usually small-scale, involving pastoralists and their employees, at times the local police (although in some regions use of auxiliary police detachments was common), and small groups of Aborigines. A few events have become the staple of Australian history books, notably the longstanding hostilities in Tas. 1804–35 which became known as the Black War and included the 'Black Line' incident of 1830 – an abortive attempt by some 3000 soldiers, settlers and convicts to round up the remaining Aboriginal population of Tas. The Myall Creek massacre of 1838 – in which 28 Aboriginal men, women and children were shot and hacked to death – is significant not for the number killed but because it marks one of few occasions in the 19th century when Europeans were put on trial and punished for the murder of Aborigines. The level of hostility on some frontiers is indicated by the taking of human remains as souvenirs: one pastoralist requested the police to supply him with the skull of a troublesome Aboriginal for use as a spittoon.

The tradition of the punitive expedition, founded on the belief that at times it was only possible to deal with Aborigines by teaching them a bloody lesson, continued well into the 20th century. The last well-documented examples occurred in the east Kimberley region of WA and in central Australia in 1926 and 1928 respectively. In the latter case, known as the Coniston massacre, a police constable acknowledged the killing of 31 Aborigines; a missionary who worked among the survivors believed the toll to be in excess of 100.

Violent confrontation is but one manifestation of racial conflict. Following their dispossession, the surviving Aborigines, particularly in northern Australia, lived within a social structure which denied them basic freedoms and assigned them a place at the bottom of the economic ladder. Friction between the black and white communities was contained by a caste system: it designated appropriate employment and places of residence for blacks, forms of deference and address, and other facets of etiquette such as eating practices. The subservient place of Aborigines in Australian society was given legal form when most States acquired the power, in the early part of the 20th century, to compel residence at a specific location such as a reserve, control the right to marriage, remove children without right of appeal, and control terms of employment and earnings. Aborigines were also denied the pension and, in most States, the right to vote.

Immigrant groups Conflict was also apparent in relations between British immigrants (and their Australian-born offspring) and immigrants from other parts of the world, notably Asia, the Pacific and southern Europe. Tolerance of cultural diversity was not a feature of life in the 19th century. On the goldfields of Vic. and NSW, and on the smaller Qld fields, there were many attacks on Chinese miners. Typically only a few miners were involved, but there were some major incidents in the declining years of the gold rush: in June 1861, for example, at Lambing Flat near the present-day city of Young in NSW, 3000 white miners took part in violent raids on Chinese camps. Nearly 70 years later, hostility was still evident on the goldfields of WA, this time directed at southern Europeans, who were perceived as members of a distinctive and inferior racial group. Members of other national groups, including the Irish, were also targets of racial hatred.

In their relations with non-European immigrants, most governments aimed not to regulate a system of inequality but to prevent the entry of people thought to be unassimilable. The Chinese were the first target in the 1850s; by 1901, under the > *White Australia Policy*, all non-European immigrants were excluded.

Recent developments Since 1945 the racist thought which underpinned discrimination has gradually lost respectability, to be replaced by a public philosophy which focuses on the individual, ignoring race as a factor in the determination of human behaviour. This change in outlook was accompanied by the dismantling of discriminatory legislation. In a gradual process which ended in the early 1970s, notional equality before the law was conferred on Aborigines and non-European immigrants. The next development was the outlawing of racial discrimination and the conferring of special rights on Aborigines: various forms of assistance for the individual, special government programs and, for a brief period, legislation in some parts of the country to return land to dispossessed Aboriginal communities.

The early 1970s were the high point of optimism that race as a factor in human relations would soon become a thing of the past. Since that time it has become evident that prejudices in areas with a significant Aboriginal population were not likely to disappear in the short term: rather, problems have been compounded by diminishing employment opportunities, as well as by resentment and apprehension aroused by legislation conferring special rights. A second factor was the revival of the politics of prejudice, evident in some responses to land-rights legislation and the removal of racially discriminatory immigration controls. This reaction has been fuelled by a phenomenon apparent throughout the western world, the attempt to give new legitimacy to racist nationalism.

Rapid change since 1945 has had the effect of opening Australian society to peoples previously denied entry or kept at the margins. But the gross disadvantage suffered by Aboriginal people, evident in a range of social indicators and perhaps most clearly summed up in life-expectancy rates 20 years below those of white Australians, demonstrates that relatively few Aborigines have been enabled to take advantage of the opportunities offered. >> *Aboriginal culture and society*; *ethnic groups*; *immigration*; *land rights, Aboriginal*; *missions and reserves*

radio > *broadcasting*

Rafferty, Chips [John William Goffage] (1909–71), actor, b. Broken Hill, NSW. Tall and lanky, Rafferty specialised in roles depicting the archetypal Australian of popular imagination in such films as *Forty Thousand Horsemen* (1940), *Rats of Tobruk* (1944) and *The Overlanders* (1946). Advocate of an independent Australian film industry, he produced – with limited success – several films including *The Phantom Stockman* (1953) and *King of the Coral Sea* (1954). Arguably his best performance was as the benevolent police sergeant in his final film, *Wake in Fright* (1970, titled *Outback* in the UK).

rails and crakes Australia has about fifteen species of these long-toed waterbirds of the family Rallidae; commonly found in swamps and marshes, one of the most widespread is the banded land-rail, bantam-sized and with black-and-white banded underparts. Crakes are the smallest of the group; with plumage generally attractively mottled, they are shy, marshland birds. The largest Australian rails are the swamphens or bald coots, with blue-black plumage and bright-red beaks; they are also known as redbills. The Tas. native hen has wings so reduced that the bird can hardly fly. Coots also are members of the rail family, distinguished by having webbed toes; they are more frequently seen on open water, and are able to dive for their food.

railways As Australia was effectively a continent of separate nations prior to Federation in 1901, its railways were developed without benefit of a master plan. The result was lasting disorder, with non-uniform rolling stock running on rails of different gauges in different parts of the continent: in fact until 1962 a rail journey from Sydney to Melbourne involved a change at Albury; and, until 1970, five changes of train were required between Brisbane and Perth. It is little wonder that in the years following World War 2, passengers took to the air and freight to the road.

Australian railways have yet to fully recover from this initial confusion and lack of foresight. Today, they are an under-used service that has been allowed to run down, being inefficient and slow by the standards of most developed nations. Other problems can be put down to neglectful government management (there are few votes and little glamour in railways any more), a demoralised workforce and, most importantly, the immense capital cost involved in improving a system that was badly conceived.

Historical development The first steam-driven railway in Australia was opened in 1854 between Melbourne and Port Melbourne. A company had earlier been formed in NSW (in 1849) with plans to run a railway between Sydney and Goulburn, but it went bankrupt. In 1855 the company was taken over by the NSW government, which managed to get a line operating as far as Parramatta; this was Australia's first government-owned railway and as such indicated the pattern for the future. By 1871 railways were operating in all the colonies, but because of a series of often trivial disagreements no uniform rail gauge allowing cross-colony links was introduced. NSW used what was called a standard gauge (1435mm); Vic. and the southern part of SA, a broad gauge (1600mm); and Qld, Tas., WA and the north of SA, a narrow gauge (1066mm). Much of the history of Australian railways since Federation involves the battle to get a standard gauge rail throughout the country, linking at least the mainland capital cities. This aim was achieved between Sydney and Melbourne in 1962, and between the other capitals with the introduction of the *Indian Pacific* transcontinental service in 1970; a broad-gauge rail still, however, connects Melbourne to Adelaide.

Today all the major rail systems in Australia are owned by their respective State governments, with the Commonwealth (through the Australian National Railways Commission) controlling the Tas. system, the non-metropolitan SA network, and the Territory networks. The *Indian Pacific* – Australia's premier passenger train – which links Sydney to Perth via Broken Hill, Port Pirie and Kalgoorlie, is controlled by NSW, SA and the Commonwealth, this trifurcation of control leading to unnecessary complexity and thus staffing and co-ordination problems. The Kalgoorlie–Port Pirie section of this line, which contains the longest stretch of straight track in the world (478km), was promised to WA as an inducement to join the Commonwealth and was completed in 1917. The eastern NSW–SA section from Port Pirie to Sydney was a natural extension of this line, but it took more than 50 years to achieve. (In the US, by comparison, the transcontinental Union Pacific railroad was authorised by Congress in 1862 and completed in 1869.)

Other long-distance Australian trains include the *Prospector*, which runs from Perth to Kalgoorlie; the *Overland*, from Melbourne to

Adelaide; the *Sunlander* from Brisbane to Cairns; and the *Sydney* (or *Melbourne*) *Express* and the *Intercapital Daylight* from Sydney to Melbourne, both controlled jointly by the NSW and Vic. governments. An enduring symbol of pioneering outback transport was the diesel-powered *Ghan*, which ran – weather permitting – from Port Augusta, SA, to Alice Springs, NT, for 50 years from 1929. Although long since replaced by an express train, in 1988 it was resurrected for a 30km tourist trip.

With the exception of the *Prospector* and the NSW XPT (Express Passenger Train) which runs between Sydney and Albury, Australia has no high-speed trains. The mean speed of Australian country and interstate services is about 56km per hour, longer journeys averaging 64 to 88km per hour; this compares unfavourably with the numerous European trains which average 150km per hour, and the Japanese Shinkansen ('Bullet') train's 210km per hour. Despite relatively cheap rail fares and reasonable accommodation, only 620 000 passengers chose to travel by rail in the Melbourne–Sydney–Adelaide triangle in 1988, compared with the 4 million who went by air – travellers have not been seduced by many of the 'improvements' to the rail system, which in many cases are cosmetic only. A proposal has been put forward for a VFT (Very Fast Train) link between Sydney and Melbourne, utilising rolling stock capable of travelling at 350km per hour along a completely new track and sponsored by a mix of government and private enterprise. While technologically feasible, the capital investment required is conservatively estimated to be $4.5 billion; a further hindrance is the interstate rivalry which has bedevilled the development of Australian railways in the past.

Today, Australia has 38 760km of government-owned railways; Qld has the largest rail network, with 10 124km of track. Some 377.5 million passenger journeys were made in 1985–6, and 172 million t of freight were carried. There is also a large non-government sector that operates freight trains for mineral haulage from mines to ports, and a network of narrow-gauge track in Queensland serving the sugar industry. As all Australian trains are now powered by diesel or electricity, there is also a growing group of steam enthusiasts running small tourist railways, such as *Puffing Billy* in the Dandenong Ranges, Vic.

rainbow-bird This species, *Merops ornatus*, is Australia's only member of the bee-eaters, a group that is widespread in Africa and Asia; as this name implies, the rainbow-bird is able to eat stinging bees and wasps, although it takes a variety of other insects as well, capturing them in flight. It is brightly coloured – plumage is predominantly blue, green and orange – and has a distinctive tail from which extend two slender plumes; to nest, a tunnel about 70cm long is excavated in sandy soil, and the eggs are laid at its end. Although more common in tropical Australia, the rainbow-bird does range down the coast into NSW.

Raine Island Qld A low coral islet lying outside the Great Barrier Reef northeast of Cape Grenville, Raine is now a sanctuary for the sea-birds that nest and breed there – in 1843 it was seen by a naturalist to be so crowded with birds and eggs that a man had barely room to walk. The island was once a source of guano, but deposits have been exhausted. In the early 19th century Raine Entrance was much used by shipping, but it is extremely dangerous and was generally avoided after the 1850s.

rainforests These closely spaced plant communities are dominated by trees but typically have a great range of shrubs, lianas and epiphytes. In Australia, rainforests are restricted to areas of high rainfall on the northern and eastern coasts; although rainfall and temperature appear to be the main determinants of rainforest distribution, a high level of soil nutrients – and fertile soils – are generally required. A range of rainforest types occurs in Australia: the most complex types have a high diversity of species and three tree layers (emergents, canopy and sub-canopy), the simpler types having only one tree layer and often dominated by a single species.

The most diverse rainforests are those of the tropical lowlands of northern Qld and are often called mesophyll vine forests. They are restricted to frost-free areas receiving a mean annual rainfall of at least 1400mm, notably the coastal plains below Mt Bellenden Ker and Mt Bartle Frere where the tallest trees reach at least 40m in height. These rainforests have yielded many primitive flowering plant families which are relicts from Gondwana, such as palms and laurels, as well as primitive representatives of other more widespread groups such as the protea family. The rainforests of the northern coast, which are scattered from Cape York Peninsula to the Kimberley Range in WA, are subject to more seasonal rainfall with relatively long dry periods. While similar to the tropical rainforests of northeastern Qld, they are often referred to as monsoon forests and accommodate a fair proportion of deciduous trees. Subtropical 'dry' rainforest occurs in areas of lower temperature and rainfall; they often have fewer lianas and epiphytes and are also characterised by smaller leaf size and fewer tree layers, with conifers and ferns as conspicuous elements. Temperate rainforests are characterised by relatively small leaf size, only one or two tree layers, and an abundance of mosses on leaves, tree-trunks, rocks and soil – giving rise to the term moss forest. In southern Australia, particularly Tas., the cool temperate rainforests are often dominated by the myrtle beech, *Nothofagus cunninghamii*, and tree-ferns such as *Dicksonia* and *Cyathea* are common understorey plants.

Natural disasters such as severe storms and fires have played an important part in determining the present-day extent of rainforests in Australia. Since European settlement, however, some two-thirds of the original rainforests have been cleared for agriculture, and timber species (such as cedar and hoop pine) have been harvested continuously. Logging in the remaining rainforests remains a controversial matter. Conservationists are concerned that some species with restricted distribution have already been lost, that many others represent an irreplacable 'gene pool', and that the clearing of rainforests may have long-term effects on the world's weather patterns; industries based on rainforest logging are, on the other hand, of great importance to local economies. Representative tracts of rainforest in all States have now been set aside as national parks and harvesting is controlled by both legislation and codes of forestry practice. By the end of the 1980s, however, the search for an appropriate balance between development and conservation was still in progress. >> *environment and conservation*; *flora*; *forests and forestry*

Ramsay, Hugh (1877–1906), painter, b. Scotland. Ramsay arrived in Australia in 1878. A contemporary of Max Meldrum and friend of George Lambert, he was an artist of great sensitivity and promise who achieved remarkable artistic maturity before his death aged 29. Trained at the Vic. National Gallery art school, he spent several years in Europe where he was influenced by the great masters – such as Velasquez – and exhibited successfully in Paris and London. His brilliant, full-length portraits demonstrate a mastery of technique, a sense of poetry and a perceptive eye for character.

RAN > *defence forces*

Ranunculaceae > *buttercup family*

rare earths > *mineral sands and rare earths*

rats and mice Australia has a diverse native fauna of true rats and mice, the latter not to be confused with > *marsupial mice*. True rodents, of the family Muridae, are relatively recent arrivals on the continent, originating in Southeast Asia within the last 10 million years. In addition to the 56 native species there are three introduced species, which probably arrived shortly after European settlement: the black rat, *Rattus rattus*; the brown rat, *Rattus norvegicus*, and the house mouse, *Mus domesticus*; these are usually found near human habitation or on agricultural land, and rarely enter undisturbed bush. Approximately eight species of native rodents have become extinct in recent times, mainly as a result of habitat destruction and predation by foxes and feral cats.

Many native rats and mice are adapted to arid conditions, being able to conserve water by excreting a highly concentrated urine; some, such as the hopping mice, are able to convert the carbohydrate of dry seeds to water. Most species are basically herbivorous, but supplement their diet with insects and other invertebrates. They are sometimes serious pests of stored foods, and occasionally there are great population explosions, especially of the house mouse in southern agricultural districts.

As well as the two introduced species of rats there are seven natives, among them the common and widespread bush rat, *R. fuscipes*, and the eastern Australian swamp rat, *R. lutreolus*. The largest Australia rodent is the water-rat, *Hydromys chrysogaster*, common in streams and swamps across much of the continent. Among the other groups of native rodents are the long-eared rabbit-rats, *Conilurus*; the rock-rats, *Zyzomys*, which store fat in their tails; and the prehensile-tailed rats, *Pogonomys*, which are able to curl their tails around branches when climbing. The hopping-mice, *Notomys*, have specially adapted hindlegs, a long, tufted tail and large ears, resembling their distant relatives, the gerbils and jerboas.

ravens > *crows and ravens*

Rawlinson Range WA Lying southeast of the Gibson Desert, this is a western extension of the crystalline Musgrave and Petermann ranges of SA and the NT. The highest point is 1200m above sea-level, with peaks rising 250m above the surrounding plain.

Raymond Terrace NSW (pop. 8793) A former port which lies on the Hunter River 196km north of Sydney, Raymond Terrace is a commuter base for workers in Newcastle 25km to the south. The surrounding district is chiefly devoted to agriculture and dairying; local industry centres on the RAAF base at Williamtown 4km to the east, an aluminium smelter at nearby Tomago, and the town's large fibre-board factory.

rays These fish are grouped with the sharks to form the class Elasmobranchii. Like sharks rays are carnivorous, but they differ in having ventral gill slits, and pectoral fins joined to the head.

The sawfish, of the genus *Pristis,* is a large tropical ray with a long, low side-lashing snout armed with saw-like teeth; it is unlikely to pursue bathers, but accidental involvement with it could be very serious. The common shovelnose or guitar-fish, *Aptychotrema banksii,* is a feeder on sandy bottoms, and of some market value; the torpedoes, or electric rays, have electrically charged organs on either side of the head – a shock of some intensity can be generated, unpleasant to a fisherman and presumably developed in order to stun prey.

True skates, of the genus *Raja,* have a very low, flat head united with the pectoral fins and with most of the body to form the wing-like disc, with a proportionately quite small, separate and rather insignificant tail. Stingrays have the main part of the body and fins in the wing-like disc, and a longish, thin tail armed with ivory-like, backward-pointing, venomous barbs. Devil rays, or great sea-bats, include the whiptail devil ray, *Mobula diabolus,* measuring as much as 3–4m and found in waters from NSW to tropical regions; despite their alarming appearance, devil rays are harmless.

Recherche Archipelago WA This archipelago consists of over 100 scattered, granitic, uninhabited islands and rocks ranging east–west for some 200km along the southern coast, east of Esperance to Cape Pasley. Chief among them are Mondrain, Termination, Figure of Eight, Middle and Salisbury. Named after one

of the ships of the 1792 expedition of Bruny d'Entrecasteaux, in the past some of the islands have been used by sealers and sheep-farmers. The islands are biologically very important, in part because the fauna seems more closely allied to that of SA than of WA. With the exception of Middle Island, the archipelago has been a nature reserve since 1948.

recreation > *sport and recreation*

red-back spider > *spiders*

Redcliffe Qld (pop. 46 130) This city is situated on a peninsula 32km from Brisbane but is virtually part of the metropolitan area. John Oxley chose it as the site of the first Qld settlement (1824), but this was moved after a few months to the site of Brisbane, and the name 'Humpybong', implying deserted dwellings, was long applied to it. It is now a growing commuter base as well as Brisbane's chief beach resort.

Red Cross Society The Australian Red Cross Society was founded in 1914, its expressed aims being to aid the sick and wounded, to render assistance in the event of disaster, and to prevent disease and relieve suffering. Its wide-ranging services to the Australian community include a blood-transfusion service, emergency-care training, and the training of instructors in first-aid skills and nursing; in recent years the Red Cross has also become involved increasingly in broader humanitarian issues, including services for refugees and other immigrants as well as local communities. The Australian Red Cross is closedly allied to the International Red Cross and helps establish and develop associated agencies in developing countries.

Reed, Joseph (1822–90), architect, b. England. The dominant 19th-century architect in Melbourne, Reed was an organised and astute businessman and excellent designer, whose prodigious output gave architectural expression to the town's yearning for respectability and culture. His prize-winning State Library (1854–70), the Independent Church (1866), Scots Church (1873), Town Hall (1867), grand Exhibition Buildings (1879–80) and sombre Trades Hall (1873) still largely define Melbourne's character. Their range of styles, from neo-classical to Gothic, reflects his extensive knowledge and diverse skills; the use of polychromatic brick-work, notably in the mansion Ripponlea (1868) in Elsternwick, Vic., was among his innovative contributions to Australian architecture.

Rees, Lloyd (1895–1988), artist, b. Brisbane. During a career spanning more than 70 years, Rees moved from formal figurative landscapes and architectural renderings of European and Australian subjects to dream-like, light-filled paintings and lithographs reminiscent of the English artist James Turner in his later years. His romantic depiction of Sydney Harbour in a 1970s series of etchings is especially well known. Rees lectured and taught art history, drawing and painting part-time at the University of Sydney 1946–70. He occupied a unique position in contemporary Australian art – critically accepted by traditionalists and modernists alike, and respected for both his sensitive handling of a wide range of media and the great serenity of his work.

referendums In Australia referendums are used principally in attempts to amend the > *Constitution*, the process being oulined in section 128 of that document. They have also been used by the federal government, although only rarely, to seek the nation's views on questions of policy: two such plebiscites were held on the controversial issue of conscription during World War 1 (1916, 1917), and one in 1977 on the preferred national song. State referendums on policy matters are, on the other hand, much more common.

As with federal and State elections, voting at constitutional referendums is compulsory. A national referendum must be initiated within the federal parliament and approved by a majority of voters overall and in at least four of the six States. It is noteworthy that of 42 federal referendums submitted between 1901 and 1988 only eight have been successful, a poor record of constitutional change which has exercised the minds of political scientists for some time. Clearly, those opposed to change have an easier task than those who support it: they may achieve only a minority vote overall but prevail if a majority of voters in three States – whatever their population – vote 'no' (which has in fact been the case on five occasions). In addition, in a country where knowledge of the Constitution is meagre a vote for the status quo has invariably seemed the safer option to many electors. It has long been held that support from both major

political parties may be a prerequisite for successful referendums. While the support of both parties by no means guarantees success, opposition from one of them almost certainly ensures failure. It seems safe to assume that the Constitution will celebrate its centenary in much the same condition as when it was first approved.

refugees > *immigration*

Reibey, Mary (1777–1855), businesswoman, b. England. Born Mary Haydeck, Reibey was transported at the age of 13 for horse-stealing. She married Thomas Reibey (1768–1811), a soldier turned trader, and helped him to acquire property in Sydney and to manage his business enterprises. After his death she continued to build up his business, becoming an extremely wealthy citizen.

Reid, Sir George Houston (1845–1918), politician, b. Scotland. Reid arrived from Scotland in 1852, destined to become premier of NSW (1894–9) and prime minister of Australia (1904–5). He was particularly influential in having secondary and technical education measures passed, and pulled NSW out of the 1890s depression by means of brilliant financial measures including the first annual budgets. He was at first opposed to Federation, protesting that it would damage NSW free trade, but having accepted the fact he led the Opposition in the first federal parliament and was briefly leader of a coalition in 1904, after successively supporting Labor to defeat Deakin and then Deakin to defeat Labor. He resigned from parliament on his appointment as first Australian high commissioner in London (1910–16) and later was a British member of parliament (1916–18).

religion In 1986 nearly three-quarters of all Australians described themselves as Christians. The two largest religious groups are the > *Anglican Church* and the > *Catholic Church*, but there are numerous minority religions – both Christian and non-Christian – which fact reflects the increasingly cosmopolitan character of the population since the 19th century. Religious affiliation has on the whole mirrored immigration patterns: the number of Anglicans has gradually declined (in percentage terms) since the mid-19th century, while the proportion of non-Christians has nearly doubled in the last 50 years.

Since the 1970s, when the census question on religious affiliation became optional, an increasing number of Australians have stated 'no religion'. This undoubtedly reflects the increasing worldwide trend towards secularism, which is generally attributed to 20th-century materialism and apathy and the decline of religious education. The increasing popularity of non-Christian sects (also since the 1970s), particularly among those in their late teens and early 20s, is equally judged to reflect the growing social and political disillusionment of that age-group. It is noteworthy that religious adherence has been more consistent in faiths such as Islam and Judaism, whose beliefs and practices are an integral part of daily life.

Historical development Before the arrival of Europeans in Australia, Aboriginal culture encompassed a complex system of religious beliefs which was inextricably bound up with the land and affected every aspect of daily life (> *Aboriginal culture and society*). In nearly every case, settlers since 1788 have brought their faith with them. The Church of England had some characteristics of an established church in the first 50 years of settlement in NSW, including a monopoly of education, which led to the unlikely but successful alliance of Irish Roman Catholics, Scottish Presbyterians and English Methodists. Today the Anglican and Catholic churches are comparatively evenly spread throughout the social strata; in the 19th century, however, the poorer communities were predominantly Catholic and the richer, ruling group was Anglican. State aid for all major denominations was introduced in NSW in 1836, followed by SA in 1851 and the other colonies thereafter.

Increasing secularism and the churches' fear of government intervention led to complete separation of church and state by the time of Federation. Section 116 of the Constitution precludes the institutionalisation of any church by the government, and prohibits religious restriction and the use of religious qualifications for public employment. In the 20th century Australia has followed the international trend towards ecumenism. The > *Australian Council of Churches* was established in 1946 as an inter-church group concerned with both evangelical and humanitarian issues; the Presbyterians (established in Australia c.1809), Methodists (c.1812) and Congregationalists (c.1798) combined in 1977 to form the > *Uniting Church* in Australia. Since the second Vatican Council (1962–5), the Catholic Church has worked to improve its relations with non-Catholics. Communication between Christian and non-Christian groups has also improved, partly in an attempt to counter the community-wide move away from conventional religion.

Today Anglicans comprise 23.9% of the population and Catholics 21.6%. The other major Christian denominations are the Uniting Church (7.6%), Presbyterians (3.6%), Orthodox Churches (2.7%), Baptists (1.3%) and Lutherans (1.3%). The Catholic Church is the fastest-growing Christian faith, largely as the result of the influx of Europeans after World War 2.

Salvation Army The Salvation Army, which originated in England and was set up in Adelaide in 1881, had some 71 000 members in 1981. Renowned as much for its unstinting welfare work as for its evangelical endeavours, it has adapted to the needs and expectations of modern society by providing alcohol and drug rehabilitation centres and refuges as well as more traditional community services.

Baptist Church The Baptist Church, introduced from England in 1831, has been influential in education (especially in Vic.) and health activities, and prominent in missionary work both in Australia and abroad.

Orthodox churches There has been a rapid growth in the Orthodox religions since World War 2, largely due to increased immigration from Greece and to a lesser degree from eastern Europe. Some 2.7% of the population belong to one of the eight recognised branches of the Orthodox Church in Australia – Greek and Russian (the two largest), Serbian, Syrian, Rumanian, Bulgarian, Antiochan and Ukrainian – the differences being cultural rather than doctrinal.

Lutheran Church German settlers brought the Lutheran faith to SA in 1838, in a period of mass emigration from their homeland which followed amalgamation of the traditional and Calvinist branches of the Lutheran Church. Early Lutheran settlers were noted for their missionary work, including the establishment of Aboriginal missions such as Hermannsburg in the NT.

Other minority Christian sects Other Christian sects in Australia include the Plymouth Brethren, Quakers (or Society of Friends), Seventh Day Adventists (who opened their first Australian church in Melbourne in 1886) and Mormons (Church of Latter Day Saints). The Jehovah's Witnesses date from 1904 in Australia: strictly neutral in times of war, they were banned from practising their faith for two years (1941–3) during World War 2.

Islam The largest non-Christian denomination is the Islamic faith, introduced to Australia by Afghan camel-drivers in the second half of the 19th century. Muslims in Australia totalled 100 000 in 1986 and their numbers are increasing in step with continuing immigration from Europe, the Middle East and Asia. There are now 25 mosques and Islamic centres throughout Australia; the activities of the Australian Federation of Islamic Councils, formed in 1976, are wide-ranging and include the provision of Islamic education for Muslim children and welfare services for Muslim immigrants.

Judaism As elsewhere in the world, Jews in Australia derive from many different countries and cultures. The first Jewish settlers were from Britain, about 1000 British Jews arriving as convicts. The largest numbers have arrived since the 1930s, escaping religious and social persecution in Europe and, more recently, the USSR and South Africa. There were more than 69 000 Jews in Australia in 1986; the majority live in the capital cities, where Jewish schools and synagogues are well established.

Other non-Christian sects Several non-Christian religions, most notably Buddhism and Hinduism, have small but well-established communities in Australia. Those of more recent origin include Baha'is, Hare Krishnas, Meher Babas and Sikhs, who tend to be concentrated in the capital cities: while numerically small, they are highly visible because of their colourful dress and religious practices. >> *missions and reserves*

remoras Several species of remora, or suckerfishes, which are members of the family Echeneidae, are found in Australian waters. The remora is either free-swimming or attached to a large fish or the hull of a ship by a powerful sucking disc on the top of the head, so formed that the fish detaches itself from the host by swimming forwards. There is fossil evidence that these fish have changed little over million of years.

Rene, Roy [Henry Van der Sluys] (1892–1954), comedian, b. Adelaide. In partnership with Nat Phillips, Rene formed the comedy duo of Stiffy and Mo, Australia's most popular vaudeville act in the 1920s. Famous for his catch-phrase 'Strike me lucky!', Rene had great success as Mo McCackie in the long-running radio series 'McCackie Mansions' in the 1940s. Frequently outrageous (for the time), Rene was a master of innuendo but rarely gave offence because of his ability to win over his audiences and his excellent timing.

reptiles Of the class Reptilia, reptiles are vertebrates which on the scale of evolution fall between the amphibians and the mammals and birds. They are cold-blooded (the body temperature dependent upon external conditions), the skin is typically scaly and thick and they either lay shelled eggs, often in terrestrial habitats, or produce live young in gelatinous masses, usually in aquatic habitats; the young are air-breathing. Australia has three orders of reptiles, Crocodilia (> *crocodiles*), Squamata (> *lizards*; *snakes*), and Chelonia (> *turtles and tortoises*).

republicanism Australia's system of government is one of constitutional monarchism, whereby the British monarch is also Queen or King of Australia and is represented by a governor-general and six State governors. A desire to sever Australia's ties with the British monarchy, and to establish a republic in its stead, has been expressed periodically since the 19th century, particularly when radical nationalism was at its height in the 1880s and 1890s. The popularity of republicanism declined after World War 1, but opinion polls in the late 1980s showed majority support for a republican Australia: the shift in opinion since World War 2 is usually explained with reference to Australia's diversified immigration policy, but it was further encouraged by the > *constitutional crisis 1975* when the governor-general dismissed from office the federal Labor government.

Popular opinion notwithstanding, recent controversies concerning the national anthem and the national flag highlight the influence of entrenched interests hostile to republican sentiment. The most popular form of republicanism advocated involves replacing the governor-general with a president elected by the people; whatever its form, converting Australia to a republic would necessitate massive alteration of the federal and State Constitutions. By 1990 the Liberal and National parties remained vehemently opposed to the idea and the Labor government had accorded it low priority. Republicanism may be inevitable, but it is certainly not imminent. >> *nationalism*

Reserve Bank of Australia > *banks and banking*

reservoirs > *dams and reservoirs; water and water resources*

Restionaceae This family of rush-like plants is confined to the southern hemisphere and is most diverse in South Africa and Australia, the latter having about 115 species in 20 genera (eighteen of which are endemic). Undistinguished plants with wiry stems sheathed by scale-like leaves, they are nevertheless an important element of the heaths and sedgelands of higher-rainfall areas on poor soils.

retail trade The retail trade is one of Australia's largest industries, employing about one million people in more than 160 000 establishments. In 1985–6, the value of goods sold (excluding motor vehicles and petrol) amounted to $52 544 million.

The development of retailing in Australia has followed the Anglo-American pattern, department stores such as the Myer Emporium being modelled on Selfridges in London and the Coles discount chain copying the US 'five and dime' stores of F.W. Woolworth. The pattern continued in the 1950s with the introduction of the supermarket, a one-stop self-service store with a vast range of convenience goods. A later development was the regional shopping centre, a kind of supermarket writ large, providing numerous stores within a single complex. Usually situated on the suburban fringe, they were made possible by universal car ownership and developed in response to increasing congestion in neighbourhood and city shopping centres. In 1974, the Trade Practices Act prohibited retail price maintenance, meaning that manufacturers could no longer place a mandatory retail price on their goods. One result was the proliferation of 'discount' shops and chains: specialising mainly in household items, many – such as Target, Venture, K Mart and Billy Guyatt's – are today part of large retailing conglomerates. Franchise arrangements, such as those operated by the bookseller Angus & Robertson, and co-operative buying chains such as Amcal chemists and Mitre 10, are also on the increase, the concepts being imported directly from the US.

By the 1970s, most central business districts (CBDs) and their traditional department stores were moribund. Concern to attract consumers back to the metropolitan area – particularly in the capital cities – encouraged governments to restore and revive their CBDs; pedestrian-oriented shopping complexes and malls have flourished and major department stores such as Coles-Myer and David Jones have been refurbished and expanded. As elsewhere in the world, notably London, much of this development has been achieved with the assistance of foreign capital: Melbourne Central, a multi-purpose complex under construction in that city in the late 1980s, will house Australia's first Japanese-owned department store. A recent retailing phenomenon is the appearance in suburban main streets of speciality shops – commonly clothing outlets – which as branches of large chains can pay high rents and often drive out independent local stores.

By the late 1980s, the opening hours of shops – for many years a contentious issue between government, management and unions – were subject to decreasing regulation and six-day trading, with limited late-night and Sunday commerce, was common. The major retailing development of the 1980s, however, was the growth of cashless shopping, through either the use of credit cards or direct debiting of shoppers' bank accounts by EFTPOS (electronic funds transfer at point of sale). While this is undoubtedly the way of the future and is already operating in many large chains, the amount of consumer debt in Australia – which in 1989 amounted to a figure of $1300 for each man, woman and child – remains of concern to both economists and the government. >> *consumer credit; service industries; trade practices legislation*

rhododendron Australia has only one native species of the large shrub and tree genus *Rhododendron*, which belongs to the family Ericaceae. The genus is centred in Asia, but numerous species and hybrids are grown as ornamental plants in temperate climates. The Australian rhododendron, *R. lochiae*, is restricted in the wild to mist-shrouded summits of the coastal ranges of northern Qld, roughly between Innisfail and Cooktown. A rangy shrub, it grows mostly as an epiphyte on trees or rocks, and has bell-shaped scarlet flowers.

ribbonfishes Greatly elongated and laterally compressed fishes of the order Lampridiformes, ribbonfishes inhabit the abyssal depths, sometimes reaching a length of over 6m. Their fins have long, slender rays and they are covered with a delicate, silvery skin; they swim with an undulating movement, and are perhaps the source of sea-serpent stories. They are found occasionally along the Australian coast, in particular the oarfish, which is distinct from the typical ribbonfish in having an extended pink crest and oar-shaped ventral fins.

ribbon worms > *marine worms*

rice Rice was first grown commercially in Australia in the 1890s, by Chinese market gardeners in the NT. The industry became established in the Murrumbidgee Irrigation Area of NSW in 1924, and NSW today produces about 97% of the country's crop; the remainder is produced around the Burdekin River in northeast Qld. Rice-growing has been attempted periodically in other parts of northern Australia, notably at Humpty Doo in the NT in the 1950s and more recently in northwestern WA, but has not been commercially successful. The NSW industry is highly efficient and State's yields per hectare, boosted by irrigation and a favourable climate, are up to five times that of tropical rice-growing countries. In 1985–6 Australia produced 716 000t of rice, with a gross value of $81 million; all standard varieties are grown and most of the crop is exported. >> *cereals and grains*

Richardson, Henry Handel [Ethel Florence Robertson] (1870–1946), novelist, b. Melbourne. Ethel Florence Lindesay Richardson, as she was born, spent an unhappy childhood which culminated in her father's admission to an asylum. She left for Europe at 17 and returned only once to Australia, in 1912, having married John George Robertson in 1895. A painstaking writer preoccupied with failure and tragedy, Richardson based much of her work on personal experience backed with detailed historical research: her first novel, *Maurice Guest* (1908) is an intense emotional tragedy based in Germany; the schoolgirl classic *The Getting of Wisdom* (1910) drew on her unhappy schooldays; and the monumental trilogy *The Fortunes of Richard Mahony* (1917–29) reflected the reality of her father's failed life. Her real identity was only revealed on publication of the final volume of the trilogy.

Richmond Tas. (pop. 693) This historic farming town lies on the Coal River some 27km northeast of Hobart. It developed from the 1820s as the centre for the colony's chief wheat-growing region. Despite its close proximity to Hobart, Richmond declined after nearby Sorell was linked with Hobart by causeway

in the 1870s. Its chief industry today is tourism, based on its fine and well-preserved colonial buildings, which include Australia's oldest extant bridge (1823) and oldest Catholic church (1837).

Richmond River NSW This river rises in the McPherson Range near the Qld border and flows south and then east to the sea at Ballina, where prawning and fishing are major activities. After flowing through mountain forests notable for timber-getting and sawmilling, it passes through grazing and farming land supporting beef and dairy cattle, and crops such as maize, sugarcane and bananas; the Richmond valley is NSW's most important producer of butter. Toonumbar dam regulates the river water and provides irrigation. Macadamia plantations are being established north of Lismore, the fertile area east of which – once forested and known as the 'Big Scrub' – was formerly an important source of cedar.

Richmond–Windsor NSW (pop. 17 088) These towns, 4km apart and about 60km west of Sydney, were originally two of Governor Macquarie's > *Five Towns*, founded in 1810 for their presumed safe location above the flood-level of the Hawkesbury River (which still inundates low parts of modern Windsor after exceptional storms). This part of the Hawkesbury shire, settled from the 1790s, has some fine early buildings including the Richmond schoolhouse (1813) and St Matthews church in Windsor (1817) which was designed by Francis Greenway. Dairying and agriculture are the chief activities in the surrounding area, and the Hawkesbury Agricultural College is situated in Richmond. Town industries include food-processing, textile and plastic factories.

riflebirds The three Australian species of riflebirds belong to the same family – Paradisaeidae – as NG's spectacular birds of paradise. They are found in rainforests along the eastern coast from the Hunter River in NSW to Cape York Peninsula. Males have purplish-black and bronze-green velvety plumage, which is said to have reminded early settlers of the uniform of rifle regiments of the British army. At least two of the species have the curious habit of wrapping discarded snakeskins around their nests; sometimes thought to be a device to repel living snakes, this is at present believed to be simply a question of utilising convenient, available materials.

ring-tailed possums > *possums*

Riverina, the NSW This is generally recognised as the area between the Murray and Lachlan rivers, extending west from a line drawn to connect Condobolin, Junee, Wagga Wagga and Albury. Wheat is produced in the undulating eastern region, and the western plains are most suitable for sheep and wool, particularly the merino. Irrigation for these industries, and also for some rice production, extends along the NSW side of the Murray River. Farther north is the extensive Murrumbidgee Irrigation Area, and south of the Murrumbidgee lies the new irrigation area of Coleambally. The northern Riverina was first crossed by John Oxley in 1817; white settlement began in the east in the 1830s, and the region has seen all stages of settlement and all degrees of intensity of land use. In the south, along the Murray River, there is evidence of Aboriginal occupation dating back 30 000 years.

river transport As Australia lacks the extensive river systems of more mountainous or wetter continents, river transport has not played an important part in the development of the country's interior. The short coastal rivers, such as the Hawkesbury and Parramatta in NSW, the Swan in WA, and the Yarra in Vic., were used for communication and the shipping of supplies and timber in the colonies' early years but, except for ferry services, never developed into major throughfares, being either too short or seasonally unnavigable. Australia's only large river system is the Murray–Darling, which was initially thought to offer great potential as a trading route. In 1852, Francis Cadell surveyed the Murray from its mouth to Swan Hill, Vic.; in the following year, J.G. and W.R. Randell in the *Mary Anne* and Cadell in the *Lady Augusta* introduced the first steam-powered boats to the Murray, the *Mary Anne* reaching as far as Moama in NSW. Cadell and the Elder family, among many, formed steam-ship companies, and by the 1870s about 200 boats and barges were plying some 8000km of waterway along the Murray–Darling system. While opening up vast areas of the interior, the steamer services were irregular owing to the variable river levels caused by frequent flood or drought; also, the sandbars at the mouth of the Murray made access to the open sea difficult. Improvements to the river system attempted by the SA government were ultimately thwarted by the arrival of the railway from Melbourne and Sydney, which captured most of the river traffic. A few paddlesteamers can still be seen on the Murray, but are only for tourist use. >> *ships and shipping*

Rivett family, eminent in several fields from journalism to science. **Albert** (1854–1934), b. England, immigrated to Australia in 1879 and was a Congregational minister in Tas., Vic. and NSW. He published the *Murray Independent* (later the *Federal Independent*) newspaper and was outspoken on many social issues. His eldest daughter **Eleanor** (1883–1972), b. Port Esperance, Tas., was a noted missionary teacher in India; her sisters **Elsie** (1887–1964) and **Mary** (1891–1962) were active youth workers in Sydney and instrumental in the formation of children's libraries. Their brother **Sir (Albert Cherbury) David** (1885–1961), b. Port Esperance, Tas., was a distinguished chemist who became the first chief executive of the Council for Scientific and Industrial Research (now the CSIRO) 1927–49. A firm advocate of self-reliance and political independence for Australian science, he oversaw the introduction of *Cactoblastis cactorum* moths to deal with prickly-pear infestation and was later a director of various pharmaceutical companies. His elder son **Rohan Deakin** (1917–77), b. Melbourne, was a journalist and author. *Behind Bamboo* (1946), his best-known work, documented his time as a prisoner of war on the Burma railway. As editor-in-chief and director of News Ltd in Adelaide during the 1950s, he was a committed campaigner for press freedom; he was director of the International Press Institute in Zurich from 1962–3, after which he worked as a free-lance journalist and commentator on foreign affairs.

roads and road transport Because of its immense size and small population, Australia's 147 000km of 'declared' main and secondary roads are generally inferior in quality to those of most other developed nations; its other 650 000km of roads comprise little more than usable tracks. In 1987, out of a total population of 16.25 million, Australia had 10.5 million licensed drivers and 9 million vehicles of all types, from motorcycles to articulated trucks. Both roads and road-users suffer because there is no nationwide controlling body able to set and maintain uniform road and licensing standards, and no uniform set of driving rules or laws governing road usage for the whole country. Control of road and licensing standards is currently shared between numerous authorities, ranging from local councils to the State and federal governments.

Historical development The first road in Australia was built by Governor Phillip in 1788, from the centre of the Sydney settlement to the Dawes Point battery. A more substantial road was built to Parramatta in 1794, but Phillip's grandiose plans for a spacious Sydney town intersected by wide streets came to nothing. His successor Lachlan Macquarie carved out Australia's first highway network, pushing well-built roads and bridges over the Blue Mountains to Bathurst and south to Goulburn. Macquarie's work was continued by Thomas Mitchell, appointed surveyor-general of NSW in 1828, who supervised construction of a road through to Melbourne, the southern part of which followed the exploratory route taken by Hamilton Hume. The main highway between Sydney and Melbourne still follows this route and is named after its discoverer. As roads were developed, coach services were introduced, the largest network being provided by Cobb & Co., which expanded north from Melbourne following the gold discoveries around Ballarat and Bendigo in 1851. In 1853, a central roads board was established in Vic. to plan a series of toll routes fanning out from Melbourne to Geelong, Portland, Gippsland and the Murray. Similar boards or departments were established in the other States, all attempting with scarce resources to create roads in difficult terrain.

Before the advent of motor vehicles, most of the money allocated to transport was spent on developing the railways. Following World War 1, the importance of road transport was acknowledged and the most important roads were placed under the control of the respective State governments, with federal assistance after 1923. It was World War 2, however, which gave the greatest impetus to road-building, with old roads being upgraded and about 6000km of new roads built, particularly in Qld and the NT. This period also saw the development of a national highway policy. In the postwar years there was a movement of freight away from railways to roads, a development which led NSW, Vic. and Qld to oppose the interstate road operators in the High Court in 1955. The challenge was defeated and, except for certain categories of loose bulk freight such as coal, the railways have never regained their previous position.

As private cars became increasingly popular, all States found it necessary to improve their road systems and most roadworks were paid for by car registration fees and fuel taxes. All the capital cities today have freeway networks radiating out from their centres, which act as short-distance traffic distributors and usually end abruptly in suburban streets or narrow rural lanes; Australia has as yet no cross-country freeway network.

The 1970s and beyond The federal government launched a national highway scheme in 1974, the aim of which was to link all State capitals (plus Adelaide–Darwin and Brisbane–Cairns) with a high-quality sealed road network. The road sealing has been completed, but the quality of the network is very patchy, particularly along the major eastern highways. The 816km Hume Highway between Sydney and Melbourne is still a national disgrace and one of the most dangerous roads in Australia, with more than 1000 heavy commercial vehicles competing daily with private cars on a carriageway that is often little better than a sealed country track; by the late 1980s, barely 50% of the highway was dual carriageway. A new roads strategy announced by the federal government in 1989 provided for major improvements to the Hume Highway, incorporating bypasses for a number of towns and cities including Euroa and Wangaratta in Vic.

The condition of the Hume Highway notwithstanding, the national scheme has had some success in improving the quality of roads in remote areas, such as the north–south Stuart Highway connecting Adelaide and Darwin. Until 1980, when sealing was completed, one-third of this 3000km highway comprised a dirt track. The main problem, as always in Australia, is the necessary spreading of scarce resources too thinly. In 1986 the federal government, through its land transport program and the Australian bicentennial road development program, spent $559.3 million on road construction and maintenance.

Road safety Regrettably, Australia has one of the worst road-accident rates, per capita, in the world – ranking from second- to fifth- highest, according to the statistical methods used. On average, some 3000 people are killed on Australian roads each year and a further 30 000 injured: this has been attributed to a variety of factors, notable among which are poor roads, badly maintained vehicles, excessive long-distance driving and drunken driving, ineffective signposting and road-marking, and inadequate testing for licences. As road casualties increased steadily during the 1960s, the poor safety record became of growing concern to the federal and State governments. Remedial initiatives in the 1970s and 1980s included public education (notably a continuing campaign against 'drink-driving'), the legal requirement to wear seatbelts, stricter traffic laws and more rigorous enforcement of them, more stringent safety standards for new vehicles, and improved design and maintenance standards for roads and roadside areas. While the accident rate has fallen in the last 20 years despite there being twice the number of cars on the road, the 'road toll' was still unacceptably high by the end of the 1980s.

Robe SA (pop. 742) A longstanding fishing and holiday resort, Robe lies on Guichen Bay 349km southeast of Adelaide. It was settled in the 1840s and was a wool port until its trade was drawn off to Adelaide, Portland and Melbourne. Thousands of Chinese disembarked at Robe in the 1850s and walked to the Vic. goldfields to avoid that colony's poll tax. The town is noted for its colonies of sea-birds, including the fairy penguin.

Robe River WA This short river of the Pilbara region drains into the Indian Ocean southeast of Barrow Island. The Robe River area developed rapidly in the 1960s with the discovery of iron ore at Mt Enid. Mining headquarters are in the town of Pannawonica, and the ore is railed to Cape Lambert for export.

Roberts, Tom (Thomas William) (1856–1931), painter, b. England. Arriving in Australia in 1869, Roberts became a major Australian artist and a founder of Australian Impressionism and *plein-air* painting. With Frederick McCubbin and Louis Abrahams, he initiated the artists' camps that led to what became known as the > *Heidelberg School*. His figure paintings and landscapes were formally composed but capture the Australian light and embodied the search for a national identity. His better-known major works, such as *Bailed Up* (1895) and *Shearing the Rams* (1890), are justly famous; he was also an accomplished portrait painter.

Robertson, George > *publishing and bookselling*

Robertson, Sir John (1816–91), politician, b. England. Robertson arrived in Australia with his family in 1820 and by the 1830s was an active campaigner for the right of squatters to use waste lands. Elected to the NSW parliament in 1856, he was premier five times in the period 1860–86 and while frequently opposed to Henry Parkes formed a coalition government with him 1878–81. Although eventually a wealthy squatter, Robertson was convinced of the need for land reforms (particularly free selection) to foster agricultural development and was generally considered a political radical. He fought in both houses of parliament for the passage of his two land Acts in 1861, which made leasehold land available for sale and introduced free selection.

Robertson-Swann, Ron(ald) (1941–), sculptor, b. Sydney. Although also an abstract painter, Robertson-Swann is best known as a sculptor of non-figurative steel works, reflecting his studies (1962) under English sculptors Anthony Caro and Phillip King. He was assistant to Henry Moore 1963–5. Since it was unveiled in 1979, his yellow-painted steel sculpture (nicknamed the 'Yellow Peril') commissioned for Melbourne's city square but later moved to a less central site, has been the most controversial public sculpture in Australian art history.

robins The Australian robin, of the family Muscicapidae, is not related to the European bird, but has a similar appeal. There are some eighteen species, in several genera, mainly of dark colours but with smart white patches or yellow or reddish breasts; males are more brightly coloured than females. Robins are insectivorous and all build open nests of bark, grass and fibres, cup-shaped and generally not high above the ground. The red and yellow robins often hold their tails vertically, and the latter, if disturbed, will cling to a tree trunk, lying flat. Other species include grey-, white-, pink-, rose- and flame-breasted robins, and hooded, dusky and red-capped robins, all of which generally remain throughout the year in specific regions of the mainland and Tas.

Robinson, George Augustus (1789–1866), colonial Protector of Aborigines, b. England. Robinson arrived in Australia in 1824 to practise his trade as a builder. As a Methodist lay preacher he soon became known for his welfare work and was appointed by Governor Arthur to look after the Bruny Island Aborigines 1829–30. Concerned at the rapidly dwindling Aboriginal population, he made a series of unarmed missions 1830–4 – assisted by Truganini – which took him all over the island and succeeded in bringing a few hundred of the decimated tribes to the Bass Strait island reserves. This proved fruitless in the event and the population died out by the 1870s. Robinson's meticulous field notes were edited by N.J.B. Plomley and published as *Friendly Mission* (1966). His term as Protector of Aborigines in the Port Phillip District (1839–49) had little impact.

rock and pop music Commercial rock and pop music were introduced to Australia from the US and Britain in the 1950s and 1960s respectively, and have since dominated the local scene. In the 1950s, the pioneer and earliest hero of rock'n'roll was Johnny O'Keefe, the 'Wild One'. In the 1960s, highly successful acts based on overseas models were developed by the Masters Apprentices, the Easybeats (who won fame in Australia and briefly in Britain) and the Bee Gees, who won a following in the US as well. By the 1970s Australian performers – more sophisticated and more professionally managed – were making a sustained impact on UK and US markets, some broadening their horizons to include Europe, Japan and Southeast Asia; leading groups of the period included Daddy Cool, Skyhooks, AC/DC and the Little River Band (LRB). These and more recent exponents such as Split Enz, Men at Work and Air Supply (who scored three number-one hits on the US charts) have made rock and pop into a large-scale – and extremely lucrative – industry in Australia in the 1980s. The political lyrics of Peter Garrett's group Midnight Oil reflect the social conscience of the 1980s and a new facet of rock music. Olivia Newton-John, popular since the 1960s and now resident in the US, and the perennially popular John Farnham, are two of the best-known individual performers in the field.

rock art > *art, Aboriginal*

rock-cods This name is commonly applied to members of several distinct families; they are found mainly in tropical Australian waters, generally lying very still among reefs and rocks, ready to pounce on passing, unwary sea creatures; they mostly have large mouths for this purpose, and are often able to change colour as camouflage. The family Epinephelidae includes several species such as the black rock-cod, *Epinephelus damelii*, and the proverbially almost inedible wirrah, *Acanthistius serratus*; the coral cod of the Barrier Reef, *Plectropomus maculatus*, has beautiful blue spots on scarlet, pink, brown or grey sides.

Rockhampton Qld (pop. 54 362) This rural city lies about 60km from the mouth of the Fitzroy River, and 660km north of Brisbane. It developed as a supply centre for pastoral industries in 1854 and as a starting-point for the abortive Canoona gold rush in 1858; development was further stimulated by the gold discoveries at Peak Downs (1861) and Mt Morgan (1882). The main factor in its growth as the chief centre for central Qld, however, was the construction of a railway over the Great Dividing Range to tap the western pastoral lands, and development of harbour and wharves at Port Alma to handle much of the region's products and imports. Local industries include meat works and railway workshops. In 1986 the city's growth rate equalled the national average, and it is an important link in the growing tourist industry.

Rockingham WA (pop. 30 635) This port and resort lies on Cockburn Sound 46km south of Perth and is both a satellite town and regional centre. It has some light industry serving nearby Kwinana and also, since surrounding lands were improved with nutrients in the 1980s, a rich dairy industry. Rockingham was named after a ship wrecked in Mangles Bay in 1830; its marine associations have persisted and despite the town's commercial and industrial focus it is noted for its boating and fishing.

rock lobsters > *crayfishes and allies*

Rocks, the NSW This 23ha historic district comprises the western shore of Sydney Cove, which developed as the commercial centre for the founding colony and by the late 19th century was noted for its colourful mix of traders, sailors and larrikin gangs. Isolated from the centre of Sydney by construction of the harbour bridge and Cahill Expressway, the Rocks area was relatively derelict until major renovation and redevelopment commenced in the 1970s. It is now the city's second most important attraction, its houses and stores having been restored as shops, restaurants and galleries.

rock wallabies > *kangaroos, wallabies and allies*

rock warbler > *cavebirds*

rodents > *rats and mice*

rodeos Originally known as bushmen's carnivals, rodeos began as informal displays of skills associated with cattle droving. The Australian Rough Riders Association, in which the bush clothier R.M. Williams played a leading role, was formed in 1944; in the following year the association staged the first Australian championship at Prospect, SA. As a result of contact with US servicemen, rodeos became influenced by American styles; the format consists of buckjumping and bullock-riding, drafting individual beasts from a mob of cattle, a variety of races, and bulldogging (in which the rider jumps from a moving horse on to a steer and brings it to the ground). National championships were initially held at different venues with ARRA approval, but since 1961 have been awarded on a points system.

Roma Qld (pop. 6069) This town lies 480km west of Brisbane and is a centre for the surrounding pastoral and agricultural region. It is noted particularly for the nearby natural-gas field, first discovered in 1900 and both used locally and piped to Brisbane. Historically, Roma is distinguished as the site of the State's first commercial vineyard (1863) and the 1879 trial of the bushranger Captain Starlight. The town was named after the wife of the State's first governor, Sir George Bowen.

Roman Catholic Church > *Catholic Church; religion*

Roper River NT The headwaters of the Roper River are in high country southeast of Katherine, and the river flows east for some 400km to Limmen Bight on the Gulf of Carpentaria. The lower section forms part of the south boundary of the Arnhem Land Aboriginal Reserve. North of the river mouth is an expanse of sandstone known as the Ruined City of Arnhem Land because the unusual, highly coloured rock formations suggested ruined buildings and streets. The river was discovered by Ludwig Leichhardt in 1845 and named after a member of his party.

Rose, Lionel Edmond > *boxing*

Rose, (Iain) Murray > *Olympic Games; swimming and diving*

Rosebery Tas. (pop. 2102) This mining town lies in the State's rugged west, 303km northwest of Hobart. Gold was first discovered there in 1893, but today the industry is based on silver, lead and zinc ores which are mined and processed by the Electrolytic Zinc Co. The town was named after the Earl of Rosebery.

rosellas > *parrots*

Rosewall, Ken(neth Robert) (1934–), tennis player, b. Sydney. After a distinguished career as a junior player, Rosewall was teamed with Lew Hoad in 1953 when, as 18-year-olds, they won the Davis Cup for Australia. Rosewall's classical court play and strong backhand won him all the major world titles with the exception of Wimbledon, where he was runner-up four times. He turned professional in 1956, and when in 1968 professionals became eligible to enter national championship tournaments the ageless 'Muscles' resumed his place at the top, winning several further titles and reaching the Wimbledon Open finals in 1970 and 1974.

Ross Tas. (pop. 283) This small rural town lies on the Macquarie River about 122km north of Hobart, in a district noted for superfine wool and beef cattle. Ross began as a military post and is best known for its carved stone bridge (1836) across the Macquarie, built by convicts to a design by architect John Lee Archer.

Rottnest Island WA A small island and a favoured holiday resort, Rottnest lies 32km west of Perth; the main settlement is Thompsons Bay, and a notable aspect of island life is the absence of motor vehicles – bicycles are the only form of transport. The island fauna includes the native quokka, and introduced pheasants, peacocks, ducks and snipe; the island's name stems from the existence of the quokka, whose nests were observed by Willem de Vlamingh in 1696 and thought to be rats' nests – 'Rottenest'. Rottnest was first settled in 1830; in the course of time it has been a prison, a pilot station, an internment camp and a military base, and it now contains many historic buildings.

Roughsey, Dick (Goobalathaldin) (1924–85), writer and artist, b. Sydney Island, Qld. A member of the Lardil tribe, Roughsey was variously a cattle-hand and seaman before taking up painting in the 1960s. He wrote and illustrated a number of children's books depicting Aboriginal myths and legends, notably *Giant Devil Dingo* (1973) and *The Quinkins* (1982), which won him international fame. Roughsey was chairman of the Aboriginal Arts Board 1973–6; his autobiography *Moon and Rainbow* was published in 1971.

roundworms > *helminths*

Rowell, Kenneth (1920–), designer, b. Melbourne. After studying as a painter, Rowell left for London in 1950, where he had a prolific and distinguished career as a set designer for numerous companies including the Royal Ballet, the Royal Shakespeare Company, the Old Vic and the Sadler's Wells Opera. Since returning to live in Australia, he has designed productions for all the major opera and ballet companies, perhaps most notably *Rites of Passage* (1974) for the Australian Opera and *La Belle Hélène* (1977) and *Orpheus* (1978) for the Vic. State Opera.

rowing and sculling Australia's first recorded rowing race took place on Sydney Harbour in 1818. The first formal regatta was held on the Derwent River at Hobart in 1827, while the inaugural Australia Day Regatta was held in Sydney in 1837. By the 1870s intercolonial and intervarsity competitions were established for both fours and eights and the major cities had annual regattas and Head of the River competitions by the early part of this century. The King's Cup (1920), Oxford and Cambridge Cup (1896) and President's Cup for sculling are the most significant events in the calendars of rowing enthusiasts, of whom 15 000 are registered in Australia. Professional sculling was enormously popular in the 19th century: Australian world champions included Edward Trickett, H.E. Searle, Peter Kemp and William Beach, who won his title on the Parramatta River in 1884 before a crowd of 100 000.

H.R. (Bobby) Pearce became Australia's first Olympic champion in 1928, outclassing all rivals with his enormous strength and fluent style. In 1931 he became the second Australian to win the Henley Diamond Sculls (C. McVilly had won in 1913), and he retained his Olympic crown in 1932; he retired undefeated as a professional in 1940. Mervyn Wood achieved the Henley–Olympic double in 1948, and won Henley again in 1952.

Stuart Mackenzie's silver medal in 1956 was the beginning of a remarkable career. He won Henley every year 1957–62, and only illness prevented him from competing in the 1960 Olympics. Mackenzie became a larger-than-life figure whose distinctive behaviour included winning Henley wearing a bowler hat.

Australia's later Olympic successes include silver in the eights in 1968; and, in 1984, silver in the quadruple sculls and bronze in the women's coxed four and the men's eight. Australian crews won world championships in the 1980–1 lightweight coxless four, and in men's eight in 1986. Adair Ferguson won the women's lightweight sculls in 1985, and Peter Antonie the men's event in 1986.

royal commissions A royal commission is an inquiry appointed by the federal or a State government to investigate and make recommendations about an issue of public moment; it is usually led by a judge or experienced lawyer, who is accorded the same protection and immunity as a judge of the Supreme Court. Unlike other fact-finding bodies appointed on an ad hoc basis (such as interdepartmental committees and 'task forces'), a royal commission has the power to compel people to give evidence and produce documents; witnesses may be questioned under oath and have no right of refusal to be sworn, but may prevent evidence unwillingly given from being used in subsequent court proceedings. People affected by the inquiry usually have legal representation, but although these procedures are similar to those of a legal hearing the commission has no power to impose discipline as the result of its findings and the government is free to reject its report and recommendations. Boards of inquiry in Vic. and Tas. have similar powers, but royal commissions enjoy greater prestige.

In the 19th century, inquiries that would now commonly be entrusted to royal commissions were often carried out by parliamentary select committees; this practice declined in tandem with the rise of highly organised political parties, as it was feared that in controversial cases the committee's conclusions would be influenced by party politics. The subjects investigated by royal commissions vary widely. Some have involved comprehensive reviews of important institutions, such as the 1929 commission on the working of the Australian Constitution, and the 1974 Coombs commission on the public service which examined most aspects of federal administration. Others have investigated more specific matters, as was the case with the 1983 Hope inquiry into

Australia's intelligence services. Many commissions – and undoubtedly those which receive most publicity – have investigated allegations of error, impropriety or criminal conduct. The collision between the Australian navy vessels HMAS *Voyager* and HMAS *Melbourne* in 1964 was the subject of two royal commissions, the first criticising and the second clearing the captain of the *Melbourne*.

Although royal commissions are generally respected for their impartiality, their terms of reference are usually set by the government and their work is in fact closely bound up with politics. Governments have on occasions used commissions to find evidence to support their policies, as in the 1949 Vic. inquiry into the activities of communists, who were a controversial force at the time because of their increasing control of major trade unions. Similarly, the appointment in 1974 of the Evatt commission on human relations helped to avoid continuing parliamentary debate on abortion and related matters which would have revealed embarrassing divisions within the major parties. On the other hand, the use of royal commissions can backfire politically: the 1980–4 Costigan inquiry into the activities of the Painters and Dockers Union, for example, which was set up by the Fraser government, found evidence of major tax evasion schemes throughout the community.

A royal commission reports directly to the governor-general or State governor, and the government decides what action – if any – will be taken. The reports are usually made public, wherein lies one unresolved problem: if a person is found to have committed a crime and the government decides not to act (perhaps because it is felt that there is insufficient evidence for a conviction), the accused person is exposed to public obloquy but has no opportunity to clear his or her name in court; this is to some extent at odds with the principles of equity that underlie Australian legal practice.

Roycroft, Bill > *equestrian sports*

RSL > *ex-service organisations*

Rubiaceae > *madder family*

rubies > *gems and gemstones*

Rudd, Steele [Arthur Hoey Davis] (1868–1935), author, b. Drayton, Qld. A farm worker and later a public servant, Rudd adopted his pseudonym in the 1890s and began contributing humorous pieces about life on a 'selection' to the *Bulletin*. These caricature studies, which came to focus on the immortal characters Dad and Dave Rudd, were first collected in *On Our Selection* (1899), the best and best known of a subsequent series of ten volumes. They were later translated to comic strips and films. While Rudd wrote several novels and plays, none achieved the popular and critical success of the Dad and Dave series and most were poor adaptations of the formula.

rugby Rugby was played informally in Sydney as early as 1864, before rules and organisation were established with the formation of the Southern Rugby Union in 1874. By 1907, 20 000 people were watching club matches and 52 000 saw an Australia–NZ event; in the same year a professional rugby league was formed. The rugby league team has thirteen players (two less than in the amateur game, rugby union), features scrums when the ball goes out of play, and requires the ball to be played backwards between the legs after a successful tackle.

With a total of 135 000 registered players, rugby union is strongest in NSW and Qld. International competitors include Britain, NZ and France; South Africa has not been included since 1971. In 1984 Australia's national team, the Wallabies, completed a Grand Slam tour of Britain, with Mark Ella becoming the first player to score a try in each Test.

Rugby league – also most popular in NSW and Qld – gained immediate popularity by securing prominent figures including 'Dally' Messenger, an unorthodox and inspired NSW player who transferred from rugby union to rugby league in 1907. Great touring league teams (called the Kangaroos) include those of 1963, and the undefeated teams of 1982 and 1986. Local competition was dominated by South Sydney under Clive Churchill, and St George – the latter winning eleven successive premierships from 1956. State-of-origin matches between NSW and Qld commenced in 1980, and have produced memorable clashes; prominent players include Johnny Raper, Reg Gasnier, Wally Lewis and Ray Price. With 158 000 registered rugby league players, the sport retains its popularity.

Rum Rebellion This is the nickname given later to the events of January 1808, when Governor > *William Bligh* was arrested and deposed from office by Major George Johnston at the request of a number of officers of the > *NSW Corps* and a group of settlers led by John Macarthur. The name derives from one of the immediate causes – the illegal importation of liquor stills – and from the NSW Corps' monopoly of all spirits, known indiscriminately as rum. Soon after his arrival in the colony in 1806, Bligh arrested Macarthur for failing to provision his ship *Parramatta*, thus forcing the sailors to come ashore, an illegal act; Macarthur's action had been a rejoinder to Bligh's demanding a £900 bond for the earlier escape of a convict on the ship. Macarthur, with the support of six officers, questioned Judge-Advocate Richard Atkins's competence to try him; Bligh threatened them with treason charges; and Johnston ordered Macarthur's release. The NSW Corps trained its guns on Government House and Johnston was petitioned to take over – Bligh refused to resign and was arrested. Bligh was upheld at Johnston's subsequent court martial in London, but the relatively light sentence indicated some sympathy with the rebels.

Ruse, James (1760–1837), pioneer farmer, b. England. Transported with the First Fleet, on expiry of his sentence Ruse was presented by Governor Phillip with seed, tools, a cleared tract of land and a promise that if he could become self-sufficient he would be given a land grant. Ruse was successful, and the promised grant – the first in the colony – was made in 1792, near Parramatta, and named Experiment Farm.

rushes The common name for any grass-like plants found in damp ground, rushes are in fact species of the worldwide genus *Juncus*, of which Australia has about 50 native species. Concentrated in the southeast, they are often seen dotting wet areas of pasture, being too tough for grazing. Most have densely clumped, cylindrical wiry stems, with leaves reduced to dry sheathing scales. Bulrushes is another popular name for these reed-like plants: the tall semi-aquatic plant > *cumbungi* is Australia's only native species of bulrush. >> *sedge family*

Russell, John Peter (1858–1930), painter, b. Sydney. Russell was Australia's first true Impressionist. A man of inherited wealth, in the 1880s he moved to Europe where he married Rodin's favourite model, Marianna Mattiocca. He befriended and worked with many of the modern masters, including Toulouse-Lautrec, Monet and Van Gogh (of whom he did a penetrating portrait in 1886). From his home on an island off the Brittany coast, he painted his luminous seascapes. He returned to Australia after World War 1, continuing to paint but never regaining the exuberance of his early work.

Rutaceae > *citrus family*

Rutherglen Vic. (pop. 1586) This town in central Vic., 274km northeast of Melbourne, developed as a gold-mining centre but is now best known as an important wine-growing region, with vineyards stretching as far south as Milawa. The surrounding farmlands produce wool and wheat, with some dairying and timber-milling, and the town has an agricultural research institute concerned with improving vines, pastures and cereals as well as animal husbandry.

rutile > *mineral sands and rare earths*

S

sailboarding > *windsurfing*

sailing and yachting Yachting involves the use of craft with keels, whereas in sailing the boat is a dinghy with a centreboard; together they represent one of the most popular forms of recreation in and around Australia. There are more than 100 000 registered participants, and many times that number are less formally involved.

The first regattas were conducted in Hobart and Sydney in 1837, using a mixture of naval and commercial craft. The formation in 1856 of the Victoria Yacht Club (later the Royal Yacht Club of Victoria) marked the first organisation concerned with purely sporting craft. Smaller organisations were formed in other colonies, but Sydney Harbour, with its unique natural advantages, became the focus for the sport. National championships commenced in 1912–13, and a world championship was conducted in 1938. Ocean racing, which had been held sporadically, was formalised in 1945 with the inaugural Sydney–Hobart race, an event that has now become a national institution. In overseas contests, Australia has since 1965 been represented in the world's premier racing event, the Admiral's Cup, winning in 1967 and 1979. It has participated in the prestigious America's Cup since 1962; in that year and in 1967, the Australian challenging yachts were captained by Jock Sturrock. In 1983, *Australia II* under captain John Bertrand won the cup for Australia – the first time that the US had been defeated since the inaugural race in 1851.

After World War 2, lighter construction materials and the greater availability of motor transport led to a rapid growth in the number of participants and their craft. Australian crews made their first Olympic Games appearance in Melbourne in 1956, resulting in a silver and a bronze medal. Gold medals came in 1964 with the 5.5m *Barrenjoey*, skippered by Bill Northam, and in the Dragon and Star classes in 1972. Australia's first world champion was Rolly Tasker, winning the title in the Flying Dutchman class in 1958. The 1988 Seoul Olympics was the first at which Australia failed to win a medal.

Sale Vic. (pop. 13 559) This city lies at the head of the Gippsland Lakes, 210km east of Melbourne. Situated on the Thomson River at the edge of an irrigation area that supports grazing, dairying and agriculture, Sale is an important regional centre for east Gippsland and for oil and gas development in Bass Strait. Industries include engineering and a processing plant at nearby Dutsun, serving the oil and gas industry and from which gas is piped to Melbourne.

salinity > *soils and soil conservation; water and water resources*

salmon, Atlantic > *fishes, introduced*

salmon, Australian This fish, of the family Arripidae, is quite distinct from the northern hemisphere salmon, family Salmonidae. It is a graceful, silver sea-fish, of which large specimens can reach 85cm long and weigh some 9.5kg. The Australian salmon migrates seasonally, and moves in large schools between offshore and inshore waters. Salmon are caught commercially in southern Australian States; they constitute a major part of ocean fisheries, but in WA reduced numbers have led to the imposing of restrictive measures on both commercial and sport fishing. Young fish are green-backed with yellow spots, while the older are black-backed without spots; the flesh is firm and dry, with a rather strong flavour when eaten fresh.

salt and sodium compounds All Australian salt production is by solar evaporation of seawater and salt lakes, with the bulk exported to Japan for the manufacture of chemicals. WA is the main producer, smaller operations being found in SA, Qld and Vic. The main companies producing salt for local use are ICI Australia Ltd (in SA and Qld), BHP (in SA), Australian Salt Co. Ltd (in SA) and Central Qld Salt Industries Ltd (in Qld). Most of the yield is used for the production of sodium carbonate, sodium hydroxide and chlorine, all vital chemicals in manufacturing industries; sodium hydroxide, for example, is used in the production of alumina from bauxite.

saltbush family The flowering-plant family Chenopodiaceae includes the saltbushes, bluebushes, copperburrs, goosefoots and samphires prominent in semi-arid vegetation of temperate Australia and in coastal saltmarshes; all are shrubs or herbs with succulent, often flabby, leaves which accumulate salt. Australia has about 300 species in 26 genera, fourteen of which are endemic. One of the largest groups is the true saltbushes, *Atriplex*, with some 60 species. These drought-resistant plants dominate the distinctive shrubby vegetation known as saltbush steppe, which is widespread on low saline ground in arid and semi-arid regions and is valued for sheep grazing. There are 57 species of bluebush, forming the genus *Maireana*: all are endemic and include dense shrubs with small succulent leaves that produce the distinctive bluish landscape of much of inland Australia. The genus *Sclerolaena* comprises 62 species of mostly spiny shrubs, often of poorer stony soils; some, such as the galvanised burr, *S. birchii,* are regarded as weeds. Samphires and glassworts, a distinct group in the saltbush family, are plants of highly saline areas with succulent, segmented stems; a common coastal species, often occurring in mangroves, is the beaded glasswort, *Sarcocornia quinqueflora.* >> *grasses and grasslands*

Salvation Army > *religion; welfare organisations*

sandalwood family The Santalaceae family of parasitic plants is present in most parts of the world; it is represented in Australia by ten native genera, of which five are endemic. The family includes trees, shrubs, climbers and herbaceous plants, most of which are root-parasites.

The most economically significant genus is *Santalum*: this includes sandalwood trees, the wood of which is distilled to yield sandalwood oil (used in incense and perfumes). Though now becoming scarce, the most valuable of the six Australian *Santalum* species is the Swan River sandalwood, *S. spicatum,* which is still gathered commercially around Kalgoorlie in WA. The quandong, *S. acuminatum,* widespread in the southern inland, is noted above all for its bright-red edible fruit enclosing an oil-bearing, nutritious 'nut' or seed. Unlike the sandalwoods, most other Australian genera in this family consist of near-leafless trees or shrubs in which the stems are responsible for photosynthesis. Best known is *Exocarpos,* some species of which are called native cherry or ballart (an Aboriginal name); the largest is the eastern *E. cupressiformis,* a cypress-like forest tree of up to 10m. The native currant, *Leptomeria acida,* which belongs to another genus of leafless shrubs, produces edible but sour fruits.

sandhoppers > *amphipods*

sand mining > *mineral sands and rare earths*

Santalaceae > *sandalwood family*

Santamaria, B.A. (Bartholomew Augustine) (1915–), Catholic activist, b. Brunswick, Vic. Santamaria has been an outspoken right-wing Catholic activist and anticommunist since the 1940s. In 1941 he formed the Catholic Social Studies Movement which, with church support, actively opposed left-wing and communist influences in trade unions. He was president of this organisation 1943–57, and has been president of its successor – the > *National Civic Council* – since 1957. Santamaria has written widely on political issues, his published works including *The Price of Freedom* (1964) and *The Defence of Australia* (1970).

Sapindaceae > *soapberry family*

sapphires > *gems and gemstones*

Sarich, Ralph (1938–), engineer, b. Perth. Sarich is best known for his invention in 1970, while running a service station and agricultural machinery business, of a revolutionary orbital engine. The engine has a single piston that follows an orbital path in a circular chamber: its main advantages are cheapness of manufacture, ease of maintenance and a dramatic increase in fuel economy. Development of the engine was started by the Orbital Engine Company, owned jointly by Sarich and BHP, in the 1970s. Worldwide production licences have been signed, and in 1988 an agreement to produce the engine was reached with the Ford Motor Company. Failure by the Australian government to support development of the engine, despite its great commercial potential, is seen by many as a reflection of the nation's general tardiness to support technological research and development.

sarsaparillas This is the common name for plants of the genus *Smilas*, which comprises climbers and shrubs found mostly in warmer parts of the world; they are unusual among monocotyledons in having broad, net-veined leaves with paired tendrils at their base. Australia has seven native species, of which two are widespread. *S. glyciphylla* is an eastern coastal species with weak stems and whitish leaf undersides; its sweet-tasting leaves were used by the early white settlers to make a beverage that was believed to prevent scurvy. *S. australis*, a more robust and prickly climber commonly called the 'lawyer vine', is widespread in eastern and northern Australia.

sassafras This is the common name traditionally used for an American tree of the laurel family but in Australia applied mainly to rainforest trees in three genera of the southern-hemisphere family Atherospermataceae. The genus *Atherosperma* consists of a single species, *A. moschatum*, generally known as the southern or black sassafras and common in Tas. and some mountain forests of Vic. and NSW. *Doryphora* consists of two species in cooler Qld and NSW rainforests, the more southern being the common or yellow sassafras, *D. sassafras*, which yields a useful timber. *Daphnandra* has four species in Qld, NSW and NG: *D. micrantha* is known as canary sassafras or socketwood, the latter for its socket-like joints between trunk and limbs. Two native members of the > *laurel family* are also called sassafras: *Cinnamomum oliveri* or Oliver's sassafras, and *C. virens* or the red-barked sassafras.

satellite communications > *broadcasting*; *communications technology*; *post and telecommunications*

Savage River Tas. This is a tributary of the Pieman River in rugged, northwest Tas. Iron ore deposits were discovered in the area last century, but only in the 1960s were mining operations begun, financed by a consortium of American, Australian and Japanese interests. The long-distance transport of the ore is unique: it is pumped as slurry through an 85km pipeline to Port Latta, on the north coast. The town of Savage River (pop. 1058) was constructed in the mid-1960s to accommodate workers at the mining project.

sawfish > *rays*

sawflies and wood-wasps These insects belong to the most primitive suborder of Hymenoptera, and are characterised by a broad-based abdomen. The caterpillar-like larvae usually feed externally on leaves, although some are miners within plant tissue. The Australian fauna has some 200 species.

The black larvae of the sawfly genus *Perga* are often found massed together on eucalypt foliage, where they sometimes cause complete defoliation; when disturbed, they secrete a noxious concentration of eucalypt oils. The introduced sirex wasp or wood-wasp, *Sirex noctilio*, has become a major pest in Australian *Pinus radiata* plantations. Females drill holes in the wood, in which they lay their eggs along with an inoculate of white rot fungus; the larvae feed on the fungus growth, and eventually the tree is killed. A biological control program using parasitic wasps and nematodes has had some success in curbing the sirex wasp.

SBS The Special Broadcasting Service was established in 1977 as a statutory body responsible for providing programs for Australia's ethnic communities. It operates the radio stations 2EA in Sydney and 3EA in Melbourne, broadcasting in 41 languages and staffed largely by volunteers. Since 1980 it has also operated a television channel, 0/28, which while beset by poor-quality transmission in some areas is noted for its outstanding programming and news service; it is the only national channel broadcasting on UHF. An amalgamation between SBS and the ABC was often mooted in the mid-1980s and is still under consideration although it is felt in many quarters that this could compromise both the independence and high quality achieved by SBS.

scale insects > *bugs*

scallops > *bivalves*; *fishing industry*

Scantlebury Brown, Vera (1889–1946), doctor of medicine, b. Linton, Vic. A pioneer in antenatal care, infant welfare and preschool child care in Vic., Scantlebury Brown was in 1926 appointed part-time director of the new infant-welfare section of the Vic. Health Department, which expanded significantly under her guidance. She encouraged links with obstetric services, introduced a compulsory course for infant-welfare sisters and fought to have pre-school children cared for by infant-welfare services.

Schepisi, Fred(eric Alan) (1939–), film director. b. Melbourne. After a career in advertising and as a maker of documentary films, Schepisi made two feature films of note, *The Devil's Playground* (1976) and *The Chant of Jimmie Blacksmith* (1978), both of which he wrote and produced as well as directed. After moving to the US at the end of the 1970s his career nearly foundered with *Barbarosa* (1981) and *Iceman* (1984), but has undergone a revival with *Evil Angels* (1988), the story of the Chamberlain case.

schools > *education*

schools of the air > *broadcasting*; *education*

science and technology Australia has made a number of distinguished contributions to world science and technology, particularly in the fields of > *medical research* and > *biotechnology*. The tradition of entrepreneurial individualism – which gave rise to Australian products such as rust-proof wheat, the mechanical harvester and, more recently, the orbital engine – has rarely been fruitfully exploited, however. This is due in part to the fact that the relatively small Australian economy has provided an inadequate base for the level of investment required to convert research into products for the market. Continuing reliance on overseas suppliers has also inhibited the development of national expertise in the creation of innovative products and services.

Scientific and technological research in Australia is primarily conducted by the universities, government departments, and specialist agencies that concentrate on areas such as medical research. In the private sector, such activities are undertaken by small innovative companies developing high-technology products and services, and the research divisions of large (often transnational) corporations. While the level of government support for science research generally matches that of other industrialised nations, backing from the private sector has been extremely poor.

Historical development Much of the early scientific work in Australia was concerned with the collection, description and classification of the new and strange phenomena, and included useful amateur anthropology. The need to introduce and acclimatise economically useful plants and animals led to further new work from the early 19th century. Organised and adequately financed research has only developed slowly and until the early 20th century most achievements were made by individuals working in isolation. Australia's contribution to international science has nevertheless been considerable in proportion to population. Outstanding early work of worldwide significance was done by > *William Farrer* in wheatbreeding, > *Hugh McKay* in agricultural machinery, > *Lawrence Hargrave* in aviation, and more recently by medical researchers such as > *Macfarlane Burnet*, > *John Carew Eccles* and Carl Wood. There have also been advances of more specifically local application, incuding the eradication of pests and weeds.

Some early researchers were in the forefront of world technology. Such was the advanced state of Australian telephony, for example, when Alexander Bell visited the colonies in the 1880s, that some of his handsets were denied patents in favour of existing local products. Indigenous researchers have, however, continued to be bedevilled by the incapacity of manufacturers to develop their products to the state where they displace imports. This has inhibited the potential of recently developed expertise in such areas as new materials research, biological control of weeds and insects, satellite remote-sensing techniques, computer software, pharmaceuticals, medical technology and genetic engineering.

The greatest growth of research and development has taken place since World War 2. The achievements of the > *CSIRO*, in particular, have been numerous and diverse in a range of fields including radio-astronomy, pest control and energy technology. Important work has also been done in universities and other educational institutions. State and federal governments have increasingly directed their attention to providing incentives for innovation, which have met with mixed success; a number of universities, some with the co-operation of State governments, have established technology 'parks' to encourage commercial development of their research breakthroughs. Research activities in government business enterprises, such as the Telecom research laboratories and the research division of the Overseas Telecommunications Corporation, play an important part in funding university research: this has resulted in a number of successful joint ventures in areas such as fibre optics and switching techniques.

The fields of research attracting most funding are biotechnology, information technology, pharmacology and medicine, based on their potential to increase the export of 'high-tech' goods and services. Attention has been focused on the production of intellectual property, because Australia (with a relatively well-educated population) is seen as a 'brain-based' economy of the future. To this end, science and technology educators are now recognising the need to increase the number of secondary and tertiary students taking natural sciences, engineering and computing. There is continuing debate about how such courses should be structured and taught, and to what extent students should be also required to undertake interdisciplinary study that embraces social and political questions.

The 1980s and beyond A range of government incentives and assistance schemes in recent years have encouraged an increase in the amount of research and development undertaken in both the public and private sectors. The Australian Research Council was established in 1988 to channel greater research funds into universities, including a number of former colleges of education, such as the University of Technology in Sydney. Federal government incentives to the private sector include 150% tax write-offs for research and development and the use of offset credits to fund joint research by local companies and the subsidiaries of transnational organisations; a controversial decision to cut the budget of research stalwarts such as the CSIRO was modified in 1989 with the restoration of some of its funds. A science-policy statement by the federal government in 1989 also included an extension of the tax write-off scheme to 1995 and the appointment of a science adviser and committee. In the field of science education, additional places have been made available in university faculties such as engineering and computing; and schools are actively encouraging more females to study science subjects at upper secondary level. The contribution of current and future generations to Australian science

and technology remains to be seen, but one likely benefit of more and better science education is a more science-literate community – increasingly essential in the post-industrial age.

In the late 1980s some areas of research continued to generate community concern, particularly the potential effects of developments such as computerisation and biotechnology. Fears that the widespread introduction of computer technology will curb individual autonomy and cause loss of privacy have been discussed in a number of recent reports commissioned by the Australian Science and Technology Council. There is also intense and continuing public debate about the moral issues surrounding genetic engineering and the use of IVF techniques.

In the 20th century, Australia has been a world leader in the adoption of new techniques, from automated banking to satellite technologies; support for the development of indigenous discoveries (particularly on the part of the business community), on the other hand, has been less than enthusiastic. As the nation's reliance on primary industries and inefficient manufacturing is increasingly called into question, the application of local research in fields such as biotechnology and information technology are likely to be an important element of its economy in the future. >> *astronomy*; *communications technology*; *electronics industry*; *post and telecommunications*

scientology This international movement, founded by US science-fiction writer L. Ron Hubbard in 1950, is one of self-styled 'applied religious philosophy'. It was introduced to Australia in 1956 and by the late 1980s claimed some 15 000 members. The movement has been controversial since its inception, largely because of its psychological techniques and unorthodox metaphysical basis. The practice and teaching of scientology were prohibited in Vic. in 1965 (without success) and later in WA and SA. The movement has been involved in periodic litigation for coercive practice and imitating religion for financial benefit, but in 1983 was ruled by the High Court to be a religion.

scorpion-flies Australia has about 20 species of these large, long-legged insects of the order Mecoptera, which have two pairs of membranous wings and a prolonged proboscis. Males feed on other insects, and females generally on nectar. Males of the genus *Harpobittacus*, having captured insect prey, hang by two legs among bushes, exuding a secretion that is attractive to females. Upon encountering a mate the male presents her with the prey as a mating gift, to ensure that the female has adequate protein for egg production.

scorpions Of the class Arachnida, a scorpion is distinguished by its pincer-like pedipalp (a modifed mouth appendage), four pairs of walking legs, and a long, slender abdomen that bears a bulbous, poison-injecting sting; it also bears a pair of unique ventral comb-like appendages known as pectines. Scorpions are carnivorous, and hunt at night; their sting is often painful, but rarely fatal to humans. Australia has some 30 species, occurring in a variety of terrestrial habitats and living in burrows or under logs, rocks or the bark of trees.

Scott, Rose (1847–1925), feminist and social reformer, b. Singleton, NSW. An energetic lobbyist for the Womanhood Suffrage League, formed in Sydney in 1891, Scott made an important contribution to the achievement of female suffrage in NSW in 1902. From 1902 to 1910 she was president of the group's successor – the Women's Political Educational League – which was instrumental in the reform of social legislation, particularly in such areas as custody and maintenance of children, and the interests of working women. Scott was also an active opponent of conscription and president of the NSW branch of the London Peace Society.

Scott, Thomas Hobbes (1783–1860). Anglican prelate, b. England. A parish rector who was secretary to John Thomas Bigge during his inquiry into conditions in the Australian colonies (1819–20), Scott was subsequently asked by the British government to plan the provision of schools and churches there. His recommendations were largely responsible for the 1825 legislation giving the Anglicans an initial monopoly of primary education, thereby arousing bitter controversy. As the first archdeacon of NSW (1824–8), Scott was arrogant and generally unpopular; he did, however, oversee substantial growth in education in the young colony.

Scottsdale Tas. (pop. 1983) This small town lies 269km north of Hobart in the heart of farmland on rich basaltic soils, and is the chief service centre for the State's northeast. It has a vegetable-processing factory and a sawmill.

Scrophulariaceae > *foxglove family*

scrub-birds The uniquely Australian genus *Atrichornis* contains two species: *A. clamosus*, the small noisy or western scrub-bird, a ground bird found only in the thick bush of southwestern WA; and *A. rufescens*, the rufous scrub-bird, equally narrowly confined to rainforest in southeastern Qld and adjacent NSW. Both possess loud voices and a talent for mimicry, in the western species this being combined with ventriloquial calling. *Atrichornis*'s distinctive anatomical features, such as the lack of a wishbone, have led to its being placed in a family by itself, next to that of the much larger lyrebird; both species build quite remarkable nests of dead leaves and grasses lined with a cardboard-like dried wood-pulp. The bird's almost mouse-like ability to run through forest litter makes it difficult to observe, but it appears that the eastern species is maintaining its numbers fairly well. The western species was for some time thought to be extinct, but in the 1960s was observed in coastal scrub near Albany, prompting the WA government to declare the area a reservation. *Atrichornis* is of great interest, not only because of its distinctive anatomy and habits, but also for the remarkable occurrence of the two species in two clearly defined areas at opposite ends of the continent. It is thought that the family once spread right across the landmass and that the two species represent peripheral groups, surviving when the dry centre was cleared of such birds by developing aridity in post-glacial times.

Scullin, James Henry (1876–1953), politician b. Trawalla, Vic. Leader of the Labor Party 1928–35 and prime minister 1929–31, Scullin was a self-educated union organiser, journalist and dedicated Labor worker. His term as prime minister was undermined by the difficulties of the 1930s depression, a Labor minority in the Senate, the lack of experienced ministers, and the campaigns of NSW premier Jack Lang, but his oratory and integrity left a lasting impression.

sculling > *rowing and sculling*

sculpture Sculpture has never captured the Australian imagination or expressed the

Australian ethos to the same extent as painting – it gave birth to no Heidelberg School, no sustained expression of nationalistic consciousness. In its first century, sculpture in Australia was principally devoted to the decoration of public buildings and spaces, or portrait commissions, and was thus largely conservative.

The first professional sculptors arrived in Australia during the gold rushes of the 1950s. Among them was Thomas Woolner, a talented Englishman of the Pre-Raphaelite school, who produced bronze medallions of the colonial wealthy while in the colonies but is best remembered for the *Captain Cook* sculpture in Sydney's Hyde Park, made in 1897 after he had returned to England. Another was Charles Summers, who built his own furnace and cast the first bronze sculpture in the colony in 1865, the impressive *Burke and Wills* monument in Melbourne. The Frenchman Lucien Henri, who arrived in Australia in 1879, although a minor talent was an inspirational teacher and helped win recognition for Australian imagery in sculpture.

The pre-eminent sculptor of the late 19th and early 20th centuries was > *Sir Bertram Mackennal*; expatriate from 1891, he was acclaimed in Paris for his mildly erotic *Circe* (1893), and later in London where he ran a successful studio and was a member of the Royal Academy. His contemporary Charles W. Gilbert, pastry-cook turned sculptor, also won recognition in both Australia and England; his heroic *Captain Matthew Flinders* (1923–5), the theatrical bronze statue outside St Paul's Cathedral in Melbourne, was his last and finest work. Englishman Paul Montford, who arrived in Australia in 1923, was an outspoken advocate of training and encouragement for young sculptors, supports which he found sadly lacking in Australia; his work included the splendid stone buttresses of the Shrine of Remembrance in Melbourne and the pensive bronze of poet Adam Lindsay Gordon (1931). In Sydney, Rayner Hoff's dramatic bronze *Sacrifice* (1930–3) in Hyde Park, and painter George Lambert's *The Unknown Soldier* (1928), in the crypt of St Mary's cathedral, were distinguished war memorials. Sydney-born Lyndon Dadswell, who worked with Montford on Melbourne's Shrine of Remembrance, became one of the country's most dedicated sculpture teachers from the 1940s, his own work moving steadily to non-figurative work and non-traditional materials.

Until the 1940s, however, sculpture generally remained staid and derivative. After World War 2, increased immigration from Europe brought new skills, sophistication and (importantly) audiences to Australian sculpture. Inge King, Clifford Last and Julius Kane (Kahn) typified the new wave of experimental sculptors who laid the groundwork for the unprecedented and highly individualistic activity of the 1960s and 1970s. Clement Meadmore, working with welding equipment, developed powerful monolithic steel sculptures; > *Robert Klippel* produced a series of assemblages of 'junk' and machinery; and Herbert Flugelman began to create his stylised, stainless-steel sculptures. The Mildura Sculpture Triennial, inaugurated in 1961, provided a further impetus and first-class venue for innovative and experimental work.

Since the 1970s the boundaries of sculpture have become blurred, with earthworks, conceptual and 'human' sculptures taking their place alongside more traditional forms. Clive Murray White, > *Ron Robertson Swann*, Ken Unsworth, and more recently Margaret Dodd, Les Kossatz and Imants Tillers are just a few of the contemporary sculptors who have helped give the art a national and international profile in the last two decades.

Sculthorpe, Peter Joshua (1929–), composer, b. Launceston, Tas. One of Australia's most successful composers of serious music, Sculthorpe has been much influenced in his work by the Australian landscape, both actual and metaphoric. Notable compositions include the *Irkanda* (1959–65) and *Sun Music* (1965–7) series, and the opera *Rites of Passage* (1974). His later compositions have shown the influence of Balinese and Japanese musical forms. Sculthorpe has also lectured in the US and UK, and since 1963 has been a member of the University of Sydney music department.

sea-anemones These marine invertebrates of the phylum Cnidaria are common along rocky seashores. The relatively sedentary, tentacled polyp stage dominates the animals' way of life; however, they can move appreciably – many by expanding and contracting the base of the body, some by floating with the current, and a few by using their tentacles for crawling or swimming. Australia has a rich diversity of sea-anemones, both along coastal rock platforms and on reefs, and they are often seen in tidal pools; some of the giant specimens of the Great Barrier Reef measure 45cm across.

sea-birds Often white or near-white in colour, the sea-birds of Australian waters and shores comprise at least 60 species, sharing the characteristic of webbed feet but varying widely in size, form and habit.

The snowy albatross, *Diomedea chionoptera*, and the wandering albatross, *D. exulans* – the latter showing more brown on wings and body – have a wingspan of over 2m and sustain their large bulk chiefly with a diet of squid, for which they patrol thousands of kilometres of the Southern Ocean. Related species tend to be smaller and browner, and are often known by the Dutch name of mollymauk. The shy or white-capped albatross, *D. cauta*, nests on inaccessible islands off Tas.

Gulls, of the genus *Larus*, are scavengers with rather thick, roundish beaks and rounded wings and tail. The true Australian members of this genus are the widespread, medium-sized silver gull, *L. novaehollandiae*, and the larger Pacific gull, *L. pacificus*, which has much more blackish-grey colouring on the back.

The sharp-beaked, diving terns of the genus *Sterna* include among them the crested tern, *S. bergii*, found over much of the Indian and Pacific Oceans, the fairy tern, *S. nereis*, and the roseate tern, *S. dougalli*. The Caspian tern is larger and is placed in a separate genus, *Hydroprogne*; it extends throughout much of Europe, the US and Australasia.

Skuas are large, stocky, often quite dark-coloured birds, with stout and often slightly down-curved beaks, which pursue other birds and force them to relinquish or even disgorge captured fish; species seen in Australian waters include the great or Antarctic skua, *Catharacta skua*, in summer an Antarctic breeder, and the Arctic skua, *Stercorarius parasiticus*, which breeds in the Arctic during the northern hemisphere summer and then flies far south to summer again.

The gannets of Australia include both sub-tropical species (such as the brown gannet or booby, *Sula leucogaster* and the red-footed gannet, *S. sula*) and also temperate-zone species such as the Australian gannet, *S. serrator*, which is very similar to those two in its markings. Gannets dive from considerable heights (15m or so), having skulls adapted and strengthened for this form of fishing and beaks capable of dealing with large fish.

Petrels are a large group of birds including storm-petrels (Mother Carey's chickens), such as the small, white-backed storm-petrel, *Pelagodroma marina*, seen skimming across the waves in the wake of ships and nesting in burrows in subantarctic islands. True petrels are quite small, oceanic birds, eating plankton or surface fish and coming to land only to breed in crevices or burrows; the diving petrel, *Pelecanoides urinatrix*, nests in islands of Bass Strait and nearby.

Distinctive sea-birds of the Australian tropics include the greater and lesser frigate-birds, *Fregata minor* and *F. ariel*, and the red-tailed and white-tailed tropic-birds of the genus *Phaethon*, although these are infrequently seen; the long tail-feathers of the red-tailed bird were formerly sought for decorative purposes. >> *birds, native*

sea-cow > *dugong*

sea-cucumbers Sluggish, sausage-shaped marine echinoderms of the class Holothuroidea, sea-cucumbers are bottom-dwellers in mainly tropical seas; the spiny plates of the echinoderm are reduced to small inclusions in the skin. A consumer of detritus, the animal may extend branched tentacles from the front of its body during feeding; it moves on tube-feet set below the body. When disturbed, some species throw out white, thread-like material, earning them the cognomen 'cotton-fish'; others may break into several pieces, or eject certain internal organs which, however, they are usually able to regenerate. Australia has more than 160 species of sea-cucumber. Several of them, gutted, smoked and dried, are marketed as bêche-de-mer or trepang, a favoured ingredient in Asian cuisine, but since World War 2 the number exported has been small. The larger species, of tropical waters, were fished by > *Macassans* in the 18th and 19th centuries.

seagrasses These aquatic flowering plants live in shallow seawater. They are not true grasses, although monocotyledonous; nor should they be confused with seaweeds, which are > *algae*. The eleven genera of seagrasses represented in Australia belong to four families: two consist exclusively of seagrasses, the others also include fresh-water aquatic plants. Most familiar along southern and eastern coasts is the eelgrass genus *Zostera*, which has ribbon-like leaves, and the strapweed genus *Posidonia*. Seagrasses are of great ecological benefit in marine environments: their creeping rhizomes stabilise shifting sediments, they are an important food source for a range of marine wildlife (constituting the sole diet of dugongs), and where they form continuous beds they provide a protective barrier against the elements. The largest and most diverse seagrass beds are in Shark Bay, WA, where they cover up to 1000sq.km and support a large dugong population. In many coastal areas, however, such as Westernport Bay in Vic., there has been extensive die-back of both seagrasses and algae due to erosion in catchment areas causing increased sedimentation.

sea-horses This remarkable family of fishes, Syngnathidae, is well represented in Australian waters and includes sea-horses and pipefishes. The sea-horse's body is enclosed in bony plates and the prehensile tail is used to cling to the weeds among which it lives; the tubular mouth is adapted to feeding on small crustaceans. The most extraordinary member of this family is the leafy sea-horse, adorned with bizarre outgrowths resembling seaweed; this species and the spiny sea-horse are confined to waters of southeastern Australia and Tas.

sea-lice > *wood-lice and sea-lice*

sea-lilies and featherstars These echinoderms comprise the class Crinoidea. Sea-lilies are marine animals superficially resembling feathery starfish, but relatively immobile at the end of a calcareous stalk and appearing somewhat flower-like – hence their name. The fragile and colourless but attractive *Metacrinus cyaneus* is sometimes brought up from deep water off southeastern Australia. Featherstars are distinguished by much more feathery and numerous arms. *Cenolia trichoptera*, a species peculiar to Australia, is sometimes found in intertidal rocks in southern waters, but much more colourful species are found in tropical waters.

seasnakes > *snakes*

sea-squirts This is the popular name applied to ascidians, a peculiar group of sessile marine organisms of the phylum Cordata, more closely related to vertebrates than to invertebrates. The free-swimming, tadpole-like larva possesses a notochord (forerunner of the backbone) and gill slits, both of which link it to primitive vertebrates. However, the mature larva attaches itself to a tidal rock and degenerates into a sac-like adult with a tough, leathery covering. Water is siphoned through the body: from it nutrients are extracted, and into it wastes are excreted. It was the forced discharge of water from specimens exposed at low tide that gave rise to the common name, 'sea-squirt'. The bright-red flesh of the common Australian species *Pyura praeputialis*, popularly known as the cunjevoi, is used as bait by rock fishermen.

sea-stars > *starfishes*

sea-urchins The sea-urchin is an echinoderm with a five-segmented, spherical to cushion-shaped, calcareous external skeleton (or test), armed with many small spines moving on ball-and-socket joints. Among the spines are a number of tube-feet, similar to those of the starfish. The test, bereft of the spines and smoothed by wave action, is often washed ashore as a 'sea-egg'. A common Australian sea-urchin is the small purple to green-brown *Heliocidaris erythrogramma*, found sometimes sheltering beneath a rock or in a small, cylindrical excavation of its own making. The tropical species include the very large-spined slate-pencil sea-urchin, *Heterocentrotus mammillatus*. *Toxopneustes pileolus*, distinguished by poisonous spines and long tube-feet, is known to have caused the deaths of several divers, but is rare in Australian waters.

sea-wasps > *jellyfishes*

seals and sealing There are three species of seal resident in Australian waters, all belonging to the family Otariidae: the Australian fur seal, *Arctocephalus pusillus doriferus*, of coastal NSW, Vic. and Tas., the largest fur seal in the world; the NZ fur seal, *A. forsteri*, of SA and WA; and the Australian sea-lion, *Neophoca cinerea*, also of SA and WA. Several species of the true (earless) seal – which belong to the family Phocidae – are occasional visitors to Australian coastal waters, including the elephant seal, *Mirounga leonina*, which breeds on Macquarie Island.

Now protected by law, seals were the basis of Australia's first commercial export industry, which began in the 1790s. Like > *whaling* it was a brutal enterprise, the seals being beaten or clubbed to death for their oil and skins. The lucrative trade attracted hunters from America and Britain as well as the Indian Ocean, and violent clashes between rival crews were common. The industry was initially centred on the islands of Bass Strait, later extending around the southern coast as the Bass Strait seal population became depleted. By the 1850s, the fur seal was virtually extinct in Australian waters and the industry came to an end; seal populations have been rebuilt only through the agency of protective measures in the 20th century.

SEATO The Southeast Asia Treaty Organisation was established in 1954, following the collapse of the French regime in Indochina. Its members were the US, UK, NZ, Australia, France, Pakistan and the Philippines; its basic aim was to prevent the spread of communist aggression in Asia, specifically in the Indochinese countries of South Vietnam, Laos and Cambodia. Australia regarded SEATO as an organisation through which it could apply a policy of 'forward defence', in which a real or imagined enemy is met and (it is hoped) defeated as far from home as possible; the US regarded it as a tool to prevent the fruition of the domino theory – a popular thesis of the 1950s and 1960s first propounded by the Eisenhower administration, that the fall to communism of one country will similarly topple its neighbours. Australia's policy of forward defence came to grief in 1962–72 during the Vietnam War, and SEATO was disbanded in 1977, the Indochinese dominoes having toppled. >> *defence*

seaweeds > *algae*

Second Fleet This was the name given to the second group of vessels bringing supplies and transporting 1267 convicts to NSW. The fleet of six ships comprised the transport *Lady Juliana* (sailed July 1789), *Surprise, Neptune* and *Scarborough* (December 1789), and the storeships *Guardian* (September 1789) and *Justinian* (January 1790). In contrast to the care taken by Arthur Phillip over the > *First Fleet*, the contract system employed in victualling led to serious abuse; 267 convicts died on the voyage and half the survivors were sick on arrival with scurvy, dysentery and fevers. The publicity given to this abuse led to some reform of the system of transportation.

secondary industry > *manufacturing industries*

sedge family The Cyperaceae family is a large worldwide group of flowering plants commonly found in bogs and other moist habitats; although they resemble grasses and > *rushes*, they are not closely related. Australia has around 650 native species of sedge in 47 genera, and quite a few more are introduced weeds. The largest genus, comprising 112 native species, is the cosmopolitan (mainly tropical) *Cyperus*, the flat sedges, typified by the tall African papyrus plant, *C. papyrus*. The inland nalgoo, *C. bulbosus*, has underground tubers prized as food by Aborigines; the introduced nutgrass, *C. rotundus*, is a serious agricultural and garden weed. Some species of the temperate and subarctic genus *Carex* dominate alpine shallow-water swamps; others are common in damp coastal grasslands and forests. There are also several endemic or near-endemic genera, mostly harsh-leaved plants concentrated on highly nutrient-deficient soils. These include the distinctive. saw-sedges, *Gahnia*, which range from 2.5cm to 3m tall but all have toothed leaves. The large genus *Schoenus* is generally confined to areas of high rainfall and includes many small mat-forming species; *Lepidosperma*, also of wet regions, includes several flat-leaved sword sedges. The small endemic genus *Caustis* is common on sandy soils of the east coast, some species also extending to the southwest of WA.

Sedgman, Frank (Francis Arthur) (1927–), tennis player, b. Melbourne. Sedgman was a popular and talented player, whose uncanny anticipation and powerful forehand brought him the Australian singles title in 1949. In 1951 he became the first Australian to win the US singles, and in the Davis Cup tie of that year won both his singles matches and teamed with Ken McGregor to win the doubles, and so the cup. In 1952 he won the singles, doubles and mixed doubles at Wimbledon; later in that year he added the US title, and successfully played again with McGregor in the Davis Cup. In 1953 he turned professional, for the then astounding sum of £44 600.

Seidler, Harry (1923–), architect, b. Austria. As a postgraduate student at Harvard 1945–6 Seidler studied under Walter Gropius, founder of the Bauhaus. He arrived in Sydney in 1948 and was subsequently responsible for introducing international modernism to Australia. His early domestic designs, including his own square, streamlined home at Turramurra (1948– 50), were opposed unsuccessfully by conservative local councils but were a seminal influence on young Australian architects. Major works include the Australia Square Tower (1967) and the MLC Centre (1977), both in Sydney, and the Australian Embassy in Paris (1973).

selectors > *free selection*; *land settlement*

Senate > *Constitution*; *government*

Serventy, Dominic (1904–), ornithologist, b. Brown Hill, WA. Educated at the universities of WA and Cambridge, Serventy joined the CSIRO in 1937, becoming officer in charge of the division of wildlife research in WA, a post he held until his retirement in 1969. His publications include *The Birds of Western Australia* (1948, with H. M. Whittell) and *The Handbook of Australian Seabirds* (1971, with his brother Vincent and John Warham), both works being seen as classics. Serventy has been honoured by the world's ornithological societies and has received numerous awards for his services to conservation. He was editor of the *Western Australian Naturalist* 1947–80.

service colleges > *defence forces*

service industries Service industries are defined variously throughout the world. In Australia they are generally categorised as non-manufacturing industries that provide services but not goods, including banking, advertising, transport and communications, tourism, the retail trade, community services, and power and water utilities; the Australian Bureau of Statistics also officially classifies building and construction as a service industry. Although generally referring to 'tertiary' industry, the service sector now includes an additional 'quaternary' level, which covers the research, processing and storage of information.

In 1987, service industries employed 4.267 million people out of a total Australian workforce of 7.073 million. It is the fastest-growing sector of industry, as the result both of increasing affluence and the concomitant demand for more and better transport and housing, and the expansion by governments of educational, health and welfare services. Within the sector as a whole the most dramatic increase has been in information industries, which incorporate everything from media outlets and advertising to business that is reliant on computer-based technology, such as banking, insurance and accountancy. Information-based industries now account for over 30% of the Australian workforce.

While service industries continue to be one of the few burgeoning sectors of the Australian economy, their future is by no means assured.

Concern has, for example, been expressed at the excessive reliance on the service sector to provide jobs for people no longer employed in the primary and manufacturing industries because of increased efficiency and mechanisation; moreover, a proportion of the community-based jobs created by governments are artificial, employment-boosting exercises of uncertain duration. Australia is also at a disadvantage in the field of computer-based technology, relying completely on hardware and software created in the US, Japan or Europe. In general, service industries are internal and make little contribution to export trade, providing instead an excessive drain on the balance of payments: increasing use by the workforce – instead of production or development – of the tools of business could leave Australia economically exposed. >> *advertising industry*; *banks and banking*; *economy*; *retail trade*; *tourism*

Seymour Vic. (pop. 6510) This commercial and industrial town lies on the Goulburn River about 98km north of Melbourne and services the surrounding grazing region. It developed as a river crossing, and an inn was constructed in 1839. A military camp was installed in the town early in the 20th century and the Puckapunyal army training camp was established during World War 2.

shags > *cormorants*

Shann, Edward Owen Giblin (1884–1935), economist, b. Hobart. Educated in Melbourne and London, Shann became a leading academic in economics in both Qld and WA. His book *The Boom of 1890 – And Now* (1927) contained a warning – unheeded – of the possibility of a depression; he subsequently wrote the now classic *Economic History of Australia* (1930), which reflected his longstanding opposition to tariff protection.

Shannon River Tas. This tributary of the Ouse flows from the south end of Great Lake, where in 1911 and 1922 dams were built (in one of Tas.'s earliest hydro-electric schemes), so increasing the volume of Shannon water. This resulted in increased breeding of the snowflake caddis moth, which in turn brought about the renowned 'Shannon Rise' – of trout, attracted by the moths in proportionately increasing numbers. Subsequent hydro-electric development depleted the Shannon and reversed the process; the last rise was in 1963.

Shark Bay WA This large, shallow inlet south of Carnarvon and about 650km north-west of Perth was named by William Dampier in 1699. Bernier, Dorre and Dirk Hartog islands lie across the entrance and the Peron peninsula divides the bay into Denham Sound (with Freycinet Estuary) and Hamelin Pool. Formerly a pearling area, it is now one of the nation's major fishing grounds; prawns, scallops and lobsters are also produced, and the area is popular for game-fishing. Salt is extracted by evaporation at Useless Loop. The bay is also famous for the presence of living stromatolites (layered blue-green algae and silt); blue-green algae were among the first forms of life, and until recently stromatolites were known only as fossils.

sharks Sharks are grouped with rays as elasmobranches, as distinct from the bony fishes that make up the vast majority of living marine species. The important differences are in the skeleton, that of the shark being not of bone but of cartilage. The tough skin of the shark is covered with denticles, and specialised denticles develop as the sharp teeth that line the jaws, these being replaced as they are damaged. Many sharks have a bird-like, whitish, movable membrane with which they can cover the eye; it is said that they use this as a protection when attacking, and that those lacking it protect the eyes by rolling them back at the moment of impact. In reproduction, the female's eggs are fertilised internally, the male having twin 'claspers' attached to the ventral fins which, when erected and clasped together, convey the sperm. The young are generally born alive, though sometimes enclosed in a sac from which they soon emerge. Sharks as a group are major scavengers, slicing or swallowing whole all manner of marine carrion but liable also to attack living creatures.

The bronze whaler, *Eulamia ahenea*, and the common or grey whaler, *Galeolamna greyi*, are large and dangerous sharks patrolling much of eastern Australia, moving into estuaries and lower rivers even beyond tidal limits; the front dorsal fin is large and pointed, the rear small and set at an obtuse angle. The grey nurse, *Carcharias arenarius*, preys on Australian salmon and is described as a relatively sluggish shark, often mistakenly blamed for attacks on bathers actually made by the grey whaler; it is a shark of temperate waters, though not un-known in Qld. The tiger shark, *Galeocerdo rayneri*, is dark grey with darker stripes and blotches, and in many tropical and subtropical waters is feared as a human-eater.

The mako or blue pointer, *Isuropsis mako*, beautifully streamlined, blue-backed and silvery-bellied, reaches a length of 5m or so and is regarded as a danger to surfboards and small craft rather than to swimmers, for it seldom comes close inshore. The white pointer, great white shark or white death, *Carcharodon albimors*, growing up to 12m, is perhaps the most dangerous shark of all; it is common off southern Australia in summer and off Qld in winter as it moves north after migrating hump-back whales, but it too is seldom seen inshore.

The thresher shark, *Alopias caudatus*, is believed to use its extraordinarily long upper tail-lobe to stun the fish on which it preys; the hammerhead shark, *Sphyrna lewini*, bears a distinctive, laterally extended head with an eye at either end and a horseshoe-shaped mouth underneath; the front of the curved 'hammer' carries very sensitive organs of smell. It is a voracious feeder on Australian salmon, mullet and other fish, mainly in open waters; poten-tially dangerous to humans, it is seldom seen inshore. The whale or checker-board shark, *Rhincodon typus*, with a white-spotted, bluish-green back and lighter belly, attains a length of 15m or more and is rather blunt-headed, like a whale. Despite its great size it is harmless, feeding on plankton which it strains through gills. The wobbegong or carpet-shark, *Orecto-lobus ornatus*, is a rather broad, flat shark, round-snouted when seen from above, brown and paisley-patterned. It lives in rocky, weedy pools and crevices and is normally sluggish, but is liable to bite severely if disturbed.

The common or piked dogfish, *Squalus megalops*, is a small harmless shark that is trawled for the market. The gummy is also commercially important; it feeds on crustaceans and is sometimes called 'Sweet William' because of its unusual odour. The shellfish-eating Port Jackson shark, *Heterodontus portusjacksoni* lays its eggs in a protective spiral of horn-like brown material; the deep-sea ghost shark, *Chimaera*, while showing many shark-like fea-tures such as the cartilaginous skeleton, also has some features of the bony fishes, such as a single gill-opening.

Shark attacks on humans always make head-lines, although the actual number of Australian fatalities in more than 150 years is less than one a year. Analysis of attacks in Australia point to two recurring patterns: almost all incidents take place in the summer months (in water at a temperature greater then 22°C); and the close proximity of certain attacks also suggests that a single 'rogue shark' may be responsible for a series of attacks.

shearing Reputedly rough and radical, shearers are the stuff of Australian legend and have long been celebrated in the nation's art and literature. While perhaps the most common image is that of shearers wielding hand blades, Australia was in fact at the forefront of shearing technology and the world's first completely mechanised shearing took place at Dunlop station in NSW, in 1888.

The structure of the industry has changed little since the 1890s, when the newly unionised shearers won great improvements in working conditions and rates of pay. Teams of itinerant shearers, working under contract for one station after another during the season, are still the norm in many parts of Australia; the majority now work close to home, however, finding other forms of employment outside the shearing season. The tradition of shearing competitions persists today; the alleged world record for blade shearing dates back to 1892, when Qld shearer Jack Howe shore 321 merino sheep in 7 hours 40 minutes.

The main change of recent years is the general acceptance of the wide shearing comb, which was long and bitterly opposed by the industry; as late as the 1980s, its introduction caused strikes in both Australia and NZ. Current research may lead to much greater technological advances which could revolutionise the industry in the 21st century, however, including robot shearers and the chemical removal of wool.

shearwater > *muttonbird*

sheep Australia produces about one-quarter of the world's wool and is also a major exporter of lamb, mutton and, increasingly if controversially, live sheep. Although flock numbers have fluctuated substantially in the last 20 years, sheep products continued to contribute 20–25% of the value of rural production in the 1980s.

Governor Phillip brought the first sheep to Australia in 1788, but the selected breed – Cape fat-tails, from the Cape of Good Hope – produced poor wool; it was not until John Macarthur began breeding from Spanish merinos in 1797 that the Australian sheep industry really began. Unlike other colonial breeders, who wanted dual-purpose sheep producing both wool and mutton, Macarthur bred his sheep for fine wool, convinced that this was the industry of the future. Others also recognised the merino's potential, and over the years it has been developed into a strain particularly suited to the Australian environment. Today the breed represents at least 85% of Australia's 167 million sheep, which are raised mainly for wool; flocks increased steadily in the 1980s, rising by 9 million in 1988 alone after several consecutive years of good seasons. After merinos, the most widespread variety is the cross-breed merino–Border Leicester; its ewes are mated with Poll Dorset rams to produce most of Australia's table lamb. Popular dual-purpose breeds are Corriedale and the NZ Polwarth, and Tukidales have been imported from NZ since the 1970s to produce carpet wool.

The export of live sheep has been growing since the 1970s and about 7 million head are transported overseas annually, mainly to the Middle East. This trade is strongly opposed by industry workers as well as animal-welfare groups. Proposals to establish a fat-tail lamb industry (storing much of its fat in the tail, this lamb has a leaner body) for Middle East markets have been met with reservations by the industry's regulating body, the Australian Wool Corporation, which fears that cross-breeding with merino ewes would introduce dark and coarse fibres into the nation's pure-white wool clip.

Blowflies are the principal pest of sheep and are estimated to cost the industry more than $50 million a year through causing sheep deaths and poorer fleece quality, combined with expensive control measures. Neither chemical nor biological controls have proved successful in the long term; although 'mulesing' – a procedure in which loose skin around the sheep's breech is cut away to prevent blowfly infestation – has proved effective, it is strongly opposed by animal-welfare groups. Internal parasites such as the liver-fluke are controlled with drenches, and in 1986 the CSIRO produced a footrot vaccine which it hoped would replace an expensive and therefore not widely used predecessor. Technology has developed rapidly in the sheep industry: artificial insemination and embryo transplants are now commonplace, and research is now being conducted into the transplantation of selected genes into breeding stock to produce bigger, leaner, faster-growing and more disease-resistant sheep. >> *wool*

Sheffield Shield > *cricket*

shells and shellfishes > *bivalves*; *cephalopods*; *chitons*; *gastropods*

she-oaks > *casuarinas*

Shepparton Vic. (pop. 24 744) This provincial city lies 182km north of Melbourne and is the service and commercial centre for the agricultural lands of the Goulburn valley; it is the State's fourth-largest city and the regional centre for many government departments. Its industry is based largely on the produce of the region, notably fruits such as apricots, peaches, pears and grapes; the city's fruit cannery is the largest in the southern hemisphere. Dairying, livestock production and vegetable-growing are also important. The settlement grew around a river crossing from the 1840s and took the name Sheppardtown 1853–5, after local property-owner, Sherbourne Sheppard. It was briefly a wool port but experienced most sustained development after the introduction of irrigation, and the consequent development of local orchards and farms, after the 1880s.

shipbuilding industry > *ships and shipping*

ships and shipping Because of Australia's size and relative isolation from the rest of the world, shipping has always been an important factor in the country's economic survival and growth. Before the development of airlines in the 1930s, shipping provided Australia's only physical link with the outside world. By the end of the 1960s the overseas passenger liners had virtually disappeared, but Australia's primary exports are still completely reliant on shipping, Today, Australia has some 30 major ports servicing about 7000 overseas shipping arrivals and departures. In 1986 Australia had 100 registered trading ships of 150 tons (gross weight) or more, of which 67 were used for internal coastal services and 33 for overseas services; the largest of these vessels are bulk or container ships. Australia's busiest ports by volume of overseas cargo loaded are Sydney, Melbourne, Newcastle, Hay Point (Qld), Dampier and Port Hedland (WA), the last three reflecting the importance to Australia of mineral exports, as cargo discharged at these ports was negligible.

A number of vessels were built in the various colonies in the 19th century – first of wood and later iron-hulled. The greatest period of shipbuilding was during World War 2, the volume of production increasing fivefold 1938–45.

Today, on average, fewer than 50 vessels are completed in Australia each year and these are mostly small cargo boats, passenger ferries, fishing boats and 'workhorses' such as dredges.

Historical development Soon after the foundation of NSW, small boats were used to transport supplies between settlements. The first boat constructed in Australia was the *Rose Hill Packet* in 1798, used for service on the Parramatta River. The construction or use of larger ocean-going ships was prohibited owing to a shipping monopoly granted to the East India Company by Britain. Ships traded with the colony nevertheless, one of the first being the American *Philadelphia* in 1792. The monopoly was ended in 1813, just as Australia was beginning to have something to export, and the shipping trade expanded dramatically. One problem was the lack of adequate port facilities, as of all the major settlements only Port Jackson provided a harbour that was not subject to silting up or blockage by sandbars. In the mid-19th century the clean-lined, fast clipper ships entered the Australian run, flying the house flags of such well-known firms as the Black Ball Line and White Star. The most famous of these was the *Cutty Sark,* which entered the Australian run in 1883 carrying wool to the UK; she is preserved today at Greenwich, London. Steamships entered service in 1852, but at first were no match in speed for the clippers. Firms such as Blue Funnel, the Peninsular and Oriental Steam Navigation Company (P & O), and Shaw Savill – as much household names in their day as airlines are now – opened up Australian runs, carrying emigrants on the outward journey and cargo on the return. Non-British firms such as Messageries Maritimes of France and Norddeutscher Lloyd of Germany appeared before the end of the 19th century, and Nippon Yusen Kaisha of Japan before World War 1.

In the face of a British-dominated external shipping industry, Australian shipping firms had to content themselves with coastal and cross-Tasman routes. Australia's first steamship company, the Hunter River Steam Navigation Company, was founded in 1839 and traded south from that river as far as Tas. Numerous other firms followed including the Adelaide Steamship Company, the Huddart Parker Line, and McIlwraith McEacharn. For a century these firms enjoyed a lucrative coastal traffic, which came to an end during World War 2 when most of their ships were commissioned for active service. Freight and passengers transferred to road and rail, and the local shipping industry never recovered.

Today, the bulk of Australian mercantile shipping is government-owned, with a few large firms such as BHP owning ore carriers and oil tankers. Government ownership came about more by default than by design. During World War 1, the Hughes government purchased a number of ships from Britain and established a shipping line, the Commonwealth Government Line. The experiment was not a success and the last ships of the line were sold in 1928. After World War 2, the government again found itself a ship-owner, leasing its ships to private companies through the Australian Shipping Board. The Menzies government wanted to sell the ships, but because of the conditions imposed on the sale this proved impossible. As a result, in 1956 the Australian Coastal Shipping Commission was formed to operate a government-owned fleet, the Australian National Line (ANL). Today, ANL has seventeen ships – twelve container ships and five bulk carriers – engaged in overseas trade, and ten ships in coastal traffic. The ANL also operates specialised freight terminals at Adelaide, Melbourne, Burnie, Sydney and Brisbane. In 1980, the Australian Shipping Commission – the 'Coastal' was dropped in 1974 – was given greater powers to enable it to operate more commercially, particularly regarding the negotiation of freight rates within the various 'conferences' (or shipping cartels) of which it is a member.

With the exception of a Bass Strait car ferry service, there are no coastal passenger services operating today. Alternative forms of transport, high labour costs and the working practices of Australia's very strong waterside unions have meant that such services would not be economically viable. For much the same reasons, there are now no regular passenger services to overseas destinations, although there is a large market in Australia for itinerant cruise ships.

Mention should be made of the mainly British and Italian liners which, from the end of World War 2 until the early 1970s, plied regularly between Australia and Europe. In often luxurious conditions, the leisurely four-week passage from Sydney or Melbourne to Southampton or Genoa via the Suez Canal or Cape of Good Hope was an experience never to be forgotten; on the Pacific route, the US Matson Line ran an equally excellent service between Sydney and San Francisco. It was,

indeed, a time 'when the going was good'.
>> *river transport*

shipwrecks Early shipwrecks off the Australian coast were mainly those of Dutch merchant vessels blown too far south on their route to the Indies, the most famous of which is the *Batavia*, which struck a reef in 1629 some 70m off what is now Geraldton, WA. The wreck was discovered in 1961. Another early wreck is the HMS *Pandora*: returning to England from Tahiti carrying some of the *Bounty* mutineers, it was wrecked on the Great Barrier Reef in 1791, near the approaches to the Torres Strait. With the founding of NSW began the long history of wrecks along the east and southeast coasts. The worst period was 1850–90, when more than 50 ships were lost. Well-known wrecks include the *Stirling Castle*, which struck a reef near the Tropic of Capricorn in 1836 and became famous as the cause of Mrs Eliza Fraser's sojourn amongst the Aborigines; and the *Dunbar*, which foundered on the rocks beneath South Head, Sydney, in 1857 with the loss of all but one of a complement of 121. Other dangerous areas for shipping were the entrance to Port Phillip Bay and the islands of the Bass Strait, particularly King Island. Today, all shipwrecks are protected under the Historic Shipwrecks Act 1976, the main aim of which is to prevent the plunder of what may be important relics of Australia's maritime heritage.

Shoalhaven River NSW This river, about 350km long, rises in the southern tablelands west of Moruya; after flowing through the Braidwood district it enters the precipitous Bungonia Gorge before reaching the coastal plain and thence the sea at Nowra. In the upland drainage, sheep and cattle grazing prevails; most of the middle section is rugged and timbered, and includes Morton National Park. The coastal district has been cleared for dairying, fodder crops and vegetables. Since the 1970s major conservation schemes on the Shoalhaven have helped to augment the Sydney and south coast water and electricity supplies. The river was named Shoals Haven in 1797 by George Bass.

Shore, Arnold Joseph Victor (1897–1963), painter and art critic, b. Melbourne. Shore was co-founder, with George Bell, of a short-lived but important Melbourne art school (c.1932–4) that introduced post-Impressionism to local artists. Like his friend Jock Frater, his early experience working with stained glass influenced his painting style. His still-lifes and bush scenes are fresh, light-coloured and richly textured.

shrimps > *mountain shrimp*; *prawns and shrimps*

Shute, Nevil [Nevil Shute Norway] (1899–1960), novelist, b. England. A successful aeronautical engineer, Shute established his name as a novelist after the publication of *Pied Piper* (1942). In 1950 he immigrated to Australia, which became the scene of some of his most famous novels, including *A Town Like Alice* (1950), *In the Wet* (1953) and *On the Beach* (1957). A perennially popular writer, Shute dealt with serious themes in a readable and lively manner.

Siding Spring Observatory > *astronomy*

silver In Australia, silver is mined mainly as a by-product of other minerals such as lead, zinc, gold, copper and nickel. Australia is the sixth-largest producer, supplying about 8% of world production. The two main centres are Broken Hill and Mt Isa, the latter providing more than 80% of national production, the bulk of which is exported in lead, zinc and copper concentrates to be refined overseas. Australia's largest refined-silver producer is the Broken Hill Associated Smelters lead refinery at Port Pirie, SA.

silver-eyes Small, insectivorous, nectar-eating birds of the genus *Zosterops*, silver-eyes are found throughout Africa, southern Asia and Australia; all have a distinctive white ring around the eye, giving rise to their alternative name, white-eyes. They nest in a cup-shaped structure composed of materials (such as grass, horsehair, moss or cobwebs) light enough to rest on slender twigs. The grey-breasted silver-eye is a frequenter of gardens; those in Tas. migrate to the mainland in winter. The common silver-eye has become established in NZ, a group presumably having been storm-blown across the Tasman Sea in the mid-19th century. Beneficial in destroying insect pests, the silver-eye can itself be a pest in destroying soft fruits; the greenie of WA, generally greenish with a flush of blue on the breast, has at times been shot in large numbers in orchards.

Simpson Desert A large expanse of uninhabited, arid land mainly in the NT but extending into Qld and SA, this desert is a triangular area, the apex pointing to Lake Eyre, bordered by the Finke River on the west and the Mulligan and Diamantina rivers on the east; the Macdonnell Ranges lie to the northeast, whence flow a number of intermittent rivers whose waters are dissipated on reaching the desert. The surface comprises apparently endless, northwest–southeast aligned sandhills about 300–400m apart; vegetation is largely spinifex. The first to enter the desert was Charles Sturt, in 1845, deterred in his attempt to reach the centre by the ridges 'stretching interminably ... like waves of the sea'. In 1929 C. T. Madigan surveyed the region from the air and named the desert after the president of the SA Geographical Society. Several expeditions have since been mounted, including the first crossing on foot, in 1973. In 1967 two national parks were proclaimed: the Simpson Desert Conservation Park in SA and Qld's Simpson Desert National Park, both of which cover sand-ridge country and, by reason of their isolation, harbour rare species of desert fauna.

Sinclair, Ian (1929–   ), politician, b. Sydney. A lawyer, Sinclair entered federal parliament in 1963 as a Country Party member; he subsequently held numerous portfolios in Liberal-Country Party coalition governments, including social services (1965–8), primary industry (1971–2), communications (1980–2) and defence (1982). Elected leader of the National (formerly Country) Party in 1984, Sinclair was an acute but abrasive leader who found it hard to escape the taint of a 1979 scandal involving his family companies (of which he was cleared of any impropriety by the NSW Supreme Court in 1981). In 1989 he was replaced as leader of the National Party by NSW backbencher, Charles Blunt.

Singleton NSW (pop. 10 990) This important coalmining centre lies on the Hunter River 230km north of Sydney; it is also a manufacturing and market centre for the surrounding region, which carries dairy and beef cattle, vegetable-growing and vineyards. The area was settled in the 1830s by Benjamin Singleton.

sirex wasp > *insect pests*; *sawflies and wood-wasps*

sittellas Of the genus *Neositta* and also known as tree-runners or nuthatches, these are small, generally black-and-white birds with straight, very sharp beaks and strong claws for vertical 'tree-running' in search of insects. They build cup-like nests in tree-forks, camouflaged to blend almost imperceptibly with the bark, making them very difficult to detect. These birds provide an interesting contrast to the tree-creepers, which commonly run head-downwards as they search for food. There are six species of sittella found across Australia.

Skase, Christopher (1948–), business entrepreneur, b. Melbourne. A journalist by training, by the early 1980s Skase was the most spectacular of Australia's younger businessmen: his company, Qintex Ltd, acquired interests in media and communication through Universal Telecasters Ltd, controller of the Channel 7 network; in hotels and leisure through Mirage Resorts, which controls a network of luxurious developments in Qld and Hawaii; and in equity and property development. Qintex America Ltd, with interests in film and television production, was launched in 1987. In 1989, however, Skase joined the decade's swelling ranks of sensational business failures when Qintex was placed in receivership.

skates > *rays*

skiing Norwegian and Austrian miners in Australia developed skiing as a sport in the 1860s, and the first ski club, at Kiandra, was formed in 1870. Subsequently, exclusive and expensive facilities were developed in the NSW and Vic. alpine regions, many ski clubs were established, and the Australian National Ski Federation was formed in 1932. Australia first competed at the Winter Olympics in 1952 and the televising of recent Games has broadened public awareness of, and interest in, the range of winter sports. Malcolm Milne's third place in the downhill event at the 1970 world championships is the best result so far achieved by an Australian. New alpine facilities are being rapidly developed, and although there are only 34 000 registered Australian skiiers, many times that number enjoy the sport informally. The three southeastern States are well served with winter snowfields: these include Thredbo and Perisher Valley in Kosciusko National Park, NSW; Mts Buller, Hotham and Buffalo and Falls Creek in Vic., and Mts Field (West) and Wellington, and Ben Lomond, in Tas.

skills training > *training programs*

skinks > *lizards*

skuas > *sea-birds*

sky sports Australia's predominantly flat terrain and extensive regions of temperate climate have combined to make a variety of sky sports more accessible in this country than in many other parts of the world. As high-profile sports such as tennis, cricket and swimming fluctuate in popularity and international success, many lesser-known sports are gaining new participants and registering world-class performances. Sky sports are prominent among them.

There are 6800 registered parachutists in this country and the Australian team won world championships in canopy-relative work in 1984 and 1986. Gliding has 4282 registered members, and in this sport Ingo Renner was world champion in 1983, 1985 and 1987. Hang-gliding has 1800 official participants; the Australian team and Steve Moyes won world championships in 1983; similarly, the Australian ballooning team took world honours in 1983, with Steve Vizzard as individual champion.

Slessor, Kenneth Adolph (1901–71), poet and journalist, b. Orange, NSW. A journalist in Sydney for most of his life, Slessor was editor of *Smith's Weekly* 1935–9 and was subsequently a war correspondent in Europe and PNG. Early volumes of his verse such as *Earth Visitors* (1926), influenced strongly by his association with the zestful Norman Lindsay, were both surrealist and evocative. His poetry later matured to a more individual, often bitter, style, but maintained its strong imagery. His magnum opus is generally acknowledged to be the meditative volume *Five Bells* (1939); while he wrote little poetry after the mid-1940s, he remained active in literary circles; *Bread and Wine* (1970), a collection of his prose writings, reflected his epicurean proclivities.

slow-worms > *lizards*

slugs > *snails and slugs*

Smart, Jeffrey (1921–), painter, b. Adelaide. An expatriate Australian artist, Smart is noted for his coolly figurative paintings which typically portray people isolated in the modern urban landscape (especially in Tuscany, where he has lived since the 1960s). He uses chilly tones with accents of lurid colour to startling effect. Smart has exhibited consistently in

England, Australia and Europe since 1957, and regularly visits Australia.

Smith, Bernard (William) (1916–), art historian and critic, b. Sydney. Smith's first book, *Place, Taste and Tradition* (1945), a survey of Australian art, was a landmark in the field of art and cultural history. A founding member of the controversial Antipodean Group in 1959, he was author of the group's catalogue manifesto. His numerous publications since that time have been both scholarly and influential: they include *European Vision and the South Pacific 1768–1850* (1960), *Australian Painting 1788–1960* (1962), *Documents on Art and Taste in Australia* (1975) and, with Rüdiger Joppien, *The Art of Captain Cook's Voyages* (1985). His autobiography, *The Boy Adeodatus*, was published in 1984.

Smith, Dick (Richard Harold) (1944–), entrepreneur and adventurer, b. Sydney. Starting his own electronic components firm in 1968, Smith built it up into a successful business. This he sold to Woolworths in 1980, using the money to finance his numerous interests, which include aviation, publishing and philanthropy. In 1983 he was the first person to circumnavigate the world in a helicopter, and in 1987 he was the first to fly a helicopter to the North Pole. In the field of publishing, he founded the *Australian Geographic* magazine (1986) and later published the revised, nine-volume *Australian Encyclopaedia* (1988).

Smith, Donald (1922–), singer, b. Bundaberg, Qld. One of Australia's best-known tenors, Smith won the 1952 Mobil Quest and after studies in Britain and Italy sang with the Sadler's Wells, Welsh and Scottish operas. After returning to Australia in 1969 as a principal of the Australian Opera, his notable roles included Don José in *Carmen*, Radames in *Aida* and Erik in *The Flying Dutchman*. He left the Australian Opera in 1980 but has since given periodic concert and opera performances.

Smith, Grace Cossington (1892–1985), painter, b. Sydney. Smith was largely instrumental in introducing post-Impressionism to Australia. A contemporary of Roy de Maistre and Roland Wakelin, she developed a distinctive style using square brush strokes and radiant colour, depicting Sydney people and scenes, and (especially in her later work) light-flooded domestic interiors. She led a quiet life outside art circles, and was not recognised for her major contribution to Australian art until her mid-70s.

Smith, Margaret > *Court, Margaret*

Smith, Sydney Ure (1887–1949), publisher and artist, b. England. Pioneer of art publishing in Australia, Smith (with Bertram Stevens) was founder of the publishing company Art in Australia and founder-editor of the periodical *Art in Australia* (1916–42). In 1939 he established Ure Smith Pty Ltd, a publishing house of exacting standards specialising in art books. Smith was also a well-known etcher, water-colourist and illustrator, inspired particularly by the Sydney region, of which he has left a fine record. Urbane and witty, he was an invaluable moral and financial support to many artists.

Smith, Tommy (Thomas John) > *horse-racing*

Smith brothers, pioneer aviators. Sir Keith Macpherson (1890–1955) and Sir Ross Macpherson (1892–1922), both b. Adelaide, served as pilots in World War 1, Keith with the Royal Flying Corps and Ross – who was to become Australia's most highly decorated airman – with the Australian Flying Corps. In 1919 the Australian government offered a prize for the first Australian-manned flight from England to Australia taking less than 30 days. The brothers won the prize in a Vickers Vimy bomber, covering the distance in 28 days; both were knighted for this accomplishment. A planned round-the-world flight was tragically aborted when Ross was killed in a plane crash in England in 1922. Keith went on to represent Vickers in Australia, subsequently becoming chairman of Vickers – Armstrong (Aust.) Pty Ltd.

snails and slugs These include both fresh-water and terrestrial representatives of the gastropods, and together total more than 600 native species. Freshwater specimens include some with gills, more closely related to marine types: these often evade drought conditions by burrowing into mud and tightly 'closing the lid'. Some may be potential alternative hosts for disease-carrying parasites such as the Chinese river fluke and the Oriental lung fluke, so justifying careful quarantine regulations.

The lunged land snails predominate; their drought-evading device is to seal off the outside world with mucus, the seal being discarded at the end of the dry period, which can be as long as several years in desert areas. They range from *Strangesta capillacea*, the carnivorous snail of some Sydney gardens, to the giant panda snail, *Hedleyella falconeri*, inhabiting the rainforests of NSW and Qld. The forests of Qld also have many colourful banded snails, such as several species of *Bentosites*, banded in brown, yellow and white and with quite an attractive shell.

Slugs are terrestrial gastropods in which the shell has vanished: most of those found in temperate rural and suburban areas are introduced; native species are few, and generally rarely observed. The native *Triboniophorus graeffei*, in which the pulmonary pore may be seen opening and shutting on the back of the animal, is also an inhabitant of NZ and some Pacific islands. Sea slugs are often brightly coloured: familiar examples include the red and blue slug, *Glossodoris bennettii*, which is sometimes seen among rocks at low tide. Sea hares of the family Aplysiidae are slug-like marine molluscs with a fragile internal shell and include the ringed sea hare, *Aplysia dactylomela*, which can measure 30cm and has two fleshy flaps on the back by means of which it can swim.

snakes Snakes are closely related to lizards (these groups together constituting the order Squamata) and might be regarded as highly specialised lizards. Australia has about 160 species, among which are some of the most venomous in the world; in fact, Australia is the only continent in which venomous species outnumber the non-venomous. Snakes are equipped with an unusual ligament that allows the lower jaw to disconnect from the skull; with this device, they are able to swallow whole exceedingly large prey. They have no outer or middle ear structure: they 'hear' only ground-transmitted vibrations to which the inner ear is sensitive, and cannot detect airborne sound.

Snake venom is a complex mixture of proteins produced in modified saliva glands at the base of hollow fangs. Depending on the species involved, venom can either destroy the linings of blood vessels, cause blood to clot, destroy red blood cells, or affect the nervous system and cause death by blocking the nerves that control the heart and lungs – neurotoxins with such effect are found in the deadly venom of Australian elapids and sea snakes. Modern treatment of snake-bite involves the administration

of antivenenes, many of which have been developed at the Commonwealth Serum Laboratories.

Six major families of snakes are found in Australia and its coastal waters. Of the family Typhlopidae, the blind or worm snakes, there are 20 species – small, burrowing, non-venomous reptiles that feed on worms and insects, chiefly ants and termites. They often have only rudimentary eyes.

The pythons, ten species of the family Boidae, also are non-poisonous and kill their small, vertebrate prey by constriction. The largest is the amethystine or rock python from northeastern Qld and NG, *Liasis amethystinus*, which has been recorded at lengths of up to 7m. The green tree python, *Chondropython viridis*, is found in the north of Cape York Peninsula and in NG, and the common carpet snake, *Morelia spilotes*, is widespread across Australia.

The family Colubridae contains eleven species and includes both non-venomous and rear-fanged venomous snakes. Among the harmless species is the green tree snake, *Dendrelaphis punctulatus*, which varies in colour from blue to yellowish and is found along the northern and eastern continental margins; the poisonous, rear-fanged species include the brown tree snake, *Boiga irregularis*, and some tropical water snakes. They are rarely dangerous to humans, partly because they cannot usually inject sufficient venom.

Also non-venomous, and allied to the colubrids, is the Acrochordidae family of file snakes, comprising only two species. The Arafura grows to 2m and is found in fresh-water streams and billabongs in northern Australia. The little file snake lives in coastal mud flats and estuaries.

All species of the family Elapidae are poisonous and front-fanged; they include species that lay eggs and species that give live birth. Among the 65 species is the taipan of northern Australia and NG, *Oxyuranus scutellatus*; the taipan is deadly, but its close relative, the giant brown snake, *Parademansia microlepidota*, has the most toxic venom of any Australian species. Tiger snakes, species of the genus *Notechis*, are found in a variety of habitats on the southeastern mainland and Tas.; the widely distributed death adder, genus *Acanthophis*, has a distinctive, triangular head and is rather sluggish. Other dangerous elapids include the red-bellied black snake, *Pseudechis porphyriacus*; the copperhead, *Austrelaps superbus*, and brown snakes, species of the genus *Pseudonaja*.

Sea snakes are derived from elapids, and form two families. Most species feed on fish. The sea snake's adaptions for marine life include a flattened, paddle-like tail and special valves on the mouth and nostrils to prevent the entry of water. The two species of the Laticaudidae, or sea-kraits, inhabit coastal waters but lay their eggs on land. Species of the Hydrophiidae, on the other hand, live entirely in the sea and give birth to live young. The striking yellow-bellied sea snake *Pelamis platurus*, is found in most Australian waters except those of the cold, southern coast.

snapper A pre-eminent commercial and sporting sea-fish related to the bream, the snapper, *Chrysophrys auratus*, in fact resembles bream until in old age it develops a marked bulge above the eyes and gills. It grows occasionally to 1.2m, weighing over 18kg, and is known by several names at different stages: as cockney when a juvenile, then later as red bream or redfish, squire and school snapper until, with development of the bulging head, it is old man snapper. It eats mainly shellfish.

snooker > *billiards and snooker*

Snowy Mountains NSW A section of the Great Dividing Range, this is Australia's highest land and most extensive alpine area. Its western escarpment is dissected and steep, drained by the Murray River, while the eastern slopes, where the Snowy River rises, are gentler. Features of the landscape give evidence of glaciation in the last ice age; residual peaks stand above a series of plateau levels, the highest point being > *Mt Kosciusko* (2228m). The higher land rises above the treeline and in summer is densely covered with alpine flora; this region was formerly used for summer grazing, now prohibited to avoid erosion. The mountains are snow-covered in winter and much frequented by skiers; snow gums extend to the treeline, beneath which are stands of alpine ash and mountain ash. Kosciusko National Park covers 645 500ha and includes the range and the river headwaters; in summer the streams provide good trout fishing, and the park is a popular attraction for bushwalkers. The mountains were first explored in 1840 by Paul Strzelecki. >> *Snowy Mountains Scheme*

Snowy Mountains Scheme A tremendous feat of engineering, this scheme diverts the south-flowing waters of the Snowy River in NSW via two tunnel systems through the rugged Snowy Mountains to provide both hydro-electricity and irrigation for southeastern Australia. Such a scheme was mooted periodically from early in the 20th century and the Snowy Mountains Authority was established in 1949. The project's sixteen dams, 150km of tunnels and 80km of aqueduct were constructed over a period of 25 years. Seven power stations provide a peak power of 4 million kW, which is shared by Vic., NSW and Canberra; the largest of the storage reservoirs is Lake Eucumbene. >> *electrical energy*; *water and water resources*

soapberry family The Sapindaceae, a large family of flowering plants found in all warmer regions of the world, consists of trees, shrubs and climbers. In Australia it is represented by 29 native genera comprising about 190 species. Most are rainforest trees of eastern and far northern coastal areas, but the largest genus, *Dodonaea*, of 60-odd species, is spread widely throughout Australia. Known as hop-bushes, these are mainly shrubs and are named for their distinctive winged fruits that can be used as a substitute for hops. Also widespread in the inland is western rosewood or boonaree, *Alectryon oleifolius*, a small crooked tree. Another important tree genus is *Harpullia*. which includes some valuable timber species such as the tulipwood, *H. pendulata*.

soccer The first soccer match was played in Sydney in 1880 and the NSW Soccer Association was formed two years later; the game spread to all colonies but was strongest among British immigrants and in the mining towns of NSW. A national body was formed in 1923 and State championships were organised in imitation of the British model. NZ and Chinese teams visited during this period, in which the leading player was A. A. (Alf) Quill, whose total goal score was 1002.

After World War 2, the influx of immigrants gave the sport an enormous boost. NSW-born player Joe Marston joined an English club in 1949 and achieved fame by playing in the 1953 FA Cup final. In 1959 Australia was banned by the world controlling body, Fédération Internationale de Football Association (FIFA), for poaching European players and was only readmitted in 1963 with the reorganisation of the game and payment of compensation to the clubs concerned by the Australian Soccer Federation.

Granted the right to compete in the World Cup, Australia made unsuccessful attempts in 1965 and 1969, but in 1973 the Socceroos under coach Rale Rasic survived elimination rounds to represent the South Pacific zone. Although the team was eliminated in the finals in Munich, players such as captain Peter Wilson and Johnny Warren, Manfred Schraeder, Attila Abonyi and John Watkiss became national heroes. Australia has not yet been successful in subsequent World Cup competition, but one of a number of players to have succeeded overseas is Craig Johnston, representing Liverpool and scoring in the 1986 FA Cup final.

Australia achieved its highest place so far in international competition when, under coach Frank Arok, the Olympic team reached the quarter-finals at the 1988 Games. After a number of false starts, a national league was formed in 1977; there are now nearly 500 000 registered male players and 22 000 female; swelling these numbers are the 100 000 or so people who play indoor soccer.

Socialist Party of Australia > *communism*

Socialist Workers Party > *communism*

social services Australia has a complex system of social services provided by the federal and State governments and voluntary organisations. The extent of government assistance has waxed and waned over the years, largely reflecting the social policies of the ruling party. The belief that state support for the needy discourages self-reliance – a feature of 19th-century laissez faire – has been upheld to the present day by many conservative governments.

Historical development In Australia in the 19th century, welfare assistance was provided mainly by voluntary organisations subsidised by charitable donations and some state funding. In 1900, NSW and Vic. introduced non-contributory but means-tested old-age pensions; this preceded the provision of similar benefits in both the UK and the US. The Commonwealth took over these responsibilities in 1909 and introduced invalid pensions in 1910 and maternity allowances in 1912. Due in part to the Commonwealth's lack of specific powers in the area, no further federal benefits were instituted for many years; a national insurance scheme was drafted in the 1920s, however, and non-financial relief was dispensed during the 1930s depression. During this hiatus, the State govern-

ments continued to subsidise voluntary welfare organisations and contributed some pensions.

World War 2, coupled with an incoming Labor government, gave new impetus to the creation of a social-security system. During the 1940s, the Commonwealth was empowered to legislate in a much wider range of welfare matters and introduced child endowment, widows' pensions, and sickness and unemployment benefits. The 1953 National Health Act introduced by the Liberal government expressly inhibited the development of universal health insurance, however, and it was not until 1975 that a national health scheme was inaugurated. Known as Medibank and initially funded from consolidated revenue, the scheme had a chequered career and was effectively dismantled by the Fraser government in the late 1970s. It was replaced in 1984 by a new system, Medicare, subsidised by a levy on taxable income (at a rate of 1.25% in 1988).

Since 1970, there has been a general expansion and rationalisation of existing social services. The appropriate level of assistance in some areas remains a matter of continuing public debate, however, and the changing demographic profile of Australia will present new challenges for forthcoming governments. The means test for age pensions has undergone significant and invariably controversial changes in recent years, an assets test being added in 1985. There have also been various, and equally controversial, moves to tie pensions and benefits to the consumer price index: in some cases indexation was granted and later rescinded, resulting in effective devaluation of the benefits as they failed to keep up with the annual inflation rate. The 'greying' of the Australian population, whose median age is predicted to rise from 29.6 years in 1981 to 34 years by 2001 – will clearly put increasing pressure on the nation's welfare system and by the late 1980s was already becoming a major consideration for welfare planners.

Also of increasing concern is the incidence of > *poverty* in Australia. A review of the social-security system in 1986 identified a number of groups that are particularly prone to poor living standards. In 1987 the federal government undertook to eradicate child poverty in Australia by 1990: this statement was greeted with initial enthusiasm, but by the end of the 1980s the social-security system had little improved the lot of the many Australian households living in poverty, most notably single-parent families headed by women. The ever-increasing number of women in the workforce is likely to make child care an important welfare issue in the future: although the federal government does provide indirect assistance for child-care facilities, the cost of such services is not yet tax-deductible – a legacy of the era when a man was assumed to be the sole breadwinner in the family.

Pensions and benefits The Social Security Act of 1947 gave the Commonwealth power to provide financial relief for the aged and infirm, widowed persons, sole parents, orphans, the unemployed, and families. Two of the most widely received allowances are the age pension, which is payable to men aged 65 and over and women 60 years and over; and unemployment and sickness benefits, paid to men aged 16–65 and women of 16–60 who are unemployed or temporarily incapacitated for work. Other forms of financial assistance include child allowances and family supplements paid to low-income families, pensions for the disabled, non-means-tested payments to parents of severely handicapped children needing constant care, and a benefit (subject to income and asset test) for sole parents.

Other support services The federal government also provides indirect assistance to State welfare services and voluntary organisations in the form of grants and cost-sharing arrangements. It subsidises a range of child-care services provided by local government and non-profit community organisations, as well as services for people with mental and physical disabilities. A home and community care program was instituted jointly in 1985 by the Commonwealth and State governments; this includes funding assistance for the Meals-on-Wheels service for aged and invalid pensioners. Other government assistance includes the provision of professional social workers, liaison officers for ethnic and Aboriginal communities, and grants to welfare agencies providing disaster relief.

Private enterprise also carries responsibility for welfare in the workplace, being required by law to insure employees against work-related injury under workers-compensation schemes, and to provide sick leave. Workers-compensation programs, which have proved both extremely costly and subject to abuse, were under review in the late 1980s. Tax incentives are provided by the government to encourage superannuation schemes, as a means of encouraging employees to save for retirement and thus easing the potential burden on the welfare system.

>> *health and health services*; *superannuation*; *welfare organisations*

soils and soil conservation Australia's land surface is very ancient, as a consequence of which its soils are quite infertile by world standards and the rate of soil formation is negligible. The combination of poor soils and relatively limited areas of reasonable rainfall (and very variable rainfall at that) substantially limits the potential for agricultural and forestry production, a fact which is belied by the size of the continent. Over the past two centuries the available arable soils have been drastically altered – usually for the worse – by European farming methods. Ecosystems that were carefully husbanded by the Aborigines for millennia have now lost much of their natural cover of trees, shrubs and largely perennial grasses, with the result that the topsoils (rich in organic content and nutrients) have been generally eroded or otherwise degraded. These processes have been accompanied by a loss of the biological activity which is so important for the maintenance of good soil structure. The widespread application of insecticides and herbicides, which frequently destroy non-target species, is another threat to the soil microfauna and microflora.

There are several very obvious forms of land degradation in Australia, from gully erosion to salinity. By the late 1980s, however, soil scientists were above all concerned with the interplay of factors that brings about more gradual and insidious forms of soil deterioration, thus making the land extremely vulnerable to the forces of erosion in the long term. These destructive processes, and the regional nature of many soil problems (such as the build-up of salt-laden watertables in irrigation areas) are encouraging scientists to examine and improve land-use practices rather than relying on the ad-hoc remedies used in the past.

Cropping The ploughing and repeated cultivation of soils, especially in crop areas such as the wheat–sheep belt of southeastern and southwestern Australia, expose them to the erosive effects of rain and wind. With each tonne of wheat produced, it is estimated that at least a tonne of soil is lost, increasing to upwards of 5t in the case of more exploitative systems (such as continuous cropping) and where rainfall is more intense. Allied with the insignificant rate of soil formation, the processes of erosion have produced truncated topsoils with not only less capacity to store rain but also crusted and structureless surfaces that hinder water infiltration and the germination of seed.

Two other symptoms of land degradation are also widespread in the wheat belt: soils becoming saline due to upward seepage of salty waters as the result of tree-clearing, especially on hills; and soils becoming more acid due to the long-term application of superphosphate to clover-rich pastures. Soil acidification, which already affects some 17 million ha, is an insidious and extremely serious problem since restoration is almost impossible once the subsoil is affected.

Grazing Land degradation is also widespread in the large higher-rainfall areas in southern Australia that are utilised for sheep and cattle grazing. Persistent overgrazing, especially in times of recurring drought, exposes the soil to the ravages of thunderstorms and flood, and soil acidification is also occurring where pastures have been 'improved' with the use of subterranean clover and superphosphate.

The vast areas of arid and semi-arid land used for grazing are similarly subject to deteriorating soils. Although generally there has been no clearing of vegetation in these regions, sheep and cattle have eliminated many of the most palatable perennial grasses, herbs and bushes: in such areas, where the soils can ill afford to lose their meagre supply of nutrients and plant cover, the result may best be described as 'desertification'. In particularly arid areas, grazing prevents plant regeneration to the extent that there is no viable seed left at all.

Irrigation The long-term fate of Australia's 1.6 million ha of irrigated and intensively farmed land, situated mainly in the Murray–Darling catchment of southeastern Australia, lies in the balance. The twin problems of soil waterlogging and salinity are becoming increasingly prevalent and only a fraction of the area has the sub-surface drainage schemes necessary for rehabilitation. Such schemes are extremely expensive to install and in addition require benign disposal of the saline effluent, as most are located hundreds of kilometres inland. Despite a wide range of measures being taken to reduce salinity in the Murray–Darling river system, the salt loads are increasing inexorably.

Forestry Plantation forestry and woodchipping take place primarily in the high-rainfall zone of southern Australia, where serious soil problems are also becoming evident as a result of the processes entailed. On the one hand, the clearfelling involved in both operations exposes the soil (which is usually on sloping land) to erosion by rain; and on the other hand, the soil's essential organic matter is lost through oxidation and the removal of nutrients with the wood. While the application of fertilisers is necessary to maintain plantations, they cause imbalances in the soil nutrients that may prove too difficult or costly to remedy.

The 1980s and beyond Many programs are under way to tackle the various manifestations of land degradation in Australia. Government agencies have been slow to respond to the complexity of the problem, however, owing in part to their narrow scientific focus but also in part to the division of responsibility between various organisations.

The problems now occurring are a clear warning that Australia's landscape and soils are ill-fitted to sustain current agricultural and forestry practices. A further and related problem is the reliance of modern agriculture on fossil fuels to power its machinery, transport produce, and manufacture commodities such as fertilisers: the diminishing supplies of Australian oil and the high cost of imported fuels, combined with the destructive environmental effects of this form of energy, is putting Australian farming methods – and soils – on notice.

Given Australia's continuing reliance on agricultural and mineral exports, pressure on the land to be productive is likely to increase in the coming decades. Such demands will not only exacerbate the existing problems of land degradation but also increase the net loss of soil nutrients through the continual export of land-based products. The wheat belt is particularly prone to this form of impoverishment, the 1986–7 wheat crop having removed 50 000t of phosphorus and 65 000t of potassium from the soil; wool, by contrast, is much more benign in its drawdown of soil nutrient reserves.

Research and conservation activities in Australia will have to take account of these global problems and responsibilities, and aim to maintain soil fertility by the exercise of a much more diverse farming-forestry system. It is essential to reintroduce significant numbers of trees and deep-rooted perennials; preserve large areas of bushland (preferably native) to provide habitat for natural predators and thus obviate the need for pesticides; and maintain the ecological diversity of the country's remaining biological resources. In the long term, soil conservation in Australia may require a much more decentralised and self-sufficient population, whose numbers are matched to the 'carrying capacity' of the land. >> *agriculture*; *environment and conservation*; *forests and forestry*; *water and water resources*

Solanaceae > *nightshade family*

Solander, Daniel (1733–82) botanist, b. Sweden. A favoured student of Carolus Linnaeus, Solander went to London in 1760 and befriended the young Joseph Banks. He was selected to accompany Banks on James Cook's first Pacific voyage, 1768–71. Rich botanical collections resulted and Solander prepared a manuscript account of them which was, however, never published. His name is commemorated in the Australian plant genus *Solandra* and in Cape Solander at Botany Bay in NSW.

Solanum > *nightshade family*

solar energy > *energy resources*

soldier settlement schemes These schemes, which operated in Australia after both World War 1 and World War 2, were intended to provide low-cost farms for returned soldiers, through government loans and credit. By 1924 more than 36 000 soldiers had taken up holdings, but most failed because of inadequate funds, lack of farming experience, and unsuitable land; the most successful were in irrigated areas. The scheme was conducted on a much smaller scale after World War 2, with fewer than 10 000 holdings being taken up, but better preparation (including training schemes) led to a greater success rate.

Sorell Tas. (pop. 2882) This municipality, which incorporates Midway Point, lies on the inlet Pitt Water 26km northeast of Hobart. One of the State's oldest towns and the centre of an early wheat-growing area, Sorell developed to the detriment of Richmond when it was linked to Hobart in 1872 by a causeway; it is now a local service centre with some fishing and tourism.

Southall, Ivan (1921–), novelist, b. Melbourne. Australia's best-known writer for children, Southall has won Britain's Carnegie Medal (1971), Holland's Zilver Griffell (1972) and four Australian Children's Book of the Year awards. His nine Simon Black air adventure stories were succeeded by the utterly different *Ash Road* (1965), which realistically explored children's problems and experiences and set the theme for some 20 serious novels and non-fiction works for young readers. He has also written adult non-fiction.

South Australia (SA) The third-largest State (excluding the NT) in terms of area and the fifth-largest in terms of population, SA is something of a poor relation among the mainland States, its industrial base having been eroded by the economic slump of the 1970s. In the 19th century, and again during the premiership of > *Don Dunstan* 1967–8 and 1970–9, it was a pioneer of enlightened social legislation, but a period of extreme conservatism intervened. With an area of 984 377sq.km (12.8% of Australia's total) and a coastline of 3700km, SA can be divided into three main zones – the arid and semi-desert north, the gulf lands, and the southeast plains. The northern sector consists of low plateau in the west, but the east is part of the Great Artesian Basin, with numerous salt lakes (almost always dry) including Lakes Eyre and Torrens; it is saltbush, mulga and sand-dune country, much of it with a rainfall of less than 250mm. The gulf lands are better watered and include Eyre Peninsula, the Mt Lofty Range, the coastal plain and the > *Barossa Valley*. Less well watered, the southeast plains are dependent on the Murray River for irrigation. The major urban centres are > *Adelaide* (the capital), Whyalla, Port Augusta, Port Pirie, Noarlunga, Gawler and Port Lincoln, all in the gulf lands, and Murray Bridge and Mt Gambier, both in the southeast plains.

Historical development European settlement in SA was resisted by sporadic Aboriginal raids, especially on overlanders from NSW, and these, in turn, led to savage European reprisals and the elimination of Aboriginal communities from the more fertile regions. Settlement was planned on free immigration, based on the theories of > *E. G. Wakefield*, and began in 1836 under the auspices of the SA Company. There was conflicting command, however, surveying did not keep pace with the arrival of settlers, and speculation in land took place instead of development; the experiment failed, and in 1842 SA became a Crown colony. Under Governor Sir George Grey the colony moved towards self-sufficiency; copper was discovered in 1845, and with wheat (especially after the gold rushes increased demand) gave rise to some prosperity. In the 1860s an economic depression resulting from drought was staved off by further copper discoveries, at Moonta in 1865, but several years of good rain then led to overborrowing and the extension of wheat-growing into marginal lands, resulting in economic collapse in the 1880s and stagnation until well after Federation. The latter initially held few benefits for SA: with very little to sell that State gained little from the abolition of tariffs. Mining of iron in the Middleback Range began in 1915 and wheat-growing revived in the new century, but with little secondary industry SA was very vulnerable to the economic depression of the 1930s. After World War 2, however, secondary industry – based on shipbuilding at Whyalla, white goods, and the manufacture of motor vehicles – expanded greatly and the State enjoyed a period of relative prosperity with a large intake of immigrants. This ended with the economic slump of the 1970s, which wiped out shipbuilding and greatly reduced the other secondary industries. Some relief was afforded by an expansion of iron-ore mining and, in the 1980s, the discovery of natural gas, further copper, and uranium.

Population and economy The population of SA at the 1986 census was 1 345 945, which showed a growth rate of only 0.02% over the five years between censuses, similar to those of Vic. and Tas., lower than that of NSW, and much lower than those of WA and Qld. This figure gives a population density of 1.37 per sq. km., which is misleading because only 1% of the population lives in the north and about 70% in Adelaide; about 76% are Australian-born. SA was unique among the Australian colonies in that only 14% of its founding Europeans came from Ireland, with about 66% from the agrarian counties of southern England and a leavening of Lutherans from Germany. The northwest of SA has been set aside for Aboriginal use, but the northeast supports a sparse population of cattle and sheep. Wheat and other grains, grown in the southern regions, are vital to the State's economy, while fruits (grown under irrigation along the Murray) and wine are also important; SA produces 60% of Australia's grapes. Coal, not of the best quality, is mined at Leigh Creek and used largely for electricity generation; iron ore from the Middleback Range is an important export; extensive deposits of uranium and copper at Roxby Downs, exploited since 1988, give some hope to the State's future; and natural gas from the Gidgealpa field is piped to cities around Australia. SA's secondary industry is situated largely in the Adelaide–Elizabeth–Salisbury area and at Whyalla, Port Pirie and Port Augusta.

Government and politics Responsible government in SA began in 1856 and initially was controlled by élite Adelaide families. From the 1890s major reforms were pioneered, including the franchise for women, compulsory arbitration, payment for parliamentarians, free education, and factory legislation; from Federation until the economic depression of the 1930s, Labor and the conservatives enjoyed approximately equal periods in office. The depression, during which unemployment in SA reached 34% (the highest in Australia), brought to office the conservative Liberal-Country League (LCL) and under R. L. Butler (1933–8) and > *Sir Thomas Playford* (1938–65) they remained there for 32 years. After World War 2 the economy boomed and there was massive immigration, but social issues were largely ignored and 19th-century restraints on social life remained in force. Don Dunstan's Labor government of 1967 and the LCL government of R. Steele Hall (1968) brought about electoral reform; Dunstan's 1970–9 regime removed restraints on drinking hours and gambling, legalised homosexuality, outlawed racial discrimination, and expanded health, education and welfare services. Neither Dunstan's Labor successor, J. D. Corcoran (1979), nor the conservative government of D. O. Tonkin (1979–82) was reform-oriented, and when Labor under John Bannon regained office in 1982 pragmatism remained the order of the day. As in the federal sphere, the distinction between Labor and conservative had become blurred.

South Australian Co. The company (1836–59) was formed, with G. F. Angas as director, to buy land in SA that was not selling at the 20 shillings per acre asked by the commissioners in charge. The company acquired considerable areas at 12 shillings per acre, and financed port, banking and whaling facilities, all of which made the settlement viable; but it also joined the subsequent disastrous speculative boom.

Southern Cross A constellation in the southern sky consisting of four conspicuous stars (forming the cross axes) and a fainter fifth star, this was first formally separated (and named *Crux Australis*) in 1679. The South Celestial Pole can be found by imagining the long axis of the cross extended beyond the base to about four times its length. Two nearby bright stars, Alpha and Beta Centauri, are also known as the Pointers, since a line drawn through them extends to intersect the head of the cross. The Southern Cross has been used frequently as a nationalistic symbol, and the constellation features on the Australian flag.

southern lights > *aurora australis*

South Pacific Forum Established in 1972, this organisation replaced the South Pacific Commission which had been set up in 1947 by the Pacific colonial powers – the UK, US, France, the Netherlands, Australia and NZ – to provide economic support to their dependent territories; when many of these territories gained their independence, the commission's importance diminished. The South Pacific Forum is the annual meeting of independent South Pacific nations, whose operating arm is the South Pacific Bureau for Economic Co-operation. Members of the forum are PNG, the Solomon Islands, Vanuatu, Nauru, Kiribati, Tuvalu, Fiji, Tonga, Western Samoa, Niue, the Cook Islands, Australia and NZ.

sparrows > *birds, introduced*

Spence, Catherine Helen (1825–1910), novelist and social reformer, b. Scotland. Spence arrived in Adelaide in 1839 and worked as a governess before her first novel, *Clara Morrison*, a woman's view of colonial life, was published in 1854. Her involvement in social and political reform became explicit in her writing from the 1860s, in both fiction (notably *Gathered In*, 1881–2) and articles; she subsequently became an active campaigner for proportional representation and female suffrage.

Spencer Gulf SA This large inlet on the State's southern coast lies between the Eyre and Yorke peninsulas. It extends about 320km northeastwards and is about 80km wide at its entrance. On its shores are located such major industrial ports as Whyalla, Port Pirie and Port Lincoln. Like neighbouring St Vincent Gulf, this inlet was discovered by Matthew Flinders in 1802 and named by him for a British admiral, in this case Earl Spencer.

Spender, Sir Percy Claude (1897–1985), politician and diplomat, b. Sydney. Spender became a barrister in 1923 and a KC in 1935. He served in the federal parliament 1937–51, holding several ministerial positions including

treasury and external affairs. In the latter position, he played an important part in the establishment of the Colombo Plan and the ANZUS treaty. He was subsequently Australian ambassador to the US 1951–8, a member of the International Court of Justice 1958–64 and its president 1964–7.

spiders Spiders, which are arachnids, have two body divisions: the cephalothorax (head) and the abdomen. The cephalothorax bears a pair of jointed chelicerae, or jaws, at the base of which is a movable fang with poison gland, used to immobilise and kill prey; it also bears a pair of palps (sensory organs) and four pairs of legs. The abdomen of all spiders bears spinnerets, silk-spinning appendages that form openings for the silk glands. Spiders' eggs are usually laid in a silken cocoon, and the young go through several moults before reaching maturity. All spiders are predators, and catch their prey either by hunting or by entangling them in silk.

Australia has a rich spider fauna with approximately 2000 described species. There are a number of suborders, the most prominent being the Mygalomorphae (funnelwebs and trapdoors), which have horizontal chelicerae, and the Araneomorphae (true spiders), which have vertical chelicerae. Of the Mygalomorphae, both sexes excavate burrows; the males, when mature, leave their burrows to search for mates. Funnelweb spiders construct silken tubes at the entrance of their burrows; species of the eastern Australian genus *Atrax* are among the most deadly spiders in the world and have been responsible for a number of human deaths. (An antidote is available but it must be administered without delay after the victim is bitten.) Trapdoor spiders seal their burrows with a plug of earth that forms a cap-like covering.

Spiders of the Araneomorphae usually capture their prey in silken snares; the family Dictynidae includes the black house-spider, whose sheet-like retreats are often found at the corners of windowsills. The orb-web spiders, the Araenidae, build elaborate webs; one of them, the St Andrew's Cross spider, constructs a characteristic, cross-like structure of white silk. The family Theridiidae includes the poisonous red-back spider, *Latrodectus mactans*, whose abdomen is marked with red in the shape of an hourglass; although human deaths have been recorded from its bites, an effective antivenene is available. The sheet-web weavers of the family Agelenidae weave sheets of silk over vegetation, and others of the Araneomorphae are hunters that stalk their prey: among these are the jumping spiders, Salticidae, which are able to pounce upon their victims; the crab spiders, Thomisidae, often cryptically coloured like the flowers on which they lie in wait; and the large huntsman spiders, Sparassidae, living under bark and stones.

Many people fear spiders, but relatively few are toxic to humans while the majority play important roles in reducing the number of insect pests.

spinebills > *honeyeaters*

spinifex > *grasses and grasslands*

spiny anteater > *monotremes*

spirits and distilling Spirits (notably rum) played a central, if infamous, role in the early years of European settlement. An essential ingredient in the Royal Navy diet, rum became for a time a substitute for legal tender and was the prime cause of the Rum Rebellion in 1808. From these questionable beginnings, based on the imported product, Australia has developed a large distilling industry producing a range of potable spirits including rum, brandy, whisky, gin, vodka and liqueurs. Industrial alcohol (ethanol) is also manufactured, mainly from molasses. Rum is produced at Bundaberg and Beenleigh in Qld, and whisky and brandy in SA. In 1986–7 overall production of potable spirits was nearly 5.8 million l. Excise duties are payable on these spirits but not on industrial alcohol, which is adulterated to make it unfit for human consumption.

Spofforth, Fred(erick Robert) (1853–1926), cricketer, b. Sydney. Nicknamed 'the demon', Spofforth is generally characterised as Australia's first great bowler and one of the finest in the history of cricket. He played in eighteen Tests against England 1877–87, taking 94 wickets for an average of eighteen runs and throughout his career captured some 1146 wickets for an average of thirteen runs. He lived in England from 1888.

sponges Aquatic, mainly marine animals of the phylum Porifera, many sponges live in colonies, sharing skeletons of spicules or fibres embedded in the tissues of the colony. Life is maintained in the adult animal by the circulation through its body of oxygen and plankton; this is achieved with the aid of inflow and outflow pores in the hollows in the sponge. Australian species are many and varied: limy sponges, species of the *Scypha* genus, are white and vase-shaped, 2–3cm high and seen at low tide on exposed, rocky coasts; the heliotrope sponge of the genus *Heliclona* inhabits rock pools and crevices near low-tide level down to 3m; and the plum sponge, *Tethya ingalli*, orange-red and about the size of a golf ball, lives underneath stones and rock ledges. Species potentially of commercial use, such as *Spongia officinalis*, are found in the Great Barrier Reef region and in other tropical waters. Some investigation was earlier made into the possibility of establishing commercial cultivation of sponges on the reef, but this project was interrupted by the outbreak of World War 2 and has not been revived. With many manufactured substitutes available, there is today little demand for natural sponges.

spoonbills > *ibises and spoonbills*

sport and recreation Sport has long occupied a central place in Australian society. Successful players and teams are afforded a prominence almost as great as that of their peers in politics, business and other cultural pursuits, and politicians of all persuasions are usually happy to be associated with sporting events, and with triumphs in particular.

Australian involvement in sport – as participants, spectators or gamblers – can be traced to the earliest days of European settlement; existing Aboriginal sports were largely disregarded, however, with the same indifference accorded to the rest of their culture. Recreational pursuits such as cricket, equestrian sports (especially racing), shooting and sailing were quickly established; the popularity of entertainment such as bare-knuckle boxing reflected the brutal nature of the early settlements.

The growth of sports through the 19th century reflected the nature of both the continent and the society being formed with it. The absence of harsh winters allowed most sports to be played all year round (although limited seasons were established); the mild climate and the concentration of population on the coast meant that water sports achieved early and wide popularity; and a generally high standard of living and ever-increasing urbanisation fostered relatively widespread participation in sports generally. Sport not only reflected the condition of society, but also helped to constitute it: many of the positive – usually male – values of the new country, such as courage, competitiveness, teamwork and moral character, were aspects of sport both drawn from and returned to the broader society. Sport played a vital role in drawing together communities, whether they were small bush settlements, crowded working-class suburbs or new developments on the edge of the expanding cities. Facilities from tennis courts and golf courses to billiard saloons were well developed by the end of the century.

Sport also contributed to the developing sense of Australia as a nation. Intercolonial matches drew the scattered settlements together; national teams in cricket and rugby were formed even before the political structure of the nation was achieved; and from 1896 onwards, Australian athletes, cyclists, scullers and swimmers brought the young nation to the attention of the world. Local variants of established sports, mostly notably Australian Rules Football, gained and have retained the following of a considerable proportion of the population. Since World War 2, sport has perhaps become an even greater focal point for Australian society, with a 'golden age' in the 1950s (its high point the 1956 Melbourne Olympic Games) that seemed to justify all the claims made for the positive aspects of sport. At the same time it has become increasingly commercialised, with major world events such as the annual Formula One Grand Prix (staged in Adelaide since 1985) attracting vast crowds and making a substantial contribution to local economies.

The 1980s and beyond Sport has been criticised, at different times and by different groups, for distracting the population from the more serious demands of intellectual excellence, work efficiency, and family formation; for its association with gambling and alcohol; and for reinforcing stereotypes and socioeconomic inequalities. By the 1980s, sport was still generally viewed as making an important contribution to good health, as compatible with achievements in other fields, and as an appropriate outlet for young people faced with contemporary ills such as economic and environmental uncertainty and drug addiction. Yet, paradoxically, sport is not immune to these and other issues: drug use by competitors is a growing problem; sport is becoming more and more an industry and media 'commodity' and thus losing its spontaneity and human scale; and many groups and individuals lack oppor-

tunities to take part. Similarly, the relation of sport and nation are not clear or fixed: cricket tours to South Africa conflict with government policy, and World Series cricket deprived Australia of many of its leading players. While the Australian Institute of Sport was established in 1980 to nurture sporting excellence, questions continue to be raised about the wisdom of judging prowess only by the highest achievement in major sports, resulting in a more balanced assessment of Australia's Olympic performance.

The role of sport in encouraging health and physical fitness has been a government concern since the 1970s, beginning with a public campaign centred on 'Norm' – a slovenly armchair sports fan who was gradually cajoled out of his chair to rediscover the delights (and merits) of recreational activities such as walking, running, swimming and cycling. Despite a fitness boom – notably in running, aerobics and gym work – in the 1980s, however, by the end of the decade only one-quarter of all Australians were taking adequate exercise. Recognition of the need for adequate recreation and exercise has emphasised problems of access to facilities and has encouraged projects such as the opening up of urban parkland and riverbanks, efforts to preserve wilderness areas for future generations, and greater care in the location and operation of other sporting and recreation resources. An ageing population will require continuing reassessment of these and other issues well into the 21st century.

squash The game of squash originated at Harrow School in about 1890. It is lightning-fast and is played in an enclosed court, using light rackets and a small ball that 'squashes' on impact. Introduced first to Qld in 1919, it remained a minority sport until after World War 2, although national championships had been established in 1931; in the postwar years thousands of courts were established either in their own right or as part of larger complexes. The domination of world competition by Australians > *Heather McKay* and > *Geoff Hunt* boosted the game's popularity in Australia, which now has the highest club and participation level in the world. By the late 1980s there were 150 000 registered players, and many more who play on a casual basis.

squatters This term was originally used in America and Europe to describe poor vagrants settling illegally on empty Crown land. In

Australia, a new class of squatter emerged as population increased, free land grants were abolished and new grazing land was discovered beyond the Nineteen Counties at the same time as demand for raw wool in England increased with the development of mechanised methods of production. Squatters were of every social origin, from ex-convicts to members of the English aristocracy, initially sharing a 'sordid, filthy' life, facing hazards of flood, drought, fire, dingoes and hostile Aborigines. A crude slab hut would be put up by a waterhole, and flocks were tended on free range: many squatters failed; others made fortunes before over-extension and drought led to a slump in the 1840s. Squatters fought for security of tenure, enraged by Sir George Gipps' scheme (1844) requiring a licence at a cost of £10 for a maximum holding of about 32sq.km (capable of holding 4000 sheep or 500 cattle), with optional puchase of the homestead block after five years. In 1847 some security of tenure was given, with longer licence periods and pre-emptive rights to buy; this made possible the setting up of more permanent homesteads. The loss of shepherds to the goldfields stimulated the use of fencing, and better organisation to reduce labour needs encouraged itinerant shearing teams. Political power waned with responsible government in the 1850s, although the 'pure merinos' or squattocracy continued to dominate the upper houses. By employing 'dummies' at land sales, or by bribery, squatters largely succeeded in ensuring the failure of the land Acts, designed to 'unlock the land' after 1860 and put it in the hands of small-scale farmers or selectors. A period of elegant prosperity lasted until the 1890s depression, after which closer settlement was more successful and application of capital allowed crop-growing to be developed alongside grazing. Today the term 'squatter' has largely been replaced by 'pastoralist' or 'grazier' when reference is made to a large landholder. >> *land settlement*

squids > *cephalopods*

St Vincent Gulf SA This is the smaller of the State's two southern inlets and is bounded by the Yorke Peninsula in the west and the coastal lowlands of the Mt Lofty Range in the east; the SA capital, Adelaide, spreads inland from its central eastern shore. St Vincent Gulf is a shallow triangular inlet that extends some 150km north–south, tapering northwards from a width of some 65km. Parts of its low sandy

shores have been developed as ports, most notably Port Adelaide. The gulf was named by Matthew Flinders in 1802, after the British admiral the Earl St Vincent.

stag-beetles > *beetles*

Stampfl, Franz (1914–), athletics coach, b. Austria. A ski instructor and art student, Stampfl first came to Australia as a refugee after having been interned in Britain at the outbreak of World War 2. He returned to Britain after the war and developed a rigorous coaching system, based on interval training designed to push athletes systematically to the peak of their ability; he was closely involved with Roger Bannister's achieving the sub-four-minute mile in 1954. Appointed to Melbourne University in 1955 as Australia's first full-time athletics coach, he developed many fine athletes, including Ron Clarke and Ralph Doubell. Rendered a quadriplegic after a car accident in 1980, Stampfl courageously overcame his injuries to continue coaching.

stamps > *postage stamps*

Standley Chasm NT A spectacular gap in the Macdonnell Ranges, Standley Chasm lies 48km west of Alice Springs. It varies in width from 6m to 9m, and the sheer walls rise to a height of 150m.

starfishes Starfishes or sea-stars, echinoderms of the class Asteroidea, have generally five arms but sometimes more, and they vary in size, form and colour. The arms carry many tube-feet used for travelling and sometimes for feeding – even for opening shells to get food, although in Australia species are not reported to be serious pests of oyster-beds, as occurs in some countries. The tropical > *crown-of-thorns starfish*, however, is a very serious predator of coral in the Great Barrier Reef. Starfishes have considerable ability to regenerate missing parts. One species, *Allostichaster polyplax*, goes so far as to use this faculty for purposes of reproduction: as an eight-armed adult it will divide into two parts, each of which will then grow four new arms.

Brittlestars, of the class Ophiuroidea, have a well-marked, disc-like central body and five long, narrow arms without obvious tube-feet; these creatures are rapid and snake-like in their movements. Habitually found under rocks or at the base of kelp groups, brittlestars with branched arms are sometimes hauled up around deep-sea bait.

starlings > *birds, introduced*

States, origins and boundaries NSW, the oldest Australian colony, reached its maximum size in 1824, growing to 5 446 000sq.km when its western boundary was moved from long. 135°E (where Governor Phillip had established it in 1788) to long. 129°E. (The move was necessary to include within the colony the new settlement at Fort Dundas on Melville Island.) From 1824 to 1915 NSW was made steadily smaller as other settlements established within it became colonies in their own right. Tas. (first known as Van Diemen's Land), discovered by George Bass in 1798 to be an island and first settled by Europeans in 1803, became a separate colony in 1825. As well as the island itself, its territories included all the Bass Strait islands (and briefly, 1844–56, Norfolk Island). WA, the only area of Australia never part of NSW, was constituted a colony in 1829 (though NSW administered the settlement at King George Sound until 1831). WA's eastern boundary abutted NSW at long. 129°E. The province of SA was proclaimed in 1836, when European settlement took place. It was bounded on the north by lat. 26°S and on east and west respectively by long. 141°E and 132°E (thus bordered on three sides by NSW), but in 1861 the western boundary was moved to the WA border. Vic., settled as the Port Phillip District of NSW in 1834–5, became a separate colony in 1851 following considerable agitation for self-government. It was 'bounded on the north and northeast by a straight line drawn from Cape Howe to the nearest source of the River Murray, and thence by the course of that river to the eastern boundary of the Colony of South Australia'. Eight years later, in 1859, the Moreton Bay District, settled by Europeans in 1824, became the colony of Qld. Its southern boundary ran from Point Danger along the McPherson, Dumaresq and Macintyre rivers, and thence along lat. 29°S to the western boundary at long. 141°E, but in 1862 Qld's area was increased by moving the western boundary to long. 138°E as far south as lat. 26°S (the SA northern border). NSW was further diminished in 1863 when the NT came under SA jurisdiction. NT was transferred to Commonwealth control in 1911, and was divided 1926–31 into two parts, North Australia and Central Australia.

It won self-government (but not statehood) in 1978.

On 1 January 1901, with Federation, all six Australian colonies became States. The ACT was established in 1911 on 2360sq.km ceded by NSW, and in 1915 was increased by a further 72sq.km at Jervis Bay.

New States No new States have been created in Australia since Federation, although provision for their establishment is made in sections 121–4 of the Constitution. The difficulties of carving new States from within existing ones are such that no developments seem likely in the foreseeable future, especially since many Australians think the country already has too many governments. From time to time there has, however, been agitation for new States, most recently in 1982 when a movement was launched to establish a State of North Qld. More powerful campaigns include those for the separation from NSW of New England (referendum defeated in 1967) and the Riverina (1920s), and J. D. Lang's 1852 proposal to split Qld into Cooksland (to include parts of NSW), Leichartsland [*sic*] and Flindersland.

Stawell Vic. (pop. 6252) This town lies 233km northwest of Melbourne near the Grampian Range, in the Wimmera region. A former gold-mining town with a population of 30 000 in the 1850s, Stawell is now a farming centre and is noted for the wines of the Great Western vineyards to the southeast and the Easter Gift foot-race (first run in 1878). The town's economy has been boosted in recent years by the re-emergence of commercial gold-mining and the establishment of a hosiery factory; other industries include woollen and timber mills.

Stead, Christina Ellen (1902–83), novelist, b. Sydney. After working as a teacher, Stead left Australia in 1928 and spent most of her life in Europe and the US. Her first collection of short stories, *The Salzburg Tales* (1934), established her literary reputation and her pre-eminence as an experimental, exploratory fiction writer; it was followed by *Seven Poor Men of Sydney* (1935), her only novel set entirely in Australia. Other novels include *Cotters' England* (1966), *The Little Hotel* (1974) and the semi-autobiographical *The Man Who Loved Children* (1940), generally considered to be her masterpiece. Although she immediately won international acclaim Stead was little acknowledged in her homeland until the late 1960s, largely because of her expatriate life; her first formal recognition occurred in 1974, when she won the Patrick White Award for literature.

steel industry > *iron and steel industry*

Stephen, Sir Ninian Martin (1923–), lawyer, b. England. Stephen completed his schooling in Australia and served with the AIF in World War 2. Admitted as solicitor (1949), barrister (1952) and QC (1966), he was appointed to the Supreme Court of Vic. in 1970, the High Court of Australia in 1972 and the Privy Council in 1979, then served as governor-general of Australia 1982–9. He has expressed the opinion – both before and after his vice-regal appointment – that the conventions underlying the Constitution, including the reserve powers of the Crown, should be codified and written into the Constitution.

sterculia family A group of flowering plants allied to the > *mallow family*, the Sterculiaceae consists mainly of trees and shrubs of warmer regions of the world and includes the cacao plant, *Theobroma cacao*. Australia has 22 native genera totalling about 180 species, many of which are endemic. The subfamily Sterculioideae includes the well-known tree genus *Brachychiton*, which has about 30 species scattered through most regions except the southern coast and Tas. and is most diverse in the far north. The kurrajong, *B. populneus*, is a shapely small tree of eastern Australia, the foliage of which is prized for stock fodder. Equally familiar are the flame tree of eastern rainforests, *B. acerifolius*, which produces spectacular coral-red blossom on bare branches, and the Qld bottle tree, *B. rupestris*, endemic to southeastern Qld. The tulip-oak genus *Argyrodendron* includes several tall rainforest trees. The other major subfamily consists of sixteen genera of mainly low, tough-stemmed shrubs which are most diverse in WA and (to a lesser degree) the far inland and monsoonal north. The genus *Commersonia* includes trees and shrubs with colourful flowers, and fibrous bark used as twine by the Aborigines; the largest genus is *Lasiopetalum*, many species of which are endemic to WA.

Stewart, Douglas Alexander (1913–85), editor and poet, b. NZ. Stewart was a prolific but undistinguished poet, his main contribution to Australian letters being as literary editor of the *Bulletin* (1940–61) and as a critic. Public-

ations include *Collected Poems 1936–67* (1967), *Writers of the Bulletin* (1977) and a volume of autobiography, *Springtime in Taranaki* (1983). He was also the author of six verse-dramas of variable quality – including *The Fire on the Snow* (1941), an account of Scott's 1912 Antarctic expedition – and co-editor of three volumes of bush ballads.

Stewart, Harold (Frederick) (1916–), poet, b. Sydney. Variously a journalist, broadcaster and lecturer after World War 2, Steward published his first volume of poetry in 1948 but is perhaps best known for his involvement in the anti-modernist Ern Malley hoax of 1944. From the 1950s his poetry, which has a limited but ardent following, reflected increasingly his interest in Asian subjects, particularly Japan where he has lived since 1965. This association is reflected in his haiku translations *A Chime of Windbells* (1969) and in *By the Old Walls of Kyoto* (1979), a twelve-part poem in which he pays homage to his adopted culture.

stick and leaf insects Plant-feeding, chewing insects of the family Phasmidae, these creatures have elongated bodies that resemble sticks or leaves; in some species the wings are either reduced or totally absent. Phasmids are very slow-moving, and often remain motionless for long periods. The spiny *Acrophylla titan* is Australia's longest insect, some specimens reaching 24cm. There are more than 140 species in all, generally found in eastern coastal forests; their seed-like eggs are dropped singly into the forest litter. Some species periodically swarm in large numbers, causing defoliation in eucalypt forests. The leaf insect, genus *Phyllium*, in Australia is found only in the rainforests of northern Qld, but has close relatives in NG and Southeastern Asia.

stinging trees These trees and shrubs of the genus *Dendrocnide*, in the nettle family, possess sharp-pointed hairs that break off under the skin and inject toxins such as histamine, causing severe pain. There are four species native to Australia, where they are largely confined to eastern coastal rainforests. The gympie or stinging shrub, *D. moroides*, most common in tropical Qld but extending to far northern NSW, grows to 4m; the slightest contact with its large heart-shaped leaves or bristly twigs causes agonising pain. The southernmost species is the giant stinging tree, *D. excelsa*, which can reach 40m and delivers a severe sting. All four species do have their uses, however, the fibrous bark providing fishing nets and lines for the Aborigines and the sweet fruits being edible if the stinging hairs are removed.

stingrays > *rays*

Stirling Range WA Extending some 80km east–west, this range rises abruptly from flat country about 60km north of Albany, on the south coast. Five peaks are above 1000m, the highest being Bluff Knoll (1073m), originally named Mt Rugged by Matthew Flinders in 1802. In 1835 the range was given the name of WA's first governor. Vegetation includes both dense scrub and, particularly on the rocky tops, a remarkable diversity of wildflowers, many of which are endemic to these mountains. The entire range is part of the Stirling Range National Park.

stock market Shares in public companies are bought and sold through an auction system centred on stock exchanges throughout the world. In Australia the system is controlled by the Australian Stock Exchange, which operates trading floors in all State capitals (formerly six separate exchanges, which were amalgamated in 1986). In Australia, as elsewhere, the stock market has long been the prime barometer of the economy and the market 'crashes' of the 1890s, 1930s and 1980s reflect the nation's perilous reliance on both overseas capital and primary-industry exports.

Trade in stocks and shares in the Australian colonies began in the 1840s, the first official stock exchange being established in Melbourne in 1861. Exchanges proliferated throughout the colonies by the end of the 19th century and some existing regional centres (such as Ballarat in Vic. and Newcastle in NSW) date from that period. Traditionally, the system for trading shares in Australia has been the 'open outcry' method, by which all buying and selling is conducted amid the hurly-burly of the trading floor. Australia is at the forefront of the world trend towards electronic stock markets, however, and trading is increasingly being conducted on computer screens.

There are about 1000 companies listed in the Australian stock market and some 115 registered brokers. About one-third of the companies are listed on the second board (for shares in small companies), the main boards being split about equally between mining and industrial stocks. The exchanges, which are owned by the brokers, are self-regulating to the extent that all listed companies must report extensively on their activities or face suspension, and brokers are monitored for ethical standards (such as the practice of 'insider trading') and solvency.

The incidence of direct share ownership by the public in Australia is lower than in most countries, largely due to the volatility of local share prices. Australian shares – especially in mining and oil – have frequently been subject to panic buying and selling, with the result that several crashes have eroded the confidence of investors; the one that did the most damage to confidence was the crash of 1970, because its severity was not shared by the rest of the world. In October 1987 world stock markets crashed in unison, and partly because of a general lack of trust in shares Australia's prices failed to recover fully. Low turnovers also produced a crisis in the stockbroking industry and the closure of many brokers during 1989. >> *business*

stone-fishes Highly poisonous, spined fishes of the family Scorpaenidae, stone-fishes inflict particularly painful stings. Those of the genus *Synanceia* are the most venomous of all fishes. Their sting, which can be fatal, is extraordinarily painful, so that a victim may lose control and risk drowning even in shallow water. Continental stone-fishes occur in estuaries and bays from northern NSW around the coast to northwest WA; reef stone-fishes live in lagoons and flats among reefs and coral rubble. Well camouflaged by their appearance, they lie in wait for prey to swim within reach. A stonefish antivenene has been developed by the Commonwealth Serum Laboratories.

stoneflies Small, elongate, usually darkcoloured insects of the order Plecoptera, stoneflies have a pair of long tail filaments, long antennae and chewing mouth-parts. These insects are rather poor fliers, but often are attracted to lights at night. They are found only near freshwater streams in cool temperate regions; their nymphal stage is aquatic. Australia has about 120 species, and they are particularly diverse in the southeastern highlands and in Tas.

stork > *jabiru*

Storm Bay Tas. This is a wide gulf on the southwest coast of Tas., between North Bruny

Island and the Tasman Peninsula, into which flows the Derwent River; it was named by Abel Tasman in 1642 when a storm prevented his ships from anchoring there. Near the mouth of the Derwent is Betsey Island Nature Reserve, where muttonbirds nest along with colonies of seals and penguins.

Storrier, Tim(othy Austin) (1949–),

painter, b. Sydney. Storrier is a fine and meticulous draughtsman and a discreet colourist, whose coolly elegant paintings and drawings combine symbolic and evocative objects. Stencilled words within a picture are a typical motif. His travels since the early 1970s in Australian country and outback areas (especially the NT and WA) have provided a rich source of subject matter.

Stow, (Julian) Randolph (1935–),

novelist, b. Geraldton, WA. After working as a lay missionary with Aborigines in WA and as an anthropologist in NG, Stow travelled widely, finally settling in the UK in 1966. His two best known novels are *To the Islands* (1958) and *Visitants* (1979), which mix realism with symbolism and display man as both oppressor and victim – a characteristic theme of Stow's work. His other writings include two opera libretti, a highly successful children's novel, *Midnite* (1967), and collections of poetry.

Stradbroke Islands Qld Stradbroke was

a single island until 1892, when during a storm the sea carved a channel to create North and South Stradbroke, lying at the south end of Moreton Bay. Mineral sand extraction is a major industry and several settlements have become holiday resorts. Plans to link the islands to the mainland with a causeway have caused concern about the effects of continued coastal development. There are many Aboriginal sites on the islands, one of which is the 'valley of shells'; the Aboriginal poet Oodgeroo Noonuccal lives on North Stradbroke, where she has established an environmental centre. Jumpinpin, the channel between the islands, is noted for bream fishing.

Strahan Tas. (pop. 516) This small town on

Macquarie Harbour lies 294km northwest of Hobart; it is a former timber-milling town and was at one stage the main port for the Mt Lyell copper mines. Today it handles Queenstown freight but relies mainly on fishing, sawmilling and tourism.

Streaky Bay SA (pop. 992) This small port

lies on a sheltered inlet on the west coast of Eyre Peninsula, 745km northwest of Adelaide. Matthew Flinders discovered the site in 1802 and gave the bay its present name for the discoloured streaking of the water. Noteworthy as the only deepwater port between Spencer Gulf and Albany in WA, Streaky Bay is also known for the seabird colonies on nearby Elba and Pigface islands.

Street family, eminent in Australian law and

politics. **Sir Philip Whistler** (1863–1938), b. Sydney, became a barrister in 1886 and was appointed a Supreme Court judge in 1907; he served as NSW chief justice 1925–33 and as lt-governor from 1930. His eldest son, **Sir Kenneth Whistler** (1890–1972), followed a similar career path. Appointed to the NSW Supreme Court in 1930, he was chief justice from 1950 until his retirement in 1959. His wife **Jessie Mary Grey** (1889–1970), despite a privileged background, was a noted social reformer who campaigned ardently for peace, women's rights and Aboriginal citizenship. A member of the ALP from 1939, she stood twice, unsuccessfully, for federal parliament (1943 and 1946). She was the only female delegate at the UN's founding conference in 1945 and was later a member of its Social and Economic Committee. Their son **Sir Laurence Whistler** (1926–), like his father and grandfather before him, became a barrister (1951), a Supreme Court judge (1965) and then chief justice of the NSW Supreme Court (1974). He played an influential role in the establishment of the Australian Commercial Disputes Centre in Sydney in 1986. **Tony (Anthony Austin)** (1926–), b. Melbourne, the son of Sir Kenneth's cousin Geoffrey, entered federal parliament in 1966. He held various portfolios before his retirement in 1984, most notably those of employment and industrial relations.

Streeton, Sir Arthur Ernest (1867–

1943), painter, b. Mt Duneed, Vic. Having studied at the Vic. National Gallery School, Streeton joined Tom Roberts and Charles Conder in establishing the group of *plein-air* painters that subsequently became known as the Heidelberg School; with Tom Roberts, he was instrumental in winning public and critical acceptance for the portrayal of the Australian landscape. He moved to Sydney in 1890 and continued his atmospheric paintings of local scenery, distinguished by their golden light and blue skies and their evocation of Australian heat and distance. Among the most poetic of his panoramas is *Still Glides the Stream and Shall Forever Glide* (1889) although it was not until much later, with *The Purple Noon's Transparent Might* (1896), that his career in Australia was established. He lived mainly overseas 1898–1923, including a productive period as official war artist during World War 1.

Strickland, Shirley (1925–), athlete, b. Perth. Strickland is Australia's most successful athlete, winning three gold, one silver and three bronze medals in the Olympic Games 1948–56. Brought up on the WA wheatfields, she was encouraged by her family to develop both academic and athletic talents but despite a brilliant junior record did not devote herself seriously to athletics until leaving university. After the 1948 Olympic Games in London she concentrated on the 80m hurdles, winning that event in 1952 and 1956.

strikes > *industrial disputes*

stringybarks > *eucalypts*

stripper harvester Invented in 1843 in SA by John Ridley, an immigrant wheat-grower and miller, this was the first workable mechanical harvester, in which combs stripped the ears and revolving beaters threshed the grain. Although the principle of beating instead of cutting heads of wheat had been previously put forward by John Wrathall Bull, Ridley is believed to have based his invention on an illustration of an ancient Roman harvester. By the 1860s, an estimated 30 000 similar machines were operating throughout Australia.

Strutt, William (1825–1915), painter, b. England. Strutt, a fine draughtsman and classically trained painter, recorded many historic events during the period (1850–62) he spent in Australia – especially in Vic. *Black Thursday*, a dramatic, neo-classical oil painting of the tragic 1851 bushfires in Vic., is his most famous Australian work. After returning to England he continued to paint (mainly religious pictures) and exhibit successfully.

Strzelecki, Sir Paul Edmund de (1797–1873), explorer, b. Poland. Strzelecki arrived in Australia in 1839. His first exploratory journey was into the Blue Mountains, where he discovered gold and reported it to Governor Gipps

(who suppressed the information). In 1840 he traversed the Snowy Mountains, climbing Mt Kosciusko and naming it after a Polish patriot, thence went south into the fertile east of Vic., which he called Gipps Land. After two years of survey in Tas., he returned to England where he wrote the detailed *Physical Description of N.S.W. and Van Diemen's Land*, published in London by public subscription in 1845. He was later knighted for his work during the Irish famine 1846–8.

Stuart, John McDouall (1815–1866), explorer, b. Scotland. Stuart arrived in Australia in 1838. He accompanied Charles Sturt on an expedition 1844–5 to the centre of Australia, and in 1860 he made the first of three attempts to cross the continent but was turned back by illness, hostile Aborigines and failing supplies. Four months after his return he set off again, but was defeated by impenetrable scrub 320km from the Victoria River. On his third and successful journey he reached Daly Waters and the Roper River, but almost died on the hard return journey. Stuart was the first explorer to cross Australia through the centre.

stump-jump plough The 1876 invention in SA of Richard Bower Smith – for which he received £500 from the grateful colonial government – this machine had three mould boards on a weighted, hinged beam that allowed them independently to jump obstacles such as stones or tree-stumps, so eliminating the costly grubbing process. Particularly suited to smaller timber of the mallee country, it was important in developing such areas in SA and Vic. in the 19th century. A modern eight-furrow version is still used in newly cleared mallee regions.

Sturrock, Jock (Alexander) > *sailing and yachting*

Sturt, Charles (1795–1869), explorer, b. India. An army officer and son of a judge, Sturt came to NSW in 1827 and in the same year led his first expedition, which discovered the Darling River. He made the greatest single contribution to Australian exploration when, the following year, he unravelled the mystery of the west-flowing rivers by sailing down the Murrumbidgee in a whaleboat to the mouth of the Murray; the return journey against the current and with little food was an epic feat that temporarily blinded him.

In 1844, having previously settled in Adelaide, he obtained permission to explore the interior – officially to find the main watershed, but in fact motivated mainly by his faith in the existence of a great inland sea. Drought and searing temperatures turned him back, half-blind and sick with scurvy. He had failed to penetrate the Simpson Desert, which lay beyond the stony desert plains between Cooper Creek and the Diamantina, the 'gloomy and burning' desert lands that bear his name. He died in England without political or financial reward of any measure, yet he was perhaps the greatest of the explorers: a humble, intensely humane man of vision, inspiring deep love and loyalty that made his great journeys possible. The earliest of these he recorded in books published in 1833, vividly written and with his own illustrations.

Sturt's desert pea This sprawling plant, *Clianthus formosus* of the legume family, bears one of Australia's most distinctive flowers, which is the floral emblem of SA. Widespread in sandy soils of dry regions from western NSW to WA, the plant has long prostrate branches with clusters of long-stalked flowers, usually crimson or scarlet but sometimes a pale white-pink. The plant was named after Charles Sturt, who collected specimens in 1844, although it was recorded as early as 1699 by William Dampier.

Sturt's Stony Desert SA/Qld This bleak region, about 750km northeast of Adelaide, extends from northeast SA into southwestern Qld. A gibber plain, it is covered with closely packed stones and is thus virtually impassable although its discoverer Charles Sturt traversed the area in 1845.

suckerfishes > *remoras*

sugar industry Australia is one of the world's leading sugar producers and the third-largest exporter (after Cuba and Brazil). Sugar cane is Australia's second most valuable crop: in 1985–6, 3.4 million t of raw sugar were produced, more than three-quarters of which was exported in both raw and refined form at a value of $613.2 million. Sugar cane is grown along the east coast from northern NSW to tropical Qld.

The first sugar was manufactured in NSW in the 1820s but commercial cultivation did not develop until a plantation was established near Brisbane in the 1860s. The industry spread rapidly in the north, initially with the assistance of indentured labour from the Pacific Islands (> *blackbirding*). The Colonial Sugar Refining Company – which, as CSR Ltd, is still Australia's largest sugar refiner – was established in 1853.

The industry, which is regarded as the most efficient and modern of all sugar-producing countries, is highly controlled: the Qld government imposes cane quotas for growers and organises the refining, marketing and exporting of sugar through CSR and Millaquin Sugar Co. Pty Ltd. Some controls on domestic prices are also exercised, through an agreement between the federal and Qld governments. Such controls are deemed necessary because of the world's recent but chronic over-supply of sugar, caused by both a vast surplus of EEC-subsidised beet sugar and falling demand. While Australia experienced a dramatic drop in sugar consumption (of some 4.2kg per head) between 1979 and 1986, Australians nevertheless still consume about 45kg of sugar per head per year, one of the highest rates in the world. While raw sugar is the main product of the industry, there are numerous by-products including molasses and the fibrous residue bagasse, commonly used as a fuel. The notorious > *cane toad,* which is now invading southeastern Australia, was introduced to Qld plantations in the 1930s as a means of controlling pest beetles that were ravaging crops.

Sulman Prize > *art awards*

sulphur There are no known deposits of elemental sulphur (brimstone) in Australia and local demand is met mainly by imports from Canada. Some sulphur is recovered from oil and from sulphur-bearing minerals, however, usually in the form of sulphuric acid. The main local producers are EZ Industries at Risdon, Tas., Broken Hill Associated Smelters at Port Pirie, SA, and the Sulphide Corporation at Cockle Creek, NSW. Four oil companies also have sulphur-recovery units, but the amount recovered has declined as low-sulphur Bass Strait crude has replaced high-sulphur imported oil.

Sumner, John > *theatre*

sunbird On mainland Australia this small, brilliantly-coloured bird, *Cyrtostomus frenatus,* is found only in northern and central Qld and is the sole Australian representative of its family, although its range also includes NG and the surrounding islands. It eats insects and extracts nectar from flowers with its long, curved bill. The male is yellowish-green, with a bright-yellow breast and a blue-marked throat, while the female is yellow on both breast and throat; their nest is constructed to hang below a tree branch or, sometimes, a window-frame or house-beam.

Sunbury Vic. (pop. 15 297) This town 39km northwest of Melbourne, on the route to Bendigo, serves farmlands devoted to agriculture, grazing and dairying. On the banks of Jacksons Creek, it was settled from the 1850s around an inn on the goldfields route, which was named the Sunbury Hotel after the village of Sunbury-on-Thames in England.

sundews These small carnivorous plants form the genus *Drosera*, which occurs world-wide but is centred in southwest WA. All are herbaceous plants that catch small insects and other animals on the sticky tips of their glandular leaf hairs, which then fold around the victim and secrete an enzyme that dissolves the creature and allows it to be digested; by thus supplementing its nutrient supply, the plant can survive in poor soils. Of Australia's 54 *Drosera* species, 40 are endemic to southwest WA; most are small, reddish rosette plants with slender spikes of flowers, some with elongated leafy stems.

Sunraysia Vic. This is the general name for the fruit-growing district centred on > *Mildura* in northern Vic. The name developed from 'Sun-Raysed', a trade name adopted in the 1920s in advertisements by the Australian Dried Fruits Association.

Sunshine Coast Qld This resort region 100–150km north of Brisbane, stretching from Caloundra to Noosa Heads, is the northerly counterpart of the State's Gold Coast. Its main urban centre is Nambour and the hinterland supports agriculture – notably sugar cane and tropical fruits – and dairying. The Sunshine Coast is noted particularly for its scenery, surf beaches and sheltered estuarine waters.

superannuation Superannuation schemes financed jointly by employers and employees have been encouraged by government tax concessions since 1915 and nearly half of the Australian workforce was covered by some such arrangement in 1986. The system was greatly expanded in the late 1980s, owing largely to an ACTU agreement with the federal government that led to a 3% productivity increase, in the form of superannuation payments, being awarded to workers in many industries; many unions established their own industry-based schemes, giving employees portability of benefits between employers for the first time. As a result, by 1988 the number of white- and blue-collar workers in superannuation schemes had increased by 25%; the percentage of part-time and women workers covered by superannuation schemes also increased. While periodic proposals for a national superannuation scheme have never been adopted, the recent extension of existing schemes is viewed by the federal government as a means of ensuring retirement income for Australia's ageing population, which would otherwise be forced to rely principally on pensions and thus put excessive strain on the national purse in the next century.

Supreme Court > *law and legal system*

surf and surfing The Australian coast has many fine beaches on which waves stirred by onshore winds break in lines of surf. The beaches of the southeast that border the Pacific, with its warm summer temperatures, are especially notable, and on one of them, at Manly, NSW, the sport of surf riding (or surfing) was first practised in Australia by Tommy Tanna, a native of the South Sea islands.

Body surfing was followed by surfboard riding, especially after the impressive demonstration of 1915 given by the Hawaiian Olympic swimming gold medallist, Duke Kahanomoku. Early boards were solid, but to allow greater length and scope hollow, plywood boards up to 5m long were developed. Since the mid-1960s these have in turn been replaced by the shorter, lightweight boards made from balsa wood and coated with fibreglass. The surf ski, an Australian variant dating from 1933, is almost a small canoe on which the rider stands, kneels or sits, and uses a paddle; the surf boat, carrying four oarsmen, is some 8m long, slim and very light. The rapid growth in the number of surfers on Australian beaches has caused some controversy owing to the danger they pose to other bathers, and in some places has led to segregation and even banning by local authorities.

Surf-racing championships were held as early as 1914, but in the 1950s the sport was boosted with the introduction of the lighter boards and in the 1960s 'Midget' Farrelly and Nat Young won world titles; it was during the 1964 championship at Manly that international title conditions were laid down. Subsequent Australian champions were Phyllis O'Donnell, Mark Richards, Wayne Bartholomew and Tom Carroll.

Surf lifesaving is a uniquely Australian development, stimulated by the manifest dangers of the waters – including shark attack, although the major hazard in surfing is the rip, an erratically flowing outward current most common at the ends of a short, curved beach and indicated often by flat water and an absence of regular and continuous lines of inflowing breakers. Some early lifesaving methods included ropes and lifebelts placed at intervals, and rescue by horseback or by human chain. In 1906 the Bondi Surf Bathers Life Saving Club was formed, soon to be followed by others that affiliated in 1907 as the NSW Surf Bathers Association, later to become the Surf Life Saving Association of NSW and then of Australia (SLSAA). Club subscriptions and functions support the purchase of equipment, and in recent years there has been some subsidy from government and business. To 1988, 324 960 people had been saved by this organisation, more than the Australian death toll for both world wars.

Surfers Paradise Qld > *Gold Coast*

Sutherland, Dame Joan (1926–), opera singer, b. Sydney. After winning the *Sun* Aria (1949) and Mobil Quest (1950) competitions, Sutherland left for London where she made her Covent Garden debut in *The Magic Flute* in 1952. Immediate acclaim followed, and in 1959 her performance in the title role in *Lucia di Lammermoor* established her as the world's leading coloratura soprano. A spectacular career followed, with Sutherland singing most of the major 'bel canto' roles in the great opera houses of the world. She performed rarely in Australia until the 1970s, but made regular appearances with the Australian Opera 1975–86 when her husband, pianist and conductor Richard Bonynge, was its musical director.

Sutherland, Margaret Ada (1897–1984), composer and pianist, b. Adelaide. After studying music in London and Vienna, Sutherland returned to Australia in 1925 and then worked as a teacher and composer. Her 90 or more

neo-classical compositions frequently drew on Australian themes and included one opera, *The Young Kabbarli* (1965), based on an incident in the life of Daisy Bates. After World War 2 she was a member of the Australian advisory council for UNESCO; later, as a council member of the National Gallery Society of Vic., she was instrumental in the development of the Vic. Arts Centre.

Swain Reefs Qld A system of reefs and cays at the south end of the Great Barrier Reef, Swain Reefs are about 190km from the coast, northeast of Rockhampton. They lie north of the Capricorn Channel, the major southern entrance to the waters within the reef, and have witnessed the wreck of a number of ships including (in 1836) the *Stirling Castle*, aboard which was the remarkable Eliza Fraser.

swallows and martins This group of birds includes many summer migrants or semi-migratory species. They are swift fliers, streamlined with a swept-back wing-position and forked tails; they catch insects on the wing, flying high in fine weather and lower if it is stormy. The swallow's bowl-shaped, mud nest is naturally built in a depression in the earth or in a rock cavity, but some birds have now also adopted the eaves of houses as home sites; others nest in tunnels in the banks of streams or in the hollows of trees. Some of the species seen in many parts of Australia are the welcome swallow, *Hirundo neoxena*, which has a bright rust flash on the head and breast upon trim brown-and-white plumage; the white-backed swallow, *Cheramoeca leucosterna*, which nests in burrows; the fairy martin, or bottle or cliff swallow, *Hylochelidon ariel*, which makes a carefully lined, bottle-shaped mud house; and the tree martin, *H. nigricans*, one of those nesting in tree-hollows or other cavities.

swamphens > *rails and crakes*

swan, black *Cygnus atratus* is the only Australian swan and the world's only black swan; early explorers were amazed by the bird, as to them a black swan was a contradiction in terms. First seen by Willem de Vlamingh on the Swan River in 1697, black swans can be found in suitable habitats across Australia, except in the far north. They give trumpet-like calls as they move in pairs or small flocks to fresh feeding-grounds, often at dusk or by moonlight; they feed upon waterplants. The nest is a large open structure on a platform of sticks or reeds, usually built on a tussock, mound or islet in a swamp. The black swan has been the symbol of WA from the time of its use on pre-Federation postage stamps until today.

Swan Hill Vic. (pop. 8831) The city of Swan Hill lies on the Murray River, at the east end of the Mallee region, 336km northwest of Melbourne; it is the commercial and market centre for an extensive region including the surrounding irrigated lands and the southern Riverina in NSW. The site was named by the explorer Thomas Mitchell in 1836 and grew as a river crossing and port in the paddle-steamer days; a moored steamer is now a museum and art gallery.

Swan River WA The city of Perth and its port of Fremantle are situated on this river, which in fact is the western course of the Avon River – the two sections being discovered independently and their common identity realised in 1834. The linking section lies in the gorges and rapids of the Darling Range, to the east of which the Avon River rises. On the coastal plains above Perth there is intensive cultivation of orchards and vineyards. Passing through Perth, the river widens to two shallow tidal basins, Perth and Melville Waters, and is joined by the Canning River. The estuary narrows in its last few kilometres through the coastal limestones to enter the Indian Ocean through Inner Harbour, at Fremantle. The Swan was discovered in 1697 by Willem de Vlamingh, and explored by James Stirling in 1827.

sweetlips This name is applied to tropical fish of several species, remarkable for their greatly thickened lips. They are deep-bodied and many are extremely ornate and diversely patterned, and can reach a considerable size. Colourful species of the genus *Plectorhynchus* include *P. goldmanni*, frequenting mangrove regions and estuaries, *P. flavimaculatus*, known as morwong, and *P. chaetodontoides*, called the harlequin.

swifts There are two species of swifts known in Australia: fork-tailed and spine-tailed. They are summer migrants from Asia, and may be seen endlessly on the wing by day – high in the air in fine weather, and low before a storm – or clinging to a cliff-face near a mud-and-saliva nest from the darkening to first light. They are generally brown-and-white, and share with swallows and martins the mode of insect-catching and the characteristic streamlined flight posture, with swept-back wings; they fly very fast, some species probably well over 160kmh. The swifts, however, have structural differences: perhaps the most obvious is that all four of a swift's toes point forwards, so that it cannot grasp a twig or wire to perch as other birds do.

swimming and diving In accordance with prevailing morality, swimming in Sydney Harbour was banned entirely in 1810, while from 1833 it was forbidden between 6 a.m. and 8 p.m. Despite these restrictions it was a popular recreation and enclosed baths were opened at the Sydney Domain in 1829, where the first swimming championships were held in 1846. However, it was not until the end of the century that swimming began to emerge from the limitations imposed on it: in 1879 the prominent English swimmer and coach Frederick Cavill came to Australia, and under his influence (and that of his sons) swimming acquired respectability. The Balmain club was formed in 1884 and the NSW Amateur Swimming Association in 1892; by the turn of the century swimming was an organised recreation in all the colonies, and was revolutionised by Alick Wickham, who introduced the crawl stroke he had learned in the Pacific islands.

In early Olympic and international competition, Freddy Lane, Barney Kieran, > *Frank Beaurepaire*, > *Fanny Durack* and Annette Kellerman all experienced success. Between the wars > *Boy Charlton* became a national hero, holding world records and winning a gold medal in the 1500m at Paris in 1924; and Claire Dennis was only 15 when she won the 200m breaststroke at Los Angeles in 1932. In 1952, John Davies won the men's event over the same distance at Helsinki, but Australia was to assume complete dominance of world swimming during the mid-1950s when a crop of naturally talented young swimmers was nurtured by an equally talented and innovative group of coaches that included Harry Gallagher and Frank Guthrie. Their goal was the Melbourne Olympic Games in 1956. The high expectations were fulfilled as Australian swimmers won eight of fourteen possible gold medals; > *Dawn Fraser*, Murray Rose, Lorraine Crapp, Jon Henricks and David Thiele were the toast of the nation. This momentum was maintained in 1960 and 1964 with further gold medals, confirming Australia's status as a nation of leading swimmers.

From that point Australia began to lag, as nations with better facilities and co-ordinated training programs began to move ahead, although gold-medal performances were recorded in 1968 by Lyn McClements and Michael Wenden, and in 1972 by Brad Cooper, Shane Gould, Gail Neal and Beverley Whitfield. The nadir was reached in 1976, when no Australian competitor achieved a first place. Australia has won medals at each of the Games since, and with the guidance of the Australian Institute of Sport seems to be achieving results in keeping with its population. Michelle Ford and the men's 4x100m medley were successful in 1980, Jon Sieben in 1984, and Duncan Armstrong (in a memorable victory in the men's 200m freestyle) in 1988. World-record holders of the period include Tracey Wickham, Karen Moras and Steven Holland.

Diving has never been a mass sport in Australia, although there are 1500 registered participants. Dick Eve won the gold medal in the high dive at Paris in 1924, and is Australia's sole Olympic medallist in that field.

swordfishes and marlins There are many species of these large, carnivorous sea-fish of the families Xiphiidae and Istiophoridae, and at least six are found in Australian waters. The strong sword, an elongated upper jaw that has been known to penetrate the timbers of ships, may be used in defence against predators such as sharks and also for speed in swimming, but it is not essential for the procuring of the fish's usual prey. Many of this group also have long, triangular fins well forward on the back, reminiscent of those of certain sharks. The broadbill swordfish of tropical waters, *Xiphias estara* or *X. gladius*, has a long, flattened sword and reaches a length of 1–2m; the tropical sail-fish, *Istiophorus ludibundus*, which can be 3m long, is related to the marlins and is named from the very large, spreading front fin on its back.

Marlins have a circular sword and a triangular fin grading into a long low one along the back; they include the black marlin, *Istiompax australis*, which may reach 4.5m and weigh 550kg, and the striped marlin, *Marlina audax zelandica*, which like the former is common seasonally; it has quite distinct, vertical bands interspersed with thin, light stripes. Marlins of the eastern Australian coast attract sport fishermen from around the world.

Sydney NSW Capital of NSW and Australia's largest city, Sydney is also the commercial, industrial and tourism capital of Australia. It is the most intensively developed of the capitals (owing largely to its splendid harbourside location) and faces grave transport and pollution problems. Because of the extremely high cost of housing in Sydney, many would-be purchasers are being forced to the city's fringes, or out of it altogether. Bounded by the Tasman Sea in the east, the Hawkesbury River in the north, the Blue Mountains in the west and the Southern Tablelands in the south, Sydney has little or no scope for further extensive development. The climate is temperate, with mean temperatures ranging from 12.6°C to 21°C, and an average annual rainfall of 1194mm, fairly evenly distributed over the year.

Sydney derives its name from Thomas Townshend, 1st Viscount Sydney, the British home secretary at the time the original settlement was founded, although it was never officially named. Arthur Phillip established the first British colony in Australia there in 1788, and the Aboriginal population (about 3000 in number) was quickly dispersed. From the 1830s the population grew rapidly and the settlement spread, although from the gold rushes of the 1850s Melbourne eclipsed Sydney in size and until the 1890s was Australia's largest city. The population initially fanned out along the railway lines as they were constructed, and from the 1880s spread also along tramlines. Following the influx of immigrants after World War 2, however, car ownership became almost universal and the spread of suburbs was no longer dependent on public transport.

At the census of 1986 the Sydney Statistical Division had a population of 3 364 858, which showed a growth rate of 5% over the five years between censuses. The greater part of this population is still housed in free-standing or semi-detached buildings, but more than 25% of Sydney's dwellings are now in units, most of them high-rise, and given that Sydney is fast running out of building space this proportion seems likely to increase. More immediately, however, little growth seems probable because of the high cost of housing. Because Sydney is the commercial capital of Australia, a large proportion of the population is engaged in administration in both the public and private sectors. Manufacturing remains important, with Sydney producing about 25% of Australia's secondary output, but it employs only about 17% of the city's workforce. Sydney's transport problems are acute, with roads clogged at every peak hour by the ever-growing number of those who prefer to commute by car, and these problems are reflected in the city's housing problems, with those on higher incomes moving to the inner suburbs to reduce driving time. This has forced the lower-paid workers and the unemployed to move to the city's fringes. In recent years State governments have been criticised for the development of the Circular Quay and Rocks area and Darling Harbour, when the money might better have been spent on public housing; it is argued on the other hand that these developments promote tourism, a major source of income for the city. Pollution arising from motor transport, manufacturing, and Sydney's antiquated sewerage system, also presents daunting problems.

Sydney Harbour Bridge The great arching edifice that links Sydney's city centre with the northern shore of Sydney Harbour was built 1923–32 and when completed was the largest single-arch bridge in the world. The central span is 503m long (the bridge itself being more than twice this length) and its crown some 135m above sea-level; the bridge decking is 49m wide and carries an eight-lane road, dual railway tracks, and pedestrian and bicycle paths. Various schemes to link northern Sydney to its southern and eastern suburbs were proposed from the 19th century; from 1912 the engineer > *John Jacob Crew Bradfield* recommended a cantilever bridge and construction by the successful tenderer, the English firm Dorman Long & Co., commenced in 1923; the cost of construction was £9.5 million. At the opening ceremony on 19 March 1932, by NSW premier Jack Lang, the tape was unofficially cut by a member of the right-wing New Guard, which was vehemently opposed to Lang's Labor administration. The bridge is still the city's prime commuter artery but ever-increasing traffic congestion has led to plans for an underwater tunnel to provide an alternative route across the harbour.

Sydney Opera House This splendid winged folly at Bennelong Point on the shores of Sydney Harbour was opened in 1973. Since that time it has vied with the Sydney Harbour Bridge as the city's most spectacular landmark, although its opera acoustics remain the subject of controversy. An opera house for Sydney was first proposed by Sir Eugene Goossens in the 1940s and a competition for its design was won by the Danish architect > *Joern Utzon* in 1957. Construction progressed in three stages, but Utzon's intricate design was greatly modified as the impracticality of its detailing became apparent and costs soared. Utzon resigned in acrimonious circumstances in 1966 and the design work was completed by local architect Peter Hall; the eventual cost of the project was $100 million, much of which was provided by the longstanding Opera House lottery. The complex comprises a major concert hall (seating 2700 and originally intended for opera), a smaller opera hall, and a number of other theatres, auditoriums and restaurants.

Syme family, influential proprietors of the Melbourne *Age* newspaper 1856–1983. **Ebenezer** (1826–60), b. Scotland, arrived in Vic. in 1853, joined the *Age* in 1854 and became its owner two years later. His brother **David** (1827–1908), b. Scotland, arrived in Vic. in 1852 and joined the *Age* in 1856. He succeeded his brother as proprietor in 1860 and built the *Age* into a vigorous, influential paper that espoused tariff protection and campaigned on many public issues including corruption; circulation reached 100 000 by the 1880s. Three of Syme's sons, (**John**) **Herbert** (1859-1939), **Geoffrey** (1873–1942) and **Oswald Julian** (1878–1967), all b. Melbourne, were successive chairmen of the family trust that controlled the *Age* until a public company, David Syme & Co., was formed in 1948. The family retained control and Herbert's son **Hugh** (1903–65) was general manager of the *Age* 1946–63. (**Kathleen**) **Alice** (1896–1977), b. Melbourne, was the daughter of David Syme's third son Arthur. An *Age* journalist 1923–43 and director 1948–71, she was active in public life and instrumental in the establishment of Women's College at Melbourne University. Oswald's grandson (**Chesborough**) **Ranald Macdonald** (1938–), b. Melbourne, led the company from 1964 until it was taken over by John Fairfax and Sons in 1983.

T

tailorbirds The small, grass-frequenting tailor-bird of the genus *Cisticola* derives its name from a remarkable ability to stitch growing green leaves and grass into the body of its nest, using fibre, spider-webbing or hair as 'thread'. It is the male that constructs the nest frame-work, while the female finishes the nest, broods the eggs and feeds the nestlings. Both male and female are buff-coloured with black mottling, although at breeding-time the male develops a golden cap. The only widely distributed species in Australia is *C. exilis*, of which considerable numbers abound in swampy areas along the eastern coast, a few reaching to Tas. *C. juncidis* is found in small groups in north Qld and NT.

taipan > *snakes*

Tait family, theatrical and concert entre-preneurs of long standing. **Charles** (1870–1933), b. Castlemaine, Vic., worked as an office boy at Allan's Music Warehouse in Melbourne and was a director by the age of 26. Although he remained with Allan's all his life, he was instrumental in the establishment of a concert bureau by his younger brothers **John Henry** (1871–1955) and **(James) Nevin** (1876–1961), both also b. Castlemaine. The two brothers arranged gramophone concerts and film show-ings, produced one of the world's first feature films – *The Story of the Kelly Gang* – in 1905, and in 1908 constituted their company as J. & N. Tait. Another brother, **E.J. (Edward Joseph)** (1878–1947) joined entrepreneur J. C. Williamson Ltd as assistant treasurer in 1900 and later became general manager, but resigned in 1916 to join J. & N. Tait. In 1920 the company merged with J. C. Williamson and henceforth – often dubbed 'the Firm' – domi-nated the staging of live theatre, opera, ballet and concerts until the 1960s. The company also established 3LO, Melbourne's second radio station. The youngest brother, **Sir Frank Samuel**

(1883–1965), b. Melbourne, joined J. & N. Tait at the age of about 20 and was a brilliant entrepreneur. He staged Joan Sutherland's first Australian performance, in *Lucia di Lammermoor*, a week before his death.

tallow-wood > *eucalypts*

Tamar River Tas. A tidal river formed by the confluence at Launceston of the North Esk and South Esk, the Tamar flows about 60km northwest to Bass Strait through Port Dalrymple, which was discovered and named by Matthew Flinders and George Bass in 1798. The Tamar takes its name from the river in southwest England; it is flanked by productive farm-ing and fruit-growing land, and the main settlements, just below Port Dalrymple, are Beaconsfield, George Town and Bell Bay, an industrial port.

Tamborine Mountain Qld This is a plateau in the Darlington Range, which branches north from the McPherson Range and reaches a height of about 550m; it is about 45km from the coast and covers an area 11km by 5km; some resi-dents commute to metropolitan Brisbane. Before being worked by timber-getters it was a region of rainforest; it now supports mixed farming but includes several small national parks that preserve remaining areas of forest. Part of the mountain was Qld's first national park, declared in 1908. The name is from an Aboriginal word, *dumberin*, meaning 'place on cliff of yams'.

Tambo River Vic. This Gippsland river rises in the Bowen Mountains – steep, forested high-lands northeast of Omeo. It flows southwards for 100km through alluvial pastures and farm-land, to form a finger-like delta in Lake King, the easternmost of the Gippsland Lakes. The river's name is from an Aboriginal word meaning 'fish'.

Tamworth NSW (pop. 30 729) The inland city of Tamworth lies 453km northwest of Sydney, on the Peel River in the New England district. It is noted both as a major transport junction and as Australia's 'country-music capital'. The city serves a rich, mixed-farming region and is the market outlet and processing centre for local produce ranging from wool, wheat and livestock to dairy products, eggs and tobacco; it also accommodates engineering and a range of manufacturing industries. Its educational and cultural facilities include an agricultural high school and a fine art gallery; the Australian Country Music Festival has been held annually at Tamworth since 1973 and attracts thousands of visitors. The area was settled by squatters from 1830 and was the headquarters of the Australian Agricultural Co. by 1841.

Tanami Desert NT This remote and extensive desert lies in the centre of the NT, west of Tennant Creek. It is composed of sand dunes in the north, and sandy plains further south which are punctuated by isolated rocky hills including the > *Granites*. It is inhospitable terrain that accommodates well-adapted mammals, such as the desert bandicoot, as well as a plethora of birds and reptiles. Much of the region is reserved as the Tanami Desert Wildlife Sanctuary, which is controlled by the local Aboriginal population.

Tangney, Dame Dorothy Margaret (1911–85), politician, b. Perth. A teacher by profession, Tangney was elected a Labor member of the Senate in 1943, the first woman to become a senator. Active in the federal executive of the Labor Party and on numerous Senate committees, she served with distinction in both capacities until her retirement in 1968. She was made a DBE in the same year.

tapestry and weaving > *craft*

tapeworms > *helminths*

Taree NSW (pop. 15 994) On the Manning River about 337km north of Sydney, Taree is a growing centre for the mid-north coast. It was settled in 1854 by Henry Flett as a private town and port, in the latter role partly displacing the nearby government town of Wingham. Local industries include the processing of dairy products and timber, boat construction, and engineering works. Tourism is also important, based on the park-lined river, nearby coastal resorts, and forested hinterland.

tariffs Although tariffs were originally introduced in Australia simply to raise revenue, their main purpose now is to protect local manufacturers from competing goods made overseas. Protectionism through tariffs has long been controversial in Australia, seen by many as providing inappropriate shelter for inefficient industries.

The debate over free trade versus protection was an intercolonial issue for many years. After Federation, however, the imposition of tariffs to protect Australian manufacturing industries from overseas competition became accepted policy and there were large increases in tariffs before and after World War 1. In 1921 a Tariff Board was established to make recommendations on tariff levels, and in 1927 the government appointed the Brigden committee to report on the overall effect of such taxes. Despite the committee's advice that high tariffs encouraged high wages and therefore excessive immigration, the ensuing depression and trade deficits 1929–31 led to substantial tariff increases; further increases were introduced in 1936, principally to discriminate against imports from Japan and the US.

In 1973 the Whitlam government reduced all tariffs by 25% and replaced the Tariff Board with the > *Industries Assistance Commission* (IAC), giving the new body wider powers; it also introduced legislation that made it impossible to alter tariffs without detailed reports from the IAC on the industries concerned. In the 1980s, influenced by the international trend towards lower tariffs, the federal government began to lower tariffs in a number of industries traditionally afforded substantial protection. >> *economy*; *manufacturing industries*; *trade*

Tasman, Abel Janszoon (?1603–1659), explorer, b. Holland. The Dutch East India Company despatched Tasman with two ships – the *Heemskerck* and the *Zeehan* – in August 1642, with eighteen months' provisions and instructions to make full exploration of the great south land. On this voyage he discovered Tas., naming it Van Diemen's Land. In 1644 he made a further voyage along the north coast of Australia, proving that the regions previously discovered in the north and the west were part of one landmass. His unfavourable reports helped to quench the Dutch hopes of wealth through trade in the south, and they lost interest.

Tasmania (Tas.) The smallest Australian State in terms of both area and population, and the second to be colonised by the British, Tas. is also notable as the nation's only island State and incorporates all the islands of Bass Strait. With chronic economic problems Tas. has, more than any other State, been embroiled in environmental debates: opposition on environmental grounds to proposals for further hydro-electric schemes, wood extraction from the native forests and the construction of a pulp mill on the northwest coast have divided the State politically between developers and conservationists for more than two decades.

With an area of 68 300sq.km (0.88% of Australia's total) and a coastline of 3200km, the mainland of Tas. consists principally of highlands. In the west the ranges rise to more than 1500m, while in the northeast the mountain mass of Ben Lomond reaches 1573m; in between is the central plateau, studded with lakes and drained by the Derwent River system, rising at Mt Ossa to 1617m. The eastern plateau averages 350–400m, while the midlands, drained by the South Esk river system, constitute the only major inland plain. The rainfall is heavy by Australian standards, decreasing from more than 2500mm in the west to less than 500mm in parts of the east; Tas. is unique among Australian States in that agriculture is confined to the drier regions. Mean summer temperatures in the north are around 18°C, while mean winter temperatures at all coastal points range from 8°C to 9°C. The main urban centres are > *Hobart* (the capital), > *Launceston*, Burnie, Devonport, Ulverstone and New Norfolk.

Historical development In Tas. the original population of full-blood Aborigines died out in the wake of European settlement (although their descendants still preserve an Aboriginal identity). This occurred partly as a result of violent conflicts between the colonisers and the Aborigines, but was completed when in the 1820s surviving tribespeople were isolated on Flinders Island and subsequently died. The initially separate settlements on the Derwent (1803) and the Tamar (1804) were united in 1825 when the colony was separated from NSW. Rapid land development took place, based on cheap convict labour, but Tas. experienced the worst of the degradations and brutalities of transportation and suffered from many bushranger escapees. Transportation ended in 1853, and this was followed by responsible government in 1856. By this time the gold rushes in Vic. were leading to an exodus from

Tas., resulting in a severe depression until the discovery of silver, gold and tin in the 1870s led to a period of stability and agricultural expansion. The economic depression of the 1890s was severe in Tas., and many left the colony; the position was improved by the development of apple-growing, following the introduction of refrigerated shipping and, from 1897, by the mining of copper at Mt Lyell. Federation was supported in Tas. as a solution to economic troubles, but at first resulted in cheap Vic. goods ruining local industry. The interwar years again were a period of stagnation and emigration, but in the 1930s the growing hydro-electric system led to some industry being attracted by cheap energy. The wood-based industries in Tas. have become increasingly important in recent years, but so has tourism – and the two are to some extent incompatible.

Population and economy The population of Tas. at the 1986 census was 436 353, which showed a growth rate of only 0.02% over the five years between censuses, similar to those of Vic. and SA and well below those of the other States. About 45% live in the southeastern coastal region around Hobart and New Norfolk, with 47% in the northern coastlands around Burnie, Launceston and Devonport; only about 6% are found in the agricultural midlands, and 2% on the west coast, mainly around Queenstown.

Because of its rugged terrain, 62% of Tas. is Crown land and only 30% is used for agriculture, although the latter employs some 7% of the population, a higher proportion than elsewhere. Products include wool and fat lambs, beef, dairy goods, vegetables, apples, hops and opium poppies (for pharmaceutical use), but timber-based primary and secondary industries yield 30% of the State's income. In the secondary sector, an electrolytic zinc plant at Risdon, an aluminium smelter and a manganese alloy plant at Bell Bay near Launceston, and a titanium pigment plant near Burnie – all based on cheap hydro-electric energy – supply 25% of Tas.'s exports. Food-processing accounts for some 25% of the manufacturing sector, and in the tertiary sector tourism, based partly on unspoiled scenic regions and partly on two casinos and associated attractions, is of growing importance.

Government and politics Until recently, development was a policy common to all Tas. political parties – at least from 1887 when a political party (Liberal) first held office. The

Labor Party, which governed briefly in 1909 and again 1914–16, was concerned more with government aid to development than with confrontation; its long period in office 1934–69 demonstrated that in this respect it had the support of its constituency. Since Federation, Tas. has always been a recipient of financial grants from the Commonwealth which exceed the revenue raised from the State in the form of taxation, and especially from the 1930s much of this money has been spent on hydro-electric development. Until the 1970s this policy remained largely unquestioned, but in that decade a proposal to increase the cheap energy available by building a dam that would flood the scenic > *Franklin River* aroused widespread opposition in Tas. and elsewhere. The issue split the State Labor Party, and when the federal Labor government successfully blocked the construction of the dam (also opposed by the federal Liberal Party) there were political repercussions in Tas. Under the Liberal government led to power by > *Robin Gray* in 1982, the clearing of native forests for the wood industry also became highly controversial and in the State election of 1989 independent 'green' candidates won a balance of power in the house of assembly; the minority Labor government of Michael Field was able to hold office only so long as it retained conservationist support.

Tasmanian devil

Tasmanian devil This powerfully built, black-and-white carnivorous marsupial, *Sarcophilus harrisii,* is found only in Tas. Fossil evidence, however, indicates that it was formerly widespread on the mainland, becoming extinct there in relatively recent times. It is thickset, coarse-furred, and measures some 30cm at shoulder-height, females being somewhat smaller than males. The forelegs are longer than the hindlegs, and the tail – rather less than a third of the animal's length – is covered with long hair that may fluff out if the devil becomes agitated. Although able to climb, it is mainly a ground-dweller and often nests in hollow logs. It feeds on carrion, small birds and animals and at times can be serious pest of poultry. The devil is common in Tas., and has become something of a State mascot.

Tasmanian tiger

Tasmanian tiger > *thylacine*

Tasman Peninsula

Tasman Peninsula Tas. The entire Tasman Peninsula, which lies in southeast Tas. and is bounded by Storm Bay and the Tasman Sea, is registered as part of the national estate. Generally wooded and hilly, the deeply indented coast exhibits much fine scenery; at Cape Pillar and Cape Raoul perpendicular columns of dolerite rise from the sea, there are several blowholes, and near Eaglehawk Neck is an extensive formation of regular blocks of rock known as the Tessellated Pavements. Best known of the small settlements, and of greatest historical interest, is > *Port Arthur*, a penal station 1830–77 and now a State reserve. The peninsula was named after Abel Tasman.

taxation At the time of Federation three-quarters of Australia's government revenue came from customs and excise duties, with little in the way of income taxes. Today the situation is reversed, 80% of tax revenue coming from individuals and most of that deriving from instalments taken out of salaries and wages through the modern system of Pay As You Earn (PAYE). The Australian tax system is the most highly centralised in the world: the federal government collects about 80% of all taxes, State governments 16% and local governments about 4%. The other unique features of the system are that there are no broadly based consumption taxes such as the Value Added Tax (VAT) in the UK, no death duties (since their abolition in the 1970s) and no general taxes on capital or wealth. Only recently has the federal government begun taxing capital gains on a systematic basis.

Historical development After 1901, all duties became exclusive to the federal government instead of being levied directly by the States. During the first ten years of the Commonwealth, the Constitution required at least three-quarters of this money to be paid to the States. By World War 1, however, the needs of public finance and the war effort prompted first the States and then the Commonwealth to concentrate much more on individual and company income taxes. The States were collecting nearly three-quarters of all income taxes by the start of World War 2, with the result that the taxation system was quite unco-ordinated apart from certain joint collection arrangements introduced in 1923. This situation became untenable after the outbreak of World War 2, when the Commonwealth had to finance its second huge war effort on a tax base that was limited by the widely differing State rates; legislation for a 'uniform taxation' system was accordingly introduced in 1942, which gave the federal government an effective monopoly over all income taxes. It imposed tax rates that were so high that they squeezed the States out, and then provided for tax reimbursement grants to the States with the proviso that they refrained from levying income taxes.

As a result of the 1942 legislation, as well as of new tax-sharing arrangements passed in 1976 and several High Court decisions excluding the States from levying sales taxes, the States have been denied access to the important direct and indirect sources of revenue available to states in most other federations. In 1971 the federal government transferred payroll taxes to the States to even up the imbalance between the two levels of government; the other main State taxes now are stamp duties, motor taxes, business franchise taxes, liquor taxes, gambling taxes, land tax, and levies on statutory corporations. The great majority of federal-government revenue comes from individual and company income taxes, minor amounts being raised from customs and excise duties and sales taxes. Local government taxes are mainly in the form of rates and other charges on residents.

During the 1970s Australian revenue from income tax was seriously eroded by a wave of tax-avoidance arrangements known as 'bottom-of-the-harbour' schemes, which were legitimised by lenient rulings from the High Court. The schemes were worked by taxpayers building up substantial cash reserves in a company that owed substantial tax, and then selling the company to an accountant or a lawyer for a price usually about 10% less than the cash reserves. The accountant or lawyer controlling the scheme would then take out the cash and send the company to 'the bottom of the harbour', usually by selling it to other companies with fictitious addresses so they could not be traced, or to bankrupts who could not meet the tax liability. A legislative crackdown in the early 1980s put an end to the practice, and further enforcement actions (both legislative and administrative) after 1984 removed virtually all opportunities for tax avoidance.

The 1980s and beyond These measures, plus the operation of 'fiscal drag' (whereby inflation takes wages into higher tax brackets and so keeps tax revenue higher than inflation) allowed the federal government to introduce significant tax cuts between 1987 and 1989.

In July 1985 the federal government convened a 'tax summit' – a meeting of representatives of governments, trade unions, business, and consumer and welfare organisations to discuss tax reform. It was in fact an attempt to shift the system away from direct taxation to a consumption tax, but little was achieved. The benefits of less tax avoidance and the effect of wage increases moving more salaries into high tax brackets have made the introduction of a broad consumption tax unnecessary; the idea has remained the subject of debate, however, because the preference of Australians for spending rather than saving tends to inhibit economic development. As a tax on spending is regarded by many economists as a desirable way of encouraging citizens to save, this option remains the most likely major tax reform of the 1990s.
>> *economy*; *federalism*

Taylor, Florence Mary (1879–1969), architect and engineer, b. England. Born Florence Parsons, she immigrated to Australia in 1883 and worked for a Sydney architect. She married inventor and journalist George Augustine Taylor in 1907 and with him founded several engineering and construction journals which she edited for 33 years. Australia's first female architect and engineer, Taylor was also an active town planner and a leading feminist; an indefatigable worker, she was an honorary member of various trade associations. The Florence Taylor Award, for outstanding services to engineering, is awarded in her honour.

Taylor, Sir Patrick Gordon (1896–1966), aviator, b. Sydney. After serving with the Royal Flying Corps in World War 1, Taylor teamed up with Charles Kingsford Smith and was a pilot with the first Australian National Airways (ANA). In 1936, while flying with Kingsford Smith across the Tasman from NZ in the *Southern Cross*, Taylor performed the feat of transferring oil from a dead starboard engine to an overheating port engine by crawling back and forth along the plane's wing. The plane thus reached Sydney and Taylor was awarded the British Empire Gallantry Medal (later George Cross). A long career in aviation followed, which included important survey flights in the Pacific, Atlantic and South America.

Taylor, Thomas Griffith (1881–1963), geographer and explorer, b. England. Arriving in Australia in 1893, Taylor was to become one of the most dynamic and controversial scientific writers. Trained in science and mining, he developed interests in meteorology, anthropology and, above all, physiography, and was a member of Scott's Antarctic expedition 1910–13. As professor of geography in Sydney (1921–9), Chicago (1929–35) and Toronto (1935–50), he wrote and taught provocatively and widely, notably on Australia; he founded the Geographical Society of NSW in 1928, and in 1959 was foundation president of the Institute of Australian Geographers.

tea Although Australians are avid tea-drinkers – consistently consuming an average of 1.5kg per head each year – commercial tea-growing has taken place only since 1970. Tea plants were brought to Australia in the late 19th century, but large-scale production dates from the 1960s, when the Nerada Tea Estate was established near Innisfail in northeast Qld. The industry, although small, is highly mechanised and leaf yields are among the highest in the world; with two new plantations established in the late 1980s, annual production was expected to reach 1 million kg by 1990.

teals > *ducks*

teatrees > *myrtle family*

technical and further education (TAFE) > *education*

technology > *biotechnology; communications technology; science and technology*

tektites > *meteorites*

telecommunications > *communications technology; post and telecommunications*

television > *broadcasting; media ownership and control*

Tench, Watkin (1758–1833), author, b. England. Tench was a marine captain-lieutenant with the First Fleet, remaining in NSW until 1792. He is best known for his keenly observed and well-written accounts of the first years of the colony, having undertaken several exploratory journeys which included the tracing of the Nepean-Hawkesbury river system. Tench later also wrote about France, when living there as a prisoner of war.

Tennant, Kylie (1912–88), novelist, b. Sydney. Attempting numerous occupations from barmaid to lecturer, Tennant often researched her novels by working among the people she portrayed. Best known for *The Battlers* (1941),

a novel about immigrant workers after the 1930s depression, and *Ride on Stranger* (1943), a semi-autobiographical novel, Tennant also wrote plays, children's books and much non-fiction, including a biography of H. V. Evatt, *Evatt: Politics and Justice* (1970). She was a fluent and witty writer who, although sympathetic to the left and writing mainly about the fringe-dwellers of society, avoided polemics and overtly political statement.

Tennant Creek NT (pop. 3503) This remote mining town 1026km south of Darwin owes its settlement to the construction of the Overland Telegraph station from 1872. It developed particularly with the discovery of gold in 1934 and copper in 1955; the gold, copper and silver from its three nearby mines dominate the NT's mineral output.

tennis Tennis was first played in Australia at the Melbourne Cricket Club in 1878. Men's and women's championships were held in the 1880s and the Lawn Tennis Association of Australasia organised the inaugural national championships in 1905.

Australasia (Australia and NZ) first entered the Davis Cup competition (founded in 1900) in 1905, and achieved its first victory in 1907 under > *Norman Brookes*, dominating the competition from then until 1923. Australia did not achieve its first victory as a separate entity until 1939, when John Bromwich and Adrian Quist defeated the US. Under the captaincy of > *Harry Hopman*, Australia again dominated the competition in the 1950s and 1960s, with memorable performances by > *Frank Sedgman*, Ken McGregor, > *Lew Hoad* and > *Ken Rosewall*. In 1986 Australia won the Cup for the 26th time (including the Australasian victories) when Pat Cash led a fighting victory over Sweden at Kooyong in Melbourne. It was a Davis Cup tie against the US that produced the record attendance figure of 25 578 at White City, Sydney, in 1954. The Federation Cup was first contested in 1963, since when Australia has won it seven times, with > *Margaret Court* dominating her matches. She is Australia's greatest woman player, winning a record eleven Australian Opens, three Wimbledon titles and the Grand Slam in 1970.

Australia has produced many Wimbledon champions. Norman Brookes, Jack Crawford, Frank Sedgman, Lew Hoad, Neale Fraser, Ashley Cooper, Roy Emerson, > *Rod Laver* and Pat Cash have achieved this honour; > *Ken*

Rosewall, in the course of an outstanding career, won all other major titles, but Wimbledon eluded him. >*Evonne Cawley* won the Wimbledon women's title in 1971 and 1980.

In 1988 the Australian Open was moved to a permanent venue at the newly constructed National Tennis Centre in Melbourne, which meant that for the first time it was not played on the traditional grass surface. Courts of a variety of surfaces, however, are widely distributed across the country to cater for the 550 000 Australians who are registered tennis players.

teraglin An excellent eating fish from the eastern coast of Australia, the teraglin, of the family Sciaenidae, is related to the mulloway. It grows to 1.3m, weighing some 9kg, and the lips and gill covers are yellow. Although it is of commercial importance little is known of its habits.

Terminalia This genus of trees belongs to the chiefly tropical family Combretaceae. Australia has about 30 native species, most endemic and only a few reaching south of the Tropic of Capricorn; in northern monsoonal forests they may form a major component of the vegetation. The fruits of some species are edible and are significant Aboriginal foods: the concentration of vitamin C in the wild plum or murunga, *T. ferdinandiana* of NT and WA, is one of the highest ever recorded.

termites These colonial and wood-eating insects of the order Isoptera are popularly called 'white ants' – a term best avoided, since they are unrelated to ants. The winged form has a long, slender body and two pairs of long, soft, transparent and gauzy wings, easily broken off. Colonies are usually originated by winged adults. They move in large numbers but are not strong fliers; after a comparatively short flight they settle, the wings are shed and they pair; having selected and excavated (in soil or wood crevice) a place for colonisation, mating takes place, and with the development of the first larvae into workers the colony grows apace.

Within each colony there is specialisation, and a distinct caste structure. The queen, often with an abdomen so swollen that she cannot move, may go on producing eggs for many years; the soldier termites have long, dark heads and formidable jaws and are sterile and blind, as are the workers, but the latters' development is specialised to obtain food by digest-

ing plant matter with the aid of protozoa, the enzymes of which are essential for the assimilation of cellulose by the insects. Termites are subterranean, working away from direct contact with the outside world. They often construct large nests, or termitariums, of earth cemented with saliva; in the NT, the north–south aligned termitariums of the magnetic termite, *Amitermes meridionalis*, serve to minimise the heat of the summer sun.

Australia has a very rich termite fauna, embracing more than 250 species; among them is *Mastotermes*, the world's most primitive known specimen, in many ways resembling the cockroach. Some termites are serious pests of structural timber, annually causing damage costing millions of dollars; however, in arid regions they are vital in the breakdown of dead plant matter, helping to recycle nutrients and themselves providing food for a variety of birds and mammals.

terns > *sea-birds*

tertiary industries > *service industries*

theatre While it was not until the 1960s that a national drama started to surface in Australia, theatre and theatre-going have long been an integral part of Australian life.
Historical development The tradition dates back to the early days of the colony when, on 4 June 1789, George Farquhar's *The Recruiting Officer* was performed by a convict cast before an audience of 60 including Governor Phillip. Six years later a former convict, Robert Sidaway, opened Australia's first theatre in Sydney; Restoration comedies were staged there until it was closed two years later, on Governor Hunter's orders, because too many robberies occurred on theatre nights. Professional theatre in Sydney dates from 1832 when Barnett Levey began performing in the saloon of the Royal Hotel. In Melbourne the first theatre, the wooden Pavilion, opened for business in 1842; in Tas. the first production took place in 1833, and Adelaide's in 1838; WA had a theatre in 1839, but Brisbane not until 1850.

A boom in theatre production followed the gold rushes – so much so that by 1860 the actor-manager George Coppin had opened six theatres in Melbourne including the Olympic (1855), better known as the Iron Pot because its metal structure was prefabricated in England. On the Vic. goldfields, performances were given of Peking and Cantonese opera by visiting troupes from China, chiefly for the benefit of the large Chinese population. In the large provincial centres and in the capital cities, vaudeville, burlesque and pantomime held sway. Later in the century the popular forms were domestic farce and sensation melodrama, with their stock casts of bushrangers, gold-diggers, gullible 'new chums' and sturdy heroines.

The first play written out of a direct experience of Australian life was probably *The Bushrangers*, by Scottish journalist David Burns, presented in Edinburgh in 1829. Early playwrights who explored Australian themes in Australian settings included Charles Harpur; the convict Edward Geogheghan, author of *The Currency Lass* (1844); and later George Cooper, best known for his *Colonial Experience* (1869). Regulations which put the licensing of plays by local authors in the hands of the colonial secretary tended to discourage plays with an Australian setting, however, particularly if they were in any way critical of the administration. As a result, most of the plays presented at this time tended to be either pale imitations of English comedies or, if set specifically in Australia, light and thoroughly innocuous entertainments. Experience showed that Australian audiences warmed to plays on local themes and subjects, but commercial managements, including J. C. Williamson, were more interested in filling their theatres with tried and tested plays from abroad or with Gilbert and Sullivan operas, often with imported stars.

The first serious attempt to create a realistic national drama occurred in 1911 – when the wells of melodrama were beginning to dry up – with Louis Esson's *Three Short Plays*. Where popular successes such as Bert Bailey's 1912 adaptation of the Steele Rudd pastoral classic *On Our Selection* relied on comic stereotypes, Esson and >*Vance Palmer* brought to their work with the Pioneer Players in Melbourne 1922–6 a seriousness of social purpose. This company was a conscious attempt to create the Australian equivalent of the Ireland's nationalist Abbey Theatre; it was also a reaction against the theatre of the day which, Esson declared, was marked by bad taste and mediocrity. In the wake of World War 1 the climate was inhospitable for pioneering playwrights, particularly those working in small makeshift halls and with limited resources, and the Pioneer Players came to an early end. In the 1930s the birth of radio gave a boost to local playwriting, encouraging experimentation and good craftsmanship. The theatre of the day remained solidly commercial, however, with promotion of the local product being left to the small repertory theatres such as the Independent in Sydney and the Little (later St Martin's) in Melbourne, and the left-leaning, politically committed New Theatre movement which was formed on a national basis during the 1950s.

The Independent (founded in 1930) was the creation of Doris Fitton, who championed the work of local writers including > *Sumner Locke Elliott*. The breakthrough came with his comedy of army life, *Rusty Bugles* (1948), originally staged at the Independent, and with > *Ray Lawler*'s now-classic study of cane-cutters and crumbling illusions, *Summer of the Seventeenth Doll* (1955). Both were vernacular plays with Australian characters and settings, and appealed greatly to Australian audiences. 'The Doll' (as it was commonly known) was also staged in London and New York by the Australian Elizabethan Theatre Trust, and did much to renew interest in indigenous Australian drama. It was the first Australian play to be presented by the Union Theatre Repertory Company (now the Melbourne Theatre Company). Founded by John Sumner in 1953 at Melbourne University, this was the first fully professional theatre company to be established in Australia: Sumner left it in the hands of Ray Lawler and then Wal Cherry until 1959 but then took over again and ran the company until his retirement in 1987, during which time the company's annual audience had grown to more than 350 000. The Old Tote Theatre Company (now defunct) followed in Sydney in 1963, the State Theatre Company of SA in 1965, and further professional theatre companies were formed in the other State capitals. Sydney also had the Ensemble, a harbourside theatre founded in the early 1960s by American-born Hayes Gordon and initially influential in that city's theatrical life. The creation of the Australian Council for the Arts (now the Australia Council) in 1968 put professional non-commercial theatre on a sound footing for the first time. Initially the council provided core funding for one major company in each capital city, but this was later expanded to include alternative theatre companies and, from the late 1970s, regional or community theatre companies. The council has also provided grants for individual writers, and most of the major writers of the last fifteen years have been among its beneficiaries. Its influence in fostering the writing and production of Australian plays has been enormous.

The 1960s saw an accelerating interest in Australian drama. Experimental seasons were held under the auspices of the National Institute for Dramatic Art (NIDA) at the tiny Jane Street Theatre in Sydney; further impetus was provided by the huge success of the historical cartoon drama, *The Legend of King O'Malley* (1970) by Bob Ellis and Michael Boddy. The upshot was the creation of two alternative theatre companies – the Nimrod in Sydney and the Australian Performing Company (APG) in Melbourne – both of them dedicated to the creation and production of Australian work and to the search for an indigenous playing style. The APG began at the tiny 50-seat La Mama coffee-house theatre in 1967, which in its early days was closely associated with the work of > *Jack Hibberd*, John Romeril and > *David Williamson*. The group later moved to the larger Pram Factory theatre, opening there with *Marvellous Melbourne* in 1970. Nine days earlier the Nimrod Street Theatre, a former stables in Darlinghurst, had opened its doors with *Biggles* by Michael Boddy, Ron Blair, Marcus Cooney and cast. The APG occupied the Pram Factory until 1981, when the building was demolished and the company went into liquidation. The Nimrod Street company moved to new quarters in 1974 – a converted tomato-sauce factory in Surry Hills, now known as the Belvoir Street Theatre – and then to the larger Seymour Centre (near the University of Sydney) in the early 1980s. The change from a predominantly Australian repertoire to a classics theatre company failed to win back audiences, however, and the Nimrod was officially wound up in 1988. While the Nimrod and the AGP reflected the differences in character of Sydney and Melbourne in their performance styles, and the AGP was more radical, both were united in their commitment to Australian writing. They also shared a playing style that was fast-paced, improvisatory and comic, with a basis in the pantomime, revue and vaudeville traditions of the past. The writers most closely associated with the Nimrod included Ron Blair, Alex Buzo and David Williamson; at the directorial level, the two most influential figures were John Bell and Richard Wherrett. The writers most closely identified with the AGP, apart from Hibberd and John Romeril, were Tim Robertson and Barry Oakley.

Contemporary theatre In the field of Australian drama, the APG and the Nimrod were the pacesetters. Their commitment to Australian plays was echoed by the various State theatre companies and even more by some of the alternative theatre companies which began to spring up in the mid-1970s. Australian drama is firmly established as a result, with a third or more of the plays presented by the funded companies now being Australian in origin. The end of the 1970s saw the beginnings of a new community theatre movement which sought to create works with particular interest and relevance to their local audiences. This period was also remarkable for the number of plays by women entering the repertoire, where hitherto Australian drama had been strongly masculine in orientation. Black theatre, which had a fitful history in the 1970s, came into its own in the 1980s with the production in Perth of the three plays that make up *The First Born* trilogy of Aboriginal playwright Jack Davis. The 1980s also saw the re-emergence in Australian drama of > *Patrick White*.

In recent years the commercial theatre in Australia has declined in importance, although big imported musicals still draw huge audiences. The Tait organisation and Garnet Carroll, who were active in the postwar period, have given way to a newer and younger breed of entrepreneurs including > *Michael Edgley* and Melbourne-based Cliff Hocking, whose interests range across the theatre spectrum. The tradition of entertainers such as > *Roy Rene* ('Mo') and George Wallace, capable of drawing large and appreciative audiences, has been followed in recent times by > *Robyn Archer*, Reg Livermore, Max Gillies and above all comedian > *Barry Humphries*, who has long been a household name in Britain as well as in Australia. There is also a great deal of activity on the comedy and cabaret circuit, which is throwing up its own team of satirists. The centre of attention for most regular theatre-goers remains the subsidised companies, however, most of which have a firm subscriber base and play to large and appreciative audiences – the Melbourne Theatre Company and the Sydney Theatre Company especially. David Williamson remains by far the best known and most popular Australian playwright, with fourteen major plays to his name since 1970, all of them box-office successes at home and most of them performed abroad as well.

Theodore, Edward Granville (1884–1950), politician, b. Adelaide. A former miner and trade unionist, as premier of Qld 1919–25 Theodore introduced far-reaching socialist legislation including abolition of the legislative

council in 1922. As a member of the federal parliament from 1927, he rose to the treasury under Scullin (1929–31); his attempt to introduce radical cures for the ills of the depression partially led to Labor's defeat in 1931. Meanwhile, a charge of fraud in relation to a mining sale in 1919 caused his resignation, but he was cleared and reinstated. Later he established successful business enterprises, including gold development in Fiji, and returned to fill a major wartime government post 1941–5.

Therry, John Joseph (1790–1864), Catholic priest, b. Ireland. Therry was one of the first two Catholic priests in the infant NSW colony, arriving in 1820. He was a man of vision who worked untiringly in the face of considerable restrictions and opposition. He established the first Catholic church (later St Mary's Cathedral) in Sydney in 1829, and was instrumental in achieving equal status for non-Anglican churches by the 1830s. He later served in Hobart and Melbourne before returning to Balmain in 1856. In directing the construction of churches in Sydney in the 1820s and 1830s he was noted for his passion for painted Gothic windows.

Thiele, Colin Milbon (1920–   ), children's author and playwright, b. Eudunda, SA. A distinguished teacher and education administrator, Thiele published the first of his seven poetry volumes in 1945 after war service with the RAAF. He is the author of more than 50 books including non-fiction, short stories and novels, but has achieved greatest prominence with his fiction for children: this includes the classic *Storm Boy* (1963), *Blue Fin* (1969), *The Fire in the Stone* (1973), and *The Valley Between* (1981), the last being named the 1981 Australian Children's Book of the Year.

Thomas family, pre-eminent in SA newspaper publishing. **Robert** (1782–1860), b. Wales, published the *South Australian Gazette and Colonial Register* in London in 1836. He subsequently immigrated to Adelaide, turning the *Register* into a weekly from 1838. He antagonised Governor Gawler by criticising his Aboriginal policy in 1839 and withdrawal of government advertising from the paper forced a transfer of ownership. His second son **William Kyffin** (1821–78), b. England, arrived in Australia with his father and joined the paper soon afterwards. He acquired an interest in the *Register* under its new ownership syndicate in the 1850s. William's sons **Sir Robert**

Kyffin (1851–1910) and **Evan Kyffin** (1866–1935), both b. Adelaide, maintained the family's involvement in the *Register*, the latter becoming its proprietor in 1899 and later chairman of Register Newspapers Ltd. His son **Archer Kyffin** (1906–78), b. Adelaide, worked on several Adelaide papers before joining the Melbourne *Herald* in 1933. He was editor of the *Herald* 1945–56 and chairman of the Herald & Weekly Times group from 1965 until his death.

Thompson, Jack (John Payne) (1940–   ), actor, b. Sydney. After various jobs including a period in the army, Thompson entered acting through television, notably in the series 'Spyforce' (1970–2). One of the major actors in the 1970s revival of the Australian film industry, Thompson added his forceful presence to such films as *Sunday Too Far Away* (1975), *Caddie* (1976), *The Chant of Jimmie Blacksmith* (1978) and *Breaker Morant* (1980), in which he gave what is perhaps his best performance to date. He is currently working mainly in international television productions.

Thomson, Peter (1929–   ), golfer, b. Melbourne. Thomson won his first club championship at 15 and the Vic. amateur title in 1948, when only 19. Turning professional in 1950, he won the first of three Australian Open championships in 1951 and was five times winner of the British Open, 1954–65. He rarely played in the US. Thomson and Kel Nagle won the Canada Cup (now known as the World Cup) in 1954 and 1959, and also in 1959 Thomson became the first Australian to play five successive rounds below 70. He won his last Australian Open in 1972.

threadfins These are mainly estuarine, tropical fishes, of the family Polynemidae, in which the lower rays of the fins below the gills are separated as thread-like feelers used for finding food in muddy waters. Threadfins are fished in NT and Qld, both commercially and for sport, but rarely appear in more southerly waters. Some species attain a length of 1.8m.

Threlkeld, Lancelot (1788–1859), missionary, b. England. Threlkeld arrived in Australia in 1817. In the service of the London Missionary Society, he administered a mission for Aborigines near Lake Macquarie in NSW 1826–8 and although dismissed because of disagreements over his expenditure he continued his work there until 1841. He published several books recording his study of the Aboriginal language of the region.

thrips Of the small, generally elongate insects of the order Thysanoptera, the 12mm brown-black, native giant thrips, *Idolothrips marginata*, is the largest known; it normally lives under eucalypt bark or leaf litter. Thrips' mouth-parts are adapted to pierce and suck; their distinctive wings, when present, are narrow and fringed with long hairs. Larval forms generally resemble wingless adults. Most thrips suck plant juices, some prey on other small insects and others feed on filaments and spores of fungi; some species abound particularly in flowers. Periodically large numbers of the endemic *Thrips imaginis* can cause much damage to apple and pear crops, and the cosmopolitan *T. tabaci* is a common pest of onions, tobacco and cotton.

thrushes > *birds, introduced*

Thunderbolt, Captain [Frederick Ward] (1835–70), bushranger, b. Windsor, NSW. Ward was twice gaoled for horse-theft. On the second occasion, 1863, he swam ashore from Cockatoo Island in Sydney Harbour; he became a 'gentle-man' robber, noted for his courtesy, fast horses and highway robbery from Maitland to the New England plateau, until he was eventually cornered and shot.

Thursday Island A small island just over 3sq.km in area, on which a central hill of 115m rises from the coastal plain, this is the administrative and commercial centre of the > *Torres Strait Islands*. For many years it was well known as a centre for pearl and trochus-shell fishing, and there is a Japanese cemetery on the island containing the graves of 19th-century pearlfishers; this activity has declined, but some production of cultured pearls has been developed and there is a freezing plant that processes fish and other marine products. The island is also a base for the pilots who take ships through the hazardous waters of the strait. It is thought that the Kala Aborigines inhabited the area before European settlement.

thylacine The extermination of the Tas. tiger, *Thylacinus cynocephalus*, is perhaps the saddest episode of Australian wildlife history. The tiger was the largest predatory marsupial at the time of European settlement, and in fact bore a strong resemblance to the placental wolf; the stripes over its rear haunch led to its being called a tiger. It resembled a wolf in its adaptation as a running carnivore, and undoubtedly ran down and killed kangaroos and wallabies using its powerful, wide-gaping jaws.

That the thylacine was once widespread on the Australian mainland is evidenced by fossil remains, some as recent as 4500 years ago, but it appears to have become extinct probably as a result of competition with the dingo. Since the dingo never reached Tas., the tiger survived there until the arrival of white settlers; then sheep became its easy prey, and this led to the imposition of a bounty on the thylacine as early as 1830.

It is possible that in addition to persecution the populations were hit by an epidemic, which hastened the decline of the species; the last known individual died in the Hobart Zoo in 1936, three months after the thylacine was granted full protection by Tas. law. The species is now almost certainly extinct, although claims of sightings or tracks still are made from time to time and carefully investigated; so far, all have proved incorrect or inconclusive. Some people hope that populations may yet exist in the wild northwest of Tas., although such wet country would be at best only a marginal habitat for the thylacine, which preferred the open eucalypt woodlands of the central regions – the very land favoured by graziers. In recognition of the unique animal and its peculiarly Tas. association, a pair of thylacines appear on the State coat-of-arms.

Tichborne case This was a famous legal case (1871–4), in which Arthur Orton, a Londoner who had settled in Wagga Wagga, NSW, as a butcher, laid claim to the inheritance of the aristocratic Tichborne family in England. He convinced many people that he was Sir Roger Tichborne, including the dowager, his alleged mother, but was convicted of perjury. Released in 1884, he died in poverty in 1898.

ticket of leave This was a certificate entitling a convict whose sentence had been remitted or reduced to work for wages. The system was instituted by Governor Phillip after 1790, abolished by Governor Macquarie (largely because of the leniency with which the system was administered), but reintroduced by Governor Brisbane. The regulations governing the system were enshrined in legislation in 1832, but their stringency encouraged the alternative practice of conditional pardons and tickets of leave had generally been abandoned by the 1850s.

ticks and mites Ticks and mites are arachnids, but are distinct from spiders in having only a single apparent body segment. They are blood-feeding ectoparasites of terrestrial vertebrates, and are usually host-specific. Since many are vectors of pathogens and some inject paralysing toxins, they are of considerable medical and veterinary concern. Most species wait on vegetation for passing hosts, which they recognise by body heat and carbon dioxide; after engorging with blood, often becoming several times their normal body size, they drop off. Australia has about 75 species of ticks, in two families.

The soft-bodied ticks, which constitute the family Argasidae, have leathery cuticles and are mostly associated with birds and bats, although one species is found on kangaroos; the fowl tick, an introduced species, is a vector of avian spirochaetosis. The hard-bodied ticks, family Ixodidae, are flattened and have a hard dorsal shield; this family includes many pest species, one of which, the introduced cattle tick, *Boophilus microplus,* causes irritation, weight loss and fever among cattle in northern Australia. Border inspection has prevented its spread to southern States, but it is of major concern to the cattle industry. The Australian paralysis tick, *Ixodes holocyclus*, occurs along the eastern coast and is especially abundant in spring or early summer. Although its normal host is the bandicoot it also attaches to stock, domestic pets and humans, and the toxin it injects can cause motor paralysis and even death, although a counteracting serum is available.

Although some 2000 species of mites have been recorded from Australia, there are considerably more still to be described. Mites show an extraordinary diversity, and include species that have become adapted to almost every conceivable terrestrial habitat. Although many are found in soil and on plants, others lodge in such specialised niches as the tracheae (air-tubes) of grasshoppers or the cloacae of turtles. Many mites, especially in their immature stages, attach themselves to flying insects as a means of transportation to other sites. Mites of the genus *Demodex* cause mange in domestic animals and poutry, and there are also several important agricultural pests, notably the red spider mite. Of the important pest species directly affecting humans, *Sarcoptes* burrows into the skin, causing scabies, and *Trombicula*, in NG, transmits scrub typhus. A number of species also can cause mild dermatits.

tiger cats > *native and tiger cats*

tiger shark > *sharks*

tiger snake > *snakes*

Tillyard, Robin (Robert) John (1881–1937), entomologist, b. England. After teaching at Sydney Grammar School Tillyard obtained higher degrees at Sydney University, where he eventually taught 1917–20. Appointed head of the department of biology at the Cawthron Institute in NZ, he worked on biological control of insect pests and is best known for the introduction of a small wasp to control woolly aphis. He was chief Commonwealth entomologist 1928–34 at the CSIR; he published numerous books and papers, especially on his favourite subjects, dragonflies and lacewings, and on the rich fossil-insect faunas discovered in Australia. His book *Insects of Australia and New Zealand* (1926) was long considered a standard reference.

timber industry > *forests and forestry*

tin Australia produces about 9000t of tin in concentrates a year, 5% of the world production. Tas. is the main producer, the Renison Bell mine being the largest underground tin mine in the world. In recent years tin prices have dropped sharply, and many smaller mines have either closed or been placed on a care-and-maintenance basis. Australia is a member of the International Tin Agreement, an organisation of consuming and producing countries aimed at balancing production and demand, and of the Association of Tin Producing Countries (established in 1983).

Titterton, Sir Ernest William (1916–), nuclear scientist, b. England. A key figure in the development of the atomic bomb by the US and Britain, Titterton was appointed professor of nuclear physics at the Australian National University (ANU) in 1951, after which he became deeply involved in Australia's defence and atomic energy policy; he monitored the British atom-bomb tests in Australia in 1952. He was research director at the school of physical sciences at the ANU 1968–73, and published numerous papers on nuclear physics, atomic energy and electronics. He was knighted in 1970.

toadoes > *porcupine fishes and toadoes*

toads > *cane toad*; *frogs and toads*

toadstools > *fungi*

tobacco Australia's first plantings of tobacco were made in NSW in about 1818, but the industry only flourished later in the century when cultivation spread to areas with more suitable climatic and soil conditions. Today the principal growing areas are around Mareeba-Dimbulah in tropical north Qld, and around Myrtleford in temperate central Vic. The annual yield supplies about half of the requirements of local manufacturers; the rest is imported, mainly from the US. Both the area under cultivation and annual production have been declining in recent years, some 14 500t of dried leaf being produced in 1980–1 compared with a figure of 10 700t in 1985–6. The anti-smoking movement has made some inroads on tobacco consumption in Australia in recent years. As taxes on tobacco are a major source of income for both the federal and State governments, however, the imposition of further restrictions on the industry remains a vexed political question.

Todd River NT Flowing only after heavy rains, this river rises in the Macdonnell Ranges and flows through Alice Springs before vanishing in the Simpson Desert, near the SA border; with its tributaries it has cut deep gorges through ridges in the Macdonnells, notably Simpsons Gap. Each year Alice Springs witnesses a remarkable event – an annual 'boat' race, the Henley-on-Todd Regatta, in which competitors run along the river bed carrying their (bottomless) boats.

Toowoomba Qld (pop. 71 362) This inland 'garden city' is situated 130km west of Brisbane, in a gap in the Main Range near the Darling Downs, for which it is the commercial, industrial and service centre. Its industries depend on the region's primary products and include dairy foods, bacon, flour, food-processing, saw-milling, tanning and agricultural engineering. Settlement dates from the late 1840s, the marshy land then known as 'The Swamp'; the city's present name derives from the original homestead of Thomas Alford, the one of earliest settlers. The town developed apace from the 1860s, with a number of factories – including the State's first brewery – being established at the same time. The city has two art galleries, several schools and the Darling Downs Institute of Advanced Education.

Torrens family, prominent in the settlement and politics of SA. **Colonel Robert** (1780–1864), b. Ireland, was a prolific writer on political economy who had an abiding interest in the settlement of both Australia and NZ. As chairman of the SA Colonisation Commission from 1835, he worked tirelessly to establish the new colony but was dismissed in 1841 for breaking the rule against its members investing in land in SA. Although he never in fact visited SA, his role in its foundation is commemorated in Lake and River Torrens. His son **Sir Robert Richard** (1814–84), b. Ireland, was appointed collector of customs in SA in 1840. Despite a stormy career marked by administrative misdemeanours, he prospered financially and became colonial treasurer and registrar-general in 1851. He was elected to the first SA parliament in 1857, principally because of his support for reform in the area of land ownership; his brief term as premier in that year ensured passage of a bill that became law in 1858 as the Real Property Act. He resigned from parliament to become first registrar-general under the Act, which although bitterly opposed by both the legal profession and the judiciary was highly successful in SA and was adopted throughout Australia by the 1870s. >> *land ownership*

Torrens River SA From the Mt Lofty Ranges near Mt Pleasant, the Torrens flows for 65km to St Vincent Gulf. The hill-gorge section has been dammed to provide part of Adelaide's water supply, and within the city construction of a weir has created a long, still stretch of water, the original marshland mouth of the river being diverted to an artificial outlet near Henley Bench. Its existence as a water supply and proximity to a natural harbour were major factors in William Light's selection of the site of Adelaide. Light named the river after Colonel Robert Torrens, chairman of the SA Colonisation Commission.

Torrens system > *land ownership*

Torres Strait Islands This archipelago of numerous islands is situated in the Torres Strait, which lies between Cape York Peninsula and NG. In form they range from the mountainous Western Islands – which are in fact a continuation of the mainland's Great Dividing Range – to the low coral cays of the central region, the volcanic outcroppings of the east, and the low alluvial islands that lie close to NG in the north. The islands and their surrounding sea were named in honour of the Portuguese navigator Luis Vaez de Torres, who discovered the strait in 1606. The commercial and administrative centre for the region is > *Thursday Island*.

Torres Strait Islanders are of Melanesian origin, with some Asian, Polynesian and European elements. Their traditional culture and society has some affinities with that of Australian Aborigines, principally in its totemic clan base and harvesting economy, although some land cultivation was practised. In the mid-19th century, the islands' extensive beds of pearl shell attracted fishermen from many countries and a pearling station was established in 1868. This industry, together with fishing, underpinned the economy of the islands until the mid-20th century when the declining world market for pearl shell deprived many islanders of their livelihood. Mass emigration to Australia began in the 1960s, and within 20 years about half of the original islands population had re-located in Qld. For statistical purposes, Torres Strait Islanders in Australia have generally been treated with Australian Aborigines, which makes precise population figures difficult, but the resident population was estimated to be about 21 500 in the late 1980s.

In 1879 the islands were proclaimed a part of the colony of Qld; most of the inhabitants remained on the islands and many were employed in the pearling industry. Under the provisions of 1897 legislation, reserves were created and the freedom of inhabitants restricted; following a strike by the island workforce in 1936, some independence was granted. Subsequent attempts to alter the boundary between Australia and NG – mainly to appropriate rights over the region's marine resources – were resisted by Torres Strait Islanders and since the 1970s there has been increasing pressure for islanders to acquire freehold title to island land and to achieve political autonomy.

tortoises > *turtles and tortoises*

tourism In Australia, as elsewhere in the world, tourism is a rapidly expanding industry. The estimated revenue from domestic and overseas tourists in 1986–7 was $22 300 million and the industry created direct and indirect employment for 405 000 people (equivalent to the figure for the textiles, clothing, footwear and motor-vehicle industries combined). Tourism in Australia, by both local and overseas travellers, is promoted by the Australian Tourist Com-

mission (established in 1967 and now trading as Tourism Australia).

Domestic tourism – once largely confined to day trips and beach holidays – is the most valuable element of the industry and the number of trips taken by Australians each year nearly doubled between the early 1970s and the mid-1980s. This resulted not only from higher personal incomes, widespread car ownership and longer holidays, but also from the fact that Australians have become more aware and more appreciative of their country's natural assets. The most favoured destinations are coastal and inland features from the islands of the Great Barrier Reef to Ayers Rock in the NT; the cities of Sydney and Canberra are also popular attractions.

In 1988, for the first time, Australia became a net 'importer' of tourists, receiving 2.25 million international visitors with only 1.7 million short-term overseas trips being made by Australians in the same period. Of foreign tourists, NZ provided the largest share (18%), followed by Japan at 14% although arrivals from Japan were up 63% and overtook arrivals from the US for the first time. This dramatic rise in the number of overseas tourists can be attributed principally to Australia's bicentennial celebrations and Expo 88 in Brisbane, and the average annual increase over the next decade is expected to remain stable at about 7%.

Australia's recent 'tourist boom' initially engendered great optimism for the industry. By the end of the 1980s, however, figures had slumped and both government and the industry were more realistic in their appraisal of tourism's potential contribution to the national economy. Most countries have enjoyed a tourist boom in the last five years: Australia's annual intake of foreign tourists is tiny when compared with that of, for example, Spain (54 170 700 tourists in 1988), and about equal to that experienced by Venice in one month during the summer season. While the current increase from a low base is spectacular, Australia continues to suffer from being far from major world population centres, from having a limited range of natural and historical attractions, from lacking the cultural variety of other countries, and from the expense of internal travel. At the same time, the relative absence of foreign tourists in Australia makes it attractive to visitors, particularly those accustomed to the congestion of European cities at the height of the tourist season; it also possesses an equable climate, relatively unpolluted beaches (at least when compared with the Mediterranean) and a friendly population, and is economically and politically stable. The main problems facing tourism in Australia in the immediate future are the shortage of high-quality accommodation and service outside main centres, and a lack of efficiency, training and forward planning in certain sectors of the industry. It is also of concern that the world trend towards developing tourist attractions such as 'theme parks' and 'arts and crafts' centres encourages sub-standard representations, and that large numbers of visitors can cause substantial damage to valued natural and cultural features.

town planning > *architecture*; *housing*; *urban planning*

Townsville Qld (pop. 96 230) Lying at the mouth of the Ross River about 1370km north of Brisbane, Townsville is the largest city in Australia's tropics and a main port and administrative centre for northern Qld. It fronts Cleveland Bay and is dominated by 290m high Castle Hill, which overlooks Magnetic Island. Townsville is the export point for lead, zinc, copper and nickel, beef, sugar and wool produced in the extensive hinterland; the artificial harbour was constructed in the late 19th century and was further expanded in the 1980s to accommodate the area's substantial fishing fleet. Industries include the processing of meat and seafood, engineering works and mineral refineries; Townsville is also an important defence centre, with the army's Lavarack Barracks and the RAAF base at Garbutt. The city is an international centre for marine research through the Australian Institute of Marine Science and the Great Barrier Reef Marine Park Authority; it has the world's largest coral-reef aquarium, at Great Barrier Reef Wonderland. James Cook University was established from a former university college, in 1971. Townsville was founded in 1864 by John Melton Black, who was commissioned by Brisbane merchant Robert Towns to find a port for the pastoralists of northern Qld.

trade Australia's unique combination of immense natural resources and small population has always made trade the backbone of the economy, even though its great distance from the world's main manufacturing centres has meant high freight costs. While trade has historically represented a high proportion of the country's gross product, it has invariably involved the exchange of raw materials for finished products (even for food, in the early days). Despite the ready availability of raw materials, manufacturers have usually found the domestic market too small to allow them to operate efficiently: goods from Europe, the US and (more recently) Asia have always been cheaper than those produced in Australia because of the economies of scale available overseas. For the first 100 years of settlement, a typical trade transaction was a shipment of wool to Britain and a return consignment of woollen suits; in Australia's second century a typical export has been iron ore shipped to Japan, subsequently returning as part of an imported Japanese motor car.

Such specialisation has been double-edged: on the one hand, it has meant otherwise unattainable prosperity and access to a very broad range of finished goods from around the world; on the other hand it has made Australia extremely vulnerable to cycles in commodity prices and – because of the relatively low intensity of employment in primary industries – has contributed to the persistent unemployment that has marked much of Australia's history.

Historical development In the 19th century, trade developed quickly in Australia because of the rapid expansion in manufacturing that accompanied the industrial revolution in Britain and Europe. In the second half of the century, exports and imports together accounted for about half of the gross national product; virtually all finished goods came from overseas, mainly from Europe. Australia's most important export, at that time and right up to the 1970s, was wool. Whaling was also very important in the early 19th century, and wheat and meat have always produced solid export revenues.

The ratio of exports and imports to gross national product fell steadily after 1900, mainly because > *tariffs* on imported goods were greatly increased in the first decades of the new century. Indeed, it was tariffs alone that made possible a substantial local manufacturing industry and prevented Australia from being dominated by its trade with the rest of the world. This was especially true during and after World War 2, when secondary industries expanded rapidly: the period 1940–55 was the first in which Australian exports were worth more than imports; the only other time that this occurred was 1975–81, when world energy commodity prices were given a dramatic and sustained boost by the rise in OPEC oil prices, and the expanding Japanese steel industry began shipping huge quantities of Australian iron ore and coking coal. Coal overtook wool as Australia's major export in 1979 and maintained this pre-eminence for almost a decade.

Trade agreements In 1947 Australia became a signatory to the General Agreement on Trade and Tariffs (GATT), instituted to provide an international forum for the resolution of trade disputes and to establish codes of conduct on subsidies and countervailing duties, custom valuation, standards, import licensing and a number of other trade issues. Apart from GATT, Australia has maintained an active presence in two other trade-related groupings: the Organisation for Economic Co-operation and Development (OECD), which was established in 1960 and is mainly aimed at collecting economic and trade information, and the United Nations Conference on Trade and Development (UNCTAD), set up in 1964 to reinforce GATT objectives on agricultural trade.

The 1980s and beyond In the mid-1980s Australia suffered a disastrous change in the relationship between the values of its imports and exports: the prices of a wide range of commodities fell, shipments of coal and iron ore slowed down and the nation's trade balance went sharply into reverse. Despite calls from some quarters to introduce more rigorous tariffs to cut imports, the government's policy was to 'trade out' of the problems by encouraging the export of locally manufactured goods. This approach was helped greatly by a substantial devaluation of the Australian dollar (hitherto floating), which provided natural protection for Australian industries and advantages for exporters.

Agricultural commodities were one of the staple exports being threatened, largely by subsidised exports from the US and Europe. Since 1986 Australia and fourteen other affected countries have been working within the framework provided by GATT to reduce these subsidies and improve access to world markets. Also in 1986, in an attempt to boost exports of manufactured goods not tied to commodity markets, the Australian Trade Commission (Austrade) was established to provide a wide range of services to exporters. Austrade combines the former functions of several statutory bodies and government departments and is now an important executor of trade policy, encouraging exporters to break into markets that would otherwise remain untapped. Trade in services is likely to become increasingly important in the 1990s, and Austrade provides incentives such as grants to further the development of overseas markets for Australian projects in this field. >> *economy*; *foreign policy*

trademarks The registration of trademarks in Australia is governed by federal legislation in the form of the Trade Marks Act 1955. Registration, which may apply to both goods and services, is permanent. The principle of distinguishing products by identifying devices derives from the industrial revolution, when the widening range of mass-produced goods led to more competition between manufacturers to distinguish their products. The first Australian laws for the registration of trademarks were enacted from the 1860s. The development of trademarks from that time vividly reflected social and political as well as economic change, and designs such as those for Vegemite or Early Kooka stoves are enduring and nostalgic national symbols.

While names of people or places cannot be registered as trademarks, they are afforded some legal protection through measures such as the Trade Practices Act 1974. This is a rapidly expanding field of law and such provisions are increasingly invoked to prevent the unauthorised use of names, or representations of cartoon and film characters or individuals.

trade practices legislation This federal legislation concerns competition in trade and commerce, the principle being that competition must not be prevented or hindered by restrictive practices either agreed to between companies that should be competing or imposed by an individual company with the economic power to do so. Australia's first such law, passed in 1906, fell into abeyance after a few years owing to constitutional problems, judicial conservatism and lack of political will. No further legislation was enacted until 1965; this appeared tentative, but laid the foundation (both constitutionally and in terms of public support) for much more rigorous legislation in 1974. This, the Trade Practices Act (which also contains provisions dealing with > *consumer protection*), has been much amended but its fundamental principles have been retained and in some cases strengthened – except in the area of mergers and take-overs, which have been encouraged provided that they do not create a monopoly or near-monopoly. The overall effect is, by means of competition, to force companies to be more efficient, with resulting benefits for consumers in terms of price, quality and service.

trade unions In 1989 there were 316 trade unions in Australia, with a membership of 3.2 million or 55% of the total labour force. Although men are more heavily unionised than women (60% and 40% respectively), female membership has increased rapidly in the last 20 years. Many Australian unions are affiliated with the > *ALP* and regard themselves as political as well as industrial agents. The main aim of the union movement is to improve the economic and working conditions of workers, which increasingly includes lobbying governments on indirectly related matters such as welfare and taxation policy. Particularly since World War 2, there has also been growing involvement by unions in non-industrial issues such as environmental protection and international relations. The major national union organisation is the > *ACTU*, formed in 1927. Its size and influence have continued to grow since that time and by 1989 it represented more than 90% of the Australian labour force.

Historical development Associations of skilled workers were formed in the colonies early in the 19th century, mainly for welfare purposes. Trade unions developed rapidly from the midcentury, with the influx of immigrants and their concentration in towns during the gold rushes; among early victories was the achievement of an eight-hour working day for many skilled workers in NSW, Vic. and Qld in the 1850s. Unions soon extended their interests beyond working conditions to issues such as the increasing competition for jobs from assisted and non-European immigrants. Intercolonial conferences were held from 1879, and in 1884 a committee was formed to lobby the parliaments on the unions' behalf. Less skilled workers began to unite after about 1885, among the earliest such groupings being the intercolonial Shearers' Union (formed 1886), precursor of the Australian Workers Union (AWU). This was a period of rapid growth and high ideals, influenced by thinkers such as > *William Lane*, although the movement was set back briefly by the depression and major strikes of the 1890s.

Political activity strengthened during the 1890s and labour leagues were formed which were instrumental in the creation of the first Labor Party. Trade unions became increasingly aggressive after World War 1, mainly in response to the hardships imposed by the war and the 1930s depression; the movement as a whole was weakened, however, by internal divisions over issues such as wages, conscription, and the increasing influence of communism. A spirit of greater co-operation developed during the Curtin Labor government of 1941–5, but the postwar period was marked by waves of > *industrial disputes* and further factionalism, which were reinforced by the economic ills of the 1970s.

The 1980s and beyond The election of the Hawke Labor government in 1983 was assisted greatly by the Prices and Incomes Accord agreed between the unions and the ALP. From the mid-1980s, the return to a centralised system of wage determination encouraged restraint on the part of unions and the number of working days lost through industrial disputes decreased markedly. Proposals to restructure the union movement were released by the ACTU in 1987, one of its major aims being to remedy the uneven distribution of workers among unions. In that year, nine large unions accounted for 34% of total union membership, a further 4.4% of which was spread between 206 small unions. The ACTU proposes to reduce the number of unions to 20 by the end of the century, but its success is questionable in the light of both apprehension on the part of employers and inter-union rivalry.

Today Australian unions represent a very wide range of occupational groupings and are often divided on matters such as political affiliation, ideology, and levels of militancy. While there was a greater unity of purpose evident in industrial negotiations in the 1980s, several issues have arisen since the 1970s on which unions have not yet established uniform policy. Central issues of the 1990s are likely to be occupational health and safety, and the needs of the ever-increasing number of women in the workforce, from real wage equality to adequate and affordable child care. >> *conciliation and arbitration*; *wage determination*

training programs The federal government operates a number of training programs, both to maintain a supply of people qualified to meet the needs of industry and to assist disadvantaged groups. The main programs are the Australian Traineeship System, which is aimed at young people who do not go on to higher education and involves a twelve-month course of both on-the-job and off-the-job training; the Commonwealth Rebate for Apprentice Fulltime Training, which provides subsidies for employers who release their apprentices to attend the technical educational component of a basic trade course; the Adult and Youth Training Programs, which provide education for the long-term unemployed in conjunction with TAFE colleges and other providers; and the Skills Training Program, which assists with the development and expansion of training centres in conjunction with industry and State governments in order to improve workforce abilities. As well as Commonwealth-sponsored programs, there are numerous others run by State and local governments.

trains > *railways*

transport > *aviation; coaches and coaching; public transport; railways; river transport; roads and road transport; ships and shipping*

transportation > *convicts and transportation*

trapdoor spiders > *spiders*

Traralgon Vic. (pop. 19 233) This city in the Latrobe Valley, 160km east of Melbourne, is the commercial and administrative centre for the region. It also has extensive industrial development associated with the provision of electricity from local coal deposits, and a cement works and pulp-and-paper mill (at nearby Maryvale). When completed, the 400MW Loy Yang power station and open-cut mine complex will be the biggest project of its kind in the southern hemisphere. Traralgon is also a base for tourists to the Latrobe Valley coalfields and to the nearby mountains and forests.

tree-creepers These birds of the genus *Climacteris* are small and brown, often with some yellow or orange on the breast, white throats, black flecking and blackish tails; there are nine species in Australia. Tree-creepers are insectivorous; their claws are strong, adapted to creeping up tree-trunks to extract insects from the bark with a quite large and slightly down-turned beak. The habit of pecking at the bark has brought them the alternative name woodpecker, but they are not related to true woodpeckers. They nest in the hollows of trees or stumps, lining the nest with soft material. Their nesting habit and curved beak distinguish tree-creepers from the sittellas, or tree-runners.

tree-ferns > *ferns and fern allies*

Tremandraceae This small family of flowering plants is endemic to Australia. Two of its three genera are confined to southwest WA: these, *Tremandra* and *Platytheca*, each consists of two species of soft subshrubs with attractive white, pink or bluish flowers. The third genus, *Tetratheca*, consists of 39 species of shrubs and subshrubs divided almost equally between the southeast (including Tas.) and southwest, but absent from the semi-arid country in between. They have small leaves and very attractive flowers with pink-purple petals and a central cluster of purplish-black stamens, giving rise to such common names as black-eyed Susan and pink-eyes. Pink-bells, *T. ciliata*, is common in open forests of Vic., making a fine spring display in areas such as the Grampians.

trepang > *sea-cucumbers*

trevallies This is the common name for several important commercial fishes of the family Carangidae; it covers more than 50 species known from Australian waters, including darts, kingfishes and yellowtails. The king or golden trevally is a swift, edible carnivore of northern reefs, beaches and estuaries, with a fairly deep, narrow, oval body; the trevally of metropolitan fish markets is a fish of more temperate waters, often moving in schools. The pennant-fish, or diamond trevally, is a deep, thin diamond-bodied fish; the young have long fin rays streaming behind them from back and belly fins, and as the fish grows the 'pennants' shorten or drop off.

trigger plants These herbaceous flowering plants or shrubs of the genus *Stylidium* consist of about 150 species, all but four of which are native to Australia. Their common name derives from the remarkable pollinating mechanism, a stiff column (comprising the stamens and style) which is bent backwards from its junction with the four petals and which, when touched by an insect, snaps across to deposit pollen on the intruder. Most *Stylidium* species are endemic to WA, where they are very diverse in habit and flower. The pink-flowering grass trigger-plant, *S. graminifolium*, is widespread in the east and particularly conspicuous in alpine areas.

Trinity Bay Qld Cairns and Port Douglas are both situated on the shore of this wide, shallow indentation on the northeast coast, stretching from Cape Kimberley to Cape Grafton, a distance of 88km. It was so named by James

Cook, since he arrived there in 1770 on the eve of Trinity Sunday. Among rivers draining into the bay are the Barron and the Daintree.

tritons > *gastropods*

trochus > *gastropods*; *pearls and pearling*

trotting and pacing In this form of racing, the horse's gait is restricted – laterally in the more popular pacing, and diagonally in trotting. A two-wheel gig with a driver is pulled around an enclosed track, an indication of the sport's origin at a time when events for tradesmen's drays and jinkers were included in race meetings.

The first Australian club was formed in NSW in 1902 and the sport was soon practised in all parts of the country; its popularity was consolidated with the introduction of night trotting after World War 2. In 1960, 50 346 people attended the Inter-Dominion final, the premier trotting event, which was established in 1936 and is held alternately in Australia and NZ. The Australian Trotting Council was established in 1973 and in 1975 introduced the 'grand circuit' of eight feature events including the Miracle Mile, the Inter-Dominion Championship and the Australian Pacing Title. Prominent drivers include Kevin Newman and Perce Hall; women drivers have officially competed since 1978. Major tracks in the capital cities are Harold Park, Sydney; Moonee Valley, Melbourne; Globe Derby Park, Adelaide; Albion Park, Brisbane; and Gloucester Park, Perth.

trout > *fishes, freshwater and marine*; *fishes, introduced*

Truganini (?1812–76), alleged to be the last full-blood Tas. Aborigine, b. Bruny Island, Tas. Daughter of the head of the Bruny island tribe, Truganini and her husband Woorraddy helped George Robinson marshal the remaining Tas. Aborigines into government protection 1830–5. They were taken to Flinders Island, where an attempt was made to teach them farming skills; the scheme failed, however, and many died. Having accompanied Robinson to Vic. in 1838, Truganini returned to Flinders Island and in 1856 moved with the sixteen remaining Aborigines to Oyster Bay on the Tas. east coast. By 1873, Truganini was the only survivor and she subsequently moved to Hobart. Against her express wish that her body be undisturbed, Truganini's skeleton was displayed in the Tas. Museum in Hobart 1904–47.

In May 1976, 100 years after her death, her bones were recovered by Aboriginal activists and her ashes scattered over the D'Entrecasteaux Channel. An enduring legendary figure, Truganini has been the subject of plays, poems and histories as well as a 1976 film, *Truganini: The Last of her People.*

Trumper, Victor (1877–1915), cricketer, b. Sydney. With Sir Donald Bradman, Trumper is generally acknowledged as Australia's greatest cricketer. He played 40 Tests against England 1899–1912, averaging 32 runs and including six centuries; he was exceptionally clever in dealing with a wet wicket, most notably in 1902 when he scored 2570 runs in such conditions. In first-class cricket he achieved 16 928 runs, including 42 centuries.

trumpeters This name is applied to a number of commercially important fishes. The Tas. trumpeter, *Latris lineata* – also known as 'stripey' – is both common and choice eating, growing to about 1.2m and weighing some 27kg. It is fished chiefly in SA and Vic. waters. The bastard trumpeter, *Latridopsis forsteri*, is more widely distributed but considered to be not so fine a food fish. It occurs in Tas., Vic., NSW, SA and NZ, and is netted when moving to shallow water for spawning. The trumpeter perch, *Pelates sexlineatus*, is a small fish found along much of the Australian coastline; it is good eating, but its size (rarely more than 20cm in length) precludes frequent marketing. The name derives from the peculiar grunting noise made when the fish is removed from the water.

Truscott, John Edward (1936–), designer, b. Melbourne. After a period as resident set-designer for the St Martin's Theatre in Melbourne 1957–64, Truscott lived and worked in the UK 1964–5 and the US 1966–79, designing both sets and costumes for theatre, ballet, opera and film; his costume and production designs for the film *Camelot* (1968) received US Academy Awards. Since returning to Australia, he has worked with the Australian Ballet and Australian Opera, as interior-design consultant for the Vic. Arts Centre and as creative director for Brisbane's Expo 88. He is currently artistic director of the Melbourne Spoleto Festival.

Tucker, Albert (1914–), painter, b. Melbourne. An artist of international repute and a contemporary of Arthur Boyd, Sidney Nolan and John Perceval, Tucker's savagely expressionist paintings – such as his crude *Victory Girls* (1943) – offended conservative sensibilities when they came to prominence in the 1940s, but accurately mirrored the warlike times; articulate and forthright, Tucker countered his critics eloquently. During his years in Europe and the US 1947–60 his distinctive, 'brutish' images of Australia crystallised, notably in his series of 'Antipodean Heads' in which bushrangers, explorers and other legendary figures are identified with their harsh bush and desert backgrounds. He subsequently exhibited to critical acclaim in Paris, Rome, London and New York.

Tuckwell, Barry Emmanuel (1931–   ), horn-player and music conductor, b. Warburton, Vic. A musical prodigy, Tuckwell played the French horn with the Melbourne Symphony Orchestra at the age of 15. He was principal horn of the London Symphony Orchestra 1955–68, and has since made a notable career as soloist and conductor throughout the world. He was editor of the complete horn literature for the music publishers Schirmer, and has written *Playing the Horn* (1978) and *The Horn* (1981). In 1982, he was appointed conductor and music director of the Maryland Symphony Orchestra.

Tuggerah Lake NSW This is the most southerly of three interconnected lakes lying south of Lake Macquarie; the others are Budgewoi and Munmorah. Tuggerah's extreme length is 18km, and it has an average width of 15km. Wyong is the main commercial centre of the district, which is popular for swimming, boating and fishing. The Entrance, containing the tourist resort Long Jetty, is situated on the southern side of the narrow channel that links Tuggerah to the sea.

tulipwood > *eucalypts*

Tully Qld (pop. 2575) This town on Banyan Creek, a tributary of the Tully River, lies some 1580km north of Brisbane. It is noted not only as the centre of an important sugar-growing region, but also as the wettest town in Australia – averaging 4550mm rainfall a year. Tourism is also important, Tully being an embarkation point for resorts such as Dunk and Hinchinbrook islands as well as lying at the heart of splendid coastal and mountain scenery.

tuna > *fishing industry; mackerels*

tungsten In 1986–7 Australia produced about 2000t of tungsten in concentrates, 4.8% of world production. A rare element with the highest melting point of all metals, the two main tungsten ores are scheelite and wolframite (or 'wolfram', which is often used as a synonym for tungsten). Tas. is Australia's main producer, the nation's largest tungsten-winning mine being on King Island in Bass Strait. Virtually all tungsten concentrates are exported for overseas refining.

turban shells > *gastropods*

Turner, Ethel Sibyl (1872–1958), novelist and children's author, b. England. Turner arrived in Australia in 1881. Her first novel, *Seven Little Australians* (1894) has become a children's classic, being translated into many languages and adapted for film, television and the stage. A prolific writer of stories for and about middle-class Australian children, Turner published at least a book a year between 1894 and 1928: the most enduring of these are *Seven Little Australians*, its sequel *The Family at Misrule* (1895), and *Miss Bobbie* (1897).

Turner, George (1916–   ), novelist, b. Melbourne. Turner won general acclaim (and shared the Miles Franklin Award) with his third novel, *The Cupboard under the Stairs* (1962), which like the rest of his 'Treelake' series is a complex study of the interaction between individuals and the social environment. Turner is perhaps best known, however, as a science-fiction writer, in which genre his trilogy *Beloved Son* (1978), *Vaneglory* (1981) and *Yesterday's Men* (1982), won wide praise both in Australia and overseas.

Turon River NSW This 110km river rises on the western slopes of the Great Dividing Range and flows through hilly country of mixed farming to join the Macquarie 80km northwest of Bathurst. Discovered in 1821 by James Blackman, the district was one of NSW's richest goldmining areas in the 1850s and 1860s. The principal centre was Sofala; others included Tambaroora and Hill End, which has now been officially listed as an historic site. A great part of the town has been restored and it is a popular tourist attraction.

turpentine tree > *myrtle family*

turtles and tortoises Australia has two major groups of the ancient order of chelonians: the large marine turtles, and the freshwater turtles, or tortoises. Turtles are characterised by a protective carapace or shell, to which the backbone and ribs are fused and which protects the reptile from predators but also restricts its movement.

Marine turtles have flippers instead of webbed, clawed feet and spend most of their time at sea, coming ashore to lay eggs. They are found only in the warmer Australian waters, feeding on various marine life and often travelling great distances; they show remarkable navigational ability, returning to the beaches at which they hatched. The largest species is the leathery turtle or luth, *Dermochelys coriacea*, which may be as long as 3m and weigh 500kg; as its name implies, it has a thick, leathery shell. The other marine specimens include the loggerhead turtle, *Caretta caretta*; green turtle, *Cheonia mydas*; hawksbill turtle, *Eretmochelys imbricata*; and Pacific Ridley turtle, *Lepidochelys olivacea*. Females returning to the shore deposit their eggs in chambers dug in the sand with the hind flippers, and it is here that both adults and young are most vulnerable; numbers in many species have declined because their nesting sites are not safe from human predation and they are caught both for their meat and for their eggs. However, most Australian populations are able to breed successfully, and some programs exist to re-establish species. An earlier attempt at farming green turtles in northern Qld was unsuccessful.

The strange pitted-shell turtle, *Carettochelys insculpta*, is known from lagoons and estuaries in NG and northern Australia. All Australia's remaining freshwater turtles belong to the family Chelidae, the side-necked turtles earning their name from the habit of curving the head sideways under the shell when alarmed; they live in streams and ponds, feeding on various invertebrates and small fish. One of the most common species is the eastern snake-necked or long-necked turtle, *Chelodina longicollis*, which may be observed crossing highways. The western swamp turtle, *Pseudemydura umbrina*, is Australia's most seriously endangered reptile, found only in a small region of swampland near Perth and believed to number only about 20 or 30 individuals.

tusk shells This is the common name of a small class of molluscs known as scaphopods; the shell is shaped like an elephant's tusk and is open at both ends. Australian waters have but a few of these burrowing marine animals, which live mostly in the mud and sand of the continental shelf. The digging foot protrudes from the shell's wider end; the mouth is surrounded by long, slender tentacles that are used in feeding on the microscopic organisms the animal extracts from sand or sea water. It has no gills, oxygen being absorbed through the mantle surface.

Tweed River NSW This is a coastal river rising in the Tweed Range, to the south of the McPherson Range. It flows for 80km through a region of fertile volcanic soils, and gemstones can be found in river gravel. The valley is the most northerly in the State; below the forested ranges, rural activities include banana and pineapple plantations, sugar cane and dairying. In the river itself, Stotts Island is a nature reserve of mangroves and rainforest. The principal inland town is Murwillumbah; at the river mouth is the town of Tweed Heads, which is now incorporated in Qld's Gold Coast. The river was discovered in 1823 by John Oxley.

twinleaf family The Zygophyllaceae family is a group of herbaceous plants, shrubs and small trees found in warmer parts of the world; it is represented in Australia by about 35 species in four genera. The largest Australian group is the genus *Zygophyllum,* which comprises about 20 species of the arid centre and semi-arid south; their succulent, bright-green two-lobed leaves provide grazing for animals. Another member of this family is the nitre-bush, *Nitraria billardierei*, a mound-like shrub of semi-arid regions, also with succulent leaves and bearing profuse sweet yellow or red-brown fruits. The genus *Tribulus*, of which there are about ten Australian species, consists of prostrate herbs with remarkable spiny fruits that can puncture bicycle tyres as well as bare feet – for which reason they are commonly called puncture vines.

Twofold Bay NSW As the name implies, this is a complex bay with curved beaches between several headlands, on which stand the fishing and former timber port of Eden and the few residual structures of the ambitious plan of Benjamin Boyd in the 1840s for the port of Boydtown, much of which is preserved in the Ben Boyd National Park. A woodchipping and pulping plant established in 1968 for export to Japan is the principal source of employment in the area, although dairying and fishing are still important. However, in the 1980s the region was the centre of a major conservation battle over the expansion of the woodchipping industry.

U

Ullathorne, William Bernard (1806–89), Catholic prelate, b. England. In 1833 Ullathorne was sent to Sydney as vicar-general in the Catholic see; he played a vital role under Bishop Polding in establishing a Catholic hierarchy in Australia by 1842 and in recruiting Irish priests. He wrote and spoke vigorously against transportation and returned to England in 1845.

Uluru > *Ayers Rock; national parks*

Ulverstone Tas. (pop. 10 055) Ulverstone is a port and tourist resort at the mouth of the Leven River, 302km north of Hobart. The centre for a dairying region that also produces vegetables, cereals, beef cattle and fodder crops, Ulverstone is a growing residential centre for workers in Burnie and Devonport. There is a small local timber industry, with some canning and freezing of vegetables.

Umbellifereae > *carrot family*

umbrella tree This small to medium-sized tree, *Schefflera actinophylla*, has large and very decorative compound leaves, the leaflet stalks resembling umbrella spokes. Native to the rainforests of Qld, the far northern NT and NG, in the wild it is mostly either epiphytic on other trees or clings to rock faces or crevices. It is perhaps the best known member of the aralia family, which is represented in Australia by seven native genera, most in rainforests.

Unaipon, David (1873–1967), Aboriginal writer and inventor, b. Tailem Bend, SA. Raised at the Point McLeay mission but spending most of his life in Adelaide, Unaipon developed an interest in engineering and acquired nineteen patents between 1909 and 1944. His inventions included improvements to shearing machinery, designs for perpetual-motion and flying machines, and laser research. His re-telling of Aboriginal legends (1925–30) were the first published writings by an Aboriginal in English; his major work was *Native Legends* (1929).

unemployment > *economy*; *employment and unemployment*

unions > *trade unions*

United Australia Party > *Liberal Party*

Uniting Church The Methodist, Congregational and Presbyterian Churches joined together to form the Uniting Church of Australia in 1977; some Congregational and Presbyterian members chose to remain outside the new denomination. The church has about 1.2 million adherents in Australia and is the third-largest Christian denomination; both men and women are accepted into the ministry.

The three member faiths have a long history in Australia. The Methodist Church had its first meetings in 1812, in a cottage in the Rocks area of Sydney. The first missionary was Samuel Leigh, in NSW from 1815, and the first church was built in Castlereagh, NSW, in 1817. The Congregational Church in Australia dates from 1798, when two Independents (as they were then called) preached in Sydney. Scottish Presbyterians built their first church in Australia in Ebenezer, NSW, in 1809 and this is the nation's oldest church still in use. The first Presbyterian minister arrived in 1822; he was followed in 1823 by the great protagonist > *John Dunmore Lang*. The church made lasting contributions in the field of education as well as inaugurating Australia's aerial medical services through its > *Australian Inland Mission*. >> *religion*

univalves > *gastropods*

universities > education

Upfield, Arthur William (1888–1964), b. England. Upfield arrived in Australia in 1911, working as a real-estate agent until 1927. He then became a full-time writer of detective fiction, based around the part-Aboriginal detective Napoleon Bonaparte. While Upfield's writing is generally undistinguished, his central character 'Bony' and his evocative outback settings made his thrillers hugely popular, particularly in the US.

uranium In 1986, Australia's economically recoverable reserves of uranium were estimated at 462kt, about 28% of the western world's resources. Production of uranium oxide (U_3O_8) in that year amounted to 4899t, of which 4164.5t, worth $373 million, were exported.

The export of uranium oxide, commonly called 'yellowcake', is rigorously controlled by the federal government, which permits exports only from the Ranger and Nabarlek mines in the NT and the Olympic Dam mine in SA; under the Nuclear Non-Proliferation (Safeguards) Act 1987, further controls over the possession and transport of uranium have been enacted. Exports are also subject to a floor price – which has been detrimental to the profitability of the industry – and may only be made to countries with which Australia has concluded a nuclear safeguards agreement. All these safeguards and controls have been instituted in response to pressure from anti-nuclear activists and environmentalists, as there has been much concern about uranium's use in nuclear arms and the problem of nuclear-waste storage. The conditions of export are that Australian uranium be used only in nuclear reactors for the generation of electricity or for the production of radio-isotopes and radio-pharmaceuticals; in practice, however, once uranium leaves Australia's shores little can be done to control its use.

Systematic exploration for uranium in Australia did not begin until 1944. Large deposits were identified in the NT and Qld, leading to the development of mines at Rum Jungle, Moline and Rockhole in the NT, Mary Kathleen in Qld, and Radium Hill in SA. The 1950s were a boom time for the industry, but as international defence-industry requirements diminished the 1960s brought a slump. With the worldwide development of nuclear energy, another boom commenced in the 1970s – a period which saw increased exploration and new discoveries at Yendirrie in WA and Roxby Downs in SA, and in the Alligator rivers area of NT, where the Ranger, Jabiluka, Nabarlek and Koongarra prospects contain about 80% of Australia's reserves.

Major companies involved in uranium mining in Australia include Pioneer International, MIM, CRA and Western Mining Corporation, all of which have had to run the gauntlet of environmentalist and Aboriginal protests, a royal commission on the industry, and confusing – often contradictory – changes in government, union and political-party policies. In the 1980s much of this protest has subsided, and the government has accepted that if the world is not given access to Australian uranium, it may turn to the immense exploitable reserves that occur in Canada, the US and various African countries.

urban planning Although the layout of most Australian cities was planned from the time of settlement, the co-ordination of land uses and public works was not undertaken by governments until well into the 20th century. After World War 2, changing social, economic and environmental conditions – and associated changes in the needs and expectations of the population – encouraged the development of statutory land-use plans.

Urban planning is primarily the responsibility of local government, although guidelines and controls are applied by State authorities. The system has often suffered from this overlap of authority; in addition it has often been characterised by conflict between the forces of conservation and development and between the aspirations of residents and the infrastructure requirements of public authorities. Many Australian ideas in planning practice and education have been derived from the UK, most notably the metropolitan 'strategies' of recent decades; in the more routine field of development control, however, planning processes have been more akin to US zoning procedures.

Colonial origins The first Australian towns were generally planned by army surveyors, using the gridiron pattern common to colonial settlements since ancient Egypt. In Sydney the planned grid was soon distorted by naturally developing tracks, and in Brisbane and Hobart its use was complicated by the steep slopes of river valleys; only on the flatter sites of Melbourne, Adelaide and Perth was it reasonably successful. Adelaide was the most celebrated case, the city being designed by > *William Light* as two grids separated by a green belt with town squares at the major intersections.

Despite the grids, land uses were unplanned and generally uncontrolled throughout the 19th century: laissez-faire industrial and housing development saw mixes of residences and noxious industries, congestion, slums and inadequate infrastructure. By the end of the century, innovations in public transport – railways, horse-drawn buses, cable trams, then electric trams – allowed residential areas to escape from the congested city cores.

Developments from the early 20th century In the 20th century, and especially after 1945, the car hastened the process of suburbanisation and allowed equally undesirable, uncontrolled, largely unsewered, and increasingly car-based suburban sprawl. From 1920 > *Canberra* provided a paradigm for planned towns, but its influence was negligible. The WA and SA governments each appointed a town planner in the 1920s, with some powers to control new land uses; elsewhere, municipalities were given authority to proclaim new residential areas from which other uses could be prohibited, and in some instances were given wider powers to zone different land uses into separate areas. Such powers were scarcely ever exercised and it was not until World War 2 that urban planning became a significant item on the public agenda.

Idealism for postwar reconstruction, expressed especially by the Curtin and Chifley governments, embraced concern for both the overall form of cities and towns and their internal quality and services, although constitutional limitations inhibited any direct federal involvement in urban planning. There were also limitations at the State level owing to the fragmented nature of local government, only Brisbane having a single metropolitan council. The 1945 Commonwealth-State agreement to fund public housing programs required the States to initiate town-planning arrangements and all eventually published metropolitan planning schemes (the first in Sydney in 1947, the last in Brisbane as late as 1964).

This first generation of planning schemes was essentially regulatory, zoning land uses throughout the city and – after a century of chaotic expansion – intent on neatness and order. At their best these plans were innovative and interventionist: the Cumberland County Council Planning Scheme for Sydney, for example, included district centres, a green belt to halt suburban sprawl, and self-contained satellite towns beyond the green belt to accommodate urban expansion.

By the 1960s the first-generation plans were under extreme pressure from unanticipated rates of population growth from the postwar 'baby boom' and greatly increased immigration, and from transport congestion. This was particularly the case with Sydney and Melbourne, but all the major cities initiated studies of land-use and transport options and in some cases produced new metropolitan plans. Notable among the latter were the Sydney Region Outline Plan (1968), new planning policies for Melbourne (1972), the Perth Corridor Plan (1970) and the Canberra 'Y-plan' (also 1970). All were more open-ended than the first-generation plans and were characterised by growth corridors along major transport routes, with green wedges between the corridors. A series of social and political changes in the 1970s compelled yet a further re-direction in urban planning. The Whitlam government focused new attention on the cities and catalysed initiatives at the State level; the declining affordability of housing after 1973 led to questions about the interaction of urban planning and land speculation. Governments were increasingly reluctant to finance infrastructure for outward urban expansion, some aspects of which were also opposed by environmentalists. The urban conservation movement resisted the destruction of historic buildings and inner-city neighbourhoods (often the slums of the 19th and early 20th centuries); and the older areas in city centres began to be reevaluated in the late 1970s, in the light of increasing oil prices and a new taste for inner-city living. Local communities became increasingly vocal in their opposition to developments such as freeways (thus thwarting the transport plans of the 1960s), public housing estates, and airport expansion. Urban planners were thus called upon to meet two new objectives that were – at least potentially – mutually exclusive: to contain urban expansion by, for example, increasing building densities, and to conserve the physical fabric and environmental quality of older neighbourhoods from the redevelopment that would accompany urban consolidation.

The 1980s and beyond The 1980s accordingly saw a third generation of planning schemes. Although preoccupied with incremental growth and urban consolidation, they were ostensibly more concerned with the processes of planning and development than with the physical form of the city, emphasising community participation, and mechanisms for objecting to developments or appealing against unfavourable planning decisions. Typical examples were the Sydney Region Outline Plan Review (1980), the Melbourne Metropolitan Strategy (1981), the Melbourne Metropolitan Policy (1987) and a new Sydney Metropolitan Strategy (1988).

The increasing frequency of revisions is symptomatic of the new age in urban planning, but there are two further trends which are even more significant. The first is the move towards negotiated planning, whereby entrepreneurs of economically important projects can bypass the formal planning system and go straight to the planning minister, who has the power to amend the planning scheme to accommodate the development. As Australian urban development is increasingly caught up in the imperatives of global economics, and as State governments compete with each other for development capital (particularly from international sources), negotiated planning becomes more common and more in conflict with the formal system. The second trend is towards integrating urban design and urban planning, in response to increasing concern for the appearance and environmental quality of both new developments and existing neighbourhoods.

Undergraduate urban planning courses are available in some universities (Melbourne, NSW, Curtin and New England) and some tertiary colleges; postgraduate courses for people entering the profession from other disciplines are also available. Planning education has tended to follow the change outlined above: concentrating on zoning and physical form in the 1940s and 1950s; moving in the 1960s towards mathematical modelling of the interaction of land use and transport; increasingly eschewing technocratic concerns in the 1970s in favour of notions such as equity, community participation and environmental responsibility; and in the 1980s exploring political processes on the one hand and urban design and landscape planning on the other. It is clear that the instability in both urban planning and its education will continue. >> *architecture*; *housing*

US bases in Australia As part of its global navigation and security network, the US has established a number of facilities in Australia since 1963. Although these are often called 'joint' facilities, Australia plays a subordinate role in most cases. All Australian governments since that of R.G. Menzies have defended the presence of the bases as both a necessary part of US defence measures against surprise attack and as a means of monitoring international use of arms. Only the Whitlam government has attempted to gain more control over the facilities, in 1974 ensuring Australia's right to be consulted before the naval communications base at North West Cape was activated in wartime, as well as the employment of more Australian staff there. Those opposed to the US presence in Australia argue, inter alia, that the facilities make Australia a nuclear target. The main facilities are North West Cape, 1000km north of Perth, which acts as a relay point for signals between US military headquarters and submarines in the Indian and western Pacific Oceans; the space-research facility at Pine Gap near Alice Springs, a satellite ground-control station used mainly by the US Central Intelligence Agency to monitor military and civil communications and radar transmissions; the space communications station at Nurrungar, situated within the Woomera 'restricted area' in SA, a main ground-control facility for the US military satellite system; and the Omega navigational transmitter at Darriman, Vic., which is a major link in a worldwide VLF air and sea navigation system.

Utzon, Joern (1918–), architect, b. Denmark. A graduate of the Copenhagen Royal Academy of Fine Arts, Utzon produced the inspired scheme that won the international design competition for the Sydney Opera House in 1957. He moved to Sydney to supervise construction and set up practice, but continual disputes over both construction of the Opera House (particularly escalating costs and modifications to the original detailing) and plans for his own house prompted him to resign in 1966.

V

Van Diemen Gulf NT A broad but partially enclosed inlet on the northwest coast of the NT, the gulf is sheltered by Cobourg Peninsula on the east and Melville Island on the west. Entrance to the Arafura Sea is through Dundas Strait, between Melville Island and the peninsula, and to the Timor Sea through Clarence Strait to the west of Melville Island. The Alligator and Mary rivers flow to estuaries on the gulf, which was discovered in 1644 by Abel Tasman and named after the governor-general of the Dutch East Indies.

Van Diemen's Land This was the name accorded to Tas. by the Dutch navigator Abel Tasman, who reached its west coast in 1642. It was named in honour of Anthony Van Diemen, governor-general of the Dutch East Indies 1636–45, who was responsible for sending Tasman on his exploratory voyages. Tas. continued to be called Van Diemen's Land until it was officially proclaimed Tas. in 1855.

Van Diemen's Land Co. Chartered in London in 1825, partly in response to J.T. Bigge's recommendation that free settlers be enticed to the colonies by the prospect of land grants and cheap convict labour, this company was established under the management of Edward Curr. It was largely responsible for exploration and development for pasture, crops and later timber extraction in northwest Tas., and still operates today, holding land in the area of its original grant at Circular Head, with headquarters in Burnie.

Van Praagh, Dame Peggy (Margaret) (1910–90), dancer and ballet administrator, b. England. Following a long and successful career in Britain, which included periods with the Ballet Rambert and the London and Sadler's Wells ballets, Van Praagh became founding artistic director of the Australian Ballet in 1962, a post she held until 1974 (in partnership with Sir Robert Helpmann from 1965) and again in 1978–9; she was an outstanding influence on the development of Australian ballet. Her publications include *How I Became a Ballet Dancer* (1954) and *Ballet in Australia* (1965).

Vassilieff, Danila Ivanovich (1897–1958), artist, b. Russia. A naive artist, Vassilieff was a flamboyant Cossack who worked on the NT railways in the 1920s, then travelled and exhibited in South America and Europe in the 1930s before settling in Warrandyte, Vic., in 1937. His vivid, childlike paintings and passionate enthusiasm inspired young artists of his day such as Sidney Nolan, Albert Tucker and Arthur Boyd. He began carving stone with great success in 1951; his polished forms in Lilydale rock – hitherto intractable to sculptors – are among his best works.

Vaux, James Hardy (1782–1853), convict, b. England. Vaux was a petty but vicious, vain and unrepentant criminal, transported three times to NSW and noted for his two-volume memoir, chiefly written to his own glory. This included a glossary of contemporary (mainly criminal) slang, *Vocabulary of the Flash Language*, which was the first dictionary published in Australia and has since been much drawn upon by students and documenters of Australian English; it was republished in 1964.

vegetable-growing European culinary vegetables were brought to Australia aboard the First Fleet; commercial production began at the time of the gold rushes of the 1850s with the operations of Chinese market gardeners, who dominated the industry for more than 50 years until their numbers dwindled because of immigration restrictions. Market gardens were traditionally located on the outskirts of towns and cities, but suburban expansion and developments in irrigation and food storage and processing have enabled the industry to extend to country areas. In 1945 the area sown with vegetables peaked at 200 000ha; this has since been reduced, as the yield per hectare for most crops has increased as a result of variety breeding, irrigation, and better control of disease and insect pests. In 1985–6, the 111 000ha under cultivation produced crops with a gross value of $714 million; potatoes were the most extensive and valuable crop, with production of 965 000t to the value of $206 million. Less than 10% of all vegetable production is exported, although Australia's capacity to grow vegetables throughout the year has encouraged exports of some speciality crops to the northern hemisphere.

vegetation > *flora*

venison > *deer*

Verge, John (1782–1861), architect, b. England. Verge arrived in NSW in 1828 to farm, but soon turned to building and architecture. In partnership with architect John Bibb 1832–7, he designed innumerable elegant buildings in the 'colonial Georgian' style, noted for their mastery of spatial composition and features such as stucco walls and shuttered openings. Fine examples include Camden Park (1834), built for the Macarthur family; and Elizabeth Bay House (1832–7), its magnificent oval stairwell commonly considered to be one of the finest interior features in colonial architecture.

Victor Harbor SA (pop. 6538) This small town 84km south of Adelaide is both a service centre for the surrounding farmlands and a popular holiday resort of long standing; it is linked by causeway to Granite Island, which was an early whaling station. Settlement dates from whaling in Encounter Bay and the town developed as a small port for the Murray basin until railways took the trade to Adelaide and Melbourne.

Victoria (Vic.) The smallest Australian mainland State in terms of area and the second-largest in terms of population, Vic. is by far the most densely populated State, has often been the richest, and is currently the dominant producer of petroleum. It is a politically conservative State which until the 1980s had never been governed by Labor over an extended period.

With an area of 227 620sq.km and a coastline of 1200km, Vic. does not divide into regions as readily as do some other States, but can be considered in four main zones – the southern lowlands, the central highlands, the Western District and the northern (Murray basin) plains, which include the Mallee and the Wimmera. On and south of the Great Dividing Range temperatures are cool to moderate and there is a reliable rainfall well distributed across the seasons, whereas the northern and western plains are drier and warmer, with droughts relatively common and frequent very high temperatures. The main coastal rivers are the Glenelg, Barwon, Hopkins, Yarra, Latrobe, Mitchell, Tambo and Snowy; inland, the Mitta Mitta, Campaspe, Ovens and Loddon flow into the Murray, while the Wimmera flows into Lake Hindmarsh and the Avoca into Lake Bael Bael. The main urban centres are > *Melbourne* (the capital), > *Geelong*, Moe and Morwell in the southern lowlands, > *Ballarat* and Bendigo in the central highlands, Warrnambool in the Western District, and Mildura, Shepparton, Horsham and Echuca in the northern plains.

Historical development Although John Batman was unique among Australia's European settlers in offering a land contract (albeit a spurious one) to the local Aborigines, it did the latter little good: the Aboriginal population at the time of settlement has been estimated at 11 500, but before the gold rushes of the 1850s it had shrunk to 3500. Settlement of Vic. – which was known as the Port Phillip District of NSW until 1851 – began in 1834, though abortive attempts had been made in 1803 and 1828. Squatters from Tas, such as Batman and John Pascoe Fawkner, were followed by others from NSW in illegally establishing themselves, and the NSW government was compelled to provide an administration in 1836. In 1851 the discovery of gold inaugurated a decade of rapid population increase and economic development. When gold-mining declined after 1865, agricultural and industrial expansion absorbed the surplus miners; the firmly entrenched squatters retained and increased their estates, and new wheatlands were opened up in the north and west; factories flourished on the growing home market and were helped by tariff protection, which was carried by Vic. into Commonwealth policy after Federation. Over-expansion and speculation based on foreign borrowings led to a disastrous slump after 1891, when many banks failed. It was not until World War 1 that Vic. fully recovered economically, which occurred largely because of the industrial production stimulated by that war. Nevertheless, the financial dominance of Melbourne over other State capitals was retained, partly because of widespread State undertakings established after 1902. Between the wars Vic. remained the wealthiest State, and after World War 2 immigration stimulated even faster growth, although the recession of the 1970s and 1980s was damaging to the manufacturing sector.

Population and economy The population of Vic. at the 1986 census was 4 019 478, which showed a growth rate of only 0.02% over the five years between censuses, similar to those of SA and Tas., lower than that of NSW, and much lower than those of WA and Qld. But with 26% of Australia's population, Vic. seems unlikely to be overtaken by any other State as the second most populous in the near future. The present figure gives a population density of 17.7 per sq.km, much higher than that of any other State. Some 67% of the population lives in Melbourne, and about 29% of Vic.'s population is overseas-born, with Greece and Italy the major sources of immigrants.

Manufacturing in Vic., despite recent declines, still produces about 34% of the Australian total, with textiles (in the Geelong region), iron and steel processing and food production as major components. Wool, wheat and dairy products are important, with orchard fruits and grapes also significant, Vic. contributing in all about 21% of Australia's agricultural production. While no black coal is produced, brown coal supplies most of Vic.'s electricity needs. From its Bass Strait reserves, the State supplies enough crude oil to satisfy 60% of Australia's refinery needs, itself refining some 38%. As elsewhere, the tertiary sector dominates the labour market, employing some 70% of the workforce, with retail trade the largest employer of the sector.

Government and politics Two main currents shaped the political development of Vic.: the first was the widespread and popular agitation in the 1840s for separation from NSW, which was achieved in 1851; the second was the gold rushes, beginning in the same year, which planted in Vic. politics a democratic strain that later manifested itself in a strong liberal tradition that took longer to merge with conservatism than was the case in other colonies. Probably this liberal tradition was a major factor in the slow growth of the Labor Party, another being the emergence of a strong Country Party based on small farmers rather than a squattocracy and which thus denied Labor a rural base. The end of World War 2 was followed by a gradual decline in the Country Party's power, the party's last premier being J.G.B. McDonald (1950–2), and a growth in strength of a conservative Liberal Party. Under > *Sir Henry Bolte* (1955–73), Sir Rupert Hamer (1973–81) and Lindsay Thompson (1981–82), successive Liberal Party governments presided over 27 years of economic growth and a population explosion due to immigration. The economic slump of the later 1970s was probably partly responsible for the election in 1982 of the Labor Government of > *John Cain*, which won an historic third term in 1989. It may, however, be attributable to the continuing dominance of a Vic. power elite that every Australian prime minister since World War 2 – with the exception of Ben Chifley, William McMahon and Gough Whitlam (all from NSW) – has come from the State of Vic.

Victoria Cross > *honours and awards*

Victoria River NT The largest river in the NT, the Victoria flows for some 640km from a source in low sandhills, through alternating basins and hills to Queens Channel in Joseph Bonaparte Gulf. It was discovered in 1839 by John Wickham of the *Beagle*, and named in honour of the Queen. In 1855–6 A.C. Gregory traced its upper course, but the land was not settled until pastoralists established cattle stations in the 1880s, several of them after epic overland journeys. There are now some 20 stations in the valley; the largest are Wave Hill and Victoria River Downs, each covering more than 13 000sq.km.

Vietnamese in Australia > *ethnic groups*

Vietnam War Australia entered the Vietnam conflict on the coat–tails of the US, the Menzies government of the early 1960s believing (as did the Americans) in a policy of 'forward defence', particularly against what it saw as Chinese-inspired communist expansion in Southeast Asia. In addition, memories of the 1950–3 Korean War were still fresh and it was held that action was required if the protective umbrella of the ANZUS pact were to have any meaning. Australian involvement began in July 1962 with a token team of 30 army advisers and increased to 100 by 1964; in May 1965, the first regular army battalion was dispatched. From modest beginnings, Australia's contribution reached a peak of 8500 military personnel by 1968, along with four RAN destroyers and three RAAF squadrons flying helicopters, Hercules transports and Canberra bombers. Australian troops were based mainly in the Phuoc Tuy province, southeast of Saigon, an area permeated with Viet Cong guerillas and regular units of the North Vietnamese army. By 1967 Australian troops had virtually cleared the province of the enemy, and during the Tet offensive of 1968 some units were called to defend the large US bases of Long Binh and Bien Hoa.

Opposition to the war was meanwhile growing in Australia. Many – particularly in the ALP – felt that both US and Australian involvement was unjustified and that it was immoral to commit conscripts to the war, > *conscription* having been reintroduced in 1965. As the patently unwinnable war dragged on, with its horrors displayed nightly on television, opposition mounted and numerous, often violent, demonstrations were held. Following the election of President Richard Nixon, the US began to withdraw its ground forces in 1969 in a policy of 'Vietnamisation' of the war, and Australia followed suit. During 1970 and 1971, the remaining Australian forces were involved in holding actions assisting the South Vietnamese army, and in civil-aid projects in the Phuoc Tuy province. All Australian combat troops were withdrawn in 1972, and after the election of the Whitlam Labor government in December of that year all defence aid to Vietnam ceased and conscription was ended.

Of a total of 50 001 Australian personnel engaged in the Vietnam War, some 496 were killed and 2398 injured, about half of whom were conscripts. Four Victoria Crosses were awarded. Of all the wars in which Australia has fought, Vietnam has left a unique legacy of confusion and bitterness, augmented by debate over the acceptance of Vietnamese refugees and reflected by the fact that Australian veterans of the war were accorded little popular recognition until more than a decade later. >> *defence*; *foreign policy*

Villiers, Alan John (1903–1982), sailor and author, b. Melbourne. Villiers went to sea as a boy and subsequently travelled the world in sailing ships, relating his experiences in vivid accounts such as *Vanished Fleets* (1931) and *Grain Vessels* (1933) which record the end of an era. In 1957, he commanded a replica of the *Mayflower* on a voyage from England to the US. Perhaps the most famous square-rigger skipper this century, Villiers published his autobiography, *The Set of the Sails*, in 1949. His writing has an unromantic and forceful quality.

violets Australia has only five native species of the small herbaceous plants that constitute the genus *Viola*; all are confined to the eastern States, the most widespread being the creeping ivy–leafed violet, *V. hederacea*, and the deeply tap–rooted showy violet, *V. betonicifolia*. This genus probably represents a specialised group in the violet family (Violaceae), some other genera of which are woodier plants of warmer climates: one found in Australia is *Hymenanthera*, comprising one species of spiny-branched shrubs with tiny yellow flowers; found in moist forest or subalpine grassland, it is sometimes called the tree violet. The spade flower (or slipper flower) genus *Hybanthus* has ten native species of shrubs and herbs, their flowers having a much-enlarged lower petal.

Vitaceae > *grape family*

von Guérard, Eugène (1811–1901), painter, b. Austria. The son of an Austrian court painter, von Guérard studied in Europe before arriving in Vic. in 1852, lured by gold. Generally considered the finest of the immigrant artists of this period, he produced many precisely detailed landscapes based on his extensive travels in the colonies, and published a volume of lithographs, *Australian Landscapes*, in 1867. Von Guérard was the first principal of the National Gallery School in Melbourne (1870–1), during which period a reaction set in against the picturesque style of landscape painting, of which he was an acknowledged master. He returned to Europe in 1882.

voting > *elections*

W

Wackett, Sir Lawrence James (1896–), aircraft designer, b. Townsville, Qld. Wackett's service with the Royal Flying Corps in World War 1, and with the RAAF from 1921, included aircraft design and development work. After leaving the RAAF in 1930 he produced several aircraft and was eventually pre-eminent among Australian aircraft designers. He was head of the Commonwealth Aircraft Corporation 1936–61.

waders Species of this very large group of birds vary considerably in body size, length of leg and neck, and habits, though most are birds of swamps or of the very fringe of land and sea. Many waders are seasonal migrants, travelling long distances that may include ocean crossings; this is done by even small and apparently frail birds such as the dotterels, species of the genus *Charadrius*, some of which come from NZ and some from Asia; such far-travelling birds tend not to belong to one country or even to one continent. Most species feed on invertebrates, plucked from sand or soil with their probing bills. The Australian fauna includes the relatively long-legged avocets of the genus *Recurvirostra* with the distinctively long, curved beak of its Latin name; the straight-beaked and fragile stilts, genera *Himantopus* and *Cladorhynchos*; and the very long-toed lotusbird or jacana, *Irediparra gallinacea*, adapted, by thus spreading its weight, to walk lightly across the large floating leaves of the lotus or water-lily. Shore-dwelling waders include the red-beaked and red-legged oyster-catchers, genus *Haematopus;* the beach curlew, genus *Orthorhamphus*; migrants from north Asia such as the greenshank, *Tringa nebularia*; the sandpiper, *T. hypoleucos*; the whimbrel, *Numenius*; the sanderling, *Crocethia alba*; the red-necked stint, *Calidris ruficollis*; and plovers of the genera *Squatarola* and *Pluvialis*. Those found further from the shore include the inland dotterel, *Peltohyas australis*; the bush curlew, *Burhinus magnirostris*; and the snipe, genera *Gallinago* and *Rostratula*. >> *bitterns, egrets and herons*

wage determination For most of this century, Australian wages have been determined by national judgments of the Court of Conciliation and Arbitration (reconstituted as the Australian Conciliation and Arbitration Commission in 1956). A 'basic wage' was first set in 1907, through the so-called > *Harvester judgment*: this established a minimum wage for unskilled male workers (based on the food and shelter needs of an average family), which was adjusted periodically to take account of changes in the real cost of living; skilled workers received an extra, negotiated amount. Although originally conceived of as sacrosanct, the basic wage was reduced by 10% during the 1930s depression and the automatic quarterly cost-of-living adjustments were abandoned in the 1950s. The basic wage for women was set at 75% of the male rate in 1950 and the principle of equal pay (still unrealised in many instances) was not introduced until 1972.

Since the 1950s, various systems of wage determination have been adopted and the notion of a basic wage was replaced in 1967 by a total (variable) wage that incorporated a minimum award rate. The combination of 'comparative wage justice', whereby increases in the skill margins for one industry were passed on to others, and individual industry awards led to a dramatic increase in both wages and inflation in the early 1970s. National wage cases were therefore reintroduced and wage increases tied to the consumer price index (wage indexation). In 1983, indexation was incorporated into the Prices and Incomes Accord between the ACTU and the federal government. >> *conciliation and arbitration*

Wagga Wagga NSW (pop. 37 577) The city of Wagga Wagga (often abbreviated to Wagga) lies on the Murrumbidgee River, 470km south-west of Sydney. It is a market, service and pro-cessing town for parts of the Riverina region and the State's western slopes and has dairy, meat and timber factories as well as foundries and a wool-combing plant. Its agricultural research station (founded in 1892) was asso-ciated with William Farrer's work on wheat-breeding. The district was settled in the 1830s and the town surveyed in 1849; growth was slow until the advent of the railway in 1878. The town's main modern growth has been to the west; to the east, Willan's Hill is the site for a lookout and nature reserve.

wagtail > *flycatchers*

Waikerie SA (pop. 1593) On the banks of the Murray River 17km northeast of Adelaide, Waikerie is the centre of an irrigated district that produces 30% of Australia's citrus fruit as well as wine grapes and stone fruits. Settlement in the region dates from the 1880s although the town was not proclaimed until 1908; farm co-operatives have fostered expansion in the past decade.

Wainewright, Thomas Griffiths (1794–1847), painter, b. England. A talented artist and essayist, Wainewright exhibited regularly at London's Royal Academy and contributed to several English literary magazines before being transported to Tas. for forgery in 1837. Allowed some freedom in Hobart, he painted a number of watercolours and portraits acknowledged for their accomplished draughtsmanship but often criticised for their genteel sameness.

Waite Agricultural Research Institute

Australia's only national research organisation in agriculture, the Waite Institute was set up in 1924 by the University of Adelaide, after re-ceiving a gift of agricultural and grazing land from pastoralist Peter Waite. It is a teaching as well as a research organisation, training staff at postgraduate level for the CSIRO and for State departments of agriculture. It consists of a campus of 160ha at the foot of the Mt Lofty Ranges, a division at the university, and the Mortlock Experiment Station near Clare, 130km north of Adelaide – the last-named being used for field experiments, particularly with crops, pasture and livestock. The institute has re-corded some notable research achievements – for example, the development of an antibiotic to inhibit cancer growth in plants, and the cul-tivation of new grain varieties, which have helped improve Australian agricultural productivity.

Wakefield, Edward Gibbon (1796–1862), theorist on colonisation, b. England. Wakefield's ideas strongly influenced Australian settle-ment, especially of SA. While in gaol in London for abduction and a runaway marriage (his second), he wrote *A Letter from Sydney* (1829) propounding a system of colonisation of ingenious yet practical simplicity: broadly, that land should be not freely or cheaply available, but sold at 'sufficient price' to be attainable only by men of capital, the proceeds to be used to pay the passages of selected free immigrants who would provide labour but also save for their own land in turn. Wakefield disassociated himself from the compromise system laid down for SA, and turned to Canada, and then NZ (where he settled) as outlets for his plans.

Wakefield system > *land settlement*; *Wakefield, Edward Gibbon*

Wakelin, Roland Shakespeare (1887–1971), painter, b. NZ. Wakelin arrived in Sydney in 1912. Inspired by the contemporary French painters, especially Cézanne, he became a prominent member of the Contemporary Group in Sydney in the 1920s and 1930s. Wakelin was an early exponent of post-Impressionism in Australia: his light-filled, formally composed paintings are serene depictions of urban Australian landscapes, seascapes and still-lifes.

Wakool River > *Edward River*

Walker, Kath > *Noonuccal, Oodgeroo*

Walkley Awards The most coveted awards in Australian journalism, the Walkleys were established in 1956 with funds provided by Sir William Gaston Walkley, founder of Ampol Petroleum. They are administered by the Australian Journalists Assocation and are award-ed, annually, to AJA members only. Bronze Walkleys are awarded in individual categories and a Gold Walkley is awarded to the best of these; Melbourne cartoonist Ron Tanberg and print journalist George Haddon have each won several Gold Walkleys.

wallabies > *kangaroos, wallabies and allies*

Wallace-Crabbe, Chris(topher Keith) (1934–   ), poet and critic, b. Melbourne. A lecturer in English at the University of Melbourne since 1968, Wallace-Crabbe is one of a group of poets of the middle ground produced by that university in the late 1950s. Eminently civilised and self-consciously understated, Wallace-Crabbe's verse lacks the flamboyance of such Sydney contemporaries as Les Murray. His poetry volumes include *The Music of Division* (1959), *Selected Poems* (1973) and *The Emotions Are Not Skilled Workers* (1980); other publications include collections of his reviews and essays, and the novel *Splinter* (1981). His brother **Robin** (1938–), b. Melbourne, was best known as an artist until the 1970s, since which time he has also turned his hand to writing. He has published a number of thrillers under the pseudonym Robert Wallace, as well as (in his own name) two novels and a semi-fictional account of his family, *Australia Australia* (1989).

Wallace's Line This term was first used in 1868 to indicate a boundary between the distinctive Australasian fauna (notably monotremes, marsupials and marine species) and that of Asia. It runs between Bali and Lombok and further north between Borneo and Sulawesi, and is named after A.R. Wallace, an English scientist who in 1860 noted that the faunas of South America and Africa (although separated by the Atlantic Ocean) differed less than those of Asia and Australia. Zoologists have since made important modifications, and the line is no longer regarded as a clearly defined boundary because there is some overlapping of the faunas.

wallaroos > *kangaroos, wallabies and allies*

Waller, (Mervyn) Napier (1894–1972), artist, b. Penshurst, Vic. Trained at the Vic. National Gallery School, Napier Waller lost his right arm during active service in World War 1 but subsequently resumed his artistic career. He worked in many media, but was outstanding as a mosaic artist and muralist. His major accomplishment was the vast commission to decorate the Hall of Fame in the Australian War Memorial: the stained-glass windows and pale-gold mural mosaics took seven years to design and execute and were completed in 1941. Art Deco, cubism and expressionism were the main influences on his work, which included murals and stained-glass windows in a number of churches and public buildings throughout Australia.

Walling, Edna (1896–1973), landscape designer, b. England. Walling arrived in Australia in about 1918 and was arguably Australia's leading landscape designer from the 1920s. Greatly influenced by the romantic cottage gardens of the English designer Gertrude Jekyll, Walling combined formal layouts with natural planting to produce many distinctive gardens. She built her own stone cottage at Mooroolbark in Vic. during the 1920s and later designed the surrounding Bickleigh Vale 'village estate' of rustic cottages and native landscaping. Her four books, which were extremely popular, included *Cottage and Garden* (1947), *A Gardener's Log* (1948) and *The Australian Roadside* (1952), the last reflecting her growing interest in Australian native plants.

Walter and Eliza Hall Institute The Walter and Eliza Hall Institute of Medical Research was established in 1916, made possible largely through an endowment made by Eliza Hall, the widow of Walter Hall (1831–1911). The institute has made major contributions to international > *medical research* since that time and has attracted grants from other sources, most notably State and federal governments (which now account for most of its funding). Early subjects of research included parasites (particularly hydatids) and poisons including snake venom and bacterial toxins; from the 1930s, the institute's investigations into viral diseases, particularly influenza, and the development of vaccines won international recognition. Under the directorship of > *Sir Gustav Nossal*, the institute has concentrated on immunological research in the last 30 years, most recently in the field of parasitic tropical diseases such as malaria. Cancer is also a major focus of study; other research projects include investigations of diabetes and arthritis.

'Waltzing Matilda' Australia's best known and emblematic song, this is a simple ballad of a swagman, a stolen sheep, and characteristically anti-police sentiment reflected in the swagman drowning rather than being arrested. Its origin has been much disputed, although it is generally believed that the song was written in about 1895 by A.B. Paterson at Dagworth Station near Winton in Qld and that his host's niece, Christina Macpherson, adapted the music from a Scottish song; its present form is attributed to Marie Cowan in 1903 and was soon thereafter disseminated in an advertisement for 'Billy Tea'. While immensely popular throughout its life and frequently mooted as the unofficial national anthem, 'Waltzing Matilda' was outvoted by 'Advance Australia Fair' in a national poll in 1977, possibly because it was deemed to be insufficiently dignified. >> *national anthems*

wandoo > *eucalypts*

Wangaratta Vic. (pop. 16 598) This city lies 237km northeast of Melbourne, at the confluence of the Ovens and King rivers, and is a prosperous regional centre. Having developed at a river crossing for cattle drovers in the 1830s, Wangaratta now serves diverse farming lands that produce cattle and sheep, cereals, tobacco, honey, fruit and wine; its longstanding textile industry base is now being diversified to include light engineering and service industries.

waratah This is the common name of Aboriginal origin for a distinctive Australian shrub, *Telopea speciosissima*, which belongs to the > *protea family*. It is endemic to the central NSW coast, extending from Newcastle in the north to Nowra in the south, and is that State's floral emblem. The shrub, which can reach 3m in height, bears spikes of crimson flowerheads, the blossom being sheathed by deep-crimson bracts; the fruit is a leathery capsule up to 10cm long, which bears flat-winged seeds.

warblers In Australia, as elsewhere, this is a name commonly applied to birds of various groups – for instance, to some thornbills, to certain wrens, and to the Australian tailorbird; it includes the sweet-voiced reedwarbler, genus *Acrocephalus*, and a small terrestrial bird known as the speckled warbler. Most commonly, Australian warblers are very small, widely distributed, insectivorous birds of the genus *Gerygone*; there are some ten species, found chiefly in northern and eastern coastal regions, not including Tas. Best known is the white-throated warbler, occurring from the tropics to Vic. and not unknown in suburban Brisbane and Sydney; with a yellow breast and a melodious voice, it appears to be migratory, appearing in the southeast in springtime. Most of these warblers nest on horizontal vines or twigs, building pear-shaped structures of fibrous material. The tropical large-billed warbler builds a nest resembling flood-debris, placed above a stream, bringing its alternative name, floodbird, while some species habitually build near

wasps' nests or in ant-infested trees, a practice apparently acceptable to the insects.

Warburton Vic. (pop. 2304) This popular tourist town on the Yarra River 77km east of Melbourne is noted for its fine treed and hilly landscape. It developed after gold was discovered in the 1860s, but today its economy relies on sawmilling and tourism; it also has a printing works and a sanatorium and health-food factory.

Warburton Range WA This ridge marks the western extremity of the crystalline ranges of central Australia and is one of a group of ranges lying between the Gibson Desert to the north and the Great Victoria Desert to the south. The region has been prospected for minerals but only minor deposits are present. The range, named after explorer Peter Egerton Warburton, is now is an Aboriginal reserve.

Ward, Russel (1914–), historian, b. Adelaide. A teacher for most of his career, Ward was appointed deputy vice-chancellor of the University of New England, NSW, in 1982. The author of numerous historical works, he is perhaps best known for *The Australian Legend* (1958) and *A Nation for a Continent: A History of Australia 1901–1975* (1977); he also edited the *Penguin Book of Australian Ballads* (1964).

Wardell, William Wilkinson (1823–99), architect, b. England. Wardell arrived in Australia in 1858 and was government architect in Vic. 1859–78. His best-known building is St Patrick's Cathedral in Melbourne (1860–97), an outstanding example of Gothic Revival architecture in Australia and reflecting Wardell's earlier association with the English pioneer of this style, Augustus Pugin. His other Melbourne buildings include the elegant St John's Church (1860–5) in Toorak and the magnificent ES&A (now ANZ) Bank (1883–7) in Collins Street. Wardell also designed several buildings in NSW and Tas., notably the fine sandstone cathedral, St Mary's, in Sydney (1855).

Warragamba River NSW This is part of the middle course of the Nepean–Hawkesbury river system – a section about 22km long, from the meeting of the Wollondilly and Cox rivers to the point at which it becomes the Nepean. The Warragamba dam, 25km upstream from Penrith, is the major source of Sydney's water supply; the waters behind the dam extend upstream through The Gorge, beyond which they form Lake Burragorang.

Warrnambool Vic. (pop. 22 706) This seaside city lies 262km southwest of Melbourne in a rich grazing and dairying region; its secondary industry is based principally on food-processing and clothing and textile manufacture. The bay was used by whalers and sealers from the early 19th century but pastoral settlement dates from the 1850s. The city is an important tourist centre noted for its sheltered beaches, parks and gardens, fine racecourse, and cultural centre; it has a number of significant historic and prehistoric sites, including an Aboriginal shell midden at Thunder Point and several offshore shipwrecks.

Warrumbungle Range NSW This is a spur of the Great Dividing Range, extending for about 130km northwest of the Liverpool Range in the east of the State. Evidence of volcanic activity 13 million years ago remains in the form of spectacular, jagged peaks created by hardening lava and from which the outer cones have been eroded. Coonabarabran is situated to the east, and the mountains also contain the British-Australian major observatory, Siding Spring. The highest peak, 1228m, is Mt Exmouth, or Wombelong; the vegetation is varied to the east and west of the range, as is the fauna. The region was first explored by John Oxley in 1818.

Warung, Price [William Astley] (1854–1911), author and journalist, b. England. Warung arrived in Australia with his family in 1859 and travelled and worked as a journalist 1875–90 before settling in Sydney. He contributed numerous short stories to the *Bulletin* in the early 1890s, after which he was actively involved in the labour movement until ill health and drug addiction forced his retirement. Many of his short stories – concentrating mainly on the horrors of the convict system – were collected and published in the 1890s; among the most notable of these volumes is *Tales of the Convict System* (1892).

war veterans, repatriation of The Australian federal government, through the Repatriation Commission and the Department of Veterans' Affairs, provides pensions, social and economic rehabilitation, medical care and other services for war veterans and their dependants; the Repatriation Commission operates under the Veterans' Entitlements Act 1986, which superseded the Repatriation Act of 1920. Personnel of the Australian defence forces from all wars or engagements in which Australia has been involved are eligible for such services; in certain cases, ex-members of allied forces, who are resident in Australia, are also eligible. There are repatriation hospitals in all State capitals and in some country centres. In 1986–7, total expenditure by all Commonwealth departments overseeing the needs of veterans was $3719 million; there were 404 794 service pensions in force, of which 170 585 were for wives and widows.

Warwick Qld (pop. 9435) This attractive city on the Condamine River, 161km southwest of Brisbane, is the main centre for the southern Darling Downs. Dairying and wheat farming have replaced the original pastoral economy established by the first settlers from NSW, led by Patrick Leslie in 1840. Industries include cheese production and wool processing. Warwick has many fine early sandstone buildings and is also noted for its scenic surrounds, much of which is set aside in national parks.

wasps The term 'wasp' is a general one covering two major divisions of these stinging insects: the parasitic wasps (> *Hymenoptera*), whose larvae develop within a free-living host, and the aculeate wasps treated in this article; females of this group usually provision burrows or specially constructed nests with paralysed prey upon which the larvae feed. Each species usually specialises in a certain insect or spider prey, which is stung so that it remains alive but immobile. Some aculeate species are social, but the majority are solitary, with a single female tending her nest; females often continue to provide nutriment until the larvae pupate. Adult wasps take nectar, and are important pollinators of plants. There are more than 2000 species of aculeate wasps in Australia, of which bees and ants are specialised derivatives.

The metallic blue-green cuckoo wasps of the family Chrysididae enter the nests of other bees or wasps to lay their eggs which, when hatched, feed on the host larvae; adults are heavily sclerotised to avoid attack by host species. Wasps of the family Thynnidae are often found on flowers, where the larger, winged male is joined in copulation to a small, wingless female; some Australian orchids, capitalising on the female's habit of waiting on a flower for the males to arrive, have developed in imitation of the appearance of the female thynnid, so that the males actually attempt to mate with the flowers, thereby facilitating pollination by pseudocopulation.

The large, active spider wasps of the family Pompilidae provision their nests with spiders, but the Sphecidae family shows a wide range of nesting behaviour and host preference; the large orange-and-black cicada-killer stocks its underground nest with cicadas, and burrows of sand wasps are often seen along sandy bush tracks. Mud-daubers gather balls of mud which they mix with saliva; this composition is used to construct a nest, which they provision with small spiders.

Wasps of the family Vespidae are social, and construct papery nests of plant matter mixed with saliva; the founding female initially produces non-reproductive female workers which help construct the nest and feed the larvae, but as the nest becomes larger, additional reproductive females are produced. Vespids will aggressively defend their nest if disturbed. The introduced European wasp, *Vespula germanica*, has become firmly established in southeastern Australia and may form colonies consisting of thousands of individuals.

Waten, Judah Leon (1911–85), author, b. Russia. Waten was the son of a Jewish family that arrived in Australia in 1914. A communist, a member of Melbourne's Realist Writers group, and a tireless political disputant, Waten published seven novels, two short-story collections, an autobiographical travel book, a children's novel and a brief history of the 1930s depression. His widely translated short stories and novels about Jewish immigrant life, notably *Alien Son* (1952), mark him as an Australian literary pioneer.

water and water resources Australia is the driest of all the inhabited continents. The main reasons for this are an average annual rainfall of 470mm (meagre by world standards), comparatively little surface run-off and very high rates of evaporation and transpiration; many of Australia's rivers are variable in flow, and one-third of the continent has no waterways at all. As a result, water conservation and irrigation have been indispensable since the first days of settlement: while urban settlement and industry draw mainly on surface water held in dams and reservoirs, these resources are available over less than two-thirds of Australia's land surface and many areas are dependent on artesian water, stored in tanks.

As the result of rapid developments in storage and distribution of water this century, Australia's water supply seems relatively secure. The main emphases of conservation in the future are thus likely to be maintaining water quality and ensuring that existing resources are used as efficiently as possible.

Surface water Surface water in Australia is both sparse and erratic in occurrence over much of the continent. Average annual rainfall decreases rapidly as one moves inland, and the semi-arid zone is reached within 300km – in many places, much less – of the seaboard. Although urban development has been concentrated in the coastal regions, the main population centres have not always been close to the major sources of surface water; moreover, as the flow from these sources varies markedly from year to year, large and expensive storages have had to be constructed to guarantee reliable supplies. In Perth and Adelaide, surface water is already limited: Perth is increasingly dependent on its limited available groundwater, and during drought Adelaide has to draw up to 70% of its water from the distant Murray River, with attendant water-quality problems.

Nearly half of the Australian land surface has no direct discharge to the sea, any run-off occurring there after storms being lost through evapotranspiration: the vast Murray–Darling river system, for example, loses more than 50% of its run-off in this way. Further inland is the huge Lake Eyre drainage basin, which extends across parts of Qld, SA, NSW and the NT; it lies some 16m below sea-level and has ephemeral streams only. Surface water has been more completely developed in the Murray–Darling system than in any other drainage basin: over 80% of its flows are controlled by storages totalling 25 400 million cu.m, the largest of which are in the Snowy Mountains region (source of the Murray) where an average of 1140 million cu.m are diverted annually into the basin from the southeast coastal drainage division. Most of this stored water is used for irrigation. Tas. also has very large surface water resources, more than 90% of the large storages being used primarily for hydro-electricity generation.

More than half of Australia's total run-off occurs in sparsely populated northeast Qld, between Cape York and Mackay. Low-lying, this region offers little opportunity for the development of storages big enough to regulate the sporadic but frequently heavy run-off generated by the summer monsoonal rains; damming of the giant Burdekin River was completed in the late 1980s, however, for irrigation development and the supply of urban water.

Groundwater The main sources of groundwater in Australia are shallow, uncompacted sediments and deeper-lying sedimentary aquifers. The unconsolidated sediments close to the earth's surface are the major and most easily developed source, although water levels vary markedly between seasons.

Sedimentary aquifers, of solid but permeable rock, often extend over large areas and may be hundreds of metres thick. When an aquifer is confined between layers of impervious rock, the resulting pressure can cause the water to rise above ground-level when tapped; these sources of artesian water have underpinned the development of Australia's inland pastoral industry. The outstanding source is the Great Artesian Basin, which underlies some 1.57 million sq.km in Qld, SA, NSW and the NT and is the largest such basin in the world: it is tapped by more than 5000 major bores and numerous smaller ones with an annual flow of about 600 000ML. The exploitation of artesian and sub-artesian water over more than a century has, however, meant that many bores now require pumping and others have dried up completely, as recharge rates are relatively low and extraction has far exceeded the rate of replenishment.

A further source of groundwater in Australia is the joints and cracks in fractured igneous and metamorphic rocks. These are geographically scattered, and the difficulty of obtaining adequate yields has discouraged exploitation.

Irrigation The establishment of large irrigation schemes, first in Vic. and then in NSW, began in the years following the severe drought of 1877–81. These early developments were seen as a means of watering and feeding stock during droughts, but it was soon realised that the best economic use of irrigation water was to maximise yearly production, thus obviating the need to accumulate reserves of water and fodder. Notable among the pioneers of irrigation in Australia were the > *Chaffey brothers*, Sir Samuel McCaughey and > *John Bradfield*. Many engineering feats were required to supply water across Australia's vast distances, one of which was the > *Goldfields and Agricultural Water Supply* scheme in WA (completed in 1903).

The greatest expansion of agricultural irrigation occurred between 1950 and 1970, when the area increased from about 600 000ha to about 1.3 million ha. Schemes now operate in every State, NSW having the largest area under irrigation (some 712 000ha, 42% of the total area). Of all irrigation water, more than 80% is drawn from rivers and canals and three-quarters is used in the Murray–Darling Basin. Other major schemes are centred on Coleambally in NSW, the Goulburn-Campaspe-Loddon rivers in northern Vic., the Dawson and Burdekin rivers in Qld and the Preston and Ord rivers in WA; in SA, most irrigation water is drawn from the Murray River. Agriculture is the greatest user, the entire yield of many crops – including rice, cotton, fruit for canning and drying, and tobacco – coming from irrigated areas. The success of irrigation depends above all on its ability to supply water at critical times of the plants' growth cycle.

Expansion has now slowed; by the late 1980s the total irrigated area was about 1.6 million ha and this figure was not expected to increase by more than another 200 000ha by the year 2000. Most of the remaining development is likely to be in the northeast coastal region.

Water quality In recent years, the maintenance of water quality has become as important as water storage and irrigation. The main problems are > *pollution* in various forms, silting and salinity – all of which are directly and indirectly caused by human activities. There are as yet no known problems in Australia comparable to the 'acid rain' occurring in parts of the northern hemisphere, although low levels of rain-borne salt have been reported in some coastal areas.

The quality of groundwater is affected by substances dissolved from the material in which it occurs. Water in the deep sedimentary aquifers is in contact with the rock for long periods, sometimes for thousands of years, and its quality ranges from excellent (as is the case with the Alice Springs town supply, which comes entirely from deep sandstone), through brackish and fit only for stock, to several times more saline than seawater (along parts of the salt-affected Murray).

The quality of surface water deteriorates for a number of reasons, most notably 'point source' pollution – the discharge of water polluted by industrial activities such as food processing or chemical production. The discharge of effluent from such industries is now strictly controlled. Since the major cities are on the coast, pollution of the water supply by urban sewage and other wastes has been minimised, as these discharges are dispatched (often with minimal treatment) into the oceans. Increasing loads on the coastal waters near urban beaches in the last decade or so have made this approach less acceptable, however, and more careful disposal schemes are being developed. The growth of large inland cities such as Canberra has caused new problems, and elaborate and costly treatment plants have been required to protect water quality for users downstream.

Water pollution is also caused by the excessive use of fertilisers, which in many parts of Australia has led to eutrophication – the presence of excess nutrients in lakes, ponds and other waterways, which alters the natural balance of resident flora and fauna. This form of pollution is extremely difficult to control, partly because its source can rarely be traced, and public education and advice are the only really effective remedies. Another problem is the accumulation of sediment loads in streams and thus increased turbidity (a longstanding problem in Melbourne's Yarra River), which sullies water supplies as well as silting up storages. This problem is often caused by soil movement caused by bare fallowing, overgrazing or overcultivation.

A particularly serious and growing problem is water salinity, arising from land development and irrigation. Large tracts of Australia's ancient landscape have been inundated by seas in the past, leaving salt deposits near the surface: the native vegetation adapted to these conditions, establishing a delicate balance between the annual input from rainfall and the output from plant transpiration, which kept the water table at depths where salt could not approach the surface and damage plant roots. Since European settlement, the replacement of native forest by shallow-rooted pastures has reduced the amount of water removed by transpiration, causing dryland salinity in southwest WA. In addition, the application of irrigation water to shallow-rooted crops has produced salt movements and sometimes waterlogging, most notably in the Murray and Murrumbidgee valleys, leaving deposited salt in the soil and killing all vegetation.

Water conservation It is now recognised that land and water management are inseparable, and water-conservation activities therefore aim to maintain the stability of whole catchments as well as waterways. Problems caused by sediment loads can sometimes be traced to particular parts of the catchment, which can be treated by such means as tree planting. Improved practices in irrigation areas include the use of drip or trickle application to avoid overuse of water, and more precise determination of the timing and amount of water supply. Salinity problems in the Murray River are being tackled by diverting groundwater effluent to artificial evaporation basins and natural salt lakes; natural flows are sometimes supplemented by pumping, as has been done in the Murrumbidgee Irrigation Area.

Although agriculture is by far the biggest user of water in Australia, much can be done to conserve it in urban areas and so postpone the need for new storage dams and reticulation works. Recommended measures include replacing lawns with native gardens, more careful watering schedules, and the use of water-efficient appliances such as dual-flush toilets. >> *agriculture*; *dams and reservoirs*

water conservation > *water and water resources*

waterfalls The majority of Australia's waterfalls occur in or near coastal regions, and in the eastern States most lie in the mountains of the Great Dividing Range. To consider as noteworthy falls of over 60m, NSW has more than 30, including Wollomombi in New England (believed to be Australia's highest) where the Wollomombi River, a tributary of the Macleay, drops 335m from the plateau into a narrow gorge. Most of these falls are found in the Macleay or Hawkesbury river systems – particularly in the Blue Mountains – or on the Shoalhaven River. Cascades of over 150m also appear in the Clarence and Hastings systems, in the northeast of the State.

Qld has about seventeen permanent falls and many on seasonal rivers. The highest, Wallaman (300m) on Stony Creek, are seasonal; the permanent, formerly spectacular Barron Falls (also 300m) have been diminished by construction of a weir. Only slightly lower are the Elizabeth Grant Falls (290m) at the head of the Tully River. Many of Qld's major falls are now contained in national parks, as are those in Tas. The Meander Falls (180m) are the highest in that State.

Vic., although containing some of the highest mountains, has few waterfalls – the longest drop being Steavenson, near Marysville – and SA has none above 60m, but the Darling Range in WA has Lesmurdie (120m), and in the NT impressive – though seasonal – falls occur on the East and South Alligator and Liverpool rivers, in the rugged country of Arnhem Land, and on the Daly and Katherine rivers.

water-fleas A popular name for a number of species of brachiopod crustaceans, this is applied most appropriately to small specimens of jumping habit, of the genus *Daphnia*, but extends to copepods and ostracods. These predominantly freshwater animals flourish in warm, equable waters; their eggs are able to withstand great cold or drought, repopulating waters with seemingly miraculous speed when warm or wet conditions return. In Australia, water-fleas in the broad sense include tadpole-shrimps in temporary high mountain pools, fairy shrimps and clam shrimps in temporary, shallow river backwaters, and brine shrimps in inland salt lakes and pools.

water-lilies These aquatic flowering plants belong to the family Nymphaeaceae, which comprises about 70 species worldwide; all are herbaceous perennials with air-filled channels in the leaves and flowers that allow them to float on the surface of water. Australia's native water-lilies are poorly known but there appear to be at least six species, occurring mainly across the tropical north. The most common northern species is *Nymphaea violaceae*; that of the subtropical east is the giant blue water-lily, *N. gigantea*, which is often confused with the introduced African variety, *N. capensis*. Also native to tropical Australia is the sacred lotus or pink water-lily, *Nelumbo nucifera*, which is generally classified in the family Nelumbonaceae. The tubers, leaf-stalks and seeds of all water-lily species are eaten by Aborigines.

water-skiing > *water sports*

water sports The formation of the Motorboat Club of Sydney in 1905 marked the beginning of water sports in Australia. Racing is conducted using craft with both inboard and outboard motors in a variety of capacities; the Griffiths Cup, usually held at Lake Eppalock in Vic., was first contested in 1910. The Power Boat Association of Australia was formed in 1927 to oversee the proliferation of local clubs, and was expanded in 1962–3 to include NZ clubs as the Australasian Power Boat Association. In 1977 Ken Warby set a world waterspeed record of 464.5kmh on Blowering Dam, NSW, and Australians have also established records in other classes.

With more than 16 000 registered competitors and an admirable record in world competition, water-skiing is a major sport. The first officially recorded attempt to water-ski was made by Bill McLaghlan and Jack Murray – both former motor racers – on the Hawkesbury River, NSW, in 1946; in 1950 the Australian Water Ski Association was formed, and has since conducted national championships. Slalom, jump and trick events are held, but it is in barefoot events that Australians have excelled: Paul McManus broke the world endurance record in 1968 and Wayne Jones set a world speed record of 121.25kmh in 1970. In the 1970s and 1980s Australia produced a string of multiple champions, including Kim Lampard, Debbie Pugh and Brett Wing, who took all five categories in a barefoot Grand Slam in 1980. The world championship was staged at Surfers Paradise in 1971. >> *surf and surfing*; *swimming and diving*; *windsurfing*

Watling, Thomas (1762–?), artist, b. Scotland. Watling, transported to Australia in 1791 for forgery, was an accomplished landscape painter and zoological artist. During his term he produced some handsome sketches and watercolours and the first oil painting in Australia, *Direct North General View of Sydney Cove, 1794*, now in the Dixson Gallery, Sydney. He was granted an absolute pardon in 1797.

Watson, John Christian (1867–1941), politician, b. Chile. Watson arrived from NZ in 1886. A former president of the Sydney Trades and Labour Council (1893) and of the Australian Labour Federation, he led the 1894 ALF conference which drew up the 'solidarity' pledge by which Labor candidates undertake to abide by majority decisions of caucus. He became the first leader of the ALP and the first Labor prime minister, April–August 1904. He was expelled from the party in 1916 during the debate over conscription, and resigned from politics.

wattle This is the common collective name for trees and shrubs in the genus *Acacia*, which belongs to the mimosa family and has up to 900 native species in Australia. The name derives from the early days of European settlement when the branches of native shrubs were used in 'wattle-and-daub' construction, although in fact the > *blackwattle* – rather than acacias – was used. The genus *Acacia* is also represented in Africa and the American tropics and the earliest named species were of northern Africa, for which reason the appropriateness of grouping all Australian species within this genus is now being questioned.

Wattles dominate the vegetation in arid regions of Australia where many thrive in environments too dry for eucalypts; elsewhere they occur as understorey plants in eucalypt forests and occasionally in rainforest. Most species are shrubs of around 1–3m tall and many become small trees up to about 15m; a few eastern coastal species of wet eucalypt forest or rainforest margins become tall trees of up to 30m. Wattles are well adapted for survival in poor soils: as with other legumes, their roots contain nitrogen-fixing bacteria which permits growth in nitrogen-deficient soils and their hard seeds, borne in bean-like pods, germinate profusely after scorching by fires. The massed cream or golden-yellow flowers are often showy, although individual flowers are minute. Each consists of a ring of tiny petals and a brush of much longer, hair-like stamens; flowers are massed either into globular heads or rod-like spikes, the latter often grouped into larger, branched sprays.

Some wattle trees are milled for timber; many inland species have dense, deeply coloured wood valued for small decorative items and tool handles and used by Aborigines for weapons and digging implements. Many have tannin-rich barks suitable for tanning leather: most of the world's tanbark now comes from a single species, A. mearnsii, which is native to southeastern Australia but is grown in plantations in southern Africa. The foliage of several species provides nutritious grazing for livestock, but most have tough inedible leaves. Aborigines used the pods and seeds of some species as food and also harvested the insects – notably witchetty grubs – that burrow into the plants' stems and roots; native bees process the pollen into protein-rich 'bee-bread', also a valued Aboriginal food.

The classification of wattles is revised periodically. Among the better-known species is the mulga, A. aneura, the dominant small tree over large areas in the 125–250mm rainfall zone; its hard cream and chocolate timber is used in ornaments. The brigalow, A. harpophyllus, is a tall tree with dense bluish foliage which dominates some semi-arid regions on fertile soils in Qld and NSW; it often forms thick scrub, much of which has been cleared for grazing and cropping. The gidgee, A cambagei, rather resembles brigalow but occurs further west; the related Georgina gidgee is a stock poison. The boree or weeping myall, A. pendula, resembles a small weeping willow; its pale-grey foliage is browsed by stock. Tree species of higher-rainfall areas include the blackwood, A. melanoxylon, which extends from southeastern SA to northern Qld; the silver wattle, A. dealbata, a slender 30m tree of the Australian Alps, with ferny foliage; and the cedar wattle, A. elata, which occurs further north in NSW. The Australian floral emblem is variously identified as the golden wattle, A. pycnantha, a common small tree or shrub of Vic., eastern SA and southwestern NSW; and the golden wreath wattle, A. saligna, of south coastal WA. Popular garden species include the Cootamundra wattle, A. baileyana, and the Qld wattle, A. pedalyriifolia, both large shrubs making a brilliant floral display in winter. The sallow wattle, A. longifolia, a vigorous shrub with yellow flowers in spikes, is widespread in coastal eastern Australia and is used in soil conservation work; a semi-prostrate form found on exposed beach dunes is valued as a sand stabiliser.

wattle-and-daub > *architecture; black-wattle; mudbrick building*

wattlebirds > *honeyeaters*

weather > *climate*

weeds In Australia, as elsewhere, most weeds are either grasses, daisies or thistles, which have numerous tiny seeds that are carried long distances by the wind, or fruit-bearing plants such as lantana, blackberry and boxthorn whose seeds are transported by birds. While some weeds (like the wax-producing jojoba plant) are economically useful, many are invasive pests that compete with crops and native plants, poison stock, or taint agricultural and grazing products.

In Australia there are a number of weeds classified as serious pests. These include widespread poisonous species such as Cape tulips, originally imported from South Africa as garden plants, which have killed large numbers of cattle in SA and WA; and another cultivated flower, St John's wort, which has produced serious (and sometimes fatal) skin inflammations in stock in the southeastern States, SA and WA. Many weeds also overrun crops, in some cases threatening production: weeds of the mustard family, notably the wild turnip and hoary cress, are major pests of cereal and grain crops from WA to the mallee areas of SA and Vic. Troublesome weeds of grazing lands include familiar invaders such as lantana, blackberries, bracken fern and Paterson's curse. While the prickly pear, which infested vast tracts of Qld and NSW from the late 19th century onwards, was virtually eliminated in the seven years 1927–34 by the introduction of the *Cactoblastis* caterpillar, other cactus plants have subsequently become serious pests in Qld. > *Algae*, which include a range of aquatic weeds, are also a serious problem in many Australian waterways, blocking drainage systems and often smothering other forms of aquatic life.

Biological control by fungi and insects has been successful with a number of weeds and is increasingly preferred to herbicides on environmental as well as economic grounds, as the destructive effects of chemicals on Australia's soils and water resources are proven. Water hyacinth, a weed that clogs drainage channels, is now, for example, being controlled by a moth released in 1977; and an introduced leaf beetle has helped reduce infestations of the pasture weed groundsel in NSW and Qld. Each State has legislation for the control of noxious weeds, and the importation of declared weeds – across State borders or from overseas – is stringently controlled.

weevils > *beetles*

Weipa Qld (pop. 2436) A former Presbyterian mission station on the northwest coast of Cape York Peninsula, this town lies on a vast bauxite deposit stretching along 160km of coastline. Weipa's development has included a new port and a town, largely built by the mining company Comalco Ltd, and a shipping channel has been dredged to the mouth of the Embley River. The Weipa bauxite mine is the world's largest, with exports to Japan and Europe, though most goes to the alumina refinery at Gladstone. Matthew Flinders noted the area's 'reddish cliffs' in 1802, but their potential as an economic source of raw material for aluminium was not recognised until 1955. The nearby Aboriginal shell middens, 2000–4000 years old, are protected archaeological relics.

Weir, Peter Lindsay (1944–), film director, b. Sydney. After working in television and for the Commonwealth Film Unit, Weir directed his first feature film, *The Cars That Ate Paris*, in 1974. Other Australian films include *Gallipoli* (1981), *The Year of Living Dangerously* (1982) and, perhaps most importantly, *Picnic at Hanging Rock* (1975), which proved to be a major commercial and artistic breakthrough for the indigenous film industry.

Now US-based, Weir has recently directed *Witness* (1985), *The Mosquito Coast* (1986), and *Dead Poets Society* (1989), all of which were both critical and commercial successes.

WEL > *Women's Electoral Lobby*

welfare organisations There are some 40 000 non-government welfare organisations in Australia, which in complementing (and supplementing) the government's formal social services make an invaluable contribution to the welfare of the community. These include major bodies such as the Australian > *Red Cross Society*, the Smith Family, religious-based organisations such as the Salvation Army, St Vincent de Paul (Catholic) and Brotherhood of St Laurence (Anglican), and a plethora of smaller organisations from advice bureaus to local self-help groups. A large part of their work is voluntary and funded by public donation, although many organisations receive some degree of government funding (62.9% of all such bodies receiving some income from the government in 1984). Traditional forms of welfare assistance include provision of accommodation, income support, social development, and health care, although services such as counselling, the provision of women's refuges and rape-crisis centres, and drug-rehabilitation have developed more recently in response to society's changing needs. Such change is also reflected in the fact that about half of the existing organisations were founded between 1970 and 1980.

Among the earliest of the existing welfare organisations is the St Vincent de Paul Society, which dates from the 1850s in Australia. The society, which is closely associated with the Catholic Church, provides spiritual and material help for homeless youth, the poor, the old and the lonely; the provision of accommodation for homeless men and aid for immigrants are major activities, although members also undertake home and hospital visits, child care and drug rehabilitation. The Salvation Army was set up in Australia in 1881 and by 1891 were corps in all Australian colonies. While membership (and support) has declined in recent years, the 'Salvos' remain highly regarded and have augmented their traditional welfare work – such as running hostels for the homeless, friendless and destitute – with undertakings such as drug-rehabilitation centres, all of which run parallel to the group's spiritual activities. The St John Ambulance, a branch of the religious Order of St John, was also established in

Australia in the 1880s, and remains the recognised authority for teaching first aid to the public and industry. Its voluntary members provide first-aid services at sports and other public gatherings, and provide assistance in the event of disasters or emergencies. Noted welfare organisations established in the 20th century include Barnardo's Australia, which was first registered in Australia as a charity in 1921 and provides help for underprivileged children with services such as foster care, day-care schemes, and vocational guidance. Australia's largest voluntary welfare organisation, the Smith Family, was set up in Sydney in 1922 and now operates in NSW, Vic. and the ACT. Its aid to the needy, provided by anonymous donations, comprises food, clothing and furniture, financial aid for rent or household bills, and professional welfare guidance. A relatively recent innovation is the telephone service Life Line, founded in Sydney in 1963 and now both national and international. As well as providing a confidential 24-hour emergency telephone service, it employs professional counsellers who attend those in emotional or financial distress and provides food and clothing in emergencies. Other large welfare organisation include Alcoholics Anonymous and Lady Gowrie Child Centres.

There are several umbrella organisations which together represent most of Australia's non-government welfare groups, providing a forum for sectional interests, affording greater lobbying power, promoting both the activities of welfare groups and the cause of community welfare in general. The main such groups are the Australian Council of Social Service (ACOSS), the Australian Council for Rehabilitation of Disabled, the Australian Council on the Ageing, the Australian Early Childhood Association and the Youth Affairs Council of Australia (YACA). >> *ex-service organisations*; *foreign aid*; *social services*; *youth organisations*

Wellesley Islands Qld This group lies at the head of the Gulf of Carpentaria, and comprises Mornington, Sweers, Bentinck, the Bountiful islands and Forsyth islands. They were first seen by Matthew Flinders in the *Investigator* voyage of 1802, and named in honour of a governor-general of India – the Earl of Mornington, later Marquis Wellesley.

Wentworth family, noted in colonial administration and politics. **D'Arcy** (?1762–1827), surgeon and magistrate, b. Ireland, was a colourful character with aristocratic connections. He sailed with the Second Fleet in 1790; after six years on Norfolk Island as superintendent of convicts, he brought his mistress (a former convict) and family to Sydney where he rose to many official positions and achieved great wealth and honour. A high point in his career was his appointment as a civil member of the Supreme Court. His son, **William Charles** (?1792–1872), explorer and politician, b. Norfolk Island, in 1813 crossed the Blue Mountains with William Lawson and Gregory Blaxland. He was the first Australian-born citizen to achieve important office, becoming the most influential politician of his day, although his views – like those of many statesmen – changed with the years. At first he was a radical, opposed to exclusivists, violently campaigning for emancipists' rights, freedom of the press and self-government, forming the Australian Patriotic Association for this purpose in 1835. He was also a precocious federalist. Later he came to favour more conservative views, supporting squatters, landed interests and continued transportation, and even proposing an Australian peerage; he also supported limited franchise based on property, thus losing the support of the increasing urban proletariat.

Werder, Felix (1922–), music composer and critic, b. Berlin. Arriving in Australia as a refugee in 1941, Werder was music critic for the Melbourne *Age* in the 1960s. A leading exponent of the avant garde in music, he has composed numerous orchestral works and operas, including *The Affair* (1969) for the Australian Opera. He also formed the group, Australia Felix, which specialises in performing contemporary music.

Wessel Islands NT A chain of elongated islands in the Arafura Sea, the Wessel Islands extend over some 120km from Point Napier, in northeast Arnhem Land. The longest is Marchimbar, more than 50km, on which bauxite deposits have been found. The islands are part of the Arnhem Land Aboriginal Reserve and famous for their rock paintings – on North Wessel is the Cave of the Rainbow Serpent, containing a striking impression of this awesome and almost universal creature of Aboriginal mythology.

West, Morris Langlo (1916–), novelist, b. Melbourne. Trained as a teacher, West wrote a number of unsuccessful novels before *Children* *of the Sun* (1957) brought him worldwide acclaim. This was followed by numerous best-selling works, including *The Devil's Advocate* (1959), *The Shoes of the Fisherman* (1963), *The Salamander* (1973) and *Cassidy* (1986), many of which have been filmed or dramatised. West's themes are usually international in scope, involving political, religious or moral dilemmas.

Westall, William (1781–1850), painter, b. England. A landscape artist, Westall was a student at the Royal Academy before being appointed topographical artist to Matthew Flinders aboard the *Investigator* for his survey of the east coast of Australia 1801–5. His work illustrates Flinders's book *A Voyage to Terra Australis* (1814).

Western Australia (WA) The largest Australian State in terms of area and the fourth-largest in terms of population, WA is also the most solitary State, the most recent to be widely explored by Europeans, and the most important producer of minerals. It is a politically conservative State but has often been headed by a Labor government.

With an area of 2 535 500sq.km. (32.9% of Australia's total) and a coastline of 12 500km, WA is largely made up of a plateau ranging from 300m to 600m above sea-level. Mountains include the Hamersley Range, within which is the State's highest point (Mt Meharry, 1244m), and the Carnarvon and Stirling ranges; coastal plains up to 60km wide border the plateau. The main urban centres, mostly but not all ports, include > *Perth* (the capital), its port > *Fremantle*, Wyndham, Yampi Sound, Port Hedland, Dampier, Carnarvon, Geraldton, Bunbury, Albany, Esperance and > *Kalgoorlie–Boulder*. The climate varies greatly: the north is tropical, with a monsoonal wet season in summer and a dry season in winter, and mean temperatures ranging from 22°C to 30°C; the southern sector has a Mediterranean climate with the rainfall mainly in winter and mean temperatures ranging from 15°C to 19°C; the intermediate zones receive light and irregular rains and there are large areas of desert. The rivers flow mainly westward and most of them are seasonal.

Historical development As elsewhere in Australia, Aborigines have inhabited WA for at least 30 000 years; the majority lived in the more fertile areas and it is only because those living in the arid regions retained their tribal identity much longer that they are commonly seen as typical. Dutch ships touched at various points on the WA coast from 1616, but there were Asian coastal visitors well before that date. Fear of French interest led to the first British settlement, at Albany in 1826, but it was James Stirling's glowing reports of the Swan River area that brought free settlement and the 1829 proclamation of the colony of WA, and thus the completion of British annexation of the continent. Early settlers had to battle with poor land, a shortage of labour and a lack of skill among what labour there was. By 1840 the European population had dropped to 1139, and the situation worsened during the economic depression of the 1840s. Between 1850 and 1868, transportation – instigated because of the desperate state of the colony – resulted in the arrival of about 10 000 convicts and some expansion of the economy, but the decade 1860–70 saw further stagnation. Growth remained slow until the gold rushes of 1885–95 brought about a population jump of 270% between 1890 and 1900; although there was antagonism between the miners and long-established coastal farmers, it was almost certainly only the presence of the former which led to the colony accepting Federation. As gold petered out the former miners took up farming, more land was cleared and manufacturing began; both sectors grew gradually, and with many setbacks, until greatly increased immigration after World War 2 led to faster growth. The present rapid growth of WA came with the exploitation of iron and nickel (from the 1960s), oil and natural gas and, since the 1980s, diamonds.

Population and economy WA is the fastest-growing State: its population at the 1986 census of 1 440 600 represents a growth rate of 0.11% in the five years between censuses, placing it above Qld (0.1%); at the same census WA's population passed that of SA, moving it into fourth position. The present figure gives a population density of 0.57 per sq. km, lower than that for any other part of Australia except the NT, but since 70% live in the Perth area and 90% in the southwest corner of the State the density of most of WA is probably much the same as that of the NT. About 71% of the population is Australian-born and 14% from the UK or Ireland (higher than any other State); Italy, with 2%, is the next most common birthplace.

Despite major developments in mining, WA's economy remains largely based on agriculture, forestry and fishing, these industries contributing some 14% of the Australian total and employing 53 000 people. Beef and wool are the main agricultural exports, which also include wheat, barley, oats, fruit, timber and fish. WA's mineral boom began slowly, iron-ore mining commencing at Yampi Sound and Koolyanobbing during 1951–2, but in 1960 the federal government lifted its embargo on iron-ore exports and huge developments in the Pilbara region began. Other mineral products include nickel (since 1967), gold, diamonds (since 1983), bauxite, and oil and natural gas from Barrow Island, Dongara and the North West Shelf. Manufacturing includes metal fabrication, the processing of minerals, engineering and food-processing, almost all centred on the Perth metropolitan area and Kwinana.

Government and politics WA was the last Australian colony to win self-government, not electing a legislative assembly until 1890 or a legislative council until 1893. Voting for the assembly was at first restricted to property owners, then from 1893 to adult (over 21) males, with women gaining the vote in 1899. The first premier, John Forrest, initiated a policy of heavy overseas borrowing to finance public works, and this policy continued under his successors – conservative and Labor – until loans were replaced by overseas investment in private enterprise, especially after World War 2. Investment greatly increased under the Liberal premiers Sir David Brand (1959–71) and Sir Charles Court (1974–82) but continued under the Labor government of Brian Burke (1983–8). Burke also initiated a policy, known as WA Inc., of modelling government enterprise on the corporate sector and investing government money in that sector; this led to a scandal under his successor, Peter Dowding, when enterprises guaranteed by the government went bankrupt. In 1990, amid resulting pressure, Dowding resigned and was replaced as premier by Carmen Lawrence – the first female leader of any State or federal government in Australia.

Western District Vic. This region occupies the southwest of the State, south of the Grampians, extending from the SA border east to Ballarat. The district was explored in 1836 by Thomas Mitchell, who named it 'Australia Felix'; first to use this land were whalers, who grew crops along the coast, and the Henty brothers established a farm at Portland in 1834.

The land is generally level and contains several volcanic lakes; the plains were natural pastures, and by 1840 squatters had taken up almost the entire area. The Western District is noted especially for production of fine merino wool; other – and still major – activities include fat lambs, dairying, and the growing of cereal crops and vegetables. Important regional centres are Warrnambool, Portland and Port Fairy on the coast, and the inland towns of Hamilton, Camperdown, Casterton and Terang. Port Fairy and other coastal centres support a fishing industry. The district's chief rivers are the Glenelg, Hopkins and Wannon.

Westernport Bay Vic. This large inlet on the south Vic. coast extends about 45km inland and in width varies from 15km to 35km; it is separated from Port Phillip Bay by the Mornington Peninsula. French Island lies in the inner section, while Phillip Island guards the entrance to the bay, which was named in 1798 by George Bass as the most westerly point of the coast then seen. An abortive attempt at settlement, to forestall possible French interests, took place on the eastern shore 1826–8. Development of the Bass Strait oil and natural gas fields in the 1960s was followed by rapid industrial development concentrated along the western shore, including oil refineries and tanker facilities. The resulting pollution of the bay is a major concern.

wetlands This term has been coined in recent years to describe a range of flooded features including lakes, swamps, and tidal flats such as > *mangroves*. Because of their distinctive characteristics and ecology – and also in part because of the paucity of damp environments in an arid continent – wetlands in Australia are now the subject of increasing attention and protection. Several thousand sites around the continent have been classified as wetlands, most of which not only constitute important wildlife habitats but also provide refuge during drought and assist in the regeneration of groundwater. Many have been modified, however – and in some cases destroyed altogether – by activities such as land reclamation and inshore dredging, and most States are now undertaking protective measures such as planning controls, improved management, and the purchase of significant sites.

whaler sharks > *sharks*

whales and dolphins Together with dolphins, whales are cetaceans – mammals adapted to a wholly aquatic existence. The species of whales most likely to be seen in Australian waters, or occasionally stranded on the shore, include members of the two main suborders, the toothless, baleen or whalebone whales and the toothed whales.

Whalebone whales, *Mysticeti*, take in huge mouthfuls of water when feeding, then filter it very efficiently through a whalebone screen, retaining krill and plankton. This group includes the southern right whale, *Eubalaena australis*, the chief target of the former > *whaling industry*, and the blue whale, *Balaenoptera musculus*, the largest known mammal (usually about 29m long, but one specimen of 40m having been recorded) and now rare. Another in this group is the humpback whale, *Megaptera novaeangliae,* the species most common in Australian waters, which has a marked hump of thick blubber and very long flippers – about 5m long in a 14m whale.

Toothed whales, *Odontoccti*, have ivory-like teeth, at least in the lower jaw, adapted for masticating food such as fish and squid or, in the case of the killer whale, other whales. They include the sperm whale, *Physeter catodon*, the largest and commercially the most important, which has an enormous, square-fronted head with numerous, large peg-teeth and feeds on giant octopuses and squids. Sperm whales were hunted almost to extinction in the last century. The killer whale, *Orcinus orca*, is a black whale with white patches; it has a scythe-like dorsal fin and 40–52 stout, peg-like teeth. Killers hunt in packs of 40 or more, preying on dolphins, seals, penguins and other whales. Beaked whales of several different genera are sometimes stranded on Australian shores; these are whales in which the upper jaw has evolved into a beak of ivory-like substance, though non-functional teeth may be embodied in it.

The dolphin derives its name from the Greek Delphinus, given to the common Mediterranean species that occurs in many other regions – including Australia – and is characterised by a distinct beak and a streamlined, spindle-shaped (fusiform) body. Small members of the Delphinidae, the family of toothed whales, they are unrelated to > *dolphin fishes*. Thirteen typical species are found in Australia, the most familiar of which is the cosmopolitan bottle-nosed dolphin, *Tursiops truncatus*, moving usually in small groups in coastal waters. Recent studies have concentrated on its communication by sound; the dolphin emits audible clicks, but calls include an ultrasonic component. The

southern section of the continent, including Tas., is the territory of the common dolphin, *Delphinus delphis*, growing to about 2m, and from a distinctive back-marking also known as saddle-back; the dusky dolphin, *Lagenorhynchus obscurus*, slightly smaller, dark-grey above and lighter below; Hector's dolphin, *Cephalorhynchus hectori*, strikingly coloured with light patterns on a purple-brown background; and the right whale dolphin, *Lissodelphis peroni* – black above, white below, and having no dorsal fin. Some species inhabit only warmer waters; among them – and the smallest of them – is the spinner dolphin, *Stenella longirostris*, so-called because it makes almost vertical leaps above the surface, rotating meanwhile at high speed.

whaling industry The closure in 1978 of Australia's last whaling station, near Albany in WA, marked the end of one of the nation's oldest – and, in later years, one of its most controversial – commercial activities.

Whaling was Australia's first primary industry and the most valuable source of exports until overtaken by wool in 1833. It began in 1791, when a fleet of re-employed convict transports killed seven whales off the southeast coast. Bases were established at Sydney, Hobart and Norfolk Island by 1803, but the East India Company's trade monopoly restricted British activity in the region and American whalers and sealers creamed off much of the industry's trade and skilled labour.

After the monopoly ended in 1813 and duties on oil were lifted in 1828, Sydney and Hobart whaling flourished. Exploring southwestern Vic. in the 1830s, Thomas Mitchell found a whaling station and settlement already established at Portland Bay; whaling was also significant in the first settlement of WA and SA. Initially the main prey were baleen (whalebone) species, particularly southern right whales, which were killed as they entered bays and estuaries to give birth; they were then towed to the various coastal stations from Eden in southern NSW to the Swan River in WA, along the whales' annual migration path between their tropical breeding grounds and Antarctica. Deep-sea whaling also developed from the late 18th century, most of the early fleets being American and British. They first targeted sperm whales, for their oil and spermaceti, but numbers and demand declined by the 1850s.

Whaling, like sealing, generally languished in the late 19th century, not least because the target populations became depleted through overfishing. Renewed activity in the early 20th century was undertaken largely by Norwegian and other foreign interests, and the federal government consulted Norway before setting up its Whaling Commission in 1949. Modern fishing methods increased catches dramatically, and the Whaling Commission allocated seasonal quotas in an unsuccessful attempt to curb the population decline of various species. Further protection was provided by the Whaling Act 1960, and by a ban on hunting humpbacks in 1963, but by this time the industry was again failing and whales in Australian waters (as elsewhere) were facing extinction.

Public pressure to protect whales increased during the 1970s. The Whale Protection Act 1980 outlawed whaling within all Australian waters, instigating fines of up to $100 000 for killing or interfering with whales, and the importing of whale products was prohibited. Since that time the number of humpback whales off the east coast is estimated to have more than doubled; ironically, a new threat to their survival is now presented by whale-watching tourists in boats and planes that threaten to disrupt migration and breeding patterns.

wheat Both domestically and in terms of exports, wheat is Australia's most important crop. While not a large producer by world standards (about 3% of the total), Australia is yet a major wheat exporter, some 80% of its annual crop being shipped overseas. In 1985–6, 16 108 million t were exported at a value of nearly $3 billion, a figure exceeded in Australian exports only by coal and wool. The largest buyers are China, Egypt, the Soviet Union and Japan.

Wheat is grown in all States, with a total of 11.7 million ha under cultivation. NSW is the largest producer and WA cultivates the greatest area. All Australian wheat is white-grained, being planted in winter and harvested from late spring through summer. Because of its harsh climate and relatively poor soil, Australia has been in the forefront of the development of drought- and disease-resistant wheat capable of early harvest, to avoid extreme summer temperatures. The Australian wheat industry owes a great debt to > *William Farrer* in this respect.

The main categories of milling wheat grown in Australia are Australian prime hard (used for bread-making, with a protein content of about 14%); Australian hard (with a protein content of 11% to 13%); Australian standard white (a general-purpose blending wheat with a protein content of 9% to 12%); and Australian soft (used for biscuit-making, with a protein content of 8% to 10%). Some specialist varieties, such as durum (used to make pasta), are also grown, and there are categories of non-milling wheats, used mainly for feedstock.

Owing to the size and complexity of the industry, all marketing and quality control is handled by one authority, the Australian Wheat Board, established by statute in 1939. In order to maintain stability, the AWB administers a guaranteed minimum price scheme for growers. It also controls domestic prices, which are related to export prices, and oversees Australia's 1000 wheat receival points and nineteen export shipping terminals. >> *agriculture*; *cereals and grains*; *soils and soil conservation*

whipbirds > *babblers and allies*

whistlers A group of small, insectivorous birds of which ten species occur in Australia, the whistlers are members of the family Pachycephalidae, and appear to be most closely related to robins. Some species are rare, but two are common and well known: the golden and the rufous whistlers. The beautiful golden whistler – yellow, with black and white – inhabits most coastal regions; the rufous whistler in spring and summer has a song that has brought it the alternative name of 'joybird'. All whistlers have pleasing songs to a greater or lesser degree; others include the olive and Gilbert whistlers and the buff-breasted whistler, the last-named limiting its territory to a small region of the Vic. mallee country. All these birds nest in cup-shaped structures of bark or twigs, built in shrubs or trees.

White, John (1756–1832), surgeon, birthplace unknown. White worked with Arthur Phillip in preparing the First Fleet and as chief surgeon to the Botany Bay settlement. His success in obtaining suitable food and ensuring some hygiene and exercise was largely responsible for the remarkable health of the convicts. In his *Journal of a Voyage to New South Wales* (London, 1790) he described it as 'a place so forbidding and hateful as only to merit curses', and resigned rather than return after his leave in 1796.

White, Patrick Victor Martindale (1912–), novelist and playwright, b. England. Of Australian parentage, White was educated in both Australia and England; his first novel,

Happy Valley, was published in 1939. After service with the RAF during World War 2, he lived in Australia from 1948. A writer of great power and observation, White has published eight novels – from the *Tree of Man* (1955) to *The Twyborn Affair* (1979) – as well as two short-story collections and nine plays; his complex use of metaphor has probably militated against the success of his work for the theatre, which includes *The Ham Funeral* and *The Season at Sarsaparilla* (both published 1965). White's querulous volume of autobiography, *Flaws in the Glass* (1981), aroused some controversy on its publication. He has received numerous awards, most notably the Nobel Prize for literature in 1973; with its proceeds he established the Patrick White Literary Award for older but inadequately recognised writers.

White Australia Policy This is the unofficial term for an early government policy, legalised in the 1901 Restrictive Immigration Act, of restricting immigration to Australia by those of non-European descent. It was based partly on racial discrimination but was generally defended on economic grounds (the maintenance of living standards by preventing cheap labour) as well as social ones (the avoidance of racial conflict). Agitation against a potential plantation economy began when squatters tried to replace convicts with Asian labourers in the 1840s, and was exacerbated by the influx of Chinese to the goldfields and Kanaka labour to Qld. The 1901 Act avoided overt exclusion of Asians, but effectively prohibited all but a very few from entry by a dictation test in a 'prescribed language'. The policy was long supported by all parties and the term 'White Australia' unashamedly used and defended by such eminent politicians as Alfred Deakin and W.M. Hughes. The policy was not officially abandoned until 1973. >> *ethnic groups*; *immigration*; *racial conflict*

whitebait This is a general name given to small fish – often only 6cm long – caught in large numbers in estuaries. Elsewhere in the world the term commonly refers to anchovies (Europe) or the young of herrings and sprats (UK); in Australia they are usually the young of jollytails, genus *Galaxias,* or of smelt, genus *Retropinna*.

white-eyes > *silver-eyes*

Whiteley, Brett (1939–), artist, b. Sydney. The most famous Australian painter of his generation, Whiteley won international acclaim as an enfant terrible in the early 1960s. He is a prolific, iconoclastic and frequently outrageous artist whose paintings, collages and sculpture exhibit powerful imagery and a destructive theme that has run through his own personal life. His sensuous nudes, Sydney Harbour views and zoo series are all dazzlingly evocative. He has twice won the Archibald Prize (1976, 1978), the Sulman Prize (1976, 1978) and the Wynne Prize (1977, 1978).

white shark > *sharks*

whitings This term is used in Australia for fishes of the family Sillaginidae, related neither to English whitings of the true cod family nor to the Australian rock whitings of the parrotfish family. They are generally fairly slender, sandy-brown estuarine fishes; the jaw has a horseshoe-shape, with small teeth. Of the ten Australian species, all choice table-fish, the sand, trumpeter, school and spotted whitings are the most important, the first three being found respectively in eastern, western and southern waters; the spotted whiting, also of the southern coasts, differs in appearance – with very small scales and blackish spots – and size, attaining a weight of some 2kg.

Whitlam, (Edward) Gough (1916–), politician, b. Melbourne. A barrister, Whitlam was elected to the federal parliament in 1952 as a Labor member and assumed leadership of the party in 1967. Becoming in 1972 the first Labor prime minister for 23 years, he set about a massive reform program that included recognition of communist China, withdrawal of military advisers from South Vietnam, the ending of conscription, and vastly increased expenditure on education, Aboriginal affairs, health and the arts. His imaginative vision was not matched by sound fiscal planning, however; nor was it helped by an ill-starred cabinet and his own impetuosity. In November 1975, on his refusal to call an election after the Senate had blocked supply, he was dismissed as prime minister by the governor-general, Sir John Kerr (> *constitutional crisis 1975*). Losing the subsequent election and another in 1977, he resigned from parliament in 1978.

Whitsunday Island > *Cumberland Islands*

Whitsunday Passage Qld This exceptionally beautiful passage lies north of Cape Conway between coastal islands, near Proserpine, and the Cumberland Island group. The passage is some 32km long and at its narrowest is 3km; it was named by James Cook on his arrival there on Whitsunday, 1770. A number of islands around the passage are tourist resorts, in particular Hayman, Lindeman, Daydream and South Molle.

Whyalla SA (pop. 26 900) This industrial city on Spencer Gulf, 396km northwest of Adelaide, was developed as a port by BHP in 1901. It is known in particular for the BHP steelworks which is the city's largest employer, but the solar salt works and engineering industries are also important; the port is an important shipment point for iron ore from the nearby Middleback Range. Shipbuilding was a major industry 1939–78, with five yards north of the town. Whyalla's desert environment is mitigated by water piped 374km from the Murray for irrigated dairy pastures and gardens; several conservation parks and historic reserves have been established to protect significant sites (including Aboriginal rock paintings) and examples of the region's vegetation and wildlife.

Wickham, John Clements (1798–1864), explorer and colonial administrator, b. Scotland. Wickham was a naval surveyor and commanded the *Beagle* (1837–41) on notable survey work on the northwest coast of Australia. He was subsequently appointed police magistrate (1842–57) and government resident (1857–9) at Moreton Bay, Qld, where he had the confidence and respect of the settlers.

Wickham, Tracy > *swimming and diving*

Wilkes > *Antarctic Territory*

Wilkinson, Leslie (1882–1973), architect, b. England. Wilkinson arrived in Australia in 1918 as the country's first professor of architecture, at the University of Sydney. His design work combined Georgian and Mediterranean styles in comfortable, elegant and occasionally whimsical houses; he was a noted advocate of the 'Spanish mission' style of sprawling and ornate buildings with features such as courtyards, eaves and verandahs well suited to Australian conditions. He received awards from the Royal Institute of Architects in Australia and England.

Willandra Lakes NSW Because of its importance in providing evidence of geological evolution over 50 000 years and of uninterrupted Aboriginal occupancy over 32 000 years, Willandra Lakes was one of the first three Australian regions to be placed on the World Heritage list (1981). It is a series of dry lakebeds and watercourses covering some 6000sq.km, having contained water between 45 000 and 13 000 years ago and formed by an overflow system along the Willandra Billabong Creek, a distributary of the Lachlan River. Research, chiefly at Lake Mungo, has established a picture of Aboriginal hunting and fishing when Mungo was 10m deep and freshwater lakes covered 1000sq.km, and presents evidence of the earliest known examples of cremation and burial rites. Lake Mungo National Park, a semi-arid area of mainly mallee vegetation, was declared in 1979.

Williams, Fred(erick Ronald) (1927–82), painter and etcher, b. Richmond, Vic. Widely acclaimed for his abstract but concentrated vision of the Australian landscape, Williams was trained at the Vic. National Gallery School and both the Chelsea Art School and the Central School of Arts and Crafts in London. Best known as a landscape painter, he was also an accomplished etcher, printmaker and portraitist. Williams exhibited consistently and successfully throughout his career (including a landmark one-man show at the Museum of Modern Art, New York, 1977) and was actively involved in the Australian art world.

Williams, John Christopher (1941–), guitarist, b. Melbourne. A musical prodigy, Williams made his debut as a classical guitarist in London in 1955, after which he was invited by Andrés Segovia to study at the Accademia Musicale Chigiana in Siena. He was professor of guitar at London's Royal College of Music 1960–73 and artistic director of the South Bank Summer Music festival in 1984 and 1985; he gives regular concerts in Australia and the UK and has made numerous recordings. Interested in broadening the range of his instrument by drawing on folk, jazz and rock music, he founded the pop group Sky in 1979 and remains an extremely eclectic musician.

Williamson, David Keith (1942–), playwright, b. Melbourne. Trained as a mechanical engineer, Williamson is Australia's most prolific and commercially successful writer for the stage and screen. His plays include *The Removalists* (1972), *Don's Party* (1973), *Travelling North* (1980) and *Emerald City* (1987), all of which have been filmed. Other screen credits included *Gallipoli* (1981) and *The Year of Living Dangerously* (1983). Although his early work ranged across a broad section of Australian society, his later plays have concentrated on examining middle-class preoccupations and values.

Williamson, J.C. > *opera*; *theatre*

Williamson, Malcolm Benjamin (1931–), composer and pianist, b. Sydney. Trained as a pianist at the NSW Conservatorium, Williamson moved permanently to London in 1953. He is a prolific composer whose eclecticism and immense facility have sometimes been held to reflect a lack of depth. His operas *Our Man in Havana* (1963) and *The Violins of Saint-Jacques* (1966), and the entertainment *English Eccentrics* (1964), won particular acclaim. In 1975 Williamson became the first Australian to be appointed to the prestigious position of Master of the Queen's Musick.

Willis group This island group lies in the Coral Sea, about 430km from the Qld coast and approximately equidistant from Cairns and Townsville. It comprises North Cay, Mid Islet and the largest, Willis Island, which since 1921 has been the site of a meteorological station of particular value to forecasters since it gives warning of approaching cyclonic storms several hours before coastal stations can detect them. The islands were discovered in 1853 by a Captain Pearson, and named after the owners of his ship.

Willmot, Eric (1936–), educator and author, b. Brisbane. A drover and rodeo rider, Willmot won a university scholarship while invalided after a riding accident. Having studied science he became a teacher and was subsequently head of the Australian Institute for Aboriginal Studies (1981–4), professor of education at James Cook University in Qld (1985) and secretary of the ACT education department (1987–). He was awarded an AM for his contribution to education and to Aboriginal studies. Also a consulting engineer, he has won several awards in this field including Australia's 1981 Inventor of the Year for his development of a stepless gear system. His novel *Pemulwuy the Rainbow Warrior* was published in 1987.

Wills, William John (1834–1861), explorer, b. England. Wills immigrated to Australia in 1852, and was appointed third in command of the Great Northern Exploration Expedition (1860–1) under Robert O'Hara Burke, later becoming second-in-command. Wills's journal is the only record of this tragic journey, during which he, Burke and Charles Gray died.

Wilpena Pound SA This is a wide, natural amphitheatre, with a ragged rim of outward-facing cliffs and an area of more than 8000ha, lying in the Flinders Ranges National Park, near Hawker. It is a major tourist attraction; the region is semi-arid, but the pound's elevation brings a higher rainfall than that of the region generally – even a rare snowfall has been recorded. The pound is of great importance in the mythology of the Flinders Ranges Aborigines, to whom the walls represent great snakes and the highest point, St Mary Peak (1189m), the giant snake head.

Wilson, William Hardy (1881–1955), architect and artist, b. Campbelltown, NSW. Having trained as an architect and travelled overseas, Wilson shared an architectural practice in Sydney 1911–27. His adaptation of the colonial Georgian style in graceful but highly individual buildings influenced Australian domestic architecture for several decades; outstanding Sydney examples include the houses Eryldene (1913) in Gordon and his own home Purulia (1915) in Warrawee. His eclectic output included a major published work on early colonial architecture (1924), furniture designs, and designs and sketches reflecting his interest in things Oriental.

Wilsons Promontory Vic. This triangular promontory – probably originally an island – lies 225km southeast of Melbourne and is the southernmost point of the Australian mainland, extending some 40km north–south and with a coastline of about 130km. The terrain is varied – from forested uplands to fern gullies, from beaches and salt marshes to the sheer cliffs of the southern tip, where the lighthouse has stood since 1859; the promontory is joined to the mainland by the narrow Yanakie Peninsula. Most of the region, now including offshore islands, is a national park, originally established in 1908; shell middens have been found, dating Aboriginal occupancy to 6800 years ago. The land was first sighted in 1798 by George Bass, and named after a merchant friend of Matthew

Flinders; in the early 19th century it was frequented by whalers and sealers.

Wiluna WA (pop. 279) This small town 944km northeast of Perth was originally a railhead and gold settlement but is now the service centre for an arid pastoral area; as elsewhere, gold-mining was revived in the 1980s. Wiluna has a majority Aboriginal shire council, believed to be the only one in Australia; to the north lies the Carnarvon Range, a rugged wilderness noted for its Aboriginal art sites.

Wimmera Vic. A region of undulating plains in western Vic., centred on Horsham, the Wimmera extends from the SA border east to St Arnaud and slopes north from the Grampians to the Mallee district. It was discovered in 1836 by Thomas Mitchell, who took its name from an Aboriginal word for a throwing-stick. European settlers appeared in the 1840s, first raising sheep, until a deficiency of zinc in the soil was realised and rectified, thus permitting development of the Wimmera as a wheat-producing area bringing the highest yields in Australia. The semi-arid northern section was an uncertain farming area until the construction of the Wimmera–Mallee domestic and live-stock water scheme, for which the Grampians are the catchment and which supplies reticulated water to many towns, and water to farms and irrigated land through 14 600km of channels. The first reservoir was built in 1887; subsequent constructions have resulted in ten inter-connected storages, the largest being Rocklands dam (1953) and the most recent Lake Bellfield (1966). Chief centres in the Wimmera are Horsham, Stawell, St Arnaud and Warrack-nabeal. Almost centred in the region, extending west from the bank of the Wimmera River, is Little Desert National Park.

Windeyer family, prominent in Australian law and public life. **Charles** (1780–1855), b. England, arrived in NSW in 1828. A journalist and parliamentary reporter, he became a police magistrate in 1833, and interim mayor of Sydney (1842) until the city's first council was elected. His brother **Richard** (1806–47), b. England, arrived in Australia in 1835. Also a parliamentary reporter, he had a large legal practice in Sydney and was elected to the NSW parliament in 1843. He was actively involved in Aboriginal welfare, education, and jury and defamation laws, and was a noted agitator for self-government. His son **Sir William Charles**

(1834–97), b. England, became a barrister and law reporter before entering the NSW parliament in 1859. During his 20-year parliamentary term, he was solicitor-general in 1870 and attorney-general 1877–8; he was also vice-chancellor of the University of Sydney 1883–7 and chancellor 1895–6. As a judge of the NSW Supreme Court 1879–96, he was a noted jurist and social reformer. His eldest son **Richard** (1868–1959), b. Sydney, was an outstanding common and criminal lawyer, becoming a QC in 1917 and an occasional judge of the NSW Supreme Court. Another son, **Sir Brian Wellingham** (1904–), b. Sydney, was professor of radiology at the University of London 1942–69, dean of the faculty of medicine 1964–8, and vice-chancellor 1969–72. Sir William's grandson **Sir William John Victor** (1900–87), b. Sydney, became a barrister in 1925. He was a lecturer in law at the University of Sydney 1929–40, and his *Lectures in Legal History* (1938) were known to generations of Australian law students. He served with distinction in the AIF during World War 2, after which he was deputy chancellor of the University of Sydney 1955–8 and an eminent High Court judge 1958–72.

Windsor NSW > *Richmond–Windsor*

windsurfing This sport, also known as sailboarding, was introduced to Australia from the US in 1976 and has since become exceedingly popular. Using a surfboard with a mast and sail attached, windsurfing is largely responsible for dramatically increased surfboard sales in the last decade. Australians, partly reflecting the nation's longstanding prowess in beach sports, have won fifteen world championships since these were inaugurated.

wine industry Although wine has been produced in Australia from the earliest years of European settlement, it is only since the 1950s that the industry has become of any real economic significance. In 1985–6, 389.2 million l of wine were produced, about three-quarters of which was (unfortified) table wine.

The days when Australians were predominantly drinkers of tea and beer are over: today they consume about 22l of wine per head every year, the highest per-capita consumption of any English-speaking country. This remarkable change in drinking patterns is owed partly to the influence of postwar immigrants from Europe; and partly to clever marketing by the industry, which has managed to break down the old prejudice that wine was just 'plonk' by emphasising both its sophistication and its harmony with food. The relative cheapness of Australian wine and the invention of the cardboard wine 'cask' have also served to boost the industry.

Exports of Australian wine are relatively insignificant, accounting for only 2–3% of annual production and being mainy restricted to wines at the top end of the market. High-quality Australian wines have been well received overseas and are judged to be on a par with the best products of South African and Californian vineyards. Australian bulk wine faces vast cost, tariff and freight disadvantages in world markets, however, at a time when all producing and consuming countries – particularly those of the EEC – are awash with an excess of potable wine. Australia is in fact a net importer of wine, and is likely to remain so as long as there is a market for expensive French champagne.

Historical development Vine cuttings were brought to Australia with the First Fleet. Small acreages of grapes for wine production were soon common, the consumption of wine being seen as less harmful than that of the colony's scourge, rum. The first commercial vineyard was planted by John Macarthur in 1817, at Camden Park near Sydney. The first scientific approach to wine production, however, was taken by the Scottish viticulturist James Busby, who planted vineyards in the Hunter Valley in the 1830s. By this time, vineyards were also being established in Vic. – in Portland and the Yarra Valley – and in SA, which rapidly became Australia's major wine producer, partly because of a plague of the insect pest *Phylloxera* that devastated the Vic. and NSW vineyards in the 1880s.

SA is still Australia's largest wine producer, with major vineyards now long established in the Barossa Valley, at Coonawarra-Padthaway, and in the Clare-Leasingham-Watervale district. In NSW, the main centres are the Hunter Valley, Mudgee and the Murrumbidgee Irrigation Area, the last being a producer of bulk wine used for blending, as are the Sunraysia and Riverland areas of Vic. and SA. The major wine areas of Vic. are Great Western, Rutherglen, and the Goulburn and Yarra valleys. More than 50 varieties of grape are grown in Australia and, for both legal and taste reasons, Australian wines are now usually named after the grape variety of their provenance rather than a European wine type (which often bears little resemblance to the local product).

For most of this century the industry has been in the hands of a few large companies such as Lindemans, Penfolds, McWilliams and Orlando, many being survivors from the early days in the Barossa Valley of SA. The large companies have grown larger, with numerous inter-industry and external take-overs, some by multinational companies such as Reckitt & Colman, Heinz and Philip Morris. In the 1960s, a new breed of wine-maker – a wine lover as opposed to a wine producer – entered the industry, which resulted in a profusion of small wineries and much experimentation. By the end of the 1980s there were more than 500 commercial wine producers in Australia, although many of the 'boutique' vineyards were feeling the pinch of over-production and cost-cutting.

Winston Churchill Memorial Trust
> *Churchill Fellowships*

Winton Qld (pop. 1281) This outback pastoral town (originally called Pelican Waterhole) lies 1340km west of Brisbane. Industries include opal-mining and tourism, and the town – which was the birthplace of the original Qantas airline, in 1920 – is also a major cattle-trucking depot.

witchetty grubs This is an Aboriginal name applied variously to large insect larvae used as a vital food source. Chiefly the name refers to the large stem- and root- boring larvae of the goat-moths, family Cossidae, and ghost-moths, family Hepialidae (whose larvae may attain a length of 13cm), although the larvae of the wood-boring jewel and longicorn beetles of the families Cerambycidae and Buprestidae are also included; the fatty grubs are either eaten raw or gently cooked in hot ashes. When raw, their taste resembles butter or scalded cream; when cooked, they are said to taste like pork rind.

Withers, Walter Herbert (1854–1914),
painter, b. England. A romantic landscape painter and illustrator who arrived in Australia in 1882, Withers was an early and influential member of the Vic. painting camps that developed into the Heidelberg School. Hazy, gentle light and broken, Impressionistic brush strokes characterise his paintings of the bush and seaside. He also designed Art Nouveau panels and marble mantlepieces for grand houses including the mansion Purrumbete at Camperdown, Vic.

Wittenoom WA (pop. 356) This small town in the Hamersley Range 450km north of Perth was built in 1947 to accommodate workers at the nearby > *asbestos* quarry. It has achieved unenviable notoriety for the toll of life and health taken by asbestos-related disease since that time; mining ceased in 1968 and the town was moved a decade later because airborne particles continued to make the original site unsafe.

wobbegong > *sharks*

Wodonga Vic. > *Albury–Wodonga*

wolfram > *tungsten*

Wollondilly River NSW > *Hawkesbury River*

Wollongong NSW (pop. 206 803) This coastal city 78km south of Sydney is the State's third-largest city and a major industrial centre, based mainly on steel-making. Cedar trade encouraged its development as a port from the 1820s; by the end of the century Port Kembla (now part of Greater Wollongong) had displaced this role but Wollongong continued to develop as an agricultural and dairying centre. Coal-mining has been important since the 1840s, and iron and steel production developed from the early 20th century; today Wollongong has Australia's largest steelworks, with a capacity of 5.5 million t a year and a staff of 20 000. Wollongong's main products are pig iron, tinplate, steel products, and coking coal. The former technical college (established in 1951) became Wollongong University in 1975. Fishing and dairying are the district's main surviving agricultural activities; tourism is increasingly important, centred on fine ocean beaches and the forested mountain scenery of the hinterland.

wombats Wombats are short, powerfully built, burrowing > *marsupials* of the family Vombatidae, which belongs to the order Diprotodonta that includes kangaroos and wallabies, and koalas. They are mostly solitary, feed primarily on grasses, and may weigh as much as 40kg; although usually nocturnal, they sometimes emerge in winter or on overcast days to graze or bask. The female has a pouch containing two teats: the young (usually single) is born in autumn, nourished in the pouch during the winter, and weaned in spring. Al-

though they are generally slow-moving, wombats can move at a fast shuffle or even a clumsy but effective gallop. There are three known species, all confined to Australia.

The common wombat, *Vombatus ursinus*, occurs in southeastern Australia and Tas. It has declined in agricultural areas, where it is considered a pest by farmers and graziers because of its burrowing habit, which may breach rabbit-proof fences or pose a hazard to horses; however, it is still abundant in forests and in other undisturbed habitats, and is protected in most areas. Generally large burrows are excavated – some up to 20m long – with several entrances and chambers.

The two species of hairy-nosed wombats are less common. The southern group, *Lasiorhinus latifrons*, once occurred as far east as the Murray River but is now confined to the Nullarbor Plain of SA and WA. The northern group, *L. krefftii*, is even rarer, and is considered an endangered species. First described from a fossil skull found in the Wellington Caves, NSW, living specimens were later discovered in isolated pockets of NSW and Qld. Today only a small and specially protected population survives in Qld, in one colony.

women in Australian society By the late 1980s, women made up 51% of the Australian population. While it is noteworthy that females in SA were given the vote in 1894, well before this right was granted to the women of most other English-speaking countries, it is only relatively recently that Australian women have achieved equality with men in many areas of legal and civil rights. Enduring myths such as mateship and egalitarianism have camouflaged the widespread prejudices and inequalities – based on sex, race and class – that developed from the early years of settlement.

Women in colonial society The British colonisation of Australia had dramatic and tragic consequences for Aboriginal society. The fact that male settlers outnumbered females four to one for many years meant that the repercussions were particularly disastrous for Aboriginal women and rape was widespread. On the whole, only white women became the legitimate wives of the colonists and the children who resulted from interracial unions were often removed forcibly from their mothers and used as cheap domestic or apprenticed labour; in some States, part-Aborigines were excluded by law from Aboriginal reserves until well into the 20th century.

The small number of females in the colonies was supplemented from the 1830s by a program of assisted immigration for young women from Britain. Their new life was strenuous and demanding, as they simultaneously raised children and laboured alongside their men in a harsh new land. The gold rushes of the 1850s further dislocated family life as men decamped en masse to the diggings; for those women and children who accompanied them, life was invariably bleak and primitive. As conditions became more stable from the mid-19th century the patriarchal society became entrenched; women, perceived as vulnerable, were afforded 'protection' by a father, brother or husband who was both morally and legally responsible for his charge. Most women accepted without question this system, with which most of them had grown up in Britain. For many it worked well enough and often it was only in the event of some misfortune – such as a husband's death or desertion – that they came face to face with the disadvantage entailed in their lack of legal status. The growth of the middle classes and of formal education in the second half of the 19th century saw the emergence of groups of articulate women demanding legal and political rights, in particular the right of married women to private property and the right to vote. Legislation was introduced by the 1890s adding desertion, drunkenness, cruelty and imprisonment to the grounds for divorce and allowing married women to acquire and dispose of property in their own right. At about the same time, the first women were admitted to Australian universities.

More than 80% of women were dependent on male support in the 1880s. Most of those who worked were in domestic service although the budding urban industries gave rise to factory-based employment and outwork. A series of articles in the Melbourne *Age* (1882) outlined the plight of the tailoresses working in a Flinders Street factory, whose wages had been reduced for a second time – at which point they went on strike. 'Small though the strike is – merely between 200 and 300 girls – it has assumed a serious aspect from the fact that the girls are helpless. Men under similar circumstances can hold indignation meetings, and publicly make known their grievances; women cannot.'

The 20th century Between the 1890s and 1909, women won the right to vote in State and federal elections; they became eligible to stand for federal parliament in 1902, and for all State

parliaments by 1924. The first female politician, Edith Cowan, was elected in WA in 1921.

Also from the early 20th century, welfare benefits such as maternity allowances were introduced and it became respectable for women to enter the workforce between school and marriage. As late as the 1950s, nevertheless, they were encouraged to give up their job after marriage, on the understanding that the male basic wage was set to allow a man to support a wife and three children. (Immigrant women, striving to make a new life in their adopted country after World War 2, were an exception to this rule.) In 1932, legislation was passed in NSW leading to the dismissal of 220 married women from the permanent staff of the Department of Public Instruction; this Act was not repealed until 1947 and it was another 22 years before women in the Australian defence forces were allowed to stay on after marriage. Similarly, although women won the right to practise law and be appointed to the judiciary early in the 20th century, it was not until 1967 that women in Vic. were allowed to serve as jurors and the first woman judge was not appointed until the 1970s.

During World War 2, the number of working women rose by about 30%, reaching 855 000 in 1944. Many joined the services and some 70 000 were mobilised into employment for the duration of the war, working in traditionally male areas. The trade unions, which had opposed equal pay for women in the past, now demanded an increase in the prewar women's wage of 54% of the male rate, as they feared that industry would acquire a taste for cheap labour and that men's wages would thus be undermined. In 1942, the Women's Employment Board awarded most women workers 90% of the male wage; some (such as clerical workers and tram conductors) received 100%, but a further 785 000 continued to receive their old wage. At the end of the war many women left paid employment: some were reluctant to relinquish their newly won financial independence, but were forced to do so because their jobs were made available to returning servicemen. The rapid expansion of industry after 1945, and the influx of immigrants to serve as factory fodder, made way for a new form of 'sweated' labour: particularly vulnerable because of their lack of English, many immigrant women – first from southern Europe and later from the Middle East, Sri Lanka and Southeast Asia – were exploited in a wide range of factory and piece-work jobs.

A 'baby boom' followed close on the heels of the war, as did a generally improved standard of living for most Australians. Children growing up in the 1950s and 1960s were better educated than those of earlier generations and increasingly began to question traditional values – first of their parents and then, partly in tandem with the new freedoms of the 1960s, those of society at large. The increasing discontent of many women found expression in the women's liberation movement of the 1970s. The feminist activism of that decade put women on the political agenda of both major parties and they have remained there ever since. Like earlier women's lobby groups, those of the 1970s, in particular the Women's Electoral Lobby (WEL), evolved among middle-class and relatively privileged women, but the ensuing changes have gone well beyond the boundaries of class: equal-opportunity legislation was introduced, as were an adult minimum wage for women and 'affirmative action' policies.

The 1980s and beyond Today women are making their presence felt in the arts, in business, in sport, in education, and on the factory floor; and in trade unions, which have finally turned their attention to traditionally female areas such as nursing and child care. Girls are being encouraged actively to complete the final years of schooling and to enter non-traditional fields such as science, engineering and the trades; women's refuges receive government funding. Ironically, many of the working conditions won by women factory workers in the 19th century are those that women in the 1980s are seeking to overturn: the limitation on weights women may lift, for example, which is seen as being used to exclude them from more lucrative, traditionally 'male' jobs such as mining. In some ways, society is being shaken to its patriarchal roots. Even religion is under siege, with the ordination of female priests in the Anglican Church now increasingly likely. Women who achieve in the workplace still, however, often face prejudice and discrimination; and many of them continue to bear sole responsibility for child care and domestic labour. In addition, although the concept of equal pay was finally introduced in 1974 it is still to take effect throughout the workforce: in 1987 full-time women workers were earning only 87% of the male wage.

Change has thus been slow and not all recent changes have been necessarily for the better. The introduction of the Family Law Act in 1975 was followed by a huge increase in the incidence of divorce, which was the fate of one in three marriages by the end of the 1980s. This social upheaval has created a new poor in Australia, women and their dependent children being the biggest recipients of welfare benefits. Laws have been passed recently to try to ensure that men take responsibility for the financial maintenance of their children, but it remains to be seen whether this will be successful. >> *Aboriginal culture and society*; *family law*; *social services*; *women's movement*

Women's Electoral Lobby (WEL) A non-partisan, feminist political group formed in Melbourne in 1972, WEL soon achieved nationwide support for its attempts to achieve change in community attitudes and in legislation affecting women, especially on issues such as family planning, divorce, child care and abortion. Its survey before the 1972 federal election revealed the conservative attitudes of many candidates, and its move to promote women for responsible positions has been more successful in the public service than in parliament. The influence of WEL declined in the 1980s. >> *women in Australian society*; *women's movement*

women's movement Over the past century, the women's movement has waxed and waned. In the 1880s Australian women, frustrated in their efforts at social reform in areas such as temperance, child welfare and the age of consent, began their campaign for the vote. The Women's Christian Temperance Union and other suffrage organisations collected thousands of signatures for petitions, lobbied MPs and rated candidates on their attitudes. By 1894, political rights had been won in SA and in 1902 Australia became the first country in the world where women were able to vote and stand for the national parliament. After this victory, Australian women carried the struggle overseas. In the huge London suffrage marches of 1908 and 1911, they carried a banner depicting the young Commonwealth of Australia pleading with Britain to 'Trust the Women, Mother, As I Have Done'. The 1911 marchers included Mrs Andrew Fisher, wife of the Australian prime minister. Australian suffragists stressed the links between women's suffrage and reforms such as old-age pensions, the maintenance of illegitimate children and deserted families, food legislation and separate children's courts.

The intensity of women's political activity subsided, however, soon after political rights were achieved. Political emancipation had been conditional on reassurances that women would not neglect their 'home duties' and early women parliamentary candidates such as > *Vida Goldstein* stressed that their role in parliament would be as 'representatives of the home'. Despite the attempt to portray women's political role as a natural extension of the maternal role, women made little headway in entering parliaments or public office. First-wave feminism survived in non-party women's political associations in different States, which were brought together by Bessie Rischbieth in 1921 in the Australian Federation of Women Voters (AFWV). This federation and the groups that made it up campaigned on issues such as the legal and political status of women, family allowances and child endowment, women's wages, divorce laws and the representation of women on government delegations. Between the wars, however, the largest women's organisations – such as the Australian Women's National League and the Country Women's Assocation – were socially and politically conservative.

In the 1930s, more radical campaigns emerged in protest against the ineligibility of women for unemployment relief and the sacking of married women. > *Muriel Heagney* published the pioneering study *Are Women Taking Men's Jobs?* (1935) and helped found the Council of Action for Equal Pay. The mobilisation of women for the war effort and their entry into previously male jobs gave renewed strength to feminist demands. Jessie Street (> *Street family*) played the leading role in the Australian Women's Charter movement, supported by some 90 organisations. The charter aimed at preserving women's wartime gains in the postwar world and covered representation of women at the peace conference, equal pay, equal rights legislation, equal employment opportunity and child care. Hopes faded after the war, as women were dispatched home. Jessie Street came under suspicion because of her pro-Soviet sympathies and the women's movement became divided by the cold war. Prime ministers Chifley and Menzies were unreceptive to Women's Charter delegations. Although the women's movement never totally disappeared, it was very quiet during the 1950s. In 1953, the AFWV appeared before the Arbitration Court to oppose the employers' application to reduce the female basic wage from 75% to 60% of the male wage.

In the 1960s, as more women entered higher education and more married women joined the paid workforce, women began mobilising again over equal pay and abortion law reform as well as joining the anti-Vietnam War demonstrations. In October 1969, Zelda D'Aprano chained herself to the doors of the Commonwealth Building in Melbourne in protest against the Arbitration Commission's 'equal pay' decision that did not apply to work usually done by women. Women caught up in the anti-war movement had experiences similar to those of their US sisters. They found that even men who supported female liberation were still dominating, exploiting and denigrating women. Ideas from the American women's liberation movement struck an immediate chord. An Australian pamphlet, *Only the Chains Have Changed*, was distributed at a Sydney anti-war march in December 1969 and women's liberation groups soon sprang up in all the major cities. Influential books included *The Female Eunuch* (1971) by Australian author > *Germaine Greer*. Women started insisting that 'the personal is the political' and that liberation must begin in the home. From the original consciousness-raising groups grew collectives providing services to other women, including refuges for women fleeing domestic violence, abortion counselling, and rape-crisis and women's health centres. > *Women's Electoral Lobby* (WEL) rated all candidates in the 1972 federal election, an idea borrowed from the National Women's Political Caucus in the US. Thanks to the lack of feminist history, WEL members were unaware that the Australian women's organisations had been rating political candidates from the days of the suffrage campaigns, up through the women's non-party political associations and the Council of Action for Equal Pay. The newly elected Labor government took up many WEL demands, including equal pay, government-subsidised child care and the removal of the luxury tax from contraceptives. WEL became the prime mover for equal-opportunity legislation around Australia and the establishment of women's policy units in government. Australia began to play an important role in the UN in seeking to improve the status of women internationally.

In the 1980s, the women's movement was no longer so politically visible as in the 1970s, but many of those involved had risen to high public office: some WEL members had become government ministers and heads of departments. Feminist networks proliferated and hundreds of women attended conferences challenging male wisdom on subjects from economics to theology. Feminist culture flourished as never before, including a boom in feminist books, films, theatre and art. The growth of women's studies in universities and colleges helped uncover the history of earlier feminist struggles. >> *women in Australian society*

Wonthaggi Vic. (pop. 5344) This regional commercial centre, which lies 132km northeast of Melbourne, developed from 1908 when the State government began to mine the local black coal for use by the Vic. railway; thin faulted seams and competition from brown coal led to closure of the town's mines by 1968. Today, industries include drop-forging, cotton spinning, and clothing manufacture.

Wood, Carl > *IVF*

wood borers Apart from some marine molluscs and crustaceans (> *marine borers*), insects are the major wood-boring pests. In nature, insect-borers work in conjunction with fungi to attack wood and return its nutrients to the soil – often mechanical destruction by insects allows the entry of fungi, which break down cellulose and thereby in turn provide food for the insects. In timber products used by humans, the borers become a source of major problems. Many beetles – longicorn, jewel, bark and pin-hole – attack living trees, and the sirex wasp is becoming a pest of exotic pine plantations in southeastern Australia. Termites often cause serious damage by entering wooden structures from underground; powder-post beetles attack sapwood of seasoned timber, and furniture beetles are sometimes found in hardwood furniture. The control and eradication of wood borers is of necessity a major concern of the timber and wood-processing industries.

woodchip industry > *forests and forestry*

wood-chopping Competition in this skill began in the sporting and drinking carnivals held by cedar-cutters in NSW in the 1820s. The first formal contests began in Tas. in the 1870s, and subsequently became an integral part of the agricultural shows held annually in settlements around the country; significant prize money, formal rules and competition structure, and trans-Tasman competitions had been organised by the turn of the century. Probably Australia's most notable axeman was Peter McLaren, who competed from the age of 16, had won Vic. and WA championships at 24 (in 1906), and remained undefeated throughout several overseas tours.

Contacts with US servicemen later led to regular competition between axemen from both nations, but although many competitions claim to establish the world title, the Sydney Easter Show always attracts a world-class fold, and as strength and experience are essential in this sport competitors tend to have long careers.

wood-lice and sea-lice These are crustacean isopods; wood-lice, the terrestrial genera, are also known as slaters, carpenters and sowbugs. The garden wood-louse or slater, slate-grey above and yellow-green below, is the introduced species *Porcellio scaber*, but there are also native species; despite their broad back and numerous legs, they can roll into a ball with great speed. Freshwater isopods include some blind subterranean species and some sighted, living in bore waters in central Australia.

Sea-lice – the marine genera – tend to be larger than the terrestrial forms, commonly measuring 5cm in Australian waters and up to 28cm in colder, Antarctic seas. The sea-slater, *Ligia oceanica*, is not unlike the terrestrial slaters; it is seen fairly often on the beaches and in the estuaries of southeastern Australia. The cosmopolitan gribble, *Limnoria*, and the marine pill-bug, *Sphaeroma*, which rolls into a ball, are marine borers that cause serious damage to wharves and other timber installations.

wood-swallows Of the genus *Artamus*, there are six species of wood-swallows in Australia, found in open woodland and savannah country. They are medium-sized birds, not related to swallows but superficially resembling them in their swift graceful flight to catch insects on the wing; they are mainly insectivorous, though some also feed on nectar. Wood-swallows are sociable birds; when not nesting, at night they usually perch close together. One species has the unique habit of hanging in a cluster, almost like a swarm of bees, close to a tree.

Woodward, Roger (1942–), pianist, b. Sydney. After winning the piano section of the ABC music competition in 1964, Woodward left for the UK and then Poland, where he studied at the Warsaw Academy of Music. He made his debut in London in 1967, and in Paris and Havana in 1969, and won the 23rd International Chopin Festival in Warsaw in 1968. He is noted particularly for his performance of Bach, Beethoven and Chopin, and for his interpretation of avant-garde scores. In 1972 he helped found the London Music Digest, a series of annual contemporary music concerts.

wood-wasps > *sawflies and wood-wasps*

wool Although Australia no longer 'rides on the sheep's back', wool is still of vital importance to the economy: some 887 000t of wool were produced in 1986–7, over 28% of the world's total clip. Among rural industries, wool vies with wheat as Australia's largest export earner, exports for 1986–7 being worth nearly $4000 million, a figure second only to coal in total export figures. An average 95% of the wool clip is exported annually, most in its natural 'greasy' state.

The bulk of the Australian clip is merino wool; NSW is the largest overall producer (33%), followed by WA (23%). Most Australian wool is sold at public auction in twelve selling centres, where there is intense competition between buyers from all over the world. The main purchasers are Japan, the EEC countries (notably France and Italy), the Soviet Union and eastern-bloc countries and, increasingly, China and Taiwan.

Marketing and promotion is controlled by the Australian Wool Corporation (AWC), a Commonwealth statutory authority whose most important role is the management of the reserve price scheme, aimed at creating price stability in a wildly fluctuating market which made life difficult for the industry. In 1950–1, for example, at the height of the Korean War, wool was selling for the equivalent of 269.90 cents per kg, but in the following year the price was halved; in 1974–5, the price had dropped to 125 cents a kilo. Today, wool sells at 400–600 cents a kilo; the AWC is empowered to set a minimum price for all grades at the commencement of each season, to purchase wool if this is necessary to maintain the price, and to sell wool back to the market if the price should rise too high. Finance for the operation of this scheme, and for the AWC's promotion and research activities, is provided by a tax on growers. >> *economy; sheep*

Woomera SA (pop. 1805) This remote town 494km northwest of Adelaide was developed from 1948 by the Australian government for weapons research and international space research programs; since the late 1960s it has also been a base for the joint Australian–US space communications station at Nurrungar, 16km to the southwest (> *US bases in Australia*). Public entry to the area is prohibited.

World War 1 (4 August 1914–11 November 1918) As a member of the British Empire, Australia was immediately in a state of war against Germany and her allies when war was declared in London on 4 August 1914. Although most Australians, like many British, were largely unaware of the complex sequence of events leading to the war's outbreak, there was a wholehearted and enthusiastic response by political parties and the people. An expeditionary army, the Australian Imperial Force (AIF), of 20000 men was formed immediately. Volunteers far exceeded this number, allowing a rigorous selection which resulted in a high degree of fitness. The AIF and the NZ troops – soon collectively called Anzacs – embarked for the Middle East on 1 November. Among the naval escort was the battle cruiser *Sydney*, which destroyed the German raider *Emden* off the Cocos Islands on 9 November.

Campaigns After training in Egypt, the Anzacs under General William Birdwood embarked in April 1915 for the Dardanelles to take part in the Gallipoli campaign, an ill-conceived venture masterminded by Winston Churchill to secure a route to the Russian grainlands and break the power of Turkey, which had entered the war on Germany's side. At dawn on 25 April, landings were made by British, French and Anzac troops along the Gallipoli peninsula, a mountainous finger of land forming the west side of the Dardanelles Straits, the narrow entrance to the Black Sea. Tenuous beachheads were made and held, but the landings had been anticipated by the Turks and all attempts to extend inland were defeated by a well-entrenched Turkish army. After eight months it was decided to withdraw. Some 80 000 Allied toops were taken off the peninsula 18–20 December, with only a handful of casualties occurring during the evacuation. This was perhaps the most impressive feat of a sideshow in which 33 532 men including 8587 Australians were killed to no end.

Four infantry divisions were now sent to the Western Front and three mounted brigades (under Major-General > *Henry George Chauvel*) remained in Egypt. Before General E.H.M. Allenby and fresh British troops arrived in 1917, the Anzacs were the main Middle East force and cleared the Turks from Sinai. During Allenby's sweep through Palestine and Syria, the Desert Mounted Corps – a combined British and Anzac force, which included the Camel Corps – made a spectacular attack on Beersheba and constantly harassed the Turks as they retreated northwards. On 1 October the Allied forces entered Damascus, and on 30 October 1918 Turkey surrendered. Allenby was Britain's best World War 1 general, and casualties during the campaign were relatively light. Less fortunate were the troops sent to France, where the war was a stalemate of attack and counter-attack based in muddy trenches under constant bombardment and attack with mustard gas. In one day's fighting on the Somme (1 July 1916), 19 000 British troops were killed – the greatest loss in a single day ever suffered by a British army. The Anzacs, who were recognised as invaluable shock troops, took part in the first battle of the Somme, losing some 21 000 men in nine weeks. In the April–June offensive of 1917, the Anzacs were involved in famous actions at Bullecourt, Bapaume and Messines; in September–October, they suffered heavy losses in the battles around Ypres and Passchendaele. In early 1918, the Australian army divisions in France were placed under the command of Lt-General > *John Monash*, with Brigadier-General > *Thomas Blamey* as his chief of staff. In the enemy offensive of March 1918, Anzac forces were outstanding in the defence of Amiens, which the Germans had hoped to capture and thereby separate the British and French armies. In the final stages of the war, the Australians were in the thick of the fighting to breach the Gemans' last line of resistance, the Hindenburg Line, where a breakthrough was made on 5 October. On 11 November 1918, an armistice was signed, ending the war. Of the 330 000 Australians who served overseas, 60 000 were killed, the highest death rate in proportion to population of any country in the Empire.

Domestic affairs A general election in Australia in 1914 returned a Labor government under Andrew Fisher, who was replaced in 1915 by W.M. Hughes, an advocate of conscription. Two referendums on conscription were defeated; after the first defeat (1916) the Labor Party was split and Hughes was expelled. In consort with the Liberals he formed a Nationalist Party, enabling him to remain prime minister. A 'war precautions' Act introduced censorship and alien internment, and tried to make Australia self-sufficient in war materials. Previous German domination of the metals industry was replaced by domestic smelting, notably by the entry of BHP into the iron and steel industry. Guaranteed government purchases of many foodstuffs gave security for the development of primary industry but, as the war dragged on and living standards were lowered, there was a series of grave industrial disputes. Tangible gains were very real nevertheless, with hundreds of previously imported articles being manufactured locally. An intangible gain was possibly the 'proving' of nationhood through the exploits of the Anzacs: the young Commonwealth had survived the strain of its first major test. >> *defence*; *defence force*; *foreign policy*

World War 2 (3 September 1939–14 August 1945)

Australia, then under a Liberal government, was at war with Germany and her allies immediately it was declared by the British prime minister, Neville Chamberlain, on 3 September 1939. The Labor opposition (led by John Curtin) concurred in this commitment, pledging the defence of Australia and the integrity of the British Empire, although it was more wholehearted in its support of the war after Germany invaded Russia in 1941. Public feeling was strongly behind Britain.

Campaigns A second AIF was formed under General > *Thomas Blamey* and sent to the Middle East, where it was involved in repulsing unsuccessful Italian thrusts towards Suez. In April–May 1940 Australian force fought as a rearguard in the disastrous Greece and Crete campaigns; in June it was landed in Syria in the successful attempt to overthrow the Vichy French regime. Australian cruisers were important in the vital Cape Matapan battle to hold open the eastern Mediterranean in March 1941. From the beginning of the war Australia had agreed to provide 10 000 airmen for service with the RAF; later, RAAF squadrons served in the European theatre, the Middle East and the Pacific. In March 1941, the gains against the Italians in North Africa were lost when General Rommel and a German army pushed the Allies back beyond the Egyptian border, cutting off a section of Allied forces in Tobruk. The mainly Australian defenders – the celebrated 'Rats of Tobruk' – held out for 242 days until relieved by a fresh British push westwards. In January 1942, Rommel counterattacked and drove the Allies back to El Alamein, only 160km from the Nile delta.

With the appointment of the British general B.L. Montgomery, the tide finally turned in the Allies' favour and in November 1942 the backbone of Rommel's army was smashed at the Battle of El Alamein, resulting in a victorious Allied sweep across North Africa. Owing to the outbreak of war with Japan in 1941, the bulk of Australian forces had been recalled for home defence prior to El Alamein, but the 9th Division remained to participate in the desert victory.

In December 1941, the Japanese attacked the US base of Pearl Harbor and simultaneously landed troops on the coast of Malaya with the aim of capturing Singapore. The Japanese advance was swift, and Singapore fell in February 1942. In all, 130 000 prisoners were taken, including 15 000 men of the Australian 8th Divison under Major-General > *H. Gordon Bennett*. In the same month the Japanese bombed Darwin, as a result of which the Australian government refused to divert the 7th Division (then on its way back from the Middle East) to Burma as requested by the British. With virtually all of Southeast Asia and numerous Pacific islands under their control, the Japanese attempted to capture Port Moresby and the major US base of Midway. They were beaten decisively in both attempts, in the former during what became known as the Battle of the Coral Sea (7–8 May), when US and Australian air and sea forces destroyed a Japanese invasion fleet. Having failed to take Port Moresby by sea, in July 1942 the Japanese began a landward attack across the Owen Stanley Range along the Kokoda Trail. After initial reverses, Australian troops held the Japanese and by September were pushing them back across the island. The war had now swung in the Allies' favour, and under the supreme command of the US general Douglas MacArthur a slow campaign of attrition followed, as island by island the Japanese were driven northwards. In the last year of the war Australian forces fought in New Britain, the Solomons and Borneo. The campaign intensified after the European victory of May 1945, and final victory was assured even before two atomic bombs were dropped on Japan. After the dropping of the second bomb, Japan surrendered on 15 August 1945.

Of a total Australian enlistment of 990 900 men and women, 35 000 were killed and 66 553 were wounded. Although nowhere near the level of slaughter seen in World War 1, one figure is perhaps more shocking: of the 22 376 prisoners taken by the Japanese, 8031 died while captive.

Domestic affairs The historical pattern of World War 1 was repeated when a Labor prime minister emerged in wartime and proved to be a leader of great stature. Curtin, with a notable team that included Ben Chifley and H.V. Evatt, was able to have unpalatable curtailments on individual liberty accepted: these included rationing of petrol and food, restrictions on travel and investment, and the extension of conscription. The economy received a stimulus in manufacturing industry but severe drought (1944–5), combined with labour and fertiliser shortages, adversely affected primary industry. The encroachment of the Commonwealth on the States' powers increased, with financial control being effected in 1942 when a uniform income tax replaced varying State taxes. On the whole, the economic results of the war were favourable and political maturity was increased by the need for Australia to redirect its alliances, away from Britain and towards the US and the Pacific. >> *defence*; *defence forces*; *foreign policy*

worms > *earthworms*; *helminths*; *marine worms*

worm snakes > *snakes*

Wran, Neville Kenneth (1926–), politician, b. Balmain, NSW. The longest continuously serving premier of NSW, 1976–86, Wran formerly practised as a lawyer. Admitted to the bar in 1957 he specialised in industrial cases, becoming a QC in 1968. He was elected to the NSW upper house as a Labor member in 1970, but resigned in 1973 and won a seat in the legislative assembly. Under his pragmatic leadership Labor won the election of 1976; as premier, he instituted a review of the legal profession and of the Crimes Act, and reforms in industry, in consumer legislation, and in the legislative council (making it a fully elective body). The last years of Wran's administration were blemished by allegations of criminal links, of which he was cleared by a royal commission; he resigned in 1986.

wrasses These are generally tropical sea-fishes of the family Labridae, medium-sized and brightly coloured. Australia has a great diversity of wrasses, found especially on coral reefs. Examples include the combfish or banana fish, rather long and graceful, cream with a broad, black mid-strip along its side, with downward strokes like a comb; the very small cleaner fish, specialised to clear larger fish of food debris and parasites, which gains it tolerance from larger species; the doubleheader, with a large hump like a forehead (absent in the juvenile form); the jawslinger, sling-jaw or telescope-fish with rather protruding lips, extensible to catch its prey; and the keelheaded wrasse, with an extremely blunt snout but a thin keel that enables it to burrow rapidly in sand.

wrens In Australia, this name is perhaps most appropriately applied to the genus *Malurus*, the fairy wrens. Of these there are about a dozen species: small, sharp-beaked, insectivorous birds of heath and shrubs. They have slender legs, a small, rounded body and a long, frequently erect tail. The males have bright plumage during the breeding season; in many species it is often blue, blue-and-white, or blue-and-red, its brilliance fading in winter. Females are predominantly a modest dark-brown, but often have a bluish tail. The usual call is a thin but vigorous warble; nests are often fur- or feather-lined domes of grass or bark set in a low bush or in tall grass, with an entrance at the side or top. Various 'blue wrens' are widely distributed in Australia.

The popular name 'wren' is extended to include the emu-wren, *Stipiturus malachurus*, of coastal eastern Australia, which has the smallest body of any Australian bird and a long, gauzy tail erected almost over its head; it often hops, mouse-like, through grass tunnels, and it builds a small, dome-shaped nest on or near the ground. Several species of grass-wrens of the genus *Amytornis* are found in central and northern Australia; their nests are globe-shaped, and built in spinifex. The scrub-wrens, genus *Sericornis*, have substantial, blunt and less erectile tails; they build dome-shaped nests near the ground, and live in undergrowth, feeding on terrestrial insects.

Wright, Edmund William (1824–88), architect and civil engineer, b. England. Wright arrived in Adelaide in 1848 and set up an architectural practice in the 1850s. In partnership with Edward Woods from 1861, he designed many of Adelaide's major 19th-century civic buildings, among them the Palladian-style Town Hall (1863–6), GPO (1867–72) and splendidly ornate ANZ Bank, now Edmund Wright House (1875–8). He also designed a number of fine churches and houses.

Wright, Judith Arundel (1915–), poet and author, b. Armidale, NSW. Wright's love for the Australian landscape is reflected in much of her early verse, notably in the collection *The Moving Image* (1946), which brought her immediate acclaim. She has since written prolifically, her later poetry volumes reflecting her preoccupations with the interdependence of all life, the evils of modern society, and the plight of Aborigines. Other works include two family histories, *The Generations of Men* (1959) and *The Cry for the Dead* (1981), as well as essays, reviews and poetry criticism. A committed conservationist, she described the fight to save the Great Barrier Reef from mineral development in *The Coral Battleground* (1977).

Wyndham WA (pop. 1329) The State's most northerly port, 70km from the entrance of Cambridge Gulf and 3227km northeast of Perth, Wyndham was established in 1886 as a port for the Kimberley goldfield. It later became the site of a government meatworks, which closed in 1985. Tourism is of increasing importance, focused on the looming (330m) Bastion Range, the Ord River nature reserve and the saltwater crocodiles that proliferate in the gulf.

Wynne Prize > *art awards*

Wynyard Tas. (pop. 4705) This service and tourist centre lies at the mouth of the Inglis River, 330km northwest of Hobart. It is a small fishing port and serves a rich dairying and mixed-farming area; the town has several sawmills and a cheese factory.

Wyperfeld > *national parks and reserves*

XYZ

yabbies > *crayfishes and allies*

yachting > *sailing and yachting*

Yallourn > *Moe*

Yampi Sound WA This is an island-studded body of water between the Buccaneer Archipelago and Collier Bay, on the West Kimberley coast and north of King Sound; with a great tidal range and a swift tidal race, it is a hazardous area. Two of the islands, Cockatoo and Koolan, contain deposits of iron ore; the latter is mined by a subsidiary of BHP Ltd. The sound was named in 1838, during the voyage of the *Beagle*, from the Aboriginal word *yampee*, meaning 'fresh water'.

yams This is the common name for plants – particularly the tuberous roots – of the genus *Dioscorea*, but is often applied to any plants with edible tubers. Australia has only three native species of *Dioscorea*, two of which are endemic. The most familiar is the long yam, *D. transversa*, widespread along the eastern and northern coasts; its long narrow tubers are both palatable and nutritious, and a regional food staple of Aborigines. The warrine, *D. hastifolia*, is endemic to the west coast of WA, and is also a traditional Aboriginal food. In Vic. the murnong, *Microseris scapigera*, an edible dandelion-like member of the daisy family, is also commonly called a yam.

Yarra River Vic. This river rises near Mt Baw Baw, not far from the sources of the Goulburn and the Thomson, and receives many tributaries from the Great Dividing Range (in the north) and the Dandenong Ranges (in the south) as it runs a winding course for some 240km, passing through Melbourne to an estuary on Port Phillip Bay. It was discovered in 1803 by Charles Grimes, and its name comes from an Aboriginal word meaning 'running water'. Since early settlement it has been important in providing Melbourne with water, and the catchment still supplies part of the city's needs. The upper section has much scenic beauty and contains many holiday resorts; on the lower reaches, reclamation works and measures for flood control have necessarily been undertaken as the city has grown. The river has become contaminated through inadequate waste disposal in growing residential areas and by industrial pollution, made worse by a reduction in the rate of flow. Late last century, excavation works and dredging made possible the construction of port facilities immediately downstream from the city area.

yellowbelly > *fishes, freshwater and marine*

Yeppoon Qld (pop. 6452) This resort on the shores of Keppel Bay, 740km north of Brisbane, is a centre for the agricultural hinterland. Its chief industries are seafood processing, brick manufacture and forestry. A 9000ha resort is being constructed by Japanese interests.

York WA (pop.1122) This town in the lush Avon valley lies on the Great Southern Highway 96km east of Perth. One of the State's oldest towns, it was settled in 1831 and developed with the farmlands around it; it also experienced a brief gold boom in the 1890s. Local industry includes wheat-growing, grazing of sheep and cattle, and tourism. The town has a fine collection of 19th-century buildings, most of which were faithfully restored after earthquake damage in 1968.

Yorke Peninsula SA A boot-shaped promontory on the State's eastern coast, Yorke Peninsula is bounded by Spencer Gulf on the west, St Vincent Gulf on the east and Investigator Strait to the south, between the peninsula and Kangaroo Island. Discovered in 1802 by Matthew Flinders and given the name of the first lord of the Admiralty, the region was inhabited first by sealers before subsequent settlers established grain crops, still the region's chief product and now bulk-handled at three deep-sea ports. From the 1860s copper was mined in the north; today the main mineral product is dolomite, at Ardrossan. There are four national parks on the peninsula of which Innes, on the southwest tip, was established chiefly because of the attraction of its vegetation for the rare mallee or western whipbird.

Young, (William) Blamire (1862–1935),
artist, b. England. A Cambridge graduate, Young arrived in Australia in 1885 to teach mathematics but soon became involved in art. He was successful as a poster artist and eventually made his mark as an accomplished watercolourist, painting lyrical scenes in iridescent colour.

youth organisations
There are some 3000 youth organisations around Australia, which provide a wide range of social and recreational activities, and in some cases spiritual development. Most offer a mix of skills training, leisure pursuits, and opportunities to do community work or simply mix with other young people. Some groups – notably the scouts, guides and religious-based movements – began with the prime aim of equipping young people to be responsible citizens; the growing sophistication and disenchantment of youth in the last 20 years have made the original values of such organisations seem outmoded and their membership has generally declined in the same period.

Many Australian youth organisations are part of an international network. The largest are the Young Men's and Young Women's Christian Associations (YMCA and YWCA), the first of which originated in Britain and was introduced to Australia in the mid-19th century; their focus is still the inculcation of Christian values in young people but their activities now include a wide range of sporting, leisure and learning activities. Also a worldwide movement is the Scout Association, which began in Australia in 1908 (only a year after its inception in Britain) and was followed in 1910 by a female counterpart, the girl guides. Both groups now accept both male and female members and the emphasis is now as much on outdoor activities as 'good works'. The Youth Hostels

Association (YHA) began in Australia in 1939, with the express aim of providing low-cost accommodation for young travellers. There are more than 100 hostels throughout Australia, one of about 60 countries affiliated with the organisation; unlike many overseas affiliates, the YHA now has no age limit on members.

Some youth organisations are attached to general welfare groups, such as the St John Ambulance and Red Cross Society. Others have been formed specifically – or have adapted in step with changing times – to combat increasing youth alienation and crime. Police clubs have been at the forefront of efforts to tackle drug and delinquency problems, with well-placed sporting and recreational facilities and, more recently, social venues. >> *welfare organisations*

You Yangs
Vic. A group of granitic hills just north of Geelong, the You Yangs are used largely as recreation grounds. In 1802 Matthew Flinders arrived in the area and climbed the highest hill (350m), which he called Station Peak, there burying a cylinder holding a record of his visit. The name was later changed to Flinders Peak, and a memorial to Flinders erected on the summit.

Yunupingu, (James) Galarrwuy
(1949–), Aboriginal advocate and leader, b. Gove Peninsula, NT. Leader of the Gumatj clan of the Gove Peninsula, Yunupingu has served several terms as chairman of the Northern Land Council, largest of the three NT organisations representing Aboriginal landowners. In this capacity he has been a central figure in land-rights negotiations on behalf of Aboriginal communities in the region, including the terms and conditions of mining agreements such as the Ranger uranium project. He was awarded an AO in 1985.

Zeehan
Tas. (pop. 1610) This former mining centre, based on silver-lead discovered in 1882, lies 287km northwest of Hobart. Mining declined early this century but the town serves the tin mines at Renison Bell 19km to the northeast, which have expanded following recent discoveries of rich reserves. Zeehan is now chiefly a sawmilling centre; tourism is of some importance, centred on the town's interesting early history, several 'boom-style' buildings and the outstanding geological collection in its museum.

zinc > *lead and zinc*

ZOOS There are five major zoos in Australia – in the cities of Sydney, Dubbo, Melbourne, Adelaide and Perth. In addition, there are many privately owned collections of native animals and three excellent government fauna parks – Cleland National Park in SA, the Sir Colin Mackenzie Zoological Park in Vic., and Currumbin Sanctuary in Qld. Like botanic gardens, until the 20th century zoos were established mainly for the keeping and breeding of exotic species that were intended to become naturalised. 'Acclimatisation societies', which were established for this purpose, developed into the zoological societies of modern times. Today, zoos function as centres of conservation, education and research as well entertainment.

The first notable zoo in NSW, Moore Park, was established after 1879 as a centre for the acclimatisation of fauna; it gradually came to incorporate native species and present permanent displays. Sydney's justly famous Taronga Zoological Park, on the shores of Sydney Harbour, was officially opened in 1916 and today covers an area of some 32ha; it has been particularly successful in breeding birds and rare reptiles, and houses the world's largest collection of chimpanzees as well as examples of extremely rare animal species. The Monarto Zoological Park in NSW is a regional annex of Taronga, used for breeding and research purposes. The other major zoo in NSW, the Western Plains Zoo at Dubbo, is an open-range park of forest, grassland and waterways, through which visitors travel by car (or the more intrepid, on foot).

The Royal Melbourne Zoological Garden dates from 1861–2, when 22ha of land were set aside for fauna display; among its original denizens were circus animals and the camels from the ill-fated Burke and Wills expedition. In recent years, major refurbishment of the zoo has allowed much of its wildlife to live in conditions approximating their natural habitat; notable features include the humid butterfly enclosure and the leafy, elevated aviary.

The Adelaide Zoo was founded in 1878 as an acclimatisation society; it has occupied its present site – an area of 8ha not far from the city centre – since 1883. As elsewhere, the zoo has recently been modified to provide natural enclosures including a rainforest aviary.

Perth Zoo, established in 1898, now includes among its unusual residents Sumatran orang-utans and several gibbon species. Warm water is supplied to enclosures from an artesian bore, to allow tropical fauna (including crocodiles) to be kept outdoors throughout the year. Perth also has a number of rare native mammals, including numbats and ghost bats, which are rarely seen outside their natural habitat.

APPENDIX: government of Australia

FEDERAL

Below are listed the governors-general and prime ministers of Australia since Federation in 1901.

The governor-general is the British sovereign's representative in Australia and is appointed by the sovereign on the recommendation of the prime minister. Administrators, who have occasionally exercised the powers of the governor-general when the latter was absent or incapacitated, have also been listed.

The prime minister is the leader of the federal government. Although officially appointed by the governor-general, the prime minister in practice becomes so through being the elected leader of the political party that wins government. The prime ministers are listed with both date of appointment and political persuasion.

Governors-general

Earl of Hopetoun, 1 Jan. 1901–9 Jan. 1903
Lord Tennyson (acting governor-general), 17 Jul. 1902–9 Jan. 1903
Lord Tennyson, 9 Jan. 1903–21 Jan. 1904
Lord Northcote, 21 Jan. 1904–9 Sep. 1908
Earl of Dudley, 9 Sep. 1908–31 Jul. 1911
Lord Chelmsford (administrator), 21 Dec. 1909–27 Jan. 1910
Lord Denman, 31 Jul. 1911–18 May 1914
Sir Ronald C. Munro-Ferguson, 18 May 1914–6 Oct. 1920
Lord Forster of Lepe, 6 Oct. 1920–8 Oct. 1925
Lord Stonehaven, 8 Oct. 1925–22 Jan. 1931
Lord Somers (administrator), 3 Oct. 1930–22 Jan. 1931
Sir Isaac Alfred Isaacs, 22 Jan. 1931–23 Jan. 1936
Lord Gowrie, 23 Jan. 1936–30 Jan. 1945
Lord Huntingfield (administrator), 29 Mar.–24 Sep. 1938
Major-General Sir Winston Dugan (administrator), 5 Sep. 1944–30 Jan. 1945
H.R.H. Duke of Gloucester, 30 Jan. 1945–11 Mar. 1947
Major-General Sir Winston Dugan (administrator), 19 Jan.–11 Mar. 1947
Sir William John McKell, 11 Mar. 1947–8 May 1953

General Sir John Northcott (administrator), 19 Jul.–14 Dec. 1951
Field Marshal Sir William J. Slim, 8 May 1953–2 Feb. 1960
General Sir John Northcott (administrator), 30 Jul.–22 Oct. 1956
General Sir Reginald A. Dallas Brooks (administrator), 8–16 Jan. 1959
Viscount Dunrossil, 2 Feb. 1960–3 Feb. 1961
General Sir Reginald A. Dallas Brooks (administrator), 4 Feb.–3 Aug. 1961
Viscount De L'Isle, 3 Aug. 1961–22 Sep. 1965
General Sir Reginald A. Dallas Brooks (administrator), 5 Jun.–3 Oct. 1962; 21 Nov.–18 Dec. 1962
Lieutenant-General Sir Eric Woodward (administrator), 16 Jun.–30 Aug. 1964
Colonel Sir Henry Abel Smith (administrator), 7 May–22 Sep. 1965
Lord Casey, 22 Sep. 1965–30 Apr. 1969
Lieutenant-General Sir Edric Bastyan (administrator), 24 Apr.–1 Jun. 1967
Sir Paul Hasluck, 30 Apr. 1969–10 Jul. 1974
Major-General Sir Rohan Delacombe (administrator), 11–18 Feb. 1971; 12–19 Oct. 1971; 29 Jun.–9 Aug. 1972
Sir John Kerr, 11 Jun. 1974–7 Dec. 1977
Sir Zelman Cowen, 8 Dec. 1977–29 Jul. 1982
Sir Ninian Stephen, 29 Jul. 1982–16 Feb. 1989
William George Hayden, 16 Feb. 1989–

Prime ministers

Sir Edmund Barton, 1 Jan. 1901: Protectionist
Alfred Deakin, 24 Sep. 1903: Protectionist
John Christian Watson, 27 Apr. 1904: Labor
Sir George Houston Reid, 18 Aug. 1904: Free
Trade/Protectionist coalition
Alfred Deakin, 5 Jul. 1905: Protectionist
Andrew Fisher, 13 Nov. 1908: Labor
Alfred Deakin, 2 Jun. 1909: Fusion (Free
Traders, Protectionists and Tariff Reformers)
Andrew Fisher, 29 Apr. 1910: Labor
Sir Joseph Cook, 24 Jun. 1913: Liberal
Andrew Fisher, 17 Sep. 1914: Labor
William Morris Hughes, 14 Nov. 1916:
National Labor
William Morris Hughes, 17 Feb. 1917:
Nationalist
Stanley Melbourne Bruce, 9 Feb. 1923:
Nationalist/Country coalition
James Henry Scullin, 22 Oct. 1929: Labor
Joseph Aloysius Lyons, 6 Jan. 1932: United
Australia
Joseph Aloysius Lyons, 7 Nov. 1938: United
Australia/Country coalition
Sir Earle Page, 7 Apr. 1939: Country/United
Australia coalition

Robert Gordon Menzies, 26 Apr. 1939: United
Australia
Robert Gordon Menzies, 14 Mar. 1940: United
Australia/Country coalition
Arthur William Fadden, 29 Aug. 1941:
Country/United Australia coalition
John Joseph Curtin, 7 Oct. 1941: Labor
Francis Michael Forde, 6 Jul. 1945: Labor
Joseph Benedict Chifley, 13 Jul. 1945: Labor
Sir Robert Gordon Menzies, 19 Dec. 1949:
Liberal/Country coalition
Harold Edward Holt, 26 Jan. 1966: Liberal/
Country coalition
Sir John McEwen, 19 Dec. 1967: Liberal/
Country coalition
John Grey Gorton, 10 Jan. 1968: Liberal/
Country coalition
William McMahon, 10 Mar. 1971: Liberal/
Country coalition
Edward Gough Whitlam, 5 Dec. 1972: Labor
John Malcolm Fraser, 11 Nov. 1975: caretaker
government
John Malcolm Fraser, 22 Dec. 1975 Liberal/
Country (later National) coalition
Robert James Lee Hawke, 11 Mar. 1983:
Labor

STATE

Below are listed the governors and premiers of each State and the administrators of the NT.

In the early years of settlement, the governor (in NSW) or lieutenant-governor (all other colonies) was the chief administrator. The governor's powers were curbed officially with the advent of nominated legislative councils prior to the achievement of self-government; after Federation, the governors legally retained executive powers but by convention they have in the main exercised ceremonial functions only. Listed are all governors (or their equivalent) from 1788 onwards, with date of appointment.

The premier is the leader of the State government. As with the prime minister, the premier is officially appointed by the sovereign's representative but in practice achieves the position by being the elected leader of the political party in government. In the NT and the ACT, this position has been designated 'chief minister' since self-government (in 1978 and 1989 respectively). The premiers (or their equivalent) are listed with both date of appointment and political persuasion. The NT, as an annex of SA 1864–1911, was administered by a government resident; when control was transferred to the Commonwealth government 1911–81, the position became that of administrator.

New South Wales

Governors

Captain Arthur Phillip, 26 Jan. 1788
Major Francis Grose, 11 Dec. 1792
Captain William Paterson, 17 Dec. 1794
Captain John Hunter, 11 Sep. 1795

Captain Philip Gidley King, 28 Sep. 1800
Captain William Bligh, 13 Aug. 1806
Lieutenant-Colonel George Johnston, 26 Jan.
1808
Lieutenant-Colonel Joseph Foveaux, 30 Jul.
1808
Colonel William Paterson, 9 Jan. 1809
Major-General Lachlan Macquarie, 1 Jan. 1810

Major-General Sir Thomas Makdougall
 Brisbane, 1 Dec. 1821
Colonel William Stewart, 1 Dec. 1825
Lieutenant-General Ralph Darling, 19 Dec.
 1825
Colonel Patrick Lindesay, 22 Oct. 1831
Major-General Sir Richard Bourke, 3 Dec.
 1831
Lieutenant-Colonel Kenneth Snodgrass, 6 Dec.
 1837
Sir George Gipps, 24 Feb. 1838
Sir Maurice O'Connell, 12 Jul. 1846
Sir Charles Fitz Roy, 3 Aug. 1846
Sir William Dension, 20 Jan. 1855
Sir John Young, 16 May 1861
Earl of Belmore, 8 Jan. 1868
Sir Hercules Robinson, 3 Jun. 1872
Sir Augustus Loftus, 4 Aug. 1879
Lord Carrington, 12 Dec. 1885
Earl of Jersey, 15 Jan. 1891
Sir Robert Duff, 29 May 1893
Viscount Hampden, 21 Nov. 1895
Earl Beauchamp, 18 May 1899
Admiral Sir Harry Rawson, 27 May 1902
Lord Chelmsford, 28 May 1909
Sir Gerald Strickland, 14 Mar. 1913
Sir Walter Davidson, 18 Feb. 1918
Admiral Sir Dudley de Chair, 28 Feb. 1924
Air Vice-Marshal Sir Philip Game, 29 May
 1930
Brigadier-General Sir Alexander Hore-
 Ruthven, 21 Feb. 1935
Admiral Sir David Anderson, 6 Aug. 1936
Lord Wakehurst, 8 Apr. 1937
General Sir John Northcott, 1 Aug. 1946
Lieutenant-General Sir Eric Woodward, 1 Aug.
 1957
Sir Arthur Roden Cutler, 20 Jan. 1966
Air Marshal Sir James Rowland, 20 Jan. 1981

Premiers

S.A. Donaldson, 6 Jun. 1856: —
C. Cowper, 26 Aug. 1856: —
H.W. Parker, 3 Oct. 1856: —
C. Cowper, 7 Sep. 1857: —
W. Forster, 27 Oct. 1859: —
J. Robertson, 9 Mar. 1860: —
C. Cowper, 10 Jan. 1861: —
J. Martin, 16 Oct. 1863: —
C. Cowper, 3 Feb. 1865: —
J. Martin, 22 Jan. 1866: —
J. Robertson, 27 Oct. 1868: —
C. Cowper, 13 Jan. 1870: —
Sir James Martin, 16 Dec. 1870: —
H. Parkes, 14 May 1872: —
J. Robertson, 9 Feb. 1875: —

H. Parkes, 22 Mar. 1877: —
Sir John Robertson, 17 Aug. 1877: —
J.S. Farnell, 18 Dec. 1877: —
Sir Henry Parkes, 21 Dec. 1878: —
A. Stuart, 5 Jan. 1883: —
G.R. Dibbs, 7 Oct. 1885: —
Sir John Robertson, 22 Dec. 1885: —
Sir Patrick Jennings, 26 Feb. 1886: —
Sir Henry Parkes, 20 Jan. 1887: —
G.R. Dibbs, 17 Jan. 1889: —
Sir Henry Parkes, 8 Mar. 1889: Free Trade
Sir George Dibbs, 23 Oct. 1891: Protectionist
G.H. Reid, 3 Aug. 1894: Free Trade
Sir William Lyne, 14 Sep. 1899: Protectionist
J. See, 28 Mar. 1901: Protectionist
T. Waddell, 15 Jun. 1904: Protectionist
J.H. Carruthers, 30 Aug. 1904: Liberal-Reform
C.G. Wade, 2 Oct. 1907: Liberal-Reform
J.S.T. McGowen, 21 Oct. 1910: Labor
W.A. Holman, 30 Jun. 1913: Labor
W.A. Holman, 15 Nov. 1916: Nationalist
J. Storey, 13 Apr. 1920: Labor
J. Dooley, 10 Oct. 1921: Labor
Sir George Fuller, 20 Dec. 1921: Nationalist/
 Progressive coalition
Sir George Fuller, 13 Apr. 1922: Nationalist/
 Progressive coalition
J.T. Lang, 17 Jun. 1925: Labor
T.R. Bavin, 18 Oct. 1927: Nationalist/Country
 coalition
J.T. Lang, 4 Nov. 1930: Labor
B.S.B. Stevens, 16 May 1932: United
 Australia/Country coalition
A. Mair, 5 Aug. 1939: United Australia/
 Country coalition
W.J. McKell, 16 May 1941: Labor
J. McGirr, 6 Feb. 1947: Labor
J.J. Cahill, 3 Apr. 1952: Labor
R.J. Heffron, 28 Oct. 1959: Labor
J.B. Renshaw, 30 Apr. 1964: Labor
Sir Robert Askin, 13 May 1965: Liberal/
 Country coalition
T.L. Lewis, 3 Jan. 1975: Liberal/Country
 coalition
Sir Eric Willis, 23 Jan. 1976: Liberal/Country
 coalition
N.K. Wran, 14 May 1976: Labor
B.J. Unsworth, 4 Jul. 1986: Labor
N.F. Greiner, 25 Mar. 1988: Liberal

Victoria

Governors

Charles Joseph La Trobe, 30 Sep. 1839
John Vesey Fitzgerald, 6 May 1854

Captain Sir Charles Hotham, 22 Jun. 1854
Captain Sir Charles Hotham, 22 May 1855
Sir Henry Barkly, 26 Dec. 1856
Sir Charles Darling, 11 Sept. 1863
Sir John Manners-Sutton, 15 Aug. 1866
Sir George Ferguson Bowen, 30 Jul. 1873
Marquess of Normanby, 29 Apr. 1879
Sir Henry Loch, 15 Jul. 1884
Earl of Hopetoun, 28 Nov. 1889
Lord Brassey, 25 Oct. 1895
Sir George Clarke, 10 Dec. 1901
Major-General Sir Reginald Talbot, 25 Apr. 1904
Sir Thomas Carmichael, 27 Jul. 1908
Sir John Fuller, 24 May 1911
Sir Arthur Stanley, 23 Feb. 1914
Earl of Stradbroke, 24 Feb. 1921
Lord Somers, 28 Jun. 1926
Lord Huntingfield, 14 May 1934
Major-General Sir Winston Dugan, 17 Jul. 1939
General Sir Reginald Dallas Brooks, 18 Oct. 1949
Major-General Sir Rohan Delacombe, 8 May 1963
Sir Henry Winneke, 3 Jun. 1974
Rear Admiral Sir Brian Stewart Murray, 1 Mar. 1982
Sir John McIntosh Young, 3 Oct. 1985
Dr John Davis McCaughey, 18 Feb. 1986

Premiers

W.C. Haines, 28 Nov. 1855: —
J. O'Shanassy: 11 Mar. 1857: —
W.C. Haines, 29 Apr. 1857: —
J. O'Shanassy, 10 Mar. 1858: —
W. Nicholson, 27 Oct. 1859: —
R. Heales, 26 Nov. 1860: —
J. O'Shanassy, 14 Nov. 1861: —
J. McCulloch, 27 Jun. 1863: —
S. Sladen, 6 May 1868: —
J. McCulloch, 11 Jul. 1868: —
J.A. MacPherson, 20 Sep. 1869: —
J. McCulloch, 9 Apr. 1870: —
C.G. Duffy, 19 Jun. 1871: —
J.G. Francis, 10 Jun. 1872: —
G.B. Kerferd, 31 Jul. 1874: —
G. Berry, 7 Aug. 1875: —
Sir James McCulloch, 20 Oct. 1875: —
G. Berry, 21 May 1877: —
J. Service, 5 May 1880: —
G. Berry, 3 Aug. 1880: —
B. O'Loghlen, 9 Jul. 1881: —
J. Service, 8 Mar. 1883: —
D. Gillies, 18 Feb. 1886: Conservative/Liberal coalition

J. Munro, 5 Nov. 1890: National/Liberal coalition
W. Shiels, 16 Feb. 1892: Liberal
J.B. Patterson, 23 Jan. 1893: Conservative
G. Turner, 27 Sept. 1894: Liberal
A. McLean, 5 Dec. 1899: Liberal
Sir George Turner, 19 Nov. 1900: Liberal
A.J. Peacock, 12 Feb. 1901: Liberal
W.H. Irvine, 10 Jun. 1902: Reform
T. Bent, 16 Feb. 1904: Reform
J. Murray, 8 Jan. 1909: Liberal
W.A. Watt, 18 May 1912: Liberal
G.A. Elmslie, 9 Dec. 1913: Labor
W.A. Watt, 22 Dec. 1913: Liberal
Sir Alexander Peacock, 18 Jun. 1914: Liberal
J. Bowser, 29 Nov. 1917: National
H.S.W. Lawson, 21 Mar. 1918: National
H.S.W. Lawson, 7 Sep. 1923: National/Country coalition
H.S.W. Lawson, 19 Mar. 1924: National
Sir Alexander Peacock, 28 Apr. 1924: National
G.M. Prendergast, 18 Jul. 1924: Labor
J. Allan, 18 Nov. 1924: Country/National coalition
E.J. Hogan, 20 May 1927: Labor
Sir William McPherson, 22 Nov. 1928: National
E.J. Hogan, 12 Dec. 1929: Labor
Sir Stanley Argyle, 19 May 1932: United Australia/Country coalition
A.A. Dunstan, 2 Apr. 1935: Country
J. Cain, 14 Sep. 1943: Labor
A.A. Dunstan, 18 Sep. 1943: Country/United Australia coalition
I. Macfarlan, 2 Oct. 1945: Liberal
J. Cain, 21 Nov. 1945: Labor
T.T. Hollway, 20 Nov. 1947: Liberal/Country coalition
T.T. Hollway, 3 Dec. 1948: Liberal
J.G.B. McDonald, 27 Jun. 1950: Country
T.T. Hollway, 28 Oct. 1952: Electoral Reform
J.G.B. McDonald, 31 Oct. 1952: Country
J. Cain, 17 Dec.1952: Labor
Sir Henry Bolte, 7 Jun. 1955: Liberal and Country
R.J. Hamer, 23 Aug. 1972: Liberal
L.H.S. Thompson, 5 Jun. 1981: Liberal
J. Cain, 8 Apr. 1982: Labor

Queensland

Governors

Sir George Ferguson Bowen, 10 Dec. 1859
Colonel Samuel Wemsley Blackall, 14 Aug. 1868

Marquess of Normanby, 12 Aug. 1871
William Wellington Cairns, 23 Jan. 1875
Sir Arthur Edward Kennedy, 20 Jul. 1877
Sir Anthony Musgrave, 6 Nov. 1883
General Sir Henry Wylie Norman, 1 May 1889
Lord Lamington, 9 Apr. 1896
Major-General Sir Herbert Chermside, 24 Mar. 1902
Lord Chelmsford, 20 Nov. 1905
Sir William Macgregor, 2 Dec. 1909
Major Sir Hamilton Goold-Adams, 15 Mar. 1915
Lieutenant-Colonel Sir Matthew Nathan, 3 Dec. 1920
Lieutenant-General Sir Thomas Goodwin, 13 Jun. 1927
Colonel Sir Leslie Orme Wilson, 13 Jun. 1932
Lieutenant-General Sir John Lavarack, 1 Oct. 1946
Colonel Sir Henry Abel Smith, 18 Mar. 1958
Sir Alan Mansfield, 21 Mar. 1966
Air Marshal Sir Colin Hannah, 21 Mar. 1972
Commodore Sir James Ramsay, 22 Apr. 1977
Sir Walter Benjamin Campbell, 22 Jul. 1985

Premiers

R.G.W. Herbert, 10 Dec. 1859: —
A. Macalister, 1 Feb. 1866: —
R.G.W. Herbert, 20 Jul. 1866: —
A. Macalister, 7 Aug. 1866: —
R.R. Mackenzie, 15 Aug. 1867: —
C. Lilley, 25 Nov. 1868: —
A.H. Palmer, 3 May 1870: —
A. Macalister, 8 Jan. 1874: —
G. Thorn, 5 Jun. 1876: —
J. Douglas, 8 Mar. 1877: —
T. McIlwraith, 21 Jan. 1879: —
S.W. Griffith, 13 Nov. 1883: —
Sir Thomas McIlwraith, 13 Jun. 1888: —
B.D. Morehead, 30 Nov. 1888: —
Sir Samuel Griffith, 12 Aug. 1890: —
Sir Thomas McIlwraith, 27 Mar. 1893: —
H.M. Nelson, 27 Oct. 1893: —
T.J. Byrnes, 13 Apr. 1898: —
J.R. Dickson, 1 Oct. 1898: —
A. Dawson, 1 Dec. 1899: Labor
R. Philp, 7 Dec. 1899: —
A. Morgan, 17 Sep. 1903: —
W. Kidston, 19 Jan. 1906: —
R. Philp, 19 Nov. 1907: —
W. Kidston, 18 Feb. 1908: —
D.F. Denham, 7 Feb. 1911: Liberal
T.J. Ryan, 1 Jun. 1915: :Labor
E.G. Theodore, 22 Oct. 1919: Labor
W.N. Gillies, 26 Feb. 1925: Labor

W. McCormack, 22 Oct. 1925: Labor
A.E. Moore, 21 May 1929: Country/National/ Progressive coalition
W. Forgan Smith, 17 Jun. 1932: Labor
F.A. Cooper, 16 Sep. 1942: Labor
E.M. Hanlon, 7 Mar. 1946: Labor
V.C. Gair, 17 Jan. 1952: Labor
G.F.R. Nicklin, 12 Aug. 1957: Country/Liberal coalition
J.C.A. Pizzey, 17 Jan. 1968: Country/Liberal coalition
G.W.W. Chalk, 1 Aug. 1968: Country/Liberal coalition
J. Bjelke-Petersen, 8 Aug. 1968: Country (later National)/Liberal coalition, later National
M.J. Ahern, 1 Dec. 1987: National
T.R. Cooper, 22 Sep. 1989: National
W. Goss, 2 Dec. 1989: Labor

South Australia

Governors

Captain John Hindmarsh, 28 Dec. 1836
George Milner Stephen, 16 Jul. 1838
Lieutenant-Colonel George Gawler, 17 Oct. 1838
Captain George Grey, 15 May 1841
Lieutenant-Colonel Frederick Holt Robe, 25 Oct. 1845
Sir Henry Edward Fox Young, 2 Aug. 1848
Boyle Travers Finniss, 20 Dec. 1854
Sir Richard Graves MacDonnell, 8 Jun. 1855
Sir Dominick Daly, 4 Mar. 1862
Sir James Fergusson, 16 Feb. 1869
Sir Anthony Musgrave, 9 Jun. 1873
Sir William Drummond, 2 Oct. 1877
Sir William Robinson, 19 Feb. 1883
Earl of Kintore, 11 Apr. 1889
Sir Thomas Buxton, 29 Oct. 1895
Lord Tennyson, 10 Apr. 1899
Sir George Le Hunte, 1 Jul. 1903
Admiral Sir Day Bosanquet, 29 Mar. 1909
Lieutenant-Colonel Sir Henry Gawley, 18 Apr. 1914
Lieutenant-Colonel Sir William Weigall, 9 Jun. 1920
Lieutenant-General Sir George Bridges, 4 Dec. 1922
Lord Gowrie, 14 May 1928
Major-General Sir Winston Dugan, 28 Jul. 1934
Sir Charles Barclay-Harvey, 12 Aug. 1939
Lieutenant-General Sir Charles Willoughby Moke Norrie, 19 Dec. 1944

Air Vice-Marshal Sir Robert George, 23 Feb. 1953

Lieutenant-General Sir Edric Bastyan, 5 Apr. 1961

Major-General Sir James Harrison, 4 Dec. 1968

Sir Mark Oliphant, 1 Dec. 1971

Sir Douglas Nicholls, 1 Dec. 1976

Rev. Sir Keith Seaman, 1 Sep. 1977

Lieutenant-General Sir Donald Dunstan, 23 Apr. 1982

Premiers

B.T. Finniss, 24 Oct. 1856: —
J. Baker, 21 Aug. 1857: —
R.R. Torrens, 1 Sep. 1857: —
R.D. Hanson, 30 Sep. 1857: —
T. Reynolds, 9 May 1860: —
G.M. Waterhouse, 8 Oct. 1861: —
F.S. Dutton, 4 Jul. 1863: —
H. Ayers, 15 Jul. 1863: —
A. Blyth, 4 Aug. 1864: —
F.S. Dutton, 22 Mar. 1865: —
H. Ayers, 20 Sep. 1865: —
J. Hart, 23 Oct. 1865: —
J.P. Boucaut, 28 Mar. 1866: —
H. Ayers, 3 May 1867: —
J. Hart, 24 Sep. 1868: —
H. Ayers, 13 Oct. 1868: —
H.B.T. Strangways, 3 Nov. 1868: —
J. Hart, 30 May 1870: —
A. Blyth, 10 Nov. 1871: —
Sir Henry Ayers, 22 Jan. 1872: —
A. Blyth, 22 Jul. 1873: —
J.P. Boucaut, 3 Jun. 1875: —
J. Colton, 6 Jun. 1876: —
J.P. Boucaut, 26 Oct. 1877: —
W. Morgan, 27 Sep. 1878: —
J.C. Bray, 24 Jun. 1881: —
J. Colton, 16 Jun. 1884: —
J.W. Downer, 16 Jun. 1885: —
T. Playford, 11 Jun. 1887: —
J.A. Cockburn, 27 Jun. 1889: —
T. Playford, 19 Aug. 1890: —
F.W. Holder, 21 Jun. 1892: —
Sir John Downer, 15 Oct. 1892: —
C.C. Kingston, 16 Jun. 1893: Liberal
V.L. Solomon, 1 Dec. 1899: Conservative
F.W. Holder, 8 Dec. 1899: Liberal
J.G. Jenkins, 15 May 1901: Liberal; Liberal/ Conservative coalition
R. Butler, 1 Mar. 1905: Conservative
T. Price, 26 Jul. 1905: Labor/Liberal coalition
A. H. Peake, 5 Jun. 1909: Liberal
J. Verran, 3 Jun. 1910: Labor

A.H. Peake, 17 Feb. 1912: Liberal
C. Vaughan, 3 Apr. 1915: :Labor
A.H. Peake, 14 Jul. 1917: Liberal until 27 Aug. 1917, thereafter Liberal/National coalition
H.N. Barwell, 8 Apr. 1920: Liberal
J. Gunn, 16 Apr. 1924: Labor
L.L. Hill, 28 Aug. 1926: Labor
R.L. Butler, 8 Apr. 1927: Liberal/Country coalition
L.L. Hill, 17 Apr. 1930: Labor
R.S. Richards, 13 Feb. 1933: Labor
R.L. Butler, 18 Apr. 1933: Liberal Country League
Sir Thomas Playford, 5 Nov. 1938: Liberal Country League
F.H. Walsh, 10 Mar. 1965: Labor
D.A. Dunstan, 1 Jun. 1967: Labor
R.S. Hall, 17 Apr. 1968: Liberal Country League
D.A. Dunstan, 2 Jun. 1970: Labor
J.D. Corcoran, 15 Feb. 1979: Labor
D. Tonkin, 18 Sep. 1979: Liberal
J.C. Bannon, 10 Nov. 1982: Labor

Western Australia

Governors

Captain James Stirling, 30 Dec. 1828
Captain James Stirling, 6 Feb. 1832
Captain Frederick Chidley Irwin, 12 Aug. 1832
Captain Richard Daniell, 14 Sep. 1833
Captain Picton Beete, 11 May 1834
Captain Richard Daniell, 24 May 1834
Captain James Stirling, 19 Aug. 1834
John Hutt, 3 Jan. 1839
Lieutenant-Colonel Andrew Clarke, 27 Jan. 1846
Lieutenant-Colonel Frederick Irwin, 12 Feb. 1847
Captain Charles Fitzgerald, 12 Aug. 1848
Arthur Edward Kennedy, 23 Jul, 1855
Lieutenant-Colonel John Bruce, 20 Feb. 1862
John Stephen Hampton, 28 Feb. 1862
Lieutenant-Colonel John Bruce, 2 Nov. 1868
Frederick Weld, 30 Sep. 1869
Lieutenant-Colonel E.D. Harvest, 4 Jan. 1875
William Cleaver Francis Robinson, 11 Jan. 1875
Lieutenant-Colonel E.D. Harvest, 7 Sep. 1877
Major-General Sir Harry St George Ord, 12 Nov. 1877
Major-General Sir Harry St George Ord, 30 Jan. 1878

Sir William Cleaver Francis Robinson, 10 Apr. 1880

Henry Thomas Wrenfordsley, 14 Feb. 1883

Sir Frederick Napier Broome, 2 Jun 1883

Sir William Cleaver Francis Robinson, 20 Oct. 1890

Lieutenant-Colonel Sir Gerard Smith, 23 Dec. 1895

Captain Sir Arthur Lawley, 1 May 1901

Admiral Sir Frederick George Denham Bedford, 24 Mar. 1903

Sir Gerald Strickland, 31 May 1909

Major-General Sir Harry Barron, 17 Mar. 1913

Sir William Grey Ellison-Macartney, 9 Apr. 1917

Sir Francis Alexander Newdigate Newdegate, 9 April 1920

Colonel Sir William Robert Campion, 28 Oct 1924

Sir James Mitchell, 5 Oct 1948

Lieutenant-General Sir Charles Henry Gairdner, 6 Nov. 1951

Major-General Sir Douglas Anthony Kendrew, 25 Oct. 1963

Air Commodore Hughie Idwal Edwards, 7 Jan. 1974

Air Chief Marshal Sir Wallace Kyle, 24 Nov. 1975

Rear Admiral Sir Richard Trowbridge, 25 Nov. 1980

Sir Francis Burt, 24 Nov. 1983

Professor Gordon Reid, 2 Jul. 1984

Premiers

J. Forrest, 29 Dec. 1890: Protectionist or Conservative

G. Throssell, 15 Feb. 1901: Conservative

G. Leake, 25 May 1901: Liberal

A.E. Morgans, 21 Nov. 1901: Conservative

G. Leake, 23 Dec. 1901: Liberal

W.H. James, 1 Jul. 1902: Liberal

H. Daglish, 10 Aug. 1904: Labor

C.H. Rason, 25 Aug. 1905: Liberal

N.J. Moore, 7 May 1906: Liberal

F. Wilson, 16 Sep. 1910: Liberal

J. Scaddan, 7 Oct. 1911: Labor

F. Wilson, 27 Jul. 1916: Liberal

H.B. Lefroy, 28 Jun. 1917: Liberal

H.P. Colebatch, 17 Apr. 1919: Liberal

J. Mitchell, 17 May 1919: National/Country coalition

P. Collier, 16 Apr. 1924: Labor

Sir James Mitchell, 24 Apr. 1930: National/ Country coalition

P. Collier, 24 Apr. 1933: Labor

J.C. Willcock, 20 Aug. 1936: Labor

F.J.S. Wise, 31 Jul. 1945: Labor

D.R. McLarty, 1 Apr. 1947: Liberal/Country coalition

A.R.G. Hawke, 23 Feb. 1953: Labor

D. Brand, 2 Apr. 1959: Liberal/Country coalition

J.T. Tonkin, 3 Mar. 1971: Labor

Sir Charles Court, 8 Apr. 1974: Liberal/ Country coalition

R.J. O'Connor, 25 Jan. 1982: Liberal/National/ Country coalition

B. Burke, 25 Feb. 1983: Labor

P.M. Dowding, 25 Feb. 1988: Labor

C. Lawrence, 12 Feb. 1990: Labor

Tasmania

Governors

Colonel David Collins, 16 Feb. 1804

Lieutenant Edward Lord and Captain John Murray, 24 Mar. 1810

Major Andrew Geils, 20 Feb. 1812

Colonel Thomas Davey, 4 Feb. 1813

Colonel William Sorell, 9 Apr. 1817

Colonel George Arthur, 14 May 1824

Lieutenant-Colonel Kenneth Snodgrass, 31 Oct. 1836

Sir John Franklin, 6 Jan. 1837

Sir John Eardley-Wilmot, 21 Aug. 1843

Charles Joseph La Trobe, 13 Oct. 1846

Sir William Thomas Denison, 26 Jan. 1847

Sir Henry Young, 8 Jan. 1855

Colonel Thomas Browne, 16 Jun. 1862

Charles Du Cane, 15 Jan. 1869

Frederick Aloysius Weld, 13 Jan. 1875

Major Sir George Strahan, 7 Dec. 1881

Sir Robert Hamilton, 11 Mar. 1887

Viscount Gormanston, 8 Aug. 1893

Captain Sir Arthur Havelock, 8 Nov. 1901

Sir Gerald Strickland, 28 Oct. 1904

Major-General Sir Harry Barron, 29 Sep. 1909

Sir William Grey Ellison-Macartney, 4 Jun. 1913

Sir Francis Alexander Newdigate Newdegate, 6 Jul. 1917

Sir William Allardyce, 16 Apr. 1920

Captain Sir James O'Grady, 23 Dec. 1924

Sir Ernest Clark, 4 Aug. 1933

Sir Hugh Binney, 24 Dec. 1945

Sir Ronald Cross, 23 Aug. 1951

Lord Rowallan, 21 Oct. 1959

Lieutenant-General Sir Charles Gairdner, 24 Sep. 1963

Lieutenant-General Sir Edric Bastyan, 2 Dec. 1968

Sir Stanley Burbury, 5 Dec. 1973
Sir James Plimsoll, 1 Oct. 1982
Sir Guy Green, 9 May 1987
General Sir Phillip Bennett, 19 Oct. 1987

Premiers

W.T.N. Champ, 1 Nov. 1856: —
T.G. Gregson, 26 Feb. 1857: —
W.P. Weston, 25 Apr. 1857: —
F. Smith, 12 May 1857: —
W.P. Weston, 1 Nov. 1860: —
T.D. Chapman, 2 Aug. 1861: —
J. Whyte, 20 Jan. 1863: —
R. Dry, 24 Nov. 1866: —
J.M. Wilson, 4 Aug. 1869: —
F.M. Innes, 4 Nov. 1872: —
A. Kennerley, 4 Aug. 1873: —
T. Reibey, 20 Jul. 1876: —
P.O. Fysh, 9 Aug. 1877: —
W.R. Giblin, 5 Mar. 1878: —
W.L. Crowther, 20 Dec. 1878: —
W.R. Giblin, 30 Oct. 1879: —
A. Douglas, 15 Aug. 1884: —
J.W. Agnew, 8 Mar. 1886: —
P.O. Fysh, 30 Mar. 1887: Liberal
H. Dobson, 17 Aug. 1892: Conservative
E. Braddon, 14 Apr. 1894: Liberal
N.E. Lewis, 12 Oct. 1899: Conservative
W.B. Propsting, 9 Apr. 1903: Liberal
    Democrat
J.W. Evans, 12 Jul. 1904: Liberal
N.E. Lewis, 19 Jun. 1909: Liberal Fusion
J. Earle, 20 Oct. 1909: Labor
N.E. Lewis, 27 Oct. 1909: Liberal
A.E. Solomon, 14 Jun. 1912: Liberal
J. Earle, 6 Apr. 1914: Labor
W. Lee, 15 Apr. 1916: Liberal; Nationalist
J.B. Hayes, 12 Aug. 1922: Nationalist
    Country
W. Lee, 14 Aug. 1923: Nationalist
J. A. Lyons, 25 Oct. 1923: Labor
J.C. McPhee, 15 Jun. 1928: Nationalist
W. Lee, 15 Mar. 1934: Nationalist
A.G. Ogilvie, 22 Jun. 1934: Labor
E. Dwyer-Gray, 11 Jun. 1939: Labor
R. Cosgrove, 18 Dec. 1939: Labor
E. Brooker, 19 Dec. 1947: Labor
R. Cosgrove, 25 Feb. 1948: Labor
E.E. Reece, 26 Aug. 1958: Labor
W.A. Bethune, 26 May 1969: Liberal/Centre
E.E. Reece, 3 May 1972: Labor
W.A. Neilson, 31 Mar. 1975: Labor
D. Lowe, 1 Dec. 1977: Labor
H.N. Holgate, 11 Nov. 1981: Labor
R.T. Gray, 26 May 1982: Liberal
M.W. Field, 29 Jun. 1989: Labor

Northern Territory

Administrators under SA 1864–1911 and under Commonwealth 1911–78

B.T. Finniss, 1864
J.T. Manton (acting), 1865
G.W. Goyder, 1868
Dr J.S. Millner (acting), 1869
Capt. W. Bloomfield Douglas, 1870
Dr. J.S. Millner (acting), 1873
G.B. Scott, 1873
E.W. Price, 1876
G.R. McMinn (acting), 1883
J. Langdon Parsons, 1884
J.G. Knight, 1890
Judge C.J. Dashwood, 1892
Judge C.E. Herbert, 1905
Judge S.J. Mitchell, 1910
Judge S.J. Mitchell (acting), 1911
Dr J.A. Gilruth, 1912
H.E. Carey (director), 1919
M.S.C. Smith (acting), 1919
M.S.C. Smith (deputy), 1921
F.C. Urquhart, 1921
E.C. Playford (acting), 1926
R.H. Weddell, 1927
J.C. Cawood, 1926
V.G. Carrington (acting), 1929
R.H. Weddell, 1931
J.A. Carrodus (acting), 1934
C.L.A. Abbott, 1937
L.H.A. Giles (acting), 1946
A.R. Driver, 1946
F.J.S. Wise, 1951
J.C. Archer, 1956
R.B. Nott, 1961
R.L. Dean, 1964
F.C. Chaney, 1970
T.A. O'Brien (acting), 1973
J.N. Nelson, 1973
E.F. Dwyer (acting), 1975
J.A. England, 1976
Commodore E.E. Johnston, 1981

Chief ministers since self-government (1978)

P.A.E. Everingham, 1978: Country/Liberal
I.L. Tuxworth, 1984: Country/Liberal
S.P. Hatton, 1986: Country/Liberal
M. Perron, 1988: Country/Liberal

Australian Capital Territory

Chief ministers since self-government (1989)

R. Follett, 1989: Labor
T.R. Kaine, 1989: Liberal

Australia and the Pacific rim

Geological formation

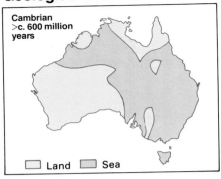

Cambrian
>c. 600 million years

☐ Land ☐ Sea

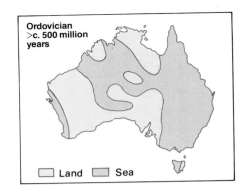

Ordovician
>c. 500 million years

☐ Land ☐ Sea

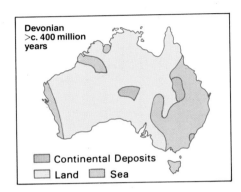

Devonian
>c. 400 million years

☐ Continental Deposits
☐ Land ☐ Sea

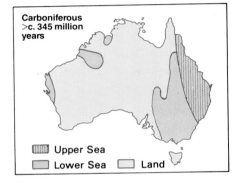

Carboniferous
>c. 345 million years

▥ Upper Sea
☐ Lower Sea ☐ Land

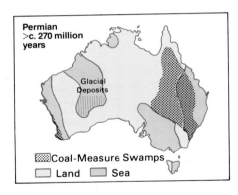

Permian
>c. 270 million years

Glacial Deposits

▨ Coal-Measure Swamps
☐ Land ☐ Sea

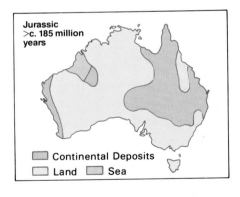

Jurassic
>c. 185 million years

☐ Continental Deposits
☐ Land ☐ Sea

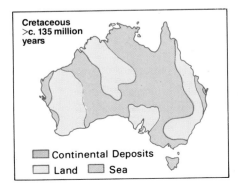

Cretaceous
>c. 135 million years

☐ Continental Deposits
☐ Land ☐ Sea

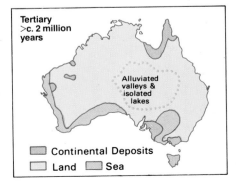

Tertiary
>c. 2 million years

Alluviated valleys & isolated lakes

☐ Continental Deposits
☐ Land ☐ Sea

Geology of Australia

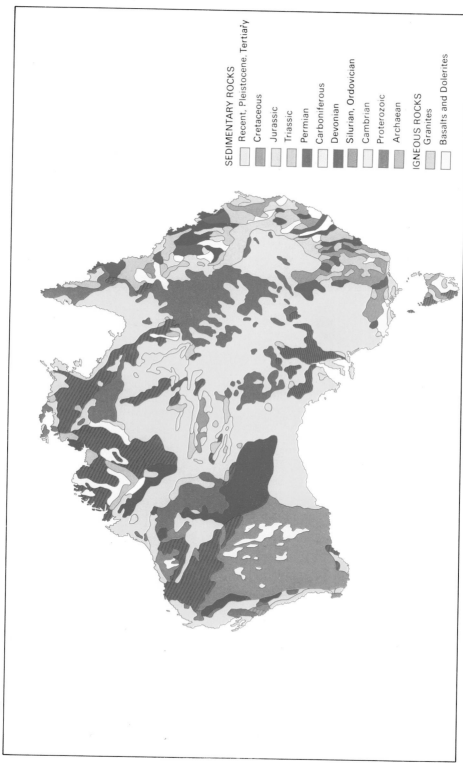

SEDIMENTARY ROCKS
Recent, Pleistocene. Tertiary
Cretaceous
Jurassic
Triassic
Permian
Carboniferous
Devonian
Silurian, Ordovician
Cambrian
Proterozoic
Archaean

IGNEOUS ROCKS
Granites
Basalts and Dolerites

Weather patterns in the major centres

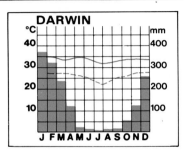

DARWIN

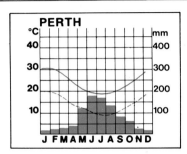

PERTH

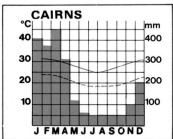

CAIRNS

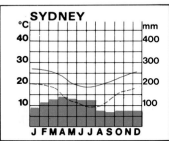

SYDNEY

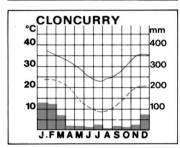

CLONCURRY

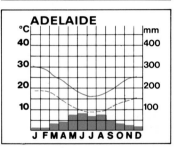

ADELAIDE

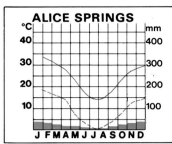

ALICE SPRINGS

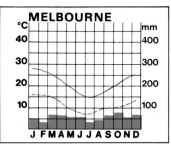

MELBOURNE

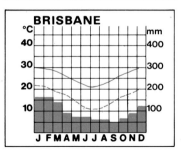

BRISBANE

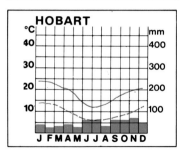

HOBART

Australian soil types

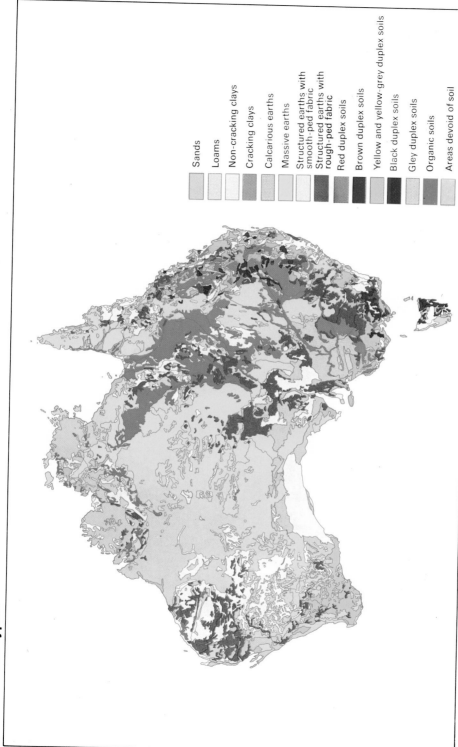

Sands
Loams
Non-cracking clays
Cracking clays
Calcarious earths
Massive earths
Structured earths with smooth-ped fabric
Structured earths with rough-ped fabric
Red duplex soils
Brown duplex soils
Yellow and yellow-grey duplex soils
Black duplex soils
Gley duplex soils
Organic soils
Areas devoid of soil

Natural vegetation

FORESTS
Rainforest
Wet sclerophyll
Dry Sclerophyll

WOODLANDS
Low layered
Savanna; tall
Savanna; medium, low
Open, low and shrub

GRASSLANDS
Grass tree savanna
Open, low tree and shrub savanna
Layered
Tussock
Low open hummock

SCRUBLANDS
Tall brigalow
Mallee
Dwarf
Heath

MISCELLANEOUS
Alpine complex
Sandy desert
Stony desert

Australia's unique wildlife

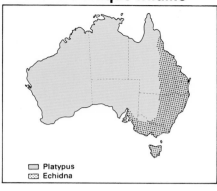

- ▨ Platypus
- ▨ Echidna

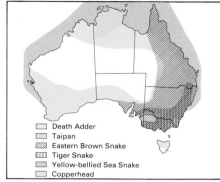

- ▨ Death Adder
- ▨ Taipan
- ▨ Eastern Brown Snake
- ▥ Tiger Snake
- ▨ Yellow-bellied Sea Snake
- ▨ Copperhead

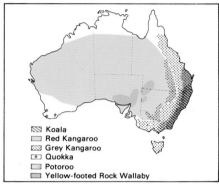

- ▨ Koala
- ▨ Red Kangaroo
- ▨ Grey Kangaroo
- ▨ Quokka
- ▨ Potoroo
- ▨ Yellow-footed Rock Wallaby

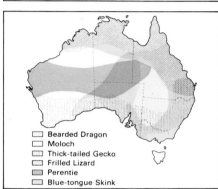

- ▨ Bearded Dragon
- ▨ Moloch
- ▥ Thick-tailed Gecko
- ▨ Frilled Lizard
- ▨ Perentie
- ▨ Blue-tongue Skink

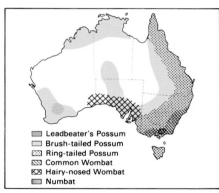

- ▨ Leadbeater's Possum
- ▨ Brush-tailed Possum
- ▨ Ring-tailed Possum
- ▨ Common Wombat
- ▨ Hairy-nosed Wombat
- ▨ Numbat

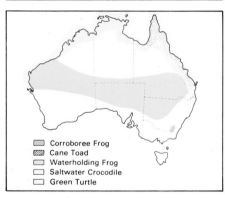

- ▨ Corroboree Frog
- ▨ Cane Toad
- ▨ Waterholding Frog
- ▨ Saltwater Crocodile
- ▨ Green Turtle

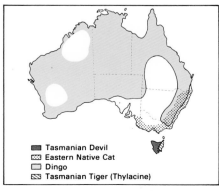

- ▨ Tasmanian Devil
- ▨ Eastern Native Cat
- ▨ Dingo
- ▨ Tasmanian Tiger (Thylacine)

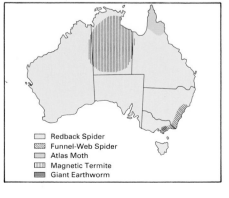

- ▨ Redback Spider
- ▨ Funnel-Web Spider
- ▨ Atlas Moth
- ▥ Magnetic Termite
- ▨ Giant Earthworm

Voyages of discovery

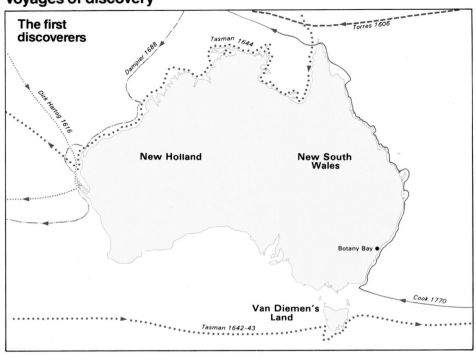

The first discoverers

Torres 1606

Dampier 1688

Tasman 1644

Dirk Hartog 1616

New Holland

New South Wales

Botany Bay ●

Cook 1770

Van Diemen's Land

Tasman 1642–43

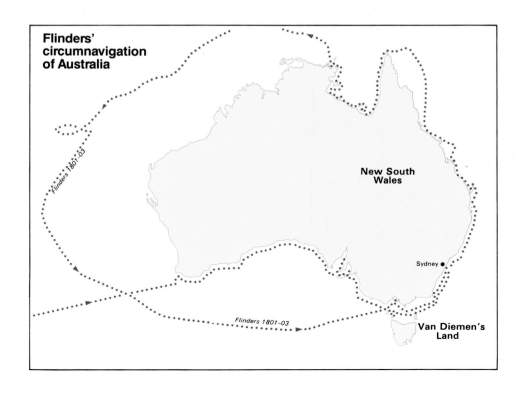

Flinders' circumnavigation of Australia

Flinders 1801–03

New South Wales

Sydney ●

Flinders 1801–03

Van Diemen's Land

The great inland explorers

How the six States developed

1786–1824

Fort Dundas 1824

long. 135°E

New South Wales

unattached

Moreton Bay 1824

Sydney 1788

Lord Howe I.

Norfolk I.

Van Diemen's Land

Hobart 1804

NZ

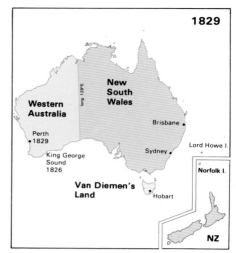

1829

long. 129°E

Western Australia

New South Wales

Brisbane

Perth 1829

King George Sound 1826

Sydney

Lord Howe I.

Norfolk I.

Van Diemen's Land

Hobart

NZ

1836

New South Wales

Western Australia

long. 132°E

South Australia

long. 141°E

Brisbane

Danger Point

Lord Howe I.

Perth

Sydney

Albany

Adelaide 1836

Melbourne 1835

Norfolk I. annexed to Van Diemen's Land 1844

Van Diemen's Land

Hobart

NZ

1851

Port Essington abandoned 1849

New South Wales

Western Australia

South Australia

Brisbane

Perth

Sydney

Adelaide

Vic.

Melbourne

Van Diemen's Land

Hobart

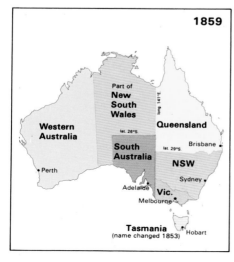

1859

Part of New South Wales

long. 141°E

Western Australia

lat. 26°S.

Queensland

South Australia

lat. 29°S.

Brisbane

NSW

Perth

Sydney

Adelaide

Vic.

Melbourne

Tasmania
(name changed 1853)

Hobart

1931

Darwin

Northern Territory

long. 138°E

Western Australia

Queensland

South Australia

Brisbane

NSW

Perth

Sydney

Adelaide

Vic.

Canberra A.C.T.

Melbourne

Tasmania

Hobart

Population growth 1788-1986

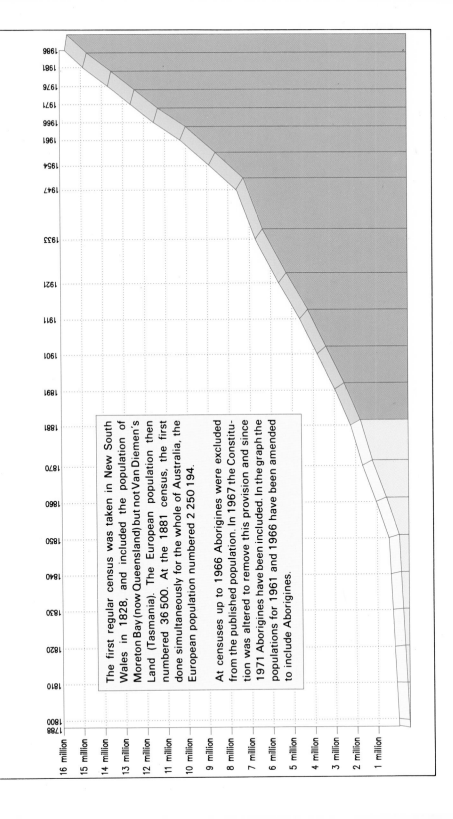

The first regular census was taken in New South Wales in 1828, and included the population of Moreton Bay (now Queensland) but not Van Diemen's Land (Tasmania). The European population then numbered 36 500. At the 1881 census, the first done simultaneously for the whole of Australia, the European population numbered 2 250 194.

At censuses up to 1966 Aborigines were excluded from the published population. In 1967 the Constitution was altered to remove this provision and since 1971 Aborigines have been included. In the graph the populations for 1961 and 1966 have been amended to include Aborigines.

Population distribution

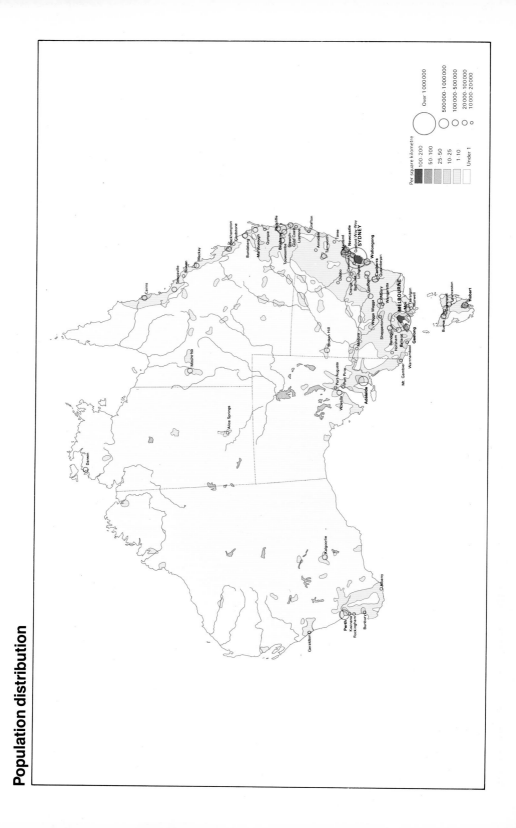

Aboriginal population by State, 1986

*Population figures projected to 1986 by Dept. of Aboriginal Affairs

Percentage scale: 25, 20, 15, 10, 5

- ACT: 900, 0.34
- NT: 32 800, 22
- Tas: 3 000, 0.68
- WA: 35 100, 2.45
- SA: 11 000, 0.8
- Qld: 50 400, 1.94
- Vic: 6 800, 0.16
- NSW: 39 900, 0.73

Population scale: 50 000, 40 000, 30 000, 20 000, 10 000

Agricultural land use

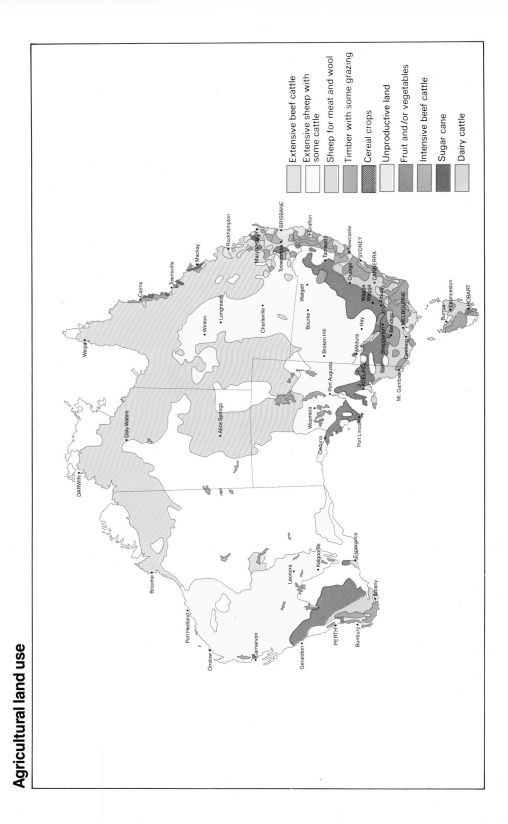

Extensive beef cattle

Extensive sheep with some cattle

Sheep for meat and wool

Timber with some grazing

Cereal crops

Unproductive land

Fruit and/or vegetables

Intensive beef cattle

Sugar cane

Dairy cattle